THE JESUITS II

THE JESUITS II

Cultures, Sciences, and the Arts
1540–1773

Edited by

John W. O'Malley, S.J.
Gauvin Alexander Bailey
Steven J. Harris
T. Frank Kennedy, S.J.

UNIVERSITY OF TORONTO PRESS
Toronto Buffalo London

© University of Toronto Press Incorporated 2006
Toronto Buffalo London
Printed in Canada

ISBN 0-8020-3861-1

Printed on acid-free paper

Library and Archives Canada Cataloguing in Publication

The Jesuits II : cultures, sciences, and the arts, 1540–1773 / edited by
John W. O'Malley ... [et al.].

Essays originally presented as papers at a conference held in 2002.
Includes index.
ISBN 0-8020-3861-1

1. Jesuits – History – Congresses.   2. Christianity and culture –
Congresses.   I. O'Malley, John W.

BX3706.3.J48 2006   271'.53   C2005-901683-3

University of Toronto Press acknowledges the financial assistance to its publishing
program of the Canada Council for the Arts and the Ontario Arts Council.

University of Toronto Press acknowledges the financial support for its
publishing activities of the Government of Canada through the
Book Publishing Industry Development Program (BPIDP).

Contents

Contents   vii

Contents   ix

Acknowledgments

As with our first conference and volume, we have incurred great debts of gratitude in the years since we began working on this project. We are first and foremost grateful to Michael J. Buckley, S.J., former director of the Jesuit Institute at Boston College, who encouraged us to undertake a second conference and provided us with the initial funding we needed to begin our task. For very generous further funding we are grateful to the Charles W. Englehard Foundation and to the Penates Foundation of the Montrone Family.

For their cooperation and labours we express our gratitude to our administrative assistant, Patricia Longbottom, and also to Patricia Fleming, administrative assistant of the Jesuit Institute; to the Jesuit community at Boston College; to the Audio-Visual and Music Departments of Boston College; and to the following members of the Society of Jesus: William P. Leahy, President of Boston College, J. Donald Monan, Chancellor of Boston College, Juan Dejo, David Hernandez, Yong Soh Kim, Hua Lee, Christopher Lockard, Christopher Soh, John R. Siberski, and Thomas H. Tjaya.

For their remarkable skills and their devotion to their tasks well beyond what we had any right to expect, we are, once again, deeply grateful to Theresa Griffin, our copy-editor, and to Patricia Gross, who constructed the index. We are also grateful to Barbara Porter of the University of Toronto Press, who so competently and graciously oversaw the progress of our volume through the press.

Contributors

Dauril Alden
University of Washington, emeritus
Seattle, Washington

Gauvin Alexander Bailey
Clark University
Worcester, Massachusetts

Ugo Baldini
Università degli Studi Gabriele
  d'Annunzio
Chieti, Italy

Peter Burke
Emmanuel College
Cambridge, England

Charlotte de Castelnau-L'Estoile
Université Paris-X
Nanterre, France

Richard Clay
University of Birmingham
Birmingham, England

David Crook
University of Wisconsin
Madison, Wisconsin

Peter Davidson
University of Aberdeen
Aberdeen, Scotland

Bruna Filippi
Università di Perugia
Perugia, Italy

Alicia Fraschina
Universidad de Buenos Aires
Buenos Aires, Argentina

Marc Fumaroli
de l'Académie Française
Collège de France
Paris, France

Steven J. Harris
Harvard University, associate
Cambridge, Massachusetts

Ronnie Po-chia Hsia
Pennsylvania State University
University Park, Pennsylvania

Olwen Hufton
Merton College
Oxford, England

T. Frank Kennedy, S.J.
Boston College
Chestnut Hill, Massachusetts

Anna C. Knaap
New York University
New York, New York

Hiromitsu Kobayashi
Sophia University
Tokyo, Japan

Franz Körndle
Friederich-Schiller-Universität Jena
Jena, Germany

Henrique Leitão
Universidade de Lisboa
Lisbon, Portugal

Judi Loach
Cardiff University
Cardiff, Wales

Sabine MacCormack
University of Notre Dame
Notre Dame, Indiana

Aliocha Maldavsky
Université Paris-X
Nanterre, France

Jeffrey Muller
Brown University
Providence, Rhode Island

Víctor Navarro Brotóns
Universidad de Valencia
Valencia, Spain

John W. O'Malley, S.J.
Weston Jesuit School of Theology
Cambridge, Massachusetts

Catherine Pagani
University of Alabama
Tuscaloosa, Alabama

Sabina Pavone
Università 'La Sapienza'
Rome, Italy

Volker R. Remmert
Universität Mainz
Mainz, Germany

Elizabeth Rhodes
Boston College
Chestnut Hill, Massachusetts

Humberto Rodríguez-Camilloni
Virginia Polytechnic Institute and
  State University
Blacksburg, Virginia

Antonella Romano
CNRS/Centre Alexandre Koyré
Paris, France

Víctor Rondón
Universidad de Chile
Santiago, Chile

Daniel L. Schlafly, Jr
Saint Louis University
Saint Louis, Missouri

Daniel Stolzenberg
Max Planck Institute for the History
  of Science
Berlin, Germany

Contributors

Dauril Alden
University of Washington, emeritus
Seattle, Washington

Gauvin Alexander Bailey
Clark University
Worcester, Massachusetts

Ugo Baldini
Università degli Studi Gabriele
   d'Annunzio
Chieti, Italy

Peter Burke
Emmanuel College
Cambridge, England

Charlotte de Castelnau-L'Estoile
Université Paris-X
Nanterre, France

Richard Clay
University of Birmingham
Birmingham, England

David Crook
University of Wisconsin
Madison, Wisconsin

Peter Davidson
University of Aberdeen
Aberdeen, Scotland

Bruna Filippi
Università di Perugia
Perugia, Italy

Alicia Fraschina
Universidad de Buenos Aires
Buenos Aires, Argentina

Marc Fumaroli
de l'Académie Française
Collège de France
Paris, France

Steven J. Harris
Harvard University, associate
Cambridge, Massachusetts

Ronnie Po-chia Hsia
Pennsylvania State University
University Park, Pennsylvania

Olwen Hufton
Merton College
Oxford, England

T. Frank Kennedy, S.J.
Boston College
Chestnut Hill, Massachusetts

Anna C. Knaap
New York University
New York, New York

Hiromitsu Kobayashi
Sophia University
Tokyo, Japan

Franz Körndle
Friederich-Schiller-Universität Jena
Jena, Germany

Henrique Leitão
Universidade de Lisboa
Lisbon, Portugal

Judi Loach
Cardiff University
Cardiff, Wales

Sabine MacCormack
University of Notre Dame
Notre Dame, Indiana

Aliocha Maldavsky
Université Paris-X
Nanterre, France

Jeffrey Muller
Brown University
Providence, Rhode Island

Víctor Navarro Brotóns
Universidad de Valencia
Valencia, Spain

John W. O'Malley, S.J.
Weston Jesuit School of Theology
Cambridge, Massachusetts

Catherine Pagani
University of Alabama
Tuscaloosa, Alabama

Sabina Pavone
Università 'La Sapienza'
Rome, Italy

Volker R. Remmert
Universität Mainz
Mainz, Germany

Elizabeth Rhodes
Boston College
Chestnut Hill, Massachusetts

Humberto Rodríguez-Camilloni
Virginia Polytechnic Institute and
    State University
Blacksburg, Virginia

Antonella Romano
CNRS/Centre Alexandre Koyré
Paris, France

Víctor Rondón
Universidad de Chile
Santiago, Chile

Daniel L. Schlafly, Jr
Saint Louis University
Saint Louis, Missouri

Daniel Stolzenberg
Max Planck Institute for the History
    of Science
Berlin, Germany

Nuno Vassallo e Silva
Fundacão Calouste Gulbenkian
Lisbon, Portugal

William A. Wallace, O.P.
The Catholic University of America,
  emeritus
Washington, District of Columbia

Haruko Nawata Ward
Columbia Theological Seminary
Decatur, Georgia

Larry Wolff
Boston College
Chestnut Hill, Massachusetts

Michael Zampelli, S.J.
Santa Clara University
Santa Clara, California

Giovanna Zanlonghi
Università Cattolica del Sacro Cuore
Milan, Italy

Preface

This volume is the second we have edited and, like the first, it grew out of an international conference we organized at Boston College in early June 2002. With sixty formal papers and scores of scholars attending from four continents, this conference was larger and longer than its predecessor. As before, our gathering was marked by a special event, the production of an opera, *Patientis Christi memoria*, composed by Johann Bernhard Staudt and originally performed in 1685 at the Jesuit college in Vienna. Our performance in the chapel of St Mary's Hall, Boston College, was produced by T. Frank Kennedy, S.J., and directed by Michael Zampelli, S.J. In the appendix to this volume T. Frank Kennedy provides an introduction to the opera and his translation of the libretto to accompany a digital videodisc (DVD) of the opera contained inside the back cover.

Our motivations for a second conference on the religious and cultural history of the 'Old Society,' that is, the Society before the general suppression of 1773, were like those for the first. We sought to bring together an ever growing community of scholars working on the Jesuits from diverse perspectives and provide them with the opportunity to discuss their work in relation to interdisciplinary themes and overarching historiographical questions. In general terms, our goal was to continue to deepen our understanding of Jesuit corporate culture and its interaction with the ambient cultural fields of Europe and the overseas missions. A leitmotif of the first conference revolved around the question of whether or to what extent the Jesuits had a distinctive approach to issues – what the Jesuits called 'our way of proceeding' (*modus noster procedendi*). A number of papers in this volume continue and enrich that discussion.

The disciplinary scope of the second conference and volume reflects, as before, the interests and proclivities of the editors, namely, the history of music, science, and art and architecture. Or, to invoke a somewhat dated but none the less useful term, the contributions in both volumes may be considered variegated explorations of Jesuit *Kulturgeschichte*. Neither in the first volume nor in this one have we sought, however, to offer a comprehensive survey of every aspect of the Society in all its multifarious activities over almost two and a half centuries. The volumes leave practically untouched, for instance, the involvement of the Jesuits in politics and diplomacy, an aspect of their activities for which, rightly or wrongly, they are perhaps best known in legend and in novels, opera, and drama. They leave practically untouched their polemics with Protestants, the administration and structure of their universities, and the internal governance of the Society. They leave untouched the Jesuits' almost countless writings on spirituality. The list could go on.

Even though the subjects covered in this volume reflect in a general way those covered in the first, we have tried in certain particulars to move the argument along. We have, for instance, organized this volume differently. Whereas in the first we wanted to show the interdisciplinary relationships within categories of Jesuit activities, in this volume we want to indicate the different expressions a given discipline might take. We have organized most of the sections accordingly. To complement the regional coverage of the first volume, we here present articles on the Flemish and Iberian provinces, and on the missions in Japan and in post-suppression Russia and the United States. The performing arts are more broadly treated than before, with essays on theatre as well as music. In addition to continued attention to painting and architecture, readers will find essays on a range of objets d'art, including statuary, reliquaries, and silver and gold pieces used in the liturgy, as well as on gardens, mechanical clocks, and related automata. Other themes unexplored in the first volume but at least touched on in this one are finances, natural theology, the Society's relationship with women, and 'adult education' in the lay confraternities and sodalities that operated under Jesuit guidance.

Perhaps most important, we have endeavoured in this volume to give more attention to the eighteenth century, which is much less well researched for the Jesuits than the seventeenth, the Society's supposed 'golden age.' A number of contributors to this volume explore the richness and complexity of the Society's activities during that later century, including its 'age of disasters'– the negative papal ruling on Chinese rites, the destruction of the Paraguay Reductions, the suppressions of the order that began in Portugal and culminated in the general suppression of 1773.

This expanded time frame raises questions about the adequacy of received categories and periodization schemes when applied to Jesuit historiography. There are historians of the eighteenth century, for instance, who now speak of a 'Catholic Enlightenment.' How do the Jesuits figure in that category? Or can we speak of an 'early modern Catholicism' that encroaches on the time and turf of the *philosophes*? In rethinking Jesuit historiography, might we not wish to revisit Jean Delumeau's periodization as set out in the title of his best-known book, *Catholicism between Luther and Voltaire*? Surely it is more than a curiosity that the years marking the death of Luther (1546) and of Voltaire (1778) bracket almost exactly the life span of the 'Old Society.' We raise such questions not with the promise that readers will find the answers to them in these pages, but rather with the persuasion that simply asking them alerts readers to issues of the relationship between religion and culture that transcend the Jesuit story. In this matter, as with the whole history of the pre-suppression Society, we are very much aware that, even with the combined efforts of our many excellent contributors to these two volumes, we offer our readers only selected glimpses into a complex and subtle historical record.

THE EDITORS

Abbreviations

Monumenta Historica Societatis Iesu

Epist. Mixt.   *Epistolae mixtae ex variis Europae locis ab anno 1537 ad 1556 scriptae*, 5 vols (Madrid, 1898–1901)

FN   *Fontes narrativi di S. Ignatio de Loyola et de Societatis Iesu initiis*, 4 vols (Rome, 1943–65)

Litt. Quad.   *Litterae quadrimestres ex universis praeter Indiam et Brasiliam locis in quibus aliqui de Societate Iesu versabuntur Romam missae*, 7 vols (Madrid and Rome, 1894–1932)

M Bras.   *Monumenta Brasiliae*, 5 vols (Rome, 1956–68)

MI Const.   *Monumenta Ignatiana. Sancti Ignatii de Loyola Constitutiones Societatis Iesu*, 3 vols (Rome, 1934–8)

MI Epp   *Monumenta Ignatiana. Sancti Ignatii de Loyola Societatis Iesu fundatoris epistolae et instructiones*, 12 vols (Madrid, 1903–11)

M Mex.   *Monumenta Mexicana*, 8 vols (Rome, 1956–91)

M Nadal   *Epistolae P. Hieronymi Nadal Societatis Iesu ab anno 1546 ad 1577*, 4 vols (Madrid, 1898–1905)

M Paed.   *Monumenta paedagogica Societatis Iesu*, 2nd ed. rev., 7 vols (Rome, 1965–92)

M Peru.   *Monumenta Peruana*, 8 vols to date (Rome, 1954–)

M Ratio   *Ratio atque Institutio studiorum Societatis Iesu* (1586, 1591, 1599) (Rome, 1986)

Po. Comp.   *Polanci complementa. Epistolae et commentaria P. Ioannis Alphonsi de Polanco*, 2 vols (Madrid, 1916–17)

Other Sources

AHSI	*Archivum Historicum Societatis Iesu*
APUG	Archivio della Pontificia Università Gregoriana, Rome
ARSI	Archivum Romanum Societatis Iesu
BA	Biblioteca Ajuda, Lisbon
Bail. 'Style'	Gauvin Alexander Bailey, '"Le style jésuite n'existe pas": Jesuit Corporate Culture and the Visual Arts,' in O'M. *Jes. Cult.*, pp. 38–89
Bald. *Leg.*	Ugo Baldini, *Legem impone subactis: Studi di filosofia e scienza dei gesuiti in Italia, 1540–1632* (Rome, 1992)
BL	British Library, London
BNL	Biblioteca Nacional, Lisbon
BNM	Biblioteca Nacional, Madrid
BNP	Bibliothèque Nationale, Paris
BNVE	Biblioteca Nazionale Centrale Vittorio Emanuele II, Rome
Fein. *Jes. Sci.*	*Jesuit Science and the Republic of Letters*, ed. Mordechai Feingold (Cambridge, MA, 2003)
Giard *Jés. Ren.*	*Les jésuites à la Renaissance: Système éducatif et production du savoir*, ed. Luce Giard (Paris, 1995)
ISI	*Institutum Societatis Iesu*, 3 vols (Florence, 1892–3)
MEFRIM	*Mélanges de l'Ecole française de Rome: Italie et Méditerranée*
O'M. *First*	John W. O'Malley, *The First Jesuits* (Cambridge, MA, 1993)
O'M. *Jes. Cult.*	*The Jesuits: Cultures, Sciences, and the Arts, 1540–1773*, ed. John W. O'Malley, Gauvin Alexander Bailey, Steven J. Harris, and T. Frank Kennedy (Toronto, Buffalo, London, 1999)
Ponc. *Hist.*	Alfred Poncelet, *Histoire de la Compagnie de Jésus dans les anciens Pays-Bas*, 2 parts (Brussels, 1926)
Rev. syn. 120	*Les jésuites dans le monde moderne. Nouvelles approches, Revue de synthèse* 120:2–3 (April–September 1999)
Rom. *Contre-réf.*	Antonella Romano, *La contre-réforme mathématique: Constitution et diffusion d'une culture mathématique jésuite à la Renaissance (1540–1640)* (Rome, 1999)
Somm. *Bib.*	Carlos Sommervogel et al., *Bibliothèque de la Compagnie de Jésus*, 12 vols (Brussels, Paris, Toulouse, 1890–1932; repr. Louvain, 1960)
Villos. *Coll. Rom.*	Ricardo G. Villoslada, *Storia del Collegio Romano dal suo inizio (1551) alla soppressione della Compagnia di Gesù (1773)*, Analecta Gregoriana 66 (Rome, 1954)

Introduction: The Pastoral, Social, Ecclesiastical, Civic, and Cultural Mission of the Society of Jesus

The foundational document of the Society of Jesus is the papal bull of 27 September 1540, *Regimini militantis ecclesiae*, issued over the signature of Pope Paul III. The bull essentially incorporated into itself a slightly revised version of a document drawn up in the spring of 1539 by the original ten companions of Paris, informally headed by Ignatius of Loyola, to indicate to the papal curia what they hoped for from their new organization and how they planned to achieve it. That document, known as the 'Five Chapters,' might well be called the five (long) paragraphs because it is only about five pages long.

The bull in the revised and somewhat expanded form of *Exposcit debitum*, approved by Pope Julius III on 21 July 1550, remains to this day the licence officially allowing the Jesuits to operate within the Catholic church. It is the charter of the Society, never superseded. As a charter it specifies, among other things, the purposes for which the order was founded and the means it will use to accomplish them. The Jesuits are free to make whatever changes in their *Constitutions* and 'way of proceeding' they deem appropriate, as long as the changes do not run counter to any major provisions of the bull. Should a proposed change run counter to the bull, the Jesuits must, even now, appeal to the Holy See for explicit permission to make the change.

Officially known as the 'Formula of the Institute,' the bull could not be more sacrosanct. It is the equivalent of 'the Rule' in other religious orders. It is the first place to look on the level of official documentation to discover what the Society of Jesus is all about. A brief revisiting of the provisions of the Formula that deal directly with Jesuit ministries will provide, I believe, a helpful framing for what follows in our volume.[1] For the readers' convenience I have appended to this introduction the text of those provisions, with indications in boldface type of changes introduced in 1540 and 1550 into this section of the 'Five Chapters.' It might be helpful to take a glance at that appendix before reading further.

The bull faithfully reproduced the purpose the ten founders set forth in the 'Chapters.' The new order was to be 'a Society founded chiefly for this purpose: to strive especially for the progress of souls in Christian life and doctrine and for the propagation of the faith.' The purpose seems generic and bland, but it deserves some explanation. 'Christian life and doctrine' can best be read as 'Christian life and Christian Doctrine,' so as to make clear that doctrine here refers to Christian Doctrine in the sense of basic truths to be lived and practised. In the sixteenth century Christian Doctrine was a synonym for catechism. 'Christian doctrine' in the Formula, therefore, is not an allusion to the advanced education in philosophy and theology the companions received at Paris; it does not presage the Jesuits' later formal cultivation of those disciplines in a number of different forms; far less is it a manifesto of orthodoxy in a Reformation context.

It implies, rather, a practice-related context. It points to a directly pastoral concern, the imparting of basic teachings as a means of spiritual progress. It is therefore intimately related to 'Christian life' because catechism, whether done by preaching, lecturing, or some other means, was conceived as an introduction to Christian living, to the ordinary obligations incumbent upon every believer, even the humblest. This meant teaching prayers, especially the Lord's Prayer. It meant teaching the Decalogue, especially as preparation for confession. It meant teaching the Apostles' Creed, usually in the form of stories about the life of Jesus. It meant, almost invariably, teaching the seven spiritual and corporal works of mercy as the expressions of what it meant to live as a Christian. 'Christian life and doctrine' meant precisely what John Van Engen has so helpfully encapsulated with the term *Christianitas* – basic beliefs and practices shared by Christians of all social classes.[2]

The second purpose was 'propagation of the faith.' Today we can hardly speak of Christianity without using the word mission, yet in the sixteenth century mission was just coming into usage in its contemporary sense of evangelization of people not yet Christian.[3] The emergence of this usage coincided with the founding of the Society, and the word in fact occurs, somewhat precociously, in other places in the Formula. The Jesuits in relatively short order would be largely responsible for its gaining currency and gradually replacing the older term, even though as late as 1622 the Roman congregation founded to deal with the overseas missions of the Catholic church was called the Congregation for the Propagation of the Faith (*De propaganda fide*).

In 1540, surely, 'propagation of the faith' (or 'journeying to the infidel') was still the technical term for the enterprise, so we should not be surprised that the companions used it here to express the fundamental missionary character of the order they were founding. They had originally banded together, after all, to travel to Palestine as 'missionaries,' even though the term missionary did not yet exist. As a result of their deliberations in 1539, they specified farther on in the Formula that they wanted to be bound by a special vow to obey the pope 'for missions,' *circa missiones.*

In their vocabulary, as time went on, 'missions' became for a while an almost distinctively Jesuit word. It recurs frequently, for instance, in Part VII of the *Constitutions*, entitled 'The Distribution of Members in the Vineyard of the Lord.' Besides pointing to overseas evangelization, the word points to the basically itinerant style of ministry the companions envisaged for themselves. Indeed, the section of Part VII dealing with missions received from the pope in fulfilment of the special vow implies that these missions would generally be of short duration, about three months. The members of the order originally saw themselves as most characteristically being on the road, with lots of comings and goings.[4]

Instead of simply 'the propagation of the faith,' the Formula was modified in the 1550 version to read 'the defense and propagation of the faith.' As has often been noted, the addition of 'defense' took account of the growing awareness among the Jesuits of the role they more and more felt called upon to assume in confrontation with Protestantism. Although the Society was not founded to confute the Reformation, as so often asserted, it soon began to take up that cause, and in certain parts of Europe, especially in Germany and England, it would become identified almost exclusively as an anti-Protestant force. In other parts of the world, such as Latin America and Asia, the Reformation entered relatively little into the Jesuits' self-understanding and practice. Unlike the other modifications *Exposcit debitum* made in the original bull and in the 'Five Chapters,' this one was not an elaboration or specification of something already present but was something new – which points to the obvious fact that the Society was an ongoing enterprise that did not assume its full identity in 1540.

The 'defense of the faith,' which in the sixteenth century often came down to defences of papal primacy, does relate to the opening statement of the 'Five Chapters,' which immediately precedes the section we have been discussing: 'Whoever wishes to serve as a soldier of God beneath the banner of the cross in our Society, which we desire to be designated by the name of Jesus, and to serve the Lord alone and his vicar on earth, should, after a solemn vow of perpetual chastity, keep what follows in mind. He is a member ...' The bull of 1540 almost verbatim repeats this mention of the pope, but the 1550 bull modifies it with mention of the church itself: '... to serve the Lord alone and the church, his spouse, under the Roman pontiff, the vicar of Christ on earth ...'

'Soldier of God' suggests the stereotype of the Jesuit as a militant, a stereotype suggested even by the title of the bull – '*militantis ecclesiae.*' Many Jesuits subsequently appropriated military imagery to describe themselves and the mode of the Society. But in the foundational documents such imagery is much less prevalent than, for instance, in the early writings of Erasmus, that great enemy of militant Christianity. It was traditional religious language. As Antonio de Aldama reminded us, moreover, in his authoritative commentary on the Formula, '"To serve as a soldier of God" (*militare Deo*) is a medieval expression meaning religious life. In the prologue to his Rule, St. Benedict addresses the novice who is "about to join battle for Christ the true King."' De Aldama goes on to suggest that in the words 'under the banner of the cross' we hear an echo of the Meditation on Two Standards in the *Spiritual Exercises*.[5]

'To serve ... his vicar on earth' indicates a connection with the papacy that is, for example, much less prominent even in the Rule of St Francis and completely absent in the Rule of St Benedict. In the 'Chapters,' however, I think the mention of the pope must be related to the pope's pastoral role, as the companions understood it, that is, the role they hoped to see him play in sending them on mission. It should not be understood in the context of Reformation controversies about the papacy and, hence, as a soft way of indicating an obligation to 'defend' the institution.

In 1550 the wording was changed, as noted earlier, to read 'to serve the church ... under the Roman pontiff, the vicar of Christ on earth.' In this shift the connection of papacy with the vow to be missionaries seems less operative, and with the appearance of the word 'church' the Jesuits imply a greater awareness of their role in the larger ecclesiastical scene. They now were explicitly claiming for themselves an ecclesiastical mission. They did so, however, according to their own 'way of proceeding.' They refused, for instance, to assume any office in the hierarchical structure, and they refused to undertake the staffing of parishes, the ecclesiastical unit under the supervision of a bishop. It is instructive to note, moreover, that in Ignatius's huge correspondence of over seven thousand letters – the largest extant collection of any sixteenth-century figure – the expression 'to serve the church' never occurs. What appears on almost every page is, instead, 'the help of souls.'

I call attention to the two adverbs in the Formula's description of purpose – 'chiefly' (*potissimum*) and 'especially' (*praecipue*). They occur in the 'Five Chapters' and are repeated in the two papal bulls. They are qualifiers, and therefore leave the door slightly ajar. I see in them an anticipation of a characteristic of Jesuit 'way of proceeding' and style that finds consistent expression in the *Constitutions*. Almost every provision in that remarkable document is accompanied by qualifications. Such and such is to be done, 'unless something else seems better in the circumstances.' It is, thus, a document filled with escape-clauses.[6] The same can be said of the directives Ignatius offered to individual

Jesuits in his correspondence. As John Bossy observed many years ago, 'Few religious superiors can have told members of their order so firmly to forget the rules and do what they thought best.'[7]

Flexibility and adjustment to circumstances were thus inculcated from the very beginning. They were principles explicit in the text of the *Spiritual Exercises* regarding the way in which individuals were to be guided in them. The Jesuits were surely not the only group in the sixteenth century to advocate and practise flexibility in their endeavours. Indeed, flexibility was a quality commended by the humanistic tradition for persons in authority. There can be no doubt, however, that it was notably present in the Jesuit ethos even though sometimes in tension with countervailing tendencies.

By what means did the first Jesuits intend to further their goal of progress of souls in Christian life and doctrine and the propagation of the faith? In the 'Five Chapters' they succinctly listed ministry of the Word, Spiritual Exercises, works of charity, and, 'specifically,' the teaching of catechism to 'children and unlettered persons.' The bull *Regimini* echoed this list but with the addition of striving for 'the spiritual consolation of Christ's faithful through the hearing of confessions,' a sacramental dimension missing in the original draft. The subsequent bull, *Exposcit*, expanded that last provision to include 'the administration of other sacraments' and then indicated further works of charity, beyond teaching catechism, that had emerged in the ensuing decade as noteworthy – 'reconciling the estranged ... devoutly assisting and serving those ... found in prisons or hospitals, and indeed performing any other works of charity, according to what will seem expedient for the glory of God and the common good.'

The primacy the first Jesuits assigned to 'ministries of the Word,' as well as its correlate, the hearing of confessions, indicates how neatly in that regard they fit into the pattern of ministry set by the great mendicant orders of the Middle Ages, especially the Dominicans and Franciscans. The list begins to diverge from the pattern with the mention of the *Exercises*, a form of ministry created by Ignatius with no precedent in the other orders. That ministry invited people to an inward journey and provided various road maps for making it, including in its most elaborate form a withdrawal for a month from the distractions of life. Although the practice of retiring from one's ordinary circumstances for reflection and meditation is older than Christianity itself, the *Exercises* was the first book to organize and codify procedures in a practical, organized, yet flexible way. In effect, it created a new ministry in Christianity, the spiritual 'retreat,' and the promotion of that ministry helped contribute to the Jesuits' self-definition and style.

What the Jesuits meant by 'works of charity' was the seven spiritual and seven corporal works of mercy, which were in large part elaborated out of the famous Last Judgment scenario in Matthew 25. One of the spiritual works was 'teaching the ignorant.' The first 'work of charity' the Jesuits specified for themselves was precisely that, 'the education of children and unlettered persons in Christianity,' the teaching of catechism, that is, Christian Doctrine, which sends us back to the statement of purpose, 'the progress of souls in Christian life and doctrine.' There is therefore circularity and considerable cohesion in these few lines of the Formula. The original grounding of the Society in simple catechesis helps explain how later, for all the Jesuits who moved in high circles, many others continued to be engaged with more humble folk in more humble pastoral enterprises. In the version of 1550, two further specifications of works of charity were added, in recognition of activities in which members had been particularly prominent in the Society's first decade: reconciling the estranged ('peace-making') and serving prisoners in jail and the sick in hospitals.

The section of the Formula we have been considering clearly established the fundamentally pastoral and missionary character of the order. As I indicated, broadly speaking the Jesuits in that regard would be doing what the Dominicans and Franciscans were doing. These two orders were active in the mission fields, for instance, long before the Jesuits arrived on the scene. But, as I also indicated, a significant difference in pastoral activity was the giving of the Exercises. Another, less obvious, was the explicit articulation of the pastoral and mission-ary character, the more explicit intentionality. The difference points to the character of the founders, to the kind of training they had received, and thus to a different cultural context. It thereby hints at further traits that would become part of the Jesuits' 'way of proceeding,' their style. The style would favour a reflec-tive and fully articulated approach to problems and their resolutions.

There was still another difference. The Formula established a commitment to works of social assistance of various kinds. In 1540, the year of the founding, Ignatius was instrumental in the creation of an orphanage in Rome and shortly thereafter of the Casa Santa Marta, a refuge for prostitutes who wanted to put their situation behind them. Although the mendicants, as well as the monks, engaged in various works of charity, for charity was intrinsic to being Christian, peculiar to the Jesuits was the explicit articulation of it as an essential element of what they were about. They were not only preachers of the Word and administra-tors of the sacraments, they were also, and professedly, agents engaged in the construction of institutions of social assistance. This commitment from the very earliest years would lead them into varied and intense relationships with confraternities, the institutions that by the sixteenth century undertook most of the ongoing commitments to the poor, the sick, and other groups on the margins of society such as prostitutes.

In the 1550 version the list of ministries ends by commending anything that contributes to 'the common good.' Up to that point the vocabulary of the section of the Formula we have been considering has been directly or indirectly derived from the Bible or from traditional Christian usage. 'Common good' derives not from those sources but from philosophy. It appears for the first time in 1550, after ten years of experience and after Juan Alfonso de Polanco became Ignatius's confidant and aide in formulating the official documents of the Society. The expression implies an openness regarding what might be included in the future in 'works of charity.' More important, it suggests, I believe, a concern for this world and its betterment, a shift away from strictly evangelical goals – the common good. The older orders doubtless had this concern and expressed it in various ways, as their histories make clear, but the up-front commitment to it in the Formula is what deserves our attention.

I mention Polanco because I believe he would be more likely to think in philosophical terms than Ignatius, and also because of the letter he wrote to Antonio de Araoz in Ignatius's name on 1 December 1551.[8] That is just a year after the publication of the revised version of the Formula, in the wording of which he played an important role. In the letter Polanco proffers fifteen goals the Society hopes to achieve through its schools. The last six are various benefits for the cities or towns in which the schools are located, and the penultimate one reads as follows: 'Jesuits will encourage and help in the establishment of hospitals, houses of *convertidas* [prostitutes seeking to change their lives], and similar institutions.' In the mind of Ignatius and the others, therefore, there was a correlation between the schools and works of social assistance, with a clear awareness of benefits for the city.

The last reason is even more comprehensive in that regard: 'Those who are now only students will grow up to be pastors, civic officials, administrators of justice, and will fill other important posts to everybody's profit and advantage.' That goal could have been written by Erasmus, Pierpaolo Vergerio the Elder, or any of the other theorists about the program of studies promoted by Renaissance humanists. The achievement of that goal is precisely what the humanists promised by their educational program. That fifteenth reason shows how profoundly the early Jesuits had appropriated the literature on the subject, and how easily they correlated it with the evolving mission of the Society.

I say 'evolving mission' because, like all social realities, the Society would continue to change in a number of ways. There was one change, however, that was of absolutely primary importance and that was already under way in 1550, when *Exposcit debitum* was published. It was the momentous impact on the Society of the decision to undertake schooling as a formal ministry, a decision first grounded in the opening of the *collegio* in Messina in 1548. The decision in very short order affected almost every aspect of the Jesuits' self-understanding up to that moment, and gave the Society an enlargement of its purpose or mission that was at best only potential at the beginning. In 1550 this change, though under way, was still too inchoate to make its way into *Exposcit debitum*.

At this point, therefore, we must abandon the Formula. Absolutely crucial though the Formula is for understanding the foundations of the Society, it fails to mention the ministry that would come almost to define the Society, and that in ways big and small had a transforming effect on all the other ministries and on almost every aspect of Jesuit procedure. With slight qualification, the *Constitutions* suffer the same major defect. They were composed at approximately the same time as the Formula of 1550 and were never adequately revised regarding the schools before their official approbation by the First General Congregation, 1558, two years after the death of Ignatius. This is a dramatic instance of how limited and misleading official and normative documentation can be for understanding a social reality. As the Jesuits had recourse to the Formula, they would get no guidance for the role the Society had in fact assumed as 'the first teaching order in the Catholic church,' and they would do only slightly better with the *Constitutions*.

In the correspondence from the Jesuit curia even during the lifetime of Ignatius, it is clear how massive the commitment to 'the colleges' had become in just a few years, but the correspondence would not be readily available to scholars or Jesuit superiors until its publication in the twentieth century. The very momentum of the commitment carried the enterprise forward without much questioning, at least at the beginning, as to whether running schools was an authentic pursuit for Jesuits. But the evangelical vocabulary of the Formula does not seem easily reconcilable with teaching horsemanship or with writing books on rhetoric or, for sure, on dance!

What we have here is a radical redefinition that was never fully articulated in official documentation and at best was only suggested in most other writings by Jesuits. What did that redefinition entail? In the first and most obvious way it entailed a shift from the Jesuits' being essentially a group of itinerant preachers and missionaries to their becoming resident schoolmasters. For the schools, moreover, the Jesuits acquired huge properties. Despite their almost Franciscan avoidance of money transactions in the beginning, they became, in order to sustain the schools, 'the first professional fundraisers,' as Olwen Hufton argues in this volume. More profoundly, they initiated for themselves a new relationship to learning and the arts in the wake of their commitment especially to the humanistic program.

What kind of schools were these schoolmasters operating, therefore, and for whom? Although some of the schools had the full course of studies eventually prescribed in the *Ratio studiorum*, 1599, which culminated in the 'higher disci-

plines' of philosophy and theology, they all taught the 'lower disciplines' of the humanistic program – grammar, rhetoric, history, drama, and so forth. They taught the program not as a preparation for theology, the traditional clerical rationale, but as a program complete in itself, with its own proper goals, that would provide laymen with the learning and skills they needed to make their way in this world. And to make their way so as to be a help to others and a benefit to the communities in which they lived. That at least was the ideal.

I believe that up to now we have not taken seriously enough how this reality entailed a redefinition of what the order was really about. Or, perhaps better, how it entailed a significant enlargement and enrichment of the mission of the order. The religious mission remained fundamental, and the other missions had to be integrated into it and even subordinated to it. As an ideal this mission remained steady through the centuries. But because of the schools the Jesuits had a commitment to culture, to urbanity, to *civiltà*, to *conversazione*, and to the *honneste homme* in the world that was new for a religious order. That commitment is one of the great themes to emerge clearly in our two volumes dealing with the Jesuits' relationship to 'cultures, sciences, and the arts.'

We still tend to look upon the Jesuit schools as church schools, as confessional schools, even as Counter-Reformation schools. That indeed they were. But what happens if we turn the picture around to look upon them as civic institutions – usually requested by the city, in some form paid for by the city, established to serve the families of the city, which service entailed listening to the expectations of those families and, when feasible, making adjustments to accommodate them? They were often the leading cultural institution, especially in the smaller cities and towns. They provided library resources in an age before public libraries, and they provided public entertainment. As especially Judi Loach and Giovanna Zanlonghi show in this volume, the cultural mission sometimes burst the walls of the classroom to effect an even more pronounced civic presence. Coordinated with this social reality, moreover, was the educational theory of the *studia humanitatis*, affirming that those *studia* were the apt instrument for producing men dedicated to the public weal, to 'the common good.'

It was this commitment to the *studia humanitatis* that distinguished the Jesuits culturally from the mendicant orders. Those orders, too, as their various programs of study unmistakably reveal, had serious commitment to 'learned ministry,' as grounded in the institutions of learning they established for their own members. But these orders were founded before the Renaissance, and their programs were already fixed before the humanists' propaganda had reintroduced the *studia* in an organized and self-conscious way into the Western world. The *studia* were not part of the *system* of the Dominicans and Franciscans, though individual Dominicans or Franciscans might be proficient in them. But they were part of the Jesuit *system*, the first studies every member of the order undertook and the subjects that almost every member taught *professionally* at some stage of his career. The Jesuit commitment to the *studia* was thorough and systemic.

There had to be repercussions. A text that every Jesuit was familiar with and that many of them taught year after year was Cicero's *De officiis* – 'On Duties,' which I translate as 'On Public Responsibility.' Here is a well-known passage: 'We are not born for ourselves alone ... Everything that the earth produces is created for our use, and we, too, as human beings are born for the sake of other human beings that we might be able mutually to help one another; we ought therefore to take Nature as our guide and contribute to the common good of humankind by reciprocal acts of kindness, by giving and receiving from one another, and thus by our skill, our industry and our talents work to bring human society together in peace and harmony' (I.7.22; my translation).

Jesuits, I opine, would easily have correlated this passage with the section opening the *Spiritual Exercises* entitled 'Principle and Foundation,' which affirms that we were created for the praise, reverence, and service of God. In the Christian context, that praise, reverence, and service, the Jesuits knew well, could not be divorced from concern for one's neighbour. Yet the passage from Cicero is directed to the betterment of this world rather than to one's eternal salvation. I suggest that the Jesuits saw this text as an amplification of the message of the 'Principle and Foundation' rather than as a contradiction of it. As an amplification, it gave the 'Principle and Foundation' an important new modality. It is not insignificant that the term 'common good' occurs in it.

We must remember, these 'pagan' texts were taught not simply as models of style but as sources of ethical inspiration. If Erasmus could invoke 'St Socrates,' I think some Jesuits, if they let themselves go, could have invoked 'St Cicero.'[9] I do not know of any who did, but Cornelius à Lapide, the Jesuit exegete, said of a passage from Epictetus, 'O wonder, these words ring of the gospel, not just moral philosophy.'[10]

The tradition of character-formation for the good of the city goes back all the way to Isocrates and is at the heart of the *paideia* that the Renaissance humanists worked so hard – and, ultimately, so successfully – to revive. I find it almost impossible to believe that teaching, day after day and year after year, the classical authors such as Cicero who inculcated this ideal did not have an impact on the Jesuits' sense of the mission of the Society and thus on their sense even of their own vocations. Did this not give them an anchor in this world and a concern for it that, for their times and particularly in the early years, was special for clerics? Partly as a result of our two conferences I have been moving towards an affirmative answer.

In making this point I am not trying to exalt the quantity and quality of the Jesuits' civic and cultural accomplishments in comparison with those of other religious orders. The cultural benefits the Benedictines have conferred upon Western civilization are incalculable. The Jesuits produced no artist of the calibre of the Dominicans' Fra Angelico. For all the importance of the Gesù in Rome, the church never had the civic significance of the Franciscans' Santa Croce in Florence. I am not, therefore, trying to say that the Jesuits did more or did it better.

I am saying, rather, that with the Jesuits their civic and cultural accomplishments assumed a new mode and were undertaken with a new rationale and a more explicit intentionality. I am saying that with the schools the Jesuits produced civic and cultural institutions that were new for a religious order and that had a more professedly this-worldly orientation in large measure because they sprang out of persuasions originating in the classical world, not the Christian world, even though they were now revived for the Christian world. I am saying that the mode of Jesuit engagement with culture in a civic context was different in that it was centred in humanistic schools. This meant that most Jesuits spent most of their day in a secular space, not in the pulpit or the cloister. This meant that they taught secular subjects – indeed, *pagan* literature, as well as mathematics, physics, and astronomy, sometimes botany and natural history. This meant that they taught secular students, not clerics or members of religious orders. This meant that, especially in teaching the classical dramatists, they were drawn into music and dance in ways new for clergy. 'Ecco, i preti delle commedie!'[11] This meant that by such engagement with 'the sciences and the arts' they shocked most notably the Jansenists, with some of the dire consequences Marc Fumaroli indicates below.

If I am correct in assigning to the Society a cultural and civic mission, it means we must re-examine that most sensitive and telling aspect of the Jesuits' reality, their spirituality. At its deepest level, Jesuit spirituality derived from the *Spiritual Exercises*. As a spiritual classic, the *Exercises* is a plastic text, open to a range of interpretations, including the highly moralizing interpretations of the nineteenth and early twentieth centuries. There can be little doubt, however, that the concluding meditation on the love of God promotes a positive appreciation of all created reality. It is a longer version of St Ignatius's exhortation to Jesuits in the *Constitutions* to 'find God in all things' (no. 288). Ignatius further exhorts them not to be afraid in their ministries to make use of 'natural' means as well as 'supernatural' (no. 814). Jesuit spirituality, as has often been remarked, has a decidedly activist, even this-worldly cast to it.

I believe that this cast provided a potential that contact with the humanistic tradition activated in a cultural and civic direction. The tradition was mediated to

Ignatius in the early years by Polanco and by Jerónimo Nadal, but it then worked its way into the very fabric of Jesuit consciousness by the sheer repetition year after year of the teaching of classical texts about civic virtue in institutions geared to the welfare of the city and its citizens.

I propose that we can begin to speak of Jesuit spirituality as a civic and culturally aware spirituality. Or we can at least say that in many Jesuits their spirituality had a civic and culturally aware dimension. This was a dimension that for the most part was more implicit than explicit. It would be manifested much more by actions than by words, by what we can infer than by what we can directly verify. This dimension, almost negated by the normative documents, can be retrieved only by the kinds of studies contained in our two volumes, studies representative of the exciting turn taken in Jesuit historiography in the past ten or fifteen years, studies that have moved away from the normative to the actual. This dimension was, moreover, too much contrary to the conventions of writing and thinking about 'spirituality' to be conceivable until we had a more capacious understanding of what spirituality might mean even in a religious-ecclesiastical context.

If by spirituality we mean something like the deep wellsprings of our motivation and the impulses within us that prompt us to make certain decisions and not others, especially as the decisions express dedication and self-transcendence, then we are here dealing with a reality absolutely critical for understanding Jesuit style, critical for understanding the Jesuit 'way of proceeding.' We are dealing with a reality altogether critical for understanding the Jesuits' relationships to 'cultures, sciences, and the arts,' and hence for understanding in their fullness the studies contained in this volume.

John W. O'Malley, S.J

APPENDIX: THE PURPOSES AND MINISTRIES OF THE SOCIETY OF JESUS ACCORDING TO THE OFFICIAL DOCUMENTS, 1539–50

I. The Five Chapters, 1539

'Whoever desires to serve as a soldier of God
   beneath the banner of the cross in our Society,
   which we desire to be designated by the name of Jesus,
and to serve the Lord alone and his vicar on earth,
should, after a solemn vow of perpetual chastity, keep what follows in mind.
He is a member of a Society founded chiefly for this purpose:
   to strive especially

for the progress of souls in Christian life and doctrine and
for the propagation of the faith
- – by ministry of the word,
- – by Spiritual Exercises
- – by works of charity, and specifically
- – by the education of children and unlettered persons in Christianity.'

II. The Formula of the Institute, 1540, *Regimini militantis ecclesiae*

'Whoever desires to serve as a soldier of God
beneath the banner of the cross in our Society,
which we desire to be designated by the name of Jesus,
and to serve the Lord alone and **the Roman pontiff**, his vicar on earth,
should, after a solemn vow of perpetual chastity, keep what follows in mind.
He is a member of a Society founded chiefly for this purpose:
to strive especially
for the progress of souls in Christian life and doctrine and
for the propagation of the faith
- – by **public preachings** and ministry of the word **of God**
- – by Spiritual Exercises
- – by works of charity, and specifically
- – by the education of children and unlettered persons in Christianity
- – **and particularly by the spiritual consolation of Christ's faithful through the hearing of confessions.**'

III. The Formula of the Institute, 1550, *Exposcit debitum*

'Whoever desires to serve as a soldier of God
beneath the banner of the cross in our Society,
which we desire to be designated by the name of Jesus,
and to serve the Lord alone and the **church**, **his spouse**,
under the Roman pontiff, the vicar **of Christ on earth**,
should, after a solemn vow of perpetual chastity, **poverty**, **and obedience**,
keep what follows in mind.
He is a member of a Society founded chiefly for this purpose:
to strive especially
for the **defense and** propagation of the faith and
for the progress of souls in Christian life and doctrine,
- – by public preachings, **lectures**, and **any other ministries whatsoever** of the word of God, and further

– by Spiritual Exercises, and
– by the education of children and unlettered persons in Christianity,
– and particularly by the spiritual consolation of Christ's faithful through the hearing of confessions and
– **by the administration of other sacraments.**
Moreover, this Society should show itself no less useful
  – **in reconciling the estranged**
  – **in devoutly assisting and serving those who are found in prisons or hospitals, and indeed**
  – **in performing any other works of charity, according to what will seem expedient for the glory of God and the common good.'**

NOTES

1 See Antonio M. de Aldama, *The Formula of the Institute: Notes for a Commentary*, trans. Ignacio Echániz (St Louis, 1990).

2 See John Van Engen, 'The Christian Middle Ages as an Historiographical Problem,' *American Historical Review* 91 (1986): 519–52.

3 See John W. O'Malley, 'Mission and the Early Jesuits,' *The Way, Supplement 79* (Spring 1994): 3–10.

4 See Mario Scaduto, 'La strada e i primi gesuiti,' *AHSI* 40 (1971): 335–90, now available in an abridged translation, 'The Early Jesuits and the Road,' *The Way* 42 (2003): 71–84.

5 De Aldama, *Formula*, p. 38.

6 The best recent study, which is essentially a study of the language and rhetoric of the *Constitutions*, is J. Carlos Coupeau, 'Beginning, Middle, and End: A Rhetorical Study of the *Constitutions of the Society of Jesus* as a Classic of Spirituality,' dissertation, Weston Jesuit School of Theology, 2001.

7 John Bossy, 'Postscript' to H. Outram Evennett, *The Spirit of the Counter-Reformation*, ed. Bossy (Cambridge, 1968), p. 130.

8 *MI Epp* 4:5–9.

9 Erasmus, *Convivium religiosum* ('The Godly Feast'), in *Opera omnia*, vol. 1/3 (Amsterdam, 1972), p. 254.

10 Quoted in François de Dainville, *La naissance de l'humanisme moderne* (Paris, 1940), p. 223.

11 See O'M. *First*, p. 224.

PART ONE

The Society in Society

For all the research on the Jesuits, there are important or at least curious aspects of their activity that have received relatively little attention but reveal some of their most interesting relationships to the milieus in which they lived and moved. Scholars in the past decade have turned their eyes in new ways to the Jesuit schools as cultural institutions. They have now begun to ask perhaps the most obvious and fundamental question: How were these institutions, some of them of great size and complexity, funded? Olwen Hufton here addresses that question and in so doing addresses the seemingly perennial issue of the 'modernity' of the Society, arguing that the Jesuits were the first of that profession we are today all too familiar with, that of the fundraiser.

In his revealing study of Jesuits as translators, Peter Burke comes close to a similar conclusion about the modernity of the Society by seeing much of the Jesuits' work as translators as a program of self-promotion for the Society, another feature of modern life with which we are very familiar today. But his study goes much deeper, showing how diligent at least a small corps of Jesuits were in introducing books written for one culture into another, engaging to some extent in what is currently known as 'cultural translation.' While such activity manifests once again the radically international ethos and sensibility of the order, it also points, somewhat paradoxically, to the grounding the Jesuits often had in the local scene and their concern for it. As Burke indicates, translations into the local vernaculars had a big impact on the development of those vernaculars, especially in East-Central Europe, where the Jesuits were especially influential in that process.

The Jesuits were the only large religious order of men not to have a women's branch, an early and adamant decision of St Ignatius. Scholars have begun to study the implications of that decision, sometimes taking as their point of departure the first and still most fundamental work on Ignatius's relationship to women, Hugo Rahner's *Saint Ignatius Loyola: Letters to Women* (Freiburg im Breisgau, 1960). As Elizabeth Rhodes here argues, from the beginning women found something that attracted them to the Society that seems to go beyond the personality of individual Jesuits whom they knew. Rhodes makes the point that it was the very masculinity of Jesuit spirituality, as codified in part in Ignatius's *Spiritual Exercises*, that drew them to the Society, for on some level they realized that, as they applied it to themselves, it moved them to a more active and dynamic role than society seemed to prescribe for them. She tellingly illustrates this point, for instance, with the story of Luisa de Carvajal y Mendoza, a self-appointed missionary to Protestant England at the turn of the seventeenth century. Aspects of women's relationship to the Society are taken up again in Part Five by Haruko Nawata Ward and in Part Six by Alicia Fraschina.

One of the special features of this second volume, as we indicated in the preface, is the attention we give in Part Six to that still unwritten history of the suppression of the Society. Many factors led up to the traumatic event, but certainly among them was the diffusion and long life of a work published a century and a half before 1773, the *Monita secreta Societatis Jesu*. This book, the magna carta of anti-Jesuit propaganda, purported to be secret instructions from the superior general of the order informing Jesuits how they were to fleece widows, work their way into the secret counsels of princes in order to advance the nefarious purposes of the Society, and do other crafty deeds. Often refuted as a crude forgery, the book shows through its publication history that it had enough verisimilitude to tap into the fears of at least certain segments of society. Despite its importance, it had never been systematically studied until Sabina Pavone recently turned her attention to it. She provides below an overview of her research on this book, which was still being published, and presumably given credence, in the late twentieth century.

Just as the Jesuits did not have a women's branch, so they did not have a 'third order' for laypersons as did older orders such as the Dominicans and Franciscans. They did have, however, their 'Marian congregations,' which functioned in largely the same way. These congregations were essentially a Jesuit adaptation of the late-medieval confraternity and, as recent scholarship has begun to show, one of the strongest ways in which the Society of Jesus reached out to affect the society in which it functioned, especially through forms of social assistance to the poor. Judi Loach here presents a striking instance, however, of a Jesuit using a congregation as a form of 'adult education' to effect what amounts to upward social mobility.

The Jesuits and the culture of the seventeenth century is the subject Peter Davidson explores in 'The Jesuit Garden' – the garden as garden, a particularly seventeenth-century fascination, the garden as a bed for exotic and newly discovered plants, the garden as expression of the symbolic mode of discourse so characteristic of that century. Davidson's article is a fitting conclusion to this section on the Society of Jesus in society, for it suggests the harmony and good order the Jesuits saw as an ideal for society that perhaps in some measure could be achieved.

1 / Every Tub on Its Own Bottom: Funding a Jesuit College in Early Modern Europe

OLWEN HUFTON

The history of the Jesuits, as the contents of this volume demonstrate, can be written in many ways, its infinite diversity contained within no single traditional subcategory of the discipline. My involvement with the Jesuits developed in the course of an ambitious research project concerned to explore the funding behind early modern Catholic social reform initiatives. That is to say, charitable, educational, and welfare concerns designed to transform, to ameliorate in every possible sense, and to discipline society. This exploration was conducted not merely as an exercise in social or economic history but as one that pursued cultural values and constraints. The approach of the Jesuits to their major educational enterprise entailed major debates and generated self-questioning as well as an exceptionally rich and varied documentation. What follows is an attempt to make some very broad working generalizations, ones open to infinite expansion and modification, about Jesuit college funding, with particular emphasis on the comparative experience of Italy, France, Spain, and the Southern Netherlands.[1] Such an exercise involves a consideration not merely of where the money came from, the question of donors or concessions made by local and national rulers, the nature, in short, of the endowment, but also of the potential and limitations of particular types of funding and the reasons for mounting debt. In particular, I shall seek to locate an understanding of the funding of colleges in the fiscal, political, intellectual or cultural, and dynastic and family history of the period 1500–1760. In so doing, I shall explore the solidity or frailty of resources by reference to the broader social and economic climate of early modern Europe.

John W. O'Malley in his landmark *The First Jesuits* remarked very pertinently that the educational mission was not the only Jesuit mission.[2] It is indeed true that a Jesuit had to preach as well as teach and to reach out to the newly colonized pagan world across the seas. However, the educational aspect of Jesuit activity could be called the mother of missions since it was intended to produce manpower, both for the order and outside it, as part of the grand design to transform secular society through the education of the young. In 'De collegiis fundandis' the first purpose, deemed to be the immediate concern, was prioritized:

Because the Company's aim and goal is travelling to various parts of the world at the commands of the vicar of Christ our Saviour, to preach, hear confessions, and show to children and other unschooled persons the commandments, mortal sins, and other foundations of our holy Catholic faith, it seemed to us convenient and indeed necessary that those who enter [the Society] be persons of good morals and some sufficiency in letters. And because people both good and lettered are few in comparison with the rest, and of the few there are those who want to rest from their past labours, most having benefices ... or important offices or other sources of livelihood ... we find it very difficult to increase the Company by such lettered persons, even good and learned, both because of the greater labour necessary in it [the Society] and because of the ... travelling even to the end of the world ... therefore it seemed to us all, desiring the conservation and augmentation of it [the Society] that we take another path, that is, of colleges.[3]

But this relatively restricted and arguably inward-turning goal by 1546 had been overtaken by the broader appeal to the second concern, the general education of youth. The early fathers of the Society of Jesus were to become the first systematized and urgent protagonists of the principle that an entire civil society is the product of its educational system, and that tomorrow's world depends on the intellectual and social development acquired in youth. Legatees of the humanist tradition conspicuous in the work of Erasmus of Rotterdam,[4] themselves honed in the Sorbonne and impressed by the rigorous intellectual training they received there, the Jesuits sought to improve the moral and intellectual formation of youth by encouraging the development of self-discipline and self-confidence. Their goal would be achieved through the structured study of the classics, the humanities, and rhetoric – the art of persuasion. This was not the full extent of the curriculum content, since development occurred, but it formed the core of the grand design. A third concern related to the college was its large building, planted conspicuously in the urban landscape, where it would stand as a powerful and substantial marker of a collusion of interests between secular and ecclesiastical powers.

Important for my particular story, the creation of colleges was the only aspect of Jesuit life for the sake of which members of the Society had authority to depart from their mendicant commitment to poverty and to raise money and make it work, own property, and build up endowment income. The process of doing this transformed the individuals forming the Society from mendicants to money raisers and managers, a conspicuous metamorphosis and one that involved a difficult learning process not completed overnight. Not all members of the Society were comfortable with the process or its implications for their life mission.[5] No Jesuit I have encountered in the records joined the order to keep the books. But having committed themselves to this work, they began to learn on their feet the discreet and less than discreet art of finding money and, having acquired it, of making it work.

The result was the creation of the biggest network of private schools Europe has known, with something in the order of five to six hundred distributed across the Continent, though most thickly in certain regions of France, the Southern Netherlands, and Italy. In Central Europe the number of schools was smaller, as indeed was the population. Moreover, these areas were theatres of war between peoples and armies of different confessions.

Even where the schools were apparently well established, their number and that of their pupils was slightly flagging in some countries by the late seventeenth century.[6] This shrinkage reflects, perhaps, as well as a reduction owing to war, something of a decline in the popularity of the collegiate model. The decline was visible in both Jesuit and Oratorian colleges (notoriously Jansenist) and thereby suggests that the struggles between Jansenists and Jesuits did not reinforce the one at the expense of the other. By that date as well, the number of teaching orders had proliferated. The didactic strategies of many of the newer orders (Piarists, Salesians, etc.) often reflected some Jesuit influence on method of teaching and structured content of learning, but these orders' schools operated on a more modest scale and were cheaper for civil authorities to fund. The Jesuit schools remained the biggest, however,[7] and the suppression of the order could not obliterate the mark they made on subsequent schooling models – not least on the laicized French *lycée* (in terms of size and approach to learning by memory). Our point of departure must be that we are looking at a huge success story, even if one pitted with frequent financial problems that were everywhere slightly different and everywhere somewhat the same. Every college tells a story, but the plot has common themes, and among these money and debt loom very conspicuously.

A basic principle informing the educational mission was that Jesuit education was to be offered free to the consumer: the Jesuits thus cut off an obvious source of revenue. Education had to be paid for, however, and the enterprise, given its scale and intensity, was not to be cheap. It is probable that the early fathers had absolutely no idea of what it might cost. They knew, however, that money would have to be courted. Indeed, it is my contention that the genesis of the Jesuit college saw the birth of the modern educational fundraiser, one instantly recognizable to the development office of a prestigious university in our time. 'Our way of proceeding' progressively had to include financial strategies and business management. The fathers in the first forty years of the enterprise evolved a mission statement that promoted an educational product so enticing and worthy as to demand consideration. It was to be attractive to those eager either to commemorate themselves or to opt for this way of fulfilling a Christian imperative. Or else the fathers offered enticements to civic governments – we can improve your citizenry, morally and intellectually, and hence the standing of your city. A recent Oxford thesis has shown that Henri IV of France, who would seem an unlikely supporter given his Protestant origins yet who probably is the royal figure who gave the most to the Jesuits, was persuaded that a Jesuit education would discipline an unruly nobility. A social transformation from a warring *noblesse* primed only by self-interest to one recognizing higher values and the good of church and state was France's main hope of avoiding perpetual conflict.[8]

Like modern fundraisers, the Jesuits wooed the potential powerful donor by means of inducements. They targeted kings, dukes, and influential churchmen, who, in the building of a college, were offered the early modern equivalent of what development offices in our own times term 'the naming opportunity'; the appeal was to the commemorative instinct. In Ignatius's own words: 'If he were thinking of leaving a monument to himself after finishing his days, it is evident that this work is quite to his purpose. It would be a great and lasting monument to his whole family.'[9] The major donor would also have the title of founder, and he and his family after him would be publicly acknowledged at the annual founder's ceremony, with its particular founder's candle. It should be noted that the Jesuit building program followed upon an important watershed in building history. Gradually, from the mid-fifteenth century, the big donor came, as it were, out of the closet, and accepted the public renown that followed the construction of an elegant building for a recognized public good. Discreet generosity (let not thy left hand know what thy right hand doeth) was an outmoded virtue in the modern baroque world. The magnificent man, in the Aristotelian model, left a visual record of his presence in the urban landscape. This development was fundamental to the Jesuits' building endeavours.[10]

The great donors, however, were tardy to present themselves without assurance that they were backing a winning program. Like a modern development office, the Jesuits from the 1540s sought to construct networks of supporters starting in the Celestial City itself and, perhaps most significantly, initially among the Spanish ambassadorial community. Court groups were obviously crucial in the long run, and success in one Catholic court, given the mobility of any supporter, could lead to developments in another. These networks have been neglected in Jesuit studies, but without them the mechanics of expansion cannot be fully understood. The group at the Palazzo Madama around Margaret of Austria, for example, progressively endorsed Jesuit aims while indulging their own Spanishness with sermons in their language and the services of Jesuit confessors.[11] In time, more complex sociability patterns developed that bound supporters together and moved them to work for targeted ends. These supporters (whom we would call the 'friends') were supplied with information specially tailored to evoke their confidence and enthusiasm, such as carefully edited (so as to preserve the enthusiasm) letters from distant Jesuits recounting developments. As the colleges took on more form, certain events such as spectacles, special sermons, and the celebration of canonizations promoted the cohesion of groups and a sense of togetherness. School performances played a particularly important role in enhancing this sentiment while also imparting spiritual information.[12] Reciprocation of favours, where possible, occurred. Finding consonance of interests and creating networks lay at the heart of the business of successful fundraising. In seeking patrons and founders, the fathers were located in a hierarchy of relationships with important families, some of whom constituted the civic government, whose input also mattered. Togetherness was of the essence.

It was also important to manage money, once acquired, to the best effect. This included both borrowing and lending at interest, and the question of at what levels this could be done taxed some of the early fathers considerably. No one thought more about the morality of money management than Juan Alfonso de Polanco and Pedro de Ribadeneira, who were seriously disturbed by the high levels of interest paid on loans in the 1560s, levels which could reach 20 per cent as governments issued bonds and became heavily involved in deficit funding to cope with the expenses of war.[13] The friars still defended a prohibition on usury, but once again the Jesuits had taken the more modern line. Nevertheless, as Polanco's agonized comments reveal, they were uncomfortable with levels exceeding 6 per cent. As borrowers they could not afford such levels, but as lenders (for both processes occurred concomitantly) they were also offended. As lenders they preferred to invest with the Monte di Pietà, which was safe and below market rates and which generated money for helping the poor.

How could colleges become a reality? Where could they start? The early band conceived of the colleges in terms of a trinity of actors – first, rulers or the ruling secular and civic elites of important families, and second, ecclesiastical authorities (princes and bishops), both as donors, along with themselves, finally, to oil the works. The lines between endowment and building costs were not clearly drawn in their minds, and the fruits of their persuasion of big donors were slow to materialize.[14] The start was very hard. The Jesuits were unknown entities, and lack of papal support in the tough formative period of the Carafa years (1555–9) was a handicap. So, in specific Italian contexts, was the predominantly Spanish constituency of the early fathers.

A working model, and one that in the long run turned out to be the dominant model in western and southern Europe, was offered to the Jesuits in 1551 by the Spanish viceroy of Sicily, Juan de Vega, who met Ignatius through his wife, Leonor Osorio de Vega, in the Palazzo Madama circle. In this model, a civic government (prompted by a king, duke, etc.) invites the Jesuits to open a college with a specified number of classes requiring a specified number of teachers, and provides a residence, classrooms, and running costs.

The City of Messina to Father Ignatius Loyola

Being well informed that in the congregation of religious of the name of Jesus, which is under the direction of Your Reverence, there are persons of learning and virtue, who by doctrine and apostolic ministry make themselves of great use in the Christian state, this city wishes very much to have some of your subjects to teach, preach, and produce the same fruit that has resulted from their labours wherever they have resided. *As it were to actuate the desire of the citizens, Our Lord has condescended to place over them as Prince and Viceroy Juan de Vega, who, with that piety, prudence, and virtue conspicuous in him, has approved our supplication to Your Reverence* [my emphasis]. Our request is that you send us five masters to teach theology, the arts, rhetoric, and grammar and another five to pursue their studies and give assistance in works of Christian zeal. The city will furnish them with food, clothing, and a residence suitably furnished: and in order to execute our will in proper form, the citizens have considered it in council and given it their unanimous sanction, to which is added that of His Excellency, the Viceroy.[15]

This is a critical text in the history of the Jesuit college, and it offered the way forward to secure financing. Where the civic government would raise the funds is not detailed, but its own revenues from indirect taxes and deficit funding can be assumed. The endowment is thus a form of public funding, but – and here we must look at the actual Sicilian model – gifts will follow and will permit a building program. Private funding thus intrudes. In due course, de Vega himself and his wife built a college at Messina, and other members of the family at Palermo and Bivona. In short, there was a development – a building program that followed the establishment of funds to ensure running costs and short-term buildings. The Jesuits themselves were expected to work with ruling dynasties and generate gifts from individuals who had been converted to the plan, and thus would accelerate the building of the great college that would grace the urban landscape.

The success in Sicily (a specific story involving Spanish elites who were office holders and generals) was impressive, but Sicily was an offshore island and did not fundamentally forward the grand plan. The big cities, first Rome and then Florence, were the main targets and were to prove difficult to crack.

The de Vega model involved one long-term problem arising from the (in)flexibility and nature of municipal funding; I will return to this issue. In the immediate term the problem was actually to secure the initiative of a ruler or dominant official that made local and national governments open to a process of negotiation. The unknown early Jesuits used the not always successful technique of sending in representatives to preach and pave the way to an accord through a supportive local network hoping to promote the desired end. They usually approached a well-disposed highly placed contact. This strategy could run into difficulties: if the ruler and civic government did not respond, the Jesuits and the local support group they had constructed could seek to accelerate the process by borrowing money for renting premises and starting a fledgling school. However, unless an official accord promising regular support followed, they could be left in a very embarrassing state. The Spanish historian Antonio Astráin graphically describes how the pilot teams could become victims of their own enthusiasm by placing too much store in the promises of individuals, and how negotiations could break down during the process of obtaining permission to start from Rome. Gifts could be disputed by the family of the donor – for example, gifts that proved to be covert attempts at tax evasion by being postponed until after the death of unborn generations of heirs. One early lesson had to be the discernment of the real offer. The worst situation occurred when the early pilot group tried to stay on and had to find interim funding for themselves and the classes they had begun. In Spain (and also in the Southern Netherlands) the local friars contested the times at which the Jesuits might preach and, by extension, appeal for gifts or raise a collection. They claimed a monopoly over peak attendance hours at mass and were sustained in their claim by Pope Paul IV. The stranded Jesuits could find themselves obliged to appeal to the parents of the children they were teaching, thereby undermining their own credibility, since they had promised education for free.[16]

The problems were not confined to Spain. The disasters in Ignatius's lifetime at Modena or even Ferrara taught the Jesuits to get an agreement with the civic authority before opening a class, or at least to have obtained some security from a patient and affluent donor to tide over the enterprise. The dreadful state of most of the thirty-two initiatives, totally precarious at the time of Ignatius's death, provided cautionary tales ranging in focus from the absolute necessity of being able to guarantee teachers enough food and rest, to the need for written evidence of committed donations. From the 1580s the Jesuits became strict archive keepers so as to have a documentary base from which to confirm their possessions.[17]

On Ignatius's death, Diego Laínez closed a handful of the weakest colleges and shifted the members of their depleted staffs elsewhere. His decision thereafter never to go in without an accord with civic authorities and never to accept a scheme for fewer than two hundred pupils made sense, if only it could be achieved. It was not always possible to keep to such principles, however, in war-ravaged regions or where reconstruction of a Catholic educational base took place in politically difficult circumstances. If the Jesuits never sought to build colleges where the national ruler was hostile, still in the 1580s they could find sections of civic elites, as in the Southern Netherlands or eastern or southern France or Rhenish Germany, overtly antagonistic. Moreover, in Central Europe their progress was constantly jeopardized by religious war until the mid-seventeenth century, and even civil authorities who welcomed the idea of a Jesuit presence lacked the means to support it. It is very difficult to point to a specific moment at which the Jesuits entered upon easier times. Furthermore, the de Vega model was not always adopted as the sine qua non in places where the Jesuits believed they were dealing with significant *frontières de catholicité*.[18]

It would seem, however, that in Italy a major break was certainly the advent of Pope Gregory XIII (1572–85), who identified the Jesuits as an important agency in Catholic reform and was prepared to build the Collegio Romano and to find for it a benefice income sufficient to constitute a plausible part of an endowment. In 1553, Ignatius gave Polanco several reasons why the Roman college was the most significant of all the colleges: first, when established it would attract many pupils to all disciplines; second, the city of Rome was in need of reforming institutions (*buone opere*); third, the college would operate to the benefit of Italy generally, where universities left much to be desired, by attracting good international professors who could teach in the Parisian model; fourth, the glory of the college would reflect upon the Apostolic City, whose intellectual and moral status needed a boost; fifth, the college would provide the pope with talented and capable people to serve the church, and missionary priests for the heretic and pagan lands. It would also serve as a model and competent authority for other colleges. A very important consideration must be that at the court of Rome were present princes, ambassadors, and bishops, who, witnessing success, would be inspired to found similar institutions in their own countries (as patrons). Finally, Ignatius pointed to the Roman institution as critical to the formation of pre-eminent Jesuits serving as leaders in other colleges; by their efforts excellence would be reproduced, and the single model, one capable of operating in all social environments, would be endorsed.[19]

Polanco needed little convincing, but the initiative was rent by broken promises and defaulting. First, Pope Julius III (1550–5) had promised an annual 1,500 scudi to help build and endow the college (insufficient but something, and from the right source). He delayed in spite of a petition from six cardinals and died before anything was handed over. The next pope, Paul IV (1555–9), gave nothing to the new institution. Francisco Borja, who on entering the order had placed about 5,000 scudi with Ignatius to refurbish a church and buy some houses to serve as a novitiate building, instructed his heirs to pay the Jesuits 1,000 scudi per annum to help endow the college. There were problems in transmitting this inheritance, and Philip II opposed the outflow of Spanish money to Rome. In 1552, debts stood at 1,200 scudi.[20] Ignatius was actively searching for a founder among noteworthy ecclesiastics and reached a certain stage of agreement with the bishop of Sora, Tommaso Giglio, one of the most influential ministers of Cardinal Alessandro Farnese. But the bishop had his own agendas, offered insufficient money, and insisted upon the founder's title.[21] Ignatius held back, knowing that once the 'naming opportunity' had been ceded the big donor in search of Aristotelian 'magnificence' would not come forward. The difficulties did not lessen in times of war, and the clerics at the college lived on alms for much of the 1550s and were decimated by fever. Cardinals and popes over the next decades were strapped for funds. The usually hopeful Polanco summed up the situation to Jerónimo Nadal in June 1561: 'The difficulty is to know where to apply.'[22] Over the next twenty years, a new builder-donor was found in the Marchese de Tolfa, who was the widow of Camillo Orsini and was intent upon erecting a building in his memory. But relationships between the widow and the Jesuits did not run smoothly. Their demands exceeded what she was prepared to give.[23] The denouement of the thirty-year saga was that Gregory XIII became the major builder and endowed the college with an abbey *in commendam*, Chiaravalle, worth 6,000 scudi a year.

After a long haul in which tenacity and Ignatius's unshaken belief that in spite of setbacks the college would come about, the flagship Collegio Romano at last acquired some solidity – at least for the next eighty years or so. The Tridentine movement also created a new generation of bishops prepared to endorse and to help, and by the early seventeenth century there were active secular as well as ecclesiastical elites, not only in Italy but in France and the Southern Netherlands, prepared to embrace education as a way forward.

If the financial history of the Roman college has some distinctive actors, the problems it experienced in its formation were replicated almost everywhere, and its ensuing history of debt accumulation likewise is typical of lesser institutions. The financial history of early modern Europe is one of shortage of specie and ready money. The wealth of kings was far from flexible and was caught up in wars and in the rewards and pensions system for their supporters. They themselves wanted to borrow, and in the second half of the sixteenth century they did so at astronomical rates (up to 20 per cent), which made borrowing difficult for others. It was a tough money market, in which there were winners (the lenders) and losers (the borrowers).

The Jesuits had expected that their major donors would be great princes, wealthy dynasties, and ecclesiastics seeking commemorative building projects. They were to discover that, in fact, only a very few among those groups could or would generate the means. The reasons in large part are attributable to the nature of inherited wealth. The wealth of great men, expressed in inherited land, was tied to the next generation; the incumbent was merely an agency through which family wealth passed in a clearly demarcated system of entail. Every father of a family knew the limitations of his disposable wealth. The part of an individual's estate that could be designated new wealth – that accruing from office, pension, or favour or made in speculative investment, from having charge of state business, for example, or the handling of the silver ships, or from generating deficit funding for the government, or from colonial position, or as a result of military involvement or naval campaigns or investment in mercantile activity – was in a different position. Even then, family costs such as the marrying of a daughter could erode the proceeds. In short, the big donor was usually childless and in a position to draw upon new wealth.

Some bishops who embraced Jesuit ideals after Trent were honoured as founders (for example, Guillaume du Prat, the bishop of Clermont, at Billom and Paris). But most, though childless, had family obligations in that they were responsible for restoring investments made by their families of origin to secure their promotion. Nor were all bishops rich, especially in southern France, where the Avignon popes had split dioceses and their revenues as a way of multiplying supporters. Moreover, for some grand churchmen who wished to make a statement of 'magnificence,' building or refurbishing a church was seen as the best statement of all.[24] Most post-Tridentine bishops were also eager to associate their names with the founding of a diocesan seminary. In short, there was an embarrassment of causes to support. Not all liked the Jesuits, and in Spain the heavy presence of the old mendicant orders in the episcopate also accounts for a holding back there.

It followed that the ecclesiastic was generally more likely to be part of a consortium of donors to a college and to be recognized as founder by agreement (rather than as a result of having contributed the largest sum) to the building or endowment. Individual bishops of the Southern Netherlands eventually became deeply involved and proved ingenious in providing sources. Gérard de Groesbeek at Liège in 1580, for example, may serve as an illustration. He considered that the income from a benefice left vacant for twelve years (not the same benefice, but six benefices for two years or four for three) would accumulate sufficient funds to endow a college.[25]

In the late sixteenth and early seventeenth centuries, a number of rulers embraced the 'naming' or commemorative opportunity (Henri IV at La Flèche, for example, or Duke Albert of Bavaria at Ingolstadt). These great flagship buildings were perhaps the exception rather than the norm, and many rulers were allowed founder status when their contribution was in fact relatively small and the main burden of financing the building had been assumed either by a consortium of donors or by someone prepared to forego the status of founder. An outstanding example of such a renunciation was at Ferrara, where the widow Maria Frassoni del Gesso put up some 70,000 scudi against the miserable 1,000 loaned by Duke Ercole d'Este, who nevertheless was given the founder's title. The Jesuits saw the ruler's name as lending an aura of distinction to the college, and as serving to encourage further gift-giving by those who sought association with initiatives of the ruler. In fact, association with a particular ruling dynasty could be crucial for sustained support. Much can be learned from certain early ventures in which women committed themselves to Jesuit college building,[26] since they reveal an eagerness on the part of the Jesuits to recognize their contribution and at the same time an anxiety to grant the honour of founder status to men.

For the Jesuits in the early days, a window of opportunity in the dynastic stranglehold on family wealth was offered by the widow. Sixteenth-century great families could put up to a fifth of the value of their estates into dowries as a way of creating links with other great families; the interest on the sum provided a usufruct enabling the bride to meet her living costs. In widowhood the whole sum could become hers to reappropriate. It was expected that such wealth would pass to her children or, in default of issue, back to her family of origin on her death. But the widow could leave a will in another direction, or use the income on her wealth freely. The extent of her power to do so varied according to national laws. Venetian and Bolognese women seem to have had more control over their resources than did Florentine or Roman women. The potentially wealthiest sixteenth-century aristocratic widows were Spanish (and this included those of Naples and Sicily) because they controlled not only their dotal wealth but 50 per cent of all new wealth accumulated after marriage by their husbands. A number of trends are to be noted. One is that wealthy women were supporters of the early fathers, and that their assets figured largely in the funding of pioneer forays to promote the establishment of sixteenth-century colleges. There were a number of women founders in the early days, but fewer later on, as families began to guard themselves by active litigation, or to push for legislation, restricting the amount of money widows could bestow on a religious order.[27] Or, in some cases, husbands gained more control of these considerable resources. Here we approach the question of the competition for women's money. Litigation over the deployment of widows' resources by anxious families threatened to blacken the Jesuit name and contributed to scandal.[28] One is struck by the disappearance of women's names over time. But it may be deceptive: ways around prohibitions could be found, and noticeable is a shift in widows' giving *post mortem* to annuities established *in vivo*, where the woman makes her investment from her dotal funds (and regards it as a gift) but receives an income in her lifetime.

In every college the construction of endowment income had to be carried out quite separately from the meeting of building costs if the institution was to survive. The triennial reports on the financial state of the house relate only – and in very broad terms – to endowment income and to expenditure; the nature of the debt is described generally, and the reader is accordingly left with tantalizing questions. How much debt came from repairs to buildings, for example?[29] Each college, as the recipient of designated gifts or civic income, had to be a tub on its own bottom.[30] Civic support in the dominant model was usually in the form of an agreed percentage of indirect taxes sometimes bolstered, especially at the beginning, by further concessions from the national ruler (notably from the profits of justice of bankruptcy cases), or, as in the case of Henri IV and his successor, by revenues from forest rights or the gabelle. It was expected that civic concessions would be topped up by gifts, and that many such gifts, cumulatively, would enhance revenues to the point where civic endowment could be reduced. If such was the expectation, as at Lyon, it did not happen. In a mature portfolio, endowment income contained land, which could be a direct gift, or could be purchased from the sale of other forms of gift, or – and perhaps most likely – could come into Jesuit hands as part of the concession of a Benedictine abbey *in commendam*. Land was less the dominant form of income in Europe than in Central and South America, though it could still represent the most valuable element in the post-suppression valuations. Theoretically, land attached to a benefice *in commendam* gave the Jesuits control of some good agricultural land, tithes, and seigneurial dues, but from the income had to be deducted the cost of a priest for the benefice, the upkeep of any ecclesiastical buildings that were part of the benefice, and sometimes the maintenance of the remaining resident Benedictines themselves. These last were invariably resentful, and claimed neglect of the upkeep of the fabric of the church and monastery. Such dissent could result in a withholding of revenues.[31] Some benefices, however, were very profitable. They usually generated grain and were the source of the supplies recorded in the triennial reports. But though grain was a valued commodity, agricultural revenues were volatile, and poor harvests produced considerable rural debt and defaultings while charges remained the same. Moreover, modest tenants might never pay them off (the *desperata* category in the triennial reports). If land did not carry tax immunities, its immediate income value was much diminished. Urban property could also constitute an active source of income, though receiving, changing, and consolidating such properties might also be part of the preliminaries to forming a site for building purposes. The intents of donors had to be respected.

For endowment purposes, the Jesuits invested in deficit funding, *juros* and *rentes*. The first, in Spain, meant lending to the monarchy against the incoming silver ships, but more generally *juros* were loans to municipalities (or other institutions) in anticipation of the product of commodity taxes for city-running costs, or of specific institutional taxes. Sometimes *juros* were given as gifts (*juros donativos*), which were specially bought by the pious to give to religious houses. It is possible to find entire Spanish colleges, Valladolid for example, the income of which was 100 per cent dependent upon the product of *juros*.[32] As well as investing income with the Monte di Pietà, where such existed, the colleges also dealt in annuities, which people considered gifts because God determined when they died. Some French colleges got involved in John Law's speculative schemes but pulled out before the crash.[33]

I would like to emphasize that the Jesuits were very active with disposable income, even when in debt. They had to be so in order to keep going and to service debts by sustaining revenue. The early modern period was a debt culture, and to be in debt was the norm provided one could service the income on any loans one had incurred.

One or two French colleges ran pharmacies to great effect, as the Jesuits were accredited with considerable pharmacological expertise emanating from their South American experience. They had, however, to avoid the imputation of trading, which could prompt considerable acrimony in particular colonial environments.

How does one explain the persistence and growing accumulation of debt? It is not universally true that actual building costs lay at the root of the problem, although there are instances in which rebuilding or unanticipated disasters during the building process lay at the root of a difficulty. The norm (true for all religious orders) was that the spectacle of a building could boost gift-giving, and that if the right names were associated with the construction of the building as it went up, others would contribute. Fires, or destruction in storms or in war – widely experienced in eastern France and in Germany during the Thirty Years' War – could deter the giving necessary for starting again. Or the repair work needed as a building aged could provoke problems.

Canonizations with spectacular ceremonies and rituals also were mechanisms for attracting gifts, and the costs of such events could be widely shared by national, local, and ecclesiastical authorities. The major enemy was simply time and familiarity. When a building has been up and running for many years and there are other good causes to promote, when the 'naming' opportunity has been used or the dynastic support of a particular family peters out, gift income can readily recede. The Condé, for example, did not prove good supporters of Bourges in the eighteenth century. The colleges had an illusory solidity, and their ceremonies betokened a deceptive affluence rather than penury.

Civic authorities, hard pressed by government taxes, were not open to appeals to enhance the endowment. They might permit a lottery, or suggest undertaking a boarding facility the profits of which could go to the school; but this latter suggestion the Jesuits did not welcome, since a boys' dormitory could generate disorder and scandal.

Fundamental to understanding the ever-mounting debt from the 1640s is a recognition of the part played by inflation and the disruption attendant upon the Thirty Years' War – what used to be called the Crisis of the Seventeenth Century. Civic endowment and privileges from the central government came either from urban indirect taxes on commodities, deficit funding, or privileges such as the profits of justice. In times of war these could be summarily appropriated by monarchies, and considerable pressure could be placed on local government. Deficit funding was particularly vulnerable. The strains placed on local populations in terms of enhanced direct taxation caused defaultings on payments to seigneurs and tithe holders and generated the risings of the 1640s, none more bitter than the Frondes of 1648.

A summary of the fundamental problems contributing to the picture of mounting debt in the triennial reports would have to recognize in first place that once a college was up and running, sustaining revenues could be difficult. It is easier to raise to build than to provide running costs. Moreover, the Jesuits suffered from being too successful at the culture of appearances: the musical and theatrical performances and the prizes, beautifully bound volumes often provided by the local Lady Bountiful, proclaimed an illusory sufficiency, as did famous libraries and silverware. The huge amount of peeling plaster and some positively danger-ous walls were less apparent.

Second, the main sources of income, the civic sources, were vulnerable and subject to the vicissitudes of the national economy. When rulers needed money, they bled the towns of their indirect taxes. Sharp withdrawal did not necessarily cause a college to close in the way that in Madrid in 1798 it provoked an almost 100 per cent mortality among foundlings, but at Valladolid in the 1630s, for example, college income fell by 50 per cent as interest on *juros* was cut from 5 per cent to 2–3 per cent.

Third, the environment was changing as the state sought to limit the slippage of land into the tax-exempt bracket. In France, from the mid-seventeenth century the monarchy sought to freeze the amount of land in mortmain (exemption from tax) in an attempt to prevent erosion of taxes. Related to this effort was a limitation on the amount of money one could leave in an individual bequest to a religious order (in France, 3,000 livres); this measure was to curtail the money that went not specifically to the Jesuits but to the new female uncloistered religious orders carrying out charitable works. Very generally, European developments favouring the greater control of women's money by husbands and the wider family (the wild card being the widow) became more apparent from the mid-seventeenth century.

Fourth, directions for charitable giving became increasingly competitive in nature, and cheaper schooling alternatives offered by various religious orders came into existence.

Financial stress within the Society as a whole had particular repercussions on the colleges as the order's only institutions that were consistent money-generating bodies. Novitiate houses state they live on *entrate*, but Delattre points out the impossibility of this given the ebbs in numbers. Jesuits also grew old and infirm and had to be sheltered by the colleges. All these considerations may explain why the question in triennial reports shifts from How many are you supporting (by agreement with the civic government), to How many are you really supporting?

A fifth problem might be summarized in the words scandal and litigation. Litigation had always haunted the shift to the Jesuits of family money. It must have been heartbreaking to be promised funds to build and then to find them delayed or denied. However, what one sees is the shift away from family money disputation to commercial issues. The Lavalette affair was far from alone among cases that reverberated through the Society as a whole. The costs of that affair before the courts prompted the French Jesuits to appeal across national boundaries for financial support. It hence raised the spectre of shifts of money across boundaries and of international rather than national priorities being set.[34]

It has not been my intention to suggest that the colleges were collapsing in advance of the particular phenomenon of the suppression. Perhaps the most permanent state in which such an institution exists is one of indebtedness. But there were real problems for those who had to manage the books and put on a brave face. Certainly, no house faced a shortage of food. There was grain, and the inhabitants of most houses were locals. This in times of hardship is a source of strength. It is my impression that in the most impoverished houses gifts of food and wine came from parents, and that certain services such as laundry and the making of habits were provided by neighbouring convents, some of which owed much to earlier Jesuit support. Rather, I would wish to emphasize that the nature and content of college revenues belonged within a broader *ancien régime* financial and institutional structure. Privileged exemptions from state taxation, the exploitation of landed privilege through tithe, the dependence upon indirect commodity taxes at the discretion of municipalities or by the grace and favour of national governments, and the vagaries of certain types of deficit funding in the medium run made for doomed sources. They were part of a financial system that was under huge strain – enough, we should remember, to provoke the Revolution.

NOTES

The research underpinning this article was funded by the Leverhulme Trust during my tenure of a Senior Research Professorship.

 1 Detailed comment on the financial history of Jesuit colleges cannot be made from the summaries in the triennial reports made to Rome but must be constructed from college archives remaining in the country of origin. The triennial reports allow generalizations on the financial health of an institution, but one learns nothing of the donors either of buildings or of the endowment income, with the revenues of which the reports are concerned. Nor does one learn anything of the provenance of grain stocks or agrarian revenues, or of where and to what end debts were generated. The destructions of war in Germany and Central Europe, beginning with the Thirty Years' War, in which the Swedes were particularly savage in their obliteration of Jesuit institutions, and the ensuing ravages and political vicissitudes of the next centuries have taken their toll on the availability of archives for all but a few flagship institutions and perhaps the special record of Bavaria. B. Duhr, *Geschichte der Jesuiten in den Ländern deutscher Zunge im XVI. Jahrhundert* (Freiburg im Breisgau, 1907) gives some account of the problems surrounding the first foundation at Cologne and particular outstanding Bavarian examples. The *Tabulae exhibentes sedes antiquae Societatis Iesu missionum stationes et collegia, 1556–1773, provinciae Bohemiae et Silesiacae* (Vienna, 1899) provides valuable listings and occasional clues to the founder's title of institutions that have now disappeared, but the information remains impressionistic. R. Pörtner, *The Counter-Reformation in Central Europe: Styria, 1580–1630* (Oxford, 2001), p. 209, offers general comments on the paucity of donations from the nobility and local elites to Graz, Judenburg, and Leoben, which were founded by Archduke Ferdinand though court officials decorated the churches as a gesture to his imperial election. She also suggests exceptions to the general behaviour of the nobility in the generosity of the Schranz and Thanhausen families.
 2 O'M. *First*, p. 6.
 3 'De collegiis fundandis,' *MI Const*. 1.
 4 On the location of the Jesuits within a humanist tradition, see D. Julia, 'L'infanzia agli inizi dell'epoca moderna,' in *Storia dell'infanzia*, ed. E. Becchi and D. Julia, vol. 1 (Bari, 1966), chap. 5, especially pp. 274–85. The Jesuits found it prudent, given Erasmus's post mortem reputation, not to hold his works in their libraries.
 5 T.H. Clancy, *Introduction to Jesuit Life* (St Louis, 1976), pp. 129, 134.

6 See the introduction to D. Julia and W. Frijhoff, *Ecole et société dans la France d'Ancien Régime: Quatre examples: Auch, Avallon, Condom, Gisors* (Paris, 1975); and M.M. Compère and D. Julia, *Les collèges français, XVIe–XVIIIe siècles* (Paris, 1984).

7 P. Bonenfant, *La suppression de la Compagnie de Jésus dans les anciens Pays Bas autrichiens (1773)* (Brussels, 1924), p. 148, gives interesting comparative data.

8 E.W. Nelson, 'The King, the Jesuits, and the French Church, 1594–1615,' dissertation, Oxford University, 1998. The involvement of the king could be intended as an incentive for emulation rather than a substantial endowment.

9 *Letters of Saint Ignatius of Loyola*, ed. W. Young (Chicago, 1959), p. 439.

10 A.D. Fraser, 'Cosimo de Medici's Patronage of Architecture and the Theory of Magnificence,' *Journal of the Warburg and Courtauld Institutes* 33 (1970): 162–70; L. Green, 'Galvano Fiamma, Azzone Visconti, and the Revival of the Classical Theory of Magnificence,' *Journal of the Warburg and Courtauld Institutes* 53 (1990): 111–12; G. Clarke,' Magnificence and the City: Giovanni II Bentivoglio and Architecture in 15th Century Bologna,' *Renaissance Studies* 13 (1999): 397–411.

11 See O. Hufton, 'Altruism and Reciprocity: The Early Jesuits and Their Female Patrons,' *Renaissance Studies* 15:3 (2001): 341.

12 *Litt. Quad.* 4:434: 'In addition to the great benefit accruing to the school by the student's display of talent ... it gave the best sort of spiritual lesson to the spectators' (Medina del Campo, 1556).

13 F. Rurale, *I gesuiti a Milano: Religione e politica nel secondo Cinquecento* (Milan, 1992), especially pp. 180–5, is an exemplary study of the anguish and triumph.

14 One can follow a developmental learning process: Ignatius recognized by the end of 1553 that an endowment for future colleges sufficient to support at least fourteen persons as teachers and the provision of a suitable house, church, and schoolrooms were the sine qua non of 'accepting' colleges in negotiation with civic authorities. Laínez's early recognition was that colleges of fewer than two hundred pupils were not viable. See W. Farrell, *The Jesuit Code of Liberal Education* (Chicago, 1938), p. 101.

15 *Epist. Mixt.* 1:450–6.

16 A. Astráin, *Historia de la Compañía de Jesús en la asistencía de España*, 7 vols (Madrid, 1902–25), II, pp. 236–7.

17 'Regulae procuratoris collegii et domus probationis,' *Regulae Societatis Iesus* (1580), pp. 188–9; E. Lamalle, 'Un livret d'instructions de 1660 pour les archives des maisons de la Compagnie,' *AHSI* 11 (1942): 113. Lamalle insists on the precocity of this body of instructions in preserving important documents from dust and vermin. Archive keeping became more of a general concern at many levels in the late seventeenth century.

18 Ponc. *Hist.*, I, p. 356, cites a letter of December 1573: 'Vouloir obtenir ici une

fondation complète dès le commencement des collèges c'est se leurrer d'un vain espoir. La Belgique est ruinée par la guerre, le peuple est écrasé sous les impôts, les nobles et les notables sont criblés de dettes, les resources des nouveaux évêchés son nulles. Quant aux villes et aux Etats, leurs charges sont si écrasantes qu'ils peuvent à peine fournir les subsides aux Roi et au salut du pays ...'

19 E. Rinaldi, *La fondazione del Collegio Romano* (Arezzo, 1914), pp. 84, 14.

20 M. Scaduto, *L'epoca di Giacomo Lainez, 1556–1565*, 2 vols (Rome, 1964–75), I, pp. 52–7 and the particularly graphic footnote, conveys the problems at Rome.

21 Interestingly, his kinswoman Margharita del Giglio was to hold the title at Bologna.

22 *M. Nadal* 1:407: letter of 6 March 1561.

23 C. Valone, 'Architecture as a Public Voice for Women in Sixteenth-Century Rome,' *Renaissance Studies* 15:3 (2001): 300–26.

24 This practice was recommended by books on the subject, such as Botero's *Della ragione di stato* (Venice, 1598), book 2, p. 96: 'stimi cosa più degna di un Principe Christiano il ristorar le chiese antiche che il fabricar le nuove. Perché la riparatione sarà sempre opera di pietà.' The restoration of the antique, suitably publicly attributed, certainly attracted cardinals.

25 Ponc. *Hist.*, I, p. 201.

26 A bibliography for the involvement of women can be found in Hufton, 'Altruism.'

27 S. Hanley, 'Social Sites of Political Practise in France: Lawsuits, Civil Rights, and the Separation of Powers in Domestic and State Government,' *American Historical Review* (1997); B. Diefendorf, 'Widowhood and Remarriage in Sixteenth-Century Paris,' *Journal of Family History* 7 (1982): 379–96.

28 An important constituent of criticism of the Jesuits and their nefarious dealings, as expressed in critical and scurrilous pamphlets and cartoons, was that they bled gullible women. See Hufton, 'The Widow's Mite and Other Strategies: Funding the Catholic Reformation,' *Transactions of the Royal Historical Society*, ser. 6, 8 (1998): 117–37; S. Pavone, *Le astuzie dei gesuiti. Le false istruzioni della Compagnia di Gesù e la polemica antigesuita nei secoli XVII e XVIII* (Rome, 2000), p. 275. 'Monito Quinto' in the *Monita secreta* deals specifically with the manipulation of widows.

29 The Jesuits may not have pioneered double-entry bookkeeping but Flori's *Trattato del modere di tenere il doppio domestico* (Palermo, 1636) was used popularly in Italy as a manual. Certainly, their records have a clarity conspicuously lacking in French old regime government records.

30 Rurale shows that the college in Milan gave investment advice to other nascent colleges, *I gesuiti a Milano*, pp. 185–7. Where there were two colleges in a single town – such as at Lyon, which had a civic foundation and one for younger pupils funded by private donors – the civic institution was concerned to the point of hysteria that the smaller, private institution might receive help from the bigger. This

concern could not be grounded in reality, since the large institution was strapped for funds. See P. Delattre, *Les établissements des jésuites en France depuis quatre siècles*, 4 vols (Enghien, 1949–57), III, on Lyon.

31 There is a tortuous history here. The Jesuits claimed that they were returning the income according to the previous intentions of the donors, and those who had previously held the benefice claimed that they were usurpers. Delattre, *Les établissements des jésuites*, vol. 1, p. xiii, deals with the implications of the acrimony

32 B. Benassar, *Valladolid au siècle d'or* (Paris and The Hague, 1967), p. 403.

33 Law was the famous financier who promised a solution to the French national debt by creating a general bank in imitation of the British and Dutch models but backed it with the presumed collateral of the Compagnie de l'Occident, which allegedly exploited the commercial potential of Louisiana. Shares to individuals and charitable institutions sold like wildfire, but after a two-year bonanza came the crash in 1719. The Jesuits' avoidance of such speculation is interesting; it suggests they were healthily sceptical.

34 Bonenfant, *La suppresson*, 42. The belief that money was crossing international boundaries to profit the Jesuits is a recurrent theme from the time of Philip II, concerning the Borja inheritance.

2 / The Jesuits and the Art of Translation in Early Modern Europe

PETER BURKE

The concept of 'cultural translation,' which once circulated in the relatively narrow circle of the British anthropologist Edward Evans-Pritchard and his pupils, has now become common currency to describe the process of adaptation through which items from one culture are domesticated in another. In the early modern period this process was often described as 'accommodation,' a concept well known to the Jesuits and their historians. When Ignatius, following St Paul, advised his own followers to be 'all things to all people,' *omnia omnibus*, he was recommending a policy of what we call the cultural translation of the Christian message.

The career of Matteo Ricci neatly exemplifies what Ignatius meant. One might describe Ricci's change of clothing on his arrival in China as an attempt to translate Christianity in the sense of dissociating it from its Western cultural baggage and searching for an 'equivalent effect' in the local culture. We might even describe Ricci's famous exchange of the robes of a bonze for those of a mandarin as a sign of his awareness that a cultural mistranslation had occurred and needed to be corrected.

In this chapter, however, the focus will be on translation in a more literal sense, translation between languages. Here too the contribution of the Jesuits, or part of their contribution, is well known. One thinks for example of the many grammars and vocabularies of non-European languages compiled by Jesuit missionaries. In the New World, famous examples include the Portuguese José de Anchieta's grammar of Tupí, for instance, published in 1595, the Italian Luigi Bertonio's grammar of Aymara (1603), and the dictionary of Guaraní compiled by the Peruvian missionary Antonio Ruiz de Montoya (1639). In the case of Asia, one thinks of João Rodrigues and his Japanese grammar, or of Florian Bahr (1706–71), a missionary in China, who helped compile a dictionary of Chinese, Latin, French, Italian, Portuguese, and German.

The contribution of Jesuit translators concerned with non-European languages is also relatively well known, as in the case of the seventeenth-century volume *Confucius Sinarum philosophus*, translated by Philippe Couplet, Prospero Intorcetta, and members of the Society, or Martino Martini's translation into Chinese of Lessius on the soul. The acute problems faced by missionaries of translating theological concepts into the language of the mission field have often been discussed, whether the people they were attempting to convert were the Chinese, the Japanese, or the Iroquois.[1]

There is still work to be done in this area, especially if one leaves the relatively well cultivated fields of China, Japan, and the Americas for other countries, to study the context in which Pierre Fromage, for instance, a missionary in Egypt and Syria, translated Emmanuel Nieremberg, Paolo Segneri, and other Jesuit writers into Arabic, while the Portuguese Luis de Azevedo, a missionary in Ethiopia, translated Jerónimo Nadal 'in sermonem Chaldaeum'; and the Bohemian Paul Clain, who worked in the Philippines, translated Dominique Bouhours into Tagalog.[2]

Roberto Bellarmino's famous *Catechism* was translated into no fewer than seventeen non-European languages, including Arabic, Bikol (a language of the Philippines), Bisaya (spoken in Borneo), 'Chaldean,' 'Congolese,' Coptic, 'Ethiopian' (now known as Ge'ez), Georgian, Hebrew, Malagasi, Maratha, Quechua, Tagalog, Tamil, and Tinigua (an Amerindian language). These translations are themselves evidence of the policy of accommodation, although they need to be studied in depth to see how much interpretative freedom this policy permitted.

Here, however, emphasis will fall on a part of the story that is paradoxically both less known and more familiar: the European part. The Jesuits were extremely active as translators from one European language into another throughout the early modern period, but this aspect of their activities has attracted relatively little attention. A few general remarks on the history of translation in early modern Europe may be useful at this point so that the work of the Jesuits can be placed in a broader context.

From the sixteenth century onwards a rapid rise of published translations becomes visible in Europe. These publications include translations from Greek into Latin, from Latin into the vernaculars, and from one vernacular into another (notably from Italian, Spanish, and French into other languages). They also include translations from the European vernaculars into Latin. More than a thousand translations from the vernaculars into Latin were produced between 1500 and 1800, of which some 40 per cent were religious books.[3] It was in the course of my research on this topic that the role of the Jesuits became apparent, and it then turned out that this role was not confined to translation into Latin. In the early modern period the Society produced more than six hundred printed translations into European languages.

The observations that follow are confined to translations into Latin and European vernaculars made by Jesuits between 1540 and 1773. It may be illuminating to approach these translations with six questions in mind. First, who was doing the translating? Second, from what language into what? Third, what kind of text? Fourth, for whom, what kind of readership? Fifth, with what intentions? And sixth, with what consequences?

It will be noticed that an extremely important question has been omitted: In what manner or style were the translations carried out? Fascinating as it would be to see whether or not the concept of *modus noster procedendi* works in the context of translation, it would be premature to venture generalizations at this point. Too little is known about different cultures of translation in early modern Europe to place the Jesuits with any accuracy. In this respect the history of translation lags behind the history of architecture, for instance, the history of science, or the history of the theatre.

Who translates? It would be good to know how many Jesuit translators were active in this period. The problem is that even an exhaustive analysis of Sommervogel's invaluable – if not always completely accurate – volumes would not be sufficient to answer this question.[4] A major difficulty is the number of anonymous translations, described on title-pages (the main source used by Sommervogel), as 'a quodam sacerdote Societatis Jesu,' 'ab alio eiusdem societatis sacerdote,' 'por otro de la misma compañia,' and so on. There are even references to what appears to be collective translation, as in the case of the *Litterae Japonicae et Chinesenses* (Antwerp, 1611), where the title-page claims that the book was translated 'by the rhetoricans of the college' ('a rhetoribus collegii').

So far, I have identified 260 individual Jesuit translators. There were probably many more, but this group may be a reasonable sample on which to base some provisional conclusions. In the case of early modern translators in general, it is useful to distinguish two groups. On one side there is a large group who produced only one or two texts in the course of a life devoted to other things. Let us call them the 'amateurs.' On the other side there was a small group who might produce as many as forty texts apiece. We might speak of them as 'professionals,' or better, as 'semi-professionals,' since they gained their living by combining the tasks of writer, interpreter, secretary, and so on.

In the case of the Jesuits, even though translating was not a way of making a living, we find a similar distinction between two groups.

A small number of translators produced a relatively large number of texts in the course of a life that might also including preaching, teaching, or writing their own books. Ten individuals produced at least 172 translations, nearly 30 per cent of the total. The highest number of texts translated by a single individual is 30 (in the case of the Fleming Frans de Smidt), followed by 23 (the Pole Simon Wysocki), 19 (the German Conrad Vetter), 18 (the northern Netherlander Jan Buys), 17 (both the Frenchman Jean Brignon and the Czech Jiři Ferus), 15 (the Italian Luigi Flori), 12 (the Dutchman Gerard Zoes), 11 (the Spaniard Joseph Echaburu), and 10 (the Czech Jiři Constanz). Most of the remaining translators may reasonably be described as amateurs.

These 260 individuals are distributed unevenly over time. It is no surprise to discover that 17 were born before 1550. What is more worthy of note is the fact that 91 were born between 1550 and 1599, the largest group in any fifty-year period. Thereafter, although the Society as a whole was growing, the number of translators steadily diminished, from 68 born in the period 1600–49 to 45 born in 1650–99 and 21 between 1700 and 1749 (total 242, the birth dates of the remaining 18 translators being unknown). It would seem that strategies or priorities were changing.

From what language into what? The principal language into which translation was made was Latin, with 77 individuals involved in the process. I have so far discovered 518 translators from the vernacular into Latin during the whole early modern period, so that the Jesuit contribution was substantial in this domain, about 15 per cent.

Next, but a long way behind, came French, with 32 translators, followed by German, with 25; Spanish, with 22; and Polish, with 20. Behind this group come translators from Italian (14), Dutch (11), Czech (11), and Hungarian (9). There were only 4 translators into English, 4 more into modern Greek, 4 into different South Slav languages or dialects (Croat, Slovene, 'Illyrian'), 3 into Portuguese (together with a number of anonymous translations), 2 into Breton, and 1 each into Basque, Irish, Lithuanian, Maltese, Romanian, and Welsh (omitting the translations of Bellarmino into Furlano and Torinese on the grounds that these 'languages' are usually classified as dialects). The importance of the Slav languages and Hungarian is worth noting, and I shall return to this topic later.

What was translated? Pending a complete quantitative study, my strategy here is to begin with the texts that had the greatest international success in the sense of being translated into many languages. It is difficult to be sure into quite how many languages, and it might be wise to treat the figures that follow, derived from Sommervogel, as minima that research in Portuguese or East-Central European libraries in particular might well amplify.

Sixteen authors were translated by Jesuits into 8 or more languages. The record is held by Bellarmino, whose *Catechism* was translated into 20 European languages (as well as 17 non-European ones, as I remarked earlier). A long way behind come three texts each of which was translated into 11 languages: the Catechism of Peter Canisius, the *Exercicio de perfeción* of Alfonso Rodrigues, and, less predictably, the *Pensées* of Dominique Bouhours (translated not only into Tagalog, as we have seen, but also, by a German Jesuit, into Greek).

Four texts were translated into nine languages apiece. One was Ignatius's *Spiritual Exercises*, which one might have expected to find at the head of the list. The remaining three works are little known today, but for this very reason worth mentioning now, the *Massime* of Gian-Battista Manni, the *Meditaciones* of Luis de la Puente, and the *Purgatorio* of Martin de Roa.

Seven texts were translated into eight languages each: a Latin grammar by Emmanuel Alvarez, the famous *Ten Reasons* by Edmund Campion, the biographies of Aloysius Gonzaga by Virgilio Cepari and of Ignatius by Pedro de Ribadeneira, the devotional work *Pia desideria* by Herman Hugo, a description of Loreto by Orazio Torsellini, and the sermons of Antonio Vieira.

It should be noted that these references are to texts rather than authors and to numbers of languages, not numbers of editions. I am not denying Carlos Eire's claim that Emmanuel Nieremberg was a best-seller – and his works were indeed translated into at least eight languages – but no one text by him, so far as I know, was translated into more than seven.

In some of these cases of multiple translation it might be prudent to avoid the term 'best-seller,' reserving it for cases of multiple editions in a given language as evidence of continuing demand. The evidence is at its best when the printer remains the same, since he would presumably have sold his stock before reprinting. A different printer in another city may pirate the book because he believes that it will sell, rather than because he knows that it has sold well.

On this criterion some works of Jesuit devotion qualify as best-sellers but others do not. The prolific translator Jan Buys was also the author of original works of devotion of which the *Meditationes* was translated into Polish (Wysocki), 1608; French, 1611; Dutch (Thielmans), 1628; second French translation (Portail), 1644; third French translation (Binet), 1669; fourth French translation, 1669; Italian (Coll'Amato), 1684; fifth French translation (Macé), 1689; sixth French translation (Brignon), 1691; Portuguese, 1751. Five languages but ten translations, suggesting the appeal of Buys in France, confirmed by the analysis of the editions of the 1644 version, at least nine by 1697 (though the sixth known edition, 1665, calls itself the 'tenth').

It is worth noting that on occasion Jesuit texts were translated by non-Jesuits, secular works such as the *Historia natural y moral* by José de Acosta, for instance, the *Uomo di lettere* by Daniello Bartoli, the *Oráculo* of Baltasar Gracián, or Martino Martini's *De bello Tartarico*, a history of the overthrow of the Ming dynasty by the Manchus.

In complementary fashion, a few Jesuits translated writers who were not members of their order, including Thomas à Kempis (four times), St François de

Sales (twice), Luis de Granada (twice), and Lorenzo Scupoli. The Bible was translated by a Polish Jesuit, Jakob Wujek, and again by a South Slav Jesuit, Bartul Kašić. Jesuits also translated a few lay writers, including Guicciardini (the maxims not the history), Richelieu's *Testament politique*, a military treatise by Montecuccoli, and the philosophy of Leibniz (like Confucius, beyond the limits of this study).[5]

All the same, to list Jesuit translations is to be impressed by the overwhelming concern of the translators for diffusing books written by their colleagues within the Society. It is possible to go still further in this direction. A substantial number of the works translated were concerned with the activities of the Jesuits themselves. Letters from the missions, for instance, were translated by Balinghem, Busaeus, Coyssard, Oranus, Simon, and others. The Jesuit Famiano Strada's well-known history of the Revolt of the Netherlands was translated into Italian by two of his colleagues, Carlo Paini and Paolo Segneri. Again, we not infrequently find that a biography of a Jesuit written by another Jesuit might be translated by a third, as in the case of biographies of Ignatius, Francis Xavier, Francisco Borja, Aloysius Gonzaga, Emond Auger, Roberto Bellarmino, Peter Canisius, Pierre Coton, Antonio Possevino, François Régis, and Pedro de Ribadeneira.

Fourth, for whom were these translations made? One of the target audiences was of course the Jesuits themselves. After all, they were a large enough group in the seventeenth century – by 1640, more than 16,000 – to consume all this literature. The fact that they would not have bought copies does not matter, since the translations did not cost anything and printing was sometimes done in house, especially in Central and Eastern Europe, where Jesuits virtually controlled higher education – in Braunsberg, for instance, Prague, Trnava, Vilnius, and so on.[6]

There was also a ready-made distribution network available through the colleges (revealed by Steven J. Harris's studies of information coming the other way, from the periphery to the centre).[7] The students in the colleges may also be regarded as virtually captive readers, and title-pages sometimes make it clear that a given text was directed towards them in particular. Some editions of the Catechism of Canisius are described as 'in usum juventutis scholasticae,' and the Würzburg 1736 Latin translation of the *Pensées* of Bouhours as 'in gratiam juventutis studiosae.'

All the same, I do not believe that all these texts were produced for internal circulation alone. Some commercial publishers were involved. It is possible that they were subsidized on occasion, but unlikely that this happened all the time. It is obviously difficult to assess the importance of the circulation of books by Jesuits outside the order, and more research on library inventories is needed, but it is clear enough that the Jesuit 'loudspeaker' was a powerful instrument. The example of Emmanuel College, Cambridge, in the seventeenth century, a strongly anti-Catholic college yet one with books by Caussin and Kircher in the library, has many parallels in the Protestant world at this time.

Fifth, with what intentions were translations made? Given the concern of Jesuits to translate works by Jesuits about Jesuits, it is only a mild exaggeration to speak of a 'conspiracy' to translate. At the very least we might speak of a 'policy' or what has been called a 'corporate strategy.'[8] Whether this strategy was devised at headquarters in Rome or whether it was originally a local initiative that was imitated elsewhere I am afraid that I am unable to say.

To put this policy in perspective, one might compare the Jesuit initiative with Christian missions in general (Wulfila and the Goths, Cyril and the Slavs, and so on), or, thinking of early modern Europe, with the translation campaigns of the Protestants, the Lutherans in particular. The first books printed in a number of European languages were Lutheran texts, as in the case of Latvian (1525), Estonian (1535, a catechism), Romanian (1542, another catechism), Lithuanian (1547, a translation of Luther's Small Catechism), and Slovene (1550, yet another catechism).

All the same, the focus by the Jesuits on the Jesuits remains distinctive. Indeed, it is my impression that other religious orders engaged in the enterprise of translation to a much smaller extent than the Jesuits did (in the case of translation into Latin, this point is easy to demonstrate). There would appear to be a link between this translation activity and what John W. O'Malley has called the 'official promotion' of the history of the Jesuits.[9]

In other words, the Society, or at least some leading figures in it, had a concern for collective self-representation, an acute sense of their 'image' relatively unusual in this period. This image-consciousness is revealed with particular clarity in the Jesuits' celebration of their centenary in 1640, including the publication of the famous *Imago primi saeculi*.[10] This enterprise was all the more remarkable because a concern for centenaries was still relatively unusual in the seventeenth century. The best-known example is that of the celebration of the centenary of Luther's 95 theses in Protestant Germany in 1617, and it may not be too fanciful to view 1640 as a Catholic reply to 1617.

The role of printers and publishers in the enterprise of translation deserves a few words, although the subject is a large one as well as little studied. Most of the texts discussed here were produced by so-called commercial printers. Certain publishers were associated quite closely with the Society in certain cities: Christophe Plantin and his successors in Antwerp, for instance, or Kink or Mylius in Cologne, all three of whom produced a good deal of Catholic devotional literature. Other names that recur include Albinus of Mainz (for Buys), Bogard of Douai (Balinghem), and Rictius of Vienna (Bucelleni).

Finally, what were the effects of this collective enterprise? It is not difficult to imagine what these effects may have been, but measuring them is rather more difficult. In certain limited fields it is possible to say something relatively precise, so this chapter ends not with a general conclusion but with a partial one, concerning East-Central Europe.

The so-called rise of the vernaculars in early modern Europe is well known, including the proliferation of printed books in more or less standard forms of certain vernaculars at the expense of both Latin and local dialects. The importance of translation for the development of these vernaculars is also well known, especially in the case of languages in which the published literature was not extensive, in Scandinavia for example, or in East-Central Europe. So far I have discovered the names of 112 early modern translators into the languages of East-Central Europe, mainly into Polish, Czech, and Hungarian. Of these 112, 51, or nearly half, were Jesuits.

One of the great defenders of the Czech language in the difficult times that followed the battle of the White Mountain was the Jesuit Bohuslav Balbín, and two more Czech Jesuits, Jiři Constanz and Jiři Ferus, published grammars of the language. 'Jesuit Slovak' (*jezúitska slovencina*) is a term still in use to refer to a kind of koine that the Jesuits adopted to reach both the Czechs and the Slovaks.[11] It might be compared to the *língua geral*, based on Tupí, which Jesuits such as José de Anchieta employed in the missions in Brazil, or the *lengua general* employed in Mexico and Peru.

It is fair to say that the Jesuit contribution to the cultural history of East-Central and indeed to that of Eastern Europe was much more important than to that of the West. This contribution is highly visible in the architecture of the Jesuits' churches and colleges. It was crucial in education. It is also clearly discernible in Jesuit translations.

NOTES

1 See Zhang Longxi, *Mighty Opposites: From Dichotomies to Differences in the Comparative Study of China* (Stanford, 1999), p. 366; George Elison, *Deus Destroyed: The Image of Christianity in Early Modern Japan* (Cambridge, MA, 1988).

2 On translation into Tagalog, see Vicente Rafael, *Contracting Colonialism: Translation and Christian Conversion in Tagalog Society under Spanish Rule* (Ithaca, 1988), a reference for which I should like to thank Luce Giard. Rafael does not mention Clain.

3 Peter Burke, 'Translations into Latin in Early Modern Europe,' forthcoming in *Cultures of Translation in Early Modern Europe*, ed. Peter Burke and Ronnie Hsia (Cambridge).

4 Somm. *Bib.*

5 Kempis was translated by Brignon, Fabricy, Kašić, and Pazmany; St François by Constanz and Lamormaini; Luis de Granada by Cuvelier and Schott; Guicciardini by Bourghesius; Leibniz by Bosses.

6 Prague, 1652, 1721 (translations by Constanz and Rogacci); Trnava, 1693 (translation by Rogacci); Vilnius, 1705 (translation by Lancicius).

7 Steven J. Harris, 'Mapping Jesuit Science: The Role of Travel in the Geography of Knowledge,' in O'M. *Jes. Cult.*, pp. 212–40.

8 Bail. 'Style,' p. 73.

9 John W. O'Malley, 'The Historiography of the Society of Jesus: Where Does It Stand Today?' in O'M. *Jes. Cult.*, pp. 3–37, at 6.

10 Marc Fumaroli, *L'école du silence: Le sentiment des images au XVIIe siècle* (Paris, 1994, 1998), pp. 445–76.

11 L'ubomir Durovic, 'Slovak,' in *The Slavic Literary Languages: Formation and Development*, ed. Alexander M. Schenker and Edward Stankiewicz (New Haven, 1980), pp. 211–28, at 212.

3 / Join the Jesuits, See the World: Early Modern Women in Spain and the Society of Jesus

ELIZABETH RHODES

The relationship between women and the Jesuits follows a trajectory remarkably parallel to that of women and the Catholic church itself. There has always been a give and take between them, and the Society of Jesus, like the church, has refused women the official, permanent, and authoritative role they have sought. Women persist in their support of both, and their efforts on behalf of Ignatius pre-date the foundation of the Society itself. Hugo Rahner is quick to point out that 'it was from the women of his time that [Ignatius] got the most abundant help, from the early years of his own spiritual development to the period of the Society's magnificent expansion.'[1] More recently, W.W. Meissner reaffirms that, 'had it not been for the assistance of important women at critical points in the early history of the Society of Jesus, that organization may have met a far different fate.'[2]

The young women who now outnumber young men as students at Jesuit universities likewise can be counted among such supporters, if less directly than the Society's original female enthusiasts, and their presence makes understanding what they need and expect especially urgent.[3] Although the prevailing attitude of the Jesuits towards women, particularly that of the early Jesuits, has been amply considered, the other side of the coin remains largely unexamined. Without treading on Freud's toes, the question is a good one: What do women want from the Society of Jesus?

From the very beginning, there has been something compelling about the Society to women. This is evident from the time of Manresa, when Ignatius is said to have offered an early version of the Exercises 'to pious women and other disciples' in 1522, and (it can be argued) when Isabel Roser won an officially recognized position as a Jesuit in 1545.[4] In what follows, as a possible explanation of why women sought out the Jesuits, I will focus on the Society's model of discernment, self-examination, and vocation itself. It may be that what distinguishes the Society from other religious orders, which did create an official space for women among them, is precisely what some women found compelling, and also precisely what kept Ignatius and his followers from welcoming them into the inner tiers of the organization.

What follows hinges on the distinction between Woman and Man, meaning the cultural construct of how human females and males are supposed to be, and women and men, meaning the ways in which individual human beings actually are.[5] I propose that the degree to which young women are socialized as Women is proportionate to the degree to which Jesuit praxis of self-development and fulfilment will be fundamentally other to them.[6] History suggests that the empowerment of the self in relationship to the world and God taught by the *Exercises* served, and serves, as a corrective for the subordinate relationship of self to other in which women are still socialized today. The extraordinary directions taken by the early women who had access to the expectations for self-development that were normative in the Society signal how powerful the combination can be, even if those women's careers were never fully 'Jesuit.'

Today we might chuckle at Anton Huonder's description of the Basque saint: 'In spite of this reserve and his powerful, masculine style – indeed, because of them – but above all on account of his virtues, pious women felt strongly drawn towards Ignatius.'[7] But there is something worth considering in this declaration. Clearly, what Huonder refers to as 'masculine style' is no longer acceptably delineated along gender lines. However, if what he refers to is considered to mean the fullness of selfhood attained through the realization of one's potential, a pursuit in which men have long been socialized, then women's desire to claim a purchase on what the Society of Jesus had to offer by accessing that 'masculinity' is understandable, admirable, and compelling.[8]

Jesuit piety seems to have held an unhappy fascination for Spanish women. I say unhappy because it was notoriously unsuccessful with many of them, particularly those who were neither wealthy nor aristocratic. In the Inquisitorial hearings of 1526 and 1527, during which the nature of Ignatius's early formulations of the *Exercises* were investigated in Alcalá, most of the witnesses were women, who were quick to point out that most of his listeners were likewise female. Among them were, for example, María de la Flor, who said of her experience with Ignatius, that 'four times there came upon this witness a very great sadness in which nothing seemed right to her' ('que cuatro veces le vino a esta que declara muy grande tristeza, que cosa ninguna le parecía bien').[9] Ana Benavente, another witness, described herself by saying that, 'reflecting upon herself and on how she had abandoned worldliness, in her manner of dress and other things, a sadness came upon her so great that she fainted; and sometimes she had entire fainting spells and lost consciousness' ('estando consigo pensando cómo se había apartado del mundo, ansí en el vestir como en otras cosas de murmurar e jugar, la tomaba una tristeza que se desmayaba; e algunas veces la tomaban desmayos e perdía el sentido').[10] Similarly, Leonora de Mena: 'When thinking about how she had left the way she used to have of laughing and joking, and thinking about in what ways she was better off than she had been before, a sadness came upon her heart, and she lost her senses' ('estando pensando cómo había dejado la manera que había tenido de reír e jugar, e pensando cómo se estaba mejor antes, le venía una tristeza al corazón, e se la quitaban los sentidos').[11]

The inner turmoil of these women was not investigated further because the Inquisitorial officers were seeking evidence of heresy rather than of what we now call depression. Such testimonies do, however, point to inherent antagonism between Feminine experience in early modern Spain and the ideals of the Jesuits. To women, attaining the discipline, self-awareness, and independence necessary to function successfully as a Jesuit, to live physically mobile, self-sufficient, and devoted to God, was perhaps as difficult as it was alluring. Since one can reasonably assume that women's contact with men of the Society was considered prestigious and spiritually beneficial by the early seventeenth century, we might also posit the ecclesiastical and political coming to power of a type of piety with which the vast majority of Spanish women were socialized to have trouble, and to which they were equally drawn. The strength of self and identity implicit in the *Exercises* offered choices where they normatively had nothing, or less.

Among the various Catholic schools of religious practice that flourished in Golden Age Spain, that of the Jesuits was certainly the one most characterized by the rhetoric of traditional Masculinity. Balbino Marcos says, 'Ignatian spirituality is distinguished by a particular character of struggle, combat, and activity' ('La espiritualidad ignaciana se distingue por un carácter particular de lucha, de combate y de actividad').[12] Aggression is perhaps the most outstanding quality of the Society and its mission, and marks the most basic Jesuit metaphors: the army of God with its militant Christian soldier on the move. Thus Bilinkoff describes the Jesuits as 'lock-stepping soldiers of the Counter-Reformation.'[13] Jesuit piety itself is decidedly aggressive; Ignatius did not call it spiritual exercise for nothing. It is, indeed, the manifestation of conviction in the world at large. Calculating in a positive sense, it reckons via a system of vigilant self-evaluation, dependent on rigorous discipline and patterns of behaviour exercised by means of a strong will.

Ignatius's religiousness is based on the ability to endure as a functioning individual even while turning over one's will to God. That is to say, one enters the spiritual fray with one's identity in place, with 'a quiet but fierce determination to accomplish results.'[14] While pursuing divine glory, one must reject the world and everything in it without losing one's grip on one's self: 'We must make ourselves indifferent to all created things' ('Es menester hacernos indiferentes a todas las cosas criadas'), according to the *Exercises*.[15] Ignatius did not have a monopoly on worldly denial; all reform movements stressed it during this period. But men such as the Franciscan Francisco de Osuna and the Dominican Luis de Granada built an affectionate, sentimental relationship between God and the worshipper, overtly structured on a nurturing piety based on passive reception of the divine, in which salvation was an acceptable goal for the individual. Better to retreat from the world than to risk sin in it, they say.[16]

Ignatius, on the other hand, thrusts his followers into the dens of iniquity and insists they carry on, like the heroes he wanted them to be. Because the prevalent form of piety in Spain during the years when Ignatius was formulating the *Exercises* was *recogimiento*,[17] a word that means precisely 'retirement from the world,' and because its proponents and practitioners, such as Luis de Granada, were constantly being accused of heresy, it is likely that Ignatius took care to *articulate* Jesuit spiritual practice in a particularly aggressive and analytic fashion as a protective contrast to the passive, sentimental rhetoric of the *recogidos*. That is not to say that, in praxis, Jesuit piety was any less heartfelt or profound than any other, although its expression is often attuned to those 'lock-stepping soldiers.'

In the contemplative process as set forth in the *Exercises*, objectives are sought, one's spiritual compass honed in on the divine north. Unlike the emotional and sensual profusion typical of the *recogidos*, makers of the Exercises were instructed to get straight to business in their prayer: the objective is, as the text states, 'to enter into contemplation always to get what I want' ('Entrar en la contemplación siempre a buscar lo que quiero').[18] The question is one of emphasis more than content, because all contemplative practice of this period emphasizes discernment of and conformity with divine will. I submit, however, that Jesuit profession was accompanied by its own concrete manifestation in the world in ways that other methods of religious experience were not. For women socialized as Women to enter into contemplation to 'get what I want,' discerning who 'I' was constituted the first, great challenge.

The difficulty derives from the fact that such goal-oriented, subjective behaviour is contrary to the socialization experienced by women of the early modern period, except those trained like men. The abundant prescriptive literature written about how females should behave makes clear the antagonism between what women were supposed to be in early modern society, and what the successful Jesuit was. Women were instructed to think of themselves as objects, not subjects, and to find fulfilment in a lack of subjectivity (the ontological equivalent of being a virgin mother). They did not make elections, they accepted the elections of others. Juan Luis Vives's 1523 treatise *De institutione feminae Christianae* reveals just how deeply conditioned the ideal Woman was against even considering herself to be an individual. Speaking to his female reader, Vives insists, 'You are to him [man] what Adam was to Eve, specifically, daughter, sister, companion, mother, and wife. And even more, if possible, because *you are another him*. And if you deceive and offend him it is as if you had laid hands upon yourself, and you had garroted or drowned yourself' ('tú eres a él lo que Adán fue a Eva, es a saber, hija, hermana, compañera, madre y mujer. Y aún más, si ser puede, porque eres otro él. El cual siendo engañado y ofendido por ti es como si hubieses puesto mano en ti misma, y te hubieses degollado o ahogado'; my emphasis).[19]

This manner of thinking did not go away, but persisted and intensified throughout subsequent centuries, resurfacing regularly in prescriptive treatises such as *The Perfect Wife* (*La perfecta casada*, 1583) by the Augustinian Luis de León, who was also the first editor of Teresa of Avila's works. Fray Luis's perfect wife testifies to the enduring nature of Vives's philosophy of Woman: 'Woman's natural occupation, and the end for which God created her, is to be a helpmate to man ... To lighten for him the burden that married life brings with it' ('el oficio natural de la mujer, y el fin para que Dios la crió, es para que sea ayudadora del marido ... Para que le alivie de los trabajos que trae consigo la vida casada').[20]

In his manual of 1580, Juan de Espinosa insisted that 'for honourable women it is not enough simply to abstain from sin, they must also free themselves from being suspected of it, and thus is behooves them to flee all those inconveniences and indications that might cause them to be perceived in that way' ('a las mugeres de honra no basta la abstinentia sola del pecado, mas aun para librarse de la sospecha del, les conuiene huir todos aquellos inconuenientes è indiçios que pueden causarla').[21] The women with whom the Jesuits had close encounters early on were women who, judging by their actions, sought a space in which to practise the fullness of selfhood in God, during a time when prescriptive literature was busily informing them that they had no self in the first place.

Precisely at the interstices of history in which men were instructed to rush forth wielding the sword of God, women were to run away, or not even be there in the first place. Gaspar de Astete's 1603 treatise insists that 'the Christian virgin do nothing but pray and keep silent, obey her parents, and live in retirement and good behaviour' ('la doncella cristiana no haga más que orar y callar, y obrar con sus manos, y obedecer a sus padres, y viuir en recogmiento y honestidad').[22] How could women fulfil the mandates that society depicted for their sex and also exercise the freedom, adventure, and self-worth that overflowed from Ignatian spirituality? The point was precisely that they could not.

Men and women socially prepared for separation and well versed in individuation were more natural fits as successful practitioners of early modern Jesuit piety than those who were not. The religious practice sustained through the Jesuit way of life and laid out in the *Exercises* is quite distinct from what is now considered to be Feminine piety, among whose early spokespeople, ironically enough, are St Francis and Henry Suso. Bynum describes the books that represent this type of devotion as 'affective, exuberant, lyrical, and filled with images.'[23] In contrast, one does not read the *Exercises*, one 'makes' them. The key to their success is not in their words but rather in their doing.

It is not difficult to imagine why women would be attracted to the Jesuit ideal; it offered alluring power and authority and freedom to move about the world, whether the physical world or that of the spirit, with confidence and with something to offer others. When seen from its most enthralling perspective, the perspective often adopted by those marginalized from inclusion in a group, the Society trained for and promoted engagement in an exciting and dangerous world among trusted and trusting companions, not silent retirement from the same. For all but the highest-class women, this was a doubly vexed enterprise, because, across the sixteenth century, they were socialized away from the spaces in which the Jesuit enterprise rightly took place, and away from the psychological and spiritual independence necessary to succeed in the relatively de-centred life in which Ignatius's soldiers of God were trained.

For example, as Rahner observes, Isabel Roser's problems began with her decision to move to Rome, abandoning her family ties in Barcelona. To Rahner's meticulous account of the difficulties that ensued for Roser and the Jesuits, I would add that a woman's removing herself from her local community in the sixteenth century had grave personal and social consequences that it did not for a man, and Roser's particular neediness, compared with that of her male companions in the Society, speaks to inequities in female and male social training as much as to personal defects of Roser or the inadequacies of women. Roser's experience reveals how fully Masculine the understanding of non-cloistered 'freedom for God' really was, and she perhaps learned what women today still struggle with: it is almost impossible for a woman to extricate herself from family and domestic obligations with anything close to the ease with which a man can accomplish the same thing.

The Society's decision not to accommodate women in its ranks is related to issues reaching well beyond gender, issues such as individual personalities (of the men as well as the women) and larger social and professional developments that made the creation of a female branch of the Jesuits an impossible dream. John W. O'Malley observes that Ignatius's small group of men had undertaken the mission to help souls; of the saint's first companions he says, 'They were primarily itinerant preachers, like Jesus and his disciples, and they were engaged in a holiness ministry.'[24] By 1550 the same group had been drawn into the larger historical wave of European religious history, and its objective, physically and conceptually centred in Rome, had changed: to defend the Catholic faith in a time of crisis. Across the same period of time and thereafter, the official mouthpieces of this Catholic faith articulated increasingly limited and limiting ideas about women's cultural, political, and social rights, which culminated in the Council of Trent's mandates regarding enclosure for female religious.[25] Although the efficacy with which the said mandates were enforced at the local level varied greatly across Christendom, for a group vowed to obedience to the pope, Trent's decrees provided a lock on the already closed door through which women wanted to pass into the Society.

The move on the part of first-generation Jesuits into the arena of civic and cultural production also worked to the detriment of the Society's relationships with women, because it eased the Society's priorities away from the social spaces where women who were potentially heroic were normatively allowed to be – listening to preachers – into places where they could not be without breaking with social protocol and calling their moral integrity into question – in colleges, in universities, in professional spaces from which 'worthy' women were excluded. O'Malley observes that after the death of Ignatius, the number of women making the Exercises diminished, as well as the quality of directors offering them: 'The best qualified people were now busy governing the growing provinces, teaching in the schools, or managing the ever-larger communities attached to them.'[26] In contradistinction, Ignatius's early experiences teaching spiritual exercise were in public and private spaces available to women, and it was largely to women that he offered the Exercises as he was refining them in Manresa and Barcelona.[27] It did not take long for Catholic authorities, and Ignatius himself, to realize that the teaching of such spiritual control and intimacy to anyone interested in and committed to the enterprise was potentially explosive, and offering such intimacies to women socially problematic. The Inquisition, then the pope, moved in where Ignatius's early female supporters had sustained him.

Education became the focus not only of the Society's professional activity, but also of the formation of its own corps. In 1556 there were 48 Jesuit colleges. In 1615 there were 372.[28] Across the sixteenth and seventeenth centuries in Spain, with every move the Jesuits made into the public arena, opting for the education of young men, the support of public cultural and civic production, physical mobility through mission, and public obedience to papal policy, they stepped farther away from the social realities of women of all classes except the highest and lowest in Spain, and probably in Europe. This left the Society with the upper and lower echelons of the female population, because only these women were free from normalized constraints on female behaviour. At the top were the wealthy royal and elite women whose intellectual experience was similar to that of the Jesuits and with whom they got along exceptionally well, even if still denying those prominent patrons a publicly recognized place in the Society.

Also important in the early Jesuit projects were the prostitutes and other female sexual sinners who so intrigued Ignatius himself, and for whom he established the Casa Santa Marta in Rome, which served as a model for others of its kind.[29] It seems likely that the pressing, basic material and spiritual needs of the women in Santa Marta probably absorbed most of the attention they received. That is to say, these sexually transgressive women were needy of things the Jesuits could provide without compromising their own mission and without any of their female charges clamouring for admission into Society ranks. Rahner describes Santa Marta as 'a house in which these women ['fallen girls and wives who were in moral danger'] could regain their self-respect and thus gradually be brought back to their husbands.'[30] Whether the said women, married or not, ever had self-respect in the first place is a good question, and if the Jesuits educated them in its exercise, the gift was invaluable. In a society which normalized the victimization of women and legalized the physical, emotional, and verbal abuse of wives, it does not seem likely that they would have learned to respect themselves in many other circumstances.[31]

Noble and royal women pose a different question. The problem with these ladies, as Isabel Roser, Juana de Austria, and Luisa de Carvajal were to prove, was precisely that they were not only educated like noble men, but thought like noble men as well: imperiously. They expected to function in the Society as the leaders they were born and educated to be, in the same fashion that a man of the social stature of Francisco Borja was called upon to perform (he was elected as general in 1565). These expectations caused problems from the beginning, in large part because they grated against the dominant culture's soft understanding of female nature as submissive and satisfied with that which happens under the roof and wing of a father or a husband, human or divine.

There is nothing new in the conflict between strong women and strong men, but it might be productive to recall that such conflict is particularly intense during periods in history, such as the Jesuits' first several decades, when society dictates silence, invisibility, and reserve for women who are naturally neither silent nor reserved and have no desire to remain invisible. The exalted class of Ignatius's female patrons might attenuate observations such as Padberg's, who implies that there was something improper about Isabel Roser's aggressive behaviour upon arriving in Rome to join the Jesuits in an official capacity: 'Roser had been a great friend and patron of Ignatius for many years, but after she took vows she made impossible demands, continued in her own ways, and demanded interminable hours of spiritual direction (more than all the rest of the Jesuits in the Roman Curia combined).'[32] It is possible that Roser's ongoing need for spiritual direction was legitimate: the Ignatian way of prayer and self-examination was – and in many ways still is – antithetical to the ways in which women of all classes were socialized to think about themselves, and so held a powerful attraction during the period in history when women were seeking out the Jesuits for instruction in how to define themselves differently.[33]

Beneath this upper echelon, where one such as Teresa of Avila was born, women's contact with the Jesuits and what they had to offer was largely a matter of coincidence *until* Teresa's own experience with the Society made history. Her twenty-year-long quest for a religious authority who could understand her ecstatic relationship with God ended happily in her encounter with the Jesuit Juan de Prádanos, who instructed her in spiritual discernment following the Jesuit paradigm: disciplined self-knowledge in God, followed by action. Teresa's spiritual life story singles out the Jesuits as the first to label her ecstatic experiences as blessings rather than curses, and also indicates that Teresa herself found Jesuit methods of discernment and discipline productive in a way that no others had been. In 1555 she gave Francisco Borja an account of her prayer, which he endorsed and instructed her to continue.[34] Her next confessor was Prádanos, who saved her religious career from the threat of exorcism under which her other superiors had sought to silence her. Almost immediately after their relationship became established, she settled into her ambitions of mysticism and Carmelite reform, unimpeded by those who had held her back for so long. The self-knowledge and discipline she acquired under the aegis of Prádanos's direction evidently enabled Teresa to define herself, rather than her confessors, as the surest authority over her relationship with God, a self-definition that literally turned her life around.[35]

What Prádanos taught Teresa, I believe, was how to take her life into her own hands. This is perhaps the essence of what Jesuit discernment offered, and still offers, women, and certainly in the sixteenth and seventeenth centuries they were sensitive to the tremendous opportunity it gave them in a time when all prevailing ideological dogma was turning them in the opposite direction, towards reactive rather than active living. Precisely because of Teresa's experience with Prádanos, and especially because she wrote compellingly about that experience in books that circulated widely in manuscript and, after 1588, in print, by the end of the sixteenth century many women in Spain with any modicum of class or authority, the professionally religious as well as devout Catholics living in the world, sought out a Jesuit as a confessor and/or spiritual director.

The question is, what happened next? Thereafter, women and Jesuits had contact largely, but not exclusively, under three rubrics, the first of which is represented by individual women's frustrated attempts at breaking with the social dictates of female enclosure for Catholic religious women, with Spain producing three in rapid succession: Isabel Roser, Juana de Austria, and Luisa de Carvajal. The second avenue was financial and political patronage. The third is exchange through confession and spiritual direction, where I believe the richest relationship developed, precisely because of the unique and equitable balance the Jesuits professed between contemplation and action, and because where other types of spirituality, such as that of the Carmelites, offered an intensification of the Female experience, the Jesuits offered an antidote to the same. St John of the Cross could no more have been a Jesuit than Ignatius of Loyola could have been a Carmelite. Choices were made, priorities were set, and larger cultural trends cemented themselves around individual men and women so that escaping them became all but impossible. Those larger cultural trends, to which I alluded above, worked much more effectively than Ignatius himself at keeping women out of the Society.

In the sixteenth and seventeenth centuries, women as a gender were subdivided into categories of sexual utility and, according to dominant constructs, signified exclusively via their relationships to men (daughter, wife, mother, widow, or nun). These constructs were employed as sounding-boards to formulate notions about masculinity and rightness by contrast. When pressed to define the wiles of the devil, for example, Ignatius wrote, 'The devil behaves like a woman, in being weak by default and strong only in fits' ('El enemigo se hace como mujer, en ser flaco por fuerza y fuerte de grado').[36] The dominant construct of Woman as evil, versus the notion of Man as struggling with evil, could not but influence the Society's workings with individual women. Inevitably, its members backed up against the equation of woman = sex, and prudently curtailed their activities with women because of the inevitable pall of sexual misconduct produced by even the most innocent intimacy with females.

Copious are the instructions dictated by Ignatius that on the surface appear to denigrate women but just as likely constitute an attempt to shield his brothers from the compromising appearances that ensued from their contact with non-royal females, or, as Raitt says, 'not because they [common and lower class women] were more dangerous in themselves but because conversation with them was more likely to be misinterpreted.'[37] O'Malley cites several cases in which the Jesuits were not only willing but eager to hear women's confessions, only to see their efforts frustrated by the overriding understanding that doing so was detrimental to the Society's reputation.[38] Ignatius's Casa Santa Marta for reformed prostitutes brought the Jesuits many headaches precisely because of the dominant understanding of non-noble women as sex objects rather than human subjects; critics of the Society referred to the Casa as the Jesuits' bordello.[39] Their relationships with women of the lower classes were especially vexed, not only because, according to Ignatius, such women's powers of discrimination were insufficient for the task at hand,[40] but also because early modern society perceived these women primarily as sexual objects and therefore tagged any association with them as necessarily sexual. In ways such as these, the hegemonic discourses of gender during this period worked against women's partnership with the Jesuits by urging them into ideological and physical enclosures that Ignatius had quite intentionally eschewed for his members from the very beginning. The social realities of women's lives, increasingly circumscribed by reproductive and contemplative objectives versus productive and active ones, accomplished the same.

Upper-class women were considered subjects with a value ascribed to their persons, a value that the entire class system was set up to defend. Juana de Austria, the emperor's daughter who took the vows of a Jesuit scholastic, could be alone with Francisco Borja *because* she was royal, not in spite of it. She, like the noblewoman Luisa de Carvajal, had subjective rights which women of lesser social classes did not.

It is in this light, I believe, that the legion of cautionary comments made by Ignatius and others about dealing with women, which later played themselves out in women's attempts to relate to the Society, are best understood. Upon entering Rome, Ignatius advised his brothers, 'We should be extremely careful and not converse with any women, unless they are of the highest rank' ('Debemos andar con mucha cautela y no tener conversaciones con mujeres, a no ser que sean ilustres').[41] Ignatius was raised in an intensely misogynist culture in which his own youthful wanderings in lust actually served to make him heroic by virtue of his having overcome them, as similar adventures had done for St Augustine. Ignatius's own history with women was evidently memorable. Juan Alfonso de Polanco said of the pre-conversion days of the Society's founder: 'Although he was affectionately devoted to the faith [as a youth], he did not live at all in conformity with it, nor did he keep himself from sin, rather he was especially naughty in gambling and dealing with women, in raising a ruckus, and in using weapons' ('aunque era aficionado a la fe, no vivía nada conforme a ella, ni se guardaba de pecados, antes era especialmente travieso en juegos y en cosas de mujeres, y en revueltas y cosas de armas').[42] Given this propensity to consider indulgence in women as indulgence in sin, it is not surprising that for Ignatius, and for the Jesuits, women sometimes seem to be considered a problem to be avoided, except in cases likely to result in financial benefit.[43]

After Roser, the Society's next encounter with a strong Spanish woman ended in another form of rejection. Around 1557, Juana de Austria began to pursue entry into the Jesuits, formally and with vows. For Ignatius, who had done all he could to keep his Society free from the clutches of women, a real dilemma ensued. How to say no to the most powerful woman in Europe, and among the richest? Juana's admission as a scholastic was rescindable at the Society's discretion. In exchange for even such conditional acceptance, absolute secrecy was demanded. Juana's courtiers scratched their heads for years trying to decipher the mystery of her veiled and severe countenance, and the unpleasantly ascetic nature of her court. Juana had been provided with an education befitting an imperial princess and her iron-clad will was unshakeable. A cog in the imperial machine, she was raised like a man. Her education and will, which tested her Jesuit companions as long as she lived, made Juana's own transformation into a Jesuit relatively easy, because she was a natural fit: Jesuit piety offered a strong-willed woman confirmation of her subjective status. However, Juana's was a short career. She died of uterine cancer in 1573, at the age of 38.[44]

One woman did manage to negotiate the frontiers of femininity and Jesuit life successfully, Luisa de Carvajal y Mendoza, rumoured to have been Ignatius's niece.[45] Born into the nobility in 1566, she was orphaned at an early age and raised until the age of 10 in the household of Juana de Austria. After the death of the aunt with whom she had lived at court, she was sent to live with her uncle, the powerful Francisco de Hurtado y Mendoza. The Jesuit influence continued; Don Francisco had made the Spiritual Exercises with Francisco Borja, and he was devoted to the Society. He also forced what are now called sado-masochistic religious exercises upon the adolescent Luisa, who submitted unquestioningly to his excesses and, not surprisingly, found herself thinking about dying.[46]

Upon the deaths of her uncle and aunt, Luisa began the crusade that was to make her life more overtly heroic: she signed over all her inheritance to the Jesuits and set about living a harshly ascetic life. Her mystical visions began at age 18, although, like most women religious, she claims she had been aware of her vocation since childhood. When she heard of the persecution of the Jesuits in England, she began to forge her plan to go there, abandoning country, family, friends, and language for God. In the meantime she took four vows: of poverty, of obedience to her Jesuit superior, to pursue perfection, and finally, in 1598, to become a martyr. This last vow is what reconciled Carvajal's womanhood, which kept her from active heroism, with her ambitions for an active apostolate, which other women had pursued through Jesuit channels before her, and would after her, without public success. If Carvajal took any vows allying her with the Jesuits specifically, they remain secret. However, her affiliation with the Society could not have been stronger, given her sex.

Freed by her religious vows as nothing else could have freed her, Carvajal actually went to England at the height of the persecution of the Catholics in London. Her penitential instruments were confiscated by customs officers upon her entry into England, and she was thereafter able to vent her considerable energies in more positive directions than in flagellating herself. After arriving, she learned English and formed an unofficial part of the persecuted Catholic population there. She instructed in the Catholic faith, ripped up anti-papist posters in the street, attended to prostitutes, and comforted the Catholics in prisons. She wrote letters and poems and probably things that have been lost. In short, she was allowed the opportunity to develop into a person, to control her own life, and to exercise authority (all while claiming obedience).

There were Catholics who were executed for lesser crimes against the English state than Carvajal committed single-handedly: she went so far as to establish a feminine version of the Society in downtown London. She surely could have got herself killed had she wanted to die, but she died in bed in London at the respectable age of 52. It seems that, once freed from the constraints of an oppressive society and emancipated by the Masculine mandates of another, this strong-willed, well-educated, and literate woman found life worth living.

Carvajal's life offers crucial evidence of something extremely important. Unable to find a space in which to exercise itself, Carvajal's spirit turned on itself. While living in Spain, she wrote of dying and of delight in pain and negation, in a mystical language typical of women religious authors of her day. Released into a space to grow and prosper, given authority and trust, her spirit flourished and her life continued to its natural end.

Some women are no different from some men: a Jesuit experience frees them to forge a self that would have remained unrealized without it. When we look at the women who wanted to become Jesuits and could not, and those who unofficially did so, that is what we see.

NOTES

1 Hugo Rahner, *Saint Ignatius Loyola: Letters to Women*, trans. Kathleen Pond and S.A.H. Weetman (New York, 1960), pp. 4–5.
2 W.W. Meissner, *Ignatius of Loyola: The Psychology of a Saint* (New Haven, 1992), p. 238.
3 'All Jesuit universities have more female than male undergraduate students. In several the female percentage approaches two-thirds of the total enrollment' (William B. Neenan, 'Sports and Jesuit Universities: A Winning Combination,' *Conversations on Jesuit Higher Education* 21 [2002]: 8).
4 About Manresa, see Ricardo García-Villoslada, *San Ignacio de Loyola, Nueva biografía* (Madrid, 1986), pp. 229. On 25 December 1545, Isabel Roser pronounced her vows as a Jesuit, with Lucrezia di Brandine and Francisca Cruyllas, in the presence of Ignatius at the church of Santa Maria della Strada in Rome (Rahner,

Letters, pp. 286–7). Within two years, Ignatius was seeking papal permission to release her from her vows, at which time he also sought and obtained papal dispensation to free the Society from having women subject to their supervision. Most studies of Roser's relationship with Ignatius are by Jesuits and reflect the interests of the Society, generally repeating Rahner's belief that Roser's feisty personality (usually referred to as 'domineering') was responsible for the initial failure of women to gain permanent acceptance as Jesuits. Roser's frustrated attempts to exercise her own will are traditionally called 'nervous disorders' (cf. ibid., p. 263), and in García-Villoslada's authoritative biography of Ignatius, Roser is considered 'a parenthesis' (pp. 237–8).

5 For refined distinctions, see Carol S. Vance, 'Social Construction Theory and Sexuality,' in *Constructing Masculinity*, ed. Maurice Berger, Brian Wallis, and Simon Watson (New York, 1995), pp. 37–48; and Judith Butler, *Gender Trouble: Feminism and the Subversion of Identity* (New York, 1990).

6 Iparraguirre notes that during the early modern period, women were guided through 'open Exercises,' thus called because they lacked precisely those related to election. Election was presumably eliminated because women were believed to be incapable of, or otherwise not responsible for, such decisions in their own lives (Ignacio Iparraguirre, *Práctica de los Ejercicios de San Ignacio de Loyola en vida de su autor* [Rome, 1946], p. 271 n173).

7 Cited in Rahner, *Letters*, p. 5; Anton Huonder, *Ignatius von Loyola. Beiträge zu seinem Charakterbild* (Cologne, 1932).

8 Less fortunate is Tellechea Igídoras's interpretation of Juan Pascual's recollection that from 1522 to 1526, honourable women, married and widowed, 'went around day and night behind him with their mouths hanging open, dying to hear the conversations and spiritual words he was always saying' ('andaban de noche y de día tras él con la boca abierta, muertas por oír las pláticas y palabras espirituales que siempre decía') as evidence that, 'as always, women are more sensitive to the attractiveness of the pilgrim, whose words are measured and true' ('Como siempre, las mujeres son más sensibles al atractivo del peregrino de palabras mesuradas y verdaderas') (José Ignacio Tellechea Idígoras, *Ignacio de Loyola, solo y a pie* [Salamanca, 1990], p. 128). Men obviously found Ignatius attractive for at least as many reasons as did women; hence the extremely popular, exclusively masculine Society.

9 Procesos de Alcalá, in Ignatius of Loyola, *Ejercicios espirituales, directorio, y documentos de S. Ignacio de Loyola*, ed. José Calveras (Barcelona, 1958), p. 337.

10 Ibid., p. 338.

11 Ibid., p. 339.

12 'Literatura religiosa en el Siglo De Oro español,' in *Historia de la Iglesia en España*, ed. Ricardo García-Villoslada, 5 vols (Madrid, 1980), III-2, p. 517.

13 Jodi Bilinkoff, 'The Many "Lives" of Pedro de Ribadeneyra,' *Renaissance Quarterly* 52:1 (1999): 185. O'Malley distinguishes between the religious and military meanings of terms such as 'general,' and cautions against over-emphasis on the military imagery in documents by the first generation of Jesuits (O'M. *First*, p. 45).

14 Bilinkoff, 'The Many Lives,' p. 194. She is describing the biographies on men and women composed by Pedro de Ribadeneira, which she finds highlight this determination. She says that Ribadeneira's biography of Ignatius constructs 'an exemplar of virtue worthy of imitation, particularly a model of sanctity applied to effective action' (p. 185).

15 Ignatius, *Ejercicios espirituales*, ed. Calveras, p. 58. This indifference and independence, to which Christ calls repeatedly in the New Testament, is often experienced by women as loneliness (versus solitude), or even abandonment. For example, Luisa de Carvajal, whose case is discussed at the end of this study, described her solitary career as a missionary in London in the early 1600s: 'I used to call solitude not only the corporeal flight from the world into religious retreat, but also, and better, being cut off from all things which the world loves and esteems; surrounded by a thousand abandonments and ignominies in following Christ, the peace with one's enemies broken and, in public declaration of this, left by all creatures and thrown from their house into the street' ('Llamaba yo soledad, no solamente a la huida corporal del siglo y al encerramiento religioso, sino también, y mejor, al estar cortada de todas las cosas que el mundo ama y estima; cercada de mil desamparos y ignominias en seguimiento de Cristo, rotas las paces con sus enemigos y con pública profesión desto, despedida de todas las criaturas y arrojada de su casa dellas en la calle') (Luisa de Carvajal y Mendoza, *Escritos autobiográficos*, ed. Camilo María Abad [Barcelona, 1966], pp. 214–15).

16 Osuna's best-known treatise is the one generally held responsible for Teresa of Avila's religious career, the *Tercer abecedario espiritual*, ed. Melquíades Andrés Martín (Madrid, 1972); in English, *The Third Spiritual Alphabet*, trans. Mary Giles (New York, 1981). Luis de Granada's books took Europe by storm in the mid-1500s. See his *Obras completas*, ed. Alvaro Huerga, 40 vols to date (Madrid, 1995–); and Elizabeth Rhodes, 'Spain's Misfired Canon: The Case of Fray Luis de Granada's Libro de la oración,' *Journal of Hispanic Philology* 15 (1990): 3–28.

17 Melquíades Andrés Martín, *Los recogidos. Nueva visión de la mística española (1500–1700)* (Madrid, 1976), p. 451.

18 Ignatius, *Ejercicios*, p. 86.

19 The first Spanish transation, of 1528, is the text Howe edits and from which I translate: Juan Luis Vives, *Instrucción de la mujer cristiana*, trans. Juan Justiniano, ed. Elizabeth Teresa Howe (Madrid, 1995), p. 212.

20 Fray Luis de León, *La perfecta casada* [1583], ed. Javier San José Lera (1938; Madrid, 1992), p. 100.

21 Juan de Espinosa, *Diálogo en laude de las mujeres* [1580], ed. Angela González Simón (Madrid, 1946), p. 268.
22 Gaspar de Astete, *Tratado del gouierno de la familia, y estado de las viudas y donzellas* (Burgos, 1603), p. 183.
23 Caroline Bynum, *Holy Feast and Holy Fast: The Religious Significance of Food to Medieval Women* (Berkeley and Los Angeles, 1987), p. 105.
24 O'M. *First*, p. 15.
25 Lisa Fullam discusses these mandates specifically; see *Juana, S.J.: The Past (and Future?) Status of Women in the Society of Jesus* (St Louis, 1999).
26 O'M. *First*, pp. 132–3.
27 The spaces where Ignatius gave the primitive versions of the Exercises are named in the Inquisitorial documents in Procesos de Alcalá, pp. 333–43.
28 See García-Villoslada, 'Colegios de la Compañía,' in *San Ignacio*, pp. 876–911.
29 The foundation was approved by the pope on 21 February 1547. According to Ignatius's autobiography, after returning to Azpeitia from Paris (1535), he busied himself controlling the activities of local prostitutes; see Ignatius of Loyola, *El peregrino. Autobiografía de San Ignacio de Loyola*, ed. Josep María Rambla Blanch (Bilbao, 1983), p. 89.
30 Rahner, *Letters*, p. 17.
31 On the status of women under early modern Spanish law, see Gregorio López, *Las siete partidas del sabio Rey Don Alonso el Nono* [*sic*], *nuevamente glosadas* (Valladolid, 1587); and Alonso de Vega, *Suma llamada Nueva Recopilación y práctica del fuero interior* (Madrid, 1606). E. Barriobero y Herrán reproduces selections of these legal codes pertinent to women in *Los delitos sexuales en las viejas leyes españolas* (Madrid, 1930).
32 John Padberg, 'Secret, Perilous Project: A Woman Jesuit,' URL http://www.companysj.com/v171/secret.html.
33 A study on the confessional influence of the Jesuits on women has yet to be done. There is evidence that women specifically sought out Jesuits for spiritual counsel, and the influence of Teresa of Avila's praise of them as spiritual directors, published in her *Life*, was quite substantial; see Charmarie J. Blaisdell, 'Calvin's and Loyola's Letters to Women: Politics and Spiritual Counsel in the Sixteenth Century,' in *Calviniana: Ideas and Influence of Jean Calvin*, ed. Robert V. Schnucker, Sixteenth Century Essays and Studies 10 (Kirksville, MO, 1988), pp. 235–54; and Jill Raitt, 'Two Spiritual Directors of Women in the Sixteenth Century: St. Ignatius of Loyola and St. Teresa of Avila,' in *In laudem Caroli: Renaissance and Reformation Studies for Charles G. Nauert*, ed. James V. Mehl, Sixteenth Century Essays and Studies 49 (Philadelphia, 1998), pp. 213–31.
34 Teresa of Avila, *The Book of Her Life*, in *Saint Teresa of Avila: Collected Works*, trans. Kieran Kavanaugh and Otilio Rodríguez, 2nd ed., vol. 1 (Washington, 1987), sec. 24.3.

35 On this long process, see Elizabeth Rhodes, 'Seasons with God and the World in Teresa of Avila's *Book*,' *Studia mystica* 22 (2001): 24–53.

36 Ignatius, *Ejercicios*, p. 203.

37 Raitt, 'Two Spiritual Directors,' p. 216. For example, 'I would not enter upon spiritual conversations with women who are young or belong to the lower classes of the people, except in church or in places which are visible to all ... A scandal, whether true or false, injures us more than the loss of half of all the spiritual progress that God achieves through us' (Rahner, *Letters*, p. 12, citing *FN* 1:440ff.).

38 O'M. *First*, pp. 147–8.

39 Rahner, *Letters*, p. 19.

40 See ibid., p. 10.

41 Ignatius, *El peregrino*, p. 97.

42 Cited in Rambla Blanch's introduction, ibid., p. 22.

43 Regarding Pedro de Ribadeneira's *Life* of Estefanía de Manrique, Bilinkoff remarks, 'This construction of an exemplary life may have also served as a guidebook for Jesuits in their dealing with elite women, suggesting ways to serve their penitents' spiritual needs, to be sure, but also to secure their donations and enlist their aid in promoting the goals of the Society of Jesus' ('The Many Lives,' p. 189).

44 On the life of Juana de Austria, see Annemarie Jordan Gschwend, 'Los retratos de Juana de Austria posteriores a 1554: La imagen de una princesa de Portgual, una regente de España y una jesuita,' *Reales sitios* 39:151 (2002): 42–65; and vol. 138 of *Reales sitios* (1998), devoted to the monastery she founded, the Descalzas Reales.

45 For a complete biography of Carvajal, see Rhodes, *This Tight Embrace: Luisa de Carvajal y Mendoza (1566–1614)* (Milwaukee, 2000).

46 Carvajal describes these practices in her spiritual life story; see ibid., pp. 81–5, 95–7.

4 / Between History and Myth:
The *Monita secreta Societatis Jesu*

SABINA PAVONE

In 1614, in Kraków, a small pamphlet was published that was destined to have a profound impact in succeeding years. Its title was *Monita privata Societatis Jesu*,[1] and its anonymous editor claimed that it contained the true instructions of the Society of Jesus, kept secret by superiors for fear that the good name of the order would be besmirched. The editor claimed that he had come into possession of the text by a stroke of luck, and had rushed to publish it so that everyone would know the true face of the Society, hidden until then beneath a veil of piety and self-abnegation. The last chapter of the *Monita* contained this passage:

Superiors should be careful to keep these *Secret Instructions* to themselves, communicating their contents to only a few of the most trustworthy fathers. Drawing upon these Instructions, they should teach others how they can profitably serve the Society, but they should do this not as if they were citing somebody else's opinion but as coming from their own considered judgment. Since, if these Instructions should fall into the hands of outsiders (may it never happen!), they will be interpreted so as to make us look bad, superiors should deny that they are genuine. They should get confirmation of the inauthenticity from some of Ours who they know for certain are ignorant of their existence. They will show how these *Secret Instructions* differ from our general procedures, and how they differ from those others that are printed and published. Finally, let them instigate an inquiry as to whether some Jesuit might not be responsible for writing them. If even the slightest suspicion should fall on somebody, they should be imputed to him, and he should be dismissed from the Society.[2]

In effect, the pamphlet read as a set of behaviour protocols for the Jesuit. It had nothing to do with religion per se, but rather invited the members of the Society to extend their political and economic power by means of a slow but steady infiltration of society at all levels. This was to be effected through domination of the conscience, with the confessor serving in the role of principal protagonist. The following passage outlines the norms of behaviour for the confessors of widows:

They should make frequent visits to the homes of widows, and they should through spiritual but pleasant conversation win their loyalty and cultivate them. They should not be too exacting with them in confession, unless it becomes clear there is nothing to gain from them. To keep them on the string, it will help very much to grant them special favours, such as easy access to our buildings, tête-à-têtes whenever and with whichever fathers they desire ... Once the widows are securely attached to us and are prepared to follow the spiritual direction they receive in confession, it should be dunned into them that their actions will be more meritorious in God's eyes if they not give alms to any religious cause without the knowledge of their confessor. They should draw up a list of those to whom they have decided to give alms and show it to him, who then will either add or delete names as seems good to him. Confessors should try to prevent members of other religious orders from visiting the widows, lest they drag the widows along their path instead of ours. Women are by nature so inconstant.[3]

At the same time, the *Monita* exhorted Jesuits to hide their real intentions whenever possible, by demonstrating humility before and submission to the reigning powers: 'They should insist with princes that the awarding of favours and dignities be in accord with the requirements of justice, and that they will greatly offend God if they sin against that virtue. They should profess that they themselves want no part in government, and that they say this not because they are of themselves unwilling but by reason of their office.'[4] Several of the chapters were dedicated to the lack of fairness with which Jesuit fathers were treated, and underlined the strong hierarchical structure of the order. In both its language and its structure,[5] the libellous pamphlet seemed to originate in the Society of Jesus, but its overemphatic picture of the Jesuits as the receptacle of every possible human vice made its defamatory intent clear. The text seemed false, even if of high quality.

Not long after its publication, the *Monita privata* was officially recognized as nothing more than anecdotal hearsay, and the Society of Jesus, with the support of the ecclesiastical authorities, took every measure possible to see that the libel was publicly denounced as such. First to intervene to that end were the Polish authorities. In July 1615 the bishop of Kraków, Piotr Tylicki, opened an inquiry: 'Lest such a great crime, which traduces an innocent religious order, go un-punished and provoke vindication from heaven, we charge Your Reverences to deal with the author of this sacrilegious text. You should inquire into the investigation carried out at our behest by proceeding first of all against the aforementioned Hieronymus Zahorowski in accordance with the prescriptions of both the law and justice.'[6] Already at that date, in other words, the Jesuits knew that the author of the pamphlet was one of them, or rather, had been one of them, as was shown by the *Diarium* of the Jesuit house of St Barbara, in Kraków,[7] from which Zahorowski had been invited to depart owing to his unseemly behaviour.[8] He had in fact already instructed his students to copy out various letters of complaint against the leadership of the Society, and had sent them to prominent figures within the Polish establishment. He was, in other words, not new to the implementing of this kind of defamatory attack. Zahorowski was born between 1582 and 1583 in Volynia. He belonged to an Orthodox family and probably became a Catholic after being enrolled in a Jesuit college. Many Orthodox young noblemen were sent to the Jesuits to receive an education appropriate to their social class. Chapter 12 of the *Monita* perhaps reflects his experience, where it summarizes the measures adopted by the Jesuits to persuade their students to join the Society: 'Both extreme zeal and great skill are necessary to attract youth of good brains, physical beauty, nobility, and wealth. To entice them, the rectors of the school shower them with kindness, keep them at arm's length from the molestations of the tutors, praise them often, offer them small gifts, and during the solemn holidays admit them to the refectory.'[9]

The *Monita privata* was quickly condemned by the Holy Office, in a decree of 28 December 1616, in which it was written: 'We declare altogether prohibited, as we have in fact prohibited, the aforementioned book, falsely attributed to the Society of Jesus. We prohibit it as filled with calumnies and defamations, and we order that henceforth it is forbidden for anybody to read, sell, or possess it.'[10] Prior to the final decision of the Holy Office, Cardinal Roberto Bellarmino, a Jesuit, produced a *consulto* in which he wrote that the *monita* 'have not been written by a good or devout person, and surely not by those who are superiors of a religious order or congregation, but by an evil liar. That is clear because in them there are many statements incompatible with genuine piety, with morality, and even with good sense. That is my judgment.'[11]

Notwithstanding the determined efforts of the Jesuits to destroy every copy they could find, the *Monita* continued to circulate clandestinely not only in Poland, but in a variety of other European nations, where new editions quickly appeared. In the seventeenth century alone, eighteen editions were published, in countries ranging from France to Italy, from England to the Netherlands. On occasion the text was mixed with anti-Jesuit material gathered from other pamphlets; the first of these miscellanies, chronologically speaking, was the *Historia Jesuitica*, written by the Protestant scholar Ludwig Lutz and published in Basel in 1627. Arriving at a moment of deep-seated anti-Jesuit feeling, the *Monita* was in fact considered by enemies of the order a striking proof of the essentially criminal intent of the Jesuits: 'The Jesuits' wrote Lutz, 'pretend that what they are about is the building up and defence of the Roman Catholic church and the conversion to it of those who have strayed or been led away ... [But] their real aim, to which they direct their gaze and all their efforts, is the subjugation of the whole world to the power of the Jesuits.'[12] These enemies seemed more or less unconcerned that the pamphlet had been almost instantly denounced as false in origin. In their minds, it was entirely possible that this denunciation sprang from the very same ecclesiastical authority that had sided with the Jesuits to begin with. From their point of view, censure was inevitable, while reality showed that the Jesuits would behave exactly as the *Monita* predicted: they would infiltrate the courts, cosy up to widows, and employ any means necessary to achieve their goal of enrolling the young nobility in their colleges. Every denial of involvement in these things by the Society seemed only to deepen their guilt. The *Monita* appeared only to add credibility to these suspicions, with its last chapter, quoted at the beginning of this essay, dwelling on how the fathers might be accused of precisely these actions and enjoining them to absolute secrecy, with the further instruction that they deny such actions had ever been contemplated within the order.

The two positions – of the Jesuits and their detractors – were completely irreconcilable, and this situation remained more or less unchanged through the centuries. The anti-Jesuit faction considered the text a fully legitimate proof of the nefarious methods of the Society.[13] On the other side, Jesuit historians, at least until the beginning of the twentieth century, believed the *Monita* so patently false that they limited their writing to proving that point and that point alone, thereby turning sterile any larger debate on this text.[14] But that debate remains of great interest, apart from the immemorial question of the text's veracity. To affirm, as is obvious, that the *Monita* is not authentic, and is therefore not the secret constitution of the Society of Jesus, cannot be considered a point of arrival. It must, if anything, be considered the starting point of any research.

Peter Burke, in a recent contribution entitled 'The Black Legend of the Jesuits,' maintains that once we concede that both structuralist and positivist approaches are *passé*, even though both have yielded valuable results in their time, it may be opportune 'to attempt a third approach to the Black Legend, viewing it as a system or at least a repertoire of stereotypes, each of which was formed at a particular moment for particular reasons, although many of them persisted for much longer to be employed in other contexts. The stereotypes might be studied not in isolation but in interaction with the events.'[15] This insight seems to me particularly fruitful as regards an analysis of a text such as the *Monita*, which, in my opinion, has a two-sided valence. The first, obviously, deals with the formation of a negative myth of the Jesuits, a myth whose origins date to the beginning of the sixteenth century.[16] This myth hung on stubbornly up until and throughout the nineteenth century, with a particular recrudescence at the time of the general suppression of the Society (1773). The second, less obvious, has to do with a particular moment in the history of the order. It was a moment of especially lively debate, debate that took place notwithstanding the face of orderly unity the Jesuits invariably turned to the world. This unity, by the way, paradoxically was only reinforced by the libel.

The famous inquiry *De detrimentis*,[17] undertaken in 1606 by General Claudio Acquaviva, did its best to credibly ground events then taking place within the order, and deserves to be studied in a more attentive and organic manner than it has been to date. Such a study would help clarify the reality within individual provinces as regards both their internal workings and their role in various national contexts. The reading of these documents shows, in fact, how in many cases it was precisely the provincial superiors who were the first to underline weaknesses and to see with clarity how these defects might create a bad impression in the surrounding areas. In the Polish case, that which interests us most about the *Monita* is the dossier drawn up by a provincial named Decio Striverio, who showed clearly that it was the intimacy of the fathers with the sovereign and his court that produced the greatest ill will towards the Society. He highlighted the fathers' bad habit of judging 'impertinent' all political debate, thereby placing themselves at the receiving end of many attacks. Striverio also portrayed negatively the attitude of submission and obedience towards superiors, the fluctuating adherence to the vow of poverty, the decline in fraternal charity among the members, and the greed of some – all of which, taken together, helped substantiate accusations that the Jesuits were far more interested in worldly goods than in spiritual good.

Having arrived in Poland in 1564, the Jesuits were rapidly integrated into the country, where they assumed an important role not only in religious but also in political life. The monarchy found itself up against the nobility, which was predisposed to a lessening of the sovereign's role and an augmentation of its own. Members such as Father Piotr Skarga,[18] the court preacher, were recognized as strenuous defenders of the monarchical cause, and for that reason the Society became a steady target of polemics by the nobility. Also weighing against the Society was its being a foreign religious order, identified with the Roman church and even the Spanish crown,[19] in view of its founder's birthplace. In consequence, the Society was seen as fundamentally extraneous and hostile to Polish interests.[20] Portions of the Polish nobility were wedded to the Calvinist cause, and sources show that Hieronim Zahorowski was tied to that world through the figure of Prince Jerzy Zbaraski.[21] Zbaraski, in turn, was described in a letter from Skarga to General Acquaviva as 'disertus ac potens,'[22] one of the most ferocious enemies of the Society during the *rokosz* of Sandomir (also known as the revolt of Zebrzydowski, the name of its leader) of 1606, when the noble party (for the most part Calvinists, though some were Catholics) tried to reduce the king's power and to expel the Jesuits from the state.

The *Monita secreta* – this was the definitive title by which the pamphlet would be known from then on[23] – seemed therefore to be the missing proof demonstrating conclusively that the Jesuits would use every means in their power to subvert the Polish state and achieve domination. From this point of view, the *Monita* was born in a particularly propitious context, one that allowed its author to escape condemnation thanks to his powerful political protection. This is an important point in understanding the facility and speed with which the text was diffused in early seventeenth-century Poland, but it does not, in and of itself, explain its success.

The *monita* are children of their time, that is to say, of a historical period strongly interested in *arcana imperii* and therefore particularly receptive to everything that had to do with this theme.[24] To cite just one example, think of the obsession of Paolo Sarpi, who was sincerely convinced that there existed secret constitutions of the Society of Jesus. Sarpi wrote to M. de l'Isle:

I have always admired the Jesuits' political astuteness, especially in the way they keep secrets. Yes, their constitutions are in print, but it is impossible to see a copy. I'm not speaking of those rules published in Lyon (they're puerile), but the real laws of their mode of government, which contain lots of secrets ... There are no other people in the world who in so great accord work for a given cause, who manage to be given directions with such precision, who are so ardent and zealous in going about their business. I believe it would be a tremendous gain to be able to get into the secrets of their governance and to discover their political outlook and views, in order to be able to confront them at the opportune moment.[25]

But it is also true that the *Monita* could not have been produced save by someone from within the order, who knew the functional mechanisms and who knew, in so many words, which buttons to press. It is undeniable that, despite being false, the *Monita* – if one excludes the avowedly satirical sections – strikes one above all for its verisimilitude. The roles of confessor and spiritual director (chaps 2–5), the mechanisms of recruitment (chap. 8), the disparity between professed (especially *professi dei quattro voti*) and spiritual coadjutors and the problem of the dismissed (chaps 14–16), and the problems of the power of the general and of delation (chap. 13) were questions that provoked differences of opinion among the Jesuits themselves.

Several *memoriali* preserved at the Archive of the Congregation for the

Doctrine of the Faith demonstrate that not only the Spanish province (whose opposition to Acquaviva was well known)[26] but also the Italian was rife with murmurs against the monarchical powers of the superior general, who alone can and does appoint all provincials, visitors, superiors, and rectors, all consultors and secretaries, down to preachers, teachers, and confessors – in a word, all superiors in every time and place. And indeed, only he designates who will become professed of the 'Fourth Vow,' that is, one of the group in whose hands the government of the order exclusively rests.[27]

Strongly criticized also was abuse of the sacrament of confession, employed as an instrument of blackmail not only within the Society but against penitents outside it, 'as happened some months ago in the Venice province, where a father of excellent quality was expelled because the penitent asserted not to have said the things they say he said, and, about the others things he confessed, he asserted not to have given permission to talk.'[28] Another request was that the *Constitutions* be changed so as to reflect the fact that certain of its provisions, such as the *correctio fraterna*, touched on matters being debated within the wider Catholic church, and certain others, such as the choice of provincials, the power of the provincial congregations, and the selection of missionaries, were the subject of debate within the Society. One of the charges repeated again and again was that, when Ignatius died, the *Constitutions* were not ready to be promulgated, but that Juan Alfonso de Polanco forced their promulgation as a way of maintaining the sway of the 'Spanish sect.'[29]

The need for reform of the order was thus felt not only by isolated Jesuits such as Juan de Mariana, the author of the noted pamphlet *Tractado de las enfermedades de la Compañía*,[30] which was drawn up but published only after his death, in Spanish (1624) and in French and Italian (1625). The controversial figure Hernando de Mendoça,[31] on the occasion of the Sixth General Congregation, wrote his *Memorial de las cosas universales y particulares que conviene remediar en la Compañía* because 'the constitution that the Society proposes is one thing; another thing entirely is that which they observe and practise. They live without laws and deceive the world.'[32] Mendoça found no sympathetic ear for his program, and he left the Society in 1608, as did Giulio Clemente Scotti, the author of numerous writings critical of the order, several years later. Scotti wrote not only *Monarchia solipsorum*,[33] an explicitly satirical work, but also *De potestate pontificia*,[34] dedicated to Innocent X and redacted before his departure from the order, in which he denounced the Society for having distanced itself from the primitive humility of its origins, and accused it of being under the sway of a tyrannical and omnipotent general.

The persons cited here all have biographies in some ways similar to that of Hieronim Zahorowski, the author of *Monita privata*. Initially, they all came into conflict with the order as a result of their own behaviour. Zahorowski and Scotti each saw their career prospects dwindle, though for different reasons: the first because, having failed to pass the theological examination, he could not proceed to full profession, and the second because the chair at the Collegio Romano went to Pietro Sforza Pallavicino, the famous historian. Their writings against the Society, therefore, could plausibly be regarded as a vendetta.

To me this seems undeniably true, but only in part. *De potestate pontificia* and the *Monita* also betray a desire on the part of their authors to enter a debate already in progress, to speak their minds about the future of the Society, by scrutinizing the process of decentralization that had already begun and by highlighting the sense of dissatisfaction among those who felt themselves underrepresented and underacknowledged by their superiors. In a *memoriale* written in 1589 and sent to the Holy Office, provincials are described thus: 'They deal with subjects as they will. They call to profession those they want and dismiss the others. And while some are professed within a few years, others are still waiting after twenty-five years ... This style of behaviour is causing great unrest throughout the order and scandalizes most of the good members. If such partiality and injustice are not remedied, the whole order will go to ruin.'[35] Dominique Julia has drawn attention to the long period of formation that fathers must undergo before being in a position to make the 'Fourth Vow' as one of the characteristics that distinguishes the Jesuits from other religious orders, and also to 'le rapport inégal qui s'introduit entre la Compagnie et ceux qui sont reçus avant leur profession definitive – la Compagnie restant a tout moment libre de renvoyer.'[36] The notion of 'unequal relation' occurs like a refrain in the text of the *Monita privata*, and is connected there to the problem of expulsion.[37] It is not by chance, I believe, that the most virulent criticisms of those years often came from the mouths of spiritual coadjutors. This fact alone testifies eloquently to what John W. O'Malley has described as 'the elitism within the brotherhood that this distinction codified ... [provoking] confusion and ... psychological toll.'[38] This idea of a 'trial phase' within the Society explains more than anything else why the *Monita* continued to be cited for so long after its publication. The fact that the text was constructed as a congeries of rules then in use by a restricted number of members reinforced the idea that the Society was above all a sect, a secret society. The image, in the middle of the eighteenth century, was potent in its suggestivity.[39]

The myth of the conspiring, power-hungry Jesuit also has other origins. First among them is the difficulty of understanding the practice of adapting to other cultures, the 'accomodarsi a tutti,' as Polanco calls it,[40] which was invariably looked upon with suspicion by critics of the Jesuits. If it is inarguable that the strategy adopted by the Jesuits caused the Society's fame to spread, it is also true that the sense or inner logic of that diffusion was not necessarily well understood. In many cases the adaptive spirit of the Jesuits was mistaken for a kind of deliberate camouflage. It seemed, in this light, nothing but another indicator of their fundamentally hypocritical character, if not an outright means of plotting to damage or overthrow the state. Fülop-Miller recounts, for example, that several Jesuits were able to enter Sweden (Lorenzo Nicolai)[41] and England (Robert Persons and Edmund Campion)[42] using similar strategies.[43]

Within the Catholic church different positions on both normative and spiritual matters of course coexist, and the Society of Jesus was often strongly criticized by other religious orders. Opposition was destined to grow bitter with respect to the Jesuits' missionary strategies – the Chinese Rites controversy offering one of the more important examples – and moral theology. It would be useful to remember that some of the stereotypes evident in the *Monita privata* were taken up within the Catholic church and used against the Jesuits. Among the most implacable sustainers of the theory of global Jesuit conspiracy are such people as the bishop of Puebla Juan Palafox,[44] the Capuchin Valeriano Magni,[45] and the Carmelite Enrico di Sant'Ignazio,[46] all authors of ferocious attacks against the Society of Jesus.

But in my opinion the *Monita* can be understood only if the text is considered in relation to the debate within the order itself. That debate helps make clear why this particular libel has exerted such sway, and why to this day it stands out amid the mass of anti-Jesuit pamphlets of the sixteenth and seventeenth centuries. It helps as well to account for the breadth of its appeal, not only among enemies of the Church of Rome, but within the same Catholic formations that looked less than happily at the methods in use by the Society, even as they marvelled at the Society's success in all the fields in which it operated.

NOTES

1 [Hieronim Zahorowski], *Privata monita Societatis Jesu* (Kraków: Notobirgae, 1614). The original pamphlet is composed of sixteen chapters; during the eighteenth century it was expanded to eighteen chapters. This 'modern' version (the first edition was *De secreten der Jesuiten. Secrete Instrucîien van de Paters der Societeyt*, 1676) is much better known and was published and translated again and again during the eighteenth and nineteenth centuries.

2 [Zahorowski], *Monita privata Societatis Jesu* ([Kraków:] Notibergae, 1615), mon. 16: 'Haec Privata Monita diligenter servent penes se superiores, et paucis idque gravibus ex Patribus communicent, ex iisque instruant alios quomodo serviant cum fructu Societati, neque ut scripta ab altero, sed ut ex peculiari prudentia deprompta aliis communicent. Quod si absit in manus externorum haec monita veniant,

quoniam sinistre ea interpretabuntur, negentur hoc sensu esse Societatis per istos confirmando e nostris, de quibus certo scitur, eos talia ignorare. Opponantur his Privatis Monitis Generalia Monita, et ordinationes impressae aut scriptae his Privatis contrariae, demum inquiretur, an non ab aliquo e nostris prodita sint (neque superior ullus eris tam negligens in asservandis tantis decretis Societatis) et si in aliquem vel leves erunt conjecturæ, illi imputentur et ex Societate dimittantur.' This is not the *editio princeps*, but the earliest edition I found in the Biblioteca Jagiellonska in Kraków, sign. 39326 I, Man. St. Dr. For a list of the editions, see Somm. *Bib.*, XI, pp. 342–56; Charles Van Acken, 'La fable des "Monita secreta" ou Instructions secrètes des jésuites. Histoire et bibliographie,' *Précis historique* 30 (1881): 261–84, 344–65, 432–46; Sabina Pavone, *Le astuzie dei gesuiti. Le false istruzioni della Compagnia di Gesù e la polemica antigesuita nei secoli XVII e XVIII* (Rome, 2000), pp. 289–99.

3 [Zahorowski], *Monita privata*, mon. 6: 'Visitentur viduae crebro, et jucundis colloquiis, spiritualibus tamen, conserventur et foveantur, non tractetur rigide cum ipsis in confessionibus, nisi tunc, cum minor est spes aliquid ab eis accipiendi. Proderit quoque ad conservandas viduas, si pleraque fiant in gratiam viduarum, ut ingressus in aedes nostras, colloquia, quando et cum quibus placete nostris ... Quare dum se viduae in nostras manus resignant, paratae sequi directionem patris spiritualis, serio inculcetur, ut maior meriti sint illarum actiones coram Deo, ne religiosis quidem personis dent eleemosinas,, inscio confessario, sed adnotatis iis quae se daturas alicui decreverunt, schedulam exhibeant confessario, qui detrahere aut addere potest, prout videbitur. Caveant confessarii frequentem aditum aliorum religiosorum ad viduas, ne post se foeminas natura inconstantes abducant.' On the relationship between Jesuits and women, see Olwen Hufton, 'Altruism and Reciprocity: The Early Jesuits and Their Female Patrons,' *Renaissance Studies* 15:3 (2001): 328–53.

4 [Zahorowski], *Monita privata*, mon. 4: 'Inculcent Principibus distributionem bonorum et dignitatum in Republica spectare ad iustitiam, graviterque Deum offendi, si contra eam a Principibus peccetur: se tamen nolle ingerere in ullam administrationem Reipublicae et haec se invitos dicere ratione sui officii.' Some editions have 'honorum' instead of 'bonorum'; see Ludwig Lutz, *Historia Jesuitica: De Jesuitarum ordinis origine, nomine, regulis, officiis, votis ... nunc etiam latine edita* (Basileae [Basel], 1627); *Monita privata Societatis Jesu* (Cosmopoli, 1668).

5 For a comparison with the Jesuit rhetorical style, see Claudio Acquaviva, *Ordinatio de confessariis principum* (1602), in *ISI*, III, pp. 281–4.

6 Letter of Piotr Tylicki, 11 July 1615, in Jacob Gretser, *Contra famosum libellum, cuius inscriptio est: Monita privata Societatis Jesu. Libri tres apologetici* (1617), in Gretser's *Opera omnia*, vol. 11 (Ratisbonae [Regensburg], 1738), pp. 1012–13: 'Ne tantum facinus, quo Ordo innocens impie traducitur, impunitum maneat, vindic-

tamque divina provocet, Reverendis D.D. vestris damus negotium super huius modi sacrilegi scripti authore, iudiciarum inquisitionem, ad instantiam instigatoris nostri faciant; in primis vero contra prædictum Hieronymum Zahorowski, judicialiter, instigatore instante, procedant, et quidquid juris et justitiae fuerit, statuant.' Piotr Tylicki wrote a second letter, 7 October 1615, to ratify the creation of a committee of inquiry; see Gretser, *Contra famosum libellum*, p. 1013.

7 Jan Wielewicki, *Historicum diarium domus professæ S.J. Ad S. Barbaram, Cracoviae,* in *Rerum Polonicarum scriptores* (Kraków, 1889), vol. 14, p. 125.

8 After his expulsion, Zahorowski was priest of Gozdiec, and before his death he was reconciled with his former order. For his biography, see Charles Sommervogel, 'Le véritable auteur des "Monita secreta,"' *Précis historique* 39 (1890): 83–8; Janusz Tazbir, 'Hieronim Zahorowski, zapomniany autor glosnego pamplefu,' *Kvartalnik historyczny* 70 (1963): 341–61, repr. in *Arianie i katolicy* (Warsaw, 1972), pp. 172–202. See also 'Hieronim Zahorowski,' *Encycklopedia wiedzy o jezuitach na ziemiach polski i litwi. 1564–1994* (Kraków, 1996), p. 777; ARSI Polon. 8, *Catalogi triennali, 1606–1622*, fol. 14v; and Ludwik Grzebien, 'Zahorowski, Hieronim,' in *Diccionario historico de la Compañia de Jesus*, ed. Charles E. O' Neill and Joaquin M. Dominguez, vol. 4 (Rome and Madrid, 2001), p. 4064.

9 [Zahorowski], *Monita privata*, mon. 12: 'Summa arte et industria opus est, ut recipiantur juvenes ingenii boni, forma non contemnenda, genere nobiles et opulenti, ut tales pertrahantur, ostendatur illis favor a scholarum præfectis, non permittantur vexari a praeceptoribus, laudentur crebrius, dentur ipsis munera ... tractentur fructis in solemnitatibus, accipi possunt ad refectorium.'

10 ARSI Instit. 175 I, fol. II: 'Praefatum Librum, utpote falso Societiati Jesu adscriptum, calumniosum, et diffamationibus plenum, omnino esse prohibendum prout de facto illum prohiberunt, et mandarunt, ne cuiquam in posterum licitum esset eum legere, vendere, vel apud se detinere.' See also *Diarium Magdaleni Capiferrei (1607–1620)*, 16 May 1616, Rome, Archivio della Congregazione per la Dottrina della Fede (hereafter ACDF), Index, *Diarii*, vol. 2, fol. 91v; and *Memoralia pro negotio Monitorum privatorum Societatis Jesu*, ACDF St. St. Protoc. B2 fol. 121.

11 ARSI Opp. NN. 244/II, *Lettere originali del S. Cardinale Bellarmino, 1604–1611*, fols 419–29: 'I *Monita* non sono stati composti da un uomo probo e religioso, né da coloro che dirigono una compagnia o un ordine religioso, ma da un uomo malevolo e maldicente, poiché in essi sono raccolte molte cose contro la pietà, i buoni costumi, e anche contro il reale buon senso, e così giudico.'

12 Ludwig Lutz, *Historia Jesuitica* (Basel, 1627), p. 345: 'Praetextum Jesuiticarum actionum omnium est Ecclesiae Catholicae Romanae reparatio ac propugnatio, errantiumque et seductorum ad illam conversio ... [Sed] scopus ... verum ipsorum, ad quem collimant ac respiciunt, est ... totius Mundi sub potestatem Jesuiticam subjugatio.'

13 Among the editions of the *Monita*, cf. [Gaspar Scioppius], *Sanctii Galindi, e Societate Jesu: Anatomia Societatis Jesu, una cum aliis opusculis, ad salutem ejusdem Societatis, et ad excitandam regum ac principum catholicorum attentionem utilissimis* (Lugduni [Leiden], 1633); [Michael Ruckert], *Constitutiones sive Monita secreta Societatis Jesu publici juris facta a Michaele Ruckert* (Groningae [Groningen], 1654); Pierre Jatrige, *Secrets instructions for the superiors of the Society of Jesus. Faithfully rendred out of the latine* [*sic*], in *A further discovery of the mistery of Jesuitisme* (London, 1658); and [Enrico di Sant'Ignazio], *Tuba magna mirum clangens somnum ad Sanctissimum D.N. Papam Clementem XI ... De necessitate longe maxima reformandi Societatem Jesu per eruditissimum Dominum D. Liberium Candidum S. Theologiae L.L.* (Argentinae [Utrecht], 1712).

14 The first Jesuit to respond to the *Monita privata* was Matthaeus Bembus, *Monita salutaria data anonymo authori scripti nuper editi cui titulus falso inditus Monita privata Societatis Jesu* (n.p., 1615). Two years later the official reply of the Society was published, commissioned by the general and entrusted to Gretser, *Contra famosum libellum*. See also Laurent Forer, *Anatomia anatomiae Societatis Jesu sive Antanatomia* (Oeniponte [Innsbruck], 1634); and Alphonsus Huylenbroucq, who replies to Enrico di Sant'Ignazio's *Tuba magna* with *Vindicationes alterae adversus famosos libellos ... sub titulo Tuba magna Argentinae 1712* (Bruxelles [Brussels], 1715). Among Jesuit historians writing against the *Monita privata*, see Paul Bernard, *Les Instructions secrètes des jèsuites. Etude critique* (Paris, 1903); Alexandre Brou, *Les jésuites de la légende*, 2 vols (Paris, 1906–7), II; Bernard Duhr, *Jesuiten-Fabeln: Ein Beitrag zur Culturgeschichte* (Freiburg im Breisgau, 1892); John Gerard, 'The "Monita Secreta" or, Secret Instructions of the Jesuits,' in *Concerning Jesuits* (London, 1902), pp. 1–19; Pietro Tacchi Venturi, 'L'autenticità dei "Monita secreta" e il prof. Raffaele Mariano,' *Civiltà cattolica* 1 (1902): 694–713.

15 Peter Burke, 'The Black Legend of the Jesuits: An Essay in the History of Social Stereotypes,' in *Christianity and Community in the West: Essays for John Bossy*, ed. Simon Ditchfield (Aldershot, UK, 2001), p. 172.

16 See John W. O'Malley, 'The Historiography of the Society of Jesus: Where Does It Stand Today?' in O'M. *Jes. Cult.*, pp. 3–37. On the Jesuit myth in France, see Michael Leroy, *Le mythe jésuite. De Béranger a Michelet* (Paris, 1992); and Geoffrey Cubbitt, *The Jesuit Myth: Conspiracy Theory and Politics in Nineteenth-Century France* (Oxford, 1993).

17 *Detrimenta Societatis ex obs. provinciis Romam missa ab 1606*, in ARSI Hist. Soc. 137.

18 His autobiography was edited by Jozef Warszawski, in *Polonica z rzymskiego kodeksu nowicjiuszy Towarzystwa Jezusowego* (Rome, 1965); see also Auguste Berga, *Un prédicateur de la Cour de Pologne sous Sigismond III, Pierre Skarga*

(1536–1612). Essai sur la Pologne du XVIe siècle et le protestantisme polonais (Paris, 1916).

19 On this topic see also the *Consilium de recuperanda et in posterum stabilienda pace Regni Poloniae, in qua demonstrantur pacem nec constitui nec stabiliri posse quamdium Jesuitae in Polonia maneant. Ad Illustres Regni Poloniae Proceres Conversum ex polonico in latinum* (Upsaliae [Uppsala], 1607). This pamphlet was condemned by the Holy Office in 1609. See Janusz Tazbir, *Literatura antyjezuicka w Polsce, 1578–1625* (Warsaw, 1963).

20 See Stanisław Obirek, 'The Jesuits and Polish Sarmatianism,' in O'M. *Jes. Cult.*, pp. 555–63; Wieslaw Müller, 'Les jésuites en Pologne aux XVIe et XVII siècles,' in *Les jésuites parmi les hommes au XVIe et XVIIe siècles. Actes du colloque de Clermont-Ferrand*, ed. Guy Demerson (Clermont-Ferrand, 1987), pp. 323–30; Claudio Madonia, 'L'intreccio tra conflitti istituzionali e conflitti confessionali nell'Europa orientale (secc. XVI–XVII),' in *Disciplina dell'anima, disciplina del corpo e disciplina della società tra medioevo ed età moderna*, ed. Paolo Prodi and Carla Penuti (Bologna, 1994), pp. 357–81; and Madonia, 'Problemi della penetrazione gesuita in Europa orientale,' in *Modernità: Definizione ed esercizi*, ed. Albano Biondi (Bologna, 1999), pp. 197–245.

21 Wielewicki, *Historicum diarium*, vol. 14, p. 198. See W. Dobrowolska, *Mlodosc Jerzego i Krzysztofa Zbaraskich* (Przemysl, 1926).

22 Quoted in Wielewicki, *Historicum diarium*, vol. 10, pp. 209–10. The letter was republished in *Listy Piotra Skargi T.J. z lat, 1566–1610*, ed. J. Syganski (Kraków, 1912), pp. 275–8. See also the letter written by Skarga to Acquaviva (20 September 1606) about the Catholic participation in the *rokosz*, 'pretextu defendendae libertatis, quam a Rege sibi eripi iactitabant,' and about the things 'atrocia quaedam, falsa et iniqua' written against the Society of Jesus. Probably he was thinking about the quoted *Consilium de recuperanda ... pace Regni Poloniae* (n19 above).

23 'Privata' was changed to 'secreta' for the first time by Gaspar Scioppius in the *Anatomia Societatis Jesu* (n13 above).

24 See Giovanni Maria Barbuto, *Il principe e l'Anticristo. Gesuiti e ideologie politiche* (Naples, 1994); Robert Bireley, *The Counter-Reformation Prince: Antimachia-vellianism or Catholic Statecraft in Early Modern Europe* (Chapel Hill, 1990); Bireley, 'The Jesuits and Politics in Time of War: A Self-Appraisal,' *Studies in the Spirituality of Jesuits* 34:5 (2002): 1–29; and Rosario Villari, *Elogio della dissimulazione* (Rome and Bari, 1993).

25 Letter to Sig. Cav ..., Venezia, 2 September 1608, BNP Cod. Italiani 508 fols 5r–6r: 'Delli gesuiti ho sempre ammirato la politica, e massimamente nel servare i segreti, gran cosa è che hanno le loro constituzioni stampate, ne però è possibile vederne un esemplare, non dico le regole che sono stampate in Lione, quelle sono puerili, ma le leggi del loro governo che tengono tanto arcane ... non vi sono altrettante persone

nel mondo che cospirino tutte in un fine, che siino maneggiate con tanta accuratezza, et usino tanto ardore, et zelo nell'operare; io crederei che fosse un grande acquisto il potere penetrare nel segreto del loro governo , et scuoprire le loro arti e tratti politici per potergleli [*sic*] opporre nella congiuntura.'

26 See José Martinez Millan, 'Transformación y crisis de la Compañía de Jésus (1578– 1594),' in *I religiosi a corte. Teologia, politica e diplomazia in Antico regime*, ed. Flavio Rurale (Rome, 1998), pp. 101–30; see also Francisco de Borja Medina, 'Intrigues of a Scottish Jesuit at the Spanish Court: Unpublished Letters of William Crichton to Claudio Acquaviva (Madrid, 1590–1592),' in *The Reckoned Expense*, ed. Thomas McCoog (Woodbridge, 1996), pp. 215–45.

27 *Del governo della Compagnia di Giesù, et sue imperfettioni,* dato dal cardinale di Camerino, 14 July 1592, ACDF S. O. St. St. N3-g: 'La Monarchia del Generale, che egli solo può fare et fa tutti i Provinciali, Visitatori, Prepositi, Rettori, Consultori, Procuratori Generali, Segretarij, infino Predicatori, Lettori, Confessori, et insomma, i superiori in qualunque luogo, a qualunque tempo, e pur egli solo tutti quei professi, che chiamiamo de' quattro voti, traquali resta e si restringe il governo della Religione.' In another *memoriale* there occurs the phrase 'con quelle persone che sono a gusto del generale si usa ogni indulgenza, ogni dispensa, e si concede loro ogni privilegio, ancorché nel resto non siano più meritevoli degli altri, anzi molto inferiori; con gli altri si osserva ogni rigore' (*Del governo della Compagnia di Giesù*, 31 May 1589, ibid.).

28 Ibid.: 'Come in questi mesi addietro è stato fatto nella provincia di Venezia ove s'è licenziato un padre di qualità in simil guisa affermando la persona penitente ed affermando con fede pubblica di non aver detto le cose che essi dicono aver detto, e di quelle che confessa aver detto non aver dato licenza di parlarne.'

29 Ibid. Many negative references to the Spanish province corroborate the thesis that these documents originated among the Italian Jesuits.

30 *Tractado de las enfermedades de la Compañía*, in *Obras del Padre Juan de Mariana*, vol. 2 (Madrid, 1854), pp. 595–618.

31 Hernando de Mendoça was born in Torecilla de las Cameros in 1561, joined the Society in 1579, and left it in 1604 with the permission 'libere transeundi ... ad regularium ordinem, ubi regulari disciplina vigeat' (see *Dimissi 1543–1640*, in ARSI Hist. Soc. 54 fol. 19). In 1611 he was made archbishop of Cuzco in Peru by Clement VIII. He died in 1617. On his involvement in affairs of state during his stay in Naples as confessor of the wife of the count of Lemos, see ARSI Neapol. 194 I, *Epist. 1601–1615*, document 15, *Lettera di B. De Angelis sulla vera storia di H. de Mendoça*, 2 May 1606.

32 Hernando de Mendoça, *Memorial de las cosas universales y particulares que conviene remediar en la Compañía, en la Congregación que se junta en Roma para su reformación* (1608). Another *memoriale* was sent by Mendoça, after his departure

from the Society, to Philip III of Spain. See Ivan De Recalde [pseud. of P. Boulin], *Les jésuites sous Acquaviva* (Paris, 1927), pp. 144–62.

33 *Lucii Cornelii Europæi Monarchia solipsorum. Ad virum clarissimum Meonem Allatium* (Venetiis [Venice], 1645). This text has been ascribed not only to Giulio Clemente Scotti but also to Melchior Inchofer (1584–1648), an Austrian Jesuit who lived for a long while in Rome and was tried by the Society because 'oltre l'haver scritta l'historia dell'ultima Congregazione Generale con stilo tanto satirico, e con tante falsità, che infamano la Compagnia: in genere, in specie, et in individuo, onde merita soggiacere alle pene tassate a scrittori di libelli famosi, ha di più avuto strettissimo commercio col p. Giulio Scotti doppo haver apostatato dalla Religione' (*Causa P. Melchior Inchofer, 1648*, ARSI Hist. Soc. 166 fol. 1). See also D. Dümmerth, 'Les combats et la tragédie du P. Melchior Inchofer S.I. à Rome (1641–1648),' *Annales Universitatis scientiarum Budapestinensis. Sectio historica* 17 (1976): 81–112. For a complete history of the attributions of the pamphlet, see Giorgio Spini, *Ricerca dei libertini. La teoria dell'impostura delle religioni nel Seicento italiano* (Rome, 1950), pp. 217–46.

34 Giulio Clemente Scotti, *De potestate pontificia in Societatem Jesu ... Ad Innocentium X, Summum Pontificem* (Parisiis [Paris], 1646). The general of the Society, Vincenzo Carafa, forbade the Jesuits to read this book and asked the pope to have the pamphlet condemned by the Holy Office. Pietro Sforza Pallavicino replied to the text with his *Vindicationes Societatis Jesu, quibus multorum accusatione in eius institutum leges ... refellentur* (Romae [Rome], 1649).

35 *Del governo della Compagnia di Giesù*: 'secondo il voler loro dispongono de'suddi, fanno professi quei che vogliono, e lascian gli altri. E dove altri in pochi anni sono promossi, altri dopo venticinque anni ancora non son professi ... Finalmente questo punto tiene inquieta tutta la religione, et scandaliza la maggior parte de' buoni. E se non si rimedia a tanta parzialità, et ingiustizia, sarà la total ruina della Religione.'

36 Dominique Julia, 'Questions posées à Louis Chatellier, Luce Giard, Dominique Julia et John O' Malley,' *Rev. syn.* 120, p. 426.

37 During Acquaviva's time as general, the problem of expulsion loomed large, owing to either the number of people expelled or the theoretical importance of his role in the expulsions. I have mentioned Zahorowski, Mascardi, Scotti, and Mendoça, but see the dossier *Dimissi 1543–1640*, ARSI Hist. Soc. 54. See also the *Instruttione del modo che si ha da osservare nel mandar fuori della Compagnia, fatta l'anno 1604*, ARSI Rom. 2 fol. 124r–v, where the rules for expelling a member are summarized: 'Consideri che qualità di colpa è questa, se sono di quelle che nosceno al ben commune, contaminando gli altri, se di quelle che scandalizzano i prossimi, se di quelle che possono apportare infamia grave alla Compagnia, se per la gravezza del peccato o per la difficoltà d'emendarsene o per risarcire il buon nome della

Compagnia, ricercano questo taglio, perché tanto il modo di maneggiar la cosa, quanto il tempo e la lunghezza della cura ricercano questa considerazione perché certo è che non si può differire lungamente dove si vede o pericolo d'appestar altri o infamia della Religione, anzi in casi pubblici sarà alle volte urgente, per ristorar il danno, eseguirlo con prestezza.'

38 O'M. *First*, p. 347.

39 Franco Venturi, *Settecento riformatore*, vol. 2, *La chiesa e la repubblica entro i propri limiti. 1758–1764* (Turin, 1976); Antonio Trampus, *I gesuiti e l'Illuminismo. Politica e religione in Austria e nell'Europa centrale (1773–1798)* (Florence, 2000).

40 The *Industriae* of Polanco draws inspiration from this principle and suggests the possibility of intervening in society with 'forme astute e coperte di penetrazione' (Adriano Prosperi, *Tribunali della coscienza* [Turin, 1999], p. 588). There are two series of *Industriae* (*12 Industrias con que se ha de ayudar la Compañía, para que mejor proceda para su fin* and *Industriæ con que uno de la Compañía de Jesus mejor consiguirà sus fines*); see *Po. Comp.* 2: 725–75, 776–807.

41 Oskar Garstein, *Rome and the Counter-Reformation in Scandinavia*, vol. 1, *Jesuit Educational Strategy, 1553–1622* (Leiden and New York, 1992).

42 Thomas M. McCoog, *The Society of Jesus in Ireland, Scotland, and England, 1541–88* (St Louis, 1995).

43 René Fülop-Miller, *Macht und Geheimnis der Jesuiten* (Munich, 1947).

44 In a letter sent to Innocent X in 1639, Palafox wrote: 'Qual altra religione ha eccitate tante turbolenze, seminate tante discordie e gelosie, suscitati tanti lamenti e tante dispute e tante liti con gli altri religiosi, col clero, co' vescovi, co' principi secolari, ancorché cristiani e cattolici? E' vero che altri regolari eziandio hanno avute varie contese; ma niun ordine ne ha giammai avute tante, quante i gesuiti con tutto il mondo,' quoted in *Istruzioni secrete della Compagnia di Gesù con aggiunte importanti* (Livorno, 1972; repr. of 'Roma 18 ...' [in reality, Florence]), p. 33.

45 See the *Apologia Valeriani Magni capuccini contra imposturas Jesuitarum ad majorem gloriam Dei* (n.p., n.d.), which contains many letters written by Valeriano Magni between 1653 and 1655. See also Jerzy Cygan, *Valerianus Magni (1586–1661). 'Vita prima,' operum recensio et bibliographia*, vol. 3 (Rome, 1989), sec. 7, pp. 427–37, 'Controversiae cum Societate Jesu.'

46 Enrico di Sant'Ignazio was in Rome during the first years of Clement XI's pontificate. Sympathetic to the Jansenists, even if not openly, he wrote many works against Jesuit casuistry. Among them, see the *Tuba magna* (n13 above). See also 'Enrico di Sant'Ignazio,' in J. Defrecheux, *Biographie nationale ... des sciences, des lettres et des beaux arts de Belgique*, vol. 21 (1911), pp. 96–104.

5 / Revolutionary Pedagogues?
How Jesuits Used Education to Change Society

JUDI LOACH

In the sixteenth century, Renaissance ideals led town councils throughout France to set up colleges to provide modern, humanist education free of charge for sons of citizens. The expense, however, soon proved too heavy for municipal budgets, so in the later sixteenth century contracts were drawn up with religious orders, who provided specified teaching more cheaply, usually for a sum determined annually.[1] The Jesuits became the dominant order in this field.[2]

The Jesuits received financial support from the state for their participation in what was thus effectively a national system of secondary education, albeit organized on a municipal basis. The principal condition for such royal support was the egalitarian nature of the education they provided, whereby 'children devoid of support might with little expense draw the same benefits and advantages as could the better off.'[3] Not only, however, was tuition free to all, but the system was meritocratic, with advancement wholly dependent upon the individual's academic progress,[4] while a spirit of emulation permeated teaching methods.[5] The educational system organized by the Jesuits thus offered genuine opportunities for upward social mobility, which were taken up by sons of the merchant, professional, and artisan classes.

Such an egalitarian and meritocratic approach towards education fitted the wider policies of an *ancien régime* state that was in fact substantially undermining the established social hierarchy, not least by selling royal offices in order to augment the national exchequer. In the seventeenth century, urban France thus witnessed a considerable degree of social mobility, particularly the ascent of educated sons from the *tiers état*.[6]

The Jesuits' enthusiasm for this initiative betrays subtly, but substantially, different motives, nevertheless compatible with those of the state. In the wake of the Council of Trent, the Catholic church in general sought to 'reconquer Catholics' at least as much as to 'conquer Protestants.'[7] It aimed to do so, in part, by supplanting Renaissance humanistic learning and culture with specifically Christian equivalents, demonstrably superior to it. It was here that the Jesuits played a crucial role, through their scholarship and teaching and through a series of initiatives ensuring that education extended beyond secondary education so as to permeate all society.[8] While they authored sermons, writings, and, most strikingly, vivid dramatic performances for the entire citizenry, their most significant contribution here was that delivered through the Marian *congrégations* (in Latin, *sodalitates*), which they ran for adult men, differentiated according to social class.[9] In college and congregation alike a spirit of emulation favoured the emergence of an elite at once studious and pious.

The continuity between college and beyond is perhaps most apparent in the existence of such congregations for both schoolboys and men, usually physically located within the same college buildings. More significant, however, is the commonality of aims throughout, namely, the parallel nurturing of soul and mind. Financial support was accorded to the Jesuits explicitly for introducing 'the youth of our kingdom' as much to 'devotion and piety' as to 'letters.'[10] In the Marian congregations, not only was training provided in devotional practices, but intellectual and cultural education was delivered.[11]

A considerable amount of research has been published about the educational system and methods employed by the Jesuits in their colleges.[12] This body of work includes coverage of cultural education, usually delivered either to the schoolboy congregations throughout the academic year, or to entire classes towards the end of it. This cultural education was made up largely of short courses, most commonly in various genres of symbolic imagery – heraldry, devices, emblems, and the like. These were delivered by the same means as were other college courses, namely, by dictation, but in French rather than the Latin of mainstream courses; presumably they followed the teaching practices of mainstream courses, and would thus have been accompanied by private study of relevant texts and by group exercises related to the same material.[13] In mainstream and cultural courses alike, the pedagogic strategies adopted would thus ensure that the individual worked actively and independently to understand the material taught, but communal exercises then ensured that this was incorporated into group – rather than individual – memory.

Much less is known, however, about the cultural education delivered to the adult congregations, because the material evidence for this is far more fragmentary. First, no exercise books containing a student's record of such courses seem to be preserved in libraries or archives, whereas many of their schoolboy equivalents survive. Second, the range of schoolboy textbooks produced is not paralleled by an equivalent range specifically designed to teach culture to adult congregations (the works published for them are ones supporting their devotional practices alone).[14] This was because the Jesuits deliberately adopted a different strategy towards reading material for these cultural courses, teaching adult congregationists how best to exploit any available literature, from a strictly Catholic perspective.

The *Idée de l'estude d'un honeste homme*

In this paper I examine the uniquely preserved course in cultural education devised for, and delivered to, a congregation attached to the town college run by the Jesuits in Lyon, the Collège de la Trinité, in the mid-seventeenth century. This course, entitled 'L'idée de l'estude d'un honeste homme,' was devised by a young Jesuit, Claude-François Menestrier,[15] in 1658, for an adult congregation there. Despite his youth, Menestrier had extensive experience of congregations, no doubt beginning when he was a schoolboy member at this college in the 1640s. He had first directed a congregation, for schoolboys, at Vienne, while teaching rhetoric there in 1656–7.[16] On returning to Lyon in the autumn of 1657, he had assisted his own teacher, Théophile Raynaud, in the direction of the most prestigious adult congregation at Lyon, the 'Grande Congrégation' or 'Congrégation des Messieurs,'[17] intended for the town's wealthiest merchants and other leading members of society, such as royal officers. Given Menestrier's background – as a teacher with experience of a range of congregations – it is not surprising to detect certain continuities between this course and both mainstream college teaching and various practices followed in congregations, schoolboy and adult alike. In fact, a few years later this course may have been delivered to the Congregation of Rhetoric and Humanities students at the Collège de la Trinité,[18] and forty years after that a major part of it would be published by the prince of Dombes at Trévoux,[19] this time seemingly with adult congregationists as the primary audience in view. During the development of the course, in 1659, Menestrier was given direction of a congregation, for artisans,[20] to whom he seems to have first delivered it.

The stated aims of this *estude d'un honeste homme* are to 'make a man of *conversation*'[21] or to enable the student to 'gain a reputation as an *honneste homme*.'[22] The term *honnête homme* had a very particular meaning in the seventeenth century, embodied in members of the *tiers état* aspiring to nobility, who emulated courtly refinement, but endowed with greater moral content. The French word *honnête*, derived from the Latin *honestus*, meaning honourable and respectable, conveyed that concept, but with an emphasis on being virtuous, in the sense of conforming to contemporary notions of virtue, probity, and honour. The term *honnête homme* combined this sense with that of an ideal participant in social gatherings, one who not only conformed to their unspoken rules but who was affable and courteous, and made pleasant conversation.[23]

This inherent interdependence between *honnêteté* and *conversation* underlies the whole of Menestrier's course, which was explicitly intended to equip the congregationist to speak competently on any subject.[24] The French word *conversation*, however, had a much wider meaning than the English; the emphasis, due to the word's etymology, lay on people's coming together and spending time in one another's company, exchanging knowledge and opinions frankly within an intimate group.[25]

Menestrier's course is divided into two parts. The first part begins by introducing the congregation member to a carefully chosen book list – entitled 'the *honnête homme*'s library' – recommending titles subject by subject,[26] so that he can read up on every subject that might arise in polite society. This is made most explicit in Menestrier's early revision of the course, where he adds an extra chapter introducing the book list, called 'Some Topics That Form the Usual Subjects of Conversation.'[27] Here he distinguishes between ephemeral chat and the more edifying discussions of *honnêtes gens*, which engage the intellect.[28] The list covers fashionable topics, notably all genres of symbolic imagery – heraldry, devices, emblems, medals, and hieroglyphs – followed by inscriptions and fables. It also details sources for 'the purity of the French language,' primarily those French-language translations of the antique classics intended to classicize the French language itself,[29] specifically because of the *honnête homme*'s need to speak a refined form of French.[30] This in turn leads to sections on antiquities and politics, before turning to Rhetoric, the subject habitually taught in the final year of the first cycle of education in Jesuit-run town colleges: for here 'Eloquence' – the principles of rhetoric – and 'Orators' – examples of good practice – are followed by shorter sections on panegyric and eulogy. The next sections cover subjects taught in the penultimate year of that cycle, the Humanities year: Geography (and, related to it, Travel), Chronology, and History. The list then covers sections on Morality and Natural Philosophy – subjects taught only in the second cycle offered in college (which few students stayed on to follow)[31] – and on Poetry.

Although compiled by a member of a religious order, the book list omits any reference to theology; the titles within each section are selected so as to comply strictly with Catholic dogma, and moreover to promote an image of Catholic culture as the most up-to-date, better informed than the Renaissance humanism that preceded it. This perhaps becomes clearest in the section on science (or rather natural philosophy), where Thomism, and therefore Aristotelianism, becomes the single deciding factor in the selection of titles.[32] Through referring to the contents of this book list, the reader will come to view the world through Jesuit-prescribed lenses, thus helping to realize the Jesuits' wider program of using erudition and culture to effect the Catholicization of society.

The course then proceeds from what to read to how to read it, first enumerating a series of study skills,[33] so that the hard-pressed congregationist can make best use of the limited time outside working hours for his cultural education; indeed, Menestrier refers to these elsewhere as 'pursuits for turning oneself into a *galant homme* in little time.'[34] Likewise, Menestrier advises his congregationist to carry a book around with him at all times so as to be able to use any spare time, which would otherwise be wasted, for reading; 'at the end of the year,' he adds, 'one finds that several odd quarter hours have brought about good progress.'[35] In the same vein he underlines the need to identify a few key texts in each field and to study these in depth[36] (thus following a distinctive principle of Jesuit college education);[37] hence his provision of a carefully selected book list, to save the congregationist wasting time on less worthwhile books.[38] He then recommends just running over the table of contents in lesser books, so as to pick out those passages that supplement key works, rather than wading through their entire text.[39]

The emphasis throughout the course is on how to read (and listen) critically, then how to ensure that one retains whatever might be of future use, and finally how to apply whatever one has learned in a social context. The first chapter after the book list, listing twenty-odd hints for private study,[40] is therefore succeeded by four chapters, each offering a 'method': the first of these chapters deals with the critical assessment of the content of any publication;[41] the second with the use of a commonplace book;[42] the third with extracting models for moral and ethical behaviour from history;[43] and the last with synthesizing and applying all these skills to express one's own views within social gatherings.[44] In his early revision of the course, Menestrier presents the book list in terms of purifying first speech, then behaviour.[45]

The first part having been devoted largely to instructing the student in how to become an *honnête homme*, the second part consists of a series of treatises intended to enable him to operate as such, so that he can participate intelligently in the creation of festivals and related decorations for his city. This series of treatises led the congregationist through the building blocks from which festivals were made:[46] inscriptions,[47] symbolic imagery (here called 'la peinture sçavante,' erudite painting: heraldry,[48] devices and emblems[49]), all culminating in festivals (*pompes sçavantes*)[50] and a genre of related performance, ballet.[51] All these subjects were considered essential, since they were deemed to be instruments of rhetoric, broadly understood by Menestrier as 'persuading through images.'[52] In his exactly contemporary 'Philosophie des Images,'

Menestrier defines three modes by which rhetoric operates: verbal images (metaphor), visual images (symbols), and enacted images (drama).[53] Within this context we might understand the series of treatises then provided in this second part as corresponding in turn to these three classes of imagery: inscriptions relating to the verbal, then symbolic imagery to the visual, and, lastly, festivals and related performances to the enacted.

While rhetoric provided the structure underlying all these propaganda media, allegory furnished the vocabulary for articulating it. Seventeenth-century French society exploited a range of such 'coded writings'[54] in its communications; in this context a variety of techniques for decipherment became essential skills for entering into social intercourse. The congregationist was taught to engage in drawing out meaning from the printed page, whether that took the form of an image for pious contemplation or a verbal text for critical exegesis.

It is therefore worth examining the way in which this course taught members of a congregation how to read, and the implications of such a manner of reading. Both the book list and the study hints reveal the author's assumption that his audience was literate enough at least to read fairly heavyweight texts fluently, and, moreover, to do so in Latin as well as in French. It therefore seems that Menestrier was addressing adults who had been taught to the level of the first cycle of education or beyond, as provided by the town college, the Collège de la Trinité, to which this congregation was attached. The fact that the book list that appeared just a few years later in a revised version of the course dropped virtually all Latin-language texts might reflect the author's pragmatic experience in teaching this course;[55] in other words, he came to realize that, regardless of his audience's college education, their practical skills in Latin had atrophied through the years in which they no longer practised those skills.

In introducing an adult learner to self-directed study, Menestrier revises disciplines inculcated earlier at college, notably through his emphasis on the need for order and method, a keynote of the *Ratio studiorum*.[56] Early on he reminds the congregationist of the need for time management, forward planning, and commitment in undertaking any study; for instance, one might rigorously set aside an hour or two in the morning before starting work, and the same again in the evening.[57] Then he implies the need to plan one's studies in an orderly way, by offering alternative strategies, either studying a single subject at a time or studying several in parallel, the latter method being one that helps to retain interest.[58] In his later version, however, he warns of this method's disadvantage: if the subjects studied together are unrelated, confusion may set in, so care must be taken in choosing them.[59] Later on he reiterates the need to plan one's study schedule before one starts.[60] Later still he criticizes those who judge the material they read in a haphazard way rather than an objective one, to the point that different readers end up praising or decrying the same title; since such ignorance should give way to knowledge and rules, he then proposes his own rational method.[61] Finally, in recommending the keeping of a commonplace book, he presupposes that whatever is set down in it will be systematically ordered. After admitting to the variety of ordering systems in use,[62] he sets out his own method in terms of one such system.[63]

Adult study, however, contrasts with schoolboy education, being dependent largely upon adults teaching themselves through reading, rather than upon their being taught by a master in a class. The need to adopt and develop a critical attitude in such reading is emphasized throughout: at the beginning of the chapter on study skills and again in its conclusion, Menestrier stresses the need to be selective as to texts.[64] His next chapter, on critical reading,[65] tacitly develops practices inculcated in college, notably those of *prélection* and *explication*,[66] which in both contexts are intended to teach how to study independently. Equally it parallels devotional practices promoted in the congregation, where texts or images were used as the catalyst for engaging the imagination (and thus the intellect) in meditational exercises.

What kind of access would congregationists really have had to the books Menestrier recommended? It is worth noting that ownership of such books is nowhere anticipated. Whenever Menestrier uses the words 'possess' or 'have' in connection with books, it is evident that he is using them to mean mental absorption of the contents rather than personal ownership.[67] The titles recommended largely match those contained in the college library.[68] It is therefore reasonable to assume that members of the congregations attached to the college had access to it; moreover, as has been indicated, the members of this congregation are likely to have been 'old boys' of the college. In any event this library – the largest by far in seventeenth-century Lyon – seems to have been considered the town's public library. This role had become widely accepted by early in the next century, and its effective recognition earlier on is reinforced by the series of major bequests made to it by leading citizens throughout the seventeenth century. Research into reading in the *ancien régime* demonstrates that the eighteenth-century public library developed from a range of earlier precedents: libraries of universities or town colleges; libraries of religious communities; libraries of such municipal bodies as guilds (and probably their affiliated confraternities as well);[69] and libraries of the philanthropic wealthy.[70] All these types are simultaneously reflected in the seventeenth-century library of the Collège de la Trinité. The bequests made to it – its material incorporation of private collections – likewise reflect the practice of facilitating public access to private libraries. All this evidence supports the supposition that this prototype public library would have been accessible to congregationists.

In addition, other – less formally organized – means of gaining access to books existed in the seventeenth century. It was common practice to borrow or share books,[71] and often to do so in quite a systematic manner. Menestrier's letters reveal how he – as a student of modest origins, probably from a family of shopkeepers – frequently asked members of the professional classes or even nobles to lend him substantial numbers of books and manuscripts, unashamedly sending long lists of those he wanted to borrow from their own libraries.[72] This correspondence proves not only that these more affluent individuals responded positively to such requests, and often sent large parcels of books to Lyon by carriage, but that they seemed to consider such loans quite natural, perhaps even a duty of those fortunate enough to possess private libraries. Against this background it seems likely that congregationists might at least have expected to benefit from comparable personal loans, perhaps from Jesuit fathers in the college, but especially from members of the wealthier congregations attached to the same college as their own.

Furthermore, since printers and booksellers would have belonged to the artisans' congregation, one might well expect them to have lent books to their fellows, not least since they often lent out books and newspapers anyway.[73] All in all, a wide variety of means were available by which even those with relatively little disposable income could access edifying texts, at least as long as they lived in towns.

Moreover, the manner in which adults – across quite a wide social range – studied in the seventeenth century rendered personal ownership of printed works less important than one might now expect. The habit of recording orally delivered material in written form pervaded society, from the practice of recording the key principles of any taught course by dictation (*cours dictés*) through to the recording of proceedings in council chambers or law courts, or of sermons heard in church.[74] It was initially inculcated in the school classroom and apparently used for congregations' cultural courses; its college origins imply something more active, however, than a passive support to rote learning, since in the classroom it followed explanatory teaching (*prélection*) in such a way as to consolidate not only the orally delivered teaching but also the individual's guided private study of prescribed texts, and to do so specifically so that the student was prepared to employ thereafter the principles learned, in creating original work of his own.[75] Likewise Menestrier's recommendation of *réflexion* each evening on whatever one had learned that day[76] continued the practice initiated in college of the evening *revue* of that day's lessons;[77] it also paralleled the Ignatian bedtime examination of conscience, prescribed for Jesuits in their *Constitutions* and promoted by them in their congregations. The same reasoning underwrote all these practices, as Menestrier effectively reminds the congregationists in saying that this will better 'imprint' the matter studied in the memory, and ensure that none of it 'escapes'; in his revised version of the course he emphasizes this mnemonic purpose, by linking such daily reflection with the practice of keeping a commonplace book.[78]

The comparatively widespread practice of making for oneself manuscript copies of printed material[79] should perhaps also be considered in this light. The material quality of some examples shows that making a copy for oneself was considered not merely a matter of economic expediency but also a means of appropriating the contents for oneself, reflecting an awareness of the mnemonic potential of writing out the text.[80] Hence Menestrier recommends this and related practices for appropriating the content of key texts (in the same way as students today are advised to 'make the material one's own'). First, he suggests writing a précis of the material read;[81] in a much later version of this passage, he adds a paragraph that links this practice directly with its use in the philosophy and theology cycles in the Jesuit educational system – levels attended by only a small minority.[82] Second, he suggests translating the work, as this will fix the contents better in one's mind.[83] Translating also forces one to study the text more seriously and pay more attention to it[84] (which was no doubt why translating – or rather paraphrasing – was practised in college); in the process one will also improve one's knowledge of the foreign language concerned,[85] another prerequisite for becoming an *honnête homme*, not least because essential texts are not necessarily translated into French.[86]

Another widespread – and perhaps again related – practice, one that Menestrier assumes his reader to follow already, is the keeping of a commonplace book, or 'livre de[s] remarques,' in a *cahier* (exercise book),[87] the word used for the exercise books in which schoolboys took down classes by dictation. The congregationist is advised to carry a pencil and *tablettes*[88] (bundles of ivory, or parchment or paper leaves)[89] at all times so as to be able to 'note down the best things,' since one should never 'let anything one reads or hears "escape."' He will then be able to transcribe these notes later into his commonplace book.[90] Not only did the keeping of such a book become the subject of a whole chapter in this course for congregationists, but an entire section of it was dedicated to an ordering system for such books.[91] The keeping of a commonplace book was a practice initially inculcated within mainstream college education; it was then practised throughout adult life, regardless of social station.[92] The rise of cheap printing led to habits of cutting and pasting printed material into one's own commonplace book or into a scrapbook-like album,[93] a practice that Menestrier himself followed.[94] As with writing in one's own hand, commonplacing was not undertaken merely to produce an *aide mémoire*; rather, Jesuit pedagogues believed that the very process of commonplacing fulfilled a mnemonic function –

and indeed broader educational purposes – the acts of selecting and ordering excerpts of text serving to engender greater attentiveness in reading, and contributing to critical reflection.

Another aspect of seventeenth-century reading practices reflected in Menestrier's course is the degree to which reading was often a collective rather than individual activity, in college and thereafter among adults.[95] This is apparent from several of the study techniques prescribed by Menestrier. For instance, he suggests sharing the reading of a book with friends, each reading a different part of it and then giving an account of that part to the others.[96] Although Menestrier explicitly recommends this as a means of saving time, he was no doubt as a teacher accustomed to *concertations* and other group exercises, and aware of the potential this technique offered for making the student reflect critically upon the matter read, in order to be able to present it adequately to his friends.

This collective character of reading is supported by Menestrier's immediately proceeding from this recommendation of shared reading to that of availing oneself of *conférences*, and then 'even' (as Menestrier himself puts it) to reading together in a group.[97] For although the French word *conférence* today is taken to mean 'lecture,' the word did not begin to acquire this sense until later in the seventeenth century. In early modern times it primarily meant a discussion, usually among a small number of people, a sense deriving from and incorporating its initial sense of comparison. By the early seventeenth century, however, the word was already being used with reference to serious issues, such as diplomatic matters. This fits with Menestrier's recommendation elsewhere of *conversations* as a locus for mutual self-improvement. It seems to be in this spirit that Menestrier recommends that such a group could also all read the same entire book together, since individuals will notice different things within the same text, so that when they subsequently share the fruits of reading, each member will get more out of the text.[98] This is echoed in one of his final hints, in which he recommends talking to others about what one has read; in this case he specifically recommends such a practice on the ground that 'it inculcates' the material read, or that 'it prints it better in the memory.'[99] These were, in fact, common practices among higher social classes,[100] which Menestrier is now introducing to a wider range of congregationists.

It is only a short step from here – encouraging congregationists to meet together for self-improvement – to urging such men to consult their better-educated fellows, and to do so specifically in order to find out which books the latter use, observe their practices, and then try to copy them;[101] indeed, throughout the course many of the means recommended to train his congregationists for entering social contexts new to them effectively introduce them to study practices that had hitherto been the preserve of higher social classes, or college classes beyond those they were likely to have attended. As before, however, the justification given here for this advice is framed in pragmatic terms, namely, its value in saving time; for Menestrier claims that by spending an hour listening to such a person one can pick up what had cost him months of study.

The communal approach to study is reiterated in one of his later points, where Menestrier recommends playing games together (a strategy reminiscent of the more ludic exercises common in college) in order to help one learn foreign languages[102] – by which he means Greek and Latin, both languages taught in the first cycle at college, together with Italian and Spanish, which were not taught in college at all.[103] Pragmatic as ever, Menestrier notes that since one is learning them specifically for the purpose of being able to read books – as opposed to speaking or writing in the language – one does not need to bother with learning grammatical rules, just immerse oneself in the language by reading.[104] He describes a game in which a group agree on a theme – such as the human body – and then try in turn to remember relevant vocabulary in the given foreign language ('head,' 'tongue,' 'arm,' hands,' 'eyes,' and so on); in another, friends would each try to name any object they could see or feel around them in this language ('house,' 'roof,' 'book,' 'stone,' 'bread,' 'wind,' 'rain').[105]

Such inherently collective study practices seem particularly appropriate for seventeenth-century artisans, if one considers how much of their activities would necessarily have been collective. Daily life offered precious little opportunity for privacy, as the artisan's household consisted of an extended family, including apprentices and sometimes other work associates, living and working together, in the comparatively cramped conditions of the densely built-up city centre. This was a milieu in which one's identity derived less from one's achievements as an individual than from one's membership of various groups: guild, *nation*, congregation. The individual identified himself with one or more groups and, by doing so, was visibly identified as such by his fellow citizens. As a member of a congregation, an artisan undertook both acts of piety and a cultural education in such a way that his participation in these activities further reinforced his own sense of identity in terms of the corporate identity of this group and of the place it occupied within larger groups, such as the citizenry or the Catholic communion.

The fact that all the books – or even the only book – owned by an individual were most likely to be books of hours is significant in that such ownership reflects the fact that private prayer might constitute the unique opportunity for privacy. Even here, however, the long print runs of such cheaply produced books ensured that their use engendered a commonality of references among a population, regardless of any individual's personal use of his own book (a feature in the related devotional books produced for members of specific congregations).[106] The practice of private devotions thus provided artisans with a commonality in even their most personal experiences, which was then echoed in the shared experience of their communal acts of piety (while the quarto prints, whether of images or of texts, continuously viewed on walls at home and work provided further common references).[107] Menestrier's book list similarly ensures a common set of textual references for his congregation, together with a series of study hints that will likewise provide a commonly held set of interpretative tools with which to decipher them. The course thus exploits reading – even critical reading – as yet another means for consolidating corporate identity.

Such an intent is confirmed by the implied purpose of the course, since this is revealed as reaching beyond any benefit to the individual undertaking it, to affect the larger bodies to which he belongs. The final goal of the first part of the course is to equip the artisan to hold his own in company by intelligently entering into *conversation* (in that wider sense mentioned earlier), and thereby to be accepted into a social milieu new to him, so that he can begin to play an active part in it. The second part seems to assume his attainment of this goal, in proceeding to equip him to enter intelligently into the creation of civic festivals proclaiming the city's propaganda.

It is in this context that Menestrier advises his congregationist to plan his study specifically according to its utility in preparing him for taking an active part in social gatherings.[108] Learning from personal observation – notably while travelling – is commended specifically because it will impress his fellows more than will repeating things he has merely read or heard.[109] Quotations and proverbs in foreign languages should be memorized so that they can be dropped into *conversations*.[110] Specialization in any single subject, particularly a recondite one, is recommended because it will impress listeners.[111] Likewise, reading lesser-known books will impress, because it will provide him with new and unusual morsels with which to entertain his hearers.[112]

Yet if this begins to sound like a 'bluffer's guide,' Menestrier's overall advice repudiates such an impression, including warnings against plagiarism[113] and affectation.[114] Moreover, he concludes by emphasizing that the display of sound literary judgment will be far more impressive[115] – in other words, that the development of the individual's critical faculty is essential. His advice thus seems to be ingenuous but pragmatic, derived from his experience as a schoolmaster.

The course of cultural education offered to congregationists in seventeenth-century Lyon was designed to turn them into *honnêtes gens*, who would thus be prepared to play an active role in provincial salon life. On acquitting themselves honourably, they would gain respect within their local community, and be included in the preparation of its festivals and decorative schemes. This course was therefore not only innovatory per se, but also had potentially subversive social consequences through – as with Jesuit college teaching – promoting an elite at once studious and pious, facilitating a social mobility favourable to ultramontanism.

Through the colleges and congregations they ran, Jesuits influenced all of society, including its elites. In seventeenth-century France, operating within a situation of perhaps unprecedented movement in the social hierarchy, the Jesuits exploited the current trend towards a meritocratic society for their own ends. The Jesuits took advantage of the Crown's initiatives, which dislodged nobles from the political elite, in preparing pious men obedient to Rome to fill this vacuum, through education. They offered men of lower social rank, but with comparable commitment to spiritual and educational advancement, opportunities for their own emancipation. Here again Jesuits made use of the contemporary social situation, notably the progressive opportunities it offered for literacy, and consequently for self-directed study, for even the artisan classes; simultaneously they exploited the eagerness of those classes to avail themselves of these opportunities, an eagerness due to widespread awareness of ensuing benefits in terms of commercial gain and social status.

By thus targeting devout men so that they would enjoy a privileged position in determining civic affairs, the Jesuits literally brought about a cultural revolution. While artisans might not accede to the council governing the citizenry, as painters, sculptors, carpenters, and the like they were responsible for realizing their city's visual propaganda in the form of festivals and decorations, not merely executing schemes devised by others but often designing artefacts themselves, albeit under the direction of a coordinating *inventeur*, responsible for the overriding rhetorical program; in seventeenth-century provincial France, this role was most commonly assumed by a Jesuit father.

The way in which the congregations under their control supplanted the self-governing, craft-, trade-, or profession-specific confraternities epitomizes the shift engendered in urban society by the Jesuits. For example, the artisans' congregation united men practising a variety of crafts or trades in a common pursuit, at first sight devotional in nature, but actually far broader. For the Jesuits' mission lay not just in converting individual souls but rather in sanctifying society. Through their range of congregations they helped individuals in each social rank to optimize their potential, not so much for their own benefit as for that of their civic community. For only by releasing a whole range of God-given talents and moulding them to these ends would the new, Christian civilization envisioned by the Jesuits become a material reality.

NOTES

1 On education in France in the sixteenth and seventeenth centuries, see François de Dainville, *Les jésuites et l'humanisme* (Paris, 1939); George Huppert, *Public Schools in Renaissance France* (Urbana and Chicago, 1984); and Aldo Scaglione, *The Liberal Arts and the Jesuit College System* (Amsterdam, 1986). See also François de Dainville, *L'éducation des jésuites (XVIe–XVIIIe siècles)* (Paris, 1978).

2 Lettres Patentes, Louis XIII, 13 October 1633, 1, in Archives Municipales de Lyon, GG 154.

3 Ibid. Such equality of treatment was also prescribed in the Jesuits' own *Constitutions* (Dainville, *Les jésuites et l'humanisme*, pp. 280–1).

4 Dainville, *Les jésuites et l'humanisme*, p. 284.

5 The Jesuits' experience in their first college, at Messina, convinced them that the competitive spirit promoted in sports and games could be usefully transferred to teaching. See also Allan Farrell, *The Jesuit 'Ratio studiorum' of 1599* (Washington, 1970), 'Common Rules for the Teaching of Lower Classes,' pp. 31ff.

6 Roland Mousnier, *Les institutions de la France sous la monarchie absolue, 1598–1789* (Paris, 1974), pp. 21–38.

7 Louis Châtellier, *L'Europe des dévots* (Paris, 1987), p. 25.

8 Louis Châtellier, 'Les jésuites et la naissance d'un type: Le dévot,' in *Les jésuites parmi les hommes aux XVIe et XVIIe siècles*, ed. Guy Demerson (Clermont-Ferrand, 1987), p. 260.

9 This classification of congregations parallels that ordained for the academies related to them in the *Ratio studiorum*, which justifies such classification on two grounds: first, keeping any group to a manageable size, and second, ensuring sufficient equivalence of level within any group to enable members to work together profitably. Hence there was to be an academy for Grammar students, another for Rhetoric and Humanities students, and another for Philosophy and Theology students: *Ratio atque Institutio studiorum Societatis Iesu* (Rome, 1599), 'Rules of the Academy,' no. 5. In mid-seventeenth century France these two institutions were in practice virtually conflated.

10 Lettres Patentes, Louis XIII, 13 October 1633, 1 (see n2 above).

11 Châtellier, *L'Europe des dévots*, p. 137.

12 See n1 above, and Gabriel Codina-Mir, *Aux sources de la pédagogie des jésuites. Le 'modus Parisiensis'* (Rome, 1968). See also studies of specific colleges, notably *L'enseignement en Provence avant la Révolution: Annales du collège Bourbon d'Aix*, ed. Edouard Méchin (Marseille, 1890); and Emile Marie Joseph Gustave Dupont-Ferrier, *Du Collège de Clermont au Lycée Louis-le-Grand* (Paris, 1921–5).

13 Judi Loach, 'The Teaching of Emblematics and Other Symbolic Imagery by Jesuits within Town Colleges in Seventeenth- and Eighteenth-Century France,' in *The*

Jesuits and the Emblem Tradition, ed. John Manning and Marc van Vaeck (Turnhout, 1999), pp. 161–86, especially 165–7.

14 Even these, being locally specific, have a poorer survival rate than school textbooks because they were printed in shorter runs. Théophile Raynaud wrote such a work, his *Pietas specialis, erga unum aliquem sanctorum prae aliis* (Lyon, 1648) (a litany invoking 'local' saints), for members of the Grande Congrégation at Lyon; it was translated by Menestrier as *Les devoirs de la ville de Lyon envers ses saints* (Lyon, 1658), again specifically for this congregation's members.

15 Two variant manuscripts, dating from c. 1658–9, contain Menestrier's own course notes: ms 1514 in the Bibliothèque Municipale de Lyon, and a manuscript in private hands, which will be referred to here as ms Baudrier; a third, dating from 1663, contains a student's *cours dictés*: Bibliothèque Municipale de Lyon, ms 2074. Full texts are contained in my critical edition of this course (Geneva, forthcoming).

16 ARSI Lugdun. Catal. Breve 1650–75 fol. 82.

17 Ibid., fol. 90v.

18 Ms 2074 (n15 above) is the *cours dicté* taken down by Jean Berthet in 1663–4, the year in which he was in the Rhetoric class.

19 Various sections from the course appear in Menestrier's *Bibliothèque curieuse et instructive*, 2 vols (Trévoux, 1704).

20 Entry for Menestrier, 1659–60: 'praef. cong. Min. Artif.,' Lugd. 15.1, ARSI Lugdun. Catal. Breve 1650–75 fol. 118v.

21 Ms 1514 fol. 1v; ms Baudrier 1; ms 2074 fol. 2.

22 Ms 1514 fol. 11v; ms Baudrier 30; ms 2074 fol. 22v.

23 In this and all subsequent cases, unless otherwise indicated, etymology draws on *Robert dictionnaire historique*, ed. Alain Rey (Paris, 1992); *Dictionnaire de l'Académie française*; Albert Dauzat, *Dictionnaire étymologique de la langue française* (Paris, 1938); and Oscar Bloch and Walther van Wartenburg, *Dictionnaire de la langue française*, 5th ed. (Paris, 1975). On the concept of the *honnête homme*, see Maurice Magendie, *La politesse mondaine et les théories de l'honnêteté au XVIIe siècle, de 1600 à 1660* (Paris, 1926); and Emmanuel Bury, *Littérature et politesse* (Paris, 1995). For Menestrier's own appreciation of *honnêteté*, see the titles he recommended to this end (ms 2074 fol. 7r–v): Nicolas Faret, *L'honneste homme ou l'Art de plaire à la Court* (Paris: Toussaincts du Bray, 1630, and many reprints); Pierre Bardin, *Le lycée ... où en plusieurs promenades il est traité des connaissances, des actions et des plaisirs d'un honnête homme*, 2 vols (Paris: J. Camusat, 1632–4); and Sr Fortin de la Hoguette, *Testament ou conseils fidèles d'un bon père à ses enfants*, 1st ed. (Paris: Antoine Vitré, 1648).

24 Ms 1514 fol. 14v; ms Baudrier 46; ms 2074 fol. 32v.

25 See n23 above.

26 Ms 1514 fols 2–11; ms Baudrier 3–30; ms 2074 fols 6–22v.

27 Ms 2074 fols 4–6. The various manuscripts order the book list differently.

28 Ms 2074 fol. 4r–v.

29 Ms 1514 fol. 4r–v; ms Baudrier 12; ms 2074 fols 6–7v. On this genre of translation, see Roger Zuber, *Les 'belles infidèles' et la formation du goût classique* (Paris, 1968).

30 Ms 2074 is most explicit here, introducing this subject as 'l'une des principales qualités qu'un honeste homme puisse avoir pour la conversation ou il ne doit iamais estre barbare. Il faut commencer par les livres les plus purs et les plus polis et par ceux qui nous fournisse [*sic*] les remarques necessaires pour le choix des mots et des locutions' (fol. 6). The list then details 'les nouvelles traductions' (6r–v), followed by 'les autres ouvrages bien françois' (6v–7), and finally publications 'pour prendre le style de la conversation ... les lettres, les entretiens, les dialogues, les conferences, les apologies' (7).

31 Mousnier, *Les institutions*, p. 553; Scaglione, *The Liberal Arts*, p. 117.

32 This section is actually headed 'La philosophie de la conversation': ms 1514 fol. 9; ms Baudrier 29–30; ms 2074 fol. 19r–v. It is specifically oriented towards conversation, covering subjects of topical interest (subjects such as magnetism and human anatomy and fashionable authors such as Descartes and Kircher) and of general curiosity value (meteors, talismans, and the subterranean realms).

33 Ms 1514 fol. 11v; ms Baudrier 30; ms 2074 fol. 22v; Menestrier, *Bibliothèque curieuse*, vol. 2, p. 20.

34 'des industries pour se faire galant homme en peu de temps': ms 1514 fol. 1v; ms Baudrier 2; ms 2074 fol. 2v. The early modern sense of *industries* was of skill or ingenuity used to achieve an end, produce something, or otherwise make a project succeed; it derived directly from the Latin *industria*, an activity using the intellect.

35 Ms 1514 fol. 12; ms Baudrier 34; ms 2074 fols 24v–25; cf. *Bibliothèque curieuse*, vol. 1, pp. 24–5.

36 Ms 1514 fol. 11v; ms Baudrier 30–1; ms 2074 fols 22v–23; cf. *Bibliothèque curieuse*, vol. 2, pp. 20–1. This point is reiterated later in the revised versions: ms 2074 fol. 5v, and *Bibliothèque curieuse*, vol. 2, p. 21.

37 Dainville, *Les jésuites et l'humanisme*, pp. 90–1.

38 Ms 2074 fols 5v–6.

39 Ms 1514 fol. 12; ms Baudrier 34; ms 2074 fol. 25.

40 Ms 1514 fols 11v–13; ms Baudrier 30–7; ms 2074 fols 22v–27v.

41 'De la methode qu'on doit tenir pour examiner les ouvrages d'un autheur': ms 1514 fols 13–14; ms Baudrier 37–43; ms 2074 fols 27v–31. (In the preface this chapter is referred to as 'les regles pour iuger prudemment de quel ouvrage que ce soit qui [luy] puisse tomber entre les mains': ms 1514 fol. 1v; ms Baudrier 2; ms 2074 fol. 2v.)

42 'De la maniere de faire des remarques': ms 1514 fols 14–15; ms Baudrier 44–51;

ms 2074 fols 31–35v. *Remarques* was the normal French term for the items collected in a commonplace book (Ann Moss, *Printed Commonplace Books and the Structuring of Renaissance Thought* [Oxford, 1996], p. 251).

43 'Methode de lire l'histoire': ms 1514 fols 15–16; ms Baudrier 52–8.

44 'Façon de dire son advis dans les assemblées': ms Baudrier 58–70.

45 Ms 2074 fol. 6.

46 Ms 1514 fol. 52; ms Baudrier 229–30 ('Traité des Pompes Sçavantes').

47 Ms 1514 fols 17–25v; ms Baudrier 201–24; ms 2074 fols 35v–49.

48 Ms 1514 fols 31–51; ms Baudrier 77–124.

49 Ms Baudrier 127–63 (devices); ms Baudrier 169–98 (emblems).

50 Ms 1514 fols 52–71v; ms Baudrier 229–57.

51 Ms 1514 fol. 78r–v; ms Baudrier 299–303.

52 Menestrier, *Recherches du blason* (Paris, 1674), sig. ã[vi] v.

53 Menestrier, *Recherches du blason* (Paris, 1673), sigs ãii r–ã[viii] v (repr. in Paul Allut, *Recherches sur la vie et sur les oeuvres du P. Claude François Menestrier de la Compagnie de Jésus* [Lyon, 1856], pp. 63–71). In the prefatory note Menestrier dates the conception of this 'Philosophie des Images' to fifteen years earlier, thus contemporary with his cultural course for congregationists (sig. ãii r).

54 Georges Couton, *Ecritures codées: Essais sur l'allégorie au XVIIe siècle* (Paris, 1990).

55 Ms 2074 fols 6–22v; cf. ms 1514 fols 2–11 / ms Baudrier 3–30.

56 On the development of the *Ratio studiorum*, see Dainville, *Les jésuites et l'humanisme*, pp. 77ff.; Farrell, *The Jesuit 'Ratio studiorum,'* 'Introduction,' p. i ff.; and Scaglione, *The Liberal Arts*, p. 83.

57 Ms 1514 fol. 11v; ms Baudrier 3; ms 2074 fol. 23r–v; cf. *Bibliothèque curieuse*, vol. 2, p. 21.

58 Ms 1514 fol. 11v; ms Baudrier 32; ms 2074 fol. 23v.

59 Ms 2074 fol. 23v; cf. *Bibliothèque curieuse*, vol. 2, p. 22.

60 Ms 1514 fol. 12; ms Baudrier 34; ms 2074 fol. 25; *Bibliothèque curieuse*, vol. 2, p. 25.

61 Ms 1514 fol. 13; ms Baudrier 37–8; ms 2074 fols 27v–28.

62 Ms 1514 fol. 14; ms Baudrier 44; ms 2074 fol. 31v.

63 Ms 1514 fols 14–15; ms Baudrier 44–52; ms 2074 fols 31v–35v.

64 See n36 above.

65 'De la methode qu'on doit tenir pour examiner les ouvrages d'un autheur': ms 1514 fols 13–14; ms Baudrier 37–43; ms 2074 fols 27–31.

66 On *prélection* and *explication*, see Dainville, *Les jésuites et l'humanisme*, pp. 94ff.; Farrell, *The Jesuit 'Ratio studiorum,'* pp. viii–ix, and 'Common Rules for the Teachers of the Lower Classes,' pp. 27ff.; Mousnier, *Les institutions*, p. 553; and Scaglione, *The Liberal Arts*, p. 80.

67 'Quelques uns lisent les livres ... pour les bien[/mieux] posseder': ms 1514 fol. 12; ms Baudrier 32; ms 2074 fol. 24; cf. *Bibliothèque curieuse*, vol. 2, p. 23. 'Il faut avoir les livres rares': ms 1514 fol. 12v; ms Baudrier 34; ms 2074 fol. 25; cf. *Bibliothèque curieuse*, vol. 2, p. 25.

68 The library of the Collège de la Trinité remained that of the town college after the suppression of the Jesuits, and following the Revolution became the kernel of today's Bibliothèque Municipale de Lyon. This contains a very high proportion of the books in this list, such that allowing for losses (largely at the Revolution) one can assume it to have contained virtually all of them.

69 The *Ratio studiorum* includes looking after the academy's books among its secretary's duties; it is ambiguous as to whether this meant a library or just its own records ('Rules of the Academy,' p. 10).

70 Roger Chartier, 'Du livre au lire: Les pratiques citadines de l'imprimé, 1660–1789,' in his *Lectures et lecteurs dans la France de l'ancien régime* (Paris, 1982), pp. 165–221, especially 166, 186–9.

71 Chartier, *Lectures et lecteurs*, pp. 184–5.

72 This is documented in Menestrier's correspondence with Samuel Guichenon, recorded in Allut's *Recherches* (pp. 247–324); in turn it indicates that he was also borrowing books and manuscripts from mutual friends.

73 Chartier, *Lectures et lecteurs*, pp. 190–6.

74 Roger Chartier, *Pratiques de la lecture* (Paris, 1985), p. 72.

75 Dainville, *Les jésuites et l'humanisme*, pp. 94ff.

76 Ms 1514 fol. 12; ms Baudrier 33; ms 2074 fol. 24v. Ms 2074 adds at the end that this provides an opportunity for catching up on one's commonplace book. In the later published version Menestrier extends the first sentence to provide more concrete detail: 'ce qu'on a vû, ce qu'on a lû, ce qu'on aura ouî dire, and consulter au plutôt les endroits des Livres and des Livres qu'ils ont loüez, alleguez, relevez de leurs erreurs, interpretez ou critiquez' (*Bibliothèque curieuse*, vol. 2, p. 24).

77 Dainville, *Les jésuites et l'humanisme*, p. 112.

78 See n76 above.

79 Even entire treatises, for example, Claude-François Menestrier, *Les ballets anciens et modernes, selon les règles du théâtre* (Paris, 1682), BNVE 40.8.H.7,6.

80 Dainville, *Les jésuites et l'humanisme*, pp. 110ff.; Chartier, *Pratiques de la lecture*, p. 72, and *Lectures et lecteurs*, p. 210; Mousnier, *Les institutions*, p. 534.

81 Ms 1514 fol. 12; ms Baudrier 32; ms 2074 fol. 24; cf. *Bibliothèque curieuse*, vol. 2, p. 23.

82 *Bibliothèque curieuse*, vol. 2, p. 23.

83 Ms 1514 fol. 12; ms Baudrier 32; ms 2074 fol. 24; only in ms 2074 does he note its mnemonic function.

84 *Bibliothèque curieuse*, vol. 2, p. 23.

85 Ms 2074 fol. 24.

86 Ms 1514 fol. 12v; ms Baudrier 35–6; ms 2074 fol. 25r–v; cf. *Bibliothèque curieuse*, vol. 2, p. 27–8.

87 Ms 1514 fol. 14v; ms Baudrier 47.

88 Ms 1514 fol. 12; ms Baudrier 33; ms 2074 fol. 24; cf. *Bibliothèque curieuse*, vol. 2, p. 24.

89 Emile Littré, *Dictionnaire de la langue française*, vol. 7 (Paris, 1958), p. 698.

90 Ms 1514 fol. 12; ms Baudrier 33; ms 2074 fol. 24; cf. *Bibliothèque curieuse*, vol. 2, p. 24.

91 'Idee des Cayer [*sic*]': ms Baudrier 49–52; ms 2074 fols 32v–35v.

92 Dainville, *Les jésuites et l'humanisme*, pp. 134–5.

93 Chartier, *Pratiques de la lecture*, p. 72, and *Lectures et lecteurs*, p. 210.

94 'Recueil de diverses armoiries, preuves de noblesse et autres pareilles choses appartenant à l'art du blason': Bibliothèque Municipale de Lyon, ms 6150. This is a calfbound, folio volume of around 360 pages, almost completely filled with engravings and drawings (some hand-coloured) of coats of arms, tombstones bearing arms, and genealogical trees.

95 Dainville, *Les jésuites et l'humanisme*, pp. 134–5.

96 Ms 1514 fol. 12; ms Baudrier 32; ms 2074 fol. 24; cf. *Bibliothèque curieuse*, vol. 1, pp. 22, 23.

97 'Les conferences sont tres avantageuses; il faut mesme lire ensemble affin que chacun puisse dire son advis [/il est bon ... de lire quelque fois ensemble afin qu'on puisse dire son advis]': ms 1514 fol. 12; ms Baudrier 32; ms 2074 fol. 24; *Bibliothèque curieuse*, vol. 2, pp. 22–3.

98 Ms 2074 fol. 24.

99 'Trouver a[d]droitement l'occasion de parler de ce qu'on a leu recemment, cela l'inculque.' Ms 2074 adds at the end: 'et l'imprime d'avantage dans la memoire.' Ms 1514 fol. 13; ms Baudrier 37; ms 2074 fol. 26v; cf. *Bibliothèque curieuse*, vol. 2, p. 26.

100 Chartier, *Lectures et lecteurs*, pp. 207–9.

101 Ms 1514 fol. 12; ms Baudrier 33; ms 2074 fol. 24v. *Bibliothèque curieuse*, vol. 2, pp. 23–4, inserts after 'servent,' 'ou qu'ils estiment le plus en chaque faculté.'

102 Ms 1514 fol. 13; ms Baudrier 38; ms 2074 fol. 26; cf. *Bibliothèque curieuse*, vol. 2, pp. 36–7.

103 Ms 1514 fol. 12v; ms Baudrier 34–5; ms 2074 fol. 25v.

104 Ms 1514 fol. 12v; ms Baudrier 35; ms 2074 fols 25v–26; cf. *Bibliothèque curieuse*, vol. 2, p. 30.

105 *Bibliothèque curieuse*, vol. 2, pp. 36–7.

106 See n14 above.

107 Chartier, *Lectures et lecteurs*, pp. 211–13.

108 'pour entretenir les compagnies des choses curieuses et nouvelles': ms 1514 fol. 12v; ms Baudrier 34; ms 2074 fol. 25. Earlier Menestrier advocates reading books specifically so as 'en pouvoir parler': ms 1514 fol. 11v; ms Baudrier 31; ms 2074 fol. 23.

109 Ms 1514 fol. 13; ms Baudrier 36–7; ms 2074 fol. 26; cf. *Bibliothèque curieuse*, vol. 2, p. 25. Ms 2074 elaborates, in vivid detail, upon the sort of things to note on one's travels. (*Bibliothèque curieuse* devotes an entire chapter to the educational potential of such visits, vol. 2, pp. 38ff., 'De l'etude des voyages.')

110 Ms 1514 fol. 12v; ms Baudrier 35; ms 2074 fol. 26. Ms 2074 adds 'belles pensées' to this list, while *Bibliothèque curieuse* adds epigrams (vol. 2, pp. 37–8).

111 Ms 1514 fol. 12v; ms Baudrier 37–8; ms 2074 fols 26v–27.

112 Ms 1514 fol. 12v; ms Baudrier 34; ms 2074 fol. 25; cf. *Bibliothèque curieuse*, vol. 2, p. 25.

113 Ibid.

114 Ms 1514 fol. 12v; ms Baudrier 35; ms 2074 fol. 26; *Bibliothèque curieuse*, vol. 2, pp. 37–8. In the last case he ends by warning that saying such things will be perceived as pedantry rather than *honnêteté*.

115 Ms 1514 fol. 13; ms Baudrier 37; ms 2074 fol. 27v; cf. *Bibliothèque curieuse*, vol. 2, p. 26.

6 / The Jesuit Garden

PETER DAVIDSON

In this article I hope to trace some plants of the Jesuit garden, using 'plants' in the archaic sense of footsteps as well as the modern sense of living herbs, trees, and flowers. I am particularly concerned with the idea of the garden, of Jesuit ways of thinking about gardens, and of the ways in which Jesuit writers of the seventeenth century related an external or veridical garden to a mental or devotional map of ideas. In the writings of the Jesuit *savants* of the seventeenth century, the old, accretive tradition of thinking about 'an interior garden' acquired a focus and precision which it had rarely attained before.

There is another aspect of the Jesuit garden which I would like to consider: the richness of Jesuit participation in the elite interest in gardens, which is such a notable international feature of the seventeenth century. The kinds of information codified by Giovanni Battista Ferrari, S.J., in his suggestions about the meanings of garden layouts, discussed below, are invaluable for decoding a number of surviving Late Renaissance gardens as spaces charged with meaning. An attentive reading of Louis Richeôme's, S.J., meditations on the Jesuit gardens of the Novitiate of Sant'Andrea al Quirinale inevitably acts as a key to seventeenth-century ways of responding to gardens: Richeôme offers an invaluable theoretical and interpretative tool for the understanding of such diverse texts as the *buitengedichten*, the country-house and estate poems of the Northern Netherlandic golden age, and even of such apparently familiar mid-seventeenth-century texts as Andrew Marvell's 'Upon Appleton House.' At the end of the century, the Jesuit Réné Rapin drew together the diverse ideas of the garden which had been so important throughout the century, and Alexander Pope, who revised the English translation of Rapin, himself made a garden and grotto which are much more closely related to the world of the seventeenth-century Jesuit *savants* and *virtuosi* than is allowed by conventional historians of landscape art.[1] Landscape art itself might also be held to be a Jesuit invention:

certainly the letters of the Chinese mission describing the gardens of Emperor Qianlong played no small part in at least the theory of the landscape garden in Europe.

While I will inevitably discuss the introduction of northern European skills and collected plants into southern Europe through the work of Giovanni Battista Ferrari, I must emphasize that it is not my intention here to trace the whole rich history of Jesuit botany and Jesuit plant collecting. I would like, rather, to offer a consideration of Jesuit ideas of the garden and of its imaginative, physical, and pedagogical possibilities.

That being said, I would like, however, to bring forward one testimony to the degree to which Jesuit plant collectors appear to have been ahead of their contemporaries, even as early as the 1590s. In the *Voyage en Italie* of Michel de Montaigne, he reports a visit to the Jesuits of Ferrara, undertaken on about 16 or 17 November 1580. Montaigne's few words seem to indicate a crucial importation from the Far Eastern missions of the Society:

Nous fûmes tout ce jour-là à Ferrare, et y vîmes plusieurs belles églises, jardins et maisons privées, et tout ce qu'on dit être remarquable, entre autres, aux Jésuates, un pied de rosier qui porte fleur tous les mois de l'an: et lors même s'y en trouva une qui fut donnée à M. de Montaigne.[2]

We saw all the notable sights of Ferrara, churches, gardens, and palaces; among others, in the house of the Jesuits we saw a rose tree which bears flowers in every month of the year; and one of these was found as a gift for M. de Montaigne.

If Montaigne's suggestion could be substantiated, this would constitute another botanical triumph for the Society of Jesus: the introduction of the remontant oriental rose a century and a half before the arrival of the 'Banksian' rose at Kew Gardens in London.

The centrality of the Garden to the concerns of early modern Europe hardly needs to be emphasized. It is not surprising to find a rich Jesuit contribution to such a central cultural phenomenon, which is also a phenomenon clearly well fitted to attract elite interest in a Jesuit college, and which could be seen too as having a place in the educational formation of the Christian citizen.

It should be noted that Jesuit poets were active in this sphere: the great Maciej Casimir Sarbiewski wrote a magically compressed ode to the family who patronized Giovanni Battista Ferrari, the Barberini of Rome, who certainly had wonderful gardens, described by Sarbiewski as the green native land, the 'viridem patriam,' of the golden age of the Barberini, over which their heraldic bees fly at will:

Laboribus quid iuvat volatibus ...
Si Barberino delicata principe
Saecula melle fluunt,
Parata vobis saecula?

What need to fly with labouring wings ... if the epoch of the Barberini flows with that delicate honey which will sweeten your years?

Sarbiewski also revisited one of the crucial sources of all subsequent writing about gardens, the *Canticum canticorum*.[3] The most celebrated Jesuit poet of Germany, Jacob Balde, also wrote charmingly of the garden world of his time, addressing an ode to one of the topiary figures in the gardens of Prince Albert of Bavaria, and predicting the reward of this modest guardian of that world:

... Te Zephyritidum
Fratrum coronabit quotannis
Et violae linet aura succo.

The sisters of the gentle wind will crown you with perfumes and violets.[4]

In another sphere of artistic endeavour, Daniel Seegers, S.J. (1590–1661), the associate of Rubens, was noted as a painter of flowers and of the *guirlandes* of flowers surrounding a sacred image which were popular in the Southern Netherlands. His celebrity was such that he drew a high praise from the Calvinist statesman and polymath Constantijn Huygens in an elegant Latin ode: '... vivus / Coram factitio flosculus umbra fuit[5] (the painted flower renders the real flower a shadow). Though early modern Jesuits made physical gardens as well as describing them, there is no space here to consider the Jesuits as makers of gardens in that sense. But the testimony of magnificent engravings of the Jesuit colleges suggests that this is a rich field for future investigation, as is the subject of Jesuits as designers of dials for gardens.[6]

It is with another institution that I would like to continue: the Collegio Romano, and the collection of the great virtuoso Athanasius Kircher, and the splendid set of optical devices from his collection.[7] What interests me here is that Kircher uses this set of kaleidoscope-like devices to multiply to infinity the image of a formal garden, producing by the adroit manipulation of light and mirrors a parterre vast beyond even the imaginings of Louis XIV or of the scenography of the Bibbiena family. Kircher himself identifies three possible locations for multiplication by his device: the garden, the library, the palace: three crucial sites of the elite baroque imagination.

Another, more familiar kind of interior garden is set forth in the Marian garden meditations, the *Parthenia sacra*, published by the English Jesuit Henry Hawkins in 1633.[8] This is a complex, transitional book. Hawkins makes us aware that he is at ease with a medieval tradition of reading the physical world allegorically. There is, after all, strong precedent for allegorical readings of a garden, reaching as far back in time as the twelfth-century Byzantine-Greek manuscript, in the Laurentian library in Florence, known as *The Symbolic Garden*, with its simple, one-to-one readings of plants as allegories of virtues set out by Christ, the master of the garden.[9]

But Hawkins's readings of objects perform a complex act of balance among traditions – of crypto-Ignatian meditation, of *ars memorativa,* and of emblematics, as well as of medieval allegory. Hawkins's mental garden is constructed in an imagined space which alters as the devout reader progresses through the book. Initially it is offered by Hawkins in small, broken-down sections, so that readers have before them a ninefold set of meditations, emblems, essays, and expositions of each element: the garden itself and its contents. But at the very end Hawkins sets the devout soul free to ramble at its own speed in the interior garden, constructed under his direction, as if it were a place now susceptible of infinite deepening, infinite recessions of new meaning, a place capable of containing everything which the devout mind can feel.

The engraved frontispiece of the book suggests the degree to which Hawkins is working from an established tradition: the enclosed garden with its roses and lilies is a constant in the tradition applying the praises of the Song of Songs to the praise of Our Lady; the house of gold and the tower of ivory are from the Litany of Loreto; and the palm and the olive are figures for Holy Wisdom in Ecclesiasticus. It is not hard to discern the essentially Edenic nature of the circular walled garden depicted here. What is fascinating in the *Parthenia sacra*, however, is the use which Hawkins makes of these garden elements. In the epistle, which he addressed to the Parthenian Sodality, who are his primary audience, he is unequivocal as to the complex status of his material. Beginning from the idea of Christ's appearance as a gardener after the Resurrection, he moves rapidly to the enumeration of ways in which the Garden is both Our Lady herself mystically considered and, also, a pattern of the soul of each spectator.

[Christ] evidently declared his good affection towards the *Garden* of the Soule, which then he came to cheer-up ... You, deerest Parthenians, yet greeued and groaning with the burden of your pressures, for his sake who is the curious *Gardener* indeed, that from the beginning planted the same for himself from al Eternitie ... you heer behold our Sacred Parthenes, who presents herselfe for your delights in Garden-attire ... in this coole and rural array, of hearbes and flowers, as if she were clothed with the Sunne, crowned with the Starres and trampling the moone ... Nor would I wish you perfunctoriously to view her only, and passe her over with a slender glance of the eye, but to enter into her garden which she is herself, and survey it well.[10]

The symbolic garden is essentially educative in a subtle way: readers are invited to participate so fully in the progressive exposition that by the end of each section they are ready to own the closing address, as it were adding their voices and their assent to the words of the author. When Hawkins comes to the description of the Garden to be contemplated, a lavish and contemporary layout is evoked rather than the simple *hortus conclusus* pictured on the frontispiece; indeed, Hawkins himself at one point compares the garden to a 'cabinet of flowerie gems,' echoing the *wunderkammer* aspect of the flower garden, expressed by Ferrari in his publication of the same year:[11]

Cast your eyes a little on those goodlie allies, as sowed over with sands of gold, drawn-forth so streight by a line. Those Cros-bowes there (be not affrayd of them) they are but crossbowes made of Bayes; and the Harquebusquiers, wrought in Rosemarie, shoot but flowers and dart forth musk ... Behold those daire and beautiful Tulips there, those rich amaranths, cerulian Hiacinths, Pansies, the gemmes of the goodlie IRIS ... O what a paradice of flowers is this! What a heaven of muskie starres, or Celestial earth al starred with flowers, empearled with gemmes and precious stones.[12]

Having established that the imaginary garden is baroque both in the way in which it is apprehended and in its collection of the fashionable bulbous plants and florists' flowers, Hawkins progresses to his discourse, and here he allegorizes these elements in a manner which is poised between tradition and innovation. A fairly brief extract gives an idea of the whole: '[Here] are faire and goodlie Allies, streight and even, strewed all with sands, that is, a streight, vertuous, and Angelical life, yet strewed with the sands and dust of her proper Humilitie; where are arbours to shadow her from the heats of concupicense; flowerie beds to repose in, with heauenlie contemplations; Mounts to ascend to, with the studie of Perfections.'[13] As the 'Discourse' continues, it becomes clear that we are indeed contemplating a baroque garden on a vast scale, perhaps not unlike the semi-sacred Paradise garden of Valsanzibio in the Veneto. 'Heer are Pooles for the harmles fry of her innocent thoughts, like fishes heer and there to passe up and downe in the heauenlie element of her mind; heer and there certain labyrinths formed in the hearbs of her endles perfections. Heer lastly are statues of her rare examples to be seen, Obelisks, Pyramids, Triumphal Arches, Aquaducts, Thermes, Pillars of Eternal Memorie, erected to her glorie on contemplation of her Admirable, Angelical, and Divine life.'[14]

When we consider the work of Louis Richeôme, S.J., particularly that section of his 1611 *La peinture spirituelle* which deals with the gardens of the Jesuit house of Sant'Andrea al Quirinale in Rome, we find some of the same perceptions and readings being applied, but, crucially, to a real and known garden[15] (fig. 6.1). His meditation upon the garden forms the sixth section of an interpreted walk through various parts of the Jesuit Novitiate. Gauvin Alexander Bailey has given splendid consideration to the paintings described in the section on the infirmary.[16] Naturally, the kind of interpretation which is offered is consistently spiritual: to Richeôme there is no visible thing which does not ring forth immediately with the overtones of its spiritual resonance.

He is patently aware of all the Reniassance modes of symbolic discourse: he was himself an emblematist and well aware of the debate on hieroglyphics, or the history of speaking pictures. It is clear too that he was aware of the kinds of medieval traditions of interpretation to which Hawkins also had access. All these traditions, as well as allegorical traditions of reading scripture, combine to give him the reservoir of material with which he can interpret the material world.

The garden section of *La peinture spirituelle* offers us a considerable insight into the mind of the seventeenth century. On the simplest level we are presented with a detailed representation of (and indeed a plant list for) an actual Jesuit garden of the beginning of the seventeenth century. If we trust that Richeôme's list of flowers and trees is specific – as the layout of his text as a walk through this specific garden would strongly suggest – rather than general, then we have a record of an extremely rich planting, almost comparable to the published plant-lists of much more celebrated institutions such as the botanic gardens of Padua or Leiden. We also have a representation, in this terraced and productive garden, of something very like the apparently unique survivor of this moment in the history of the Italian garden, the Giardini Buonaccorsi near Macerata, which I will consider in some detail later.

As well as providing a fascinating documentation of one garden (complete with sundials and a symbolic obelisk already contributing an extra layer of meaning to the layout), Richeôme's text offers a clear insight into a process of mental training in right perception of the world: nothing, no single object observed in the garden, is allowed to pass without being at once supplied with a spiritual reading, an interpretation concerned with the virtuosity and mercy of the Creator as well as with the perceptions and spiritual growth of the observer. This flow of interpretation is itself virtuosic: there is hardly a strained interpretation in the whole course of Richeôme's spiritual perambulation of the garden.

It is perhaps not necessary to follow the complete course of his progression, from the garden gate at the top to the pyramid or obelisk in the lowest terrace, but it is useful to give some indication of the nature of the complex process of

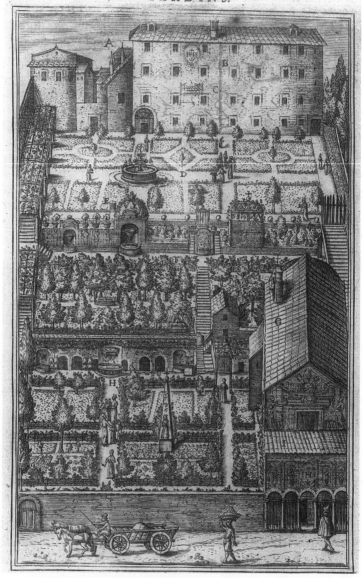

6.1. Illustration of the gardens of Sant'Andrea al Quirinale from Louis Richeôme,
La peinture spirituelle (Lyon, 1611).
Photo courtesy of Aberdeen University Photographic Services.

education (literal training of the mind to a set of responses) which Richeôme sets forth for the walk through the gardens.

The essential conjunction of physical and spiritual is offered early – unsurprisingly, with a pun on fruits as results of a process of maturation – by means of an immediate contrast between the fugacity of the earthly and the eternity of the heavenly: 'et vous donnant interieurement l'adresse de cueillir non seulement les fruits temporels, mais encore les fruicts spirituels d'incorruption.' As in the Giardini Buonaccorsi, the central position of the fountain on the upper terrace at once evokes the earthly paradise, Eden. This symbolic perception is common in the recorded layouts of many early modern botanic gardens, in accordance with the idea of the sacrality of the botanic garden as a divinely sanctioned reassemblage of the flora of the earthly paradise, scattered at the fall. Richeôme's response to the florists' flowers of the upper garden is simply one of humble contemplation of the inexhaustable riches of divine creation: 'ne sentez-vous pas vostre ame rauie a l'admiration, & amour du Createur, qui les a produictes?'

The sundials of the upper garden offer an intriguing moment of contemplation of the light orbiting the globe (clearly these are superb Jesuit dials, offering readings of the hour at different places on earth) as an image of the universality and endless wakefulness of the Universal Church: 'facon qui se garde encor en l'eglise Romaine, & partoute la Chrestienité, [d]és festes & iours mysterieux.'

The fountains of the lower garden, by contrast, are read as symbols of the humility and usefulness of water. Then the 'arbre triste' of Goa (presumably sent back to Rome by the established Jesuit mission there) is read as a symbol of the true Christian in penitence, in that it casts its night-borne flowers at the moment when the sun rises, and so represents the triumph of penitence in the religious soul. This kind of allegorization of newly introduced trees leads us, of course, to an emblem book of the later seventeenth century, *Ashrea, or The Grove of Beatitude* (London 1665), possibly a Jesuit product, which offers a highly ingenious set of readings of exotic trees, overlaid with a contemplation of the limbs of Christ on the cross.

Finally, Richeôme dwells upon the pyramid or obelisk in the lower gardens, which is already supplied with imprese, one of which, incidentally, is identical to that on the tomb of the ex-Catholic English poet John Donne: the eastern face with the figure of Christ and the sun and the words 'His name is Orient,' 'L'Orient est son nom,' 'Cuius nomen est oriens.'

If Richeôme's description of the garden is indeed accurate in its itemization of an extensive Jesuit flower collection, then we can see how the culture of the Roman houses would foster the work of the last Jesuit writer to be surveyed here: Giovanni Battista Ferrari, who published his central work, *De florum cultura*, in 1633, the same year as Hawkins's *Parthenia*.[17]

Ferrari was born in Siena in the early 1580s, entered the Society of Jesus at Rome in 1602, and was professed in May 1621. He had studied in the Collegio Romano from 1606 to 1611 and he taught Hebrew there from 1618 until he retired on the ground of ill health in 1647. He published *De florum cultura*, a treatise on the flower garden, under the patronage of Cardinal Francesco Barberini in 1633. This beautifully produced book includes designs engraved after Pietro da Cortona[18] and Guido Reni. In 1646, Ferrari published an equally lavish and encyclopaedic work on the history, cultivation, and uses of citrus fruits: *Hesperides, sive De malorum aureum cultura*. After his retirement he returned to his native city, where, after the publication of his virtuoso's jottings in *Collocutiones*[19] in 1652, he died in February 1655.

His garden writing is encyclopaedic in the best sense: a summary of what is known. His *Hesperides* of 1646 records all ancient records of the golden apples of the Hesperides, and all representations of them in surviving classical art. From there it offers a treatise on the types and cultivars of citrus trees, with beautifully detailed notes on their culture (including magnificent plates of orangeries) and also a dissertation on why the citrus has been identified with the biblical apple of Adam. A thought which would bear further investigation is the degree to which the iconography and layout of this work coincides with that of the Villa d'Este at Tivoli, outside Rome. The educative function of the book is confirmed by an exhaustive concluding section on the uses of citrus fruits, which includes what looks like an early recipe for a type of lemon marmalade.

Ferarri's *De florum cultura* of 1633 is a remarkable work. It covers all matters to do with the layout of a garden, including the symbolic force of different ground-plans). It details the florists' flowers of the seventeenth century, with some emphasis on the newer introductions of bulbous plants. It concludes with a section – of the highest interest for what it records – on the use of flowers as well as on subtle baroque tricks which can be played with the scent or colour of flowers. In addition to the recording of marmalade, we must credit the Society with being the first to record the green carnation.[20] The book has magnificent engraved plates, including an allegorical representation of Flora banishing slugs and common garden pests from the garden (fig. 6.2). As well as these allegorical plates, there are numerous illustrations of flowers and, indeed, of garden tools. The whole feeling of the book is one of a new aspect of civil life being introduced to Italian society from the (in these years, literally) flower-mad Northern Netherlands. In Ferrari's work, the garden is seen very much as a living *wunderkammer*, an outdoor extension of the global scope of the *Musaeum Kircherianum*. There may also be found in Ferrari's work, I suspect, a reluctance to allow the primacy in horticulture, horticultural collecting, or horticultural innovation to pass to the Protestant Netherlands.

6.2. Flora banishes garden pests. Illustration from Giovanni Battista Ferrari,
De florum cultura (Rome, 1633). Photo courtesy of Peter Davidson.

Like the *Hesperides, De florum cultura* ends with a lengthy section on the uses of flowers. Here the sense of a real transplantation of a culture is palpable, in the numerous and fascinating plates offered for the arrangement of flowers, the transportation of flowers, and the ingenious vases for the reception of flowers or flower heads, so that they may form a wreathed column, or so that you may pick out the badge of the Society in the heads of your best tulips (figs 6.3, 6.4). As well as these baroque 'subtleties,' Ferrari records a strange ephemeral work of Bernini's: the coat of arms of the Barberini formed in flowers, with realistic Barberini bees formed out of wax and stuck with flower heads of broom and African marigolds to simulate their stripes.[21] The effect can have been comparable only to the flower sculptures which today accompany the better class of gangland funerals in the East End of London.

But it is to Ferrrari's itemization of symbolic garden plans that I would now like to turn. When the English poet Andrew Marvell wrote of 'Paradise's only map,' the image in his mind may have been a specific one, for in *De florum cultura* are five plans which assign specific meanings to what might otherwise be taken for purely abstract patterns (fig. 6.5). These patterns for intricate garden cut-works of geometric flower bed and paths offer a casual revelation about the workings of the baroque imagination: many garden parterres all over Europe which hitherto have been thought of as purely decorative may prove yet to be bearers of meaning as fully as any statue or inscription. As so often, a little studied treatise (though one certainly known in seventeenth-century Britain, as John Evelyn's surviving, annotated copy testifies) provides a 'key to the garden' by recording information about ways of thinking and feeling once all but universal and now forgotten. Here are four examples. The first described a square plan of four quarters:

Si cui volupe sit caelestis civitatis beatissimam sedem aeternae stabilitas in quadro positam terrenae amoenitatis hortensi ambito designare, caeloque quodammodo in terris assuescere: hoc illi proponitur, quod in quadratos hortos quadrat, exemplar. (p. 25)

If it might be a pleasure to someone to design within the bounds of a garden the blessed seat of the Holy City in its eternal stability, laid out in four quarters of celestial beauty, and to acclimatize something heavenly on the earth, this is proposed here, since the diagram divides the garden into patterns of fours.

The second interprets a circular garden:

Si mundi ornatissimam rotunditatem hortensis ornatus rotunda imagine lubet aemulari, vel aetati florum novum orbem condere: orbiculatum habes rudimentum quadrata in area

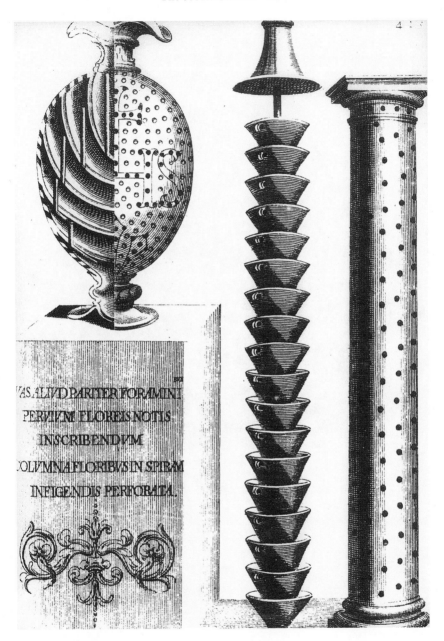

VAS ALIVD PARITER FORAMINI
PERVIVM FLOREIS NOTIS
INSCRIBENDVM
COLVMNA FLORIBVS IN SPIRAM
INFIGENDIS PERFORATA.

6.3. Vases from Ferrari. Photo courtesy of Peter Davidson.

6.4. Flower arrangement from Ferrari. Photo courtesy of Peter Davidson.

Consimilium triangularium cellarum quadrata in area opportuni-
tas erit, si angulos octonos habeant horti, quorum aliquod hic spe-
cimen subijcio: ut plures tibi ubiq̄; parabiles, quàm venusino po-
etæ in Tiburte recessu, amœnitatis anguli rideant.

6.5. Octagonal garden plan from Ferrari. Photo courtesy of Peter Davidson.

lineatum; cuius continenti muro circumseptae superuacaneis quatuor in angulis tum hortensis supellectilis cellas, tum congruentia floribus aviaria poteris excitare: ut florea in silva silvestres Orphei ne desint. Cavebis tamen, ne munimentum circa extructum vel altitudine nimia, vel minimo intervallo areolas incommode opacet. Quare caute excitandum. Et latiore ambulacro distinendum erit [*sic*]. (p. 29)

If you wish to imitate the rotundity of the world with a round image in a garden, or in a flowering (or flourishing) age to found a new world, here you have a little world outlined within a square, of which, inside the surrounding wall, you have four little chambers, in which you may place aviaries to complement the flowers, so that as in a flowery wood there is no lack of woodland Orpheuses. Be careful, however, that the surrounding defences are not built too tall or that there is so little space between them that they overshadow the garden beds: they should be raised circumspectly, and the encircling path should be broad.

The third is an oval scheme:

Si circense spectaculum non olim procurrentium equorum fugitiva, sed assidue vernantium florum stataria voluptate exhibere mavis: en tibi ovati circuitus commodum circum honestissimae Florae novus Aedilis aperio, iisdemque cellis extruendis opportunos simillimos angulos propono. (p. 33)

If you wish to set forth the spectacle of a circus, not (as once) with the flight of swiftly running horses but with the fixed delight of blooming flowers, here I open to you a new structure for flowers of elegant roundness, oval in form, and I set down external structures of the same form in the equivalent corners.

The fourth represents a labyrinth:

Si velis denique florae curae quam facilem aditum, tam difficilem exitum hortensi representare simulacro: tuos hortos in labyrinthi arcolae vel caeterarum instar humiles subsidere, ut oculi tantum implicatis flexibus irretiantur: vel as quatuor circiter palmoslateritia structura excitari, ut pedes quoque inter flores errabundi iucundissume impediantur. (p. 37)

If you would like to represent in an image the easy entrance to the growing of flowers but the difficult exit [from such a beguiling study], entwine your garden into a labyrinth, the image of which is set forth here. The 'hedges' of the labyrinth may be sunk down or represented by low-set plants, so that the eye can take in the whole design at one glance; or alternatively the beds can be raised about four palms' width above the earth, so that feet wandering among the flowers may be delayed in the most pleasant way.

At once, these plans serve to identify the ancient botanic garden at Padua as a microcosm of the world, and the botanic garden at Leiden as a combination of the Celestial City plan with an evocation of the Garden of Eden and its central fountain; and they offer a rich set of possible readings for that most ambitious of Late Renaissance gardens, the Hortus Palatinus at Heidelberg, laid out by the savant Salomon de Caus for the illuminatus Elector Palatine and his bride, Elizabeth Stuart. This garden, described in lavish contemporary engravings, brings us neatly full circle as the most probable source for many elements in Marvell's poem 'The Garden,' including his famous 'flowering Zodiac.'

By an extraordinary series of coincidences, a flower garden laid out on one of Ferrari's plans survives in Italy to this day. The Giardini Buonaccorsi near Macerata are famous for their extraordinary statuary and for their preservation of a layout dating generally from the early eighteenth century. They also preserve on the uppermost terrace, between the villa itself and its chapel, a mid-seventeenth-century *giardino segreto* laid out from Ferrari's plans and maintained in accordance with his precepts. Lower terraces extend this original layout into a superb eighteenth-century flower garden very much working within the aesthetic defined by Ferrari and Rapin.

The source is unequivocal: the Conte Buonaccorsi's copy of the 1637 Italian reprint of *De florum cultura* survives in the section of the Biblioteca Nazionale da Napoli kept at Macerata.[22] This layout, with its statues and little obelisks and stone-edged geometrical beds, gives the fullest sense possible of the ambitions and pleasures of the baroque flower garden which Ferarri sought to transplant from the Low Countries to Italy (figs 6.6, 6.7, 6.8).

This upper terrace is laid out from the first of Ferrari's plans: it evokes both the Celestial City and the Garden of Eden, in that the central part of Ferrari's plate 25 is repeated four times, symmetrical about a central fountain which evokes the unfallen garden with its central fountain, whence flowed the four rivers of Paradise, while the whole in its symmetries of fours answers to Ferrari's apprehension of the 'mystical mathematics of the city of heaven.'

The rare visitor to the Giardini Buonaccorsi is privileged to experience an aspect of baroque thought and aesthetics which survives nowhere else. Deserted but not abandoned, kept in wonderful order by its local custodians, the garden spreads in terraces down the slope. Flora's bouquet and crown still spray water at the unsuspecting visitor, and in the grotto at the bottom of the slopes the skeletal automata of Turk and Pierrot still stand in their eighteenth-century rags. But the most remarkable survival of all is the original *giardino segreto,* the three-and-a-half-century survival of an ephemeral flower garden laid out on one of the symbolic plans of Ferrari's treatise.

The Jesuit writer on gardens who was best known in the eighteenth century was the French Jesuit Réné Rapin (1621–87), whose didactic Latin poem

6.6. The *giardino segreto* of the Villa Buonaccorsi, Marche, Italy.
Photo courtesy of Jane Stevenson.

Hortorum libri quatuor, published in Paris in 1665, was translated successfully into English heroic verse by Gardiner and (tradition at least asserts) polished for its third edition by no less a poet than Alexander Pope.[23] Slightly less well known is that much of Rapin's first book clearly derives from *De florum cultura*, certainly in the lists of flowers cited; and indeed its aesthetics are clearly fixed in the flower garden of the seventeenth century as Ferrara codified it. Even the frontispiece, which seems to have travelled with editions and translations of Rapin (it faces page 1 of the English translation), is very clearly derived from Ferrari's plate of a rectangular flower-garden layout, even if Rapin's own instructions tend to point instead to a box-edged arrangement with *plat-bandes*, perhaps rather like the restored garden of Het Loo at Appledoorn in the Netherlands.

It is not, I hope, a perverse ending to this survey to focus on a celebrated, if vanished, English garden, and to speculate for a moment on its Catholicity and on the Jesuit horticultural and scientific atmosphere which it retained. I refer – with an element of paradox – to the famous garden at Twickenham, near London, of the poet and aesthetic theorist Alexander Pope (1688–1744), the

6.7. The *giardino segreto* of the Villa Buonaccorsi, Marche, Italy.
Photo courtesy of Jane Stevenson.

reviser of Gardiner's translation of Rapin. As well as being the most celebrated poet of early Georgian England, Pope was one of Georgian England's most visible Catholic laymen. Indeed, his *Rape of the Lock* can sensibly be interpreted as an epic of the proscribed recusants and Jacobites of Hanoverian England, its central figure of deflationary bathos as the accurate response to the symbolic powerlessness in every part of life to which they were condemned by the penal laws.

I said 'paradox' a moment ago because Pope is generally credited with having at least been a godfather to the new development of the landscape garden of the English eighteenth century, a movement which began in the imitation of classical antiquity and ended in the simulation of the random sublimity of nature. This movement could also be seen to trace a trajectory away from the encodement of meaning in a place, towards a condition in which only the aesthetic impact of place was deemed to be of significance. The eighteenth century began with the construction of Pope's grotto, but it ended in the demolition of 'columns erected only to receive quotations.'[24]

6.8. The *giardino segreto* of the Villa Buonaccorsi, Marche, Italy.
Photo courtesy of Jane Stevenson.

Yet even in the landscape movement we may discern Jesuit influence. A constant point of reference for early theorists of the landscape garden was the Chinese garden, accounts of which inevitably (despite the unproved assertions of the English architect Chambers that he had himself visited China) derive from the Jesuit missions in Pekin. The classic text is the letter from the Jesuit Jean-Denis Attiret, published in Paris in 1749, with its description of the Yuan Ming Yuan of the Qianlong emperor, and the emphasis in that description of the extent to which everything (trees, rocks, and water) is meant to appear natural, however much thought has gone into its positioning.[25]

And yet my contention still would be that Pope's practice as a deviser of gardens was infinitely closer to the Renaissance and baroque tradition which we have been considering than to the 'natural' landscapes which may have been the ultimate outcome of his innovations, and, indeed, of the letters from the Pekin mission. His garden functioned as a place for contemplation of the passage of time and of the succession of generations, focused as it was on a long, hedged green space, closed at the furthest point by an obelisk, inscribed in Latin, to the memory of the poet's mother, with her gentry and recusant ancestry.

Pope's celebrated grotto is a place as much retrospective as prospective in its meaning and arrangement. It is essential to remember that the grotto was remodelled in the last few years of Pope's life as an imitation, however mannered, of the natural arrangement of rocks and minerals within a cave. Even in this naturalistic state the roof of the grotto bears two carved slabs dating from the seventeenth century. These show respectively the crown of thorns and the *arma Christi*, that arrangement of the Five Wounds which constituted the badge of the last Catholic rising, the Pilgrimage of Grace. These seem, at a reasoned guess, to be from the North, and definitely from the recusant North: we can conjecture that they are remnants from a house associated with the family of Pope's mother. So in this sense the grotto is associated with the Catholic tradition of houses such as Harvington, Stonor, Scarisbrick, and Little Crosby. It is also associated with one palpably Catholic, unmistakably sacred grotto of the English eighteenth century, one which commemorates the site of the martyrdom of St Kenelm at Winchcombe in Gloucestershire.[26] Alison Shell has also discovered that at least one contemporary of Pope's, Thomas Gent of York, appears to have associated Pope's grotto with the pilgrimage site of St Winifred's Well in Flintshire.[27]

The state of the grotto as it was for most of Pope's lifetime, and before the naturalistic rearrangement which we see, bore clearer relation to the world of the seventeenth-century virtuoso. Originally, spars, shells, fossils, and precious minerals were displayed as in a virtuoso's cabinet, albeit one masquerading as an enchanted cave in a late baroque romance. We are not far from the world of the Collegio Romano, of Athanasius Kircher's wonderful and prodigious stones. The original grotto reminds us even more of the world of the seventeenth-century Jesuit virtuoso in its insets of mirror to catch reflections from the proximate river, as well as in a most Kircherian device, a lens set into the door which transformed the grotto into a camera obscura. The space as originally conceived owed, I suggest, not a little to the moment in scientific and aesthetic history embodied by Kircher's *Mundus subterraneus* (1665) or *Ars magna lucis et umbrae* (1646).

I have concluded with Pope's garden to demonstrate that those aspects of the seventeenth-century Jesuit interest in gardens which I have been considering had distinct echoes as late as the Augustan eighteenth century. The questions of place, meaning, and meditation which occupy Richeôme and Hawkins are no less long-lived than are the elements of symbolism and virtuoso collecting which distinguish the works of Ferrari. As so often in seventeenth-century cultural history, the members of the Society of Jesus were not only early participants in a cultural movement but also peerless codifiers and describers of the often fugitive essentials of early modern intellectual and aesthetic experience.

NOTES

1 While Mavis Batey's *Alexander Pope: The Poet and the Landscape* (Barn Elms, 1999) offers wonderful illustrations, it is itself a telling illustration of a general reluctance to read Pope's gardens as closely modelled on seventeenth-century precedents, as also of a general refusal to consider Pope's Catholicism.

2 Michel de Montaigne, *Journal de Voyage en Italie*, ed. Paul Faure (Paris, 1948), p. 89.

3 *Jesuit Latin Poets*, ed. James M. Martz, John P. Murphy, and Jozef Ijsewijn (Wauconda, IL, 1989), pp. 30–1, 20–3.

4 Ibid., pp. 116–19.

5 See *A Selection of the Poems of Sir Constantijn Huygens (1596–1687),* ed. Peter Davidson and Adriaan van der Weel (Amsterdam, 1996), p. 128.

6 See especially Ludwig Schwab, *Das Jesuitenkollegium des 16. und 17. Jahrhunderts der Oberdeutchen Ordensprovinz* (Darmstadt, 2001); for at least one fascinating instance of a Jesuit as diallist (and possibly mediator between Charles II and his illegitimate son), see David R. Coffin, *The English Garden: Meditation and Memorial* (Princeton, 1994), pp. 15–16.

7 [Athanasius Kircher], *Collegii Rom: Sac: Jesu musaeum* (Amsterdam, 1678), pp. 35–7.

8 Henry Hawkins, *Parthenia sacra, or The Mysterious and Delicious Garden of the Sacred Parthenes, Set Forth and Enriched wih Pious Devices and Emblemes* (Rouen, 1633).

9 *The Symbolic Garden, Reflections Drawn from a Garden of Virtues*, ed. and trans. Margaret H. Thomson (York, ON, 1989).

10 Ibid., 'The Epistle to the Parthenian Sodalitie,' sigs A1r–2r.

11 Ibid., p. 6.

12 Ibid., pp. 8–9.

13 Ibid., p. 11.

14 Ibid., p. 13.

15 Louis Richeôme, *La peinture spirituelle* (Lyon, 1611). 'Le sixieme livre ... des Iardins,' from which I quote below in the text, describes the gardens.

16 Gauvin Alexander Bailey, *Between Renaissance and Baroque: Jesuit Art in Rome, 1565–1610* (Toronto, Buffalo, London, 2003), pp. 74–106.

17 Giovanni Battista Ferrari, *De florum cultura libri VI* (Rome, 1633). Quotations below in the text are from this edition.

18 Cortona was also in receipt of Barberini partonage, especially in the commission for the heroic fresco *The Triumph of Divine Providence* (with particular reference to the care of Divine Providence for the Barberini) in the Palazzo Barberini, Rome.

19 Including a very early commentary on a match at ur-football.

20 Ferrari, *De florum cultura*, pp. 458–9.

21 Ibid., p. 426.

22 By the great kindness of Dott Gabriele Cingolani of the University of Macerata, who arranged my access to the gardens, I am able also to report that this copy (preserved in the section of the Biblioteca Nazionale da Napoli at Macerata) was definitely in the possession of the Buonaccorsi family by the time the top terrace of the garden was laid out. Unfortunately, it is not annotated.

23 *Rapin of Gardens, a Latin Poem, Englished by Mr Gardiner, the Third Edition, Revised and finish'd* (London, 1728). Book 1, the section which describes the garden proper, occupies pp. 1–63.

24 Thomas Whatley, *Observations on Modern Gardening, 1770,* quoted in Coffin, *The English Garden*, p. 222. Coffin's beautifully nuanced discussion of the fading of signification from the English garden is highly relevant in this context.

25 Quoted in Maggie Keswick, *The Chinese Garden* (London, 1978), pp. 9–11.

26 Now in the back garden of Bleby House, Abbey Terrace, Winchcombe, Gloucs.

27 *British Piety Display'd in the Glorious Life, Suffering, and Death of the Blessed St Winefred ... Part the Fifth* (York, 1742), p. 12.

PART TWO

The Visual Arts and the Arts of Persuasion

The propagation of the faith took many forms, and it brought the Jesuits to the ends of the earth. One of the most celebrated ways in which even the earliest Jesuits tried to communicate the basic truths to be lived and practised by Christians was through the visual arts. Like our first volume, this one explores how architecture, painting, sculpture, and the decorative arts were used to serve as a vehicle for catechism, teaching, and other ministries, and as a mirror for good behaviour. Two of the papers, those by Gauvin Alexander Bailey and Hiromitsu Kobayashi, also consider the ways in which the non-European recipients of these art forms used and transformed them, thereby creating new acculturative visual and architectural languages.

We begin in Antwerp with Jeffrey Muller's call for a new art-historical approach to the field of Jesuit visual arts in Flanders. One of the ironies of the field is that Antwerp, recognized as the 'second city' of Jesuit art activity after Rome, has received from art historians only piecemeal and, as Muller argues, inadequate study. Muller calls upon art historians to apply a more interdisciplinary approach to the wealth of documentary evidence that survives, as in the rich archives of the Antwerp sodalities. The main part of Muller's paper is taken up by an engaging conceit: he uses the Jesuits' own illustrated allegory of their spiritual conquest of Flanders, book 6 of the *Imago primi saeculi*, as a framework for illustrating how the Jesuits used the visual arts in their ministries.

The focus stays on Antwerp in Anna C. Knaap's reassessment of the original painting cycle of the Jesuit church of the city, particularly the famous high altarpieces and the thirty-nine ceiling paintings (now destroyed) by Rubens. Instead of merely reconstructing lost imagery, as others have done before her, Knaap goes beyond stylistic reconstruction to ask how these images would have worked on their viewers. She show how paintings interacted across the space of the church interior to create a framework of meditative prayer and doctrine for the laity, and how they also promoted an image of the Society of Jesus as a leading reform order of the Catholic church.

Lost or scattered evidence also forms the subject of Nuno Vassallo e Silva's pioneering article on the Jesuits' use of the decorative arts, particularly work in gold and silver, as a way of enhancing the sacred spaces of their churches in Portugal. It is paradoxical that although there are few parts of the world where the Jesuits had such an early and prolonged impact as in Portugal, the field remains virtually unknown outside Portuguese scholarship. Vassallo e Silva introduces us to this rich world of art patronage, focusing on the mother church of São Roque in Lisbon. The extraordinary concentration there of visual and decorative arts (one of its paintings was on the dust jacket of our first volume) makes it an example of what baroque art historians, in a nod to Richard Wagner, call a *Gesamtkunstwerk* (a fusion of the arts). Vassallo e Silva opens our eyes to media the Jesuit connection with which has never been studied in depth for any country. Silver and gold objects, such as monstrances and chalices, were especially important to Jesuit devotions because they directly related to the Eucharist and helped promote that sacrament in the post-Tridentine era.

We then move to a global perspective. Bailey's article supplements his earlier work by examining one of the least-known and most distant Jesuit mission enterprises in the world – the furthest south any missionaries went before modern times – the archipelago of Chiloé in Chilean Patagonia. The mission reveals a visual and architectural culture unlike anything else found in Spanish America. It resulted from a meeting between Central European Jesuits and Amerindians from the Huilliche and Chono tribes. Bailey goes against the grain of recent scholarship by asserting that the unique Chilote style was forged in the Jesuit era, not after 1767, when the Franciscans and diocesan priests succeeded the Jesuits in the Chiloé mission.

Humberto Rodríguez-Camilloni takes us farther up the Pacific coast in his study of a little-known but important form of Jesuit architectural patronage in Latin America: the farms, or haciendas, that helped finance the more famous missions and colleges. He explores three of the haciendas in coastal Peru. The Jesuits were one of the largest landowners in Peru, and their haciendas were the backbone of the colony's agrarian economy. Rodríguez-Camilloni reveals the everyday functioning of these farms using a wealth of contemporary documentation. One of the most unexpected discoveries in his paper is how lavish these complexes were. Rodríguez-Camilloni explains that the churches were emphasized because they were built to serve as a symbolic reminder of the spiritual basis of farm life. The processions and festivals held in front of the churches were meant to inculcate Christian devotion in the workers and African slaves who tended the land.

Festivals and their decorations are also the subject of the last paper in this part of our volume. Here, however, Hiromitsu Kobayashi focuses on how a non-Christian festival adopted a type of image developed by the Jesuits for Christian purposes. Kobayashi's study is a welcome respite from the attention that has been paid to the superstars of Jesuit mission art, men such as Giuseppe Castiglione and Jean-Denis Attiret, who toiled at the art workshops of the Qing court of the Qianlong emperor. Kobayashi takes us south to the prosperous city of Suzhou, the economic capital of China, where a wealthy middle class reacted to the stimulus of Western perspective in a unique way. Between the 1730s and the 1750s, large woodblock prints of landscapes and cityscapes using linear perspective techniques derived from Jesuit court art became the vogue during the annual New Year's festival. Entirely devoid of any Christian meaning, the visual techniques of Castiglione and his colleagues enjoyed an unexpected afterlife as the backdrop to a quintessentially Chinese event.

7 / Jesuit Uses of Art in the Province of Flanders

JEFFREY MULLER

After Rome, Antwerp was the second great centre of the Jesuits during the early
modern period. Gauvin Alexander Bailey was right to make that point in his
essay on the historiography of the term 'Jesuit style' and what has been called
Jesuit corporate culture in relation to the visual arts.[1] Yet his essay shows as well
how little is known about the use of art by the Jesuits, not only in Antwerp but in
the whole province of Flanders. Outside Belgium, recent work has concentrated
almost exclusively either on the two illustrated books published by the Jesuits in
Antwerp that exerted worldwide and decades-long influence, Jéronimo Nadal's
Adnotationes et meditationes in evangelia of 1593 and the *Imago primi saeculi*
of 1640, or on Rubens's paintings and drawings for the Jesuits, especially for the
new church of the Professed House in Antwerp, the first church ever dedicated to
St Ignatius of Loyola.[2] But the Jesuits' uses of visual images and signs were
richly varied, dynamically innovative, widespread, and integral to a much larger
historical process: the revolution in media, forms, functions, and content that
was instrumental to the conversion of Southern Netherlands society starting in
1585, and paradigmatic as well for Jesuit practice throughout the world.

Given the extraordinary significance of this development, it seems necessary
first to ask why it has been so neglected in comparison with what happened in
other European countries and now, remarkably, in Latin America, India, and East
Asia. Art history in Belgium is the product of a tangled historiography and
politics that have rigorously excluded truly interdisciplinary methods and innovative questions.[3] American, British, and German art historians approach the
material from geographical and intellectual distances that result in encounters
with secondary literature, where the answers and even the questions contained in
the abundance of primary sources can never be found. Artificially complicated
interpretations of well-known art works substitute for real discovery. There are,
of course, exceptions. But it is highly symptomatic that the most stimulating

recent contributions are by historians, a literary historian, and a team of graduate students of architectural history. It also is characteristic of many art historians that they do not read precisely the writings that could give impetus to their work in promising new directions. I would like to open a dialogue between art history and other disciplines that would make fruitful the vast and rich field that has been so neglected.

First, an integrated and global approach has to be crafted if the goal is to link together with all their apostolic missions and means of persuasion the diverse uses of art made by the Jesuits. It so happens that for their Flemish province the Jesuits themselves provided the perfect framework ready at hand for this purpose of incorporating the Jesuit uses of art into their larger project of individual conversion and, more profoundly, the transformation of society. The sixth book of the *Imago primi saeculi* is, after all, an epic of their Herculean labours in killing the monsters who had laid Flanders to waste, making it a hell on earth where salvation was impossible to find.[4] The trick, of course, is to take this narrative in good faith, accept the presence of God in it, and, at the same time, treat it critically, without imposing the assumptions about power and politics divorced from religion that make reductive even the best analysis of Jesuit language and strategies.[5]

The sixth book of the *Imago primi saeculi* recounts the troubled years of war and heresy that began in 1566 with the iconoclastic fury and the outbreak of Protestant-driven revolution against Philip II and ended in 1585, when the Spanish army under the command of Duke Alessandro Farnese reimposed Roman Catholic and Habsburg control over most of what is now Belgium. In these times of troubles, true religion in the province of Flanders had been destroyed by heresy, war, and ignorance. When they returned at the invitation of Farnese in 1585, the Jesuits entered a spiritual wilderness that, by 1640, they claimed to have transformed into a paradise.[6] Without false modesty they cast this effort as the twelve labours of Hercules, a well-known story of antiquity that they told as the twelve daily labours of the Society.[7] These are ordered in a sequence of precedence, indicating a structure built on the foundation of catechism, reaching its greatest glory in the administration of the sacraments of penance and the Eucharist, and crowned by the ornament of the twelfth labour, which is writing books.

How was visual material integral to the accomplishment of these twelve labours? I want to answer the question without extracting the pictures and other sacred objects from the contexts of word, ritual, and social exchange in which they were embedded, and also without exaggerating their importance.

Take catechism, the first labour. If Martin Luther had published the first catechism in 1529, the Council of Trent responded in kind with a call to systematic instruction in the faith.[8] The *Imago primi saeculi* tells us that in Flanders, because of what the Jesuits have impressed upon the minds (*ingenia*) of children, which are *tabulae rasae* retaining whatever is engraved on them, 'religion today stands uncorrupted in Belgium, peace stands with religion, felicity with peace.'[9] Through the remarkable, exuberant union of different rhetorical genres, in which Marc Fumaroli has recognized one distinctive character of the *Imago primi saeculi*, the Society was able to support the narrative of heroic effort with gargantuan numbers that introduce the matter-of-fact historical truth – *res gestae*. In the space of one year the catechism has been taught 10,045 times to 32,508 catechumens.[10]

It is the Flemish historian Alfons Thijs, interested in gaining access to the experiences of workers, women, and children as well as to what the elite knew, who has most paid attention to what pictures can tell us in this regard, in the tradition of leftist historians such as Richard Trexler and Robert Scribner, for whom visual sources have been so vital. Thijs observes that in 1618, when the Jesuits in Antwerp organized their Congregation for Christian Instruction for the purpose of teaching poor children at Sunday school, they received a gift from one lay member, Johannes Bruegels, who paid for 3,000 prints of the congregation's patron saint, Carlo Borromeo – one image for each of the 3,000 some students who attended – confirmation of a remarkably high number in a city with a population of around 45,000 at that time.[11] These prints may have enticed and rewarded the children, but there is no evidence that pictures were used at that time to teach Christian Doctrine.

It was precisely for the illiterate, the slow of understanding, and the persecuted who lived where they could not receive the normal instruction of the Roman Catholic church that Father Guilielmus Steegius invented in 1647 his *Christian Doctrine More Accessibly Explained through a Picture-Language, Necessary for Children as well as Adults Who Cannot Read* (figs 7.1, 7.2), which was published in Antwerp and dedicated to the bishop of Bruges, and was written in Dutch and thus exclusively for the Flemish province.[12] Divine signs sanctified this new method to win souls. As if God wanted to spur him on, sitting at table four or five days after he began the work, Steegius heard read aloud a story from Father Jacobus Damianus's Latin history of the first hundred years of the Society. Studying divinity in Lima, Diego Martinez asked Christ what he most wanted. When the Saviour through his image on a crucifix answered aloud, 'Save souls,' Martinez burned all his writings and entered the wild forest, where the people were impervious to explanation through words but could grasp the main points of Christian doctrine painted on panels: the horrors of hellfire depicted in vermilion were firmly impressed on the mind; and the joys of heaven by illustrations of meats, dainties, cakes, and wine.[13] In all these exchanges,

7.1. Guilielmus Steegius, *De Christelycke Leeringhe* (Antwerp, 1640), title-page.
Copy in Antwerp, Stadsbibliotheek. Photo courtesy of Jeffrey Muller.

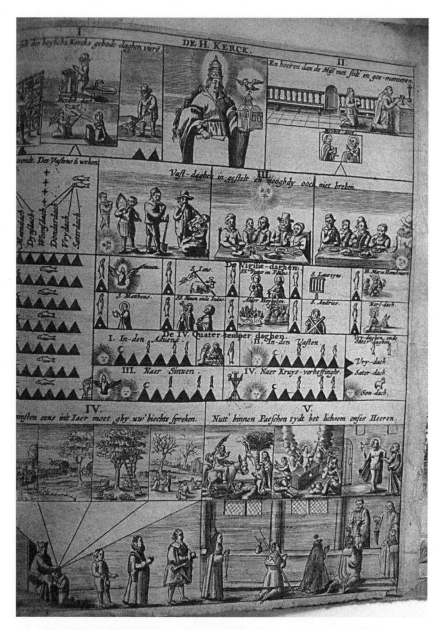

7.2.   Steegius, *De Christelycke Leeringhe*, p. 21: The Five Commandments of the Holy Church. Copy in Antwerp, Stadsbibliotheek. Photo courtesy of Jeffrey Muller.

images and voices are more important than reading silently, and the chain of divine messages linked by Jesuit texts from Paraguay to Antwerp suggests, of course, an equivalence between the indigenous people of Paraguay and Flemish peasants. But the actual strategy of accommodation to teach illiterates through pictures has much more in common with the reproduction in China of compositions taken from Nadal's *Adnotationes*, but supplied instead with texts in Chinese and rendered in the style and technique of Chinese woodcuts – images, that is, that adapted the visual conventions of the intended audience.[14]

In his foreword Steegius says that to teach illiterates he has devised 'a special Farmers' and Shepherds' Almanac; from which they, even though not able to read, could nevertheless understand through picture-signs that which others learn from reading in the letter-almanac.'[15] His intended audience was, of course, those who could read and would teach his catechism. Through his desire to win souls, Steegius became the first real ethnographer of Flemish folk culture.[16] If he wanted to invent an effective picture-language to teach Christian Doctrine, then he had to master the semiotic conventions, symbols, and drawing style through which his intended audience was conditioned to understand their world as set out in almanacs. Steegius broke down the components of this language into three parts: narrative or figural representations (*verbeeldingen*), likenesses in the metaphorical sense of parables, and symbol signs.[17]

How he derived and manipulated them is evident in a comparison between the page from his catechism that teaches the Five Commandments of the Holy Church and the presentation of December in the Farmers' or Shepherds' Alamanac for 1791, published in Amsterdam (figs 7.1, 7.2, 7.3).[18] Steegius in the text on the facing page prompts the instructor to ask: What is ordered by the third commandment? / A. To fast on designated days. / Q. What is fasting? / A. To go without certain kinds of food; and to eat a full meal only once a day. / Q. What are these foods? / A. Meat, and (*altemets*) eggs, and dairy are excluded by the fast unless permitted. / Q. Which are the days on which it is commanded to fast? / A. Those indicated in the picture, taken from the Shepherds' Almanac.[19]

After the forty days of Lent, the student adds the four times of year called Quartertemper, when one fasts on the Wednesday, Friday, and Saturday of the week, recognizable by the inclusion of symbols. These are, of course, fishes, used to mark the quartertemper days in both the almanac and the catechism.[20]

Other kinds of picture-signs also are taken from the almanac. Conventional scenes of the seasons, which measure the cycle of agricultural work in the almanacs, now mark a kind of one-point perspective in which time is transformed into space by positioning the vanishing-point below on the penitent who obeys the church's fourth commandment, to confess at least once a year – although the implication of the picture is made explicit in the text, where the

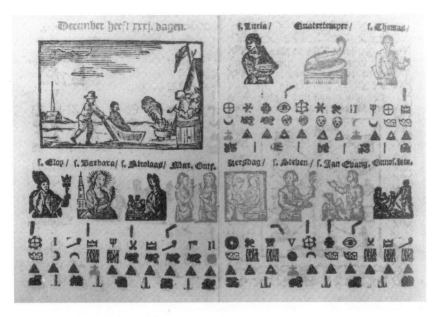

7.3. December, from *Den Boeren of Schapers Almanach voor't Jaar ons Heeren Jesu Christi, 1791* (Amsterdam). Museum't Oude Slot, Veldhoven.

catechumen acknowledges that it is better to confess frequently.[21] By placing the young penitent on his knees in front of the Jesuit confessor, who lays his hand on the child's head in a sign of absolution, Steegius likely was reproducing the conditions of rural churches, where the separation required in 1607 by the Provincial Council of Mechelen and imposed in the cities by the new confessionals had not yet penetrated, and might even have unsettled tradition-bound parishioners.[22] Easily recognizable figure representations – of the Resurrection, for example – separate out Easter as the most important time, when all Roman Catholics must participate fully in the sacrament of the Eucharist.[23]

On a larger scale, Steegius emulated the organization and density of different kinds of information presented in the typical layout of an almanac page. His picture-language setting out the commandments of the church is to be scanned left to right, top to bottom, like reading, with symbol signs integrated into countable rows of days and weeks; rectangular picture-panels of varied size are separated in clear sequences, few words serve as prompts, and many pictures are crammed together; the graphic style-medium is simple and cool in contrast to the density of the page.[24]

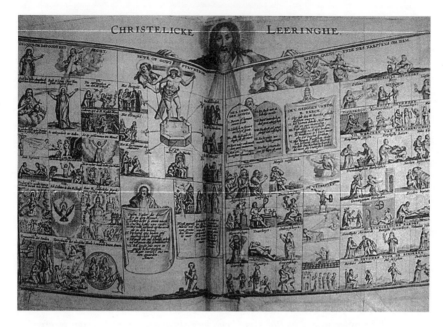

7.4. Steegius, *De Christelycke Leeringhe*, summary table of Christian Doctrine.
Copy in Antwerp, Stadsbibliotheek. Photo courtesy of Jeffrey Muller.

Steegius understood the need to adapt not only the picture-language of the almanacs but also the way they were used in social exchanges that combined looking at images, reading words, and listening to oral explanations. Illiterates, children, and the slow-of-mind would grasp the picture-language if assisted 'now and then by someone who can read, or who already has mastered the material, as happens in reading aloud the Farmers' almanacs.'[25] I have already given an example of the kind of question-and-answer dialogues based on the pictures that Steegius provided for his teachers of Christian Doctrine. Reinforcement of memory comes in a summary table of pictures at the end, repeating all major points in the numerical sequences that made them easier to remember in the first place (fig. 7.4).

Steegius's attempt to use picture-language for catechism in the Flemish province was unique. Learning and adapting a new language and also, I think, rural and peasant practices, for the purpose of conversion, represented a distinctly Jesuit accommodation. But the mass production that would have indicated real success never came, and a second edition appeared only in 1839, published in Groningen.[26] Steegius's effort was aimed at the stray sheep who could not be brought into the fold by the usual method of teaching with texts – proof that images were of secondary importance in the Society of Jesus. John W. O'Malley's argument that the Society was an order of the word does not apply only to the first Jesuits.[27]

This holds even more for the second labour, that of schools, accomplished by the Flemish province. Alfred Poncelet, S.J., in what remains by far the best history of the Jesuits in Belgium (1926), counts thirty-seven colleges in the whole Belgian province, before it was split into Dutch- and French-speaking halves in 1612.[28] In 1640 the *Imago primi saeculi* boasted that 'where few had been educated before, letters now flourish, and the Republic glitters with a greater number of learned men than the sky is filled with stars.'[29] And with the free education offered to the poor, the authors ask proudly, 'how many thousands of Belgians do you think have been instructed by us in good arts?'[30]

It was only in the most sophisticated display of wit, in their emblems exhibited at some colleges once or twice a year as one of the means, along with plays, of demonstrating the fruits of Jesuit education to the public, that students actively combined images with words in their literary exercises. These emblems recently have been analysed thoroughly and perceptively by the literary historian Karel Porteman, who places them in the mainstream of Jesuit pedagogy.[31]

Porteman centres his study on the unique collection of manuscripts commemorating the emblematic exhibitions held by the Jesuit college in Brussels between 1630 and 1685, now in the Royal Library at Brussels. Each year professional painters and calligraphers reproduced on a reduced scale a selection of the best emblems conceived by the rhetoric and poetry classes on one or two related themes. Two themes especially offered the opportunity for direct, self-reflective commentary on the more general question of Jesuit uses of art (figs 7.5, 7.6). In 1652 Carolus Baert, a member of the senior poetry class in the Brussels college, invented the title-page for emblems that would visualize quotations from Horace, and in particular the dictum 'ut pictura poesis' from the *Art of Poetry*.[32] And in 1683 one sees a bookbinder tacking silver clasps to a cover, an image suggesting that external splendour will make learning attractive – a central principle of Jesuit teaching, rhetoric, and art.[33]

The contexts of Spanish court, emblematic traditions, poetic style, topical references, competition among classes within the college, and address to public audiences all are convincingly set up by Porteman. He also relates the emblems to the annual religious feast on which they were exhibited, that of the Miracle of the Blessed Sacrament – a major celebration in Brussels, commemorating the consecrated hosts that bled miraculously when Jews stabbed them in 1370. Luc Dequeker has reconstructed a history of the broader and chronic anti-Semitism associated with this miracle and its subsequent cult.[34]

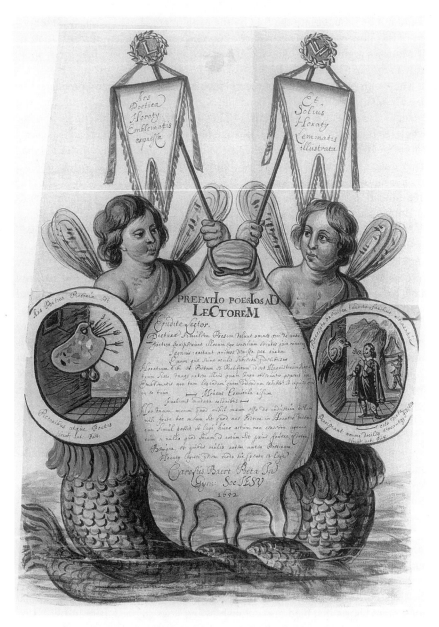

7.5. *Ars poetica Horatij Emblematis expressa*, 1652, title-page, recording *affixio* of the Jesuit college in Brussels. Brussels, Royal Library, ms 20.310 fol. 1r.

DOCTRINÆ
vt magis placeat, ſplendor quidam
externus addendus.

Splendet, vr alliciat

7.6. *Ineffabili divinae sapientiae Sacramento haec de doctrina ... emblemata*, 1683.
Emblem invented by Judocus van Obberghen, watercolour and calligraphy by
Joannes Carolus van Deijnum, recording *affixio* of the Jesuit college in Brussels.
Brussels, Royal Library, ms 20.327 fol. 84v.

In a strange contradiction within his own work, Porteman says in his introduction that 'in the affixiones anti-Semitism was kept at bay.' But in his catalogue entry for the commemorative manuscript of 1658, when the theme was the miraculous Blessed Sacrament itself, he points out two sharply anti-Semitic emblems. In the first, the sacrament brings glory to the handsome Christian and shame to the ugly Jew who look into the mirror of their souls. In the second, a Jewish owl, evil bird of the night, is chased by all the others (fig. 7.7): the emblem thus praises the banishment of the Jews, thought to have occurred in 1370, and refers as well to Philip IV's recent veto against the establishment of a separate quarter for Jews in Antwerp where they could practice their religion openly.[35]

Poncelet in 1926 dismissed the *affixiones* of emblems at Brussels as frivolous because in them sumptuous painting – useless ornament – threatened to overwhelm literary content.[36] He was taking sides, echoing a refrain voiced more and more frequently by Jesuit visitors to the Belgian province in the late sixteenth and early seventeenth centuries, and by the fathers general, who took seriously these warnings. Concern over an encroaching luxury that violated the Society's spirit of poverty was raised not only by the lavish decoration of emblems, but, much more gravely, by the practice of music and, as we shall see, by the building of churches.[37] I think this dialectic between actual practice and stated ideal in the use of art is key to understanding the Jesuit accommodation in Flanders.

It was the triumph of ornate splendour that the *Imago primi saeculi* trumpeted in its account of sodalities, the third labour of the Flemish Jesuits. 'Our Province has ninety sodalities with 13,727 members. Antwerp alone boasts ten sodalities with easily 3,000 members. And here you will see (as no where else on earth) an ample and splendid edifice built completely of magnificent stone by and for the collective membership' (fig. 7.8).[38] If fixation on paintings by Rubens and Van Dyck explains why art historians neglect catechisms and emblems, it gives all the more reason to wonder why no integrated history exists of the architecture and decoration of the Antwerp Jesuit Sodality House. Perhaps this is because the one attempt is a thesis that has been published only in part.[39] After all, even though no more than the shell of the original building survives, this shell in itself represents a remarkable innovation in the history of architecture. Everyone knows that Rubens's *Annunciation* for the altar of the downstairs Latin sodality, and Van Dyck's two paintings for the upstairs sodality, of unmarried young men – his *Virgin and Child Crowning St Rosalia, with Sts Peter and Paul*, as altarpiece, and his *Virgin Appearing to the Celibate Blessed Brother Joseph Herman*, which hung to the right of the altar – still survive in Vienna, where they were taken by the Austrians after the suppression of the Society in 1773.[40]

But most art historians are not aware that the whole archive of these sodalities still exists to reconstruct membership, religious practice, income, and expenses,

7.7. *A cunctis expellitur*, emblem, 1658, recording *affixio* of the Jesuit college in
Brussels. Brussels, Royal Library, ms 20.316 fol. 46v.

7.8. Former Sodality Building of the Professed House at Antwerp, now part of the Stadsbibliotheek. Constructed 1622. Photo courtesy of Jeffrey Muller.

and that abundant visual and textual evidence makes possible a precise reconstruction of the interior spaces.[41] For example, two eighteenth-century plans of the two storeys, each keyed to a descriptive table of paintings and sculptures, survive in the Antwerp City Archive, making possible a close reconstruction of the interiors. Nevertheless, only the plan of the upstairs sodality has been published (figs 7.9, 7.10).[42] At the same time, Zirka Zaremba Filipczak's fine study of the picture-narrative of the life of St Rosalia, invented along with the inception of the cult of this plague saint and centred around her relic and Van Dyck's picture in the upstairs sodality, gives an inkling of the rich iconographical material that can be related to the decoration as a whole – for example, meditation books published for use by sodality members.[43]

A deeper failure of training and method prevents even those art historians who might use the archives and consult primary iconographical sources from taking seriously the Jesuit project stated so clearly in the *Imago primi saeculi*, to win souls and transform society through religion. Given the foundation in social history provided by Louis Châtellier's Weberian *The Europe of the Devout*, in which he is exclusively interested in weighing the effect of the Jesuit sodalities on society, it seems to me that art history easily could undertake a study of how visual environments were integral to the process throughout the Flemish prov-

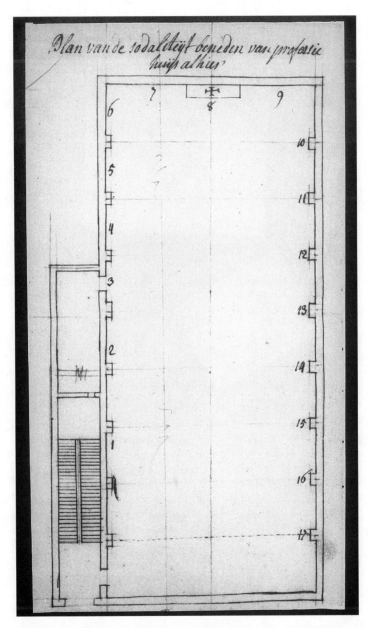

7.9. Plan of the downstairs sodality house in Antwerp. Pen and ink. Antwerp, Stadsarchief, Kerken en Kloosters 589.

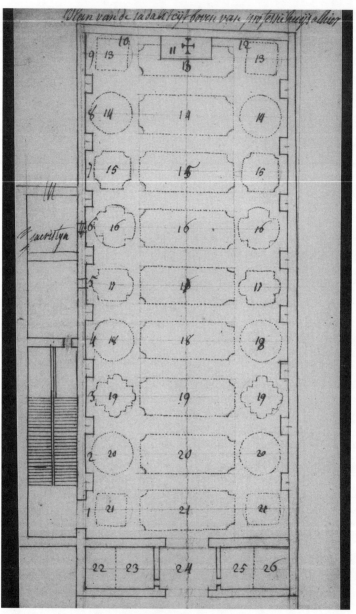

7.10. Plan of the upstairs sodality house in Antwerp. Pen and ink.
Antwerp, Stadsarchief, Kerken en Kloosters 589.

ince, not only in Antwerp but in other major cities as well.[44] Take Mechelen, for example, the seat of the archbishop, where the Jesuit sodality chapel of Our Lady was dedicated in 1633 to the Virgin of the Immaculate Conception, as the *Imago primi saeculi* tells us.[45] I would add here that the iconography and politics of the Immaculate Conception as played out during the seventeenth century in the Spanish Netherlands is in itself an issue of major importance that has been ignored.[46]

Because the sodalities all were dedicated to various aspects of the Virgin, the *Imago primi saeculi* included in this labour the Jesuits' larger support for the cult of the Virgin, referring to the central pilgrimage shrines of miraculous images at Scherpenheuvel and Halle, which the Jesuits were instrumental in founding and managing.[47] Just as important, they claim credit for the proliferation of an infinite number of statues of Our Lady expressing 'popular' (the Jesuits' word) devotion in every city of Flanders, 'with their candles, votive tablets, and miracles.' Further praise is given to those images 'in the churches of our colleges, and also others erected by the Society in public squares and streets; of which easily the principal is that which watches over the city hall of Antwerp.'[48] This is an extremely important claim, because it involves sacralization of the whole urban environment. By the end of the eighteenth century, more than five hundred images of the Virgin and other saints watched over Antwerp's streets and squares, most of them placed on corners above the ground storey, thereby inserting a constant divine presence hovering between heaven and earth, covering the city just as powerfully as did the waves of sympathetic vibrations from all the church bells pealing together.

Certainly, the example given, the image of the Virgin as protectress of the city, placed with public celebration in 1587 on the Antwerp City Hall by the Jesuit sodality under the leadership of Franciscus Costerus, was a forceful statement of Roman Catholic religious and political restitution after the years of Protestant control, during which the pagan image of the hero Brabo had taken the Virgin's place (fig. 7.11).[49] More daring and innovative, the Jesuits opened a corridor of charged sacred space between their new church and the City Hall when, in 1621, they dedicated the church to the Virgin as well as to St Ignatius and placed a relief of Mary in the pediment of the facade looking directly at her counterpart on the City Hall (fig. 7.12). A year later, in 1622, the Jesuit Father Grisius observed joyfully how 'Our Lady, over the roofs and into the distance, surveys the City Hall, so that she might protect it without cease,' thereby providing evidence that the connection was planned from the beginning.[50] Whether the Jesuits set the decisive example for this kind of devotion, as they claimed, remains an open question, which Nancy Kay currently is attempting to answer in a dissertation about the outdoor sacred images of early modern Antwerp.

7.11. View of the Antwerp City Hall, with image by Philippus de Vos, *Our Lady Patroness of Antwerp*, 1587, seen from the direction of the Antwerp Jesuit church. Photo courtesy of Jeffrey Muller.

Preaching, the fourth labour, brings us inside the Jesuit churches of the Flemish province, which, since Joseph Braun's *Die belgischen Jesuitenkirchen* of 1907, have served as the first proof that there was no such thing as a Jesuit style.[51] This of course is true, if one conceives of style in the Hegelian sense as the monolithic expression of the dialectic of Zeitgeist.[52] However, the most authoritative voice of the time on artistic matters, Rubens, associated Jesuit churches with a revolution in style – a historical phenomenon that cannot be ignored, but instead requires historical explanation. In his book reproducing the ground-plans of exemplary palaces of Genoa, printed first at Antwerp in 1622, Rubens told his intended audience, the gentlemen of the Spanish Netherlands, 'We see in this region the gradual obsolescence and rejection of the manner of architecture called Barbaric or Gothic, and that several of the finest minds introduce the true symmetry of that style, conforming to the rules of the ancients, Greek and Roman, with the greatest splendour and ornament for the country; as is evident in the famous temples recently constructed by the venerable Society of Jesus, in the cities of Brussels and Antwerp.'[53]

7.12. View of the triangular pediment on the facade of the former Jesuit church,
Antwerp, taken from the Grote Markt in front of the City Hall.
Photo courtesy of Jeffrey Muller.

The two churches were built simultaneously. In Brussels the college church
was constructed in 1617–21 after the design of the Italian-trained court architect
Jacques Francart, recruited by Archdukes Albert and Isabella, who financially
supported this church and in general aggressively promoted the adoption of
Italian style in ecclesiastical architecture, not only that of the Jesuits, but that of
other orders as well.[54] In this case, as Thomas DaCosta Kaufmann has observed
for the Italianate Jesuit churches of Poland, patronage was decisive in persuading the Jesuits to introduce radical innovation that broke with local tradition.[55]
Francart's design for the facade may follow Giacomo della Porta's example at
the mother church, Il Gesù, but it introduces the original and distinctly vertical
and Flemish element of a third storey.[56]

In the church of St Ignatius at Antwerp, however, the impetus came from
within, developed by two Jesuit architects, François de Aguilon, superior of the
Professed House, the centre of Jesuit activity in the province of Flanders, and
then Pieter Huyssens, the greatest Flemish Jesuit architect (fig. 7.13).[57] The
ornate splendour and exorbitant costs of their project were fought tooth and nail

7.13. Facade of the former Jesuit church, Antwerp. Photo courtesy of Jeffrey Muller.

by the father general and landed the Antwerp Jesuits in serious debt, which, snowballing, threatened the existence of the settlement.[58] So the choice was deliberate and tenaciously followed, suggesting in this case not so much an accommodation to the taste for luxury of Spanish Brabander merchants as a self-conscious attempt to form their taste in new directions, in the way that Rubens presented the church as an example to emulate in domestic architecture as well. Deficit spending in this case also fits into what Olwen Hufton has shown to be the normal Jesuit practice of investing in magnificence to attract new wealth.[59] Once again, there is abundant written and visual documentation in the Jesuit archives that would allow for a deep analysis of this decisive conflict within the Society of Jesus, as significant as that fought between Fathers Roberto De Nobili and Gonçalo Fernandez over strategies of conversion in early seventeenth-century India.

Koen Ottenheym recently has shown that Rubens, who was deeply involved with the decoration of the church, also provided contemporary terms for the distinctive manner in which its facade exemplified the rules of the ancient Greeks and Romans.[60] In 1639, when Constantijn Huygens, virtuoso and secretary to the Prince of Orange, sent etchings of his new house in The Hague to Rubens, the painter responded with detailed criticisms based on the common ground of Vitruvius's theory of architecture. Among other faults, Rubens thought the house facade too simple, and that the addition of half-round pilasters and a deeper cornice on the middle bay would have given 'greater dignity and relief to the whole facade,' a view recalling precisely the elements that give depth and strength to the facade of the Jesuit church, and the ideal of dignity in architecture that Rubens associated with the church.[61]

Later Jesuit churches in the Flemish province are immediately recognizable by the profiles and muscular sculptural articulation of their facades, which stand like corporate signs in the cities. Indeed, the St Francis Xavier church built at Mechelen starting in 1670 is an inbred hybrid (fig. 7.14). Designed by the amateur architect Father Antoon Losson, whose family paid for it, and intended first as the second Jesuit church of Antwerp, it is above all a copy of the now destroyed Jesuit college church in Yper, which Losson's family also supported. The outline plan of that church depended in turn on the Jesuit churches of Bruges and Namur, both designed by Pieter Huyssens, architect of the completed Antwerp church. Most original in Mechelen is the facade, which resembles the Brussels side of the family, mediated through a later generation of Jesuit churches, above all the church at Leuven, designed by Father Willem Hesius, who may have lent a more professional hand to completion of the church at Mechelen.[62]

A team of graduate students of architectural history under the direction of Krista de Jonge at the Catholic University, Leuven, has taken another approach

7.14. Facade of the former Jesuit church, Mechelen. Photo courtesy of Jeffrey Muller.

to discovering what might be unique or distinctive in Jesuit church architecture by isolating different elements and tracing their genealogies.[63] One group, for example, focuses on oratoria, balcony-like openings facing onto the high altars that allowed Jesuits and privileged laypersons the opportunity of private prayer (fig. 7.15). These are traced from Italian Jesuit architecture and then found in Belgium exclusively and consistently in Jesuit churches.[64] Likewise distinct to the Jesuits was the shift of the bell tower from the west front, where it was incorporated in Brabant Gothic churches, to the east, either the southeast corner or directly behind the church. At Antwerp the bell tower, now ascribed to Rubens, vertically marks the end of the main west–east axis, and served as a distribution point, connecting the residence of the Jesuits to the church, allowing access to the oratoria, and also housing the hidden machinery used to change the four altarpieces painted by Rubens and two other artists for the high altar.[65]

What led us into the churches was the fourth Jesuit labour, preaching. Again, the *Imago primi saeculi* tells us, they have been so stupendously successful that the ample spaces of their churches are too narrow to contain the crowds they attract. The voice of the Society issuing from sacred pulpits is a sound most welcome to Belgian Roman Catholics, formidable to heretics, and fruitful for both. In their Flemish province the Jesuits have preached to the people 15,206 times in the space of a single year.[66]

It is hard for us, conditioned by rows of chairs lined up facing the east, where mass and sermon are spoken together through a microphone, to imagine how emphatically separate a place was dedicated to the word in early modern Roman Catholic churches. At least in urban Flemish churches of the seventeenth century, the sermon was scheduled as an event independent of the mass, and the pulpit most often was set facing into the centre of the nave against a column of the south aisle, so that listeners formed a circle centred exclusively on the preacher, crossing the main west–east axis, distant from the altar.[67]

It is distinctive of Flemish early modern church decoration, especially that of Antwerp, that the most important elements of Roman Catholic worship were incorporated into progressively more elaborate ritual and symbolic forms. The pulpit built in the nave of the Antwerp Jesuit church was lost in the fire that destroyed most of the nave decoration in 1718, but is visible in several seventeenth-century paintings (fig. 7.16). From what we can see, it was very similar in design to the pulpit carved for the St Gummaruskerk in Lier by Artus Quellinus the Elder and Peter Verbruggen the Elder between 1640 and 1642.[68] This Jesuit pulpit is relatively simple in profile, figural ornament, and iconography when compared to the animated, organic allegory of the Roman Catholic Faith spread across the four continents, replacing any semblance of architectural structure in the pulpit of the former St Francis Xavier church at Mechelen,

7.15. Oratorium in the east end of the former Jesuit church, Antwerp.
Photo courtesy of Jeffrey Muller.

7.16. Wilhelm von Ehrenberg, *Interior of the Jesuit Church*, Antwerp, 1667.
Brussels, Koninklijke Musea voor Schone Kunsten, Inv. 3603.
Photo courtesy of A.C.L. Brussels.

designed in 1700 by the Antwerp sculptor Hendrik Frans Verbrugghen (fig. 7.17).[69]

While the role played in this development by the Jesuits still is unclear, I can demonstrate that their fervent effort to accomplish the sixth labour, of administering the sacraments of penance and the Eucharist, stimulated the introduction of paradigmatic new elements, imitated and rivalled for a century. The *Imago primi saeculi* proclaims that the Society, from its inception, has worked for the restitution of confession, than which there is no greater bridle to restrain liberty of life (*libertas vitae*), mother of all vices. And this effort has met with such great success, the authors continue, that an infinite number confess to us in Antwerp, to the degree that in the church of our Professed House twenty-six priests lend their ears to penitents; and other auxiliaries do so in the college.[70]

By 1635 the Jesuits in Antwerp had incorporated at least eleven confessionals into the decoration of their church to serve as distinct ritual frames for the thousands of penitents who flocked there. Unlike the simple, isolated boxes perfected by St Carlo Borromeo in Milan, these were built into the wainscoting that lined either side of the church.[71] Although destroyed by the fire of 1718,

7.17. Hendrik Frans Verbrugghen, pulpit, former Jesuit church, Mechelen, 1700.
Photo courtesy of Jeffrey Muller.

Willem von Ehrenburg's picture of 1667 records their appearance and number (see fig. 7.16). Similar confessionals carved around 1640 that survive in the Chapel of Our Lady off the south aisle demonstrate the beauty of the newly introduced figural ornaments (fig. 7.18). Seraphic angels flank the confessor's chair, and engaged Ionic columns grace the penitent's stool on either side.[72]

This innovation was made in competitive response to rival orders, especially the Antwerp Dominicans, who had built similar walls of confessionals and then, in 1658–60, increased the stakes with replacements more densely ornamented and boasting full-figure images of penitent saints.[73] The Jesuits themselves kept pace, as one can see in the row of confessionals at Mechelen, carved under the supervision of Nikolaas van der Veken in 1683–4 (fig. 7.19).[74]

I think the claim to suppress liberty of life through confession raises the issue currently most important in the historiography of the Counter Reformation in the Spanish Netherlands, that of the actual control on individual behaviour exercised by the Roman Catholic church and the consequences of that control on society.[75] Wietse de Boer already has integrated an excellent 'archaeology' of the confessional into a well-balanced investigation of penance and social discipline in the Milan of Carlo and Federico Borromeo.[76] Nevertheless, he also comes up against the insurmountable obstacle that most evidence depends on the official account of the church. A truly effective study of the Jesuits and their uses of art would take de Boer's approach and maybe add to it statistics on levels and kinds of crime.

Framing reception of the Eucharist in the Antwerp Jesuit church also stimulated artistic innovation. In one year before 1640, the sacrament was administered 240,00 times, and in 1649, 300,000 times, in a city of around 65,000 people.[77] The Jesuits were, of course, not monks. Unlike the Franciscans, the Dominicans, and the other regular orders, they did not chant the liturgical hours, so there was no need for the rood screen that separates laity from the high altar.[78] What they substituted was the ornate communion rail, drawing a barrier between the space of the laity and the altar, low enough to see over, and decorated at the eye level of the kneeling recipients (see fig. 7.16). The splendour of the original communion rail for the high altar of St Ignatius can be guessed from the one still intact in the adjacent Chapel of Our Lady, with its symbolic garlands of wheat, grapes, and corn (fig. 7.20). In 1695, when the parish church of St Jacob commissioned a communion rail for its Eucharist Chapel, the contract cited the Jesuit example as the standard for measurements and quality.[79] In turn, the communion rail for the Eucharist Chapel in Antwerp Cathedral was patterned on that at St Jacob's. Successive generations thus descended directly from the Jesuit church.[80]

The fifth labour was missions, not only in the Protestant United Provinces of the Netherlands, but also in the rural parts of Flanders.[81] Most striking in the

7.18. Confessionals in the Chapel of Our Lady, former Jesuit church, Antwerp.
Photo courtesy of Jeffrey Muller.

7.19. Nikolaas van der Veken, confessionals in the former Jesuit church,
Mechelen, 1683–4. Photo courtesy of Jeffrey Muller.

United Provinces were the Jesuit 'hidden churches' (*schuilkerken*), some grandly decorated on a large scale, and hidden only in the sense that they did not proclaim their existence publicly. What emerges from recent articles by Xander van Eck on these churches, none of which survives intact, is the overwhelming dependence on Flemish Jesuit models of architecture and decoration, displayed, for example, in the 1788 drawing by A. de Lelie of the interior of the Krijtberg church at Amsterdam.[82] In general, I suggest that the resemblance of the hidden Jesuit churches in the Netherlands to Flemish churches was a positive choice, not merely passive acknowledgment of a dearth of local talent, and that the reasons for the choice should be investigated further.

As far as I know, the Flemish Jesuits did not employ visual communication in their seventh labour, of ministering to prisoners, or their eighth, of promoting peace and conciliation, especially among merchants in cities.[83]

Images were, however, central to the ninth labour, of leading people in the practice of spiritual exercises, above all in guided sequences of meditation.[84] Steegius justified his picture catechism with the precedent of meditations, during which the passion of Christ was displayed, vividly painted.[85] Jesuit Lenten meditations in the Flemish province, introduced at Leuven in 1626, displayed

7.20. Communion rail in the Chapel of Our Lady, former Jesuit church, Antwerp.
Photo courtesy of Jeffrey Muller.

images in order to heighten the desired responses.[86] Above all, the illustrations in Jesuit meditation books have received the most recent attention from art historians. Peter van Dael, Manuel Insolera, Walter Melion, and now Christine Göttler have developed the argument that the Jesuit use of illustrations for meditation was a direct outgrowth of St Ignatius's *Spiritual Exercises*, and therefore particular to Jesuit spirituality.[87] It would be fruitful to investigate further the different ways in which Jesuit techniques of meditation learned through spiritual exercises, sermons, books, group prayer, and varied kinds of images were coordinated to reinforce the impact of the experience.

To accomplish their tenth labour, of fostering pious institutions such as the Stations of the Cross, the cult of the Virgin, and devotion to saints, the Flemish Jesuits put in play a range of visual objects. Medallions, crucifixes, and rosaries all stimulated Christian piety.[88] Thijs has fully documented and analysed Antwerp's position as the publishing centre of what the *Imago primi saeculi* calls 'pious images representing the mysteries of the faith, features and acts of saints, engraved in copper, disseminated through all Belgium and the world.'[89] Cheap devotional prints, like those inserted at the back of Steegius's picture catechism, were printed and distributed in editions of thousands, a true mass medium (fig. 7.21). Over

7.21. Steegius, *De Christelycke Leeringhe*, devotional prints bound at the back of the book. Copy in Antwerp, Stadsbibliotheek. Photo courtesy of Jeffrey Muller.

three years during the 1660s, the Jesuits at Mechelen handed out 36,000 prints of Francis Xavier, whom they were promoting as a plague saint.[90] Nevertheless, Thijs warns against exaggerating the importance of the Jesuits in the production of devotional prints before the late seventeenth century. He also shows how the Bollandists, starting in 1692, obtained exclusive privileges, set up their own retail shop in 1717, and finally ran their own printing press in 1735, thus controlling all stages in the production and sale of the prints. From that date they were the only regular order to operate a full-fledged publishing enterprise.[91]

While the eleventh labour, of winning souls through private conversation, did not require visual communication, the twelfth, of writing books, certainly did.[92] This topic is enormous, and expands outwards into the whole world of Jesuit knowledge, as, for example, François de Aguilon's *Opticorum libri sex* of 1614, with its illustrations by Rubens.[93]

I have presented the extraordinarily innovative and diverse uses of the visual arts by which Jesuits accomplished their labours in Flanders. Once again, the most important and stimulating recent work has been done by historians, literary historians, and architectural historians, the latter elaborating the strong tradition of Braun and Plantenga.[94] Art historians have not yet learned to ask the questions and use the sources that could break new ground in this rich and important field.

NOTES

I gratefully acknowledge the Netherlands Insitute for Advanced Study, where I wrote this essay during my tenure as fellow-in-residence. Joost van der Auwera kindly sent me the photo of figure 16, and Brooke Hammerle developed my own photos.

1 Bail. 'Style,' p. 69.
2 See, for example, Walter S. Melion, 'Artifice, Memory, and *Reformatio* in Hierony-mus Natalis's *Adnotationes et meditationes in evangelia,*' *Renaissance and Reformation* 22 (1998): 5–34; Marc Fumaroli, 'Baroque et classicisme: *L'Imago primi saeculi Societatis Jesu* (1640) et ses adversaires,' in *L'école du silence: Le sentiment des images au XVIIe siècle* (Paris, 1994, 1998), pp. 343–65; and Christine Göttler, '"Actio" in Peter Paul Rubens' Hochaltarbildern für die Jesuitenkirche in Antwerpen,' in *Barocke Inszenierung*, ed. Joseph Imorde, Fritz Neumeyer, and Tristan Weddigen (Berlin, 1999), pp. 10–31.
3 I have addressed this historiography in a lecture entitled 'The Catholic Negative in the History of Flemish Art,' delivered at the annual meeting of the Renaissance Society of America, Chicago, 29–31 March 2001. I intend to undertake the additional research necessary to do justice to so complex a topic.
4 *Imago primi saeculi societatis Iesu a provincia Flandro-Belgica eivsdem societatis*

repraesentata (Antwerp, 1640), p. 769: 'Liber sextus, Societas Flandro-Belgica, caput Tertium. De functionibus ac laboribus Societatis per Flandro-Belgium.' For brevity's sake I will, like the poet with Hercules, reduce many labours to twelve.

5 Here I heed the call by John W. O'Malley, *Trent and All That: Renaming Catholicism in the Early Modern Era* (Cambridge, MA, 2000, 2002), pp. 138–42, to recognize and consider the yearning for the transcendent and the human comfort at the heart of religion; and the criticism directed by Jean-Claude Galey in his 'Politiques de conversion et conversion au politique. L'Inde des jésuites et de l'histoire,' review of Ines G. Zupanov, *Disputed Mission: Jesuit Experiments and Brahmanical Knowledge in Seventeenth-Century India* (Oxford and New Delhi, 1999), against the reduction of religion to a politics of power.

6 *Imago primi saeculi*, p. 769.

7 See n4 above.

8 See Alfons K.L. Thijs, *Van Geuzenstad tot Katholiek Bolwerk: Maatschappelijke betekenis van de Kerk in contrareformatorisch Antwerpen* (Turnhout, 1990), p. 140.

9 See *Imago primi saeculi*, p. 769, as explanation of the first labour, of catechism: 'Tabulae rasae sunt ingenia pauulorum; quidquid insculpitur, tenent ...' Because of Jesuit catechism, 'staret hodieque Belgis incorrupto Religio (sic omnes sentiunt) staret cum Religione pax, cum pace felicitas ...'

10 See ibid., p. 771: 'Explicatur Catechismus vnius anni spatio, decies millies, septingenties, quinies & quadragesies: numerantur catechumeni duo & triginta millia quingenti & octo.'

11 See Alfons K.L. Thijs, *Antwerpen Internationaal Uitgeverscentrum van Devotieprenten 17de–18de Eeuw* (Leuven, 1993), p. 13. At the same time, Thijs, p. 83, in reaction to Adolf Spamer, *Das kleine Andachtsbild vom XIV. bis zum XX. Jahrhundert* (Munich, 1930), p. 62, warns against overestimating the active role played by the Jesuits in the production of devotional prints in Antwerp during the seventeenth century. Thijs does, however, credit the Jesuits with providing strong encouragement in the use of these prints. On this issue, see further below. See Richard C. Trexler, *Public Life in Renaissance Florence* (New York, 1980); and R.W. Scribner, *For the Sake of Simple Folk: Popular Propaganda for the German Reformation*, Cambridge Studies in Oral and Literate Culture 2 (Cambridge, 1981). See Herman van der Wee and Jan Materné, 'De Antwerpse wereldmarkt tijdens de 16de en 17de eeuw,' in *Antwerpen verhaal van een metropool 16de–17de eeuw*, ed. Jan van der Stock (Antwerp, 1993), p. 21, for Antwerp population figures.

12 P. Ioannes Gvilielmvs Steegivs, Priester der Societyet Iesv, *De Christelycke Leeringhe verstaenelycker vyt-geleyt door eene Beelden-Sprake noodigh soo voor kinders als groote die niet kvnnen lesen, gherievigh voor een ieder om beter te vatten ende t'onthovden* (Antwerp, 1647).

13 Steegius, *De Christelycke Leeringhe* (n12 above), Voor-Reden tot den Leser, fol. 3v:

'*Ende siet; soo ick nauwelijcks hadde begonst myne haendt aen dit werck te slaen den 4. ofte 5. dagh, als ofte Godt by daer toe had willen aendryven, my wordt op syn onverwachts tot voordere beweghinghe over tafel ghelesen uyt het kort begryp* der geschiedenissen onser Societeyt geduerende haere eerste 100. jaeren beschreven, in 't Latijn door P. Iacobus Damianus *dit navolghende in 'tlaetste van den 5. boeck:* Godt makte de Patres in Paraquarien bequaem tot het ziele-ghewin der wilde menschen, ende namentlijck Iacobum Martinez, Christus selver van een Crucifix hem toe-sprekende. Desen studeerde in de Godtheyt te Lima, een man wel ghe-knocht ende ghesondt: hy vraeght van Christus wat hy 't meeste op hem versochte: ende soo den Salighmaker antwoorde stemmelijck: de saligheyt der menschen, worpt hy op staende voet alle sijne schriften in 't vier; ende aldus gelijck ontlast zijnde gaet naer de wilde bosche. Sy waren plomp ende hardt om iet vatten: aen hem ende d'andere is ingestort menigher vernuftheyt om zielen te winnen. hunne ingheborene bot-sinnigheyt bleef haer aaen; nochte ghedooghde dat sy haer wat soude vertoonen, ofte door het ghehoir vatten de uytgheleede leeringhen. Men heeft se hen moeten aen dienen door hunne ooghen: want den wegh hier door tot inwaerts korter ende sekerder is; ende het ghemoedt hem lichtelijcker laet beweghen door de verbeeldinghen der saken. Hierom schilderden sy de hooft-stucken van de Christelijcke wet op tafereelen. Daer wiert vaster inghedruckt het vier der Hellen door sijne vertoonde schrickelijckheyt met meni-verwe: ende de ghenoechten des Hemels door de verbeeldinghe van vleesch, spijsen, koecken, ende wijn.'

14 Hui-Hung Chen, 'Encounters in People, Religions, and Science: Jesuit Visual Culture in Seventeenth-Century China,' dissertation, Brown University, Providence, 2004.

15 Steegius, *De Christelycke Leeringhe*, Voor-Reden tot den Leser, fol. 3r: '*eenen bysonderen Boeren-almanach: uyt den welcken sy, alhoe wel niet kunnende lesen, souden niet te min vermoghen te verstaen door* Beelde-teeckens, '*tghene andere weten met te lesen in den Letter-almanach.*'

16 See Tom Dekker, 'Ideologie en volkscultuur: Een geschiedenis van de Nederlandse volkskunde,' in *Volkscultuur: Een inleiding in de Nederlandse etnologie*, ed. Tom Dekker, Herman Roodenburg, and Gerard Rooijakkers (Nijmegen, 2000), pp. 13–65, where no mention is made of Steegius.

17 See Steegius, *De Christelycke Leeringhe*, Voor-Reden tot den Leser, fol. 3r, where he says that he has, for the purpose of teaching the illiterate, '*gaen versieren oock eene* Beelden-sprake, *vertoonende door verbeeldinghen, ghelijckenißen, ende teeckenen de gheheele* Christelijcke leeringhe ...'

18 See Gerard Rooijakkers, ''Opereren op het snijpunt van culturen: Middelaars en media in Zuid-Nederland,' in *Cultuur en maatschappij in Nederland 1500–1800: Een historisch-antropologisch perspectief*, ed. Peter te Boekhorst, Peter Burke, and Willem Frijhoff (Heerlen, 1992), pp. 273–80, on almanacs as mediators between cultural circuits in seventeenth- and eighteenth-century Netherlands.

19 See Steegius, *De Christelycke Leeringhe*, p. 21, 'Van de V. Gheboden der H. Kercke':
'Vr. Wat wortter bevolen in het III. Ghebodt?/ Te vasten op de ghestelde daghen./
Vr. Wat is Vasten?/ Ant. Derven sekere soorten van spijsen; ende maer eens volko-
mentlijck op den dagh eten./ Vr. Welcke zijn die spijsen?/ Ant. Vleesch; ende
altemets eyeren/ ende suyvel/ te weten in den Vasten/ ten zy daer het toe-ghelaeten
wort./ Vr. Welcke zijn nu die daghen, op de welcke het gheboden is te Vasten?/
Antw. Die daer ghestelt staen in het beeldt/ zijnde ghetrocken uyt den Schaep-
herders-Almanch.'

20 See ibid.: 'Ten 3. de 4. tijden in het Jaer/ die-men Quarter-temper heet/ dat is/ de
Woensdaghen/ Vrydaghen/ Saterdaghen van die sekere 4. weken/ die welcke ken-
baer ghemaeckt zijn in het beeldt door het by-voeghen van sommighe teeckenen.'

21 See ibid.: 'Vr. Wat ghebiedt ons de H. kerck door het IV. Ghebodt?/ Ant. Te minsten
eens in het Jaer te Biechten/ ghelijck dat wort uytghedruckt het laetste beeldeken op
een naer de 4. tijden des Jaers/ die 't samen in een linie worpen op de Biechte. al-
hoe-wel het seer gheraedtsaem is; jae gheheel in 't ghebruyck/ dickwils te biechten
door het Jaer.'

22 *Synodicon belgicum, sive acta omnium ecclesiarum Belgii a celebrato concilio
Tridentino usque ad concordatum anni 1801*, ed. P.F.X. de Ram, 4 vols (Leuven and
Mechelen, 1828–58), I, p. 372, decrees and statutes of the Provincial Council,
Mechelen, 1607, sacrament of penance, chap. 3: 'Ubi erecta necdum sunt confessionalia, quae Confessarium à asserculo cancellato, ac poenitentem à sequentibus
alio asserculo disjungant, intra tres menses à publicatione decretorum hujus Concilii
sumptibus fabricarum eriganturet ab eo tempore nemo sine licentia ordinarii extra
ejusmodii confessionalia foeminarum confessiones audiere praesumat, nisi in casu
necessitatis.' The introduction of confessionals was resisted in the suburban parish
of Berchem, outside Antwerp, where penitents objected to confessing through
grates, which were subsequently removed; see Kristin de Raeymaecker, *Het
Godsdienstig Leven in de Landdekenij Antwerpen (1610–1650)*, Belgisch Centrum
voor Landelijke Geschiedenis Publikatie 52 (Leuven, 1977), p. 59 n138.

23 See Steegius, *De Christelycke Leeringhe*, p. 21, 'Van de V. Gheboden der H.
Kercke': 'Vr. Wat wortter gheboden in het laeste V./ Ant. Eens oock t'ontfanghen
het hoogh-weerdigh Sacrament, des Autaers/ ende dat omtrent den Paeschen/
welcken tijdt daer staet te kennen ghegheven op het laetste beeldeken door den
Palmen-Sondagh, Paesch-dagh, ende Beloke-Paeschen.'

24 See Marshall McLuhan, 'Media Hot and Cold,' in *Understanding Media: The
Extensions of Man* (New York, 1965), pp. 22–3: 'A cool medium like hieroglyphic
or ideogrammic written characters has very different effects from the hot and
explosive medium of the phonetic alphabet.'

25 See Steegius, *De Christelycke Leeringhe*, Voor-Reden tot den Leser, fol. 3r–v:
through the picture-language, the illiterate will be able to grasp everything contained

in text catechisms, '*alsoo dat sy hier ende daer wat gheholpen zynde met eene lichte uyt-legghinghe door iemandt, die lesen kan, oft de ghemelde wetenschap nu vast heeft, gelyck dat geschiedt in het voort-leeren des Boeren-almanachs, sal seer ghemackelyck kunnen ghevat worden van kinders, minverstandighe menschen, ende alle die niet en kunnen lesen, jae van alder-taelighe volcken.*' Early modern practices combining public reading, oral explanation, and visual illustration for the illiterate and semi-literate are documented and analysed in Scribner, *For the Sake of Simple Folk* (n11 above), pp. 211–16; and in Tessa Watt, *Cheap Print and Popular Piety, 1550–1640* (Cambridge, 1991), p. 227.

26 See Peter van Dael, 'Geillustreerde boeken van jezuïeten uit de 15de en 17de eeuw: De verhouding tussen woord en beeld,' in *Jezuïeten in Nederland*, Rijksmuseum Het Catharijneconvent (Utrecht, 1991), pp. 30–40, where the Groningen edition is illustrated.

27 John W. O'Malley, in O'M. *First*, p. 358, observing that Jesuits ignored the controversy around Michelangelo's *Last Judgment* and most other art, concludes that 'for all the Jesuits' cultivating of the imagination, their culture was most directly a culture of the book and the word.'

28 Ponc. *Hist.*, I, pp. 352–412, on the foundation of colleges in both Belgian provinces.

29 See *Imago primi saeculi*, p. 771, under 'Secundus labor, Scholae': while previously few had been educated, 'nunc autem florere doctrinam, viris magno numero litteratis, tamquam pleno sideribus caelo, splendente Republicâ.'

30 See ibid., p. 772: 'Quot millia Belgarum putas per nos bonis artis instituta?'

31 See Karel Porteman, *Emblematic Exhibitions (affixiones) at the Brussels Jesuit College (1630–1685): A Study of the Commemorative Manuscripts (Royal Library, Brussels)* (Brussels, 1996), p. 11. The *affixiones* were, he says, an outgrowth of exercises – *exercitationes* – central to the *humaniora* studies of rhetoric and poetry, leading to perfect command of *eloquentia* 'in its widest sense, namely: literary and moral command of words in the service of Church, Ruler, and Country.'

32 See Porteman, *Emblematic Exhibitions*, p. 59, colour illustration, and pp. 121–2, English translations of texts: Emblem of Affixiones, 1652, Brussels, KB, Horace Art of Poetry: title-page with chimerical creatures invented by painters and poets. All who have written on the art of poetry assert that poetry resembles painting: following their advice, 'yet considering that / more slowly moves the heart what / seeps in through the ear than what is set / before the trusty eye (*Ars*, vv. 180–1), I offer you Horace, the poet and trainer of poets, that is, the instructor of instructors, and at the same time I put his art (nourished by long observation) before you in emblems, not so much to read as to view them.'

33 See ibid., p. 59, colour illustration, and pp. 164–7, commentary and texts, 1683, on the theme of piety combined with wisdom and learning, watercolours and calligraphy by Carolus van Deijnum: 'splendet ut alliciat.'

34 See Luc Dequeker, *Het Sacrament van Mirakel: Jodenhaat in de Middeleeuwen* (Leuven, 2000).

35 See Porteman, *Emblematic Exhibitions*, pp. 29–32, on the link between the Brussels *affixiones* and the Miracle of the Sacrament; p. 31, on the issue of anti-Semitism; and p. 135, on the explicitly anti-Semitic emblems I have mentioned.

36 Ponc. *Hist.*, II, p. 70.

37 See ibid., pp. 81–9, on internal debate over Jesuit theatre and festivities, and pp. 358–61, on the gradual increase of luxury in Jesuit music.

38 See *Imago primi saeculi*, p. 774: 'Habet nostra Provincia Sodalitates nonaginta: numerus Sodalium 13727. Antuerpia sola decem Sodalitatiibus gaudet; in iis tria facilè millia Sodales. Atque hîc videas (quod terrarum nusquam) congregandis Sodalibus amplum splendidumque aedificium augusto lapide ab ipsis ductum fundamentis.'

39 See Rudi Mannaerts, 'De artistieke expressie van de mariale devotie der Jezuïeten te Antwerpen (1562–1773): Een iconografisch onderzoek,' 3 vols, licenciaat thesis, Catholic University, Leuven, 1983, copy in the library of the Ruusbroecgenootschap, University of Antwerp.

40 See, for Rubens's *Annunciation*, *Peter Paul Rubens, 1577–1640: Ausstellung zur 400. Wiederkehr seines Geburtstages 15. April bis 19. Juni 1977*, Kunsthistorisches Museum (Vienna, 1977), pp. 56–8, no. 7; and for Van Dyck's two pictures, Hans Vlieghe in *Van Dyck, 1599–1641*, ed. Christopher Brown and Hans Vlieghe (Antwerp and London, 1999), p. 218, no. 56.

41 As noted in Ponc. *Hist.*, II, chaps 7–9; and Louis Châtellier, *The Europe of the Devout: The Catholic Reformation and the Formation of a New Society*, trans. Jean Birrell (Cambridge, 1989), pp. 55–9.

42 Rudi Mannaerts, 'Het Sodaliteitsgebouw en zijn decoratie (1623–1773). Een reconstructie van twee barokke Mariakapellen,' in *De Notteboomzaal boek en mecenaat*, Publikaties van de Stadsbibliotheek en het Archief en Museum voor het Vlaamse Cultuurleven 34–6 (Antwerp, 1993), pp. 63–81, consults the drawings but does not publish them. For the drawings, see Stadsarchief Antwerpen, Kerken en Kloosters 589: Jesuites: two folios glued together and folded closed: 18th century, c. 1760?, pen and ink:
fol. 1r: on cover: Plan van de boven sodaliteyt der Paters Jesuwieten
fol. 1v: Plan van de sadaliteyt [*sic*] boven van professiehuys alhier
with exact plan in pencil, reinforced in pen and ink, below:
fol. 2r: *Beschryvinge van de sodalityt boven van de Paters Jesueten alhier*
dese is gebouwt in jaer 1622 uyt reden van den voorgevel der kerke dat dese naer de konst was gebout ende niet tegenstaeende volgens de breede van den voorgevel de hooghte niet en hadt die hy moest hebbe zoo heeft Rubbens dese genoemde sodaliteyt doen op rechten om het gesicht te beletten van den mislacht die aen den

selve gedaen was dese is verciert in kostelycke witten marber steen van onder tot boven

N 1 boven den inganck van de sodaliteyt staet het Portret van Pater arckenroede geschildert door

N 2 stuck representeert maria inde hemelsche glorie geschildert door fransciscus Boeyermans geteekent FB

N 3 stuck representeert de martelie van den h: laurentius geschildert door Garibaldi

N 4 stuck representeert den h: ignatius by den paus approberende den Regel van het order der societydt [*sic*] geschildert door arregauts

N 5 stuck representeert h: xaverius en h: ignatius geschildert door arregauts

N 6 boven de Deur van sacristyn staet de religui van h: rosalia

N 7 stuck representeert een battaillie geschildert door van heck

N 8 stuck representeert een lantschap geschildert door gasper de wit de figueren door goubau

N 9 stuck representeert maria toevlucht der seeckenen en krancke geschildert door

N 10 stuck representeert h: alowisius gonsager met den leelitack van suyverheyt tot maria geschildert door gerardus segers

N 11 den autaer is van composita ordre ter ordinantie van het stuck representeert met het kindeken op haeren schoet ende daer neffens staende petrus en paulus voor h: kindken is knielend de h: maeghet rosalia het hr kindeken stellende een kroone op haer hooft geschildert door A van dyck

N 12 het stuck representeert maria met den h: hermanus joseph uyt het order der premonstreyt syn hant uytstekende voor maria en ontfancke van

fol. 2v: haer eenen rinck van trouw voor de suyverheyt geschildert door A van dyck gaet in print uyt gesneden door

N 13 Blason representeert

two folios glued together and folded closed: 18th century, c. 1760?, pen and ink:

fol. 1r: on cover: Plan van de beneden sodaliteyt der Paters jesuwieten

fol. 1v: Plan van de sodaliteyt beneden van professie huys alhier

with exact plan in pencil, reinforced in pen and ink, below:

fol. 2r: *Beschryvinghe van de schilderyen van de benede sodaliteyt der Paters jesuiten tot antwerpen*

N 1 stuck representeert de offerhande van de 3 konighen geschildert door deodate delmont

N 2 stuck representeert daer maria gekront woort door de h: dryvuldigheyt geschildert door

N 3 stuck representeert Christus aen het Cruys geschildert door

N 4 stuck representeert Christus sittende met syn riet in d'hant en synen purpuren mantel om ringelt met engelen die teeckens der passie hebben geschildert door

N 5 stuck representeert Christus syn Cruys draegende geschildert door deodate del mont was discipiel van Rubbens waer meede hy gereys heeft naer italien en andere plaetsen

N 6 stuck representeert de trouw van maria met st joseph geschildert door

N 7 stuck representeert maria haer veropenbaerende aen den h: ignatius geschildert door gerard segers

N 8 autaer is van composita ordre ten ordinantie

het stuck representeert de bootschap door den engel aen maria geschildert door Rubens gaet in print uyt gesneden door

N 9 stuck representeert daer franciscus xaverius de duyvelen wegh jaeght geschildert door gerard segers

N 11 stuck representeert

43 See Zirka Zaremba Filipczak, 'Van Dyck's "Life of St Rosalie,"' *Burlington Magazine* 131 (1989): 693–8; M. Insolera, 'Les caractéristiques spécifiques du livre illustré dans la spiritualité jésuite flamande,' in Manuel Insolera and Lydia Salviucci Insolera, *La spiritualité en images aux Pays-Bas Méridionaux dans les livres imprimés des XVIe et XVIIe siècles conservés à la Bibliotheca Wittockiana*, Miscellanea Neerlandica 13 (Leuven, 1996), pp. 13–18; and, in particular, pp. 150–2, cat. no. 50, entry on Thomas Saillius, *Thesaurus precum et exercitiorum spiritualium, in usum pr[a]esertim Sodalitatis Partheniae. Additae breves apologiae, eidem subservientes* (Antwerp, 1609); and pp. 177–80, cat. no. 63, entry on Andreas Brunner, *Fasti Mariani cum divorum elogiis in singulos anni dies distributis* (Antwerp, 1660).

44 Châtellier, *The Europe of the Devout* (n41 above).

45 See *Imago primi saeculi*, p. 779. On this chapel, see L. Brouwers, *De Jezuïeten te Mechelen in de 17e en 18e eeuw en hun Xavieruskerk, de huidige Parochiekerk S.S. Petrus en Paulus* (Mechelen, 1977), p. 35: this chapel of Our Lady of the Immaculate Conception was built out of necessity, to accommodate the growing crowds that pressed into the church. Drawings are reproduced on p. 34; the exterior on p. 36; the interior, by J.B. De Noter, is now Stadsarchief van Mechelen, Akwarellen verzameling Schoeffer B6701 no. 186. Pp. 35–7 n3 indicates that these drawings were made after the interior was completely stripped in 1773, so reconstructions are based on the still standing structure and some remnants of the interior decoration. The dedication is on p. 40: 'Mariae absque labe originali conceptae,' used by the seven Marian sodalities of the city,

46 This issue involves the Jesuits in conflict with Jansenists and Dominicans. The most important published source is *La fin de la première période du Jansénisme: Sources des années, 1654–1660*, ed. Lucien Ceyssens, 2 vols, Bibliothèque de l'Institut Historique Belge de Rome 12–13 (Brussels and Rome, 1963–5).

47 See *Imago primi saeculi*, p. 775. The Jesuit role at Scherpenheuvel is documented in Luc Duerloo and Marc Wingens, *Scherpenheuvel, Het Jeruzalem van de Lage Landen* (Leuven, 2002), which I have not yet been able to consult.

48 See *Imago primi saeculi*, p. 778: 'Infinitus sim, si statuas singularum vrbium populari pietate, luminibus, votiuis tabellis, miraculis illustres recensere studeam'; 'Praeter has in Collegiorum templis, alias quoque in plateis locisque publicis poni curauit Societas; quarum facilè princeps quae Antuerpiensem Curiam servat.' The best account of these images remains Aug. Thijssen, *Onderpastoor in St. Antonius, Antwerpen vermaard door den Eeredienst van Maria: Geschiedkundige Aanmerkingen over de 500 Mariabeelden in de straten der stad*, 2nd ed. (Antwerp, 1922). Currently Nancy Kay is writing a dissertation on the topic.

49 Documentation on the festive installation of the image is given in Thijssen, *Antwerpen vermaard* (n48 above), pp. 147–53. See Thijs, *Van Geuzenstad tot Katholiek Bolwerk* (n8 above), p. 107, who stresses the symbolic importance of this means of displaying Roman Catholic triumph.

50 See Thijssen, *Antwerpen vermaard*, p. 273: 'Over de daken heen, aanschouwt O.L. Vrouw het stadhuis, opdat Zij het zonder ophouden bescherme.'

51 Joseph Braun, *Die belgischen Jesuitenkirchen. Ein Beitrag zur Geschichte des Kampfes zwischen Gotik und Renaissance* (Freiburg im Breisgau, 1907), p. 3, who challenged the concept of a Jesuit style by proving that the first churches in the Southern Netherlands were built in Gothic style, and that their later churches participated in the larger turn of Belgian ecclesiastical architecture towards Italian models.

52 For an eloquent challenge to this restrictive concept of style, see E.H. Gombrich, *In Search of Cultural History* (Oxford, 1967).

53 Peter Paul Rubens, *Palazzi antichi di Genova, Palazzi moderni di Genova*, intro. Alan A. Tait (1622; repr. New York and London, 1968), 'Al Benigno Lettore': 'Vediamo che in queste parti, si và poco à poco inuecchiando & abolendo la maniera d'Architettura, che si chiama Barbara, ò Gothica; & che alcuni bellißimi ingegni introducono la vera simmetria di quella, conforme le regole de gli antichi, Graeci e Romani, con grandißimo splendore & ornamento della Patria; come appare nelli Tempij famosi fatti di fresco dalla venerabil Società di Iesv, nelle città Brusselles & Anuersa. Li quali se per la dignità del Vfficio diuino meritamente doveano essere i primi à cangiarse in meglio.'

54 On the Jesuit church in Brussels, see J.H. Plantenga, *L'architecture religieuse dans l'ancien duché de Brabant depuis le règne des archiducs jusqu'au gouvernement autrichien (1598–1713)* (The Hague, 1926), pp. 57–65. See Krista de Jonge et al., 'Building Policy and Urbanisation during the Reign of the Archdukes: The Court and Its Architects,' in *Albert & Isabella, 1598–1621: Essays*, ed. Werner Thomas and Luc Duerloo (Brussels, 1998), pp. 191–220, on the archdukes' patronage of architecture.

55 See Thomas DaCosta Kaufmann, 'Jesuit Art: Central Europe and the Americas,' in O'M. *Jes. Cult.*, pp. 284–7.

56 Plantenga, *L'architecture*, pp. 63–4.

57 The best account to date is ibid., pp. 83–115. It will be very interesting to find out what kind of use will be made of archives and visual material by Marie Juliette Marinus in *Antwerpen en de Jezuïten, 1562–2002*, ed. Herman van Goethem (Antwerp), announced to appear after completion of this paper.

58 See the account of building the church in Ponc. *Hist.*, I, pp. 457–83. Poncelet, on p. 458, echoes the disapproval of luxury provoked by the church during its construction.

59 See Olwen Hufton, '"Every Tub on Its Own Bottom": Funding a Jesuit College in Early Modern Europe,' in this volume. Hufton observes that the Jesuits operated in a debt culture in which spectacular building attracted donations; that deficit funding was vulnerable in times of crisis; and that subsequent maintenance of what had become less glamorous always presented a problem.

60 Koen Ottenheym, 'De correspondentie tussen Rubens en Huygens over architectuur (1635–'40),' *Bulletin Koninklijke Nederlandse Oudheidkundige Bond* 96 (1997): 1–11.

61 Ibid., p. 7.

62 See Plantenga, *L'architecture*, pp. 192–5; and Brouwers, *De Jezuïeten te Mechelen*, pp. 52–4.

63 See *Bellissimi ingegni, grandissimo splendore. Studies over de religieuze architectuur in de Zuidelijke Nederlanden tijdens de 17de eeuw*, ed. Krista de Jonge et al., Symbolae, Faculatatis Litterarum Lovaniensis, ser. B, 15 (Leuven, 2000).

64 See Philip De Mesmaecker, Liesbet Haghenbeek, and Griet van Opstal, 'Oratoria in de jezuïetenkerken van de Zuidelijke Nederlanden. Een fenomeen eigen aan de Contrareformatie,' in *Bellissimi ingegni*, ed. de Jonge et al., pp. 79–90.

65 Bert Daelemans, Jamina Koninckx, and Sofie van Loo, 'De verplaatsing van de klokkentorens in de 17de-eeuwse kerkarchitectuur,' in *Bellissimi ingegni*, ed. de Jonge et al., pp. 67–78.

66 See *Imago primi saeculi*, p. 781: 'Illud constat, Societatis vocem è sacris adhuc pulpitis gratissimam sonare Belgis Catholicis, haereticis formidandum, vtrisque interim fructuosam. Dicitur in Prouinciâ ad populum à nostris, intra anni spatium, qundecies millies ducenties & sexies.'

67 Hans Storme, *Preekboeken en Prediking in de Mechelse Kerkprovincie in de 17e en de 18e Eeuw* (Brussels, 1991), pp. 161–2, demonstrates this with a passage from a sermon delivered by Rumoldus Backx at Antwerp Cathedral in 1685, and published in 1711: 'Ten tweede soo can het Gebodt van op Sondagen en Heylighdagen Sermoon te hooren, oock wel begrepen worden in het Gebodt van Misse te hooren: want in vorige tyden pleegh men altyt het Sermoon te doen onder de Misse, gelijck den H. Paus Clemens getuyght in sijn 8. boeck van d'Apostolike instellingen aen het 4. Capittel. En gelijck men noch op vele plaetsen in't gebruyck siet, principaelijck in de buyten Parochien te platte Lande.' St Carlo Borromeo actually gives instructions

opposed to Flemish practice. If there is one pulpit in the church, he says, it should
be on the north or Gospel side and not far from the high altar, so that it can be
reached conveniently by the priest when he delivers the sermon during solemn
mass (Carlo Borromeo, *Instructiones fabricae ecclesiasticae*, in *Trattati d'arte del
Cinquecento fra manierismo e controriforma*, ed. Paola Barocchi, 3 vols [Bari,
1962], III, p. 62: 'Si unus tantum ambo in ecclesia constituendus sit, is a latere
evangelii statuatur'; and p. 63: pulpits should be situated 'in gremio ecclesiae, loco
conspicuo, unde vel concionator vel lector ab omnibus et conspici et audiri possit,
apte collocati, ab altari maiori, ut pro ecclesiae ratione fier decore potest, non longe
admodum sint: quo sacerdoti, ut decretum est, intra Missarum solemnia,
concionanti, commodiori usui esse queant').

68 See *De Sint-Gummaruskerk te Lier, Inventaris van Het Kunstpatrimonium van de
Provincie Antwerpen*, ed. Hertha Leemans, vol. 1 (Antwerp and Utrecht, 1972),
pp. 177–8, inv. no. 90.

69 See the recent summary in Lieve Lettany, *Sint-Pieter en Sint-Pauluskerk, Torens
aan de Dijle* (Mechelen, n.d.), pp. 26–9.

70 See *Imago primi saeculi*, pp. 783–4: 'Ante Societatis adventum rarus Belgis & ferè
exosus Confessionis vsus: qui primus ad haereses gradus fuit. Confessione, nullo
magis freno compescitur vitae libertas, mater omnium vitiorum.'

71 See Wietse de Boer, *The Conquest of the Soul: Confession, Discipline, and Public
Order in Counter-Reformation Milan* (Leiden, 2001), pp. 84–105, for the best
account of Borromeo's innovative confessionals.

72 S. Zajadacz-Hastenrath, *Das Beichtgestühl der Antwerpener St. Pauluskirche und
der Barockbeichtstuhl in den südlichen Niederlanden*, Monographien des Nationaal
Centrum voor de Plastische Kunsten van de XVIde en XVIIde Eeuw 3 (Brussels,
1970), p. 172, no. 7, on the confessionals in the Chapel of Our Lady and the nave of
the Antwerp Jesuit church.

73 See ibid., pp. 176–7, nos 14–15. See Marie Juliette Marinus, *De Contrareformatie
te Antwerpen (1585–1676), Kerkelijk Leven in een Grootstad* (Brussels, 1995),
pp. 194–202, for the larger context of inter-order rivalry.

74 See Brouwers, *De Jezuïeten te Mechelen*, (n45 above), p. 70; and Zajadacz-
Hastenrath, *Das Beichtgestühl*, pp. 199–200, no. 89.

75 See Thijs, *Van Geuzenstad tot Katholiek Bolwerk* (n8 above), who argues that the
Roman Catholic church, Spanish government, and Antwerp patrician-merchant elite
conspired to keep the growing poor and proletariat docile and exploitable, and thus
were imposing a conspiracy to repress the masses. Châtellier, *The Europe of the
Devout*, pp. 25–39, using a variety of primary sources, establishes the importance of
Jesuit sodalities in changing the normative behaviour of members. He documents
the imposition of what he calls an oppressive, strict, and prudish morality, and
control of the imagination. On the other hand, on pp. 121–9, Châtellier also suggests

that the organization of sodalities into separate units for each segment of urban society resulted in the formation of new, cohesive group identity. This was especially important for journeymen, who met apart from their masters, and may have produced revolutionary uprisings in both Naples and Antwerp. Throughout his work, however, Châtellier consistently sees the Jesuit sodalities, especially in the Southern Netherlands, as a particularly effective means 'to wield – under the cloak of religion – general influence over all classes of people.' By contrast, Marinus, in *De Contrareformatie te Antwerpen* (n73 above), takes what she claims is a more neutral, objective, archive-based position, and which, in the end, is uncritical of the Roman Catholic church and the Jesuits. These are, of course, only a representative sample among recent contributions.

76 See n71 above.

77 See *Imago primi saeculi*, p. 785: 'Antuerpiae Professa Domus intra anni spatium supra ducenta & quadraginta communicantium milla numerauit.' See Marinus, *De Contrareformatie te Antwerpen*, p. 280, table 19, for annual statistics of select years between 1636 and 1675.

78 See Jan Steppe, *Het Koordoksaal in de Nederlanden* (Brussels, 1952), pp. 44–5, on Jesuit opposition to rood screens.

79 Archive, St Jacob's church, Antwerp, Oud no. 560, Theodore van Lerius, 'Beschryving der parochiale en voor heen vermaarde Collegiale Kerk van St. Jacobo te Antwerpen. begonnen in Oct 1846' : 'bylage 46: Extract uyt zekere Boeck berustende in Venerabel Capel der Parochiale Kerk van St. Jacobs. De Conditien van de Communi Banck van witten marber voor de Cappel van het Alderheylichste in de Collegiale kerc van St Jacop. 1695' (with many thanks to Dr J. van den Nieuwenhuizen for making this document accessible to me).

80 See Frans Baudouin, 'Het Kunstpatrimonium: De 17de en de 18de eeuw,' in *De Onze-Lieve Vrouwekathedraal van Antwerpen*, ed. W. Aerts (Antwerp, 1993), pp. 252, and 400 n168.

81 *Imago primi saeculi*, p. 782. See, on the mission to the United Provinces, Paul Begheyn, 'Geschiedenis van de jezuïeten in Nederland,' in *Jezuïeten in Nederland* (n26 above), pp. 6–9.

82 See Xander van Eck, '"Haar uitstekend huis, en hoge kerke": Enkele gegevens over de bouw, inrichting en aankleding van schuilkerken der jezuïeten in Gouda en andere Noordnederlandse steden,' in *Jezuïeten in Nederland*, p. 48, who draws this conclusion in regard to the churches in Amsterdam and Utrecht. See also van Eck, 'De jezuïeten en het wervende wisselaltaarstuk,' *De zeventiende eeuw* 14 (1998): 81–94, in which the practice of changeable altarpieces used in Dutch hidden churches is derived from the mechanism in the Antwerp Jesuit church.

83 See *Imago primi saeculi*, pp. 785–8.

84 See ibid., pp. 789–91.

85 See Steegius, *De Christelycke Leeringhe* (n12 above), Voor-Reden tot den Leser, fol. 3v.

86 See Ponc. *Hist.*, II, p. 380.

87 See van Dael, 'Geillustreerde boeken' (n26 above); Peter van Dael, '"De christelijcke leeringhe met vermaeck gevat": De functie van illustraties in boeken van jezuïeten in de Nederlanden tijdens de zeventiende eeuw,' *De zeventiende eeuw* 14 (1998): 119–34; Insolera, 'Les caractéristiques spécifiques' (n43 above); Melion, 'Artifice, Memory' (n2 above); and Christine Göttler, 'Artifices of the Afterlife: Eschatological Imagery in Jesuit Meditation,' abstract of paper read at the conference 'The Jesuits II: Cultures, Sciences, and the Arts, 1540–1773,' Boston College, 5–9 June 2002, pp. 27–8.

88 See *Imago primi saeculi*, p. 791.

89 See Thijs, *Antwerpen Internationaal Uitgeverscentrum* (n11 above).

90 Ibid., p. 21.

91 Ibid., pp. 83–6.

92 See *Imago primi saeculi*, p. 795.

93 See *The Illustration of Books Published by the Moretuses*, ed. D. Imhof, Publications of the Plantin-Moretus Museum and the Stedelijk Prentenkabinet (Municipal Printroom), Antwerp 36 (Antwerp, 1996), pp. 137–8, no. 41.

94 See n51 above for Braun; n54 above for Plantenga.

8 / Meditation, Ministry, and Visual Rhetoric in Peter Paul Rubens's Program for the Jesuit Church in Antwerp

ANNA C. KNAAP

Pieter Neeffs's small panel painting of the interior of the Jesuit church in Antwerp (fig. 8.1) offers us a glimpse of the original splendour of one of the most important Counter-Reformation monuments built north of the Alps in the early seventeenth century. What made this church of particular interest was its lavish interior, boasting polychrome Italian marble and a spectacular decorative program by Peter Paul Rubens, which consisted of two high altarpieces dedicated to the famous Jesuits Ignatius of Loyola and Francis Xavier, as well as a series of thirty-nine ceiling paintings installed in the vaults of the aisles and galleries. Unfortunately, Rubens's program can no longer be appreciated *in situ*. In 1718 a fire destroyed the nave of the church, including all the ceiling paintings, leaving intact only the church's facade, choir, and side chapels. In addition, Rubens's high altarpieces, which had survived the fire, were transferred to Vienna towards the end of the eighteenth century.

In consequence of these losses, scholars have had to rely on the artist's preparatory oil sketches and later copies by others to reconstruct the initial appearance and layout of Rubens's ensemble.[1] Beyond such reconstructive efforts and various attempts to place the Jesuit paintings within Rubens's artistic development, little attention has been given to the program's original function. Indeed, there has been scant effort to analyse how Rubens's paintings actually worked within their original architectural context and how they articulated, both visually and spatially, the concerns of the Jesuits.[2] It is my premise that Rubens's altarpieces and ceiling paintings were conceived as a unified program that guided the viewer through sacred space. Drawing on the artist's preparatory sketches, later copies, the surviving architecture, and the evidence of Neeffs's interior view, I will demonstrate that Rubens devised an intricate network of visual, rhetorical, and thematic relationships that interacted across the actual space of the church. This sophisticated program, I will argue, created an entirely

8.1. Pieter Neeffs and Sebastiaan Vrancx, *Interior of the Jesuit Church in Antwerp,*
mid-seventeenth century, oil on panel. Kunsthistorisches Museum, Vienna.
Photo courtesy of the Kunsthistorisches Museum.

new visual experience for the viewer and was meant to fulfil a tripartite function. Besides acting as a framework for meditative prayer and an instrument of teaching doctrine to the laity, it constituted a larger propagandistic statement portraying the Jesuits as a leading reform order, whose doctrinal beliefs and pastoral goals were predicated on the teaching and ministry of Christ and the early Church Fathers.[3]

The Monument: Updating the Early Christian Basilica

Designed by the Jesuit architects François de Aguilon and Pieter Huyssens, the Jesuit church of St Ignatius was begun in 1615 and consecrated in 1621.[4] The building of the church was part of a larger campaign, sponsored by Archdukes Albert and Isabella, to restore the Catholic identity of Antwerp, which had been severely weakened during the iconoclastic outbursts of the previous century. Located in the centre of town not far from the cathedral, the Jesuit church featured a monumental classical facade and ostentatious interior ideally suited to attract and impress a wide audience. As Koen Ottenheym has demonstrated, the interior showed striking similarities to Vitruvius's plan for a basilica, which was illustrated by Andrea Palladio in the famous edition of Daniele Barbaro.[5] Like Vitruvius's plan, the Jesuit church contained three aisles, with the nave terminating in an apse at the east end. Both buildings also displayed a similar elevation consisting of side aisles surmounted by galleries, with Doric columns on the lower level and Ionic columns on the upper.

The choice of a basilica ground-plan and the profuse use of ornament and Italian marble are reminiscent of early Christian churches. Such conscious references to the primitive church were part of an Early Christian revival that took place during the Counter Reformation. Catholic reformers studied the writings of the Church Fathers and examined the material remains of the apostolic age in an effort to lay claim to the legacy of the *ecclesia primitiva*. As the centre of the Catholic world and the site of numerous early Christian monuments, Rome became the focus of such research into the church's history. Not only were various early Christian churches renovated, but the evidence made available through archaeological research also inspired new church programs patterned after these venerable models of the past.[6] What makes the example of the Jesuit church in Antwerp so exceptional is the conscious effort to re-create the aura and sanctity of the primitive church by constructing an Early Christian basilica outside Rome itself.

Apart from introducing a new architectural and artistic vocabulary, the Jesuit church also presented a newly conceived sacred space that reflected the order's pastoral and liturgical activities. As John W. O'Malley has shown, the Jesuits engaged in a form of ministry that was distinct from that of the parish.[7] While parish priests ministered to their own congregations, the Jesuits actively went out into the community to convert heretics and recruit non-observant Catholics. In devising this outward-looking ministry, the Jesuits modelled themselves after the itinerant Jesus and the apostles, often travelling to remote places and encouraging spiritual conversion of the individual through preaching, catechism, guidance in the Spiritual Exercises, and the administering of the sacraments of confession and communion.

The unique character of the Jesuit ministry was reflected in the open and spacious nave of the Antwerp church, which was intended to hold a great many visitors. By opening up the choir to the laity, the Jesuits broke with the traditional practice of physically enclosing the high altar behind a rood screen, which allowed the clergy to chant the liturgical hours in private. The absence of such an enclosure signalled the Jesuits' communal mission and encouraged a wider participation of the laity in the celebration of the mass. The emphasis on the high altar was intensified by the prominent display of Rubens's high altarpieces and by the reduced number of side altars. Of the six side altars dedicated to the Virgin, Joseph, and the four celebrated Jesuits Ignatius of Loyola, Francis Xavier, Stanislas Kostka, and Aloysius Gonzaga, four were situated in the apsidal ends of the aisles and galleries, while the other two were placed in the side chapels. The distribution of the altars over two floors allowed the Jesuits to celebrate several masses at the same time, and so administer the Eucharist simultaneously to a large number of worshippers.[8] Jesuit support for the sacrament of confession, in turn, was lent architectural definition in the row of confessional booths along the walls of the side aisles. The church also accommodated the Jesuit ministry of preaching. Like the mother church of the Gesù in Rome, the Antwerp basilica featured a large barrel vault for better acoustics and a prominent wooden pulpit situated halfway down the nave.

The ample space of the Antwerp church was thus ideally suited to the Jesuit goals of ministering to the masses and converting Protestant visitors, who frequently travelled to the Southern Netherlands from the nearby Calvinist territories.[9] Despite its communal character, the church also housed more private spaces, such as the oratoria in the choir, which were used exclusively by the Jesuits themselves for prayer. Screened off to assure privacy, these oratoria communicated with the sacristy and offered a direct view of the Eucharist on the high altar.[10] Other spaces reserved for private worship included the two side chapels, and the upper gallery, which could be accessed from the outside as well as from the sacristy and the side aisles. Although documentation about its religious function is scarce, the evidence of other Jesuit churches suggests that the Antwerp gallery was a restricted space intended for private meditation, private masses, and sacred lectures for special members of the congregation, including schoolchildren and confraternity members.[11]

Rubens's pictorial program was carefully arranged to respond to the functions and audiences of the Antwerp monument. The Jesuit fathers were directly involved in devising the iconography, as is confirmed by the survival of a copy of the contract for the ceiling paintings, signed in 1620, which included a list of subjects that Rubens was to execute with the help of his large studio.[12] The Antwerp scheme consisted of a series of thirty-nine typological and hagiographic ceiling paintings that were visually and thematically tied to the altarpieces at the east end. The Venetian-inspired paintings, which were conceived as if seen from below, were divided over two floors into four parallel sequences of nine paintings. An additional group of three hagiographic paintings was placed on the vaults of the narthex.

In order to determine the full function of the ceilings, it is important to realize that they could be viewed from different positions within the church. Although scholars have rightly argued that the ceilings' perspective was oriented towards a viewer entering the church, they have mistakenly assumed that one had to physically enter the galleries in order to comfortably take in the array of images overhead. Indeed, it has generally been overlooked that the gallery ceilings – owing to their large size and relatively high position – were also visible to viewers on the ground floor.[13] The ceilings could thus have served both as teaching tools during sermons being preached in the nave and as instruments for the private devotion of those who had access to the more secluded galleries.

Typology: A Discourse on the Eucharist

A closer look at the images themselves will illuminate these devotional and didactic functions. As stipulated in the contract, Rubens was to execute eighteen biblical narratives for the vaults in the galleries. The north gallery displayed a sequence of events from the earthly life of Christ alternating with Old Testament prototypes. The nine scenes in the south gallery detailed the heavenly life of Christ together with Old Testament types. Typological cycles like this were fairly common in the Counter-Reformation period, which saw a rise in the scholarship on and visualization of concordances between the two dispensations. The revival of this typological mode accorded with the church's renewed focus on the Bible as propagated during the fourth session of the Council of Trent.[14] Within Jesuit discourse, typology was used for various purposes, but it took on an especially important role in devotional literature. The Jesuit Louis Richeôme, for example, advised readers of his pilgrim guide to Loreto to start their meditations on the life of the Virgin with a contemplation of Old Testament prophecies.[15] Apart from providing a deeper understanding of the Bible, the Jesuits believed that type-antitype connections could stimulate a greater love of God. As Richeôme put it, '[The Figures] inflame our love towards God, because this contemplation of the ancient Figures, which prophesy the truth, makes us see the eternal charity with which God loves us.'[16]

In keeping with these traditions, Rubens's gallery ceilings are likely to have functioned as instruments for meditative prayer.[17] This proposition is confirmed not only by the range of Christological subjects that echo those in Jesuit devotional literature, but also by the cycle's spatial organization and visual logic. Like the sequential arrangement of Ignatius's *Spiritual Exercises*, which invited the reader to dwell on the places, figures, and actions of Christ's life, Rubens's typological paintings were structured as a progressive exposition of related images, encouraging the viewer to draw mystical connections between various details in the life of Christ and the Old Testament narratives that prefigured them.[18] While the prevalence of typological thinking in this period would have provided viewers with the knowledge to draw connections between episodes from the Old and New Testaments, it was especially Rubens's coordination of visual and rhetorical relationships that compelled viewers to engage in a deeper level of meditative practice.

Standing at the western side of the church, whether in the gallery itself or the nave below, viewers would have been able to take in two-thirds of the painting sequence, or six of the nine ceiling panels in the north gallery. The first cluster to come into view included *Moses in Prayer*, the *Last Supper*, *Abraham and Melchisedek*, the *Temptation of Christ*, *David and Goliath*, and the *Adoration of the Magi*. Walking farther down, a viewer would have encountered *Solomon and the Queen of Sheba*, the *Adoration of the Shepherds,* and *Michael Casting Satan Out of Heaven*. While looking upwards and progressing from the entrance towards the altar, one would thus trace the history of salvation backwards in time.

In reconsidering the layout of the north sequence, it becomes clear that Rubens employed various visual cues to underscore the Eucharistic meaning of the images represented. The formal element that set this chain of relationships in motion was the gesture of Moses. Occupying the westernmost compartment in the series, *Moses in Prayer* (fig. 8.2) formed the starting point for a viewer upon entering the gallery. The perspective of this scene, which is recorded in an early eighteenth-century copy by Jacob de Wit, directed the eye of the viewer towards the prophet's raised arms, which were supported on either side by Aaron and Hur. This emphatic pose had long been interpreted as a prefiguration of the cross and a prophecy of the gesture of the priest elevating the host during the mass.[19] Proceeding down the gallery, viewers would have seen this gesture repeated in the extended arm of Christ offering the bread to Peter in the *Last Supper* (fig. 8.3) and in Melchisedek's offering of bread to Abraham and his troops. The careful arrangement of objects and gestures also applied to the subsequent scene, the *Temptation* (fig. 8.4), which showed the devil tempting Christ to turn stones into bread. Deviating from the conventional formula, which pictured the devil pointing towards stones on the ground, Rubens represented the devil extending them towards Christ, and thereby created an eloquent visual rhyme between the stones and the bread. The rich exegetical tradition that identified rocks with the body of Christ suggests that Rubens aligned these objects to emphasize Eucharistic associations.[20] It is significant, too, that we can extend this revelatory chain of carefully orchestrated similes towards the scenes situated near the altar. In the *Adoration of the Magi* and the *Adoration of the Shepherds*, for example, Rubens placed the Christ child on the same axis as the bread and the rocks to alert the viewer to the Christian significance shared by these objects and figures. We may surmise, then, that Rubens's choreography of visual and symbolic cues did not

8.2. Jacob de Wit after Peter Paul Rubens, *Moses in Prayer,* c. 1718, watercolour.
Copy after ceiling painting in the Jesuit church in Antwerp. Courtauld Institute Gallery,
Somerset House, London. Photo courtesy of the Courtauld Institute Gallery.

merely establish compositional balance within the cycle, but also created a
visual pathway that involved the viewer in a process of meditation on the nature
of Christ's presence in the Eucharist.

In addition to serving as an aid to private devotion, Rubens's typological
ceilings may be interpreted as didactic in nature.[21] The Council of Trent had
underscored the value of representations of salvation history for teaching doctrinal truths to the laity.[22] The doctrine enshrined in the images under discussion
was that of the Eucharist, which had become the central issue dividing Catholics
and Protestants. The Jesuits fiercely argued for its importance to human salvation. Among others, they staged an open debate on the topic with Protestant
theologians in 1609 and wrote numerous polemical tracts to defend this central
doctrine of Catholic faith.[23] Citing the writings of the revered Church Fathers,
the Jesuits had recourse to typology to demonstrate the significance of the

8.3. Peter Paul Rubens, *The Last Supper*, 1620–1, oil on panel. *Modello* for ceiling painting in the Jesuit church in Antwerp. Seattle Art Museum, Seattle, gift of the Samuel H. Kress Foundation. Photo courtesy of the Seattle Art Museum.

Eucharist. For example, in his Eucharistic tract of 1601, Louis Richeôme examined fourteen Old and New Testament parallels to the Blessed Sacrament. He explained the effectiveness of these typologies in defending doctrine, stating, 'For when our mysteries are declared to us by figures and prophecies developed many ages ago, our faith is consolidated by the authority and certainty of things past.'[24]

In accordance with these traditions, Rubens's ceilings can be interpreted as aiding the post-Tridentine mission of teaching the doctrine of the Eucharist to

8.4. Peter Paul Rubens, *The Temptation of Christ*, 1620–1, oil on panel.
Modello for ceiling painting in the Jesuit church in Antwerp. Courtauld Institute Gallery,
Somerset House, London. Photo courtesy of the Courtauld Institute Gallery.

the laity. The Last Supper was the key event in Christ's life that served to justify
the Eucharist as a sacrament instituted by Christ himself. Rubens clearly emphasized this doctrinal point by eliminating all references to the betrayal of Judas
and focusing on Christ's offering of the bread to Peter. He further stressed the
Eucharistic significance of the scene by placing a bread basket and wine jug in
the immediate foreground. The typological ceiling paintings surrounding the
Last Supper also helped to persuade the viewer of the validity of the Blessed
Sacrament, for they established that Christ's institution of the Eucharist was

already foreshadowed in the actions of the Old Testament figures of Moses and Melchisedek.

Apart from promoting Catholic teaching on the Eucharist, the Jesuits were eager to bolster their own pastoral activities. More than any other contemporaneous order, the Jesuits advocated frequent reception of communion by the laity. This position may help explain why Rubens in the Jesuit ceiling departed from his usual representation of the Last Supper. In contrast to other depictions of the theme, where Christ is shown blessing the bread and the apostles are depicted as responding to the announcement of the prophesied betrayal, Rubens focused instead on the communion of St Peter. By depicting this rarely visualized moment of the story, Rubens followed an illustration of the Last Supper in the well-known Jesuit devotional tract by Jerónimo Nadal, *Adnotationes et meditationes in evangelia*, which was published in 1595.[25] By this choice, Rubens reminded the viewer that in administering communion the Jesuit fathers were continuing the labours of Christ and the apostles.

Saints: Orthodoxy, Eloquence, and Conversion

The attempt to support the Jesuit ministry visually was also the guiding principle behind the thematic choices represented in the hagiographic ceilings situated in the side aisles. The north sequence included four depictions of the Greek Church Fathers: St John Chrysostom, St Gregory of Nazianzus, St Basil, and St Athanasius. These alternated with four representations of early Christian female martyrs, while the central scene was devoted to the monogram of Christ (IHS). In the south aisle, the viewer encountered the four Latin Church Fathers – St Gregory the Great, St Ambrose, St Augustine, and St Jerome – together with four female martyrs and the monogram of the Virgin (MAR). Just as in the gallery ceilings, these paintings articulated a sophisticated rhetoric of pictorial relationships that orchestrated symbolic meaning across the actual space of the church. While the spectator's natural progression from west to east would compel him or her to connect images along a longitudinal axis, Rubens also intended his audience to discover parallels between ceilings positioned on opposite sides of the nave.

Representations of saints were a common component of Jesuit church programs and functioned in the first place as aids to devotion. In the scheme for the Gesù, for example, chapels featuring images of the life of Christ along with others containing images of the lives of the apostles provided stations for contemplative prayer.[26] Located in the aisles close to the confessional booths, the hagiographic scenes in the Antwerp church also offered the congregation a range of appropriate exempla on which to meditate. The emphasis on the veneration of saints corresponded to the Catholic belief that the exemplary deeds

8.5. Peter Paul Rubens, *St Gregory of Nazianzus,* 1620–1, oil on panel. *Modello* for
ceiling painting in the Jesuit church in Antwerp. Albright-Knox Art Gallery,
Buffalo, New York, Georges B. Mathews Fund, 1952.
Photo courtesy of the Albright-Knox Art Gallery.

of the saints could lead the beholder to a more pious life. As the Jesuit Jan David
observed, 'When we see in images how [the saints] have lived and how they
acted and suffered in the name of Christ, we are encouraged and moved in the
heart to do the same and to follow them in their virtuous life, so that we too may
arrive where they now are: in the glory of heaven.'[27]

As Margit Thøfner has shown, Rubens reminded the viewer of the spiritual
rewards of a life lived in imitation of the saints by employing a strong *di sotto in
su* perspective and by situating some of the saints in a heavenly realm.[28] The
visual affirmation of the role of the saints as mediators between heaven and earth
is especially strong in *St Gregory of Nazianzus* (fig. 8.5), for which a preparatory
sketch by Rubens survives. This ceiling represented the fourth-century bishop
of Constantinople pushing a devilish figure out of heaven. Looking up at this
image from below, the viewer was virtually harassed by the devil, as though Evil

incarnate were about to tumble into the aisle. The ceiling thus visually reinforced the message that a believer should follow the actions of the saints and resist the temptations of the devil in order to successfully quit the terrestrial world of demons for the glorious realm of heaven. In conveying this message, Rubens's ceiling functioned as a visual equivalent of a Jesuit sermon or meditation, which likewise depended on vivid language and dramatic exempla to inspire strong emotions in the worshipper and direct him or her to a life of virtue.[29]

The hagiographic imagery takes on further significance, however, when it is related to the Society's vocation and program of reform. The lives of the saints provided Catholic reformers with extensive evidence that could be used to legitimize their own mission and doctrinal teachings.[30] Recognizing the propagandistic value of saints' *vitae*, the Jesuit Heribert Rosweyde started a project of publishing a complete and authoritative hagiography that might function as the ultimate source for Catholic priests, preachers, and polemicists.[31] To strengthen their position in the face of Protestant attacks, the Jesuits relied especially on the lives and writings of saints of the early church.[32] In studying such sources, they followed the advice of Ignatius, who had declared in his 'Rules for Thinking with the Church' (an appendix to the *Spiritual Exercises*) that his fellow Jesuits should praise the theology of the Fathers, such as St Jerome, St Augustine, and St Gregory, since they had the ability 'to rouse the affections so that we are moved to love and serve God our Lord in all things.'[33] The same idea was expressed in a late sixteenth-century print by the Flemish engraver Hieronymus Wierix, *Christ Teaching the Doctors of the Church* (fig. 8.6), which showed Ignatius and two other Jesuits in the company of St Jerome, St Augustine, and St Gregory the Great. Both the Jesuits and the Church Fathers are pictured as writers inspired by the teachings of the young Christ, who appears in the cloud above. The image thus not only stresses the orthodoxy of Jesuit teaching, but also presents the early Jesuits as latter-day Church Fathers whose writings and educational goals were founded on the ideals and authority of Christ and the early church.

Rubens would have been familiar with the visual and textual discourse on hagiography. He had spent several years in Rome (1600–9) during a period when many decorative church programs featuring early Christian saints were being erected. In addition, he maintained close contact with Jesuit scholars in Flanders and Italy and designed various title-pages for their publications on the lives of the saints, including Rosweyde's *Lives of the Fathers* ('*t Vaders Boeck*) of 1617.

Particularly striking in Rubens's hagiographic cycle is that three of the four Greek Church Fathers are involved in battling enemies of the church, and five of the female martyrs are shown overcoming the persecution of pagan rulers and

8.6. Hieronymus Wierix, *Christ as a Child Teaching the Doctors of the Church*,
late sixteenth century, engraving. Metropolitan Museum of Art, New York,
Harris Brisbane Dick Fund, 1953. Photo courtesy of the Metropolitan Museum of Art.

oppressors. For example, the last three paintings of the north aisle, which
appeared closest to the entrance, all showed the towering presence of a triumphant saint toppling an adversary: St John Chrysostom orders the overturning of
the pagan statue of Empress Eudoxia; St Catherine, one of the female martyrs,
tramples Emperor Maxentius; and St Gregory of Nazianzus uses his crozier to
push a demon out of heaven. The cumulative effect of seeing this group in
sequence enhanced the already powerful impression of the individual deed of
each saint, thereby involving the viewer more directly in the narratives depicted.

To keep the viewer engaged, Rubens may also have intended a comic effect in
these works.[34] For example, in the ceiling painting *St Catherine* (fig. 8.7), which

8.7. Peter Paul Rubens, *St Catherine*, early 1620s, etching, counter proof, with pen indications by Rubens. Metropolitan Museum of Art, New York, Rogers Fund, 1922. Photo courtesy of the Metropolitan Museum of Art.

is recorded in a slightly altered state in an etching by Rubens himself, the perspective of the scene leads the eye upward along the saint's attractive body, encouraging the viewer to peek under her skirt.[35] This tantalizing effect would have been even more impressive in the original ceiling, which included the prostrate figure of Maxentius gazing upwards at St Catherine's voluptuous body. Similarly, Rubens manipulated the perspective of the ceiling paintings *St John Chrysostom* (fig. 8.8) and *St Gregory of Nazianzus* (fig. 8.5) so that the Eudoxia statue and the devilish figure seem about to fall on top of the viewer. Such visual tricks had a long history within illusionistic painting, and they lent the ceilings a sense of wit that would have appealed to a wide audience. Although such humour may seem out of place in a cycle of sacred polemical content, it would have been entirely in keeping with the diverse modes of Jesuit persuasion.[36] As various authors have demonstrated, the Jesuits sought to delight diverse audiences by employing the richest mode of rhetoric in their speeches and sermons.[37] Like Jesuit preachers, Rubens smartly enlivened the message of his ceilings by making full use of the rhetorical figure wit (*argutia*).

The message contained in this cluster of images speaks to the Jesuit vocation to battle heresy, which the Antwerp Jesuits in particular regarded as one of their primary tasks.[38] To convert the Protestant heretics from the northern provinces, the Jesuits actively participated in the Holland mission by sending numerous priests to heretical territories. They also directed their attention to the city of Antwerp itself, where non-observant Catholics and Protestant tourists from the north formed a ready target for their missionary activity. In light of this activity, the Church Fathers who had courageously defended Christian doctrine and aggressively confronted those who had deviated from orthodox teaching would come to serve as especially appropriate exemplars for the Jesuit order in the seventeenth century.[39]

St John Chrysostom, St Catherine, and St Gregory of Nazianzus were known not only for their fighting spirit, however. Indeed, their appeal to the Jesuits can also be ascribed to the extraordinary preaching talents with which they confronted their adversaries. St Catherine, for example, was famed for converting fifty philosophers to Christianity through erudite argumentation.[40] Eloquence and oratory were also the hallmarks of St John Chrysostom (the 'golden-mouthed') and Gregory of Nazianzus. The writings of these early Fathers served as a primary source of inspiration for the Jesuits, who considered preaching fundamental to their ministry.[41] Basing themselves on these models, the Jesuits utilized rich rhetorical language and employed the arguments of their predecessors to justify their own doctrinal positions.[42]

While the ingenious disposition of Rubens's ceilings encouraged viewers to discover visual and thematic conjunctions among successive images in a single

8.8. Jacob de Wit after Peter Paul Rubens, *St John Chrysostom*, c. 1718, watercolour.
Copy after ceiling painting in the Jesuit church in Antwerp. Courtauld Institute Gallery,
Somerset House, London. Photo courtesy of the Courtauld Institute Gallery.

aisle, it should also be noted that Rubens forged meaningful connections across
the nave. One of the most powerful examples of such lateral pairings are the
ceilings depicting St John Chrysostom and St Gregory the Great (fig. 8.9), which
occupied parallel positions in the north and in the south aisle respectively. This
charged juxtaposition, which has gone unnoticed to date, framed a larger interpretation that alluded to contemporary reform issues.

Standing on a flight of steps, St John Chrysostom (fig. 8.8) orders the taking
down of a statue of Empress Eudoxia. A dramatic diagonal is formed by the
thrust of his right hand that continues in his forward-bending body and ends
with his right leg at the foot of his throne. A young deacon, seen from the back,
strikes a complex turning pose that connects the standing bishop on the left
with the falling statue on the right. While the left side of the image is
dominated by signs of stability, the right side represents instability and loss of

8.9. Jacob de Wit after Peter Paul Rubens, *St Gregory the Great*, c. 1718, watercolour.
Copy after ceiling painting in the Jesuit church in Antwerp.
Photo courtesy of the Courtauld Institute Gallery, London.

authority. Here, five muscular men are using ropes and crowbars to overthrow Eudoxia's statue.

Although St John Chrysostom had criticized the erection of images in honour of the pagan Empress Eudoxia, there is no evidence that he actually ordered the removal of her statue. Instead of depicting a specific episode in the saint's life, Rubens is likely to have referenced St John Chrysostom's influential text *Homilies on the Statues*.[43] Composed in 387, the discourse describes an uprising of the people of Antioch, which culminated in an attack on imperial images and statues. This episode had great relevance to the current reform climate in Antwerp. Antwerp had experienced a wave of iconoclasm in the late sixteenth century, and the debate over the proper use of images in churches was one of the key issues dividing Catholics and Protestants.[44] By showing St John Chrysostom taking down a pagan idol, Rubens offered a painted rebuttal against the Protestant charge that Catholics engaged in idolatry.[45] By invoking St John Chrysostom's *Homilies*, the Jesuits thus propagated their own efforts to defend the proper use of images.

St John Chrysostom's removal of Eudoxia's statue fitted perfectly into the sequence of the north aisle that presented the Greek Church Fathers as active eradicators of heresy and representatives of the Church Militant. In contrast to their Greek counterparts, the Latin Church Fathers located in the south aisle are engaged in various states of contemplative prayer. For example, the ceiling panel of St Gregory, preserved in an eighteenth-century copy by Jacob de Wit (fig. 8.9), shows the saint in a heavenly realm enrapt in a vision of the Virgin and Child.

In the post-Tridentine period, St Gregory was celebrated for his devotion to the Virgin. Church reformers popularized several legends about St Gregory and miraculous images of the Virgin in an effort to counter Protestant attacks against the use of images and the notion that the Virgin had a role in salvation history. According to one legend, a Marian icon, which was kept at the monastery of Santo Gregorio Magno in Rome, began to speak when St Gregory prayed in front of it. In 1600–3 a new altar ensemble was erected in the monastery, consisting of Annibale Carracci's painting of Pope Gregory directing his pious gaze across the chapel towards the icon mounted on the opposite wall. Perhaps inspired by this commission, Rubens himself created an altarpiece for the Chiesa Nuova in Rome in 1606–8 that likewise showed St Gregory adoring a miraculous image of the Virgin.[46]

In his ceiling panel for the Antwerp church, Rubens did not show St Gregory adoring an icon, but experiencing a vision of the Virgin in heaven. This representation served to emphasize St Gregory's devotion to the Virgin and his testimony to the Assumption and the Immaculate Conception.[47] Appropriately, St Gregory's vision of the Virgin appeared right underneath the upper-level ceiling painting, the *Coronation of the Virgin*.[48] Together, these ceiling panels confirmed the doctrines of the Virgin's assumption and immaculate conception, which were supported by the Jesuits and contested by the Protestants.

The image of St Gregory takes on further significance when it is seen in conjunction with the image of St John Chrysostom. Both Church Fathers are shown in official garb and have directed their attention upward towards a female figure occupying the opposite side of the image. These female figures are presented as moral and stylistic opposites. The Virgin, rendered in brilliant red and blue, is placed in the clouds and surrounded by a radiant light. Eudoxia, on the other hand, topples downward and is removed from her architectural support. Not only does her unstable position contrast with the lofty presence of the Virgin, but her greyish white colours are in contrast to the saturated colours of the Virgin. Contemporary viewers are likely to have understood this antithetical pairing as symbolizing the triumph of Christianity over paganism, which, in turn, signified the current triumph of Catholicism over Protestantism.[49] Thus, the Jesuits consciously placed their own actions as true defenders of orthodoxy in the revered tradition of the Church Fathers. More specifically, the ceiling panels of St John Chrysostom and St Gregory proclaimed the active and contemplative strands of the Jesuit mission: to convert Protestants and disbelievers and to guide the faithful Christian towards union with God through meditation and spiritual exercises.

The Jesuits' consciousness of themselves as latter-day Church Fathers further-ing the mission of Christ and the apostles was not only implied by Rubens's iconographic choices, but also lent visual affirmation by the carefully choreo-graphed relationship between the Jesuit altarpieces and the ceiling paintings. As is clear from Neeffs's picture, Rubens's high altarpieces dedicated to Ignatius (fig. 8.10) and Francis Xavier visually dominated the interior. Set within a monumental altar frame designed by Rubens and executed by Hans van Mildert, the altarpieces could be alternated by means of a pulley system, which allowed the paintings to be shown in accordance with the liturgical calendar. This dramatic and theatrical presentation of the altarpieces belied the status of Ignatius and Francis, who, by the time of the commissioning in 1617–18, had not yet been canonized by the church. Indeed, the depiction of Ignatius and Francis on the high altar breached church protocol, which ruled that men and women could not be depicted as saints before they were officially canonized.

With little visual tradition to draw upon, Rubens relied on recent biographies to invent an iconography that elevated the standing of the Jesuit figures.[50] In the first altarpiece, the artist represented Ignatius as a saint with a halo celebrating the mass and performing various miracles, such as freeing a possessed woman from demons. Francis Xavier is depicted in his role as apostle to the East, curing the sick and converting non-believers. Behind him, a ray of divine light effects the fall of idols from a pagan temple, a reference to a story recounted by his biographer in which Francis encouraged recent converts to raze an old pagan temple. Several authors have convincingly demonstrated that the rhetorical power of Rubens's altarpieces constituted a propagandistic argument to aid the Jesuit campaign for the canonization of both men. It has generally been over-looked, however, that the spatial and pictorial ambience of the altarpieces also served to enhance their visual and political impact.

Visitors entering the church would have seen the illustrious Jesuits on the high altar in a direct line with the ceiling paintings of the aisles and galleries. They would also have recognized the actions of Ignatius and Francis Xavier as continuing the virtues of Christ and the early Fathers. In showing Ignatius

8.10. Peter Paul Rubens, *The Miracles of St Ignatius of Loyola*, 1617–18,
oil on canvas. Kunsthistorisches Museum, Vienna.
Photo courtesy of the Kunsthistorisches Museum.

standing before an altar celebrating the mass, for example, Rubens emphasized that the founder of the order was implementing the very ritual that was inaugurated by Christ at the Last Supper. Moreover, Ignatius is represented as a mediator between heaven and earth and as purifying the church of demonic forces, a clear reference to St Gregory of Nazianzus, who was depicted as casting a devilish figure out of heaven. Francis Xavier's actions of preaching, eradicating heresy, and opposing the worship of idols likewise reiterated the heroic deeds of the Church Fathers as they were represented in the aisles. In coordinating altarpieces and ceiling paintings, then, Rubens created a tripartite program that showed Ignatius and Francis as the legitimate successors of Christ and the early Church.

Rubens's program for the church of St Ignatius in Antwerp provides valuable evidence of the way in which the Jesuits used works of art to further their own interests and pastoral goals. A reconstruction of the program within its original environment suggests that Rubens's ceilings and altarpieces were conceived as an integrated statement that served to involve the beholder in meditative practice and instruct diverse audiences in doctrines contested during the Counter Reformation. By creating a pictorial network of inter-compositional connections, Rubens invited the viewer to lavish meditative attention on Old and New Testament narratives and the lives of the early saints, and, at the same time, offered a visual framework that could substantiate the polemical message of a public sermon. Rubens thus devised a program that simultaneously engaged loyal followers and targeted wayward believers, who had left the Catholic church in the wake of the religious upheavals. Apart from fulfilling these meditative and didactic functions, Rubens's concerted imagery also served to bolster the Jesuits' public image. With very little history of their own to build upon, the Jesuits presented themselves in the Antwerp church as preachers, fighters of heresy, defenders of images, guardians of orthodoxy, and promoters of frequent communion, who actively and dynamically continued the ministry and vocation of Christ and the early church. Capitalizing on the rhetorical power of Rubens's images, which so directly implicated the viewer, the Jesuits ensured that their mission would triumph over that of all other religious institutions in Antwerp, with which they fiercely competed for public attention.

NOTES

I am very grateful to Egbert Haverkamp-Begemann, David Freedberg, and Ivan Gaskell for their insightful comments and to Barbara Haeger and Gregory Galligan for their helpful remarks on an earlier draft of this article. My research was sponsored by a

Robert H. and Clarice Smith fellowship from the Center for Advanced Studies in the Visual Arts, National Gallery of Art, Washington.

1 On the ceilings, see John Rupert Martin, *The Ceiling Paintings for the Jesuit Church in Antwerp* (London, 1968); and Julius Held, *The Oil Sketches of Peter Paul Rubens*, vol. 1 (Princeton, 1980), pp. 33–62. On the altarpieces, see Graham Smith, 'Rubens' Altargemälde des Hl. Ignatius von Loyola und des Hl. Franz Xaver für die Jesuiten-kirche Antwerpen,' *Jahrbuch der kunsthistorischen Sammlungen in Wien* 65 (1969): 39–60; and Frans Baudouin, 'De datering van de twee schilderijen van Rubens voor het hoofdaltaar van de Antwerpse Jezuïetenkerk en enkele aantekeningen over Hans van Mildert,' in *Miscellanea Josef Duverger*, vol. 1 (Ghent, 1968), pp. 301–22.

2 The notable exceptions are Christine Göttler, '"Actio" in Peter Paul Rubens' Hochaltarbildern für die Jesuitenkirche in Antwerpen,' in *Barocke Inszenierung*, ed. Joseph Imorde, Fritz Neumeyer, and Tristan Weddigen (Berlin, 1999), pp. 10–31; and Margit Thøfner, '"The Bearing of Images": Femininity, Sovereignty, and Religion in the Spanish Netherlands, 1599–1635,' dissertation, University of Sussex, 1996, pp. 115–54. Neither author discusses the program in its entirety, however.

3 For the role of Jesuit imagery in reinforcing the message of ministry, see Walter S. Melion, 'Artifice, Memory, and *Reformatio* in Hieronymus Natalis's *Adnotationes et meditationes in evangelia*,' *Renaissance and Reformation* 22 (1998): 5–34. I am very grateful to Walter Melion for drawing my attention to the importance of the Jesuit vocation for Rubens's ceilings. On the history of the Jesuits in Flanders, see Ponc. *Hist.*; Jeanine de Landtsheer, '*Historia Domus Antverpiensis*. De Jezuïeten te Antwerpen voor het Prille Begin tot het Eerste Kwart van de Zeventiende Eeuw,' *De zeventiende eeuw* 14 (1998): 15–26; and Marie Juliette Marinus, *De Contra-reformatie te Antwerpen (1585–1676). Kerkelijk Leven in een Grootstad* (Brussels, 1995), pp. 155–171.

4 For the church's building history, see Joseph Braun, *Die belgischen Jesuitenkirchen. Ein Beitrag zur Geschichte des Kampfes zwischen Gotik und Renaissance* (Freiburg im Breisgau, 1907), pp. 151–6; and Joris Snaet, 'De Bouwprojecten voor de Antwerpse Jezuïetenkerk,' in *Bellissimi ingegni, grandissimo splendore. Studies over de religieuze architectuur in de Zuidelijke Nederlanden tijdens de 17de eeuw*, ed. Krista de Jonge et al. (Leuven, 2000), pp. 43–66.

5 Koen Ottenheym, 'De correspondentie tussen Rubens en Huygens over architectuur (1635–'40),' *Bulletin Koninklijke Nederlandse Oudheidkundige Bond* 96 (1997): 1–11.

6 For the Jesuit involvement in the restoration of early Christian monuments, see Evonne Levy, '"A Noble Medley and Concert of Materials and Artifice": Jesuit Church Interiors in Rome, 1567–1700,' in *Saint, Site, and Sacred Strategy: Ignatius, Rome, and Jesuit Urbanism*, ed. Thomas Lucas (Vatican City, 1990), pp. 46–61.

7 O'M. *First*, pp. 17–18, 51–90, 134–5, 284–7, 303–6, 321–7.

8 On feast days, mass was celebrated at four separate altars in the Jesuit church. See Marinus, *De Contrareformatie*, p. 170.

9 On the presence of Protestants in the Catholic Antwerp, see ibid., pp. 61–2, 69, 161–2, 164.

10 Philip De Mesmaecker, Liesbet Haghenbeek, and Griet Van Opstal, 'Oratoria in de jezuïetenkerken van de Zuidelijke Nederlanden. Een fenomeen eigen aan de Contrareformatie,' in *Bellissimi ingegni*, ed. de Jonge et al., pp. 79–90.

11 On the use of galleries in German Jesuit churches, see Jeffrey Chipps Smith, *Sensuous Worship: Jesuits and the Art of the Early Catholic Reformation in Germany* (Princeton, 2002), pp. 109, 122, 124–7. I thank the author for discussing this topic with me.

12 For a transcription of the contract, see Martin, *The Jesuit Ceilings*, pp. 213–19.

13 Since the nave of the church was restored in the eighteenth century according to the seventeeth-century plan, today's experience of the building can serve as a reliable indication of original viewing conditions. This experience confirms that the original ceilings would have been legible from the ground floor.

14 *The Canons of the Council of Trent*, trans. H.J. Schroeder (Rockford, IL, 1978), pp. 17–18.

15 Louis Richeôme, *Le pèlerin de Lorete* (Paris, 1607), p. 170.

16 Louis Richeôme, *Tableaux sacrez des figures mystiques du tres Auguste Sacrament & Sacrifice de l'Eucharistie* (Paris, 1601), p. 17.

17 Several authors have drawn attention to the devotional role of works of art in Jesuit churches. See, for example, Jeffrey Chipps Smith, 'The Art of Salvation in Bavaria,' in O'M. *Jes. Cult.*, pp. 568–99.

18 Although I see general similarities between Rubens's upper-level program and Ignatius's *Spiritual Exercises*, I am not convinced that the program's singular role was to act as a visual counterpart to Ignatius's text. Instead, I believe the program's function was multivalent.

19 Held, *The Oil Sketches*, pp. 36–7. That this interpretation still held currency in the sixteenth and seventeeth centuries is evidenced by numerous Jesuit commentaries. See, for example, Franciscus Costerus's sermon on Luke 18 in *Catholiicke Sermoonen op de Evangelien van de Sondaghen naer Sinxen tot den Advent* (Antwerp, 1598), p. 114.

20 Daniel J. O'Connor, 'The Stone the Builders Rejected: Psalm 118 (117):22 in Carvaggio's Deposition,' *Irish Theological Quarterly* 1 (1994): 2–13.

21 On the didactic role of sacred art in the post-Tridentine period, see Pamela Jones, *Federico Borromeo and the Ambrosiana: Art Patronage and Reform in Seventeenth-Century Milan* (Cambridge, 1993), pp. 96–167.

22 *The Canons of the Council of Trent*, trans. Schroeder, p. 216.

23 Cynthia Lawrence, 'Before the *Raising of the Cross*: The Origins of Rubens's Earliest Antwerp Altarpieces,' *Art Bulletin* 81 (1999): 276.

24 Louis Richeôme, *Tableaux sacrez*, p. 16.

25 Hieronymus Natalis [Jerónimo Nadal], *Adnotationes et meditationes in evangelia* (Antwerp, 1595), pp. 246–250, plate 202.

26 Howard Hibbard, 'Ut picturae sermones: The First Painted Decorations of the Gesù,' in *Baroque Art: The Jesuit Contribution*, ed. Rudolf Wittkower et al. (New York, 1972), pp. 29–50; and Gauvin Alexander Bailey, 'The Jesuits and Painting in Italy, 1550–1690: The Art of Catholic Reform,' in *Saints and Sinners: Caravaggio and the Baroque Image,* ed. Franco Mormando (Boston, 1999), exhib. cat., pp. 151–78.

27 Joannes David [Jan David], *Den Bloemhof der Kerckelicker Cerimonien* (Antwerp, 1607) p. 34.

28 Thøfner, 'The Bearing of Images,' pp. 126–7.

29 On exempla in post-Tridentine preaching, see Frederick McGinness, *Right Thinking and Sacred Oratory in Counter Reformation Rome* (Princeton, 1995), pp. 99–104.

30 Simon Ditchfield, *Liturgy, Sanctity, and History in Tridentine Italy* (Cambridge, 1995), pp. 117–34, especially 125–7.

31 One of the first publications was devoted to the desert fathers. See Heribert Rosweyde, *Vitae patrum* (Antwerp, 1615). A Dutch translation appeared two years later.

32 Dominique Bertrand, 'The Society of Jesus and the Church Fathers in the Sixteenth and Seventeenth Century,' in *Reception of the Church Fathers in the West: From the Carolingians to the Maurists,* ed. Irena Backus (Leiden, 1997), pp. 889–950.

33 O'M. *First*, p. 260.

34 I am grateful to Graham Larkin for discussing the topic of irony in Rubens's paintings with me.

35 In comparison with the drawn copies of the now lost ceiling painting of St Catherine, it appears, Rubens's etching gives a reliable impression of the figure of the saint. He did, however, introduce a few changes in the setting, by eliminating the figure of Maxentius, shifting the position of the wheel, and placing St Catherine on a cloud.

36 Göttler has likewise drawn attention to the comic character of the high altarpieces for the Jesuit church. See 'Actio in Peter Paul Rubens,' pp. 25–7.

37 See Marc Fumaroli, 'Définition et description: Scholastique et rhétorique chez les jésuites des XVI et XVIIe siècles,' *Travaux de linguistique et littérature* 18 (1980): 37–48; and Melion, 'Artifice, Memory and *Reformatio*,' pp. 5–34.

38 Martin has also observed the anti-heretical character of these scenes. See *The Jesuit Ceilings*, pp. 202–4.

39 An interesting parallel to this is Rubens's program for St Michael's in Antwerp, which presented the Norbertines as continuing the anti-heretical actions of their twelfth-century founder. See Barbara Haeger, 'Abbot Van der Sterre and St. Michael's Abbey: The Restoration of Its Church, Its Images, and Its Place in Antwerp,' in *Sponsors of the Past: Flemish Art and Patronage, 1500–1700*, ed. Hans Vlieghe et al. (Turnhout, 2005), pp. 157–79.

40 The Jesuits staged various plays dedicated to St Catherine that emphasized her Christian *sapientia* and *eloquentia*. See Barbara Bauer, *Jesuitische 'Ars Rhetorica' im Zeitalter der Glaubenskämpfe* (Frankfurt, 1986), pp. 333–40.

41 The other Church Fathers represented in the program were also known for their preaching talents. Rubens emphasized this aspect by showing St Ambrose with a beehive, a reference to the legend that bees alighted on his mouth when he was in the cradle.

42 McGinness, *Right Thinking*, pp. 15–17, 43–4.

43 The importance of St John Chrysostom's *Homilies* for an understanding of Rubens's ceiling panel is rightly pointed out by Martin, *The Jesuit Ceiling*, pp. 203–4.

44 David Freedberg, 'The Hidden God: Image and Interdiction in the Netherlands in the Sixteenth Century,' *Art History* 5 (1982): 133–53.

45 For the debate on images, see Steven F. Ostrow, *Art and Spirituality in Counter-Reformation Rome: The Sistine and Pauline Chapels in S. Maria Maggiore* (Cambridge, 1996), p. 234.

46 On the relationship between Rubens's Chiesa Nuova altarpiece and Annibale Carracci's ensemble for Santo Gregorio Magno, see Ilse von zur Mühlen, 'Nachtridentische Bildauffassungen. Cesare Baronio und Rubens' Gemälde für S. Maria in Valicella in Rom,' *Münchner Jahrbuch der bildenden Kunst* 41 (1990): 23–50, especially 34–8.

47 Significantly, an antiphon attributed to St Gregory was used to celebrate the feast of the Assumption. In this text, St Gregory glorified the Virgin's role as heavenly intercessor and co-redemptrix (Ostrow, *Art and Spirituality*, p. 168).

48 Martin was the first to observe the vertical correspondence between *St Gregory* and the *Coronation of the Virgin*. See Martin, *The Jesuit Ceiling*, p. 204.

49 The juxtaposition of the heavenly vision of the Virgin and the pagan statue of Eudoxia also raises the question of the efficacy of images in Catholic worship, an important topic that is beyond the scope of this study.

50 On Rubens's invention of a new icongraphic formula, see Göttler, 'Actio in Peter Paul Rubens,' pp. 11–31; and Christine Boeckl, 'Plague Imagery as a Metaphor for Heresy in Rubens' *The Miracles of Saint Francis Xavier*,' *Sixteenth Century Journal* 27 (1996): 979–95.

9 / Art in the Service of God: The Impact of the Society of Jesus on the Decorative Arts in Portugal

NUNO VASSALLO E SILVA

In this article I examine the art produced in Portugal under the patronage of the Society of Jesus. Particular emphasis will be placed on the so-called decorative arts, especially the metalwork in silver and gold that was used in the celebration of the Eucharist.

The history of art in Portugal cannot be recounted without underlining the central role played by the Society of Jesus. From 1540, when the Society reached Portugal – under the patronage of King João III – until 1759, when the Jesuits were expelled, they were among the leading patrons of art. As is well known, the Jesuits' impact was due not merely to the quality and quantity of the work they commissioned, but, above all, to the innovative role they assigned to the arts, one that soon spread beyond the Society to influence all religious art in Portugal.

As José Eduardo Horta Correia has accurately noted, two major and novel aspects of the Society would have a direct influence on subsequent artistic programs in Portugal. First, the order is fundamentally a priestly one, centred on the altar, the confessional, and the pulpit. Second, the followers of St Ignatius of Loyola considered education of particular importance and had adopted the pedagogical achievements and educational reforms of humanism.[1] Both these aspects of the Society meant that art would become a sophisticated tool in the teaching of doctrine.

The Glory of the Eucharist: Wood Carving, Tiles, Textiles, and Furniture

A visit to the church of the Casa Professa of São Roque in Lisbon (built 1555–73), which includes the essential elements that enable us to speak of Jesuit architectural design and has a significant number of works of art, offers an overview of the Jesuits' use of the decorative arts in Portugal. In contrast to other

Jesuit colleges and churches, São Roque and its works of art escaped almost unscathed after the expulsion of the Jesuits in 1759. The first pieces to be lost were those made of precious metals, which were unable to withstand the depredations of human avarice, specifically the war tax imposed by the French during their first invasion of Portugal in 1808, and again following the triumph of the liberal forces in 1834. None the less, some reliquaries did manage to survive.

The remaining altars, carvings, tiles, hardstone inlays, reliquaries, balustrades, and sacristy furnishings all combine to create a unique and visually striking atmosphere. It is difficult (if not impossible) to gain a complete understanding of or to contextualize this concentration of the visual arts, since it is an authentic example of the 'total work of art,' or *Gesamtkunstwerk*. As such, however, the church with its contents can be used to establish parallels with other works of art in other churches built by the Society in Portugal and the Portuguese colonies. Using a little artistic licence, we can claim that it allows us to 'visualize' the art described in the inventories of the Jesuit colleges drawn up in 1759, when the Society was expelled from Portugal. These inventories, now at the Arquivo do Tribunal de Contas (Public Accounts Archive) in Lisbon, are the only source available for any attempted reconstitution of the interiors and decoration of Jesuit churches. All the items described share rich and varied decoration and materials, demonstrating a magnificent use of ornament and a high level of decorative sophistication under the Jesuits.

Wood Carving

The carved altars in the Jesuit churches in Portugal almost all date from after the first quarter of the seventeenth century.

The large altarpiece in the main chapel at São Roque was produced between 1625 and 1628, some fifty years after the church was built (fig. 9.1). The Late Renaissance decorative grammar, later copied in many Jesuit churches, could lead an unwary observer to think the altarpiece was from an earlier period.

The pairs of Corinthian-composite columns at the outer sides, the tondos, and the niches holding figures of the Society's saints suggest that some artistic options reflected on the exterior stone facades were projected into the interior of the church. Altarpieces of this kind cannot legitimately be claimed to have originated with the Jesuits, since earlier examples are known, but there can be no doubt that the Jesuits knew how to maximize their effect so as to heighten the importance of their saints and to emphasize the sacrarium.

Baltazar Telles's description, published in 1645, lists the altarpiece's components and the suitably adapted classical roots that would be recognized by everyone: 'It is the most delightful and imposing altarpiece in Lisbon; it consists

9.1. Altarpiece of the main chapel at São Roque, Lisbon, 1625–8.
Photo courtesy of Museu de S. Roque.

of two sections and their respective finishes, with several columns, whose fluted shafts are finely worked, and there are magnificent Corinthian capitals and architraves on the columns. The friezes are carved in good Roman style, and the ornamental cornices are in fine relief. There are fluted niches between the columns, which are also fluted, and their half-domes are decorated with fleurons, while the bases have curious borders with excellent relief foliage and fruit.'[2]

In addition to the sculptures, which perhaps represent the chief innovation introduced by the Jesuits, the São Roque altarpiece has a tribune in the centre for displaying the Blessed Sacrament. Although the tribune was uncovered only during the Corpus Christi celebration, its central importance justifies the altar's entire structure and the decorative magnificence of the classical architectural orders, which were deemed the most appropriate.[3] Seven large canvases by seventeenth-century Portuguese masters, showing scenes from the life of Christ that marked the liturgical calendar, covered the tribune during the year, creating a spectacular setting that has - surprisingly – survived until today.

The same model would be used – albeit without the same scenographic impact – in other altarpieces at São Roque, namely, those in the Chapel of the Holy Family, built in 1634, and the Chapel of St Francis Xavier, presumably from the same date. Both altarpieces reveal exceptional levels of architectural and decorative sophistication. Churches outside São Roque also adopted this model. Two examples are the main chapel of the church at the Colégio do Espírito Santo, Evora, and the church of the former Colégio das Onze Mil Virgens, Coimbra, founded in 1542, which became the city's cathedral after the expulsion of the Jesuits in 1759.[4]

The main altarpieces in the cathedral's side chapels (of the Blessed Sacrament, St Ignatius, St Anthony, the Resurrection, and Our Lady of the Immaculate Conception) were produced between 1640 and 1670, and all adopt the model from the Casa Professa in Lisbon (fig. 9.2)[5] – confirmation that successful models were consistently adopted. Rather than establishing an artistic canon, the Jesuits took the highly practical approach of using tried and true formulas, a feature commonly found in Jesuit artistic programs. Significantly, there is an enormous contrast between the decoration of Jesuit churches and the *estilo chão*, or 'plain style,' to quote George Kubler, of the architecture that flourished under the same order.[6] The eminently functional architecture contrasts with the wealth of the interior decoration, but only in formal, not symbolic, terms.

The influence of São Roque is also perfectly evident at the Colégio de São João Evangelista, Funchal (Madeira). Building work on the college started in 1599, and the result is an eloquent homage to the decorative options used in the Lisbon church.[7] Both the carving and the 'decorative paintings,' produced using inlaid marble and patterned tiles, attempt to re-create the visual experience of São Roque (fig. 9.3).

9.2. Chapel of St Ignatius at Coimbra Cathedral (former Colégio das Onze Mil Virgens), Coimbra, 1640–70. From Robert C. Smith, *A talha em Portugal* (Lisbon, 1962).

9.3. Altarpiece of the main chapel at the church of the Colégio de São João Evangelista, Funchal (Madeira). From Smith, *A talha*.

The chapel in the Colégio Jesuítico on Ilha de Moçambique, on the far western border of the Portuguese State of India, confirms that the Lisbon model spread through the Portuguese colonial empire well after the end of the seventeenth century.[8]

The structure of the Jesuit altarpieces would be adapted to produce reliquaries in ebony and gilded bronze. These altarpiece-style pieces had flanking columns and lintels, the form of which varied according to fashion, surmounted with pediments. Some of these reliquaries, which look like small altarpieces, can be seen in the collection at São Roque, as will be shown below.

The eighteenth century saw the art of gilded wood-carving in Portugal reach one of its high points. The Jesuits adopted the models found in the rest of Portugal's churches, carved in the so-called national style, as can be seen in the large altarpiece of the main chapel at the Colégio de Coimbra (c. 1698) and in those of the church's colossal transept chapels, flanked by shrines with reliquaries (fig. 9.4). The altarpieces of these chapels feature the characteristic Solomonic columns decorated with plant motifs as well as putti and birds, supporting an entablature under concentric arches that crown the altar. The keystone is decorated with a spectacular medallion bearing the arms of the Society, flanked by angels and surmounted by the royal crown. The Coimbra work, which naturally includes, in lateral niches, the iconographic constant of figures depicting the Society's most important saints, is a close copy of the altarpiece produced shortly before for the Colégio de Jesus in Elvas (1692).[9] The same 'national style' would also be adopted at São Roque, specifically for the new altarpieces built in the last decades of the seventeenth century. The chapels of Our Lady of Doctrine (1688–90), of the Assumption of Our Lady (c. 1690) – now the Chapel of the Blessed Sacrament – and of Our Lady of Piety (1709) are all examples.

The erudite style of the Jesuits' early projects was diluted in the eighteenth century, as it blended with the large-scale Portuguese production of altarpieces, apparently losing its individuality. But its special character was preserved in the distinctive iconography of the Society and its saints. Images of St Ignatius and St Francis Xavier were a constant presence, their numbers followed by those of images of St Aloysius Gonzaga and St Francisco Borja.

Tiles

Apart from those at São Roque, the Jesuits are not known to have commissioned any tiles in the sixteenth century. The panels on the walls of the lower choir are especially noteworthy (fig. 9.5). Produced in Lisbon and dated 1595, the majolica painting combined the symbols of Christ's passion with the arms of the Society to produce a magnificent decorative effect. [10]

9.4. Transept chapels in the Colégio das Onze Mil Virgens, Coimbra, c. 1700.
From Smith, *A talha*.

9.5. Tile panels in the church of São Roque, Lisbon, dated 1595.
Photo courtesy of Museu de S. Roque.

Tiles became a common decorative element in seventeenth-century Portuguese churches, specifically those using the 'diamond-tip' pattern, which was
often commissioned from workshops in Seville when they were not made in
Portugal. Chequered black and white tiles were also used to cover large areas
and create an appealing aesthetic effect that maintained a sense of sobriety and
decorative grandeur.

The Jesuits did make some significant commissions of tiles in the eighteenth
century, for the two Lisbon colleges of Santo Antão and Arroios. As with the
altarpieces, the iconography used causes the tiles to stand out among the other
decorative features found in Portuguese churches of that period.

The Colégio de Santo Antão, built in 1579 to replace the oldest Jesuit house in
the world, has a small panel of seventeenth-century polychrome tiles showing an
altar between the figures of St Ignatius and St Francis Xavier (fig. 9.6).[11] The
college's main hall, long ago converted into a hospital, has several allegories of
the subjects taught, especially in the so-called sphere class, which focused on
astronomy and cosmography. There are eight panels of blue and white tiles
showing 'Archimedes' Mirror at the Siege of Syracuse,' as well as allegories of
Geometry, Optics, Geography, Geometry, Ballistics, and Astronomy. Portugal

9.6. Tile panel *St Ignatius and St Francis Xavier*, Portugal, first quarter of the seventeenth century, Hospital de São José (former Colégio de Santo Antão), Lisbon. Photo courtesy of Luís Pavão.

had a colonial empire, and there is also a panel showing ships flying the Portuguese flag and a transcription of the first line of Camões's *Lusiads*, 'On seas ne'er before sailed.'[12]

A depiction of the subjects taught by the Jesuits also appears on the panels at the Colégio do Espírito Santo in Evora, which was founded in 1559 and became the first Jesuit university, teaching mathematics, geography, and physics as well as science and military architecture. The blue and white tile panels, mostly produced in the 1740s, depict the sciences but also include allegories of literary genres in a unique iconographic summary of the Jesuit teaching program.[13]

The Colégio de Arroios, founded in 1705 by Catherine of Bragança, was established to train Jesuit priests for the missions in India. The tiled imagery shows the lives of three Jesuit saints: Ignatius, at the entrance, and Francis Xavier and Stanislas Kostka, in what was formerly the main hall. These pieces are among the most important in the Jesuit pantheon, second only to the series on the lives of Ignatius and Francis Xavier produced by André Reinoso and Domingos da Cunha, or 'Cabrinha,' in the first half of the seventeenth century.

The Arroios series depicting the life of Ignatius, attributed to the Lisbon tile painter Bartolomeu Antunes and symbolically located at the entrance to the

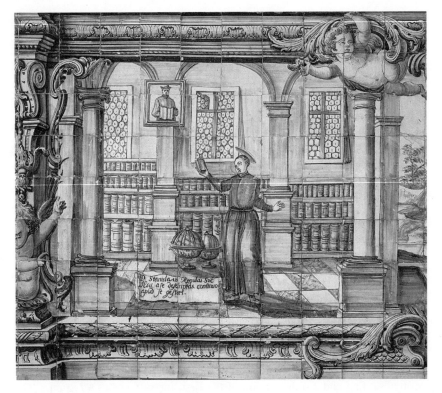

9.7. Tile panel from the series *Life of St Stanislas Kostka*, Portugal, second quarter of the eighteenth century, Colégio de Arroios, Lisbon. Photo courtesy of Luís Pavão.

college, originally consisted of five panels.[14] Four have survived: the *Apparition of St Peter to St Ignatius*, the *Gift of Chastity to Our Lady*, the *Conversion in the Frozen Water*, and *Giving Clothes to a Poor Man*. Significantly, more than a hundred years later these works were followed by a series of images produced by Jean-Baptiste Barbé after drawings by Rubens for the *Vita Beati P. Ignatii Loiolae Societatis Jesu*, published in 1609.

Six scenes from the lives of St Francis Xavier and St Stanislas Kostka are depicted along the walls of what was probably the main hall, on the first and main floor of the college (fig. 9.7).[15] The tiles date from the second quarter of the eighteenth century and are part of the so-called *grande produção*. Almost all the stages in the two saints' life stories are accompanied by captions in Latin. But the series on the life of Francis Xavier, one source for which was probably Dominique Bouhours's *Vie de Saint François Xavier*, also includes a small panel without a caption showing a baptismal ceremony – perhaps evidence of how popular the saint was in Portugal.[16]

Textiles

A consideration of today's churches gives us no real sense of the important role once played by textiles. As well as being exceptionally decorative, textiles provided colour as a visual reflection of the liturgical calendar.

The use of textiles in Jesuit churches went beyond the liturgical vestments worn by the celebrants of the mass to include items, some of them very large, that decorated the chapels; some of these, especially those used on the most solemn occasions, were also richly embroidered.

Besides altar frontals, there were curtains, canopies, and wall- and door-hangings, as well as tapestries and even precious carpets. The significance of textiles was so great that the ceiling of São Roque, painted after 1588 by Francisco Venegas and in the early seventeenth century by Amaro do Vale, shows painted *trompe l'oeil* tapestries depicting biblical scenes: 'Gathering the Manna,' 'Jewish Easter,' 'Abraham Meeting Melchisedek,' and 'The Sacrifice of Isaac.'[17]

Owing to the fragility of the materials – among the decorative arts, textiles have always suffered the worst ravages of time – few pieces from before the eighteenth century have survived.

Portugal has preserved, once again at the church and museum of São Roque, an almost complete seventeenth-century set of paraments produced at Portuguese workshops, evidence of Jesuit commissions for textiles. This set of ten altar frontals is richly embroidered with gold, silver, and silk and decorated in places with pieces of glass cut and set to imitate precious stones (figs 9.8, 9.9). Its grammar is late mannerist, with rich cartouches and 'ferroneries' in the earlier pieces, and baroque-style entwining plant motifs in those from the second half of the seventeenth century.[18]

Many of the carpets that covered the chapel floors at São Roque were made in the Far East, as was an almost complete set of polychrome silk and gold vestments, probably from China, for use at mass. It consists of two dalmatics, one chasuble, one chalice veil, one pall, two stoles, and three maniples. The inventories record the pieces from at least 1695, when they are described as 'vestments in Indian satin and yellow cloth.'[19]

The altar frontal that belonged to the Cotovia novitiate, founded in Lisbon in 1619, was another Asian piece produced in China, probably in Macao.[20] The Society's arms are the only religious symbol found on the embroidered silk decoration, which also shows dogs of Fo and gazelles. The piece now belongs to

9.8. Altar frontal, first quarter of the seventeenth century, Museu de São Roque, Lisbon.
Photo courtesy of Museu de S. Roque.

the Museu da Ciência of the University of Lisbon, formerly the Nobles' College, which was built on the site of the original Jesuit novitiate.[21]

As indicated below in the sections on furniture and jewellery, the Funchal church houses some rare examples of the last Jesuit commissions before the expulsion. Despite their poor condition, a pair of door-curtains embroidered with the Society's arms was still in use until recently. The depiction of the arms of the Society under the Portuguese crown is similar to that on the coronas of the monumental transept chapels in the church at the Coimbra college. The Museu de Arte Sacra in Funchal has a set of paraments, consisting of a chasuble, maniple, stole, pallium, veil, and altar frontal, all in red damask with gold embroidery, that is believed to have come from the Jesuit college.[22]

Furniture

The chest in São Roque's sacristy is by far the most important surviving piece of furniture commissioned by the Jesuits. Made around 1600 and recorded in the church inventories as from 1604, it has a broad rosewood surface on an oak carcass. The doors and drawers are decorated with geometrical ivory fillets the

9.9. Altar frontal, last quarter of the seventeenth century, Museu de São Roque, Lisbon.
Photo courtesy of Museu de S. Roque.

great sobriety of which produces a superb decorative effect (fig. 9.10). The decoration cannot be described as characteristically Jesuit, since it is also found on other Portuguese furniture of the period. But the pieces with similar decoration are smaller in size, and there are no known similar chests.

The balustrades in São Roque's chapels also reveal the use of precious ornamental woods, demonstrating a taste that to some extent can be linked to the Jesuits. The ebony balustrades in the Chapel of Our Lady of Doctrine have 'waves and twists,' produced by incising highly decorative parallel, gently undulating flutes. Many similar pieces from the period are known. The side doors of the same chapel are inlaid with precious woods that recall the furniture produced in Portuguese India. The doors show the iconography of the Confraternity of Christian Doctrine, namely, a missal and a rosary, an exceptional piece of late seventeenth-century Portuguese marquetry.

Unfortunately, except for some chests, almost all the furniture of the Jesuit colleges has been lost.

One of the last major Jesuit works commissioned from Portuguese joiners is in the sacristy of the Funchal college: a chest with an upright back in gilded wood and paintings on canvas. According to Rui Carita, who has conducted an

9.10. Chest, c. 1600, sacristy at São Roque, Lisbon.
Photo courtesy of Museu de S. Roque.

exhaustive study of the college, it can be dated to 1730. The sacristy also contains three magnificent wall wardrobes framed in inlaid polychrome marble and crowned with the Society's insignia. The doors and inner panelling are in jacaranda. The wardrobes display a synthesis of materials and techniques that recalls the Chapel of Our Lady of Doctrine at São Roque.

The chests and large wardrobes in the Bom Jesus sacristy, in Old Goa, India, are the finest achievements of Jesuit art in the Portuguese Empire. Produced in the 1650s and 1660s by exclusively local craftsmen, these pieces are made of wood inlaid with precious woods and ivory. They belong, however, to a different chapter in the history of the decorative arts.[23]

Precious Celebrations: Gold and Silverware

The pieces in gold and silver produced for the Jesuits, particularly those related to divine worship and the Eucharist, reflect an era when the cult of the Blessed Sacrament, actively spread by the Jesuits, was at its peak. This form of art enjoyed the Jesuits' special attention, the natural result of the Society's presence in a country with a centuries-old tradition in such wares.

Documents show that the faithful were soon making gifts of money and silver objects to the first Jesuit institutions in Portugal. After São Roque was built in the 1580s, these highly valuable gifts were used chiefly to produce the pieces used in the liturgy. It is also known that pewter images were cast at São Roque, from moulds imported from Spain in 1588. These pieces, which unfortunately have not survived and the subjects of which are unknown – they probably depicted Christ or the Virgin – would later have been sold or used as gifts. The following section examines some of the most significant Jesuit commissions for pieces of silver and gold in chronological order. All but one have survived.

Two of the earliest gold pieces found at Jesuit churches in Portugal are now part of the collection of reliquaries at São Roque. Both items, a reliquary and the centrepiece of a monstrance, date from the late sixteenth century and are made of enamelled gold and rock crystal. The reliquary holds a piece of Christ's crown of thorns and was originally hung among the leaves of a silver tree next to the image of St Ignatius of Loyola in the main chapel (fig. 9.11). It probably started life as a scent bottle; it later was donated to the Lisbon Jesuits by Don Francisco de Bragança (?–1634). The centrepiece came from an imposing monstrance that has been lost and perhaps was melted down. The monstrance consisted of two silver angels supporting an ostensory that held the surviving enamelled gold piece, in micro-architectural Renaissance style and containing a small fragment of the Holy Cross that had belonged to Holy Roman Emperor Charles IV. It was

9.11. Reliquary, c. 1600, Museu de São Roque, Lisbon.
Photo courtesy of Museu de S. Roque.

later given, in Bohemia, to Dom João de Borja, the celebrated benefactor of the Lisbon Jesuits and the son of St Francisco Borja.

The much larger Reliquary of the Crib, dated 1615, was commissioned by a bequest in the will of Maria Rolim, the wife of Dom Luís da Gama, the grandson of Vasco da Gama (fig. 9.12). The reliquary is made of gilded bronze and silver, and the centre of the exceptional sculptural group showing the Holy Family contains a relic from the manger of the Christ child, which came from Santa Maria Maggiore in Rome. It closely follows the model of carved altarpieces. The fact that it dates from ten years before the main chapel at São Roque suggests that the new model adopted for Jesuit altarpieces in Portugal may have been introduced via works of jewellery, specifically the reliquaries that probably

9.12. Reliquary of the Crib, dated 1615, Museu de São Roque, Lisbon.
Photo courtesy of Museu de S. Roque.

originated in Italy and Spain. This is yet another open question, having to do
with the influence of mobile objects in spreading artistic models.

The architectural nature of this new model, which was clearly influenced by
wooden altarpieces, is evident in the reliquary from the church of the Onze Mil
Virgens, now Coimbra Cathedral, kept at the Museu Nacional de Machado de
Castro (fig. 9.13). The sides have composite-Corinthian columns that support a
triangular pediment bearing the Jesuit IHS emblem. Like the da Gama family
reliquaries at São Roque, this one confirms the rise of the Late Renaissance
artistic grammar, with the architectural features that spread throughout the
Jesuit-influenced decorative arts, especially during the first half of the seventeenth century.

9.13. Reliquary from the church of the Colégio das Onze Mil Virgens, first quarter of
the seventeenth century, Museu Nacional Machado de Castro, Coimbra.
Photo courtesy of IPM.

The same college owns an architectural-style reliquary containing a relic of
unknown origin, probably of St Lucy (fig. 9.14). This extremely sober piece, the
geometrical pattern of which recalls the decoration of the São Roque chest,
probably dates from the first quarter of the seventeenth century. The monstrance-
chalice originally from the Altar de Jesus at the church of the college of São João
Evangelista, Funchal, and now at the Museu de Arte Sacra is of slightly later
date.[24] It has a baluster-like foot, and the upper part has a canopy supported by
columns and crowned with a cross (fig. 9.15).

The sacrarium of the church of Santo Nome de Jesus is part of the group of
pieces from the main chapel at the college of the Onze Mil Virgens, Coimbra
(fig. 9.16). The goldsmith João Rodrigues made the sacrarium, including the

9.14. Reliquary of St Lucy (?) from the church of the Colégio das Onze Mil Virgens,
first quarter of the seventeenth century, Museu Nacional Machado de Castro, Coimbra.
Photo courtesy of IPM.

throne and frontal, in silver and bronze between c. 1675 and 1685.[25] Like almost
all the surviving silverware from this college, it is now at the Museu Nacional de
Machado de Castro, having come from the treasury of Coimbra Cathedral.
Along with paintings and furniture, it was numbered among the most important
Jesuit pieces for use in worship that the bishop-count incorporated into the
cathedral's treasury after the expulsion of the Society. He had all signs or
emblems of the Jesuits removed from the pieces so that they could not be
identified and incorporated into the royal treasury[26] – which is why the pieces
have survived. Significantly, the use of silver and gilded bronze, found here on
the Coimbra sacrarium, is also recorded at other Jesuit colleges such as São
Lourenço in Oporto and São Roque and Santo Antão in Lisbon, whereas it is not

9.15. Monstrance, second quarter of the seventeenth century,
Museu de Arte Sacra, Funchal.
Photo courtesy of Cintra, Castro Caldas.

usual in the treasuries of other Portuguese churches. It may be yet another Roman influence introduced by the Jesuits.

The Coimbra college also owned other important pieces of silverware that were saved by the bishop-count. A seventeenth-century silver cross believed to have belonged to St Francis Xavier can still be seen at the Museu Nacional de Machado de Castro. It is decorated with a highly naturalistic silver crab, representing the crustacean that is supposed to have given the saint the crucifix on the island of Ceram. The inscription states, 'This holy crucifix is the same that the crab brought to St Xavier on the beach' (ESTE STO CRUCIFIXO É O MESMO QUE O CARANGUEJO TROUXE Á PRAYA AO STO XAVIER). The miracle was one of the most celebrated at the time of Francis Xavier's beatification.

9.16. João Rodrigues, sacrarium from the church of the Colégio das Onze Mil Virgens, Coimbra, 1675–85, Museu Nacional Machado de Castro, Coimbra.
Photo courtesy of IPM.

São Roque has a silver book-cover and halo from a figure of St Francis Xavier that was originally on the main altar. Entirely decorated with floral motifs in the late seventeenth-century style, it was commissioned in 1696 from the Lisbon goldsmith António da Cruz, one of the leading craftsmen from whom the Lisbon Jesuits commissioned work.[27]

One of the most important pieces produced for the Portuguese Jesuits was the majestic silver sacrarium at the college of Santo Antão, Lisbon. This colossal structure in silver and gilded bronze was shaped like a globe surmounted by a cross with Christ crucified and supported by two angels. It originally included several other elements such as busts and the canon of the mass. It was destroyed by the Lisbon earthquake of 1755; though some badly damaged parts were known to be still in existence four years later, no further record of them remains.[28]

The Jesuits had initially commissioned António da Cruz to make this sacrarium, since he had worked before at São Roque, but shortly thereafter they went in search of foreign craftsmen who might create a more modern work for this allegory of the Blessed Sacrament. In due course, two such men came to Lisbon. The first was Jacomo Smith, who was of Flemish origin and who came via Rome to work on the sacrarium in August 1700. The other was Francisco Ludovice, a goldsmith of German origin (the original family name was Ludwig) who had also worked for the Jesuits in Rome – at the Gesù, in association with Johan Adolf Gaap of Augsburg.

Ludovice's arrival in Lisbon in 1701 opened a new chapter in the history of art in Portugal. It is significant that both Smith and Ludovice had studied in Rome; their background reveals that there was interest in introducing a modern Roman baroque–style decorative language into Portugal. This interest is confirmed by the many pieces of silverware that King João V commissioned in Rome and gave to churches throughout Portugal to stimulate a change in the dominant taste for what he called 'village work' (*obra de aldeia* [*sic*]). The finest such pieces are in the treasury in the chapel of São João Baptista, in São Roque; they were produced in Rome between 1742 and 1747. Other religious commissions of Italian silver can be found at the Lisbon Cathedral Museum and the Museu Nacional de Arte Antiga. Under the patronage of King João V, Ludovice would become a leading figure in the history of art in Portugal. Shortly after his arrival, without completing his seven-year exclusive contract, he abandoned his Jesuit patrons and started work as the king's architect; he designed the monumental monastery and palace of Mafra, to be a reflection of the monarch's magnificence.

The silver frontal originally in the chapel of Nossa Senhora do Pópulo at the former Jesuit college in Funchal, now Funchal Cathedral, also dates from the first half of the eighteenth century. Its aesthetic model can be found in embroidery.[29]

The 'six new silver candlesticks in Roman style'[30] now at the Museu de Arte Sacra in Funchal and recorded in the inventory of the chapel of Nossa Senhora do Socorro at the local college were very probably the last of the Madeira Jesuits' commissions. They were produced in Lisbon in the second quarter of the eighteenth century by the silversmith IF, who used Roman style for the candlesticks and decorated them with the IHS emblem on the base, an acknowledgment that the commission was from the Jesuits.

Since the Jesuits were part of a nation with a large colonial empire, their treasures included a significant number of Asian pieces in precious metals, mainly from India and China. Among the most important surviving examples is a seventeenth-century Indian processional cross made of ivory and *lignum vitae*, the silver mounts of which were made in Portugal. It belonged to the Casa Professa de São João Evangelista, Vila Viçosa, formerly a Jesuit college and now the parish church. The Casa Professa of São Roque assembled the most significant group of pieces brought from the Jesuit missions in the Far East. The most important to have survived, owing to its use as a reliquary, is a tortoiseshell and silver casket recorded at São Roque before 1588. This monstrance-shaped reliquary may have come from Macao, but the absence of similar pieces or any documentation on the reliquary makes it impossible to date or classify this extremely interesting piece with any accuracy.

Another of the finest Jesuit treasuries, perhaps second only to São Roque's, can be found in the former Portuguese territories in India, specifically at the basilica of the Bom Jesus, in Old Goa. This church houses the body of the 'Apostle of the Indies' and, formerly, works that were at the Rachol Museum until their recent move to the new museum in the Santa Monica monastery, Old Goa. The overwhelming majority of the pieces date from the seventeenth and eighteenth centuries. The Marquis of Pombal had them sent to Portugal, but after the ascent of Queen Maria I to the throne in 1779 and the consequent fall of the dead king's chief minister, they were immediately returned to Goa, without even having been unpacked. The reliquary cross, containing a fragment of the wood of the Holy Cross, was produced around 1650, when the new sacristy was built at the Bom Jesus. It is of particular note became it made direct reference to the architecture – in this case, a facade – of a Jesuit church. In addition, it used the Society's emblem, which can also be found on a fine reliquary-monstrance and a censer boat.[31]

The question of whether or not there was a Jesuit style has not been definitively answered, as Gauvin Alexander Bailey has noted.[32] The importance of the decorative arts, which in this case derive their partly functional nature from their role in liturgy, is demonstrated by the uses to which they were characteristically put in the program of the Society of Jesus. Certain features consistently appear in the models adopted by the Jesuits, thereby demonstrating that the Society pragmatically and systematically retained models that proved to be both functional and successful, such as the carved altarpieces discussed above. Sometimes, however, there was a search for novelty and modernity, as when Roman-trained artists were hired to work on the Santo Antão sacrarium. I believe a clear link can be established between pragmatism and art through study of the work produced for the Society of Jesus, especially the wood carving, tiles, textiles, furniture, and silverware.

Reliquaries were among the Jesuits' principal cult objects. They can be seen as a synthesis of all the arts, in their fabulous combination of materials such as precious metals, gems, wood, and even textiles and painting to produce some of the most creative art of the Counter Reformation. Fortunately, art history is now beginning to study them properly. São Roque has by far the finest example of the phenomenon of reliquary collection in Portugal, with around 240 pieces. These mostly date from the sixteenth and seventeenth centuries and were produced in a wide range of locations, from Europe to the Far East.[33]

The techniques and materials were also combined on a far larger scale, as in São Roque's Chapel of Our Lady of Doctrine, where the various decorative arts work together to establish a highly individual iconographic program (figs 9.17, 9.18). The carving, stone, and other inlays in exotic woods on the gates, executed during the redecoration of the chapel in 1688, as well as the frontal in embroidered silk, all feature a rosary encircling a missal that bears the inscription DOCTRINA, ET VERITAS LEVIT, which serves as an ornamental 'leitmotif' for the chapel. The paintings that covered the reliquaries on the two large lateral-wall shrines are the work of Bento Coelho da Silveira, a painter who worked for several Jesuit churches in Portugal. The paintings are the *Apparition of Christ to Our Lady* and the *Ascension of Christ*, a clear reference to St Ignatius's *Spiritual Exercises*, specifically the contemplations of the Fourth Week, as recently identified by Luís de Moura Sobral.[34]

The Jesuits achieved their most spectacular results in temporary decoration. Unfortunately, only signs of these, many of them literary, have survived, such as descriptions of festivals and ceremonies. Yet these reports help us reconstruct, to some degree, the use of ornaments, especially those made of precious materials, which were of great importance for creating a theatrical setting and for promoting the cult of saints and their relics within a liturgical ceremony. While celebrations and festivals were necessarily ephemeral, they represent the high point in the Jesuits' use of ornament. One of the most spectacular public events in Lisbon took place when twelve litters bearing relics and precious reliquaries donated by Dom João de Borja, some of them made especially for the occasion, were taken to São Roque in 1588.[35] The celebrations are recorded in a description by Manuel de Campos that was published in Lisbon in 1588 and in Alcalá the following year, translated by Alvaro de Veanncos.[36] Only later would such ostentation be matched, by a magnificent play performed at the college of Santo Antão when Philip II of Portugal (III of Spain) visited Lisbon in 1619. It involved more than three hundred actors and a wardrobe of Oriental finery studded with precious stones. In all, 1,090 diamonds, 3,000 pearls, 248 emeralds, 1,139 rubies, and precious furnishings from royal and noble palaces, monasteries, and churches were used.[37]

9.17. Chapel of Our Lady of Doctrine, c. 1688, São Roque, Lisbon.
Photo courtesy of Museu de S. Roque.

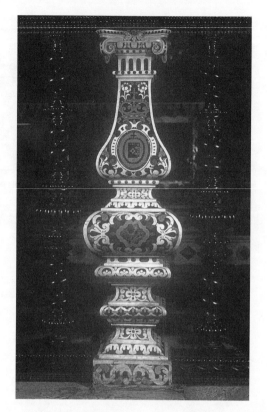

9.18. Balustrade, Chapel of Our Lady of Doctrine, c. 1688, São Roque, Lisbon.
Photo courtesy of Museu de S. Roque.

The celebrations to mark the canonization of Francis Xavier and Ignatius of Loyola in 1622 were equally spectacular and had an enormous impact on the collective imagination of the people of Lisbon. There were allegories with paintings and sculptures on triumphal arches, tableaux vivants, and a host of artistic and emblematic decorations accompanying poetry, dance, and music.

The precious materials all combined to produce a spectacular and intensely visual atmosphere. The Jesuits evidently used gold, silver and precious stones to help create such an atmosphere, and to sacralize it – the materials having an undeniable evocative power, especially in the cult of relics and the Blessed Sacrament.

The so-called decorative arts were the most successful plastic expression of sacred eloquence ever achieved by the Jesuits. Unfortunately, the destruction and dispersal after 1759 of the artefacts concerned has made it impossible to gain a clear picture of the extent of their impact. Only by cross-referencing objects and works of art, such as those at São Roque, with others in other museums and collections and with documentary and literary descriptions will it be possible to re-create, to some extent, a visual universe that has otherwise been lost for good.

NOTES

This article was translated by Richard Trewinnard.

1 José Eduardo Horta Correia, 'A arquitectura – maneirismo e "estilo chão,"' in *História da arte em Portugal*, vol. 7 (Lisbon, 1986), pp. 110–14.

2 Baltazar Telles, *Chronica da Companhia de Jesu, na provincia de Portugal,* vol. 1 (Lisbon, 1645–7), p. 115.

3 For the adaptation of the Corinthian-composite style as a reflection of triumphalism on the part of the church, see David M. Kowal, 'Innovation and Assimilation: The Jesuit Contribution to Architectural Development in Portuguese India,' in O'M. *Jes. Cult.,* p. 484.

4 Robert C. Smith, *A talha em Portugal* (Lisbon, 1962), pp. 58–62.

5 Teresa Freitas Morna, 'Os jesuítas e a arte,' in *O púlpito e a imagem. Os jesuítas e a arte* (Lisbon, 1997), exhib. cat., p. 30.

6 George Kubler, *A arquitectura portuguesa chã entre as especiarias e os diamantes, 1521–1706* (Lisbon, 1988).

7 Rui Carita, *O colégio dos jesuítas do Funchal* (Funchal, 1987).

8 José Meco, 'As artes decorativas,' in *História da arte em Portugal*, vol. 7, p. 161.

9 See Smith, *A talha*, p. 76.

10 Julio Parra, *Azulejos. Painéis do século XVI ao XVII* (Lisbon, 1994), cat. nos 5 and 6.

11 A.J. Barros Veloso and Isabel Almasqué, *Hospitais civis de Lisboa. História e azulejos* (Lisbon, 1996).

12 M. dos Santos Simões, *Azulejaria em Portugal no século XVIII* (Lisbon, 1979), p. 207.

13 José Filipe Mendeiros, *The Tiles of the University of Evora* (Evora, 2002).

14 Santos Simões, *Azulejaria*, p. 211.

15 Veloso and Almasqué, *Hospitais civis*, pp. 75–85 (these panels are currently undergoing conservation work at the Museu Nacional do Azulejo, Lisbon).

16 Victor Serrão, *A lenda de São Francisco Xavier pelo pintor André Reinoso* (Lisbon, 1993), pp. 49–54.

17 See Joaquim Oliveira Caetano, 'O tecto de São Roque,' in *O tecto da Igreja de S. Roque: História, conservação e restauro* (Lisbon, 2002), pp. 32–6.

18 *Frontais de altar seiscentistas da Igreja de S. Roque* (Lisbon, 1994), exhib. cat.

19 'vestimenta de cetim da India e tela amarela': see *No caminho do Japão: Arte oriental nas colecções da Santa Casa da Misericórdia de Lisboa* (Lisbon, 1993), exhib. cat. nos 19–28.

20 Nuno Vassallo e Silva, 'Missions and Merchants: Christian Art in Macao,' *Oriental Art* 46:3 (2000): 84–91.

21 *Encontro de culturas: Oito séculos de missionação portuguesa*, ed. Maria Natália Correia Guedes (Lisbon, 1994), exhib. cat., no. 362.

22 Carita, *O colégio dos jesuítas*, p. 186.

23 Pedro Dias, *História da arte portuguesa no mundo (1415–1822). O espaço do Indico* (Lisbon, 1998), p. 333.

24 *Documentos para a história da arte em Portugal*, vol. 13 (Lisbon, 1975), p. 81; Carita, *O colégio dos jesuítas*, p. 171–6.

25 Fausto Santos Martins, 'A arquitectura dos primeiros colégios jesuítas de Portugal. 1542–1759,' dissertation, University of Oporto, 1994, p. 759; António Nogueira Gonçalves, 'O altar de prata da Sé Nova de Coimbra,' in *Estudos de ourivesaria* (Porto, 1984), pp. 204–10.

26 *Documentos para a história da arte em Portugal*, vol. 3 (Lisbon, 1969), p. 21.

27 Vassallo e Silva 'Aspectos da arte da prata na Companhia de Jesus (séculos XVI a XVII),' in *O púlpito e a imagem* (n5 above), pp. 62–3.

28 *Documentos para a história da arte em Portugal*, vol. 5 (Lisbon, 1969), p. 6.

29 Carita, *O colégio dos jesuítas*, p. 175.

30 *Documentos para a história da arte em Portugal*, vol. 13 (Lisbon, 1975), p. 79; Carita, *O colégio dos jesuítas*, p. 174.

31 Vassallo e Silva, 'A arte da prata nas casas jesuíticas de Goa,' in *A Companhia de Jesus e a missionação no Oriente*, ed. Nuno Silva Gonçalves (Lisbon, 2000), pp. 367–85.

32 Bail. 'Style.'

33 Nuno Vassallo e Silva and Júlio Parra Martínez, *Esplendor e devoção: Os relicários de S. Roque* (Lisbon, 1998), exhib. cat.

34 Luís de Moura Sobral, '*Un bel composto*: A obra de arte total do primeiro barroco português,' in *Struggle for Synthesis*, vol. 1 (Lisbon, 1999), pp. 308–9.

35 William Telfer, *The Treasure of São Roque: A Sidelight on the Counter-Reformation* (London, 1932), pp. 31–52.

36 Manuel de Campos, *Relaçam do solenne recebimento que se fez em Lisbon às santas reliquias q[ue] se leuáram à igreja de S. Roque da companhia de Iesu aos 25 de Ianeiro de 1588* (Lisbon, 1588); *Relacion del solene recebimiento que se hizo en Lisbon a las santas reliquias que se llevaron a la Iglesia de San Roque de la Compañia de Iesus* (Alcalá, 1589).

37 José Sasportes, *História da dança em Portugal* (Lisbon, 1970), p. 121.

10 / Cultural Convergence at the Ends of the Earth: The Unique Art and Architecture of the Jesuit Missions to the Chiloé Archipelago (1608–1767)

GAUVIN ALEXANDER BAILEY

As John W. O'Malley reminds us in the preface to this volume, the 'propagation of the faith' was one of the principal goals set down in the 'Formula of the Institute.' Little did the first companions realize, when drafting that document, how quickly the Society would take that exhortation to heart, by extending their missionary enterprise to the furthest reaches of the globe – to Tibet, Paraguay, and Huronia. Recent studies, including several in both volumes of *The Jesuits: Cultures, Sciences, and the Arts*, have revealed how important the visual arts and architecture were to these ventures, in providing a bridge between languages, a visual explanation for tricky points of doctrine, and a roof over people's heads. Yet it has been only in the last decade that scholars have begun to pay serious attention to the artistic activities of one of the most distant and fascinating missions attempted by the Society: the missions in Chiloé on the frontier of Chilean Patagonia, the southernmost Catholic missions in the world before modern times.

Very few people – including specialists in mission history and culture – are familiar with Chiloé. While this might not be an issue were Chiloé merely distant and not interesting, the missions to that archipelago turn out to have inspired one of the most intriguing and acculturative artistic traditions of the early modern world, comparable to those of the much more celebrated Reductions in Paraguay. I, for one, wish that I had encountered this missionary episode in time to include it in my own study of Jesuit mission art.[1] This article, which draws upon a wealth of unpublished source material in the National Archives of Chile, is my way of trying to make amends.

The Chiloé missions are unique because both sides of the exchange were different from the norm in colonial Latin America. On the one hand, the Chiloé missions accommodated profoundly to an indigenous woodland culture that has more in common with North American Amerindian culture than it has with that of more familiar indigenous groups in South America. On the other hand, the missionaries who staffed these outposts during their height came primarily from non-Iberian regions, particularly from Central and Eastern Europe. As a result, the art and architecture of Chiloé was a blend of Germanic forms with those of a people with extraordinary aptitude for woodworking and carpentry. One thing at least the architecture of Chiloé did not resemble was anything else in Latin America.

Chilote churches are plain, barnlike structures with pitched roofs and shingled siding, raised on stone foundations and fronted with a single elegant arcade and steepled bell tower. This profile – more akin to that of a Tyrolean wayside chapel than a Spanish colonial mission church – makes these churches look right at home in their alpine setting. Their interiors are more richly decorated, with classical columns, inventive mouldings and rib vaults, and delicately carved wooden altarpieces. They also house a striking collection of wooden statuary, in which rigid bearing, passive expressions, and schematic treatment of anatomy and drapery recall the art of the Paraguay Reductions, and have given rise to the designation of a separate 'Hispano-Chilote school of carving.'[2] Owing to the efforts of a local charity called the 'Friends of the Churches of Chiloé' (founded 1993) and especially to UNESCO's decision in 2000 to declare sixteen of the sixty wooden churches of Chiloé World Patrimony Sites, scholars are beginning to devote serious study to these treasures, and they have been the subject of several recent books, photography exhibitions, and Internet sites.[3]

Nevertheless, these same studies have played down the importance of the Jesuit era, and emphasized instead the role played by the Franciscan and diocesan priests who took over the missions after the Society was expelled in 1767. There is no doubt, as the Chilean scholar Hernán Montecinos Barrientos is now demonstrating, that most of the churches and sacred art that survive today in Chiloé post-date the Jesuit era, and that credit for some of their most familiar architectural novelties – from the neo-Gothic pointed arches in the porticos to the column-like octagonal central towers – is due to the Jesuits' successors in the mission field. But it would be a mistake to underestimate the Jesuit era's impact on these remarkable buildings and their contents. Archival and published documents from that epoch leave no doubt that most of the basic elements of the Chilote style were established by the Jesuits, particularly a group of Germanic priests and brother artisans who had travelled to Chile with Carlos (Karl) Haimbhausen (1692–1728), the founder of the famed crafts workshops of the Calera de Tango, which I have treated elsewhere.[4] In collaboration with the Huilliche and Chono Indians of the archipelago, the Jesuits created a syncretic visual arts tradition that relied as much on indigenous techniques as it did on those of Europe. The most compelling document to support this hypothesis is not

10.1. Church of Santa María de Loreto, Achao, exterior.
Photo courtesy of Gauvin Alexander Bailey.

to be found in the archives. Called 'a veritable architectural jewel in wood,' the church of Santa María de Loreto at Achao survives almost intact from the Jesuit mission era, giving us precious insight into the creative capacity of these missions built so far from the settled colonial heartland (figs 10.1, 10.2).[5] I will examine this church in much greater detail below.

Although the Spanish first occupied Chiloé in 1567, and founded the capital at Castro the next year, the islands were isolated from the colonial settlements in central Chile by the vast territories of the hostile Mapuche tribes and the equally intimidating winds and storms of the South Pacific, and settlement was slow and sporadic. The densely forested archipelago extends from the Chacao Canal in the north to the Gulf of Corcovado in the south, and its largest island, the Isla Grande de Chiloé is – at 8,394 square kilometres – the largest island in South America outside Tierra del Fuego. Several different indigenous groups lived on the islands, but the most prominent were the Huilliche and Chono peoples, who supplemented their diet of potatoes with the fish they caught in small wooden canoes called *piraguas* or *dalcas*. The young colony bore the brunt of several attacks from foreign pirates in the seventeenth century, particularly the Dutch,

10.2. Church of Santa María de Loreto, Achao, interior.
Photo courtesy of Gauvin Alexander Bailey.

who sacked Castro twice, in 1600 and 1642, and burned it to the ground on both occasions.

The Jesuits arrived early on the scene, although the Franciscans and Mercedarians had beaten them to it. In 1595, Father Luis de Valdivia found the tiny colony already served by three churches, a parish church and the conventual churches of the two mendicant orders.[6] The Jesuits founded their first permanent mission in Castro in 1608, under the supervision of Melchor Venegas and Juan Bautista Ferrufino, and this institution would eventually head three other permanent missions, in Achao, Chonchi, and Cailín.[7] Venegas and Ferrufino also introduced one of the most noteworthy features of the Chiloé missions: the itinerant missions. These extraordinarily exhausting eight-month, 4,000-kilometre canoe tours of the archipelago's most distant indigenous villages took place annually between 17 September and 17 May. Fighting fierce winds, cold, and starvation, the priests supervised the construction of makeshift chapels in each of the villages and appointed *fiscales*, or lay catechists, to manage the missions in their absence.[8] A few decades later, in 1646, the Jesuit chronicler Alonso de Ovalle could write with pride that these missions were 'the most distant in this province, and the most apostolic that our Society has in all the Indies.'[9]

The earliest chapels on the itinerant missions were built by Amerindian carpenters and acculturated profoundly to indigenous traditions of domestic architecture. They were built of boards and planks and roofed with cypress beams and straw, which was later replaced by shingles made of the *alerce* (larch) tree, a water-resistant answer to the islands' heavy rainfalls. Instead of nails, the builders used strong wooden dowels, and they supported the churches on stone foundations to protect them from the humidity of the soil. Itinerant churches were also built next to the beach, for easy access by the canoes of the missionaries. As the eighteenth-century Jesuit chronicler Miguel de Olivares commented:

The said chapels are placed next to the beaches, so that the fathers can arrive there with their *piraguas*, [and] can begin their ministries right away without much trouble ... Each community raises its own church, which is composed of some wooden posts, with other boards which are placed next to them, forming the walls; and the roof [is] covered with straw on some beams, so that not a single nail was used in its construction, because everything is bound with roots and vines, which climb the trees.[10]

These rectangular structures on stone bases resembled the traditional family homes of the Huilliche Indians, which were also large rectangular halls with a platform in the front where the family lived during the day and the eaves of which protected them from rain.[11] Much of the woodworking knowledge that went into these chapels also derived from the making of canoes, which were constructed from large wooden planks bound together with vines called *paupué*, and other fibres.[12] The chapels were decorated with the natural produce of the forest. A passage in the Jesuit Annual Letter for 1611 describes how they were decorated to greet the visiting missionaries: 'We arrived at the church, which is a straw hut, but well made, and adorned with flowers and laurel branches, of which there is quite an abundance here.'[13] The number of these *visita* chapels increased steadily. In 1611 the Jesuits had already established thirty-six of them, and by the time of the expulsion there were almost eighty. The basic features of these early chapels, from the materials and building methods to the rectangular shape, pitched roof, and porch at the front, already form the essence of what would become the distinctive Chilote style of architecture.

The architecture of the Jesuits in Castro was a different story. Since they ministered there primarily to the Spanish community, they built their churches and residences on a grander scale to compete with those of their mendicant rivals. A 1611 description, which proudly calls the Jesuit church and residence of Santa María de Loreto 'the best house in the town,' describes a wooden structure with a tiled roof that occupied a quarter of a city block. The account continues by saying that the compound also had

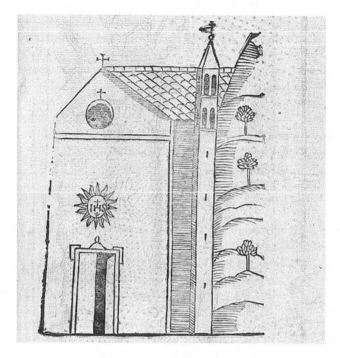

10.3. *Residenza di Ciloe*, from Alonso de Ovalle, *Historia relatione del Regno di Cile*
(Rome, 1646), plate 11.

an orchard garden, which surrounds us nicely, and another patio ... In the complex we have
built two parts, and in the best and biggest we built the church with its grand portal onto
the street, and, in the other two, living quarters for the two [fathers], a dispensary [and] a
refectory, and a nook for the sacristy – very small – and made of wickerwork enforced
with straw ... In the garden, on one side of it, we built another little hut that serves as a
kitchen, where we have a boy who accompanies and serves us.[14]

In 1649, when three missionaries were living there, Alonso de Ovalle published
a woodcut illustration of the Castro residence and church (fig. 10.3).[15] Although
the Italianate Late Renaissance structure in the print has more to do with the
fantasies of the printmaker than the actual structure in Castro, it nevertheless
demonstrates the church's key civic role in the city, as the basis of a ministry that
extended to Spaniard and Amerindian alike.

By the early eighteenth century the Jesuits had founded a college at the Castro
residence to train missionaries in the Huilliche and Chono languages, and four

missionaries were based there, two responsible for ministry in Castro and two designated for the itinerant missions.[16] By the end of the eighteenth century, the 'beautiful college and large church all of wood' supported eight missionaries in the winter months and three in the summer, compared to two Franciscans at the Franciscan church and the single Mercedarian who maintained La Merced.[17] Our last descriptions of the Jesuit foundation come from the suppression documents, beginning with this mundane report dated 11 December 1776, which deals with the college alone:

Item: The said house [i.e., the college], which is twenty-three *varas* [a unit equivalent to about 83 centimetres] long and nine wide with a roof of planks and walls made of the same kind of planking, divided into two sections, the smaller one for the living quarters has two windows in it with small latches and a door with the usual lock and key, with a plank roof, the said dwelling having beams with mouldings and linings, and the floor laid with rough planks, the other section which is larger does not have planks on the floor nor in the upper part, [and] it has a large double door with bolt and lock, and a small padlock.[18]

A further description of the whole complex is dated 12 December of the same year:

Item: The rectangular college with its frame of boards and palisade of cypress.
Item: Four rectangular houses with the church, of three aisles, all done in wood, and houses, and their roofs made of clapboard, with its corresponding rooms, warehouse, larder, refectory, and school.
Item: Five houses farther inside the said college, two of large proportion, and the three small ones with the same roof as the former serve as the kitchen, dispensary, ovens, and other functions ...
Item: three medium-sized houses for [making the Spiritual] Exercises, made of similar woods.[19]

According to the suppression documents, the high altar retablo of the church could accommodate five statues. There were two lateral altars, dedicated to Christ in Agony and St Michael, and additional side altars dedicated to St Joseph, Our Lady of the Assumption, and St Anne. There were also seven niches on the sides of the nave housing further sculptures, seven confessionals, and a pulpit and baptismal font.[20] The Jesuit church in Castro was made the cathedral in 1772, and the building lasted until an 1857 fire burned it to the ground.[21] The delightful neo-Gothic structure that replaced it was built in 1910.

In the eighteenth century the Chilote styles of architecture and carving reached their maturity. It was in this period that the first Central European priests and brothers made the perilous trip south from Santiago, many of them hailing from the original 1722 expedition from Central Europe that also brought Haimbhausen and many of the artists and architects of the Calera de Tango and Santiago workshops. These men included Father Franz Khuen, from the Upper Rhine, who radically expanded missionary activity on the islands; Arnold Yaspers, who enlarged the Castro college and improved its living quarters; the Austrian Father Michael Choller, who became superior of the mission at Achao; his compatriot Brother Anton Miller, a carpenter and cabinetmaker who joined Choller at Achao; and Father Anton Friedl, the only member of the 1722 expedition still alive (although barely, at the age of 83) at the time of the 1767 expulsion.[22] Other Germanic missionaries followed, mostly from the 1747 expedition from Central Europe, including Fathers Melchor Strasser from Bavaria, Franz Xavier Kisling from Franconia, Michael Mayer from the Upper Rhine, and the Bohemian Johann Nepomuk Walter (or Erlager). All these men were still alive in 1767.[23]

Khuen promoted the itinerant missions, and the number of village chapels slowly increased to accommodate the growing congregations. In 1717 there were already 69 village chapels and 6,120 neophytes on the islands; by 1734–5 the number had grown to 72 chapels and 9,400 neophytes; and by 1757 there were 76 chapels and 11,047 neophytes. When Melchor Strasser and Michael Mayer travelled through Chiloé in 1758–9, they found the Jesuits ministering in an astonishing 80 chapels throughout the islands.[24] The chapels were listed in an anonymous manuscript from 1769–70 now in the Jesuit archives in Rome, although it gives few detailed descriptions.[25] In some cases, as for the villages of Pudeto, Caipulli, Peldehuetu, Huitu, Vilupulli, Añihue, Chegniau, Vutachauqui, the island of Chaulinec, and the settlements of Ichoac, Pucolon, Alachildu, and Detif on Lemuy Island, the report merely states that a chapel was there. Other references give more of an idea of the churches' appearance, as in the village of Lacuy, which had 'a fine chapel, all of wood, and of three naves'; Manao, the church of which was 'well proportioned'; Quilquico, Rillan, Quenac, Apeao, and Quehui, each of which had a 'beautiful church'; or – at the other extreme – the towns of Huilad, which had a 'small church,' Linlin, with its 'average church,' and Caucahue, with its 'poor church.' The description of the chapel at Lacuy shows that some of these chapels were built as three-aisled basilicas, more like the typical Chilote prototype found at the permanent mission centres of Achao, Cailín, and Chonchi, which would remain the model throughout the post-Jesuit era. Each of the missions also had a little catechism school, the largest of which was the Colegio de Caciques in Chillán, which functioned for twenty-three years, teaching indigenous children to read and write Spanish.

More evidence has survived to help us reconstruct the appearance and devotional activities of the three main permanent missions, at Cailín, Chonchi, and Achao. Scattered documentary references exist for Cailín; more detailed descriptions illuminate Chonchi – the most important and populous foundation outside Castro; and the original church still survives at Achao. The Cailín mission, home to the Caucahue tribe, was founded in 1764 by royal decree, and as the southernmost mission it also served as a base for annual excursions into unexplored territories as far south as the Straits of Magellan and Cape Horn.[26] The Real Audiencia of Chile assigned each mission an initial 500 pesos for building costs, and gave each missionary an annual salary of 300 pesos, with an additional 30 pesos for wine and candle wax.[27] In 1764, Johann Nepomuk Walter described the veneration of an image of the Carmen at the Cailín church, at the time still under construction by Amerindian carpenters:

They maintain their church ... which they themselves built through their own industry and personal labour. They venerate in the said church a precious statue of Nuestra Señora del Carmen, for which they exhibit singular devotion, and calling it their mother they invoke her in a very heartfelt way in their tribulations and labours; and to make themselves more worthy of her patronage they take it out in procession through the streets on some of their feast days, garnished with laurel branches, which they set up for greater decorum, and having done the rounds of the village they return to the church in the same order in which they left it.[28]

I will return to the veneration of carved images of saints when I consider the Chilote sculptural tradition. The expulsion references to Cailín are quite perfunctory, merely mentioning 'a chapel, three houses with straw roofs, [and] their corresponding rooms.'[29]

The mission at Chonchi, just south of Castro on the Isla Grande, was founded by the same royal decree in 1764 to minister to Amerindians of various ethnicities who had settled in this extremely populous region of four thousand inhabitants. Walter describes bustling building activity, as the Indians 'quickly built a very spacious living quarters for the father, all of them working spontaneously; and they are still progressing with determination in finishing a large section which serves for the school for children, in which many children from this village and neighbouring villages are already learning to read and write.' He continues by noting that the elites of the town and surrounding communities 'graciously and voluntarily' paid the 3,000 pesos that the complex cost to construct – much more than the stingy Audiencia had granted them.[30] The anonymous report from 1769–70 describes the Chonchi church in more detail: 'Here the Jesuit fathers had begun to build a larger church than that at Castro, completely of wood, with squared columns all of one piece, which draw admiration because of their thickness.'[31] The suppression report calls it a 'church of three aisles, completely of wood and a roof of clapboard,' and mentions three outbuildings as well.[32] Francisco Enrich, describing the church as it looked in the mid-nineteenth century, wrote of a 'beautiful church, of seventy *varas* in length, and a width corresponding to a church of three aisles. The columns that form [the aisles] rest on bases and plinths of stone, which extend for about one *vara* into the earth.'[33] The handsome church that stands there today, with its brightly painted corrugated iron sheeting and elegant neo-Gothic arcade, is entirely a product of the late nineteenth and early twentieth centuries.

It is hard to determine the exact foundation date of the church of Santa María de Loreto at Achao, the oldest church in Chiloé (see figs 10.1, 10.2). An itinerant mission was established there as early as 1690 with a makeshift chapel, and in 1723 the superior, Michael Choller, wrote that the Jesuits were constructing a permanent mission, specifically mentioning the Austrian furniture maker Anton Miller and a lathe operator called Miguel, who likely supervised the Amerindian carpenters working on the project.[34] A Jesuit visitation report shows that the church was finished by 1734–5, and in 1743 it was already being praised as 'a large and beautiful church,' the first of a long litany of accolades the church would enjoy over the course of the century.[35] The anonymous report from 1769–70 provides more detail, describing 'a beautiful church of wood, of three aisles, with columns all of one piece,' which is roughly what the present building looks like.[36] The expulsion documents (December 1776) note the remarkable mouldings that make the central vault the finest in Chiloé: '[The church is] of three aisles, all of wood, and a roof of clapboard, adorned inside with mouldings.'[37] A much later testimony, written in 1791 by the Franciscan Pedro Gonzáles de Agüeros, again praises the church, calling it 'the finest that they made in the whole archipelago.'[38] He goes on to say, 'The church, which has three aisles ... although of wood, is of noteworthy and detailed architecture, and the dwellings for the two religious [are made] with all possible commodiousness and with spacious offices to house provisions.'

The Achao church testifies not only to the skills of the Huilliche carpenters but also to their ability to make the best use of the natural resources on hand. It is built entirely of local wood such as *alerce* and cypress, using traditional methods that had been employed for centuries for constructing homes. Unlike cypress, which grew in abundance in Chiloé's dense forests, *alerce* had to be obtained by undertaking long canoe trips to the mainland coast and weeks of back-breaking labour. According to the 1769–70 account, teams of six to eight Amerindians would go for three-week periods in their canoes and set up camp on the mainland, felling the giant trees and splitting them into planks using hatchets and wedges.[39] These same methods of splitting and carving, which the Huilliche also employed to make their wooden canoes, were used to prepare and dress the building materials of the Achao church; and the preference for strong wooden dowels over nails (the church at Achao used no nails) also derives from indigenous building traditions, as already noted.

The expulsion documents reveal that there were several major woodworking shops at the Chiloé missions, furnished with a panoply of tools including handsaws, regular saws, chisels, scrub brushes, files, hammers, jointers, gouges, tools for making grooves, machetes, drills, hatchets and axes, awls, knives, compasses, and quadrants, which were used both for building the churches and for carving the sculptures and retablos that went in them. Achao had one of the largest workshops,[40] although there were also substantial collections of tools and unused wooden planks at Cailín, Chonchi, and Castro. The Cailín workshop, which still possessed 275 unused *alerce* planks at the time of the expulsion, also had several unfinished faces from statues of saints, indicating that it was one of the sculpture ateliers as well.[41] At Castro, where a comparable collection of tools was kept, there is also evidence of sculptural and painting activity, since the private quarters of Franz Xavier Kisling included a mortar for grinding colour pigments as well as several unfinished saints' faces and hands.[42] Chonchi had the least number of tools, but the mission did have four hundred unused planks of *alerce* at the time of the expulsion.[43] Planks of alerce were even stored at the estancias, or farms, such as the estancia at Meulin (belonging to the college of Castro), which had fifty planks at the time of the expulsion.[44]

The facade of Santa María at Achao features a graceful arcade of five arches, the central arch wider than the flanking ones (see fig. 10.1). The proportions are classical, each arch hemispherical in shape and supported by classical piers resting on plinths with plain wooden capitals. Above the arcade, three arched windows let onto the choir, and two more windows adorn the tower, but no other ornamentation of any kind disturbs the unrelentingly flat walls with their surface of overlapping shingles, a fish-scale appearance appropriate to a community that gains most of its living from the sea. The austere, almost cubist bell tower rises directly above the portico, and is proportional with the rest of the facade. Its sober, blocklike base supports a pyramidal roof that is itself crowned by a delicate octagonal cupola and spire (the different levels of Chilote towers are called *cañas*).[45] The barnlike main body of the church contains only nine small arched windows on each side and one lateral door. Six rectangular windows let light into the sacristy behind the flat apse. The church faces a large open plaza known as the *explanada* that was used for processionals and other theatrical events, and that gives the church a prominence over the mission's urban space comparable to that developed on the Paraguay Reductions at the same time.[46] The sides of the church were once adjoined by wide eaves to protect the faithful

10.4. A wayside chapel near the Benedictine shrine of Einsiedeln, Switzerland.
Photo courtesy of Gauvin Alexander Bailey.

during downpours, a feature derived from Huilliche domestic architecture, but these have been removed.[47]

The architectural prototype found at Achao – and undoubtedly at Chonchi and Cailín – became the standard followed for the next century and a half; it is now known as the Chilota School of Wooden Religious Architecture and is protected by UNESCO. It combines the indigenous techniques of carpentry and carving that we have just observed with an architectural style derived from the South German rococo. Elsewhere I have shown that the basic profile of the tower and its location in the centre of the facade recall South German examples, such as the seventeenth-century tower of the Peterskirche in Munich or the late medieval St Margaret's Chapel in Salzburg (1491); and versions with an arcaded porch at the front and a small central tower at the back are common in the Tyrol and in Switzerland, for example in the wayside chapels outside the eighteenth-century pilgrimage shrine of Einsiedeln (fig. 10.4).[48] This kind of central tower appeared soon afterward in the Jesuits' principal church in Santiago, San Miguel

10.5. Church of San Miguel, Santiago. From a drawing by Juan Mauricio Rugendas
(1839). Photo courtesy of Staatliche Graphische Sammlung, Berlin.

(1751–66), which the Jesuit architect Franz Grueber built in a hybrid Bavarian style (fig. 10.5). The San Miguel tower, now destroyed but preserved in drawings, had a gambrel roof, corbelled cupola, and finials. This manner of building facades became typical of later architecture in central Chile, and is distinct from that of neighbouring Argentina. Later examples can be found in Santa Ana (begun 1806) in Santiago and in a plethora of provincial nineteenth-century churches, such as the Franciscan church in Curimón, the Convento del Buen Pastor at San Felipe, and the delightful pilgrimage church of San Antonio del Almendral, the last three all made of painted wood.

Montecinos Barrientos has pointed out that the facade and tower at Achao are not original to the church, but date from an 1873 reconstruction.[49] I am also convinced by his arguments that the octagonal shape of the top *caña* of the new tower at Achao was updated to echo that of nearby Quinchao, which was constructed in 1861. Nevertheless, the new tower and facade at Achao almost certainly maintained the basic profile of the original structure, with its central tower rising from the peak of the facade, and its classical portico below. The most important evidence that the Achao church had a facade with a central tower can be found at San Miguel in Santiago, and the classical lines of Achao's arcade, so different from the Gothic-inspired porches of its successors on the archipelago, also point towards an eighteenth-century origin. No scholars have denied that the appearance of the Achao church is Central European. Montecinos Barrientos has noted strong similarities with South German churches such as the Sebastiankirche in Binzwagen and the Marienkirche at Kloster Schultz; Ignacio Modiano traces the design to a 1520 engraving of the church of the Immaculate Conception in Regensburg, and also found commonalities with the architecture of Zagreb (Croatia); and Gabriel Guarda has made references to the architecture of Poland.[50] It would have been strange indeed had the Franciscans imported these Germanic styles, since they were primarily of Iberian or Iberian-American extraction. These later missionaries brought with them a taste for neo-Gothic pointed arches and traceried altarpieces as at Dalcahue (nineteenth century), and for the tall, spindly towers found at churches such as Villupulli (late eighteenth century).

The interior of Santa María in Achao (fig. 10.2) is more typically Latin American, in its echoing of a type of mission church that originated in the first years of colonial New Spain in the 1530s and survived in places such as the eighteenth-century Jesuit missions in Chiquitanía (Bolivia) (fig. 10.6), and the original churches of the Paraguay Reductions, as well as the Franciscan mission of Yaguaron (Paraguay).[51] The basic shape is rectangular, with three aisles of columns creating a basilical form. This kind of building served two functions, since it both was relatively easy to build – crucial in a world of amateur architects – and also recalled the era of the early church, considered a golden age by missionaries in colonial times.

The columns dividing the aisles at Achao, constructed by joining several planks together, are made to follow simple classical prototypes, with plinths, plain capitals, and entablatures. The latter are particularly inventive, since they imitate the horizontal divisions of Graeco-Roman entablatures by making each horizontal plank step forward as they move upward, and they even imitate triglyphs by having an additional staircase-like projection from the entablature jut out above each column. The pilasters on the walls, which correspond to the main columns, are even more classicizing, with their fluting and mouldings. The wide planks of the floor, with their coarse chiselled surfaces – similar to those mentioned in documents – contrast sharply with the intricate carved foliage and geometric patterns on the ceiling, altars, tabernacle, and pulpit.

The main difference between the Chilote interiors and those of, say, the

10.6. Church of San Rafael, Chiquitanía (Bolivia), eighteenth century, interior.
Photo courtesy of Gauvin Alexander Bailey.

Chiquitos missions is that the central aisle is vaulted, in the case of Achao in a delicate and complex net-vault adorned with scalloped mouldings, recalling the light-hearted stucco decoration of South German church vaults of the eighteenth century. Similar vaults appear, for example, at the former Premonstratensian abbey church at Obermarchtal in Bavaria (1686–1701). The vault ribs at Achao criss-cross the roof from the tops of the arches below and are adorned at their intersection points with peony-like flowers (fig. 10.7). A giant, multi-layered flower also appears in the centre of the ceiling. With these ribs, the architect has created the impression that the entire ceiling is covered with a large garden trellis, and so a structural element is transformed into a purely decorative one – an approach that is very rococo in spirit.

The far end of the church focuses on three inventive wooden retablos, done in a style that harmonizes with the rest of the church. The high altar consists of three sections enclosing statue niches. Its shape is very simple – it is essentially three boxes set next to each other; however, there is a hint of rococo style in the concave profile of the central niche, as well as in the delicately twisting Solomonic columns that frame that and the two lateral niches. The most ingenious features of this altar result from the woodworkers' need to substitute wood for rarer

10.7. Church of Santa María de Loreto, Achao, detail of net vault.
Photo courtesy of Gauvin Alexander Bailey.

media. For example, instead of taffeta curtains or silver finials, the artist has given us an expertly rendered false pair of curtains in the central niche, and has added flat, scalloped finials and crowns to all three sections, including the monogram of the Society of Jesus and of the Virgin Mary. The tabernacle is especially elegant, with its relief carvings of Sts Ignatius of Loyola and Francis Xavier, polychrome painted and surrounded by a plethora of scrolls and other rococo ornamentation, and the delightful palm capitals on the retablo columns. Scholars in the past have maintained that the central part of the high altar is a later reconstruction by the Franciscan friar Alonso Reyna of Andalusia, but its style is too perfectly consonant with the rest of the church for this to be likely, and, as Pereira Salas points out, the altar depicts Jesuit saints and the Jesuit emblem.[52]

The side altars, also undoubtedly original to the church, are equally interesting. On the left one, the artists have created a sense of volume not by carving deeply into a log of wood, but by layering planks of wood on top of one another, their edges decorated by the same kind of scalloped plant decoration as seen on the ceiling ribs, although here with a repeating tulip motif. The result is highly ornamental, with considerable texture and variety. On the right-hand side, the altar has another pair of artificial curtains made of wood, with classical-style columns on either side and expressive rococo scrolls at the top. In addition to these two side altars, side niches open up on both sides, framed by wooden curtains and crowned by miniature cupolas set into the vaulting of the aisles. The fine pulpit, with its cone-shaped base and feather headdress–like crown, also picks up the leafy decorative strips used in the ceiling and altars, giving the entire interior a tremendous sense of unity that is remarkable in view of the builder's constraints.

Although it has not yet received the attention garnered by the UNESCO-endorsed churches, Chilote sculpture is also a unique expression of cultural convergence that is, at its best, tremendously moving. I can only provide a glimpse here, as no one has seriously studied these works beyond a brief overview in 1955, but they are highly intriguing and merit further research. I have already noted evidence for sculpture production on the missions in Chiloé, particularly at Cailín, Achao, and the college of Castro, where Father Kisling may have taught sculpture and perhaps painting – although the expulsion documents suggest that very little painting was taught on the Chiloé missions.[53] Isidoro Vazquez de Acuña's pioneering 1955 study of what he called the 'Hispano-Chilote school of carving' divided it into four different categories depending upon characteristics such as size and subject.[54] Made by elders in the community (called *santeros*) – both men and women – Chilote sculpture is often chiselled from a single piece of wood, and it includes larger figures (between 80 cm and 160 cm in height) with plain, rough trunks but finished and painted hands and faces, as well as smaller figures (no taller than 90 cm) in which the body is roughly sketched out, sometimes with inventive draperies. Although full-figure statues in wood are rare, there is an especially important group of Christ figures (25 cm to 150 cm) that have movable arms attached with pieces of leather. These appear in many of the main churches (Achao and Dalcahue have two of the finest [fig. 10.8]), and they were hung on the cross until Good Friday, when the parishioners would take the Christ figure down and lay it in a coffin or on a table until Holy Saturday.

In style, Chilote sculpture has much in common with that of the contemporary Paraguay Reductions, which I have studied elsewhere.[55] Although there are many fewer examples of Chilote sculpture to use by way of comparison – and we must keep in mind that most of what survives today is likely post-Jesuit – it is clear that the two traditions have striking similarities. Both favour images carved out of a large, single block of wood, and both schematize drapery and anatomical features (such as rib-cages and shoulder blades), turning them more into geo-metrical patterns than natural forms. Both also display very little emotion. The

10.8. *Christ Crucified*, polychrome wood and leather, eighteenth century (?), church at Dalcahue, Chiloé. Photo courtesy of Gauvin Alexander Bailey.

Christ figures in particular, while lacerated and covered in blood, stare impassively out at the viewer in a way that paradoxically creates a feeling of intense pathos. Such is the Achao Crucifixion, with its rigid lines, schematic treatment of drapery, and calm facial expression. The lower body, which seems to be carved from a single log, has column-like legs that are countered by the horizontal lines of the loincloth. Christ's hair is also braided into parallel lines, which hang from the part on his forehead. The Dalcahue Christ is very similar (see fig. 10.8), although its head is more tilted to the side, and the zigzag drapery is livelier. Both Christs bear a certain resemblance to some of the earliest Guaraní sculptures, particularly the Passion figures at the Santa Ana museum or the crucified Christ at San Cosmé y Damián (seventeenth or early eighteenth century) (fig. 10.9).

The expulsion inventories list full-figure statues, as well as faces and hands used for *imágenes de vestir* (figures to be dressed). Most common are statues of Christ, which were found at Achao, Cailín, Chonchi, Castro, and the estancia at Lemuy, followed by images of Our Lady, including the Assumption, the Immaculate Conception, Our Lady of Sorrows, and the Virgin of Loreto, and Sts Anne and Joseph.[56] Naturally, Jesuit saints were also common, not only Ignatius of Loyola and Francis Xavier but also Aloysius Gonzaga and Stanislas Kostka,

10.9. *Christ Crucified*, polychrome wood, seventeenth or early eighteenth century, church at San Cosmé y Damián, Paraguay. Photo courtesy of Gauvin Alexander Bailey.

and there were statues of St Rose of Lima, St Teresa, and St Michael, and one of a soul in purgatory. At least a few of the statues were imported, most notably an ivory *Immaculate Conception* that was probably brought from the Philippines or China, but there is no reason to doubt that most of them were made in Chiloé. The inventories also list a substantial collection of clothing for the statues, gathered together from the churches at Castro, Achao, Chonchi, and Cailín, reminding us that most of them would have been displayed wearing vestments – which is why even the full-figure statues tend to have very basic bodies.[57]

Walter's description of veneration of the statue of Nuestra Señora del Carmen in the town of Cailín hints at the intimate role religious sculpture played in the devotions of the Chilote communities. One of the most remarkable and moving examples of this interaction between worshippers and statues took place during the annual rounds made by the itinerant missionaries. The *Noticia breve* of 1769–70 gives the most detailed description of this tradition, which is worth quoting in full:

On 17 September two *piraguas* come from Ichoac to the college of Castro, with some Indians from that village, in search of the missionary fathers. These, who are ready for them, depart from that city in a procession, which goes to the beach, where the following statues of saints embark [on the *piraguas*]: St Isidore, St John the Evangelist, St Notburga, the Virgin, and a large [statue of] Our Crucified Lord. In addition to these are the furnishings for the masses, tables, boxes, and whatever is necessary in a land where there is nothing ... When the *piraguas* arrive [in a village], the saints are disembarked and conducted to the church in procession with the missionary fathers, where [the statues] are placed, each one in its appointed niche. They light the candles, which are not extinguished from this point until the departure. An elderly Indian is the patron of the Holy Christ, and he has the privilege of going in procession with a banner, and has two assistants to take care of the same high altar; and St Notburga has her patroness, who also looks after the same. All must obey these patrons in matters pertaining to their altars, and the women must obey the patroness ... On the day of departure the saints are placed in their boxes and carried in procession to the beach, where the missionary makes a brief sermon, [and] gives the benediction. The saints embark on the two *piraguas*, which arrived the day before from the [next] chapel [they will visit], and when they set off [the Indians] shout from the beach three times, 'Buen viaje!'[58]

During their stay at the village, the statues also participated in other processions, depending upon the size of the village and the length of stay. One can only imagine how upsetting it must have been to these communities to have these annual missions cut off by the expulsion in 1767. And indeed, listed in the inventory made nine years later in the college of Castro, are the very saints who embarked upon this annual voyage, including the large Christ figure, the Virgin of Sorrows, St John the Evangelist, St Isidore, and St Notburga (a Tyrolean saint, who reflected the Germanic origins of the missionaries), all resting in their boxes ready for a voyage they would probably never make again.[59]

Churches such as Achao and the carvings of the Chilote sculptors are reminders that the art and architecture of the Jesuit missions embraced the widest possible range of styles and techniques, one reflecting the global nature of their enterprise. By merging a Central European style that was quite distinct from the Iberian and Italian influence in most of the rest of Latin America with a unique Amerindian tradition of woodwork and architecture, the Jesuits and Amerindians of the Chiloé missions created a distinctive prototype that would survive and flourish on the islands for almost two hundred years after the Society of Jesus was expelled from Spanish territories in 1767, and be continually enriched and updated by later influences and traditions.

NOTES

The research for this article was made possible by the Higgins School of the Humanities at Clark University. I would also like to express my gratitude to Walter Hanisch, S.J., who shared his research with me in late 1999, shortly before his death, and to Gustavo Barros, who helped me obtain documents at the National Archives of Chile. A different version of this study is being published by the Pontifica Universidad Católica del Perú, *El rostro de la tierra encantada: Religión, evangelización y sincretismo en el Nuevo Mundo*, ed. Marco Curatola Petrocchi and José Sánchez Paredes (Lima, forthcoming).

1 Gauvin Alexander Bailey, *Art on the Jesuit Missions in Asia and Latin America, 1542–1773* (Toronto, 1999).

2 The term 'escuela hispano-chilota de imaginería' was coined in 1955 by Isidoro Vazquez de Acuña; see Isidoro Vazquez de Acuña, *Costumbres religiosas de Chiloé y su raigumbre hispana* (Santiago, 1955), p. 51. For a typology of Paraguay Reduction sculpture, see Bailey, *Art on the Jesuit Missions*, pp. 173–82.

3 Recent works include Gabriel Guarda, *Iglesias de Chiloé* (Santiago, 1984); Ignacio Modiano, *Iglesias de Chiloé: Riqueza iconográfica dentro de una acción racionalista* (Santiago, 1988); Modiano, *Las experiencias arquitectónicas de los jesuitas en la misión de Chiloé durante los siglos XVII y XVIII* (Santiago, 1993); *Las iglesias misionales de Chiloé. Documentos*, ed. Hernán Montecinos Barrientos, Ignacio Salinas, and Patricio Basáez (Santiago, 1995); *Chiloé: Un legado universal* (Santiago, 2001); *Iglesias chilotas: Patrimonio de la Humanidad* (Santiago, 2001); and Bailey, 'Iglesia de Santa María Achao (Chiloé), Chile,' in *Fundaciones jesuíticas en iberoamérica*, ed. Luisa Elena Alcalá (Madrid, 2002), pp. 282–91. The best Internet sites at the time of writing are www.iglesiaschilotas.cl and www.iglesiasdechiloe.cl.

4 Bailey, 'La Calera de Tango (1741–1767) y los otros talleres de arte misional de la Compañía de Jesús en Chile colonial,' in *Los jesuitas y la modernidad en iberoamérica, 1549–1773*, ed. Felipe Portocarrero Suarez (Lima, forthcoming); Bailey, 'The Calera de Tango of Chile (1741–67): The Last Great Mission Art Studio of the Society of Jesus,' *AHSI* 74: 147 (January–June 2005): 175–212; Walter Hanisch Espíndola, 'Calera de Tango, cuna industrial de Chile,' *Boletín de la Academia chilena de la historia* 93 (1982): 159–89; Hanisch Espíndola, 'El P. Carlos Haimbhausen S.J. precursor de la industria chilena,' *Jahrbuch für Geschichte von Staat, Wirtschaft und Gesellschaft Latein Amerikas* 10 (1973): 133–206.

5 Walter Hanisch Espíndola, *Historia de la Compañía de Jesús en Chile* (Santiago,

1974), p. 141. Although its facade and tower were rebuilt in 1873, they preserved the basic profile of the original building – one that would become the prototype for the entire archipelago, as I will discuss below.

6 From the Jesuit Annual Letter for the Paraguay province from 1611, published in Facultad de Filosofía y Letras, *Documentos para la historia Argentina XIX: Iglesia, Cartas anuas de la provincia del Paraguay, Chile, y Tucumán, de la Compañía de Jesús* (Buenos Aires, 1929), pp. 109–10. See also Miguel de Olivares, *Historia de la Compañía de Jesús en Chile, 1593–1786*, ed. Diego Barros Arana (Santiago, 1874), p. 364.

7 From the Jesuit Annual Letter of 1611, published in *Documentos para la historia Argentina XIX*, p. 107. See also *Chiloé: Un legado universal*; Roberto Maldonado, *Estudios geográficos é hidrográficos sobre Chiloé* (Santiago, 1897), p. xxxv; Olivares, *Historia*, p. 367; Francisco Enrich, *Historia de la Compañía de Jesús en Chile*, 2 vols (Barcelona, 1891), I, p. 141.

8 *Documentos para la historia Argentina XIX*, p. 379; Facultad de Filosofía y Letras, *Documentos para la historia Argentina XX: Iglesia, Cartas anuas de la provincia del Paraguay, Chile, y Tucumán, de la Compañía de Jesús* (Buenos Aires, 1929), pp. 165–6; Walter Hanisch, *La isla de Chiloé, Capitanía de rutas australes* (Santiago, 1982), p. 45. See also *Chiloé: Un legado universal*, pp. 24–7; Olivares, *Historia*, pp. 368–78; Alonso de Ovalle, *Historia relatione del Regno di Cile* (Rome, 1646), pp. 337–8, 354–5.

9 Ovalle, *Historia*, p. 354. All translations from Spanish or Italian in this paper are my own.

10 Olivares, *Historia*, pp. 373–4.

11 Maldonado, *Estudios*, p. 356.

12 Hanisch, *La isla de Chiloé*, p. 57.

13 *Documentos para la historia Argentina XIX*, p. 118.

14 Ibid., pp. 109–10.

15 Ovalle, *Historia*, plate 11; see also p. 331.

16 Hanisch, *La isla de Chiloé*, p. 198.

17 *Noticia breve y moderna del Archipiélago de Chiloé, de su terreno, costumbres de los indios, misiones, escrita por un misionero de aquellas islas en el año 1769 y 70*, published in Hanisch, *La isla de Chiloé*, p. 226.

18 'Ittn. d[ic]ha casa q. consta de veinte y tres varas de largo y nuebe de ancho con la techumbre de tablas y las pared.s de la misma especie en tabicaras, dibisida en dos cañones el uno q. es menor para bibiensa constan en el dos bentanas con aldabas pequeñas y una puerta con seradura y llabe corriente, entablada por la techumbre d[ic]ha bibienda con forraje y molduras tod.s las bigas, yel suelo entablado con tablas toscas, el otro cañon q. es mas grande sin entablar el suelo ni la parte sup.or de el, consta, de una puerta grande de dos manos con serrojo y serradura, y un

candado pequeño' (Archivo Nacional de Chile, Santiago [hereafter ANC], Jesuitas 3 [Inventories of the Jesuit Missions in Chiloé] fol. 271a).

19 'Itt. el colegio en quadro con serco de tablas y estacada de sipres; Itt. quatro casas en quadro con la Yglesia, de tres naves, obra toda de madera, y casas, y sus techos de tabla de pizarritta con sus corresponientes aposentos, almacen, vodega, refictorio y escuela; Itt. Sinco casas mas dentro de d[ic]ho colegio dos de proporsionado grandes, y las tres pequeñas con el mismo techo que las primeras sirben de cosina, despensas, ornos, y otras oficinas ... Itt. tres casas a medio haver para exercicios con maderas correspondientes' (ibid., fol. 227a).

20 'Altares: Ittn. El Mayor con sinco nichos cada uno con su velo de perciana azul, los tres, y los dos de perciana vende; Ittn. un sagrario de torno con tres nichos, el uno aforrado con espejos y los dos con damasco colorado; Ittn otro sagrario pequeño abajo del mayor tambien de torno para el copon; Itt. otro altar colateral del Señor de Agonia con un sagrario pequeño tiene ensima un corazon de Jesus; con su doselito, y su velo de calamaco p.a el nicho del Señor; Ittn. otro altar colateral de S. Mig[ue]l sin velos; Ittn. otro altar de S.n Joseph con su velo de raso colorado y su medindre de plata echisso; Ittn. otro altar de N.ra S.a de la Asuncion; Ittn. seite repissas a los lados de la media nave con las estatuas ya dichas; Ittn. otra de S.ta Ana en la nave colateral; Ittn. un pulpito con sus cortinas de persiana; Ittn. seis bancas, y quatro medianos mas; Ittn. seis cillas forradas en bagueta, quatro mas llanas de madera; Ittn. una pila baptismal y su tapa de cobre estañada; Ittn. dos mesas grandes y otra mediana, otras demas; Ittn. dos andas grandes viejas otra dos pequeñas todas de madera; Ittn. tres atarimas postisas y un sagrario postisso sin llave forrado en tafetan blanco, un baulin chico, tres escaparates, sin llave, otro pequeño; Ittn. la messa de la sacristia forrada en cordoban con sus competentes caxones; Ittn. tres caxas con sus chapas y llaves donde estan andados la ropa de yglesia y ornam.tos la una de el ... grande; Ittn. un caxoncillo de ornam.tos sin llave; Ittn. todas las puertas de la yglesia con llaves; Ittn. siete confesonarios, seis atriles de madera' (ibid., fol. 256a–b).

21 *Chiloé: Un legado universal*, p. 68.

22 Eugenio Pereira Salas, *Historia del arte en el reino de Chile* (Santiago, 1965), pp. 81, 263; Hanisch Espíndola, 'El P. Carlos Haimbhausen' (n4 above), p. 146; Hanisch Espíndola, *Historia* (n5 above), p. 109; Hanisch, *La isla de Chiloé*, p. 166; Vicente D. Sierra, *Los jesuitas germanos en la conquista espiritual de Hispano-América* (Buenos Aires, 1944), pp. 243–51; Claudio A. Ferrari Peña, 'La influencia de los jesuitas bávaros en la arquitectura y el arte chilenos del siglo XVIII,' in *Symposium internazionale sul barocco latino americano* (Rome, 1980), pp. 200–25; Mario Buschiazzo, *Historia de la arquitectura colonial en iberoamérica* (Buenos Aires, 1961), pp. 128–9; Damián Bayón and Murillo Marx, *History of South American Colonial Art and Architecture* (New York, 1992), p. 233; Enrich, *Historia*, vol. 2, p. 153. There are references to Haimbhausen and his companions in the personnel

records of the Society of Jesus in the Jesuit archives in Rome: ARSI, Chil. 2 (Triennial Catalogue, 1640–1726) fols 322a–b, 326b, 330a; and Chil. 3 (Triennial Catalogue, 1729–55) fols 70a, 241b, 245b, 246a, 249b, 251b, 252a, 255b, 256a.

23 ANC, Jesuitas 3 fols 250b–251a.

24 Hanisch Espíndola, *Historia,* pp. 65, 67–8; Hanisch, *La isla de Chiloé*, pp. 172–3, 198.

25 *Noticia breve*, in Hanisch, *La isla de Chiloé*, pp. 225–30.

26 Hanisch, *La isla de Chiloé*, pp. 67, 201; Enrich, *Historia*, vol. 1, p. 264.

27 Hanisch, *La isla de Chiloé*, p. 210; see also 211–17.

28 Ibid., p. 202.

29 'Ittn. se compone d[ic]ha Micion de una capilla, tres casas con techo de paja, sus apocentos correspond.tes' (ANC Jesuitas 3 fol. 233a).

30 Hanisch, *La isla de Chiloé*, pp. 203–4.

31 *Noticia breve*, ibid., p. 227.

32 'Itt. la Iglesia de tres naves obra toda de madera y techo e pisarritta de tabla; Itt. tres casas de vivienda con el mismo techo ... distribuidas en aposentos, con correspondientes sillas, mesas, estantes, y canseles, despensa, y escuela' (ANC Jesuitas 3 fol. 231a).

33 Enrich, *Historia*, vol. 2, p. 250.

34 Pereira Salas, *Historia*, pp. 113–14.

35 Enrich, *Historia*, vol. 2, p. 154, 182.

36 *Noticia breve*, in Hanisch, *La isla de Chiloé*, pp. 229–30.

37 'Itt. la Yglesia, de tre naves, toda de madera, y techo de tabla de pisarritta, adornada por dentro de molduras' (ANC Jesuitas 3 fol. 228b).

38 Pereira Salas, *Historia*, p. 114.

39 *Noticia breve*, in Hanisch, *La isla de Chiloé*, p. 244.

40 The following tools were inventoried at Achao itself in 1776: '9 Hachas; 3 Serruchos de 2 manos; 3 Seruchos de una mano; 2 Sierras medianas; 2 Chiquitas; 6 Escoplos grandes. 1 mediano. 4 chiquitos; 1 Zepillo; 2 Acanaladores; 2 Junteras; 2 Azuelas de una mano, y otra de 2 manos; 1 Compas; 3 Barrenas g[ran]des 3 medianas, 2 menores y 3 chiquitas; 1 Yunque; 2 Bigonias; It. 1 yunque y 1 tornillo tiene Don Juan de Loayza; 3 Tenazas; 3 Limas; 1 Clavera; 1 Tornillo gr[an]de otro chiquito p[ar]a la messa; 4 Martillos' (ANC Jesuitas 3 fol. 202a–b). Even more tools originally from the Achao mission had been moved to the college at Castro for safekeeping, including the following: 'Itt. ocho hachas, herrameintas fragua; Itt. un yunque, dos viornias quatro machos los tres grandes y uno pequeño, un tornillo grande; Itt. otro tornillo grande, y yunque del mismo grandor que el sitado arriba esta prestado al S.r Juan Loayza se manda la recojer; Itt. otro tornillito pequeño con su yunquesito y vigornia; Itt. onse sierras, y quatro de ellas pequeñas y las demas grandes que se componen de tres serruchos, dos grandes y dos medianos; Itt. quatro

martillos, y un machetito; Itt. dos tenasas un alicate, una entenalla, una vasqueta y
una clavera, tres limas viejas, un compas; Itt. ocho varrenas sinco de ellas grandes y
las tres chicas; Itt. sinco escoplos de maior a menor, los tres de todo fierro; Itt. una
urbia chica, tres junteras una de molduras un guillamen, un sepillo, un acanalador,
otro mas; Itt. dos asuelas de una mano, y otra de dos; Itt. dos gramilles, dos fierros,
sueltos e junteritas; Itt. una plancha de fierro, dos chapas viejas, y once ur[...]; Itt. un
escarcador, un tajonsito, y una claverita para hacer clavos chicos; Itt. un acanalador
con su fierro' (ibid., fols 227b–228a).

41 The following tools were listed at Cailín: 'Ittn. por una petaca unos pocos clavos y
    unas alforjas son 26 clavos; Ittn. por 4 sierras; Ittn. dos machetes; Ittn. por 275
    tablas de alerse las tabl[a]s son de este colegio ... Nota lo que sigue aqui apuntado se
    allaria con el ymbentario que se hizo de lo que pertenece desta casa en la ciudad de
    Castro 22 de diciembre de 1767. Dos rostros de santos, onse junteras, un acanalador
    y una moldura todo con sus cajas, dos sepillos con caxas, 7 gurbias con su caxa,
    entre grandes y chicas, 9 escoplos con cax. de madera las 8 uno de fierro, 8 varren-
    itas, 3 compases, 4 fierros de tornear, unas tenasas, 4 limas con una quebrada, una
    sacabroca, 3 fierros sueltos de picostera y sepillo, una barrena descora, un martillo,
    3 punsones de fierros chicos, una asuela de dos manos, y otra de una mano, una oja
    de sierra vieja, 9 limas nueb., 9 escoplitos chicos, otra asuela de dos manos, una
    hachita ynglesa con su pico, siete fierros de molduras con sus caxas, dos sepillos
    con sus caxas de madera, un guillamen con caxa, tres herramientas de tornar' (ibid.,
    fols 212b–214b). The following items belonging to the Cailín mission were kept at
    the college in Castro: 'Ittn. docientas y ochenta tablas de alerse pertenecen al este
    colegio de Castro; Ittn. dos rostros de santos; Ittn. erramientas q.e se hallaron en los
    cajones sitados onse junteras, un acanalador, una moldura todo con sus cajas de
    madera, dos cepillos con cajas, siete inbias, entre grandes y pequeñas; Ittn. nueve
    escoplos con cavos de madera los ocho menos uno; Ittn ocho varrenitas, tres com-
    pases, y quatro fierros de tornear, unas benasas, quatro limas, con una quebrada;
    Ittn. una sacabroca, tres fierros sueltos de juntera y sepillo, una varrena de cocona,
    un martillo, tres punsones y dos fierros chicos; Ittn. dos asuelas de dos manos y otra
    de una, una oja de cierra vieja; Ittn. sinco limas mas, quatro escoplos pequeños; Ittn
    una acha pequeña con su pico, siete fierros de molduras con sus cajas, dos cepillos
    con sus cajas toda madera; Ittn. un guillamen con caja, y tres erramientas mas de
    tornear, otra varrena y dos quebradas pequeñas' (ibid., fols 232a–233a).

42 'Itt. quinse hachas nuebas, trese d[ic]has mas viejas, y veinte y ocho hachas mas que
    dise el R.do P.e Vd. estan en las hasiendas las que se recojeran en el poder de los
    sujetos que las tienen; Itt. otra hacha mas; Itt. seis varrenas sin cavos, y seis limitas
    sin cavos; Itt. una caxeta de madera con varias menudencias de reliquias, estampitas,
    y medallas; Itt. sinco varrenas entre chicas y grandes, una asuela de una mano, un
    escoplo con cavo de madera; Itt. sinco herramientas de molduras con sus caxas; Itt.

un limpiador de fierro, quatro fierresitos de carpintería, un alicate, dos fierros de sepillo, una varrenita, una oja de sierra vieja; Itt. quatro limas sin cavos, un tacho viejo, un pedaso de fierro como de dos libras, un barretonsillo de sero; Itt. una juntera, un martillo grande, un formon, un escoplillo, otro formon quebrado, una asuela de una mano; Itt. dos fierros con sus cavos que llaman maichiques; Itt. unas tenasas, dos urbias viejas, un anillo de grillete; Itt. las hachas y amencionadas son en el todo sinquento y seis con catorse nuebas, y no quinse como se dijo antes; Itt. de d[ic]has hachas quatro estan en la estancia de Meulín dos en poder del capatas, y dos as cargo de los pastores en la estancia de Lemuy otras dos hachas, una d[ic]ha en poder del molinero que hasen sinquenta y sinco, fuera de una hacha que se le dío al yndio sacristan en parte de pago; Itt. herramientas de fragua, un yunque, un tornillo, un macho, dos martillos, uno grande, y otro pequeño, unas corbas, una tenasa, un alicate pequeño una clavera, nuebe limas, dos contadores, quatro medianos, tres sinselitas; [in the rooms of Franz Xavier Kisling] una lima grande, un martillo pequeño, dos barrones pequeñas, un alicate quebrado, tres basitos de christal, un candado de viuda con llave, una escrivanía con su erraje y llabe, una piedra grande con su mano para moler colores; Itt. seis rostros de santos con sus manos sin encarnar, y otra estatua, y un niño sin encarnar; [in the rooms of Francisco Xavier Pietas] Itt. quarenta y dos limas nuebas de todos tamaños; Itt. nuebe d[ic]has con cavos; Itt. dos sepillos, una juntera sin caxas; [in the rooms of Michael Mayer] Itt. seis machetes, quatro gurbias; Itt.una barrena, y tres fierros de torno; Itt. una juntera armada; Itt. dos fierros con un sepillo y acanalador; Itt. un guillamen; Itt. un sepillo grande con su caxa; Itt. un compasito de alquimia; [in the rooms of Joseph García] Itt. un compas grande, y una tenasa; Itt. siete limas sin cavos, un sepillo, tres fierros pequeños de carpintería; Itt. un martillo, una barrenita, una sierra pequeña; Itt. un quadrante de observasión descompuesto, otro quadrante hechiso' (ibid., fols 222b–227a).

43 'Ittn. Un cajonsillo de clavos echos de varias vitolas; Ittn. Dos sierras; y dos serruchos; y dose varrenas; Ittn. Tres escoplos y una urbia; Ittn. Seis ores; Ittn. Un juntera; Itt. quatro sientas tablas de alerse' (ibid., fols 205b–206a, 231a).

44 'Ittn sinquenta tab.s de alerse buenas' (ibid., fol. 217b).

45 *Chiloé: Un legado universal*, p. 37; *Las iglesias misionales*, ed. Montecinos Barrientos et al. (n3 above); Hernán Montecinos Barrientos, 'Las iglesias de madera de Chiloé, Chile: La constante tarca de conservas,' paper delivered at the World Monuments Fund Conference, São Paulo, Brazil, April 2002.

46 *Las iglesias misionales*, ed. Montecinos Barrientos et al. See also Ramón Gutiérrez and Graciela María Viñuales, 'Architettura in Paraguay e nelle missioni gesuitiche (secoli XVII e XVIII),' in *L'arte cristiana del nuovo mondo*, ed. Ramón Gutiérrez (Milan, 1997), pp. 375–84.

47 *Chiloé: Un legado universal*, p. 98; *Las iglesias misionales*, ed. Montecinos Barrientos et al.

48 Bailey, 'La Calera de Tango' and 'The Calera de Tango' (n4 above).

49 *Las iglesias misionales*, ed. Montecinos Barrientos et al.; Montecinos Barrientos, 'Las iglesias de madera.'

50 Guarda, *Iglesias* (n3 above); Modiano, *Iglesias de Chiloé* and *Las experiencias arquitectónicas* (n3 above); *Las iglesias misionales*, ed. Montecinos Barrientos et al.; *Chiloé: Un legado universal.*

51 Bailey, *Art on the Jesuit Missions* (n1 above), pp. 11, 32, 38, 44, 64.

52 Pereira Salas, *Historia* (n22 above), pp. 114–15.

53 In contrast to sculpture, the inventories list very few paintings, and the fathers seem to have made do mostly with engravings. At Cailín, for example: 'Ittn. dos laminas la una S.n Fran.co Xavier y la otra S.n Ygnasio; Ittn. dies y seis estampas de humo y colores, entre grandes y pequeñas' (ANC Jesuitas 3 fols 210a, 232b). At the estancia of Meulin: 'Ittn. mas seis estampas grandes en el dormitorio' (fol. 217b). At the estancia of Lemuy: 'Ittn. una lamina con su marco dorado de media bara de alto, seis estampas grandes; y quarenta y dos menores; una cruz esta de firme puesta en la pared; y un cajonsito de qu[...] belas' (fol. 220b). At Castro: 'Itt. una estampa de S.n Fran.co de Vorja con su marco de madera; Itt. un cajonsito de estampas y reliquias; Itt. un lienso de Sn. Fran.co Xavier' (fols 223b–224b). The following formerly belonged to the church at Castro and the missions of Achao, Chonchi, and Cailín and were kept at the college of Castro: 'Quadros: Ittn. uno de S.n Joseph en su Altar; Ittn. otros dos de S.n Agustin, y S.ta Ana con sus marcos dorados viejos; Ittn. otro de S.ta Maria Magdalena con marcos tallados de madera esta en la Capilla del S.r del Agonia; Ittn. una estampa de S.n Fran.co de Asis; Ittn. dos quadros viejos de S.n Blas y S.n Pablo; Ittn. otro del Corazon de Jesus; Ittn. un quadro pequeño viejo de N.ra S.a con su marco dorado; Ittn. una lamina con marco dorado de plata de Bolonia esta arriva del Sagrario; Ittn. seis laminitas con marcos del espejos, y una estampa de S.n Franc.co Xavier esta en el pulpito; Ittn. seis estampas de la pasion arriva de los pilares de la nave de la iglecia' (fols 254b–255a).

54 Vazquez de Acuña, *Costumbres religiosas* (n2 above), pp. 51–9; see also Pereira Salas, *Historia*, p. 264.

55 Bailey, *Art on the Jesuit Missions*, pp. 164–9.

56 The following belonged to the church at Castro and the missions of Achao, Chonchi, and Cailín, and they were gathered together in the college at Castro: 'Estatuas: Primeramente N.ra S.a del Rosario con su niño de cuerpo entero; Ittn. S.n Ign.cio y S.n Fran.co Xavier de cuerpo entero; Ittn. un Señor en la Cruz esta en su altar; Ittn. S.n Miguel de cuerpo entero algo maltratado; Ittn. N.ra S.a de la Asuncion de rostro manos y pies en su altar; Ittn. N.ra S.a de la Purissima Concepción de cuerpo entero tiene tres quartas algo mas de alto esta en el altar del S.r S.n Joseph; Ittn. un Señor de la columna esta en una repisa; Ittn. un bulto de N.ra S.a de los Dolores esta en su repisa; Ittn. otro de S.n Juan Nepomuceno en su repissa; Ittn. dos bultos de S.ta Theressa y S.ta Rosa con su niño Jesus estan en sus repissas; Ittn. un Señor encar-

selado esta en una repissa; Ittn. una anima del purgatorio de medio cuerpo esta en una repissa; Ittn. dos pares de rostros y manos p.a N.ra S.a y S.n J.ph y para otros santos; Ittn. S.ta Ana y su niña componense de rostro y manos; Ittn. otras dos estatuas del S.n Ign.cio y S.n Fran.co Xav.r componense de rostro y manos; Ittn. otras dos estatuas de S.n Luis Gonsaga y S.n Stanislao tiene el uno un Santo Christo en las manos, y el otro un Niño Jesus, estan en los nichos colaterales del altar mayor; Ittn. un Santo Christo de pasta en la Sacristia puesto en un nicho a manera de corazon forrado p.r de dentro con turpi asul; Ittn. una imagen pequeña de la Purissima Concepción de marfil q.e esta arriva de la repissa de S.ta Rosa; Ittn. dos Santos Christos de Alquimia medianos que sirven a S.n Fran.co Xav.r y a S.n Juan Nepomuceno; Ittn. otro de lo mismo pequeño q.e sirve en el altar de N.ra S.a de la Asumpcion; Ittn. otro d[ic]ho de guesso pequeño en el altar mayor; Ittn. una cruz en la pila bautismal con sus puntas de plata; Ittn. otra cruz de madera; Ittn. un rostro y manos de S.n Ign.cio' (ANC Jesuitas 3 fol. 254a–b). The following were found at Cailín: 'Ittn. un santo cristo chico; Ittn. mas un santo cristo con su cajon; Ittn. un S.to Xpto con su caxa de madera; Ittn. dos rostros de santos' (fols 210b–233a). These objects were inventoried at Lemuy: 'Ittn. otra d[ic]ha casa con dos bibiendas la una que sirve de oratorio y ai en el una de N.ro Señor de bulto de una bara de alto' (fol. 220a). This piece was listed for Castro: 'Itt. un santo Christo que se hallo en el aposento rectoral como de dos tersias de largo con su dosel de raso negro guarnecido con ojacillo de plata, y sinta llana amarilla angosta' (fol. 224a). And at Chonchi the inventory recorded these: 'Itt. dos rostros de ymajenes' (fol. 229b).

57   'Ropa y Vestido de las Estatuas: Ittn. quatro mantos de N.ra S.a del Rosario, uno de tissù con frang[a]s finas de oro, otro de brocato, con frangas de oro, y flecos de ylo de oro, otro de lama amarilla con encajes falsos de ylo de plata, otro morado de ala buelta con perciana nacar por delante; Ittn. sinco tunicas o vestidos de N.ra S.a Ittn. dos tuniquitos del niño Jesus; Ittn. un capillo bueno con frang[a]s finas de plata y sintas finas y una joita de oro; Ittn. tres niños Jesuses, uno en el sagrario, otro q. esta en brasos S.ta Rosa y el otro S.n Estanislao tienen su vestidos desentes, ademas de los d[ic]hos arriva puesto[...] Ittn. dos mantos de N.ra S.a de los Dolores el uno de perciana azul con puntas negras, el otro de tela negra bordado alrrededor con seda blanca tiene lo puesto; Ittn. dos tunicas con sus mangas, una de perciana y otra de damasco negro y senefa amarilla tiene lo puesto; Ittn. S.n Juan Nepomuceno, tiene su vestido completo y puesto de brocato negro, su roquete y esclavina de azul; Ittn. las estatuas de S.ta Theresa, y S.ta Rossa tienen sus vestidos puestos, el de S.ta Theressa se compone de un manto blanco de lana y tunico de pico de oro y escapulario de lo mesmo; el de S.ta Rossa avito blanco escapulario y manto negro; Ittn. dos bestidos de N.ra S.a de la Asuncion q.e se componen de dos mantos el uno de rasso y el otro de lustrina y de lo mismo las tunicas Ittn. N.ra S.a de Belem con bestido de persiana colorada sin manto; Ittn. un bestido de S.n J.ph; Ittn. bestido

entero de S.ta Ana y su niña tienen lo puesto componece de manto y escapolaria de rasso; Ittn. un estandarte de glasè con franja de oro fina y su Jesus q.e le sirve a S.n Ign.cio p.a su fiesta; Ittn. un pendon de damasco carmesi viejo otro de rasso Ittn. un palio verde con senefa colorada de damasco y heco de lana; Ittn. onse alfombras entre grandes y chicas; Ittn. quatro paños negros, y otros mas; Ittn. dos vandas coloradas, y un pano de facistol negro; Ittn. dos liensos de anganipola, de a quatro varas Ittn. dos colgaduras de seda coloradas con listas amarillas viejas, dos cojines uno de terciop.lo carmeci viejo y otro listado; Ittn unos retasos de anganipola q.e estan en el altar de N.ra S.a de la Asuncion; Ittn. el nicho de S.n Mig[ue]l esta aforrado con un retaso de calamaco de seda viejo; Ittn. quatro sotanillas p.a los acolitos, dos de ellas de sanga con felpa azul en sus estremidades; Ittn. dos retasos cortos de pañete colorado' (ibid., fols 253b–254a).

58 *Noticia breve*, in Hanisch, *La isla de Chiloé*, pp. 249–52.
59 'Razon de los ornament.s, vassos sagrados y estatuas q.e sirven p.a la mision circular de esta prov[inci]a; Primeramente un Santo Christo grande con su caxa forrado por de fuera con cordovan y por de dentro con tripi colorado y caracolillo de plata con dos cornas de rasso; Ittn. una imagen de N.ra S.a de los Dolores y otra de S.n Juan, ambas con mantes de perciana asul y tunicas de persiana colorada, y un niño Jesus pequeño; Ittn. un corazon de Jesus grande con rayos dorados; Ittn.una peaña con sus senefas de tripi coloradas y guarnecido con caracol de plata; Ittn. un coponcito de plata p.a tener a N.ro amo colcado durante el tiempo de la Micion de cada capilla; Ittn. una estatua de S.n Isidro, y otra de S.ta Noburg con sus caxones y cortinas; Ittn. tres colchitas chicas de la tierra' (ANC Jesuitas 3 fol. 256b).

11 / The Rural Churches of the Jesuit Haciendas on the Southern Peruvian Coast

HUMBERTO RODRÍGUEZ-CAMILLONI

During the Spanish colonial period in Peru, the hacienda became the backbone of the agrarian economy, but it represented more than just an economic enterprise. As Pablo Macera has noted, the productivity of every hacienda depended on the fulfilment of religious, demographic, and fiscal functions that made it a complex institution, which in many places substituted for and at the same time complemented the Spanish colonial city and the Indian pueblo.[1] The Jesuits, in particular, were destined to play a major role in its development when the Society became one of the largest landholders of Peru as a result of sound investment and efficient administration. Between their arrival in Peru in 1568 and their expulsion in 1767, the Jesuits accumulated impressive wealth that amounted to a veritable economic empire managed by the college of San Pablo in Lima.[2] The Jesuits succeeded in maximizing the agricultural production of their haciendas while diversifying crops, to deliver to the Peruvian and other markets of the continent some of the best wine, flour, sugar, oil, and honey available in the viceroyalty. The resulting wealth made possible the creation of beautiful churches and adjacent structures that often rivalled in formal and decorative splendour the buildings erected in the urban centres. More than a few churches belonging to former Jesuit haciendas on the southern Peruvian coast have survived in different states of conservation, and here I will discuss three notable examples: San Juan de Surco, in the province of Lima, just south of the viceregal capital, and San José and San Xavier at Ingenio, in the Nazca valley, Ica. First, however, I will address some important matters concerning the internal administration of the haciendas, the communities they served, and the labour force that contributed to their growth.

Even though the college of San Pablo in Lima served as the seat of the Jesuit province in the viceroyalty, an intelligent policy of decentralization allowed each college to administer directly the judicial, technical, and commercial affairs pertaining to its own haciendas and landholdings. In charge of each hacienda was the *administrador de hacienda, hermano y coadjutor*, always a member of the order, who was responsible for the enforcement of rules and procedures dictated by the provincial superior, and also was the day-to-day administrator of the agricultural work.[3] The central administration in turn checked the running of the hacienda periodically through a system of *visitas* – not unlike those conducted by the secular government – in which a *visitador* made an audit of the *libros de la hacienda* and ultimately recorded his findings in a special *libro de órdenes, memoriales e instrucciones.*

In their management of the haciendas, the Society of Jesus acted as both a commercial entrepreneur and a religious institution, always striving to identify common ground where the demands of the two would be met. Nature itself and the natural laws that governed the land being worked were viewed as products of divine creation, and as such believed to exist subject to the will of God. The agrarian worker was bound by the rules dictated by experience, common sense, and tradition; but above all he had to pray, hoping and trusting in God, who would bless the fruit of his labour.

The Jesuit community of the hacienda was committed to a daily schedule of arduous work interrupted only by prayer and sleep. According to Macera,

The typical day in the country for the Jesuit began at 4 o'clock in the morning and ended at 9 o'clock at night. During this time, he would spend at least an hour in prayer at dawn, attend mass at 5:00 AM, pray the rosary later in the day, and make the examination of conscience before going to bed; during meals he would listen to readings from the *Contento mundis* and the martyrology. Moreover, every year he was required to travel to his college to make the Spiritual Exercises, which lasted eight days.[4]

This rigorous discipline served as a model for the Indians and African slaves, and at the same time was intended to protect the priests, especially the *administrador*, from dangerous worldly temptations.

Religion and agriculture were inextricably bound, and the evangelical mission of the Jesuits was restated time and again in the *libros de instrucciones y visitas*. Aside from the rules governing the lives of the Jesuits living in the haciendas, there were clear instructions concerning the lives of the slaves and the work in the offices and fields. For example, the orders imparted by the *visitadores* to the hacienda of Ingenio at Huaura, north of Lima, in 1684 stipulated, 'The brothers who live in this hacienda should understand that they are obliged not only to oversee the work of the slaves, but also to preach to them what they need to know in order to live a good Christian life according to the examples and teachings of the Lord.'[5] And again in 1707: 'The care in teaching African slaves their catechism and Christian Doctrine is most properly our duty; and so our brothers in charge of them should make sure they conscientiously fulfil this obligation by teaching them their lessons on a daily basis.'[6]

Work in the fields was forbidden on religious holidays, and any violation of this observance brought immediate sanction by the authorities. The daily schedule also contained a variety of religious services to be provided for the slaves; catechetical instruction for Africans who had recently arrived in the colony; weekly religious instruction for children and adults; community prayer; ten memorial masses upon the death of a slave; Easter Sunday services; confession and communion at least twice a year; Lenten services; and other celebrations. As in the Spanish colonial city, continuous observance of the liturgical calendar itself became a lengthy catechetical service, in which the entire population of the hacienda learned the contents of the New Testament through direct participation in its festivals.

The Jesuits derived their largest revenues from the sugar cane haciendas on the Peruvian coast, located mainly in the northern and central regions, with Chincha on the southern coast a notable exception. Vineyards were second in importance. Slaves provided most of the labour in the sugar cane plantations. As has been shown by Frederick P. Bowser, however, it would be erroneous to think of the slaves exclusively as tilling the fields or serving deferentially in the master's house. Many Africans were highly esteemed skilled artisans who contributed extensively to the building of the Spanish colonial cities of Peru and also made significant contributions in the rural areas. As Browser has pointed out:

By the late sixteenth century most Peruvian vineyards and sugar plantations possessed blacks skilled in the operations essential to the function of these agricultural enterprises. For example, the black slave population of the sugar hacienda of San José de Quipico in the corregimiento of Chircay in 1636 included a sugarmaster and six assistants, three purgers, two carpenters, two potters, one blacksmith, and one charcoal-maker. Some of the southern vineyards obtained their earthenware jugs from large factories located in the village of Córdoba, between Ica and Pisco, whose skilled black workers were valued at 4,000 pesos each. And many other vineyards kept slaves of their own to make the jugs or wineskins they needed. Slaves adept at masonry and adobe-making were a common feature of the Peruvian plantation, as were charcoal-makers.[7]

The Jesuits also played a key role in the religious education of the African population, a responsibility they assumed with exemplary zeal. From the very moment of their arrival on Peruvian soil in 1568, the Jesuits understood that since the Africans had been imported to make up for the shortage of Indians to serve the Spaniards, the Spaniards had an obligation to show equal concern for the spiritual welfare of both servile groups. One of the best indicators of the special care with which the Jesuits pursued proselytism among the Africans was the serious consideration given to the establishment of courses in the African languages at the college of San Pablo in Lima, and to the printing of a simple dictionary and grammar in the 'language of Angola.' According to Luis Martín, '[Already by] 1629 San Pablo was using and distributing, even to the furthest ends of the viceroyalty, prayer leaflets, catechisms, and instructions printed in Lima in the language of the slaves. In 1630, fourteen hundred and forty copies of a simple grammar came off the press, and the Jesuits of San Pablo were furnished with the essential tools to begin the systematic study of the "language of Angola."'[8]

San Juan de Surco (fig. 11.1) was one of the first haciendas acquired by the college of San Pablo; it was a direct donation in 1581 from Diego Porras Sagredo.[9] In subsequent years the agricultural land was significantly increased through the leasing of tracts belonging to Indian chieftains of the region. During the seventeenth century, part of the property was used for grazing 800 head of cattle and 250 goats, and part was reserved for growing sugar cane – the product for which it came to be best known. In the 1620s the sugar cane yield was substantially increased by irrigation, with the construction of a large reservoir and an aqueduct. Among the decisive improvements made by the Jesuits was the installation of a good *trapiche*, or sugar mill, to produce sugar and honey. San Juan also benefited from the new techniques invented in the 1630s by Brother Bernardo Lete, who succeeded in making *trapiches* work faster and produce more, while at the same time decreasing their deafening noise.[10]

The extant buildings of San Juan, partially restored in 1991–2, constitute the essential components of the *casco*, or architectural nucleus, of the hacienda: the church and the adjoining house and other service quarters define the western front of a large open plaza. Other secondary original structures once facing this space have long since disappeared. A distinctive feature of the elevation is the second-storey loggia of wooden arches, which give a strong sense of direction, articulation, and coherence. The loggia would have provided a privileged observation post onto the plaza below.

Most prominent, however, is the church, with its twin-towered facade serving as a vertical counterpoint to the adjacent horizontal wing. It is located in the southwestern corner of the complex so as to offer a monumental three-quarter view of its mass from the plaza. Traces of an old road suggest that the major ceremonial approach to the plaza would have provided this view – an important feature of the layout of the buildings, whereby the church became the visual

11.1. Church of San Juan de Surco, Surco, Lima, exterior, 1752.
Photo, taken in 1972, courtesy of Humberto Rodríguez-Camilloni.

symbol of the entire complex. The desire to highlight the church in this fashion
perhaps explains why this arrangement of the buildings was adopted in several
hacienda complexes during the Spanish colonial period. It conforms, for instance, to the prototypical hacienda complex as depicted in the coloured drawings commissioned by Martínez de Compañón for the work *Trujillo del Perú*
(1779–91), even though in these representations the actual size of the church
may have been exaggerated.[11]

A clear geometric order is also apparent in the plan (fig. 11.2), revealing a
strict orthogonal organization of interior and exterior spaces. In the centre, the
large square courtyard, reminiscent of a monastic cloister, would have provided
a semi-private space complementary to that of the exterior plaza. The repetition
of similar measurements in the string of single and double rectangular rooms
aligning the northern and western sides strongly suggests a modular design.
Administrative offices and storage rooms associated with the daily activities of
the hacienda appear to have been housed in the western wing, with direct access
from the exterior plaza. The piano nobile of the western wing contained the cells
of the religious community, including professors and novices from the college of
San Pablo, who used the hacienda as a country house. The administrator's rooms
were located to the far right, enjoying the distinction of having a separate
balcony overlooking the enclosed atrium of the church.

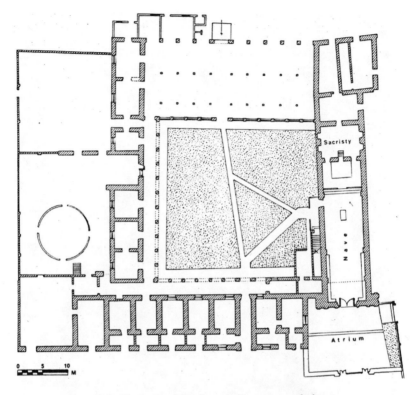

11.2. Hacienda of San Juan de Surco, general plan.
Drawing by Humberto Rodríguez-Camilloni.

The church (fig. 11.3) has a single nave covered by a *quincha* barrel vault that terminates in a dome above the sanctuary. The structural elements of this remarkable antiseismic method of construction can best be seen in a photograph of the dilapidated building (see fig. 11.1), taken in 1972. Here are visible the thick adobe brick walls, covered with plaster, that support the structure of the roof, consisting of a wooden frame of transverse arches covered with cane mats, and finished with a layer of adobe and plaster on the exterior and wooden boards and stucco in the interior.[12]

The dome of San Juan, also made out of *quincha*, is a daring structure supported by transverse arches above the sanctuary that are pierced by lunette windows. Lack of maintenance undoubtedly contributed to its progressive deterioration over time and final collapse during the earthquake of 1966, when the wooden retablo, or main altarpiece, was destroyed. Only fragments of this

11.3. Church of San Juan de Surco, interior nave after the restoration of 1991–2.
Photo courtesy of Humberto Rodríguez-Camilloni.

original eighteenth-century retablo survive today. However, it is known that the church 'had a beautiful retablo on the main altar with thirteen wooden carved panels; two lateral retablos; two paintings in the apse described in the inventories as *very large*; six paintings in the nave, and twelve other small paintings of the Passion; in addition to a bronze baptismal font, and an elaborate architectural decoration.'[13]

The newly restored interior of San Juan (fig. 11.3) permits us to appreciate its unified longitudinal space, with the major focus provided by the sanctuary, raised by three steps from the floor of the nave. A series of four lunette windows evenly spaced between transverse arches at either side of the nave allows even illumination, which is complemented by a dramatic spotlight over the altar supplied by the lantern of the dome. A certain movement in depth is found at the cornice level in the rhythmic articulation of ornamental corbels that mark the axes of the lunette windows and alternate with the capitals of the engaged pilasters and the corbel that supports the third major transverse arch of the nave. It should be noted that the special condition of this transverse arch helps to emphasize visually the axis of the lunette windows and the exact mid-point of the nave measured beyond the choir loft over the main entrance.

An inscription on the face of the choir loft bears the date 1752, which is that of the completion of the church in its present form; but it is very likely that this latest colonial design incorporated significant portions of one or more earlier structures. Evidence of such incorporation is provided by fragments of mural paintings that decorate the walls of the nave and the sanctuary and were discovered during the restoration work of 1991–2. Most typical are the horizontal and vertical bands containing cherubs and foliate scrollwork of Renaissance origin derived from European prints. On the walls of the sanctuary, however, a striking illusionistic painting in perspective suggesting the arms of a transept is depicted. This painted decorative scheme also included a sculptural cherub font for holy water next to the side door, which gave direct access to the interior courtyard; the scheme was extended to the walls and niches of the *camarín* (vestry and sacristy) behind the high altar.

Even though the *camarín* is a separate, single-storey rectangular room, it appears to have been an integral part of the original church design. It is spatially connected to the sanctuary by two small doors at either side of the high altar and a raised central opening permitting access to the high altar retablo from the rear. The *camarín* and the sanctuary also have the same dimensions in the plan, their measurement yielding the ratio 3:4. The use of simple ratios elsewhere in the church so as to achieve harmonious integration of the parts, such as the 1:3 ratio of the width to the length of the nave (including the wall thickness), and the 1:1 ratio of the width to the height of the nave (again including the wall thickness), suggests the intervention of an architect familiar with Renaissance design principles.

The main facade of the church is a similarly balanced, symmetrical composition that can be inscribed in a perfect square (excluding the tower cupolas). The width of each tower measured from pilaster to pilaster serves as the module, repeated six times across the width of the entire facade, or a side of the square. Another, smaller square, four modules to the side, contains the frontispiece, which presents a simplified variation with different architectural elements of facade schemes found in Lima churches such as San Francisco (1657–74) and San Agustín (1720). It is divided into two storeys symmetrically arranged. On the first storey, the doorway is flanked by single rusticated pilasters and shell niches, and these are echoed by the same elements, but in diminishing height, on the second storey. The larger pilasters are topped by a complete entablature block, in which the cornice steps forward and curves upward at the middle to embrace the central niche of the second storey, which most likely contained the statue of the patron saint. This niche, flanked by two oval windows, is the focus of the entire composition and is crowned by a curvilinear entablature that rises slightly above the bases of the towers. Finally, above the cornice runs a horizontal wooden balustrade divided into three parts corresponding to the vertical bays of the frontispiece; it establishes a visual connection with the balustraded balconies of the belfries.

A distinctive motif is the stucco arabesque that appears above the rusticated frame of the doorway. This sculptural ornament, probably derived from European prints, would have been complemented by the figures of saints that once filled the empty niches. In addition, the painted ornamentation on the bases of the towers along with the other floral panels, unknown until their recent discovery, would have added a variety of colouristic effects.

Like those of its urban counterparts, the plaza of the rural hacienda must have served as a stage during outdoor religious ceremonies. Dominating the space, the elaborate church facade provided a focus and a fitting backdrop. Here the Jesuits made good use of the pomp and ceremony of the church, with processions carrying multicoloured standards, garlands, incense, and, especially, music to attract Africans and Indians. Dialogues with a Christian message were set to music, and the slaves quickly developed a reputation for fine performances. Not surprisingly, in the seventeenth century the college of San Pablo boasted a band of talented African musicians, 'accomplished players of clarinets and *chirimias*, the Spanish version of the Scottish bagpipe. The Negro musicians performed at the festivities organized by the sodalities and became so famous that they were in great demand even outside the [college].'[14] In this way, by oratorical, visual, and musical means, the fundamental Christian mission of the Society was reasserted.

In contrast with San Juan de Surco, the churches of the haciendas of San José (fig. 11.5) and San Xavier (fig. 11.9) at Ingenio, in the Nazca valley – perhaps the best known among the Jesuit hacienda churches – remain among the most threatened today. Harold E. Wethey found these churches in ruinous condition in 1949,[15] and I documented their progressive deterioration with photographs taken during my visits in 1972 and 2000. They are both extraordinary, high-quality designs that betray the hand of accomplished architect-sculptors of the period. Despite their physical proximity, San Xavier was under the jurisdiction of the college of San Pablo in Lima, whereas San José was under the jurisdiction of the college of San Bernardo in Cuzco – a fact that may be of importance when considering the skilled labour that went into their construction. San Xavier was donated to the Jesuits in 1668 by Francisco Cabezas. San José was purchased from Juan Francisco Arias Maldonado in 1619, but it was enlarged the following year with a donation of land by Juan de Madrid.[16]

At the time of the Jesuit expulsion in 1767, San José and San Xavier were appraised at 247,729 pesos and 198,992 pesos respectively, an indication of their value as top-producing vineyards of the southern Peruvian coast.[17] The ever increasing productivity of these haciendas was achieved largely through the successful reclamation of marshy lands by the Jesuits. According to one source, 'the vineyards of San Xavier and [San José] produced, in 1750, more than eleven thousand jars of several kinds of wine, which were sold in the public markets of the viceroyalty. Three hundred slaves were engaged full time there picking and pressing the grapes, and producing the well-known Jesuit wines.'[18]

An aerial view of 1945 shows the *casco* of the San José complex (fig. 11.4), with the church occupying the northeastern corner of the rectangular plaza. The church stands on a raised platform with a staircase extending the whole width of the facade. The arcaded loggia of the main house (missing its roof) can be seen on the opposite side of the plaza, though not directly on an axis with the church. The collapsed first half of the *quincha* roof of the church may be owing to the severely destructive earthquake of 1940.

The western front of the San José church (fig. 11.5) reiterates the theme of the twin-towered facade, but is an original monumental ensemble of which the most distinguishing feature is the fully developed Solomonic portal, resembling an altarpiece. The columns of the first storey stand on individual pedestals arranged in pairs flanking shell niches, occupied by Jesuit saints, that are repeated on the second storey. In the centre, above the doorway, the entablature bends upward to form an elongated curvilinear pediment that breaks to embrace a horizontal oval window, surmounted yet by another shell niche.

The use of the Solomonic order is most unexpected here: although frequently found in seventeenth- and eighteenth-century retablos, it is rarely used in colonial church exteriors on the Peruvian coast. As Wethey noted, 'this Solomonic

11.4. Hacienda of San José, Ingenio, Nazca, aerial view in 1945.
Photo courtesy of Servicio Aerofotográfico Nacional.

retable on the exterior of a church has no exact parallel in Peru,' the portals of La Merced (1697–1704) and San Agustín (1720) in Lima notwithstanding.[19] The columns of San José in fact follow Vignola's rule (1562) in that the spirals make six complete turns; but they are divided by rings of acanthus leaves into three sections of equal height, the centre one smooth and the others striated, suggesting later models such as those of Caramuel de Lobkowitz (1678) and Guarini (1737).[20] Elsewhere in South America, the closest parallels to the Solomonic columns of San José are probably those of the facade of La Compañía in Quito (1722–5), designed by the Jesuit Leonhard Deubler (1689–1769), who evidently had no connection with the Nazca church. But it appears that, like Deubler, the designer of the San José portal may have followed the Spanish theoretician Fray Juan Ricci (1662) in considering the Solomonic order 'a supreme order, the highest of all.'[21]

The arabesques and scrollwork of the middle section of the frontispiece and around the oval window reveal a familiarity with European pattern books and prints, and these have been translated into a robust composition of great vitality. The towers, with their two-storeyed belfries and hemispherical cupolas, also

11.5. Church of San José, Ingenio, Nazca, facade, 1744.
Photo, taken in 2000, courtesy of Humberto Rodríguez-Camilloni.

recall the church of La Compañía at Pisco (1723), except that here the bases are further embellished with a rusticated surface and engaged pilasters with *mudéjar* patterns of interlocking square links. The bold projections and deep recessions of the cornices and other mouldings intensify the pictorial effects. Despite the decorative exuberance of the facade as a whole, however, the design is controlled by classical proportions based on the square. The module is again the width of the tower measured at its base, which is repeated exactly five times along the width of the entire facade and five times along the height of the towers, excluding the belfry cupolas. The date 1744, inscribed on the facade and still readable in 1945, is confirmed by another inscription in the sacristy stating that the church was begun in 1740 and completed on 19 March 1744, the feast of St Joseph, the patron saint of the church.

The crumbling facade (see fig. 11.5) reveals the structure to be made of a combination of different materials. Brick and adobe covered with plaster form the lower tiers of the facade, including the bases of the towers. In the upper parts, however, *quincha* construction with stucco facing is used throughout. The wooden framework of the belfries is also visible from within, as are the cane mats that cover the surviving transverse arches of the raised choir.

The exterior decorative scheme of San José was extended to the side portal of the church and the entrance to the sacristy, both of which deserve to be revisited here. The side portal (fig. 11.6) has an arch *in alfiz* flanked by curious segments of columns – not half columns as noted by Wethey in 1949[22] – supported by small corbels. Not previously mentioned, however, is the painted wooden statue *de vestir* that fills the central niche above the door. Its appearance and evident function would explain the missing statues in many Spanish colonial portals and should be taken into consideration when analytical reconstructions of their original appearance are made. My photograph of this side portal taken in 1972 (fig. 11.6) clearly shows that the statue was a delicate carved construction of a torso on staves, by then much deteriorated owing to exposure to the elements. In its original condition, the statue would have been dressed with gesso-stiffened cloth or textile garments and very likely also been used as a lightweight processional figure.

The sacristy portal illustrates the kind of misinterpretation that can result from an incorrect reading of the iconographic elements. The stucco work in high relief on the lintel of the rectangular doorway features a cartouche of the Holy Eucharist, with heraldic angels flanked by grotesque masks with projecting tongues set on miniature pilasters suspended on tiny corbels. A similar symmetrical arrangement consisting of an arabesque and *groteschi* is found on the frieze immediately above. Foliate borders containing dragon heads at either side of the portal (fig. 11.7) provide a vertical counterpoint. For Wethey, such motifs

11.6. Church of San José, side portal.
Photo, taken in 1972, courtesy of Humberto Rodríguez-Camilloni.

signified 'an undeniable case of the reappearance or survival of an ancient pre-Columbian theme, so thoroughly characteristic of Nazca pottery and textiles, which were produced in the same valley many centuries before the arrival of the Spaniards.'[23] The problem with this interpretation is that it assumes the eighteenth-century colonial designer would have had access to archaeological material of a pre-Inca culture that flourished in 100–800 CE, while ignoring the overwhelming evidence of the most likely source, namely, European prints. To cite two examples: the anthropomorphic head with plumed headdress is frequently found in designs by Vredeman de Vries (1562); the foliate border with dragon heads may be associated with designs by Gabriel Krammer (1611) (fig. 11.8).

The plan and reconstructed section drawings of the church show the single nave with its *quincha* barrel vault pierced by four pairs of lunette windows that culminate in the sanctuary, elevated by five steps and then one step. Behind the high altar is a rectangular *camarín*, recalling that of San Juan de Surco, lit by a large window in the rear wall. The sacristy, also rectangular in plan, abuts the northern wall of the church along its major axis, and communicates with the sanctuary through a splayed doorway. On the southern side is the square baptistery, which can be entered from the nave through an arched doorway just beyond the *sotocoro* (the space under the choir loft). Finally, as was common in the hacienda churches, a crypt was located under the nave, and was used for the burial of members of the religious community.

Even in its present ruinous condition, the interior of San José reveals another similarity with La Compañía at Pisco in the broad moulded cornice running the length of the nave, with each individual window having its separate cedar balustrade resting on a decorative console. Unlike at La Compañía, however, at San José consoles rather than pilasters mark the separation into bays above the wall niches where the side retablos were set. The high altar had a very fine Solomonic retablo captured *in situ* in some old photographs; but this was removed in 1949 and reassembled inside the modern church of La Virgen del Pilar in San Isidro, Lima, where it can still be viewed today.

The stucco decoration of the interior is most exuberant in the spandrels of the *sotocoro* arch, featuring masks with plumed headdresses of coiled foliage and dragons growing from their mouths. Again, it is unnecessary to interpret these forms as deriving from pre-Columbian motifs, since they appear in a variety of European prints (mainly non-Hispanic) dating from the sixteenth century and later. Similarly, the floral bands and strapwork that decorate the intrados surfaces of the transverse arches and lunette ribs point to German garment-hem patterns or prints. The beautiful shell tympanums that decorate the inside door of the church and the interior door of the sacristy – also typical of the Lima school – probably owed their popularity to the wide diffusion of printed architectural frontispieces with this design.[24]

11.7. Church of San José, exterior portal of sacristy, detail.
Photo, taken in 2000, courtesy of Humberto Rodríguez-Camilloni.

At San Xavier (fig. 11.9), also located in the Nazca valley, the single-nave church and L-shaped hacienda house front are separated by an open passageway that permits the church to be appreciated as an almost free-standing monument dominating the western end of the plaza. The arrangement recalls that of the hacienda of San José at Chincha (1754), but the traditional orientation of the church is reversed, so that the facade faces east. In plan and elevation, San Xavier differs in several important respects from San José at Nazca and indeed from all the other Jesuit hacienda churches on the southern Peruvian coast. Most conspicuous are the massive circular towers with internal spiral staircases leading to the choir loft and belfries, the absence of the *camarín* behind the high altar, and the rectangular storage room and square sacristy surmounted by a dome on pendentives flanking the sanctuary. The bays down the nave are clearly indicated by protruding pilasters that correspond to the transverse arches of the nave barrel vault (fig. 11.10). The uniform rhythm of four identical lunette windows beyond the choir loft at either side of the nave is broken only at the western end, where

11.8. Border designs from Gabriel Krammer, *Schweiff Buchlein* (Cologne, 1611), fol. 18.

11.9. Church of San Xavier, Ingenio, Nazca, facade, 1745–6.
Photo, taken in 1972, courtesy of Humberto Rodríguez-Camilloni.

an additional pair of wider lunette windows extends the depth of the sanctuary. Directly underneath the sanctuary, which is raised by four and two steps, is the crypt, ingeniously lit by a splayed window cutting across the rear wall, which is three metres thick.

The church of San Xavier can be firmly dated to 1745–6 by the inscription on a contemporary painting in the hacienda, unknown to Wethey, which clearly states that its first religious service was celebrated on Christmas Day, 1746. This is a remarkable fact, since it indicates that the church survived the devastating earthquake of 28 October 1746; it is even more extraordinary given that adobe brick construction was used throughout the building, *including* in the barrel vault of the nave and in the dome above the sacristy. Though seriously damaged, these structures were still standing when I photographed and measured them in 1972.

Like San José in the same valley, San Xavier (see fig. 11.10) has lost its interior artwork, including the retablo of the main altar. There remains, however, the superb stucco work, unrivalled among the other hacienda churches. The rich high-relief ornament is concentrated upon the pilasters, frieze, transverse arches, and face of the choir loft, containing fantastic combinations of anthropomorphic animal and vegetable forms that have suggested pre-Columbian and even Asian derivations. Here too, however, one must proceed with caution, since close European models can readily be identified. These designs must have provided a stunning architectural backdrop to the gilded retablos and religious paintings that once decorated the walls. As Wethey wrote in 1949, 'the stucco work throughout the interior is of surpassing beauty. Even the font for holy water is part of the unified scheme which was originally complemented by a series of large paintings upon the walls, now alas, in ruinous condition.'[25]

Wethey read the main facade of San Xavier as a hybrid work, 'the product of crossed influences from Lima and Arequipa.'[26] He based this conclusion on a formal comparison between the towers of San Xavier and the tower of Santo Domingo in Arequipa (1649 and later), a good example of the planiform style characteristic of that region. He drew special attention, once again, to the grotesque masks with plumed headdresses, also found on the Arequipa monument. Yet, as I have suggested, these iconographic parallels can be explained by the mutual debt of Nazca and Arequipa to common sources of inspiration in European prints and pattern books. And such masks also appear on Lima monuments such as the sacristy portal of San Francisco, by Lucas Meléndez, of 1729. At the same time, the frontispiece of San Xavier, with its curved broken pediments and oval window, is certainly derived from a scheme already developed by the Lima school, perhaps inspired by Italian designs such as those by Bernardino Radi (1618) and adopted in church facades such as those of Santa

11.10. Church of San Xavier, interior nave.
Photo, taken in 2000, courtesy of Humberto Rodríguez-Camilloni.

Rosa de los Padres (1669–85) and Las Trinitarias (1708–22). The different aesthetic results between Nazca and Arequipa, however, merit recognition as a reflection of the talent of the colonial designers and craftsmen, who time and again were able to translate those common sources of inspiration into truly original designs.

Through an analysis of these three rural churches belonging to former Jesuit haciendas on the southern Peruvian coast, I have tried to demonstrate that these monuments constitute an architectural corpus of singular importance in the history of South American colonial architecture. San Juan de Surco, just to the south of Lima, has been partially restored in modern times and has now been incorporated into a new urban district; San José and San Xavier at Ingenio in the Nazca valley face an uncertain future. To be sure, several other hacienda churches have been lost to earthquakes, years of neglect, or virtual abandonment following the ill-fated agrarian reform undertaken by the Peruvian government in the early 1970s, and still others have deteriorated to a condition beyond repair. Yet, whenever and wherever possible, the extant examples merit the investment of every effort to ensure their preservation. I hope this study will serve as a modest contribution towards a better appreciation of them and towards their definitive conservation.

NOTES

1 Pablo Macera, *Mapas coloniales de haciendas cuzqueñas* (Lima, 1968), p. xi.
2 For a history of this institution, see Luis Martín, *The Intellectual Conquest of Peru: The Jesuit College of San Pablo, 1568–1767* (New York, 1968).
3 See Pablo Macera, *Instrucciones para el manejo de las haciendas jesuitas del Perú (ss. XVII–XVIII)* (Lima 1966), pp. 24–6.
4 Macera, *Instrucciones*, p. 31.
5 Ibid., p. 30 n40.
6 Ibid., p. 73.
7 Frederick P. Bowser, *The African Slave in Colonial Peru, 1524–1650* (Stanford, 1974), p. 126.
8 Martín, *The Intellectual Conquest*, p. 51.
9 Ibid., p. 173.
10 Ibid., p. 174.
11 See, for example, plates 88 and 89 in *La Obra del Obispo Martínez Compañón sobre Trujillo del Perú en el siglo XVIII*, vol. 2 (Madrid, 1985).
12 Light and elastic enough to withstand the dreaded frequent earthquakes, the system of *quincha* construction was introduced by the Portuguese architect Constantino de

Vasconcelos in the church of San Francisco in Lima (1657–74) and widely used along the Peruvian coast thereafter. See Humberto Rodríguez-Camilloni, 'Tradición e innovación en la arquitectura del virreinato del Perú: Constantino de Vasconcelos y la invención de la arquitectura de Quincha en Lima durante el siglo XVII,' in Universidad Nacional Autónoma de México, Instituto de Investigaciones Estéticas, *Arte, historia e identidad en América: Visiones comparativas*, XVII Coloquio Internacional de Historia del Arte, vol. 2 (México 1994), pp. 387–403.

13 Luis Villacorta Santamato, 'Iglesias rurales en Lima,' *Huaca* 2 (Lima, 1988): 61.

14 Martín, *The Intellectual Conquest*, p. 137.

15 Harold E. Wethey, *Colonial Architecture and Sculpture in Peru* (Cambridge, 1949), pp. 95–7. In later studies, only San José is briefly mentioned by Enrique Marco Dorta, *La arquitectura barroca en el Perú* (Madrid, 1957), p. 18, and p. 44, note to plate 19; whereas both San José and San Xavier are succinctly described, and illustrated with old photographs, in Damián Bayón and Murillo Marx, *History of South American Colonial Art and Architecture* (New York, 1989, 1992), p. 152, figs 383 and 384. More recently, Carlos Garayer et al., *La hacienda en el Perú: Historia y leyenda* (Lima and Cali, 1997), p. 127, includes San José and San Xavier in a list of Jesuit haciendas, and reproduces a few photographs of San Xavier, on pp. 185, 186, and 301.

16 See Michel Piaget Mazzetti and Jaime Lecca Roe, 'Iglesias de las haciendas San José y San Javier de Nazca,' B. Arch. thesis, Universidad Nacional de Ingeniería, Programa Académico de Arquitectura, Urbanismo y Artes Lima, 1974. This important study, under the direction of Professor José García Bryce, remains the most comprehensive research on the two churches to date. It includes a useful photographic survey and measured drawings.

17 Macera, *Instrucciones*, table 1.

18 Martín, *The Intellectual Conquest*, p. 174.

19 Wethey, *Colonial Architecture*, p. 95.

20 See Giacomo Barozzi da Vignola, *Regola delli cinque ordini d'architettura* (Rome, 1562); Juan Caramuel de Lobkowitz, *Architectura civil, recta y obliqua* (Vigevano, 1678); and Guarino Guarini, *Architettura civile* (Turin, 1737).

21 See Juan Antonio Ramírez, 'Guarino Guarini, Fray Juan Ricci, and the "Complete Salomonic Order,"' *Art History* 4:2 (June 1981): 176.

22 Wethey, *Colonial Architecture*, p. 95.

23 Ibid.

24 For example, Antonio de Leon Pinelo, *Questión moral si el chocolate quebranta el ayuno eclesiástico* (Madrid, 1636).

25 Wethey, *Colonial Architecture*, p. 97.

26 Ibid.

12 / Suzhou Prints and Western Perspective: The Painting Techniques of Jesuit Artists at the Qing Court, and Dissemination of the Contemporary Court Style of Painting to Mid-Eighteenth-Century Chinese Society through Woodblock Prints

HIROMITSU KOBAYASHI

Several talented Jesuit missionary artists, such as Giuseppe Castiglione (Lang Shining, active in China 1715–66), Jean-Denis Attiret (Wang Qicheng, active 1738–68), and Ignace Sichelbarth (Ai Chimeng, active 1745–80), worked in the eighteenth-century Qing court. The genius of one of them, Castiglione, helped to establish a Sino-Western style of painting that is recognized today as one of the styles representative of the imperial court during the mid-Qing dynasty. Owing to the strong association of these Jesuit painters with imperial art, there is a tendency to believe that the works they produced rarely reached the larger population. But there is evidence of a strong Western influence in the style of a popular type of luxury print made during this same period in Suzhou. In this study I will present some possible routes by which Sino-Western painting techniques were disseminated to the public from the court, and so gave rise to the production of large Suzhou prints employing Western perspective.[1]

The Creation of the Sino-Western Style of Painting at the Qing Court

The first phase of Sino-European interrelation in art[2] resulted from the introduction by Matteo Ricci (Li Matou, 1552–1610) and other Jesuit missionaries of oil paintings and copper engravings into China in the late Ming period. The penetration of Western art into Chinese society in this first encounter stimulated interest among the Chinese, but new styles or schools of art were not born of this primary encounter. The second phase, with which I am concerned in this study, produced a completely new style of Sino-Western art that gained many followers. The dynastic change from the Ming to the Qing and the existence and persistence of Castiglione at the Qing court resulted in the formation of this new style.

The second phase was initiated with Emperor Kangxi's (1662–1722) intense interest in Western science. Kangxi did not allow missionary work in China, but he recognized the greatness of Western science and the superb talents of the Jesuit missionaries. He created an environment in which Western ideas could flourish within the court. Kangxi himself was an enthusiastic student of Western science and culture, and often summoned the Jesuits to teach him natural science, anatomy, and mathematics. He also took an interest in the scientific mechanisms of Western perspective drawing, as we know from his approval of the painter Jiao Bingzhen (c. 1650–after1726), who pioneered a new Sino-Western style in painting[3] by acquiring a knowledge of perspective drawing from Western scholars working at the court. Jiao was an officer at the Imperial Astronomical Observatory, where Ferdinand Verbiest (Nan Huairen, 1623–88) and other Jesuit missionaries were employed. His work at the Observatory provided Jiao with a unique opportunity to learn Western science and perspective from the missionaries. Both Kangxi and his artist were interested in the scientific aspect of Western art, and they were especially stimulated by the realistic ambience produced by the use of perspective.

Jiao's study of Western perspective resulted in the design of forty-six illustrations for the printed imperial edition of *Rice Farming and Sericulture* (*Gonqitu*) (fig. 12.1),[4] published in 1696 and engraved by the renowned woodblock carver Zhu Gui.[5] Clearly foreshortened views of rice fields, houses, and fences and diagonally extended roads enhance the realism of scenes depicting the daily activities of farmers. Paintings such as *Classical Ladies*,[6] also by Jiao, demonstrate how his hybrid style works in the genre of figures in architectural settings. *View of Venice* (fig. 12.2), another interesting painting on silk, featuring a European landscape with figures, employs the same kind of Western perspective. The work is ascribed to Jiao, but attached to it are two small seals of doubtful origin reading 'Jiao Bingzhen' and 'Attending the Court,' and the work bears neither signature nor inscription.

A strange style of composition and selection of motifs in *View of Venice*, including eighteen figures in Western attire, provide an exotic atmosphere. In the foreground a gruesome though tame beast accompanied by five gentlemen walks over a bridge. The scene reminds the viewer of the classical theme of tribute to China from an unidentified distant country. It is noticeable that the animal wears a cross around its neck, perhaps symbolizing the religious beliefs of the entourage. The building topped with a solar clock at the far left side of the picture may be an observatory. The facial features of the female figures resemble those painted by Jiao. Other motifs, such as the trees, are painted in the Chinese style. The painter of this work has not yet been identified definitively, but it is obvious that the artist was seriously attempting a Western-style painting with a single vanishing-point, yet was unable to employ the technique with perfect accuracy. The further development of Western painting techniques among Chi-

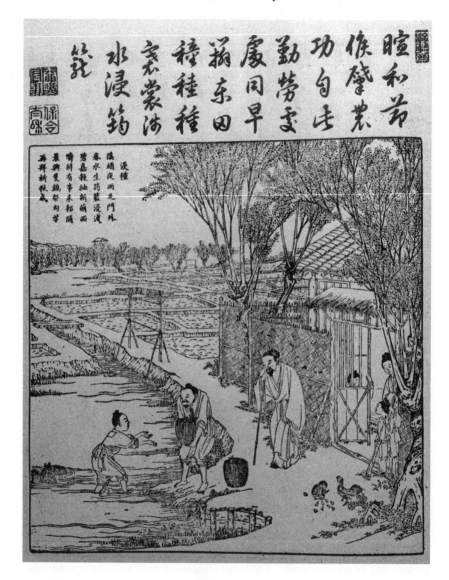

12.1. Jiao Bingzhen, 'First Sprout,' in *Rice Farming and Sericulture*, preface dated 1696. Leaf from woodblock printed album, c. 24 cm × 24 cm.
From a nineteenth-century reprint.

12.2. Ascribed to Jiao Bingzhen, *View of Venice*, eighteenth century. Hanging scroll,
ink and colour on silk, 129 cm × 50 cm. Yamato Bunkakan, Nara.

nese artists would not take place until a later period, with the publication of Chinese manuals on Western painting techniques based on newly imported European books on perspective, and the beginning of organized instruction by the Jesuit painters in the Qing Imperial Painting Academy.

Jiao's work and style were carried on in the interim period by court artists such as Leng Mei (active late seventeenth- to mid-eighteenth century), who painted an album of ten leaves entitled *Ten Court Poetries*, dated 1735;[7] it was created to accompany poems by Prince Bao, the future Emperor Qianlong (r. 1736–95). In this work, Leng Mei employed perspective to depict lively figures in courtly scenes representing ancient states and dynasties. Kangxi was also interested in the techniques involved in oil painting.[8] Under the instruction of Jesuit missionary artists, Chinese court painters also produced oil paintings, such as the eightfold screen entitled *Beauties in the Shade of the Phoenix Tree*.[9] The picture has a single focal point, and shadows are used effectively to render a scene in dimming sunlight. The style of the court ladies' faces resembles that used by Jiao Bingzhen.

During the reign of Emperor Yongzheng (r. 1723–35), stronger prohibition was placed on the teaching of Christianity, but Jesuit missionaries continued their activities at the court. There are no extant works by Castiglione from the Kangxi reign and only a handful of signed works from the Yongzheng period, but the missionary's diligence seems to have won him friends within the elite circle at the court. It is in this period that Castiglione edited the first Chinese-language book on the mechanics of perspective, entitled *Shixue* (Visual Learning). The book was published in cooperation with Nian Xiyao (d. 1738/9), a painter,[10] mathematician, and government official.[11] It adapted sections of the first volume of a contemporary study of perspective entitled *Perspectiva pictorum et architectorum* by Andrea Pozzo (1642–1709), published in 1693. Pozzo was a celebrated Italian Jesuit painter, architect, and, above all, champion of the theory of perspective in the baroque age. Castiglione and Nian's book was first published in 1729;[12] a second, enlarged edition appeared in 1735. The second edition explicated the use of perspective by including an illustration of a miniature stage set with a furnished interior scene (fig. 12.3). The stage setting was divided horizontally into six sections, with each section receding farther into the background than the one in front of it; objects and figures were depicted in correct perspective, that is, according to their distance from the audience or the viewer of the illustration. The publication of *Shixue* represented the first formal dissemination of techniques and mechanisms used in Western art from a Western artist at the Qing court to the Chinese public.

Nian Xiyao states the significance of publishing the *Shixue* in the 1735 preface: 'China has cultivated a great tradition of depicting nature in landscape paintings but neglected the accurate representation of projection and the meas-

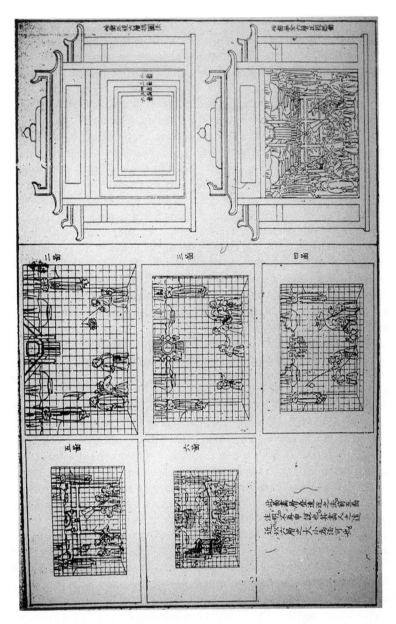

12.3. Leaf from Giuseppe Castiglione and Nian Xiyao, *Shixue*, preface dated 1735,
woodblock printed book, Bodleian Library, Oxford University. From *Chugokuno yofuga
ten*, ed. Shigeru Aoki and Hiromitsu Kobayashi (Machida, 1995).

urement of buildings and implements. If one desires to depict these objects correctly [in a composition], one must use the Western technique.' It is clear that Nian, like Kangxi and Jiao, was interested in the production of realism and accuracy within a depicted space, and not in changing the stylistic foundations of Chinese landscape painting.

Simultaneous with the inauguration of Emperor Qianlong's reign in 1736 was the establishment of a formal Imperial Painting Academy.[13] Many talented artists from various localities came to work under the emperor. In 1737 three established artists from Suzhou, including Zhou Kun,[14] were summoned to the court by Qianlong as academy painters. Zhou Kun was a literati-style landscape specialist, and upon his entry into the court he produced a painting entitled *Auspicious Grand Bell*.[15] This large hanging scroll, on which Qianlong inscribed a verse, represented a Beijing scene; it employed a moderated single-point perspective, creating naturalistic space. Since the Yongzheng period the print shops of Zhou's home city had been producing large landscape prints using the techniques of Western perspective known to the public, but the prime period of their production would arrive in the next decade.[16] From at least the thirteenth century, Suzhou had been home to many professional and literati artists.[17] The affluence of this area and its abundance of talented artists made Suzhou a supply base for master painters of a calibre qualifying them to work as artists in Qianlong's Academy. At the same time, men such as Zhou, having worked at the court, returned to their native city with a newly acquired knowledge of Western art. This knowledge further influenced the stylistic development of the Suzhou landscape prints.

Emperor Qianlong selected Castiglione as his official portrait painter. Qianlong preferred Castiglione's realistic depiction of human faces, animals, birds, and flowers, but did not employ him to paint landscapes. Court records, memorandums, and passages from the letters of the Jesuit missionaries indicate that Qianlong exercised firm control over how things were depicted in the paintings he ordered. This was especially true with respect to figure paintings, including imperial portraits. Castiglione followed the imperial orders faithfully and adapted his style to create a new form of Sino-Western art to suit the taste of the emperor. Works such as *Qianlong Enjoying Snow* (fig. 12.4), dated 1738, and *Qianlong Inspecting Horses in a Spring Field*,[18] dated 1745, are fine examples of this new style of Sino-Western art at the Qing Academy. In these paintings Castiglione collaborated with Chinese artists, who in many cases painted the backgrounds, clothing, and other accessories, while Castiglione painted the faces of the figures, and any animals. The naturalism in the proportions of the figures, in the use of light and shadow, and in the treatment of space introduced a realistic ambience into the scene – it depicted the world as one saw it in real life. This kind of realism was not emphasized in traditional Chinese figure and landscape

12.4. Giuseppe Castiglione in collaboration with anonymous court artists,
Qianlong Enjoying Snow, dated 1738. Hanging scroll, ink and colour on silk,
289.5 cm × 196.7 cm. Palace Museum, Beijing. From *Empresses and Their Court Arts
in the Forbidden City* (Tokyo, 1997).

painting, but it must have interested artists naturally looking for new facets of their art. Works such as *Record of the Year's Holidays*[19] were most probably created by the artists who painted the backgrounds in many of Castiglione's large compositions of figures in a landscape setting.

While producing numerous works of art by imperial order, Castiglione was also given the job of teaching Western methods of painting to the artists of the Academy and also of training young apprentices selected among the bannermen[20] as specialists in the Western style.[21] In the classrooms there were supposedly no limitations as to genre, and both oil painting and painting using traditional Chinese materials but in the Western style were taught by Castiglione. Unfortunately, not one of these apprentices was talented enough to become a leading court painter in the Academy, and their known extant works are scarce. The Academy had a large staff, and the artists competed for the attention of the emperor by presenting him with paintings on the occasion of special celebrations, which were not many.[22] There was a high turnover among the court painters,[23] and those who learned from Castiglione or from his art brought the style home with them.

Suzhou Prints and the Court Style

The prints known to us today as Suzhou prints were also called Gusu prints, Gusu being the old name of the Suzhou area. The prints have many subjects and styles, but in this study I will focus on those showing natural landscapes and cityscapes using Western perspective, which flourished mainly from the 1730s to the 1750s. These prints are on average about 1 metre high and 50 centimetres wide, and are either plain monochrome woodblock prints or monochrome prints to which bright colours have been applied manually. They were usually sold in pairs as New Year's decorations. The works are meticulously rendered, with human figures, architecture and architectural objects, landscapes, and other elements. The Suzhou prints came from the studios of artists living in the city, but their creation was made possible by the nurturing of the Sino-Western style of art at the Qing court and by the dissemination of the styles and techniques mastered by former court artists to professional artists working in the cities.

It was in Suzhou, the leading economic and cultural city of China in the early to mid-Qing period, that the large and meticulously rendered luxury prints were produced using Western perspective. This city was also known for its publishing business, which supplied illustrated books in abundance to the Chinese public. In the early Qing period, many craftsmen who had previously engaged in print making moved to Suzhou from other centres of production[24] and manufactured the first relatively large multi-coloured woodblock prints – featuring, for example, 'beauties,' or beautiful women, with auspicious motifs celebrating the coming of the new year. These are called New Year's prints (*nianhua*);[25] they were large in size but were not landscapes or cityscapes, and did not depict architecture showing hints of Sino-Western stylistic influence.

In the early eighteenth century the print shops in the districts of Taohuawu and Shantang[26] in Suzhou initiated the production of some completely new types of New Year's print – intricately composed, meticulously engraved, and including figures in landscapes. They employ the Sino-Western mixture of styles found at court, using a fixed-focus perspective and shading. *Auspicious Dwelling of Minister Taozhu*,[27] *Ladies and Boys in an Elegant Garden*,[28] and *Noble Family Celebrating the New Year*[29] are examples of the new type of Suzhou print. The use of shading undoubtedly came from Western copper engravings, which had been imported into the country beginning in the late Ming period, but the use of single-point perspective in landscape prints was an innovation. Nor had large commercial prints of landscapes been produced previously. Engraved inscriptions reading 'in the manner of Western painting' are sometimes found on these prints.

The prints feature city scenes, popular scenic or tourist spots in Suzhou and other areas, imaginary versions of sites with historical or cultural associations, scenes from popular dramas or novels, and compositions containing auspicious images for the New Year's celebrations. These themes, subjects, and motifs had previously been found in Chinese art: what was new, and what gave rise to a new subject for New Year's prints, was their treatment in landscape-with-architecture settings.[30] The realism with which the setting was depicted marked an innovation in the art of the Qing period. The traditional artistic emphasis in woodblock printing on the forming of images by employing smooth and clear unbroken lines – as opposed to the freehand brush-strokes used in painting – enhanced the linearity characteristic of composition using Western perspective. The period in which these Suzhou landscape prints were being produced coincides with the period in which Castiglione and the Chinese painters at court were actively cooperating to produce paintings in the Sino-Western style that has come to mark the court art of that era.

The earliest-dated pair of Suzhou prints and one of the most celebrated of those extant today is *Encyclopaedic View of Jobs in the City* (*Sanbailiushiixing tu*) (fig. 12.5); it was drafted and printed by the Master of Baohuijian in 1734. The pair of prints vividly articulates the prosperity of Suzhou, in depicting the area around Changmeng (Heaven's Gate), the busiest water gate and commercial district of the city. It employs the conventional bird's-eye-view perspective, traditional in Chinese art, by looking eastward from outside the gate, but it also

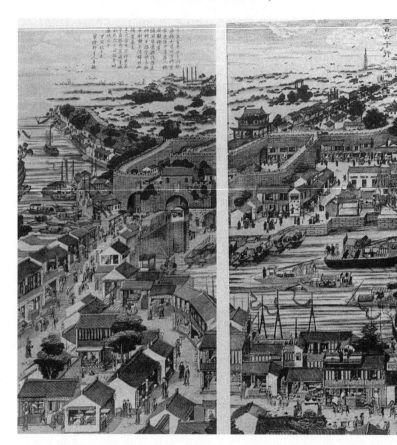

12.5. Master of Baohuijian, *Encyclopaedic View of Jobs in the City* (right)
and *Changmeng Gate in Suzhou*, dated 1734. Hand-painted woodblock prints: right,
108.7 cm × 55.6 cm; left, 108.6 cm × 55.6 cm. Ohsha'joh Museum of Art,
Hiroshima, Japan. Photo courtesy of the Ohsha'joh Museum of Art.

adapts the fixed focal point of Western perspective to portray the city realisti-
cally, in smooth diagonal recessions. Though the artist draws the buildings in a
typically Chinese isometric manner, the shadows of the houses are cast on the
streets, implying the presence of a single source of light from the upper left side.
Such a shading technique undoubtedly was appropriated from the hatching seen
in Western copper engravings. This calculated shading and the use of a constant
single source of light were new in Chinese art, having been uncommon in
traditional painting up to this period. The engraved inscription in the upper left

corner of the print eulogizes the city: 'It [Suzhou] gathers commercial goods from all over the world, and its urban affluence can be compared to that of Kaifeng, the capital of the Northern Song.' A bit of regional pride can be found in both the verse and the visual presentation, which uses the most contemporary techniques found in China at the time.

A print that can be traced to an illustrator who had a relative working as a court artist in the early Qianlong Academy is the work entitled *One Hundred Children* (*Baizitu*) (fig. 12.6). It was designed by Zhang Shuchu[31] and issued by Zhang Xingzhu at Taohuawu in 1743. Zhang Shuchu was a student from Suzhou who is recorded as having produced landscapes[32] in a manner identical to that of his cousin Zhang Zongcang (1686–1756), a literati-style landscape painter of Suzhou, who later became a leading court artist[33] in the early Qianlong era. The theme of *One Hundred Children* is one of the most popular auspicious subjects for New Year's prints, symbolizing wishes for abundance of offspring and prosperity among one's descendants.

Zhang Shuchu shows a joyful gathering of children in the evening. The composition is filled with boys and girls in every corner. Lanterns lit and hanging on the eaves indicate the time of day, and plum blossoms covered with snow identify the season. The artist combines two scenes, rendered in different styles. The lower half of the composition depicts children riding hobby horses, children playing military general inside a well-decorated house, and children playing with toys shaped like animals with auspicious associations, such as rabbits and fish, in the garden. This lower half is in the conventional Chinese manner. The upper half of the composition, however, which serves as a backdrop for the scene below, uses a mixture of Western and traditional Chinese perspective. On the upper left side, boys are climbing steps towards a viewing terrace, and on the right boys with their maids are in the pavilion cheering the ascending boys. The traditional Chinese perspective of high distance has been used for the viewing terrace, and the Western technique of foreshortening for the pavilion on the right.

The details prove Zhang to be a painter of some calibre. The hanging landscape scroll in the pavilion, in ink bamboo, and the plants and wall painting of trees in the house are drawn with minute attention to detail and a convincing brush. Zhang's treatment of rocks such as those at the base of the terrace and the marvellous garden rock in the left foreground attests to his familiarity with contemporary landscape painting. The formation of the garden rock especially resembles the rock formation typical in the works of Yuan Jiang, a leading landscape painter of Yangzhou, who painted at the court during the Yongzheng era. An inscription at the top bears the sobriquet of Zhang Shuchu and mentions that the artist employed the Western style.

12.6. Zhang Shunchu, *One Hundred Children*, dated 1743.
Woodblock print, 102.2 cm × 56.5 cm. Collection unknown.

A large painted hanging scroll that reminds the viewer of the Suzhou prints that use Western perspective is entitled *A Poetic Thought of a New Spring in the Capital*.[34] The work was created by a leading Academy painter, Xu Yang, who came from the Changmeng Gate district of Suzhou. He had already won fame locally as a painter before Emperor Qianlong summoned him to court in 1751. In his hanging scroll Xu employs the same compositional device – a combination of fixed focal point and bird's-eye view – that we have seen in *Encyclopaedic View of Jobs in the City*. The work depicts the city of Beijing, covered with light snow, with hundreds of minute figures going about their activities in the Forbidden City. The artist creates a lively New-Year's-morning atmosphere within an otherwise soundless and austere cityscape. Although it is unlikely that Xu Yang himself designed Suzhou prints, some minor court artists may have returned to Suzhou after their tenure and could have played a role in the production of the new landscape prints by appropriating from painted compositions such as those of Xu. There are no written records of Suzhou print draftsmen being summoned to court, but according to Wang Shucun, draftsmen from Yangliuqing, another major centre of New Year's prints near Tianjin, were summoned to serve at the court during the Qianlong era.[35] It is most likely that artists involved in print making in Suzhou were also called to the service of the emperor at court.

Another work bearing an inscription mentioning that Western style has been used is *The Romance of the Western Chamber (Xixiangji)*,[36] dated 1747. The title was the name of a popular novel, of which there were many editions, and also of a stage drama. The composition features a bird's-eye view of a temple complex, employing a fixed single focal point. The artist depicts several scenes in the one composition by separating the scenes within architectural structures. This printed composition presents the first seven acts of the drama, and the artist intelligently highlights one of the most significant scenes, in which the hero and heroine first encounter each other at a ceremony, commemorating her late father, in a temple. The two young lovers-to-be, along with other main characters of the drama, are shown inside the Buddha hall, the largest building in the picture, placed in the upper right section. The building is situated closest to the focal point of the composition, and its placement means that the viewer is led to the first climax in this tale of romance.

A perspective with a single focal point is employed in a symmetrical pair of prints entitled *Afanggong Palace* (fig. 12.7). The date is unknown, but the work was produced by Guan Yuduan's print shop of Shijiaxiang in Suzhou. The printed composition portrays the imaginary garden of a palace built by the first emperor of the Qin in 212 BCE. The artist is a certain Guan Lian. The buildings on both sides are depicted in smooth recessions that give realistic depth to the picture. The shadows of the figures and of the piers of the bridge imply a source

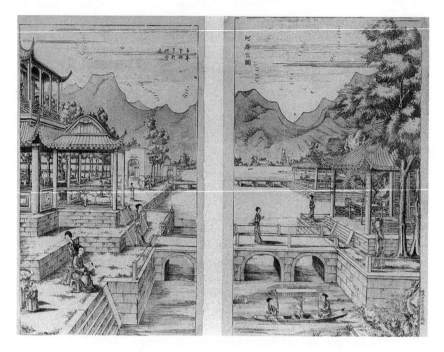

12.7. Guan Lian, *Afanggong Palace*, eighteenth century. Woodblock prints,
each 36 cm × 28 cm. Ohsha'joh Museum of Art, Hiroshima, Japan.
Photo courtesy of the Ohsha'joh Museum of Art.

of light on the upper left side. A pair of prints entitled *Playing at the Lotus Pavilion*[37] is similarly composed, but the scene is viewed from the inside of a room in which the ceiling and floor are drawn using Western perspective. The viewer, viewing a blooming lotus pond from inside a pavilion, is given a unique and stunning visual experience – it is as if the viewer is actually in the interior of the room looking out. The realistic treatment of space and depth here and the accurate rendition of the architectural setting may be a good example of the technique of perspective that was acquired from the miniature stage set illustrations in the *Shixue*.

Chinese artists specializing in Western-style portrait painting also created landscape prints. *West Lake* (*Xihu*) (fig. 12.8) was designed by Ding Yingtai[38] from Qianjian, today's Hangzhou, and issued by Dinglaijian of Suzhou. He and his daughter, Ding Yu, were known for their ink and colour portraits in the Western style. The print portrays a dwelling by the West Lake in which two

12.8. Ding Yingtai, *West Lake*, early eighteenth century. Woodblock print,
36 cm × 28 cm. Ohsha'joh Museum of Art, Hiroshima, Japan.
Photo courtesy of the Ohsha'joh Museum of Art.

ladies are conversing. A little boy is climbing a fence assisted by a maid, and other boys are playing in the house. The quality of the work indicates that Ding Yingtai made a serious study of Western perspective. In fact, we know that Ding studied Jiao Bingzhen's *Rice Farming and Sericulture*, because he has appropriated motifs from Jiao's art in *West Lake*. The most apparent of these motifs in Ding's composition is the little boy being held by his lady attendant, looking over a fence: an almost exactly similar pair of figures appears in Jiao's work (fig. 12.9). In Ding's work, an effective and painstaking use of hatching on the surfaces of objects and on the shadows represented in the picture gives the illusion that this woodblock print might have been produced from a copper engraving. Also noteworthy is the three-dimensional effect of even small motifs such as potted plants on a table, a dog, and trees, which is enhanced by the careful rendering of shadows produced from a single light source on the upper right side of the composition.

Tengwangge Pavilion (fig. 12.10),[39] undated, and printed by a certain Mr Guan of Taohuawu, is another work typical in its employment of Western techniques to create a realistic depiction of a scene. The work also combines the scholar-artist's tradition of *shiyitu* (poetic thought painting), which had been popular among literati artists in Suzhou since the middle Ming period. The print visualizes a poem about Tengwangge by Wang Bo, a celebrated poet of the Tang dynasty; the poem is engraved on the upper right side of the composition with calligraphic strokes, and the scholar-artists' ideal of combining the 'three perfections' of poetry, painting, and calligraphy is thereby realized. However, unlike in the works of literati painting, here the combination of the three arts is made clearer to a wider audience by the actual illustration of what is read in the verses reproduced within the picture itself. Many Suzhou prints were engraved with verses composed and signed by the draftsmen themselves. They indicate that in the mid-eighteenth century, professional painters, often called mere 'artisans,' were educated enough to compose poetry, even though their verses may not have been as refined as Wang Bo's.

In *Tengwangge Pavilion*, scenes of lively activity generate a joyous atmosphere celebrating the coming of spring. Ladies in the pavilion and the courtyard amuse themselves by enjoying the view over the Hanjiang River or by watching a boy flying a kite. The foreshortening employed for the pavilion and the hatching used to create shadows on figures and buildings introduce a naturalistic and realistic effect. In the background boats sail on the river, ruffled by the wind. The waves are left blank at intervals, as if to portray the reflections of sunlight.

New Year's Morning (*Suizhaotu*),[40] rendered in the Sino-Western style, is another fine example of a poetic thought picture adorned with auspicious motifs celebrating the new year. Cai Weiyuan of Taohuawu designed the picture to

12.9. Jiao Bingzhen, 'Reeling Silk Thread' (detail), in *Rice Farming and Sericulture*.
Leaf from woodblock printed album, c. 24 cm × 24 cm. From a nineteenth-century reprint.

12.10.   Anonymous, *Tengwangge Pavilion,* eighteenth century. Hand-painted woodblock print, 106.8 cm × 54.5 cm. Akita City Akarenga-Kan Museum, Katsuhira Tokushi Memorial Gallery, Akita, Japan. Photo courtesy of Akita City Akarenga-Kan Museum.

correspond to the lines of the poem engraved at the top. The picture portrays a section of the city of Suzhou covered lightly with snow. Houses and streets along a canal are depicted in the foreground, a garden with a viewing terrace in the middle ground, and distant snow-covered mountains beyond a river in the background. The sunlight shines from the upper right side, and the shadows cast by the houses on the surface of the water in the canal are depicted using the hatching technique.

The verses engraved above the mountains read 'Plum blossoms and snow compete with each other for the spring; the sound of fireworks announces the coming of the new year; charcoals burning red in the brazier please boys; and an old gentleman walks towards the viewing terrace with a staff.' The picture represents a clear morning scene after snow. Ladies in the foreground break the branches of plum blossoms, and a boy at the lower left corner lights a firecracker. Inside the house, in the middle ground of the picture, a boy warms his hands over a charcoal brazier. In the back yard by the river, an old gentleman with a staff approaches the terrace. As in the case of *Tengwengge Pavilion*, the picture visualizes exactly what is written in each line of the poetry, and the verses describe exactly what is depicted in the corresponding illustration. This well-designed composition reminds us of Academy paintings in the Sino-Western style such as *Record of the Year's Holidays*. The print is a visual record of how imperial painting styles of the period were assimilated into conventional literati painting.

Prints of any type are difficult to study owing to the lack of specific information on such things as date of production and the background of the artists who produced them. Information is scattered throughout miscellaneous sources, if it can be found anywhere. There have been short references by recent scholars to the fact that the Suzhou prints were produced under the influence of art works imported from the West through the trading ports of Guangdong (Canton), but neither specific examples of such stylistic influence nor specific dating has been offered. In this study I have attempted to present as many dates and names of artists as possible, along with any reliable background information on the artists. More concrete information must be found if we are to reconstruct the cultural and art historical situation of the period. Further study will aid our understanding of the dissemination of court culture to the Qing public.

Large Suzhou prints employing Western perspective were created in the city ateliers, but much circumstantial evidence points to the stylistic influence of court art and to the dissemination of the Sino-Western style by Chinese artists who acquired Western techniques in the Qing Imperial Painting Academy. The Suzhou area produced many talented men for both officialdom and the world of art and had consequently built strong ties with the court circle by the mid-Qing period. The creation of the Sino-Western style of art would not have been possible without the Qing emperors' acceptance of the art introduced by the Jesuit missionaries; these emperors provided an environment for the nurturing of an innovative style. The Sino-Western style would not have been born without artists such as Castiglione, who persisted in his work through three imperial reigns and accepted and understood Chinese preferences in art. The development of the woodblock printed form of Sino-Western art was possible only in a city such as Suzhou, which had both a long tradition of print making and artists receptive and educated enough to recognize and value the mechanics of the innovative Sino-Western style being developed at the court. The printed works would not have flourished without a sufficient number of customers educated and affluent enough to purchase such luxury goods, which were used only during the holiday seasons. All these factors made possible the development in the cities of Suzhou of prints with landscapes using Western perspective, under the strong influence of a contemporary Sino-Western style of painting representative of court art in the mid-Qing period.

NOTES

1   The word perspective is used in a broad sense in this article. Perspective as understood in Western art is different from perspective as used in traditional Chinese art. Traditional Chinese perspective has been referred to in English by words such as 'vista,' 'distance,' and 'view.' The most significant difference between the perspective drawings of the two cultures is the fact that traditional Chinese perspective used a moving focus or multiple focal points in a single composition. In this article, both Western and Chinese perspective are referred to by the single term 'perspective' and are differentiated by the specification 'Western' or 'Chinese.'

2   For a discussion of the first phase, see Hiromitsu Kobayashi, 'Chinese Painting and Western Art Introduced by the Jesuit Missionaries,' in *St. Francis Xavier – An Apostle of the West: The Encounter between Europe and Asia during the Period of the Great Navigations*, vol. 1 (Tokyo, 1999,) pp. 172–84.

3   Jiao's new style was approved by Kangxi when he created a landscape painting for the emperor in the spring of 1689. Pleased with the accurate calculation of the distances among the components of the landscape, the emperor praised him: 'Jiao Bingzhen, who truly understood astronomy and perspective, successfully assimilated Western styles into Chinese painting.' See Hu Jing, *Guozhao Yuanhualu*, preface dated 1816, vol. 1, reproduced in *Huashi Congshu*, vol. 5 (Shanghai, 1962), pp. 1–2.

4   A later edition of the *Gonqitu* was printed in 1808, and similar painted versions by

Leng Mei and Chen Mei are found in the collection of the National Palace Museum, Taibei.

5 Zhu Gui was best known as a carver for the *Lingyangetu* (Portraits of the Meritorious Retainers of the Hall of Fame), preface dated 1669, illustrations by Liu Yuan. Zhu meticulously engraved twenty-four meritorious retainers of the Tang emperor Taizong for the illustrations for the printed book.

6 *Classical Ladies* is a set of twelve album leaves, ink and colour on silk, 30 cm × 21.2 cm, in the collection of the National Palace Museum, Beijing. For a reproduction, see *Court Paintings and Court Painters of the Qing Dynasty, Qingdai gongting huihua*, comp. and ed. National Palace Museum (Beijing, 1992), plate 1.

7 *Ten Court Poetries* is an album painting consisting of a set of ten double-spread album leaves with paintings in ink and colour on silk on the right and verses by Prince Hongli (Bao) on the left. The prince's poems were inscribed on the leaves by an official, Liang Shizheng. Each leaf measures 32.2 cm × 42.3 cm. The album is in the collection of the National Palace Museum, Beijing. For a reproduction, see *Court Paintings and Court Painters* (n6 above), plate 3.

8 It is recorded that in 1721 Kangxi examined ten oil paintings by Chinese artists. See Takeyoshi Tsuruta, 'Banreki-Kenryukan no Seiyoga no ryunyu to Yofuga,' in *Chugokuno yofuga ten*, ed. Shigeru Aoki and Hiromitsu Kobayashi (Machida, 1995), p. 443.

9 *Beauties in the Shade of the Phoenix Tree* is an eightfold screen, oil on paper, 128.5 cm × 326 cm, in the collection of the National Palace Museum, Beijing. For a reproduction, see *Court Paintings and Court Painters*, plate 30.

10 There is a record of a painting by Nian entitled *Four Mynah Birds on a Branch of Loquat* and dated 1734. The written descriptions of the painting imply a stylistic resemblance to Castiglione's realistic rendition of birds. See Zuo Lang, *Huzhong Huachuanlu*, preface dated 1795, reproduced in the compendium *Meishu Congshu* ser. 1, book 10 (Taibei, 1969), p. 196.

11 Nian Xiyao was once the superintendent of the Imperial Porcelain Factory. Under his supervision the imperial kiln at Jingdezhen produced fine ceramic works for the court and other purchasers in the early Qing period. Castiglione is believed to have produced designs for ceramic works during the period in which the factory was supervised by Nian. See Cécile and Michel Beurdeley, *Giuseppe Castiglione: A Jesuit Painter at the Court of the Chinese Emperors,* trans. Michael Bullock (Rutland, VT, and Tokyo, 1971), p. 47. Western shading and realism are found in some of the motifs on the wares and porcelain, which later came to be known as *Nianyao* (Nian's porcelain). For an example of *Nianyao* porcelain, see plate 111 in *From Beijing to Versailles: Artistic Relations between China and France* (Hong Kong, 1997), pp. 284–5. Nian Xiyao was also a junior vice-president of the Board

of Works and a minister of the Imperial Household. See *Eminent Chinese of the Ch'ing Period*, ed. Arthur W. Hummel (Washington, 1943; repr. Taibei, 1975), pp. 588, 590.

12 In his preface to the 1729 edition Nian writes that he was able to use Western techniques for Chinese subjects after receiving frequent advice from Castiglione. This preface is reproduced in the 1735 edition of the *Shixue*, a copy of which is in the collection of Bodleian Library, Oxford University.

13 For further reading on this topic, see Yang Boda, 'The Development of the Ch'ien-lung Painting Academy,' trans. Jonathan Hay, in *Words and Images: Chinese Poetry, Calligraphy, and Painting*, ed. Alfreda Murck and Wen C. Fong (Princeton, 1991), pp. 333–56.

14 Two other artists were Yu Xing and Yu Zhi. See Yang Boda, 'The Development,' p. 341.

15 *Auspicious Grand Bell* is a hanging scroll, ink and colour on silk, 180.2 cm × 105.6 cm, in the collection of the National Palace Museum, Taibei. For a reproduction, see *Gugong shuhua tulu*, ed. National Palace Museum, vol. 12 (Taibei, 1993), p. 379.

16 The dates of extant known works range from 1734 to 1747, but undated works show further developments in style.

17 The literati were scholar-gentlemen, the educated elite, who often held government posts. Literati artists in theory were distinct from professionals in that they painted as amateurs; in other words, their paintings were not for sale. By the Ming and Qing periods, however, there were many literati painters who sold their art discreetly, and many professionals who painted according to literati tastes and in literati styles.

18 *Qianlong Inspecting Horses in a Spring Field* is a hand scroll painting created by Castiglione in collaboration with Tang Dai. The work is 46 cm × 446 cm and is in the collection of Fujii Yurinkan, Kyoto. For a reproduction, see the exhibition catalogue entitled *Chugokuno yofuga ten* (n8 above), plate 58.

19 *Record of the Year's Holidays* is a hanging scroll, ink and colour on silk, 195 cm × 97 cm, in the collection of the National Palace Museum, Taibei. For reproductions, see *Gugong shuhua tulu*, vol. 14 (Taibei, 1994), pp. 275–97.

20 *Baqi* (Eight Banners), established in the Qing dynasty, was a basic administrative and military system consisting of eight units distinguished by the colour of the flags symbolizing each unit. There were eight banners each for the Manchus and for the Mongols and the Chinese. For further information on *Baqi*, see Charles O. Hucker, *A Dictionary of Official Titles in Imperial China* (Stanford, 1985), p. 134, no. 611. Yang Boda has discovered that the apprentices in the Imperial Painting Academy were originally *sula*, or workmen from the top three Manchu banners. For further reading on this topic, see Yang Boda, 'The Development,' pp. 343–4.

21 Ibid., pp. 338, 343.

22 Ibid., p. 343.

23 Ibid.

24 Craftsmen came to work in Suzhou in the late Ming and early Qing periods from Xin'an, Hangzhou, and Nanjing. In the Qing period the number of such craftsmen in the area increased because the publication of vernacular literature was banned in 1652, 1709, and 1714 as part of an attempt to uphold Confucian morality in society, and experienced craftsmen employed in producing illustrations for vernacular literature in other centres lost their jobs. Many of them found positions in which they could utilize their expertise in Suzhou print shops. For further discussion of this topic, see Wang Shucun, *Chungguo minjian nianhuashi tule*, vol. 1 (Shanghai, 1991), pp. 10–11

25 New Year's pictures could be either paintings or prints. *Emperor Qianlong Enjoying Snow*, mentioned in the text, is a good example of a painted work. Today the term *nianhua,* or New Year's pictures, generally means printed works in the tradition of popular folk art that are produced by unknown local craftsmen from all over China before the holiday seasons. In the Northern Song period, New Year's prints illustrating such images as door-gods and the demon-queller Zhonggui were sold at city markets in the capital, Kaifeng, at the end of the year. These printed images were believed to expel bad spirits and to prevent children from succumbing to diseases. Among the prints made in the Jin period (1115–1234) can be found the earliest extant New Year's prints. Two significant examples are *Four Beauties* and *General Guan Wu*. In the Ming and Qing periods, a variety of subjects, including beauties, boys, animals, plants, and other miscellaneous auspicious motifs, were employed in the prints. They all expressed good wishes for long life, wealth, distinction, successful careers, the prosperity of one's descendants, and soon on, as befitting the New Year's celebration. In the early Qing period, Suzhou and Yangliuqing, near Tianjin in Hubei province, became major centres of production of New Year's prints and were known for their high-quality work. Other well-known centres of production in the Ming and Qing periods included Weifang and Yangjiabu in Shandong province, Fengxiang in Shaanxi province, Wuqiang in Hebei province, and Mianzhu in Sichuan province. For further information on the history of New Year's prints, see Wang Shucun, *Chungguo minjian nianhuashi tule*, vols 1 and 2 (n24 above).

26 During the Yongzheng and Qianlong eras, there were more than fifty print shops in the districts of Taohuawu and Shantang, which manufactured more than a million prints a year. See *Suzhou Shihua, Jiangsu renmin chubanshe*, ed. Liao Jiao et al. (Suzhou, 1980), p. 193.

27 *Auspicious Dwelling of Minister Taozhu*, 107.2 cm × 53.9 cm, is in the collection of the Ohsha'joh Museum of Art, Hiroshima. For a reproduction, see *Chugokuno yofuga ten* (n8 above), p. 398.

28 *Ladies and Boys in an Elegant Garden*, 100.1 cm × 50.5 cm, is in the collection of the Ohsha'joh Museum of Art. For a reproduction, see ibid., p. 57.

29 *Noble Family Celebrating the New Year*, 105.7 cm × 55.3 cm, is in the collection of the Ohsha'joh Museum of Art. For a reproduction, see ibid, p. 400.

30 Although Suzhou prints are for the most part New Year's pictures, extant examples suggest that some were used to celebrate other events, such as the Harvest Moon or the construction of a new bridge.

31 For a biography of Zhang Shuchu and Zhang Zongcang, see Zhang Geng, *Guozhao Huazhengxulu*, vol. 2, prefaces dated 1735 and 1739, vol. 2, reproduced in *Huashi Congshu* (n3 above), pp. 104–5.

32 Ibid.

33 When Qianlong visited Suzhou in 1751 on the first of his southern inspection tours, Zhang Zongcang presented him with an album of landscapes depicting the scenery of Suzhou and its vicinity. He was immediately summoned to the court. See Yang Boda, 'The Development,' p. 345.

34 *A Poetic Thought of a New Spring in the Capital* is a hanging scroll, ink and colour on silk, 255 cm × 233.8 cm, in the collection of the National Palace Museum, Beijing. For a reproduction, see *Court Paintings and Court Painters* (n6 above), plate 106.

35 See Wang Shucun, *Chungguo minjian nianhuashe tule*, vol. 1, p. 13.

36 *The Romance of the Western Chamber*, 96.5 cm × 53 cm, is in a private collection in Kyoto, Japan. For a reproduction, see *Chugokuno yofuga ten*, p. 61.

37 The prints that make up the pair entitled *Playing at the Lotus Pavilion* are 73.6 cm × 56 cm (right print) and 74.6 cm × 56.3 cm (left print). The pair is in the collection of the Ohsha'joh Museum of Art. For a reproduction, see the exhibition catalogue entitled *Chugoku kodaihanga ten* (Machida, 1988), p. 261.

38 For a biography of Ding Yingtai and Ding Yu, see *Guozhao Huazhengxulu*, vol. 2, pp. 116–17.

39 Tengwangge pavilion, near Nanchang, was built by Li Yuanying, the twenty-second son of Tang Gaozu, when he became King Teng. For biographical accounts of King Teng, see the reproduction of *Jiu Tangshu*, vol. 64, Liezhuan 14, Gaozi Ershierzi, in *Ershi wu Shi* [Histories of Twenty-five Successive Dynasties], vol. 5 (Shanghai, 1986), p. 293. The poet Wang Bo visited the pavilion and composed the poem in 659 CE. For further information on the poem, see *Toshi Sen*, ed. Maeno Naoaki (Tokyo, 1961), pp. 62–4.

40 *New Year's Morning*, 97.8 cm × 53.9 cm, is in the collection of the Ohsha'joh Museum of Art. For a reproduction, see *Chugokuno yofuga ten*, p. 385.

PART THREE

Scientific Knowledge, the Order of Nature, and Natural Theology

Twenty years ago a small group of historians of science were able to surprise many of their mostly Anglo-American colleagues with evidence of Jesuit involvement in early modern science. The clichés of an older historiography, grounded in the metaphors of conflict between science and religion, had led historians of science to focus largely on the role of Jesuits as obstructionists. Jesuits had been known primarily as opponents in debates with Galileo over heliocentric planetary theory, with Descartes over philosophical materialism, and with Newton over the nature of light and gravitation. In the context of the received opinion of two decades ago, that initial surprise took two forms: acknowledgment of the sophistication and intellectual fruitfulness of Jesuits' debates with figures such as Galileo, Descartes, and Newton, and the recognition of the range and diversity of Jesuit scientific activity. The essays in Part Three show that studies of the Jesuit scientific tradition can still generate surprise. In addition to diversity and sophistication, what we see here is evidence of the complexity and durability of that tradition: the complexity of institutional niches involving education, publication, censorship, and disciplinary authority; and the durability of teaching and publication practices across time and space.

Several Jesuit astronomers attempted to set boundaries in turbulent arenas. Christoph Clavius was the Society's first and one of its more famous mathematical astronomers, a champion of geocentric astronomy, yet a friend of Galileo. Volker R. Remmert's analysis of the engraved title-page of Clavius's collected works (1612) leads him to a careful study of Jesuit scriptural exegesis. He concludes that Clavius's astronomical opinion exercised considerable influence on Jesuit interpreters of the Bible and that well before the condemnation of Copernicus's heliocentric theory (1616) and the trial and condemnation of Galileo (1633), Jesuit exegetes had already come to a consensus: rejection of astronomical theories that put the earth in motion as damnable and heretical.

William A. Wallace's, O.P., painstaking archival research presents us with what is surely one of the most ironic twists in the scientific exchange between Galileo and Jesuit natural philosophers. Wallace is able to demonstrate a direct line of influence running from Jesuits who taught natural philosophy and mathematics to Galileo's experiments and publications on free-fall. Moreover, Wallace is able to show that the method that guided Galileo's experiments, the so-called demonstrative *regressus*, depended directly on the Roman Jesuits' Aristotelian commentaries. The irony, of course, is that Galileo's experimental method and mathematical approach to motion were fundamental elements of the 'new science' employed in the defence of heliocentric astronomy.

Daniel Stolzenberg reveals the complexities of the Society's process for reviewing, revising, and censoring manuscripts that Jesuit authors submitted in order to obtain permission to publish. His choice of sites goes to the heart of the matter: the reports of the principal revisers in Rome for Athanasius Kircher's controversial work on magical practices and Hermetic esoterica. He finds that a famous, well-connected, and determined author such as Kircher was able to circumvent the restrictions the revisers repeatedly sought to impose on him.

Beginning with the Jesuits' first school in Messina, mathematics had an important place in the curriculum. But what went on in the classroom? Antonella Romano examines a range of sources, especially lecture notes, to answer that question for seventeenth-century France. She finds (among other things) that Jesuits taught a richer array of mathematical topics, especially in the fields of 'mixed' (or applied) mathematics, than one would expect simply from perusing the *Ratio studiorum*. This phenomenon was perhaps in part a response to the generally more pragmatic interests of the Jesuits' well-born students.

Henrique Leitâo takes up the much-studied question of Jesuits' engagement with the 'science of the heavens.' We must recall that in the seventeenth century science consisted of the intertwined teachings of astronomy, which had to do with determining the position and motion of the stars and planets, and astrology, which sought to trace the influence of celestial configurations on terrestrial events. We must also recall that both astronomy and astrology presupposed a geocentric cosmos. As willing (or obligatory) geocentrists, were Jesuits, then, favourably disposed to astrology? Jesuits were generally opposed to the teaching of astrology since foretelling future human events smacked of predetermination and thus undercut human moral responsibility. In a surprising discovery, however, Leitâo shows how Jesuit mathematicians, working in the Society's most prestigious college in Portugal, openly taught judicial astrology, even as other Jesuit mathematicians in other provinces condemned it.

Víctor Navarro Brotóns examines the state of the Society's scientific tradition on the eve of its extinction in Portugal. In the late seventeenth century, the *novatores* (the name given Spaniards who sought to introduce and promote in Spain the most recent advances of the 'new science') found Jesuits to be their strongest supporters. Until the national expulsion in 1767, Jesuits taught courses in mathematics (including calculus), experimental and theoretical physics (including Newtonian mechanics), optics, geography, and military science. What is striking is that Jesuits continued to be appointed to high-level teaching positions in the sciences right up through the 1750s and 1760s, and some were able to continue to write and publish even after the expulsion, as Navarro Brotóns shows for Juan Andrés.

With Ugo Baldini's contribution we turn our attention to Roger Boscovich (Ruđer Bošković), perhaps the most accomplished of all Jesuit scientists, who died in 1787, fourteen years after the Society was suppressed. Baldini examines Boscovich's theory of an attraction-repulsion force producing all physical phenomena from two points of view: first, as a purely scientific product of a man who happened to be a Jesuit, and second, as a Jesuit's attempt to forge, in a partially new form, an agreement between contemporary science and theological ontology. Baldini shows through a wide-ranging survey of publications the resistance to Boscovich's theory from both those who came at it as scientists and those who came at it as theologians, and shows as well the prejudices behind the resistance. Even today assessments of the theory differ widely. Boscovich appears again in Part Six in the contribution by Larry Wolff.

13 / Picturing Jesuit Anti-Copernican Consensus: Astronomy and Biblical Exegesis in the Engraved Title-Page of Clavius's *Opera mathematica* (1612)

VOLKER R. REMMERT

The debate over the Copernican theory held a prominent place in the so-called scientific revolution of the sixteenth and seventeenth centuries. It culminated in the trial of Galileo Galilei and his conviction in June 1633. Much has been written about the context of this trial, its motivations, and its rationale. This article is concerned not with these issues, but rather with the prehistory of the 'first trial' of 1616. Here my particular focus is on the position adopted by Jesuit biblical exegesis on Copernican theory and its connection, in turn, with the views of the leading Jesuit mathematician and astronomer Christoph Clavius, whose writings had a fundamental influence on the Jesuit exegetes.[1]

The relationship between Copernican theory and biblical exegesis has received unsystematic attention from historians. In particular, only a few studies have given detailed attention to Catholic or Jesuit biblical exegesis before 1610,[2] although this is precisely the field that needs to be investigated if we are to understand the situation between 1610 and 1616, when Galileo composed his famous letter to Christina.

In this paper I make no claim to fill that gap in the historical record. My theme is the treatment of terrestrial motion in Jesuit biblical exegesis, particularly in the light of the astronomical miracles of the Sun standing still in Joshua 10:12 and the Sun reversing its course in 2 Kings 20:8–11 (*Horologium Ahas*), both portrayed in the engraved title-page of Clavius's *Opera mathematica* of 1612. By interpreting the title-page in the context of the exegetic and scientific traditions of the Jesuits and in the light of their interaction with the post-Tridentine Counter-Reformation project, I will show that Clavius played a decisive role in the rejection of terrestrial motion by Jesuit exegetes.

In February 1616 the Holy Office condemned two principal features of the Copernican system. First, the idea that the sun rested at the centre of the universe was rejected as stupid, absurd, and, moreover, formally heretical, because it contradicted a number of passages in Holy Scripture, both in their literal sense and as they had been interpreted by the Church Fathers and learned theologians. Second, the claim that the earth was not the immobile centre of the universe was likewise declared stupid and absurd from the standpoint of philosophy; from a theological standpoint it was held to be at least an error of faith ('ad minus esse in Fide erroneam').[3] This provided the basis for placing Copernicus's principal work, *De revolutionibus orbium coelestium* of 1543, on the Index of Prohibited Books until it had been corrected. In precisely what form the Jesuit cardinal Roberto Bellarmino had personally admonished Galileo to abandon Copernicanism, or at least his propaganda for Copernicus's theory, was an object of controversy at the 1633 trial, since no unambiguous record of what had passed between them could be found. But there is no doubt that Galileo was aware of the Roman church's objections to the Copernican system and its effective ban on teaching or defending it.

Although the various versions of the prehistory of this so-called first trial differ in details, most agree that the Jesuit order played only a small role, and the leading Jesuit astronomer, Christoph Clavius, none at all.[4] But in his commentary of 1570 on Sacrobosco, *In Sphaeram Ioannis de Sacro Bosco commentarius*, an introduction to contemporary astronomical science that went through numerous editions, Clavius set out biblical arguments against Copernican theory that became part of Jesuit and Catholic biblical exegesis. At the turn from the sixteenth to the seventeenth century, Jesuit exegetes were finally unanimous in rejecting Copernicanism. This rejection in its turn became binding on Jesuit astronomers whenever they were required to take a position in the contemporary cosmological debate. The compulsion to reject Copernicanism, however, was rooted not in the authority of the theologians of the Society of Jesus, but in that of its leading mathematician, Clavius.

A valuable window onto this interweaving of astronomy and exegesis is provided by the engraved title-page of Clavius's *Opera mathematica* of 1612. But before I turn to considering this programmatic image, some remarks about Clavius and the context for biblical exegesis are in order.

Christoph Clavius (1538–1612)

Clavius was regarded as the Euclid of the sixteenth century. A native of Bamberg, he joined the society of Jesus in Rome in 1555 and became the force behind the blossoming of the mathematical sciences that took place among the Jesuits in the late sixteenth and early seventeenth centuries. He was the last important Ptolemaic astronomer.[5] Some historians have proposed that Clavius may have been beginning to distance himself from the Ptolemaic view of the universe shortly before his death. In the last edition of his Sacrobosco commentary, which appeared in 1611 in the third volume of his *Opera mathematica*, he gave an account of Galileo's most recent discoveries and ended by calling on astronomers to 'consider how the heavenly spheres would have to be arranged so as to save these phenomena.'[6] In his other published writings, however, he invariably showed a preference for the geocentric view, although he also presented Copernicus's theories.

Clavius's Sacrobosco commentary, first published in 1570, became a classic in his lifetime. In the chapter on the immobility of the earth, Copernicus was cited by name as a proponent of the idea that the earth moves. Clavius emphasized in the same paragraph 'the common opinion of the astronomers and philosophers that the earth is devoid of either rectilinear or circular motion, and that on the contrary the heavens themselves are constantly in motion around it.' He based his conclusion in particular on the fact that such an account made it 'much easier to explain all [celestial] phenomena without any inconsistencies.'[7] Copernican theory was thus rejected, and this was justified not only on grounds of physics or astronomy; Clavius proceeded to add biblical arguments as well:

The meanings of the scriptures affirm in many places that the earth is immobile and that the sun and the rest of the stars move. Thus we read in Psalm 104:5, 'Who laid the foundations of the Earth, that it should not be removed for ever.' Similarly in Ecclesiastes 1:4–6: 'The Earth abideth for ever. The Sun also ariseth, and the Sun goeth down, and hasteth to his place where he arose: and there rising againe, compasseth by the South, and bendeth to the North.' What could be clearer? Also, the testimony presented to us in Psalm 19:4–6 states very clearly that the sun moves. There we read: 'In them hath he set a tabernacle for the Sun, which is as a bridegroom coming out of his chamber, and rejoiceth as a strong man to run a race. His going forth is from the end of the heaven, and his circuit unto the ends of it: and there is nothing hid from the heat thereof.' And again, it is recounted among the miracles that God sometimes causes the sun to go back or to stand still altogether.[8]

The last comment refers to the miracles of the Sun reversing its course in 2 Kings 20:8–11 and the Sun standing still in Joshua 10:12. Both miracles are represented on the engraved title-page of Clavius's *Opera mathematica* of 1612, which thus presents an anti-Copernican message in a prominent position.

It has been maintained that Clavius never mentioned Copernicus in his discussion of the immobility of the earth, so that the biblical arguments cited above cannot be interpreted as being directed against the Copernican system.[9] It is difficult to follow this argument, since Copernicus was invoked on the very same page as the principal witness for terrestrial motion. However, this opinion tends to exculpate Clavius, and implicitly the Society of Jesus as well, as but one among many who used biblical arguments in the Copernican debate. Indeed, even before 1570, numerous biblical arguments against the motion of the earth had been discussed in print.[10] But it was in Clavius's work that they were printed and reprinted in a prominent place, although the conclusion was not drawn there that Copernican theory could be dangerous to true faith. It was left to Jesuit exegesis to make that connection, with consequences that were not limited to the Jesuit order.

'Sun, stand thou still': Anti-Copernican Biblical Exegesis and the Engraved Title-Page of Clavius's *Opera mathematica*

The beginnings of title-page graphics go back to the fifteenth century, but within the Jesuit order title-pages came into their own only in the 1620s. As early as the first years of the seventeenth century it was customary among students in the Collegio Romano to design sheets elaborately decorated with emblematic figures on which to publish their theses. The students' enthusiasm for this was so great that the professors openly complained about the time they wasted on it and tried to call a halt to this form of theatrical self-advertisement, or at least to regulate the thesis print industry.[11] Among Jesuit mathematicians it was above all Christoph Scheiner who promoted such visual extravaganzas, in the 1620s and 1630s;[12] they reached their apogee in the middle of the century in the hands of Athanasius Kircher, Kaspar Schott, and Mario Bettini, whose title-pages are carefully staged artefacts of patronage.[13] In comparison to these histrionics, the engraved title-page of Clavius's *Opera mathematica* seems very modest (fig. 13.1).

The story of how the *Opera mathematica* came to be published has come down to us only in fragmentary form. Clavius's fellow Jesuit Johann Reinhard Ziegler arranged for the printing of the five volumes of the *Opera mathematica* in Mainz. It was he who suggested in 1608 that a title-page be designed for the work. It is not clear what part Clavius himself had in the design because the idea is not mentioned again in the surviving correspondence between Ziegler and Clavius. In a letter of 1611 to his fellow Jesuit Paul Guldin, Ziegler merely reports that the bishop of Bamberg, Johann Gottfried von Aschhausen, to whom the *Opera mathematica* was dedicated, has had the title-page engraved in Bamberg.[14] Even though the exact circumstances of the origin of this engraved title-page are obscure, it seems improbable that it could have been published without Clavius's consent.

The title-page takes the form of an early baroque funerary monument, with three axes and three storeys clearly divided among pedestal, title space, and

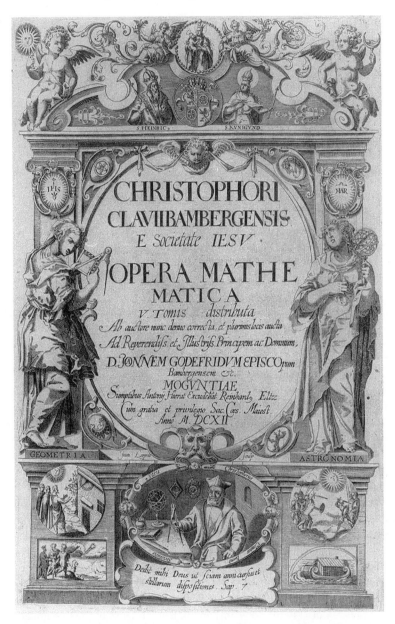

13.1. Johann Leypoldt, engraved title-page for Clavius's *Opera mathematica* (Mainz, 1612). Photo courtesy of Herzog August Bibliothek, Wolfenbüttel.

tympanum. The dedication to Johann Gottfried von Aschhausen (1575–1622), who had been made bishop of Bamberg in 1609, reflects Clavius's attachment to his birthplace, but it also evokes the depth of the Jesuits' involvement in the Counter Reformation, as Aschhausen stood in high favour in Rome, especially among the Jesuits, as a paragon of the Counter-Reformation clergy in Germany. In 1609 Bellarmino congratulated Aschhausen on his election, which he described as a divine miracle, and in 1611 he dedicated his commentary on the Psalms to the bishop.[15] In various dedicatory texts in the *Opera mathematica*, Clavius, too, shows himself well informed about Aschhausen's achievements. The close tie with Bamberg is further reflected in the tympanum, where the patron of the Bamberg bishopric, Henry II, and his wife, Cunegunde, are portrayed on either side of the episcopal arms of Bamberg. To the left and right of the title stand personifications of Geometry and Astronomy.

In the centre of the pedestal an oval medallion shows Clavius in his study with a compass and an armillary sphere representing his mathematical and astronomical interests. Below the portrait is printed a heavily abbreviated quotation from the Wisdom of Solomon, which refers directly to Clavius but also alludes to the astronomical signification of the title-page: 'For God gave me to know the cycles of the years and the position of the stars' ('Dedit mihi Deus ut sciam anni cursus et stellarum dispositiones'). An unabbreviated version of the text (Wisd. of Sol. 7:7–19) reveals considerably less modesty: 'For it was He who gave me unerring knowledge of existent being, to know the structure of the universe and the operation of the elements; the beginning, and end, and middle of times, the changes of the solstices and the vicissitudes of the seasons; the cycles of the years and the position of the stars.'

God had given man true knowledge ('scientiam veram') about the stars, or, to be exact, about astronomy and the system of the universe. As one endowed with this true knowledge, Clavius is, in allusion to his important role in the 1582 reform of the calendar, simultaneously portrayed as representing Jesuit, and thus Catholic, astronomy.[16] That system of the universe that God had given Clavius to know was definitively geocentric and thus anti-Copernican; so much is made clear in the circular vignettes to the left and right of the author, which portray the *Horologium Ahas* and the Sun standing still over Gibeon. The two rectangular vignettes show (on the left) the three Wise Men with the star of Bethlehem and (on the right) the ark with the rainbow, the sign of the covenant God made with Noah after the Flood (Gen. 9:12–13). The star of Bethlehem can be interpreted as the counterpart of the rainbow, a symbol of the renewal of the covenant through Jesus Christ in the New Testament. But the sense of the two images lies deeper. As the best known of the four astronomical miracles in the Bible, the star of Bethlehem was the common point of reference for late sixteenth-century discussion of whether new stars could come into being and what comets were. Among astronomers it was completely unclear where in the heavens comets and new stars were positioned, that is, which of the spheres they should be assigned to, what their path was, and, above all, how they had got there, because until the nova of 1572 it was assumed that the heavenly spheres were immutable.

Beginning with the 1585 edition, Clavius's Sacrobosco commentary contained a discussion of the 1572 nova in which he wrote that in his opinion the new star was located in the eighth sphere of the fixed stars. He made two suggestions about how such phenomena might be explained, namely, 'that the nova was either produced by almighty God in the eighth sphere of heaven in order to announce a great event (although what that might be remains unknown), or that in that sphere comets can be generated, as in a vapour, although this happens quite rarely.'[17] Clavius, then, seemed inclined to ascribe power over astronomical events to almighty God, who was able to produce celestial effects entirely at will. This falling back on God's omnipotence recalls the 'medicina del fine' in Galileo's *Dialogue on the Two World Systems* of 1632. There, a similar train of thought, also propounded by Pope Urban VIII, was placed in the mouth of the Aristotelian Simplicio. Luca Bianchi has provided convincing support for the hypothesis that Galileo took this argument, with which Clavius aimed to rescue God's omnipotence as an explanation of final resort in astronomy, directly from his Sacrobosco commentary.[18]

While the star of Bethlehem was thus associated with fundamental considerations of the limits of the explanatory power of astronomy and natural philosophy, the rainbow referred to the realm of biblical exegesis. There, the rainbow, as a divine sign, stood in an intimate relationship to the astronomical miracles of the *Horologium Ahas* and the Sun standing still over Gibeon.

It is reported in Genesis 9 that, as a sign of his promise that there would be no more floods, God placed the rainbow in the sky. In sixteenth-century biblical exegesis, as among the Church Fathers, the ark was regarded as a symbol of the church: the damned outside the ark and the saved within. The true church stood in perpetual covenant with God; this was the sense of the emblem of ark and rainbow.

But the symbolism of the rainbow, seemingly so simple, posed a serious problem for biblical exegesis, because it could be interpreted at one and the same time as a natural phenomenon and as a sign given by God. In the seventeenth century, Jesuit exegetes were agreed that while there had certainly been rainbows before the Flood (since they were natural phenomena), Noah's rainbow had not been an act of nature but a divine sign.

In his Genesis commentary of 1592, Benito Pereira gave extensive attention to the rainbow. To the question 'whether the rainbow was a natural sign of the

Flood,' Pereira answered that 'it was not and could not be' but had been brought about 'through the omnipotence of God alone.'[19] Just as with the rainbow, Pereira argued in detail, God was able to bring about the Flood with or without rain, entirely according to his will.[20] Both propositions reflect the standard argument, already used by Clavius and later satirized by Galileo, that many phenomena, even if they could be explained in scientific or rational terms, could nevertheless rest on divine intervention. Pereira emphasized that, like the rainbow, the phenomenon of the Sun reversing its course was to be counted among the divine signs.[21] Before Pereira, though in a similar context, Roberto Bellarmino had discussed signs in his *Disputationes de controversiis Christianae fidei*. He also mentioned the rainbow in the same breath as the *Horologium Ahas*.[22]

These remarks about the engraved title-page of the *Opera mathematica* underline the importance it assigns to biblical exegesis. The history of exegetic positions in relation to the Copernican problem, and in particular the history of interpretations of the passages in 2 Kings 20 and Joshua 10, are discussed below.

Catholic Biblical Exegesis between the Council of Trent and 1616

The question of how the Bible should be understood, and who had the right to decide how to establish a binding interpretation, had presented a serious problem since the beginning of the Reformation. It was on the agenda at the fourth session of the Council of Trent. In April 1546 two decrees were issued that had a key place in the history of the Catholic interpretation of the Bible and of Catholic exegesis. The decree on Holy Scripture and tradition was ostensibly about establishing which books constituted Holy Writ. This was a reaction to Luther's doubts about the character of the canon. It was stated in the introduction to the decree that the sources of faith consisted of both the written books and unwritten traditions. Luther's principle of *sola scriptura* had excluded such unwritten, apostolic traditions from the category of sources of faith.[23]

The decree on the vulgate edition of the Bible and the interpretation of Holy Scripture included clear advice about the interpretation of the Bible:

Furthermore, to control petulant spirits, the Council decrees that, in matters of faith and morals pertaining to the edification of Christian doctrine, no one, relying on his own judgement and distorting the Sacred Scriptures according to his own conceptions, shall dare to interpret them contrary to that sense which Holy Mother Church, to whom it belongs to judge their true sense and meaning, has held and does hold, or even contrary to the unanimous agreement of the Fathers, even though such interpretations should never at any time be published.[24]

This explicit warning confirmed the claim that the interpretation of scripture was the business of the church alone. However, it did not explain how the church should reach a reliable interpretation: ecclesiastical traditions, conciliar decisions, Church Fathers – any and all of these could be called upon as authorities in the case of dispute. The central question of the relative evidential power of the various theological sources and their relation to philosophical reflection had exercised theologians even before the Reformation. But their discussions were finally recorded only after the decrees of 1546, in the treatise *De locis theologicis* by the Dominican theologian Melchior Cano (1509–60). Cano developed a hierarchy of authorities that was generally accepted as a guide in the succeeding centuries.

Cano gave no particular weight to particular arguments, but ordered them in terms of the places (*loci*) in which they were to be found. Theological argumentation, he argued, could rest on ten *loci*, the first seven of which relied on authority and were theological in the narrower sense: 1) written books; 2) unwritten traditions; 3) the Catholic church; 4) the general councils; 5) the Roman church; 6) the Church Fathers; and 7) the scholastic theologians. The other three *loci* were grounded on reason: 8) human reason; 9) the philosophers; and 10) history. Cano's treatise devoted a book to each of these *loci*, but his plan of adding a book on how they should be deployed in interpreting the Bible was frustrated by his premature death. In the twelfth book he did set out rules on how to proceed when the sense of scripture was not unambiguous but obscure. Here, he gave an important role to the shared views of the Church Fathers and scholastic theologians. For, according to Cano's eighth rule, 'if all scholastic theologians have established the same firm and fixed conclusion with one voice ... then the faithful certainly should embrace it as a Catholic truth.'[25] Notwithstanding Cano's suggestions, for post-Tridentine theologians there was no firmly established procedure on how to find a consensus where exegetical opinions did differ. However, such a consensus of the exegetes emerged in the Copernican question by the late sixteenth century and would later become a commonly cited argument against Copernican theory.

The positions of the two Jesuits Benito Pereira and Roberto Bellarmino were also central to the development of Catholic exegesis in the sixteenth and seventeenth centuries. But already Cano had left no doubt that the arguments of the natural philosophers would play a subordinate role. As its proponents consistently maintained, Copernican theory was not primarily a question of faith, and it was not mentioned at all at the Council or in any related publications. At the same time, it was clearly incompatible with the literal sense of Holy Scripture and thus bound to present serious problems for the theologians.

Through the comprehensive four-volume commentary on Genesis based on his lectures at the Collegio Romano, Benito Pereira (1535–1610) established himself as one of the most prominent exegetes around 1600.[26] In the first volume of his Genesis commentary he set down four basic rules for exegesis, which were often cited and which Galileo in particular referred to in his letter to Christina. Pereira declared that 1) the Mosaic account of creation was to be understood as historical, that is, in its literal sense, and 2) interpretations of this account should avoid having recourse without good reason to miracles or divine omnipotence. He exhorted exegetes 3) to subject their own interpretations to critical scrutiny before they rejected alternative views, for scripture was very broad and open to different readings. Finally, he considered 4) the meaning of non-theological disciplines, especially philosophy and natural philosophy, for biblical exegesis: 'This also must be carefully observed and completely avoided: in dealing with the teachings of Moses, do not think or say anything affirmatively and asser- tively that is contrary to the manifest evidence and arguments of philosophy or the other disciplines. For since every truth agrees with every other truth, the truth of Sacred Scripture cannot be contrary to the true arguments and evidence of the human sciences.'[27] Here Pereira, invoking Augustine, elaborated an exegetic position that Cano had only sketched out in *De locis theologicis*. Cano had expressly given the arguments of reason a subordinate status, but had allowed for exceptions as long as the issues involved had little or nothing to do with faith. In his explanation of the fourth rule, Pereira provided concrete examples of how insisting on the literal sense of the Bible could contradict 'manifest truths and necessary arguments,' for example, if one were to conclude from the wording that the 'stars [actually] move through the heavens in the same way as fish move through the water and birds through the air.'[28] Galileo cited Pereira's fourth rule directly in his letter to Christina, and the principle that two truths could not contradict each other was an important element in his accommoda- tion theory.

The determination of the 'true' meaning of Holy Scripture also played an important part in the work of the most influential contemporary theological controversialist, the Jesuit cardinal Roberto Bellarmino. His principal work, the multivolume *Disputationes de controversiis Christianae fidei* (1586–93), a mon- ument of Counter-Reformation eloquence and erudition, was composed in the years following the Council of Trent as the result of intensive study of the positions of Protestant theologians.[29] The confessional controversy made it essential to arrive at a clear view of divine revelation and the authorities through which it was transmitted. In this context, great importance was attached not only to the correct interpretation of the Bible but also to the question of who should decide whether an interpretation was binding.

For Bellarmino there was no doubt that scripture was obscure and that it was therefore vital to name a final arbiter in matters of scriptural interpretation. But before he turned to consider how such an arbiter might be identified, he devoted a separate section to expounding the doctrine of the multiple meanings of scripture, drawing heavily on Aquinas.[30] He began by making a fundamental distinction between a literal or historical meaning and a spiritual or mystical one. Establishing the spiritual meaning of any given passage seemed largely unproblematic. This was anything but the case for the literal meaning, which was the most relevant for the interpretation of scripture.[31] The ambiguity and obscurity of scripture engendered the need for a legitimate interpreter, a judge whose verdict could bring light in the darkness. This judge, Bellarmino argued, could not be scripture itself, nor could it be 'the revealing spirit of private individuals,' but only the ecclesiastical prince, alone or in conjunction with a council.[32] In the third disputation Bellarmino goes on to give an extensive justification for what was only hinted at in his discussion of the role of the judge, namely, that the pope was the supreme judge in disputes over matters of faith. Bellarmino's account had an important implication for biblical exegesis: rational arguments could not finally establish the validity of any particular interpretation, for the ultimate decision in exegetic disputes lay with the pope.[33] His comments made possible a crucial distinction between academic exegesis, which applied the tools of scholarship to analysing the Bible line by line, and official exegesis, which was based on academic interpretation but in the end was up to the pope and his advisers. There remained only a very narrow space in which the interpretation of the Bible was open to debate. Anybody who deviated from the interpretation of the Bible that had been adjudged correct was exposed to the suspicion of heresy.

When Galileo in his 1615 letter to Christina insisted that parts of Holy Scripture would have to be reinterpreted in the light of the strong arguments for the Copernican system, not only was he lacking real proof for that system, he was also setting himself against the consensus of Catholic exegetes.

Copernican Theory and Catholic Exegesis

The Bible recounts four astronomical miracles: the Sun standing still, the Sun returning in its path, the eclipse of the Sun at Jesus' crucifixion (Matt. 27:45, Mark 15:33, Luke 23:44–5), and the star of Bethlehem (Matt. 2:2–11). The eclipse was of no interest for exegetical discussions of terrestrial motion. The interpretation of the star of Bethlehem had cosmological implications, which have been discussed above. But the two miracles involving the motion of the sun had a role to play in the discussion of views of the universe.

The Book of Joshua recounts how the Israelites conquered the land of Canaan.

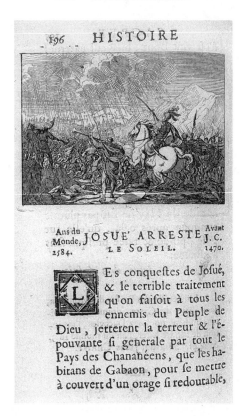

13.2. Sébastien LeClerc, *Josué arreste le soleil*, in Claude Oronce Finé de Brianville,
Histoire sacrée en tableaux, vol. 1 (Paris, 1677), p. 196.
Photo courtesy of Herzog August Bibliothek, Wolfenbüttel.

This required God's help, especially in the conflict with the Amorites, when 'the Sun stood still, and the Moon stayed, until the people had avenged themselves upon their enemies' (Josh. 10:12–13). This had long been one of the standard arguments against the Copernican system, as it referred explicitly to the motion of the sun. The scene of 'Joshua stopping the Sun' was one of the most spectacular miracles in the Bible and, being an ideal subject for graphic representation, was ubiquitous in art throughout the Middle Ages and well into the eighteenth century, and appeared regularly in illustrated Bibles (see fig. 13.2).

In the Second Book of Kings the prophet Isaiah announces to the dying King Hezekiah that he will recover and live a further fifteen years. But Hezekiah is

88   HISTOIRE

<table>
<tr><td>Ans du
Monde,
3309.</td><td>EZECHIAS.</td><td>Avant
J.C.
745.</td></tr>
</table>

Rois de Iuda. Ezechias 29 ans.
Rois d'Israël. Osée 18 ans.

E bon Roy n'eut rien
tant à cœur que de
démolir tous les au-
tels profanes & tou-
tes les idoles des faul-
ses divinités, dont ses predecesseurs
avoient rempli tout le Royaume
de Judée, & son zele fut si agreable

13.3. Sébastien LeClerc, *Ezechias*, in Claude Oronce Finé de Brianville,
Histoire sacrée en tableaux, vol. 2 (Paris, 1677), p. 88.
Photo courtesy of Herzog August Bibliothek, Wolfenbüttel.

unconvinced, and demands as a sign from God that 'the shadow return backward ten degrees. And Isaiah the prophet cried unto the Lord: and he brought the shadow ten degrees backward, by which it had gone down in the dial of Ahas' (2 Kings 20:9–11). This passage was known by the phrase *Horologium Ahas*, because the majority of commentators were of the opinion that the measure of the sun's retreat referred to a sundial. By the beginning of the seventeenth century this passage, too, had become a standard argument against Copernican theory. This miracle of the sun going backward made as good a picture as the stopping of the sun over Gibeon (see figs 13.3 and 13.4). The exegetes often mentioned the two miracles together. They stood side by side in Clavius's

13.4. *Sciatericum Ahas*, in Johann Jakob Scheuchzer, *Kupfer-Bibel* (Augsburg and Ulm, 1731–3), plate 494. Photo courtesy of Herzog August Bibliothek, Wolfenbüttel.

Sacrobosco commentary of 1570, just as they did in the engraved title-page of his *Opera mathematica* of 1612.

Of course, these two passages were not all that the exegetes could use to challenge the Copernican system. The Spanish Jesuit theologian Juan de Pineda (1557–1637) chose another point of attack in his two-volume commentary on Job, which was first published in Seville in 1598 and 1602.[34] Pineda rejected the motion of the earth in the context of an interpretation of Job 9:6 ('Which shaketh the Earth out of her place, and the pillars thereof tremble'), in which he referred to Clavius. At the same time, he expressly distanced himself from the commentary on Job written by the Spanish Augustinian Diego de Zuñiga (1536–c. 1598). Zuñiga, whose work was placed on the Index along with that of Copernicus in

1616, had maintained in his own commentary on this passage that it did not contradict Copernican theory but could easily be reconciled with it.[35]

Pineda rejected Zuñiga's view as 'plainly false.' According to him, others regarded it as 'foolish, frivolous, reckless, and dangerous to the faith' ('deliram, nugatoriam, temerariam, & in fide periculosam'). The last two censures explicitly invoke the threat to true belief, thereby opening the way for a condemnation of this view by the church.[36] Pineda reinforced his rejection of Zuñiga's view with a concluding reference to Clavius's Sacrobosco commentary, in which Clavius had demonstrated the falsehood of the Copernican thesis with 'philosophical and astronomical arguments.'

Twenty years later Pineda provided a much more comprehensive biblical refutation of the motion of the earth, in his commentary on Ecclesiastes, *In Ecclesiasten commentariorum liber unus* (Seville, 1619). But his interpretation in the Job commentary had already set an example, for his fellow Jesuit Jean Lorin (1559–1634) published a commentary on Acts in 1605 in which he based his rejection of territorial motion on Pineda's arguments. Lorin rejected the theory summarily and invoked the authority of 'our Clavius' and Pineda to confirm its 'falseness and recklessness' ('falsitatis ac temeritatis'). He appears to have got his information from Pineda, however, without looking at the original texts, for as the source for Copernicus he cited his 'Resolutionibus' (*sic*).[37] It is noteworthy that of Pineda's catalogue of critical terms for Copernican theory, only 'temeritas' remained in Lorin's vocabulary to signal the danger involved in propagating it.

The most extensive contemporary commentary on the Sun standing still over Gibeon was written by the Jesuit Nicolaus Serarius (1555–1609), whose wide-ranging erudition and literary productivity made him one of the most important exegetes of the late sixteenth and early seventeenth centuries. At the suggestion of the superior general of the Jesuit order, Claudio Acquaviva, Serarius planned to write exegetic commentaries on all the books of the Bible, but this mammoth undertaking was frustrated by his death.[38] In the year Serarius died, 1609, there appeared the first part of his commentaries on the Old Testament, in particular on the Book of Joshua. More than twenty pages were devoted to the miracle at Gibeon. In *quaestio XIV*, Serarius dealt with the question of whether 'Sun and Moon can naturally stand still.' He cited 'the famous astronomer of our day, Nicolaus Copernicus,' also known as 'a second Ptolemy,' as a proponent of the teaching that 'the sun always stood still and was the centre of the whole universe ... Not only Clavius, in his Sacrobosco commentary, praised [Copernicus], but also and in particular Giovanni Antonio Magini in the work *De theoricis*, and many others.'[39] Despite his generous references to Copernicus, Serarius left his readers in no doubt that Copernican theory posed serious problems for faith. He made a clear distinction between the hypotheses on the universe and their truth content. He said he could not see 'how these [Copernicus's] hypotheses could escape the charge of heresy, if anyone so to speak claimed they were true.'[40] For Holy Scripture always ascribed rest to the earth and motion to the sun and moon. Serarius underpinned this statement with biblical quotations and ended by emphasizing the consensus of Church Fathers and theologians in this matter; not only had all philosophers condemned this theory, but also all Church Fathers and all theologians. Serarius's view that the Copernican system was heretical in so far as any claims to truth were made on its behalf was very similar to Bellarmino's 1615 warning to Foscarini and Galileo to present the Copernican system only as a hypothesis, and not as truth, because it was 'likely not only to irritate all scholastic philosophers and theologians, but also to harm the holy faith by rendering Holy Scripture false.'[41] Bellarmino was merely invoking a well-established position.

Pineda and Serarius, two of the most influential and widely read Jesuit theologians, rejected Copernican theory as incompatible with scripture. Both, like Jean Lorin, cited Clavius's Sacrobosco commentary and left no doubt that the Copernican hypotheses contained a germ of heresy, long before this topos came to be more or less politicized between 1610 and 1616. Later exegetes had in common that they presumed a geocentric view of the universe and reflected this view in their biblical commentaries, but hardly made any mention of Copernicus and his hypotheses. The Portuguese Jesuit Cosme de Magalhaens (1551–1624), for example, published a two-volume commentary on Joshua in 1612 entitled *In sacram Iosue historiam commentarium*. In it the Sun standing still over Gibeon was discussed at length and considered in connection with the *Horologium Ahas*, but neither the name of Copernicus nor the danger to faith implicit in his theory was mentioned. Galileo cited this commentary in the context of his Copernican interpretation of Joshua 10:12 in the letter to Christina.[42] It may be that Magalhaens's silence on the issue lured Galileo into a false sense of security about the status of the Copernican question among theologians – a misapprehension of which a reading of Serarius would have cured him. All in all the position of Catholic biblical exegesis on the Copernican question on the eve of the Galileo affair was unambiguous: with the united authority of the Church Fathers, Copernicus's theory was unanimously rejected, in so far as it was taken into account at all.

Although it remains uncertain just how the anti-Copernican exegetical consensus developed among Jesuit theologians, the examples of Juan de Pineda and Nicolaus Serarius make clear that the views of Christoph Clavius had an important function in the process. The engraved title-page of his *Opera mathematica* of 1612 alluded to an anti-Copernican exegesis, by now canonical, to whose establishment Clavius had made a decisive contribution through the various editions of his Sacrobosco commentary.

Results of the Interpretation

The analysis of the four biblical images in the pedestal of the engraved title-page has revealed a web of meanings and allusions, which would have been only incompletely understood outside the circles of the theologically knowledgable. While the references to the *Horologium Ahas* and the Sun standing still over Gibeon left no room for speculation as to their meaning, the connection with the other two images was not self-evident. In each case – and this is the decisive point – the charge of heresy lay in the air: a charge laid by the Jesuit exegetes who set the tone within the Catholic church against anybody who expressed doubts about the truth of the events depicted or the correctness of the official Catholic interpretation of them. When these four pictures were brought together, what appeared on the page were not simply arguments against Copernicanism, but the clear sense that these astronomical issues, far from being a private matter for the astronomers, touched on central questions of faith.

It is true that, from 1570 on, Clavius used the Sun standing still over Gibeon and the *Horologium Ahas* as arguments against the motion of the earth. But the various forewords and dedications of the *Opera mathematica* gave no help in decoding the engraved title-page or the interplay among the four pictures in the pedestal. Only in the foreword to the reprint of the first of four essays on the theory of sundials, *Gnominices libri octo* (1st ed. Rome, 1581), which figured unchanged in the 1612 publication of the fourth volume of the *Opera mathematica*, was brief reference made in an unlikely place to Clavius's cosmological position. Before addressing the importance of sundials and their theory as astronomical aids, Clavius commented on the nature of mathematics and astronomy, emphasizing that they were 'so certain that they make no room for mere probability, but prove everything with clear and necessary arguments' ('Cum enim ipsae sint ita exploratae, ut nihil probabile admittant, sed illustribus omnia argumentis necessariisque demonstrent'). He saw this as the foundation of astronomy, whose tasks included the study of 'the heavenly spheres created by the hand of God' and of the 'utterly immutable movement of the sun.' Clavius left readers in no doubt that the universe was geocentric.[43]

The exclusion of probabilistic arguments and the insistence on necessary demonstrations was directly linked to the Copernican debate. In his Genesis commentary, Pereira had left open the possibility of interpretations of the Bible that deviated from the literal sense, in cases where a literal reading would contradict 'manifest proofs and necessary arguments.' Necessary demonstrations for the Copernican system were what Galileo thought he had after 1610. On this basis he thought he had legitimate grounds to call for a reinterpretation of the biblical passages that appeared to contradict Copernican theory.[44] For Clavius, however, as for Bellarmino, Galileo's arguments were not necessary, but merely probable. The Bible could not be challenged on this basis. But – and this is often misrepresented in the historiography – Bellarmino did not reject Copernicanism on biblical grounds; rather, he rejected reinterpretation of the Bible in accordance with the Copernican system while no definitive proofs were available.[45]

With the engraved title-page of the *Opera mathematica*, Clavius's full authority as a leading mathematician and astronomer was visibly mobilized in support of a geocentric cosmology. What is notable here is not the rejection of the Copernican view of the universe, but the peculiar amalgam of mathematical science and theology. It looked as though astronomy was citing biblical exegesis as an authority. This observation directly contradicts the view, often presented in the historiography, that it was the intervention of the theologians that shifted the Copernican debate from the realm of natural philosophy and mathematics to that of theology between 1610 and 1616. The engraved title-page of the *Opera mathematica* reveals a contrary development. It reflects the connections, sketched above, among Clavius, Jesuit biblical exegesis, and the positions the Catholic church finally adopted in 1616 with the ban on the Copernican system.

The engraved title-page of the *Opera mathematica* records a long history, stretching from Clavius's anti-Copernican remarks in the Sacrobosco commentaries of 1570 and after, through the Jesuit biblical exegesis of the late sixteenth century and the church positions on the Copernican question informed by it, up to the first trial of 1616. But the title-page could not be effective as anti-Copernican propaganda, especially since it was not accompanied by an *explicatio frontispicii*, which might have put readers on the right track.

Many questions remain open. With regard to Clavius it is not clear why he included biblical arguments against Copernicanism in his Sacrobosco commentary at all. In the context of discussions of the syllabus of the Collegio Romano, Clavius was intensively engaged in trying to improve the status of the mathematical sciences and establish their independence of other disciplines. But the theological arguments against Copernicanism rebounded against the independence of astronomy, arguments made in the name of astronomy's Nestor, Clavius.

We also need a closer investigation of the history of Jesuit biblical exegesis, in particular of the relations among theologians, exegetes, philosophers, mathematicians, and astronomers within the Jesuit order that existed at the turn to the seventeenth century, if we are to answer the many open questions still associated with the Catholic church's reaction to the so-called scientific revolution and the role of the Jesuits in it.

In Galileo research of the 1990s, the trial of 1633 is often understood as the result of an inevitable clash between Galileo and the church, or, more generally, between the new science and the church. An important component of this argument is the view that the post-Tridentine Catholic church and above all Cardinal Bellarmino were characterized by 'authoritarian' and 'fundamentalist' tendencies epitomized by the Catholic attitude to biblical exegesis. In an article on Galileo and the church, Rivka Feldhay has subjected this approach, and the associated diagnoses of authoritarianism and fundamentalism, to an extensive critique. She emphasizes that while the post-Tridentine church gave a high priority to controlling the interpretation of the Bible, 'interpretive pluralism' persisted in practice.[46]

The exegetic principles formulated by one such as Pereira did indeed include the exhortation to be careful and open-minded, but in the Copernican question Catholic exegesis proved relatively closed. At the same time, there is a qualitative difference between rejecting terrestrial motion on biblical grounds and branding it, and with it Copernican theory, as heretical and damnable. Long before the first Galileo trial of 1616, the exegetic consensus among Jesuits was tending towards the latter. But this was without reference to Galileo's Copernican propaganda, which is often invoked to explain the 1616 condemnation of Copernicus's theory; nor did it lead in itself to a clash. In the emergence of this exegetical consensus, authoritarianism or fundamentalism as such played no significant role.

NOTES

1 The literature on Galileo is vast; excellent introductions are *The Galileo Affair: A Documentary History*, ed. Maurice A. Finocchiaro (Berkeley, 1989); and *The Cambridge Companion to Galileo*, ed. Peter Machamer (Cambridge, 1998). Galileo's works are cited below by volume and page number (III 289) from *Le opere di Galileo Galilei,* ed. Antonio Favaro, 20 vols in 21 (Florence, 1890–1909; repr. 1968).

2 See, most recently, Corrado Dollo, 'Le ragioni del geocentrismo nel Collegio romano,' in *La diffusione del Copernicanismo in Italia, 1543–1610*, ed. Massimo Bucciantini and Maurizio Torrini (Florence, 1997), pp. 99–167, especially 102–21; Rinaldo Fabris, *Galileo Galilei e gli orientamenti esegetici del suo tempo* (Vatican City, 1986); Irving A. Kelter, 'The Refusal to Accommodate: Jesuit Exegetes and the Copernican System,' *Sixteenth Century Journal* 26 (1995): 273–83; and Paolo Ponzio, *Copernicanismo e teologia. Scrittura e natura in Campanella, Galilei e Foscarini* (Bari, 1998).

3 Galileo, XIX 321.

4 For presentations of these established facts, cf. *The Galileo Affair*, ed. Finocchiaro;
   Volker R. Remmert, '"Sonne steh still über Gibeon." Galileo Galilei, Christoph
   Clavius, katholische Bibelexegese und die Mahnung der Bilder,' *Zeitschrift für
   historische Forschung* 28 (2001): 538–80, on 541–43.
5 On Clavius, cf. Ugo Baldini, 'Christoph Clavius and the Scientific Scene in Rome,'
   in *Gregorian Reform of the Calendar*, ed. George V. Coyne, M.A. Hoskin, and
   Olaf Pedersen (Vatican City, 1983), pp. 137–70; Eberhard Knobloch, 'Sur la vie et
   l'oeuvre de Christophore Clavius,' *Revue d'histoire des sciences* 41 (1988): 331–56;
   Knobloch, 'L'oeuvre de Clavius et ses sources scientifiques,' in Giard *Jés. Ren.*,
   pp. 263–83; James M. Lattis, *Between Copernicus and Galileo: Christoph Clavius
   and the Collapse of Ptolemaic Cosmology* (Chicago, 1994); Michel-Pierre Lerner,
   'L'entrée de Tycho Brahe chez les jésuites ou le chant du cygne de Clavius,' in
   Giard *Jés. Ren.*, pp. 145–85; Rom. *Contre-réf.*, pp. 85–180; and *Christoph Clavius:
   Corrispondenza*, ed. Ugo Baldini and Pier Daniele Napolitani, 4 vols (Pisa, 1992), I,
   pp. 33–58.
6 Christoph Clavius, *Opera mathematica*, 5 vols (Mainz 1611/12), III, p. 75. Cf.
   Richard J. Blackwell, *Galileo, Bellarmine, and the Bible* (Notre Dame and London,
   1991), pp. 25f.; Annibale Fantoli, *Galileo: For Copernicanism and for the Church*
   (Vatican, City 1994), p. 126; Lattis, *Between Copernicus and Galileo*, pp. 181, 198;
   and Lerner, 'L'entrée de Tycho Brahe,' p. 164.
7 Christoph Clavius, *In sphaeram Ioannis de Sacro Bosco commentarius* (Rome,
   1570), pp. 244–50.
8 Clavius, *In sphaeram*, pp. 247f. Biblical translations are from the King James
   version.
9 Lattis, *Between Copernicus and Galileo*, pp. 123f. Cf. Blackwell, *Galileo*, pp. 25f.
10 See, for example, Philipp Melanchton, *Initia doctrinae physicae* (Wittenberg, 1549),
   fols 48r f.; and Jean Pierre de Mesmes, *Les institutions astronomiques* (Paris, 1557),
   pp. 57f.
11 On this, see Louise Rice, 'Jesuit Thesis Prints and the Festive Academic Defence at
   the Collegio Romano,' in O'M. *Jes. Cult.*, pp. 148–69.
12 On this, see Volker R. Remmert, 'Die Einheit von Theologie und Astronomie: Zur
   visuellen Auseinandersetzung mit dem kopernikanischen System bei jesuitischen
   Autoren in der ersten Hälfte des 17. Jahrhunderts,' *AHSI* 72 (2003): 247–95.
13 On Jesuit title-pages, see Remmert, *Widmung, Welterklärung und Wissenschafts-
   legitimierung: Titelbilder und ihre Funktionen in der Wissenschaftlichen Revolution*
   (Wiesbaden, 2005), chap. 7.
14 Ziegler to Clavius, 13 April 1608, in *Clavius: Corrispondenza*, ed. Baldini and
   Napolitani, vol. 4(1), p. 83; Ziegler to Guldin, 14 May 1611, ibid., vol. 4(2), p. 9.
15 Roberto Bellarmino, *Explanatio in Psalmos* (Cologne, 1611). On Aschhausen, see

Heinrich Weber, *Johann Gottfried von Aschhausen, Fürstbischof von Bamberg und Würzburg, Herzog zu Franken* (Würzburg, 1889).

16 Baldini, 'Christoph Clavius and the Scientific Scene in Rome,' pp. 146–54; Lattis, *Between Copernicus and Galileo*, pp. 20f.

17 Clavius, *Opera mathematica*, vol. 3, p. 105. On Clavius's views about new stars and comets, see Lattis, *Between Copernicus and Galileo*, pp. 147–60.

18 Galileo Galilei, *Dialogue on the World Systems: A New Abridged Translation and Guide*, ed. Maurice A. Finocchiaro (Berkeley, 1997), p. 307; Luca Bianchi, 'Galileo fra Aristotele, Clavio e Scheiner. La nuova edizione del "Dialogo" e il problema delle fonti galileiane,' *Rivista di storia della filosofia* 54 (1999): 189–227, on 214–27.

19 Benito Pereira, *Commentariorum et disputationum in Genesim tomi quatuor* (Cologne, 1601), 527.

20 Pereira, *Commentariorum*, p. 528.

21 The marginal heading to this passage reads 'The variety of signs by which God seals his promises, Judges 6:4, Kings 20; Genesis 17' (Pereira, *Commentariorum*, p. 525).

22 Roberto Bellarmino, *Disputationes Roberti Bellarmini Politiani, Societatis Iesu, de controversiis Christianae fidei, adversus huius temporis haereticos*, 3 vols (Ingolstadt, 1587–93), II, pp. 191–204.

23 On the Council of Trent, the standard work is still Hubert Jedin, *Geschichte des Konzils von Trient*, 4 vols (Freiburg im Breisgau, 1949–75). On the council in the context of the Galileo affair, see Blackwell, *Galileo*, pp. 5–10; Fabris, *Galileo*, pp. 23–5.

24 Blackwell, *Galileo*, p. 183. On the development of the decree, see Jedin, *Geschichte*, vol. 2, pp. 42–82.

25 Book 12, quoted from Blackwell, *Galileo*, p. 18. On Cano and his doctrine of *loci*, see above all Charles H. Lohr, 'Modelle für die Überlieferung theologischer Doktrin: Von Thomas von Aquin bis Melchior Cano,' in *Dogmengeschichte und katholische Theologie*, ed. Werner Löser et al. (Würzburg, 1988), pp. 148–67, on 148f.; cf. Blackwell, *Galileo*, pp. 15–19.

26 On Pereira, see Blackwell, *Galileo*, pp. 20–2, 101–2, 258–60; Fabris, *Galileo*, pp. 29–33; Rivka Feldhay, *Galileo and the Church: Political Inquisition or Critical Dialogue?* (Cambridge, 1995), pp. 136–9, 164–6; Lattis, *Between Copernicus and Galileo*, pp. 34–6, 91–8, 109–11; and Klaus Reinhardt, *Bibelkommentare spanischer Autoren (1500–1700)*, vol. 2 (Madrid, 1999), pp. 176–83.

27 Benito Pereira, *Prior tomus commentariorum et disputationum in Genesim* (Ingolstadt, 1590), p. 27. Cf. Galileo, 'Letter to Christina', V 320; Blackwell, *Galileo*, p. 22.

28 Pereira, *Prior tomus*, pp. 27f.

29 On Bellarmino, see Blackwell, *Galileo*; *Bellarmino e la controriforma. Atti del*

simposio internazionale di studi, Sora 15–18 ottobre 1986, ed. R. DeMaio et al. (Sora, 1990); Thomas Dietrich, *Die Theologie der Kirche bei Robert Bellarmin (1542–1621). Systematische Voraussetzungen des Kontroverstheologen* (Paderborn, 1999); *Roberto Bellarmino arcivescovo di Capua, teologo e pastore della Riforma cattolica. Atti del Convegno internazionale di studie, Capua 18 settembre–1 ottobre 1988*, ed. G. Galeota, 2 vols (Capua, 1990); Richard S. Westfall, 'Bellarmine, Galileo, and the Clash of Two World Views,' in his *Essays on the Trial of Galileo* (Vatican City, 1989), pp. 3–10.

30 Bellarmino, *De Verbi Dei interpretatione liber tertius, cap. III: Proponitur quaestio de iudice controversiarum; & simul disseritur de sensibus Scripturarum*, in Bellarmino, *Disputationes*, vol. 1, pp. 211–17. On the doctrine of the multiple meanings of scripture, see Blackwell, *Galileo*, pp. 33–5; and Dietrich, *Theologie der Kirche*, pp. 129–32, 164–74; and cf. Francesco Beretta, *Galilée devant le Tribunal de l'Inquisition. Une relecture des sources* (Fribourg, 1998), pp. 114–28.

31 Bellarmine, *Disputationes*, vol. 1, pp. 212, 214f.

32 Ibid., p. 237.

33 Ibid., p. 248.

34 On Pineda, cf. Estanislao Olivares, 'Juan de Pineda S.I. (1557–1637) Biografía. Escritos. Bibliografía,' *Archivo teológico granadino* 51 (1988): 5–132; and Reinhardt, *Bibelkommentare*, pp. 192–6.

35 Diego de Zuñiga, *In Iob commentaria* (Toledo, 1584; repr: Rome, 1591), pp. 205–7; the index to the volume refers to this passage under the phrase 'terram moveri non est contra scripturam sanctam' (the motion of the earth is not against Holy Scripture). For an English translation, see Blackwell, *Galileo*, pp. 185f. On Zuñiga, cf. Francesco Barone, 'Diego de Zuñiga e Galileo Galilei: Astronomia eliostatica ed esegesi biblica,' *Critica storica* 19 (1982): 319–34; Víctor Navarro Brotóns, 'The Reception of Copernicus's Work in Sixteenth-Century Spain: The Case of Diego de Zuñiga,' *Isis* 86 (1995): 52–78; Reinhardt, *Bibelkommentare*, pp. 424–6; and Robert S. Westman, 'The Copernicans and the Churches,' in *God & Nature: Historical Essays on the Encounter between Christianity and Science*, ed. David C. Lindberg and Ronald L. Numbers (Berkeley, Los Angeles, London, 1986), pp. 76–113, especially 99–103.

36 Juan de Pineda, *Commentariorum in Iob libri tredecim* (Cologne, 1600), p. 339. On the system of ratings that could be formally applied to theological propositions, see Lohr, 'Modelle' (n25 above).

37 Jean Lorin, *In Acta Apostolorum commentaria* (Lyon, 1605), p. 215.

38 Serarius's exegetic principles are discussed by Fabris, *Galileo*, pp. 33f; cf. Serarius's own remarks in chapter 21, 'De sacrorum Bibliorum exegetica interpretatione,' of his *Prolegomena biblica* (Mainz, 1612), pp. 138–56.

39 Nicolaus Serarius, *Iosue, ab utero ad ipsum usque tumulum, e Moysis Exodo*,

Levitico, Numeris, Deuteronomio; & e proprio ipsius libro toto, ac Paralipomenis, libris quinque explanatus, 2 vols (Mainz, 1609/10; repr. Paris, 1610/11; Mainz, 1622/26), II, p. 237.

40 Serarius, *Iosue*, vol. 2, p. 238.

41 Bellarmino to Foscarini, 12 April 1615, in *The Galileo Affair*, ed. Finocchiaro, p. 67; Galileo, XII 171f.

42 Cosmas Magalhaens, *In sacram Iosue historiam commentarium* (Tours, 1612), pp. 342–54; Bernard R. Goldstein, 'Galileo's Account of Astronomical Miracles in the Bible: A Confusion of Sources,' *Nuncius: Annali di storia della scienza* 5 (1990): 3–16, has convincingly identified Magalhaens's commentary as the principal source for Galileo's remarks in the letter to Christina (V 347).

43 Clavius, *Opera mathematica*, vol. 4, first page of the unpaginated foreword to *Gnominices libri octo*. The identical wording is in *Gnominices libri octo* (Rome, 1581).

44 He made this explicit in the letter to Christina: 'Because of this, and because (as we said before) two truths cannot contradict one another, the task of a wise interpreter is to strive to fathom the true meaning of the sacred texts; this will undoubtedly agree with those physical conclusions of which we are already certain and sure through clear observations or necessary demonstrations' (*The Galileo Affair*, ed. Finocchiaro, p. 96). On this, see Remmert, 'Galileo, God, and Mathematics,' in *Mathematics and the Divine: A Historical Study*, ed. Luc Bergmans and Teun Koetsier (Amsterdam, 2005).

45 Cf. Blackwell, *Galileo*, p. 172; Ernan McMullin, 'Galileo on Science and Scripture,' in *Companion to Galileo*, ed. Machamer (n1 above), pp. 271–347, especially 273.

46 Rivka Feldhay, 'Recent Narratives on Galileo and the Church: or, The Three Dogmas of the Counter-Reformation,' *Science in Context* 13 (2000): 489–507, on 496.

14 / Jesuit Influences on Galileo's Science

WILLIAM A. WALLACE, O.P.

The casual reader, when noting this essay, might wonder whether a mistake has been made in its title. Shouldn't it read, 'Galileo's Influences on Jesuit Science'? That would be a workable title, but it is not the topic intended here. No mistake has been made. There were Jesuit influences on Galileo's science, but they are not 'writ large' in the history of science, nor are they widely appreciated today by scholars, even among historians and philosophers of science.

There are several reasons for this, among which only two need be mentioned. The first is that the evidence to be adduced is not readily available – it dates from the late sixteenth and early seventeenth centuries and is contained mainly in Latin manuscripts and early printed books.[1] The second is that what evidence there is has been made available only gradually and in bits and pieces.[2]

The following is an overview of my sources and the conclusions to which I have come. For Galileo I have worked mainly from four of his manuscripts, all autographs, contained in the Galileo collection in the National Library in Florence. These are ms Gal. 27, concerned mainly with logic and scientific demonstration; ms Gal. 46, containing questions on the heavens and the elements; and mss Gal. 71 and Gal. 72, dealing with local motion.[3] My interest has been in Galileo's use of scholastic terminology, and particularly that of fourteenth-century thinkers at Oxford and Paris. Key Latin terms for which I have searched in his notebooks include *calculatores* and *doctores Parisienses; resolutio, compositio,* and *regressus demonstrativus* for scientific reasoning; and *impetus, uniformiter difformis, gradus velocitatis,* and *motus gravium et levium* for local motion. Galileo's handwriting is easy to read once one gets used to it, and his manuscripts containing these expressions posed no problem.

The Jesuit materials presented another situation entirely. These consisted of lecture notes for philosophy courses given at the Collegio Romano between 1559 and 1599, many of which are in the archives of the Gregorian University in

Rome, while others are scattered in different libraries throughout Europe.[4] All are in different hands and in various states of preservation. They have taken an enormous amount of time to locate, transcribe, and translate, and have been the main hurdle to be overcome in all my investigations.

The conclusions from all this are basically two. The first is definite and beyond doubt, whereas the second is partly conjectural and still open to fuller study. The first conclusion is that Galileo's knowledge of scientific methodology, as set forth in his ms 27, lay behind all his claims for 'necessary demonstrations' throughout his life, including those made in his *Sidereus nuncius* of 1610, his *Dialogo* of 1632, and his *Discorsi* on 'two new sciences' of 1638.[5] Galileo was never the hypothetico-deductivist he is painted to be by some in the present day. In his logic he was very much an Aristotelian, despite his repudiation of other aspects of Aristotle's teachings. In that mind-set he was influenced by the Jesuits, and in a unique and distinctive way.

The second conclusion is that Galileo's arrival at the basic proposition that underlies his second science in the *Discorsi*, the science of local motion, namely, that the motion of falling bodies is uniformly accelerated, or *unformiter difformis* with respect to time, was influenced by a tradition deriving from a teaching of Domingo de Soto, first proposed at Salamanca around 1551.[6] That tradition was constant among the Jesuits for a hundred years, down to Giambattista Riccioli's *Almagestum novum* of 1651. Here the Jesuit influence is circumstantial, but still worthy of serious consideration.

In offering the evidence for these two conclusions, rather than following the order of its discovery I present it in synoptic fashion. I also explain the conclusion with respect to Galileo's 'logical questions' of ms 27 first, although the support for that was not uncovered until after considerable work had already been done on his 'physical questions' of mss 46, 71, and 72.

Jesuit Course Materials[7]

Table 14.1, based on a sixteenth-century *rotulus*, shows the principal professors who taught philosophy courses at the Collegio Romano from 1559 to 1599. During that time philosophy was taught on a three-year cycle, the first year being devoted to logic, the second year to the *Physics* and *De caelo*, and the third year to metaphysics and the tract on the elements, as shown in the captions along the top of the table. Usually a professor would stay with a particular class throughout the cycle, thus assuring the course's completeness. The basic program was laid out by Francisco de Toledo (Franciscus Toletus), a Spaniard who had studied at Salamanca under Domingo de Soto before becoming a Jesuit.[8] In the 1570s Toledo published several manuals of philosophy that were often reprinted. These

Table 14.1
Philosophy courses at the Collegio Romano, 1559–99

Years	Logic	Physics On the Heavens	Metaphysics On the Elements
1559–60	F. de Toledo		
1560–1		F. de Toledo	
1561–2	B. Pereira		F. de Toledo
1562–3		B. Pereira	
1563–4			B. Pereira
1564–5	B. Pereira		
1565–6		B. Pereira	
1566–7			B. Pereira
...			
1577–8		A. Menù	
1578–9			A. Menù
1579–80	A. Menù		
1580–1		A. Menù	
1581–2			A. Menù
1583–4	J. Lorin		
1585–6	J. Lorin		P. Vallius
1586–7			P. Vallius
1587–8	P. Vallius		
1588–9	M. Vitelleschi	P. Vallius	
1589–90	L. Ruggiero	M. Vitelleschi	P. Vallius
1590–1		L. Ruggiero	M. Vitelleschi
1591–2	R. Jones		L. Ruggiero
1592–3		R. Jones	
1593–4			R. Jones
1595–6	S. Del Bufalo		
1596–7	A. Eudaemon	S. Del Bufalo	
1597–8		A. Eudaemon	S. Del Bufalo
1598–9			A. Eudaemon

Philosophy professors: Francisco de Toledo (Franciscus Toletus); Benito Pereira (Benedictus Pererius); Antonio Menù (Antonius Menutius); Jean Lorin (Ioannes Lorinus); Paulus Vallius (de la Valle); Muzio Vitelleschi (Mutius Vitelleschus); Ludovico Ruggiero (Ludovicus Rugerius); Robert (Robertus) Jones; Stefano (Stephanus) Del Bufalo; Andreas Eudaemon (or Eudaemon-Ioannis)
Mathematics professors: Christoph Clavius (1564–95); Christoph Grienberger (1595–8)
Censors: Lorin was one of the Jesuit censors who reviewed the manuscripts for Vallius's *Logica* in 1612 and again in 1615, and for the first two books of his *Physica* in 1621. The *Logica* was published in two volumes at Lyon in 1622. Lohr lists the publication of the *Physica* at Lyon in 1624 (Draud); but Vallius died in 1622, and the *Physica* may never have been published.

are important because they were supplemented, and improved upon, in the lectures of later Jesuits. Toledo was followed by Benito Pereira (Benedictus Pererius), a Valencian who later made his mark as a scripture scholar.[9] Less Thomistic than Toledo, Pereira subscribed to a number of Averroist theses, among which was a strongly expressed opposition to the use of mathematics in the study of nature. On this he clashed with the Collegio's celebrated mathematician Christoph Clavius, and was soon 'promoted' out of philosophy to another faculty of the institution.[10]

In natural philosophy the notes of Antonio Menù (Antonius Menutius) are the indispensable starting point for the study of influences on Galileo.[11] Menù, a Roman, broke radically with the path being pursued by Pereira. In place of a conservative Averroist stance, Menù imported into a general Thomistic framework a progressive Aristotelianism that owed much to the calculatory traditions of Oxford and Paris. On this account he was more open than Pereira to the use of mathematics in physics. Indeed, he initiated a period of concord between the philosophers and the mathematicians at the Collegio lasting well up to Galileo's discoveries with the telescope in 1610.

Many of Menù's ideas in physics, particularly his teachings on *impetus*, were taken up by a successor, Paulus Vallius (or de la Valle), also a Roman.[12] Vallius taught *De elementis*, a tract on the elements wherein the motion of heavy and light bodies was treated, from 1585 to 1587. Then, in 1587, Vallius began teaching the full three-year philosophy cycle, from 1587 to 1590. Muzio Vitelleschi (Mutius Vitelleschus), yet another Roman, who was later to become general of the Society, pursued the same cycle from 1588 to 1591.[13] And Ludovico Ruggiero (Ludovicus Rugerius), a Florentine, did the same from 1589 to 1592.[14] Vitelleschi and Ruggiero are important because complete sets of their lectures have been preserved, and these are in remarkable continuity with the portions of the courses of Menù and Vallius that are still extant. This is particularly true of most of the matters that show up in Galileo's Latin notebooks. Strong evidence has been accumulated, in fact, to show that much of the contents of Galileo's notebooks were appropriated from the lectures notes of Vallius (and possibly his colleagues) between 1589 and 1591, precisely the time when Galileo was beginning his own teaching career at the University of Pisa.

Details of the Philosophy Course

Until fairly recently it has been hard to know precisely what was covered in the philosophy courses at the Collegio Romano, for textbooks were not used and each professor worked from his own notes. Fortunately in my researches I turned up Ruggiero's notebooks for his entire course of philosophy, now conserved in seven volumes of manuscripts in the Staatsbibliothek in Bamberg, Germany.[15] Ruggiero was meticulous in detail, and he numbered his lectures in the margins of his notebooks. In addition he entered the dates on which he began or finished various tracts in the course. I have summarized much of the information he provides in figure 14.1.

During the year beginning on 3 November 1589 and ending on 24 August 1590, Ruggiero gave 310 lectures on the *Organon* of Aristotle, ending with 94 lectures devoted exclusively to the *Posterior Analytics*.[16] The following year, again starting on 3 November, he delivered 207 lectures on Aristotle's *Physics*, up to 21 May 1591.[17] Following that Ruggiero gave 74 lectures on the *De caelo*, finishing its last book on 7 August of the same year. Concurrently, starting on 7 July, he covered the *Meteorology* in about 75 lectures. Aristotle's *De genera-tione* he did not teach until his third year; he began on 4 November 1591 and completed its last book on 12 February 1592, with a total of 125 lectures. In the same month, finally, he began two concurrent courses, one consisting of about 200 lectures on the *De anima* and another of 99 lectures on the *Metaphysics*, which brought him to mid-September 1592 and the end of the philosophy cycle, some 1,100 lectures in all.

I have transcribed goodly portions of these manuscripts: the erudition, clarity, and detail of Ruggiero's teaching are incredible. Even a cursory examination of his work will enable one to see why the years between 1587 and 1592 are regarded as the 'golden age' of the Collegio Romano. How old was Ruggiero when he did this? He was born in 1558, so he was 31, six years older than Galileo, when he began the philosophy cycle. His two colleagues, Vallius and Vitelleschi, were only 25 when they began teaching the cycle and so were about the same age Galileo was when he began teaching at Pisa.

According to the *Ratio studiorum* of St Ignatius, philosophy was to be covered in three and a half years, but it seems that by 1589 the half year had been dropped for many students and was used by others for exams and reviews.[18] Classes ran roughly from 9:30 to 12:00 AM and from 3:00 to 6:00 PM. Jesuit scholastics were given the two extra hours before supper, which was at about 8:00 PM, for recitations and to complete their notes from the professor's lectures or other source materials. Usually there would be an hour-long lecture in the morning on the major subject, followed by a half-hour review, and then another hour in the afternoon on the same, followed by another half-hour review. On the basis of Ruggiero's numbering of his lectures, he must have lectured morning and afternoon every day through most of the school year to cover the matter he did. Truly a back-breaking task, and one can only wonder how he and the others were able to sustain that pace over a three-year period.

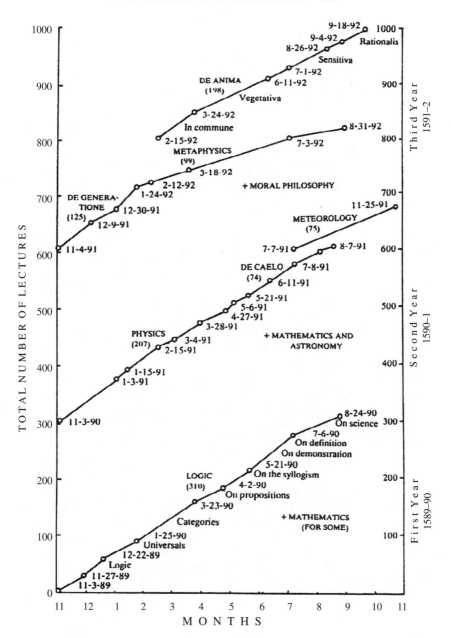

14.1. Ruggiero's lectures at the Collegio Romano, 1589–92.

Sources of Galileo's *Logical Questions* (ms 27)

Next to consider are Galileo's manuscripts. This material is difficult. The exposition here is brief, intended only to give an impression of how the analysis was done. The tables provided will allow the reader to puzzle out the details.

As shown in table 14.2, Galileo's *Logical Questions* contain only two treatises, the first concerned with the knowledge one must possess before attempting a demonstration, that is, with foreknowledge, and the second with demonstration itself.[19] At the Collegio these treatises would be taught in the last two months of the year devoted to logic, and thus they are but a part of the logic course – yet an important part, indeed its culmination. Galileo's treatise on foreknowledge contains three disputations, each composed of a series of questions, 11 questions in all. His treatise on demonstration is longer and likewise contains three disputations composed of a series of questions, here 17. When these are added to the questions on foreknowledge, the total is 28 questions. Listed across the top of the table are, first, the contents of Galileo's manuscript, and then, from left to right, the correlations between Galileo's questions and those of five Jesuits who taught the logic course between 1584 and 1592. These are shown as Lorin, Vallius-Carbone, Vitelleschi, Ruggiero, Jones, and Vallius again.

Three of the entries here require further explanation. At the Collegio Romano during this period, Jean Lorin (Ioannes Lorinus), who taught the logic course twice (1583–4 and 1585–6), stood at the head of the logic tradition there.[20] Two dates are given for Lorin, 1584 and 1620, one under the other. The first is the manuscript for his logic course that ended in 1584, and the second is the date of publication of his textbook *Logica*, printed at Cologne in 1620. Comparison of the two reveals that the textbook reproduces exactly the matter contained in the manuscript. Thus they may be treated as one, with the X's of the first column indicating that 24 of Galileo's 28 questions had been covered in Lorin's course.

The entries for Vallius are more complex, since they involve Vallius's relationships with Ludovico Carbone.[21] They are entitled 'Vallius-Carbone (1588–1597)' over the third column and 'Vallius (1622)' over the last column. The hyphenated entry over the third column indicates Vallius's manuscript for his logic lectures in 1587–8 (which has been lost), and Carbone's plagiarism of Vallius's manuscript, which Carbone published under his own name as 'Additions to Toledo's Commentary on the Logic of Aristotle' at Venice in 1597. The last column, entitled 'Vallius (1622),' then stands for Vallius's two-volume text *Logica*, which Vallius himself published at Lyon in 1622. In the prefaces to these two volumes, Vallius points out that Carbone, in his 'Additions,' had plagiarized the logic course he taught in 1588, and that he had now changed the wording in his 1622 account so that one could see in the 'Additions,' as Vallius wrote, what

Table 14.2
Correlations of ms Gal. 27 with logic courses at the Collegio Romano

Galileo ms 27	Lorin (1584) (1620)	Vallius-Carbone (1588–97)	Vitelleschi (1589)	Ruggiero (1590)	Jones (1592)	Vallius (1622)
		Treatise on Foreknowledges and Foreknowns				
		On foreknowledges of principles				
F.2.1	X	**[X]**		X	X	X
F.2.2	X	**[X]**		X		X
F.2.3		**[X]**			X	X
F.2.4	X	**[X]**				X
		On foreknowledges of the subject				
F.3.1	X	**[X]**		X	X	X
F.3.2	X	**[X]**			X	X
F.3.4	X	**[X]**				X
F.3.5		**[X]**				X
F.3.6	X	**[X]**		X		X
		On foreknowledges of property and conclusion				
F.4.1	X	**[X]**		X	X	X
F.4.2	X	**[X]**	X	X	X	X
11	9	11	1	6	6	11
		Treatise on Demonstration				
		On the nature and importance of demonstration				
D1.1	X		X	X	X	X
D.1.2		**[X]**				X
		On the properties of demonstration				
D.2.1	X		X		X	X
D2.2	X			X	X	X
D2.3	X		X	X	X	X
D2.4	X		X			X
D2.5	X				X	X
D2.6	X		X	X		X
D2.7	X		X	X	X	X
D2.8	X		X	X	X	X
D2.9	X			X		X
D2.10	X		X	X		X
D2.11	X		X			X
D2.12				X		X
		On the species of demonstration				
D3.1	X			X	X	X
D3.2	X			X	X	X
D3.3	X			X	X	X
17	15	1	9	12	10	17
		Total number of paragraphs in agreement:				
28	24	(12)	(10)	18	16	28

Note: Boldface type indicates word-for-word similarity; totals in parentheses are for only a portion of the course.

Carbone 'took from me, and in this what I have prepared more fully and at length.'[22] In our table 14.2, the X's in the column for Vallius-Carbone are registered in boldface type, to indicate that they show word-for-word correspondences with Galileo's questions F2.1 through F4.2, and also D1.2. Carbone apparently had intended to publish only the tract on foreknowledge, but by accident, as it were, he appropriated one question from Vallius's second treatise, that on demonstration (D1.2). This is a clue that the exemplar Carbone worked from originally contained both treatises. Galileo obviously worked from the same manuscript or from a copy of it.

With regard to the remaining columns, Vitelleschi covered the least matter in his logic course, omitting the first treatise almost entirely and covering only about half the material in the second. Robert (Robertus) Jones was somewhat better, touching on 16 of the 28 questions in Galileo's manuscript, but even when discussing a question he did so in sparser detail than any of his predecessors.[23] Ruggiero emerges as the best conserver of the tradition, by showing the highest number of questions, 18 of 28, and covering each in significant detail. The last column on the right, that of Vallius's reworked version, is the only column that lists correspondences for all 28 of Galileo's questions. In some questions there is word-for-word agreement, but this is not generally the case, nor is it to be expected, since by his own admission Vallius changed the wording so as to differentiate his final work from Carbone's plagiarization.

Sources of Galileo's Physical Questions (ms 46)

Being now acquainted with this method of tracing correlations, we turn to the materials in Galileo's ms 46. These contain what I have called his physical questions, most of which Galileo wrote shortly after he had composed the logic of ms 27. Their contents are shown in table 14.3.[24] Ms 46 contains six treatises, three from commentaries on Aristotle's *De caelo* (introduction, on the universe, and on the heavens) and three from his *De generatione* (on alteration, on the elements, and on primary qualities). An important difference is that the table for the logical questions showed only generic agreement by means of an 'X,' whereas this one records the fine structure in two ways. The first is by recording the total number of paragraphs in each of the author's questions that correspond to Galileo's, and the second by indicating, in parentheses, how many of these paragraphs contain passages that register word-for-word agreement. Otherwise the Jesuit authors listed along the top are similar: Menù for his course on natural philosophy in 1578, Clavius for an excerpt from his *Sphaera* of 1581, Vallius for his courses from 1585 to 1589, Vitelleschi for his course of 1590, and Ruggiero for his course in 1591.

Table 14.3
Correlations of ms Gal. 46 with physics courses at the Collegio Romano

Galileo ms 46	Menù 1578	Clavius 1581	Vallius 1585–9	Vitelleschi 1590	Ruggiero 1591	Carbone 1594
			On the books *De caelo* Introduction			
[A](21)				13	18	X
[B](9)					5	X
			On the universe			
[C](9)	**9(8)**			5	8	X
[D](8)	**8(7)**			3	4	X
[E](23)	**23(11)**			13		
[F](27)	5			**14(4)**	21	
			On the heavens			
[G](34)		**34(34)**				X
[H](36)		**36(36)**				X
[I](47)	**35(2)**			29	18	X
[J](36)	17			25	18	X
[K](183)	106			34	28	X
[L](41)	22			**32(3)**	24	
474	*225(28)*	*70(70)*		*168(7)*	*144*	
			On the books *De generatione* On alteration			
[M](2)	1			1	1	X
[N](32)	2			25	23	X
[O](9)	5			7	6	
			On the elements			
[P](15	**12(1)**			14	2	**11(4)**	X
[Q](17)	12			**13(6)**	3	12	X
[R](6)	**6(4)**			6		
[S](17)	13			**15(2)**	**12(4)**	4	X
[T](21)	**10(1)**			**14(2)**		11	X
[U](80)	**33(1)**			**44(8)**	42	23	X
			On primary qualities			
[V](10)				6	4	7	X
[W](17)	**10(2)**			**14(7)**	15	**15(2)**	X
[X](21)	6			10	**15(2)**	**8(4)**	X
[Y](25)	4			9	**14(1)**	7	
272	*114(9)*			*145(25)*	*140(7)*	*128(10)*	
746	*339(37)*	*70(70)*		*145(25)*	*308(14)*	*272(10)*	
Number of questions in agreement:						
25	20	2	10	20	21	20

Note: Boldface type and number of paragraphs in parentheses indicate word-for-word similarity.

A striking feature of table 14.3 is the role played by Menù in setting up the physics course in 1578, much the same as the role of Lorin in setting up the logic course of 1584. A number of Menù's questions in the *De caelo* portion of the course show strong correlations with Galileo's questions [C] through [L], suggesting either that Menù's notes were available to Galileo, or else that they were appropriated by a successor and passed on to him indirectly. Such a successor was probably Vallius, whose lectures of 1589 on *De caelo* and *De generatione* were then available to Vitelleschi and Ruggiero, as seems to have been the case with Vallius's notes of the previous year on the *Posterior Analytics*. Note here that there are no counterparts for Galileo's question [A] prior to 1590, when Vitelleschi has 13 of its 21 paragraphs. Similarly there are no counterparts for Galileo's question [B] prior to 1591, when Ruggiero has 5 of its 9 paragraphs. Again, only Menù has any parallels for Galileo's questions [P] through [U] prior to those in Vallius's *De elementis*, for which there were three versions between 1585 and 1589, only one of which, undated, is still extant. It is difficult to draw firm conclusions from such sparse data. Yet Vallius is still the most promising candidate for being the Collegio professor behind the composition of ms 46, just as we know him to have been the professor behind the composition of ms 27.[25]

Galileo's Logical Methodology

We leave textual correlations at this point and return to the first conclusion I wish to establish regarding Galileo's logical methodology. This is that Galileo learned from these Jesuit notes how to construct a valid scientific demonstration with the type of rigour sought by Aristotle, which was that expected of a *scientia* in Galileo's day. One could do this by employing a technique known as the demonstrative *regressus* (or regress). The technique was developed over a long period, from the fourteenth century onward, mainly at the University of Padua.[26] As Galileo explained it in ms 27, the regressus is made up of two progressions, one going from effect to cause, the other from cause to effect. It is called a regress because the second progression reverses the direction of the first, with effect and cause then being interchanged. To avoid circularity, however, the two progressions must be separated by an intermediate stage during which the researcher passes from grasping the cause in a provisional way to seeing it formally and distinctly as the proper cause of the particular effect.[27]

How Galileo used this technique is best illustrated in the astronomical demonstrations he first proposed in the *Sidereus nuncius* of 1610 and later in the *Dialogo* of 1632. My first instance is the telescopic observations that led him to affirm that there are mountains on the moon. Here the first progression went from effect to cause in a provisional way: shadows on the moon's surface suggest that they are the effect of a mountainous terrain. This insight led directly to the intermediate stage, a period of observational and even experimental activity, to see whether or not this is the proper explanation. We know that Galileo constructed a model of the lunar surface, illuminated it in various ways, viewed it from different angles, and finally came to see that mountains are the only plausible explanation. The final step, the second progression, then affirmed that there *are* mountains on the moon, which we do *not* see, and these are the cause of the shadows we *do* see on the moon's surface.[28]

Galileo's discovery of the satellites of Jupiter involved a similar application of the same method. The discovery of 'the four Medicean stars' and their changes of place with respect to Jupiter set up the first progression, in which the movements of these newly discovered points of light prompted the suspicion that they might not be 'stars' at all, but wandering heavenly bodies. In the intermediate stage a detailed study of their seemingly erratic motions led to the conviction that they result from the bodies' actually revolving around the planet, at different periods according to their distances from its centre. This brought on the second progression, wherein these revolutions (which we do *not* see) were recognized formally as the proper cause of the changes of position of the new bodies (which we *do* see), with the conclusion further implied that they are actually moons of Jupiter.[29]

The same *regressus* could be applied to Galileo's discovering the phases of Venus and showing how these prove that Venus revolves around the sun and not the earth.[30] All three of these demonstrations belong to a 'mixed science' (*scientia mixta*) that makes use of physical and mathematical premises to establish its conclusions and so can, with reason, be spoken of as a mathematical physics. The physical premises are the more problematic, since they suppose that the appearances seen through a telescope are not optical illusions but factual states of affairs. The mathematical premises are supplied by projective geometry, based on the supposition that light travels in straight lines and thus that optical phenomena can be analysed using geometrical principles. On this account each proof may be seen as a *demonstratio ex suppositione*. But a proof from a supposition is a rigorous proof if the supposition is true, and this was the case for Galileo.[31]

How regressive methodology could be applied to the study of motion is more complex: in order to understand it we require a quick look at the remaining professors on our *rotulus* for the Collegio Romano (see table 14.1).

Galileo and the Jesuit Calculatory Tradition (mss 46 and 71)

Of the natural philosophers who taught physics at the Collegio after Ruggiero, lecture notes for three other Jesuits are available: Robert Jones, an Englishman, who taught in 1592–3; Stefano Del Bufalo, who taught in 1596–7 and again in

1598–9; and Andreas Eudaemon-Ioannis, who taught in the intervening year, 1597–8. Of these, Jones shows the least concern with the calculatory tradition. Del Bufalo, on the other hand, has a full discussion of alteration, degrees of qualities, intension and remission of forms, and action and reaction. In the last of these he mentions the teaching of the *calculator* Richard Swineshead and contrasts it with those of Pietro Pomponazzi, Ludovicus Buccaferreus, Flaminio Nobili, and Jacopo Zabarella. In his discussions of *gravitas* and *levitas*, moreover, he cites the *doctores Parisienses* and compares their teachings with those of Girolamo Borro and Francesco Buonamici, both of whom were among Galileo's teachers at the University of Pisa.[32]

The remaining Collegio Jesuit is Eudaemon, who had even greater calculatory interests than Del Bufalo.[33] In addition to his lectures of 1597–8 on the *Physics*, *De caelo*, and *De generatione*, Eudaemon left a *tractatus* in two books on action and passion and a question on the motion of projectiles. A key expression in these works was *uniformiter difformis*, which Eudaemon saw as applicable not only to falling motion but to all physical actions throughout the universe. As he put it, 'When close, an agent acts more vehemently, and when farther away, less so; therefore, the closer the greater, the farther the lesser; therefore, as the distance increases the action decreases; therefore the action is *uniformiter difformis*.'[34]

Finally, attention should be directed to a related Jesuit, not at the Collegio Romano, who made extensive use of calculatory expressions. This was François de Aguilon (Franciscus Aquilonis), a Belgian, who published six books on optics at Antwerp in 1613.[35] Aguilon taught mathematics and philosophy in Belgium before completing his theological studies at Salamanca in the early 1590s. In his discussion of the propagation of light, Aguilon uses the language of the *calculatores*, as can be seen in his statement 'Light when diffused over long distances ... weakens by proportional decrements in equal spaces ... [i.e.,] with a *difformitate uniformi* ...'[36] Other passages in this context are so close to Eudaemon's in his analysis of natural agency that it is difficult to believe that Aguilon did not have access to Eudaemon's treatise on this subject.

Consider, then, the situation at the Collegio Romano from the time of Pereira, say 1566, when he taught, or 1576, when his textbook was published, to that of Eudaemon in 1599 and Aguilon in 1613. In all that time there were many references to the calculatory tradition and how it impacted on theses in natural philosophy. Not one, apart from Aguilon's text on optics, is to be found in a printed text – all occur only in manuscript sources. So it is not surprising that Jesuit acquaintance with the *calculatores* has been overlooked by scholars and not seen as part of the significant growth of mathematical physics among the Jesuits up to the end of the sixteenth century.

Galileo and the Jesuit *Studium* at Padua (ms 72)

To finish the story we must now move from the Collegio Romano to the Jesuit *studium* in Padua. This had been established in the mid-sixteenth century and by 1589 was offering a three-year course in philosophy similar to that offered in Rome.[37] Shortly thereafter Galileo had come to Padua from Pisa, and there continued his researches on motion. Who were the Jesuit professors staffing their college at Padua? The names of a few are known, and they truly are a surprise. They were Antonio Menù, Paulus Vallius, Andreas Eudaemon-Ioannis, and a younger Jesuit thus far not mentioned, Giuseppe Biancani (Josephus Blancanus).[38]

Biancani is important because he had studied under Clavius at Rome in the 1590s, and later wrote treatises on mathematics and mathematical physics as sciences in the Aristotelian sense.[39] In these he showed considerable competence as both a philosopher and a mathematician. His works were directed explicitly against Pereira and the *Conimbricenses*, the authors of the Jesuit *cursus philosophicus* published at Coimbra, who had refused to accept the mathematical disciplines as true sciences. Biancani defended Galileo's stand regarding mountains on the moon, and this elicited a letter from Galileo stating that he was 'infinitely obliged' to Biancani.[40] Later Biancani taught at Parma, where Giambattista Riccioli was his student. And Riccioli, working at Bologna around 1630, experimentally verified Galileo's law of falling bodies, showing that their velocity increased *uniformiter difformiter* during their time of fall.[41] Riccioli's co-worker in these tests was Francesco Grimaldi, who later discovered optical diffraction and was the most celebrated Jesuit scientist of the seventeenth century.[42]

Did Galileo have any contact with the Jesuits at Padua? Presumably he did. Years later, Galileo's friend Mario Guiducci reminded him that he had discussed the famous 'ship's mast' experiment with Father Eudaemon at Padua around 1604, an experiment concerned with impetus and the fall of heavy bodies.[43] Still another contact was John Schreck, who worked with Galileo at Padua and later entered the Jesuits. When Galileo heard of this he wrote that Schreck had exchanged one *compagnia* (the Lincei) for another, the Compagnia di Gesù, one to which Galileo acknowledged he 'owed much.'[44] Clearly Galileo was on good terms with the Jesuits up to 1606, when they were forced to leave Padua because of protests that they were competing there with the University of Padua.[45]

Which brings us back to the second conclusion proposed at the beginning of this essay. In 1604, Galileo was speculating that the speed of fall of a body varies *uniformiter difformiter* with its distance of fall, not with its time of fall, as we now know it to do. The two – velocity increase with respect to time and velocity increase with respect to distance – are not the same. Domingo de Soto was the first to recognize this, and his teaching was known to the Jesuits for some sixty years.[46] Shortly after 1604, Galileo became aware of his mistake. How did he learn of the error? Quite probably he got it from the Jesuits then teaching at Padua – Menù, Vallius, Eudaemon, and Biancani, all of whom clearly knew that falling motion was *uniformiter difformiter* with respect to time.

Precisely at this time Galileo performed new experiments at Padua that discriminated between the two possibilities and so arrived at the correct laws of falling bodies. The experiments, now referred to as 'table-top experiments,' were never published and were hidden for some 360 years, finally being uncovered by Stillman Drake in 1972. Drake found them in folios of ms 72, the last of the Galileo manuscripts to be treated in this paper. Figure 14.2 provides diagrams of these experiments as they have been reconstructed and performed in the present day.[47]

As shown in the diagrams, Galileo's program made use of four different, but connected, types of experiment, probably made in the order shown from top to bottom. The first type, diagram *a*, was designed to show that the distance of horizontal projection after different distances of roll down an incline varies as the square root of the distance of roll and not as that distance itself. With this established, the next type, diagram *b*, attempted to define the curves that result when the angle of inclination is varied. The curves shown there approach more and more a semi-parabolic form the smaller the angle of incline. The next type, diagram *c*, shows Galileo's experimenting with different kinds of deflectors to produce a variety of curves in projection. And the final type, diagram *d*, shows the deflector he finally used to achieve horizontal projection, along with the series of semi-parabolic curves he eventually produced. The conclusion that emerges from the experiments is that the speed of bodies in free fall, instantiated by balls that are no longer on the incline but have left it and are falling naturally, varies directly as their time of fall.[48]

The demonstrative regress that established this conclusion was first sketched out by Galileo in 1609.[49] The conclusion itself was not published until 1638, when it appeared in his *Discorsi* on the 'two new sciences,' but without its supporting data.[50] In the *Discorsi* it provided the basis for all the propositions of the Third Day relating to what Galileo called 'naturally accelerated motion.' The demonstration itself was made *ex suppositione*, namely, on the supposition that all impediments to the falling motion, such as friction and air resistance, were either removed or small enough to be neglected. And, of course, the precise measurements made by Riccioli and Grimaldi some years later, dropping balls from the Torre di Asinelli in Bologna, showed that these suppositions were justified and that Galileo had truly arrived at a scientific conclusion.

Were the Jesuits an influence in his coming to that result? Readers will have to make that judgment for themselves. Admittedly the evidence is not apodictic, but clearly it is worth serious consideration.[51]

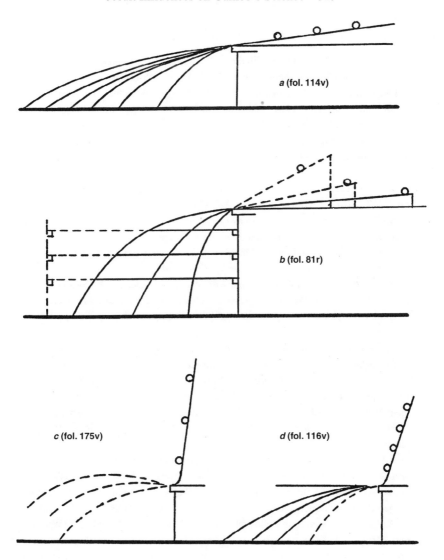

14.2. Galileo's table-top experiments, ms Gal. 72, Padua, 1604–9.

NOTES

1 The basic sources are listed in Willaim A. Wallace, *Galileo and His Sources: The Heritage of the Collegio Romano in Galileo's Science* (Princeton, 1984), pp. 351–5.

2 As one of the principal investigators, I have been working on the topic since the late 1960s. During that time I have had many other duties and have never been able to work on it steadily. My publications relating to this subject, however, include 9 books and 27 articles, widely spaced over time, the most recent being *Domingo de Soto and the Early Galileo*, Variorum Collected Studies Series 783 (Aldershot, UK, 2004).

3 A description of the manuscripts is given in the introduction to Wallace, *Galileo's Logical Treatises: A Translation, with Notes and Commentary, of His Appropriated Latin Questions on Aristotle's Posterior Analytics*, Boston Studies in the Philosophy of Science 138 (Dordrecht, Boston, London, 1992), pp. 4–63.

4 A listing of many of the libraries I have visited is given in the acknowledgments to Wallace, *Prelude to Galileo: Essays on Medieval and Sixteenth-Century Sources of Galileo's Thought*, Boston Studies in the Philosophy of Science 62 (Dordrecht and Boston, 1981); and in Wallace, 'Late Sixteenth-Century Portuguese Manuscripts Relating to Galileo's Early Notebooks,' *Revista portuguesa de filosofia* 51 (1995): 677–98.

5 The fullest argument in support of these conclusions will be found in Wallace, *Galileo's Logic of Discovery and Proof: The Background, Content, and Use of His Appropriated Treatises on Aristotle's Posterior Analytics*, Boston Studies in the Philosophy of Science 137 (Dordrecht, Boston, London, 1992); a summary statement is given in Wallace, 'Galileo's Pisan Studies in Science and Philosophy,' in *The Cambridge Companion to Galileo*, ed. Peter Machamer (Cambridge, 1998), pp. 27–52.

6 Details are given in Wallace, 'The Enigma of Domingo de Soto: *Uniformiter difformis* and Falling Bodies in Late Medieval Physics,' *Isis* 59 (1968): 384–401. For an overview of Soto and his influence, see Wallace, 'Domingo de Soto and the Iberian Roots of Galileo's Science,' in *Hispanic Philosophy in the Age of Discovery*, ed. Kevin White, Studies in Philosophy and the History of Philosophy 29 (Washington, 1997), pp. 113–29.

7 For access to the Jesuit course materials on which my studies have been based I am indebted to many Jesuit scholars. Principal among these are Edmund Lamalle, S.J., archivist of the Curia Generalizia in Rome; Vincenzo Monachino, S.J., archivist of the Pontifical Gregorian University, also in Rome; and Charles H. Lohr, S.J., of the Raimundus-Lullus-Institut of the University of Freiburg im Breisgau. On 1 June 1975, at the Curia Generalizia, Lamalle showed me a *rotulus* of professors at the Collegio Romano in the last half of the sixteenth century, along with a listing by

number of all the manuscripts then conserved in the archive, with only a generic description of their contents. I made notes on the *rotulus* and the numbers of the codices in Lamalle's listing that interested me, and took them across Rome to the Gregorian University, where the codices were then stored under the designation 'Fondo Curia.' There Monachino gave me full access to the sought-after manuscripts, and then, when I had identified a number of codices I wished to have copied, graciously arranged for their microfilming. Without that initial store of information, obtained in the summer of 1975, I could never have got as far as I have in the study of Jesuit teaching notes. Later, Lohr's extensive knowledge of Latin Aristotle commentaries assisted me greatly in locating libraries in which many of these notes are still extant; see Charles Lohr, *Latin Aristotle Commentaries II. Renaissance Authors* (Florence, 1988). In the intervening years, before this work appeared, Lohr published preliminary listings of his findings, in the journals *Studies in the Renaissance* and *Renaissance Quarterly*, and these got me started on my search.

 8 For some details on Toledo, see Wallace, *Galileo's Early Notebooks: The Physical Questions. A Translation from the Latin, with Historical and Paleographical Commentary* (Notre Dame, 1977), pp. 13–14 and passim; Wallace, *Galileo and His Sources*, pp. 10–14; and Wallace, 'The Early Jesuits and the Heritage of Domingo de Soto,' *History and Technology* 4 (1987): 301–20, especially 302–4, repr. as Essay VI in Wallace, *Galileo, the Jesuits, and the Medieval Aristotle,* Variorum Collected Studies Series 346 (Aldershot, UK, 1991).

 9 Further information on Pereira is in Wallace, *Galileo's Early Notebooks*, pp. 14–15 and passim; Wallace, *Prelude to Galileo*, pp. 207–9, 255–62, and passim; and Wallace, 'The Early Jesuits,' pp. 302–3.

10 References to Clavius are in Wallace, 'Galileo's Early Arguments for Geocentrism and His Later Rejection of Them,' *Novità celesti e crisi del sapere*, ed. Paolo Galluzzi (Florence, 1983), pp. 31–40 and passim; Wallace, *Galileo and His Sources*, pp. 91–2, 136–41, 282–4, and passim; and Wallace, *Galileo's Logical Treatises*.

11 Little is known about Menù in literature on the Jesuits. For the results of my research on him, see Wallace, *Galileo's Early Notebooks*, pp. 16–17 and passim; Wallace, *Prelude to Galileo*, pp. 243–5 and passim; Wallace, 'Aristotelian Influences on Galileo's Thought,' *Aristotelismo Veneto e scienza moderna*, ed. Luigi Olivieri, 2 vols (Padua, 1983), I, pp. 349–78, repr. as Essay I in Wallace, *Galileo, the Jesuits, and the Medieval Aristotle*; and Wallace, *Galileo and His Sources*, pp. 61–3, 150–5, 158–60, 191–6. The key source for Menù is a manuscript contained in the Leopold-Sophien-Bibliothek, Überlingen, Germany, Cod. 138, described in *Galileo and His Sources*, p. 352. Charles Lohr used his facilities at the University of Freiburg im Breisgau to obtain for me a microfilm of this manuscript, which has proved indispensable for my researches.

12 In my publications up to 1988, I refer to this author as Paulus Valla, since this is the name under which he appears in Lamalle's *rotulus*. In this and later publications I refer to him as Paulus Vallius, the name he himself used when publishing his *Logica* of 1622. Alternate versions of his name are Paulus de Valle and Paulus de la Valle. For details on Vallius, see Wallace, *Galileo's Early Notebooks*, pp. 17–18 and passim; Wallace, *Prelude to Galileo*, pp. 245–7 and passim; Wallace, *Galileo and His Sources*, pp. 63–6, 168–70, 178–80, 196–9; and Wallace, 'Randall Redivivus: Galileo and the Paduan Aristotelians,' *Journal of the History of Ideas* 49 (1988): 133–49 and passim, repr. as Essay V in Wallace, *Galileo, the Jesuits, and the Medieval Aristotle.*

13 On Vitelleschi, see Wallace, *Galileo's Early Notebooks*, pp. 18–19 and passim; Wallace, 'Causes and Forces in Sixteenth-Century Physics,' *Isis* 69 (1978): 400–12 and passim, repr. in Wallace, *Prelude to Galileo*, pp. 110–26; Wallace, *Prelude to Galileo*, pp. 111–25, 247–9, 289–90, 330–6; Wallace, 'Aristotelian Influences,' pp. 364–7; and Wallace, *Galileo and His Sources*, pp. 66–8, 155–7, 160–7, 173–8, 180–9, 201–2.

14 For details on Ruggiero, see Wallace, *Galileo's Early Notebooks*, pp. 19–20 and passim; Wallace, *Prelude to Galileo*, pp. 249–51, 311–14, 334–6; and Wallace, *Galileo and His Sources*, pp. 69–70, 170–2, 189–91, 199–201.

15 The catalogue number there is Cod. Msc. Class. 62.

16 I have taught the *Posterior Analytics* many times in graduate courses at The Catholic University of America in Washington, D.C., and covered it in 28 lectures – less than a third of the time given it by Ruggiero.

17 Again, I have covered the whole of the *Physics* in graduate courses at Catholic University in 28 lectures – about a seventh of his time.

18 The basic source of information on philosophy courses at the Collegio Romano is Villos. *Coll. Rom.*, pp. 84–115. Fuller details on materials relating to Galileo's Latin manuscripts are given in Wallace, *Galileo and His Sources*, pp. 6–96.

19 This table is adapted from table 9 in Wallace, *Galileo's Logical Treatises*, p. 32. See also the discussion of this table there, on pp. 31–7.

20 On Lorin, see Wallace, *Galileo and His Sources*, pp. 14–16 and passim; and Wallace, *Galileo's Logical Treatises*, pp. 17–19 and passim.

21 For details on Carbone, see Wallace, *Galileo and His Sources*, pp. 12–14, 16–23, 89–95, 223–5; and Wallace, *Galileo's Logical Treatises*, pp. 11–13, 20–3.

22 Wallace, *Galileo and His Sources*, p. 19.

23 On Jones, see ibid., pp. 26–7; and Wallace, *Galileo's Logical Treatises*, pp. 25–7.

24 This table is adapted from table 14 in Wallace, *Galileo's Logical Treatises*, p. 48, and is explained on pp. 47–50.

25 For a fuller discussion, see ibid., pp. 50–7.

26 A historical overview of the development can be found in Wallace, 'Circularity and

the Demonstrative *Regressus*: From Pietro d'Abano to Galileo Galilei,' *Vivarium* 33 (1995): 76–97.

27 This is the way the *regressus* was understood by Vallius and so passed on to Galileo, as explained in Wallace, 'Randall Redivivus,' pp. 141–5.

28 For a complete analysis of this argument, see Wallace, *Galileo's Logic of Discovery*, pp. 197–201.

29 Again, for a fuller analysis of the argument, see ibid., pp. 201–3.

30 Ibid., pp. 203–7.

31 More details on Jesuit teachings concerning the mixed sciences are given ibid., pp. 97–114.

32 On Del Bufalo, see Wallace, *Galileo and His Sources*, pp. 87–9; Wallace, 'The Early Jesuits'; and Wallace, 'Portuguese Manuscripts,' pp. 690–4.

33 On Eudaemon-Ioannis, see Wallace, *Galileo and His Sources*, pp. 27–8, 269–71; and Wallace, 'The Early Jesuits,' pp. 306–8, 312.

34 Wallace, 'The Early Jesuits,' p. 307.

35 On Aguilon, see ibid., pp. 311–12; and August Ziggelaar, *François de Aguilon, S.J. (1567–1617), Scientist and Architect*, Bibliotheca Instituti Historici S.I. 44 (Rome, 1983).

36 Wallace, 'The Early Jesuits,' p. 311.

37 On the Jesuit foundation at Padua, see Paul F. Grendler, *The Universities of the Italian Renaissance* (Baltimore and London, 2002), pp. 479–83. In his researches Grendler discovered that the Jesuit establishment began in Padua in 1542 and took the form of a college the next year, making this the fourth oldest *studium* in the order. The foundation seems to have been established to enable young Jesuits to study at the University of Padua. But in 1552, not satisfied with lectures at the university, the Jesuits established a school for external students, and then, in 1589, began to offer higher studies. For documentation, see John Patrick Donnelly, 'The Jesuit College at Padua: Growth, Suppression, Attempts at Restoration, 1552–1606,' *AHSI* 51 (1982): 46ff. The title of Donnelly's article seems to suggest that there was a Jesuit college at Padua from 1552 to 1606, but this title refers only to that for external students, not to the Jesuit community, which began in 1542.

38 On Biancani, see Wallace, *Galileo and His Sources*, pp. 141–8, 206–8, and passim; and Wallace, 'The Early Jesuits,' pp. 313–14.

39 Biancani's treatises were two, both published in Bologna, one in 1615, the other in 1620. The full titles are given Wallace, *Galileo and His Sources*, p. 354, and their teachings are described on pp. 141–8. The first volume documents all Aristotle's references to mathematics as a science, and then gives Biancani's own Aristotelian view of the nature of the mathematical sciences. The second volume is a treatise on cosmology, citing all the new discoveries of Tycho Brahe, Johann Kepler, and Galileo Galilei, with very favourable evaluations of Galileo's *Sidereus nuncius*,

De maculis solaribus, and *De iis quae natantur aut moventur in aqua*. The last of these Biancani refers to as a 'very intelligent treatise.'

40 The text in which Galileo does so is cited in Wallace, *Galileo and His Sources*, p. 269.

41 Of his early work on falling motion, Riccioli writes in his *Almagestum novum* (Bologna, 1651), 'At that time I had not yet come to the better and more evident experiments manifesting not only an inequality in the motion of heavy bodies but the true increment of their velocity, increasing *uniformiter difformiter* toward the end of the motion' (cited in Wallace, 'The Early Jesuits,' p. 19).

42 These experiments are described in Alexandre Koyré, *Metaphysics and Measurement: Essays in the Scientific Revolution* (Cambridge, MA, 1968), pp. 102–8.

43 The incident is described in Wallace, *Galileo and His Sources*, pp. 269–70.

44 Galileo to Federico Cesi (in Rome), from Florence, 19 December 1611, in *Le Opere di Galileo Galilei*, ed. Antonio Favaro, 20 vols in 21 (Florence, 1890–1909, repr. 1968), XI, p. 247: 'La nuova del S. Terenzio m' è altrettanto dispiaciuta per la gran perdita della nostra Compagnia, quanto all'incontro piaciuta per la santa resoluzione e per l'aqquisto dell'altra Compagnia, alla qual io devo molto …' Schreck's name in religion was Terrentius, so the reference to him in Galileo's letter is to 'Signor Terenzio.' The Lincei was a scientific academy founded by Cesi to which Galileo also belonged, and the pun on *compagnia* was that Schreck had exchanged one society, that of the Lincei, for the Society of Jesus. Schreck was later posted to China and was responsible for the first introduction of the telescope and Galilean ideas into China. For details on the China mission, see Pasquale M. d'Elia, *Galileo in China*, trans. R. Suter and M. Sciascia (Cambridge, MA, 1960).

45 See Grendler, *Universities*, pp. 480–3.

46 On Soto's teaching, see Wallace, 'Enigma of Domingo de Soto'; for his influence on the Jesuits, see Wallace, 'Domingo de Soto and the Iberian Roots.'

47 The diagrams are adapted from those in Wallace, *The Modeling of Nature: Philosophy of Science and Philosophy of Nature in Synthesis* (Washington, 1996), pp. 345–7; and Wallace, 'Dialectics, Experiments, and Mathematics in Galileo,' in *Scientific Controversies: Philosophical and Historical Perspectives*, ed. Peter Machamer, Marcello Pera, and Aristides Baltas (New York and Oxford, 2000), pp. 111–14. Apart from Drake, the principal investigators involved in duplicating Galileo's experiments are Ronald Naylor and David K. Hill, whose results are there summarized, pp. 121–2 nn 3–6.

48 A simple mathematical proof of this conclusion is presented in Wallace, *Prelude to Galileo*, pp. 153–6.

49 The document in which the regress is sketched is referred to as the *De motu accelerato* fragment and is now bound in with the related materials of ms 71. For a

detailed analysis of the fragment, see Wallace, *Galileo's Logic of Discovery*, pp. 268–73.

50 The *Discorsi* materials, and their connection with the *De motu accelerato* fragment, are further analysed *ibid.*, pp. 284–95.

51 For a fuller development of the arguments presented in this essay, see Wallace, 'Galileo's Jesuit Connections and Their Influence on His Science,' in Fein. *Jes. Sci.*, pp. 99–126, which bears a title similar to that of this essay. Actually the 2003 essay was written late in 1997, but its publication was held up for many years because of changes of plans for the anthology in which it has finally appeared. The two essays are related but none the less different, in view of their contexts and the readers to whom they are addressed.

15 / Utility, Edification, and Superstition: Jesuit Censorship and Athanasius Kircher's *Oedipus Aegyptiacus*

DANIEL STOLZENBERG

It is a singular fact that one of the most detailed compendiums of magical practices and esoteric traditions published in early modern Europe was written by a Jesuit and printed in Rome in the 1650s. In *Oedipus Aegyptiacus* (1652–4), Athanasius Kircher (1602–80) purported to translate the Egyptian hieroglyphs, which he believed to conceal a mixture of esoteric wisdom and superstitious magic.[1] He prefaced his translations with a three-volume interpretative apparatus that explained the 'hieroglyphic doctrine' by reference to the various occult traditions associated with medieval magic and late antique and Renaissance Neoplatonism. Kircher treated at length the ancient pagan theologies of figures such as Zoroaster, Orpheus, and Hermes Trismegistus, arguing that they had understood, if imperfectly, Christian mysteries such as the Trinity. More daringly, long sections of the *Oedipus* described illicit magical practices with the detail of an instruction manual. While works containing similar material, such as Cornelius Agrippa's *De occulta philosophia*, were placed on the Index of Prohibited Books, Kircher sent his works to press with the imprimaturs of his ecclesiastical superiors and enjoyed a prestigious position at the Collegio Romano. In this article, which examines the Jesuit censorship of Kircher's *Oedipus* and its companion volume, *Obeliscus Pamphilius* (1650), I aim to shed light on this enigma.

Previous studies of Jesuit censorship have focused primarily on natural-philosophical works and the Society's efforts to enforce scientific orthodoxy among its members.[2] Specifically regarding Kircher, articles by Carlos Ziller Camenietzki and Marcus Hellyer have examined the case of his 1656 astronomical dialogue, *Itinerarium exstaticum*, which generated intense controversy owing to its overtly anti-Aristotelian content, but publication of which was none the less permitted.[3] The case of the *Oedipus* and *Obeliscus*, which deal extensively with magical practices and non-Christian religions, shows how the Society responded to other kinds of heterodoxy. The revisers' duty was not limited to policing orthodoxy, however, and this article also examines their efforts to control quality and enforce authorial decorum. It ends with discussions of the limits of the revisers' power and of the influence of censorship on Kircher's studies. Because of the constraints that ecclesiastical censorship exerted on the free expression of early modern authors, interpreting texts that treat heterodox subject-matter is inherently difficult. The case of the *Oedipus* – for which, in addition to the printed text, there survive censors' reports, the manuscript of half the work,[4] and letters by the author discussing censorship – allows us to see concretely how one such work was shaped by these pressures and thereby offers insight into how to read the published work.

Discussing 'the Errors of the Ancients'

Like every Jesuit author, Kircher was required to submit his works to superiors for internal review prior to publication.[5] After 1601, this task was entrusted to the College of Revisers, a panel of five theologians, which made recommendations to the father general, who ultimately decided whether a book could be printed. The primary purpose of Jesuit censorship was to maintain the 'soundness and uniformity of doctrine' required by the Society's constitutions – in other words, to police doctrinal orthodoxy, represented by Aquinas in theology and Aristotle in philosophy. To this end the revisers were guided by a set of Rules of the Revisers-General, which required that nothing be admitted 'which is not entirely congruent with Christian faith and piety; or which might rightly offend others, or which seems inappropriate for the reputation of the Society'; and which forbade 'new opinions disagreeing with common doctrine' and anything 'that overturns the common reasons which theologians [above all, Aquinas] confirm about Christian dogma.'[6]

In both *Oedipus Aegyptiacus* and *Obeliscus Pamphilius*, the revisers found clear-cut, but easily remedied, conflicts with Catholic theology. For example, the manuscript of the *Oedipus* called attention to the imperfect understanding of the Trinity in the Chaldean oracles, which fail to acknowledge the primacy of the Father, and declared that 'according to orthodox theology there is no origin of divine emanations except the Father.' The revisers censured this statement, commenting, 'as if the Holy Spirit didn't proceed from the Son.'[7] Elsewhere, the revisers asked Kircher to clarify his exposition of a supposed Egyptian teaching about the reception of divine gifts, lest it be read as supporting semi-Pelagianism.[8] In other passages they asked him 'to correct that way of speaking that seems to make God the author of sin,' as well as statements seeming to suggest that souls are mortal or material.[9]

A much larger part of Kircher's text fell into a greyer area. The heterodox, non-Christian beliefs and practices that constituted the subject-matter of the *Oedipus* and the *Obeliscus* could be discussed, of course. But the revisers required that such topics be presented in a particular manner and within certain limits, which varied for different kinds of heterodox material. The principal distinction visible in the judgments is between the treatment of erroneous *beliefs* and that of magical *practices*, with the latter perceived as a greater danger and thus in need of more aggressive censorship. That there should be such a distinction is by no means obvious, as the Tridentine church considered questions of belief as important as those of practice. The relative permissiveness shown towards the discussion of heterodox beliefs was likely due to the church's well-established tradition of opposing heresy by exposing and refuting it.[10] Kircher himself invoked this tradition in the preface of *Oedipus* II, defending his discussions of unorthodox doctrines by comparison with Irenaeus's writings against the Gnostics.[11] No comparable tradition supported the pious exposition of illicit magical practices.[12]

In the realm of descriptions of pagan theology, the revisers were troubled by such things as Kircher's suggestion that the Egyptians had worshiped the Nile 'not without reason'[13] and depiction of Hermes Trismegistus as a holy man despite his having introduced superstitious rites and having believed in sensible gods.[14] Where Kircher discussed Psellus's opinion that souls are produced from seed, he was instructed to indicate that this was an error *in fide*.[15] The treatment in the *Oedipus* of the Chaldean oracles, the Orphic verses, and the sayings of Pythagoras, which contain unorthodox doctrines about theologically sensitive matters, such as the creation of souls and the process of divine emanation, received special attention from the revisers. Here as elsewhere the revisers were primarily concerned that Kircher make clear that erroneous and superstitious beliefs were such and that he not appear to endorse them. Thus he was not to say that Zoroaster was divinely inspired, or that Orpheus took many things from the book of Moses, or that the followers of Pythagoras lived a 'heavenly life on earth.'[16]

Kircher's dependence on Jewish and Arab sources was especially problematic, not only because of their content, but because of their very provenance. Such texts did not describe the beliefs and practices of extinct pagan peoples, but those of living infidels whose presence was all too closely felt, whether in the form of Europe's barely tolerated Jewish minority or that of the Turkish empire that threatened Christendom from the east. In his judgment of *Obeliscus Pamphilius*, the reviser Honoré Fabri complained that Kircher placed too much value on Hebrew and Arab authors, even seeming to prefer them to familiar Christian authors – a criticism that ignored, or at least called into question, the whole rationale of Kircher's study, which was explicitly to bring to light knowledge hidden in 'oriental monuments,' especially those of the Arabs and the Jews.[17] The second volume of the *Oedipus* contained a lengthy treatise on the Jewish Kabbalah, followed by one on Arabic magic, which the revisers commanded Kircher to rewrite completely and then resubmit for a new judgment.[18]

The status of Jewish literature was vexed owing to the 1592 bull of Clement VIII, included in the 1596 edition of the Tridentine Index of Prohibited Books, which removed the exceptions to the ban on the Talmud that had been granted in the previous edition of the Index and forbade outright all books by 'Talmudists, Kabbalists, and other impious Jews.'[19] But despite its sweeping language, the ban was generally interpreted in more nuanced terms. Catholic theologians widely acknowledged that there was a good Kabbalah and a bad one, and that the ban applied only to the latter. Within the Society of Jesus there was a literary tradition that sought to clarify this question, which found its most authoritative expression in the work of Jacques Bonfrère, to whom the revisers appealed as a guide.[20] Thus the revisers were not opposed in principle to Kircher's positive assessment of parts of the Kabbalah, but they were dissatisfied with his definition of good and bad Kabbalah. They called on Kircher 'to show clearly what Kabbalah is legitimate and what prohibited; so that he may not seem to contravene the bull of Clement VIII ... and also the Index of Prohibited Books itself; which includes the Kabbalah of Johannes Reuchlin ... Therefore let the author distinguish, with Bonfrère in *Praeloquiis de Pentateuchum* ... and with others, among a good kabbalah, an indifferent kabbalah, and a bad kabbalah.'[21]

The more substantive problem, however, was not that Kircher didn't distinguish adequately between the good and bad Kabbalah – though he was inconsistent on this matter – but that he improperly discussed many beliefs and practices that by his own assessment belonged to the illicit Kabbalah. The revisers demanded that Kircher omit, or at least greatly abbreviate, substantial sections of the treatise, in which the subject-matter fell into this category. With regard to kabbalistic beliefs, including erroneous ones (as with the pagan theologies of Zoroaster, Hermes, Orpheus, and Pythagoras), there was room for discussion as long as the material was presented in the correct way. In their judgment of the first volume of the *Oedipus*, the revisers reprimanded the author for 'repeatedly ... cit[ing] too respectfully [*honorificé*] the Talmud and other Jews, which are despised names or persons, as is to be seen in the Index of the Council of Trent.'[22] The problem, then, was not that Kircher cited the Talmud and other Jewish authors despised by the Index, but that he did so *too respectfully*. The revisers advised Kircher to treat these authors in the circumspect manner that the *Ratio studiorum* prescribed for teaching Averroes and other theologically problematic interpreters of Aristotle.[23]

There were certain linguistic rules that a Jesuit author had to obey if he wanted to discuss certain topics. Already in his initial manuscript, Kircher accompanied his discussions of pagan, Jewish, and Muslim beliefs and practices with refutations of their superstitious errors and stern warnings to Christian readers 'not to try this at home.' The revisers accepted the principle that some heterodox ideas could be presented if they were framed with such language. But they found the author negligent for not distinguishing adequately between his own convictions and the false opinions of his sources, for not condemning superstitions forcefully enough, and for sometimes even seeming to endorse them. They called on Kircher to remedy these problems by modifying the tone of his presentation, by making more frequent use of expressions such as 'inquiunt' ('they say') to better distinguish the opinions of his sources from his own,[24] by augmenting his refutations of falsehood, and in certain cases by abbreviating his discussions of superstitious material.[25]

There is no way of knowing to what extent Kircher really believed in the perfidious, superstitious character of the beliefs and practices he so condemned. It is evident, however, that he was not much troubled by the danger that such material posed to readers and that he used such language because censorship required him to do so. There was a tradition of early modern writers on heterodox subjects employing such expressions in order to inoculate themselves against censorship and the charge of unorthodoxy. A classic example is Agrippa's preface to his famous guide to magic, *De occulta philosophia* (1531), in which he protests that the views expressed in the book are written 'more narratively than affirmatively.'[26] Experienced early modern readers understood these tactics and knew to take such expressions with a grain of salt. Agrippa's disclaimers did not save his work from the Index.

Kircher's use of similar expressions often rings hollow and may seem like a linguistic trick employed to smuggle illicit material past the gate. But the revisers did not view the matter in that way. In the case of heterodox beliefs, they were willing to take such language at face value, accepted its efficacy, and even offered Kircher advice on the kind of phrases he needed to insert in order to receive their stamp of approval. In his judgment of *Obeliscus Pamphilius*, Nicolaus Wysing (probably the most scrupulous reviser of these works) accepted the inevitability that such a work would contain 'some things, not only contrary to the intention of the author, but also contrary to truth, which nevertheless are to be tolerated by a certain necessity on account of the goal of proving things in that same context.'[27] To mitigate the danger posed by such material, Wysing gave instructions for a series of disclaimers to be placed at the beginning of the work, which would explain to readers how to understand such material. For example, he directed that 'warning is to be given beforehand that authority is to be granted to [ancient authors] only to the extent that they demonstrate that on account of which they are cited, although they may happen to mix in something inconsistent.' Furthermore, readers should be told that

in that way of speaking used sometimes by the ancient authors, it is not to be thought from this that in matters so obvious (in the light of faith ...) the author believes otherwise than is received in the church. But he uses the very words of the authors, even those far from the truth, both so that it may appear how far they attained in such secret matters, and because it would be too difficult and irksome to reduce those ways of speaking, repeated so many times, to the words customary today. Examples include places where there is discussion with the ancients about the soul of the world ... about the shape of the Trinity, about the triform God ... For although they may sometimes have a sound meaning, they nevertheless sometimes seem to be wrongly understood by these authors, and can draw into similar suspicion those who may read them without an attached disclaimer [*animadversio*].[28]

Wysing was no doubt sincere in his effort to maintain orthodoxy and protect readers. But while the careful use of language that he prescribed would keep a work technically orthodox, it risked sending an ambiguous message to readers, who might perceive the author to be speaking out of both sides of his mouth. Kircher's treatment of chronology, for example, which assembled evidence that implied a heretical view of antediluvian history, was allowed to stand unchanged as long as the introduction of the work informed the reader that statements about chronology and genealogy 'should be understood as things said only in passing,' unless they agreed with opinions that Kircher explicitly endorsed as his own.[29]

There was other material, however, that posed such danger to 'curious souls' that, in the opinion of the revisers, no kind of language was sufficient to render it safe for publication. The revisers demanded that Kircher's discussion of the 'practical Kabbalah' be entirely omitted from the *Oedipus* since it was 'filled with dangerous superstition.'[30] They permitted him to preserve a semblance of the section on Arabic magic called the 'Kabbalah of the Saracens' (because it constituted an entire subdivision of the work, deleting it entirely would have upset the book's structure) but demanded that he drastically shorten it, by removing all specific details of magical practices. Thereby, they said, readers might have a taste of the Saracenic Kabbalah without entering into it in depth.[31] A similar verdict was pronounced regarding the lengthy treatment of Arabic planetary magic seals in the treatise 'Hieroglyphic Astronomy.'[32]

The linguistic strategies for discussing heterodox subjects that the revisers sanctioned in the case of superstitious beliefs were deemed insufficient in the case of Jewish and Arabic magical practices. In the manuscript submitted to the revisers, Kircher had already wrapped his discussions of magical practices in all manner of disclaimers, reprobation, and invective, but the revisers were not persuaded. In assessing the permissibility of questionable material, they frequently invoked the principle of utility laid out in the eighth Rule of the Revisers-General, justifying their decisions by weighing the potential danger of the material in question against its usefulness. 'In the correction of [the treatises on the Hebrew and Saracenic Kabbalah],' they wrote, 'it will be enough (for the author's purpose) for the whole thing to contain much less, seeing as it is undoubtedly for the most part useless, if not also dangerous.'[33] The judgment of the first volume of *Oedipus* II concluded with this warning:

Finally, the author must carefully beware, lest in this work he recklessly spills onto the page everything he has drawn from the Platonists, Pythagoreans, Kabbalists, Talmudists, and other authors of similar character, and thrusts on the world things long buried, and which should always remain buried. Therefore let him adduce these authors in such a way, where it is necessary, that he may explain doubtful things clearly, condemn blameworthy things, not assert magical or superstitious matters in detail, establish a definite purpose for his allegations, and let him be convinced that from the treatment of such things, by no means may so much of utility among the general public be expected, compared to the danger that must be feared among some curious men.[34]

For his part, Kircher tried to establish the religious utility of his descriptions of superstitious amulets, claiming that they would teach Christian readers, who might happen on such an object, to recognize its dangerous character. He even asserted that for this reason the Holy Office had requested him to publish such a description.[35] Kircher probably hoped that invoking the authority of the Inquisition would lend his discussion of magical seals a sheen of propriety in the eyes of the revisers. It didn't. 'It is not enough,' the revisers insisted, that, after describing minutely how such things are used in practice, Kircher 'reproves them as superstitions that should be avoided, since over-curious and insufficiently pious individuals might esteem them and put them to use.'[36]

The revisers deemed another category of material unfit for print. In chapter 5 of *Oedipus* I, they instructed Kircher to remove 'everything that was said about the disgraceful cult of Priapus; even though it may ... be taken from respectable authors or even from the holy Fathers themselves; especially since it is not necessary for his purpose, and therefore among certain people may well cause offence.'[37] A similar sense of propriety led the revisers to ask Kircher to be more discreet in discussing the allegorical interpretation of the sexual liaisons of the gods and goddesses, by treating such matters 'only generally and in passing.'[38]

In a sense, there was a scholarly culture-clash between Kircher and the revisers regarding the utility and edification to be had from studying ancient superstition.[39] Kircher believed it was worthwhile to investigate such matters in detail in order to gain knowledge of the past – an endeavour that was inherently valuable, that is, useful and edifying. Like other antiquarian scholars, he was dedicated to as total a recovery of knowledge of antiquity as possible; no part of the past should remain buried. As he wrote about the lost teachings of the 'hieroglyphic doctrine,' 'They are buried so that they may rise again more full of life; they hide so that they may be revealed more clearly.'[40] The revisers, however, thought that much of this material, because false and superstitious, was ipso facto useless and unnecessary. At best, they allowed that some of it might have a certain value for scholars, but this possibility was outweighed by the danger it posed to curious souls – a danger that did not much worry Kircher.

Censorship as Peer Review

To end discussion here would present an incomplete picture of Jesuit censorship, for the revisers' mandate was not limited to policing orthodoxy. The eighth Rule of the Revisers-General stipulated that Jesuit books should be useful and edifying, not seem merely to repeat things that others have already written, and be better than average of their kind.[41] Therefore, the judgments of Kircher's works, like those of other authors, devoted considerable attention to criteria such as scholarly merit, literary quality, and authorial decorum, which did not directly pertain to 'the soundness and uniformity of doctrine.'

In the *Oedipus*, Kircher's efforts to clarify enigmatic esoteric doctrines were often found wanting. 'The author boastfully claims to explain certain sayings of Pico,' the revisers commented, 'which however he by no means adequately accomplishes, except perhaps about the seventh saying: the rest have the usual obscurity.'[42] Concerning the Chaldean oracles, they similarly complained that Kircher 'offers explanations of the Zoroastrian sayings, which nevertheless are so very obscure, or too unsuitable, so that they cannot be printed unless they are rewritten ... and again reviewed.'[43] In his judgment of *Obeliscus Pamphilius*, Wysing conceded that a certain amount of confusion was inevitable owing to the diversity of sources adduced in the work, but requested that Kircher do his best to disentangle inconsistencies.[44]

The revisers also called Kircher to task for repeating verbatim long passages from his earlier volumes, or even from elsewhere in the same volume.[45] Many criticisms simply signalled factual errors: he calls Ezekias king of Israel when he was only king of Judaea;[46] 'he says that the Rhône passes through the middle of Lake Zürich, which anyone who has looked at a geographical atlas, even in passing, knows to be false';[47] he states that there exists no nation so barbarous that it does not possess letters, which is contradicted by the example of the Indians of Canada;[48] and so forth. Kircher was also chastised for inadequacies in his scholarly apparatus: quotations are given only in Latin and not in the original language, or in other cases only in the original language without translation, 'as if everyone were expert in Greek'; when there are Latin translations, sometimes they are inadequate, translating 'word for word' rather than 'sense for sense';[49] in certain places citations of original texts are missing or incomplete.[50] (However, in the cases of certain dangerous authors, the revisers ordered Kircher *not* to give precise citations that would help readers consult the original.)[51] Where Kircher spoke in his own voice, a 'remarkable unevenness of style' was noted, 'for sometimes he speaks very elegantly and sometimes very lowly.'[52] Honoré Fabri simply worried that 'someone will perhaps laugh, when he hears that Aristotle got his philosophy from the obelisks.'[53]

Last but not least, Kircher's lack of modesty recurred like a leitmotif in the judgments of his books. The judgment of a preliminary outline of the *Oedipus* concentrated entirely on the author's 'puffed-up [*exaggeratum*] way of speaking' and asked him to moderate his extravagant claims. 'It shall be more honourable to the author to deliver more than he promises,' wrote the revisers, 'and it shall be more pleasing to the reader if he discovers more things in the work than he expected.'[54] The judgment of *Oedipus* I noted that the author 'very often praises his own work, and seeks renown for his uncommon skill, and the name of the first discoverer of abstruse things.' There followed a litany of specific transgressions of modesty, including that Kircher 'pronounces that singular men are sent by God for restoring sciences, just as for sustaining the faith at certain times. Here, any smart person will presume that the author speaks boastfully about himself.'[55]

There is a common denominator to the sundry forms of criticism found in the judgments of Kircher's works. For the Society, books were not only potential vehicles of dangerous ideas, which had to be controlled out of concern for public safety, but also bearers of the Society's good name. A book by a Jesuit author that was heterodox, indecent, controversial, immodest, or of poor quality would reflect badly on the order, and it was the duty of the revisers to prevent the publication of 'anything that seems to dishonour the reputation of the Society.'[56]

The Limits of Censorship

As we have seen, the Revisers-General demanded extensive revisions to every volume of *Obeliscus Pamphilius* and *Oedipus Aegyptiacus* before they would be fit to print. It remains to be seen how Kircher responded. Comparison of the censorship records with the printed books, as well as with the surviving mansucripts, reveals that the revisers' interventions had but a limited influence on the texts that were ultimately published.

As for modesty, Kircher may have made some small changes in response to the revisers, but the text that went to press was still remarkably self-aggrandizing. Some, but not all, of the passages repeated from earlier volumes were removed and replaced with cross-references, and most of the minor factual errors that had been noted by the revisers were corrected. In response to the complaints of obscurity, Kircher considerably rewrote his interpretation of the Chaldean oracles, by making quotations from Psellus and Pletho evident as such, extending his glosses in the interest of greater clarity, and deleting certain passages that apparently he thought he could not adequately elucidate.[57] In his interpretation of the Orphic verses, however, which had been subject to similar criticism, he changed much less.[58] Aristotle remained a student of hieroglyphic wisdom.

How Kircher responded to concerns about the presentation of doctrinally questionable material is most clearly seen in the case of the second 'tome' of *Oedipus Aegyptiacus*, the manuscript of which survives and bears the changes made by Kircher in response to the revisers.[59] For the most part, specific requests for minor changes were dutifully carried out. In his statement about the orthodox dogma of the Trinity, for example, Kircher specified that the Father is *originally* the only source of divine emanations,[60] and he deleted the words 'in fide' from the statement that it was certain *in fide* that Adam was the inventor of letters.[61] Similarly, in both the *Obeliscus* and the *Oedipus*, Kircher obeyed the revisers' instructions to remove the statement that it was certain *de fide* that Enoch wrote books, contenting himself with declaring that to doubt the fact was 'at least presumptuous and rash.'[62] Elsewhere, however, Kircher ignored similar orders: the statement that Orpheus received many things from the book of Moses, for example, appeared in the printed version, despite the revisers' call for its deletion.[63] Kircher added more of the kind of language (already present in the original draft) requested by the censors to distinguish his own opinions from those of his impious sources, by inserting phrases such as 'as the Platonists say,' 'so say the Rabbis,' and 'according to the opinion of the Arabs.' In many cases, particularly in the treatise on the Kabbalah, he merely inserted an asterisk next to an opinion that had been singled out for correction and placed a note in the margins labelling it a 'ridiculous rabbinic superstition' or something similar. Along the same lines, he added passages refuting specific errors, as well as more general disclaimers, such as 'if anything heterodox occurs in these things, I wish readers to know that it is not asserted by my judgment, but from the opinion of the ancients.'[64]

But while Kircher generally complied with requests for such small alterations to his text, the revisers' most urgent demands – most notably their order to remove large portions of the treatises on the Kabbalah and on Arabic magic – went unheeded. With respect to the descriptions of magical practices that the revisers had demanded be completely deleted, Kircher responded by doing more of exactly what the revisers had declared inadequate. That is to say, he left these sections intact but added more of the kind of language that has been described above. The section on the practical Kabbalah remained as long and detailed in the printed book as in the original draft; but Kircher added marginalia and new phrases in the body of the text stating that he spoke 'not according to my own opinion, but according to the Jewish theologians.'[65] Likewise, the indecent passages concerning Priapus and the unions of the gods were left unchanged.[66]

And so, in a form much closer to Kircher's original drafts than to that desired by the revisers-general, the five volumes of *Obeliscus Pamphilius* and *Oedipus Aegyptiacus* one by one went to press, raising the question, Why was Kircher allowed to publish the *Oedipus* and *Obeliscus* without addressing the revisers' most urgent demands?

If the books were published with many of the revisers' orders disregarded, this seems to have happened with the blessing of the father general, who gave the works his imprimatur. In this case, one cannot rightly say that Kircher evaded the censorship system, since according to the rules governing that system, the reports of the revisers were simply recommendations addressed to the father general, who had complete discretion in making a final decision. It was the duty of the father revisers rigorously to apply the rules governing Jesuit publications to submitted texts. It was then the duty of the father general to make a decision, and this decision, while taking account of the revisers' judgments, could also be based on other factors. Although the Jesuit *Constitutions* contained rules for the father revisers (which make reference to the ultimate authority of the general), there were no such rules laying out the criteria by which the father general should make his decision. One assumes that the guidelines laid out in the Rules of the Revisers-General were implicitly understood to be those criteria, and that in most cases the general was intended to follow the recommendation of the revisers, especially when their opinion was unanimous. But ultimately, in granting permission to publish books as in other matters, the father general was at liberty to consider extenuating circumstances and to make exceptions.[67]

If this is the correct way to understand what happened, it is interesting that *formally* the scenario did not play out with the general overriding the revisers. Rather, the revisers attested to the adequacy of Kircher's revisions before the general signed a standard imprimatur stating that the work could be published *because* it had been approved by the revisers. None the less, it seems unlikely that the decision to approve Kircher's manifestly inadequate revisions was made by the revisers without the general's knowledge.[68] Indeed, at the time of the review of the first volume of *Oedipus Aegyptiacus*, one reviser wrote to the father general to warn him of the likelihood that Kircher would ignore the revisers' instructions, as he had done before.[69] The censorship process did not take place entirely on paper, at least for an author like Kircher, who was a colleague of the revisers at the Collegio Romano. There may have been conversations and negotiations, involving the author, the revisers, and the father general, between the time of the initial judgments and the approval of the corrected manuscript.[70] (A glimpse of the face-to-face dimension of the process, which by its nature has left few traces in the archive, can be caught in Nicolaus Wysing's judgment of *Obeliscus Pamphilius*, which refers to the changes requested in his report as being 'in addition to those that I have discussed personally with the author.')[71] This leaves the question, Why would the father general have allowed Kircher to publish the books in the form he did?

The Society of Jesus had various goals, which could conflict with one another, and in such cases one had to be chosen over the other. The author Athanasius Kircher brought advantages and disadvantages for the Society, which put up with the latter because it valued the former. If his works often contained arguably heterodox material, they simultaneously supported the Society's cause in other respects. In the case of the *Obeliscus* and *Oedipus*, one may suppose that the affinity of their central argument – that a common spiritual past united all mankind – to the Society's missionary goals and, more generally, to the universal claims of the Catholic church may have mitigated the reaction to the questionable means by which Kircher supported that argument. Apart from the specific content of his books, the Society no doubt valued Kircher's prominence as a Jesuit author widely recognized in the world of European learning, and, in particular, a favourite among European princes. Kircher's megalomania may have been unbecoming to a Jesuit priest, but it played quite well in the aristocratic culture the Society so consciously sought to engage. The Holy Roman emperor Ferdinand III underwrote and received the dedication of *Oedipus Aegyptiacus*; Pope Innocent X played a similar role with respect to *Obeliscus Pamphilius*. Whether or not there was direct communication between these mighty patrons and the father general, it is not hard to imagine that knowledge of their support for Kircher's enterprise might have influenced his attitude towards the revision of the manuscripts. Upon receiving news that the emperor would provide funds for the very costly printing of the *Oedipus*, Kircher wrote to his go-between at the imperial court, Grand Burgrave Bernard Martinic, 'The Father General was stunned by the emperor's largesse in offering so much help, and he earnestly instructed me to put all other things aside and apply myself exclusively [to the preparation of the *Oedipus*], so that the Holy Roman Majesty shall be completely satisfied by the said work.[72]

But even if it is likely that such factors were at play, their explanatory power is limited to a general level of analysis and cannot be considered decisive. Other works by Kircher supported by powerful patrons were treated less liberally.[73] Indeed, the fact that a publication had an illustrious patron could argue in favour of *stricter* control of its orthodoxy, since heterodox material would be all the more pernicious if published with the stamp of approval of a royal or papal dedicatee.[74] Nor did Kircher's own eminence necessarily lead his superiors to grant him more leeway. Kircher's value to the Society as a celebrated Jesuit author depended on his reputation, so allowing him to publish works that would damage it would have been counterproductive. This logic can be seen behind the judgments of *Iter Etruria, Ars magna sciendi, Diatribe de prodigiosis crucibus*, and *Scrutinium pestis*, all of which were rejected on their initial submission owing to concern for 'the credit of the Society and the author.'[75]

Despite Kircher's victory over the revisers in the publication of *Oedipus Aegyptiacus* and *Obeliscus Pamphilius*, this case should not be taken as evidence that the censorship of material pertaining to magic and superstition was not a serious business in seventeenth-century Rome, or that the threat of censorship did not affect Kircher's studies. In the first years after his arrival in Rome at the end of 1633, Kircher was studying several Arabic manuscripts relating to Egypt and the hieroglyphs, which his mentor, the French antiquarian Nicolas-Claude Fabri de Peiresc, encouraged him to translate and publish. But the threat of censorship weighed heavily on the young scholar's mind. In 1635 he wrote to Peiresc about the difficulty of publishing such works. 'It is sure,' he declared, 'that the whole [text] cannot be published, since it treats many magical things, and in many places entirely concerns incantations, which neither the Holy Office nor our Society will permit, because of the danger that that they could pose to souls.'[76] Peiresc continued to insist, and in 1636, Kircher explained the situation at greater length: 'Since books of this sort are full of superstitious magical seals and other opinions condemned by the church ... [and] the magic arts are so mixed up with the hieroglyphic works ... that [the authors] seem not to recite but to teach, indeed they seem to pave the way to reviving the necromancy of the ancients ... surely these things will never be permitted and cannot be permitted; especially here in Rome, where the censorship [*censura*] of all books is so strict that not even the least straw of error or false opinion is tolerated.'[77] It will not do, he continued, to publish an expurgated version that removes the controversial parts, since 'these books are by their nature such that they can serve me nowhere better than where they treat the worst things. For in books of this sort I do not seek Catholic truths, which infinitely many other authors may provide, but the errors of the ancients, and teachings or whatever opinions are expressed in hieroglyphic notes, and their use.' Kircher explained that to overcome these obstacles he devised the *Oedipus Aegyptiacus*, in which

all the said authors are introduced in such an order that the authors' words may be sincerely and faithfully alleged, but, the scandalous parts having been prudently and discreetely refuted, the errors of the ancients may be like witnesses, and nothing which may be of use for emending antiquity may be omitted from the cited authors ... I have shared this plan of mine with excellent friends and most learned men ... And all judiciously proclaim this to be the only way that these authors can be delivered from eternal darkness, perhaps even the flames ... For in this way hidden truth shall be made known, the dangerous rocks of scandal shall be avoided and, what I wish most of all, greater gain will be added to the Republic of Letters.[78]

As Kircher tells it in this letter, *Oedipus Aegyptiacus* was originally conceived as a means to publish certain oriental texts about pagan religion and magic in a manner acceptable to the organs of ecclesiastical censorship. He argues that publication of the texts on their own will never be permitted because of their superstitious content, and that the only way around this is for him to present passages from these texts within a larger interpretative work so that he can properly contextualize them and refute their errors – in other words, to employ the linguistic strategies that we have examined. When Kircher finally executed this plan years later, the censors intimidated him rather less. And when the revisers found Kircher's 'refutations of the scandalous parts' insufficient to render certain parts of his books innocuous, he ignored them, confident that he could prevail over their judgments.

The revisers were also aware of the limits of their power. In a postscript to the judgment of the first volume of the *Oedipus*, the reviser Nicolaus Wysing addressed a poignant personal plea to Father General Alessandro Gottifreddi: 'I fear,' he wrote,

that the work expended by the father revisers in the judgment of this book may be of little use with Father Athanasius; for even recently in that Synopsis, he followed the judgment of these fathers only as much and in the manner that he wished. Then, he once said to me that he had significantly enlarged the book on the Pamphilian Obelisk after the judgment;[79] and I even hear elsewhere that he boasted, on account of experience in these matters, that he can safely [engage in] practices of this sort. Further, I know from personal experience that things in a work to be printed (i.e., at the time of printing) are sometimes changed by Father Athanasius, at least with respect to order, so that it cannot easily be determined whether he has followed the judgment or rather has neglected it.[80] Indeed, as these things seem to me capable of highly prejudicing our judgments, I have decided they should be deferred to the providence of Your Paternity ... I entrust myself most humbly to Your Father's paternal benevolence.[81]

Wysing knew that Kircher knew that he need not comply with all the revisers' demands. And he knew that real power lay with the father general, whose intervention alone could compel Kircher. All evidence indicates that General Gottifreddi (like Vicar General Florentius de Montmorency, with respect to *Obeliscus Pamphilius*, and General Goswin Nickel, with respect to the subsequent volumes of the *Oedipus*) chose not to exercise that power.[82] A week after the original judgment was submitted with the plea just quoted, Wysing and the other revisers dutifully signed a statement attesting that Kircher had satisfactorily corrected the manuscript, and the first volume of *Oedipus Aegyptiacus* was sent to press.[83]

NOTES

The complete Latin texts of the censorship documents analysed here are printed with annotations in Daniel Stolzenberg, 'Oedipus Censored: *Censurae* of Athanasius Kircher's Works in the Archivum Romanum Societatis Iesu,' *AHSI* 73 (2004): 3–52, which also provides other information that complements this article. This article uses the abbreviations *OA* (Athanasius Kircher, *Oedipus Aegyptiacus* [Rome, 1652–4]), and *OP* (Kircher, *Obeliscus Pamphilius* [Rome, 1650]). I wish to thank Paula Findlen, Gabriel Stolzenberg, the editors of this volume, and especially Brad Gregory for their helpful comments.

1 A number of new works are devoted to Kircher: *Athanasius Kircher: The Last Man Who Knew Everything*, ed. Paula Findlen (London, 2004); *Athanasius Kircher: Il museo del mondo*, ed. Eugenio Lo Sardo (Rome, 2001); Ingrid Rowland, *The Ecstatic Journey: Athanasius Kircher in Baroque Rome* (Chicago, 2001); and *The Great Art of Knowing: The Baroque Encyclopedia of Athanasius Kircher*, ed. Daniel Stolzenberg (Stanford, 2001). See these for references to earlier studies.

2 E.g., Bald. *Leg.*, chap. 2; Marcus Hellyer, '"Because the Authority of My Superiors Commands": Censorship, Physics, and the German Jesuits,' *Early Science and Medicine* 1 (1996): 319–54; and Michael John Gorman, 'A Matter of Faith? Christoph Scheiner, Jesuit Censorship, and the Trial of Galileo,' *Perspectives on Science* 4 (1996): 283–320.

3 Carlos Ziller Camenietzki, 'L'extase interplanetaire d'Athanasius Kircher: Philosophie, cosmologie et discipline dans la Compagnie de Jésus au XVIIe siècle,'

Nuncius (1995): 3–32; and Hellyer, 'Censorship.' Cf. Ingrid Rowland, 'Athanasius Kircher, Giordano Bruno, and the *Panspermia* of the Infinite Universe,' in *Kircher*, ed. Findlen, p. 198. Harald Siebert, 'Kircher and His Critics: Censorial Practice and Pragmatic Disregard in the Society of Jesus,' in *Kircher*, ed. Findlen, pp. 79–104, came to my attention after I had written this article. Siebert and I exchanged notes on some of the Kircher *censurae*.

4　BNVE Ges. 1235. See n59 below.

5　On Jesuit censorship and its institutional and doctrinal context, see Bald., *Leg.*; Hellyer, 'Censorship'; and Antonella Romano, 'Pratiques d'enseignement et orthodoxie intellectuelle en milieu jésuite (seconde moitié du XVIe siècle),' in *Orthodoxie, christianisme, histoire*, ed. S. Elm et al. (Rome, 2000) pp. 241–60.

6　'Regulae revisorum generalum,' in *ISI*, III, pp. 65–8. The Rules are discussed at greater length in Stolzenberg, 'Oedipus Censored.'

7　ARSI FG 668 fol. 391.

8　Ibid., fol. 391v. Critics of Molinism – the Jesuit teaching about divine grace that emphasized the role of free will – accused its Jesuit exponents of advocating 'semi-Pelagianism.' The term invokes Pelagianism, an early Christian heresy (which Molinism and semi-Pelagianism in fact refute) that denies original sin and the orthodox doctrine of divine grace. See *New Catholic Encyclopedia*, 16 vols (New York, 1967–88), s.v. Semi-Pelagianism, XIII, pp. 75–6.

9　ARSI FG 668 fol. 391v.

10　The outstanding early modern Jesuit representative of this tradition is Roberto Bellarmino.

11　*OA* II.1, p. 3.

12　Such practices were, furthermore, no mere theoretical issue. During this period, the Holy Office and other authorities actively prosecuted illicit magic, both learned and popular. For examples in Rome, see Luigi Fiorani, 'Astrologi, superstiziosi e devoti nella società romana del seicento,' *Ricerche per la storia religiosa di Roma* 2 (1978): 97–162; and Thomas Cohen, *Words and Deeds in Renaissance Rome* (Toronto, 1993). Cf. Guido Ruggiero, *Binding Passions: Tales of Magic, Marriage, and Power at the End of the Renaissance* (Oxford, 1993), on Venice.

13　ARSI FG 668 fol. 398.

14　Ibid., fol. 390; cf. fol. 394v.

15　Ibid., fol. 390.

16　Ibid., fol. 391r–v.

17　Fabri excluded from this censure Jewish and Arab 'philosophers, physicians, and mathematicians,' who formed part of the scholastic canon (ARSI FG 668 fol. 394). Fabri (1607–88) was not an official member of the College of Revisers but occasionally served as a reviser of particular books. He was himself a noteworthy natural philosopher and mathematician, as well as a theologian, and no stranger to the other side of censorship and controversy. His acceptance of certain Cartesian ideas had led to difficulties with his superiors when he taught in Lyon; his soft attitude towards the heliocentric hypothesis earned him a prison sentence from Alexander VII; and the 1672 edition of his work on probabilist ethics was placed on the Index of Prohibited Books shortly after publicaton. See *Dictionary of Scientific Biography*, 18 vols (New York, 1970–90), IV, pp. 505–7; and *Catholic Encyclopedia*, 16 vols (1907–22), V, pp. 743–4. Cf. E. Caruso, 'Honoré Fabri, gesuità e scienzato,' in *Miscellanea secentesca. Saggi su Descartes, Fabri, White* (Milan, 1987), pp. 85–126.

18 ARSI FG 668 fol. 391v.

19 *Index librorum prohibitorum ... Clementis PP. VIII* (Rome, 1596); facsimile printed in *Index des livres interdits*, vol. 9, ed. J.M. De Bujanda et al. (Sherbrooke, 1994), p. 930.

20 Jacques Bonfrère, *Pentateuchus Moysis commmentario ... praemissis ... Praeloquiis perutilibus* (Antwerp, 1625). See François Secret, 'Les jésuites et le kabbalisme chrétien à la renaissance,' *Bibliothèque d'humanisme et renaissance* 20 (1958): 543–55.

21 ARSI FG 668 fol. 391v. Cf. ibid., fol. 390v (regarding *OP*).

22 Ibid., fol. 398.

23 See 'Regulae professoris philosophiae,' 3–5, in *ISI*, III pp. 189–90; cf. Stolzenberg, 'Oedipus Censored,' p. 23 n69.

24 See especially ARSI FG 668 fol. 396v.

25 These linguistic strategies parallel those used by Jesuit authors to discuss unorthodox natural-philosophical theories, as discussed by Hellyer, 'Censorship,' pp. 336ff., who calls attention to the importance of the judicious use of words such as 'true,' 'false,' 'probable,' and 'hypothesis.'

26 Cornelius Agrippa, *De occulta philosophia*, ed. V. Perrone Compagni (Leiden, 1992), p. 66.

27 ARSI FG 668 fol. 390r–v.

28 Ibid., fol. 390v.

29 Ibid. On Kircher's heterodox chronology, see Anthony Grafton, 'Kircher's Chronology,' in *Kircher*, ed. Findlen, pp. 171–87.

30 Ibid., ARSI FG 668 fol. 392.

31 Ibid.

32 Ibid., fol. 396.

33 Ibid., fol. 391v; cf. fol. 392r.

34 Ibid., fol. 392r–v.

35 *OA* II.2, p. 474; cf. ibid., p. 211.

36 ARSI FG 668 fol. 396; cf. ibid., p. 392.

37 Ibid., fols 399, 391v.

38 Ibid., fol. 391v; cf. *OA* II.1, class 3, chap. 10.

39 I use the word 'superstition' in its early modern sense, which refers to the morality of beliefs and practices, not necessarily to their irrationality or inefficacy.

40 *OA* I, p. a4v.

41 *ISI*, III, p. 67.

42 ARSI FG 668 fol. 391v.

43 Ibid., fol. 391.

44 Ibid., fol. 390.

45 Inter alia, ibid., fols 391, 396.

46 Ibid., fol. 396v.

47 Ibid., fol. 398v.

48 Ibid., fol. 400v.

49 Ibid., fol. 398.

50 Ibid., fols 398v, 396v, 392.

51 Ibid., fol. 392.

52 Ibid., fol. 400.

53 Ibid., fol. 394.

54 Ibid., fol. 389r–v.

55 Ibid., fol. 398v. Similar concerns are found in the judgments of *OP* and the other volumes of *OA*.

56 *ISI*, III, p. 67, Rule 6.

57 BNVE Ges. 1235 fols 89v–96.

58 Ibid., fols 104–10v.

59 BNVE Ges. 1235. This consists of the fair copies of parts 1 and 2 of *Oedipus Aegyptiacus*, tome 2, which Kircher submitted to the revisers and which he subsequently revised and sent to the printer. For details see Stolzenberg, 'Oedipus Censored,' p. 14 n42.

60 BNVE Ges. 1235 fol. 87; cf. *OA* II.1, p. 133. See n7 above.

61 ARSI FG 668 fol. 391; *OA* II.1, p. 43; BNVE Ges. 1235 fol. 24v.

62 ARSI FG 668 fol. 390; *OP*, p. 6. ARSI FG 668 fol. 391; *OA* II.1, p. 68; BNVE Ges. 1235 fol. 44.

63 See n16 above.

64 BNVE Ges. 1235 fol. 85; cf. *OA* II.1, p. 130.

65 BNVE Ges. 1235 fol. 335.

66 Ibid., fol. 109; cf. *OA* II.1, p. 155.

67 My interpretation here is in line with Baldini (Bald. *Leg.*, p. 87), who remarks that the generals often possessed a greater 'political-cultural' sensitivity than the revisers, and thus were relatively more tolerant of innovative propositions, sometimes mediating between authors and revisers and occasionally even permitting works that the revisers had condemned.

68 Based on the appearance of the revised manuscript of *OA* II, I do not believe that

Kircher could have hidden his disobedience from the revisers by playing with the manuscript (e.g., by removing sections and then reinserting them before sending the text to press), and thus I conclude that the revisers knew that Kircher had not made all the changes they had required. For additional evidence that the revisers may sometimes have approved works against their better judgment because of pressure from above, see François Duneau's dutiful approval of the corrections of Kircher's *Iter exstaticum II* (ARSI FG 661 fol. 32), following his plea to the father general not to allow the work to be published (ARSI FG 661 fols 30, 34); Stolzenberg, 'Oedipus Censored,' appendix, items 29–30.

69 See the letter from Wysing to Gottifreddi quoted at the end of this essay.

70 See Hellyer, 'Censorship,' pp. 339–41, on cases of authors appealing to the general to override the revisers.

71 ARSI FG 668 fol. 390.

72 Kircher to Bernard Ignac Martinic, 30 December 1650, APUG 561 fol. 70.

73 E.g., Kircher's ill-fated *Iter Etruria*, dedicated to the Grand Duke of Tuscany, which was refused approval in 1660; ARSI FG 663 fols 312–18.

74 See Hellyer, 'Censorship,' pp. 342–3.

75 Quotation from ARSI FG 663 fol. 135. The latter three works were ultimately published despite the initial rejections of the revisers. See Stolzenberg, 'Oedipus Censored,' for details.

76 Kircher to Peiresc, 8 February 1635, BNP NAFr 5173 fol. 25v; cf. BNP FF 9362 fol. 13v (copy). The Latin text of the excerpts from this and the following letter are printed in Stolzenberg, 'Oedipus Censored.'

77 Kircher to Peiresc, 3 December 1636, BNP FF 9538 fol. 236.

78 Ibid., fols 236v–7.

79 Adding to a work after the text had been approved for publication was a serious violation of the rules of Jesuit publishing. See *ISI*, III, p. 68 (Rule 15).

80 In his denouncement of *Iter exstaticum II*, Duneau later likewise stated that 'it is known from experience' that Kircher has often not corrected his books as instructed (ARSI FG 661 fols 30, 34.)

81 ARSI FG 668 fol. 399.

82 Thus, the dynamic in Rome between the revisers and the general, specifically with regard to this case, seems to be the opposite of the dynamic described by Hellyer between the general and the provincial revisers, whose lack of vigilance in enforcing the 1651 ordination aroused General Nickel's frustration and anger. See Hellyer, 'Censorship,' pp. 335–6.

83 ARSI FG 668 fol. 397 (approval of corrections of *OA* I).

16 / Teaching Mathematics in Jesuit Schools: Programs, Course Content, and Classroom Practices

ANTONELLA ROMANO

In today's efflorescent scholarship on the Society of Jesus, which I have ob-served and analysed on a Europe-wide scale on several occasions,[1] it seems that the history of teaching and that of education in general are two areas that have barely been investigated. The exceptions are the close readings of the *Ratio studiorum*, particularly by French scholars;[2] and the collection of essays pub-lished following the 2001 conference in Parma on the Jesuits and the university,[3] which provides an inventory of the relevant issues mostly for Italy, where the historiographical tradition of local studies has ensured continuity in research relating to the history of the Society's establishments.[4]

To put the matter in another way, if one were to characterize the output of recent years, one would focus first on a monographic research axis, and second, on an axis relating to normative texts, sometimes in relation to local contexts. The same would apply to the output dealing with scientific courses, the study of which, as I have argued elsewhere, has helped boost interest in the history of teaching and of education.

The panorama I have briefly sketched highlights the gaps and limitations that still hinder the writing of history. Among these, the most evident is the issue of classroom practices. The attempt to revisit the Society's history by forsaking the exclusive vantage point of normative texts – and therefore that of institutional history – has proved especially crucial during the last decade in some areas of Jesuit history;[5] but when it comes to the history of course content, this attempt has stopped short, namely, on the doorstep of the classroom.

This observation is especially true of the work I carried out five years ago concerning the teaching of mathematics in Jesuit colleges. At the time I was especially interested in the way in which a mathematics culture had evolved from the Collegio Romano, and the way in which this culture had been imple-mented in the Society's intellectual space. During my research, which focused on discussion of an institutional and historiographical model based on the centre-periphery coupling, I found myself having to bridge from norms into the area of practices. From the profuse sources that were available, I discovered that I ought to delineate the singularity of local contexts, in searching for 'site-related constraints' that might account for the uniqueness of classroom practices and induce a new reading of the status of norms in Jesuit culture.[6] Within this framework, I was struck by one group of sources, namely, manuscript lecture notes.[7] My approach to these was not exhaustive: instead, it relied on a selective analysis of their contents, through which I hoped to retrieve traces and echoes of the local cultures that Jesuit participants must have integrated into the cultures they were both inheriting and contributing to.

If I have continued to work on the question of the 'Jesuit mathematics culture' and thus partly moved away from the question of 'teaching', I nevertheless think that research in this area should be articulated with the approaches of intellectual history and the history of education. Indeed, beyond what we still ignore and need to find out about the tasks of establishments or about disciplines,[8] the figure of the Jesuit scholar conjured up in research relating to such diverse topics as textual production, scientific practices, and scholarly exchanges has its roots in the profession of teaching and the legitimacy conferred by the status of professor, in this case that of mathematics professor. From this point of view, manuscript lecture notes make up an original group of sources[9] that could help us develop this articulation and shed light not only on an important episode in the Society's history, but also on the construction of professional identities in the early modern period.

My goal is not to write the history of the Collège de Clermont, which became the Collège-Louis-le-Grand during the late seventeenth century, even though the question of the mathematics and philosophy lectures at the Clermont college would necessitate starting all over with that history.[10] Instead, I propose to read the manuscripts as indications of classroom practices, and to do so I will analyse three manuscripts that can be used as landmarks in the development of those practices from the 1560s to the 1660s.

In the Bibliothèque Nationale, Paris, there is an untitled manuscript the first part of which bears the following subtitle: *Annotationes in regullas arithmetices dictatae per dominum Vallentinum in collegio claromontano dicto des Jesuites in via jacobea et in hanc papirum scriptae per nobillem virum Andream Bedellum parrochia de Benero prope urbem Cadomum, scriptum Lutetiae parissierum Anno Domini 1567.*[11] As far as we know, this is the first tangible trace of a mathematics course taught by the Jesuits in Paris, only three years after they had settled there. The prosy subtitle enables us to see that we are dealing with notes taken during the year 1567 at the dictation of Jacques Valentin, whose identity can be confirmed by another much relied upon source, the lists of individuals working for Jesuit establishments that had been drawn up and sent to Rome by the colleges' directors.[12] There Valentin was listed as a professor of logic.

The folio, as its title makes clear, contains the notes taken under dictation by a student auditing the Logic lecture – his name appears several times on the document. The layout suggests that the succession of subjects corresponds to the order of the lectures, a suggestion that leads us to infer that the first year of training in Logic started with lectures in mathematics. The order was as follows: after a general introduction, which spans the first four folios, the professor dealt first with arithmetic, which corresponds to seven short chapters (fols 4v–11r); then geometry (fols 15r–20v); and finally astronomy. Following mathematics was Aristotelian logic.

The second manuscript I will use in my analysis is the mechanics course[13] taught by Jean François:[14] it was given in 1621, that is, three years after the reopening of the college.[15] The document is made up of 104 folios, which include ink drawings of machines. After an introduction, which consists in a defence of the mechanical sciences, the course content is divided into two parts, ordered as follows. In the first part, a few definitions (fols 2–3v); the world's centre, and a few conclusions drawn from the natural fall of heavy bodies (fols 3v–14v); the principle of 'movement from an indeterminate cause' (fols 14v–17v); the principles of vacuum and penetration (fols 48–55v); the principles of condensation and rarefaction (fols 22v–30); the 'reason for placing weights at various distances from the centre of the scales' (fols 30v–42v); the principle of inclined plane (fols 43–8); the principle of fluid bodies (fols 48–55v); and the principle of the force of movement (fols 56–7). In the second part: perpetual motion (fols 57v–64); a description of a few machines (fols 64–73); and hydraulics (fols 73–100).

The structure of this manuscript gives evidence of the important phenomenon of specialization, and in fact the document is the first known French testimony concerning teaching of such a topic as mechanics. We can note at this stage that it does not point to an exceptional situation, but instead suggests a slight adaptation of the mathematics course content, as is further evidenced by the bills announcing the theses defended in the same year.[16]

The third manuscript[17] bears a title that has little to do with a lecture: *L'art de fortifier les places régulières et irrégulières, expliqué, pratiqué et démonstré d'une façon agréable et facile a la noblesse françoise par le RP. Bourdin de la Compagnie de Jésus, a Paris, 1654.*[18] It is, however, of the greatest interest, principally because the place where it was housed – the Jesuit archive of the province of Toulouse[19] – points to the phenomenon of text circulation, which should be taken into account in the analysis of classroom practices.

This document, made up of 90 recto and verso folios bound together, is without pagination, table of contents, tables, and conclusion; it consists of numerous hand-drawn figures and is organized according to a simple principle: the text on the verso, and the figures on the facing recto of each new page. Furthermore, several plates of a larger size have been added, folded and inserted, without page reference or specific numbering, into the binding. The author of the treatise, Pierre Bourdin,[20] who held the chair of mathematics at the Collège de Clermont for an extensive period, died that same year, 1654; nothing is known about the manuscript's copyist.

Thanks to their differing contexts, these three manuscripts are most helpful in that they shed an unusual light on the history of mathematics teaching in Paris between 1560 and 1660. In particular, they allow for fresh insights precisely where normative texts remain silent. Until the publication of the *Ratio studiorum* in 1599, in the regulations that were available – whether they had a general character, such as the *Constitutions,* or a local one, such as the local *ratio*, which multiplied on a more or less explicit Roman pattern – little seemed to be said about mathematics, as though the teaching of this discipline began only with the creation of chairs. A document describing the situation in Paris in 1567–8 allows us to grasp the immediate preoccupations of the board of directors of the college:

Regulations concerning studies at the college are as follows:
In Theology there shall be one lesson a day, as well as a catechism lesson on feast days. In Philosophy there have been only two professors hitherto. The dialectician shall teach four hours a day, two in the morning and two in the afternoon. The physicist [*physicus*] shall teach less. Repetitions shall be organized for training dialecticians during the last half-hour of the morning and the afternoon, although it is difficult to keep the day students. Boarding students in Dialectics and Philosophy shall repeat every evening. On Saturdays, from 3 o'clock to 5 o'clock, classes for training physicists and dialecticians shall assemble in the same place and hold public disputations, except during weeks of two or more feastdays.

Furthermore, on Sundays from 4 o'clock to 6 o'clock, boarding students in Dialectics and Philosophy shall challenge their professors in a disputation.

The professor of dialectics customarily provides a commentary in the first-year course on all of Aristotle's works and on Porphyry's *Dialectics*, with the exception of a few chapters of the *Prior Analytics*; as well as a summary of Dialectics before class resumes. During the same year, generally at the beginning, he shall explain Aristotle's *Ethics*.

The physicist shall teach all Aristotle's works relating to nature, the treatise *On the Heavens*, the treatise *On the Soul*, the *Meteorology*, and the treatise *On Generation and Corruption*, as well as some books of the *Metaphysics*.[21]

By placing emphasis on Theology and Philosophy courses, the fathers were evidently targeting an academic audience; their effort focused on higher education, and the drive was to compete with the university. A comparison of this document with documents describing the situation in other establishments at the same time enables us to grasp more fully the significance of the fathers' effort in Paris. We can therefore conclude that this was a deliberate choice on their part, despite the restrictions imposed on educational activities by Rome, implicit in the instructions left by Jerónimo Nadal during his visit to Paris between 15 June and 15 July 1568: 'It does not appear useful, at the present time, to organize at the Paris college more classes than those already existing, nor more than are sufficient for our patrons; these, as was reported by the provincial, are satisfied with the golden mean we currently provide; that is why they shall not have a *lector* in Greek, nor another theologian, nor a *mathematician* [my emphasis].'[22]

Jacques Valentin's manuscript allows us to see that the choice was not to entrust a specialist with the teaching of mathematics, and also enables us to get a sense of what this teaching may have been like, devolved as it was to a philosophy professor, that is, a non-specialist. At this stage it is important to note that during this early phase, when colleges were opening and no unifying normative text existed, the curriculum in Philosophy very seldom included mathematics – Rome and Messina should be viewed as exceptions.[23] Conversely, the fact that mathematics lectures were given in some cases must be examined carefully. Concerning Jacques Valentin's lectures, a detailed reading reveals that the course dealt with the discipline only superficially. The superficiality is recognizable in the preface, which consists in a lengthy introduction to the course – a sort of *prolegomena*, as it were – with no epistemological dimension, and resting instead on a long exposition of the tradition concerning the origins of the discipline and the authors who passed on the tradition, namely, Pythagoras, Aristotle, Boethius, and Isidore of Seville,[24] all of whom are the author's main intellectual references. The preface manifests the characteristics of a culture still imbued by medieval references, which undoubtedly were also those of the intellectual community of the time: more than a thousand manuscripts of Isidore's *Ethymologia* were circulating in Europe after 1470.[25] The same can be said of Boethius's work, which benefited from large circulation on account of the early editorial interest he received.[26]

In short, one is left with the impression that it is the silences that truly matter, much more than the question of references. Indeed, given that an abundant mathematics output was available, especially in Paris, where the professors who moved in the circle of the Collège Royal had already printed many texts – whether Jacques Pelletier or Claude Oronce Finé de Brianville, not to mention Italians such as Cardano – Jacques Valentin's course must have appeared that of a non-specialist, who for all his firm knowledge of scholastic tradition displayed little awareness of the issues involved in the discipline he dealt with. The medieval influence behind the lectures given in Paris is evidenced by the structure of the course, which was based on the quadrivium, the transmission of which was guaranteed by the Parisian professor.[27]

More than fifty years later, in Jean François's days, the institutional situation of mathematics in the Society had changed radically, thanks notably to the prolonged effort by Christoph Clavius to defend its role in the curriculum of superior studies. Without dwelling too long on this development, which is already well documented,[28] I would like to emphasize the fact that neither the *Ratio* nor any of the other sources gives us insight into the nature of the lectures. The 1621 manuscript gives us a description of a course content far different from what was known until recently and points to a clear orientation towards mixed mathematics.[29] Was this choice individual, local, and isolated? Even if that question remains partly unanswered, it indicates that the structure of Jean François's course was the reflection on an intellectual plane of a policy the institutional enforcement of which led to the creation of specific chairs in mathematics.

When courses started to stabilize, from the year 1603 in France, and when Clavius's books started to circulate and France started to recruit mathematics professors, that is, Jesuits who in the course of their career had been able to benefit from a more thorough training in the discipline, then the phase of book production began. I will not develop this aspect here, but simply point out that the trend was initiated, rather slowly, in the early 1620s, precisely when Jean François's manuscript was dictated, and that it met with real success from the 1640s on.

Thus, beginning in this period, course content in mathematics general classes, designed for all the students enrolled in Philosophy, can be documented by comparing three main types of sources, namely, textbooks, lecture manuscripts, and bills of theses. Those available in France lead us to reflect on the early diversification of courses, in comparison both to normative texts and to the attention paid to mixed mathematics in these classes. This diversification is confirmed by Jean François's course in a clearer way than is allowed by the thesis prints, which give no indication of the proficiency attained in the classes, and in a more precise way than is allowed by printed books, which remained scarce throughout this period in France.[30] Moreover, printed books confront us with an important methodological problem: the study of mathematics books has often avoided in-depth analysis of the connections between books and classes on the assumption that those books were systematically used as textbooks, but this was seldom the case.[31]

If one were to trace course content through books only, one would be unable to identify the interests of the professors, in particular those of Jean François. Mechanics was a topic of prime concern in the scientific context of the 1620s. The work of Galileo and Stevin was changing ideas on movement, while experimental protocols, which ushered in the 'scientific revolution'[32] during the following decades, were being developed in relation to the question of vacuum. If one relied solely on the published output of Jean François – the same would be true of Pierre Bourdin's output thirty years later – one would fail to grasp adequacy or irrelevance, the latency periods that separated debates within the scientific community from classroom discussions, the rhythms and the progress of the motifs of the 'new science.' It seems to me, therefore, that the debate on the scientific modernity of the Society of Jesus should be completely reassessed through the lens of manuscript lecture notes and *in situ*. Thus the methodological slant I propose would consist in restating the question of scale as well as in refocusing on practice, as evidenced in manuscripts.

Manuscript lecture notes raise an issue I have not yet addressed, that of their purpose. Although this issue has often been touched upon by scholars reflecting on the dissemination of scientific knowledge and references in the Jesuit community, it has never been studied for its own sake. The sample presented here will enable us to re-examine two notions related to this topic.

The first notion interprets the manuscript as an indicator of the professors' specialization. The abundance of this kind of source for the period preceding the creation of chairs has enabled scholars to postulate that the transmission of a manuscript course from one professor to another made up for the frequent turnover of chair holders, a phenomenon that was itself synonymous with a low degree of specialization. That postulation is what I contributed as the result of a prosopographic study of the first chair holders up to 1640. That study makes clear the link that existed in the minds of stable chair holders between teaching and printed output: most of them, indeed, wrote fairly important scientific treatises. Conversely, those who held a chair temporarily, in most cases for less than three years, showed no further interest in the discipline, a fact that leads us to surmise that they were without competence in the field. For them, the lecture dictated by a previous professor was probably a prop enabling them to carry out a short-term mission. Although this hypothesis cannot be confirmed, one could interpret manuscript lecture notes as indicators of professionalization and take them into account in the analysis of the 'personnel management' implemented by the Society in its teaching activity. This 'management' articulated several problems, which were each of a different kind and which fostered internal tensions between the universality of the Jesuits' apostolate (as expressed in the bull of foundation and the *Constitutions*) and the need for specialization (which concerned not just mathematics), between external demands and internal aspirations, between means and needs. Because being a Jesuit meant going anywhere in the world in response to any type of external need, there is no evidence in the Society of a choice being made to train specialists for a discipline (especially the scientific disciplines). The Society's goals were distinct from those of a scientific institution, and consequently the two institutions cannot be compared, though historiography is sometimes tempted to make the comparison.

The second notion approaches manuscript course notes as material relevant to a reflection upon doctrinal unity.[33] But it is difficult to allow that manuscript course notes might have been used as a means of controlling teaching activities. Such a hypothesis is highly improbable, since very few of these documents can be found in Rome, either in the archive of the Society (AHSI) or in that of the Collegio Romano (APUG), in which college resided the censors of the College of Revisers-General.

But it is quite likely that manuscripts were circulated from one college to another, less for censorship reasons than for the technical purpose of sharing information. In this connection, the third manuscript I have referred to raises an issue that so far has barely been highlighted, namely, the fact that dissemination of manuscripts went on while printed books were already in existence and being circulated. Pierre Bourdin's work was varied and long established, in that it spanned the years 1639–61.[34] The topic of fortification is not addressed in his work on general mathematics, as is revealed by L'introduction à la mathématique of 1643. Yet a manuscript dating to 1636–9 – the manuscript of his courses at the Clermont college[35] – gives evidence of his long-standing interest in this subject. In 1636 the course opened with a series of geometry lessons,[36] including a brief excursus on mechanics:[37] all the lectures bore a direct relation to the military art of fortification. The same is true of the arithmetic lectures that followed: 'Arithmeticus militaris Tractatus'[38] and 'Tractatus Armentarium sive Machinatrix Militaris hellicas Machinas ...'. Last is a more classic component: astronomy and cosmography[39] as well as complementary mixed disciplines such as hydraulics, gnomonics, and optics.[40] In 1637, the mathematics course dealt with geometry: it relied on a series of figures, printed on separate sheets and inserted between the student's notes. A second series of lecture notes was then added: 'Geometria militaris. Primus nomenclator militaris.'[41] The following year the course focused on optics, as is shown by the manuscript.[42] Thanks to this document, we can construct the link between teaching and written output, even though the chronological discrepancy between those activities should not be overlooked.

Still, how did it come about that the 1654 manuscript, which followed its author's death by a year, was found in the province of Toulouse? Could it be that this was the early version of the book published by the printer Benard the following year, in 1655, namely, *Le dessein ou la perspective militaire. Piece tres-facile et tres-necessaire à tous ceux qui desirent de pratiquer l'Art de fortifier. Par le feu P. Pierre Bourdin de la Compagnie de Iesus?*[43] A comparison of the two texts deflates this hypothesis. But another possibility is that Bourdin's text was being circulated in the colleges in an abridged version, while an early version of the book that would be printed was in existence in Paris. From the documents we have, it is difficult to decide which is the correct hypothesis; most likely the printer's papers would be of help here.

Something else calls for attention: in 1654, there was available a book by a Jesuit on the same subject, the *Traite des fortifications ou Architecture militaire. Tiree des places les plus estimées de ce temps, pour leurs fortifications. Divisé en deux parties. La premiere vous met en main les Plans, Coupes et Elevations des quantités de Places fort estimées, & tenües pour tres-bien fortifiées: La Seconde vous fournit des pratiques faciles pour en faire de semblables.*[44] The book was published in Paris by Jean Hénault in 1648, in duodecimo, consisting of 190 pages; it was written by Georges Fournier.[45] Like Bourdin's work, it conspicuously addressed a large readership of aristocrats training to be soldiers. The readership was identified explicitly in the opening dedication to Louis XIII of Fournier's previous work, *Hydrographie* (1643), in which military topics were featured.

The book on fortifications returned to these topics in a most exemplary way. In addition to the explanatory title, the lengthy preface, 'containing many facts useful to all soldiering people,' identified the readers to whom the book was addressed. Those aristocrats were indeed those attending the classes of the mathematics professor.

Pierre Bourdin's two posthumous books, published in 1655, less than ten years after Georges Fournier's book, seem far less ambitious in their handling of the same topic. The two books – *L'architecture militaire, ou l'art de fortifier les places régulières et irrégulières. Expliqué, pratiqué et démontré d'une façon facile & agreable. Avec un Abregé de la pratique de la Géometrie militaire*[46] and *Le dessein ou la perspective militaire. Piece tres-facile et tres-necessaire à tous ceux qui desirent de pratiquer l'Art de fortifier* – could be described as works of popularization for the use of the aristocracy. The publisher's foreword explains as follows:

To the reader.
Here is a short work that is an excellent summary of the great and lengthy treatises by several good authors. My praises will fall short of doing it justice: only experience can convince you of how much you will value it. To give you some satisfaction and pay tribute to its author's memory, I will venture to say this much: it is the work of a fine mind, who,

being capable of delving into the subtlest parts of mathematics, deemed his time would be put to good use if he were to employ it to compose this piece, since he clearly foresaw that, in penning in the space of a few pages all the greatest lessons contained in the large volumes of other authors, and in offering them using a very easy method, this piece would be most useful to many a nobleman now desiring to join the army and serve the king and the glory of France. For this author's dearest wish was to serve, after God's interests, his prince and his country with all his might. Accept the fruit of his labour, and pray that God may reward him in heaven and lead us there hereafter. For after all is said and done, a man's paramount task is his redemption.

This comparison between Bourdin's and Fournier's books triggers two sets of comments. The first has to do with the printing of the books, which may not have been the work of the authors but an initiative of the printers undertaken in order to meet a larger market than that of the colleges' students: that hypothesis would explain why Bourdin's texts were published in addition to those by Fournier. Second, the fact that a manuscript of Bourdin's text turned up in Toulouse seems to confirm the idea that the rise of printing did not end the circulation of the manuscript copy, which might have been used as a prop by a non-specialist professor teaching the subjects concerned. For scholars dealing with the history of cultural practices, here is an example that both qualifies the thesis of a 'print revolution' and paves the way for finer interrogations of the interactions of manuscripts and books, of authors, institutions, and publishers.[47]

My object in addressing the issue of manuscript courses in mathematics has been to emphasize a kind of course-content history – particularly scientific course content – that would attend as much to practices as to normative discourses. I am aware that I have tackled only part of this topic, and have left aside the more strictly pedagogical dimension. By way of conclusion, I would like to point to three research leads that might enable us to articulate, *in situ*, the history of ideas with the histories of teaching and of pedagogy – to which the Jesuits made such a decisive contribution[48] – and help us, furthermore, to engage fresh work for a history of practices and practical knowledge.

The first project would deal with exercises, and relates to a question that has seldom been worked on, namely, objects and modalities of assessment in addition to examinations. Manuscripts, more than books and thesis prints, might be of evidential value.

The second project, which ties in with the previous one, would lead us to pay close attention to the drawings and figures that accompany a manuscript text. Such attention would help us appraise the requirements of 'mixed mathematics,' which demanded more representations than pure mathematics; it would also raise the more concrete issue of course organization. How did the professor give his lectures? Were the classrooms equipped with blackboards? Did the teacher draw diagrams of the machines or devices he was explaining on the blackboard? Or did he make copies of these machines or devices from existing drawings in printed books (one should bear in mind the machine theatres, the success of which was growing rapidly during this period)? Did he teach in a room equipped with machines? Or did he ask his students to bring instruments to class?

Such questions take us to the third and final project I wish to point to, namely, the links between course and instruments. François de Dainville emphasized the rise of physics cabinets in the colleges over the course of the seventeenth century;[49] more recent research on the development of experimental science has helped historians identify a process of experiment dissemination that often took place in the Jesuit colleges outside class hours and beyond the student community. What was the influence of these experimental practices on course organization? Even if books bear traces of an 'experimental contamination,' as is evidenced by many book titles, it remains that work in the classrooms cannot be accessed through this type of source, and that only manuscripts can provide an account of it, however partially.

NOTES

1 See my summary of topics in the history of sciences and the history of education in *Rev. syn.* 120, pp. 440–55, and Antonella Romano, 'Les jésuites dans la culture scientifique française de l'époque moderne,' in *Gesuiti e università in Europa (secoli XVI–XVII)*, ed. G.P. Brizzi and R. Greci (Bologna, 2002), pp. 335–52. A more thorough analysis can be found in Romano, 'I gesuiti e le scienze in età moderna: Fonti, storia, storiografia,' in *Anatomia di un corpo religioso. L'identità dei gesuiti in età moderna*, special issue of *Annali di storia dell'esegesi* 19:2 (2003): 437–49.

2 As is shown by Giard *Jés. Ren.*; by the annotated translation of the *Ratio, Ratio studiorum. Plan raisonné et institution des études dans la Compagnie de Jésus*, ed. Dominique Julia at al. (Paris, 1997); and by the contributions in the recent volume *Tradition jésuite et pratique pédagogique. Histoire et actualité*, ed. Étienne Ganty et al. (Namur and Brussels, 2002).

3 *Gesuiti e università*, ed. Brizzi and Greci (n1 above).

4 See, among others, Maurizio Sangalli, *Università, accademie, gesuiti. Cultura e religione a Padova tra Cinque e Seicento* (Padua, 2001); and *Alle origini dell'Università dell'Aquila. Cultura, università, collegi gesuitici all'inizio dell'età moderna in Italia meridionale*, ed. Filippo Iappelli et al. (Rome, 2000). The discussion of Jesuits as 'savants' is opened by Mordechai Feingold in Fein. *Jes. Sci.*, pp. 1–45.

5 I have especially in mind the history of missions, which has often been written using the sole testimony of the *Litterae annuae* or official decrees, in the way the *Monumenta* have written the history of many provinces. The point of view provided by other sources (*indipetae, litterae soli, memoriales* addressed to the general) is developed in *Histoire culturelle et histoire sociale. Les missions ibériques*, ed. Pierre-Antoine Fabre et al. (forthcoming); and in *Mission et diffusion des sciences européennes en Amérique et en Asie: Le cas jésuite (XVIe–XVIIIe s.)*, ed. Romano, *Archives internationales d'histoire des sciences* 148 (2002).

6 This hypothesis has been developed in Romano, 'Pratiques d'enseignement et orthodoxie intellectuelle en milieu jésuite (seconde moitié du XVIe siècle),' in *Orthodoxie, christianisme, histoire*, ed. S. Elm et al. (Rome, 2000), pp. 241–60.

7 Here we could develop a detailed analysis of Jesuit sources; their richness, quantitative importance, and variety partly account for the popularity of the Society as a subject of general history. Especially in the history of science, the correspondences are fundamental. The major example is that of Kircher's correspondence, but his model, apart from Ignatius, was Clavius, whose correspondence was first edited by Ugo Baldini and Pier Daniele Napolitani. For Kircher, see Michael John Gorman's Kircher website, URL: http://www.stanford.edu/group/STS/gorman/nuovepaginekircher/.

8 See, more particularly, Annie Bruter, *L'histoire enseignée au Grand Siècle. Naissance d'une pédagogie* (Paris, 1997).

9 It is important to stress the originality of this type of source: throughout the modern period, the Society had no monopoly on its production. French archives, for instance, abound in this type of document. Readers will find a tentative inventory in the repertory of French colleges established by Marie Madeleine Compère and Dominique Julia, *Les collèges français, XVIe–XVIIIe siècle*, vol. 1, *La France du midi* (Paris, 1984); vol. 2, *La France du Nord et de l'Ouest* (Paris, 1988); vol. 3, Paris (Paris, 2002). But the quantitative importance of these sources enables us to appraise the importance of their use and circulation especially within the order. In the case of philosophy, the hypothesis of an external circulation of the manuscript courses is provided by William A. Wallace, especially in *Galileo and His Sources: The Heritage of the Collegio Romano in Galileo's Science* (Princeton, 1984).

10 The monograph by Gustave Dupont-Ferrier, *La vie quotidienne d'un collège parisien pendant plus de 350 ans. Du Collège de Clermont au Lycée Louis le Grand (1563–1920)*, 3 vols (Paris, 1921–5), does not attempt the history of the scientific teaching. Some indications of that history can be found in François de Dainville, *L'éducation des jésuites (XVIe–XVIIIe siècles)* (Paris, 1978). The investigations of LaurenceW. Brockliss remain indispensable; see, among other works, Brockliss, *French Higher Education in the Seventeenth and Eighteenth Centuries: A Cultural History* (Oxford, 1987). I have set forth the chronological frames of the development of mathematics courses in Rom. *Contre-réf.*, pp. 194–206, 287–352, 365–92.

Some of the works of the principal who held the chair, Pierre Bourdin, have been studied by Roger Ariew, 'Pierre Bourdin and the Seventeenth Objection,' in *Descartes and His Contemporaries: Meditations, Objections, and Replies*, ed. Ariew et al. (Chicago, 1995), pp. 208–25. Finally, interesting indications can be found in Didier Kahn, 'Entre atomisme, alchimie et théologie: La réception des thèses d'Antoine de Villon et Etienne de Clave contre Aristote, Paracelse et les "cabalistes" (24–25 août 1624),' *Annals of Science* 58 (2001): 241–86.

11 BNP Lat. 11243. The existence of another manuscript by Jacques Valentin (ms 31), in the municipal library of Loches, confirms that the following year, 1568, he was still teaching mathematics – arithmetic, music, geometry, optics, a treatise on the sphere. I have not yet been able to consult it, but hope to compare it with the Parisian copy soon. One reason for consulting this second manuscript is that it might reveal an interest in optics, although the general conception of mathematics that inspired Valentin was that of the medieval quadrivium.

12 On these catalogues, whether annual or triannual, see my critical presentation in Rom. *Contre-réf.*, pp. 10–27, and the supporting bibliography.

13 BNP Lat. 14081.

14 No study is available of Jean François (1582–1668), but sorting through the catalogues of the French province enables us to reconstruct the itinerary of a Jesuit representative of the first French generation of mathematics professors; see Rom. *Contre-réf.*, s.v. François.

15 A specific trait of the Parisian establishment, in a chronology marked in France by the first ban of the Society between 1593 and 1603, lies in the extension there of this ban on Jesuit teaching, which was allowed to resume only in 1618, after a twenty-five-year period. For a general reflection on this topic, see Dominique Julia, 'Jésuites et universités: Les logiques d'une politique d'après les textes normatifs,' in *Gesuiti e università*, ed. Brizzi and Greci, pp. 13–36. On mathematics chairs, see Rom. *Contre-réf.*, pp. 311–33, 542–3.

16 Mathematics theses defended in Paris in 1622, printed poster, 70 cm × 40 cm, BNP, Département des imprimés, V 8665. They were defended as part of the events organized in celebration of the canonization of Ignatius and Francis Xavier. They developed propositions in general mathematics, arithmetic, geometry, mechanics, music, astronomy, optics, and gnomonics.

17 It is in the Jesuit archive in Vanves, ref. H 223 94.

18 'The Art of Fortifying Regular and Irregular Fortress Towns, Explained, Practised, and Demonstrated in a Pleasant and Accessible Way for the Use of the French Aristocracy, by the Reverend Father Bourdin of the Society of Jesus.'

19 It was kept there until it was taken back to Vanves, in the 1990s, during the reorganization of the Society's archives in France.

20 On Pierre Bourdin (1595–1653), who belonged to the same generation as Jean

François, see the work by Ariew, n10 above; and Rom. *Contre-réf.*, s.v. Bourdin and pp. 563–4.

21 ARSI Franc. 37 fol. 121r, 'Fundatio Parisii, Regula generalis quibus diebus docendum sint (1567).'

22 Quoted by Ladislau Lukacs in *M. Paed.* 3:161–3.

23 On mathematics in these two establishments, see Bald. *Leg.*; Ugo Baldini, *Saggi sulla cultura della Compagnia di Gesù (secoli XVI–XVIII)* (Padua, 2000); and Rosario Moscheo, *I gesuiti e le matematiche nel secolo XVI. Mauroilico, Clavio e l'esperienza siciliana* (Messina, 1998).

24 BNP Lat. 11243 fol. 1r–v.

25 See 'The Availability of Ancient Works,' in *The Cambridge History of Renaissance Philosophy*, ed. C.B. Schmitt et al. (Cambridge, 1988), p. 784.

26 *The Cambridge History*, ed. Schmitt et al., p. 778. For a general commentary on these medieval references, see Edward Grant, *La physique au moyen âge* (Paris, 1995), pp. 11ff.

27 For a global analysis of the state of mathematics courses in the Middle Ages, see John North, 'The Quadrivium,' in *A History of the University in Europe: Universities in the Middle Ages*, ed. Hilde de Ridder-Simoens (Cambridge, 1992), pp. 337–59.

28 See Bald. *Leg*; Moscheo, *I gesuiti e le matematiche*; Rom. *Contre-réf.*; Romano Gatto, *Tra scienza e immaginazione. Le matematiche presso il collegio gesuitico napoletano (1552–1670 ca.)* (Florence, 1994); and Peter Dear, *Discipline and Experience: The Mathematical Way of the Scientific Revolution* (Chicago, 1995).

29 As Dear's research in *Discipline and Experience* has shown.

30 On the general topic of Society's mathematics library, see Steven J. Harris, 'Les chaires de mathématiques,' in Giard *Jés. Ren.*, pp. 239–61. For an analysis of this French library, see Rom. *Contre-réf.*, pp. 415–74. On mathematics books in France in the seventeenth century, see Aude Le Dividich, 'L'enseignement des mathématiques en France (1600–1670),' dissertation, Ecole Nationale des Chartes, 1996. On the rise of mixed mathematics in this production, see Romano, 'Les jésuites dans la culture scientifique française.'

31 On this issue, see Rom. *Contre-réf.*, pp. 415–34.

32 Of the extensive scholarship on this issue, see, regarding Jesuits, Dear, *Discipline and Experience*; Michael John Gorman, 'The Scientific Counter-Revolution: Mathematics, Natural Philosophy, and Experimentalism in Jesuit Culture, 1580–c. 1670,' dissertation, European Academic Institute, 1999; Gorman, 'Jesuit Explorations of the Torricellian Space: Cap-Bladders and Sulphurous Fumes,' *MEFRIM* 106 (1994): 7–32; and Gorman, 'L'académie invisible de Francesco Lana Terzi. Les jésuites, l'expérimentation et la sociabilité scientifique au XVIIe siècle,' in *Académies et sociétés savantes en Europe, 1650–1800* (Paris, 2000), pp. 409–32.

On the Collegio Romano and France, see Romano, 'Les jésuites dans la culture scientifique romaine au temps de Borromini,' in *Francesco Borromini* (Milan, 2000), pp. 237–43; and Romano, 'Enseignement des mathématiques et de la philosophie naturelle au collège jésuite de Rouen dans les années 1640,' in *Les Pascal à Rouen 1640–1648*, ed. J.P. Clérs (Rouen, 2001), pp. 217–35.

33 This subject has been treated mostly in Bald. *Leg.*; see also Romano, 'Pratiques d'enseignement et orthodoxie intellectuelle.'

34 His principal works are *Prima geometriae elementa. Ad usum academiae mathematicae Collegiis Claromontani Societatis Iesu* (Paris, 1639); *L'introduction à la mathématique. Contenant les connoissances, & pratiques necessaires à ceux qui commencent d'apprendre les Mathematiques. Le tout tiré des Elements d'Euclide rengez et demontrez d'une façon plus briefve, & plus facile que l'ordinaire* (Paris, 1643); *Sol flamma, sive tractatus de sole, ut flamma est, eiusque pabulo. Sol exurens montes, & radios igneos exsufflans. Aphorismi analogici parvi mundi ad magnum magni ad parvum* (Paris, 1646); *L'architecture militaire, ou l'art de fortifier les places régulières et irrégulières. Expliqué, pratiqué et démontré d'une façon facile & agreable. Avec un Abregé de la pratique de la Géometrie militaire* (Paris, 1655); *Le dessein ou la perspective militaire. Piece tres-facile et tres-necessaire à tous ceux qui desirent de pratiquer l'Art de fortifier. Par le feu P. Pierre Bourdin de la Compagnie de Iesus* (Paris, 1655); and *Le cours de mathématiques contenant en cent figures une idée générale de toutes les parties de cette science, l'usage de ses instruments, diverses manières de prendre les distances, l'art d'arpenter, divers moyens de lever et tracer un plan, la réduction des figures par les triangles de rapport, la trigono-métrie, les fortifications régulières et irrégulières, leur dehors, profil, évolution et sciagraphie. Contenant de plus un traité de l'usage du globe terrestre et un autre de l'optique, dioptrique et catoptrique, dédié à la noblesse* (3rd ed., Paris, 1661).

35 See BNP Lat. 17861 and 17862. The first volume consists of 792 folios, of which only a third directly relates to my work. The notes were taken by Paul Le Mercier, from fol. 353r. The second volume was also Paul Le Mercier's own copy of the mathematics course, which he had attended the previous year, in 1636–7. Consisting of 989 folios, this manuscript deals only with mathematics.

36 BNP Lat. 17862 fols 2r–91v; fols 108–233.

37 Ibid., fols 92r–107v, 'Tractatus de ponderibus et machinis, sive de Mechanica.'

38 Ibid., fols 262r–425v.

39 Ibid., fols 486r–592v.

40 Ibid., fols 594r–989v. The chronological indications on the manuscript do not allow us to ascertain the exact length of the lectures, and it is difficult to know whether they represent one or two years of teaching. One should probably regard the two manuscripts as corresponding to an order of presentation different from that of the lectures.

41 BNP Lat. 17861 fols 386r–517v.

42 Ibid., fols 534r–561v.

43 'Drawing or Military Perspective. A Most Easy and Useful Work Intended for All Those Wishing to Practise the Art of Fortification. By the Late Father Pierre Bourdin of the Society of Jesus.'

44 'A Treatise on Fortifications or Military Architecture. Drawn from the Fortress Towns Most Esteemed in This Time for Their Fortifications. Divided into Two Parts. The First Part Gives the Reader Maps, Cross Sections, and Elevations of a Great Many Towns Highly Esteemed and Deemed to Be Well Fortified: The Second Part Provides Easy Practices for Building Similar Fortresses.'

45 Fournier (1595–1652) belonged to Pierre Bourdin's generation. He taught mathematics at La Flèche and left a mathematical production similar to Bourdin's: *Euclidis sex primi Elementorum Geometricorum libri, in commodiorem formam contracti et demonstrati* (Paris, 1643); *Hydrographie contenant la theorie et la practique de toutes les parties de la navigation* (Paris, 1643); the work on fortifications discussed in the text (1648); *Asiae nova descriptio, in qua praeter provinciarum situs, et populorum mores, mira deteguntur, et hactenus inedita. Opus recens exit in lucem* (Paris, 1656); and *Geographica orbis notitia. Per litora maris & ripas fluviorum* (Paris, 1667).

46 'Military Architecture, or the Art of Fortifying Regular and Irregular Fortress Towns. Explained, Practised, and Demonstrated in a Pleasant and Accessible Way. Including a Summary of the Technique of Military Geometry.'

47 This issue still needs research, but Stephane Van Damme's work has already shed new light on it in presenting the case of Lyon. See Van Damme, 'Savoirs, culture écrite et sociabilité urbaine. L'action des enseignants jésuites du Collège de la Trinité de Lyon (1630–1730),' dissertation, University of Paris I, 2000, to be published as *Le temple de la sagesse* (Paris, 2005).

48 See the indispensable study by G. Codina-Mir, *Aux sources de la pédagogie des jésuites. Le 'modus Parisiensis'* (Rome, 1968).

49 See n10 above.

17 / Entering Dangerous Ground: Jesuits Teaching Astrology and Chiromancy in Lisbon

HENRIQUE LEITÃO

As any teacher knows, lecturing is always done under the constraint of time limits. The choice of what to teach is also implicitly a choice of what to omit, because the time available (one hour, one semester) is never sufficient to cover everything. In this sense, lecturing is very different from writing a book. Authors face other constraints, but these are not as inexorable as the limits imposed by time. Thus lecturing is always an exercise in the definition of what is more and what is less important. Lecture notes are statements on the hierarchy of knowledge; that is one reason why they are so important to historians.

My objective is to discuss a series of lecture notes confirming the teaching of astrology and chiromancy (palmistry) in the mathematics classes at the Jesuit college of Santo Antão in Lisbon, in the seventeenth and eighteenth centuries.[1] I believe their existence is surprising enough to merit some inspection. It is certainly not equivalent to the well-known fact that some Jesuits *wrote* about those subjects.

An important caveat is necessary at the outset. The mathematics teaching of the Jesuits in Lisbon was, in a sense, rather normal. That is, the vast majority of subjects taught were geometry, astronomy, cosmography, geography, and so on. To be more precise, there are peculiarities in the mathematics curriculum in Lisbon as compared with that in other Jesuit colleges in Europe at the same period, but these peculiarities exist within a 'canonical' set of disciplines. The presence of 'non-standard' subjects such as astrology and chiromancy was something of an exception and does not in any way reflect the usual teaching of the majority of the professors of mathematics.

Having said this, I must also specify in what sense it was an exception. Astrology and chiromancy were taught by only a few of the many teachers of the Santo Antão college, but certainly by more than one. Lecture notes on astrology, from four different teachers, are extant, dating from the early to mid-seventeenth century. Furthermore, the lecture notes that have survived seem to indicate that the astrology taught was part of the mathematics curriculum. For example, while addressing the more technical parts of astrology, teachers sometimes referred to astronomical or mathematical matters they had previously taught.[2] All this is anomalous, for, as far as I know, in no other province of the Society were astrology and chiromancy taught in what appear to have been public classes. Chiromancy was taught in Lisbon by at least two different teachers, in the early eighteenth century.[3]

Under the name astrology there can always be found a highly complex set of ideas and techniques, supported by an equally broad and complex set of beliefs and philosophical notions. For our purposes it is sufficient to keep in mind that two very important subdivisions were natural astrology and judiciary (or judicial) astrology. These two types of astrology are radically different in a fundamental point. Although both natural and judicial astrology are based on the notion that heavenly bodies affect events on the earth, natural astrology limits this influence to natural effects – in nature or humankind – and thus essentially allows the freedom of human acts (presumed independent of natural causes). Judicial astrology, however, claims to predict the course of events that are the result of human actions and choices, and hence, to a greater or lesser extent, implicitly assumes that heavenly bodies determine the outcome of one's actions and life; the notion of personal freedom is thereby undermined. This very schematic description is sufficient to enable us to understand why in Catholic culture these two types of astrology were, in general, evaluated in very different terms. Whereas natural astrology was usually considered licit, judiciary astrology was not.[4]

Judicial astrology and, in a more general sense, all 'divinatory arts' have a long history of formal suppression in Catholic culture. In the sixteenth century they had been explicitly condemned in several documents issued at the highest level of the church's magisterium. The Index of Pope Paul IV, published in 1559, banned many books on different divinatory arts including chiromancy, and also books related to judicial astrology. These prohibitions were further confirmed in the Indexes published in the following decades. In the documents of the Council of Trent, among the rules concerning prohibited books, one reads: 'All books and writings dealing with geomancy, hydromancy, aeromancy, pyromancy, oneiromancy, chiromancy, necromancy, or with sortilege, mixing of poisons, augury, auspices, sorcery, magic arts, are absolutely repudiated. The bishops shall diligently see to it that books, treatises, catalogues determining destiny by astrology, which in the matter of future events, consequences, or fortuitous occurrences, or of actions that depend on the human will, attempt to affirm something as certain to take place, are not read or possessed.'[5] Of much more significance than these prohibitions was the famous bull *Coeli et terrae* of Pope Sixtus V, issued on 5 January 1586, condemning astrology. It was followed by the condemnations, in even stricter terms, in the bull of Pope Urban VIII *Inscrutabilis judiciorum Dei*, of 31 March 1631.

Following these papal condemnations, several members of the Society of Jesus wrote important anti-astrological and anti-divinatory books. Among the various Jesuit works against these practices the two most famous and influential were the *Adversus fallaces et superstitiosas artes* (1591) by Benito Pereira, and the *In astrologos coniectores libri quinque* (1615) by Alessandro de Angelis. It is known that some Jesuits seem to have been interested in astrology, but the practice of it received a severe blow with Sixtus V's condemnation, which led to a general refusal within the Society to allow its members to engage in such activity. By and large, after 1586 the Society expelled all forms of astrological teaching from its classes, and, at most, astrology was treated marginally in private courses.

This atmosphere of condemnation of astrological practice was characteristic of the situation throughtout Christendom, and there is no indication that things were very different in Portugal.[6] In fact, to the books and documents previously mentioned condemning astrology one might add the important *Contra os juízos dos astrólogos* (Against the Judgments of Astrologers), published in Lisbon in 1523, by Friar António de Beja, a work responding to the controversy surrounding the prediction of a universal deluge in 1524. The *Contra os juízos dos astrólogos* is deeply rooted in the famous *Disputationes adversus astrologiam divinatricem* of Pico de la Mirandola, and in Agostino Nifo's *De falsa diluuii prognosticatione*. It was widely distributed in Portugal all through the sixteenth century.[7]

Of course, the question of astrology and, to a lesser extent, that of chiromancy is extremely complex, for it is well known that even when the prohibition was stated in the most explicit terms, compliance was not universal in everyday life.[8] Nevertheless, in view of the explicit and harsh condemnations of judicial astrology and chiromancy, it is striking that Jesuits in Lisbon taught these subjects in what seem to have been public classes. Two questions therefore need to be considered. The first has to do with the contents of the lessons: How were these subjects taught? What, exactly, was being taught? The second is related to the motive: Why did Jesuits teach such subjects, against papal determinations? And also, Why in Lisbon?

The college of Santo Antão was the first college founded by the Jesuits in Portugal. Originally established in a house the Jesuits had had in Lisbon since 1542, it held its first classes in 1553. It was to attain a deserved reputation as a leading cultural institution in Portugal. A course on mathematical sciences –

known as the *aula da esfera*,[9] 'class on the sphere' – started around 1590 and continued regularly until 1759. A considerable number of lecture notes from these mathematics classes have been preserved, spanning a period from the end of the sixteenth to the mid-eighteenth century.[10] It is therefore possible to ascertain with some precision the nature of the courses given there. Notably, lectures in the *aula da esfera* placed considerable emphasis on matters related to cosmography, geography, and nautical science. They included topics not usually taught in the mathematics courses of the Society (such as navigation techniques) and differed somewhat from the traditional mathematics courses in other provinces. The fact that these classes were held in Portuguese – all the surviving lecture notes are in Portuguese – is also anomalous in the teaching of mathematics. It is a clear indication that non-Jesuits with poor educational levels – not necessarily from low social strata – were attending the classes.

Teaching Astrology

Astrology was taught in Santo Antão by the mathematics professors João Delgado (who taught mathematics in 1590–3, 1595–9, and 1605–8); Francisco da Costa (who taught in 1603–5, and sometimes replaced Delgado in previous years); Simon Fallon (who taught in Lisbon in 1638–41, and had previously taught mathematics at the Coimbra college); and Luís Gonzaga (who taught mathematics in 1701–5).[11] In the lecture notes also of several other professors passing references to astrology can be found.

I will follow the arguments set forth by one of the teachers of mathematics.[12] The notes of the other teachers' lessons are not much different; indeed they are identical in the most important parts – possibly the consequence of a sort of tradition in the teaching of these subjects. I will concentrate solely on the justification for and the initial remarks about astrology and its status that can be found in all the sets of lecture notes, and omit consideration of the technical part of the lectures.

The teacher gave the title 'Judiciary Astrology' to his classes and began his couse of lessons by making brief reference to the importance of astrology (fig. 17.1). His doing so is justified not only because such is the usual practice when starting a new subject but especially because in this particular case, as he says, 'astrology is generally considered of poor value.' This initial statement is interesting. It provides information as to both astrology's reputation (low) and the students' expectations. The teacher goes on to declare that his lectures are directed to those who, with 'sincere mind and catholic curiosity devote themselves to this noble science,' thus immediately revealing that, despite its critics, there is a 'nobility' in these investigations. He then systematically deals with a

17.1. First page of the lecture notes of the course on 'judiciary astrology' taught at the Jesuit college in Lisbon, in 1640, by Simon Fallon. BNL Cod. 4246.

number of 'introductory questions,' the first being astrology's distinctness from the other sciences: 'Judiciary astrology is distinguished from other sciences in that it is a natural science considering the nature and influence of the stars, planets, and other celestial bodies, whereby it teaches to judge and prognosticate the natural effects that depend on them. This is because although Our Lord disposes everything in an orderly manner by himself, with regard to the execution, he governs the lower bodies by means of the superior ones.' This classification of astrology as a natural science is then clarified by its being inserted into the standard Aristotelian division of the sciences: 'From which it follows that astrology is one of the sciences that Aristotle calls mixed sciences, by which is meant that they are partly philosophical and partly mathematical. Philosophical because it considers the celestial bodies as mobile beings. Mathematical because it regulates this movement and considers it certain and determined.' The Jesuit teacher then addresses the difference between astronomy and astrology. This is an important point, because prior to being exposed to these lessons on astrology the students had studied cosmography and astronomy. 'Astronomy is a science that speculatively considers the number, order, and movement of the starry bodies using the certain and evident demonstrations of geometry and arithmetic. Astrology is like a practical science that, from these speculations, declares the effects that the celestial bodies cause.' Thus, one more clarification: astrology is a practical science. The epistemological content of astrology is not questioned, but it is clearly distinguished from the 'certain and evident' mathematical foundation of astronomy. Astrology is therefore defined by its triple characterization as a natural, mixed, and practical science. Moreover, astrology is subordinate to astronomy, because it is from the 'speculations' of astronomy that the effects of the planetary configurations can be established.

Having defined astrology, the author probes somewhat deeper into his previous statements, addressing the important question of 'whether astrology is a science or not.' In typical scholastic fashion he proceeds by stating the reasons against, which he will afterwards refute by showing their inconsistency and error.

Invoking the authority of Pico de la Mirandola, Alessandro de Angelis, and Benito Pereira, the author lists six reasons against astrology's being considered a science:

1 True science is that by which, from the knowledge of causes, effects are deduced. Astrology cannot do that.
2 There is no uniformity in the astrologers' judgments; on the contrary, they hold the most diverse opinions.
3 Gross errors in astrological predictions are well known. No true science can generate such errors.
4 Astrological judgments depend on extremely precise determinations of planetary positions. The degree of precision required appears to be impossible for the human intellect.
5 If, as Ptolemy asserts, all born under a certain conjugation of the sun and moon will become kings, many more kings would exist. By the same reasoning, all twins would have the same fate – which is not observed to be the case.
6 The stars and planets today have the same virtues they had in the state of innocence (i.e., in Paradise, prior to the fall). How, then, can they prognosticate diseases and death?

But after supplying these weighty arguments the teacher declares that astrology is indeed a true and natural science and proceeds to refute the reasons against, one by one.

The (philosophical) theoretical background underlying astrological speculation was well known and was set forth in many treatises of natural philosophy. The teacher frequently refers to the *Cursus Conimbricenses*, where these matters are treated. In the commentary on Aristotle's *De caelo* in this famous *Cursus* (1593),[13] the core of all astrological speculation, that is, the theory of celestial influence, is treated in detail. Celestial bodies, according to the commentary, can affect the sublunar world in three ways: by movement, light, and *influentia*. In the mathematics notes of the classes at the college of Santo Antão this theoretical background is assumed, and teachers spend little time on it, merely directing students to the relevant works.

Having assured himself and his audience that astrology is a true science, the teacher addresses a much more delicate issue: Is astrology licit or not?

Again proceeding in typical scholastic fashion, the teacher starts by listing the reasons for astrology's being considered not licit. The ancient Romans declared it illicit; Holy Scripture in many places condemns it; canon law castigates it; most important, Pope Sixtus V condemned it in the bull *Coeli et terrae*, which condemnation was strengthened by the even stricter bull of Urban VIII; finally, many saints and Doctors of the Church have condemned it. Undeterred by the magnitude, at first sight insurmountable, of these objections, the teacher moves ahead by refuting the criticisms one by one. The lawfulness of astrology is defended not only by Aristotle, Ptolemy, and many other ancient astrologers, but also by many Catholic authors of the present time, such as Luca Gaurico, Giuntini, Miguel de Petrasancta, Cardano, Firmico, Stöfler, and Stadius. Among the ancient Fathers can be found important eulogies of astrology. The list of these is impressive: Eusebius, Origen, Jerome, Albert the Great, Bonaventure, and, above all, Thomas Aquinas. But this contest of authorities seems to leave the question undecided, for the teacher goes on to say that in order to understand the question it is essential to know some of the errors that have been made. 'The first of these errors was that some have extended the jurisdiction of astrology to more than it truly says. Some have termed astrology the opinion of the Stoics, who argue that everything that happens in this world proceeds as a necessary effect of the celestial bodies.' Others have adulterated it by adding superstitions. Thus, the source of many misunderstandings is the action of those who have 'profaned true astrology by mixing it with vain and superstitious arts such as necromancy, geomancy, and so on.' And in this fashion the teacher arrives at the fundamental point: 'When the authors quoted above reprove astrology, it is to be understood that they are referring to vain and superstitious astrology and not to the true and natural science we are about to treat.' With this distinction all previous difficulties are solved. The ancient Romans persecuted the false astronomers, but they held the true ones in high esteem. Civil and canon law condemn the false astrology, not the true one. Holy Scripture, the ancient Fathers and Doctors all refer to the false and superstitious astrology. But none of this was taken in to account by 'the modern calumniators who, without making any distinction, have gravely reprehended astrology.'

What about the papal bulls? the Jesuit teacher asks, quite sensibly. He answers that here too what is being condemned is false and superstitious astrology. According to this Jesuit, 'it is clear that the pope is not condemning all astrology, but merely the *vanam falsamque*,' and this is further confirmed by the fact that in the same document the pope himself says there are many future events that can be known beforehand as natural effects.

This is all very well, but how, asks the Jesuit teacher, do we distinguish the true and sane astrology from the bad and superstitious one? Drawing from the papal text, he explains, 'True astrology is only that which teaches to prognosticate the effects that have either a necessary and natural connection with their causes or at least a very frequent and ordinary connection with such causes.' In practice, true astrology is the ability to predict beforehand 'the calms, tempests, sterilities, and so on' of nature and 'the good or bad dispositions, the few or many diseases, this or that inclination, and so on' of individuals.

Once again, the strictly 'natural' character of astrology is underlined. It is also interesting to note that astrological prognostications of two kinds are accepted: those based on necessary connections, and hence connections that one can know and 'explain'; and those based on at least very frequent connections. It seems to be implied that some astrological knowledge is (as one would put it today) inferred statistically, that is, without a precise understanding of the cause-effect relation.

He concludes this most important section on the lawfulness of astrology by insisting on a fundamental point: 'There is no astrology that can guess human actions because these depend on our free will. Therefore, those who by setting horoscopes affirm that a certain newborn will become a criminal, and the like, are not true astrologers, but false and superstitious ones. And as such they deserve to be severely punished.' The teacher concludes his introductory paragraphs by addressing one final topic, 'the need, nobility, and benefits of astrology.' Referring to the importance of astrology in relation to the other sciences, he says, 'Hippocrates calls the doctor ignorant of astrology a one-eyed doctor. As for nautical science and agriculture, the importance of astrology is evident.' The nobility of astrology is derived from its object – the celestial bodies – and from the great reputation of many astrologers. Commenting on the benefits of astrology, the teacher mentions the rather prosaic, but by no means unimportant, fact that, 'with astrology, Thales of Miletus was able to guess the scarcity of olive oil, and in that way was able to make so much money that he became extremely wealthy.'

It is apparent that, despite the surprising title 'Judiciary Astrology,' the Jesuit teacher in reality is making a case for *natural* astrology. Hesitations can be detected, especially in the section of the course devoted to 'nativities,' that is, the interpretation of horoscopes cast at the time of a person's birth, but there is no doubt that natural astrology is what is being proposed. What is peculiar in the case of the astrology taught in Lisbon is not so much the arguments invoked to distinguish 'good' from 'bad' astrology and in defence of the lawfulness and practice of 'good' (i.e., natural) astrology. Most of these arguments can be found – as the Jesuit teacher repeatedly insists – in literature of good and sound doctrine, including many works with explicitly anti-astrological objectives. The peculiarity of the situation in the Lisbon college lies in the fact that the Jesuits did teach astrology, at the risk of misunderstanding and scandal, and even at the risk of incurring Inquisitorial attention. That is, although no doubt Jesuits in most European colleges would subscribe to the arguments put forward by their Portuguese confreres, it was only in Lisbon (as far as I am aware) that astrology was included in the Jesuits' public classes. This demands an explanation. Why was astrology taught in the Lisbon college? What could motivate teachers to deal with such a delicate subject?

The answer perhaps lies in the specificities of the teaching at this college. As I have noted, the Santo Antão college offered a scientific curriculum with some distinctive features, the most prominent of which was the attention given to matters of practical interest, especially related to navigation. Subjects such as cosmography, geography, nautical science, and so on received a great deal more attention in this college than in other Jesuit colleges around Europe. It is no surprise, therefore, to note that a link with nautical activities is explicitly and repeatedly made during the discussion of astrology. While arguing for the scientific status of astrology, the teacher answers the critique that the astrologer often cannot explain the exact reason why certain planetary configurations will lead to certain effects by saying: 'The same happens in navigation. Pilots are able to predict the approaching storm but they are unable to penetrate totally the secrets of the element water.'

The connection between astrology and the practice of navigation is also made explicit when the teacher explains the importance of astrology in relation to the other sciences. In fact, this application of astrology was traditionally accepted in Christendom, and its usefulness is mentioned in Thomas Aquinas's *De judiciis astrorum*. It was also allowed in the sixteenth century anti-astrological documents. In the document issued by the Council of Trent regarding prohibited books was this statement: 'Permitted, on the other hand, are the opinions and natural observations that have been written in the interest of navigation, agriculture, or the medical art.'[14] Agriculture and medicine were not what the Jesuits had in mind, but the teaching of navigation was indeed one of the objectives of the mathematics classes at the Santo Antão college.

One can speculate that the attention devoted to astrology in Lisbon is related to the fact that astrology was a reservoir of much useful information, of important traditions about the operations of the natural world. Even more, astrology provided a theoretical framework in which to place numerous empirical rules, those, for example, known and used by sailors and farmers; indeed, it gave credibility to those rules. It conferred the respectability of the scientific assertion on knowledge, usually expressed in the form of popular sayings or traditional dictums, that had many important practical applications. It allowed the incorporation of numerous obviously useful rules, the true (or scientific) cause of which was not known at the time. As I have indicated, all this was made explicit by the teacher. Astrology thus enlarged the field of acceptable and useful knowledge beyond what could be mathematically proved or scientifically explained. In a sense, it made it possible for popular knowledge to rise to the level of 'scientific' knowledge, and thus was of the utmost importance for an audience interested especially in useful and practical knowledge.

The inclusion of astrology in the Jesuit courses is probably related to the importance of practical science, especially nautical science, in Portugal at this time. During the sixteenth and seventeenth centuries, several authors called for the transformation of navigation from an art into a science (*ratio*). In 1573, Pedro Nunes, the best-known mathematician in Portugal, published a work the title of which reflected this development: *De arte atque ratione navigandi* (On the Art and Method [that is, science] of Navigation). The transformation of navigation into a science should not, it was felt, be at the expense of having to acquire knowledge of great importance, the truth of which could not be established on a sound 'scientific' basis; that is where astrology came in. The fact that Nunes, an adversary of astrology, was involved in constant polemics and controversies with pilots and sailors seems to confirm a deep aversion on the part of 'practical men' to knowledge of a more theoretical nature.

There is also certainly a connection between the teaching of astrology and the level of the mathematics teaching in Santo Antão. In general, mathematics classes in Lisbon were of lower technical sophistication than those at Jesuit colleges in other European countries. To the poorly educated students attending the mathematics classes, astrology surely offered a much more efficacious and appealing way of presenting the fundamentals of the operations of the heavens than did a discourse in dry mathematical terms. Indeed, an important part of the lessons is devoted to strictly technical (i.e., astronomical) procedures, and inserting these in a course on astrology was possibly a successful pedagogical approach.[15]

This solution was not confined to the Society of Jesus. From the late sixteenth to the eighteenth century, many works published in Portugal reflect an interest in compilations of practical and useful knowledge, frequently in the guise of astrological information. One finds an abundant literature of *repertórios* (or almanacs), 'poor man's encyclopaedias,' with general astronomical explanations, information on tides and lunations, basic data of relevance to navigation and agriculture, simple tables, and so on.[16] These very popular booklets were addressed to a readership with low levels of education, and, to a greater or lesser extent, all of them adopt the language and concepts of astrology. Along with strictly natural knowledge (of the seasons, or weather forecasting, for example) one usually finds astrological content, such as rules on how to cast horoscopes. Sometimes clear excesses in the direction of 'forbidden' astrology are evident, and these hardly ever escaped the scrutiny of the book censors and the Inquisition.

This phenomenon was not confined to the realm of popular or unsophisticated culture. The university was also engaged in the process. Astrology was taught in mathematics classes at the University of Coimbra, which stressed its practical applications, in an approach similar to that adopted at the Jesuit college.[17]

Teaching Chiromancy

A case for astrology can thus be made. But what about the much more disreputable chiromancy, the presence of which in the mathematics courses of the Jesuits in Lisbon can be confirmed by the lecture notes of Luís Gonzaga (who taught mathematics in Lisbon in 1701–5) and Inácio Vieira (who taught in Lisbon in 1710–9)?[18] It is true that, as far as can be ascertained today, only two teachers lectured on chiromancy. This represents much less attention than that given to astrology, but even so it is conspicuous enough to merit the historian's attention.

Not so famed as astrology, but nevertheless one of the most important of the divinatory arts, chiromancy is the practice of telling fortunes from the lines, marks, and patterns of the hands, particularly the palms. Like astrology, chiromancy has a long history traceable to antiquity. In general, it can be considered a branch of physiognomy, a discipline claiming to predict personality traits and future events from an individual's physical aspect.

Condemnation of chiromancy was implicit in all documents that prohibited the practice of 'divinatory arts,' and in some cases, such as in the document issued by the Council of Trent, it was explicitly mentioned; the document declared that the practice should be 'absolutely repudiated.' Surprisingly, at least two Jesuit teachers addressed the subject at length in their lectures.

I will follow the course of chiromancy taught by Inácio Vieira in Lisbon in 1712, lecture notes of which were written down by the student João Barbosa de Araújo, about whom more will be said below.[19] The Jesuit professor of mathematics begins his course in the usual fashion by defining the subject he will address. Chiromancy is 'not a small part and no less certain a part of physiognomy. However, bad use and false applications have made it hateful. We will free chiromancy from this charge, by declaring certain what is proved and false what is false.'

As in the case of astrology, the first observations confirm the bad reputation of chiromancy and immediately establish a dichotomy between 'good' and 'bad' chiromancy. This distinction confirms the teacher's awareness that he is entering controversial ground. He then goes on to explain that there are two types of chiromancy: 'One of them is concerned with the lines of the hand, the asperities, the smoothness, the size, the figure, the proportion of the hand, and from this it investigates what are the probable passions of the soul and inclinations of the subject. This is called physical chiromancy. The other type is that by which to the hills and lines of the hand and fingers one attaches certain planets, in such a way that it is affirmed that knowledge of future events becomes possible … This is called astrological chiromancy.' Although a very different evaluation of these two different types of chiromancy will be made in the end, the lecture notes treat the two types in comparable detail and devote roughly the same space to each.

Then follows a eulogy of the hand, a lengthy praise of the immense importance of the hand, its privileged place in the human body and in all human actions, its power. The hand makes war, and it makes peace; there is nothing of human importance in which the hand is not involved. The hand signifies friendship (shaking hands) and denotes veneration and obedience (kissing the hand of kings and prelates). The hand blesses and is also a symbol of faith. The importance of the hand is acknowledged by Christians and heathens alike.

After extolling the virtues of, the importance of, and the meaning attached to the hand, the Jesuit teacher describes the parts of the hand, with its two faces and its fingers, each of these divided into different parts. The description continues with a naming of the many marks, lines, and hills of the hand. In astrological chiromancy, each of these signs is associated with celestial configurations. Despite the care that has gone into the exposition, the author concludes that this astrological chiromancy is not worthy of much credence: 'It is in reality a mere fiction, to entertain frivolous persons, or to cheat ignorant ones.' But, he continues, there is another sort of chiromancy, called physical chiromancy, which, by considering the physical aspect of all the signs in the hand, attaches to them some tendencies and conditions of the person.

Physical chiromancy is licit. This is proved by several authors and, most specifically, by stating the objective of this type of chiromancy. Physical chiromancy allows one to deduce the temperament of the body and consequently make a probable judgment about the inclinations of the soul. A second argument in favour of the lawfulness of physical chiromancy is based on the fact that chiromancy is part of physiognomy. Although physiognomy refers particularly to the study of the form and appearance of the face of a person, its object is wider and is related to the appearance of all parts of the body. Thus, since physiognomy is licit, that part of physiognomy called physical chiromancy is licit.

What is the justification and the theoretical explanation for the success of physical chiromancy? Is there a theoretical equivalent to the notion of celestial *influentia*, which in astrology provides the fundamental explanation? Using arguments borrowed from the more general science of physiognomy, the teacher explains: 'The basis of this art or science comes from the similitude that man has with other animals, such as can be appreciated in the schemes and figures shown in Giovanni Battista dalla Porta's *Libro de phisionomia humana*, in which he compares the face and forms of man with that of animals and from this extracts information about the temperament, conditions, and natural inclinations of men.' For example, 'men who have very small eyes are full of envy,' because sea-animals that are known to be full of envy also have small eyes; 'persons who have big eyes are stupid, like the stupid big-eyed ox'; and so on. The reasoning behind these inferences is that God Almighty knew what tendencies of character each of his creatures would have, and to each gave the instruments most appropriate to the expression of those tendencies. Other physical characteristics express the differences among the various peoples who inhabit the earth, by means of which they adapt to the type of life they live; moreover, different physical characteristics are associated with the different sexes. The external physical traits of a person, therefore, are correlated with the inner personality and the humours of the person.

Many learned authorities, in particular medical doctors, have accepted these ideas. The scriptures accept them, when, for example, robust men are compared to lions. Civil law also accepts them: according to the Jesuit teacher, the law prescribes that when several suspects of a crime are arrested, the most ugly and deformed of them should be tortured into confessing, for it is probable that the person with the worst looks also has the worst inner disposition. All these different authorities accept these notions, and all agree that physiognomy is licit. Hence, any part of it, such as physical chiromancy, is also licit.

The precise explanation of the correlation between the marks and lines of the hand and the inner disposition of a person is, however, somewhat ambiguous and open to dispute. At this stage the Portuguese Jesuit differs from the opinion of Kaspar Schott. This well-known Jesuit wrote about chiromancy, but expressed some doubts concerning its efficacy. Commenting on the opinions of Schott, the Portuguese Jesuit counters that the principle underlying chiromancy is the same as that underlying physiognomy (accepted by Schott). Accordingly, the specific characteristics of a person's hand provide information about his or her personality.

The Jesuit teacher then strives for greater precision: physiognomy – and hence physical chiromancy – is not infallible; it merely asserts a probability. In the case of the beasts it is much more certain, since these have their actions determined by their physical characteristics. But in the case of man that is not so, because man is free. So great caution must be used when drawing conclusions: 'It is not licit to form a judgment about the final destiny or the actual life of a certain man. One is allowed only to state his propensities and his natural inclinations.' By the same reasoning, 'chiromancy cannot express judgments about supernatural things, because these are granted by God as he pleases, nor about things that are totally extrinsic to man or controlled by the will of other men – violent death, for example … If chiromantic predictions have been right in these cases, it was by mere chance and because God allowed it, and not by any inference drawn from the physical examination of a person.' Chiromancy is therefore presented as having a strictly natural basis, and as being a source of probable knowledge about a person's disposition.

Interestingly, these lecture notes on chiromancy end with two lengthy appendices, entitled 'Arithmetical Chiromancy' and 'Chiromantic Calendar.' They consist of practical rules on the use of the hand and fingers in numerical calculations and as aids to solving many problems related to the calendar. There is nothing illicit in this application of chiromancy, and the teacher is clearly at ease in addressing the topics concerned.

Despite the great care he takes to distinguish 'good' from 'bad' chiromancy, and despite his effort to place chiromancy in the context of the natural or to present it as merely an operational technique, it is impossible for this Jesuit teacher to conceal his sympathy for the subject. The plethora of authors mentioned and the precision of the definitions and arguments create a vivid sense of the discipline's respectability, a sense the teacher clearly wanted to instil in his audience. It is interesting to note that although the teacher in the end declares astrological chiromancy devoid of truth, he devotes quite a substantial section of the course to it. One is left to wondering as to his true sentiments.

This general attitude towards chiromancy is similar to that towards astrology, and is expressed in the writers' tendency to refute 'astrological chiromancy' while approving 'natural chiromancy.' As in the case of natural astrology, chiromancy is presented as a tool for the description of a person's inclinations and tendencies rather than as an instrument of prognostication.[20]

The views of chiromancy taught at the Jesuit college in Lisbon were widely disseminated in Portugal, beyond what the original school context would imply, because a certain student of the college, who attended the lectures, turned out to be one of the most celebrated Portuguese mythographers of the eighteenth century. This was João Barbosa de Araújo (1675–?), the student who took the notes of Vieira's lessons on chiromancy at Santo Antão.

In his own works, Barbosa de Araújo advances arguments and defends a position on chiromantic knowledge with evident similarities to those expressed by his former teacher.

The arguments I have ventured to account for the presence of astrology in the mathematics classes in Lisbon do not apply, or apply only marginally, to the teaching of chiromancy. In fact, only the material contained in the two appendices to the course of lectures has any practical relevance, and, particularly, any relevance to navigation or seafaring techniques. That is perhaps why only two of the mathematics teachers lectured on chiromancy. The former student Barbosa de Araújo offered one very interesting suggestion as to why the Jesuit Vieira dealt with such matters:

Astrological chiromancy – popularly termed *Buena-dicha* or *Buena-ventura* – is considered here as a mere fable and mere game. Its principles are a pure lie – such as in fables – with no probability. This has been demonstrated by many authors with solid arguments, such as the Rev. Father Inácio Vieira in the chiromancy course he delivered at the college of Santo Antão in Western Lisbon in the year 1712. [He gave this course] to provide some rest from the speculative matters he had been teaching, or to attract a larger audience, since that [mathematics] class was poorly attended, having only four students. [21]

So according to Barbosa de Araújo, lecturing on chiromancy was a way of making the mathematics classes more appealing and thus attracting more students – a bold and surprising strategy when one considers the risks involved.

Despite the fact that hesitations and ambiguities can be detected in the courses devoted to astrology and chiromancy, it is evident that the Jesuit teachers presented these subjects as offering an instrument for the investigation of the natural world. They invariably took great pains to distinguish 'good' and licit practices from 'bad' and illicit ones, thereby staying within the boundaries of accepted orthodoxy. Human freedom was never questioned, and a strict determinism was refuted. Even so, it is surprising to find Jesuit teachers entering such dangerous ground.

The teaching of astrology can be accounted for as an attempt to teach facts of practical relevance, but for which a precise 'scientific' explanation could not be provided. It is more difficult to see the teaching of chiromancy in the same light. With the exception of arithmetical and calendrical chiromancy, the subject could hardly have practical applications. Both astrology and chiromancy seem to have been taught in order to stimulate the interest of the students and thus attract larger audiences – an objective that led some Jesuits to the limits of orthodoxy.

The case of astrology and chiromancy in the Jesuit classes in Lisbon prompts a further reflection. An examination of the Prohibitory and Expurgatory Indexes in Portugal in this period clearly shows that a strict control of the literature on these subjects was in force. All printed works with even a remote affinity to any type of 'occultist' or divinatory material were harshly prohibited. It is true that a careful inspection of the Indexes in Portugal shows that the condemnation of astrology was pursued with great care. Many books dealing with the topics in question were not prohibited outright, but subjected to expurgation of those parts revealing some kind of allegiance to the 'false and hollow' sort of astrology.[22] Nevertheless, it is obvious that a measure of risk was associated with the subject. That was the situation with respect to printed materials. But the oral tradition – as these lecture notes suggest – was a different matter. Here there was considerably more freedom. It is perhaps no coincidence that although more than one Jesuit in Portugal taught astrology – very likely in his public courses – none ever published a book on the subject.

NOTES

I thank Ugo Baldini and Steven J. Harris for helpful comments and observations on preliminary versions of this paper.

1   I am not the first to note the curious appearance of astrology in these courses. Luís de Albuquerque, 'A "Aula da Esfera" do Colégio de Santo Antão no século XVII,' *Anais da Academia portuguesa de história* 21 (1972): 335–91, and Ugo Baldini, 'L'insegnamento della matematica nel Collegio di S. Antão a Lisbona, 1590–1640,' in *A Companhia de Jesus e a missionação no Oriente* (Lisbon, 2000), pp. 275–310, have also noted its appearance, but without entering into a detailed analysis of it. L.M. Carolino, 'Aristotelianism, Occult Qualities, and Astrological Belief in Counter-Reformation Portugal,' in *Actas. 1º Congresso Luso-Brasileiro de história da ciência e da técnica* (Evora, 2001), pp. 83–94, addresses the subject, but pursues a completely different analysis from the one I am presenting here. No author that I am aware of has noted the presence of chiromancy.

2 For example, in his course on judicial astrology (c. 1640), BNL AT/L–9, Simon Fallon, while addressing an issue related to setting a chart, observes, 'This can be done according to the rules I gave on the course on the sphere' (fol. 11v). A continuity between the lectures on the sphere and astrology is evident in other passages.

3 All the evidence leads me to assume as very probable that the astrology lecture notes are a record of *public* lessons and not private ones. (See n2 above and also n11 below). However, this evidence, though compelling, does not constitute strict proof. With regard to the chiromancy notes, the testimony of one former student (see text, and n21 below) implies that the classes were public. The fact that the highly disreputable chiromancy was taught in public classes in Lisbon, at least by one teacher, further supports the likelihood that the more 'acceptable' astrology was also taught in public classes. All this seems to have been characteristic only of Portugal, since neither astrology nor chiromancy makes an appearance in Jesuit mathematics courses in other provinces. See, for example, Albert Krayer, *Mathematik im Studienplan der Jesuiten: Die Vorlesungen von Otto Catenius an der Universität Mainz 1610/11* (Stuttgart, 1991); Bald. *Leg.*; Romano Gatto, *Tra scienza e immaginazione. Le matematiche presso il collegio gesuitico napoletano* (1552–1670 ca.) (Florence, 1994); and Rom. *Contre-réf.*

4 Obviously, my description is very schematic. For a detailed analysis, see Ugo Baldini, 'The Roman Inquisition's Condemnation of Astrology: Antecedents, Reasons, and Consequences,' in *Church, Censorship, and Culture in Early Modern Italy*, ed. Gigliola Fragnito (Cambridge, 2001), pp. 79–110.

5 Council of Trent, Session XXV. Ten rules concerning prohibited books drawn up by the fathers chosen by the Council of Trent and approved by Pope Pius.

6 As far as I can see, the belief in and practice of astrology in Portugal show no specific features when compared with those in other European countries. However, a particular historical circumstance needs to be kept in mind. In Portugal, the appearance of the comet of 1577 was soon followed by a series of dramatic events, possibly the most traumatic in all of Portuguese history. In 1578 the Portuguese suffered their worst military disaster, in a battle in North Africa in which thousands perished, including the king and many noblemen of the highest rank. As a direct consequence of this dramatic defeat, Portugal lost its independence; it was united with the crown of Castile in 1580, under Philip II. These events reverberated throughout Europe, and a connection with the comet of 1577 was inevitably drawn. Understandably, to the seventeenth-century Portuguese, celestial signs such as comets came to be seen as harbingers of great affliction, and their 'meaning' gave rise to an enormous amount of speculation and generated an enormous quantity of publications.

7 See José V. Pina Martins, *Frei António de Beja contra a astrologia judiciária* (Lisbon, 1962).

8 The literature on astrology is immense. I have relied for the general background on

Jim Tester, *A History of Western Astrology* (Woodbridge, UK, 1987); Lynn Thorndike, *A History of Magic and Experimental Science*, 8 vols (New York, 1923–58); *Astrology, Science, and Society*, ed. Patrick Curry (Woodbridge, UK, 1987); Theodore Otto Wedel, *The Medieval Attitude toward Astrology, Particularly in England* (New Haven, 1920); *Astrologi hallucinati: Stars and the End of the World in Luther's Time*, ed. P. Zambelli (Berlin, 1986); J.D. North, *Horoscopes and History* (London, 1986); and Keith Thomas, *Religion and the Decline of Magic* (London, 1971).

9 See Albuquerque, 'A "Aula da Esfera" do Colégio de Santo Antão'; and Baldini, 'L'insegnamento della matematica.'

10 See Albuquerque, 'A "Aula da Esfera" do Colégio de Santo Antão,' in which lists of teachers and descriptions of the manuscripts of their lecture notes are provided. See also Baldini, 'L'insegnamento della matematica,' where corrections and additions to these lists are made, and further essential information is provided.

11 The following notes on astrology are extant; dates are given in parentheses. The astrology courses taught by João Delgado survive in three copies: BNL Cods 2130 (1607) and 6353 (undated); and BNM 8931 (undated). The couse taught by Francisco da Costa is BL Egerton 2063 (undated). Of the courses by Simon Fallon, there are four copies from classes at Santo Antão: BNL Cods 4246 (1640), 4331 (c. 1640), 5161 (c. 1640), and A.T.9/L (c. 1640); there are also lecture notes of a course taught elsewhere, presumably at the college in Coimbra: BNL Cod. 2127 (1631). The lecture notes of Luís Gonzaga's course are BA ms 46.VIII.21–3 (undated). The fact that multiple copies have survived – which is quite rare – suggests a large audience. Certain other elements suggest that astrology made up part of the standard public mathematics classes (for example, Fallon's astrology notes of 1631 are contained in a manuscript dealing with other mathematical matters – in fact, the whole manuscript is entitled 'Materias mathematicas'; and Gonzaga's notes on astrology are part of a three-volume set of lecture notes containing other mathematical matters).

12 I use the astrology notes by the Jesuit Simon Fallon, BNL Cod. 4331. All quotations are from fols 1–11v. A brief description of the contents is as follows: Judicial astrology. Introductory questions (fols 1–11v); First treatise: On celestial figures (fols 11v–46r); Second treatise: General principles for forming astrological judgment (fols 46r–65v); Third treatise: Astrological judgment on the times (fols 66r–107v); Fourth treatise: On birth (nativities; fols 107v–121r); Fifth treatise: On directions, profections, and revolutions (fols 121v–131r). The manuscript ends with some explanation of how to use ephemerides (fols 132r–136v). The figure provided in the text is from another copy of Fallon's notes (BNL Cod. 4246). Simon Fallon was born in Ireland, around 1604, and entered the Society in 1619. He completed his studies and lived in Portugal. In addition to teaching within the Society, in 1640 he was named chief engineer of Portugal by King João IV. Fallon died in Lisbon in

1642. For further information on Fallon and his work, see Baldini, 'L'insegnamento della matematica.'

13 *Commentarii coleggii Conimbricensis Societatis Iesu in quatuor libros De coelo Aristotelis Stagiritae* (Lisbon, 1593).

14 Council of Trent, Session XXV (n5 above).

15 All the surviving lecture notes show that a considerable part of the Jesuit courses on astrology was devoted to technical (i.e., astronomical) matters. The issues covered range from simple astronomical notions about planetary motions to more sophisticated subjects, such as the principles of stereographic projection necessary for the division of the houses, and calculations using spherical trigonometry.

16 See Rui Grilo Capelo, *Profetismo e esoterismo. A arte do prognóstico em Portugal* (Coimbra, 1994). The situation in Portugal has interesting parallels with that in England; see Bernard Capp, *Astrology and the Popular Press: English Almanacs, 1500–1800* (London, 1979).

17 André de Avelar (1546– after 16??), a professor of mathematics at the university in the last decade of the sixteenth century, in 1590 published a *Repertorio dos tempos*, which went through many editions and was widely known. Avelar's sympathy towards astrology seems to have exceeded the limits of what was acceptable, and he was persecuted and convicted for practising astrology.

18 The lecture notes on chiromancy by Luís Gonzaga are in Porto, Biblioteca Municipal, ms 769 (undated). Those by Inácio Vieira are in BNL Cods 4324 (1712) and 7782 (1710).

19 I am following the lecture notes on chiromancy by the Jesuit Inácio Vieira of 1712, BNL Cod. 4324.

20 The appearance of chiromancy in lectures at the beginning of the eighteenth century may be related to a resurgence of these studies in Italy in the second half of the seventeenth century. In 1639, Augustinus Mascardus had published in Rome a work on chiromancy and physiognomy. In 1662 the influential *Studio di curiosita* by Nicola Spadoni, which dealt with many aspects of chiromancy, had been published in Venice.

21 BNL Cod. 322 fol. 235v. On Barbosa de Araújo and the cultural relevance of his work, see Maria Helena Prieto, *João Barbosa de Araújo, mitógrafo português dos sécs. XVII–XVIII* (Lisbon, 2001).

22 For example, in one of the most complete and massive Indexes ever published in Portugal, the *Index auctorum damnatae memoriae* (Lisbon, 1624), by Inquisitor-General Fernando Martins Mascarenhas, many books containing astrological notions were ordered to undergo expurgation, not prohibited *in toto*.

18 / Science and Enlightenment in Eighteenth-Century Spain: The Contribution of the Jesuits before and after the Expulsion

VÍCTOR NAVARRO BROTÓNS

Spain, as is only too well known, participated hardly at all in the achievements and advances of European science in the seventeenth century. Owing to a confluence of political, social, economic, and ideological factors, Spain was increasingly distanced from the scientific activity that marked the century elsewhere in Europe. Ideological isolation, initially imposed in order to preserve religious orthodoxy, acted increasingly as a barrier to new philosophical and scientific ideas.[1]

Notwithstanding this marked decline, scientific isolation was never complete; the knowledge emanating from the scientific revolution continued to trickle into a small number of Spanish institutions, encouraged by persons or groups who made singular efforts to assimilate it. In so far as physics and mathematics were concerned, the Jesuits played a major role in this process, for a number of reasons. First, the only institutions that displayed any vitality in scientific studies in the central decades of the seventeenth century, especially in mathematics and in the framework of Jesuit ideology,[2] were some of the colleges established by the Society in Spain, especially the Colegio Imperial in Madrid beginning in 1624, when the Reales Estudios were established there.[3] Second, membership in the Society permitted Spanish professors, or foreign professors stationed in Spain, to maintain contact with European Jesuit scientists and through that contact to keep abreast of European science generally. Finally, Jesuit eclecticism and the cautious but progressive manner in which European Jesuit scientists approached modern science were well suited to the Spanish environment, which was resistant, if not indifferent, to innovations. Thus, Spanish scientists who favoured innovation, even those who were not members of the Society, embraced the Jesuits for their effort to introduce the new science in Spain.

In the last decades of the seventeenth century, those in Spain who wished to break with traditional knowledge and its suppositions adopted a clearly delineated program of systematic assimilation of modern science. At the heart of this program was an awareness, which Spanish scientists made explicit, of the scientific backwardness of the country and Spain's marginal status with respect to modern science. Valencia, Zaragoza, Madrid, Barcelona, Seville, and a few other cities were the stages on which the so-called *novatores* of the turn of the century performed. Naturally, these groups were in a distinct minority and had frequently to confront the opposition of the dominant conservatives. Nevertheless, the *novator* movement (so named by its detractors) was able to consolidate and expand its area of influence, setting the bases for the significant scientific developments of the Enlightenment.

As regards the disciplines of mathematics and physics and their applications, this renewal movement can, however, be considered as the continuation of the work carried out by the Jesuit mathematicians of the Colegio Imperial in Madrid in the central decades of the seventeenth century, along with that of authors such as Vicente Mut, who was in close contact with the Jesuits. The work of other Spanish authors must also be taken into account, such as that of Juan Caramuel de Lobkowitz, who, despite having produced most of his oeuvre outside Spain, kept in close contact with Spanish authors and influenced many of them. Indeed, the Spanish *novatores* saw their predecessors as teachers, directly or indirectly, and considered themselves part of and steeped in a tradition. For example, the origin of the movement of scientific renewal in mathematics and physics, in which Valencia was one of the most outstanding centres, lay in the activity carried out in that city by the Valencian Jesuit José de Zaragoza, who was subsequently a professor of Reales Estudios at the Colegio Imperial in Madrid. Similarly, one of the most widely read texts used as a model by *novatores*, was the *Cursus seu mundus mathematicus* by Claude-François Milliet Dechalles, together with the works of mathematics, 'pure' and 'mixed' or physico-mathematics, by Giambattista Riccioli, Honoré Fabri, Francesco Maria Grimaldi, Athanasius Kircher, Andreas Tacquet, Francesco Lana Terzi, and other Jesuit authors from elsewhere in Europe, which enlarged the scope and subject-matter of the mathematical disciplines, incorporating and spreading new ideas, discoveries, procedures, methods, and instruments.[4]

It was under the initial impulse of this renewal movement that scientific activity experienced considerable development in Spain throughout the eighteenth century, right up to the reign of Ferdinand VII. This scientific development was in part a continuation of the process of renewal begun in the previous century, and in part a consequence of the requirements and objectives of the new Bourbon state and the reformist policies of its leaders. Moreover, the different phases of scientific growth during this period correspond to a general process of diffusion, European in nature, of which Spain constitutes a particular case.[5]

Jesuit scientists participated actively in this new phase of Spanish science from the beginning of the eighteenth century until the Society's expulsion in 1767, although they lost the leadership role they had enjoyed in the previous century.[6] Besides holding the chairs of the Reales Estudios of the Colegio Imperial, along with the associated post of Cosmographer of the Indies, the fathers of the Society imparted scientific instruction in the Seminary of Nobles, founded in Madrid in 1725.[7] In Barcelona, in the College of Nobles, or Cordelles college, operated by the Society, chairs of physics and mathematics were endowed around 1754, one of which was held by the Jesuit Tomás Cerdá, one of the best mathematicians in eighteenth-century Spain.[8] The Jesuit presence was also pronounced at the University of Cervera, created by Philip V after the suppression of the traditional Catalan universities.[9] In this university, several Jesuit professors, including Cerdá, attempted to revivify philosophy by introducing new scientific and philosophical perspectives. In the University of Gandía, directed by the Jesuits from its foundation in 1547, three chairs of medicine were established in 1700, to which were added another in anatomy in 1747 and another in surgery prior to 1767.[10] We also have notices on the introduction of science education in other Spanish Jesuit centres of the period, especially in mathematical subjects and descriptive geography.[11]

In the first decades of the century, the teaching staff of the Reales Estudios of the Colegio Imperial and the Seminary of Nobles included Pedro de Ulloa (1663–1721), José Cassani (1673–1750), Carlos de la Reguera (1679–1742), Pedro Fresneda, and Gaspar Alvarez. Although none of them made outstanding contributions, they published diverse works in mathematics, astronomy, geography, and military arts, generally oriented towards teaching.

Renewal in the content of instruction in the Colegio Imperial and the Seminary of Nobles began in the 1750s with the incorporation of Newton's theories, experimental physics, and infinitesimal calculus. It was owing to the confluence of several factors. First was the impact of the expedition sent by the Paris Académie des Sciences to the Viceroyalty of Peru to measure an arc of the meridian and test the various theories on the shape of the earth. As is well known, two Spaniards, Jorge Juan and Antonio de Ulloa, participated in this expedition.[12] Jorge Juan subsequently became the principal science and technology adviser to the secretary of the navy, the Marquis of Ensenada, who put him in charge of the reform of the navy and sent him to London to collect information on ship construction, hire technicians, and acquire instruments. Upon his return from London, Juan both directed the reorganization of naval construction and served as director, from 1752, of the Academia de Guardias Marinas of Cádiz, where he established an astronomical observatory.

Besides the reorganization of the navy, there was a general effort at mid-century to improve the quality of military instruction. A 'Hall of Mathematics' was founded in Madrid in 1750 in the barracks of the royal guard, where mathematics, including the algebraic study of conics and differential calculus, was taught.[13] Likewise, mathematical schools for artillerymen were created in Barcelona and Cádiz (1751), and instruction was upgraded in the military engineering schools in Barcelona and other cities.

The Jesuits did not remain on the sidelines of these new developments in science in Spain. In 1746–7, when he was named director of the Seminary of Nobles, the Jesuit Andrés Marcos Burriel tried to modernize instruction in the centre. The new scientific spirit in the Seminary and Juan's influence on Burriel can be detected in the 'Conclusions,' held in 1748 and presided over by the professor of mathematics Esteban Terreros y Pando.[14] In them the seminarians took up the question of the shape of the earth, explicitly referring to the expeditions to Lapland and Peru and, in the astronomy section, not only to the Copernican system – as a 'hypothesis' – but also to Newtonian celestial mechanics. The new *Constitutions* of the Seminary, published in 1755, provided for instruction in philosophy 'in such a way that it be useful to the public'; logic, metaphysics, general physics (where the 'opinions of Gassendi, Descartes, Maignan, Newton, and Leibniz' were to be taught 'without omitting those of the chemists, adopting the most true, with the appropriate critiques'), 'particular' physics, the sphere, astronomy, moral philosophy, and experimental physics are all included as components of the course of study. With regard to experimental physics, King Ferdinand VI had bestowed on the Seminary a collection of instruments. The chair of mathematics was responsible for the entire discipline, including 'Cartesian' and infinitesimal calculus, in addition to the 'mixed' subjects – fortification, optics, astronomy, and navigation.[15]

To carry out this program, the Jesuits called upon some foreign Jesuit professors. Around 1750, the Czech Juan [Johannes] Wendlingen (1715–90),[16] apparently on the recommendation of the king's confessor, Francisco Rávago, and, some years later, the Austrian Christian Rieger were appointed professors of mathematics at the Colegio Imperial. After being named Cosmographer of the Indies, Wendlingen addressed a memorial to the king in which he indicated that it would be 'more useful and necessary for the greater service of Your Majesty to teach mathematics in exactly the way it is done in Europe today,' at the same time suggesting that a 'useful and instructive philosophy' be taught in all the universities. In addition, Wendlingen made a series of recommendations related to his office of cosmographer 'to arrange and display the maps.'[17] Under the patronage of Ensenada, Wendlingen directed the construction of a new astronomical observatory in the Colegio Imperial for which he had access to the instruments acquired by Jorge Juan in London. He also had a special classroom, acquired books to support his teaching, and planned the development and publication of a course of mathematics in several volumes, of which four appeared (1753–6). The work merited the praise of Jorge Juan.[18] Wendlingen likewise made a number of astronomical observations summarized in the *Philosophical Transactions*.[19]

The other foreign Jesuit mentioned, the Austrian Rieger (1714–80), who had been professor of mathematics, physics, and architecture in Görz and Vienna, probably arrived in Madrid at the end of the 1760s.[20] In Madrid, Rieger published some *Observaciones del tránsito de Venus por el disco del Sol* (1761), a treatise on civil architecture (1763), and a treatise on electricity (1763), the first text published in Spain that presented the ideas of Franklin (though as interpreted by Wilcke, Beccaria, and other European authors). Moreover, Rieger has left a series of manuscripts on mechanics, mathematics, and astronomy, probably drawn up for his lectures at the Colegio Imperial at the beginning of the 1760s and designed, no doubt, for an encyclopaedic course on physical science and mathematics.[21]

As we have noted, modern science was not generally taught in Spanish universities until the reign of Charles III. Nevertheless, in certain centres such as Valencia and Cervera, some professors of philosophy, or, in the case of Valencia, of philosophy and mathematics, strove to modernize their instruction by eclectically incorporating aspects of the doctrines of Gassendi, Maignan, and Descartes, or of recent work in physics and mathematics.[22] In Cervera, where the professorate consisted principally of Jesuits, the most outstanding instructors in this respect were Mateo Aymerich (1715–99) and Tomás Cerdá (1715–91). Aymerich insisted on the need to introduce students to advances in experimental physics, to which he devoted a portion of his writings.[23] The same interest in promoting recent scientific knowledge is reflected, to a greater degree than in the works of Aymerich, in the *Jesuiticae philosophiae theses* (1753) of Cerdá, in which he raised questions belonging to physics, astronomy, and mathematics, citing, among other authors, Kepler, Descartes, Gassendi, Huygens, Cassini, Clairaut, Jorge Juan, Nollet, and Newton.[24]

In 1755, after completing his term as professor in Cervera, Cerdá moved on to Marseille to further his scientific education with the French Jesuit Esprit Pezenas, the author of the French version (1749) of MacLaurin's *Treatise of Fluxions*. Upon his return to Barcelona, he occupied (between 1757 and 1764) the chair of mathematics in the College of Nobles, or Cordelles college, a chair created expressly for him.[25] Cerdá composed various works on mathematics, physics, and astronomy, attempting to place the study of these sciences on the level 'where they now are in England and France ... selecting the best from their books.'[26] Some of these works were published between 1758 and 1760; others were never published. Among the latter there exist drafts on differential calculus in which are explained problems of maxima and minima and of radii of curvature and of evolutes; a manuscript of Newtonian mechanics in which Cerdá makes ample use of differential calculus; and a treatise on astronomy in which he expounds Newtonian celestial mechanics.[27] This last work is essentially a Spanish translation of the *Philosophia Britannica, or A New System of the Newtonian Philosophy, Astronomy, and Geography* (1747) by Newton's follower Benjamin Martin, with some minor changes and additions by Cerdá.

In 1762 the inspector-general of artillery, the Count of Gazola, merged the two existing artillery schools of Cádiz and Barcelona into a consolidated institution now located in Segovia. It opened its doors in 1764 with an inaugural lecture by the Valencian Jesuit Antonio Eximeno, 'first professor' of the centre, on 'the need for theory in order to sustain practice,' replete with references to Newton on the form of the earth as confirmed by the expeditions to Lapland and Peru, and to Newton's works on the resistance of air to the motion of projectiles.[28] For instruction in the new Segovian academy, Cerdá published *Artillery Lessons* (1764), probably commissioned by Gazola, to whom the text is dedicated. In the prologue Cerdá suggested (as had Jorge Juan, Wendlingen, and others before him) the creation of a National Academy of Sciences, a project left unrealized in this period.

In 1764, Cerdá was summoned to Madrid, where he remained until the expulsion of the Society. The king entrusted him with teaching mathematics to the royal princes and named him Chief Cosmographer of the Indies. Cerdá probably also held a chair of mathematics at the Colegio Imperial.

After the expulsion of the Society in 1767, the majority of its members emigrated to Italy, where they continued to be active in different areas of learning.[29] Some, such as Francisco Llampillas and Juan Francisco Masdeu, participated in a polemic with Girolamo Tiraboschi, Saverio Bettinelli, and other Italian authors over Spanish contributions to culture, philosophy, and science, which can be linked to the famous 'polemic of Spanish science' begun in the eighteenth century. According to Tiraboschi and Bettinelli, from the time of Seneca and Martial the Spanish had brought to Rome the bad taste that had corrupted Latin letters, and in modern times Gongora and his followers had introduced the same kind of corruption into Italian literature.

In his reply, entitled *Saggio storico apologetico della letteratura spagnuola contro le preggiudicate opinioni di alcuni moderni scritori italiani* (6 vols, 1778–81), particularly in the section concerning the Renaissance, Llampillas not only addressed religious studies, poetry, and the theatre, but also provided an in-depth analysis of Spanish contributions to medicine, navigation, military art, natural philosophy, and humanism, in all its different trends and schools, including those related to science. While Llampillas acknowledged that Spain had not made noteworthy progress in mathematics and physics in the most recent period, he ruled out his opponents' attribution of this lack of progress to factors such as climate, and also rejected the concept of a supposedly unchanging 'national temperament.' In the face of such notions, the Spanish Jesuit introduced a historical perspective and adopted a relativist point of view.[30]

As François López has pointed out, the Spanish Enlightenment was, to a great extent, a revision of the legacy of the past and of national traditions. Never before had the image projected by Spain in other countries had such influence on the thought and activities of its educated elite. Probably none of the great intellectual undertakings of this period were executed without the declared (or deliberate) aim of rehabilitating the Spanish nation, denigrated as it was by foreigners, and of opening the eyes of the Spanish themselves. From this point of view and within this context, the contribution made by expelled Jesuits was particularly noteworthy.[31] Indeed, the first to react on Italian soil against the anti-Hispanic legend and to argue with Tiraboschi and Bettinelli was Juan Andrés. In 1777, Andrés published a letter in Cremona addressed to Cayetano Valenti Gonzaga in which he defended his nation in such measured and courteous terms that his adversary Tiraboschi paid him tribute.

This author, Juan Andrés, was born in Planes (in an area in the south of the Valencian country) in 1740 and entered the Society of Jesus in 1754. He taught rhetoric in Gandía University until 1767 and was in contact with the outstanding Valencian scholar Gregorio Mayáns. Following the expulsion of the Jesuits, he left for Italy, where he spent the rest of his life. He settled in Ferrara; there he taught the sensist school of philosophy and published a book on the subject. He lived subsequently in Mantua, Parma, Pavia, Naples, and finally Rome, where he died. He was known chiefly as the author of the monumental work *Dell'origine, de' progressi e dello stato attuale d'ogni letteratura* (Parma, 1782–99), an ambitious history of culture in seven volumes that by 1844 had been republished eleven times in full (apart from the section on ecclesiastical literature, which is missing from the Spanish edition) and six times in part, in Italian, Spanish, and French.[32] The Spanish version, by Carlos Andrés, the author's brother, appeared in ten volumes between 1784 and 1806, and was used as a textbook of the history of literature in the Reales Estudios in Madrid. The volumes of this work that concern the history of philosophical and scientific literature constitute the first history of science written by a Spanish author.[33] Andrés addressed the history of mathematics, mechanics, hydrostatics, navigation, acoustics, optics, astronomy, physics (general and particular), chemistry, botany, natural history, anatomy, and medicine. He openly acknowledged his debt to Montucla, Bailly, Priestley, Leclerc, Freind, Portal, and other contemporary historians of science. At the same time he assumed and situated himself among the currents of interest in that learned period in order to outline the historical development of scientific knowledge. Since this is not the place for an analysis of the work, I will simply mention two of its most noteworthy aspects. One is the incorporation of Arab science and culture and the prominent place assigned to it; Andrés made use of Casiri's exceptional *Bibliotheca Arabico-Hispanica Escurialensis* (1760–70), which had been given to him by Charles III himself, as a present. The other is the meticulousness with which Andrés points out the Spanish contributions to science and their applications in each of the periods studied, but also weighs their importance so as to avoid proffering simply an apologia.

Andrés entered the Mantua Academy of Science in 1776 (where he had already presented a comprehensive work on the dynamics of fluids) thanks to his *Saggio della filosofia del Galileo*. In this study, Andrés examined the different subjects encompassed by Galileo's work: mechanics (accelerated motion, descent by inclined planes, resistance of means, the pendulum, ballistics, etc.), statics (simple machines, hydrostatics, hydraulics), properties of matter (cohesion of bodies), astronomy and cosmology, ebb and tide of seas, meteorology, music, optics, and magnetism. His express aim was to demonstrate what he deemed to be the philosophical method of the Pisan author, 'to study particular facts rather than create a general system; to follow the traces of nature by means of geometry, experimentation, and observation, and not to put forward vague ideas or aerial plans about how nature may or may not proceed, and not to aim to be a teacher of others.'[34] According to Andrés, Galileo refused to build a philosophical system and demonstrated the true manner of philosophising; had he adopted a system, he would have attracted many followers, but that would have meant 'giving blind men a better leader while not freeing them from their blindness.'

He continued to study the work of Galileo, and in 1779 he published a study entitled *Sopra una dimostrazione del Galileo* on the challenged passage of the *Discorsi*, in which Galileo attempted to demonstrate that it was impossible for the speed of the motion of falling bodies to be proportional to the distance travelled, which Galileo deemed a belief 'as false and impossible as saying that motion takes place instantaneously.' Andrés provided a good historical summary of the different interpretations of this argument put forward by Fermat, Gassendi, Blondel, Riccati, and Montucla, and ended with his own interpretation. Andrés's work is particularly interesting because of the light it casts on the history of this question and the effort put into reconstructing Galileo's thought. Nevertheless, he left the question formulated in the same terms in which Fermat had formulated it when he wrote, 'Providing it is true, one may concede to this "Linceo" the conclusion he has not demonstrated. However, if he has seen or believed he has seen the demonstration in the dark then it will surprise no one that it is demanded by his readers, who are not *linceos*'[35] – and more or less in the same terms in which it continues to be formulated.

From his exile in Italy, Andrés followed with interest and optimism the stimulus given to culture and the sciences in Spain: 'Spain, once a tenacious supporter of scholastic subtleties, has expelled them from her schools and has wisely applied useful knowledge in their place. Feijóo, Juan, Ulloa, Ortega (Casimiro Gómez Ortega, director of the Botanical Garden), and other physicists, mathematicians, and naturalists; Luzán, Montiano, and Mayáns, adorners of the language, rhetoric, poetry, and theatre; Martí, Flórez, Finestres, the two Mayáns, Pérez Bayer, the two (García) Mohedano, and other antiquarians and scholars of every kind provide clear·proof of the ardour that animates Spain to good scholarship.'[36]

The important scientific and cultural development in Spain in the eighteenth century underlined by Juan Andrés continued until the war of the independence and the reign of Ferdinand VII, events that involved a deep crisis in that development. But the roots of the crisis were already present in the contradictions and insufficiencies of the Spanish Enlightenment and of monarchical absolutism. The expulsion of the Jesuits was a clear manifestation of those contradictions and insufficiencies; one of its results was to deprive Spanish society of an important group of intellectuals active in all branches of the culture, including science. These intellectuals continued to make a contribution to culture and science from their exile in Italy.

NOTES

1 In considering the topic of Spain and the scientific revolution, it is useful to distinguish between two periods that correspond more or less to the sixteenth and seventeenth centuries. In the sixteenth century, Spanish achievements (that is, achievements by Spaniards, or by others living in Spain) in fields such as geography, cartography, terrestrial magnetism, astronomy (especially, but not only, connected with navigation), medicine, and natural history were notable; although the secrecy imposed by the government limited the spread of such development, it did not stop it, and through various channels it became part of the European patrimony of knowledge. There were also notable contributions in the field of technology. During the sixteenth century, then, the development of scientific fields and technological activity in Spain was consonant with those of Europe as a whole (with some peculiarities, and with emphasis on certain activities, such as those related to maritime expansion). In the seventeenth century, on the contrary, Spain hardly participated at all in the achievements and advances of European science. On Spanish scientific and

technological activity in the sixteenth century, see J.M. López Piñero, *Ciencia y técnica en la sociedad española de los siglos XVI y XVII* (Barcelona, 1979); D. Goodman, *Power and Penury* (Cambridge, 1988); N. García Tapia, *Ingeniería y arquitectura en el Renacimiento español* (Valladolid, 1990); M.I. Vicente Maroto and M. Esteban Piñeiro, *Aspectos de la ciencia aplicada en la España del Siglo de Oro* (Valladolid, 1991); *Medicinas, drogas y alimentos vegetales del Nuevo Mundo. Textos e imágenes españolas que los introdujeron en Europa*, ed. J.M. López Piñero (Madrid, 1992); V. Navarro Brotóns, 'The Reception of Copernicus's Work in Sixteenth-Century Spain: The Case of Diego de Zúñiga,' *Isis* 86 (1995), 52–78; V. Navarro and E. Rodríguez, *Matemáticas, cosmología y humanismo en la España del siglo XVI. Los* Comentarios al segundo libro de la 'Historia Natural' de Plinio *de Jerónimo Muñoz*, (Valencia, 1998); *Historia de la ciencia y la técnica en la corona de Castilla*, vol. 3, *Siglos XVI y XVII* (Valladolid, 2002); and Navarro Brotóns, 'Astronomía y cosmografia entre 1561 y 1625. Aspectos de la actividad de los matemáticos y cosmógrafos espñaoles y portugueses,' *Cronos* 3 (2000): 349–81.

2 In the sense expressed by Steven J. Harris in 'Transposing the Merton Thesis: Apostolic Spirituality and the Establishment of the Jesuit Scientific Tradition,' *Science in Context* 3 (1989): 29–67. Harris expands upon Rivka Feldhay's proposal 'to cover more than just the Jesuit educational program, developing the value-structure of the Society, and exploring further the institutional ramifications of the Jesuit image of knowledge' (ibid., p. 48); see also Harris, 'Jesuit Ideology and Jesuit Science: Scientific Activity in the Society of Jesus, 1540–1773, dissertation, University of Wisconsin–Madison, 1988; Rivka Feldhay, 'Knowledge and Salvation in Jesuit Culture,' *Science in Context* 1 (1987): 195–213; Bald. *Leg.*; and Rom. *Contre-réf.*

3 And, at the end of the century, the Jesuit college in Cádiz. We lack information as to whether scientific instruction was introduced in other colleges of the Society. According to Alberto Dou, 'Las matemáticas en la España de los austrias,' in *Estudios sobre Julio Rey Pastor* (1888–1962), ed. Luis Español González (Logroño, 1990), pp. 151–72, mathematics was also taught at the Real Colegio de Santa María y San Jaime (Cordelles) in Barcelona, in the College of Nobles in Calatayud, and in that in Bilbao, all directed by Jesuits, but probably only in the eighteenth century. See also Dou, 'Matemáticos españoles jesuitas de los siglos XVI y XVII,' *AHSI* 66 (1997): 300–21. In the University of Gandía, the only teaching centre of the Society permitted to grant degrees, there was no chair of mathematics. In 1700 three chairs of medicine were established there. See below in the text.

4 On the Jesuits and scientific activity in Spain in the seventeenth century, see Navarro Brotóns, 'Los jesuitas y la renovación científica en la España del siglo XVII,' *Studia historica. Historia moderna* 14 (1996): 15–44; Navarro Brotóns, 'La ciencia en la España del siglo XVII: El cultivo de las disciplinas físico-

matemàtiques,' *Arbor* 604–5:153 (1996): 197–252; and Navarro Brotóns, 'Tradition and Scientific Change in Early Modern Spain: The Role of the Jesuits,' in Fein. *Jes. Sci.*, pp. 331–89. On the renewal movement, see López Piñero, *Ciencia y técnica* (n1 above).

5 On science in eighteenth-century Spain, see the synthesis by Antonio Lafuente and José Luis Peset, 'El conocimiento y el dominio de la naturaleza: La ciencia y la técnica,' in *Historia de España*, ed. José María Zamora, vol. 30(1) (Madrid, 1988), pp. 349–394. See also the volume *Carlos III y la ciencia de la Ilustración*, ed. Manuel Sellés, J.L. Peset, and A. Lafuente (Madrid, 1988); the relevant chapters by Vernet in *Historia de la ciencia española* (Madrid, 1975); and the section covering the eighteenth century in J.M. López Piñero, V. Navarro, and E. Portela, 'La actividad científica y tecnológica,' in *Enciclopedia de historia de España*, ed. M. Artola, vol. 3 (Madrid, 1988), pp. 273–327. On the diffusion of scientific and philosophical ideas, there is some interesting information in Francisco Sánchez-Blanco Parody, *Europa y el pensamiento español del siglo XVIII* (Madrid, 1991). For physics, see Navarro Brotóns, 'La física en la España del siglo XVIII,' in *Historia de la física hasta el siglo XIX* (Madrid, 1983), pp. 327–42. The classic work by Jean Sarrailh, *L'Espagne eclairée de la seconde moitée du XVIII siècle* (Paris, 1954), if used judiciously, is a source of valuable information.

6 Between the end of the seventeenth century and the reign of Charles III, the two powers, civil and ecclesiastical, struggled to delimit their jurisdictions, and the Spanish clergy began to enter, at the slowest of paces, a process of modernization that would bring them up to the level of the intellectual elite. In this period, and until their expulsion in 1767, the Jesuits passed from a position of power to one of opposition. The Jesuits' loss of key positions in the power structure began with the fall of their protector, the Marquis of Ensenada, and the subsequent fall of the king's confessor, Francisco Rávago (1755). See T. Egido, *Oposición pública y oposición al poder en la España del siglo XVIII* (Valladolid, 1971); and François López, 'El pensamiento tradicionalista,' in *Historia de España*, ed. Zamora (n5 above), pp. 813–51. Here I cannot deal comprehensively with the political and scientific policy of the Jesuits, which was not monolithic; instead, I will summarize the most notable aspects of the participation of the scientists of the Society in Spanish scientific development in the period.

7 On the foundation of the Seminary of Nobles, see Simón Díaz, *Historia del Colegio Imperial de Madrid*, vol. 1(Madrid, 1952) pp. 165ff. See also Antonio Lafuente, 'La enseñanza de las ciencias durante la primera mitad del siglo XVIII,' in *Estudios dedicados a Juan Peset Aleixandre*, vol. 2 (Valencia, 1982), pp. 477–95.

8 On the Cordelles college, so called in honour of its founder, Juan de Cordelles (1538), which was directed by the Jesuits from 1658, see José Iglésies Fort, *La Real Academia de Ciencias Naturales y Artes en el siglo XVIII* (Barcelona, 1964).

Besides this college, intended for the education of the nobility, the Jesuits ran the college of Belén, so called because it is next to the present-day church of Belén, the construction of which was begun in 1681. On Cerdá, see below in the text.

9 On the University of Cervera, see M. Peset and J.L. Peset, *La universidad española* (Madrid, 1924), pp. 65–85; and M. Rubio y Borrás, *Historia de la real y pontificia Universidad de Cervera*, 2 vols (Barcelona, 1915–16).

10 See Mario Martínez Gómez, 'Gandía ante la reforma carolina: El proyecto de plan de estudios de 1767,' in *Claustros y estudiantes*, vol. 2 (Valencia, 1989), pp. 45–69.

11 Antonio Eximeno probably also taught mathematics at the college of St Paul in Valencia, although for only a few years. On public examinations, see H. Capel, 'La geografía en los exámenes públicos y el proceso de diferenciación entre geografía y matemáticas en la enseñanza durante el siglo XVIII,' *Areas. Revista de ciencias sociales* (Murcia) 1 (1981): 91–112.

12 On this expedition and the participation of Spaniards in it, see Antonio Lafuente and Antonio J. Delgado, *La geometrización de la tierra* (1735–1744) (Madrid, 1984); and Antonio Lafuente and Antonio Mazuecos, *Los caballeros del punto fijo. Ciencia, política y aventura en la expedición geodésica hispanofrancesa al virreinato del Perú en el siglo XVIII* (Barcelona and Madrid, 1987). The technical and scientific aspects of the expedition have been studied also by James R. Smith, *From Plane to Spheroid: Determining the Figure of the Earth from 3000 B.C. to the 18th Century Lapland and Peruvian Survey Expeditions* (Rancho Cordoba, CA, 1986).

13 See the *Conclusiones mathemáticas ... defendidas en el Quartel de Guardias de Corps* (Madrid, 1752). These *Conclusiones* were presented by Captain Pedro Padilla, the author of *Curso militar de mathemáticas*, 4 vols (Madrid, 1753–6), the first Spanish text to discuss differential calculus. For a description of Padilla's work, see Norberto Cuesta Dutari, *Historia de la invención del cálculo infinitesimal y de su introducción en España* (Salamanca, 1983), pp. 120–37. On the Academia de Guardias de Corps, see also Antonio Lafuente and José Luis Peset, 'Las academias militares y la inversión en ciencia en la España ilustrada,' *Dynamis* 2 (1982): 193–208; and Horacio Capel, Joan Eugeni Sánchez, and Omar Moncada, *De Palas a Minerva. La formación científica y la estructura institucional de los ingenieros militares en el siglo XVIII* (Barcelona and Madrid, 1988), pp. 147–8 and passim.

14 *Conclusiones mathemáticas ... por el Seminario de Nobles ... presididas por el R.P. Mro. de Mathemáticas en el mismo Real Seminario* (Madrid, 1748). According to the Jesuit Manuel de Larramendi, *Corografía o descripción general de la ... Provincia de Guipúzcoa* (Barcelona, 1882), p. 283, the animator of this presentation of mathematical 'conclusions' was Burriel (cited by Capel, 'La geografía en los exámenes públicos,' [n11 above], p. 98).

15 The *Constituciones* were published in Madrid together with a 'Memoria histórica de

la fundación del Real Seminario de Nobles,' in which it is indicated (p. 18) that Philip V funded this centre, inasmuch as he 'did not find any seminary devoted to the education of those nobles who normally did not attend universities but were employed in the service of the palace and court, in the administration of the business of the state; and of those who remained in their cities administering their houses and estates and who ought to be, owing to their birth, leaders of their regions.' The memorandum also states that this seminary was modelled after the one that Louis 'the Great' had established in France.

16 Wendlingen was professor of humanities in the Jesuit college in Prague. After the expulsion of the Jesuits from Spain, he returned to Prague, where he was inspector of mathematics and director of a science museum. See J.C. Poggendorff, *Biographisch-Literarisches Handwörterbuch (zur Geschichte) der Naturwissenschaften* (Leipzig, 1863–), vol. 2, p. 1296.

17 A copy of this memorandum is conserved in the Archivo General de Simancas, Marina, Negociado Indiferente, leg. 712.

18 In the Archivo General de Simancas, Marina, Negociado Indiferente, legs 712 and 713, are found various letters and documents by Wendlingen on all these matters, along with reports and letters by Juan and Ulloa. Some of the letters refer to instruments requested by Wendlingen and acquired by Juan in London.

19 See Díaz, *Historia del Colegio Imperial* (n7 above), p. 576.

20 See Poggendorf, *Handwörterbuch*, vol. 2, p. 640.

21 Rieger's manuscripts are conserved in the Academia de Historia, in a thick folder in the Cortes collection, 9/2792.

22 On the University of Valencia, see Salvador Albiñana, *Universidad e Ilustración. Valencia en la época de Carlos III* (Valencia, 1988); V. Navarro, 'La ciència il.lustrada,' in *Història del País Valencià*, vol. 4, ed. Manuel Ardit (Barcelona, 1990), pp. 277–97; J.M. López Piñero and V. Navarro, *Historia de la ciència al País Valencià* (Valencia, 1995), pp. 295–326; López Piñero and Navarro, 'Estudio histórico,' in J.M. López Piñero et al., *La actividad valenciana de la Ilustración*, 2 vols (Valencia, 1998), I, pp.11–108; and Navarro, 'Filosofía y ciencias,' in *Historia de la Universidad de Valencia*, ed. Mariano Peset, vol. 2 (Valencia, 2000), pp. 189–215.

23 M. Aymerich, *Systema antiquo-novum Jesuiticae philosophicae contentiosam, et experimentalem philosophandi methodum complectens* (Cervera, 1747). See Ignacio Casanovas, *La cultura catalana en el siglo XVIII. Finestres y la Universidad de Cervera* (Barcelona, 1953), p. 172.

24 See Cuesta Dutari, *Historia de la invención* (n13 above), pp. 240–54. On Cerdá, see also Iglésies Fort, *La Real Academia de Ciencias Naturales*, pp. 41–7 and passim; Santiago Garma Pons, 'Cerdà,' in *Diccionario histórico de la ciencia moderna en España*, ed. José María López Piñero, Thomas F. Glick, Víctor Navarro Brotóns,

and Eugenio Portela Marco, vol. 1(Barcelona, 1983), pp. 206–7; and Lluís Gassiot, 'Tomàs Cerdà els inicis de l'Acadèmia de Ciències de Barcelona,' in *La Reial Acadèmia de Ciències i Arts de Barcelona als segles XVIII i XIX*, ed. Agustí Nieto Galán and Antoni Roca (Barcelona, 2001), pp. 125–33.

25 The chair was solicited by the rector of the college with the support of the municipal government. See Iglésies Fort, *La Real Academia de Ciencias Naturales*, p. 23. Among the manuscripts by Cerdá there is a description of the city of Barcelona in which he states that there were two chairs of mathematics. There is also a letter from Cerdá to Thomas Simpson, dated 1758, in which he provides information on his teaching activities in the Cordelles college.

26 T. Cerdá, *Liciones de mathemática o elementos generales de arithmética y algebra para el uso de la clase*, 2 vols (Barcelona, 1758), I, p. [2].

27 Cerdá's manuscripts are conserved in the Academia de la Historia of Madrid. See Santiago Garma Pons, 'Cultura matemática en la España de los siglos XVIII y XIX,' in *Ciencia y sociedad en España: De la Ilustración a la Guerra Civil*,' ed. J.M. Sánchez Ron (Madrid, 1988), pp. 93–129; Navarro Brotóns, *Tradition and Scientific Change*; and Gassiot, 'Tomàs Cerdà.' The treatise on astronomy has been edited recently by Lluís Gassiot i Matas in Tomás Cerdá, *Tratado de astronomía* (Barcelona, 1999). This work must have been written around 1760, since in it Cerdá alludes to the 'present [year] 1760' (see fols 69r, 69v, 70v).

28 Antonio Eximeno (1729–1808) taught rhetoric in the Seminary of Nobles in Valencia and mathematics at the college of St Paul in the same city. After the expulsion, he went to Italy and became an important musicologist. He published two works on philosophy and mathematics, *De studiis philosophicis et mathematicis instituendis* (Madrid, 1789) and *Institutiones philosophicae et mathematicae* (Madrid, 1796), which display his advanced mathematical formation. Like his fellow Jesuit and compatriot Juan Andrés, to whom he dedicated the first of the two works cited, he inclined towards the sensualism of Bonet and Condillac in philosophy. See Miguel de Guzmán Ozamiz and Santiago Garma Pons, 'El pensamiento matemático de Antonio Eximeno,' *Llull* 3:1 (1980): 3–38. Eximeno's lecture has been edited by Enrique Pardo Canalís, *El Padre Eximeno, profesor primario del Real Colegio de Artillería de Segovia* (Segovia, 1987).

29 See Miguel Batllori, *La cultura hispano-italiana de los jesuitas expulsos* (Madrid, 1966). The destinations of the Jesuits in Italy were, as is known, the Pontifical States and particularly Bologna (where the nucleus was formed by Jesuits from the province of Castille), Ferrara (where prevailed Jesuits of the province of Aragon), Rome, and some other cities. Around the end of the century, many Jesuits were sheltered in the Parmesan duchies under the protection of Duke Ferdinand of Bourbon. The occupations of the expelled Jesuits were very various. Some assumed professorships in universities, such as Ferrara and Bologna, mainly in the humani-

ties; others took up positions as librarians; still others became tutors of the nobility. Those who engaged in scientific activity include Antonio Eximeno, Juan Andrés, Lorenzo Hervás y Panduro, and Antonio Ludeña.

30 See François Lopez, *Juan Pablo Forner y la crisis de la conciencia española en el siglo XVIII* (Salamanca, 1999).

31 It has been said that the Spanish Jesuits thought the censures of the Italian authors more insulting than they actually were, and that their counterattacks accordingly were out of proportion (see Batllori, *La cultura*, p. 415). But as Roberto Mantelli has observed ('Nationalism, Xenophobia, and Catalanism in the Writings of an Enlightened Catholic Historian: Juan Francisco Masdeu, S.J. [1744–1817],' *Analecta sacra Tarraconensis* 55–6 [1982–83]: 209–60), their over-sensitivity may be accounted for by the continuous attacks made by eighteenth-century *philosophes* on Spanish culture and institutions. Voltaire's repeated strictures against Spanish colonization and the Inquisition are typical of a general Enlightenment view of Spain as characterized by religiosity at best and intolerance at worst. Eighteenth-century Italians showed little interest in Spanish life and culture; for them, Spain was a poor and uncultured country.

32 The Spanish edition consisted of several partial editions until the work was complete, with the exception of the two last Italian volumes, on ecclesiatical literature, which were not translated into Spanish.

33 See Navarro Brotóns, 'Juan Andrés y la historia de las ciencias,' in *Estudios dedicados a Juan Peset Aleixandre* (n7 above), pp. 81–93; Manuel Garrido Palazón, *Historia literaria, enciclopedia y ciencia en el literato jesuita Juan Andrés* (Alicante, 1995).

34 J. Andrés, *Saggio della filosofia del Galileo* (Mantua, 1776), pp. 3–4.

35 P. Fermat, letter to Gassendi, 1646 (?), in *Oeuvres*, vol. 3 (Paris, 1896), pp. 302–9, on 303. 'Linceos' refers to the Accademia dei Lincei, or Academy of Lynxes, founded in Rome by Federico Cesi (1585–1630); its aims were to cultivate the scientific disciplines, encourage collaboration, and make known the results of research. Galileo was a member of the Lincei from 1611.

36 J. Andrés, *Dell'origin, de' progressi e dello stato attuale d'ogni letteratura*, 10 vols (Spanish ed., Madrid, 1784–1806), II, pp. 361–2.

19 / The Reception of a Theory: A Provisional Syllabus of Boscovich Literature, 1746–1800

UGO BALDINI

1. The Question

The theory of an attraction-repulsion force producing all physical phenomena appeared progressively in some of R.J. Boscovich's works: *De viribus vivis* (1745), *De lumine* (1748), *De continuitatis lege* (1754), *De lege virium in natura existentium* (1755), the notes to B. Stay's *Philosophia recentior*,[1] *De materiae divisibilitate et principiis corporum* (1757),[2] and *Philosophiae naturalis theoria* (1758), with slightly different titles in later editions.[3] Boscovich's theory may be looked at in two ways, one 'technical' and the other 'institutional' and 'philosophical,' that is, with a focus on the metaphysics and the 'ideological' aims of the body of which Boscovich was a member, the Society of Jesus.

The theory assumed that the various natural forces are cases of a single, general force, and that the laws governing them derive – given some special restrictions – from the general law, as asserted in the title of Boscovich's principal work, *Naturalis philosophiae theoria ... redacta ad unicam legem virium in natura existentium*. Boscovich generalized Newton's law of gravitational attraction, making it capable of accounting for apparently non-mechanical facts. While using a matter-space (mechanistic) language, he introduced the notion of infinitesimal force-points that attract or repel each other as a function of distances. According to some, Boscovich's theory paved the way for Faraday and post-Faraday field theory. So this by-product of Newtonian science provided a conceptual framework alternative to the prevailing mechanistic one, which considered itself the only legitimate offspring of that science.

From the first point of view, the theory was the product of a scientist who was a Jesuit. From the second, it was the attempt of a Jesuit, who was a scientist, to bring contemporary science and natural theology into agreement. The writings of later Jesuit scientists also present both these aspects (consider Teilhard de

Chardin's paleontology and his 'omega point theory'). Boscovich, however, combined them into a *unified* theory, so that the second element (often dismissed as anti-scientific or unscientific) influenced the first. He conserved the scholastic idea of a 'total' knowledge including theology, metaphysics, and physics by attempting to show that the progress of the third did not exclude the legitimacy of the first and second. In fact, the conceptual matrix he provided retained some aspects of scholastic cosmology and physical ontology as well (which had been abandoned by the new science as unscientific or even meaningless), thereby 'extending' them in the manner of some present-day theoretical physics and cosmology.[4]

Its truth apart, the theory was the boldest attempt made in theoretical physics, in so far as it aimed to explain all physical reality as the product of a single force, ruled by a law represented in a graphical form.[5] It was sufficiently different from academic physics and from traditional *philosophia naturalis* to produce something between perplexity and hostility among many representatives of both fields. Those of the first group who opposed metaphysics and were agnostics or atheists dismissed it as unscientific; those of the second, several Jesuits included, perceived this radical reshaping of old doctrines as a renunciation of their purpose. Many thought the theory absurd because it questioned some everyday appearances (such as the contact of bodies). Taking these sources of resistance into consideration makes it possible to explain some peculiarities of the theory's reception, which have few analogues, if any, in the history of science. Here it suffices to describe them briefly:

A) Boscovich's 'normal' scientific work was highly regarded; he met some of the best scientists of his era, and, important scientific academies admitted him and published his writings in their proceedings. However, *in continental Europe* no outstanding scientist devoted a paper to what he considered his main contribution; it was not discussed in any *advanced* scientific work or taught in any university (a few Jesuit ones excepted); and no academy, including those of which Boscovich was a member, promoted discussion of it.[6] Learned journals such as the *Mémoires de Trévoux* and the *Acta eruditorum* reviewed some of his works, but not the *Naturalis philosophiae theoria*; a review of it in the *Journal des savants* did not produce a public debate.[7] This was not owing to lack of information, because Boscovich had done his best to circulate the work, and several scientists and philosophers had read it.[8]

B) By contrast, in Britain his theory was soon discussed by scientists, some of whom accepted it in various ways; it even entered the universities, mainly in Scotland. In fact, almost all scientists who later acknowledged it as a source of inspiration were British.[9]

C) The theory's diffusion did not conform to the pattern typical in modern science. For forty years it inspired no substantial scientific work; the work came after 1800, in a different scientific panorama. Moreover, the revival was not the outcome of an enduring tradition, because it came after the last defenders of the theory had disappeared.

D) Strictly speaking, no 'Boscovich school' existed. His supporters did not control important chairs in Italy's principal Jesuit colleges or universities;[10] none was an original scientist or added something really new to his ideas. After 1757, Boscovich was not rooted stably in an institution, so his followers lacked an official reference point, and none succeeded him; a second generation of supporters failed to emerge, with the result that by 1800 in Italy, Boscovichianism was already a purely historical fact.[11]

E) The theory was the most sophisticated scientific product of a Catholic priest in the mid-eighteenth century and offered a new way of connecting science, metaphysics, and theology. However, it did not become standard for Catholic scientists and philosophers, nor was it adopted as a 'paradigm' in the principal schools of Catholic Europe.[12]

Are these facts accounted for simply by saying that since the theory was the work of a Jesuit, its failure was a consequence of the Society's collapse? Some distinctions are needed. The theory was 'Jesuit' in the trivial sense that the author himself was a Jesuit. But it was not a *direct* outcome of the Society's learning, and it was not generally accepted within it. Nevertheless, it was 'Jesuit' in the following senses:

1 it appeared in a typical vehicle of Jesuit discourse, that is, college dissertations;
2 from 1750 to 1758 it was known and discussed mainly in Jesuit circles;
3 it was opposed by the Society's leadership in Rome and by older professors, though defended by some younger ones;
4 in a sophisticated and sometimes disguised way, it echoed some conceptual and terminological traits of Jesuit natural philosophy and natural theology.

Since the Society of Jesus had been expelled from most European countries between 1759 and 1768, the theory's primary audience was very soon restricted to some parts of Italy and of the Holy Roman Empire, and after the Society's suppression in 1773 it disappeared altogether. Boscovich's vicissitudes, whether personal or connected to his identity as a Jesuit, were of no help in making his theory a stable presence in scientific discussions. More generally, suppression of the Society reduced the support for the traditional thesis of a *rational* integration of science and theology, which Boscovich had tried to maintain, and made it easier to place him on the margins of scientific discussion, leaving the mechanistic-Laplacian interpretation of Newtonian science at its centre. The immediate fate of his ideas was determined, therefore, by a mixture of scientific, ideological, and institutional factors. Had they been evidently true and independent of metaphysical options, they could still have had a role; they might also have had a role if they had been institutionally supported. Things being different, they passed into the nineteenth century as something puzzling, esoteric, and different from 'normal' science.

This seems the general pattern, but a detailed description of the reception of Boscovich's theory is still a desideratum. The theory's life-history went from 1745 (when Boscovich began to develop it) to c. 1799, when E.G. Gil published his *Disquisitio in causam physicam recentium chemicorum*, the last work expounding and defending the theory as a full and adequate explanation of all physical phenomena. What follows is a chronological list of writings (different in kind, length, and scientific level), divided into national sections, or cultural-geographic areas. It excludes works written and published by English and Scottish scientists, because they have been described much more completely than those produced on the Continent, and also because the paths of diffusion of Boscovich's ideas in Britain were markedly different, in both their institutional and their 'ideological' components. This list is meant to provide only a (partial) textual ground for future reconstructions of the period.

2. Boscovich's Theory in Works Published in Continental Europe (1746–1800)[13]

The following lists do not include all discussions of Boscovich's scientific works, but only those treating the fundamentals of his 'system.'[14] A notable portion of them are theses of students in colleges or universities.[15] The few theses that were published were printed in only a few exemplars and were not intended for the normal book market, so generally they are found only in libraries or archives in their area of origin.[16] Although they are often catalogued under students' names, their real authors were the teachers, so they inform us of the ideas of persons who often published nothing on the subject concerned, and whose manuscript lecture notes, when they have been preserved, often deal with it in a brief or vague fashion. The theses were also a favourite channel for new or even unorthodox ideas.[17] Accordingly they can reveal tensions within the Society that were usually removed from the eyes of the world, as well as tensions with other orders, which usually appeared only in the course of theological debate. Discussions of Boscovich's theory are not found primarily in theses on mathematics, the discipline he taught, but in those on philosophy, a discipline on which, according to conventions rooted in medieval gnosiology and epistemology, he lacked formal authority to speak. Those conventions divided philosophy (physics) from mathematics in such a way as to assign the theory to the former; so in the lists below, the number of 'philosophical' works exceeds the number of 'mathematical.' Most mathematicians belonging to the regular clergy left discussion of the theory to men who often lacked adequate knowledge of the sophisticated mathematical-physical tools and concepts employed by Boscovich.[18]

This division influenced the reactions to his ideas and the typology of the works in which these reactions were expressed. In the mid-eighteenth century, most Jesuit philosophers were still producing – theses and academic dissertations apart – general treatises, while mathematicians were replacing them with handbooks on single parts of mathematics or writings on special subjects. Only a few analyses of Boscovich's ideas were published separately (mostly by enthusiastic supporters), a majority being inserted in various sections of general works. The fact that a new theory was placed in the pigeonholes provided by an old pedagogical structure meant that some discussed it in sections on continuous entities, others in sections on the structure of matter, and still others in places concerning forces acting in nature or the existence of repulsive phenomena. In each case, some aspects of the theory were given more attention than others, and its inner structure was often represented inadequately.[19]

Italy

1746

1 [T. Correa, S.J.?], *Theses ex physica generali selectae, a Nicolao Cauccio ... ad disputandum propositae ...*, Romae.[20]

1749[21]

1750

2 N. Arrighetti, S.J., *Ignis theoria solidis observationibus deducta*, Senis.[22]
3 [D. Troili, S.J.], review of the *Dissertatio de lumine* in *Storia letteraria d'Italia*, ed. F.A. Zaccaria, S.J., 2nd ed., vol. 1 (Venezia), pp. 129–33.[23]

1751

4 F.L. Balassi, *Epistola in qua Legem continuitatis in collisionibus corporum servari ostenditur, etsi non prius velocitas incipiat extingui, quam eorum primae partes sese contingant*, Lucae.[24]

1752

5 [S. Guidi, S.J.], *Propositiones ex universa philosophia selectae ...*
propositae ab Equite Jacopo Trotti ..., Romae.[25]
6 [Idem], *Propositiones ex universa philosophia selectae et ad disputandum*
propositae ab Equite Hierosolymitano M. Antonio Ansidei, Romae.[26]
7 [Idem], *Theses ex universa philosophia ad disputandum selectas*
Franciscus Cennini ... dicat, Romae.[27]
8 [F.M. Gaudio, O.S.P.?], *Ex physica selectas propositiones ... publice*
disputandas proponit ... Andreas Maruffius ... in novo Scholarum Piarum
collegio convictor, philosophiae et matheseos auditor, Romae.[28]
9 [Idem], *Ex physica selectas propositiones ... publice disputandas proponit*
... Philippus Cionius ..., Romae.[29]

1753[30]

1753–6[31]

1754

10 [C. Benvenuti, S.J.], *Synopsis physicae generalis, quam ... proponit D.*
Joseph Joachimus a Vereterra ..., Romae.[32]
11 Idem, *De lumine dissertatio physica, quam ... proponit D. Joseph*
Joachimus a Vereterra ..., Romae.
12 Idem, *Conclusiones philosophicae* [Romae].[33]
13 [F.M. Gaudio, O.S.P.], *Propositiones physicae, et astronomicae quas ...*
publice disputandas proponit Vincentius Costantius ..., Romae.[34]
14 [Idem], *Propositiones physicae, et astronomicae quas ... publice*
disputandas proponit ... Vincentius Martinius ..., Romae.[35]
15 L. Fassoni, O.S.P., *De Leibnitiano rationis sufficientis principio dissertatio*
philosophica, Senogalliae.[36]
16 [Anon., S.J.], *Propositiones ex institutionibus philosophicis excerptae et a*
Paullo Simoni ad disputandum propositae ... in collegio Interamnensi Soc.
Jesu, Romae.[37]
17 [G.M. Francolini, S.J.], *Philosophicae theses publice propugnandas*
Joannes O'Kelly ... [dicat], Florentiae.[38]

1755

18 [O.G. Lunardi S.J.], *Theses ex universa philosophia selectae ... a Aloysio*
Leonori ... Accedit dissertatio physica de naturali electricismo, ejusque ad
auroram borealem applicatione, Romae.[39]
19 Idem, *Theses ex universa philosophia selectae ... a ... Joachimo Canali ...*

propositae. Accedit dissertatio physica de meteoris a naturali electricismo pendentibus, Romae.[40]

20 [Idem?], *Theses ex universa philosophia selectas Ignatius Calvestrani ... [dicat]*, Romae.[41]

21 [F.M. Gaudio, O.S.P.], *De natura extensionis dissertatio ... nuncupata, et publice propugnata ... a Paschali de Petra Sulmonensi. In Collegio novo Calasanctio Scholarum Piarum Convictore, et Philosophiae, ac Matheseos Auditore...*, Romae.[42]

22 [Anon., O.S.P.], *Propositiones ex universa metaphysica quas ... publice propugnandas exhibet Nicolaus Cruciani ... philosophiae ac matheseos auditor*, Romae.[43]

1756

23 F.M. Gaudio, O.S.P., *De naturae vi, et lege generali dissertatio*, Romae 1756.[44]

24 [Anon., O.S.P.], *Ex physica selectae propositiones publice disputandas proponit ... Michael Antonius Toti lucensis in novo Calasanctio Scholarum Piarum Collegio Convictor ... Accedit tractatio de artificiali electricismo ex Beniamini Franklini theoria quam expolivit ... Joannes Baptista Beccaria ex Scholis Piis*, Romae.[45]

25 G.B. Scarella, C.R.T., *Physicae generalis methodo mathematica tractatae ... tomus secundus*, Brixiae.[46]

1757

26 [F.M. Gaudio, O.S.P.], *Physicas propositiones nuncupat ... Dominicus Dionigi Romanus in Collegio Calasanctio Scholarum Piarum philosophiae, et matheseos auditor*, Romae.[47]

27 [Anon., O.F.M.], *Hanc logices et somatologiae synopsin ... F. Hieronymus Vectianensis Minorita ... in Aracoelitano Gymnasio Philosophiae Auditor dicat consecratque*, Lucae.[48]

1758

28 [Anon., S.J.], *Universam philosophiam ... [dicat] ... Joseph Paganus*, Cremonae.[49]

29 [Anon., O.S.P.], *Propositiones ex universa philosophia selectas publice disputandas proponit Johannes Laurentius De Saporitis ...*, Genuae.[50]

1759[51]

30 [F.M. Gaudio, O.S.P.], *Propositiones physicae quas ... publice propugnat Vincentius Cassini Romanus. In Collegio Calasanctio Scholarum Piarum Philosophiae, et Matheseos Auditor*, Romae.[52]

1760

31 [F.M. Gaudio, O.S.P.], *Propositiones physicae, et mathematicae quas ...*
propugnat Joachimus Pessuti Romanus in Collegio Calasanctio Scholarum
Piarum philosophiae, et matheseos auditor, Romae.[53]

32 Idem, *De rectilinea lucis propagatione dissertatio*, Romae.[54]

33 Idem, *De Altitudine athmospherae dissertatio*, Romae.[55]

34 [I. Gaetani, S.J.], *Propositiones philosophicas publice propugnandas*
indiscriminatim exponit Dominicus Damis Epirota ..., Romae.[56]

35 [Idem], *Propositiones philosophicae quas ... publice propugnandas*
exponit ... in Collegio Anglorum de Urbe Gulielmus Winter ..., Romae.[57]

36 [Idem], *Philosophicas theses publice propugnandas Apollonius Belli ...*
dicat, Romae.[58]

37 [Idem], *Philosophicas theses publice propugnandas Vincentius Benucci ...*
dicat, Romae.[59]

38 [Idem], *Philosophicas theses publice propugnandas Petrus Frazer ....*
dicat, Romae.[60]

39 [Idem], *Philosophicas theses publice propugnandas Aloysius Calvini dicat*,
Romae.[61]

40 [Idem], *Philosophicas theses publice propugnandas Joseph Maria Sozzi ...*
dicat, Romae.[62]

41 [G. Stoppini, S.J.], *Sapientissimae Errantium Academiae Propositiones ex*
universa philosophia Firmi in Templo PP. Societatis Jesu publice
propugnandas dicat Dominicus Cardinali ..., Firmi.[63]

42 [Idem], *Philosophicas theses Firmi in Templo PP. Societatis Jesu publice*
propugnandas dicat Nicolaus Petrarca ..., Firmi.[64]

1761

43 [F.M. Gaudio, O.S.P.], *Propositiones ex universa philosophia selectae quas*
... publice propugnat Aloysius Cerroni In Collegio Calasanctio Scholarum
Piarum Convictor, Romae.[65]

44 [G.M. Francolini, S.J.], *Synopsim physicae newtoniano-boscovichianae*
[dicat] Aloysius Panelli ex Aquaviva, Asculi, 1761.[66]

45 [I. Castani, S.J.], *Theses ex universa philosophia selectae quas, ...*
Vincentius Mannius ... publice ad disserendum proponit ... Romae.[67]

46 [I. Nava, O.S.B. Cist.], *Theses philosophicae quas ... D. Edmundus Appiani*
Mediolanensis Sacri Cisterciensis Ordinis monachus ... publice D.D.
proponit, Mediolani, 1761.[68]

47 D. Troili, S.J., a review of B. Stay's poem *Philosophia recentior* and
Boscovich's notes to it, in *Storia letteraria d'Italia*, ed. F.A. Zaccaria, S.J.,
2nd ed., vol. 12 (Venezia), pp. 119–32.

1762

48 [G.B. Pareti, S.J.], *Theses philosophicae quas ... Alexander Mattheius ... publice defendendas proponit*, Romae.[69]

49 [Anon., O.S.P.], *Theoremata ex universa philosophia selecta atque elementa Architecturae civilis et militaris quae ... publice per biduum propugnanda exponit Julius Caesar Maria Capicius Anghillara*, Romae.[70]

1763

50 [G. Bozzoli, S.J.], *Selectae Theses ex universa philosophia quas publice indiscriminatim propugnandas exponit ... D. Ferdinandus Saluzzo e Ducibus Coriliani ... pridie cal. Septembris MDLXIII*, Romae.[71]

51 [Idem], *Selectae propositiones ex universa philosophia quas ... publice indiscriminatim propugnandas exponit Baro Carolus De Aste ...*, Romae.[72]

52 [Idem], *Selectae propositiones ex universa philosophia quas ... publice indiscriminatim propugnandas exponit ... Franciscus Clarelli*, Romae.[73]

53 [Idem], *Selectae propositiones ex universa philosophia quas ... publice indiscriminatim propugnandas exponit ... Joseph Gavotti ...*, Romae.[74]

54 A. Rota, *Ragionamento ... su la teoria fisico-matematica del P. Ruggiero Giuseppe Boscovich ... esposto in una publica adunanza di eruditi signori*, Roma.[75]

55 [Anon., S.J.], *Propositiones philosophicae, quas ... dicat ... Hyacinthus Rapaccioli ...*, Viterbii.[76]

56 [Anon., C.R.S.], *Analysis elementorum Philosophiae, cuius Propositiones publice propugnat in Pontificio Collegio Gallio Julius Guglielmi ejusdem collegii alumnus*, Novo-Comi.[77]

1765

57 [G. Stoppini, S.J.], *Philosophicae theses ... propugnandae [ab] ... Antonius Gregori*, Romae.[78]

58 [Idem], *Philosophicas theses publice in Collegio Romano indiscriminatim propugnandas [dicat] Comes Alamannus Isolani*, Romae.[79]

59 [Idem], *Philosophicas theses ... dicat Felix De Grassis ...*, Romae.[80]

60 [Anon., S.J.], *Sancto Aloysio Gonzagae ... se suasque philosophicas theses publice propugnandas Joannes Paulus Maggi ... dicat*, Florentiae.[81]

1766

61 [Anon., S.J.], *Electricitatis synopsis juxta Franklini theoriam deque eadem Electricitate ad Auroram Borealem non applicanda dissertatio quas ... publico exponit certamini Josephus Travigi ... in Perusino Soc. Jesu Collegio*, Perusiae.[82]

62 [G. Vanni, C.R.M.I.], *Theses ex universa philosophia depromptas dicat Joseph Melchior De Risenfeldt*, Mantuae.[83]

63 [Anon., S.J.], *Cardinali amplissimo Urbano Paracciano ... philosophicam disputationem ... Theodorus Ercolanus ... [dicat]*, Venezia.[84]

1767

64 G. Vittori, S.J., *Institutiones philosophicae carminibus explicatae et adnotationibus illustratae*, Romae.[85]

65 [C. Crespi, O.S.B.], *Theses philosophicae quas in Imperiali Monasterio S. Ambrosii Majoris Mediolani publice D.D. proponit D. Amadaeus Pavarini Mediolanensis ... Assist. Adm. R. PP. D. Christophoro Crespi in eodem Caenobio Philosophiae Lectore*, Mediolani.[86]

1768

66 [G. Romano, S.J.], *Propositiones ex logica et physica a Joanne Widmann ... exhibitae in Seminario Romano*, Romae.[87]

67 [Idem], *Conclusiones ex universa philosophia selectae, quas Joseph Corari ... publice propugnandas indiscriminatim exponit ...*, Romae.[88]

68 [Idem], *Conclusiones ex universa philosophia selectae, quas Angelus Maria Tinelli ... publice propugnandas ... exponit ...*, Romae.[89]

1769

69 B. Corti, *Institutiones physicae*, vol. 1, Mutinae.[90]

1771

70 L. Altieri, O.F.M., *Elementa philosophiae in Adolescentium usum adornata. Tomus alter. In quo traduntur elementa metaphysicae, et physicae generalis*, Ferrariae.[91]

71 [Anon., S.J.], *Synopsis universae philosophiae quam ... ad disuputandum proponit Comes Cajetanus Boari ...*, Florentiae.[92]

72 [G. Pizzati, S.J.], *Exercitatio ex logica, physica, et metaphysica habita in Nobili Collegio Ptolemaeo ab Antonio Potenziani ...*, Senis.[93]

73 [Anon. (a secular priest?)], *D.D. Antonio Lantes ... Julianus Tozzi ... Venerabilis Seminarii ... S. Salvatoris Majoris alumnus ... se suasque philosophicas theses ... [dicat]*, Reate.[94]

74 [Anon. (a secular priest?)], *D.D. Ferdinando Mariae De Rubeis ... Bernardinus Mascetti ... se, suasque philosophicas theses ... [dicat]*, Reate.[95]

75 G. Barbarigo, C.R.S., *Elementa physicae generalis*, vol. 1, Venetiis.[96]

76 A. Volta, *Novus ac simplicissimus electricorum tentaminum apparatus: seu de corporibus eteroelectricis quae fiunt idioelectrica esperimenta, atque observationes*, Novocomi.[97]

1772

77 [F. Cittadelli, S.J.?], *Argumenta e logica, physicis, metaphysicis singula ad disputandum proposita apud Coll. Rom. Soc. Jes.*, Romae, 1772.[98]

78 [Idem], *Propositiones philosophicae a Josepho Smit Romano ... ad disputandum publice exhibitae ap. Colleg. Romanum ...*, Romae.[99]

79 [D. Troili, S.J.], *Ex universa philosophia selectae propositiones ... [propugnat] Paulus a Furno*, Mutinae.[100]

1773

80 C. Vitale, S.J., *Lex virium in materiam dominatrix illustrata, et ad physicas institutiones accomodata*, Mediolani.[101]

81 D. Troili, S.J., *Philosophiae universae institutiones ... Tomus I. Dissertationes proemiales de philosophia continens*, Mutinae.[102]

1778

82 C. Vitale, S.J., *L'unione dell'anima col corpo esaminata ne' suoi principi, e nelle sue conseguenze*, Milano.[103]

1779

83 D. Troili, S.J., 'Lettera a' Signori Giornalisti di Modena,' *Nuovo giornale de' letterati* 17 (Modena): 186–235.[104]

1780

84 C. Vitale, S.J., 'Lettera ... a' Signori Giornalisti di Modena su una controversia metafisica,' *Nuovo giornale de' letterati* 19 (Modena): 85–127.[105]

[1781]

85 D. Troili, S.J., 'Lettera a' Signori Giornalisti di Modena,' *Nuovo giornale de' letterati* 22 (Modena, 1781 or 1782): 51–81.[106]

[1782]

86 Idem, 'Lettera II à Signori Giornalisti di Modena,' *Nuovo giornale de' letterati* 23 (Modena, 1782 or 1783): 247–79.

[1783]

87 Idem, 'Lettera III à Signori Giornalisti di Modena,' *Nuovo giornale de'*
    letterati 24 (Modena, 1783 or 1784): 111–34.
88 G.B. Lascaris Guarini, S.J., *Ragionamenti filosofici. Parte prima*, Roma.[107]

1787

89 G. Calandrelli, *Physicae elementa*, Romae.[108]
90 *Elenchus rerum in triennio philosophico pertractandarum et quaestionum*
    pro Baccalaureatus assecutione exponendarum jussu Reverendissimi
    Patris Magistri Gregorii Clementi Ordinis Servorum Prioris Generalis
    editus, Romae.[109]

1789

91 [Anon., O.S.P.], *Conspectus propositionum philosophicarum quas publice*
    propugnandas exponit Petrus Saetone ..., Genuae.[110]
92 [Anon.], review of A. Fabroni's biography of Boscovich, *Giornale de'*
    letterati (Pisa): 126ff.[111]

1791

93 E.G. Gil, S.J., *Theoria boscovichiana vindicata et defensa*, Fulginiae.[112]

1794

94 A. Ludena, S.J., *Universae Philosophiae elementa*, Camerini.[113]

1798

95 O. Del Giudice, O.F.M.Obs., *Physicae generalis eclecticae elementa ad*
    usum studiosae juventuti [!] *accommodata*, vol. 1, Perusiae.[114]
96 [E.G. Gil, S.J.], *Dissertatio de viribus repulsivis in natura existentibus.*
    Propugnabitur a ... Carolo Anguissola, Josepho Bellotti, Dominico
    Lusardi, Placentiae.[115]

1799

97 Idem, *Disquisitio in causam physicam recentium chemicorum pro*
    elasticitate aeris, Placentiae.[116]

[Date unknown; post-1773]

98 Anon., *Theoriae Philosophiae Naturalis Patris Rogerii Josephi Boscovich*
    Epitome.[117]

The preceding list is probably very incomplete.[118] However, it makes possible
some inferences. Of the roughly 50 authors of the works, only 4 (nos 54, 69, 76,

96) were not clerics; at least 2 of the 4 (including A. Volta) had studied in Jesuit colleges; and roughly 25 of the others were Jesuits. This shows that discussion of Boscovich's ideas developed in small and specific circles; his colleagues in Bologna's Accademia delle Scienze, in the Società Italiana delle Scienze (the most renowned Italian scientific body), and at the university in Pavia never pronounced publicly on his theory. The same is true for teachers in Roman institutions of higher education, such as the university and the college De Propaganda Fide.[119] But public discussion was limited not only because it was restricted to Jesuit schools (Calasanzio college being the only notable exception). In mid-eighteenth-century Italy, philosophy and mathematics were taught in at least forty colleges of the Society, attended every year by some thousands of students; had Boscovich's ideas been considered in most of them, in the four decades from 1746 to his death, they would have become so well known that non-Jesuit teachers and scientists would have had to consider them. Boscovich's efforts to have the theory received in Jesuit schools were successful only in some colleges of the Roman province (central Italy and Tuscany). Normally the scientific and philosophical specialists of a province were trained within the province; most of Boscovich's students who later taught philosophy remained in the Roman province. Even there, however, superiors and professors did not allow the theory to replace the standard content of physics courses, a mixture of eclectic Aristotelianism and Galilean-Newtonian physics: the theses, the manuscript lecture notes, and other information show that it was expounded, or simply mentioned, only in some courses before 1773.[120]

Sometimes silence meant hostility. Within a few years, conservative Jesuits had largely succeeded in expelling Boscovich and his followers from their chairs. In 1754 two philosophy theses defended in the Collegio Romano under the direction of Carlo Benvenuti, one of Boscovich's pupils (the theses were in fact written by him and by the master himself), triggered a bitter reaction from the superiors in the order, which eventually led to intercession by Pope Benedict XIV on Benvenuti's behalf. In 1760, during Boscovich's absence from Italy, his opponents in the Collegio Romano met in order to work on a common strategy to thwart the diffusion of his ideas.[121] In the same year, when his brother Baro, who substituted for him in the Collegio's mathematics chair, fell ill, his replacement, G.M. Asclepi, was immediately made an ordinary professor, so that Boscovich could not hold the chair again when he returned to Rome. Asclepi's works never mentioned his illustrious predecessor.

We may conclude that while Boscovich's theory suffered in being the production of a Jesuit even in the increasingly 'enlightened' climate, it also lacked the advantages of full support within the Society's system of schools. It had been structured as a bridge connecting the new science and some parts of the scholastic tradition, but a majority of people on both sides regarded such a bridge as favouring the enemy.

Reactions by other religious orders are still largely unexplored. Some titles show that a hostile front existed among the Piarists.[122] Very little, however, is known about the philosophical-physical teaching in other orders. Individual cases apart, it is plausible that those competing with the Jesuits in teaching were critical, while others – especially the minor orders, without school systems of their own, who frequently used that of the Jesuits – had no standard position.[123]

The German Empire, Prussia, and Poland

1750
99 Review of Boscovich's *Dissertatio de lumine* (1748), in *Acta eruditorum*, pp. 462–9.

1752
100 K. Scherffer, S.J., *Institutionum physicae pars prima, seu physica generalis, conscripta in usum suorum D.D. Auditorum*, Viennae.[124]

1756
101 J. Mangold, S.J., *Philosophia rationalis et experimentalis hodiernis discentium studiis accomodata ... Tomus II. Physicam generalem complectens*, Ingolstadii et Monachii.[125]

1757
102 Review of F.M. Gaudio, 1756 (no. 23), in *Acta eruditorum*, p. 648.

1758
103 B. Hauser, S.J., *Elementa philosophiae ad rationis et experientiae ductum conscripta, atque usibus scholasticis accommodata ... Tomus IV. Physica Generalis*, Augustae Vindelicorum et Oeniponti.[126]

1759
104 J. Stepling, S.J., *Miscellanea philosophica tam mathematica, quam physica*, Pragae.
105 M. Mendelssohn, review of Boscovich's *Theoria*.[127]

1761
106 Review of *De solis ac lunae defectibus*, in *Acta eruditorum*, pp. 168–74.

107 J. Diesbach, S.J., *Institutiones philosophicae de corporum attributis ad mentem Rogerii Boscowichii*, Pragae.

1762 [or 1763]

108 Idem, *Expositio systematis Boscowichiani de lege virium*, Pragae.
109 P. Mako de Kerk-Gede, S.J., *Compendiaria physicae institutio*, Vindobonae.

1763

110 K. Scherffer, S.J., *Institutionum physicae pars prima, seu physica generalis conscripta in usum tyronum philosophiae ... Editio altera*, Vindobonae.[128]
111 M. Mangold, S.J., *Philosophia recentior praelectionibus publicis accommodata*, vol. 1, Monachii.[129]
112 [B. Stattler, S.J.], *Tractatio cosmologica de viribus et natura corporum, publice proposita; cum ... positiones ex universa philosophia et pluribus partibus matheseos ... in Electorali Lyceo Monacensi publice propugnaret ... Josephus Fuchs ...*, [Monachii].[130]

1765

113 [Anon., S.J.], *Propositiones philosophicae* [defended by Ant. Grothusz], Vilnae.[131]
114 M. Krammer, S.J., *Theoria de lege virium in natura existentium. Phaenomena applicata*, Pragae.
115 Idem, *Theoria de lege virium in natura existentium, curva quidam legitime exhibita*, Pragae.
116 A. Radics (Radits), S.J., *Introductio in Philosophiam Naturalem, Theoriae P. Rogerii Boscovich ... accommodata*, [Budae].

1766

117 Idem, *Institutiones physicae in usum discipulorum*, Budae.
118 J. Pawlik, S.J., *Compendiaria physicae generalis et specialis doctrina*, Olomucii.
119 [J.B. Zallinger zum Thurn, S.J.], *Conspectus assertionum ex universa philosophia ... [quas defendet] ... P.F. von Volkenstein*, Tridenti.[132]

1767

120 F. Tessanek, S.J., *Institutiones physicae*, 2 vols, Olomucii.[133]
121 L. Biwald, S.J., *Physica generalis*, Graecii.

122 Idem, *Assertiones ex universa philosophia* [with the name of a student of his, C. Priebling], Graecii.
123 J.B. Horvath, S.J., *Institutiones metaphysicae*, Tyrnaviae.[134]

1768

124 M. Mendelssohn, introduction to the second edition of *Phädon oder über die Unsterblichkeit der Seele.*[135]

1769

125 L. Biwald, S.J., *Institutiones physicae in usum Philosophiae auditorum* [ed. by M. dal Pozzo], Graecii.
126 [J.A. Zallinger, S.J.], *Lex gravitatis universalis ac mutuae cum Theoria de sectione coni, potissimum elliptica proposita, cum ... praeside P. Jacopo Zallinger S.J. Philosophiae Professore ... Theses philosophicas propugnarent ... Marcellinus Hendl ... et Philippus Schmid ...*, Monachii.[136]
127 A. Zeplichal, S.J., *Entwurf der Boscowichschen Naturlehre*, Breslau.

1770

128 [I. Windisch, S.J.], *Theses logicae et metaphysicae quas ... propugnabunt ... Georgius Hübschmann, ..., Joannes Reuther ..., Franciscus Benedictus Hanauer ..., Franciscus Hettrich ...*, Bambergae.[137]
129 J.B. Horvath, S.J., *Physica generalis*, Tyrnaviae.[138]
130 N. Burkhäuser, S.J., *Theoria corporis naturalis principiis Boscovichii confirmata*, Wirceburgi.

1771

131 Idem, *Institutiones metaphysicae*, Wirceburgi.
132 S. von Storchenau, S.J., *Institutiones metaphysicae*, Vindobonae.[139]
133 J.B. Zallinger zum Thurn, S.J., *De viribus materiae dissertatio physica*, Oeniponti.

1772

134 L. Biwald, S.J., an edition of J.B. Zallinger's *De viribus materiae dissertatio*, Graecii.
135 [Anon., S.J.], *Philosophia rationalis et experimentalis proposita in Alma, Catholica, et Electorali Anglipolitana, propugnata a sex Religiosis Soc. Jesu. Mense Martio MDCCLXXII*, [Monachii].[140]
136 [L. Biwald, S.J.], *Anmerkungen über den Auszug, und die Kritik eines berlinischen Herrn Recensenten das Boscovische System betreffend. Herausgegeben, als aus der Kaiserl. Königl. Vorderösterreichischen*

hochen Schule zu Freyburg einigen die Magisterwürde in der
Weltweisheit ertheilet wurde im Augustmonate 1772. 61. Fortsetzung
der Anmerkungen über den Auszug, und die Kritik ..., im Augustmonate
1772 [trans. into Latin, *Animadversiones in Extractum et Crisin Censoris*
Berolin, circa Systema Boscovich, Graecii, 1773].[141]

137 B. Stattler, S.J., *Philosophia methodo scientiis propria exposita ... Pars*
VII. Physica particularis corporum totalium huius mundi, Augustae
Vindelicorum.[142]

1773

138 J.A. Zallinger zum Thurn, S.J., *Interpretatio naturae, seu Philosophia*
Newtoniana methodo exposita, 3 vols, Augustae Vindelicorum.

139 Review of Burkhäuser, 1770 (no. 130), in *Nova acta eruditorum*,
pp. 114–16.

1782

140 I.N. Alber, O.S.P., *Cogitationes philosophicae de immediato corporum*
contactu, Theoriam Cl. Jos. Roger. Boscovichii respicientes, Viennae.

1805

141 F.S. Zallinger zum Thurn, S.J., *Praelectiones ex physica theoretica, et*
experimentali, Oeniponte.[143]

[Date unknown]

142 J.N. Alber, O.S.P., *De natura extensionis*, [?].[144]

The list confirms that Central Europe was, along with Italy, an area in which
Boscovich was more successful; but his success there was centred in Jesuit
schools even more than it was in Italy (only Alber, Mendelssohn, and the
reviewers in *Acta eruditorum* were not Jesuits). A look at the geographical
distribution of supporters of the theory is instructive. They taught and published
in Hungary (Budapest), Slovakia (Trnava, Breslau), Bohemia (Olomouc, Prague),
Austria-Tyrol (Vienna, Graz, Innsbruck, Trent), and Bavaria (Munich, Augsburg,
Ingolstadt, Würzburg, Bamberg).[145] All these localities belonged to just three
provinces of the German assistancy of the Society: Austria (Austria, Hungary,
Transylvania, Slovenia, Principality of Trent), Bohemia (Bohemia, Moravia,
Silesia), and *Germania superior* (Bavaria). In the Jesuit provinces along the
Rhine (Upper Rhine, Lower Rhine, Gallo-Belgica, Flandro-Belgica), no rel-
evant work is known so far. Finally, one work was written and published in
Vilnius (no. 111), then in the Jesuit assistancy of Poland.

In part this geography has biographical logic. Boscovich's stay in Vienna in 1757–8 and 1763 was decisive for the editorial history of the *Theoria*; Scherffer, his most active supporter, taught there.[146] Boscovich had been in Bavaria during 1761 and in Bohemia in early 1763; Jesuit professors in Bohemia, Slovakia, and Hungary had often studied in Vienna; Austrian and Bavarian Jesuits had been closely connected since the sixteenth century.[147] Even the Vilnius publication is accounted for by Boscovich's stay in Poland (1762), where he was in close contact with some Jesuit philosophers and mathematicians; a better knowledge of publications in that area would probably turn up a number of relevant texts.[148] However, his personal influence and propaganda do not explain everything. From late 1760 to April 1761, he also was in Flanders, in the Netherlands, and on the eastern bank of the Rhine from Cologne to Augsburg, visiting Jesuit houses and colleges and surely advocating his theory. So the seemingly total lack of response in these provinces cannot be accounted for in terms of an absence of information; some specific intellectual factors must be considered.

a) During the eighteenth century, German Jesuit philosophers increasingly adopted Leibnizian/Wolffian concepts and, even more, the Wolffian structure of the *cursus philosophicus* in place of the scholastic one.[149] This favoured reception of Boscovich. His hypothesis on the structure of matter resembled that of the monads; that is, both Boscovich's point-atomism and Leibniz's monads provided an arrangement in which modern mechanics was favoured but philosophical mechanism was denied in principle; accordingly, in so far as Boscovich's theory coupled some quasi-Leibnizian features with Newtonian mechanics, it made contact between the two traditions easier.

b) Jesuit colleges in Belgium and the Rhine region were within or contiguous to a 'Cartesian' area. Cartesian metaphysics had not been accepted there, nor had those parts of physics that had (or seemed to have) heterodox theological implications, but Cartesian cosmology and epistemology had entered the colleges and were still influential in the middle of the eighteenth century.[150] In that region the metaphysical dualism the Society regarded as essential to its religious aims was guaranteed, but not in a Leibnizian way, and a mechanistic epistemology still opposed the adoption of Newtonian physics and the extended notion of force so essential to Boscovich's model.

c) In 'deep' Catholic Germany, from Bavaria to Bohemia, the Jesuit influence in the universities was much stronger (most theological, philosophical, and mathematical chairs were controlled by the Society), so whatever prevailed in Jesuit learning also influenced the universities, and something like a distinctly 'lay' judgment could hardly prevail. For geographical and historical reasons, the Jesuits' role was less exclusive in Flanders and western Germany, where their physical teaching had been sufficiently permeated by mechanistic approaches to configure Boscovich's metaphysical premises as sophistic or obsolete. Such a partially laicized situation made reception difficult: the link between classical metaphysics and modern physics (maintained by Boscovich in a refined way) looked like the symptom of an anti-scientific or pre-modern bias, which made a purely 'factual' evaluation of the theory seem useless. It is worth noting that the impact of this was so extensive that before 1800 not a single case is known on the Continent of an agnostic scientist who adhered to the theory, or even discussed it abstracted from the modes of its presentation.

d) The scarcity of appreciable responses by scientific and academic circles in Protestant Germany, where the background was still Leibnizian/Wolffian, may be attributed partly to strong anti-Jesuit feelings, and partly to the fact that the academies, especially Berlin's Academy of Sciences, were unfavourable to Boscovich.[151]

So Boscovich could be successful only in scientific and educational institutions where epistemological, ideological, and religious positions did not prevent his ideas from being discussed in purely scientific terms (the more so because his purely qualitative law of force could not be tested precisely). Unfortunately for him, this was not the situation in the principal scientific centres, in Germany as elsewhere; he had an audience where it was less decisive to have one, and, being mostly Jesuit, that audience disappeared within a few years.

France

1750

143 Review of Boscovich's *De lumine*, in *Mémoires pour l'histoire des sciences et des beaux arts* ('Mémoires de Trévoux'), pp. 1642–57.[152]

1754

144 H.-S. Gerdil, C.R.S.P., *Dissertations sur l'incompatibilité de l'attraction ... avec les Phénomenes, et sur les tuyaux capillaires*, Paris.[153]

1756

145 Review of vol. 1 of B. Stay's *Philosophia recentior* and Boscovich's notes to it, in *Mémoires pour l'histoire des sciences et des beaux arts* ('Mémoires de Trévoux'), pp. 80–108.[154]

1757

146 Review of the same work, in *Journal des savants*, pp. 259–65.[155]

1760

147 F.B. de Felice, abstract of Boscovich's *Theoria, Estratto della letteratura europea per l'anno MDCCLX* 4: 3–29.[156]

1761

148 Review of *De solis ac lunae defectibus*, in *Journal des savants*, p. 764.[157]
149 Review of the same work, in *Journal étranger* (July), pp. 65–88, (August), pp. 81–103.
150 Review of vol. 2 of Stay's poem and Boscovich's notes to it, in *Mémoires pour l'histoire des sciences et des beaux arts* ('Mémoires de Trévoux'), pp. 1232–54, 1393–1411, 2117–32, 2714–38.

1764

151 Anonymous review of the *Theoria, Gazette littéraire de l'Europe*, suppl. to vol. 5 (4 April): 1, 118–20.

1766

152 Anonymous review of the first two editions of *Naturalis philosophiae theoria*, in *Journal des savants* (January), pp. 9–14.[158]

1771

153 J.J. de Lalande, *Astronomie*, 2nd ed.[159]

1772

154 F. Para du Phanjas, S.J., *Theorie des êtres sensibles, ou cours complet de Physique, spéculative, expérimentale, systématique et géométrique*, Paris.[160]

1774

155 J. Saury, *Cours complet de mathématiques*, Paris.[161]

1776

156 Idem, *Cours de physique expérimentale et théorique*, Paris.[162]

1777

157 J.-J. Rossignol, S.J. *Plan d' étude á l'usage des collèges*, Embrun.[163]

1779

158 A. Barruel, S.J., French translation of Boscovich, *Les éclipses, Poëme en six chants ...*, Paris.[164]

1780

159 Review of *Les éclipses* (no. 158), *Année littéraire* (3): 73–98.

1802

160 J.-J. Rossignol, S.J., *Pshysique générale. Première partie*, Turin.[165]

What kept Boscovich's theory out of the academic establishments in France? In Protestant Germany the prejudices against a Catholic and Jesuit author, the geographical distance from Rome, and the tenuousness of the links with the Roman cultural milieu could – reviews in *Acta eruditorum* notwithstanding – be seen as obstacles to the circulation of his works, and could conceal his originality with respect to Leibniz and Wolff. In France, however, these factors were less in play. Anti-Jesuit attitudes were frequent among academic scientists, but not unanimous (Lalande is a possible example). The Society was suppressed in France in 1762, but the individual Jesuits were not expelled, and many remained on the intellectual scene. Boscovich tried very early to have his writings circulated in France, was active during his two visits there (1759–60 and 1769–70), and lived in the country from 1773 to 1782.[166] Finally, he enjoyed good relations with Clairaut, La Condamine, Lalande, Messier, and Bezout, to mention only a few of the leading scientists of the day. So institutional or religious factors could not have played a decisive role. A puzzling fact is the French Jesuits' attitude. From 1750 to 1762, no fewer than two hundred Jesuits taught mathematics and philosophy in at least twenty-five schools;[167] it seems no accident, therefore, that, Rossignol apart, in half a century only Para du Phanjas discussed (unfavourably) Boscovich's ideas in a published work (no. 154).[168] The authoritative Jesuit journal *Mémoires de Trévoux* was cautious, but its editor, Guillaume François Berthier, decidely opposed Boscovich.[169]

Traditionalism was not responsible: Jesuit education in France was relatively advanced, and most metaphysical-epistemological barriers had collapsed. If a common attitude towards the new theory existed among scientists – those who were also *philosophes*, those who were pure specialists, the members of the Society, and the members of other religious orders – it could have come only from a shared idea of science. Boscovich's model was Newtonian in two basic senses. It accepted the law of attraction as a description of macroscopic events; and it shared the assumption that physical reality includes a non-material element, force, but extended the role of force so as to reverse Descartes's thesis. The Cartesian world consisted of matter only; that of Boscovich, of force only. French scientists had reluctantly accepted the first aspect of Newtonianism but still opposed the second (i.e., a not entirely mechanistic world picture), mechanism being the residue of the old Cartesian ideal. Obviously, differences existed: philosophical mechanists such as d'Alembert, Condorcet, and Laplace believed that matter constituted not only all physical reality, but all reality whatsoever; religious scientists, the Jesuits among them, admitted spiritual entities. That difference, however, did not affect their view of natural science; as violent as the polemic between the two parties could be, both reacted against a theory contradicting that view.

This interpretation of events seems confirmed by known episodes, even if each of those episodes also had a more specific motivation.[170] A French Jesuit in the Collegio Romano, J.-B. Faure, opposed Boscovich in order to defend not scholastic cosmology, but an anti-Newtonian idea of physics.[171] If this was what was at stake, then a foreign and relatively insulated theorist could only lose. Mechanism would be questioned only at a subsequent stage.

The Iberian Countries

Boscovich had almost no personal contacts in Portugal and Spain, and his works were not disseminated in those countries; his ideas are not mentioned by local Jesuits before the suppression of the Society in Portugal in 1759 and in Spain in 1767–8.[172] The suppressions came just a few years after the first presentations of the theory, and Boscovich was never in the Iberian Peninsula. But in France and Germany some information as to his theory spread before 1755, whereas no debate on it is documented in Spain and Portugal even after 1770. So an explanation is needed.

Some simple matters of fact must be taken into account. For both Spain and Portugal, very few Jesuit scientific and philosophical theses or manuscript lecture notes of the mid-eighteenth century have been studied. In both countries, unlike in France, Italy, and the German world, the members of the Society were imprisoned or expelled after the suppression; so greater discontinuity took place in these regions and in certain areas of intellectual life. Most of the expelled Portuguese and Spanish Jesuits were young enough to be influenced by the state of learning in the countries to which they went (mostly Italy), so it is problematic to use their works as documents of the situations from which they came.[173] Owing to their partially 'enlightened' frame of mind, the leaders of the anti-Jesuit action in Spain and Portugal gave the school system a strong anti-metaphysical bias, insisted on application (in both countries much of the modern teaching of science was in military schools), and reduced the scope of fundamental science. So the standard picture within which science was taught and practised during these decades was the mechanistic one, substantially deprived of its foundational and theoretical aspects.

This state of affairs was surely unfavourable for consideration, to say nothing of acceptance, of the theory, and makes it probable that the now growing study of edited and unedited writings will not change the picture substantially. An obvious possibility is that until 1790–1800, Boscovichian ideas were diffused by the writings of the expelled Iberian Jesuits that were published abroad or published after their authors returned to their own countries; only a small portion of these writings (very small in the case of manuscripts and correspondence) has been studied for its bearing on scientific history.[174]

3. A Summary Analysis of the Data and Some Final Remarks

The works listed for the three regions Italy, the Empire–Poland, and France differ markedly in number: 97, 44, and 15 titles respectively. Since the number of educational institutions (particularly of the religious orders) in these areas was comparable, the fact that relevant texts (especially Jesuit texts) have been researched more in Italy than in the German world, and very little in France, does not suffice as an explanation. Nor does the fact that the Society was suppressed in these areas in different years (1768–73 in Italy, 1773 in the German world, and 1762–4 in France), because differences show no correlation with chronology: before 1762, the numbers of relevant works are, respectively, 49, 11, and 8; after the general suppression (1773), they are 16, 3, and 5 (four of the French being from two authors, and the fifth being the translation of a poem that dealt with the theory only marginally). Moreover, differences in absolute numbers are perhaps less revealing than those among types of works:

	Italy	German world	France
theses	65 (90.2%)	7 (9.8%)	0
dissertations	15 (57.7%)	9 (34.6%)	2 (7.7%)
treatises, handbooks	9 (25.7%)	21 (60%)	5 (14.3%)
reviews, articles, translations	8 (32%)	7 (28%)	10 (40%)

Other differences may be observed in chronology, both in general and from region to region. The appearance of most of the writings between 1760 and 1770 is accounted for by the fact of the suppression, which had an immediate impact on the production of theses (a major component of the literature on Boscovich, especially in Italy). For other aspects of the chronology, however, there is no ready explanation. An analysis of the factors responsible for the differences, both regional and chronological, is beyond the scope of this essay, and moreover, at present would be certainly premature and probably misleading, because the differences (in both the absolute and the regional numbers) also reflect the current state of textual research, which is uneven across national and cultural contexts. It will be sufficient to hint at some factors that possibly were influential. Because a dissertation focused on a single subject, those on the theory were, in general, the most specialized evaluations of it. So the fact that all dissertations but one appeared in the Italian and German assistancies reflects the substantial ostracism to which French professional science subjected the theory, and shows that sensitivity to it was comparable in Italy and the German world (even if it was present in those areas for different reasons). The great difference in the number of theses is a highly uncertain datum, because theses are by far the most difficult texts to find. So perhaps the most telling difference is that in the number of treatises and handbooks, particularly between Italy and the German world. Very roughly, it may be attributed to two facts: first, the smaller production in Italy was party due to the smaller geographical distances involved and the relatively few regional divisions – the nearness of the Roman vertex, which induced conformity; and second, in half the peninsula the Society was suppressed in 1768 (six German treatises were published between 1769 and 1773). But a much deeper immersion in the currents of Jesuit culture in the mid-eighteenth century and in the educational, hierarchical, and logistical dimensions of the question – and their interconnections – is required before adequate assessment becomes possible.

Every reconstruction of factors affecting the diffusion and reception of Boscovich's ideas must agree with a map of those processes, which may be derived only from the geography of the texts treating the ideas. To the extent that the number of texts known remains smaller than their real number, the map may change, and so may the factors relevant to the formulation of a hypothesis. That, however, is not the only limitation of the analysis offered in this paper. A more conceptual one is that it has looked at the theory as something unchanging and, consequently, at the reactions to it as fixed and stable. This could be wrong: Boscovich developed his theory over time, from 1745 to after 1780 (i.e., in his last notes to B. Stay's *Philosophia recentior*); his principles and basic explanations remained the same, but he illustrated them differently, he extended his examples, and he rectified some previous assertions in response to criticism. So the theory could have a history, in both its external and – perhaps – its internal traits. The same could be said of the writings of Boscovich's followers: the case of A. Volta has been mentioned; E.G. Gil's *Disquisitio in causam physicam recentium chemicorum pro elasticitate aeris* came after Lavoisier's revolution in chemistry, so it is yet to be ascertained whether he tried to explain the new doctrines in terms of his theory. The criticisms too could be regarded as 'historical.' Studies of Boscovich, however, have considered texts written at various moments (if usually not the later ones) as slightly different expressions of a single theory. So a future shift of focus, from the theory's statics to its dynamics, is desirable. This, however, will only make a mapping more essential: history needs a reliable geography as much as a reliable chronology.

If the original theory had a history, so did its uses in the nineteenth century, though the two histories were not of the same kind. Externally, the fate of Boscovichianism may appear similar to that of, say, Copernicanism: in both cases, most contemporaries considered the theory as the eccentric product of one man, and the theory was accepted only decades later. The inner process, however, was profoundly different. Copernicanism was accepted in Kepler's version, but its principles had not changed, and that version applied to the same phenomena, although it was much more clearly defined. Boscovich's theory, however, incorporated many more phenomenological and logical levels. From 1780 to 1820, the range of physical facts to which it was applied was restructured by advances in chemistry, thermodynamics, optics, magnetism, and electricity; so the phenomena were not the 'same' as those Boscovich considered. What some nineteenth-century scientists found inspiring (not literally 'true') were the theory's assumptions about unobservable space-matter relations and the implications of a continuity principle at a microphysical level. So there is no question about its having been 'proved,' or about certain nineteenth-century results in optics or electricity being 'preceded' by it. Therefore, whereas before c. 1800 the theory may be dealt with as the primary subject-matter of a history, after that date it may be considered only as an element in the development of other theories (as it has been for some). This is perhaps the chief reason why the place of the theory in the history of physics has not been entirely defined, and why current assessments of its author differ so widely – he is regarded as everything from a talented visionary to a scientific revolutionary. Only an integrated reconstruction of the role of Boscovich's ideas can prove whether he more resembles a Velikovsky or an Einstein.

NOTES

1 *Philosophiae recentioris a Benedicto Stay ... versibus traditae libri X ... cum adnotationibus, et supplementis P. Rogerii Josephi Boscovich SJ ... Tomus I* (Romae, 1755), pp. 332–3, 354–6. Boscovich gave a larger exposition in vol. 3 (Romae, 1792).

2 Not listed among Boscovich's works in Somm. *Bib.*, I, pp. 1828–50. It was published in *Memorie sopra la fisica e istoria naturale*, ed. C.A. Giuliani, vol. 4 (Lucca, 1757).

3 For bibliography on Boscovich, see P. Casini, 'Boscovich, Ruggiero Giuseppe,' in *Dizionario biografico degli Italiani* (Rome, 1960–) (hereafter *DBI*), XIII, pp. 221–30; Ž. Marković, 'Bošković, R.J.,' in *Dictionary of Scientific Biography*, 18 vols (New York, 1970–90), II, pp. 326–32; *R.J. Boscovich: Vita e attività scientifica: His Life and Scientific Work*, ed. P. Bursill-Hall (Rome, 1993), pp. 620–6; *Isis Cumulative Bibliography, 1986–95: A Bibliography of the History of Science Formed from the Annual Isis Current Bibliographies*, ed. John Neu, vol. 1 (Canton, MA, 1997).

4 The theory entails the possibility of 'parallel' universes having no spatial relation; isomorphic transformations or movements of a universe, imperceptible to its inhabitants; and continuous dimensional changes of a universe, also imperceptible to its inhabitants.

5 Boscovich did not represent the law as a formula but as a curve. The lack of numerical parameters was serious, making it impossible to test it exactly.

6 The Académie des Sciences had the Jesuit as a *correspondant* since 1748, but never made him an *associé* (to say nothing of an ordinary member), mainly because of d'Alembert's hostility; see R. Hahn, 'The Ideological and Institutional Difficulties of a Jesuit Scientist in Paris,' in *R.J. Boscovich*, ed. Bursill-Hall, pp. 1–12; J. Pappas, 'R.J. Boscovich et l'Académie des sciences de Paris,' *Revue d'histoire des sciences* 49 (1996): 401–14.

7 See work no. 152. Most *éloges* of Boscovich focused on his technical contributions and discoveries, omitting his general conception, or else describing it briefly, as something eccentric that diminished rather than increased his merit (two Italian exceptions are F. Ricca, *Elogio storico dell'abate Ruggiero Giuseppe Boscovich* [Milano, 1789], pp. 15–22; and D. Troili, 'Elogio del Sig. Abate Ruggiergiuseppe Boscovich,' *Nuovo giornale de' letterati di Modena* 28 [1787]: 184–215, and 29 [1788]: 131–59). A. Fabroni, a former pupil of Boscovich, in the portrait in his *Vitae Italorum doctrina excellentium*, vol. 14 (Pisis, 1789), pp. 278–381, and in a necrology in *Memorie di matematica e di fisica della Società italiana delle scienze*, vol. 4 (1788), pp. vii ff., came close to describing the theory as the master's obsession.

8 One was Diderot, who received (1760) the work from the author; see J. Pappas, 'Les relations entre Boscovich and d'Alembert,' in *Bicentennial Commemoration of R.G. Boscovich: Proceedings*, ed. M. Bossi and P. Tucci (Milan, 1988), p. 123; for d'Alembert see the same essay. In a letter to Frisi (1770), the latter defined Boscovich as a 'charlatan orgueilleux'; see J. Pappas, 'Les relations entre Frisi et d'Alembert,' in *Ideologia e scienza nell'opera di Paolo Frisi (1728–1784)*, ed. G. Barbarisi, vol. 2 (Milan, 1987), p. 160.

9　M. Feingold, 'A Jesuit among Protestants: Boscovich in England, c. 1745–1820,' in
　　R.J. Boscovich, ed. Bursill-Hall, pp. 511–26. As a consequence, British Boscovich-
　　ianism has been more studied than that in continental Europe; so this essay will deal
　　only with the latter. The reasons for the difference deserve a paper of their own; I
　　believe they had to do with the lesser philosophical and ideological constraints
　　present in the British context.

10　Italian Jesuit writings (see the list for Italy) show that – the Collegio Romano
　　apart – his followers were present in some minor colleges of the Roman province
　　and in very few others; none of these writings was produced in the *collegium
　　maximum* of another province (Milan, Parma, Bologna, Naples, and Palermo).

11　'[Now the system of Boscovich is], like all others, forgotten and neglected':
　　J. Andrés, *Dell'origine, de' progressi e dello stato attuale d'ogni letteratura*, vol. 4
　　(Parma, 1790), p. 431.

12　The curially inspired Accademia di Religione Cattolica, which devoted many papers
　　to the relations between science and religion, never analysed the theory; see U.
　　Baldini, 'Filosofia naturale e scienza nell'Academia di religione cattolica,' in
　　Simposio internazionale di studi filosofici e storici in onore di Antonio Rosmini ...,
　　vol. 2, *Rosmini e Roma*, ed. L. Malusa and P. De Lucia (Stresa, 2000), pp. 173–225.

13　Biographical and bibliographical information is given only when necessary; on
　　Jesuit authors, see Somm. *Bib.*

14　Letters, 'éloges,' biographies, necrologies, historical memoirs, etc. are excluded.
　　Owing to the rarity of the student theses, the site of an exemplar for each has been
　　indicated, chiefly Rome's Biblioteca Nazionale Centrale Vittorio Emanuele II
　　(BNVE) and Biblioteca Apostolica Vaticana (hereafter BAV).

15　In Italian Jesuit colleges 'thesis' was a name for 1) an anonymous list of proposi-
　　tions to be 'defended' by all students of a discipline in a certain college and year;
　　2) the same list, with respect to a single student; 3) a longer work (from 10–20
　　pages to a book-length volume) with both the propositions and their 'defences.'
　　Texts of type 3 may be divided into a) theses on a part of a discipline (as astronomy
　　in mathematics or ontology theses, 'general physics' or psychology in philosophy
　　theses); b) theses on the whole of a discipline. Usually, those of type 3a were
　　defended in the year in which the relevant subject was dealt with (those of math-
　　ematics and 'general physics' in the second year of philosophy); those of type 3b
　　at the end of the last year (the third in the case of philosophy). The defence was
　　usually presided over by the teacher of the discipline; in Italian theses his name was
　　indicated rarely, but since the theses were printed for the purposes of the defence,
　　if the names of those teaching in a college or university are known the professor in
　　question is readily identifiable. Professors were usually the real authors, as I will
　　mention below, so the theses offer a way of reconstructing a school's history in
　　terms of what was being taught.

16 Catalogues attribute the theses to the students, who are unknown. Most type 1 and type 2 texts have been lost; those that survive are not catalogued independently, and are found mostly inside manuscript lecture notes written by the student who would be defending the propositions. Full-length theses were printed only by affluent students or those with a patron, so this very valuable kind of source is rare.

17 A Jesuit's work had to be submitted to the Society's revisers-general; only if approved could it proceed to the Inquisition for the *imprimatur*; see Bald. *Leg.*, chap. 2. A thesis, printed under the student's name, was usually approved by the rector of the college – often after a superficial examination – and as an educational text was not the principal focus of the Inquisition.

18 Boscovich's violation of the traditional boundary had probably prompted reactions from philosophers. By the middle of the eighteenth century, the boundary had largely been abandoned by advanced scientists and (in part) in the universities, but not in the religious schools. So the reactions could be informed by a mixture of intellectual opposition and corporate defensiveness.

19 The lists expand preceding ones, such as that in Steven J. Harris, 'Boscovich, the "Boscovich Circle," and the Revival of Jesuit Science,' in *R.J. Boscovich*, ed. Bursill-Hall, pp. 546–8. The teacher is indicated as the author of the thesis; when his name is not on the title-page but may be inferred from another source, it is in brackets. The names of regular clerics are followed by the acronyms of their orders, so as to reveal some interesting facts. Manuscripts (lecture notes or other) are excluded, because their role in the diffusion of the theory was smaller and is difficult to assess. In some cases they were more explicit than the printed works: see G.S. Conti's evaluation of Boscovich's system in G. Arrighi, 'La inestendibilità de' primi elementi della materia nella teoria boscovichiana (un manoscritto inedito di G.S. Conti),' *Physis* 5 (1963): 78–96. A shorter, negative evaluation can be found in the philosophy lecture notes of L. Fortis (1790–1800), APUG FC 1198/1 fols 269ff.); it is not to be confused with his 'Confutatio systematis Boscovichiani' (Somm. *Bib.*, III, p. 897 M), not found so far. Other relevant manuscripts are mentioned in the notes.

20 BNVE 34–2–L–3, 3. Theses reflecting the pre-Boscovich teaching of physics in the Collegio Romano. One point, however, probably represents the first printed reaction to his ideas: the author denies that the constituents of bodies are 'physical inextended points,' but considers it possible that impenetrability is produced by a 'vis repulsiva' (p. 9), and considers elasticity a combined effect of it and the 'vis attractiva' (p. 24). These theses deal only with *physica generalis*, which in 1745–6 was taught by Correa (1706–70). However, Caucci could have discussed them at the end of his course; he had been a pupil of G.P. Bartolucci, who taught that subject in 1744–5 (Villos. *Coll. Rom.*, p. 331; Baldini, 'Boscovich e la tradizione gesuitica in filosofia naturale: Continuità e cambiamento,' in *R.J. Boscovich*, ed. Bursill-Hall,

p. 130). This could be decided by comparing the theses with the lecture notes of both teachers: Somm. *Bib.*, II, p. 1482; Baldini, 'Boscovich e la tradizione,' p. 130 nn 34, 35.

21 In this year a philosophy graduate at the Collegio Romano was Andrea Archetti, the nominal author of the first part of Boscovich's *De lumine* (Romae, 1748; the second part was published anonymously in the same year and reprinted by Boscovich in Vienna in 1766). Archetti's theses (*Theses ex universa philosophia selectas, quas ... ad disceptandum proponit ... Andreas Archetti ...* [Romae, 1749], BNVE Misc. Valenti 783, 3) reflected the anti-Boscovich views of his philosophy teacher, P.A. Raffagni, by ignoring the mathematician's ideas, perhaps in order to avoid having to deal with contrasting treatments of the same topic by the same person at the interval of just one year. On Archetti (1731–1805), later a bishop, *nuncio*, and cardinal, see *DBI,* III, pp. 754–6. Raffagni is known only as the last rector of the Collegio Romano before the suppression of the Society. The same pattern is seen in the *Selectae ex universa philosophia theses ...* of L. della Porta and in the *Theses ex universa philosophia selectae* of B. Ridolfi, also defended in the Collegio Romano in 1749 (BAV Racc. Gen. Filosofia I, 15/15; BNVE 34-2-K-10, 2).

22 BNVE Misc. Valenti 854, 6; BAV Misc. C 23, 5. Siena, Tolomei Jesuit college. Thesis 51 (pp. 56–8) praises Boscovich for having extended Newton's physics by his doctrine of force.

23 The mathematical and physical reviews in the *Storia letteraria* were written by Troili and another Jesuit, Leonardo Ximenes; the former was a student and supporter of Boscovich (see n102 below), so is more probably the author. The final part (pp. 132–3) contains a sketchy exposition of the theory, the first outside the Collegio Romano along with the one in *Acta eruditorum* (see no. 99).

24 Appendix to his *De viribus vivis opusculum* (Lucae, 1751). Balassi (1723–1809), a regular cleric, denied that if bodies do touch, continuity (a universal principle according to Boscovich) is broken.

25 BNVE 34-5-K-23, 8. Collegio Romano. Theses 17–22 (pp. x–xii) expound Boscovich's system and accept it.

26 BNVE 34-2-K-18, 11. Collegio Romano. Same text as no. 5.

27 BNVE 34-2-K-24, 6. Collegio Romano. Same text as no. 5.

28 BNVE 34-8-G-8, 4. Rome, Calasanzio college (Piarists). The author should have been the professor of philosophy in the Piarists' new Roman college (the older one being the Nazareno); however, Maruffi was qualified as a student of mathematics himself, and in the following years some physics theses in the college were certainly supervised by Gaudio, who taught mathematics there (see n34 below). Note 9 to thesis 12 says that Boscovich avoids some of the difficulties of Lebniz's and Wolff's ideas on the structure of matter, but that his theory contradicts the law of attraction (p. 13). Note 20 to thesis 27 (pp. 24–5) criticizes his remarks on rectilinear motions.

29 BNVE 34–8–D–3, 19. Rome, Calasanzio college. Same text as no. 8.

30 A second anti-Boscovich year at the Collegio Romano. The theses of at least five students, identical in title and text, reject the resolution of matter into points (G.B. Vincentini, F. Landi, A. Baldelli, N. Trulli, G. Apolloni, *Institutiones philosophicae*, BNVE 34-6-G-7/6; Misc. Valenti 785/1, 34–7–H–10/3, 34–8–D–3/5; BAV Racc. Gen. Filosofia IV, 1269/8). The teacher was Gregorio Vittori, a declared opponent of Boscovich (see under the year 1767).

31 During these years Boscovich's ideas were discussed by Paolo Frisi in his philosophy lectures in the Arcimbolde schools, in Milan, as shown by the manuscript in which they are preserved, the *Institutiones philosophiae* (Milan, Biblioteca della Facoltà di Ingegneria del Politecnico, Fondo Frisi, ms 28). Frisi referred to *De viribus vivis* and to the second part of *De lumine*; his judgment was negative, mainly on the ground that the continuity principle – a kind of ontological pillar of the theory – was universal logically, but not physically (pp. 318–21: 'Sisthema Patris Boscovich'; pp. 587–91: 'Propositio octava. Attractiva ... vis minimorum terrestrium corpusculorum pro variis eorundem distantiis non mutatur in repulsivam'). It is most probable that Frisi also discussed the theory when teaching philosophy at the University of Pisa (1756–64), but this does not seem to be documented. From 1764 he taught mathematics at the Scuole Palatine in Milan, and from 1768 he had Boscovich as a colleague. Their relations were strictly formal, and in his biographies of scientists the Barnabite strongly criticized both the Society of Jesus and its scientific tradition (Baldini, 'Frisi, Paolo,' in *DBI*, L, pp. 558–68).

32 BNVE Misc. Valenti 784, 2. This and the following text were written under Boscovich's supervision, and in part directly by him.

33 BNVE Misc. Valenti 784, 5. Collegio Romano. Unlike nos 10 and 11 (theses on general physics and optics, considered in the second philosophy year), these deal with the subjects of all three years; the absence of a student's name may mean that they were written for all Benvenuti's students. Their content is pure Boscovich.

34 BNVE 34-2-K-24, 4. Rome, Calasanzio college. Thesis 6 (pp. 9–10) criticizes Boscovich's theory. This Piarist (1726–93) was his most decided critic in Rome; see nos 14, 21, 23, 26, 30–3, and 43. From 1768 to 1787 he taught mathematics at the university in Rome; P. Riccardi, *Biblioteca matematica italiana*, vol. 1 (repr. Milan, 1952), p. 576, lists some of his writings. Only a biographical sketch exists: A. Amoretti, *Elogio di P. Gaudio* (Nice, 1848).

35 BNVE 34–6–G–13, 7. Rome, Calasanzio college. Same text as no. 13.

36 Fassoni, a teacher in the Piarist college of Senigallia, criticizes (pp. xviii–xx) Boscovich's dismissal of the Leibnizian principle of sufficient reason and discusses his view of the structure of matter. He discusses the theory again at pp. lxiv–lxv, inclining to the negative and quoting Balassi (no. 4).

37 BAV Racc. Gen. Filosofia IV, 1269/7. Paragraph 14 (p. xxvi n39) accepts Boscovich's hypothesis on the structure of matter.

38 Prato, Jesuit college. Francolini is indicated as the professor in Somm. *Bib.*, III, p. 946. I could not find an exemplar; if he was the teacher, it is highly probable that O'Kelly expounded Boscovich's ideas, because Francolini supported them (see no. 44).

39 BNVE Misc. Valenti 784, 12. Collegio Romano. Leonori was a student of Boscovich; in the same year the master used his name under which to publish his *De lentibus et telescopiis dioptricis* (another edition in that year appeared under Boscovich's name: BNVE 34-5-K-18, 1). The theses say (p. ix) that matter is made up of indivisibles, that bodies do not touch, and that both an attractive and a repulsive force exist. Lunardi's lecture notes are in Imola, Bibl. Comunale (Somm. *Bib.*, V, p. 187 A).

40 BNVE 34-2-K-20, 1. Collegio Romano. Theses 13–14 (p. 4) and the dissertation on atmospherical electricity (pp. 22–4) adopt the theory's central ideas.

41 BNVE 34-5-K-23, 8. Collegio Romano. Thesis 9 (p. 10) asserts the theory. The theses are followed by a notable *De meteoris a naturali electrismo pendentibus dissertatio physica*, different from that attached to no. 19. This does not prove that Calvestrani's teacher was someone else: although theses defended in the same year by students of the same teacher were usually the same in content, sometimes professors tailored theses to students' abilities, with the result that the theses were sometimes the same and sometimes different. Similar theses by different students (from the same school and year) that differ somewhat in content do not prove that different professors were involved.

42 BNVE 34-6-G-8, 1. Rome, Calasanzio college. A high-level text, surely by Gaudio. Theses 19–20 (pp. 17–20) criticize Boscovich's interpretation of inertia; thesis 29 (pp. 28–9) expounds his denial of contact among matter-points; theses 30–2 (pp. 29–30) refer to criticisms by Balassi (no. 4) and Gerdil (no. 144). The theory is examined more generally on pp. 30–48.

43 BNVE 34-2-K-24, 9. Rome, Calasanzio college. These theses, like those of no. 24, show that the teachers in the college were not unanimous. Gaudio, the professor of mathematics, was engaged in a long anti-Boscovich battle; but the metaphysics professor writes in thesis 43 (p. 15) that the elements of bodies are unextended and that forces acting on matter may be reduced to one, which has opposite effects at different distances.

44 BNVE 34-6-G-23, 4. First, Gaudio observes that Boscovich's curve expresses graphically a general equation for cases in which attraction is a function of distance, without providing numerical values. Second he criticizes Boscovich's deduction of the impossibility of contact from the principle of continuity, referring to his *De natura extensionis* (no. 21).

45 BNVE 34-6-G-23, 5. Rome, Calasanzio college. The most Boscovichian Roman Piarist theses. Like all Piarist texts on Boscovich, this one names him in relation to specific scientific questions, but only alludes to him when dealing with the theory.

Theses 14–15 (pp. 6–7) maintain an energetist idea of substances, taking Boscovich's curve as ingenious and probable; thesis 19 (pp. 8–9) agrees that bodies result from unextended points; thesis 22 (p. 10) considers impenetrability as a possible result of a repulsive force. Pp. 60–1 and 63–4 consider two other Boscovich themes: the rectilinear path of light rays and the density of light. Perhaps the appendix on 'artificial electricism,' one of the first Roman texts considering Franklin's work, was written not by a philosophy teacher in the college, but by Gaudio; see n55 below.

46 Scarella's discussion was one of the most ample and detailed early Italian reactions to the theory. Pp. 35–40 discuss Boscovich's ideas about the continuum; pp. 487–9 consider his explanation of the fact that stars do not approach; pp. 605–35 examine the theory itself, and reject it. The first volume of the work (1754) expounded Scarella's own system, which partly resembles that of Boscovich (he accepts a repulsive force, but maintains that the parts of the bodies are extended).

47 BNVE 34-6-G-23, 6. Rome, Calasanzio college.

48 BNVE 34-7-E-14, 3. Rome, convent of Santa Maria in Aracoeli. The title-page describes Hieronymus as a friar of the province of Genoa; nothing is known about him. The text is notable; its author knew mathematics and recent mathematical physics. Theses 9–14 (pp. 24–8) expound Boscovich's ideas on the discontinuity of matter and the attractive-repulsive force, without discussing them; thesis 24 (pp. 33–5) discusses the penetrability of bodies as viewed by A. Genovesi, Gaudio (*De natura extensionis*), and Boscovich; thesis 54 (pp. 49–50) accepts Boscovich's explanation of elasticity.

49 BNVE 34-2-K-5, 8. Cremona, Jesuit college. Theses entirely Boscovichian.

50 Genoa, Piarist college. Thesis 70 (p. xviii) mentions a 'vis repulsionis' introduced by Newton 'et alii' that makes contact impossible. According to the author, some experiments seem to prove its existence, but he inclines against it, because certain of the phenomena could be produced by other mechanisms.

51 This was a third anti-Boscovich year at the Collegio Romano, as is shown by the silence on him in the *Philosophicae theses* of T. Facciotti (BNVE 34-2-K-3/6). The professor was Francesco Asquasciati (b. 1724; Somm. *Bib.*, I, pp. 603–4), a declared opponent of Boscovich (see n121 below).

52 BNVE 34-6-G-23, 8. Rome, Calasanzio college. In the section 'De luce' (p. 1), Boscovich's criticisms of the rectilinearity of light rays are rejected, and his estimate of the matter expelled by the sun is accepted.

53 BNVE 34-6-G-23, 9. Rome, Calasanzio college. Although the title is slightly different, the text is the same as Cassini's (no. 30). As far as the history of science is concerned, Pessuti (1743–1814) is the most important of the Italian authors listed. Later, he taught mathematics in the military academy of St Petersburg, where he met Euler; and then he was professor of mathematics at the university in Rome until his death. A noted analyst and a member of many academies, he was also important in

Roman intellectual life owing to his involvement in some local journals, and he was the most important Roman student collaborator with the French during their occupation of the city. See E. de Tipaldo, *Biografia degli Italiani illustri*, vol. 3 (Venice, 1836), pp. 266–9; G. Ferretto, *Note storico-biografiche di archeologia cristiana* (Vatican City, 1942), s.v. Pessuti; and M. Caffiero, 'Le "Efemeridi letterarie" di Roma (1772–1798),' *Dimensioni e problemi della ricerca storical* (1997): 77–8. Some unpublished papers of his, entitled *Schede di Gioacchino Pessuti*, are in BAV Vat. Lat. 9828; interesting information on his mathematical work and his debates with G. Calandrelli (no. 89) may be found in A. Eximeno,
De studiis philosophicis et mathematicis instituendis (Madrid, 1789), part 2, passim.

54 BNVE 34-6-G-23, 11. Gaudio's replies to Boscovich's doubts on the rectilinearity of light rays reveal good scientific information, but partly miss its epistemological bearing. He writes (p. 32) that he has discovered 'how dangerous it is to part from common opinions,' so has persuaded himself 'to abstain from the love of novelties': 'If I conceive something new, I rather look for arguments against it than for others supporting it; and, if I am not able to prove it is false, I prefer to be silent about it rather than to make it public.'

55 BNVE 34-6-G-23, 10. Gaudio writes that, three years before, there appeared in Rome a dissertation, *De naturali electricismo, ejusque ad Auroram Borealem explicandam applicatione*, critical of his presentation of G.B. Beccaria'a ideas on Franklin's discoveries (he probably refers to the 'tractatio de naturali electricismo' attached to the theses of a Calasanzio student, 1756; see no. 24). He adds that since a reply by Beccaria has been published, he can devote himself to one topic, the height of the atmosphere. The Jesuit dissertation he mentions has almost the same title as that attached to no. 24, but that one was published five years earlier, whereas the dissertation referred to here followed Gaudio's work. It should have been published in 1757, but no known work of the Collegio Romano in that year deals with the subject. If the anonymous dissertation exists (perhaps as an appendix to theses not found so far), it could be Boscovich's (or inspired by him), because a reply to Gaudio would have had to be the work of an expert.

56 BNVE 34-2-K-9, 3. Collegio Romano. These theses (pp. 14–15 and 18–19) accept Boscovich's curve and his matter-points (point-atomism), but reject some theological criticism. Gaetani was born in 1720 (Somm. *Bib.*, III, pp. 1084–5), so it is probable that he had been a pupil of Boscovich.

57 BNVE 34-2-K-20, 9. Collegio Romano: the students of Rome's colleges for foreigners (Greek, English, Maronite, etc.) attended classes in the Jesuit school. Same text as no. 34.

58 BNVE 34-2-K-24, 2. Collegio Romano. Same text as no. 34.

59 BNVE 34-5-K-23, 12. Collegio Romano. Same text as no. 34.

60 BNVE 34-2-K-18, 4. Collegio Romano. Same text as no. 34.

61 BNVE 34-2-K-19, 8. Collegio Romano. Same text as no. 34.

62 BNVE 34–2–K–24, 8. Collegio Romano. Same text as no. 34.

63 BNVE, 34-6-G-7, 5. Fermo, Jesuit college. Theses 78–85 (pp. 15–17) accept
    Boscovich's theory. Like the following text (no. 42), this text is attributed to
    Stoppini in Somm. *Bib.*, III, pp. 641 nn 5, 7, and VII, p. 1597. Stoppini later taught
    in the Collegio Romano, where he also expounded the theory from the chair and had
    it described in his students' theses; see under the year 1765.

64 BNVE 34-6-G-7, 7. Fermo, Jesuit college. Same text as no. 41.

65 BNVE, 34-2-K-18, 10. Rome, Calasanzio college. Boscovich's criticism of the
    rectilinearity of light rays is rejected (p. 1); his calculation of matter expelled from
    the sun and his ideas on the lunar atmosphere are approved (thesis 15, p. 2; thesis
    187, p. 20).

66 BNVE 34-2-K-19, 1. Ascoli Piceno, Jesuit college. The professor is identified in
    Somm. *Bib.*, III, p. 945. The physics portion entirely follows Boscovich, who is said
    to have completed Newton's work (pp. 4–5) by providing a system in which all
    phenomena are derived from one principle and the parts fit together.

67 BNVE 34-2-K-3, 2. Collegio Romano. Boscovich's ideas on matter, the relativity of
    motion, and the repulsive force are accepted (pp. 18, 25–6, 29).

68 BNVE 34-8-B-1, 2. Milan, monastery of Sant'Ambrogio Maggiore (Cistercians).
    Nava appears as the teacher on the title-page. Boscovich's theory is called beautiful
    and ingenious but false, because the continuity principle on which it rests has not
    been shown to be valid universally (p. 13). The author partly misunderstood
    Boscovich's ideas.

69 BNVE 34-2-K-9, 2. Collegio Romano. The theory is accepted on the ground that it
    is the 'simplest' (p. 11).

70 BNVE 34-7-G-2, 1. Rome, Nazareno college (Piarist). The theory is rejected (pp.
    10, 12) on the grounds that simplicity and extension are incompatible and that
    matter cannot be infinitely divided.

71 BNVE 34–2–K–3, 1. Collegio Romano. The unextended matter-points and the
    repulsive force are accepted (pp. 9–11); subsequently the theory is applied to some
    classes of phenomena (pp. 12–14). Bozzoli's lectures in physics (1762; 4 manuscript
    vols in APUG FC 788) summarize Boscovich's ideas (vol. 2, pp. 122–3); perhaps
    out of caution Bozzoli does not accept them openly, but says only that they have not
    been (and perhaps cannot be) shown to be false.

72 BNVE Misc. C 223, 4. Collegio Romano. Same text as no. 50.

73 BNVE 34-8-G-10, 7. Collegio Romano. Same text as no. 50.

74 BNVE 34-2-K-16, 2. Collegio Romano. Same text as no. 50.

75 BNVE Misc. C 143, 5. A notable dissertation, connected to the Collegio Romano
    because Rota was a boarder at the Seminario Romano, the students of which
    attended Jesuit schools. The first part (pp. 5–26) describes the theory, sometimes in

original terms; the second (pp. 27–49) shows it to be compatible with certain classes of phenomena in such fields as electricity, magnetism, and capillarity. Then (pp. 51–63) follows a list of questions asked by the public, with Rota's answers.

76 BNVE 34-2-K-24, 11. Viterbo, Jesuit college. The author expounds a modification of Boscovich's theory without naming him; he holds the parts of matter to be extended, but applies the curve of force to them (pp. viii–xiv).

77 BAV Racc. Gen. Filosofia IV, 1269/2. Como, Gallio college. Boscovich's idea on the structure of matter is accepted (p. 16). This is interesting, because Alessandro Volta (a former pupil of the Jesuits) began his research on electricity in Como during this period, so the discussion of these theses could have drawn his attention to Boscovich's works (see no. 76).

78   BAV Racc. Gen. Misc. A 47, 12. Collegio Romano. Theses 59–61 (pp. 17–19) assert that matter is compounded by Boscovich's force-points. Gregori's teacher, Stoppini, had already inserted these ideas in theses defended by his students in Fermo (see nos 41 and 42). The reviewer of Boscovich's *Theoria* in the *Journal des savants* (no. 152) writes (pp. 9, 13–14) that in that year Stoppini divulged them using the theses of fourteen students; only two others are known (nos 58 and 59), so eleven remain to be found.

79 BNVE 34-2-K-9, 5. Collegio Romano. The section 'De corporum principiis' (theses 59–69, pp. 17–19) accepts Boscovich's ideas on matter and force.

80 BNVE 34-2-K-25, 1. Collegio Romano. This text is almost identical with the preceding one (only the numbers of the relevant theses and pages change: here they are theses 54–64 and pp. 18–20).

81 BNVE 34-4-I-17, 13. Prato, Cicognini Jesuit college. Theses 67–75 (pp. 16–18) entirely accept the theory.

82 BNVE 34-2-K-5, 10. Perugia, Jesuit college. Travigi accepts Franklin's and Beccaria's experiments, but observes that the deep cause of electrical phenomena can be found only in Boscovich's theory, which 'explains them wonderfully by means of attractions and repulsions at various distances' (pp. 10–11); he goes on to illustrate it.

83 BNVE 34-6-I-10, 6. An unknown school in Mantua. Vanni was a Camillian. Theses 8–12 (p. 10) maintain that bodies do not consist of unextended points; and that Newtonian attraction lacks a physical (mechanical) explanation and is not the same in all phenomena; and that the same is true for the 'vis repulsiva,' so its simplicity does not prove it is real.

84 Probably Fermo, Jesuit college. The part on *physica generalis* (theses 41–166, pp. v–xviii) is thoroughtly Boscovichian.

85 Vittori had taught philosophy at the Collegio Romano (1750–6), where his students defended anti-Boscovich theses (see n30 above). In this poetic exposition of the whole of philosophy, perhaps rivalling that of B. Stay, which had been annotated by Boscovich, he made his opposition explicit.

86 BNVE Misc. C 220, 17. Milan, convent of Sant'Ambrogio Maggiore (Cistercians). Boscovich is considered among authors who hold that matter is made up of un-extended parts (pp. 11–12). His 'system' is said to involve inextricable difficulties. Thesis 40 (pp. 16–17) vaguely admits a repulsive force.

87 BNVE 34-2-K-18, 9. Collegio Romano. *Physica generalis* theses (pp. xii–xxxi) completely adhere to Boscovich; some objections are discussed, including those of Gaudio and Vittori. Boscovich's ideas are also considered on pp. xxxii–xl. Romano also taught the theory in his classes (Somm. *Bib.*, VII, p. 34).

88 BNVE 34-2-K-25, 6. Collegio Romano. Corari too was a student of Romano, but his text differs from Widmann's. Boscovich's arguments on the infinite divisibility of matter and the discontinuty of its parts are said to be valid (pp. vi–vii), but the whole question is said to have no direct scientific bearing. However, Boscovich's interpretation of inertia is accepted (p. vii).

89 BNVE Misc. C 207, 22. Collegio Romano. Same text as no. 67.

90 Pp. 222–3 refer to 'some' who maintain that corpuscles are endowed with a force that changes from attractive to repulsive and vice versa, as distance varies.

91 The theory is criticized in the *Physica generalis* sections (58 and 211–12). Altieri taught scholastic theology at the Lyceum in Ferrara.

92 BNVE 34-7-H-10, 1. Prato, Cicognini Jesuit college. Theses 1–32 (pp. xv–xxi) are openly Boscovichian.

93 BNVE 34-2-K-3, 5. Siena, Tolomei Jesuit college. The teacher is identified as Pizzati in Somm. *Bib.*, VI, p. 868. At pp. v–vi he criticizes those maintaining that bodies are composed of unextended and discontinuous parts; on p. xvi Boscovich's estimate of the density of the sun's light is mentioned.

94 BNVE 34-2-K-3, 8. Rieti, seminary of San Salvatore Maggiore. A provincial text, but containing some up-to-date information. Boscovich's interpretation of inertia is accepted (pp. 13–14), but not his conception of matter or his force theory.

95 BNVE 34-4-L-17, 10. Rieti, seminary of San Salvatore Maggiore. Same text as no. 73.

96 Pp. 59–61 expound the repulsive-attractive force and its curve, accepting both after some corrections.

97 In this juvenile work the future inventor of the 'voltaic pile' applies Boscovich's law to electricity; see L. Fregonese, 'Gli influssi di Boscovich e della chimica delle affinità nelle prime fasi dell'elettrologia di A. Volta,' in *Atti del XII Congresso nazionale di storia della fisica*, ed. F. Bevilacqua (Milan, 1993), pp. 91–106.

98 BNVE 34-2-K 3, 4. Collegio Romano. A list of theses to be defended by the students who completed their philosophy course in 1772; their professor was Filippo Cittadelli. Theses 34 and 36 (p. ix) leave undecided whether matter results from extended atoms or unextended points (in Boscovich's sense), and whether bodies are continuous or discontinuous (again in Boscovich's sense).

99 BNVE 34-2-K-9, 1. Collegio Romano. Same text as no. 77.

100 These theses of the Jesuit college in Modena are registered as Troili's in Somm. *Bib.*, VIII, p. 252. I could not find them, so it is uncertain whether they discuss Boscovich's most characteristic ideas. Troili, however, was a decided supporter, and in the following year he taught Boscovich's ideas at the university in Modena. (see n102 below).

101 BNVE 12-1-I-15. Vitale taught philosophy at the Jesuit college in Milan. He declares he has written this handbook according to Boscovich's ideas, which he has taught from the chair; this makes it almost unique among Jesuit pre-suppression works (a similar handbook was planned by Troili in the same year, but the relevant part was not published: see n102 below). Vitale admits that the theory is not yet widespread, but affirms it is not a 'mera hypothesis' but a 'theoria satis demonstrata.' The work's three parts deal with the theory itself, its ability to account for the general properties of matter, and experimental proofs of its truth. A fourth part, on the ability of the theory to account for phenomena other than those for which it was formulated, was not published. Five years later Vitale provided an examination of the theory's impact on some parts of Catholic theology; see n103 below.

102 Troili had been a pupil of Boscovich at the Collegio Romano, and he supported the master until his death (nos 3, 47, 79, 83, and 85–7). See F. Barbieri and M. Zuccoli, 'Domenico Troili da Macerata (1722–1793),' in *Scienziati e tecnologi marchigiani nel tempo: Convegno storico-scientifico* (Ancona, 2001), pp. 168–84. The *Institutiones* were written for Troili's courses on philosophy at the university in Modena (from 1772); however, he was replaced only a year later, so published only the first two volumes – not that on physics, which, he declares, was designed according to Boscovich's law of force. In vol. 1 a paragraph lists the master's published works and hints at his physical ideas (pp. 366–76).

103 In the fourth appendix to this work, without correcting his previous total acceptance of the theory (see no. 80), Vitale considers its bearing on the debate on mind-body relationship, judging it – its truth apart – unsuitable for a defence of Catholic doctrine on the subject. This started a polemic with Troili; see nos 83–7.

104 A reply to Vitale's partial criticism of Boscovich.

105 A reply to Troili's reply.

106 A new reply to Vitale, preceding two others also by Troili (nos 86 and 87). It is possible, though this has not been demonstrated so far, that they were partially inspired by Boscovich.

107 The work expounds and approves Boscovich's 'system' (pp. 110–15).

108 E.G. Gil (no. 93) and others mention this work as containing a criticism of Boscovich's ideas. However, the work cannot be found in any of the principal Italian libraries or in lists of works by Calandrelli (1749–1827). He was teaching mathematics at the Seminario Romano, and perhaps the title pertains to unpublished lecture materials there (Baldini, 'Calandrelli, Giuseppe,' in *DBI*, XVI, pp. 440–2).

109 BNVE 34-6-B-29, 3. A 44-page list of themes to discuss, theses to maintain, and handbooks to use in the schools of the Servites. Boscovich is not mentioned explicitly, but (pp. 19 and 21) discussion of the 'vis repulsiva' is said to be requisite; moreover, among the books suggested are those by Boscovich, Para du Phanjas (no. 154), Saury (nos 155 and 156), and Horvath (nos 123 and 129), 'which now are in the hands of everyone.'

110 BNVE 34-8-K-2, 4. Genoa, Piarist college. Bodies are said not to consist of unextended points, but Boscovich's law is accepted, without mention of him (pp. iii–iv).

111 The biography was in Fabroni's *Vitae italorum* (n7 above). The reviewer is mostly critical of the theory, while recognizing it as a work of genius.

112 Gil (1745–1807), a former missionary in Paraguay, went to Italy after the Society's expulsion from Spain, and became a teacher at the seminary in Cremona and then in Piacenza. His philosophical and mathematical studies were probably mostly Italian; there he encountered Boscovich's ideas, of which he was the last decided supporter. This first book of his (the others are nos 96 and 97) was probably the most ample work on the theory by someone other than Boscovich.

113 Vol. 2, book 2, chap. 3, pp. 189–210: 'De virium corporearum origine, et principio, deque toto Boscovichii de lege continuitatis systemate.' Boscovich's curve is said to be an adequate mechanical representation of known phenomena, but wrong at a causal, physical level. Gil's defence of Boscovich (no. 93) is also criticized. Ludena (also Ludenna, Ludeña, 1740–1820), one of the Spanish Jesuits who lived in Italy after the expulsion of the Society in 1767–8, taught philosophy and mathematics in Camerino, Parma, and Cremona; he published other interesting works, mainly in pure and applied mathematics (Somm. *Bib.*, V, pp. 168–9).

114 Del Giudice taught philosophy in Perugia. He expounded Boscovich's ideas with approbation (pp. 28–53, 185–6, 227–34, 259–64).

115 Piacenza, St Peter's school. After 1800, Boscovich's ideas are still found in a few theses of religious schools, such as the *Positiones ex universa philosophia* (Romae, 1805), and the *Theses ex universa philosophia* (Romae, 1807) (both of Lazarist students: BNVE 34-8-K-4, 7 and 9). The 1805 theses (pp. 41–2) accept the theory, but refer it to extended parts of matter and accept the changes in the curve of forces introduced by B. Stattler (nos 112 and 137). The 1807 theses assert that a repulsive force produces extension, impenetrability, and elasticity, and that its law has been represented by Boscovich as a special curve (p. 23).

116 An attempt to show that Boscovich's model accounts for recent developments in the physical chemistry of gases.

117 An exemplar, without the title-page, is in Parma, Bibl. Palatina, Misc. Erudita in quarto, 199/7. The author, who totally agreed with Boscovich, lived in Ferrara and addressed himself to the 'Philosophiae professores Ferrarienses.'

118   Only some of the Jesuit theses are known so far, and that is even more true of those
        of other orders and of the universities. In particular, very little is known about
        teaching in Benedictine monasteries; some members of the Vallombrosa branch
        were Boscovich's students, but the manuscripts of one of them, Vitaliano Riva
        (1741–1808), a scientist of repute, have never been studied; see M. Mazzucotelli,
        Cultura scientifica e tecnica del monachesimo in Italia, 2 vols (Seregno, 1999), s.v.
        Boscovich and V. Riva.

119   F.M. Gaudio ceased his anti-Boscovichian polemic when he became a lecturer in
        mathematics at the university in Rome (1768). A notable fact is the silence of the
        French Minim friars of the monastery of SS. Trinità dei Monti, Thomas Le Seur
        and François Jacquier, who were for decades – with Boscovich himself – the poles
        of mathematical physics in Rome. From c. 1745 they taught philosophy and
        mathematics in both the university and the college De Propaganda Fide, enjoyed
        good formal relations with Boscovich, and cooperated with him in some projects.
        Jacquier even wrote a necrology of him, but none of his works (including the large
        physics section in his *Institutiones philosophicae ad studia theological potissimum
        accommodatae*, 1757, edited many times with additions) refers to the Jesuit's ideas.

120   The texts of the Collegio Romano in the list are for only eleven years. For some
        of the other years no thesis has been found, but in most cases the theses that have
        been found ignore Boscovich. Some belong to years in which philosophy profes-
        sors were notoriously hostile to his thought (such as 1749, 1753, and 1759).

121   See nos 10 and 11. On the 'Benvenuti case,' see Baldini, *Saggi sulla cultura della
        Compagnia di Gesù (secoli XVI–XVIII)* (Padua, 2000) pp. 281–301; on the profes-
        sors' meeting, called by F. Asquasciati (n51 above), see Paoli, *Ruggiero Giuseppe
        Boscovich*, p. 489; on Asclepi (1706–76), see Somm. *Bib.*, I, pp. 599–602.

122   From 1754 to 1760 the general of the Piarists was Edoardo Corsini (1702–65), a
        mathematician and philosopher (Baldini in *DBI*, XXIX, pp. 620–5). So Gaudio's
        criticisms and those of others in the order may reflect not just the responses of
        individuals, but, perhaps, a history of differences between Calasanz's order and that
        of Ignatius.

123   A contrary attitude was probably behind the silence of four students of another
        important school in Rome, the Collegio Clementino (Somaschi): G. Lucchesi Palli,
        Philosophicae theses (Romae, 1762; BNVE 34-8-G-10, 5); Alberto and Girolamo
        Litta, *Praelectiones mechanicae practicae, globi terraquei historia naturalis,
        atmospherae telluris* (Romae, 1777; BNVE 34-6-G-1, 20) and *De igne electrici-
        tate luce et de quibusdam elementaribus geometriae usibus exercitatio physico-
        geometrica* (Romae, 1779; BNVE 34-6-G-1, 16); and L. Caccia Piatti, *Elementa
        quarumdam physices partium summatim exposita* (Romae, 1783; BNVE 34-2-I-
        12, 8). Girolamo Litta mentions some of Boscovich's works only to criticize his
        ideas on the *aurora borealis* and the rays of light. But the rather poor theses of a

student at the Dominican school in Rome suggest that in his case silence came merely from obsolete information: *Se, suasque selectas conclusiones philo-sophicas ... Fr. Thomas Mac-Donagh Hibernus ... in Collegio et Studio Generali SS. Sixti, et Clementis ... philosophiae studens ... [dicat] ...* (Romae, 1761; BNVE 34-6-F-7, 7).

124 Later, Scherffer edited Boscovich's *Theoria* and was perhaps his most enthusiastic supporter in the German area (see no. 110, and n146 below). Another important supporter was J. Liesganig, whose letters remain in the Boscovich archive at Berkeley; however, this noted Jesuit cartographer and geodesist was absorbed in his technical work and never published anything theoretical in the field of physics (see Somm. *Bib.*, IV, pp. 1823–25). This first edition of Scherffer's *Institutiones* asserts (pp. 400–1) that the 'vis repulsiva' does not oppose the 'attractiva,' because they act alternately according to a single law. This could be the first recorded echo of the theory outside Italy (reviews of Boscovich's works excluded).

125 Paragraphs 143–50 criticize Boscovich's ideas on physical continuum; par. 303 expounds his interpretation of Newton's concept of gravity. Mangold (a brother of Maxim, no. 111) taught philosophy in Ingolstadt.

126 A sketch of the theory on pp. 147–50; Hauser is mainly critical.

127 In *Briefe, die neueste Litteratur betreffend*; now in his *Gesammelte Schriften,* vol. 5-1, *Rezenzionsartikel in Briefe, die neueste Litteratur betreffend (1759–1765)*, ed. Eva J. Engel (Stuttgart and Bad Cannstatt, 1991), pp. 58–88.

128 This edition expounds the theory more amply than the first (no. 2), presenting it as demonstrated (pp. 360–72).

129 Boscovich's ideas and some applications are expounded but not formally accepted (pp. 236–41, 244–6, 291–2). Mangold writes that he is describing them only for 'teachers wishing to adopt them.'

130 BNVE 12-1-M-10, 1. Chap. 3 deals with Boscovich's ideas, which essentially are rejected (for Stattler's later attitude, see no. 137).

131 Parma, Bibl. Palatina, Misc. Erudita in folio, VIII, 1. Vilnius, Jesuit college. The teacher is not indicated; the most important Jesuit professors in Vilnius were B. Dobszewicz (1722–94) and J. Nakcyanowicz (1725–96); see Somm. *Bib.*, III, p. 110, and V, p. 1554. However, the most likely source for knowledge of the theory in Lithuania was J.-J. Rossignol; see n163 below. Boscovich could have been considered also in Dobszewicz's *Placita recentiorum philosophorum explanata nec non phenomenis physicis adornata* (Vilnius, 1760), which I was unable to see. Grothusz adheres to Boscovich's ideas without naming him (pp. 27–44).

132 Trent, Biblioteca Comunale, TS I D 18. Trent, Jesuit college. The theses confirm Zallinger's attitude in his *De viribus materiae* (no. 133). Johann Baptist is not to be confused with his brothers, Franz Seraphim (no. 141) and Jakob Anton (nos 126 and 138). On their relations with Boscovich, see A. Trampus, *I gesuiti e l'illuminismo.*

Politica e religione in Austria e nell'Europa centrale (1773–1798) (Florence, 2000), pp. 269–70; see also pp. 80–1 for Scherffer, Mako, Biwald, and Liesganig.

133 The second volume was published in 1768. I was unable to see this work, which has a section on the theory.

134 United to his *Institutiones logicae*. Chaps 2, 3, and 6 of dissertation 2 are pure Boscovich, but he is mentioned only in relation to certain points, without acknowledgment that the whole approach is his. Horvath uses the theory even more extensively in his *Institutiones physicae generalis* (no. 129).

135 A short reference to Boscovich's *De continuitatis lege* and *Philosophiae naturalis theoria*. This, and Mendelssohn's former discussion of Boscovich (no. 105), are a likely source for Kant's knowledge of the Jesuit. Kant never mentioned Boscovich, but some influence of the *Theoria* on his *Metaphysische Anfangsgründe der Naturwissenschaft* (Riga, 1786; mainly in chap. 2, theorems 1–7) and *Opus postumum* has seemed probable. As is well known, in his *Kritik der reinen Vernunft* (1781; section on 'transcendental dialectic') Kant maintained that human mind basically aspires to a definitive and total understanding of reality, as a synthesis of all psychological phenomena (soul), all natural phenomena (universe), all phenomena whatsoever (God). As for the second, an 'antinomy' exists between the thesis that bodies consist of unextended parts and the thesis that they consist of extended and indivisible ones. Kant named the supporters of the first 'monadists,' a term that has been seen as referring to Leibniz's school and, possibly, to Boscovich; see *Critique of Pure Reason*, trans. and ed. Paul Guyer and Allen W. Wood (Cambridge, MA, 1998), p. 744 n62. But the Jesuit could be a reference also because his was the most recent and most specific attempt to make that fundamental human aspiration scientific. The date of Kant's first *Kritik* is compatible with that of influence by both of Mendelssohn's writings. However, if the Jesuit's influence could be found – some maintain it is present – also in Kant's pre-critical works (*Kant's Werke*, vol. 1, *Vorkritische Schriften I, 1747–1756* [Berlin, 1902], p. 16), the source could not be Mendelssohn or even Boscovich's *Theoria*, but his previous writings.

136 BNVE 12-22-D-5. Munich, Jesuit college. The first part is an up-to-date exposition of celestial mechanics, surely written by the professor (who also wrote the unsigned *prefatio*). Zallinger adopts Newton's method, because 'all other systems are mainly speculative' (pp. 5–6); however, he says, Boscovich's law of forces is useful, consistent, and compatible with phenomena. He has not made the law a basis for his exposition because it is difficult for students; however, if ultimate explanations have to be introduced, nothing is superior to it. Zallinger expounds it and the curve of forces in a special section (pp. 232–5).

137 Bamberg, Jesuit college. In 1769–70 Windisch taught physics according to Boscovich's theory, as shown by a manuscript (*Physica utraque theoretica et*

practica explicatione illustrata et ad systema celeberrimi viri Rogerii Josephi Boscovichii S.J. ordinata); see I. Pauler–van Hofer, *Personalbibliographien der Professoren an der Philosophischen Fakultät der Academia Ottoniana und Universitas Ottoniano-Fridericiana Bambergensis von 1646–1664 und 1770–1803* (Erlangen, 1971), pp. 71, 193.

138 As in *Institutiones metaphysicae* (no. 123), Horvath expounds Boscovich's theses (chap. 1, prop. 2; chap. 2) without saying that all the essentials come from him. His works had a large diffusion and went through several editions. I could not see two others: *Elementa physicae* (Budae, 1790) and *Summarium elementorum physicae* (Budae, 1794).

139 Paragraphs 49–55 of chap. 4 entirely accept Boscovich's ideas.

140 BNVE 34-4-I-17, 7. Munich, Jesuit college. Bodies are said to consist of 'puncta,' endowed with forces ruled by a law 'unica et simplicissima,' represented by a curve (pp. 12–13).

141 The work is attributed to Biwald in Somm. *Bib.*, I, p. 1530 n14.

142 Stattler considers the theory a mere hypothesis, and partly objects to it (pp. 306–23); he says little more than is said in the theses of one of his pupils (no. 112).

143 Here the younger brother of Jakob Anton and Johann Baptist accepts the 'vis repulsiva,' explaining elasticity as its interplay with a 'vis attractiva.' He knew Boscovich's ideas through the works of his brothers and Scherffer, and partly misunderstood them. Boscovich (and Benvenuti) are quoted only on optical questions (pp. 7–11, 25–9, 432–61).

144 Somm. *Bib.*, I, p. 1842, includes this in a list of works on Boscovich's theory, together with the *Cogitationes* by the same author (no. 140). However, no work by Alber with this title seems to exist.

145 Since most of their works were handbooks, they brought about a wider diffusion of Boscovich's ideas; Horvath's books were adopted also in Italian schools east of Venice, and Biwald's *Physica* was used in Klagenfurt. See A. Trampus, 'I gesuiti e la riforma delle università austriache nel secondo Settecento,' in *Gesuiti e università in Europa (secoli XVI–XVIII)*, ed. G.P. Brizzi and R. Greci (Bologna, 2002), p. 174.

146 All non-Italian editions of Boscovich's relevant works appeared in Austria: *Dissertatio de viribus vivis* (Viennae, 1752; ed. K. de Reuttern and his teacher, F. Gindhoer, S.J.); *Philosophiae naturalis theoria* (Viennae, 1758; ed. K. Scherffer); *Philosophiae naturalis theoria* (Viennae, 1759; ed. K. Scherffer); *Philosophiae naturalis theoria* (Viennae, 1764; ed. K. Scherffer); *Theoria philosophiae naturalis* (Graecii, 1765; ed. L. Biwald); *Dissertatio de lumine* (Viennae, 1766); *Dissertatio de lumine* (Graecii, 1767); and C. Benvenuti, *Dissertatio physica de lumine* (no. 11; partly written by Boscovich, who also edited it in Vienna, 1761 and 1766).

147 Some other Bohemian professors could be relevant; see A. Boll (Bratislava), K. Cardell, and S. Schmidt (Olomouc), in Somm. *Bib.*, I, pp. 1622–3; II, p. 732; VII, p. 806.

148 A notable name is Stefan Luskina (1725–93), who taught mathematics in Warsaw (Somm. *Bib.*, V, pp. 194–6; Paoli, *Ruggiero Giuseppe Boscovich*, p. 165). Immediately after Boscovich's departure from Poland, Luskina's students defended some *Propositiones ex universa philosophia*; I could not find them, or other Polish texts after 1760. On mentions of Boscovich in Polish-Lithuanian Jesuit works, see R. Darowski, 'La philosophie des jésuites en Pologne du XVIe au XVIIIe siècle. Essai de synthèse,' *Forum philosophicum* 2 (1997): 211–43.

149 M. Hellyer, 'Jesuit Physics in Eighteenth-Century Germany: Some Important Continuities,' in O'M. *Jes. Cult.*, pp. 538–54.

150 See the assertions of P. Friedrich, a Jesuit professor in Mainz (1745), in Hellyer, 'Jesuit physics,' p. 548. As for Belgium, Jesuit reactions to Cartesianism have been a topic of study since G. Monchamp's *Histoire du cartésianisme en Belgique* (Brussels, 1886).

151 Until 1759 the Berlin academy was directed by Maupertuis, who had subjected the Jesuit's *De telluris figura* to haughty criticism. He was succeeded by Euler, who correspondend with Boscovich but had a different scientific outlook. In 1766, Euler was replaced by Lagrange, who was on good formal terms with Boscovich but was an adherent of an even more different scientific 'paradigm'; in his letters to d'Alembert he never contradicted the French writer's sharp evaluations of the Jesuit.

152 A purely descriptive review, not considering those parts of the dissertation that were connected to the theory. In 1749 (pp. 304–24, 1155–78) and 1750 (pp. 416–35), the *Mémoires* also reviewed C. Noceti's *De iride et aurora boreali carmina* and Boscovich's annotations (Romae, 1747).

153 The future cardinal discusses Boscovich's theory (pp. 39–47, 54–70) as presented in *De lumine* without naming him. First, he advances two objections: the continuity principle does not prove that the contact of bodies is impossible; it cannot be proved through induction. Second, he says that two of Boscovich's theses are contradictory: the thesis that one continuous entity (motion) is real and the other (space) 'imaginary'; and the thesis that two 'simple' parts cannot touch without penetrating each other. In 1754 the theory was already known in France; in that year C. Maire, an English Jesuit cooperating with Boscovich on geodetic and cartographical matters, mentioned it in a letter to J.-N. Delisle, saying that in Italy some Jesuits opposed it (Paoli, *Ruggiero Giuseppe Boscovich*, p. 489).

154 The reviewer does not discuss the final part of Boscovich's notes, which expound some of his most characteristic ideas. He qualifies these as 'unique,' promising to discuss them in a supplement, but it never appeared.

155 In this year the *Mémoires de Trévoux* (fasc. 4, pp. 581–600) reviewed G.B. Scar-
     ella's *Physica generalis* (no. 25), which dealt extensively with Boscovich's ideas.
156 De Felice had studied in Rome under Boscovich and Jacquier. His journal may be
     considered French because it was printed in Berne, but it was written to inform
     Italian readers about new books published in Europe.
157 Boscovich had drawn the main lines of his theory in a note to book 3, l. 62.
158 By far the most positive French review of a work by Boscovich. The author, surely
     a scientist, has not been identified with certainty. The review shows that he was
     informed as to the intellectual life at the Collegio Romano, and perhaps a corre-
     spondent of Boscovich; a possible name is Lalande.
159 'Le P. Boscovich dans l'ouvrage qui a pour titre, *Philosophiae naturalis theoria ...*
     Ce ... ouvrage contient des idées très-ingénieuses et très-singulières; l'attraction, la
     répulsion, la cohésion, l'élasticité y sont déduites d'une seule loi; je voudrais qu'il
     me fût permis de m'étendre sur ce sujet; mais il faut consulter l'ouvrage même de
     cet illustre Auteur' (p. 536). Lalande, who had travelled with Boscovich during his
     Italian journey and was one of his few friends among French scientists, never
     discussed his ideas (a possible partial exception being the 1766 review), and only
     mentioned them again in his necrology of Boscovich (*Journal de Paris*, 13 March
     1787, p. 310). In a note to the second edition of J.E. Montucla's *Histoire des
     mathématiques*, vol. 4 (Paris, 1802), p. 188 n1, he deplored d'Alembert's attitude
     towards the Jesuit.
160 Vol. 1, pp. 62–5: 'Les points sans contact de Boscovitz.' A partial and superficial
     analysis, designed more to ridicule the author than to understand his reasons. This
     remained in the Latin translation published in Venice (*Theoria entium sensibilium*,
     1782–7).
161 The essentials of the theory are described in vol. 5, p. 566–607.
162 This work follows Boscovich's *Theoria* almost literally and reproduces the original
     drawing of the curve of forces, without mentioning the author.
163 In 1773, immediately after the suppression of the Society, the bishop of Embrun
     offered Rossignol the direction of the city's high school. Rossignol wrote an
     analytical program of studies for it, which was adopted that year but published only
     in 1777. For general physics, the plan requested the teacher to discuss 'de la nature
     de la matérie; pourquoi elle n'est pas connue; de ses propriétés; de l'inertie. De
     l'attraction, de la répulsion. Manière de réduire ces deux loix à une loi simple et
     unique.' The *Plan* was published again by Rossignol in 1803, in Turin, with the
     title *Plan d'un cours de philosophie*. How faithful the teachers were to it needs
     investigation, but they were required to adopt the scientific handbooks Rossignol
     published in those years, and he wrote that the plan was not changed until the
     Revolution; so the school in Embrun could offer the only instance in which the
     theory was an officially prescribed and lasting part of the teaching. Rossignol had

met Boscovich in Marseille during the latter's first stay in France (1759–60); in 1761 he had been sent as a professor of philosophy or mathematics to the college in Vilnius, where he probably taught the theory (see no. 113). From 1764 or 1765 to 1773 he had been in Milan as a teacher first of history and geography and then of philosophy in the Jesuit College of Nobles; there he had collaborated with Boscovich ('qui a été mon Maître, qui m'a servi de père, et qui a consenti à être mon ami': *Histoire des oeuvres de M. Rossignol* [Turin, 1804], pp. 11–12). Following Embrun he was in the Delphinate and then in Turin, where after 1800 he published a complete collection of his works (see titles in Somm. *Bib.*, VII, pp. 179–86); given that many had been written – and published in part – in France years before, they document the knowledge of Boscovich's ideas in that country in the late eighteenth century. Rossignol has been studied partially, and mostly for his political and anti-revolutionary ideas; for a biographical sketch, see A. Bianchi, *Scuola e lumi in Italia nell' età delle riforme (1750–1780). La modernizzazione dei piani degli studi nei collegi delgli ordini religiosi* (Brescia, 1996), pp. 151–89.

164 The volume has a list of works written by Boscovich. Although in frequent contact with Boscovich during his stay in France, Barruel made no use of his ideas in *Les helviennes* (1781), where they could have served a function.

165 The chapter 'Des qualités réelles des corps' follows Boscovich strictly, but does not refer to him.

166 In 1745, Mme de Châtelet learned from F. Jacquier of Boscovich's *De viribus vivis* and received a copy (H. Bedarida, *Amitiés françaises du Père Boscovich* [Dubrovnik, 1931], p. 9); in 1746, Voltaire corresponded with the Jesuit; during his French travel in 1759–60, Boscovich established contacts with Rossignol and other Jesuit scientists in various cities (P. Bianchini, *Educazione, cultura e politica nell' età dei Lumi. I gesuiti e l'insegnamento dopo la soppressione della Compagnia de Gesù* [Turin, 2001], pp. 103–8); in 1760 he sent his *Theoria* to Diderot (whose response is unknown); and in 1769 he became an associate of the academy in Lyon.

167 There were about fifty-five mathematics professors; see K.A.F. Fischer, 'Jesuitenmathematiker in der Französischen und Italienischen Assistenz bis 1762 bzw. 1773,' *AHSI* 52 (1983): 55–66. Mathematics was taught only where philosophy was; every year, however, a school had one professor of the former and three of the latter.

168 Some sources also mention J.B. de la Borde (1730–77; Somm. *Bib.*, I, pp. 1784–5); I was unable to check all his scientific works.

169 Boscovich indicated this in 1760 to his brother Baro (Paoli, *Ruggiero Giuseppe Boscovich*, p. 489).

170 For instance, d'Alembert's attitude towards Boscovich was shaped by a mixture of scientific polemic, personal dislike, and philosophical dissent. This, and the general French scientific climate, have been analysed many times, so bibliographical citations are unnecessary.

171 For the works of Faure (1702–79), see Somm. *Bib.*, III, pp. 558–68 (he also wrote
     an *Opuscolo anti-newtoniano*). On his relations with Boscovich, see Baldini, *Saggi
     sulla cultura della Compagnia di Gesù*, p. 292; on his anti-Newtonian, and implic-
     itly anti-Boscovichian, scientific work, see P. Nastasi, 'I primi studi sull'elettricità
     a Napoli e in Sicilia,' *Physis* 24 (1982): 255, 258–60.

172 Studies on Jesuit science in Portugal are synthesized in Baldini, 'The Teaching of
     Mathematics in the Jesuit Colleges of Portugal, from 1640 to Pombal,' in the
     proceedings of the colloquium held in Obidos, 16–18 November 2000, *A pratica
     de matematica em Portugal* (Coimbra, 2004), pp. 293–465. For Spain, see V.
     Navarro Brotóns, 'Tradition and Scientific Change in Early Modern Spain: The
     Role of the Jesuits,' in Fein. *Jes. Sci.*, pp. 331–87. Boscovich was named in the
     Conclusiones analytico-eclecticas pro universa philosophia (Evora, 1758) by some
     students of Evora university, but only as a Jesuit who did not swear by Aristotle;
     see A.A. Banha de Andrade, *Vernei e a cultura do seu tempo* (Coimbra, 1966),
     p. 235. The most important scientific-philosophical work by a Portuguese Jesuit
     in the mid-eighteenth century, Inácio Monteiro's *Philosophia libera seu eclectica
     rationalis et meccanica sensuum*, written in Portugal but published in Italy (7 vols;
     Venetiis, 1766), ignores Boscovich. In Spain, some of his works were mentioned
     by C. Rieger in his scientific manuscripts (Navarro Brotóns, 'Tradition and Scien-
     tific Change,' p. 362); notably, Rieger was sent to Madrid from Vienna (then a
     centre of Boscovichianism) in 1760.

173 Among those relevant, Andrés (n11 above), Gil (nos 93, 96, and 97), and Eximeno
     (n53 above and n174 below) may be considered Iberian-Italian authors. This
     categorization is extended to many others by M. Batllori, *La cultura hispano-
     italiana de los jesuitas expulsos* (Madrid, 1966). Monteiro represents a somewhat
     different case (see n172 above).

174 There is no evidence that Gil's and Ludena's works (nos 93, 94, 96, and 97) had an
     audience in Spain. A possibility may be Eximeno (1729–1808), a good mathemati-
     cian who was in Rome for some time; however, his *De studiis philosophicis et
     mathematicis instituendis* (Madrid, 1789) does not mention Boscovich, and the
     physics part of his *Institutiones philosophicae, et mathematicae* (Madrid, 1796)
     was not published. Unlike his *Philosophia libera*, Monteiro's *Principia
     philosophica theologiae, atque religionis naturalis* was written and published in
     Italy (Venetiis, 1778), but Boscovich is quoted there only for some optical results.
     Another Portuguese philosopher living abroad, L.A. Verney (not a Jesuit), whose
     books were widely known in his native land, omits Boscovich's ideas from his *De
     re physica* (Romae, 1769).

PART FOUR

Music, Theatre, and the Uses of Performance

The Jesuits' decision to operate schools opened them up to an engagement with music and theatre that no religious order had ever had before and in general led to their cultivating these 'arts' in remarkably intense and fruitful ways. That is the theme of this part of our volume. Yet a further theme runs through it, a recurring Jesuit ambivalence towards precisely this engagement. How and to what extent were music and theatre appropriate to priests, to the Jesuits' 'way of proceeding' – or even to Christians? We open this part with two case studies regarding music, both of which implicitly raise a third theme that also recurs in these pages, the relationship between actual practice and official norms. David Crook and Franz Körndle expertly analyse some of the rare manuscript sources that throw light on all three themes. Crook writes about the Collège de Clermont, Paris, in the late sixteenth century, and Körndle about a number of Jesuit schools in Germany in the same period. It is interesting to note that in so doing they must both deal also with the Jesuits' use of the music of Orlando di Lasso.

At least after the first few years of the Society's existence, the Jesuits had no hesitation about using music as a vehicle for catechesis and other forms of evangelization. This has long been known, but what Víctor Rondón provides is another case study of the precise kind of music the Jesuits used and its relationship to the correlative texts in the indigenous languages of colonial Chile. He goes on to contrast this music with the relatively sophisticated music required for the operas the Jesuits produced for more sophisticated audiences – themselves, their students, and the urban public.

We here therefore call your attention once again to T. Frank Kennedy's, S.J., presentation of Johann Bernhard Staudt's opera *Patientis Christi memoria*, first performed in Vienna during Holy Week, 1685, and to the DVD contained in the back cover of this volume. There is no better way, we believe, of conveying some sense of what opera sounded like (and to some extent even looked like) on the stages of the Jesuit colleges around the world.

That said, our DVD is perhaps a little misleading. It does not convey how elaborate some of the Jesuit theatrical productions were, especially in major cities, but the articles by Bruna Filippi and Giovanna Zanlonghi compensate for that deficiency with their descriptions of the sets, the 'sound effects,' and the other physical apparatus of Jesuit theatre, which sometimes spilled off the stages to be simply one small part of much larger productions and spectacles. The celebration in 1622 at the Collegio Romano of the canonization of Ignatius of Loyola and Francis Xavier, for instance, took up almost the whole public space of the institution, and the celebrations the Jesuits staged for great political occasions in Milan during the seventeenth and eighteenth centuries give substance to the claim that the Jesuits at least implicitly saw themselves as carrying out a civic mission. Both these articles stress and illustrate the close relationship the Jesuits assumed between literature/rhetoric and performance.

We end this part of our volume with Michael Zampelli's, S.J., article and thus with a theme raised at the beginning of it, the ambivalence or even negativity some Jesuits felt about the 'arts' (here, theatre) and the limits they tried to impose for themselves or others. The two Jesuit authors Zampelli studies directed their criticism to the professional stage, which they saw as undermining the morals of the members of the audience and hence as posing a great danger to their eternal salvation. Zampelli suggests that Jesuit theatre was to some degree a creative response in that it provided a healthy and helpful alternative.

20 / 'A Certain Indulgence': Music at the Jesuit College in Paris, 1575–1590

DAVID CROOK

The practice of ecclesiastical visitation, wherein an ordinary of the church makes official visits to persons and institutions subject to his authority, originated in the early centuries of the Christian era and is well documented in the decrees of the church councils of the Middle Ages.[1] Such visits, most commonly undertaken by bishops and superiors of religious orders, provided opportunities to monitor local practices, identify abuses, and propose reforms. And although its use declined during the late Middle Ages, visitation constituted, according to Hubert Jedin, the most important instrument of control over both the cure of souls and the maintenance of church property.[2] In the sixteenth century, the Council of Trent endorsed and encouraged the practice, and the surviving reports of the resulting visitations provide a rich source of information on the thought and practice of early modern Catholicism.

Early official documents of the Society of Jesus provide little specific information concerning the practice of visitation: the 'Formula' does not mention it at all; the *Constitutions* do so only in passing. The latter direct the superior general, or a commissary appointed by him, to visit his subjects 'according to the circumstances and necessities which arise.' The provincial superior should also undertake such visits, for they are 'something quite proper to his office.'[3] The First General Congregation, which approved the *Constitutions* in 1558–9, also decreed that provincials should visit houses and colleges in their provinces on an annual basis.[4] And in 1565 the Second General Congregation called for the appointment by the general of special visitors every three to four years, or as often as he deemed appropriate.[5]

Within these modest guidelines, visitation appears to have developed during the sixteenth century into an important component of the Jesuit 'way of proceeding.' The written reports prepared by visitors document the practices they encountered, the changes they advocated, and in some instances the local responses they elicited. With their unique blend of (sometimes dismayingly detailed) description and (in the best cases, thoughtful and well-reasoned) prescription, they offer a form of access to the lived experience of Jesuits absent from both the official documents of the Society and the more personal correspondence of its members. The value of these reports seems clear, yet they have received relatively little attention from historians in general and musicologists in particular. One reason for their neglect by the latter is obvious: visitors had many issues to address, and music almost never rose to the top of their lists of concerns. Accordingly, information on musical practices tends to be sparse and widely scattered in the sources. In what follows, I hope to demonstrate how comments contained in one set of visitation reports contribute to our understanding of both the day-to-day cultivation of music in a Jesuit college and larger questions concerning the role of music in Jesuit ministries and culture.

The reports in question come from the Jesuit college in Paris, the Collège de Clermont, founded in 1561 with funds left by Guillaume du Prat, the bishop of Clermont, upon his death the previous year.[6] The manuscript that preserves these reports, Paris, Bibliothèque Nationale, ms latin 10989, falls into two sections, the first of which contains reports of nine visitations carried out between 1562 and 1593. Table 20.1 lists the dates and authors of these reports, with the five containing discussions of music shown in boldface type. Appendix 1 provides a transcription and translation of the passages pertaining to music. Although a visitation always included two main procedures – investigation and recommendation – the final written reports assumed a variety of forms. The numbered items contained in some of the reports evidently indicate responses to questions contained in formal questionnaires drawn up as guides for the visitors. A visitor's questions typically led to dialogue and discussion, elements most obvious in the three-column format of the 1579 report prepared by Juan Maldonado, where column 1 presents 'what the rector said' in response to specific questions or 'proposed of his own accord'; column 2, 'what the advisers said when asked about the things under consideration'; and column 3, 'what the visitor decided' (see appendix 1, fol. 41). At the other end of the continuum stands the 1587 report of Lorenzo Maggio, in which all elements of interrogation, discussion, and recommendation have been distilled into a single well-ordered set of instructions.

The second part of ms latin 10989 preserves copies of ordinances issued by the Society's generals from 1575 to 1591. Appendix 2 gives a transcription and translation of one of these, a brief directive on music issued in 1575 by the Society's fourth general, Everard Mercurian. It concerns, according to the title given in the Paris manuscript, 'those things to be observed with respect to the

Table 20.1
Chronology of visitation reports for the
Jesuit college in Paris
(BNP Lat. 10989)

1562	Jerónimo Nadal
1570	Everard Mercurian
1575	Claude Matthieu
1576	**Claude Matthieu**
1578	**Claude Matthieu**
1579	**Juan Maldonado**
1585	**Odon Pigenat**
1587	**Lorenzo Maggio**
1593	Clément Dupuy

music books, which members of the Society sometimes use for the relaxation of the soul' ('Quae visa sunt observanda in libris Musices quibus aliquando Nostrj in Societate utuntur ad animi laxationem'). Mercurian allows sacred music, 'the kind called motets, masses, and hymns,' to be sung at any time and directs that songs with 'shameful text and music' be destroyed. Music of dubious nature – presumably, all music that does not fall clearly within the general category of sacred motets, masses, and hymns – must undergo an examination by the superior to determine whether or not it should be allowed within the college.

Sent out to colleges all across Europe, this ordinance elicited different responses in different places. It inspired an official at the Jesuit college in Munich, for example, to draw up a detailed list of approved and prohibited compositions, evidently compiled in conjunction with a thorough review of the college's music collection.[7] In the Parisian manuscript we find no such catalogue of specific compositions, nor explicit reference to Mercurian's ordinance in any of the various visitation reports. Indeed, despite their chronological proximity, I would hesitate to draw any causal connection between the 1575 ordinance and the first mention of music in a Parisian visitation report the following year – the concerns expressed in the two documents simply differ too much from one another. Nevertheless, I cannot help wondering if the appearance of both in the mid-1570s might reflect a more general perception at that time of the need to control and discipline musical practices within the Society.

The 1576 visitation report comes from the pen of Claude Matthieu, the provincial of France from 1574 to 1582 (see appendix 1, fol. 49). He directs that on 'those days on which the sacred rite is done at the ninth hour,' the psalms should be sung with alternate verses in falsobordone, the Magnificat in polyphony with a motet appended to it, and the mass in either polyphony or falsobordone. On other days, the psalms should be performed alternatim, the

Magnificat in falsobordone, and the mass in Gregorian chant, except for the Credo, which should be rendered in falsobordone. Matthieu here articulates the parameters of much of the discussion that follows in later reports. He distinguishes between two categories of feast – the more important, when mass is sung at the ninth hour, and the less important, when it is sung at the normal time – and three styles of music: polyphony, falsobordone, and Gregorian chant. Implicit in his discussion is the assumption that more elaborate music should adorn the more important portions of the liturgy. He associates the simpler styles of Gregorian chant and falsobordone with liturgical genres and feasts of lesser rank and reserves polyphony, the most elaborate style, for the most important items.

Most interesting, however, is his description of the singing of motets directly following the Magnificat at vespers. When and where Renaissance musicians actually performed the immense corpus of motets that survives from the sixteenth century remains a question for which very little specific information has come down to us. Matthieu's explicit reference to the singing of motets in an unambiguous, liturgical context nicely complements other recent research in this area by T. Frank Kennedy, Anthony M. Cummings, and others.[8] But Matthieu also seems to have had second thoughts about the singing of motets after the Magnificat. A marginal annotation states laconically, 'Sustulit motetum postea' ('He later did away with the motet').

This restriction on the use of motets finds confirmation in the visitation report that follows two years later, in 1578 (see appendix 1, fol. 51v). Matthieu now asks that the singing be done in falsobordone and the motet eliminated entirely unless special permission be granted by the rector. In lieu of the motet, a Marian antiphon should be performed. Here Matthieu appears to have two goals in mind. First, the post-Tridentine liturgy allowed for the singing of the Marian antiphon at the end of vespers when compline did not follow.[9] In calling for the substitution of the Marian antiphon for the traditional singing of motets, Matthieu seems to have sought a higher level of liturgical propriety. Second, with his recommendation that the singing be done in 'common falsobordone and not otherwise without permission,' he seems implicitly to advocate a general abandonment of polyphony.

Further concerns about the performance of polyphony combine with exasperation over the recalcitrance of singers in the visitation report prepared by Juan Maldonado one year later, in 1579 (see appendix 1, fol. 43). In column 1 of his report, Maldonado records the comments of the rector of the college, Odon Pigenat: there had already been many warnings against the singing of polyphony, and past experience clearly demonstrated that 'singers can scarcely be restrained from going beyond the kind of music that has already been prescribed by the superiors many times.' Given this state of affairs, Pigenat asked if the college should perhaps eliminate polyphony altogether. Others, whom the visitor consulted, proposed a trial period without polyphony, during which nothing would be decided one way or the other. Maldonado, however, rejected the latter proposal and instead asked that arguments both for and against the elimination of polyphony be submitted to the general, who would then rule one way or the other on the matter. Although nothing in Maldonado's report indicates what decision was reached, the next report, prepared six years later by Pigenat himself, shows that those in favour of polyphony had won a decisive victory.

Pigenat completed his 1585 visitation of the Collège de Clermont in his capacity as provincial of France, an office to which he had been appointed in 1582. Having served as rector of the college from 1575 to 1582, the period during which all three of the previously discussed visitations had been completed, he possessed both first-hand knowledge of the institution's musical traditions and evident respect for the rulings of previous visitors. Indeed, he begins his discussion of music by asking that greater care be paid to those things prescribed in the past (see appendix 1, fol. 53v). But the recommendations that follow signal a fundamental change in attitude: no longer is there talk of the possible elimination of polyphony. Instead, the visitor endeavours to define those aspects of musical style that render a polyphonic composition inappropriate: 'Let those things concerning the manner of singing prescribed in other visitations be observed more diligently, but especially on feasts of the second class, let the music not be so ornate and long-winded, either at mass or at vespers. Let that music be abandoned, in which the same words are repeated so many times. Let neither the masses nor the Magnificats of Orlando [di Lasso] be sung. Let the antiphons of the Blessed Virgin be rather brief. In short, let all things be directed towards devotion and sweetness.'

Here we encounter a level of specificity entirely absent from earlier reports. Music should not be too fancy; it should not exhibit too much word repetition; and finally, it should not be composed by Orlando di Lasso. This last injunction, of course, remains the most intriguing: what was it about Lasso's music that prompted Pigenat to single him out in this way? It was not, I think it is safe to say, that Lasso's music was so transgressive, but rather that it was so popular. The surviving publications of Lasso's music far outnumber those of any other sixteenth-century composer; by the 1580s, thousands of people – including a fair number of Jesuits, it seems – were clamouring for his music. The visitor and former rector of the Collège de Clermont focused on the masses and Magnificats of Lasso because they were what the college had in its library and what the Jesuits and their students enjoyed singing.

Interestingly enough, publications of Lasso masses and Magnificats prior to

Table 20.2
Principal publications of masses and Magnificats by Orlando di Lasso issued prior to 1585

1566	*Liber missarum ... liber primus*	Venice
1567	*Magnificat octo tonorum*	Nuremberg
1570	*Quinque missae suavissimis modulationibus*	Venice
1574	*Patrocinium musices ... missa aliquot, secunda pars*	Munich
1576	*Patrocinium musices ... Magnificat aliquot, quinta pars*	Munich
1577–8	*Missae variis concentibus ornatae*	Paris
1578	*Octo cantica ... Magnificat*	Paris
1581	*Liber missarum*	Nuremberg

1585, when Pigenat filed his report, are actually not that numerous. For all his international popularity, Lasso at that time would have been known – especially in France – primarily as a composer of motets and chansons. Table 20.2 lists the principal mass and Magnificat publications up through 1585. We cannot know, of course, which of these publications the Jesuit college in Paris possessed. (And although it seems unlikely to me, we also cannot rule out the possibility that they performed this music from manuscripts.) Nevertheless, I find it difficult to escape the conclusion that the two collections printed in Paris are the most likely sources of the music that drew Pigenat's criticisms.

The 1578 Magnificat print presents a cycle of eight Magnificats written in a richly imitative style, replete with the complex counterpoint and text repetitions Pigenat seems to be describing. The mass publication of the previous year, outlined in table 20.3, is both larger and stylistically more varied. Fifteen of the eighteen settings contained in it are so-called parody or imitation masses, based on pre-existent polyphonic compositions: three on Italian madrigals, five on Lasso's own Latin motets, and seven on French chansons. From such diverse models Lasso derived equally varied mass settings. Some, such as the masses on Lasso's own motets *Surge propera* and *In te Domine speravi*, present a luxuriant and contrapuntally complex web of sound. In other masses, such as those based on Certon's *Frère Thibault* and Sermisy's *La la maistre Pierre*, he cultivated a remarkably concise, transparent, and largely homophonic style. Ironically, the masses based on secular music generally come closer to the modest polyphonic style Pigenat seems to have sought. Indeed, some of the shortest and simplest settings derive from irreverent models that must have offended some Jesuit sensibilities. Even the publishers of the *Missae variis concentibus ornatae* felt the need to suppress some of the original titles. Mass no. 5, for example, which is based on a chanson about the adventures of a lecherous priest, appears here simply as the *Missa sine nomine*.[10] Pigenat, of course, neither mentions the

Table 20.3
Contents of Orlando di Lasso, *Missae variis concentibus ornatae* (Paris: Le Roy and Ballard, n.d. [1577–8])

	Title	No. of voices	Model
1.	*Doulce memoire*	4	Sandrin's chanson
2.	*Puis que i'ay perdu*	4	Lupi's chanson
3.	*O passi sparsi*	4	S. Festa's madrigal
4.	*Iager*	4	
5.	*Sine nomine* [= *Frère Thibault*]	4	Certon's chanson
6.	*Ad placitum* [= *La la maistre Pierre*]	4	Sermisy's chanson
7.	*De feria*	4	
8.	*Pro defunctis*	4	
9.	*Le berger*	5	Gombert's chanson
10.	*Ite, rime dolenti*	5	Rore's madrigal
11.	*Credidi*	5	his own motet
12.	*Sydus ex claro*	5	his own motet
13.	*Susanne un iour*	5	his own chanson
14.	*Credidi propter* [= *Scarco di doglia*]	5	Rore's madrigal
15.	*Surge propera*	6	his own motet
16.	*Tous les regretz*	6	Gombert's chanson
17.	*In te Domine speravi*	6	his own motet
18.	*Verbum bonum* [= *Vinum bonum*]	8	his own motet

models of Lasso's masses nor distinguishes between secular and sacred styles of music. That distinction first surfaces in a report penned by Lorenzo Maggio two years later, in 1587.

Serious factional discord among Jesuits in Paris and increasing concern about the involvement of certain Jesuits in affairs of state cast a dark cloud over activities at the Collège de Clermont beginning around 1583.[11] By 1586 the situation had deteriorated to the point where the Jesuit general in Rome, Claudio Acquaviva, found himself responding to demands by King Henri III that a visitor be sent to Paris to stem the rising tide of Jesuit involvement in political affairs. Acquaviva's initial appointment of Pigenat as official visitor elicited vehement objections from the French monarch, and it was only after months of negotiation, correspondence, and political brinkmanship that Acquaviva, on 9 February 1587, named the Venetian Lorenzo Maggio as Visitor to France. Delighted with this new choice, Henri issued the necessary passport, and on 3 June Maggio arrived in Paris.

If the reduction of internal strife and political involvement formed the primary focus of Maggio's visitation, he nevertheless found time for a thorough evaluation of the college's musical practices. His thoughtful and well-ordered discussion, which he presented in a series of twenty short paragraphs, surely ranks as one of the most valuable statements on the function and practice of music from the pen of a sixteenth-century Jesuit[12] (see appendix 1, fols 63–64v). Maggio both begins and ends his discussion with a clarification of the role of music in the college. Music is potentially dangerous in that it threatens to distract Jesuits from their more important duties. It is tolerated only on account of the *convictores* or boarding students, and for this reason they should assume responsibility for its continuation, by hiring a man skilled in music and of good character, who, like a chapel master, will instruct and direct them. The Jesuits themselves should neither compose music nor involve themselves in any way in the music of the chapel.

Although Maggio never invokes the Council of Trent explicitly, common post-Tridentine concerns are addressed. All ceremonies should be performed according to the Use of Rome, and one should beware, lest profane elements corrupt the sacred rites: 'With respect to the nature of the music, let care be taken in general that nothing be sung based on enticing songs of a trivial and secular nature, much less lascivious songs, or songs of war, as they are called, for it is not at all fitting to mix such profane things into divine worship. But let all the music be serious, suited to the occasion, not long-winded; and let it exude piety and inspire devotion.'

In the remainder of his rules on music, Maggio enumerates the days of the year on which music is to be performed; ranks those days according to their solemnity; indicates which liturgical items may be sung on the aforementioned days; and explains how both the liturgical genre and the degree of solemnity determine which of the three styles of music – polyphony, falsobordone, or chant – is to be used. In all classes of feasts, mass and vespers provided the principal contexts for music. Matins and lauds were celebrated only on Christmas Eve and the Triduum Sacrum of Holy Week. The Office of the Dead was sung entirely in chant, with the possible exception of the psalms, which could be rendered in falsobordone. Finally, for a handful of feasts, Maggio was at pains to indicate no sung mass and no sung vespers. Obviously there would have been many other feasts without sung mass and vespers. Why these were singled out remains unclear. Perhaps these feasts had formerly been celebrated with music and Maggio wished to ensure that the practice stopped.

The fragmentary description of music at the Parisian college that emerges from the five visitation reports discussed here leaves many questions unanswered and gaps unfilled. Nevertheless, much of the discussion contained in these reports is unmistakably coloured by a distinctive characteristic of the Jesuits' musical *modus procedendi*. What shaped sixteenth-century Jesuit musical thought and practice above all else was an extreme ambivalence about the role of music in the Society's ministries – an ambivalence firmly in place from the beginning, as the fifth chapter of the 1539 version of the 'Formula' so clearly demonstrates.

All the members who are in holy orders, even though they can acquire no right to benefices and revenues, should nonetheless be obliged to recite the office according to the rite of the Church, but not in choir lest they be diverted from the works of charity to which we have fully dedicated ourselves. Hence too they should use neither organs nor singing in their Masses and other religious ceremonies; for these laudably enhance the divine worship of other clerics and religious and have been found to arouse and move souls, by bringing them into harmony with the hymns and rites, but we have experienced them to be a considerable hindrance to us, since according to the nature of our vocation, besides the other necessary duties, we must frequently be engaged a great part of the day and even of the night in comforting the sick both in body and in spirit.[13]

Here, side by side, we find the Society's much-discussed eschewal of the singing of the Office in choir on the one hand, and a less frequently acknowledged Jesuit appreciation of the profound power of music to 'arouse and move souls' on the other. Today we struggle to appreciate the radical nature of the Jesuits' exemption from singing the Divine Office or canonical hours in choir, but as John W. O'Malley has noted, 'in the sixteenth century most Catholics could not conceive of a religious order without choral chanting of the Hours and, indeed, tended to see it as what most clearly distinguished members of religious orders from the rest of the population.'[14] Instituted for entirely practical reasons, the exemption from choir had a profound effect on Jesuit thought. Certainly it contributed to what Kennedy has characterized as 'an institutional bias against musical practice,'[15] but it also invited Jesuits to rethink music's function and construct a new philosophy of music largely 'from the ground up.' To an extent unparalleled in other early modern Catholic institutions, within the Society, thinking about music carried more weight than musical tradition. That is not to say that Jesuit attitudes about music derived entirely from initial policy and subsequent philosophizing: the actual experiences of many early Jesuits also demonstrated that liturgical music was not an indispensable component of spiritual life.

The freedom to think about music in new ways proved nowhere more valuable than in the schools. Ever mindful of the need to resist the seductive powers of music lest they be diverted from their primary vocations, sixteenth-century Jesuits nevertheless embraced music's ability to arouse and move the souls of their students. At once both deeply suspicious and profoundly respectful of its power, Jesuits came to define music almost exclusively in terms of its function within their pastoral and pedagogical ministries. Maggio expressed this attitude most directly when he asked that Jesuits not involve themselves in the music of the chapel and called for a hired chapel master supported by the boarding students, 'on account of whom these things are chiefly done' (appendix 1, fol. 63, item 2). Indeed, at the close of his report, he asserted that the college would be able to abandon music altogether if a change in circumstances were to free it from the care of these students. Calling for diligent oversight by the superiors, Maggio concluded that music in the college was to be understood as a certain indulgence granted by the administrators and tolerated only for the sake of the students (appendix 1, fol. 64r–v, item 20).

In Maggio's attitude we recognize the kind of accommodation more commonly associated with Jesuit missions in Asia and the New World. Indeed, sixteenth-century Jesuits sometimes drew this connection themselves. In 1587, for example, a representative of the Austrian provincial council informed the general in Rome that the 'voice of the people demands the reintroduction of the organ; its elimination has led to annoyance, grumbling, and bitterness. Our people in India have been granted many things for the conversion of the infidels; likewise, in Germany, which in many ways can be compared to India, one must allow the organ.'[16]

If the Parisian reports reveal certain fundamental priorities and values that defined a common Jesuit musical identity, they also remind us that specific expressions of that identity exhibited considerable variation. To take just one example, in 1566, Jerónimo Nadal, principal assistant to the general in Rome, issued a set of instructions for the college in Vienna, in which he approved of polyphony for the mass ordinary and Magnificat, falsobordone for the vespers psalms, and Gregorian chant for everything else. On higher feast days, according to Nadal, the rector of the college could make exceptions to this rule and allow somewhat more polyphony. This is the earliest reference to the performance of liturgical music in a Jesuit college, and as Kennedy has pointed out, previous research has suggested that in subsequent years musical practices permitted in other Jesuit colleges more or less conformed to Nadal's instructions.[17] As we have seen, Claude Matthieu discussed music in similar terms in his 1576 visitation report, allowing for the Magnificat in polyphony, the mass also in polyphony (or falsobordone), alternate verses of the vespers psalms in falsobordone, with the rest in chant. But Matthieu's instructions actually differ significantly from Nadal's in that the plan outlined above was intended for the highest feasts. On other days, Matthieu called for a greatly simplified observance consisting entirely of chant except for the Magnificat and the Credo, which could be rendered in falsobordone. And eleven years later Lorenzo Maggio offered a far more detailed plan for Paris that differed in many of its particulars from the instructions of both Nadal and Matthieu. More significant than these discrepancies, however, is the variability of musical observance that the Parisian visitation reports reveal. Far from adopting the instructions of Nadal and sticking to them, the Jesuits in Paris between the years 1576 and 1587 tried a variety of approaches, including serious consideration in 1579 of the abandonment of polyphony altogether.

It is the capacity of early visitation reports to capture such moments of evaluation and reflection and the opportunities they provide to chart the evolution of local thought and practice during a crucial period for the formation of Jesuit identity that most strongly recommend their further study. They will not serve us well, of course, if we merely mine them uncritically for the 'truth of the matter': visitors' perceptions were probably not always accurate, their prescriptions not always realized. And we should resist the temptation to transform them into 'official' statements of general policy. Their value to us lies rather in their ability to show us how individual members of the Society analysed and responded to specific situations, and in so doing, took stock of their own enterprise. We need to read them, in other words, because they allow us to meet early Jesuits at moments when they thought carefully about who they were and how they should proceed.

APPENDIX I:

DISCUSSIONS OF MUSIC IN BNP LAT. 10989

[fol. 41]

Decima sexta mensis Martij 1579 venit in Collegiu[m] Parisiense R[everendus] Pater M Joan[n]es Maldonatus a R[everendo] P[atre] pr[aeposit]o Generali Everardo Mercuriano visitator provinciae constitutus; suasq[ue] l[itte]ras ostendit quae sequuntur.

VISITATIO COLLEGIJ PARISIENSIS FACTA PER R[EVERENDUM] P[ATREM] M JOHANNEM MALDONATU[M] ANNO D[OMI]NI 1579 [SPACE LEFT TO FILL IN THE DATE] MENSIS

[column 1] Quae Rector in singulis regulis aut interrogat[us] respondit, aut sponte proposuit.

On 16 March 1579, Reverend Father Juan Maldonado, appointed visitor of the province by Reverend Father General Everard Mercurian, came to the Parisian college and issued his report, which follows.

VISITATION OF THE PARISIAN COLLEGE MADE BY REVEREND FATHER JUAN MALDONADO [ON 16 MARCH] IN THE YEAR OF OUR LORD 1579.

[column 1] What the rector said, or proposed of his own accord, in the matter of individual rules.

[column 2] Quae consultores in rebus dubijs interrogati responderu[n]t.

[column 3] Quae visitator constituit.
[fol. 42v]
REGULAE PRAEFECTI ECCL[ES]IAE

[fol. 43]
[column 1]
28. Quia exp[er]ie[n]tia docuit, vix posse coerceri ca[n]tores, quin exceda[n]t modu[m] musice, qui s[a]epe ia[m] a superiorib[us] praescriptus fuit, et q[ui]a saepe ia[m] nos amici monueru[n]t, ne musice canerem[us], sed solo ca[n]tu Gregoriano et falsis vocib[us]; propositu[m] e[st:] An Musica in hoc collegio e[ss]et o[mn]i[n]o tollenda, solo ca[n]tu Gregoriano et falsis vocib[us] rete[n]tis.
[column 2]
28. Consultores iudicaru[n]t exp[er]ie[n]du[m] e[ss]e quomodo res succedet per aliquod tempus relicta musica, et retentis falsis vocibus; nihil interim statuendum in una[m] vel alteram partem.

[column 3]
28. scribantur ad P[atrem] N[ostrum] r[ati]o[nes] in utra[m]q[ue] partem & servetur diligenter, quod prescripserit.

[28 bis, column 1]
Deni[que] quaesitu[m] e[s]t quot Psalmi cane[n]di e[ss]ent falsis vocibus.
[28 bis, column 2]
Visu[m] e[st] co[n]sultoribus diebus

[column 2] What the advisers said when asked about the things under consideration.
[column 3] What the visitor decided.

RULES OF THE SUPERINTENDENT OF
THE CHURCH

[column 1]
28. Because experience has taught that singers can scarcely be restrained from going beyond the kind of music that has already been prescribed by the superiors many times, and because friends have already warned us many times not to sing polyphony but only Gregorian chant and falsobordone, the question was raised, whether in this college polyphony should be eliminated entirely, with only Gregorian chant and falsobordone retained.
[column 2]
28. The advisers judged that it should be tested how the matter will come out after polyphony has been relinquished for a while and falsobordone retained, [and] that nothing should be decided one way or the other in the meantime.
[column 3]
28. Let the arguments both pro and con be written to Our Father [General], and let whatever he prescribes be diligently maintained.
[28 bis, column 1]
Finally, it was asked how many psalms should be sung in falsobordone.
[28 bis, column 2]
It seemed good to the advisers if only

D[omi]nicis, t[antu]m canendu[m]
e[ss]e unu[m] et hymnu[m]
Magnificat Diebus a[u]t[em]
solemniorib[us] duos psalmos cu[m]
Magnificat Diebus a[u]t[em]
solemnissimis o[mn]es psalmos
alternis vocibus.
[28 bis, column 3: blank]
[column 1]
29. Dubitatu[m] et[iam] e[st], An
expediret n[ost]ros cu[m] faciu[n]t
primu[m] sacru[m], illud ca[n]tare,
cu[m] pauci sint qui sciant canere, et
videatur e[ss]e invidiosa dissimilitudo
si alij cana[n]t, alij no[n] cana[n]t.

[column 2]
29. Visu[m] e[st] co[n]sultoribus no[n]
expedire.

[column 3]
29. Possu[n]t canere Missam
ordinariam, no[n] t[ame]n ideo canere
quia nova est quod intelligatur si sit
aliqua necessitas, alioqui melius est
no[n] canere.

[fol. 46]
Quae in tertia columna mea manu
scripta sunt partim a R[everendo]
P[atre] N[ostro] praeposito generali
Everardo Mercuriano constituta,
partim a me eius nomine ordinata et
ab ipso visa et approbata sunt.
J[ohannes] Maldonatus
[fol. 48]
EXCERPTA EX VISITATIONE ~~ANNI 1575~~
R[EVERENDI] P[ATRIS] CLAUDIJ ANNI
1575

one [psalm] and the hymn Magnificat
be sung on Sundays; on more solemn
days, however, two psalms with the
Magnificat; and on the most solemn
days, all the psalms in alternating
voices.
[this paragraph later crossed out]
[28 bis, column 3: blank]
[column 1]
29. It was also questioned whether it
was advantageous for our people,
when they perform the first holy rite,
to sing it, seeing that there are only a
few who know how to sing, and that it
seems to be an invidious discrepancy
if some sing, and others do not.
[this paragraph later crossed out]
[column 2]
It seemed to the advisers that it was
not advantageous. [this paragraph
later crossed out]
[column 3]
29. They may sing the mass ordinary,
but [should] not sing it just because it
is new. In other words, [they can sing it]
if there be some necessity; otherwise it is
better not to sing. [this paragraph later
crossed out]

Those things written in my own hand
in the third column were in part
decided by Our Reverend Father
General Everard Mercurian and in
part drafted by myself in his name
and seen and approved by him.
Juan Maldonado

EXCERPTS FROM THE VISITATION OF
REVEREND FATHER CLAUDE IN THE
YEAR 1575

[fol. 49]

EX VISITATIONE EUISDEM
V[ISITATO]RIS ANNI 1576

FROM THE VISITATION OF THE SAME
VISITOR IN THE YEAR 1576

[fol. 49v]

SACELLUM

CHAPEL

Iis dieb[us] quibus fit sacrum hora
nona cantabunt[u]r psalmi a
faulxbourdone alternib[us] versibus et
magnificat musice cum *uno moteto* in
fine: missa vero cantabit[u]r
sole[m]niter id est musice vel a
faulxbourdone. Alijs v[er]o dieb[us]
cantabunt[u]r psalmi alternatim et
magnificat a faulxbourdo[n]e missa
v[er]o cantu Gregoriano t[antu]m et
Credo a faulxbourdoni.

Those days on which the sacred rite is
done at the ninth hour, the psalms will
be sung with alternate verses in
falsobordone, and the Magnificat will
be sung in polyphony with a motet at
the end. But the mass will be sung
solemnly, that is, in polyphony or in
falsobordone. On the other days,
however, the psalms will be sung
alternatim and the Magnificat in
falsobordone, but the mass only in
Gregorian chant and the Credo in
falsobordone.

[marginal annotation:] Sustulit motetum
postea.

[marginal annotation:] He later did
away with the motet.

In ~~matitum~~ matutinis p[re]cibus, nulla
fit musica, benedictus a faulxbourdone
et Te Deum.

At matins, nothing is done in polyphony; the Benedictus and Te Deum
are done in falsobordone.

In matutinis heb[domad]ae s[anc]tae
3es Lectiones Hieremye musice et
miserere a faulxbourdone.

At matins during Holy Week, the
three Readings [i.e., Lamentations] of
Jeremiah are sung in polyphony and
the Miserere is sung in falsobordone.

Non videtur e[ss]e opus ut officium
fiat in vigilia pentecostes. Iudicet
t[ame]n p[ater] n[oster].

It does not seem necessary that the
office should be done on the vigil of
Pentecost. But let Our Father decide.

[marginal annotation:] Anno 1586 et
aliis [1585, 1587, 88, 89 added above]
in[ter]cede[n]tib[us] non est fact[um].

[marginal annotation:] In 1586 (and
also in 1585, 1587, 1588, and 1589),
with other factors intervening, it was
not done.

[previous paragraphs – from 'Iis dieb[us] quibus fit sacrum hora nona' to
'Iudicet t[a]m[en] p[ater] n[oster]' – later crossed out]

[fol. 51v]

EX VISITATIONE ANNI 1578

Lon chantera avec les faulx bourdons
co[m]munes et non aultrement sans
licence lon ostera les motez du tout, si
ce n'est avec conge du Recteur et au
lieu d'iceulx lon dira une antiphone
de la vierge Marie avec faulxbour-
dons.
[this paragraph later crossed out]
[fol. 53]
VISITATIO R[EVERENDI] P[ATRIS]
ODONIS PROVINCIALIS ANNJ 1585
[fol. 53v]
SACELLUM
3. Quae de ra[tio]ne cantus in alijs
visitationibus praescripta sunt,
diligentius serventur praesertim vero
 in festis secundae classis non sit tam
celebris et longa musica, nec in sacro,
nec in Vespertinis pr[ec]ibus.
Relinquatur ea musica, ubi toties e
adem verba repetunt[ur]. Non
canant[ur] Orlandi missae, nec
magnificat. Antiphonae B[eatae]
Virg[inis] sint breviores, omnia
deniq[ue] ad devotionem et
suavitatem dirigantur.

[this paragraph later crossed out]
[fol. 56]
Die 6 Julij 1587 venit in Collegium
Parisiense R[everendus] Pater
Laurentius Magius a R[everendo]
P[atre] n[ost]ro Generali Claudio
Aquaviva visitator Provinciaru[m]
Gallicarum constitutus, suasq[ue]
Literas ostendit quae sequuntur.

FROM THE VISITATION IN THE YEAR
1578
One will sing with common
falsobordone and not otherwise
without permission. One will eliminate motets entirely unless with the
permission of the rector. And in lieu
of these, one will sing an antiphon of
the Virgin Mary in falsobordone.
[this paragraph later crossed out]

VISITATION OF REVEREND FATHER
PROVINCIAL ODON IN THE YEAR 1585

CHAPEL
3. Let those things concerning the
manner of singing prescribed in other
visitations be observed more diligently, but especially on feasts of the
second class, let the music not be so
ornate and long-winded, either at
mass or at vespers. Let that music be
abandoned, in which the same word
s are repeated so many times. Let
neither the masses nor the Magnificats
of Orlando [di Lasso] be sung. Let the
antiphons of the Blessed Virgin be
rather brief. In short, let all things be
directed towards devotion and sweetness.
[this paragraph later crossed out]

On 6 July 1587, Reverend Father
Lorenzo Maggio, appointed Visitor of
the French Provinces by Our Reverend Father General Claudio
Acquaviva, came to the Parisian
college, and he issued his report,
which follows.

VISITATIO COLLEGIJ PARISIENSIS FACTA
PER R[EVERENDUM] P[ATREM]
LAURENTIU[M] MAGIUM ANNO
D[OMI]NI 1587
[fol. 63]
CIRCA CANTU[M] SACELLI INFERIORIS
ETC.

1. Cantus in Collegij sacello, quo
Convictores ad suae pietatis exercitia
utuntur, et externis co[m]mune est, ea
ratione ac moderatione quae sequitur,
servata, et non aliter retineri poterit.

2. In cantu sacelli deinceps nostri
nullo modo occupari, aut et[iam]
misceri, nec sine Rectoris falcultate
musice componere permittantur, sed
convictores, regiiq[ue] Pauperes, et
Claromontani hoc cantandi munus
sustineant, conducto aliquo viro bono
musices perito, qui tanqua[m]
mag[iste]r capellae illos instruat, ac
dirigat, et cantuj sacelli praesit. Hic
vero apud Convictores p[ro]p[te]r
quos praesertim haec fiunt, alatur,
a quibus et[iam], si quos canere
docuerit, mercedem sui laboris
accipiet.

3. Totum officiu[m], et Caeremoniae
o[mn]es s[ecundu]m Usum
Romanu[m] semper fiant, et nullus
summo sacro (ad quod cantandum
sacerdos e[x] n[ost]ris adhibeatur)
ministret, ep[istu]lamve cantet, nisi
clericus et superpellices indutus fuerit,
quod ordinarie pauperes ipsi
praestent.

VISITATION OF THE PARISIAN COLLEGE
MADE BY REVEREND FATHER LORENZO
MAGGIO IN THE YEAR OF OUR LORD
1587

CONCERNING MUSIC OF THE LOWER
CHAPEL

1. Song in the college chapel, which
the boarding students use for their
pious exercises and share with the
externs, may be retained in the manner, and with the moderation, described below, and in no other way.

2. Let our people henceforth in no
way be permitted to take up, or be
involved in, the music of the chapel,
and let them not be permitted to
compose music without the approval
of the rector. Let rather the boarding
students, the poor students of the
king, and the Clermont students
support this duty of singing, having
hired a good man skilled in music to
instruct and direct them as a chapel
master and preside over the music of
the chapel. Let him, in fact, be supported by the boarding students, on
account of whom these things are
chiefly done, and from whom, if he
teaches anyone to sing, he will receive
payment for his labour.

3. Let the entire office and all ceremonies be done always according to
Roman Use, and let no one minister at
high mass (for the singing of which a
priest from our people is employed)
or sing the epistle, unless he is a cleric
and dressed in a surplice. For this, let
the poor students ordinarily assume
responsibility.

4. Porrò sequentia t[antu]m p[rae]scriptis diebus cantari licebit, v[idelicet] matutinas preces in nocte Natalis ×[i] cum toto officio fieri solito; et in Commemoratione o[mn]ium fideliu[m] defunctoru[m] post Vesperas o[mn]ium sanctorum: Officiu[m] quoq[ue], quod tenebraru[m] dici solet, cum suis Ceremonijs in hebdomada sancta tam manè, qua[m] à prandio pro consueto more fieri poterit. Alias huiusmodi matutinalia officia nunqua[m] fiant.

[fol. 63v]

5. Vespertinas preces in solis pervigiliis Christi D[omi]ni, Beat[issi]mae virginis Mariae, Pentecostes; et o[mn]ium sanctorum cantari liceat. In alioru[m] quoru[m]cumq[ue] festoru[m] pervigiliis nullae o[mn]i[n]o vespertinae preces, nulla item in ullo festi ullius pervigilio completoria decantentur. Quae praeterea diebus festis Quadragesimae ante prandiu[m] cantari solent, deinceps o[mn]i[n]o ne cantentur, neq[ue] ulla penitus completoria, excepto die festo Annunciationis B[eatae] Virginis Mariae.

6. Caeteris diebus d[omi]nicis, et festis per totum annum Vespertinae preces retineri possunt, q[ua]n[do] festa per totam Civitatem ab o[mn]ibus servantur, et non al[ite]r. Excipiuntur sequentia festa, v[idelicet] SS. fabiani, et sebastiani 20 Januarij: S. Benedicti 21 Martij: translationis eiusdem 11 Julij:

4. Furthermore, the following may be sung only on the prescribed days: viz., matins may be sung on Christmas Eve, with all the office that is usually done; at the Commemoration of All the Faithful Departed, following vespers on All Saints' Day; and also during the office, which is customarily called Tenebrae, it can be done with its ceremonies during Holy Week, either in the morning or after lunch, according to the usual practice. Let no other matins office of this kind be done.

5. Let vespers be sung only on the vigils of Christ Our Lord, the Most Blessed Virgin Mary, Pentecost, and All Saints. Let no vespers whatsoever be sung on the vigils of any other feasts, and likewise let no compline be sung on any vigil of any feast. Furthermore, on the feast days within Lent, let none of those things that are commonly sung before lunch, nor any compline whatsoever, be sung, except on the feast of the Annunciation of the Blessed Virgin Mary.

6. On other Sundays and feasts throughout the entire year vespers can be retained when the feasts are observed by everyone throughout the entire city, and not otherwise. The following feasts are excepted, namely, Sts Fabian and Sebastian on 20 January; St Benedict on 21 March; his Translation on 11 July; St Roch on

S. Rochi 16 Augusti: SS. Mauritij et
Socioru[m] 22 Septembris:
Commemorationis o[mn]ium
fideliu[m] defunctoru[m] 2 Nov-
emb[ris] quibus nullae
Vespertinae preces cantabuntur.
7. Sacra cantentur solum in
solemnibus festis, v[idelicet] Chr[ist]i
D[omi]ni n[ost]rj (et quidem in eius
Natali primum tantum, et tertium)
Beatiss[imae] Virg[inis] Mariae,
Pentecostes, Trinitatis, Sanctorum 12
Ap[osto]lorum, D[ivi] Stephani,
D[ivi] Jo[hann]is Bapt[ist]ae, D[ivi]
Laurentij, D[ivae] Catharinae, D[ivi]
Nicolai in decembri, o[mn]ium
Sanctoru[m], Commemorationis
o[mn]ium fideliu[m] defunctorum,
D[omi]nicae palmarum; alias
nunqua[m], nec initio renovationis
studiorum, nec in die Cinerum.
8. Hymnus Veni Creator Sp[irit]us,
diebus d[omini]cis, et antiphonae
Salve Regina, atq[ue] aliae quotidianae
alijs diebus, quae vesperi a Convictoribus pro tempore cantari solent;
Benedictio quoq[ue] candelaru[m] in
Purificationis festo, et palmaru[m],
in D[ome]nica Palmaru[m] cum suo
cantu retineri possunt: sicut et Miserere, feria 4. et 6. Quadrag[esim]ae,
p[ro]p[ter] Congreg[atione]m
B[eatae] Virginis. Cerei et[iam]
benedictio in Sabbato sancto cum
prophetijs more solito.

9. Quod ad rationem cantus attinet,
illud generatim o[mn]i[n]o caveatur,

16 August; St Maurice and his Companions on 22 September; the Commemoration of All the Faithful
Departed on 2 November, on which
days no vespers will be sung.

7. Let the mass be sung only on
solemn feasts, namely, on the feasts of
Christ Our Lord (and, indeed, on
Christmas only the first and third
[masses]), the Most Blessed Virgin
Mary, Pentecost, Trinity, the Twelve
Holy Apostles, St Stephen, St John the
Baptist, St Laurence, St Catherine,
St Nicholas in December, All Saints,
the Commemoration of All the Faithful
Departed, Palm Sunday; and on no
others, neither at the start of the
school year nor on Ash Wednesday.

8. On Sundays the hymn Veni Creator
Spiritus and on the other days the
Salve Regina and the other daily
antiphons, which are customarily
sung in the evening by the boarding
students as the occasion demands,
also the Blessing of the Candles on
the Feast of the Purification, and the
Blessing of the Palms on Palm Sunday can be retained with their music;
likewise, the Miserere on Wednesdays
and Fridays of Lent on account of the
Congregation of the Blessed Virgin;
also the blessing of the taper on Holy
Saturday with the prophets [i.e., the
Old Testament readings] according to
the usual custom.

9. With respect to the nature of the
music, let care be taken in general that

ne quippiam cantetur compositu[m]
ad leves cantiunculas seculares,
multoq[ue] minus lascivas, aut et[iam]
ad cantionem belli, ut vocant, cum in
cultu divino h[uius]mo[d]i profana
misceri minime deceat, sed tota musica
gravis sit, t[em]p[o]ri accom[m]odata,
non prolixa, quaeq[ue] pietatem
redoleat, et excitet devotionem.
10. Servetur proportionis mensura
inter maiores minoresq[ue] festos
dies, ut sc[ilicet] in his minus
musices, quam in illis admisceatur, in
quibus t[ame]n excessus cavendus est,
ne ostentationem potius, auriumq[ue]
pruritu[m], quam a[n]i[m]orum
devotione[m] affectare videamur.

11. Nulli sumptus in musicis
instrumentis conducendis fieri
permittantur, neq[ue] et[iam] si qui
cu[m] illis se venturos offerent
ornandi causa sacelli cantum,
admittantur, quantumvis festa celebria
fuerint.
12. In particularj haec ratio cantus
observetur. In natalitijs matutinis
tertius t[antu]m cuiusq[ue] nocturnj,
et laudu[m] quintus psalmus
falsobordono: Te Deum verò,
Hymnus, et Benedictus musice cani
poterunt.
13. Officiu[m] defunctoru[m] vel
Gregoriano cantu totu[m] fiat, vel
certe psalmi tono simplici, reliqua
Gregorianice canantur.

14. Officiu[m] tenebraru[m] sic fiat
tertius cuiusq[ue] nocturni psalmus
falsobordono,

nothing be sung based on enticing
songs of a trivial and secular nature,
much less lascivious songs, or songs
of war, as they are called, for it is not
at all fitting to mix such profane
things into divine worship. But let all
the music be serious, suited to the
occasion, not long-winded; and let it
exude piety and inspire devotion.
10. Let due proportion be kept between the major and minor feast days,
so that less polyphony may be included on the latter than the former, in
which nevertheless an excess must be
avoided, lest we be perceived as
striving more for ostentation and
stimulation of the ears than devotion
of the soul.
11. Let no expenses be allowed for
the hiring of musical instruments, nor
should even any who offer to come
with them be admitted for the sake of
decorating the chapel's music, no
matter how well attended the feasts
will be.
12. In particular, let this rule of song
be observed. At Christmas matins
only the third psalm of each nocturn
and at lauds only the fifth psalm may
be sung in falsobordone; but the Te
Deum, the hymn, and the Benedictus
may be sung in polyphony.
13. Let the Office of the Dead be done
either entirely in Gregorian chant, or
at least with the psalms done to a
simple tone and the rest sung in
Gregorian chant.
14. Let the Office of Tenebrae be
done thus: the third psalm of each
nocturn in falsobordone,

[fol. 64]

nisi malint ut o[mn]es psalmi triu[m]
nocturnoru[m] gregorianice: haec
lamenta[ti]o[n]es vel pluribus vocibus
lugubrj musica cu[m] responsoriis
cantu gregoriano, vel una voce
gregorianice cum responsoriis musicè
(quod et[iam] fieri poterit in
responsorijs sequentu[m] lectionu[m])
decantentur. In laudibus ultimus
psalmus laudate D[omin]um de caelis
e[t]c. falsobordono: Benedictus
autem, et ultimu[m] Miserere, musicè:
Antiphona verò, Chr[ist]us factus est
pro nobis e[t]c. gregorianicè canantur.

15. Officiu[m] verò quod manè
celebratur in hebdomada sancta, fiat
hoc modo: In sacro quintae feriae,
Kyrie, Gloria, Credo, Sanctus, Agnus
Dei musicè cani poterunt. Sexta feria
musicè nihil praeter passionem, quae
à pluribus personis et in quibusdam
eius partibus musicè pronuntiarj
poterit, nisi malint à sacerdote solo
cantu gregoriano, vel à diacono, vel
ab utróq[ue] praetermissa musica.
Sabbato Kyrie, Gloria, Sanctus,
Agnus Dei, Magnificat, musicè;
Laudate D[omin]um o[mn]es gentes,
falsobordono.

16. In sacris peragendis haec cantus
mensura observetur. In festis Chr[ist]i
D[omin]i, Beatiss. Virginis,
Pentecostes, Ap[osto]lorum Petri et

unless they prefer all psalms of the
three nocturns in Gregorian chant; let
these lamentations be sung either in
many-voiced solemn polyphony with
the responsories in Gregorian chant
or with one voice singing Gregorian
chant and the responsories in polyphony (which can also be done in
the responsories of the following
readings). At lauds, let the last psalm,
'Laudate Dominum de caelis, etc.,' be
sung in falsobordone; let the
Benedictus and the last Miserere,
however, be sung in polyphony, but
the antiphon 'Christus factus est pro
nobis, etc.' in Gregorian chant.

15. But let the office that is celebrated
in the morning during Holy Week be
done in the following manner: at mass
on the fifth feria [i.e., Maundy Thurs-
day], the Kyrie, Gloria, Credo,
Sanctus, and Agnus Dei may be sung
in polyphony. On feria six [i.e., Good
Friday], nothing in polyphony except
the Passion, which may be performed
by several people and in some parts
polyphonically, unless they prefer it
performed by a single priest in
Gregorian chant or by a deacon, or by
both, with polyphony being omitted.
On Saturday, the Kyrie, Gloria,
Sanctus, Agnus Dei, and Magnificat
in polyphony; [the psalm] 'Laudate
Dominum omnes gentes' in
falsobordone.

16. In performing the rites, let this
amount of music be observed. On the
feasts of Christ the Lord, the Most
Blessed Virgin, Pentecost, the Apostles

Pauli, D[ivi] Jo[hann]is Bapt[ist]ae, O[mn]ium Sanctoru[m], Kyrie, Gloria, Credo, Sanctus, Agnus Dei, Deo gr[ati]as: In alijs Gloria, Sanctus, Agnus Dei, musicè, Credo et[iam] falsobordono; [illegible word crossed out] cani poterunt. In die Commemorationis defunctorum Missa cantu gregoriano canenda est, exceptis, Dies irae, et ad elevatione[m] Pie Jesu, quae lugubrj, et simplici musica decantari poterunt.

Peter and Paul, St John the Baptist, [and] All Saints, the Kyrie, Gloria, Credo, Sanctus, Agnus Dei, and Deo gratias [may be sung] in polyphony; on other [feasts] the Gloria, Sanctus, [and] Agnus Dei in polyphony; the Credo also in falsobordone. On the day of the Commemoration of the Dead, the mass is to be sung in Gregorian chant, except for the Dies irae and, at the elevation, the Pie Jesu, [both of] which may be delivered in solemn, simple polyphony.

17. Vespertinae preces, quae in supradictis n° 5° pervigiliis permittuntur hac ra[ti]o[n]e decantentur, ut o[mn]es quinq[ue] psalmi falsobordono, Hymnus, et Magnificat musicè canantur, et finitis vesperis, Antiphona consueta B[eatae] Virginis sine moteto retineatur.

17. Let vespers, which is permitted on the vigils mentioned above in number 5, be sung according to this rule: let all five psalms be sung in falsobordone, the hymn and Magnificat in polyphony, and at the end of vespers, let the usual antiphon of the Blessed Virgin be retained without a motet.

18. Caeterorum dierum quibus vespertin[ae] preces conceduntur, tres sunt Classes: prima eorum, qui sunt valde solemnes, vi[delicet] festorum Xpī D[omi]ni, Pentecostes, Trinitatis, festorum item B[eatae] Virginis Mariae, SS. Ap[osto]lorum Petri et Pauli, D[ivi] Jo[hann]is Bapt[ist]ae, Omniu[m] Sanctoru[m]. 2ᵃ minus solemniu[m], cuiusmodi sunt caeteri o[mn]es s[an]ctorum dies festi. 3ᵃ Co[mmun]ium, quales sunt dies Dominici. In his di[e]bus hac ratio cantus teneatur. In festis p[rim]ae classis psalmi o[mn]es falsobordono: Hymnus verò et Magnificat musicè cantarj possunt. In festis 2ᵃᵉ classis p[rimus] 3. 5. psalmi falsobordono,

18. The other days on which the vespers prayers are allowed are of three classes: the first of these [consists] of those [days] that are very solemn, viz., the feasts of Christ the Lord, Pentecost, Trinity, and likewise the feasts of the Blessed Virgin Mary, of the Holy Apostles Peter and Paul, of St John the Baptist, [and] All Saints. The second [consists] of the less solemn ones, of which sort are the feast days of all the other saints. The third [consists] of the common ones, which are Sundays. On these days, let this manner of singing be maintained. On feasts of the first class, all the psalms in falsobordone, but the hymn and Magnificat in

Magnificat musicè cani poterunt. In festis demu[m] 3ᵃᵉ Classis p[rimus] vel 2. et 4. aut 5. psalmi; praeterea Magnificat falsobordono decantarj possunt.

19. In Vespertinis precibus, quae apud S[anctum] Ludovicu[m] in domo n[ost]ra professa, quibus diebus pomeridiana concio h[abetu]r, decantantur, eadem moderatio servetur. Eas verò cantent aliquot ex Pauperibus qui m[onaste]rij fuerint, quibus t[ame]n unus, aut alter è n[ost]ris adesse poterit, qui eas deducat, ac et[iam] in cantu dirigat, quandiu aliquis eoru[m] huic regendi illic cantus muneri idoneus non erit.
20. Haec o[mn]ia supradicta superioribus diligenter observanda commendantur, qui serio cavebunt ne quippia[m] introducatur, quod societatis instituto ulla ra[ti]o[n]e adversetur, aut concessionis metas excedat: et illud p[rae]terea curabunt, ut hoc cantandi onus Convictoribus, et Pauperibus p[ro]p[ter] quos praesertim toleratur, ita relinquatur tanquam proprium, ut si quando contingat societatem eorum cura liberari, Collegiu[m] n[ost]rum illud sustinere non

[fol. 64v]
cogatur, cum meminisse debeant, cantum in Societate quadam dispensationis indulgentia tolerari, et ob eam c[aus]am restringendum potius esse quam extendendu[m].

polyphony. On feasts of the second class, the first, third, and fifth psalms may be sung in falsobordone, the Magnificat in polyphony. Finally, on feasts of the third class, the first or second and the fourth or fifth psalms, and in addition the Magnificat, may be sung in falsobordone.
19. At vespers, which is sung at St Louis in our professed house on those days when an assembly is held in the afternoon, let the same moderation be observed. But let some of the poor students in the monastery sing it. Nevertheless, one or the other of our people may be present to lead them and even direct them in singing, as long as one of them [the poor students] is not suited to this task of directing the music there.
20. All the things mentioned above are committed to the diligent care of the superiors, who will earnestly beware lest anything be introduced that is in any way adverse to the institute of the Society, or exceeds the boundaries of concession. And beyond this, they will take care that this burden of singing be left exclusively to the boarding students and the poor students, on account of whom especially it is tolerated. [Thus,] if sometime it should befall the Society to be freed from their care, our college would not be forced to keep it up,

since they ought to remember that music is tolerated in the Society by a certain indulgence of the administration, and for this reason should be restricted rather than extended.

APPENDIX 2: EVERARD MERCURIAN, ORDINANCE ON MUSIC,
1575 (BNP LAT. 10989 FOL. 86v)

QUAE VISA SUNT OBSERVANDA IN
LIBRIS MUSICES QUIBUS ALIQUANDO
NOSTRJ IN SOCIETATE UTUNTUR AD
ANIMI LAXATIONEM.

THOSE THINGS TO BE OBSERVED WITH
RESPECT TO THE MUSIC BOOKS, WHICH
MEMBERS OF THE SOCIETY SOMETIMES
USE FOR THE RELAXATION OF THE
SOUL.

Cantus ecclesiastici qui nempe origine sua ecclesiastici sunt et sanctae sedis Apostolicae seu Ep[iscop]or[um] et Inquisitorum p[er]missu typis excusi vel scripto quidem solum evulgati sed tamen à Superioribus approbati sunt neque ab haereticis prodierunt poterunt aliquando cantari à n[ost]ris quales sunt qui dicuntur Motteti, missae, hymni, piaeque aliae id genus cantiones.

Ecclesiastical songs, which truly by their origin are of the church and the holy Apostolic See – whether printed with the permission of the bishops and inquisitors or indeed merely promulgated in manuscript with the approval of the superiors – and have not been produced by heretics, may sometimes be sung by our people. They are the kind called motets, masses, and hymns, and other pious songs of this sort.

Quae turpem habent dictionem et sonum sive eum cantandi modum cui etiam subesse obscaena aut vana putentur comburantur.

Let [those songs] be burned that have shameful text and music or a manner of singing that obscene or vain things are thought to underlie.

Quae dubia sunt examinet diligenter Superior atque aedifica[ti]o[n]is o[mn]is ra[ti]o habeatur.

Let the superior examine carefully those [songs] that are questionable, and let every principle of edification be borne in mind.

Idem v[er]ò Sup[er]ior neque emi neque à quoquam huiusmodi libros legi aut haberi sinat, quos ipse diligenter prius non examinaverit.

Indeed, let the same superior allow no books of this sort that he himself has not first examined carefully to be bought, or to be read or kept by anyone.

NOTES

I wish to thank Leofranc Holford-Strevens, who provided invaluable assistance with the transcription and translation of a number of problematic passages in the documents on which this study is based.

1 On the history of visitation, see J. Gilchrist, 'Visitation, Canonical, History of,' in

New Catholic Encyclopedia, 16 vols (New York, 1967–88); Hubert Jedin, 'Einführung,' in *Die Visitation im Dienst der kirchlichen Reform*, ed. Ernst Walter Zeeden and Hansgeorg Molitor (Münster, 1967), pp. 4–9; Ernst Walter Zeeden, 'Vorwort,' in *Repertorium der Kirchenvisitationsakten aus dem 16. und 17. Jahrhundert in Archiven der Bundesrepublik Deutschland*, vol. 1, *Hessen*, ed. Zeeden (Stuttgart, 1982), pp. 9–14; Gerald Strauss, 'Visitations,' in *The Oxford Encyclopedia of the Reformation*, ed. Hans J. Hillerbrand (New York, 1996).

2 See Jedin, 'Einführung,' p. 5.

3 *Constitutions*, part VIII, chap. 2, *The Constitutions of the Society of Jesus and Their Complementary Norms: A Complete English Translation of the Official Latin Texts* (St Louis, 1996), p. 324.

4 'Actum est deinde de visitatione Praepositorum Provincialium; et visum est: committendum id esse Praeposito Generali, qui poterit Provincialibus iniungere, ut quotannis visitent Domos et Collegia suarum Provinciarum, vel eorum arbitrio id relinquet. Itaque ipsemet Praepositus Generalis Constitutiones interpretetur in hac parte' (*ISI*, II, p. 182).

5 'Commissarios ad visitandas Provincias tertio vel quarto quoque anno, vel quando Praeposito Generali videbitur, et cum qua auctoritate ac iurisdictione videbitur, mittendos esse' (ibid., p. 196).

6 On du Prat and the foundation of the college, see Paul Schmitt, *La réforme catholique: Le combat de Maldonat* (Paris, 1985), pp. 191–7.

7 I discussed the Munich document in 'An Instance of Counter-Reformation Music Censorship,' a paper presented at the 1993 meeting of the American Musicological Society in Montreal.

8 See Anthony M. Cummings, 'Towards an Interpretation of the Sixteenth-Century Motet,' *Journal of the American Musicological Society* 34 (1981): 43–59; and T. Frank Kennedy, 'Jesuit Colleges and Chapels: Motet Function in the Late Sixteenth and Early Seventeenth Centuries,' *AHSI* 65 (1996): 197–213. Kennedy's n1 provides a concise overview of other recent studies of motet function.

9 The *Caeremoniale episcoporum* (Rome, 1600), book 2, chap. 3, p. 139, states, 'Si completoriu[m] continuetur, salutatis canonicis ab utraque parte chori, discedit cum praedictis paratis ordine, quo venerat; si verò non sequatur Completoriu[m], dicit Antiphonam beatae mariae genuflexus, pariter.' On the use of the Marian antiphons in the late sixteenth century, see John Harper, *The Forms and Orders of Western Liturgy* (Oxford, 1991), p. 132; Jerome Roche, 'Musica diversa di compietà: Compline and Its Music in Seventeenth-Century Italy,' *Proceedings of the Royal Musical Association* 109 (1982–3): 63; and John Bettley, '"L'ultima hora canonica del giorno": Music for the Office of Compline in Northern Italy in the Second Half of the Sixteenth Century,' *Music and Letters* 74 (1993): 166.

10 The *Missae variis concentibus ornatae* forms no anomaly in this respect: composi-

tions based on irreverent or salacious chansons appear in all of Lasso's early mass publications.

11 On the political situation, see Lynn A. Martin, *Henry III and the Jesuit Politicians* (Geneva, 1973), especially pp. 187–207.

12 For an early (and unreliable) French translation of Maggio's report, see Henri Fouqueray, *Histoire de la Compagnie de Jésus en France des origines à la suppression (1528–1762)*, 5 vols (Paris 1910–25), II, pp. 192–5. Fouqueray's translation is reproduced in Pierre Guillot, *Les jésuites et la musique: Le Collège de la Trinité à Lyon (1565–1762)* (Liège, 1991), pp. 67–9. Translations of Maggio's item no. 9, as well as brief statements from the reports of Matthieu (1578, fol. 51v) and Pigenat (1585, fol. 53), are included in François Lesure, 'France in the Sixteenth Century (1520–1610),' in *The Age of Humanism, 1540–1630*, New Oxford History of Music 4, ed. Gerald Abraham (London, 1968), pp. 250–1. Isabelle Cazeaux's brief discussion of ms lat. 10989 in *French Music in the Fifteenth and Sixteenth Centuries* (New York, 1975), p. 192, derives from Lesure.

13 See Antonio M. de Aldama, *The Formula of the Institute: Notes for a Commentary*, trans. Ignacio Echániz (St Louis, 1990), p. 18.

14 See O'M. *First*, p. 136.

15 See T. Frank Kennedy, 'Jesuits,' in *The New Grove Dictionary of Music and Musicians*, 2nd ed., ed. Stanley Sadie and John Tyrrell (London, 2001).

16 See Bernhard Duhr, *Geschichte der Jesuiten in den Ländern deutscher Zunge im XVI. Jahrhundert* (Freiburg im Breisgau, 1907), p. 443.

17 See Kennedy, 'Jesuits.'

21 / Between Stage and Divine Service: Jesuits and Theatrical Music

FRANZ KÖRNDLE

In reflecting on the attitude of the Society of Jesus to music and theatre, one seems continually to meet with contradictions. The problem manifests itself in the scepticism towards music in the early days of the order on the one hand, and the intensive cultivation of music in several of the colleges on the other. Often these contradictions give the impression of utter utilitarianism: music is cultivated where it appears to be profitable, and takes a back seat where the Society of Jesus has more important or at least broader concerns. In reality, there is much more than utilitarianism behind the discrepancies.

The notion of a common identity, expressed in theological, anthropological, and cultural convictions, goes back to the founder of the Society, Ignatius of Loyola himself. This common identity was guided by official rules; it was, however, permitted to impose patterns of thought, feeling, and method on existing situations in an almost spontaneous manner, depending on the time and place. Ignatius called this 'our way of proceeding.'[1]

The various applications of music to theatrical performances exemplify the 'Jesuit way of proceeding.' In accordance with humanistic ideals of education, drama with music and dance was cultivated in many colleges from about 1560,[2] primarily for educational purposes. But theatrical effects were also used in Counter-Reformation propaganda, with public performances involving up to 1,000 actors. We know that in 1568 and 1589 no less a person than Orlando di Lasso, a leading composer of polyphony during the second half of the sixteenth century, was commissioned to write choruses and music for such plays.[3] In spite of such obvious promotion, theatre music remained problematic, always a threat to liturgical music, and especially to music for the setting of the mass ordinary. All these dramatic texts need to be seen in the context of the tension between the educational use of theatre music, and the negative influence this music could have on church music, and consequently on the devotion of the faithful. Part 1 of this article considers theatre music and its function. Part 2 introduces a particular drama, which has music itself as its theme and leads in a surprising way to the subject of church music. Part 3 is concerned with the theological discussion of music for the theatre.

1. Music in the Theatre

Music was an integral part of many Jesuit dramas. Recently discovered material enables us to get a sense of the role it played in these dramas.[4] The *Litterae annuae* of most colleges regularly refer to performances of the more important plays. In Munich these annual letters, which are more or less complete for the years 1574–6, 1580, 1591, and 1593–4, frequently refer to performances of longer plays: *Josaphat and Barlaam, Constantinus Magnus, St Clement, Nebuchadnezzar*, and *Cassian Martyr*.[5] The lively interest taken by the ducal court in these performances is recorded with particular care. The college's connection with the court during these years justifies the assumption that the master of the ducal choir, Orlando di Lasso, was involved in the productions.

In 1577 the play *Hester. Comoedia sacra ex biblicis [sic] historijs desumpta* was performed in various places in the old city of Munich. In the document Munich, Bayerische Staatsbibliothek, Clm 524, fols 157ff., there is a complete index of the participants in the play,[6] and indication that trumpets, kettle drums, cornets, and trombones were used, as well as bagpipers, drummers, and pipers. According to Horst Leuchtmann, at least nine trumpeters and the six town musicians were involved. In addition, a carriage for the musicians[7] is mentioned, along with a prefect of singers, three boys, and musicians with instruments and books.[8] Unfortunately, we do not know whether Lasso's motet on the subject of the drama, *O decus celsi*, was sung, nor can we be sure whether 'praefectus' means the master of the ducal chapel or the Jesuit prefect of music.

In addition to the *Esther* of 1577, *Samson* by Andreas Fabricius, performed in 1568 as part of the celebration of the marriage of Wilhelm V and Renata of Lorraine, has been of interest to Lasso scholars. On 6 January of that year, Fabricius wrote a letter to Chancellor Simon Eck in which he asked that the texts of the choruses be passed on to Orlando di Lasso so that he could set them to music.[9]

Lasso scholars have grappled with almost insoluble problems in connection with these remarks on *Esther* and *Samson*. If Lasso did indeed compose choruses for Fabricius's *Samson*, then we have to regard them as lost, for not a single chorus from *Samson* is to be found among Lasso's known motets.[10] Conversely, the fact that *O decus celsi*, which Lasso did compose, is missing from the *Esther* of 1577 leads us to ask whether such motets were indeed an integral part of Jesuit plays, or whether, perhaps, they were simply included as interludes. If that was their role, it will be impossible to establish their exact place within the drama because the directives themselves are much too vague. As a rule we find instructions such as 'fit cantus' or 'fit musica.'[11] Very occasionally the manuscripts contain more specific references about the type of pieces set to music, such as a 'double chorus' or 'echo.'[12] Other instructions may appear: 'The angels sing. Here a song of the Blessed Virgin can be inserted,'[13] or 'Something appropriate to the feast day may be sung, e.g., a Nunc Dimittis or something else.'[14] Or, some final examples: 'Something artistic is sung here, a piece with echoes or two choirs alternating with an Ave Maria,'[15] and 'All sing a hymn in praise of the Blessed Virgin.'[16]

These are rare exceptions. Real strokes of luck are the stage directions contained in some manuscripts, which occasionally mention the additional music. Jacob Gretser's play *Lazarus resuscitatus*, written in 1584 and performed in Fribourg, contains a number of such stage directions in the margins.[17] At the end of Act IV, a motet by Orlando di Lasso is required: 'Here the motet *Fremuit Spiritus* by Orlando should be sung, the one that is to be found in the Thesaurus for six voices, or something by Palestrina, who composed motets on the same subject.'[18] This *cantio* is the Lasso motet *Fremuit Spiritus Jesus*, which was first published in the so-called Antwerp Motet Book[19] in 1556 and again in another work, *Thesaurus musicus tomus tertius*, published by Montanus and Neuber in Nuremberg[20] in 1564. Lamentably, the motet by Palestrina is not mentioned here by name.

Another codex from the Dillingen Studienbibliothek, Cod. XV, 225, contains the first version of Gretser's *Udo of Magdeburg*, performed at Ingolstadt in 1587.[21] At a certain point in the play the profligate bishop and his companions visit a tavern, where they abandon themselves to wine and music. After all, a bishop, as Udo himself remarks, is a man, not an angel. Then the musicians are called upon to play: 'Come, you players, harpists and musicians, play and sing! Today shall be a holy day of joy, as well tomorrow and the day after. And may all the Fates be willing to shine upon us.'[22] According to the marginal notes, several songs were to be sung: 'Here should be sung Orlando's *Omnis enim homo* or *Fertur in conviviis*, or *A solis orto sidere*, or *Si bene perpendi*, etc., or some other jolly song. In the meantime the bishop and his retinue call out, "Io, io, this is a joyful day, etc."'[23]

The scene contains more notes on the music. When Phormio, the sponger, proposes a toast to the bishop, his companion Gnatho begins to sing the German lines 'Aus – so wirdt ein fröhlicher man drauß' ('Out – so will a happy man go!'),[24] a slightly modified quotation from the song *Ist keiner hie*, which appeared in 1570 with music by Christian Hollander[25] and Ivo de Vento.[26] It ends, 'Trincks gar aus suffs gar auß so wird ein voller bruder drauß' ('Bottoms up! That should do, and so will a brother do!'). Udo's answer, 'Vinum quae pars, verstehst du das, etc.' ('Do you understand that wine is what it's all about!'), with the stage direction 'He sings one or other of the verses,'[27] refers to a song by Ivo de Vento published in 1571.[28] The scene ends with a refrain, 'Dummel dich guottes weinle' ('Get yourself a good wine!'), from the song *Frisch auff gut Gsell, laß rummer gahn*, composed by Jacob Meiland.[29]

While Udo of Magdeburg is beheaded for his sins before the throne of Christ and carried off by the devil – a rather uncompromising scene[30] – the Prodigal Son from the biblical parable is spared a similar fate, and instead taken again into his father's favour. However, in the Fulda *Acolastus* ('Libertine' or 'Spendthrift'), there is a similar passage that shows the Prodigal Son carousing with his companions and the two girls Lais and Flora. The stage directions here require the motet *Ave color vini clari*.[31]

The use of these drinking songs, which at first sight seems appropriate, appears in a new light when we realize that three of them were placed on an index of forbidden works in the 1590s by the rector of the Munich Jesuits, Ferdinand Alber, as David Crook has pointed out.[32] This index gives precise instructions for implementing the rules set out by the general of the Society, Everard Mercurian, in 1575. Bad music was to be burned[33] – 'Songs that have been prohibited because of their texts or music.'[34] The three songs *Jam lucis orto*, *Ave color vini*, and *Fertur in conviviis* were prohibited because of their texts or music ('Cantiones quo ad textum et notas prohibitae'), that is, they were considered by the censors vile enough to warrant that those who sang them would roast in hell. But as we can conclude from their use in the play, the exhortation to obey the censors and burn the songs was not followed.

While pieces of music are fitted in at suitable moments in the plays, the choruses peculiar to the plays are of a completely new type. They are mostly placed at the end of an act or scene, and they follow a traditional verse-form, the anapaestic metre, for example, or the sapphic strophe. Clearly the intention was to re-create classical Greek drama, with texts set for a chorus within the play as part of the play itself, and probably written by the author.

Little is known about the music of these choruses. The assumption that the pieces were more or less similar to the humanistic odes we are familiar with seemed a promising lead.[35] Indeed, occasionally the texts provide musical notation that permits us to describe the compositions more precisely. The choruses of the *Acolastus* manuscript are very similar to humanistic odes. A play from Regensburg, *Herodus defunctus*, dated 1598 and now preserved in Vienna, contains choruses of this kind[36] (fig. 21.1). But the choruses in several Dillingen manuscripts are quite different.[37] Codex XV 223 contains three choruses from

Example1: Herodes defunctus (Regensburg 1598)
Vienna, Österreichische Nationalbibliothek, Cod. Vind. 13231, fol. 50v-51r

21.1. Chorus 'Quanta mundi dignitas' from *Herodus defunctus*, Regensburg, 1598.
Vienna, Österreichische Nationalbibliothek, Cod. Vind. 13231 fols 50v–51r.

Timon, performed in Fribourg in 1584, of which 'Plute tu solus'[38] (fig. 21.2) and
'Cordaqui curis'[39] (fig. 21.3) can be regarded as typical. The key signatures in
the latter indicate that some of these choruses were intended for treble voices.
Even settings for four soprano voices have been found (fig. 21.4).

The substitution of other texts in the choral verses (*contrafactum*) is governed
by the metre. In the aforementioned choruses, the new material is sapphic/
anapaestic; hexameter verses, for example, could not possibly be substituted. So
if the choruses in the neo-Latin plays are mostly sapphic or hymnlike in verse
construction while the spoken texts contain a variety of metres, that is because
the use of the same music in several choruses has necessitated the use of
metrically similar texts. We shall never be able to find out how many similar
settings actually existed; those extant could well have been used in many
different plays. But the number of simple sapphic/anapaestic settings should not

Example 2: Timon (Fribourg 1584)
Dillingen, Studienbibliothek, Cod. XV 223, fol. 73v-74r

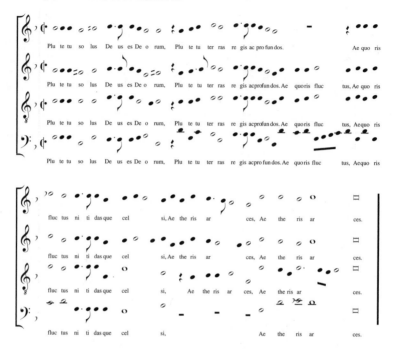

21.2. Chorus 'Plute tu solus' from *Timon*, Fribourg, 1584. Dillingen,
Studienbibliothek, Cod. XV 223 fols 73v–74r.

lead us to conclude that the choruses always used a simple verse-form; some relevant poetic texts are quite complex, and changes of metre as well as musical imitation of the text metre are found.

Compositions with neo-Latin texts are especially numerous in the *Magnum opus musicum*, the complete edition of Orlando di Lasso's motets, which appeared in 1604.[40] In his new edition of 1908, Franz Xaver Haberl called them 'secular occasional compositions.'[41] Since the appearance of Haberl's edition, two scholars, Wolfgang Boetticher and Philip Weller, have suggested that these choruses could form part of dramatic presentations,[42] but no proof for their suggestions has been found to date. The chief evidence – the plays for which Lasso is supposed to have composed these motets – has not been uncovered. Some years ago, however, I succeeded in tracing a play containing six such motets by Lasso and in discovering its author and the site of its performance.[43] The play is *Christus Iudex* by the Italian Jesuit Stefano Tucci (1540–97). It was

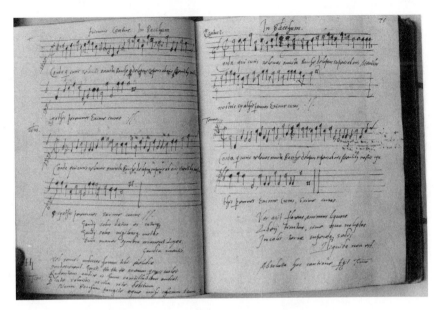

21.3. Chorus 'Cordaqui curis' from *Timon*, fols 74v–75r.

performed in Messina in 1569 and in Rome in 1574.[44] The first performance in Austria, which may be relevant to Lasso's compositions, was on 14 May 1589 at the Jesuit theatre in Graz.[45] The choruses are inserted as in table 21.1.

The *Litterae annuae* of the Jesuit college in Graz reported on the performance. The letters have now been lost, but they were still available in 1719, when a chronicle of the University of Graz quoted from them (see appendix, document 1). The performance on 14 May 1589, according to this text, must have made a very strong impression on the audience. They saw the sun and the moon growing dark and the stars falling from heaven. Graves opened to the sound of trumpets, the dead arose, and the Judge appeared on a cloud of glory. There followed the triumph of the Blessed and their ascent to heaven. They heard the howls of the Damned when the ground opened, spitting flames, and swallowed them. Finally, the very earth collapsed in flames. All this was shown in such lively fashion and so successfully that both wonder and terror gripped the audience, who did not know whether to praise more highly the talents of the young actors or the art of the engineers and pyrotechnicians.[46] When the sister of Archduchess Maria, Maximiliana of Bavaria, visited Graz two months later, Archduke Karl had the play performed again at his own expense.[47]

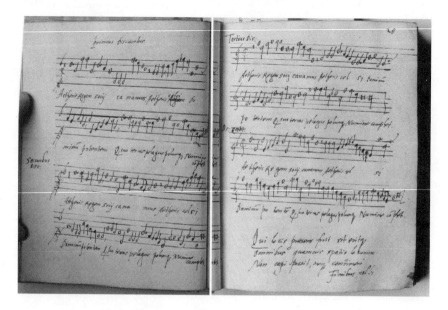

21.4. Chorus 'Aetheris Regem,' for four soprano voices. Dillingen, Studienbibliothek, Cod. XV 245 fols 20v–21r.

Even if Tucci's play was never actually performed in Munich, *Christus Iudex* was certainly known there. Near the end of the manuscript Munich, Bayerische Staatsbibliothek, Clm 19757$_2$ is the well-known *Triumphus divi Michaelis Archangeli Bavarici*, first performed at the dedication of St Michael's church in Munich in 1597. The music is thought to be by Georg Viktorin,[48] though since it has disappeared we cannot be certain as to its composer. It is possible that at the end of the play a chorus by Lasso was performed, namely, 'Tibi progenies,' which was the final chorus in the Last Judgment scene in *Christus Iudex*.[49]

This discovery demonstrates the context in which Lasso composed at least six of his motets. It also gives us an insight into early Jesuit theatre and music as often bearing a formal resemblance to ancient Greek drama, in that it included choruses as integral parts of the action, not only as interludes between scenes or acts.

2. Music as the Subject of a Play

In 1583 the Jesuit college in Fulda staged an extremely comical new play, *Dialogus musicae*,[50] full of pointed references, in which six cuckoos and six

Table 21.1
Choruses in *Christus Iudex*

Type of chorus (persons)	Text	Stage direction
Chorus Prophetarum (Choir of the Prophets)	'Flemus extremos hominum labores'	
Sybillarum Chorus (Choir of the Sybils)	'Heu quis armorum furor in tyranno est?'	
Elias, Enoch, Joannes	'Ad te perenne gaudium'	Hymnus ascendentium in coelum (Hymn of those ascending into heaven)
Chorus Angelorum (Choir of the Angels)	'Tragico tecti'	
Chorus Nocent[ium] (Choir of the Damned)	'Heu quos dabimus miseranda cohors'	
Chorus	'Tibi progenies'	Ascendunt beati cum choro canentes primam stropham / Ascendunt beati canentes reliquas strophas. (The Blessed rise up with a choir and sing the first verse / The Blessed rise up and sing the other verses)

nightingales argue the pros and cons of music, including, of course, the question of whether cuckoo music or nightingale music is better. In the end the cuckoos and nightingales can agree only that a judge must be found to settle the quarrel. The dialogue is as follows (see appendix, document 2):

3rd Nightingale:	But who shall we call on to be judge? The dog?
1st Cuckoo:	No, for he barks. [the alto]
4th Nightingale:	The horse?
2nd Cuckoo:	No, for he whinnies. [the descant]
5th Nightingale:	The ox?
3rd Cuckoo:	On no account, for he moos. [the tenor]
6th Nightingale:	The boar?
4th Cuckoo:	Under no circumstances whatsoever, for he grunts. [the bass]
6th Nightingale:	The donkey?
1st Cuckoo:	The donkey, the donkey, yes, I want the donkey as judge.

Amusing as this text sounds, it has a serious background. The dialogue imitates a passage from a treatise by Cornelius Agrippa of Nettesheim, *De vanitate scientiarum*, printed in 1531 (see appendix, document 3). In the chapter entitled 'De musica,' Agrippa makes an extremely critical contribution in his assessment of church music:

Now a daies the vnlo[o]ful libertie of Musicke, is so muche vsed in Churches, that together with the Canon of the Mass, very filthie songes haue like tunes in the Organs, and the Diuine Seruice is songe by lasciuious Musitians hired for a greate stipende, not for the vnderstandinge of the hearers, but for the stirringe vp of the minde: But for dishoneste lasciuiousnesse, not with manly voices, but with beastely skeekinge, while the children braie the Discante, somme bellowe the Tenoure, somme barke the Conterpointe, some howle the Treble, some grunte the Base, and cause many soundes to be hearde, and no woordes and sentences to be vnderstoode, but in thes sorte the authoritie of iudgement is taken both from the eares, and minde.[51]

But we must ask, what on earth was Agrippa's criticism of the state of church music doing in a piece of comic dialogue? If we look at the dialogue more closely, we see that all the references to Agrippa come from the cuckoos; they are the ones who speak Agrippa's words and appear to concur with his criticism. Finally, the donkey appears and pronounces judgment in favour of the cuckoos, principally because the song of the cuckoos is nearest to the sounds the donkey himself produces. The attentive observer has of course already noted that the cuckoos' song is monophonic, whereas the nightingales sing in parts. The donkey confirms this difference when he admires the cuckoos' singing of chant. So it is clear that the cuckoos represent liturgical unison singing, but the nightingales, figural music. We recall, too, the proposals of the Council of Trent aimed at controlling polyphony in the church and preserving pride of place for Gregorian chant.[52] This seems to be the meaning of the dialogue of the cuckoos and nightingales as well. But there is a surprise in store: the nightingales appeal to an impartial *iudex Spirensis*, who, after a brief examination of the donkey, revokes his judgment and orders Longears back to his shed. From a musicological perspective, the reference clearly touches upon contemporary church debates concerning musical style. The Council of Trent had called for strict control over polyphonic music, but the fact is that very few composers stopped writing polyphony. The question here may point towards the problematic reception of the Trent directive. The *iudex Spirensis* is the judge of the *Reichskammergericht*, the imperial 'supreme court.' So though the directive of Trent favours the cuckoos and the plainchant tradition, the directive of the state from the judge of the supreme court of the land favours the nightingales, or figural singing.

With the rehabilitation of the nightingales the place of polyphony is secured without detracting from the cuckoos' chant (see appendix, document 4). And yet the comic effect of the dialogue, which in the end goes against the donkey, cannot hide the fact that we really have found ourselves amused by the cuckoos' simple chanting. Indeed, the dialogue expresses strong sympathy for polyphonic music. Here, the question once again involves demonstrating the use that can be made of polyphonic music, and how it can be employed to support an ideology. So it may not be surprising that in the period following the Council of Trent the Jesuits continued to use polyphonic music, especially of a homophonic, falsobordone style, in their services and dramas, and propagated this in their writings.

3. Theatrical Music in Jesuit Treatises

A pronounced change occurred around the year 1600 in the development of plays with music. Up to this point only the choruses had been provided with music. From now on, however, it was not unusual to find some spoken parts set as solo recitative and aria. This change coincides with the development of opera as a musical genre. The fact that the intelligibility of the text could be challenged by the musical setting was a concern in the educational or rhetorical plan of the Jesuits in their plays, and of course was a concern of the early writers of opera as well. But by the 1630s opera had become available to the public, in that musicians and composers sold tickets to performances in theatres, rather than being the closed preserve of wealthy courts or of the students, faculty, and associates in the academies; and naturally enough, the general public was rather more in favour of the opera than of traditional Jesuit drama. At the same time the operatic solo style invaded church music, and not only in Italy. Criticism was voiced above all in the writings of Jesuit authors in the neo-Thomist tradition. According to the teachings of Thomas Aquinas, the human voice is the most important instrument of knowledge.[53] For this reason many of the tracts by authors belonging to the order are to be understood as commentaries on the *Summa theologiae* of Aquinas, and particularly the 'Secunda secundae.' The new conflict was naturally fought partly on the basis of older literature on the subject. Often quoted are Tommaso De Vio, Cardinal Cajetan, and Bartolomeo Fumo, both Italian Dominicans writing in the first half of the sixteenth century. The neo-Thomist tradition gave rise to numerous treatises on the five senses: how they are influenced, and where the dangers to touch, taste, smell, sight, and hearing lie. The last two senses are the most important for our subject, in which the context is theatre and music. Note how the texts gradually adapt to contemporary practice in their sections on music. Table 21.2 lists some tracts that at least in part comment on the *Summa theologiae* of Aquinas.

In his *Rhetorica caelestis*, published in 1638, the Munich Jesuit Jeremias

Table 21.2
Sixteenth- and early seventeenth-century commentaries on Thomas Aquinas's *Summa theologiae*

Author	Treatise	Printed
Fumo, Bartolomeo, O.P. (d.1545)	*Summa aurea armilla nuncupata*	1550
De Vio, Tommaso, Cardinal Cajetan, O.P. (1469–1534)	*Commentarius*	1554
Bellarmino, Roberto, S.J. (1542–1621)	*Disputationes*	1586
Henriquez, Henrique, S.J. (1536–1608)	*Theologia moralis*	1588
Valencia, Gregor de, S.J. (1549–1603)	*Commentarii theologici*	1591
Suárez, Francisco, S.J. (1548–1619)	*De religione*	1609
Sanchez, Tomás, S.J. (1550–1610)	*Opus morale*	1613
Cressolles, Louis, S.J. (1568–1634)	*Mystagogus*	1629
	Anthologia sacra	1632
Drexel, Jeremias, S.J. (1581–1639)	*Rhetorica caelestis*	1638
Persico, Pietro A., S.J. (1564–1644)	*De sacerdotis officio*	1639

Drexel in no uncertain terms criticized 'operas,' that is, comedies with an entirely sung text, popular in Italy at that time (see appendix, document 5).[54] In doing so Drexel was one of a whole line of Christian – and latterly, mainly Jesuit – authors who would have liked to see everything that could be considered 'theatrical' banned from music. It was not that the Jesuits were against music in the theatre; they were against the influence of theatrical music in the liturgy. There it detracted from and troubled the devotion of the faithful. The treatise *De primo ac praecipuo sacerdotis officio libri tres* by Pietro A. Persico, S.J., published in Naples in 1639, quotes numerous ancient texts on the subject, by Jerome, Augustine, and Thomas Aquinas; the bull *Docta sanctorum patrum* of Pope John XXII; and the fourteenth-century writing of Petrus de Palude. From the sixteenth and early seventeenth centuries Persico quotes Cardinal Cajetan, Martín de Azpilcueta, Gregor of Valencia, and Francisco Suárez.[55] Persico's text (see appendix, document 6) is about the disapproval of polyphonic music and the prohibition against its use in the liturgy, especially by Pope John XXII in 1324/5. But Persico then goes on to explain why polyphonic music was cultivated in the liturgy even after the resolutions passed by the Council of Trent.[56]

Jesuit literature not least of all pleaded for a liberal attitude to church music. At the same time it also seemed important to the Jesuits to find a way to justify music and theatre in general. A few years before Persico, the Paris Jesuit Louis Cresolles had formulated in his *Mystagogus* what was probably the most elegant legitimation of music and theatre. Theatre was often vulgar, and therefore for the rabble; spectacular theatricals and music were to be condemned. Cressolles is not writing of those pieces, however, but of noble works, of true actors rather than of vagabonds, of serious, experienced persons of sound judgment who would stage the fine and sober dramas that would entertain and at the same time nourish the human spirit.[57] In writing thus, Cressolles gives expression to the 'Jesuit way of proceeding' as it applies to music and theatre.

APPENDIX

Document 1: *Lustrum primum almae ac celeberrimae Universitatis Graecensis, Societatis Jesu* (Graz, 1719), pp. 38–9

... alterum de Christo judice venturo spectaculum die decima quarta Maji repraesentatum est. Expallescente sole, ac luna, siderum de coelo praecipitantium, ipsóque in lapsu extinctorum ruina; sepulchrorum, insonante buccina, dehiscentium, & dissilientium fragor, diversus è mortuali cinere surgentium, judicem praestolantium affectus, advenientis in nube fulgurante redemproris, sententiámque ex iride pronunciantis majestas; triumphalis beatorum ad fulgentissimas empyrij sedes è terris progredientium ascensus, avernalis barathri flammas eructantis, impijsque absorbentis vorago, ultimúmque mundi conflagrantis incendium, adeò felici successu exhibita, ut spectantium oculis, animisque mixtum voluptate horrorem altè impresserint, relicto problemate, majorémne sibi laudem Poëta, tragoediaeque actrix juventus academica, an machinarum, igniúmque missilium artifex vendicârit. Interim Serenissimo Fundatoriusque adeo placuit, ut repetitis liberaliter impensis theatrum restaurari jusserit, dum mense Julio Fundatricem Serenissimam Maximiliana soror, dux Boica inviseret. Inter hosce Palladis mansuetioris labores, suum quoque theatrum, severior aperuit. Etenim die nona Martij geminos ex Archiducali Convictorum collegio alumnos, Georgium Frisan, Carniolum, & Bartholomaeum Balen, Prutenum philosophico pallio donavit ...

Document 2: *Dialogus musicae*, Fulda, Hessische Landesbibliothek, 4° C 13 fol. 152v (performed Fulda, 1583)

Philomela 3.	Quem autem vis iudicem appellemus ? Canem ?
Cucullus 1.	Non, quia latrat altum.
Philomela 4.	Equum ?
Cucullus 2.	Non, quia discantum hinnit.
Philomela 5.	Bovem?
Cucullus 3.	Minime gentium, quia tenorem mugit.
Philomela 6.	Aprum?
Cucullus 4.	Nihil minus, quia frendet baßum.
Philomena 6.	Asinum?
Cucullus 1.	Asinum, asinum, sic, asinum volo iudicem.

Document 3: Heinrich Cornelius Agrippa of Nettesheim, *De incertitudine et vanitate scientiarum* (Cologne, 1531), chap. 17, 'De musica'

Hodie vero tanta in ecclesijs musicae licentia est, vt etiam vna cum missae ipsius canone obscoenae quaeque cantiunculae interim in organis pares vices habeant, ipsaque diuina officia & sacrae orationum preces, conductis magno aere lasciuius musicis, non ad audientium intelligentiam, non ad spiritus eleuationem: sed ad fornicariam pruriginem, non humanis vocibus, sed bel[l]uinis strepitibus cantillant, dum hinniunt discantum pueri, mugiunt alij tenorem, alij latrant contrapunctum, alij boant altum, alij frendent bassum, faciuntque vt sonorum plurimum quidem audiatur, vt verborum & orationis intelligatur nihil, sed auribus pariter & animo iudicij subtrahit autoritas.

Document 4: *Dialogus musicae*, fol. 150v

> *Philomela 1a.*   Me una cum socijs cantibus & symphonijs afficere, et his
>   adminiculis animos recreare.
> *Cucullus 1us.*   Cantum laudo, musicam aut symphoniam minime probo.
> *Omnes Cuculli.* Simul. Non symphoniam tanti non facimus.
> *Cucullus 1us.*   Nam & ego fallendi temporis causa cum meis cantibus
>   indulgebo, sed symphoniam quidem non conabor attingere.

Document 5: Jeremias Drexel, *Rhetorica caelestis* (Munich, 1638), book 1, chap. 5

Crebrae sunt in Italiâ comoediae, quae voce tantùm modulatâ, solòque cantu peraguntur: ijs simillimus est hic musteus cantandi modus, qui specie rerioris artificij, sacris aedibus infert comoedias. Adòne noua omnia tam pulchra sunt & honesta, vt eâ jure omnibus & vbique debeant placere? Fuerunt aeuo superiore praestantissimi Musici, sed reuerâ, vel vobis testibus ij aliter (& liceat dicere) religiosiùs cecinerunt: sed eorum libros Musicos vestrum jam fastidium pridem sepeliuit. Reuiuiscat, obsecro, saltem aliquid priscae religiositatis in sacrâ Musicâ. Quòd si cordi est & curae diuinus honor, hoc agite viri, hoc laborate, vt quae cantantur, verbo simul etiam intelligantur. Quid mihi varius in templo sonus, quid multiplex concentus, si desit ei nucleus, si sensum & verba, quae concentu sunt instillanda, percipere nequeam? Aliud est choreis, aliud Christianis sacris accinere; illis satis est symphonia, in his etiam symphoniae sensus desideratur. Nimirum talibus flabellis excitanda est pietas, vt quod canitur, etiam cogitetur.

Document 6: Pietro A. Persico, *De primo ac praecipuo sacerdotis officio libri tres* (Naples, 1639), book 3, *dubium* 5

Circa primam igitur difficultatem, sunt duae sententiae. Prima docet cantum organicum, seu figuratum esse omnino illicitum, ac proinde prohibitum in diuinis officijs; praesertim in celebratione Missae; ratio est; quia S. Hieroymus lib. 3. comment. in cap. 5. Epistolae ad Ephesios, monet cantores Ecclesia, ne in *tragoedorum modum*

guttur, & fauces, dulci medicamine, liniant, vt in Ecclesia theatrales moduli, audiantur,
& cantica, refertur c. cantantes 92. d. vbi Glossa, verbo, liniendae, ait, *vt populum*
delectent; & Ioannes XXII. in extrauaganti vnica de vita, & honestate clericorum, solum
permittit, *vt in diebus festis, praecipue, siue solemnibus, in Missis aliquae consonantiae,*
quae melodiam sapiunt; puta actauae, quintae, & huiusmodi, supra cantum Ecclesiasti-
cum simplicem proferantur: sic tamen, vt in ipsius cantus integritas illibata permaneant;
& districte praecipit, *vt nullus deinceps alios cantus praesertim, tum motetis vulgaribus,*
cum Missarum solemnia celebrantur; attentare praesumant. Ratio praedictae
prohibitionis est; quia in officio diuino, & Missae celebratione cantus permissus fuit; vt
augeretur attentio, & deuotio fidelium, vt expresse docet Ioannes XXII. in praedicta
extrauaganti. Vbi ait; *In ecclesijs Dei psalmodia cantanda praecipitur, vt fidelium*
deuotio excitetur; & S. Tho. 22. q. 92.a.2. corp. ait; *salubriter fuit institutum, vt in*
divinas laudes cantus assumeretur, vt animi infirmorum, magis prouocarentur ad
deuotionem, sed cantus organicus , seu figuratus; est causa, vt nec audiantur, nec bene
intelligantur verba, quae canuntur; ac proinde non solum non excitant; sed potius
adimunt attentionem, & deuotionem debitam; ergo operatur contrarium eo, ob quod
permissus est, & per consequens frequenter est abusus; & ideo grauis culpa. Hanc
sententiam expresse docet Nauarrus, in tract. de oratione cap. 16. n. 32. dicto 19. vbi ait
peccare communiter cantores, qui in Missa canunt cantum organicum, & intelligit de
peccato mortali, vt patet ex ipsius rationibus, & nu. 33. probat esse prohibitum in
praedicta extrauaganti Ioannis 22. confirmat hoc ex S. Augustino lib. 10 confessionum
cap. 33. vbi accusans se de aurium voluptatibus subiungit; *eum mihi accidit, vt me*
amplius cantus, quam res, quae canitur moueat; poenaliter me peccare confiteor; &
tunc mallem non audire cantantem; eandem sententiam docuit idem Nauarrus in
Manuali cap. 12 num. 87. §. quarto; huic sententiae fauet Caietanus in summa v.
Organorum vsus; vbi ait: *quod Ecclesia prohibuit prophanos cantus, vt theatrales.*
Paludan. 4.d.15.q.5.a.2. concl. I. motetos damnat ...

Haec est communis sententia; quam docet S. Tho. 22.q.91.a.2. corp. Caietanus ibi in
principio, & in summa v. Organorum vsus; vbi ait *ecclesiam prohibuisse cantus*
profanos, vt theatrales; quare admittit honestos, & moderatos, idem docet Armilla v.
cantus nu. 4. Nauarrus tract. de oratione cap. 16.nu. 35 *ait praedictam extrauagantem*
non comprehendere, cantum oranicum illorum, qui ita modeste, & deuote canunt, vt nec
auditum, & intellectum verborum, quae cantantur impediant, & in sequentibus
corollarijs semper abusus reprehendit; P. Henriqu. lib.9. de Missa cap. 31.n.8. P. Suarius
to. 2. de Religione lib.4. de horis canonicis cap. 8. nu.2. P Gregorius de Valentia to. 3.
disp. 6. qu. 9. puncto vnico: hanc sententiam sequuntur ...

Hanc sententiam non solum confirmat vniuersalis vsus omnium Ecclesiarum, non
solum saecularium clericorum; sed, etiam multorum Religiosorum, Monialium; sed
etiam concilium Tridentinum sess. 22. in Decreto de obseruandis, & euitandis in
celebratione Missae; vbi solum prohibet abusus; dicens, *Ab Ecclesij vero musicus eas*

vbi, siue organo, siue cantu, lasciuum, aut impurum aliquid miscetur; arceant. ergo Concilium probat, & confirmat reliquas musicas, in quibus nihil impurum aut lasciuum miscetur; & in hoc sensu intelligenda sunt iura citata pro prima sententia ...

NOTES

This article was translated by Marian Lampe.

1 John W. O'Malley, 'Die frühe Gesellschaft Jesu,' in *Rom in Bayern. Kunst und Spiritualität der ersten Jesuiten,* ed. Reinhold Baumstark (Munich, 1997), pp. 31–40, on 35.

2 O'Malley, 'Die frühe Gesellschaft Jesu,' p. 34. The foundational studies of the music and theatre of the Jesuits are Max Wittwer, *Die Musikpflege im Jesuitenorden unter besunderer Berücksichtigung des Länder deutscher Zunge* (Greifswald, 1934); Thomas D. Culley, *Jesuits and Music,* vol. 1, *A Study of the Musicians Connected with the German College in Rome during the 17th Century and of Their Activities in Northern Europe* (Rome, 1970); and T. Frank Kennedy, 'Jesuits and Music: The European Tradition, 1547–1622,' dissertation, University of California–Santa Barbara, 1982.

3 Franz Körndle, '"Ad te perenne gaudium." Lassos Musik zum "Vltimum Judicium,"' *Die Musikforschung* 53 (2000): 68–70.

4 Körndle, 'Ad te perenne gaudium.'

5 Munich, Archiv der oberdeutschen Jesuitenprovinz, XIII. Hc.

6 'Verzaichnis des ganntzen Aufzugs der vorsteenden comoedie.'

7 'Currus cum musica.'

8 'Cantorum praefectus cum tribus pueris clausa instrumenta et libros portantes musicos'; see Horst Leuchtmann, *Orlando di Lasso,* vol. 1, *Sein Leben* (Wiesbaden, 1976), pp. 193–4.

9 Philip Weller, 'Lasso, Man of the Theatre,' in *Orlandus Lassus and His Time: Colloquium Proceedings, Antwerp 24–26.08.1994,* ed. Ignace Bossuyt, Eugeen Schreurs, and Annelies Wouters (Peer, 1995), pp. 89–127.

10 See Munich, University Library, P. lat. rec. 171. This copy was formerly part of 'Bibl. Acad. Ingolstad.' On p. 1 there is a handwritten indication: 'Clarißimo ac Magnifico uiro Simonj Eckio, Ill^{mi} Bauariae Ducis Alberti Cancellario, Dno suo obseruandis°, autor DD,' which means that the book was a present from Fabricius to Eck.

11 Munich, Bayerische Staatsbibliothek, Clm 611 (*Hercules in bivio*), fols 58v, 59r.

12 Munich, Bayerische Staatsbibliothek, Clm 19757$_2$ (drama without title), pp. 318, 329, 344, 358 (*Dialogus: De cultu B. Virginis*).

13 'Canunt Angeli. Potest ex quunque cantio de B. Virg.'

14 'Canitur aliquid de festo; Nunc dimittis uel aliud.'

15 'Canitur aliquid artificiosum, Echo, uel duo chori alternatim. Aue Maria.'

16 'Omnes canunt hymnum B. Virginis.'

17 Dillingen, Studienbibliothek, Cod. XV 223 fols 29v, 52r, 58v.

18 'Hic cantetur cantio Orlandi Fremuit spiritus Jesus quae est in Thesauro 6 uocum vel Praenestini qui de eadem materia cantiones composuit.'

19 Orlando di Lasso, *Sämtliche Werke: Supplement, Seine Werke in zeitgenössischen Drucken, 1555–1687*, ed. Horst Leuchtmann and Bernhold Schmid, 3 vols (Kassel, 2001), I, pp. 49–50.

20 Lasso, *Sämtliche Werke: Supplement*, vol. 1, pp. 126–8.

21 Anton Dürrwaechter, *Jakob Gretser und seine Dramen* (Freiburg im Breisgau, 1912), p. 135.

22 'Vos Ludiones, citharoedi atque Musicj / Ludite, canite, hodiernus laetitiae dies / Sacer erit, etiam crastinus et perendinus / Et quotquot nobis fata illucescere uolent.'

23 'Canatur Ex Orlando: Omnis enim homo. Aut: Fertur in conuiuijs. Aut: A solis orto sidere. Aut: Si bene perpendi aut alia laeta cantio. Episcopus interim cum suis exclamat io io, dies est laetitiae' (fol. 169r). See *Lateinische Ordensdramen des XVI. Jahrhunderts, mit deutschen Übersetzungen,* ed. Fidel Rädle (Berlin and New York, 1979), pp. 398–403.

24 *Lateinische Ordensdramen*, ed. Rädle, p. 400, l. 268.

25 Christian Hollander, *Newe teutsche, geistliche und weltliche Liedlein, 4–8vv* (Munich, 1570); 2nd ed. Munich, 1574, as *Neue ausserlesene teutsche Lieder.*

26 Ivo de Vento, *Neue teutsche Lieder, 4–6vv* (Munich, 1569, 1571).

27 'Cantat unum aut alterum versiculum.' See *Lateinische Ordensdramen*, ed. Rädle, p. 400, l. 269.

28 Ivo de Vento, *Neue teutsche Lieder, 4 vv, samt zweien Dialogen* (Munich, 1571). I owe a particular debt to Nicole Schwindt for drawing my attention to the songs of de Vento and Hollander.

29 Jacob Meiland, *Neuwe außerlesene Teusche Gesäng, 4–5vv* (Frankfurt, 1575). See *Lateinische Ordensdramen*, ed. Rädle, p. 402.

30 *Lateinische Ordensdramen*, ed. Rädle, p. 573.

31 Fulda, Hessische Landesbibliothek, C 18 fol. 18r–v. See Fidel Rädle, 'Über mittelalterliche lyrische Formen im neulateinische Drama,' in *Litterae Medii Aevi, Festschrift für Johanne Autenrieth zu ihrem 65. Geburtstag*, ed. Michael Borgolte and Herrad Spilling (Sigmaringen, 1988), pp. 339–62, on 348–50; Rädle, 'Acolastus – Der Verlorene Sohn: Zwei lateinische Bibeldraman des 16. Jahrhunderts,' in *Gattungsinnovation und Motivstruktur: Bericht über Kolloquien der Kommission für literaturwissenschaftliche Motiv- und Themenforschung, 1986–1989*, part 2, ed. Theodor Wolpers (Göttingen, 1992), pp. 15–34, on 29; and Rädle, 'Musik und Musiker auf der Bühne des frühen Jesuitentheaters,' in *Musikalische Quellen –*

Quellen zur Musikgeschichte. Festschrift für Martin Staehelin zum 65. Geburtstag, ed. Ulrich Konrad, Jürgen Heidrich, and Hans Joachim Marx (Göttingen, 2002), pp. 187–202.

32 David Crook, 'An Instance of Counter-Reformation Music Censorship,' paper read at the conference of the American Musicological Society in Montreal, 1993. I thank David Crook for allowing me to use his material prior to its publication.

33 Munich, Bayerische Staatsbibliothek, Clm 9201 fol. 8r, and Clm 9237 pp. 31–2. See Wittwer, *Die Musikpflege im Jesuitenorden*, pp. 13–15.

34 'Quae turpem habent dictionem et sonum, sive eum cantandi modum, cui etiam subesse obscaena, aut vana putentur, comburantur.'

35 See Weller, 'Lasso, Man of the Theatre,' pp. 108–10.

36 Vienna, Österreichische Nationalbibliothek, Cod. Vind. 13231 fols 50v–51r.

37 Cod. XV 221 fols 97v–98r; Cod. XV 223 fols 27v–28r and 73v–75r; and Cod. XV 245, fols 183v–186r.

38 Fols 73v–74r. See Wittwer, *Die Musikpflege im Jesuitenorden*, appendix 2.

39 Fols 74v–75r.

40 See Lasso, *Sämtliche Werke: Supplement*, vol. 2, pp. 287–306.

41 See Orlando di Lasso, *Sämmtliche Werke*, ed. Franz Xaver Haberl and Adolf Sandberger, 21 vols (Leipzig, 1908), XIX, preface, p. viii.

42 See Wolfgang Boetticher, *Orlando di Lasso und seine Zeit, 1532–1594* (Kassel, 1958), p. 571: 'Sie sind freie Dichtung mit großem sezenischen Aufwand und scheinen Reste zur Frühgeschichte der Oper darzustellen'; p. 572: 'vielleicht ... zu einem verschollenen szenischen Werk um 1585 gehörig.' See Weller, 'Lasso, Man of the Theatre,' pp. 89–127.

43 See Körndle, 'Ad te, perenne gaudium.'

44 See Fidel Rädle, 'Italienische Jesuitendramen auf bayerischen Bühnen des 16. Jahrhunderts,' *Acta Conventus neo-Latini Bononiensis: Proceedings of the Fourth International Congress of Neo-Latin Studies, Bologna 26 August to 1 September 1979*, ed. R.J. Schoeck (Binghamton, 1985), pp. 303–12.

45 See Jean-Marie Valentin, *Le théâtre des jésuites dans les pays de langue allemande. Répertoire chronologique des pièces représentées et des documents conservés (1555–1773)*, 2 vols (Stuttgart, 1983–4), I, pp. 32–3.

46 See R. Peinlich, *Geschichte des Gymnasiums in Graz, Programm* (Graz, 1869), p. 33.

47 Munich, Geheimes Hausarchiv, Korr. Akt 597 VII. See Bertha Antonia Wallner, *Musikalische Denkmäler der Steinätzkunst des 16. und 17. Jahrhunderts nebst Beiträgen zur Musikpflege dieser Zeit* (Munich, 1912), p. 103. The shelf mark given in Wallner's book is incorrect and obviously a misprint.

48 See *Die Jesuiten in Bayern, 1549–1773. Ausstellung des Bayerischen Hauptstaatsarchivs und der Oberdeutschen Provinz der Gesellschaft Jesu*, ed. Generaldirektion der Staatlichen Archive Bayerns (Weißenhorn, 1991), p. 178.

49 See *Triumphus divi Michaelis Archangeli Bavarici. Triumph des heiligen Michael, Patron Bayerns (München, 1597)*, ed. Barbara Bauer and Jürgen Leonhardt (Munich, 2000), pp. 96–7, 290–5.

50 Fulda, Hessische Landesbibliothek, 4° C 13 fols 150r–155.

51 Henrie Cornelius Agrippa, *Of the Vanitie and vncertaintie of Artes and Sciences, Englished by Ja. San. Gent* (London, 1569), fol. 30r.

52 See Körndle, 'Was wußte Hoffmann? Neues zur altbekannten Geschichte von der Rettung der Kirchenmusik auf dem Konzil zu Trient,' in *Musikalisches Jahrbuch*, vol. 83 (1999), pp. 65–90.

53 *Die Jesuiten in Bayern,* ed. Staatlichen Archive Bayerns, p. 190.

54 Jeremias Drexel, *Rhetorica caelestis* (Munich, 1638), book 1, chap. 5, p. 106.

55 Pietro A. Persico, *De primo ac praecipuo sacerdotis officio libri tres* (Naples, 1639), book 3, *dubium* 5, pp. 667–9.

56 See Körndle, 'Was wußte Hoffmann?' pp. 65–90.

57 Louis Cressolles, *Mystagogus* (Paris, 1629), pp. 1017–18.

22 / Sung Catechism and College Opera: Two Musical Genres in the Jesuit Evangelization of Colonial Chile

VÍCTOR RONDÓN

Traces of Music in the Evangelization of Indians: The Influence of José de Acosta

Although some socio-historical studies interpret the period of Chilean culture that runs from the mid-seventeenth century to the expulsion of the Society of Jesus as the 'Jesuit century,'[1] the evangelizing influence of the Jesuits had been felt in the country since before the end of the sixteenth century. Many years before the order established itself there in 1593, it had radiated from Ciudad de los Reyes (Lima), which, as capital of the Viceroyalty of Peru, exercised permanent control over the religious, cultural, and political life of an immense territory, of which the Captaincy of Chile was a part during the whole of the period.

Through his role as editor and compiler of its constitutions, the Jesuit José de Acosta earned an important and now recognized position within early missionary ideology in South America. In the implementation of the goals of the decisive and far-reaching Third Council of Lima (1582–3), he found an opportunity to introduce an Ignatian ethos to the region.[2]

Chapter 29 of the council's constitutions was devoted to the roles of the college teacher and the cantor, both of whom performed a pedagogical labour on behalf of the ecclesiastical ideology they served. If this decree could not be observed in every place owing to lack of means, even in the chapels farthest from the metropolis the early relationship between the church and the teaching of reading, writing, and music can be verified.

It is in this environment of incipient urbanity that the first books containing words and music were found, and in which music was performed and heard. Processions began and ended here, and the environment constituted the first site of Christian ritual. Chapter 44 of the council's constitutions, which dealt with the confraternities, attempted to stop their spread among the indigenous and African communities. The public presence of the confraternities in the festive and ritual spaces was manifested in the procession, which constituted a symbolic, plastic, musical, and choreographic complex representing a particular ethnic and social sector. The confraternities, the council decided, would be recognized by the colonial power only if they were controlled by a member of the clergy.

In 1584, as a direct product of the council, the first South American book was printed in Lima, *Doctrina Christiana y catecismo para la instrucción de Indios* (Christian Doctrine and Catechism for the Instruction of Indians), also supervised by Acosta.[3] One difference in strategy that distinguished the prescriptions of the Third Council of Lima from earlier ones[4] concerned language. Before this, the use of either Spanish or the indigenous language had been prescribed for catechesis; now the prescription was for the exclusive use of Quechua or Aymara, the most widely used languages in Peru, and never again a language unknown to the Indians.[5] A model catechetical manual was to be drawn up in Spanish, and on it were to be based translations into the South Andean Amerindian languages.

Profiting by his missionary experience, in 1588 José de Acosta published his *De procuranda Indorum salute*, in which chapter 22 of book 5 set forth methodologies for the teaching and learning of catechism. Its recommendation of constant repetition through chanting and recitation is well known, and led to the development in the mission field of a large repertoire of catechetical chants that in turn gave birth to a religious poetry closely tied to singing. Chapter 19 of book 6, as well as setting forth the inappropriateness of the priestly ordination of Indians, prescribed subordinate roles for them[6] – among others, those of acolyte, sacristan, and cantor.

Two years later, in 1590, Acosta published in Seville his treatise *Historia natural y moral de las Indias*. In chapter 28 of book 6, he returned to a subject that worried him deeply: the indigenous feasts and celebrations. He began by recognizing that in all human societies there is an admissible space for such things, and that music and dance form part of them. And he indicated right from the start that an infinite number of mimic dances and others that he regarded as demoniac, particularly owing to their use of masks, were known in Peru. The majority of the latter, in his judgment, were superstitious manifestations associated with the veneration of idols and *guacas*. He also pointed out that the ecclesiastical authority made an effort to suppress them, but that it tolerated those considered only an entertainment and those that had been adapted to conform to catechetical objectives. With respect to native chant, he recorded the existence of a responsorial form, in which one or two soloists sang some strophes, each of which was answered by all the participants.[7]

Such a responsorial form – which survives today – was used by the missionaries to adapt catechetical texts with great benefit, according to Acosta, because of the liking for it shown by the Indians, who would repeat the chants for whole days without becoming weary of them. Acosta went on to note in some detail that not only were autochthonous melodies with evangelizing texts in the indigenous languages used, but the missionaries 'have translated into their tongue our compositions and tunes, as well as eight-line stanzas (octaves) and songs, ballads in octosyllabic metre (romances), [and] redondillas.'[8] According to Acosta, antiphonal chant was customary among the South Andeans prior to the arrival of the Europeans. Thus, rather than introducing a new practice, he combined a preexisting practice with the new catechetical chant in a manner that became so powerfully rooted in popular religious traditions that it endures to the present day.[9]

In Chile, it was mainly the Jesuit missionaries who adapted Spanish songs, translated into Mapudungun, to the catechetical council's texts. The missionaries incorporated these songs into their treatises on indigenous Chilean languages published between the beginning of the seventeenth century and the middle of the eighteenth century.

The Catechetical Repertoire of Songs for the Missions to the Mapuche during the Seventeenth and Eighteenth Centuries

The missionary territories of Arauco and Chiloé were restored in 1608, and their evangelization constituted one of the first works of the recently formed province of Paraguay, of which Chile was a part until 1625. Yet if evangelization efforts were rewarded with early success in Chiloé, this was not the case in Arauco. Nevertheless, in order to protect the principal indigenous group of the Chilean territory, the Jesuit treatises were written in Mapundungun, from the start considered the general language of the Captaincy of Chile.

As I pointed out earlier, it was the Third Council of Lima that made possible the conjunction of a determined Jesuit presence in missionary ideology in the South Andean region and a commitment to evangelization in the indigenous language. As a result, throughout the archbishopric a prolific work of elaborating treatises in various indigenous languages got under way, with the labour assumed chiefly by members of the Society of Jesus who were willing to contribute to their fellow Jesuits' education in these languages.[10] Since the purpose of the whole undertaking was to improve evangelization, frequently the treatises contained, besides grammatical and lexicographical content, such things as important prayers, catechism, and even short sermons and edifying dialogues. A modality or didactic strategy for the teaching of the prayers and the catechism was singing, and that is why the catechetical repertoire of songs is part of these works.

In the case of Chile, three Jesuit treatises on the Mapudungun language contain songs belonging to the catechetical repertoire. The first of these, *Arte y gramática general de la lengua que corre en todo el Reyno de Chile* (Art and General Grammar of the Language Used throughout the Kingdom of Chile), was written by Father Luis de Valdivia and published in Lima in 1606. The second, *Arte de la lengua general del Reyno de Chile* (Art of the General Language of the Kingdom of Chile), was written by Father Andrés Febrés and printed in Lima in 1765. The third had a Latin name, *Chilidúgú, sive Tractatus linguae Chilensis*, and was written by a Jesuit of German origin, Bernardo Havestadt, who published it only after the expulsion when he was already back in his homeland, in Münster in 1777.

Because I have elsewhere alluded to the principal characteristics of the repertoire included in these sources,[11] here I would like to develop some considerations surrounding the text-music relationship in the works. Valdivia includes in his work four texts dealing with, respectively, the newborn Christ child, the Virgin Mary, the catechetical contents of the Ten Commandments, and the sacrament of confession. The only indication that we are dealing with songs is the title 'Couplets to Sing after Catechism.' Neither melodies in musical notation nor the names of tunes to which the words could be sung are given. Why do these texts appear separated from their melodies, and how then was the directive that they be sung to be fulfilled? A possible answer is that a strong oral tradition was still being kept alive among a number of individuals. Father Valdivia's influence on and knowledge of the Chilean Jesuit group during this period of establishment and consolidation of the order in this territory made him consider the identification of the melodic component of the couplets unnecessary, since these were transmitted orally among the Jesuit missionaries, who by then were a reduced group consisting mainly of Spaniards, native Peruvians, and native Chileans educated in the Spanish tradition. The melodies that were used, therefore, were probably of Spanish origin, both religious and secular in character, with instances of the latter reflecting the process known as 'divinization,' although here the term applies only to the melodic component of the songs in question.[12]

Probably this group of couplets was still in use when the chroniclers of the order, Alonso de Ovalle in 1646 and Diego Rosales[13] two decades later, gave an account of the practice of such musical catechesis. But as the seventeenth century progressed, to the Spanish were added other European influences, a process that was favoured both by Chile's belonging to the province of Paraguay – which meant routine changes of personnel among the missionary group during the very early stage – and by the gradual increase in the number of Jesuits of diverse origin as the number of Spaniards decreased. Be that as it may, the work of Father Valdivia retained its standing until the middle of the eighteenth century, and it first encountered an objection only a few years before the expulsion. But without doubt the catechetical repertoire grew and became more diverse.

In the work of Febrés are twelve songs without written melody, but unlike his predecessor the author indicates the tunes to which they are to be sung. Again, a living oral tradition with an ample repertoire is implied, whereby it is necessary only to mention the name or *incipit* of a song or hymn to indicate the melodic component of a song included here. That means that the melodies of Febrés's songbook were not unique or exclusive to the texts he wrote down. My intention here is not to focus on the very common practice in the oral tradition of the period of using pre-existent melodies to sing diverse texts, but simply to state that the melodies in question had no identity relationship with the texts of the songbook – a state of affairs that in some cases permitted the indication of more than one melodic option for the same text.[14]

In the case of the nineteen catechetical songs proposed by Havestadt, we find that both melody and text are notated, though in separate sections of the book (fig. 22.1). Even here the melodies correspond to those of a pre-existent repertoire, derived mainly from the old religious songbook of Cologne, the missionary's place of origin.

In comparing the repertoires of Febrés and Havestadt, I found some coincidences in the melodies used (mentioned in the work of the former, and written in musical notation in that of the latter).[15] Since I had the opportunity to study Havestadt's repertoire in more detail, I was able to verify that he did use melodies from the German Catholic milieu for his catechetical texts in the Mapuche language. It is noteworthy, therefore, that the Spaniard Febrés also uses those melodies in almost half of his repertoire.[16] The presence of melodies of German origin in the repertoire of the Spaniard could be proof that Febrés copied some materials from Havestadt, a practice denounced by the latter in a *nota bene* at the beginning of part 5 of his work: 'Benevolent reader, if you find the things herein contained somewhere else, in manuscripts or in printed books, you must know that I did not take them from him, but that he took them from me.'[17]

Febrés's 'El Bendito' (The Blessed One), furthermore, coincides with Havestadt's 'Ufchigepe,' which has as its basis the *paraquayensis tone*. But this coincidence can be understood as reflecting a sense of common ownership of the repertoire of the province of Paraguay, which served as a model for the Chilean Jesuits, and the missionary results of which constituted an ideal.[18] As for how the melody came into the hands of Havestadt, it has been stated that it was supplied to him by Father Anton Sepp – but that is hardly possible, since Sepp died fifteen years before Havestadt arrived in South America.

22.1 'Quiñe Dios,' from Bernardo Havestadt, *Chilidúgú, sive Tractatus linguae Chilensis* (Westphalia, 1777). Photo courtesy of Víctor Rondón.

If these three Chilean Jesuit sources of catechetical repertoire are taken as a whole (see the appendix), we can observe that in general the early Spanish influence was followed by a later, German one. In addition to an increase in the number of songs, there was also a growing tendency to specify melodies and instrumentation. None of the authors could boast any specialized musical training beyond that acquired within the limits of a general education.

Finally, with respect to the text-music relationship, we can observe that the text was an ever present and an explicit element, whereas the music was absent most of the time, or present only implicitly. Havestadt's repertoire constituted a rather happy exception, but even there the text preceded the music. The most important common characteristic of the items that made up this corpus is that the catechetical texts did not possess melodies of their own but borrowed pre-existent melodies, which thereupon were adapted to a new text in a new language.

Both the authors' lack of specific musical qualifications and the weak and unstable text-music relationship have caused me to reconsider these 'catechetical songs' as forming a musical repertoire, because they really represent a kind of 'sung catechesis,' in which the relevant thing is the text. Accordingly, if the practice of sung catechesis is evidence of a specific Jesuit missionary methodology,[19] the musical setting is not the appropriate place in which to look for an ideology characteristic of the Jesuits in the period.

The sung catechesis, in other words, is not representative of Jesuit music if by that term we understand a symbolical system reflecting Jesuit aesthetics and Jesuit ideology through sounds and in which a text-music relationship gives proof of intentional correspondence. But the question of correspondence leads us to the topic of music as representation and therefore as being naturally associated with the theatre.

College Opera during the Eighteenth Century

The seventeenth-century history of the Society of Jesus in Chile incorporates various accounts of theatrical representations demonstrating Spanish influence, performed by students in the schools of the order. These performances were of a public character – that is why records of them were retained – and in them the music was secondary to the moral message, so much so that no information is given as to the melodies that were employed or the manner in which they were executed.

Apart from this seventeenth-century Jesuit public theatre, directed to the general society of the period, there were eighteenth-century forms of representation in music directed to the college community, that is, the community inside the institution. Such works, because of their scenographic, dramatic, and musical elements, are the ones I call 'college opera.' In the case of Chile, they reveal a German origin.

If the sources for our knowledge of the public theatrical representations of the seventeenth century in general consist of chronicles and similar documents, in which contextual data abound but specifically musical information is lacking, the sources for our knowledge of the college opera of the next century are the musical works themselves, for which to date we have no major contextual data.

Two such sources are collections of works entitled *Theatrum affectuum humanorum* and *Theatrum doloris et amoris*, edited by the Jesuit Franz Lang in 1717 in Munich, which arrived in Chile probably in 1748, through the offices of the then attorney of the order, Carlos (Karl) Haimbhausen, from the German provinces.

The *Theatrum affectuum humanorum* contains nineteen works with Latin texts written by Lang himself and set to music by more than a dozen composers of the Munich Jesuit circle of the early eighteenth century.[20] The *Theatrum doloris et amoris*[21] contains the Passion in twenty-three works with text by Lang and music by Francisco Mathia Delaman. Franz Lang (1654–1725) was also the author of the most important book on dramaturgy of the period, *Dissertatio de actione scenica cum figuris eandem explicantibus, et observationibus de arte comica* (Dissertation on Dramatic Action, with Its Figures Explained and with Observations about the Art of Theatre), published in Munich in 1727.

It is precisely the significance of the author of the texts, the existence of complementary sources, and the use of symbolic characterization in the works, particularly the one first mentioned, that enables us to see reflected in them the Jesuit ideology of the period and an aesthetic attempt to articulate that ideology in musical works written specifically for the sake of such articulation.

The full title of the first source is *Theatrum affectuum humanorum, sive Considerationes morales ad scenam accomodatae*, that is, 'Theatre of Human Affections, or Moral Considerations Accommodated to the Stage.' In the list of the vocal and instrumental cast of characters the point is made that these 'considerations' are semi-melodic, that is, that the texts, which are rhetorical in character, are to be alternately recited and sung (figs 22.2, 22.3). Accordingly, there are characters who only recite (*personae*) and others who sing (*personae musicae*) their text. Among the latter are the Angel, the Demon, Christ, the Virgin, the Soul, Death, Justice, Fatherly Love, Conscience, Penitence, the Genii, and the Shadows. The voices, all of which are masculine, are alto, tenor, and bass register soloists, and a choir.

The instrumentation is made up of an unspecified basso continuo and strings (generally two violins and a viola, occasionally a *viola d'amore* duplicating the first violin). The wind instruments are scarcely used and have a symbolic and colouring function.[22] The same low range is reserved for the character of Death, sung by a bass, although the personified Demon is often sung by a tenor. The parts of the good characters such as the Soul, the Conscience, Christ, and the Virgin are always sung by high voices.

This, together with the theatrical and scenographic elements, constitutes a symbolic complex of the highest interest for an understanding of the 'Jesuit' music and performance arts of the period. When I can begin the transcription of these works, and when analysis and interpretation of the resulting score allows some access to the purely musical level, perhaps it will be possible to advance in a less speculative way in our understanding of the early eighteenth-century Jesuit symbolic sound universe that had its origins in the German provinces. Also awaiting further study are the artistic connections between the Jesuits of those provinces and their Chilean brothers, and the circle of composers around the important figure of the Jesuit Franz Lang in Munich, along with his role in Jesuit baroque art.

The principal objective of the catechetical repertoire directed towards indigenous neophytes in their own language was to promote their conversion and to maintain the evangelical territories. Melodies were thus subordinate to texts, which, of course, carried the message; that is why texts were fixed and melodies

22.2. *Consideratio* 1, 'Daemonium Mutum' (*symphonia*), from Franz Lang, *Theatrum affectuum humanorum, sive Considerationes morales ad scenam accomodatae* (Munich, 1717). Photo courtesy of Víctor Rondón.

changed. As Jesuits' evangelizing efforts increased, so too did the repertoire of songs; and the origin of their melodies was always directly related to that of the missionary himself, who, as I have pointed out, had no specialized musical training.

The college opera, created with a higher degree of aesthetic refinement, was directed to educated Christians – the college students and the Jesuits themselves. It assumes a more advanced training in matters of faith, and its theological component is more sophisticated. There is coherence between the message, here in Latin, and the artistic forms that contain it (music, poetry, and scenographic representation), and there are correspondences among these symbolic systems.

Sung catechesis represents a particular component of the Jesuit use of music in the evangelization of the indigenous South American peoples, in which singing was nothing more than a pedagogical tool, a substitute for or an alternative to the written word. In the study of this corpus of songs, then, aesthetic, artistic, or purely musical estimations are not relevant. They are relevant, however, in the study of college opera, where characters represent values whose discourse is both transmitted and reinforced by a specific sonorous medium (voices and instruments).

22.3. *Consideratio* 1, 'Daemonium Mutum' (*recitativo*), from Lang,
Theatrum affectuum humanorum. Photo courtesy of Víctor Rondón.

For this musical and dramatic manifestation of religious art, the sources and materials that have been found exist in response to a creative will, and so make possible a consideration of the concept of the work. That concept enables us to integrate this particular Jesuit artistic production within the wider picture of the Western art of the baroque period, because the music theory of the period distinguished as one of the three types of repertoire precisely the *stylus scenicus seu theatralis*.[23] Both the creation and the interpretation of the operas required, however, specialized musical training, unlike the sung catechesis, which, as we have seen, was brought into being by the indigenous peoples and the missionaries without musical training. If sung catechesis informs us about local aspects of Jesuit activity in Chile, college opera offers more generalized insights into Ignatian practice around the world. Taken together, they contribute to our understanding of the Jesuits of this period and allow us to pinpoint some of the factors that achieved for the Jesuits a privileged position within its culture.

APPENDIX

The following chart lists Chilean Jesuit sources of sung cathechesis in the Mapudungun language during the seventeenth and eighteenth centuries.

Source	Repertoire	Melody/instrumentation
		Unspecified/voice
Luis de Valdivia, *Arte y gramática general* (Lima, 1606)	1. A.N.S. iesu Xpò Jesus Pellebichi	
	2. A Nuestra Señora, para despedirse en acabando la doctrina Virgen santa Dios ni ñuque	
	3. De los mandamientos Dios (Peñi) no ayuabimi	
	4. De la confesión Dios ta peme duamalu	
		Implicit/voice
Andrés Febrés, *Arte de la lengua general* (Lima, 1765)	1. El Bendito	– al tono de las misiones del Paraguay
	2. A Nuestra Señora	– por el tono 'Omni die dic Mariae'
	3. Acto de caridad y contricion	– al tono 'O anima par coelo spiritus'
	4. Acto de contricion y atricion	– por el tono 'Horrenda mors, tremenda mors &c.'
	5. Al Niño Dios recién nacido, en la noche buena	– por el tono 'Véante mis ojos &c.'
	6. Al sagrado Corazon de Jesus	– por el tono 'O cor divinissim &c. u otro semejante'
	7. A Maria santa madre de la Luz	– por los mismos tonos [anteriores]
	8. Al glorioso patriarca S. Joseph	– el Hymno 'Te Joseph celebrent & c. Por el tono de Mi, bi, mi, fa, re &c.
	9. A San Juan Bautista	– los himnos 'Ut queant, Antra deserti y O nimis felix &c. Por el tono y metro de El Atractivo &c.'
	10. Al grande patriarca san Ignacio de Loyola	– la marcha 'Fundador sois, San Ignacio'
	11. Al nuevo taumaturgo San Francisco Xavier	– por [el tono de] 'La Amable'
	12. A San Luis Gonzaga	– por el tono de 'Quondam simpliculi' u otro semejante
		Explicit/voice and basso continuo
Bernardo Havestadt, *Chilidúgú, sive Tractatus* (Westphalia, 1777)	1. Quiñe Dios	– Vervum supernum prodiens
	2. Dios ñi Votmm	– Creator alme siderum
	3. Cume que che ñi	– Jesu mae delicae
	4. Vill dgu mo	– O Deus ego amo te
	5. Ufchigepe	– Sono paraquayensi
	6. Quiñe Dios	– Cur mundus militat
	7. Duamtumn vill	– Sonus militaris Austriacus
	8. Ventenlu	– Joannes magna Lux Bohemiae

Source	Repertoire	Melody/instrumentation
Bernardo Havestadt,	9. Duamtumn vill	– Sonus Austriacus
Chilidúgú, sive	10. A Señor Dios	– O Anima par caelo Spiritus
Tractatus	11. Hueda que che	– Sonus Austriacus
(Westphalia, 1777)	12. Ayueimi	– Omni die dic Mariae
	13. Jesus cad	– Rhatgeberi
	14. Aiubige Dios	– Omni die dic Mariae
	15. Mari Mari	– Xaveri rumpe moras
	16. Santo Angel	– Defensor noster aspice
	17. Cad Burenyeve	– S. Joanne Nepomuc
	18. Acui ta	– unspecified
	19. Vau mlei	– unspecified

NOTES

1 See Hernán Godoy, *La cultura chilena* (Santiago de Chile, 1982), especially chap. 3, 'La hegemonía cultural jesuita y el barroco,' pp. 99–148.

2 José de Acosta was also sent on the long errands of obtaining the approval of the Consejo de Indias in Spain, and of the Holy See in Rome. The decree of Vatican approval was obtained in October 1588, and the authorized printing was done in Madrid in 1590. The royal edict that decreed its execution, sent by Philip II to the viceroy, tribunals, governors and magistrates, and archbishops and bishops of the ecclesiastical province of Peru, is dated September 1591.

3 The printing was done owing to the Jesuit effort of bringing from Mexico the printer Antonio Ricardo, with all his equipment and machinery – which were installed in the offices of the order – to serve their work of evangelization. See José Toribio Medina, *La imprenta en Lima (1584–1824)*, vol. 1 (Santiago de Chile, 1904), pp. 3–20.

4 Especially the 'Constituciones para Indios' of the first council, of 1552.

5 This idea would be complemented later by the disposition requiring an ordained person operating in missionary territory to have prior and through knowledge of the language of his catechumens.

6 The natives held these roles in great esteem, because they conferred social prestige.

7 He gave some additional details concerning the music accompanying the dances, mentioning the use of various flutes, tambourines, and trumpets (*caracoles*).

8 José de Acosta, *Historia natural y moral de las Indias* (Seville, 1590), book 6, chap. 28, 'Of the Dances and Feasts of the Indian.' The 'redondilla' in colonial sources was a quatrain with the rhyme scheme a-b-b-a.

9 On the survival of the practice, see Víctor Rondón, 'Una interpretación de los bailes *chinos* como modelo de reproducción de evangelización misional, en Chile central,' paper presented at the Fourth International Latin American Symposium of Musicol-

ogy, Curitiba, Brazil, January 2000. The proceedings of the conference are forth-coming.

10 For an in-depth study of the missionaries' linguistic works, see *La descripción de las lenguas amerindias en la época colonial*, ed. Klaus Zimmerman (Madrid, 1997), especially the contribution by Zimmerman entitled 'Introducción: Apuntes para la historia de la linguística de las lenguas amerindias,' pp. 9–17.

11 See Rondón, 'Música y evangelización en el cancionero "Chilidúgú" (1777) del padre Havestadt, misionero jesuita en la Araucanía durante el siglo XVIII,' in *Los jesuitas españoles expulsos. Su imagen y su contribución al saber en el mundo hispánico en la Europa del siglo XVIII,* ed. Manfred Tietz (Madrid and Frankfurt, 2001), pp. 557–79.

12 The process of divinization – whereby a secular theme is changed to a religious one – finds its most polished expression in the replacement of profane terms by pious ones while retaining metre and rhyme, and always within the boundaries of the same language. In South America the process was employed by the Jesuit missionary José de Anchieta, who evangelized in Brazil in the mid-sixteenth century. See Rogelio Budasz, 'O cancionero ibérico em José de Anchieta – Un enfoque musicológico,' dissertation, Universidade de São Paulo, 1996.

13 The first edition of the work by Rosales, *Historia general del Reyno de Chile Flandes Indiano*, was published by Benjamín Vicuña Mackenna, in Valparaíso, in three volumes in 1877–8.

14 For example, he writes, 'To the Sacred Heart of Jesus, for the tune "O cor divinissim &c" or any similar one.'

15 We must remember that these works, though published twelve years apart, were written at the same time.

16 As an example, I can point out that the melody for 'Canción a Nuestra Señora' (Song to Our Lady) in the work of the Spanish Jesuit is the same as that for the 'Aiubige Dios' in the work of the German Jesuit; similarly, the melody for Febrés's 'Acto de caridad y contrición' (Act of Charity and Contrition) is the same as that for Havestadt's 'A Señor Dios' (To the Lord God).

17 This is the opinion of the historian Walter Hanisch in *Itinerario y pensamiento de los jesuitas expulsos de Chile (1767–1815)* (Santiago de Chile, 1972), p. 236.

18 Febrés includes at the end of his work an imaginary dialogue between two Mapuche *caciques*, one of whom, just returned from a trip to the country of the Guaraní, recounts the marvels he saw there, and ponders their state as an ideal for the Mapuche.

19 The practice was not exclusive to the Jesuits; other religious orders used it in their catechetical work.

20 Among those about whom it has been possible to obtain information are Florianus Ott (probably an Augustinian); Giuseppe Antonio Bernabei (1649–1732; of Italian

origin, he arrived in Munich with his father, Ercole Bernabei); Rupert Ignaz Mayr (1646–1712; a chapel master outside Munich); and J.C. Pez (1664–1716; a pupil of the Jesuit school in Munich and afterwards a musician at Jesuit institutions). Others less well known are Johann Andreas Rauscher, D. Deichel, A. Deichel, M. Duerr, Francisco Mathia Delaman, J.T. Holl, J.G. Steingriebler, J.P. Weiss, and M. Praunsperger.

21 The complete title is *Theatrum doloris et amoris, sive Considerationes mysteriorum Christi patientis, et Mariae matris dolorosae sub cruce condolentis filio piis affectibus conceptae.* The title does not specify that the 'considerations' are *ad scenam accomodatae.*

22 As, for example, in the first work, 'Daemonium Mutum,' in which it is thought necessary to have two trombones and two bassoons to produce a dark timbre that would seem to describe the depths of the empire of evil.

23 See Paul Henry Lang, *Music in Western Civilization* (New York, 1941), p. 437. The other styles, the names of which referred to the spaces for which the works were produced, were liturgical music (*stylus ecclesiasticus*) and chamber music, which was mainly instrumental (*stylus cubicularis*). The practice of these styles is documented also in South American Jesuit sources of the period, but they constitute another world. Similarly, I regard the so-called missionary music, that is, the music and drama practised in missionary towns, as constituting another type of repertoire, different from those I have focused on here.

23 / The Orator's Performance: Gesture, Word, and Image in Theatre at the Collegio Romano

BRUNA FILIPPI

The Festival of Theatre

In March 1622, on the occasion of the canonization of Sts Ignatius of Loyola and Francis Xavier, the ecclesiastical rites celebrated with great pomp in the Vatican were joined by a festival of literary ceremonies staged in the Collegio Romano, or, to use the words of Father Famiano Strada, in the 'Palace of Learning,' where 'erudite allusions and ancient Apotheoses' were represented in magnificent style.[1]

The ancient funeral rite of the glorification of Roman emperors, reproposed in its various phases and locations, was the main theme of the whole program of festivities, and it effected a total redesign of the college's interior space: the atrium and porticoes of the Collegio Romano represented the Forum, which in ancient times hosted statues of illustrious men and images of dead emperors; the ceremonial hall became the Campus Martius, where the Apotheosis was celebrated, and the classrooms of the various scholastic disciplines were transformed into rostrums, where the praises and merits of the saints were declaimed and illustrated.

At the main entrance visitors were met with two large globes representing the Old and New Worlds, where several characters personifying Fame invited them to participate in the ceremony. The arches of the porticoes were adorned with painted armour and shields representing the conversion of St Ignatius, while other paintings and festoons represented the world's thirty-four Jesuit provinces, with all the houses and colleges then belonging to the Society of Jesus. Here, a group of fifty-four young men, wearing crowns, classical garb, and medals of St Ignatius, danced and sang a dithyramb, the lyrics of which could be read on a banner hanging on the walls.[2] Evoking the classical locations and faithfully following the sequence of the ancient imperial rite – with, of course, the necessary superimposition of new contents and new symbolic meanings – the Company of Jesus and the Collegio Romano celebrated the fame of their founding princes, now saints.

This way of appropriating a single feature of classical culture was certainly nothing new for the Jesuits of the time, who, as St Ignatius himself had indicated in reference to the 'spoils of Egypt,'[3] believed in the legitimacy of salvaging ancient and pagan culture for religious, and therefore superior, ends. On this particular occasion, the ceremonial structure of the Apotheosis, completely emptied of its original significance and referents, became a formal shell within which to arrange the symbolic contents of the triumph of the Faith through the theatrical description of the exploits of the two new saints.

In the attempt to provide a worthy and exhaustive account of the life and works of the two saints, the theatre aspects of the celebration dominated and conditioned every other aspect of it; that is, while the festivities occupied and transformed the entire space of the college, the central part of the celebration of St Ignatius and St Francis Xavier was entrusted to three theatrical representations, which succeeded one another in the ceremonial hall, and which dictated continual changes in the enormous scenographic apparatus that invaded and changed the appearance of the college. One could say that the magnificence and grandiosity of this all-encompassing 'theatre' of the festival – in the spatial sense of 'theatre' – actually ended up creating a veritable 'festival of the theatre,' in that the dramatic representations, entitled *Apotheosis, Ignatio in Monserrato*, and *Pirimalus*, constituted the central attraction around which rotated all the other ceremonies and performances.

The surprising dramatic inventions proposed by the three theatrical productions allowed visitors to appreciate the creative skill of Jesuit playwrights, the mastery of the student-actors, and the astounding technical and scenic experimentations of the set designers. This memorable theatrical event, staged by teachers and students of the Collegio Romano, brought the forms and methods of Jesuit theatre and its pedagogical efficacy an extraordinary and enduring public recognition.

By the time of the canonization the college's theatrical practices had already been well established for decades. Although the *Ratio studiorum* provided no more than a skeletal normative framework, regarding only the regulation of public performances and the insertion of theatre as a scholastic exercise in classes on rhetoric, there were numerous occasions for theatrical performance at the college. In the remarkable chronicle of 'scholastic activities, of things studied, and of students' contained in the *Annals* of the Seminario Romano written by Father Girolamo Nappi, mention is made of several kinds of theatrical performances.[4] In the Seminario, where most of the students of the Collegio

Romano lived, theatre was an integral part not only of the academic program but also of the students' daily lives and even of institutional social events. There were public performances during Carnival, improvised plays and contests between the various dormitories of the college, and private performances on the occasion of visits by important patrons or guests.[5] The frequency and diversity of theatrical productions in Roman Jesuit circles demonstrates the key role of theatre, not only as a tool for training students in perfect eloquence, but also as a complement to the pedagogical program that, combining utility and recreation, became a characteristic feature of community life.

The 'festival of theatre' organized on the occasion of the canonization undoubtedly brought Roman Jesuit theatre to the apex of its visibility and fame outside the institution, both as a demonstration of its pedagogical efficacy and as an exhibition of the high degree of dramatic experimentation and scenographic magnificence it had achieved.

In historical terms, this 'apotheosis' of the theatre can be understood as the manifestation of the central and transversal role of a cultural practice, or rather of a universe of practices that contributed to the construction of dramatic works. We cannot, in fact, limit ourselves to the consideration and analysis of the dramatic works and performances of the 'theatre of the college' as defined only as definitive artistic and literary products. On the contrary, Jesuit dramatic works and their stage productions must be analysed first of all as complex productive processes that involve and at the same time represent an entire pedagogical institution. Our intention and our method is, therefore, to identify in the works those features that bear witness to the broader cultural process that gave rise to and supported their creation. This means, on the one hand, abandoning the idea or the ideology of a triumphant dramaturgic and production model that was coherent with the norms and provisions of the Jesuit pedagogical institution, in order to analyse the variations and adaptations, the technical innovations and theoretical discussions that demonstrate the complexity and the vitality of Jesuit theatre. And it also means, on the other hand, paying constant attention to the changes and ferment animating the cultural debate in the environment in which the theatre operated and on which it ultimately depended. From this perspective, one clearly discerns, even in the 'festival of the theatre' that we have examined up to now, the symptoms of a transition towards a different way of organizing the practice of theatre and making it work.[6]

During its early seventeenth-century flowering, Roman Jesuit theatre showed indications of production theatricals and a rhetorical culture that went beyond the prescriptions of the *Ratio studiorum*. Taken as a whole, these indications reveal a significant divergence between official rules and cultural practices. Already in the early years of the century, for example, the precept requiring the use of Latin in theatrical productions was violated by the introduction of the vernacular in private or 'domestic' performances – as productions staged within the walls of the Collegio and the Seminario Romano were called at the time. Beginning in the 1630s, the use of Italian would be extended to public performances as well. By the same token, with the profusion of visual effects and the recourse to emblematic representations, Jesuit productions were more and more marked by a 'poetics of marvel and invention' that changed both the process of composition and the procedures for staging dramatic works, until that time subject to the Renaissance poetics of *mimesis* and *iudicium*.

In the teaching of rhetoric, furthermore, the old models of Cicero for prose and Virgil for poetry were joined by other examples, chosen from among both classical writers such as Tacitus, Valerius Maximus, Apuleius, and Seneca, and the more recent contributions of Lipsius, Puteanus, and Rodiginus. At the same time, rhetoric classes dedicated more space and gave more importance to the invention of emblems and the composition of epigrams, while the introduction of new authors produced substantial changes in repertories of rhetorical commonplaces.

These internal changes in the teaching of rhetoric gave rise to a type of oratory that not only reintroduced unusual and obsolete Latin words and expressions but also moved towards a style that was more concise and obscure, and no longer respectful of the old canons of the elegant phrase typical of Cicero. This new style was known as the *peregrino* or *lipsiano* style; it spread above all in the Jesuit colleges of northern Europe, and it was criticized by Father Alber, named vicar in 1615 upon the death of Father General Claudio Acquaviva, in the official document *De stilo vitioso in provinciis corrigendo et Cicerone sequendo*.[7] Though it confirmed the fact of the spread of the new style of teaching, this document required prefects of the curriculum to prohibit new authors, to choose 'lovers of Cicero' as teachers for the students, and to supervise the compilation of the catalogue of authors.

Apart from its institutional effect, the document's proposed return to the original model of oratory reveals a state of crisis in Jesuit rhetoric. Even if the colleges returned to a didactics based on the Ciceronian model, fidelity to Cicero did not eliminate the trend towards flowery eloquence and the rhetorical procedures of wit. Moreover, the crisis testifies to Jesuit participation in the wider cultural movement against Ciceronianism, which spread throughout Europe in the last decades of the sixteenth century, and which would eventually lead to the creation of two opposite stylistic alternatives: on the one hand, an intense style, dry and without ornament, known as *acutus*, inspired by Tacitus and Seneca and proposed and defined by Justus Lipsius; on the other, the *argutus,* derived from the ornate style and inspired by the masters of the second school of Sophists. To the density and sharpness of the Senecan school the Jesuits preferred pomp and flourish, and they became the proponents of a broader and wittier style of elocution.[8]

In the first decades of the seventeenth century, however, the distinction was still not well defined, and the two terms – acuteness and wit – were used interchangeably. This was the case at the Collegio Romano at least until the years 1622–5, when the young Polish Jesuit Maciej Casimir Sarbiewski,[9] in a highly charged atmosphere of polemical debate, gave a series of lectures that were crowned with success. Attended by prestigious scholars and masters of rhetoric, the lectures, entitled 'De acuto e de arguto,' distinguished the 'acuteness' of operations of invention from the 'wit' of procedures derived from ornament.

The crisis in rhetoric affected Jesuit theatre both directly and indirectly, because of the breach it opened in the normative organization of the schools and because of the innovations it introduced in the teaching of the discipline more akin than any other to dramatic writing and representation. The same period, however, saw other significant changes in the cultural and political context in which the Jesuits of the Collegio Romano lived and worked. There was, for example, the favourable atmosphere for Jesuit culture created by the papacy of Urban VIII, which also had repercussions on the audience for the theatrical performances of the Collegio Romano, now attended for the first time by noblewomen from the papal court.[10] Furthermore, we must recall the renewed cultural interest in ecclesiastical history and science exemplified by the publication and diffusion of a work such as the *Annales* of Cesare Baronio, a true milestone in Catholic historiography, which would provide the historical basis and serve as a constant reference for the construction of the sacred story lines for the Jesuits' seventeenth-century Christian tragedies.

A contribution to the expanding religious and cultural role of theatre in Roman society also came from the keen-eyed cultural activity of the Jesuit fathers, who elaborated a strategy for the publication of dramatic texts and began writing theoretical treatises aimed at specifying and codifying the compositional canons of 'Christian tragedy.' Moreover, beginning in 1616, theatre attendance was promoted by the publication of plot summaries to be distributed to the audience to facilitate their understanding and enjoyment of what was represented on stage.[11]

The Recovery of the Visible

Contrary to widespread and anachronistic contemporary critical opinion, for the Jesuits of the Collegio Romano in the first half of the seventeenth century dramatic literature did not yet constitute an autonomous literary genre. The distinction between a dramatic text as written and the same text as performed served, if anything, to underline the greater importance of the latter. The various parts that – like the dramatic text – went into the composition of the theatrical phenomenon remained strongly anchored in stage practice and were judged for their effect on the audience. As late as 1649, Pietro Sforza Pallavicino, in his *Vindicationes*, praised *Crispus* by Bernardino Stefonio, to which he attributed the merit of having brought tragedy to Rome, recalling that 'it won applause from all nations, because it was often performed and still more often read.'[12] This distinction between the two ways of experiencing and appreciating the theatre of the great playwright, however, is followed immediately by the comment that only those who were able to see the performance in person received the greatest pleasure and were able truly to admire it.

Thus the audience's admiration and wonder became the criterion for evaluating dramatic composition. What made a dramatic text fully enjoyable was the mastery of the student-actors in 'giving body' to the text in the course of the performance, of the choragus in organizing the staging of the play, and of the architect or the painter in conceiving its scenographic effects. The priority assigned to the moment and the technique of performance is also an indication of the double purpose of this theatre, which combined the pedagogic objective of acquiring and exhibiting the 'know-how' of the actors and the creators of the performance with the apologetic necessity of 'making the audience see' the edifying examples of heroes of the faith.

Active proponents of the 'recovery of the visible'[13] that the Council of Trent had promoted in both pastoral care and doctrinal development, the Roman Jesuits – especially the seventeenth-century generation of Fathers Galluzzi, Donati, Santi, and Sforza Pallavicino – dedicated themselves, in their publishing work and in their theatrical experimentation, to defining the expressive and compositional criteria of theatrical representation.

In his 1621 commentary on tragedy, Tarquinio Galluzzi[14] showed himself highly attentive to the technical aspects of stage production and to the persuasive function of performance. His theoretical reflections were centred around two poles – composition and stage production – that the humanist exegetic tradition of Vitruvius and Aristotle had treated as separate and independent levels. This close connection between the unfolding of the dramatic action and the place and manner of its staging demonstrates, yet again, the Jesuit author's primarily performative conception of the dramatic arts.

Referring to both ancient and modern authors, Galluzzi believes it is indispensable that dramatic composition be combined with the apparatus, defined as 'the first element of the structure of the theatre' in so far as it includes all those things that 'are placed before the eyes of the spectator: the decoration of the set, the costumes of the actors, the characters in action, and all things of that nature that are used when one acts out a fable.'[15] Particularly significant are his references to the scenic space of Vitruvius and the iconographic illustration of Fra Giocondo's edition of him, and he also includes minutely detailed descriptions of how this scenic space – perfectly reconstructed with its doors, the royal palace, and its stairways – must be managed in order to accommodate the entrances and exits of the various characters in the drama: 'from the right the wayfarers and the guests ... from the left ... only the aquatic divinities. The Eumenides and all other gods of the nether world exit by the lower stairs; the shadows and the spirits of the dead enter from the stairs known as Charon's staircase ...'[16]

This is followed by illustrations of machines used to create transformations and metamorphoses: the machine by which celestial gods descended suddenly onto the stage, the one that 'quickly snatched mortals from the earth and carried them off to the gods,' the one that 'flashes lightning in the thunderous sky, and the rumbling vibrations of which re-create an earthquake on the stage,' and then 'pictures, paintings, signs, fountains, or machines that diffused odorous latices, ivory, silver, gold, and sumptuous streams of flowers, waters yellow with saffron powder, vapours wafting through the air, and similar insalubrious, prodigious, and luxurious additions.'[17]

While displaying the author's taste for erudition, these detailed reconstructions also expressed his emphasis on the know-how and techniques of a stage production characterized by the use of numerous inventions and frequent and stupefying changes of scene. In Jesuit productions, the set was continually transformed by the constant interplay of *apparenze* and *lontananze* that alternated 'seaside settings' with the city, the forest, gardens, and military camps.

As Leone Santi would recall several years later, 'As far as concerns the things involved with the sets, the moderns have gone far beyond' the ancients by making 'fake scenes with the use of perspective to show the distances between places with much greater artistry and taste.'[18] This consciousness of a new way of constructing the 'visible,' inherent in perspective and its paradigm, had become an imperative and allows Santi to come down on the side of the moderns, for whom the visible had by now become an instrument of discovery and demonstration.[19] It was precisely this 'greater artistry,' in fact, that would allow the seventeenth-century Jesuit stage to embrace 'heaven, earth, and hell' and finally to represent the conflict between the forces of Good and Evil, which the subjects of their tragedies put at the centre of their dramaturgy.

The need to represent sacred themes and subjects is the motivation for the 'renewal of ancient tragedy' promoted by Galluzzi, who declared his intention to 'follow Plato with regard to purpose and character and to obey Aristotle in the story and the arrangement of the other parts.'[20] This Platonic option or correction allows the play to represent the extraordinary lives of the saints and martyrs, proposing them as examples of heroic virtue. The objective of Jesuit tragedy, therefore, would no longer be catharsis, that is, to 'move to compassion and terror, and to purge, that is to cure and diminish, these two passions,'[21] but edification: to instil courage in the spectator and reinforce his or her faith through the viewing of cruel and inhuman acts against the faithful, representing 'above all the countless martyrs of all ages and both sexes, who [went to their deaths] with steadfast and happy faces, with intrepid hearts, and often accompanied by unheard of wonders of nature, such as fire that did not burn them, water that did not drown them, iron that did not cut them, winds sent whirling by their deaths, tremors of the earth showing its empathy and pain, and with other clearer and more wondrous signs of their true Faith.'[22] Thus Aristotle's identification of the audience with a 'middling' character (excessive in neither virtue nor vice) is replaced by the projection of the spectator onto a hero of the faith, a witness to the surprising power of religion. The spectator will have to be moved by the reflection and by the consideration that a great tragedy 'can even fall down upon us and hurl itself against us like a lightning bolt, but the more powerful such consideration and such reflection will be, the more innocent and good will be the person fallen in misery and affliction right before our eyes.'[23]

To better persuade and edify the spectators, therefore, it is important to exalt and amplify what they see by showing openly on stage the crudest situations and the cruellest actions, as Alessandro Donati suggests in his *Poetica*.[24] In the chapter on the dramatic role of the passions in animating and complicating the plot of the tragedy with the constant movement from one state of mind to another, Donati ponders whether it is opportune to represent killings on stage. Refuting the classical canon that preferred the use of messengers charged with recounting killings that had happened elsewhere, Donati proposes that Christian tragedies represent killings on stage. This choice is motivated by two dramaturgic considerations: the first regards the importance of real time in giving force to the performance event and specifies that 'no death-carrying act can be entrusted to narration since the act has already happened';[25] the second is the necessity of giving maximum visibility to the act itself, the apex of the dramatic event. Killings must 'happen' on stage so that the viewing of them can disturb and move the audience. In Christian tragedy, death means martyrdom, and the viewing of the martyr's suffering and death allows the spectator to reflect on the exemplary fate of the martyr and thus to promote his or her own spiritual elevation.

In the final scene of Donati's tragedy *Pirimalus Celiani princeps*, presented during the canonization festival of 1622, the protagonist, Pirimalo, is 'forcefully seized and imprisoned in a cloud, where, with barbarous cruelty, he is killed by his father'; then St Francis Xavier appears and 'forbids the audience to cry for the regal and glorious martyr Pirimalo.'[26]

The martyr's death scene often used another staging device: immediately following the death, light would erupt into the place of sacrifice. This sudden illumination of the scene prolongs the moment of sacrificial death and highlights the religious meaning of the drama, inverting the classical tragic ending by crowning the death of the martyr with the manifestation of the 'glory' of God.[27] The final scene for the tragedy *Sigismondo* describes the illumination of the martyr's death scene as 'revealing in the glory of the place of death, the glory that it has in heaven.'[28]

The eruption of light into the place of sacrificial death is, therefore, the theatrical representation of a complex theological concept: it 'brings to light,' as it were, the fundamental cooperative tie between God and Man by which the sacrificial act passes to the 'stage' of the supernatural. This commingling of the earthly act of martyrdom and the higher level of divine meaning is characteristic of both ancient and Christian tragedies. And yet, in classical culture, the connection between human and divine has a different value, represented with stage devices of a different orientation: the *deus ex machina* unties the dramatic knot by descending onto the stage, while the 'glory' machine indicates a direction of ascent. Although the drama concludes with the death of the hero, this final ascent places the mournful ending within Christian eschatology, conceiving death as an opening to and a prolongation of life in eternal salvation. What we have, if you will, is a sort of *happy ending* where the prevailing element is not final recognition and surprise but the providential reading of history that transforms momentary defeats into glorious sacrifices.

Instruments of Stage Performance

The favourite subjects of the Collegio Romano's seventeenth-century 'Christian tragedies' were the lives of the Christian princes, for the most part taken from Greek and Byzantine ecclesiastical writers, although the tragedies certainly did not neglect the lives of the saints and martyrs recounted in the numerous hagiographies revisited by the most recent Christian historiography and contained primarily in the previously cited *Annales* by Cesare Baronio.

The sources having been discovered and the stories recovered, the latter had to be given a form that could be performed on stage using the techniques and materials, the instruments and the practices of the dramatic arts. Just as painters use colour and sculptors marble, so the poetic instruments adopted for the staging of a play, Alessandro Donati recalled, were three: *oratio, harmonia,* and *rhytmus.*[29] While the exposition of the word was based on poetry and metrics, harmony consisted in the *musicus concentus*, that is, the sounds and songs of the musicians accompanying the action of the scenes. In the most common arrangement, the musicians in the pulpit accompanied the recitation of the actors on stage. Rhythm, on the other hand, was provided by the *mimorum saltatio*, the dance of the mimes, who, 'with clever gesticulation, movement, and dance,' repeated in the orchestra what the actors had recited on stage.

While generally faithful to these customary practices, seventeenth-century Jesuit stage productions combined the three components or instruments of the drama in multiple ways that were also subject to variation between productions of the same work. It is still possible, however, to trace some specific developmental trends through the various productions, especially with regard to movement and dance. In the first decades of the century, the collective entrances of the chorus 'with promenades' rather quickly become 'evolutions and intertwinings' that compose geometric figures on the stage. In the first chorus of the 1622 production of *Ignatio in Monserrato*, for example, there are some young men accompanied by four queens who 'partly with a song, partly with a promenade' represent 'the ancient chorus in the movements of the heavens and stillness of the earth, doubling themselves now in a semicircle, now in a line, with evolutions, dances, labyrinths, knots, spirals, and other martial movements transferred to the stage. Adding to all this, other figures of stars, moons, lilies, and coats of arms of the Ludovisi family, for variety and embellishment of the chorus.'[30] Clearly, what we have here is a description of 'figurative dance,' which later on, beginning in the 1630s, would give rise to complex narrative choreographies that came to take the form of pantomimes with songs and music.

Song, music, and dance were not adjunct instruments but structural components of the art of theatre. They were used not only in the chorus to mark the passage from one act to the next, but also in the prologue and as solemn accompaniment to the triumphant entrances of the characters, or, integrated with or superimposed on other actions, to underline, amplify, or illustrate the dramatic situation.

In productions the subject of which was the lives of the 'Christian princes' or in scenes representing armed conflict or knightly combat, military games such as 'barriers' or 'batterings' took on an important role. These games, as can once again be seen in *Ignatio in Monserrato,* were staged in accordance with precise rules 'regarding both the use and handling of arms and steps and manoeuvres, and the entrances and exits of everyone who is represented in a military manner.'[31] In these parades and battles the cavaliers identified themselves by exhibiting their own insignia and emblems.

There were other ways of and other occasions for inserting emblems into the narrative structure of the work, the use of which touched off a linguistic and visual amplification tied to the more immediate perception of images. The use of emblems thus contributed to an accentuated development of the *illustratio*, which in the classical rhetorical tradition was defined as a choice to show rather than tell in order to provoke in viewers 'the same affections that strike us when we are present at events.'[32] Illustrative elements of representation, such as emblems and visual effects, thus open up a space for evocation while introducing a suspension of time into the narration; they provoke, that is, an effect that could be described as estrangement or distraction with respect to the flow of the story that depends on the words recited by an actor.

Emblems were iconographic-verbal compositions that, by virtue of the special relationships and reciprocal qualification between word and image, involved complex operations of rhetoric and brought into play contents that were both moral and spiritual. The association between the image – the body – and the textual parts (*inscriptio* and *subscriptio*) – the soul – was supposed to achieve a unity of meaning, which rendered the two elements of the emblem mutually penetrating and complementary. It was precisely this operation of putting the two parts into relation that constituted the foundation of emblematic language. This form of expression was left concealed by the rhetorical procedures that constructed it since the emblem was nothing more than the act of ideation of the person who wrote it. It was a 'signification of the concept of the soul, which is performed with appropriate similar images,' as Torquato Tasso once explained to a certain count from Aversa.[33]

As a reification of a concept, an emblem was meant to establish a close correspondence between the idea and the two parts – visual and verbal – of the composition, by resorting to any semantic code or any rhetorical link that might allow for their association. The bold juxtapositions and the erudite associations brought into play in their composition produced an ingenious construction of illuminating synthesis. The *ingenium* that supported this process made use of and at the same time developed that 'marvellous force of the intellect' that Emanuele Tesauro[34] called wit.

Wit effected a semantic transfer by syllogism, or, through example or paradigm, by induction. With regard to the relationship between emblems and wit – a word and virtue born of the *argumentum* – Tesauro declared that emblematic compositions are metaphors, that is, they 'signify one thing by another and not by its own terms'; metaphors, 'by leading the mind no less than words, from one genre to another, express a concept by means of another very different concept, finding the similarity in the dissimilar.'[35] This metaphorical essence of the emblem, proposed by Tesauro, attributes a function to reasoning in the composition of metaphorical discourse, thus producing a substantial reversal of the tradition of classical rhetoric, for which the metaphor belonged to the *ornatus*, which was added as ornament to or simple revival of an already formed idea. According to Tesauro, the metaphor, although still anchored in the *elocutio*, becomes a figure of thought rather than a figure of discourse, precisely because the metaphor becomes a constitutive element of argument. The conception of metaphor as a figure of thought is even more distinct in the analysis of a contemporary of Tesauro, the German Jesuit Jacob Masen, outlined in his book *Speculum imaginum veritatis occultae*, published in Cologne in 1650.[36] With regard to the construction of emblematic compositions, Masen too refers to wit – or, as he himself defines it, to the 'ars nova argutiarum'[37] – as the highest genre of the first part of rhetoric, the *inventio*. It was not a question, therefore, even for Masen, of having recourse to a figure of style tied to elocution, but rather of utilizing the places of comparison and contrast (*similia atque contraria*), which have their foundation in thought.

Of all the architecture employed in these elaborate rhetorical processes, however, the only part that remained visible was the facade, or rather the emblem, so that to the deciphering ability or the erudite sensibility of the most expert spectators was left the pleasure or the task of figuring out the key and identifying the hidden structures. The spectator's enjoyment was all in the difficulty of discovering and therefore in the pleasure of resolving the refined riddles of composition – in 'recognizing' the steps in the composition process and in retracing, in the opposite direction, the route travelled by the author. This mechanism gave rise to the 'double pleasure' referred to by Tesauro, between 'he who creates it' and 'he who perceives it,' 'because the one takes pleasure in giving life in the intellect of the other to his noble creation, while the other takes delight in stealing with his own invention that which the invention of the first had so furtively concealed.'[38] This reciprocal interaction, rooted in the discovery of what had been hidden, in what is unsaid, or in what is only sketched rather than fully drawn, was the soul of emblematic expression.

Masen addresses the spectator's deciphering of the emblem in chapter 4 of his *Speculum*. He identifies in the reciprocal interaction between image and epigram a relationship analogous to that which makes complementary opposites of the composition and the resolution of the drama, revealing how the theatrical contradiction between appearance and substance, between the figure shown and the thing signified, is concentrated and repeated in the synthesis of every emblem. 'In truth, the deciphering of the emblem,' writes the German author, 'whether it takes the form of verse or prose, explains the thing represented through the figure that is shown and establishes a comparison between the *protasis* and the *apodosis*.'[39] In classical rhetoric, the two rhetorical procedures, *protasis* and *apodosis,* correspond to the composition and the successive resolution of the dramatic knot or intrigue. The *protasis*, in fact, is the phase of preparation and information that creates a situation, or rather it is that part of the dramatic composition in which the subject of the work is developed; by providing the characterizing elements of the situation it performs the function of creating tension and expectation in the spectator. The *apodosis*, on the other hand, is the phase in which the tension is resolved and relaxed.

With regard to the emblem, the process of the *expositio*, or rather of its deciphering, takes place when the *protasis*, which obviously corresponds to the image shown, and the *apodosis*, constituted by the thing signified, are brought together in the *collatio*, the operation of comparison of the two parts carried out by the spectator.

The homology of the rhetorical processes used in both dramatic and emblematic composition suggests how emblems, inserted in theatrical productions as linguistic or visual amplifications, amount to so many dramatic syntheses proposed to the audience as 'portraits' or 'reflections' of the drama, in an amazing game of mirrors on the stage.

These visual-verbal amplifications are nevertheless inserted in the main structure of the representation, where the dramatic story line and the recitation of the actors obviously have the dominant role, and where the *oratio*, or the instrument of the word and of oral expression, though accompanied by the *harmonia* and the *rhytmus*, imposes itself as the principal poetic component of the language of theatre.

In the Italian edition of *Il gigante*, Father Leone Santi declared it necessary to use the 'vernacular' because the use of Italian 'opens up, facilitates, and ensures understanding of the sacred enterprises of the ancient Heroes.'[40] Justified by the need to communicate with the audience, Italian was thus introduced into public performances after having already been adopted since the beginning of the century – as we have said – in 'domestic' productions and in the recreational competitions between dormitories in the Seminario Romano. Italian would be used again in 1644 by the prestigious Sforza Pallavicino, whose publication of *Ermenegildo*[41] definitively sanctioned its diffusion. From this point on, tragedies performed in Latin exclusively by future priests would alternate with those performed in Italian by lay residents of the dormitories. For several decades, however, the Italian versions of dramatic texts continued to be translations of the original Latin. Not until the early 1670s were plays composed in Italian.

There is certainly a close connection between the emergence and expanded use of the Italian language in Jesuit dramaturgy and the literary and linguistic commitment of the Roman Jesuits, which would reach its apogee in 1655, with the critical and polemical *summa* against the prescriptions of the Accademia della Crusca, written by Father Daniello Bartoli and entitled *Il torto e il dritto del non si può*.[42]

This dichotomy leads to two further, closely related considerations. First, we must take account of some observations regarding orality in reference to verse recitation and the application of the rules of prosody and metrics on the part of the actor. Second, some evaluation must be made concerning the consequences for Jesuit theatre, and particularly for its pedagogical function, of the passage to recitation in Italian.

In dramatic compositions, the *numerus* – understood as the rhythmic division in which quantitative values and accents alternate with regularity – constitutes the basic structure on which one composes and subsequently performs the verses; both the author and the actor are evidently aware of the oral quality of a text composed in verses. The oral quality and character of the composition is further reinforced by the variety of the verses (and therefore of rhythms) used in the dramatic literature of the Jesuits. A recent study has highlighted the ample freedom of versification exercised by Jesuit authors, who were able to use equally well the metrics of tragedy and of comedy, and who often created 'mixed forms' derived from the combination of two different metrics.[43]

In the tragedies written in Italian by Leone Santi and Pietro Sforza Pallavicino, hendecasyllabic verses are mixed with septenarii, and, as the verse develops, the rhyme scheme accentuates the harmony produced by the succession of long and short verses. Sforza Pallavicino defended the frequent recourse to rhyme in his *Ermenegildo* on the ground that it 'brings delight to the ear, wonder to the intellect, and aid to memory.'[44] The metric structure of his work, and its free alternation of hendecasyllables, septenarii, and rhyme, endow the text with a vivaciously descriptive quality, accentuating the visual effects of the stage production. At the same time, the primary objective of this variety of versification was to give maximum play to the musicality of the recited text.

It is well known that the Jesuit schools placed high value on exercises tied to prosody and metrics. Through exercises related to the *numerus oratorius*, based on the alternation of numerical groups of feet, pauses, and caesurae, the teaching of rhetoric enters into relationship with the structure of language and the metrics of verse. Versification, as the union of syntax and arithmetic, taught students the habit of achieving musical rhythm through artificial measure and abstraction from meaning. This exercise effected an important change in verse recitation, as actors learned to respect and highlight structure and rhythm rather than meaning and the logical nexus of the words. For the actor, syllables and rhythms count (even in the literal sense) more than words. In the attempt to come to terms with the verse, the actor finds that the verbs 'to understand' and 'to feel' present themselves as verbs separate from and complementary to the verb 'to listen'; the actor must listen to the verse before he speaks it because 'understanding' is first of all knowing and recognizing the metrics of the verse.

Paradoxically, this suspension of meaning to the advantage of musicality is what ensures greater comprehension of the dramatic text; the more the vocal action of the actor embraces the metrics of the verse, the better the audience understands its meaning. The paradox of the greater intelligibility of the dramatic text in relation to a greater musicality of its recitation in verses had been discovered by Cicero, who observed that 'entire theatres rebel against the pronunciation of a verse if one syllable is longer or shorter, and yet the crowd doesn't know anything about the feet or the metre of the verses.'[45]

The application of these sophisticated rhetorical procedures in the context of the Collegio Romano suggests a relationship between the choice of Italian and the attempt to achieve a more authentic orality and a more refined musicality. The orality and the musicality of verse thus become the two greatest contributions that practical theatrical experience brings to the training of the modern orator, who must enrich his command of the language that is used in the life of society.

This brief journey through the Jesuits' 'way of proceeding'[46] in the world of theatre – from production techniques to rhetorical procedures, from emblematic forms to methods of recitation – has allowed us to recapitulate the development of a 'theatre practice,' born as a pedagogical complement, which extended its scope to become, over the course of the seventeenth century, a complement to the school and the life of the Jesuit college. This important cultural phenomenon, however, has left nothing more than a labile memory in Italian culture, and historical studies showing an appreciation of its importance are rare. A major factor in this operation of cultural repression has certainly been the severe judgment of Jesuit culture, considered an expression of the Counter Reformation and a decisive element of baroque 'decadence' compared to the glorious Renaissance, expressed by Benedetto Croce,[47] the most influential Italian historian of the twentieth century.

And yet, paradoxically, Croce himself attenuates his attribution of decadence, when he admits that such a definition is the product of comparison and is, therefore, 'an empirical and relative fact.' Furthermore – as Giovanni Getto[48] has observed – his evaluation does not preclude Croce from highlighting several positive aspects of Jesuit culture. Despite its decadence, he recognizes and highly values the contribution of all those who dedicated themselves to the elaboration and divulgation of extremely significant artistic and cultural activities: the heritage of 'stylistic training,' 'initiation in the secrets of art,' 'literary and artistic education' that Italian masters of rhetoric, court poets, painters and architects, choir directors, singers, and actors spread throughout Europe was, in Croce's words, 'a kind of last benefit that old Italy bestowed on European culture.'[49]

The degree to which the Jesuit fathers were among the architects and promoters of this 'benefit' seems evident. To be sure, this does not authorize us to attribute to Croce an implicit and involuntary recognition of their contribution; but the enormous amount of activity performed and the great cultural influence exercised by the most powerful and most vital pedagogical institution of the time are indisputable – and Croce certainly knew it. In any event, with regard to our field and methods of research, we need not hesitate to place his name, and his indubitable prestige, among those who have highlighted the value of these cultural practices and ultimately of the theatre that contained and diffused them in the climate of a century marked by its reinvention and affirmation.

NOTES

1 Famiano Strada, *Saggio delle feste che si apparecchiano nel Collegio Romano in honore de' Santi Ignatio, Francesco ...* (Rome, 1622).
2 Strada, *Saggio*, pp. 2–6.
3 'spoils of Egypt': expression used by St Ignatius in a letter to Diego Laínez on 30 March 1555, to indicate the use of pagan culture in a Christian key; see *MI Epp* 8:618 and 9:122. On expurgation of classical texts, see Pierre-Antoine Fabre, 'Dépouille d'Egipte, l'expurgation des auteurs ...,' Giard *Jés. Ren.*, pp. 54–76.
4 APUG 2800, 2801, 2802, Girolamo Nappi, *Annali del Seminario Romano*.
5 On theatrical life of the Seminario Romano, see Luigi Mezzadri, *Il Seminario Romano. Storia di un'istituzione di cultura e di pietà* (Turin, 2001), pp. 259–81.
6 This methodological approach owes much to Michel de Certeau's work, particularly to the reading of a chapter that was described by Dominique Julia as 'one of the most difficult chapters, but maybe the most foundational for some generations of historians': 'La formalité des pratiques du système religieux à l'éthique des Lumières (XVII–XVIII),' in *L'écriture de l'histoire* (Paris, 1975), pp. 153–212; cf. Dominique Julia, 'Un histoire en acte,' in *Le voyage mystique, Michel de Certeau*, ed. Luce Giard (Paris, 1988), pp. 103–23.
7 *M Paed.* 7:428–30; on the crisis in the teaching of rhetoric, see *M Paed.* 6:25*–31*; on the institutional and cultural impact of this crisis, see Mario Zanardi, 'Sulla genesi del "Cannocchiale aristotelico" di Emanuele Tesauro,' *Studi seicenteschi* 23 (1982): 3–61.
8 For this distinction, see Andrea Battistini and Ezio Raimondi, *Le figure della retorica* (Turin, 1990), pp. 147–91; and Florence Vuilleumier, 'Les conceptismes,' in *Histoire de la rhétorique dans l'Europe moderne (1450–1950)*, ed. Marc Fumaroli (Paris, 1999), pp. 517–37.
9 On Sarbiewski's work and his stay in Rome, see Irene Mamczarz, 'La trattatistica dei gesuiti e la pratica teatrale ...,' in *I gesuiti e i primordi del teatro barocco in*

Europa, ed. Miriam Chiabò and Federico Doglio (Rome, 1995), pp. 349–60; the preface by Jean-Marie Valentin in Matthias Casimir Sarbiewski, *Choix de poèmes lyriques* (Paris, 1995); and Vuilleumier, 'Les conceptismes,' pp. 524–5.

10 According to Nappi, the presence of Roman noblewomen dates from 1629 (APUG 2801, 803); on the Jesuits during the papacy of Urban VIII, see Marc Fumaroli, 'Cicero Pontifex Romanus: La tradition rhétorique du Collège Romain et les principes inspirateurs du mécenat des Barberini,' *Mélanges de l'Ecole française de Rome: Moyen âge – temps modernes* 90 (1978): 798–835; and Fumaroli, *L'âge de l'éloquence* (Geneva, 1980), pp. 202–26.

11 For an analysis of one seventeenth-century summer's collection for the Collegio Romano and Seminario Romano, see Bruna Filippi, *Il teatro degli argomenti. Gli scenari seicenteschi del teatro gesuitico romano, Catalogo analitico*, Bibliotheca Instituti Historici S.I. 54 (Rome, 2001).

12 Pietro Sforza Pallavicino, *Vindicationes Societatis Iesu* ... (Rome, 1649), p. 118.

13 For the 'visible' and its recovery after the Council of Trent, see especially Alphonse Dupront, 'Le concile de Trente,' in his *Le Concile et les conciles* (Chevetogne, 1960), pp. 195–243.

14 Tarquinio Galluzzi, *Virgiliane vindicationes et commentarii tres de tragoedia, comoedia, elegia* (Rome, 1621).

15 Galluzzi, *Virgiliane*, p. 266.

16 Ibid., p. 271.

17 Ibid., p. 272.

18 Leone Santi, *Il gigante* (Rome, 1632), p. 7.

19 On perspective and its paradigm, see the work of synthesis and anthology edited by Philippe Hamou, *La vision perspective (1435–1740). L'art et la science du regard, de la Renaissance à l'âge classique* (Paris, 1995); on visual culture and its transformations in the seventeenth century, see Carl Havelange, *De l'oeil et du monde. Une histoire du regard au seuil de la modernité* (Paris, 1998).

20 Tarquinio Galluzzi, *Rinovazione dell'antica tragedia e difesa del Crispo* (Rome, 1633), p. 59.

21 Galluzzi, *Rinovazione*, p. 48.

22 Ibid., p. 63.

23 Ibid., p. 50.

24 Allessandro Donati, *Ars Poetica libri tres* (Bologna, 1659; Rome, 1931).

25 Donati, *Ars Poetica*, p. 210.

26 Allessandro Donati, *Scenario del Pirimalo* (Rome, 1623), p. 14; see Filippi, *Il teatro*, pp. 104–12.

27 For a review of the theme of light and glory with respect to the biblical imagination in the Christian tradition, see Jean Robert Armogathe, 'Le Grand Siècle et la Bible,' in *Bible de tous le temps*, ed. Jean Robert Armogathe (Paris, 1989); and Hans Urs von Balthasar, *Gloria. Un'estetica teologica*, vol. 2 (Milan, 1964).

28 *Argomento del Sigismondo* (Rome, 1617), p. 8; see Filippi, *Il teatro*, pp. 79–83.

29 Donati, *Ars Poetica*, pp. 138–9.

30 *Soggetto d'Ignatio in Monserrato* (Rome, 1623), p. 4: see Filippi, *Il teatro*, p. 100.

31 *Soggetto d'Ignatio*, p. 6; see Filippi, '"Grandes et petites actions" au Collège Romain. Formation rhétorique et théâtre jésuite au XVIIe siècle,' in *Cérémonial et rituel à Rome (XVI–XIX siècle)*, ed. Maria Antonetta Visceglia and Catherine Brice (Rome, 1997), pp. 177–99.

32 Quintilian, Institutio Oratoria VI 32.

33 Torquato Tasso, *Dialogo delle imprese* (Naples, 1594), p. 17.

34 Emanuele Tesauro, *Il cannocchiale aristotelico o sia, Idea dell'arguta* (Venice, 1682; 1st ed. Turin, 1654), p. 51.

35 Tesauro, *Il cannocchiale*, p. 164.

36 Jacob Masen, *Speculum imaginum veritatis occultæ, exhibens symbola* (Cologne, 1650); see Barbara Bauer, *Jesuitische 'Ars Rhetorica' im Zeitalter der Glaubenskämpfe* (Frankfurt, 1986), pp. 461–541.

37 Jacob Masen, *Ars nova argutiarum* (Cologne, 1649).

38 Tesauro, *Il cannocchiale*, p. 11.

39 'Expositio vero, sive illa versibus, sive oratione soluta absolvatur, rem per figuram significatam explicat, ac comparationem protasis cum apodosi instituit': Masen, *Speculum*, p. 561.

40 Santi, *Il gigante*, p. 3.

41 Pietro Sforza Pallavicino, *Ermenegildo martire* (Rome, 1644).

42 Daniello Bartoli, *Il torto e il dritto del non si può* (Rome, 1655).

43 *Triumphus divi Michaelis Archangeli Bavarici. Triumph des heiligen Michael, Patron Bayerns (München, 1597)*, ed. Barbara Bauer and Jürgen Leonhardt (Munich, 2000), pp. 104–6.

44 Sforza Pallavicino, *Ermenegildo*, p. 146.

45 Cicero, *De oratore,* p. 51.

46 For this interpretative category, see O'M. *Jes. Cult.*, pp. 27–9.

47 Benedetto Croce, *Storia dell'età barocca in Italia* (Bari, 1929); on Croce, Counter Reformation, and the baroque age, see John W. O'Malley, *Trent and All That: Renaming Catholicism in the Early Modern Era* (Cambridge, MA, 2000), pp. 34–5; for an in-depth study of the idea of 'decadence' in Croce's work, see Filippi, 'Benedetto Croce et le vide de la décadence du Seicento,' *Cahiers du Centre de recherches historiques* 28–9 (2002): 215–22.

48 Giovanni Getto, 'La polemica sul barocco,' in his *Il barocco letterario in Italia* (Milan, 2000), pp. 377–470.

49 Benedetto Croce, *Storia*, ed. Guiseppe Galasso (Milan, 1993), p. 62.

24 / The Jesuit Stage and Theatre in Milan during the Eighteenth Century

GIOVANNA ZANLONGHI

Introduction: Dramatic Texts and 'Apparati: The Two Faces of Jesuit Theatricality

A consideration of the theatre of the Jesuits in Milan during the eighteenth century can benefit from inquiry into what the theatre had been for the Society of Jesus in the previous century, in order to allow a focus on the dialectic between continuity and change. The central question is whether the Jesuit theatre was merely a series of plays performed by the Jesuits' students, an experience confined within the school walls, and nothing else. My research concerning the history of Brera University shows that it may be restrictive to consider the theatre only from that point of view. A rich and homogeneous array of documents suggests that the college performances and the parallel spectacle of the *apparati*, both generated by the same historical occasion and dedicated to the city, should be seen in close connection. In fact, the Jesuits' theatre was one with the life of the city in which it developed.

Recent historiography has shown that Milan was then a strategic centre in the Spanish Empire. When the city was called upon to celebrate a special civic event, the authorities would set the Jesuits the task of orchestrating the celebration. The celebrations were invariably spectacular, designed to enhance the political status of the city of Milan. They were displays of civic pride and civic hope articulated in great *apparati*, around which were centred long and elaborate festivities. Such displays are so far from our present-day experience that on the surface they might seem merely formal commemorations of the death of a king or of an important wedding, but in fact they were symbolic constructions designed to exhibit and strengthen civic and religious values. The Jesuits – and more specifically the professors of rhetoric at Brera University – were regularly involved in organizing both theatrical performances in their schools and *teatri effimeri,* 'ephemeral theatres,' built for the occasion and later dismantled. The school theatre was the 'private' aspect of these public spectacles. The plays were performed in the universities at the same time that the *apparati* were on display, and to celebrate the same event. We cannot possibly study or understand the Jesuit theatre if we sever the link between the Jesuits' stage and the city's festive celebrations. As Michel de Certeau suggested in *La fable mystique,* we can imagine a triangle consisting of an event, a festivity, and a symbolic-rhetorical performance. As a community that shared and reflected the high culture of Milan, the Jesuits became the centre of gravity of this symbolic triangle.

More precisely, it was the same purpose that nourished the relationship and exchanges between the two. On the occasion of an event of significance for the city, the 'all-inclusive' Jesuit rhetoric was called upon to become the 'grammar' of symbolic presentations. It is my belief that the Jesuits' contribution founded itself on the notion of the rhetoric of the image as a sort of language that could communicate to the person as a totality, body, soul, and heart. Such a conclusion is perfectly in line with the Jesuits' anthropology, of which the fundamental notion of the human person as a unity is of special interest in our day.

I shall therefore focus on the so-far unexplored relationship between the Jesuits' theatre, traditionally connected to the teaching activity of the college, and the creation of *apparati effimeri* in the baroque period. I shall then consider how the Jesuits in Milan faced the challenge of opening up to the novel features introduced by the Century of Lights, when their theatre was confined to the college stage. To that end, I shall examine a cross-section of the theatrical activity at Milan's Collegio dei Nobili, and the interplay between Jesuit culture and the culture of the Enlightenment in Milan and beyond.

An Example of Seventeenth-Century Interpretation: Emanuele Tesauro and the Commemoration of the Death of King Philip III

The Ephemeral Apparatus: A 'Pantheon of Virtues'

A great celebration was held in Milan on 7 June 1621 to commemorate King Philip III of Spain, who had died on 31 March. The civic authorities assigned the rhetorical *inventio* to Emanuele Tesauro, who was professor of rhetoric at Brera,[1] and the design of the catafalque to Giovanni Leonardo Rinaldi[2] (fig. 24.1). A description of the event has survived in a report written by Tesauro himself,[3] and the iconographic document is to be found in the engraving by Cesare Bassano, which today belongs to the Civica Raccolta delle Stampe Achille Bertarelli di Milano.[4]

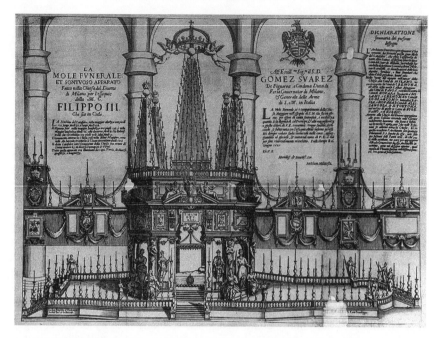

24.1. Giovanni Leonardo Rinaldi, catafalque for Philip III. From *Racconto delle sontuose essequie fatte in Milano alli 7 di giugno l'anno 1621* (Milan, 1621). Photo courtesy of Civica Raccolta delle Stampe Achille Bertarelli, Milan.

Several things combined to make the 1621 event one of extraordinary relevance. From the historical point of view, it was the first Milanese funeral ceremony for a Spanish king in the seventeenth century. From the rhetorical point of view, it was even more prestigious in being created by Emanuele Tesauro. This celebrated Jesuit had already written two dramatic texts and had ushered in the new rhetorical trends, which in the early seventeenth century bore the mark of *concettismo* and a taste for wittiness. He was also a keen emblematist, as testified by his *Idea delle perfette imprese*, written during the same period.[5] The authorship of the rhetorical creation was acknowledged by the great connoisseur Father Claude-François Menestrier, who mentioned it in his book *Des décorations funèbres* as an example to be imitated when writing funerary inscriptions.[6]

Last but not least, the 1621 event offers a rare example of a celebration in which the *apparatus* can be illuminated by an ample theoretical re-elaboration.

Connections can be made with both Tesauro's *Il cannocchiale aristotelico*, probably completed during these years, and his later *Filosofia morale*, the ultimate systematization of the traditional Aristotelian-Thomistic thought the Society had assimilated.

Using Tesauro's account as a guide, we shall analyse the *dispositio*, so as to show the internal articulation of the *apparatus*, or, in Tesauro's words, the *ossatura* (skeleton) of a strategic plan designed to involve the intellect and the *potentia imaginativa*, and based on an awareness that 'ogni persuasione si fa con le ragioni,' all persuasion can be brought about by giving reasons.[7]

The facade of Milan Cathedral, where the 1621 ceremony was held, was covered for the occasion with black and silver-coloured velvet palls, bearing figures of skeletons and of two angels blowing the trumpets of the Last Judgment. The rhetorical function of such paraments was the *triumphum mortis*, the proclamation of the king's death, which would penetrate to the consciences of the Milanese people and arouse their reflection on the meaning of life. Hence the depiction of virtues inside the church, as a means of restoring a sense of the significance of individual and collective life and of history itself, which death had apparently obliterated. The dead king was the symbolic figure embodying the virtues of the 'body politic.'

While the facade served as an *exordium*, the rhetorical distribution of the various parts in the indoor display – emblems, statues, pictures – was much more complex. The displays of the *apparatus* can be considered a visual moral discourse. The vehicle for this picture language was provided by the careful symbolic arrangement of the virtues in the space of the church. Here, I shall concentrate on the ephemeral constructions in the central nave. When people entered the church, they were steeped in a symbolic ambience. In the long and fascinating array of statues and emblems thronging the nave, transept, and choir, the succession of cardinal virtues, in their double incarnations of 'daughter virtues'[8] and corresponding to the pillars, alternated regularly with the figures of the several dominions of the empire, placed in the intercolumns (fig. 24.2). The order of appearance of the eight 'daughter virtues' clearly confirms the argumentative character of the *apparatus*, in turn suggested by the moral hierarchy it portrayed. Justice and Prudence, the two virtues of the intellect, occupied the whole of the central nave in a pre-eminent position. In a secondary position in the transepts, being morally subordinate, were displayed Temperance and Fortitude, the two virtues regulating the *anima sensitiva*. By placing the virtues of the *anima intellectiva* in a pre-eminent position, Tesauro suggested the educational intention behind the whole operation: to propose a well-defined ethos valid for the civic life of the individual as well as a metaphorical *institutio principis*.

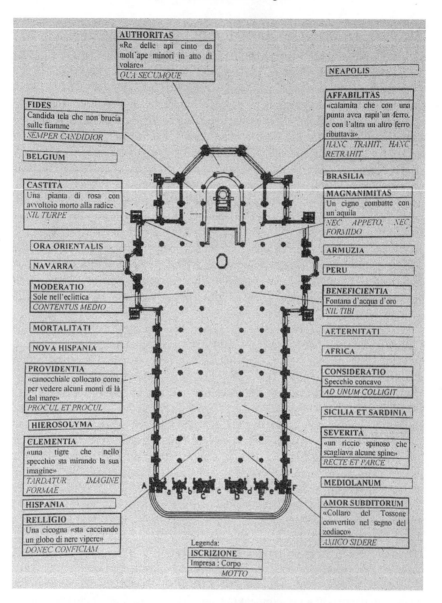

24.2. The obsequies of Philip III in Milan Cathedral, 1621: the parade of the virtues in the central nave. From *Racconto delle sontuose essequie*.

The inspirational theme of the rhetorical *inventio* was the cardinal virtues, and Prudence in particular. Prudence was the only one of the four cardinal virtues to appear in the central nave, where it was presented in the double form of the two 'virtù potenziali od integrali' (potential or integral virtues)[9] of Providence and Consideration, as well as on the catafalque. Here Prudence was placed on the side of the octagon facing the altar, thereby representing the civic and military Prudence the virtuous sovereign had earned through *industria* and had offered to God. According to scholastic teaching, Prudence nourishes the manifold tasks of civic and political life – 'ella comunica il ben consigliare, il ben giudicare, il ben commandare,' it is conducive to good advice, good judgment, and good command.[10] In politics, Prudence is therefore the 'scienza de' regi,' the science of kings, and as such it enables the prince to combine justice and wisdom, thus making him similar to God.[11]

Prudence, however, in being a virtue 'imagine della divina,' also reverberates down onto lower levels of morality; it is therefore a virtue for the father, in the form of 'economic prudence,' and for the single individual, in the form of 'monastic prudence.' A man can be a good sovereign only if he is a good father. Economic prudence, meant as the virtue of family or the virtue of amicable and social relations, found its specific 'application' in the virtues of Liberality and Affability, which are indispensable to social life. Prudence, in short, forms the individual conscience at various levels, from that belonging to the highest dignity of a sovereign down to everyday 'monastic prudence.'[12] It even encompasses the most intimate human virtues, such as Chastity and Moderation, which demand an appropriate measure of emotion obtained through a sensible use of passion and an alert 'politics of the soul.' An ethical-political scheme of this kind was relevant not only to the public conduct of those in high political circles but to the behaviour of every individual.

Yet, once again, Prudence was not merely the moral object of the *apparatus*: prudent individuals were also the ideal spectators of this *teatro effimero* – those who, by purifying themselves of their passions, become capable of judgment. In fact, while non-prudent creatures such as animals and children are merely moved by 'imagini singolari, corporee e sensibili' (singular, concrete, and perceptible images) and do not turn them into 'regole della ragione' (rules of reason), prudent individuals compare and connect until they are able to formulate 'proposizioni generali.' The combination of all the images of moral virtues ostentatiously submitted to the audience's view by the *apparatus* formed a well-organized microcosm of 'imagini singolari, corporee e sensibili' by means of which prudent individuals could deduce and judge, observe and learn, exercising intellect and will, through the help of images.

The Production of the Tragedy Hermenegildus:
The Theme of the Prince-Saint

The tragedy *Hermenegildus* was performed at the Collegio di Brera on 26 August 1621, approximately two months after the celebration of Philip III's funeral in Milan Cathedral. The only extant trace of the performance is to be found in the manuscript preserved in Turin's Royal Library. The title, *Hermenegildus. Tragoedia Emanuele Tesauro in Braydensi collegio rhetoricae professore auctore. Habita die 26 Aug. anno 1621 D. Hermenegildo votum auctoris*, makes explicit reference to the occasion of the stage production.

As was customary, the tragedy is written in Latin verse, and keeps to the structural canons of the genre – five acts of six scenes each, with choruses concluding each act. The story of St Hermenegild had long been circulating in the network of Jesuit colleges. The earliest known version was probably the one written by Father Pedro de Acevedo and performed in Seville in 1580. The play incorporated several different motives: veneration of local patron saint; opposition to the Arian heresy, hinting at the topical subject of the conflict between Catholicism and Protestantism; and lastly, celebration of the historical foundation of the Spanish monarchy. The text probably became popular thanks to Father Nicolas Caussin's version, performed at La Flèche in 1615, published in the collection *Tragoediae sacrae* in Paris in 1620, and subsequently adapted several times even in German- and Italian-speaking colleges.[13] Within this tradition, Tesauro's work stands out on account of its depth and original style. The author mentions the historiographical sources for his subject-matter: Isidore, Pope Gregory I, Gregory of Tours, and Cesare Baronio.[14] From the dramatic point of view, however, the tragedy is indebted to the model of Seneca's *Thyestes*.

The plot narrates the story of Hermenegild, a sixth-century prince of the Visigoths. Having converted from Arianism to Christian orthodoxy, he is sent into exile by his father, King Leovigild of Spain, at the instigation of his wife, a staunch Arian, and the wicked counsellor Mysio. Hermenegild is later readmitted to the kingdom after the siege of Seville and a civil war against his father and his brother Reccared, and he is designated for succession to the throne provided he resumes his Arian faith. He refuses and is sentenced to death, and his brother is crowned king. After Hermenegild's death, however, Reccared realizes his wrongdoing, converts to Catholic Christianity, and makes Spain a Catholic kingdom.

The plot elaborates the motive behind martyrdom, weaving together scriptural elements – the martyr as representing Christ – and historical ones – the struggle against heresy. In tune with the themes dealt with in the funerary apparatus, the tragedy presents the exemplum of a prudent and saintly king, worthy of ruling over a Catholic kingdom. Thus the tragedy, like the *apparatus*, presents a reflection on prudence and imprudence, of which the various characters embody specific aspects.

Reccared talks, decides, and acts under the promptings of the 'imagini singolari, corporee e sensibili,' which nourish the *anima sensitiva*. He is unable to turn these images into 'rules of reason,' and he is imprudence itself, a slave to his passions, unable to move beyond a pre-rational state. Mysio, on the contrary, is a lucid, rational plotter who manipulates Reccared – another facet of culpable imprudence, in which the ability to 'dedurre e connettere dalle imagini particolari' is put to a negative use.

At times the 'prudence of the flesh' is generated by the inability to discern. Practical reason is consequently clumsy and unable to cope with the situation. This is the case of Leovigild, who in the face of events attempts some kind of solution but chooses the wrong strategy because he lacks full discernment.

Hermenegild is the only character in the tragedy to follow the true line of prudence. But even he reaches virtuous prudence only gradually. At first his behaviour simply follows natural prudence, that is, good discernment, but with the passage of time, when he has to choose between the values of politics and those of faith at the cost of his own life, his political prudence turns into 'infused virtue.' Hermenegild seeks strength in prayer and becomes progressively estranged with respect to human bonds, whether family affections or the desire for power.[15] The sanctifying catharsis undergone by the character is expressed in words that turn into prayer.[16]

The two 'texts' here, the *apparatus* and the play, present two parallel routes from contradiction to catharsis. The symbolic itineraries lead the intellect from contradiction to truth, and guide the emotions from disquietude to peace. In both cases prudence helps the individual to achieve full ability to judge reality and to exercise the 'virtù eroica,' or magnanimity. The latter, being an epitome of all the virtues, is the expression of human nature brought to the highest degree of perfection.[17] The figurative and the dramatic representation of this virtue are in perfect unison.

The Anthropological Foundations of Jesuit Theatre

A few questions will help illuminate the Jesuits' broad notion of theatre. What was the real purpose of this medium in Jesuit universities and colleges in the *ancien régime*? Why was it so frequently used as a pedagogical instrument?

What were its deep meaning and anthropological foundations? How do we account for such great emphasis on non-verbal language in a Tridentine culture, which was supposedly against any expression of corporeal language?

Some assumptions also need to be reconsidered, and the point made that the Roman Catholic church was no enemy of the theatre as such. The church was of course against 'lascivi spettacoli,' for the simple reason that such performances did not show the human spiritual dimension but only the most material aspects of the body. But a noble level of theatricality was accepted and even promoted. Behind it stood a notion of the human being that synthesized the various traditions that converged in the Jesuit system. Among these traditions was of course that of the *studia humanitatis*, of which rhetoric was the culmination. Rhetoric, as the examples here have shown, was not a mere ornament of discourse but a device that could ideally operate a profound change in the individual conscience. The Jesuits' 'total' rhetoric became an instrument towards an ideal of the person in which all that pertains to the senses – memory, fantasy, imagination – plays an active role in the cognitive life, thereby combining the psychological and emotional with the intellectual.

Rhetoric filters emotions and passions through words, images, and *actio*. It is able to reach the conscience and to fertilize society through imagination. This idea of language as tradition and transmission of moral treasures made the Jesuits' theatrical language a laboratory of memory, education, and pedagogy.

But how could the Jesuits expect to shape the students' consciences through words? By stressing the necessity of the 'phantasm' in the process of understanding, scholastic epistemology taught that the language of the senses is necessary to the human mind. Human beings are *Geist in Welt*. This famous and exhaustive definition by Karl Rahner means that whatever one thinks needs to be supported by 'fantastic,' that is, imaginative, language. It also means – and this is even more important – that one must return to imaginative language after abstraction, because the person is conscience at one with the body. *Phantasia, imaginatio, memoria, facultas cogitativa, sensus interior* need to be continuously referred to. They support the individual's approach to reality, which is a sort of 'work in progress.' The passage from the senses to the concept is not completed once and for all. After abstraction, the human intellect must return to the *phantasma*.[18] Against such a background, recourse to theatrics may be interpreted as the creation of a special psychological and cognitive space – that of the stage and that of the apparatus. This space was designed to provide formative activities in which imaginative re-creation, by activating memory, imagination, *adfectus*, and intelligence, taught the students to observe and judge reality in an orderly, conscious, well-oriented fashion. That is the reason why the theatre was so widely used. It was a way to assert, encourage, and express the anthropological unity of the human person. This is the special contribution of Jesuit spirituality, with its optimism and faith in human nature. Drama was called upon to ensure the full promotion of the human.[19]

Having outlined the principal features of the Jesuits' theatre in the seventeenth century, we can now move on to the new century and attempt to ascertain whether it was a period of decline, stasis, or growth.

The Jesuits' Theatre in Milan during the Eighteenth Century

From the Seventeenth to the Eighteenth Century

In the early eighteenth century there was continuity with the past. Recent historiography can guide our approach to the culture of this part of the century. Italian historians used to be conditioned by the category of 'pre-Enlightenment,' a term coined by Franco Venturi.[20] This category suggested that the first few years of the century should be interpreted as a sort of step towards the Enlightenment, in the wake of what John W. O'Malley calls 'a kind of cultural Darwinism.'

A rich harvest of information suggests, however, that we can now go beyond the sweeping generalization that the eighteenth century must be identified with liberation from superstition and political-ecclesiastical repression. In fact, changes ripened on the tree of classical culture, and the old and the new lived together. Thanks to its geographical position and political status, Milan can be a good observation point for such developments, as new ideas reached the city from Paris and London, the intellectual capitals of Europe, as well as from Vienna and the German lands.

The early eighteenth century is therefore double-faced. The studies of Paola Vismara on devotion in Milan, for instance, show that popular attachment to religion and the church was strong up to the 1750s.[21] Religious processions to pray for rain or for victory in battle were as frequent as in the previous century. At the same time, Ludovico Antonio Muratori, one of the most important Italian thinkers of the time, who lived and worked in Milan from 1690 to 1695, began to question the *regolata divozione*. *Buon gusto* became the leitmotif of the newborn poetic of the Arcadia, and a strong desire for rationalization and simplification was already spreading among the intelligentsia.

Milan was a city in which cultural academies were springing up. A colony of Arcadia met regularly in Carlo Pertusati's garden, where heated greenhouses were used in winter. One of the visitors to this circle in the 1710s was Father Tommaso Ceva, a poet, a member of Arcadia, and a literary critic of great insight. After entering the Society of Jesus as an adolescent, he devoted himself to teaching and to mathematical studies, a field in which he achieved important scientific results.[22] Yet he never abandoned his inclination to the humanities. Following his belief in an integrated model of learning, he also produced *inventiones* and accounts of festivities, epigrams and inscriptions, and numerous 'oratorios,' all published in Milan, as well as poetic compositions, collected in his *Carmina*.[23]

Ceva serves as a case in point of the cultural scenario at the turn of the century. His letters to Muratori reflect the whole intellectual dilemma of his time. The two horns of this dilemma were reason and the affections, *iudicium* and imagination, the verisimilar and the marvellous. On the one hand, Ceva shared the emerging sympathy for rationality, precision, and clarity, owing to his scientific mentality and practice; on the other, he was attracted by the new taste for obscurity and the imagination. His famous statement 'poetry is a dream made *in the presence* of reason'[24] reveals a divarication between reason and imagination. The predilection for what was 'small' and 'particular,' the defence of 'vagueness' and 'gracefulness' show a need to express 'naturalness' and 'evidence' as opposed to sixteenth-century magniloquence. Ceva was aware that the balance between the two was hard to reach. He believed that the verisimilar and the marvellous were the two souls of poetry, which he compared to two horses galloping in opposite directions. This made the poet 'un essere dimidiato: un po' pazzo e un po' savio,' a twofold creature, partly mad and partly sane.

One of Ceva's most significant creations was the funeral ceremony for Maria Anna of Austria in 1696. In the rhetorical *inventio* the images were clearly separated from the words: in the catafalque, the emotional impact was entrusted only to the image (fig. 24.3), whereas in the nave, words in the form of emblems and inscriptions added explicit commentaries to the portraits and statues of the queen's ancestors. This treatment represents a more rational approach to the use of figurative language, in tune with the desire for simplification typical of the era. Fiction and reason come together as complementary, but the pendulum was now definitely swinging towards rationalization.

Around the middle of the eighteenth century, Milanese political and cultural life reached a turning point. From the political point of view, 1741 ushered in an era of Austrian domination. The rise of a new patrician aristocracy open to jurisdictionalism and to anti-clerical attitudes reduced the Jesuits' involvement in public events. In the field of culture the break came around 1760, when Milan had already assimilated the philosophy of France and England. Empiricism and sensism from the English and rationalism from the French front undermined the traditional anthropological foundations of the Society. I shall briefly touch on the nature of the Jesuits' reaction to these changes and on the extent to which they accepted the challenge posed.

24.3. Giovanni Ruggeri, catafalque for Maria Anna of Austria. From Tommaso Ceva,
Esequie celebrate alla gloriosissima memoria della Serenissima Maria Anna Reina
di Spagna nel duomo di Milano il giorno 3 settembre 1696 …
Photo courtesy of Biblioteca Nazionale Braidense, Milan.

A key fact is that the Society of Jesus definitely lost its cultural monopoly in the city, at the same time as the Barnabite schools were springing up. The political authorities entrusted the Jesuits with the organization of civic festivities until 1741, when they orchestrated the public mourning for the death of Emperor Charles VI, Maria Theresa's father. But when, after that last public exhibition, the curtain dropped over the Jesuits' civic stage, another curtain was raised in their Collegio dei Nobili.

This college, founded in Milan in 1682, was now one of the most important schools in Milan. The curriculum offered was first-class, and there were celebrated teachers. Some, such as Roger Boscovich, came from across the Alps. Jean-Jacques Rossignol came from France and proposed a reform of the curriculum: French and German were introduced besides Latin; music, astronomy, mathematics, physics, history, geography, hydrography, and the equestrian arts were regularly taught. As reported by Serviliano Latuada, the author of a famous eighteenth-century guidebook on the city of Milan, there hundreds of students were 'equally well educated, and with the greatest care, in the humanities as in the equestrian arts, being attended to by the most experienced teachers to be found in this city, as they publicly prove in the Academies and in the stage performances, where their training and learning can be admired.'[25] The plays were performed in the college's own theatre by boarders who were members of the college's academy.

All this goes to prove that the equation between the eighteenth century and a decline in and crisis of Jesuit culture is to be refuted. The fact remains that complex processes were under way, and the efforts to transform and adapt in the face of provocations from outside were not always made with the same degree of flexibility and open-mindedness. But the closure of the city stage did not imply the closure of the Jesuits' cultural interests and horizons.

The Accademia dei Vigorosi and Its Theatre

The rise of the academies has been acknowledged by Amedeo Quondam as one of the most relevant phenomena in the culture of the modern age, especially in Italy.[26] The academies provided one of the principal contexts for the elaboration and circulation of ideas, to the point that they can be considered a true 'vehicle' of culture. The *Ratio studiorum* of 1599 had already set out the rules and purposes of the school academies. Aiming at the all-round education of the individual, the academies undertook to offer opportunities for 'exercitationes ad studia pertinentes.' In fact, their activity served a twofold purpose. On the one hand, they were designed 'ad pietatem promovendam,' in tune with the entire pedagogical project of the Society of Jesus, in which even grammar was meant to shape the *civis* of the *respublica Christiana:* on the other hand, they were intended to cultivate the more technical aspects of education.[27]

One element of interest stands out, however. Although each activity at the academy was supposed to cultivate the mastery of speech, during the eighteenth century the emphasis gradually shifted towards the so-called equestrian arts. The decisive factor, as Quondam remarks, was that these colleges were meant *per nobili*, for the sons of noble families. Even ancillary subjects such as horse-riding, fencing, dancing, and exercising with pikes and flags were designed, like geography, history, and the modern languages, to provide a young man with an education that was in step with his era. The choice of those subjects derived from the non-dualistic idea of the individual that has repeatedly been referred to and that in this century was taking on a new colouring, thus making the common good of society the final goal of education.

The Milan community also modelled itself along these pedagogical lines. The activity of the Accademia dei Vigorosi at the Collegio dei Nobili most probably began in 1707, when *Lo scetro di Giove* was performed, and perhaps even as early as 1700.[28] We do not know what 'Vigorosi' refers to, and we know very little about the theatre building itself. Giuliana Ricci supposes the theatre may have been provided with boxes.[29] The plays were performed on the stage, and the equestrian arts were practised in the wide space of the parterre. The stage too must have been wide enough to contain the engines needed for rather complex and sophisticated scenarios featuring such things as sudden apparitions of deities, the gushing of water springs, the making and breaking of spells. Hardly anything is known about costumes, except for the brief and unspecific mention of a 'tragico abbigliamento,' tragic attire, to be worn for a performance held in 1765.[30]

What we do know for certain is that the Jesuits regularly put on two plays a year: a drama for Carnival and an *accademia* for the election of the Prince of the Academy at the end of the year. Then there were extraordinary performances marking particular events: one of these was the election of Ignazio Visconti as superior general of the Jesuits on 12 August 1752. The *accademia* performed on the occasion is an example of the structure of this genre, its main feature being that the script had become less important, whereas the non-verbal part had acquired greater pre-eminence. The performance in fact was an exhibition of ballet, songs, poetry with accompaniment, numerous equestrian exercises, dancing, and jousting. The actor on the stage was 'a body in action.' *Actio debet praecedere locutionem*, wrote Franz Lang in his essay of 1727. In Spanish theology, the human being is a unity of body and soul growing together. *Actio* fashions *adfectus*; rhetoric forms gesture, language, and self-discipline. The shift of emphasis towards *actio* is the eighteenth-century version of the Jesuits' educational theatre.

The *argumenta* preserved at the Brera National Library in Milan, in particular those of the plays performed between 1748 and 1768, prove that new, 'modern' interests now stood side by side with classical themes on the stage. The students' performances included dramatized readings and musical or choral exhibitions on a wide range of new subjects such as travel, holiday-making, dancing, the entertainment of the nobility, and even physics – by now a standing teaching subject – as well as the role of classical culture in a nobleman's education. Some performances in 1755 were recitations in verse on problems of optics, on the origin of water springs, on atmospheric phenomena, on opinions of Galileo and Leibniz, and, finally, on astronomical questions such as the formation of comets and planets. The theatre was still meant to serve the ancient unitary notion of the human person, in opposition to an overspecialization in the different fields of learning, but the needle was now pointing towards a more modern approach. Even equestrian practice was introduced into dramatic performances. The firm idea of the seventeenth-century college theatre as an instrument for education was gradually being softened by more lay and mundane forms of expression. The shift towards spectacular performance tended to make the written text less important, with the result that the language used grew more essential and less rhetorical – in line, for that matter, with the general trend towards simplification of style in the writing of the period.

The repertoire of the Milan college theatre shows that Jesuit culture was neither moribund nor myopically retrospective. On the contrary, it constantly updated its subject-matter and themes. The programs, for instance, included a vernacular comedy by Carlo Maria Maggi, a few comedies inspired by Molière (*Le malade imaginaire* and *Les fourberies de Scapin*), and a tragedy derived from *Rodogune* by Corneille. Tragedies focusing on a martyr (e.g., *Hermenegildus*) were replaced by biblical tragedies, written according to the ancient classical rules, with Racine's *Athalie* serving as a model. In Italy this type of drama was theorized by Giovanni Granelli, who wrote many plays for the students of Bologna's Collegio San Luigi. Three of his tragedies were first successfully performed in Milan in the 1730s and then repeatedly until almost the end of the century.[31] A comparison of the various texts shows how easily the plays circulated from one college to another, and how they were adapted to local tastes and needs. For example, the tragedy *Temistocle* was first performed in 1714, presented again in 1745, produced a third time in 1757 along with the comedy *Zanetto*, and finally performed in French in 1767. The play performed in 1745 was a translation of the French original, *Thémistocle* by Father Folard, which had been performed by the students of the Grand Collège de la Compagnie de Jésus in Lyon on 23 May 1728.[32] The author had an excellent reputation within the Society, so much so that Saverio Bettinelli indicated him as a model in his *Discorso sul teatro italiano*.[33] In the theoretical introduction to his play, Folard argues that the intrinsic value of the tragedy consists in its ability to sound the psychology of the characters. The tragic conflict shifted to the psychological level, in the 'flus et reflus de pensées et de sentiments opposés' designed to capture the spectator's emotions. The result is a tragedy indebted to the classical tradition but offering a great potential for introspection. In 1767 the times were ripe for *Thémistocle* to reach the Milanese stage in its original language, a further proof of the vitality and flexibility of the Jesuits' culture.

The novel feature, which becomes apparent as the century progresses, is that the hero of the plays possesses a 'modern' sensibility. When his behaviour shows tenderness and sweetness, he is more like the hero of eighteenth-century melodrama than the martyr of seventeenth-century baroque drama. Though the emphasis is still on the pedagogical function of the theatre, the model suggested by these plays is no longer that of the ascetic and martyr, but that of the man of civic and social virtue. The identical seventeenth-century values are now presented in a new light, as virtue leaves the citadel of individual heroism and is placed at the service of society and of public happiness.

As a consequence of these changes, drama was also taking on a new formal structure, becoming increasingly similar to a *libretto* in blank hendecasyllables, with three acts instead of five and no chorus. And the heroic character was being replaced by a weak and doubtful one, for whom love, not religion, was the main problem and in whom feelings replaced passions. A good example is the play *Dardano*, performed at the college in 1772 to celebrate the wedding of Archduke Ferdinand, Maria Theresa's son, to Beatrice d'Este. Though the plot was taken from the Greek tradition, the main character, Dardano, was now a young and sorrowful man in search of love.

The crucial question, then, is whether the Jesuits' pedagogical theatre could survive when psychological categories were changing, and whether college theatre could be adapted to what the French called *l'homme sensitif* and *les mouvements*. Modern philosophies had ploughed deep into the ground where the Jesuit theatre had taken root.

If we consider *Dardano*, we can conclude that in any case the pedagogical aim of the theatre was still very much alive. It is Dardano's virtue that brings about the happy ending. The penetration of *sensiblerie* could fascinate but not undermine the ancient moral and anthropological model.

The Jesuits' culture – by then represented in Milan by men such as Andrea Draghetti and Giovanbattista Noghera[34] – opened up to the new philosophical developments but continued to stress its original tenet of the unity of the human person. In the face of materialism the Jesuits saved the heart and the self; in the face of rationalism they saved imagination and fantasy. This culture was constantly able to shape a correlation between soul and body, between the intellect and the heart. When the suppression of the order caused the curtain of Jesuit theatre to drop forever, there remained on the stage, in the very century of rationalism, what the famous phrase by Giambattista Vico defined as *un cuore che pensa*, 'a thinking heart.'

NOTES

1 Emanuele Tesauro, formerly a student at the Turin college, then a Jesuit of the *provincia Mediolanensis* from 1611, was *magister rhetoricae* first in Cremona and then at the Milan college (1619–20 and 1620–1). For biographical details, see Mario Zanardi, 'Vita ed esperienza di Emanuele Tesauro nella Compagnia di Gesù,' *AHSI* 47 (1978): 3–96.

2 Giovanni Leonardo Rainaldi (or Rinaldi) belonged to the Rainaldi family of Rome. His father, Tolomeo, arrived in Milan towards the end of the sixteenth century and initiated a dynasty of architects, then called *dei Tolomei*, which was naturalized in Milan and held the field for a century in architecture and in civil and military engineering. For the architecture of the catafalque, see Olga Berendesen, 'The Italian Sixteenth and Seventeenth Century Catafalques,' dissertation, New York University, 1961, pp. 61–5, 194–5.

3 The report is ascribed to Tesauro in Somm. *Bib.*, VII, p. 1943.

4 Cesare Bassano (or Bassani or Bassanio; Milan, 1584–1648) can boast an abundant production of engravings, the best consisting precisely of the official engravings commissioned by the city. See *Dizionario enciclopedico dei pittori e degli incisori italiani dall'XI al XX secolo* (Turin, 1972).

5 In 1618–21, Tesauro tried his hand at dramatic work with *Hermenegildus* and *Il libero arbitrio*. His essay *Idea delle perfette imprese esaminata secondo gli principii di Aristotele* (Florence, 1975) was written, according to its editor Maria Luisa Doglio, between 1622 and 1629. Mario Zanardi puts it at a later date, certainly during the years when Tesauro was teaching rhetoric at Cremona and Milan. See Zanardi, 'Vita ed esperienza,' p. 40 n118; 'Sulla genesi del "Cannocchiale aristotelico" di Emanuele Tesauro,' *Studi seicenteschi* 23 (1982): 12–15. There is evidence that Tesauro was involved with emblematics as early as 1619 (see Zanardi, 'Sulla genesi,' p. 14 n26).

6 Claude-François Menestrier, *Des décorations funèbres* (Paris, 1684), pp. 235, 262.

7 Emanuele Tesauro, *Dell' arte delle lettere missive* (Venice, 1674), p. 25.

8 The double nature of each virtue was shown as follows:

In the nave:	JUSTICE:	Severity (right)
		Clemency (left)
	PRUDENCE:	Consideration (right)
		Providence (left)
In the left transept:	TEMPERANCE:	Chastity (right)
		Moderation (left)
In the right transept:	FORTITUDE:	Liberality (right)
		Magnanimity (left)

See *Racconto delle sontuose essequie fatte in Milano alli 7 di giugno l'anno 1621* (Milan, 1621), fols 15r ff.

9 Tesauro, *Dell'arte*, p. 111.

10 Emanuele Tesauro, *Filosofia morale* (Turin, 1670), p. 388.

11 'Ciò ch'è Iddio nel mondo, è il principe nella republica: deve dunque la providenza umana regolar la republica, come la providenza divina regola i cieli': Tesauro, *Dell'arte*, p. 108.

12 Tesauro, *Filosofia morale*, p. 409.

13 See Jean-Marie Valentin, *Les jésuites et le théâtre (1554–1680). Contribution à l'histoire culturelle du monde catholique dans le Saint-Empire romain germanique* (Paris, 2001), pp. 637–41. Valentin lists at least thirty-two plays written between 1622 and 1769 on the subject of St Hermenegild. Among those worth mentioning are Tesauro's Italian translation (Turin, 1661) and the new version by Father Pietro Sforza Pallavicino (Rome, 1644).

14 *Hermenegildus,* ms Cod. 59 Vario bis, Biblioteca Reale, Turin, fol. 92v.

15 Ibid., fol. 110r: 'Dehisce tellus, patria rebellis, tuis / noverca natis. Regia o Regi brevis, / ex urbe vasta denique haud restat locus / quo lateat infans. Quid manum ferro admoves? / Tegisque clamide? Cassa praesidia occupas. / Est haec nefasta purpura parenti brevis. / Iam, nate, fugias: patriam tecum feras.'

16 Ibid., fol. 114v: 'Morior: paterni morior opprobrium fori / ne sancta turpem iura concipiant notam. / Beata mors, secunda mors, accepta mors: / o mors amoris, una solamen boni; / o mors doloris, una sedamen mali.'

17 Tesauro devoted the whole of chap. 19 of his *Filosofia morale* to the heroic virtue that makes man 'un uomo deificato o un dio umano' (a deified man or a human god) and is cultivated through the example of 'famosi eroi.'

18 Karl Rahner, *Geist in Welt. Zur Metaphysik der endlichen Erkenntnis bei Thomas von Aquin* (Munich, 1964; Italian trans. Milan, 1989), pp. 255ff.

19 On the philosophical foundation of these statements, see Giovanna Zanlonghi, *Teatri di formazione. Actio, parola e immagine nella scena gesuitica del Sei–Settecento a Milano* (Milan, 2002), pp. 195–231.

20 See Franco Venturi, *Settecento riformatore*, vol. 1 (Turin, 1969), pp. 161–86.

21 See Paola Vismara, 'Secolo empio o devoto? La religione a Milano,' in her *L'Europa riconosciuta. Anche Milano accende i suoi lumi (1706–1796)* (Milan, 1987), pp. 137–63.

22 Tommaso Ceva was born in Milan in 1648 and joined the Society of Jesus in 1663. He taught rhetoric and mathematics at Brera from 1675 until his death in 1737 (ARSI Med. 55 fol. 128 no. 128). His *Opuscula mathematica* (1699), which brought him international fame, summed up his studies in mathematics, geometry, and gravity.

23 His *Carmina* were favourably reviewed in *Actorum eruditorum quae Lipsiae publicantur. Supplementa* 3 (1702): 423–5. For a full catalogue of his works, see Somm. *Bib*, II, pp. 1015–24.

24 See Tommaso Ceva, *Memorie d'alcune virtù del Signor Conte Francesco De Lemene con alcune riflessioni su le sue poesie* (Milan, 1706), p. 140.

25 See Serviliano Latuada, *Descrizione di Milano* (Milan, 1738), pp. 290–1.

26 See Amedeo Quondam, '*L'Accademia*,' in *Letteratura italiana,* vol. 1, *Il letterato e le istituzioni* (Turin, 1982), pp. 823–86; and Frances Amalia Yates, 'The Italian Academies,' in *Renaissance and Reform: The Italian Contribution*, ed. Yates (London, Boston, Melbourne, Henley, 1983), pp. 6–29.

27 *M Paed.* 5:448.

28 The foreword to the text of the 1707 *accademia* states: 'nella galleria ... vi sono i ritratti di quei signori che dal mille settecento in qua ebbero l'onore d'esser principi della Accademia [de' Vigorosi]' (*Lo scetro di Giove* [Milan, 1707], fol. 2r). For further details, see Zanlonghi, *Teatri di formazione*, pp. 293–4.

29 See *1776–1815. Teatri a Milano (tra utopia e realtà)*, ed. Giuliana Ricci (Milan, 1973), p. 32.

30 *La tragica poesia* (Milan, 1765), fol. 2r.

31 Granelli's *Manasse re di Giuda* was performed in Milan in 1733, 1743, and 1756; *Dione siracusano* was performed for Carnival in 1744 and 1751; and *Sedecia* had a single performance in 1763.

32 Melchior de Folard (b. Avignon, 1683; d. Lyon, 1739) joined the Society in 1699. He taught rhetoric in Lyon, where he was a member of the Académie des Sciences et Belles Lettres. Besides *Oedipe,* published in Lyon and Paris in 1722 and translated into Italian by Father Antonio Bernardo Barbieri, he wrote *Thémistocle* (Lyon, 1729). Both tragedies were very favourably reviewed in *Mémoires de Trévoux*, in March 1722 (p. 929) and August 1729 (pp. 1519–21) respectively.

33 Saverio Bettinelli, *Discorso sopra il teatro italiano*, in *Illuministi italiani*, vol. 2, ed. Ettore Bonora (Milan and Naples, 1969), p. 1126. Further praise can be found on pp. 1137–8, where Folard is called one of the best modern tragedians.

34 Draghetti wrote *Psychologiae specimen* (Milan, 1771–2), in which he attempted
a synthesis of the scholastic tradition and English and French modern philosophy.
Noghera wrote a number of apologetic essays meant to strike a balance between 'gli
spiriti di novità e di antichità' (the words of the title of an essay published in Milan
in 1779).

25 / '*Lascivi Spettacoli*': Jesuits and Theatre (from the Underside)

MICHAEL ZAMPELLI, S.J.

Even among general theatre historians, the relationship between Jesuits and theatre is usually reckoned in positive terms. The 'Jesuit school drama' and its related entertainments (e.g., opera, music drama, ballet, etc.) attest to the very significant investment made by the pre-suppression Society in performance. Even English-language reference works, frequently less sophisticated in their appreciation of non-English theatrical traditions, have included ample statements on Jesuit contributions to the performing arts. The third edition of the *Oxford Companion to the Theatre*, edited by Phyllis Hartnoll, for example, included an entry on Jesuit drama by Edna Purdie that ran 7 pages, longer than almost every other single entry except those treating the history of theatre in particular countries.[1] In the last several years, scholars of the sixteenth, seventeenth, and eighteenth centuries have laboured mightily to extend our appreciation of the 'Jesuit style' of theatre in the early modern world and have underscored the critical role played by Jesuit performance in the construction not only of Catholic but also of local cultures within the ambit of Jesuit colleges.[2]

Less well known and less appreciated, by historians both of the Society and of performance, is the extensive shadow side of the Jesuit converse with the theatre. Alongside the elaborate dramas in their colleges, the fathers and brothers of the Society also staged their suspicions about spectacles. In advice manuals, devotional books, moral theology texts, sermons, and letters, Jesuits advanced strong arguments *against* theatrical representation. Since Jesuits clearly did not eschew theatre (or theatricality) in the exercise of their own ministries, their antitheatrical sentiments do not attack theatre per se but rather a particularly potent manifestation of the theatrical impulse: the public professional theatre that was, throughout the sixteenth and seventeenth centuries, migrating from Italy to Spain to France and back to Italy and other parts of Europe. For those interested in the evolution of the theatrical profession and the construction of early modern culture, the Jesuit critique of professional theatricality proves particularly revelatory because it is rooted not only in theory but also in praxis. Jesuits 'do' theatre with particular ends in view; hence, they are particularly well placed to discern the power inherent in 'playing.' Jesuit criticisms of the professional theatre foreground the apparently competing ends of the *comici* and reveal what is 'at stake' in professional performance, socially, culturally, and in terms of religion.

Scholarly awareness of this antitheatrical anxiety on the part of the Jesuits goes back many years. Professor Marc Fumaroli and the Jesuit historian Mario Scaduto discussed it as far back as 1970,[3] just at the time the Italian theatre historian Ferdinando Taviani published with commentary a compendium of significant antitheatrical texts relating to the shifting social position of the *commedia dell'arte* in the baroque world.[4] In this essay, I propose that we spend more time examining – not 'in general,' but from a particularly Jesuit point of view – what Jonas Barish has called 'the antitheatrical prejudice,' that markedly persistent hostility to the theatre that emerges regularly in the history of Western performance.[5] I advocate the project not because antitheatrical writing necessarily proves a reliable source in documenting developments in the history of theatre practice, nor even because antitheatrical writing clarifies primarily theoretical understandings of play and performance, but because antitheatrical writing communicates identifiable anxieties that take seriously theatre's intersection with a particular culture, especially a culture in crisis.

In his most recent book, *The Waning of the Renaissance, 1550–1640*, William Bouwsma provocatively considers the Renaissance theatre as 'symbol, catalyst, and focus for what was felt – if not understood – to have gone deeply wrong in the culture of the age.'[6] The antitheatricality of early Jesuits warrants a new and more sustained investigation in order to 1) explore the professional theatre's influence in fashioning early modern culture, and 2) thicken our understanding of the Society of Jesus' perception of how that emerging culture should be consolidated. The temporal correspondence between the founding of the Society of Jesus in 1540 and the beginnings of the Italian professional theatre, the first hard evidence of which appears in a Paduan contract of 1545, suggests that the relational experiment between religion and theatre, between theatre and culture, could find a privileged laboratory in the history of the Society of Jesus. The danger that must be avoided, however, is the reduction of the project to composing a catalogue aria of negative Jesuit attitudes towards theatre, which would surely prove a tired song with limited value.[7] Hence, the exploration must maintain its focus on those elements that lend energy and excitement to any good drama: the action, the dialogue, the oscillation between the characters – in this case, two cultural actors taking their places on the stage of early modernity.

In this essay I attempt a first pass at revisiting Jesuit hostilities towards the professional theatre. I begin by relating what some Jesuits were saying about professional performers and performances while others were busy staging elaborate theatrical fare. I then venture to consider what the antitheatrical writing might indicate about the state of the professional theatre, the Jesuits themselves, and the movements within early modern culture. I conclude by troubling the distinctions between Jesuit and professional theatre by pointing all too briefly at the dramaturgy of Giovan Battista Andreini, a successful actor, a prolific dramatist, and an eloquent defender of the theatrical profession. The focus of the article remains the later sixteenth and early seventeenth centuries, not only a time associated with the expansion of the Society and its work but also a time known as the 'golden age' of the *commedia dell'arte*.[8]

Jesuit Antitheatrical Writing

The years after the Council of Trent saw an increase in written hostilities towards the Italian theatre. That the theatre had become a professional enterprise increasingly visible in *piazze*, *stanze*, and other performance venues remains the most important explanation of this rise in antitheatrical sentiment. Simply put, after 1563 there *is* a vibrant professional theatre of which to be critical. The archiepiscopal reign in Milan of Carlo Borromeo – the exemplum of a Tridentine pastor – produced a relatively large body of antitheatrical literature affirming time and again that comedies and the actors who perform them tear at the social fabric of the *civitas Christiana*.[9] Though Carlo Borromeo did not provide a definitive *summa* of early modern antitheatricalism, he did transpose long-standing antitheatrical prejudices into a new key. Theatrical play set itself in competition with liturgical celebration, causing what the cardinal archbishop saw as a potentially fatal arrhythmia in the heart of Milan. For Borromeo, the theatrical play that disrupted holy days, that indulged the imagination to no useful (i.e., religious) purpose, that literally wasted time, acquired, in Ferdinando Taviani's words, 'the value of demonic liturgy.'[10]

Acutely aware of cultural happenings everywhere they were professionally engaged, Jesuits also began reflecting on the nature of the theatre and its effects on early modern society. We might understand their efforts as revealing a Borromean provenance in that Jesuit antitheatrical writing, at least in part, attempts to safeguard the ends of Catholic reform in the post-Tridentine era. John W. O'Malley's *The First Jesuits* reminds us that the Jesuit ministries of the Word took place in city streets, piazzas, churches, and eventually schools.[11] Public religious 'performances' such as catechesis, missions, Quarant'ore celebrations, and regular preaching took place in venues quite close to (if not identical with) the venues hospitable to professional performance. That Jesuits would perceive some kind of competition with professional acting troupes whose performative ends were manifestly different remains likely. However, O'Malley's observation that the agenda of the early Jesuits was not the agenda of the Council of Trent forces us to recognize that Jesuit antitheatricality may not be entirely accounted for by the oft-invoked principles of 'Tridentine reform' or 'Counter-Reformation Catholicism.' According to O'Malley,

the Society was founded for 'the defense and propagation of the faith' and for 'the progress of souls in Christian life and doctrine.' It was founded 'for the greater glory of God' – *ad majorem Dei gloriam* ... [The Jesuits] saw themselves as teachers of 'Christianity' (*Christianitas* or *Christianismum*), that is, of basic beliefs and practices. But of such expressions none occurs more frequently in Jesuit documentation – on practically every page – than 'to help souls.'... By 'soul' Jesuits meant the whole person. Thus they could help souls in a number of ways, for instance, by providing food for the body or learning for the mind. That is why their list of ministries was so long, why at first glance it seems to be without limits. No doubt, however, the Jesuits primarily wanted to help the person achieve an even better relationship with God. They sought to be mediators of an immediate experience of God that would lead to an inner change of heart or a deepening of religious sensibilities already present. With varying degrees of clarity, that purpose shines through all they wrote and said as the ultimate goal they had in mind when they spoke of helping souls, whether through the simple *Christianitas* of their catechesis or through something more profound.[12]

Hence, situating Jesuit antitheatricality within the self-understanding of Jesuits in particular evolving ministries remains crucial in discerning the import of these writings.

At this juncture a consideration of the antitheatrical writing of particular Jesuits is finally in order. In what follows we do well to ask what this material reveals and/or conceals about 1) the professional theatre, 2) the interests of the Society of Jesus, and 3) the state of early modern culture. In hopes that the comparison will prove illuminating, I have chosen to examine two different kinds of antitheatrical texts produced by Jesuits from two different countries in the later sixteenth and early seventeenth centuries.[13]

Francisco Arias, S.J., Aprovechamento spiritual *(1587)*

The antitheatrical writing of some influential Spanish Jesuits managed to make its way out of the Iberian Peninsula and into the rest of the continent; the *Aprovechamento spiritual* of the Jesuit Francisco Arias (1533–1605) is a case in point. It was translated into Italian in 1599 by Giulio Zanchini as the *Profitto spirituale* and enjoyed five printings by 1613. Arias, having entered the Society at 26, worked as a professor of theology in Cordova and then in the Jesuit college in Trigueros, where he became rector. Also rector of the college in Cádiz, Arias was well known for his erudition and apostolic zeal, and for the integrity with which he lived the religious life.[14] In particular, Arias came to be considered a leader in the spiritual life, with his written works, either whole or in part, being translated into Latin, Italian, French, German, English, and Polish.[15] Arias advanced a spiritual program clearly inspired by his Ignatian formation in the young Society of Jesus: he began with the presumption that all people could have access to genuine religious experience. For Arias, as Ferdinando Taviani notes, individual and intimate participation in Christological and Marian mysteries required a devotion to mental prayer and a constant cultivation of the inner spiritual life. This attention to interiority, a particular mark of the religious culture of the Renaissance and early modern world,[16] implied a corresponding mortification of exteriority, of the outer, sensual life.[17]

The *Aprovechamento spiritual*, dedicated to the archbishop of Valencia Don Juan de Ribera, is a long work exceeding 800 pages originally published in two parts.[18] From the outset Arias makes it clear that the book is intended for all persons in any state of life – religious or lay – who desire to deepen their spiritual lives and grow in the service of God.[19] Since the aim of the piece is 'to cultivate and perfect with sound virtues the interior of the soul,' Arias recommends that his audience savour the work by reading it not once but many times, so that the mind might be given the luxury of pondering the virtues and the heart the time in which to be moved by them.[20] The anticipated result is the actual living of a life dedicated to God's service.

Arias divides the piece into six major sections and an appendix, the subjects of which clarify the author's presiding interest: outlining a program by which any and all persons may deepen their religious experience with the aim of living more virtuously as servants of God. The work foregrounds the process of 'improvement' and 'progress' in the spiritual life, implying that one's contemplative and active lives could always bear more fruit. The first section introduces 'the necessity and importance' of improving one's 'divine service' and 'growing in all the virtues.'[21] The second suggests that one cultivates true confidence in God by being suspicious of oneself. The third focuses on the profitable use of the Rosary in the process of spiritual growth. The fourth tract moves to a consideration of the Virgin as a model of virtue worthy of imitation. The fifth concerns 'mental prayer,' that is, the more interior 'meditation on those sacred mysteries of Christ our Lord and his glorious mother' for those who seek to grow – even more – in the spiritual life.[22] The sixth deals with the 'mortification of one's own will, the passions of the soul, and all the other things that impede spiritual progress.'[23] The tripartite appendix presents Father Arias's thoughts on the sacraments, their use (and abuse), as well as 'a very profitable spiritual exercise about the presence of God, in which one is taught to make to God present, yearning for him with arduous desires of the heart.'[24]

Predictably, Arias situates his critique of the professional theatre in the sixth segment, in which he discusses the 'holy exercise of mortification.' Faithful to Ignatius's rules for the discernment of spirits, Arias reminds his readers that efforts at spiritual growth are always accompanied by counter-movements governed by their own internal dynamics. These countervailing forces boast a will of their own and, at least in Arias's reckoning, are most often grounded in the sensual passions. Hence, Arias ends the main body of the *Aprovechamento* with an exploration of mortification, by which 'all the impediments to spiritual improvement are gotten rid of.'[25] In his prologue to the reader, Arias admits that this section is longer than any other because the material is so important for those who wish to progress in the spiritual life.[26]

The professional theatre, then, proved problematic for Arias because it embodied a movement away from progress in the devout life, an impediment to the 'aprovechamiento espiritual.' In the fifteenth chapter of the section on mortification, Arias considers 'the mortification of the eyes, particularly in seeing performances, dances, and other things that cause evil.'[27] Though he deals with the sinful tendencies inherent in each of the bodily senses, Arias emphasizes the particular dangers of sight because its objects are more easily accessible. That is to say, one can look at something without occasioning as much publicity as one would, for example, in touching or tasting it. Sight remains the sense by which sinful human nature most consistently seeks the satisfaction of its sensual desires. In its disordered state, sight seduces people into attending visually pleasing spectacles, including 'comedies and other vain representations,' for their own sake. Further, because they are performed by generally disreputable performers in the presence of a mixed audience that includes women, such spectacles are always 'accompanied by many occasions for vice.' Mortifying the sense of sight, then, would aid the Christian in short-circuiting the potentially destructive dynamics inherent in such indulgence, a dynamic that results in 'forgetting God' for the sake of 'imaginings.'[28]

Further, Arias criticizes public persons of authority who patronize these spectacles, 'things so pernicious to virtue,' because they give bad example and damage their reputations.[29] After all, not only Christian thinkers such as Cyprian and Augustine condemned such public shows, but also pagans such as Cato and Cicero. For Arias, all Christians who seriously await the day of divine judgment must 'flee with great vigilance those things that are for them occasions of sin,' most especially public professional performances, seedbeds of vanity and dishonesty at which one literally wastes time in idleness.[30] Arias treats these *spettacoli* as schools of vice in which 'from *seeing* a representation of something dishonest, or of revenge that someone took, or of the ambition of a vain man, the heart goes along tasting dishonesty, vengeance, ambition and becomes fond of them.'[31] Arias is well aware that the public professional theatre instructs and educates its audiences. For him, though, the instruction leads to changes that disrupt the journey towards spiritual integrity.

The presence of women in the professional theatre companies in Italy, Spain, and France proved neuralgic to many antitheatrical writers, including Arias. Identifying the practice of women acting with men as yet 'another abuse of these times,' Arias rehearses the major tropes of Christian misogyny deriving from scriptural and patristic authors:

Sacred Scripture warns us that the sight of a seemly woman scandalizes and murders the hearts of many, that her pleasing discourse is like the fire that excites hearts to dishonest love, and that like a two-edged sword wounds and kills the soul with the death of error and eternal pain. For this reason St Augustine said that it is more tolerable to hear the whistling of a basilisk than to hear the singing of a woman, because the basilisk with its look may kill the body, but the woman, with her lascivious songs, making one consent to desires, kills the soul. Now, if with this are joined the movements and the gestures that women make while they are acting, which all breathe and send forth inconstancy and dishonesty, what effects will take place in the hearts of weak people who look at and listen to them if not that which befell Holofernes looking at the departure of Judith, [a man] the scripture says remained prisoner and slave of dishonest love – the cause of his temporal and eternal death?[32]

Given this attitude, it is not surprising that Arias invokes the Pauline injunction against women speaking in public to condemn professional actresses further. The gender inclusivity of professional companies convinces Arias that this particular theatre sabotages the project of human sanctification.

Arias goes on to note that theatrical representation can indeed be praiseworthy and licit, especially when it concerns 'holy and devout things,' and when care has been taken to 'end those harmful occasions that bring about the concurrence of men and women.'[33] This acknowledgment certainly opens up the possibility that particular kinds of theatre, especially Jesuit educational theatre, can continue to function with a clear conscience. But Arias is very insistent that professional players, even when they claim to be performing material meant to stir devotion, are bound by a craft that trades in 'vain and lascivious things.'[34] Arias would go so far as to claim that any attempt by professional performers to stage virtuous entertainments remains a crafty ploy to justify their scurrility by playing with the laudable. In this way, they entice the virtuous to attend their shows and thus establish a good reputation for themselves. For Arias the mixture of the holy with the profane is nothing less than an artifice of the devil, who aims at subverting spiritual progress by masquerading as piety. The things of God must be mediated only by the instruments of God.[35]

What, then, are we to make of Arias's critique of the theatre as it appears in the *Aprovechamento spiritual / Profitto spirituale*? What might it indicate about the professional theatre, Arias's own interests as well as the interests of the Society of Jesus, and the state of early modern culture on the cusp of the seventeenth century? Arias's antitheatrical writing indicates that the most significant elements of the public professional theatre are the actors and the audiences. The social converse among and between these groups in a public venue sets the professional theatre apart from other theatrical manifestations such as, for example, school drama. Though Arias mentions generally the lasciviousness of professional performances, he never dwells on the details of plot or character in contemporary plays. His focus remains on the people who are the *sine qua non* of the early modern professional theatre – not texts but rather actors and their paying audiences. Further, Arias's writing makes it clear that the theatrical experience, even as manufactured by professional actors for a public audience, can effect substantial change. Even though Arias cautions his readers to beware this power, he implicitly acknowledges the power of the form to communicate and educate.

It is important that we not over-dramatize Arias's antitheatricality. His comments on the theatre occupy only about 8 of the 800 pages of the *Aprovechamento*. Arias, unlike some of the more extreme antitheatrical writers, hardly writes out of an obsession with the theatre.[36] His remarks about the theatre remain potent because they publicize his attitudes towards professional theatre beyond a circle of theological specialists to a more wide-ranging readership. In this regard, we must remember that the entire context for Arias's judgments on the theatre is improvement in the spiritual life, and that the antitheatrical attitudes discussed here reveal as much about this Jesuit's way of seeing the spiritual cosmos as they do about his way of seeing the professional theatre. Arias assumes a continuity between the spiritual and the physical. He encourages his readers to mortify the latter for the sake of the former, affirming that physical realities affect spiritual ones. If, in other words, progress in the devout life can be derailed by seeing a farce or by hearing a song, then the activity of the body is never insignificant in the education of the spirit. Spiritual improvement depends upon the proper formation of both the spirit *and* the body.

Lastly, Arias's anxieties about the professional theatre reveal the tensions besetting early modern culture. Though Arias's writing argues that spiritual improvement ought to be available to anyone irrespective of state in life, it also inscribes with its theatrical commentary the need to police and reinforce existing social and religious boundaries. Spiritual egalitarianism aside, women in Arias's work stand in need of monitoring, public interaction between the sexes must be controlled, and the pearls of religious devotion cannot be cast before infamous professional actors. If Arias's attempts at making improvement in the spiritual life possible for all people implies an optimism in the power of God to draw people towards the good, his antitheatrical commentary implies that such an optimism (characteristic of the Jesuit way of proceeding) has its limits. As William Bouwsma argues, increasing cultural freedoms generate diffuse cultural anxieties that are eventually specified in particular fears. In Arias's case, the fear of professional theatrical representation concerns the dangers in blurring the boundaries between male and female, between reputable persons and disreputable ones, between holy and profane.[37]

Similarly, the new-found respect for physicality, affect, and imagination in early modern culture results in an increased emphasis on bodily gesture, emotional movement, and effective invention even in Catholic culture.[38] Despite the already developed Jesuit traditions in rhetoric, preaching, theatre, and the like, Arias asserts the need to monitor these elements of human experience because they may prove 'too much' for ordinary people, especially when they are manipulated by the likes of professional actors. Arias's antitheatrical writing suggests that for human life not to career out of control it must be ordered hierarchically towards particular ends, especially the union with God and the cultivation of virtue. The professional theatre, as far as Arias can tell, boasts no such commitment to final causes; hence, it sows the seeds of chaos.

My hope is that the foregoing analysis of Francisco Arias's antitheatrical writing makes the case that religious critiques of the theatre – at any time, but especially in the early modern world – are not simply one more manifestation of the repressive tactics of Catholic clerics and therefore easily dismissed. More careful consideration of antitheatrical writing such Arias's succeeds in laying bare the contours of a particular world view, a particular understanding of culture, a particular social and spiritual program undertaken at a particular historical moment. A fuller, richer understanding of both theatre and Jesuit ministry depends upon a growing appreciation of these emerging shapes not always evident at first glance.

Paolo Comitoli, S.J., Responsa moralia *(1609)*

Whereas Father Arias wrote his *Aprovechamento spiritual* in the vernacular for the sake of a wide readership, Paolo Comitoli (1544–1626) wrote the *Responsa moralia* in Latin for use by a more specific, but no less significant, Catholic population. A native of Perugia, Comitoli entered the Society of Jesus in 1559 and spent his life teaching rhetoric and 'explicating questions of public and private morals.'[39] In 1609 this 'Perugian theologian of the Society of Jesus' published the *Responsa moralia*, a Latin handbook of 'answers' to particularly thorny and potentially confusing moral questions arising in conjunction with Christian life.[40] That the text is written in Latin and boasts an easily consulted index suggests that the work was intended mainly for religious professionals – pastors and educators in particular. As is apparent in the full Latin title of the work, Comitoli distributes his thoughts on these difficult moral cases into seven books that consider 1) sacraments, 2) vows and oaths, 3) legal agreements, 4) crimes and criminals, 5) shameful ignorance, 6) censures, and 7) wills and ownership.

Father Comitoli's consideration of 'obscene comedies' (i.e., professional ones) appears in the fifth book of the *Responsa*, which concerns 'shameful ignorance.'[41] Intentionally practical, Comitoli's analysis of theatre aims at determining whether 'the actors who perform [in comedies] and the spectators who attend them are guilty of mortal sin.'[42] He resolves the issue in the affirmative by marshalling the force of five categories of authoritative source material: 1) ecclesiastical decrees and civil laws, 2) opinions of the Fathers and Doctors of the Church, 3) writings of theologians concerned with the principles of Christian obligation, 4) concepts from Christian moral philosophy and theology, and 5) the 'thought of the philosophers who were deprived of the light of Christian wisdom.'[43] Most of the time, Comitoli cites the pertinent authorities within each category and notes the kernel of their arguments, thus making his work a rather handy compendium of antitheatrical source material.[44]

In the section concerned with moral philosophy and theology, Comitoli enumerates the arguments by which the moral culpability of both actors and spectators at a theatrical performance is demonstrated. All the arguments deal in some way with theatre's effect on social interaction and a person's spiritual progress. Actors sin mortally in the exercise of their craft for ten reasons, most of which focus on obscenity, that is, impurity and lewdness made flesh by virtue of theatrical artifice.

1 Actors sin mortally in the exercise of their profession because they willingly and pointedly 'reproduce obscene things in public' and so 'deprive themselves and others of the purity of heart without which no one will see God.'[45]

2 Actors and charlatans undermine the foundations upon which a virtuous state is established because by reason of their trade they 'banish restraint, modesty, and temperance from the cities.'[46]

3 'Those most corrupt actors of obscene comedies' obstruct the education of children in honesty and decorum by providing them with bad example.[47]

4 The actors rob adolescents of their innocence because they provoke the youth 'to search for dishonest lovers and friends.'[48]

5 Dishonest mimes and actors 'infuse vice and lust' into a city, thus depriving it of virtue, 'the only road to happiness.'[49]

6 Professional performers entertain audiences with obscene productions; hence, they commit 'spiritual murder' because they cause others to give themselves over to mortally sinful activities.[50]

7 Actors are in many places denied the sacraments. Since such denial results only from the commission of faults 'worthy of eternal damnation,' their sin is obviously mortal.[51]

8 Professional actors 'light and burn the spectators' souls with torches of vice' not simply by poetic suggestion but by performative incarnation, the voice 'exhaling passion' and the body 'vibrating with immodesty and lust.'[52]

9 Professional actors of 'indecent comedies' do serious spiritual harm to themselves and others because they 'scorn God and his august laws in an unmistakable way.'[53]

10 Since so many noble and learned persons have already condemned both actors and comedies, Comitoli and his readers can do nothing but assent to the proposition that actors commit mortal sin in exercising their profession.

Father Comitoli spends less time in dealing with the sin of the spectator, which reveals that his more urgent concern is the condemnation of the professional actors. Yet most of the points Comitoli makes with regard to actors find their correlate in the audience. Unmistakably, those who attend professional comedies sin mortally for the following four reasons:

1 Patrons of professional performance provide an occasion of mortal sin for the actors, who, in response to their audience's demands, stage their 'shameful imitations and actions' in order to make money.[54]

2 In giving money to professional performers, audience members offer sacrifice to the devil, who is finally responsible for the pagan origins of public theatre.

3 Since taking pleasure in the sin of another is itself sinful, audiences who delight in the actor's craft (mortally sinful for them) also commit sin.

4 Church authorities have already established that those who attend spectacles commit mortal sin; 'hence it is not right that we should believe or think differently.'[55]

Like that of his Spanish confrère, Comitoli's critique of professional performance communicates implicit assumptions about the professional theatre, the
Society of Jesus, and the condition of early modern culture. Comitoli, in line
with Arias, implicitly affirms the power of the theatre to exert a physical and
spiritual influence on both individuals and society. When a fiction is mediated to
an audience theatrically, an incarnation of sorts takes place and fiction comes
ever so close to becoming a convincing reality. Hence, for Comitoli, the content
of the theatrical fiction becomes a fixation. Whereas in Arias's case the emphasis
fell on the actors themselves, Comitoli places the accent on the kinds of comedy
the professional performers make their bread and butter: the plays about cuck-
olded husbands, duped masters, young lovers who sidestep their parents, and
servants who are almost exclusively concerned with the earthier pleasures of
human living. In this case, the power of theatrical artifice to affect an audience –
to change or educate – is placed in the service of what Comitoli sees as only
excess, immodesty, and lack of restraint. Finally, Comitoli ends up at the same
place as Arias: the professional theatre indeed educates, but it educates badly.

Again, as with Arias's writing on the theatre, we do well not to over-dramatize
Comitoli's pique regarding professional performance. His answers to the vexing
questions about the morality of the public theatre occupy a relatively small
segment of one of the seven books of the *Responsa moralia*. More significant is
the fact that he treats the professional theatre at all. Clearly, it would not be
possible for Comitoli to provide a contemporary audience with an orientating
compass for living the moral life without engaging the increasingly present
cultural reality of theatre. Relegating his remarks to the 'typical' Counter-
Reformation 'hang-ups' impoverishes our appreciation of the professional theatre's effects – real or perceived – on early modern culture. Further, that Comitoli
treats the question of the theatre in the context of *criminosa ignorantia* highlights the relative novelty of this kind of reflection. The nature of public
performance, its practitioners, its audience, its way of proceeding cannot, for the
audience of the *Responsa moralia*, remain unknown or unknowable; hence,
Comitoli and Jesuits of his ilk shine a spotlight on the professional theatre and
engage in a relatively substantial reflection on its role in early modern culture.
Ironically, Jesuit attacks on the professional theatre publicize its power even as
they provide actors with an incentive to compose and publish their own defences
of the profession.[56]

Finally, in addition to the implicit affirmation of theatre's social potency noted
above, Comitoli's critique reminds us that the professional theatre, precisely
because it is professional, embeds itself in the structures of early modern public
life. In his observations on the sin of the spectators, Comitoli returns to the
notion that the exchange of money defines professional performance; hence, it

functions according to the basic laws of supply and demand. Were there no demand, no audience eager to pay for the services rendered (performative or otherwise), the professional theatre would cease to exist. The audiences who patronize such performances bear some responsibility for further strengthening the position of the profession in urban cultures.

Jesuit Theatre and Professional Theatre: Points of Contact

The foregoing critiques of the professional theatre by Jesuits highlight the salient features of their own theatrical practice and ultimately direct our attention to the dialogue that must have been consistently occurring between Jesuits and theatre – their own and the professional variety. As the self-understanding of the Society of Jesus was increasingly shaped by its commitment to education, antitheatrical writers such as Arias and Comitoli were quick to recognize the transformative potential of all kinds of performance. Convinced of the theatre's power to educate for particular ends, Jesuits incorporate theatrical production into their own pedagogical enterprises. Taking note of the similarities and the differences between the Jesuit theatre and its professional counterpart aids us, then, in appreciating their distinctive roles in early modern culture. Though there are clear similarities and differences between the two forms, there are also some more ambiguous points of contact that urge us to be careful in the ways we finally construct 'Jesuit' and 'professional' theatricality.

As we have already seen, Jesuit antitheatrical writing criticizes the professional theatre for its consistent and unrestrained appeal to the senses, in stimulating not just one but all of them, and thereby giving Lucifer a wide path on which to journey towards the human soul. Yet, at the same time, Jesuit theatrical production in no way eschews the sensual. It relies upon a performative language that includes gesture and spectacle sometimes so elaborate that it threatens to overwhelm the audience. In the foreword to William McCabe's *An Introduction to the Jesuit Theater*, Louis Oldani reminds us:

Jesuit theater distinguished itself from other kinds of school theater by its practice of uniting well-nigh all the arts in the service of drama. It evolved from simple student exercises in delivering dialogue and presenting single scenes to the mounting of elaborate, often ostentatious, stage productions that rivaled contemporary court and public theaters in style, complex scenery, special effects, and technical skill. Latest developments in scenic properties and mechanical devices, usually initiated in Italy, sometimes progressed from Jesuit school productions to the court and public theaters. Characteristically Jesuit plays conveyed their message to the audience by means of potent appeals to the eye and ear, enhancing dialogue and action with music, orchestras, dance, ballet, incidental songs, and spectacle (riding scenes, for instance, and magnificent processions); with interludes, intermezzos, and other forms of entr'acte; with elegant décor and costumes; and with use of the magic lantern and such various contraptions of staging as ghost apparitions, vanishing acts, cloud apparatus, and even flying machines. Thus, following art's way, Jesuit plays helped the audience to grasp abstractions through the senses.[57]

Arguably, the Jesuit theatre appears even more sensual than the professional theatre, which did not boast the financial or personnel resources that made such sumptuousness possible. The Jesuits understand the difference between these battling 'sensualities,' however, in terms of their final causes. In the Jesuit theatre, the end of such an assault on the senses is to teach the actors eloquence in word and in deed and to educate them and their audience in religious and civic virtue. Jesuit antitheatrical writers construct and then interpret the professional stage as a foil to their own: the professional theatre indulges sensuality for its own sake especially in its exploitation of the love plot, the stock-in-trade of the professional comedy.[58]

As is apparent in the appeal to the senses, the Jesuits distinguish their theatre from the professional theatre by underscoring educational aims. Jesuit antitheatrical writing likens the public theatre to a school of vice. Because the theatre is 'embodied' and 'imitative,' the professional *commedia* effectively teaches audiences how to lust after potential lovers, how to cuckold husbands, how to undermine the authority of masters, and how to indulge the basest longings of the flesh. By contrast, Jesuit theatre remains quite literally a school of virtue. Likewise 'embodied' and 'imitative,' the Jesuit theatre effectively teaches audiences how to live virtuously and honourably in a world created by and ordered towards God. The Jesuit theatre is not obscene, because of its eloquence, its 'reason-made-flesh.' The Jesuit theatre is not obscene, because it aims to 'mean' something, because it looks to catapult its audience beyond the surface of its language, movement, and scenography to something more. Jesuit dramaturgy operates in a thoroughly incarnational way: transcendence is achieved through the physical, through words-made-flesh.

We might be tempted to think, then, that all professional theatre is exactly what Jesuit antitheatrical writers say it is, especially because the Jesuits are characteristically observant of cultural phenomena, and because they themselves are relatively sophisticated practitioners of the dramatic arts. However, in the same way that we have attempted to avoid a fundamentalist reading of antitheatrical writing by considering it in a wider context, so must we avoid such a reading of professional theatre by placing Jesuit antitheatrical writing alongside actual trends in the professional theatre. Not all theatrical professionals are what Fathers Arias and Comitoli make them out to be.

At present it must suffice simply to allude to the celebrated Andreini family, who, over the course of two generations, succeeded in constructing themselves and their profession as virtuous, learned, and respectable servants of the common good.[59] In fact, the career of Giovan Battista Andreini (1576–1654) suggests a convergence between the dramatic activities of a particular breed of theatrical professional and those of the Society of Jesus.[60] Like Jesuit critics, Andreini also insisted that the sensuality of the theatre must not be aimless, chaotic, or voyeuristic. Instead it must be orchestrated by a knowing *capo* and executed by capable actors so as to provide the audience with an experience of transformative wonder. The key dramaturgical principle separating Andreini's brand of *commedia* from the primarily physical buffoonery of charlatans and mountebanks remains one dear to the heart of Jesuit critics: eloquence, reason made flesh in word and gesture.[61] In all his defences of the professional theatre, Andreini continually affirms the contribution made by his profession to early modern society: the professional theatre educates and humanizes its audience. The case of Giovan Battista Andreini – a professional through and through – suggests that the wall separating the professional and Jesuit theatres is, at points, exceedingly thin. And the communication occurring at these particular points calls for more sustained investigation.

Any antitheatrical writing invites a consideration of what is 'at stake' in performance. Jesuit antitheatrical writing foregrounds particular issues pertinent to early modern Catholic culture. The educational program of the Society prepared Jesuits to assert that theatre changes people, forming in them particular habits of being in the world. It seems less likely that Jesuits attacked the public theatre because of 'their zealous regard for the demands of Christian righteousness'[62] and more likely that they perceived real competition from the popular theatre in the education and care of souls. Further, Jesuit antitheatrical writing reveals the Society's investment in the human imagination. Not only key to the Jesuit practice of prayer but also critical in the formation of conscience, the early modern imagination proved to be territory for which Jesuits were prepared to do battle – even with the public, professional theatre.

NOTES

1 Phyllis Hartnoll, *The Oxford Companion to the Theatre*, 3rd ed. (Oxford, 1967).
2 Particularly significant are these recent publications: Giovanna Zanlonghi, *Teatri di formazione. Actio, parola e immagine nella scena gesuitica del Sei–Settecento a Milano*, La Città e lo Spettacolo 13 (Milan, 2002); and Bruna Filippi, *Il teatro degli argomenti. Gli scenari seicenteschi del teatro gesuitico romano, Catalogo analitico*, Bibliotheca Instituti Historici S. I. 54 (Rome, 2001). The bibliography on Jesuit

theatre is immense; some of the more helpful sources for those seeking to orient themselves are J.-M. Valentin, *Les jésuites et le théâtre (1554–1680). Contribution à l'histoire culturelle du monde catholique dans le Saint-Empire romaine germanique* (Paris, 2001); and William H. McCabe, *An Introduction to Jesuit Theater: A Posthumous Work*, ed. Louis J. Oldani (St. Louis, 1983). More extensive bibliography may be found in all the works above, and in L.J. Oldani and M.J. Bredeck, 'Jesuit Theater in Italy: A Bibliography,' *AHSI* 66 (1996): 185–235; and Nigel Griffin, *Jesuit School Drama: A Checklist of Critical Literature* (London, 1976; supplement 1986).

3 See Marc Fumaroli, 'La querelle de la moralité du théâtre avant Nicole et Bossuet,' *Revue d'histoire littéraire de la France* 70 (1970): 1007–30; and Mario Scaduto, 'Momenti di storia religiosa e di storia culturale italiana tra '500 e '700,' *AHSI* 46 (1977): 431–56, especially 452ff., where Scaduto treats the issue in his review of Taviani (n4 below).

4 Ferdinando Taviani, *La commedia dell'arte e la società barocca: La fascinazione del teatro*, La commedia dell'arte: Storia testi documenti, ed. Ferruccio Marotti, 1* (Rome, 1969). In this volume Taviani considers the antitheatrical writing of twenty early modern personalities (including Carlo Borromeo); of these, half are Jesuits.

5 Jonas Barish, *The Antitheatrical Prejudice* (Berkeley, 1981).

6 William J. Bouwsma, *The Waning of the Renaissance, 1550–1640*, Yale Intellectual History of the West, ed. J.W. Burrow et al. (New Haven, 2000), p. 142. See the entirety of chap. 9, 'The Renaissance Theater and the Crisis of the Self,' pp. 129–42.

7 I am indebted to Professor Giovanna Zanlonghi for counselling me to be wary of considering Jesuit antitheatrical writing in isolation from theatrical praxis. It is her insight that prompts me to suggest that it is precisely Jesuit theatre practice that endows Jesuit antitheatrical writing with its particularly revelatory possibilities.

8 The choice to limit the temporal parameters will result in my not treating here the very important work of some of the best-known Jesuit critics of the theatre, among them Giovanni Paolo Oliva (1600–81), Paolo Segneri (1624–94), and Giovan Domenico Ottonelli (1584–1670). Ottonelli's work in particular remains very significant in gauging the evolving relationship between the professional theatre and religion. His *Della Christiana moderatione del theatro* is a six-volume series published between 1646 and 1652 by Bonardi in Florence; the monumental work was republished as a set by Bonardi in 1655. Other pertinent sources include Giovan Domenico Ottonelli and Pietro da Cortona, *Trattato della pittura, e scultura, uso, et abuso loro. Composto da un theologo, e da un pittore ...* (Florence, 1652; ed. Vittorio Casale, Treviso, 1973); Marco Collareta, 'L'Ottonelli-Berrettini e la critica moralistica,' *Annali della Scuola normale superiore di Pisa,* Classe di Lettere e di Filosofia, ser. 3, 5/1 (1975): 177–96; Vittorio Casale, 'Poetica di Pietro da Cortona e teoria del barocco nel *Trattato della pittura e scultura*,' in *Pietro da Cortona, 1597–*

1669, ed. Anna Lo Bianco (Milan, 1997), exhib. cat., pp. 107–16. I am grateful to Professor Gauvin Alexander Bailey for these last three references.

9 Taviani's collection, n4 above, remains the primary source for the antitheatrical literature under examination. Regarding Carlo Borromeo (as well as his cousin Federico Borromeo) and the *Acta ecclesiae Mediolanensis*, see Taviani, *La commedia dell'arte*, pp. 5–43.

10 Ibid., p. lii ('il valore di liturgia demonica').

11 O'M. *First*. The bulk of O'Malley's work consists in exploring how the first Jesuits saw themselves by examining the details of their ministries; for a discussion of these ministries, see especially pp. 91–242.

12 Ibid., pp. 18–19. On the issue of Jesuits and 'reform,' see also O'Malley's earlier article, 'Was Ignatius Loyola a Church Reformer? How to Look at Early Modern Catholicism,' *Catholic Historical Review* 77:2 (April 1991): 177–93.

13 My concern, however, remains the antitheatrical ambience generated particularly in Italy, since the Italian professional theatre (variously known in the early modern period as the *commedia mercenaria*, the *commedia all'improvviso*, the *commedia degli zanni*, and the *commedia italiana*, and only later as the *commedia dell'arte*) is my area of interest.

14 See, for example, Pedro de Ribadeneira, *Bibliotheca scriptorum Societatis Iesu* (Antwerp, 1643): 'Fuit vir cum varia eruditione, tum vitae integritate admirandus, et inter viros non huius solum aetatis, sed venerandae etiam antiquitatis, opinione sanctitatis, qua floruit, numerandus. Religiosae pauperitatis tam amans fuit, ut euis verum spiritum videretur esse assecutus. Vestes, praesertim internas attritas semper, et laceras, suisque resartas minibus gestabat. Obedietiae tenax, Maiorum placita tuebatur apud alio egregie. Salutis proximorum cupidus, eorum praecipue, qui tenuioris essent fortunae, et ope magis destituti ...'

15 See Somm. *Bib.*, I, pp. 540–9. See also Ludwig Koch, *Jesuiten-Lexicon: Die Gesellschaft Jesu einst und jetzt* (Paderborn, 1934), p. 88.

16 See Bouwsma, *The Waning of the Renaissance*, p. 105.

17 Arias in Taviani, *La commedia dell'arte*, p. 127

18 The frontmatter of the *Aprovechamento spiritual* (i.e., the dedication to the archbishop, Arias's prologue to the reader, and the formal approbation by the Jesuit provincial) indicates that Arias finished the piece in 1587. According to Sommervogel, however, the earliest published edition seems to have been produced in 1592–3 in Valladolid. The third edition, consulted in the preparation of this essay, was published in Seville in 1596 by Juan de Leon. References to the work (that are not in Taviani's excerpt from the Italian edition) are to this 1596 Spanish printing.

19 See Arias, *Aprovechamento*, fols 5–6.

20 Ibid., fol. 6: 'Y advertimos a todos, que si dessean de versa aprovecharse de la lecion deste libro, que no so contenten le leello una vez, porque como es libro de

doctrina y avisos espirituales, y endereçados principalmente a labrar y perficionar con virtudes solidas lo interior del anima: conviene mucho para que se perciban bien, y se ponderen, y el coraçon se mueva, y ancione a la practica y execucion dellos, no passar por ellos ligeramente y de corrida, sino leellos y considerallos de espacio muchas vezes.'

21 Ibid., fol. 2r: 'El primero Exhortacian [*sic*] al Aprovechamiento espiritual, en el qual se trata de la necessidad y importancia que es a los que començado a servir a Dios, y aprovechando en su divino servicio, y creciendo en todas las virtudes.'

22 Ibid., fol. 2r–v: 'El quinto de la oracion Mental. En que se da instruccion a los que para mas aprovechar en el servicio de Dios, se exercitan en la meditacion destos sagrados mysterios de Christo nuestro Señor y de su gloriosa madre.'

23 Ibid., fol. 2v: 'El sexto de la mortificacion de la propria voluntad y de las passions del alma, y de todas las demas cosas, que impiden el aprovechamiento espiritual.'

24 Ibid.: 'Y con un exercicio muy provechoso de la presencia de Dios, en el qual se enseña a traer a Dios presente, aspirando a el con encendidos desseos del coraçon.'

25 Ibid., fol. 4: 'Y porque el aprovechamiento espiritual tiene sus contrarios, y sus impedimentos, que son el juyzio proprio, y la propria voluntad, y proprio amor, y las passions de la parte sensitive, por esta causa hezimos un tratado de la mortificacion, y lo ponemos en el ultimo lugar, que es como quien enseñada la verdad, responde ultimamente a los argumentos contrarios, porque este exercicio santo de la mortificacion es el instrumento, con que se quitan todos los impedimentos del aprovechamiento espiritual ...'

26 Ibid.: '... y aunque en los demas tratados avemos procedido con particular cuydado de ser breves ... en este ultimo de la mortificacion nos alargamos.'

27 Ibid., fols 692–8: 'De la mortificacion de los ojos, particularmente en ver representaciones, bayles y otras cosas que provocan a mal.' See also Arias in Taviani, *La commedia dell'arte*, pp. 128–32: 'Della mortificazione de gli occhi particolarmente in vedere rappresentazione, balli, et altre cose che provocano a male.'

28 Arias in Taviani, *La commedia dell'arte*, p. 128: '... comedie e altre rappresentazioni vani ... cose accompagnate da molte occasioni di vizii, cagionano grandissimo danno dall'anima, distraggono quella e la fanno dimenticare di Dio e di ogni buona considerazione, la empiono di imaginazioni e di desiderii di varii peccati ...'

29 Ibid., p. 129: '... cose tanto perniziose alla virtù ...'

30 Ibid., p. 129: '... fuggano con gran vigilanza quelle cose che gli sono occasione di peccato ...' Father Arias's concern with the wasting of time echoes a trope continually sounded by Carlo Borromeo. The Christian, in this view, must be engaged in useful and efficacious activity in the journey towards God. One of Arias's main problems with 'seeing' public shows is the manifest lack of purpose in the activity: one looks, not for the sake of any useful end but solely for the sake of looking.

31 Ibid., p. 129: '... da vedere una rappresentazione d'una cosa disonesta o di una vendetta che uno fece, o di un'ambizione d'un uomo vano, il cuore va gustando della disonestà e della vendetta e dell'ambizione e vi si affeziona.'

32 Ibid., p. 130: 'Si congiunge con questo un altro abuso di questi tempi, che in queste comedie recitano le donne tra gl'uomini. Avisaci la sacra scrittura che la veduta della donna acconcia scandaleza et uccide i cuori di molti; che il suo ragionar piacevole è come il fuoco che accende i cuori all'amore disonesto, e che è come coltello di due tagli, che ferisce et amazza l'anima con morte di colpa e di pena eternal. Per la qual cosa disse S. Agostino che è cosa molto più tolerabile l'udire fischiare un basilisco che udire cantare una donna, percioché il basilisco con la sua vista uccide il corpo, e la donna co' suoi canti lascivi, facendo consentire a rei desiderii, uccide l'anima. Ora, se con questo si aggiungono i movimenti et i gesti che fanno recitando, che tutti spirano e mandano fuori leggerezze e disonestà, che effetti hanno a seguire ne' cuori deboli che le guardano e che le odono se non quello che succedette ad Oloferne dal guardare l'andare di Giudit, che come dice la scrittura rimase pregione e schiavo di disonesto amore che gli fu cagione della morte temporale et eterna?'

33 Ibid: '... rappresentare alcune cose sante e divote è cosa lodevole e che quando cessano le occasioni nocive, che cagiona il concorso d'uomini e di donne, si possono vedere lecitamente ...'

34 Ibid.: '... cose vane e lascive ...'

35 Ibid., pp. 130–1. See also Arias, *Aprovechamento*, fols 417–20. In this latter segment of the appendix treating the 'good use of the sacraments' ('buen uso de los Sacramentos'), Arias continues this line of thought. In chap. 8 of the appendix he discusses 'the sins of gaming; and of seeing vain and harmful things' ('peccados de juegos; y de ver cosas vanas'). Herein he argues that the apparently little sins of gaming are, in reality, quite grave precisely because they seem harmless. Meant as a diversion for a hard-working person, they result in a wasting of time, of hard-earned money, and of respect for family. Gaming, though in itself clearly not as evil as murder or adultery, remains a seedbed of more serious sin. Arias places 'seeing farces' ('ver farsas') in this same category; though it seems harmless, it in fact leads to greater spiritual dangers.

36 See, for example, William Prynne's rather hysterical *Histriomastix* (1633), written during the reign of England's Charles I. It runs to 1,000 pages, is heavily annotated with references to scripture, the Fathers of the Church, ecumenical councils, and other classical sources, and dwells entirely on 'the scourge of playing.'

37 See Bouwsma, *The Waning of the Renaissance*, pp. 146–50.

38 See ibid., particularly chap. 2, 'The Liberation of the Self,' pp. 20–34, and chap. 11, 'The Reordered Self,' pp. 165–78.

39 See Ribadeneira, *Bibliotheca* (n14 above), pp. 362–3: 'Quaestiones de Moribus publice et privatim explicavit.' Information on Comitoli's life and career is scarce. There remain

inconsistencies in the biographical data as presented by Ribadeneira and Sommervogel. Comitoli is listed as having been on the faculty of rhetoric at the Collegio Romano during the 1568–9 academic year. See Villos. *Coll. Rom.*, p. 335. Though the *Responsa* was published in Lyon, France, in 1609, the provincial approbation was given by Bernardino Confalonieri, the provincial of Venice, in 1607. See Paolo Comitoli, *Responsa moralia, in VII libros digesta: quibus, quae in Christiani officij rationibus videntur ardua ac difficilia, enucleantur*, 3 vols (Lyon, 1609). Though I am yet unable to place Comitoli during this time, it is worth remembering that both the Veneto and Lyon were very significant regions for professional acting companies.

40 Comitoli, *Responsa moralia*, title-page. The title-page identifies Comitoli as 'Perusini Societatis Iesu Theologi.'

41 Comitoli, *Responsa moralia*, book 5, 'De Criminosa Ignorantia, de Metu iusto ac de tuta elegenda Opinione.' This book considers ignorance as the cause of sin and discusses moral issues arising in conjunction with, among other things, drunkenness and anger. The consideration of theatre takes place in question 11.

42 Comitoli in Taviani, *La commedia dell'arte*, p. 147: 'Utrum ne earum actores et spectatores sint mortiferi criminis rei.'

43 Ibid., p. 148: '... illorum Philosophorum, qui Christianae sapientiae luce orbati fuerunt.'

44 The first three of these sections as well as the last (i.e., concerning ecclesiastical and civil law, the Fathers and Doctors of the Church, theologians, and classical philosophers) find Comitoli simply presenting the standard arguments against theatrical representation. It is in the fourth section that he constructs an argument by drawing on the principles of Christian moral philosophy and theology.

45 Comitoli in Taviani, *La commedia dell'arte*, p. 150: '... cordis munditia, sine qua nemo videbit Deum, sponte se, et alios privat, qui palam in obscoenarum rerum imitatione versatur ...'

46 Ibid.: '... cum pudorem, modestiam, temperantiam, pudicitiam e civitatibus exterminant ...'

47 Ibid., p. 151: '... impurarum comoediarum impurissimi actores ...'

48 Ibid.: '... prolectant ad inhonestos amatores, amatosque quaerendos ...'

49 Ibid.: '... cum pro virtute, quae sola est ad felicitatem via, vitium et libidinem in civitatem infundunt ...'

50 Ibid.: '... homicidii spiritualis ...'

51 Ibid., p. 152: '... aeterna damnatione dignum ...'

52 Ibid.: '... spectantium animos vitiorum taedis incendit et exurit ...'; '... spirante libidinem ... impudicitiam omnem, atque lasciviam vibrante ...'

53 Ibid.: 'Verum impudicarum fabularum actores et Deum illiusque augustas leges insigniter contemnunt ...'

54 Ibid.: '... sed spectatores suo accessu et praesentia causam adferunt scenicis illa turpia imitandi et agendi ...'

55 Ibid.: '... ergo nos secus credere, aut opinari fas not est.'

56 The effort of professional performers to dispel the myths of their *arte* is considerable. Their explications and defences function as clarifying conversation partners to
all antitheatrical writing. Some of the more noteworthy are Francesco Andreini, *Le
bravura del Capitano Spavento divise in molti ragionamenti in forma di dialogo*
(Venice: Somasco, 1607); Giovan Battista Andreini, *La ferza contro le accuse date
alla commedia e a'professionisti di lei* (Paris: Callemont, 1625); Nicolò Barbieri, *La
supplico, discorso famigliare di Nicolò Barbieri detto Beltrame diretto a color che
scrivendo o parlando de' comici trascurando i meriti delle azzioni virtuose. Letture
per que' galantuomini che non sono in tutto critici né affatto balordi* (Venice:
Ginammi, 1634); and Pier Maria Cecchini, *Brevi discorsi intorno alla comedia,
comedianti & spettatori di P.M. Cecchini comico acceso et gentilhuomo di S.M.
Cesarea dove si comprende quali rappresentationi si possino ascoltare e permettere*
(Naples: Roncagliolo, 1616).

57 Oldani, foreword to McCabe, *An Introduction to Jesuit Theater* (n2 above), p. vi.

58 Though Jesuit plays tend assiduously to avoid the sensuality of human love, they
cannot do entirely without it. In a performance context, heroes in Jesuit performance pieces love something – faith, Christ, the church. I would like to suggest that
although the sensuality of this love is domesticated by the use of allegory, the
performance context continues to embody that love in human terms. For example, in
the 1685 Jesuit opera *Patientis Christi memoria* (music by Johann Staudt), Memoria
Passionis (the Memory of the Passion) spends the first part of the opera desperately
trying to find someone who will fall in love with him/it. Eventually, the beloved
turns out to be Pietas Christiana (Christian Duty). Their dialogue with each other is
clearly and distinctly that of two lovers. Though they are allegorical characters in
the text, on the stage they are human beings reaching out to each other in deep
desire. This phenomenon will receive further exploration in a forthcoming article on
the effects of contemporary staging on our appreciation of such historical pieces.

59 Francesco (1548–1624) and Isabella Andreini (c. 1562–1604) were perhaps the most
celebrated professional actors of the Cinquecento. They exercised their craft not
only with technical virtuosity but also with a breadth of intellectual understanding.
The couple associated with contemporary literary figures, belonged to learned
academies, and published both prose and poetry; hence, they began a process of
constructing themselves, their family, and their profession as virtuous, learned, and
respectable. As the first-born son, Giovan Battista Andreini would be the primary
heir of his parents' celebrity.

60 For more information on Giovan Battista Andreini, see *Comici dell'arte:
Corrispondenze,* ed. Claudia Burattelli, Domenica Landolfi, and Anna Zinanni, 2
vols, Storia dello Spettacolo, Fonti, ed. Siro Ferrone (Florence, 1993); Siro Ferrone,
Attori mercanti corsair: La commedia dell'arte in Europa tra Cinque e Seicento

(Turin, 1993); and Maurizio Rebaudengo, *Giovan Battista Andreini: Tra poetica e drammaturgia* (Turin, 1994).

61 See especially Giovan Battista Andreini, *La saggia egiziana. Dialogo spettante alla lode dell'arte scenica* ... (Florence: Timan, 1604); *Prologo in dialogo fra Momo e la Verità, spettante alla lode dell'arte comica* ... (Ferrara: Baldini, 1612); and *La Ferza. Ragionamento secondo contra l'accuse date alla commedia* (Paris: Callemont, 1625).

62 Thomas Austin O'Connor, *Love in the 'Corral': Conjugal Spirituality and Anti-theatrical Polemic in Early Modern Spain*, ed. A. Robert Lauer, Ibérica 31 (Boston, 2000), p. 190. I am suspicious of O'Connor's conclusion that 'jesuits [*sic*] began to take hard moral positions on the issue of commercial theatre, principally due to their zealous regard for the demands of Christian righteousness, whereas augustinians [*sic*] championed a more moderate approach.' Antitheatrical criticism – Jesuit or otherwise – begs to be read within a specific context. Antitheatricality is rarely just about what it claims to be about; like theatre post-Freud there is always a much more interesting, driving subtext that gives antitheatrical writing its power. In the Jesuit instance, there needs to be more work on the subtext. Despite the sometimes very plodding nature of the work, O'Connor's book remains valuable in its attempt to provide a synthetic reading of Spanish antitheatrical literature and for its identification of sources.

PART FIVE

The Overseas Missions:
Challenges and Strategies

When, in 1539, St Ignatius and his companions from Paris drew up their 'Formula,' they made provision in it for a certain flexibility in the future they envisaged for themselves. None the less, they saw themselves as particularly devoted to 'the propagation of the faith,' whether they should be sent for that purpose 'among the Turks, or to the New World, or to the Lutherans, or to any others whether infidels or the faithful.' Even when the schools qualified the itinerant ideal that animated the first Jesuits, the Society continued all through its history to assign high, even the highest priority to its overseas missions, where it often effected a working synthesis between its evangelizing and its educational objectives. Moreover, the linguistic skill that was a product of the Jesuits' devotion to the *studia humanitatis* served them well in their dealings with the strange, and to them exotic, languages they encountered overseas.

Sabine MacCormack's article about the Jesuits in Peru ranges over many decades and touches on a number of important topics, including the severely critical attitude of some Jesuits to the Spanish conquest. Besides taking account of well-known Jesuits such as José de Acosta, the article introduces others who deserve to be better known. It centres, however, not only on how the Jesuits learned and codified the languages of the Andean peoples but on the relationship they saw between the disciplined study of language and the inculcation of virtue, a traditional theme and concern of the *studia*. In the end, however, as some Jesuits realized, it was the Indians who were teaching the Jesuits.

How many Jesuits in Peru worked with the Indians, and what difficulties did the Society encounter as a result of its directive that all members of the province learn the indigenous languages of the region? Those are the more corporate questions related to the phenomenon addressed by Aliocha Maldavsky, who takes us into some of the tensions within the province, and into disagreements about the whole project of evangelization of the Indians and about official Jesuit policy regarding it. At the same time she deals with another sensitive issue in the Society at the time, the admission of non-Europeans.

Learning the indigenous languages was only one of the problems the Jesuits faced on the overseas missions, and it was only the first step in getting their message across what sometimes seemed impassable cultural barriers. Charlotte de Castelnau-L'Estoile examines the extraordinary career of Francisco Pinto, a Jesuit in Brazil in the late sixteenth and early seventeenth centuries who had a profound understanding of how deep the chasm was between the cultural world of the Europeans and that of the Amerindians. To bridge it, he adopted postures and procedures that prompted the Indians to dub him a 'rainmaker' and regard him as a saint – but a saint according to their own norms. He was, granted, 'a marginal figure,' but not therefore unimportant for helping us grasp 'the variety of missionary behaviours and practices' and the extremes to which the Jesuit policy of adaptation might go.

In the sophisticated cultures of China and Japan, the missionaries faced different problems, but nowhere was a policy of adaptation more fully articulated and more consistently carried out. Implicit in the policy was winning the admiration and favour of the persons the Jesuits hoped to influence towards Christianity. As is well known, for the Jesuits in China that meant impressing the emperor and his court with the accomplishments of European science and mechanics. Catherine Pagani examines how Matteo Ricci and his successors used the clock in this enterprise, and how it brought them, as did their general policy, both renown and troubles.

A recognized but practically unexplored aspect of Jesuit missionary practice was inducing lay men and women to work alongside the members of the Society and even to venture alone into milieus where the Jesuits could not go. Haruko Nawata Ward has uncovered fascinating evidence of the activities of about a dozen women catechists in Japan, and here she presents in some detail the careers of three of them. She thus adds another valuable piece to our understanding of the relationship of the Society to women, but in the process she also points to the lively engagement of the native population in the missionaries' enterprise, which helped Christianity survive in some form in Japan even through centuries of suppression and persecution.

26 / Grammar and Virtue: The Formulation of a Cultural and Missionary Program by the Jesuits in Early Colonial Peru

SABINE MACCORMACK

In 1571, just three years after the first Jesuits arrived in Peru,[1] they managed to acquire one of the most desirable pieces of real estate in Cuzco, the ancient capital of the Incas. This was Amarucancha, where – as many people believed – the Inca emperor Guayna Capac had resided.[2] Here, not without much threatened litigation, financial crisis, and conflict with the clergy of Cuzco's cathedral, the Jesuits built their church, still known to all as La Compañía. Thanks to its location and its splendid design, the church defines the square as powerfully as the much larger cathedral does, and it became a focal point in the ritual life of the city, the hub of Jesuit preaching in Spanish and Quechua and of an elaborate network of processions and missionary journeys.[3]

Next door to the church was the college, now the University of Cuzco,[4] where the study of Latin grammar was to tame the insolence – as one Jesuit saw it – of the young creole students, and was to further their progress in religion and piety.[5] The discipline of learning Latin grammar and the liberal arts, it was felt, would lay the groundwork for the good customs that were the precondition for living a truly Christian life. Whether it was Latin, arts, or Christian Doctrine, the method of teaching was similar.[6] In Peru, as in Europe, there was indeed formal instruction both in the classroom and in sermons in church, but much of the teaching was accomplished dialogically – in the form of plays and colloquies, epistles and orations composed by students, and in responses and chants sung by different choirs during religious processions.[7]

The regular timetable of secular and sacred knowledge acquisition was punctuated by major ceremonial and civic events on feast days,[8] as, for example, for the Immaculate Conception of Mary in Lima in 1570, when the students of the college performed a play representing the triumph of work over idleness. The play marked Viceroy Toledo's first visit to the Jesuit house and with its appropriately moralizing message was such a success that a repeat performance was organized for the archbishop.[9]

Ritual projections of Jesuit activities, duly enhanced by being enacted in a dignified architectural setting,[10] could thus be useful in very practical ways: in making an impact on public life, and in gaining the Jesuits reputation and patronage. But that was not their only, or even their primary purpose.[11] Architecture likewise was in a sense secondary, because as the Society's general Francisco Borja succinctly expressed it, 'It is spiritual works we lay claim to, not material ones.'[12] In effect, what the Jesuits were looking for was a general change and improvement in manners and customs, 'a universal reformation of all kinds of people,'[13] of which plays, declamations, processions, and architecture could be no more than outward expressions. And with respect to manners and customs, there seemed to be much room for improvement. Peru was a land of 'tigers and dragons,' Luis López, who was one of the first group of Jesuits to be sent from Spain, wrote from Lima in 1569, a land of excess, cruelty, greed, avarice, and idolatry.[14] Other Jesuits were alarmed by the rebellious and conflictive ethos that pervaded Peruvian society, the excessive 'liberty,' as they perceived it, that people arrogated to themselves – whether this was in the feuds and rivalries of men, the provocative dress and demeanour of women, or the insouciance and venality of the clergy in Indian and Spanish parishes. It was thus with some satisfaction that in Lima and Cuzco, and in the other cities where they established colleges, and also in the places where they conducted missions, the Jesuits felt that they were observing a certain amelioration of these many social ills. Inveterate enemies were reconciled, couples living scandalously were reformed and got married, and hardened conquistadors made restitution of their evilly gotten riches.[15]

To accomplish such goals over the long run, however, was a tall order. In the first instance, it required that the Society remain on good terms with the Crown, and especially the viceroy, and next, it required that members of the Society live and act in accordance with what they described, in a kind of shorthand, as 'our way of proceeding.'[16]

In some respects, these two issues were interdependent. Ignatius had placed the Society under the jurisdiction of the pope. Jesuits thus preferred not to accept cures of souls and become parish priests because it would bring them under episcopal jurisdiction, and because, furthermore, it would restrict their freedom of movement. In addition, within the Spanish monarchy, by virtue of the *patronato real*, the royal prerogative of making episcopal appointments, accepting cures of souls meant that Jesuits would ultimately be under royal jurisdiction as well. Adding to the entanglement, the first Jesuits were sent to Peru at the insistent request of Philip II of Spain, there being a shortage of qualified priests to undertake the evangelization of Andean people, which the king and many others viewed not only as a sacred obligation, but also as the legitimation of the Spanish presence in the Andes.[17]

In a sense, therefore, the Jesuits went to Peru in the king's service. As one of them said, 'We are going in the sight of the king and kingdom of Spain.'[18] Furthermore, if the mission was to succeed, it was crucial that the Jesuits not join the chorus of clerical vituperation of the conduct of the invaders of Peru that had been resonating throughout the Spanish monarchy ever since Bartolomé de Las Casas and Francisco de Vitoria had first drawn public attention to the issue.[19] Borja as general of the order thus urged the Jesuits in Peru to practise the virtue of reticence: 'I advise you most urgently ... not to undertake either to absolve or to condemn the first conquerors of the Indies and their successors ... The religious orders who have been in the Indies for many years have experienced the greatest difficulty in resolving this issue, and it would be temerity if we, having only just arrived, claimed to act as judges.'[20] Even so, it was a discouraging topic. Early in 1574 a group of Jesuits destined for Peru nearly perished in a shipwreck and had to return to Seville, which was a sign to some of them that aspects of Spanish dominion in Peru 'cannot be tolerated in good conscience, and cannot be remedied or discussed without causing scandal,' so that it was best to leave Peru altogether.[21] This is also what Luis López felt, who, in a moment of desperation in 1572, appealed to Borja 'to give the order that we may flee from these princes of the world because for sure they will destroy us.'[22]

Although Borja did not live to respond to this letter, his successor, Everard Mercurian, repeated the familiar warning not to meddle in politics.[23] Luis López, however, found the advice hard to square with his conscience, and his experience as rector of the college in Cuzco did not help. He taught Latin in the college, while Alfonso de Barzana from Granada, who was rapidly becoming the Society's most admired Quechua linguist, dedicated himself to teaching Christian Doctrine to Indians and Spaniards and hearing their confessions. But the major event of those years was political. In September 1572, Tupac Amaru, the last Inca emperor, was brought captive to the old Inca capital and executed in the main square, in front of the building believed to have been the palace of his grandfather, Guayna Capac, which had become the home of the Jesuits. Barzana was one of several priests to catechize Tupac Amaru, and López along with the heads of all the other religious houses in Cuzco implored Viceroy Toledo on their knees to desist from the execution; but all to no purpose.[24]

Forty years after the Spanish invasion, this event highlighted the contradictions of policy and conscience that continued to torment a good many people. At some point during those years, Luis López compiled a memorandum listing everything that was wrong with the Spanish conquest and government of Peru. The king himself, the viceroy, local governors, the courts of appeal, and the clergy all came in for uncompromising and well-informed criticism.[25] Somehow, this document found its way into the hands of the Inquisition. López was imprisoned, and, by way of trying to hush up the incident, was sent back to Spain, and spent his final years caring for victims of the plague in Seville.[26] López was not alone in having discarded Borja's advice to avoid getting involved in politics,[27] although he did it in more uncompromising terms than many, and as a consequence breached those tacit rules of conduct that were described as 'our way of proceeding.'

Some of López's fellow Jesuits were perhaps not entirely surprised by such a termination of his career in Peru. This possibility, at any rate, emerges from the judgments that his colleagues and superiors made of him in their periodic reports to Rome. In Spain, Luis López had studied Latin and Greek as well as theology, and wanted to go to Japan,[28] but when the first Jesuits were sent to Peru with Viceroy Toledo in 1568, López was among them.[29] In a memorial that was sent to Rome in 1571, López was described in this way: 'He is very learned and has excellent judgment. His talent is in dealing with his neighbours and hearing confessions. He is of a severe disposition and little adjusted to the mould of the Society, and he is very self-willed and little devoted to matters of mortification.'[30] By this time, or soon thereafter, López was in Cuzco, where as rector of the newly established college he attracted another harsh judgment: 'He was made rector in order to soothe him, because when in the ranks, he gives much trouble to those who deal with him, and when in a position of authority, he will needs give more.'[31] Four years later, Juan de la Plaza, who had been sent from Rome to report on the Peruvian province, wrote a little more gently and also observed, almost prophetically, that when sending men to the Indies it was crucial to be sure that they were of proven virtue and had a vocation for such a life, or at least 'firm obedience.' For otherwise, 'apart from achieving no good, they will live here disconsolately [desconsolados], and will occasion no small disedification.'[32]

The judgments the Jesuits were accustomed to make of one another, themselves, their penitents, and the world around them were, more often than not, concise, sharp, and to the point. They were also deeply realistic and humane, all this being the result, perhaps, of the authors of these judgments working their way through the Spiritual Exercises on a regular basis.[33] They thus understood, in an intimate, profound way, the importance of consolation and of being, in whatever situation, consoled.[34] Luis López appears to have found himself very far from consolation.

In 1588, after López had returned to Spain, Alfonso de Barzana wrote him a letter. The two of them had repeatedly worked together: in Lima and Cuzco to begin with, and later in Potosí and Arequipa. During those years López was Barzana's confessor. They were both present in 1578, when by order of Viceroy Toledo the house the Jesuits had founded in Arequipa was confiscated because of various alleged breaches of protocol. The two of them ended up, quite literally, on the street.[35] By 1588, when he wrote to López, Barzana had found his way to a consoled life, or maybe he had had it all along. After the two of them separated, Barzana had increasingly devoted himself to work with Andean people and to missionary journeys. When he wrote to Luis López, he was in Tucuman, a journey of some six hundred leagues from Cuzco. 'How much I want this letter to reach the hands of Your Reverence,' he wrote.

And on the other hand, a letter without sound little satisfies my hunger; the hunger would be somewhat assuaged if for a week, maybe, I could give Your Reverence a long account, face to face, of my peregrinations ... yet that, I hope in Jesus, will be in the land where neither weeks nor years have a measure, where Your Reverence will forever bless your creator ... And I also shall praise him, for, taking from me the love I had of ministering to Spaniards, he changed my eyes so that I found contentment only in helping the utterly helpless, these abandoned Indians. You have always known in me the thirst to work for the healing of the Indians, but until we separated, I was always divided between these ministries, helping Spaniards, and helping these others.[36]

Barzana the linguist was a master not just of spoken but of unspoken words, for between these lines he inserted a wordless memory of his old friend as a wise and trusted spiritual guide – a dimension in López's personality that is also present, in however clipped a fashion, in the impersonal evaluations of him in reports sent to Rome. Barzana went on to describe his own work and his journeys, which had removed him far from the centres of power, and from the torments of conscience that the 'bodily and spiritual servitude'[37] of Andean people living among and under Spaniards brought upon López and so many others among his brothers in religion.

His was a very different temperament from that of López, and this was evident from early on.[38] In 1566 he wrote to Borja asking to be sent to the Indies. He had initially thought of working with the Jews, but the right moment, he felt, either had not yet come or had passed. But regarding the gentiles, it seemed that the time of the early church had returned, and that by living, as he yearned to do, an 'unvarnished life,' he could perform in Peru whatever ministry would be called for. Barzana arrived in Lima in 1569 and immediately threw himself into work with Andean people. In the report of 1571 he was described as 'a devoted servant of God, a good preacher, [who] has the ability to hold a university chair, but has no talent for government.'[39] The writer of the next report expressed a certain disappointment: 'He is a good preacher and confessor and a very good theologian, but he is not adjusted to the Institute of the Society; he is good only for preaching and hearing confessions. He knows the language of the Indians well.'[40] In 1576, Juan de la Plaza, as he did so often, judged more expansively: 'He is adviser to the provincial, and lector of the Indian language, has good intelligence and judgment, has good health, talent to preach to Indians and Spaniards, to hear confessions and teach Indians in the two general languages of this kingdom; he is a sufficient preacher. He has humility and obedience, is dedicated to prayer and practises it with feeling; is well disposed to our Institute.'[41]

By this time, Barzana had composed, in both Quechua and Aymara, a vocabulary and grammar, and a short and long catechism. The short catechism was designed for the instruction of the elderly and the very unlearned, and the long one for more advanced students of Christian Doctrine and for the the missionaries themselves. In that same year, the general congregation of the Jesuits in Peru was contemplating the publication of these books.[42] They were to be sent to Rome, but somehow disappeared,[43] as did all of Barzana's other writings about indigenous languages. But his influence was very much alive among the Jesuits and other missionaries of his time, and among those of a subsequent generation.

In November 1576, Barzana, having been given a tearful farewell by the Andean people of Cuzco,[44] helped to set up the Jesuit missionary parish, *doctrina*, of Juli on Lake Titicaca. The Society took this step in compliance with the mandate of the viceroy, but with deep misgivings about becoming involved in the daily practicalities of running a *doctrina* – about possible conflicts with bishops and competition with secular clergy, about entanglements concerning material survival and the exercise of authority over Andean people, and, not least, about the implied contravention of the Society's constitutions.[45] Some of these fears, however, proved to be groundless. Juli had its problems, but it also became a model both for teaching Christianity to Andean people and for learning from them not only their language, but also something of their culture. [46]

The routines of daily life and of the festivals of the Christian calendar unfolded in Juli much as they did elsewhere, with processions and sermons, with children reciting Christian Docrine antiphonally, while on occasion Barzana and a Jesuit brother staged dialogues with each other 'of things accommodated to the Indians, which they enjoy and from which they derive more benefit [than from sermons].'[47] What distinguished Juli from other Jesuit houses was a distinctly Andean dimension to almost everything.[48] On the feast day of St Thomas in 1576, José de Acosta, who as provincial of the Jesuits in Peru had come to visit Juli, was honoured with a solemn ceremony of reception. It was only just over seven years since the first Jesuits had arrived in Lima, their orientation inevitably Spanish and peninsular. But in Juli, where Andean students memorized what they learned with the help of quipus, the knot records used by the Incas, and where the Creed, the Ave Maria, the Salve Regina, and other prayers were recited in Aymara, and children sang Christian songs, also in Aymara,[49] a rather different mental and spiritual world was coming into existence, as was evident in the reception ceremony honouring Acosta: 'The schoolboys walked a long way ahead [of the rest], singing in their language and in their manner. Next came the men, in great numbers, performing two dances, dressed in silk clothes of Indian style, and dancing in the Spanish manner, and another dance was of some children who hardly knew yet how to walk. Next came their *pingullos*, or music of flutes, and some twenty-five or thirty crosses with their banners (carried by the heads of *ayllus*), and then the lords of the village with our fathers.'[50]

The Jesuits were masters at teaching Latin, and a number of them were superb Latinists who wrote in lucid, elegant classical prose – as is evident from some of the correspondence that was sent from Peru, for example the official documents that were translated into Latin by Luis López. [51] In presenting their agenda to the world, the Jesuits were fond of linking the study of letters, by which they meant Latin letters, with virtue.[52] The study of Latin tamed the uproarious impulses of boys and young men, and prepared them to become virtuous, useful members of society, this being the program that in due course would culminate in the mature practice of piety and the service of God.[53]

In Juli, the program was extended to include the study of Aymara by the Jesuits themselves. José de Acosta, who, in the face of much heart-searching and anxiety by his fellow Jesuits, was strongly in favour of taking up the *doctrina* of Juli and keeping it, saw as one of its advantages that there members of the Society could learn Aymara really well. [54] In effect, Juli, while in the strict sense it was merely a *doctrina*, a missionary parish, really functioned as a college in which the religious life, formal learning and instruction, and pastoral work went hand in hand. Work at Juli made it clear that there was practical and spiritual advantage not just in studying and teaching Latin, but, for somewhat different reasons, in studying and teaching indigenous languages. Nor was this all. In 1586, Juan de Atienza, who was then provincial, wrote a set of instructions for the Jesuits at Juli, and also described their working day, which was long and arduous.[55] It was thus crucial that the fathers and brothers should periodically enjoy some respite. The respite, as Atienza saw it, was studying Aymara: 'It is most appropriate that in the time they have left from ordinary occupations they should be free to study the language and other things, and to re-create themselves within themselves through the exercise of study and virtue, in order thus to attend with greater energy to the good of the Indians and the assistance of their neighbour.'[56]

By 1586, when Atienza wrote these words, the Jesuit had made a considerable impact in Peru, and that not only in the gradual and sometimes hesitant formulation of a policy of mission to Andean people and of the revitalization of Christian virtues among Spaniards and creoles, but also in a more public and explicit sense. In April 1572, José de Acosta arrived in Lima. He had joined the Society at the age of 12 in 1552,[57] and in 1569 he expressed his desire to be sent to the Indies in a letter addressed to Francisco Borja that is a model of balanced and tranquil self-scrutiny. He was already an admired teacher, preacher, Latinist, and theologian, and feared, so he wrote to Borja, the dangers of vanity in continuing such a career in Europe. Yet if Acosta thought that by going to Peru he would escape fame and honour, he was mistaken, for he was welcomed in Lima as a veritable god-sent. As one of the Jesuits already in Lima wrote, 'I understand the arrival of Father Joseph in these kingdoms to have been by the command of the Lord.'[58] Acosta's reputation as an inspired preacher spread at once, and between 1576 and 1581 he was provincial.

But his attention was focused primarily on the responsibility of the Society and of the church at large in the conversion of Andean people.[59] In the face of frequent assertions by missionary clergy, who knew no Quechua or Aymara, that the natural dispositions of Andean people made them incapable of comprehending Christian teaching, Acosta was convinced of the opposite. Not only did experience at Juli demonstrate that Christianity could be successfully taught in the Andes, he maintained, but also, when the scriptures spoke of the calling of all human beings, this did not refer merely to those who lived when the scriptures were written, but should be understood prophetically of all future times.[60] This did not mean that Acosta was ready to idealize Andean people. Just as so often the Jesuits applied a cool, intelligent reasonableness in judging their own and one another's qualities, so Acosta did here. It was true that communicating the gospel took time, that Andean people were often slow of understanding,[61] but it was also true that experience in Spain and everywhere else demonstrated that education and good examples proffered from infancy infinitely outweighed the forces of inheritance and ethnic origin[62] – which was of course also the reason why the Jesuits in Peru and elsewhere were so firmly dedicated to instilling in the young 'letters and virtue.'[63]

Nor did Acosta have illusions about his fellow Spaniards. The invaders and their descendants constituted a huge obstacle to evangelization. The remedy, as Acosta saw it, was that priests should be seen to lead exemplary lives, that they should be learned, and that they should, above all, speak to the Indians in their own language: 'for faith comes from hearing, and hearing by the word of God.'[64] What was also needed, Acosta thought, was a short catechism that the Indians could learn by heart, and a longer one, explaining matters more spaciously, that the teacher could use – where perhaps he had in mind Barzana's short and long catechisms.[65] There were thus no short cuts whereby to avoid either the labour of learning grammar and practising the language daily, or the labour of working patiently for the gradual conversion of Andean people,[66] just as Christ had patiently taught his disciples.[67] All this had consequences for the Society, because notwithstanding the many entanglements likely to result from running *doctrinas*, Acosta thought that the Jesuits ought to accept their share of this responsibility,[68] all the more so because, like Barzana, he believed that the time was propitious.[69]

That Acosta was profoundly critical of many aspects of Peruvian governance did not escape the attention of Mercurian, who in December 1576, and on two subsequent occasions, repeated to him the already familiar reminder not to give cause for offence to the viceroy.[70] If ever there was a *casus conscientiae*, this was it. Acosta was regarded by many of his fellow Jesuits as an exemplary religious, he had been nurtured in the Society from a very early age, and he was devoted to the virtue of obedience.[71] None the less, he not only stuck to his ideas about the past and continuing detrimental impact of the Spaniards on Andean people and advocated programs for change, all of which was bound to cause offence, but also wrote about these ideas in his Latin treatise *De procuranda Indorum salute*.[72] Mercurian approved the work, but required that passages on the cruelty of the conquerors of Peru, and any others that might give offence, be removed before publication.[73] In spite of what was perhaps a quite extensive toning down of troublesome views, the published *De procuranda* still contains many uncompromising statements about the invaders and their successors, and also about the missionary clergy of Acosta's own day.

In this sense, the book is a companion piece to the decrees of the Third Council of Lima, which met in 1583 and endeavoured to reform the conduct of the clergy.[74] The council also prepared a volume of texts collectively described as *Doctrina Christiana,* designed for teaching Christianity to Andean people.[75] Two of these texts, the 'Short Catechism for Uneducated and Busy People' and the 'Longer Catechism for Those Who Are More Capable,' each in a trilingual version in Quechua, Aymara, and Spanish, appear to be versions of Barzana's earlier work.[76]

The Third Council of Lima and the years following it marked the passing of an epoch in Peru at large, and for the Jesuits those years saw the passing of a generation, and the emergence of a new one. After the council disbanded, Acosta laboured hard in making the publication of the *Doctrina Christiana* a reality. The book consisted of the short and long catechisms that Acosta had thought should be in every missionary's hands, a manual for confession, and a collection of sermons, all in Quechua, Aymara, and Spanish; comments about certain grammatical and semantic peculiarities of Quechua and Aymara, to assist learners of those languages and to explain the translators' choice of vocabulary; and finally, brief descriptions of Andean religious practice. All this was printed under the supervision and with the help of Acosta and other Jesuits. In 1587, Acosta returned to Spain. Diego de Bracamonte, who had been rector in Cuzco and Juli, died in 1584,[77] and Jerónimo Ruiz de Portillo, who had headed the first group of Jesuits to land in Lima, died in 1590, mourned by many.[78]

Alfonso de Barzana died in Cuzco on 1 January 1598,[79] having walked the six hundred leagues from Paraguay to spend his last days among his fellow Jesuits. His epitaph was written by Gregorio Cisneros, who had joined the Society in 1579.[80] For this younger man, Barzana was the stuff of legend. On one of his missionary journeys, so Cisneros wrote in the epitaph, Barzana was speaking with some people who were most unwilling to listen to him, and in that place he met the devil. 'As soon as Barzana recognized [the devil], he got up from where he was sitting, and went to meet him on the path, and said to him, "Why don't you sit down here, because this place, you deserve it much better than I." He said it so simply and with such humility that the devil with a great uproar took himself off and disappeared.' As Cisneros wrote in the words of the psalm, thinking of Barzana's multilingual peregrinations all over the Andean world, 'We passed through fire and water and you have led us forth into rest.'[81]

When Barzana first learned Quechua, he probably used the vocabulary and grammar by Domingo de Santo Tomás, published in 1560. Fray Domingo of the Order of Preachers had taken Latin as the framework within which to set up Quechua grammar, with the intention of demonstrating that Quechua, being a civilized langage like Latin, was orderly and elegant and therefore both learnable and worthy of being learned. But Latin grammar could not provide a full framework for the description and analysis of Andean languages, and the linguistic notes in the *Doctrina Christiana* made a start at addressing this problem. However, those brief remarks could not begin to answer the question as to how this much more ample material might be presented.[82] That task was taken on by two of the next generation's Jesuits, Ludovico Bertonio[83] and Diego González Holguín.

They may have arrived in Peru in the same year, 1582, and were of roughly the same age, but they were very different in other ways. Bertonio was Italian and received his Jesuit training in the Collegio Romano.[84] After teaching Latin poetry in Lima for a few years, he spent the rest of his life in Juli, dedicating his free time to work on an Aymara grammar and dictionary.[85] These were published by the Jesuit press in Juli in 1612. [86] People liked Bertonio: 'He is an angel,' Juan de Atienza, then provincial of Peru, who was not given to such statements, wrote about him.[87] González Holguín's life as a Jesuit was more complicated,[88] and so was his temperament: when young, he was thought to be 'a little hard in his judgment,' and in his later years his disposition was described as 'phlegmatic and melancholic.'[89] But he became, as another fellow Jesuit wrote, 'one of the best linguists we have here.'[90] He was from Cáceres, studied Latin and theology, and perhaps began learning Quechua while still in Spain. In any case, he was caring for Andean people shortly after he arrived in Lima,[91] and he continued this work in Quito, where he witnessed the terrible earthquake of 1587 and the tax riots of 1589. By 1601 he was in Arequipa, ministering to both Quechua and Aymara speakers, [92] having picked up Aymara along the way. His repeated requests for time to devote to his linguistic work went for the most part unheard, but his Quechua grammar was published in Lima in 1607, followed by the dictionary in 1608.

The writings of Bertonio and González Holguín share certain features in being the direct outcome of the Jesuits' commitment to the study of indigenous languages and of their experience of teaching Christian Doctrine. Both of them listened to Andean people attentively and laboured to devise a systematic orthography that reflected pronunciation, especially with regard to the sounds that Spanish lacked. As Bertonio observed, the task in hand was not just to say things oneself, but also to understand what was said in response, and what Andean people said in their own right. Language was not just the statements of one person, but dialogue. Language as dialogue, at the same time, was part of the experience of every Jesuit in studying and teaching Latin. In the colleges, students and teachers conversed in Latin, and that not only during formal instruction but all the time; and when the attainments of erudition were displayed in public, it was again dialogically, in declamations, colloquies, dialogues, and plays. This same dialogic method was used in teaching Christian Doctrine,[93] and entered into the creation of the linguistic works of Bertonio and González Holguín.

When Domingo de Santo Tomás wrote his grammar, he described his work as 'reducing Quechua into an *Arte*,' a grammatical work. This amounted to discerning the principles of order in the language, and hence defining the way it worked. From this perspective, all languages were alike, all had an order, and for that reason all were intelligible. González Holguín and Bertonio also described their grammars as *Arte*, but they saw the task of the grammarian and lexicographer a little differently. For reducing a living language to grammar, making it systematically accessible to learners, was not the same thing as reducing Latin, or even reducing Christian doctrine. With Latin and Christian doctrine, what was to be reduced was in some sense fixed: Latin was learned from Roman and ecclesiastical texts, and Christian doctrine had most recently been defined and fixed by the Council of Trent. Both could be read in books. Quechua and Aymara, by contrast, were not written in books, but were spoken, remembered, and recorded on quipus. In a sense, therefore, the language had to be re-created before it could be reduced into an *Arte* and a dictionary in alphabetic script. That, at any rate, is what Bertonio thought. He therefore asked the people of Juli, many of whom had learned to read and write in the Jesuit school, to compose in Aymara texts that he could use as his sample of the language:

We arranged that they should write in their Aymara langage, with all possible accuracy, the principal mysteries of the life of Christ, a large number of rules of conduct[94] and lives of the saints, many sermons about diverse subjects, various comparisons relating to virtues and vices, some treatises on the mass and about confession and communion, and about many other things that it would take too long to enumerate. And since Our Lord wished to make use of this work, he likewise deigned to assist these Indians, so that they were able to arrive at a very complete comprehension of all these sacred subjects, also using some books in Spanish, which language they understand very well, and with this intelligence they wrote so well in their language, and with such propriety and elegance, that it is an admirable thing for those who understand the language.[95]

Bertonio's linguistic work is thus the product of Jesuit pastoral practice in Juli. In the Spanish world, in Spanish Peru, grammar, the learning of Latin, was a step towards learning virtue, and the same was the case in Juli, except that, in this missionary context, the two processes became inextricably joined. The teacher, the Jesuit Bertonio, became the student, and the students, the Aymara people, were the teachers, instructing Bertonio how to give voice to virtue in their language.

To get to that point, as Acosta had seen so well, it was necessary in the first place for the missionary teacher to accommodate his message to his hearers, and Bertonio agreed. In terms of language, this meant that Christian virtue was accommodated to Aymara grammar and ways of speaking, and the grammar and ways of speaking were accommodated to virtue.[96]

The conceptual coherence of Bertonio's work documents the conceptual coherence of the Jesuit program at Juli and, in more general terms, of the Jesuit missionary program in Peru at large. González Holguín, who did not spend his life in the protected environment of a model missionary *doctrina*, experienced language rather differently, although like Bertonio he wrote for purposes of evangelization. To make this point, Bertonio told the parable of the Good Samaritan: the missionary priests who refused to learn the Indians' language were like the priest and Levite in the parable, who passed by on the other side.[97] González Holguín, the man whose judgment had been felt to be 'a little hard,' expressed himself more sharply and passionately, at the same time echoing Acosta:[98]

We say the Indians die of their idolatries, and what are they dying of? Of hunger for the word of God, because 'faith comes from hearing, and hearing is through the word of

Christ.' And what kills them? Not having anyone who will give them the pasture for the soul that is the word of God, and this ... is explained by Jeremiah ... who says, 'The little ones asked for bread, and there was no one to give it to them,' as when a father of many little children who ask him for bread does not want to give it to them, although his storehouse is full. How cruel a father this is, if the Indians die in their idolatries ... If you did not feed them, you killed them.[99]

In the introduction to his Quechua grammar, González Holguín explained that at the beginning of Christian history Christ had given to the church, his bride, as her dowry, the gift of languages, so that the apostles were able to preach in the languages of all nations, 'and the nations shall walk in your light.' However, now that the church was no longer a young girl but a mature mother of many children, languages were no longer infused as a gift without work, because the task of the church now was to raise her new Andean children in the labour of love. 'Love never fails,' as St Paul had said. The labour of love consisted of studying languages, thereby entering into the gift that had been given to the apostles, and preaching with conviction as they had done. [100]

Here was a different way from Bertonio's of joining grammar with virtue, although the concrete linguistic and scholarly tasks that González Holguín thought had to be accomplished were similar or the same. As well as seeing, as Bertonio did, the need for an orthography that reflected pronunciation as closely as possible, like Bertonio he did not attempt to fit Quechua grammar into the structure of Latin grammar, although he did periodically draw the student's attention to instances where Latin provided a helpful analogy, or where Latin was different. Also, like Bertonio, he was aware that frequently there were no direct Spanish equivalents of Quechua terms and vice versa, and that one language in given areas supplied more or less than the other, and he offered alternatives to bridge these deficiencies and exuberances. In short, he listened to Quechua speakers with focused attention, and over many years.

But not having lived long years in the daily and recurring rhythms of the *doctrina* of Juli, González Holguín envisioned his public differently from Bertonio. Like Bertonio, he wrote for prospective priests of Andean parishes; but unlike Bertonio he composed his dictionary not only for them but also for 'the Indians who would like to learn the Castilian language.'[101] Second, he did not have a corpus of texts that had been prepared for his own specific purposes to draw on. Instead, his source was the speech of everyone and of every day, which yielded a superabundance of material. Where Bertonio thus saw his public in terms of the missionary parish as exemplified by Juli, González Holguín identified with the traditions and the work of the Society of Jesus in broader terms, and also with Andean people wherever he found them.

González Holguín thought that all the material he had gathered during some twenty-five years of talking with Indians who were 'wonderful linguists' was 'important for the perfect understanding of the language, and could not be left aside.'[102] But as a compromise with the reader, he divided his *Arte* into four books, the first two providing the necessary grammar, and the last two providing 'what is more for the building up and perfection of the language,' that is, the derivation of words from one another, and their composition in an elegant manner. The student might thus choose to master just the first two books, or continue to the fourth.[103] Within this order of books, the *Arte* is arranged as a dialogue between student and teacher, to allow for the student's participation, in the familiar Jesuit way. Also, by way of achieving greater clarity, as González Holguín pointed out, he arranged the material as main paragraphs each followed by commentary, a feature that makes for a certain formal resemblance between the *Arte* and the *Constitutions of the Society of Jesus*, which Ignatius of Loyola arranged in a similar way, in order to make them easier to remember.[104]

Even so, both the *Arte* and the *Vocabulario* of González Holguín, because of the abundance of material, have a certain tendency to want to burst out of the framework of the printed book. This is the case especially with the *Vocabulario*, where many entries are much more than dictionary entries. Some offer synonyms, and via the synonyms explore possible contexts of a given word. Other entries form groups, exploring semantic fields. Elsewhere, the *Vocabulario* provides glimpses of how Quechua was changing by having Spanish as a neighbouring language.[105] The *Vocabulario*, in short, records what people had said, which was why González Holguín thought that 'just as I myself am not convinced that this work is primarily my own, but rather is the work of the many Indians of Cuzco, whom I have asked again and again, and have ascertained from them the meaning of each word, and from them I have learned it, so they are the principal authors of this work, and to them should be attributed all that is good in it, after the primary author, who is God. And to me as the instrument of those Indians should be attributed everything that might not be as fitting, perfect, and correct as it should be.'[106]

And where was virtue now? In the speech of the people who by means of the book in the reader's hands – their own book – were going to be taught. This shift of the role of the teacher towards that of the student, and the accompanying, albeit only implied, shift of the virtue that was inculcated in the pursuit of grammar and letters from teacher to student, took place in the course of the multifarious contacts between Jesuits and Andean people during the early years of the Society's work in the Andes. Concurrently, several Jesuits in Peru, especially José de Acosta, thought that mestizos, sons of Spaniards or creole fathers and Andean women, should be full partners, in the work of evangelization, of Jesuits from Europe and of Peruvian Jesuits of European descent.[107] The plan, however, met with much opposition in both secular and ecclesiastical circles, and from within the Society, and did not come to fruition.[108] Furthermore, throughout the colonial period and even now, Andean people play a subordinate role in church and state.

But the aspiration of the early colonial Jesuit grammarians, of Acosta and men of similar outlook, was perhaps not entirely forgotten. In the later seventeenth century, the Jesuits in Cuzco commissioned a painting, which now graces the narthex of La Compañía in that city.[109] The painting shows the wedding of Martín García de Loyola, a kinsman of St Ignatius, and Doña Beatriz Clara Coya, a granddaughter of the Inca Guayna Capac. Behind the couple are the bride's parents and the Inca Tupac Amaru, for whose life Luis López had interceded in vain. On the other side, the child of this union is marrying a kinsman of Francisco Borja, under whose direction the first Jesuits had come to Peru. Also depicted are Ignatius of Loyola and Francisco Borja with the emblem of the Society. Admittedly, this painting gives an idealized vision of a past that in any case could not be recovered, how ever deeply Andean viewers may have identified with the Inca personages being depicted. But the vision did connect with a reality that had been alive during the first decades of the Society in Peru, and that left a legacy in the alliance between grammar and virtue that speaks in the work of Bertonio and González Holguín.

NOTES

1 Ruben Vargas Ugarte, *Historia de la Compañía de Jesús en el Perú*, 4 vols (Burgos, 1963–5), is a comprehensive and well-documented survey. For the foundation of the first Jesuit house in Lima in 1568, see vol. 1, chap. 3.

2 The topography of Inca Cuzco remains full of puzzles. There are reasons for thinking that Amarucancha was not the dwelling of Guayna Capac, even though it was generally believed to have been so by sixteenth-century Spanish inhabitants of Cuzco. Well-informed Andean witnesses in the Probanza of Melchor Carlos Inca (BNM 20193) all stated that the buildings used by Guayna Capac were Casana, Collcampata, and Ucchullu, which was also described as the 'palacio dormitorio' on the site of the 'iglesia mayor.' Amarucancha is never mentioned.

3 The first church of the Jesuits on the site of Amarucancha was destroyed in the earthquake of 1650, and was replaced by the building standing there now. See Ruben Vargas Ugarte, *Los jesuitas del Perú y el arte* (Lima, 1963), pp. 66–73. See also Antonio de Vega, *Historia o enarración de las cosas sucedidas en este colegio del Cuzco destos Reynos del Perú desde su fundación hasta hoy primero de noviembre Día de Todos Santos año de 1600,* ed. Ruben Vargas Ugarte under

the title *Historia del Colegio y universidad de San Ignacio de Loyola de la ciudad del Cuzco*, Biblioteca Historica Peruana 6 (Lima, 1948).

4 This was anticipated by Francisco Borja (letter to Jerónimo Ruiz de Portillo, 14 November 1570, *M Peru*. 1 document 79), and the foundation had begun by 19 April 1572; Bartolomé Hernandez mentioned it in his letter to Juan de Ovando, *M Peru*. 1 document 97 sec. 14.

5 Annual Letter, by José de Acosta, Lima, 1 March 1576, *M Peru*. 2 document 2 sec. 11.

6 Luis Antonio Eguiguren, *Las huellas de la Compañía de Jesús en el Perú* (Lima, 1956) includes several inventories of Jesuit libraries made at the time of the expulsion in 1767. A significant number of the books date from the sixteenth and early seventeenth centuries and were probably acquired then.

7 *M Peru*. 1 document 57 sec. 12, written by Diego de Bracamonte on 21 January 1569, on Bracamonte's activities in Lima; for Indians, the dialogues and responses had already been composed in Quechua at this early date.

8 See, for example, the description of Corpus Christi in Huarochiri (then a Jesuit *doctrina*), *M Peru*. 1 document 85 sec. 20, with songs in Quechua honouring the Blessed Sacrament and a dance of 'nobles que se llaman ingas,' who said that the praises 'que antiguamente daban al sol y a su Rey, ésos conbertían en loor de Jesuchristo tomando matheria de lo que oían predicar.'

9 *M Peru*. 1 document 69 sec. 20.

10 Cf. David M. Kowal, 'Innovation and Assimilation: The Jesuit Contribution to Architectural Development in Portuguese India,' in O'M. *Jes. Cult.*, pp. 480–504.

11 The Jesuits did not favour ritual for ritual's sake. Note the stance taken on exorcism, a ritual procedure that was very popular in Peru at the time, Borja to Portillo, 14 November 1570, *M Peru*. 1 document 79. Much effort had been expended, Borja had learned, in exorcizing a 'donzella endemoniada'; he observes, 'V.R. advierta que este ministerio no le tenemos por proprio de nuestro Instituto, el qual es endereçado a sacar los demonios de las animas mas que de los cuerpos.' For in the latter, Borja added, the 'obra de charidad' can easily become 'obra scandalosa.' The instruction was repeated in a further letter by Borja to Portillo, ibid., document 80 sec. 6.

12 *M Peru*. 1 document 80 sec. 2: 'Las obras espirituales son las que pretendemos, y no las materiales.'

13 Bracamonte, in *M Peru*. 1 document 57 sec. 22: 'El fructo que de los sermones se a seguido, a sido una reformación universal en toda suerte de gentes.'

14 *M Peru*. 1 document 68.

15 *M Peru*. 1 document 57 sec. 22, concerning 'bandos' and enmities; see also document 61; and document 69 concerning restitution – and disagreement with a member of the secular clergy about the need for restitution. The Annual Letter of 1579, written by Acosta, reviews the accomplishments of the Society in this vein, *M Peru*.

592   Sabine MacCormack

2 document 123. See, on these pastoral and social aspirations of the Jesuits, O'M.
   First, chap. 5.

16 'Nuestro modo de proceder.' The phrase recurs often in Jesuit documentation,
   for example in the report on the Peruvian province by Juan de la Plaza, Cuzco,
   12 December 1576, *M Peru*. 2 document 20 sec. 17.

17 See *Provisiones cedulas, capitulos de ordenanças, instruciones, y cartas*, vol. 1
   (Madrid: En la Imprenta Real, 1596 – this being the *cedulario* of Diego de Encinas;
   repr. Madrid, 1945), pp. 31–4, reproducing the bull of Alexander VI *Noverint
   universi*, and a part of the testament of Isabella, both asserting the primacy of
   evangelization in the Americas. The inclusion of these documents in a compilation
   of legislation highlights the political importance of this issue. The *Recopilación de
   las leyes de las Indias* (Madrid, 1681, 1973), book 1, title 1, reiterates this theme by
   reproducing legislation mandating the preaching of Christianity. Viceroy Toledo, in
   whose company some of the first group of Jesuits to come to Peru had travelled, was
   deeply aware of the shortage of priests in missionary parishes; see Francisco de
   Toledo, *Memorial espiritual*, in Francisco de Zabálburu and José Sancho Rayon,
   Nueva colección de documentos ineditos para la historia de España y sus Indias,
   vol. 6 (Madrid, 1896), pp. 306–23 (on p. 306 the *Memorial* is attributed to 'Francisco de Mendoza'; the error is corrected in the table of contents). Toledo was
   accordingly most impatient with Jesuit reluctance to accept the care of parishes; see
   Plaza to Toledo, 1576, *M Peru*. 2 document 20 sec. 22. See also document 53, on
   the problems entailed by *doctrinas*. This was one of the several areas of conflict that
   made for poor relations between the Society and the viceroy; cf. *M Peru*. 1 documents 83, 91, and 92; *M Peru*. 2 document 126 sec. 47. Relations between the
   Jesuits and the Crown were much less fraught in Mexico; see Peggy Liss, 'Jesuit
   Contributions to the Ideology of Spanish Empire in Mexico,' part 1, *The Americas*,
   19:3 (1973): 314–33; part 2, *The Americas* 19:4 (1973): 449–70.

18 Portillo to Borja, January 1567, *M Peru*. document 3.

19 Juan Belda Plans, *La escuela de Salamanca* (Madrid, 2000), pp. 379ff.; Gustavo
   Gutiérrez, *Las Casas: In Search of the Poor of Jesus Christ* (Maryknoll, NY, 1993).

20 Borja to Portillo, 1567, *M Peru*. 1 document 29 sec. 3: 'Ya e avisado y torno a
   encomendar por ser muy importante que no se determinen en absolver ni condenar
   a los primeros conquestadores de las Indias y successores ... porque tienen muy
   honesto titulo para eximirse deste cargo diziendo que las Religiones, que tantos años
   han estado en las Indias, allan tanta difficultad en la determinación, y ansí sería
   temeridad que nosotros, acabando de llegar, quisiésemos ser juezes.'

21 Plaza to Everard Mercurian, *M Peru*. 1 document 144 sec. 5 p. 608; and more to the
   same effect in another letter by Plaza to Mercurian, written in Seville, June 1574,
   document 158 sec. 5.

22 Luis López to Borja, Cuzco, 12 October 1572, *M Peru*. 1 document 103 sec. 3.

23 Letters to Acosta, *M Peru.* 2 documents 15, 83, and 97; letter to Plaza, document 126.

24 López refers to this event in a letter to Borja, 12 October 1572, *M Peru.* 1 document 103 sec. 3. For a detailed account by an eyewitness, see Baltasar de Ocampo Conejeros, *Descripción y sucesos históricos de la provincia de Vilcabamba,* in Víctor Maurtua, *Juicio de límites entre el Perú y Bolivia. Prueba peruana presentada al gobierno de Argentina. Tomo séptimo. Vilcabamba* (Barcelona, 1906), pp. 306–44, on 324–7. For other problems involving Luis López, see *M Peru.* 1 document 88.

25 'Capítulos hechos por el maestro Luis López ... en deservicio de S.M. y del gobierno del virey y audiencias,' in *Colección de documentos inéditos para la historia de España,* vol. 94 (Madrid, 1889), pp. 472–86, with Toledo's rebuttal, pp. 486–525. For López's letters, see *M Peru.* 1 documents 68 and 71; regarding Borja's reaction, see document 79 sec. 9.

26 *M Peru.* 4 p. 420 n57.

27 See, for example, the letter by Hernandez, the former confessor of Francisco de Toledo, to Ovando, *M Peru.* 1 document 97. The letter leaves little unsaid, but Hernandez was a much more circumspect person than López, expressed himself with extreme care, and saw to it that his information was handled confidentially.

28 *M Peru.* 1, p. 139.

29 During the Atlantic crossing, he devoted himself to teaching and 'consoling' some thirty African slaves, and once arrived in Lima, he continued working with Africans; see *M Peru.* 1 document 33 sec. 6 (Cartagena, 1568); document 57 sec. 11 (Lima, 1569).

30 Catalogue of the Province, 1571, composed by Juan de Zúñiga, *M Peru.* 1 document 90. P. 444: 'El Padre Maestro Luis López. Tiene muchas letras y gran juicio; su talento es para tratar con proximos y confesar; es recio de condicion y poco amoldado al talle de la Compañía, y es muy libre y poco afficionado a cosas de mortificacion.' The writer of this catalogue succeeded López as rector of Cuzco (ibid., document 178 sec. 11).

31 Catalogue of the Province, 1572, by Zúñiga, *M Peru.* 1 document 108. P. 514: Luis López is currently rector ... 'sepa V.P. que el hazerle rector a sido porque sosiegue, porque siendo inferior da mucho trabajo a los que tratan con el, y sinedo Superior, deve de dar mas; necessidad ay que V.P. ponga remedio en esto.' The person being addressed is Francisco Borja, the general of the Society.

32 *M Peru.* 2 document 19 sec. 4. The sentence is almost impossible to translate: 'Que los que ovieren de venir a estas partes, sean de virtud probada y se conozca en ellos vocación de las Indias, o a lo menos firme obedienzia; porque de otra manera, de más de no hazer fruto, acá ellos bivirán desconsolados y darán no poca desedificazión.'

33 O'M. *First,* pp. 37ff., 372ff.

34 The topic pervades the Jesuit letters. *M Peru*. 1 document 85 sec. 11, about
    Barzana's preaching: 'in el Cercado Lima, con el qual sermon consoló a los indios
    que alli estaban.' Ibid., document 112, Juan Alfonso de Polanco to Portillo, in 1573,
    reporting that Ortuno was troubled by hearing confessions; have him study cases of
    conscience, Polanco advised, 'teniendo para ello capacidad; y si no, de consolarle.'
    See also Acosta on this topic, ibid., document 63 sec. 5, about himself, and sec. 6,
    about Luis de Guzman. *M Peru*. 2 document 26 sec. 66: Alfonso de Barzana experi-
    ences 'gran consuelo' when baptizing a mortally ill Andean woman, because 'vió en
    ella claras muestras de querella para Sí Dios nuestro Señor.'
35 *M Peru*. 2 documents 89–91.
36 *M Peru*. 4 document 101 sec. 4.
37 The phrase is Acosta's, *M Peru*. 2 document 2 sec. 19: the Indians are a nation
    'corporis et animi servitute oppressa.'
38 On his life, see the summary by Antonio de Egaña in *M Peru*. 1 p. 83.
39 *M Peru*. 1 document 90 p. 444.
40 *M Peru*. 1 document 109 p. 514.
41 *M Peru*. 2 document 20 pp. 118–19: 'Consultor de provincial and lector de la lengua
    indica, tiene buen ingenio y juizio, tiene buena salud, talento para predicar a indios y
    españoles, para confesar y doctrinar indios en las dos lenguas generales, es pre-
    dicador sufficiente. Tiene humildad y obediencia, es aplicaco a oración y exercitala
    con sentimiento. Es bien affecto a nuestro Instituto.'
42 Mercurian to Barzana, 19 November 1576, congratulating him on the work, *M
    Peru*. 2 document 19; Mercurian to Plaza, 28 November, about possible publication,
    document 14 sec. 19; document 17 sec. 18 and document 18 sec. 21, where Barzana
    is mentioned as the author. See also *Recopilación* (n17 above), book 1, title 24, law
    1, regarding the need for the royal licence. See further Plaza to Mercurian asking for
    help obtaining the licence to publish, *M Peru*. 2 document 19 sec. 26.
43 Mercurian to Acosta, 25 September 1578, *M Peru*. 2 document 60 sec. 4. Whether
    this disappearance of materials had anything to do with the troubles of Blas Valera
    merits some thought. On Blas Valera, see Sabine Hyland, *The Jesuit and the Incas:
    The Extraordinary Life of Padre Blas Valera, S.J.* (Ann Arbor, 2003).
44 *M Peru*. 2 document 26 sec. 61; Valera was to leave Cuzco at the same time, but
    this generated so much resistance from the Indians that his departure was post-
    poned.
45 The problems are listed at some length by Plaza in his report on the Peruvian
    province, Cuzco, 12 December 1576, *M Peru*. 2 document 20 secs 24–8. For the
    Jesuit architecture of Juli, see Ramon Gutiérrez, Carlos Pernaut, et al., *Arquitectura
    del altiplano peruano* (Buenos Aires, 1978), pp. 323–69.
46 For a list of problems at Juli as recorded by Andrés López on 6 August 1578, see *M
    Peru*. 2 document 55. He weighs the advantages of Juli against the disadvantages,

and proposes some remedies. See also Manuel Marzal, 'Las misiones jesuitas, una utopía posible,' in *Un reino en la frontera. Las misiones jesuitas en la América colonial*, ed. Sandra Negro and Manuel M. Marzal (Lima, 1999), pp. 489–504.

47 Annual Letter written by Acosta to Mercurian, 15 February 1577, *M Peru*. 2 document 26 sec. 72 p. 281.

48 See further ibid., secs 66–7: Eight days after the Jesuits arrived in Juli, they assembled the entire community, and Barzana preached to them in Aymara, at which 'they were attentive and surprised ... to see that he spoke to them in their own language and with spirit from heaven.' Next, after mass, the fathers invited the lords of the community to eat with them in order to discuss how Sunday observance would unfold, and how the alms would be distributed, this being another cause for surprise, 'because for these Indians it amounts to performing a miracle, when they see that [Spaniards] give to them, rather than taking from them.' Both the eating together and the redistribution of alms to the community conformed in some respects with Andean tradition.

49 For the prayers, ibid., sec. 69; for the songs, sec.72 p. 281.

50 Ibid., sec. 72.

51 See, for example, *M Peru*. 2 documents 17 and 18, the 'Acta' of the first provincial congregation of Peru, in 1576. Another fine stylist was José de Acosta.

52 See, for example, *M Peru*. 3 document 45 sec. 1, of 11August 1582, in which the viceroy Martin Henriquez responds to a petition by the Jesuits on behalf of their college, repeating their own wording: they would work 'en la instrucción de la juventud,' and 'aunque de su trabajo se servía Nuestro Señor y esta republica con el aprovechamiento de los studiantes en letras y virtud'; this purpose, so the petition ran, would be achieved even better with the granting of the favour being sought.

53 For an extended justification of the program, see Pedro de Ribadeneira, *Vida del Padre Ignacio de Loyola*, in Ribadeneira, *Obras escogidas*, ed. Vicente de la Fuente, Biblioteca de Autores Españoles 60 (Madrid, 1952), book 3, chap. 22. The course of study was pioneered by Ignatius himself during his time in Paris; see book 2, chap. 1.

54 Even critics of the enterprise agreed on this point, among them Andrés López, report on Juli, 6 August 1578, *M Peru*. 2 document 55 sec. 2: 'Fructos de la doctrina de Juli ... el criar la Compañía con brevedad muchas y muy buenas lenguas, el hazer cathesismos y enseñar la doctrina y cosas de la fe a nuestro modo, sin contradición de clérigos ni Ordinarios.' See also Acosta's very strong plea for Juli in a letter to Mercurian, *M Peru*. 3 document 141 sec. 2. Acosta, the soul of discretion, rarely wrote in criticism of anyone, but he did here. If Juli were given up, he thought, the Society would lose the language teaching that was offered there, and hence the ability to work with and for Andean people. He expressed appreciation for the way in which Diego de Torres, superior of Juli, was running the *doctrina*, and finally he

observed that Miguel de Fuentes, a critic of Juli, 'tiene muy poca afficción a los indios y siente y habla muy cortamente de sus cosas.'

55 *M Peru.* 4 documents 18 and 19.

56 *M Peru.* 4 document 18 sec. 4, written in 1586.

57 León Lopetegui, *El Padre José de Acosta y las misiones* (Madrid, 1942), chap. 1; and Claudio M. Burgaleta, *José de Acosta, S.J. (1540–1600): His Life and Thought* (Chicago, 1999), pp. 8–11, 12–31, on Acosta's Jesuit education.

58 Zúñiga to Borja, Lima, 31 December 1572, *M Peru.* 1 document 107.

59 For the topic as a whole, see Javier Albó, 'Jesuitas y culturas indígenas. Perú 1568–1606. Su actitud, métodos y criterios de aculturación,' *América indígena* 26:3 (1966): 249–308; 26:4 (1966): 395–445; and Albó, 'Notas sobre jesuitas y lengua Aymara,' in *Un reino en la frontera.* ed. Negro and Marzal (n46 above), pp. 397–413.

60 José de Acosta, *De procuranda Indorum salute,* ed. Luciano Pereña, 2 vols (Madrid, 1987), book 4, chap. 4:2, quoting Titus 2:14 and Isa. 11:6–9, as well as other scriptural passages. Acosta wrote to Mercurian (*M Peru.* 2 document 27) that he had long reflected on how to apply the scriptures, the writings of the Church Fathers, and the earlier history of Christian mission to the Americas. In actually doing so himself, he argued that Indians were not a second class of humanity; in fact, there was no such thing. This had earlier been argued by Las Casas and others, but for different reasons and with different arguments; cf. Sabine MacCormack, *Religion in the Andes: Vision and Imagination in Early Colonial Peru* (Princeton, 1991).

61 Acosta, *De procuranda,* book 1, chap. 8:1: '... istam ineptitudinem animi morumque indicorum feritatem ... consuetudinem bestiarum vita non valde dissimilem' are strong words.

62 Ibid., book 1, chap. 8:1: 'etsi enim vim habet non parvam genus et patria ... tamen infinitis partibus superat vitae institutio et exempla ab ipsa infantia per sensus inscilpata rudi adhic et tenero animo ...'

63 The phrase was used by Ribadeneira when describing Jesuit educational aims (n53 above).

64 Acosta, *De procuranda,* book 4, chap. 6:1, quoting Rom. 10:17: 'ergo fides ex auditu, auditus autem per verbum Christi.' See also book 1, chap. 4:5, quoting Rom. 10:14: 'Quomodo credent, si non audiunt? Quomodo vero audient sine praedicante?'

65 Acosta, *De procuranda,* book 5, chap. 14:2–3; in addition, priests would need a manual for confession that was accommodated to the consciences of the Indians. All these items were included in the *Doctrina Christiana* published by the Third Council of Lima; see below in the text.

66 Acosta, *De procuranda,* book 4, chap. 6:2.

67 Ibid., book 5, chap. 15:4.

68 Ibid., book 4, chap. 6:3, and book 5, chaps 17–20.

69 Some of the first Jesuits to come to Peru saw their task in almost apocalyptic terms: Barzana thought the days of the primitive church were returning, and Bracamonte believed that the solar eclipse and earthquake that occurred just as he and his companions were arriving in Lima were signs that 'God wanted to inspire us by giving us hope that he wanted to use us as instruments to help the souls of these kingdoms'; see Bracamonte to the Society in Rome, Lima, 21 January 1569, *M Peru*. 1 document 57 sec. 2. Such thoughts harmonize well with the apocalyptic hopes and expectations that moved so many people in the mid-sixteenth century, and also with the enthusiasm of those beginning a new enterprise. Acosta took a more sober view. He had a sense of mission, and *De procuranda* was a sustained meditation on the significance of the 'teachings of Scripture and the Holy Fathers' in a New World context (*M Peru*. 2 document 27 sec. 4), but he did not perceive any apocalyptic significance in his own time; see *De temporibus novissimis* and *De Christo revelato*, and also the writings of Delgado.

70 Mercurian to Acosta, Rome, 1 October 1578, *M Peru*. 2 document 15 sec. 2 – this letter was written for the sole purpose of telling Acosta not to offend the viceroy; Rome, 15 November 1578, document 97 sec. 2.

71 See the protracted correspondence about when and whether Acosta should return to Europe. Given Acosta's eminence and the importance of his work wherever he was, his superiors did not want to give him orders, whereas Acosta himself preferred to live by holy obedience. See Acosta to Claudio Acquaviva, *M Peru*. 3 document 99. Note especially document 115, in which Acquaviva wrote to Juan de Atienza asking him to find out what Acosta wanted, and then to order Acosta to do it.

72 'On Achieving the Salvation of the Indians.'

73 Mercurian to Acosta, Rome, 25 September 1578, *M Peru*. 2 document 60 sec. 6; Mecurian to Gil Gonzalez, provincial of Peru, 8 November 1582, *M Peru*. 3 document 46.

74 The decrees of the council met with much opposition from those whose conduct they were designed to reform, and who sent procurators to Madrid charged with persuading Philip II to abrogate the decrees and prohibit their publication. Acosta submitted a carefully drafted memorial in defence of the council's decrees (published in *Obras del Padre José de Acosta*, ed. J. Mateos [Madrid, 1954], pp. 321–30) and succeeded in obtaining the king's approval for the council, whose decrees were thereupon published.

75 Several of these documents, in particular the *Instrucción* of Polo de Ondegardo, drew on earlier materials dating as far back as the 1560s, before the Jesuits had come to Peru.

76 See nn 42 and 43 above; for the council's version of the two catechisms, see *Doctrina Christiana y catecismo para instruccion de los Indios y de las demas personas que han de ser enseñadas en nuestra sancta Fé ...* (Lima, 1584; facs. ed.

Madrid, 1985). The short catechism is on fols 13–18, at the beginning of the book – the pages are not numbered consecutively, but in several batches. Next comes a 'Platica breve,' and then the 'Catecismo mayor,' on fols 25–82v. On the council, see further Francesco Leonardo Lisi, *El tercer concilio Limense y la aculturación de los indígenas sudamericanos* (Salamanca, 1990). For the short and the long catechism in Juli, see Acosta to Mercurian, 11 April 1579, *M Peru.* 2 document 123 sec. 22: the boys in school 'aprenden el cathecismo breve y largo y enséñanle a los viejos y a los demás.' It is tempting to suppose that these were the catechisms of Barzana. Vega, *Historia o enarración* (n3 above), pp. 11–12, attributes the 'Confesionario' and 'Sermonario' to Barzana, Bartolomé de Santiago, and Blas Valera, the latter two of whom were mestizos, as well as 'otros algunos versados en esta tierra y buenas lenguas.' On Valera, see Hyland, *The Jesuit and the Incas* (n43 above); and Francisco Borja de Medina, 'Blas Valera y la dialéctica "exclusión-integración del otro,"' *AHSI* 68:136 (1999): 229–67.

77 Baltasar Piñas to Acquaviva, *M Peru.* 3 document 77 sec. 3.

78 Annual Letter, *M Peru.* 4 document 140 sec. 9.

79 Gregorio Cisneros to Acquaviva, Cuzco, 2 January 1599, *M Peru.* 6 document 186 sec. 25, with note *ad loc.* about alternative dates.

80 *M Peru.* 3 p. 232, and n98.

81 *M Peru.* 6 document 186 sec. 30: 'transivimus per ignem at aquam et eduxisti nos in refrigerium,' Ps. 65:12.

82 Neither did the dictionary published for the council by the printer Ricardo, which is usually referred to under his name. In large part, this dictionary is a version of the dictionary by Domingo de Santo Tomás.

83 Ludovico Bertonio is first mentioned in Peru in the official list of members of the Jesuit house in Lima for the year 1582. In the customary laconic style, the entry says, 'aged 26 years, energetic, ten years in the Society, studied arts for three years, theology for four, not graduated, minister, preacher, and confessor' (*M Peru.* 3 document 48 sec. 30 p. 226). He was in Sanlucar, ready to leave for Peru, in February 1578, but it is not clear when exactly he did leave (*M Peru.* 2 p. 343 n6, where he is referred to as Juan Ludovico). On Bertonio's linguistic work, cf. Albó, 'Notas sobre jesuitas' (n59 above), pp. 397–413.

84 To Acquaviva, *M Peru.* 3 document 151 sec. 25.

85 *M Peru.* 5 document 187 (14 March 1595) p. 778; this is the catalogue of the Peruvian province. The document states that he also taught cases of conscience. At his own request, Bertonio while at Juli was given time for further studies (Acquaviva to Bertonio, 3 August 1592, ibid., document 42; see also document 56, Juan Sebastian to Acquaviva, of the same year), but what these studies were is not stated.

86 By 1596, Bertonio had written a book 'in the language of the land,' which Acquaviva, then general of the Society, recommended be published (*M Peru.* 6

documents 55 and 65, both written in October 1596). Whatever this book was, in 1603, Bertonio's Aymara grammar was published in Rome; cf. *M Peru*. 8 document 40, Acquaviva to Bertonio, who was in Potosí at the time, 10 March 1603, with editor's note on the publications. A corrected edition, along with his Aymara dictionary, emerged from the printing press of the Jesuits in Juli in 1612. The dictionary is entitled *Vocabulario de la lengua Aymara. Primera parte, donde por abecedario se ponen en primer lugar los vocablos de la lengua Española para buscar los que les corresponden en la lengua Aymara ... Impresso en la casa de la Compañía de Jesus de Juli Pueblo en la provincia de Chucuito* (Juli: Francisco del Canto, 1612).

87 Atienza to Acquaviva, 7 August 1587, *M Peru*. 3 document 151 sec. 15.

88 In *M Peru*. 3 document 48 p. 227, Diego González Holguín is described as having 'buenas fuerzas,' as coming from Cáceres, and as having studied arts and theology. For his voyage to Peru, see *M Peru*. 2 p. 343 n6, where the person being described as Diego González is perhaps González Holguín. But there was another Diego González, and it is not clear which of the two is referred to here. Regarding the Diego González who is referred to as being in Juli, see *M Peru*. 2 p. 372 n10. For more on the other Diego González, see ibid., document 20 p. 128, where it is clear that this is not González Holguín.

89 *M Peru*. 4 document 30 sec. 23 (24 February 1587); *M Peru*. 7 pp. 255 and 272 (15 March 1601). González Holguín was not alone in his melancholy; Acosta suffered from it also, *M Peru*. 3 document 51 sec. 4 (1583), and document 63 sec. 5 (1583).

90 *M Peru*. 7 p. 610.

91 *M Peru*. 3 document 48 p. 227 says that he was hearing the confessions of Spaniards and Indians.

92 *M Peru*. 7 document 50 sec. 13 p. 255 (15 March 1601).

93 For example, Acosta to Mercurian, 11 April 1579, *M Peru*. 2 document 123 sec. 22, about the school in Juli: 'han representado este año dos o tres colloquios o comedias, en su lengua, de cosas muy utiles a la edifficación de los indios.'

94 Translating Bertonio's 'exemplos.'

95 Bertonio, *Vocabulario* (n86 above). See also *M Peru*. 5 document 181 (1595) sec. 7 p. 709, mentioning that the fathers in Juli 'tienen començado un libro de sermones y otro de exemplos en la lengua aumara ... y tambien tienen hecho un bocabulario,' and that these might be published. Perhaps these are the preparatory materials for his lexical and grammatical works that Bertonio mentions here.

96 Bertonio, *Vocabulario*, fol. A3v: 'acomodandose el predicador a la capacidad de los oyentes, abriendo camino al entendimiento con algunas comparaciones faciles y claras, y en fin dando mamar la leche de la docrina Evangelica Quasi nutris fovens filios suos.' See further the 'Approbación' of the book by Hernando de Herrera, Pedro de Oñate, and Diego de Torres (who also wrote a grammar), praising the

Vocabulario because it provides 'vocablos acomodados a la lengua Española y modo nuestro de hablar; y en las phrasis muchos modos de dezir acomodados a lo Espiritual.'

97 Bertonio, *Vocabulario*, fols A2v–A3.

98 The echo is González Holguín's appeal to the passage 'fides ex auditu,' n64 above.

99 Diego González Holguín, *Vocabulario*, dedication to Hernando Arias de Ugarte.

100 *Gramática y arte nueva de la lengua general de todo el Peru llamada lengua Qquichua o lengua del Inca. Añadida y cumplida en todo lo que le faltaba de tiempos, y de la Gramática y recogido en forma de Arte lo mas cecesario en los dos primeros libros. Con mas otros dos libros posteros de adiciones al Arte para mas perficionarla el uno para alcanzar la copia de vocablos, y el otro para la elegancia y ornato. Compuesta por el Padre Diego González Holguín de la Compañía de Jesús natural de Cáceres. Nueva edición revista y corregida 1842,* dedication to Hernando Arias Ugarte.

101 González Holguín, *Vocabulario*, point 9 in the 'Suma de las cosas ...' in the introductory material.

102 Contrast Bertonio, in the introduction to his *Vocabulario*, explaining that he left aside much of the vocabulary that would not be needed for missionary teaching.

103 González Holguín, *Arte*, p. xii.

104 Ibid., p. xii; and Ignatius of Loyola, *The Constitutions of the Society of Jesus*, trans. George E. Ganss (St Louis, 1970), sec. 136 (p. 121): the *Constitutions* should be complete, clear, and brief, so that they can be readily remembered. The 'Declarations' and 'Annotations' that were added to them 'possess the same binding force as the other Constitutions'; just as in the *Arte*, the commentaries were part and parcel of the whole.

105 See, for example, the *Vocabulario*, p. 270: 'Pacha camac. El templo que el Inca dedico a Dios criador junto a lima, para hazer alto sus exercitos, y el Demonio de embidia se entro y se hizo poner un idolo que porque hablava en el mucho le llamaron rimak, que dize hablador y es ya el nombre de Lima corrompido de rimak.'

106 Ibid.: 'Al Christiano Lector: assi como yo no estoy perusadido para mi a que esta obra sea mia principalmente sino de los muchos indios del Cuzco a quienes yo he repreguntado y averiguado con ellos cada vocablo, y de ellos lo he sacado, assi ellos son los principales autores desta obra, y a ellos se deve atribuir todo lo bueno que uviere en ella despues del autor principal que es Dios, y a mi como a instrumento de ellos no mas todo lo que no fuere tan acertado cumplido y ajustado.'

107 *M Peru.* 3 document 58, opinions of Acosta to that effect.

108 The failure of the plan is most saliently manifest in the career of Blas Valera, on whom see n76 above.

109 José de Mesa and Teresa Gisbert, *Historia de la pintura cuzqueña*, 2 vols (Lima,

1982), I, p. 180; II, figs 246 and 247. See also Marie Timberlake, 'The Painted Image and the Fabrication of Colonial Andean History: Jesuit and Andean Visions in Conflict in *Matrimonio de García de Loyola con Nusta Beatriz*,' dissertation, University of California–Los Angeles, 2001, *inter alia* making a convincing case for the Andean message of the painting.

27 / The Problematic Acquisition of Indigenous Languages: Practices and Contentions in Missionary Specialization in the Jesuit Province of Peru (1568–1640)

ALIOCHA MALDAVSKY

Without indigenous languages, 'here theology would be speechless in preaching the gospel,' wrote a Jesuit about Peru in 1636.[1] The Jesuits left behind many printed documents that attest to their linguistic endeavours in the Americas. The memory of authors such as Juan Ruiz de Montoya and Diego González Holguín lives on through these written fragments, which include catechisms and confession manuals as well as grammar and vocabulary books in indigenous languages, especially Quechua and Aymara. However, these eminent linguists represent only the visible tip of the iceberg. In the 1580s, General Claudio Acquaviva requested that indigenous languages be taught throughout Brazil, Peru, and Mexico to Jesuits preparing for priesthood. My analysis focuses on the ways in which this widespread instruction about local languages was carried out in the Viceroyalty of Peru during the first sixty years of the Jesuit province's existence, on the evidence of documents that have been little studied and for the most part remain unpublished. The study highlights the reluctance and hesitation such instruction encountered, and its significance for missionary identity in the province. The debates among the members of the Peruvian province emphasize the difficult relationship that often existed between the missions and colonial society.

Learning Indigenous Languages in Peru

The General Situation in Peru

In 1568, when the Society of Jesus arrived in Peru, the Spanish policy was to encourage friars and priests to learn the indigenous languages, especially when they were responsible for the evangelization of Indians in their parishes, called *doctrinas* in Spanish America. Even if the Crown encouraged the 'castilianization' of elites, it encouraged the use of local languages in catechesis and preaching, which was in accord with the dictates of the Council of Trent (1545–63). These dictates reinforced an existing trend. As early as 1215, Lateran Council IV had insisted on the importance of preaching in vernacular languages. Peruvian councils and synods reiterated this point when ordering priests to learn local languages. In Peru, the languages in question were Quechua and Aymara, those most spoken by the Andean people. As Robert Ricard wrote about the Nahuatl language in New Spain, these languages were used as 'auxiliary' languages in the evangelization of Peru. The first Quechua lessons were given in 1551 in the cathedral of Lima. Among the Dominicans who were in charge of this instruction, the most important was Domingo de Santo Tomás, the author of the first Quechua grammar. A chair of Quechua was founded at the University of San Marcos in Lima in 1579.

Language and Local Recruitment in the Society of Jesus

Jesuits could not avoid learning Indian languages, since their method of evangelization was based on teaching Christian Doctrine and administering sacraments, particularly confession. They maintained contact with Andean Indians first in the cities where they had their colleges, and then – especially – during the 'flying' missions they made periodically in teams of two into the Andean highlands and along the Peruvian coast. They also undertook remote missions, as far away as the borders of modern-day Chile and Paraguay. But unlike the other religious orders, the Jesuits of Peru refused at first to assume responsibility for *doctrinas* as ordinary priests. Nevertheless, in the 1570s, Viceroy Francisco de Toledo forced them to do so in Santiago del Cercado, on the outskirts of Lima, and in Juli, on the shores of Lake Titicaca. By the time of his arrival in Peru, the Society of Jesus had already been confronted with linguistic challenges in other places, such as Brazil and India. In order to ensure their linguistic efficiency, they adopted a strategy in Peru that focused on local recruitment. Local *criollos* (native Peruvians of European descent) or mestizos (Peruvians of mixed blood) who mastered indigenous languages could act as interpreters or share their knowledge with the Jesuits who came from Europe. This skill-sharing had been theorized as early as the 1550s by Jesuit authorities in Rome. The locals would offer their knowledge, while the Europeans would form them in the Society's 'way of proceeding.' This approach aimed to adapt the Society of Jesus to local conditions and ensure its unity in spite of challenging geographical distances.

In 1568, the provincial superior Diego de Bracamonte justified the recruitment of 'colonial-born young people' on the ground that 'all of them knew the language and were used to the country.' He gave the example of Brother Pizarro, a scholar who taught catechism in Quechua in Lima. The documents have not revealed whether this descendant of a conquistador was a mestizo or a Spaniard.[2] Later, in the catalogue of 1576, Father Juan de la Plaza abundantly praised the linguistic skills of the American-born Jesuits, as though doing so would help to justify their presence in the Society amid a general atmosphere of racial discrimination. Among them there were five mestizos given the title of 'lengua' (tongue), without any further indication of their level of linguistic knowledge. This title referred to the individual's ability to communicate in Quechua or Aymara. The mestizo himself was the 'tongue,' because he filled the role of spokesman for the Jesuits. There is no doubt that the admission of Blas Valera (in November 1568) and Bartolomé de Santiago (in 1574) gave a first impulse to the policy of indigenous language–learning in the Society of Jesus in Peru.[3] These two mestizos went on to translate the catechism of the Third Council of Lima (1583), under the supervision of José de Acosta.

The Circle of Language: From Learning to Teaching

Language chairs were quickly established in the Jesuit colleges of the viceroyalty to deal with instruction in linguistic theory. Approved by the civil and religious authorities, this teaching applied to members of the order and the local clergy alike. The teaching of Quechua began in Lima at least as early as 1575. Later on, at the end of the sixteenth century, it reached Potosí and La Plata (Sucre). Very quickly, owing to their mastery of the local languages, which was acknowledged and demonstrated beyond a doubt by their books, the Jesuits took on the role of linguistic experts for the viceregal authorities. In 1599 the viceroy called upon some Jesuits in Cuzco to test the knowledge of men who wished to become priests, in Quechua, Ayamara, and Puquina, the last being another language of the highlands. Even if this role was reserved for a minority of Jesuits, their reputation was based on a language-learning policy derived from frequent contact with the indigenous population. This interaction took place in the *doctrinas*, which were the true language schools for the Jesuits in Peru.

The provincial congregation of 1576 clearly differentiated between the theoretical and the practical conditions of language learning: 'Both general languages, Quechua and Aymara, of such an extended kingdom, must be industriously learned by Ours, because they are really necessary for the Lord's benefit. At least a smattering of them, firmly established by learning the art, will be taught in the colleges. But then Ours must gain the perfect linguistic talent in the Indian *doctrinas* through practising and training. The Indian *doctrinas* are the easiest and the most convenient place for that, and there is no other shortest and most suitable way to the ministry of preaching.'[4] The Juli *doctrina* very soon became a centre for learning Aymara. At the beginning of the seventeenth century, the Jesuits of Peru considered diversifying their learning policy by taking on another *doctrina* to found a Quechua school.

The experience here was very similar to the experiences the Jesuits had in Brazil, with the aldeias, and in New Spain, where they had two parishes – one outside Mexico City called Tepozotlán, where Indians spoke Nahuatl, and the other in Pátzcuaro (Michoacán), where Indians spoke the Tarascan language. The learning methods were actually more intensive and practical in the *doctrinas* than in the colleges, where they tended to be theoretical. In Juli the method focused mostly on preaching, as the provincial wrote in 1579: 'They practise a lot, and every day they meet for one or two hours in order to talk and do numerous composition and translation exercises. And it is our experience that, by this method, in four or five months Ours can learn the Indian language sufficiently to hear confessions and teach catechism. Then, after a year, they are able to preach. This way, five of Ours now preach with great facility and eloquence. And we pay great attention to this, because experience shows that this is the way to convert Indians.'[5] Some personal letters also refer to the stay in the *doctrina* to learn Indian languages. In 1625, Buonaventura Beati, a brother from Italy, wrote from La Paz after he had gained proficiency:

It has already been a year since I began learning the Aymara language, to help the gentiles; praise be to God, I can hear confessions and preach in the Indian language, even if it is not easy because I have just started doing it. With God's help, it will be easier in a while, and if not, we can suffer everything for such a good God. Thank God I am healthy, healthier than in Italy. In a few days I will be sent on mission for the first time. I am living in the college of Chuquiabo [La Paz] for the time being, and I spent ten months in the residence of Juli in order to learn the language after I left Lima, where I took my third year after the end of studies. I cannot write any longer because my time is taken up by continual confessions.[6]

We cannot say for sure whether the Jesuits of Peru all went to Juli to learn Aymara, because there were never more than ten residents in that *doctrina* at any one time. The time required to become a preacher (at least one year) left little room for rotation. The more gifted were certainly sent to Juli, and most of the others had a smattering of Quechua, which they acquired in the colleges. Nevertheless, it is difficult to determine the number of Jesuits who were proficient in an indigenous language, since such information was not systematically recorded in the catalogues. Why did the Peruvian catalogues leave out this information, when language skill was a crucial component of the Brazilian catalogues? Was it to conceal the unequal distribution of this skill among the members of the province? Because learning was long and arduous, the question of indigenous language facility leads to the question of specialization in missionary activity. Language was an instrument of evangelization. Accordingly, the degree of linguistic facility among the Jesuits in a given province or college reflected the importance of missionary activity in that province or college. During the seventeenth century a debate on language-learning developed in the Peruvian province, and documents demonstrate that it was possible for students to avoid learning the indigenous languages in any depth. This evidence clearly demonstrates that missionary goals were not accepted unanimously by the members of the Society of Jesus in Peru.

Language and Missionary Specialization: Questioning the Mission

The Debate over Acquaviva's Order: The Missionary and the Professor

In the late 1570s, Jesuit authorities in Rome enjoined the members of overseas provinces to learn local languages systematically as an instrument of evangelization. Francisco Borja wrote to the province of New Spain in 1579, 'It would be a good thing if nobody were ordained before he had learned one of the general languages spoken in those kingdoms.'[7] In 1583, Claudio Acquaviva reiterated this order in his instructions to the Peruvian province.[8] In 1594, thanks to the Fifth General Congregation, knowledge of indigenous languages became compulsory for Jesuits living in the Indies. The provincial congregations in Peru frequently repeated this decree. It was also one of the requirements incorporated by José de Acosta in his *De procuranda Indorum salute*, which he was preparing in the 1570s and 1580s. But elements of a polemic concerning indigenous language–learning are to be found in letters written at the beginning of the seventeenth century. At that time, Jesuits in Peru began questioning the validity of having all members in the province learn Quechua and Aymara.

In March 1601, Nicolas Durán, the superior of Juli and the founder of the province of Paraguay some years later, complained about superiors who failed to learn indigenous languages. He wrote, 'In houses where the superior does not know the language, the Indian ministries are so lethargic that they are nothing like the colleges of the Society.'[9] Some Jesuits 'fear inferior occupations, especially when they are in touch with Indians,' and refuse to be assigned to them by stating their dislike.[10] Such behaviour ran counter to the obedience that was supposed to prevail throughout the Society of Jesus. In Nicolas Durán's opinion, the consequence was that 'peace cannot prevail in this province without equal division of labour, because it frequently comes to pass that those who know the language work day and night, and those who do not know it, since there is very little work to do among the Spanish people, spend their time studying or talking with the lay people.'[11] Their duty, however, was to help others; furthermore, 'the language is very easy to learn, and whoever wants to learn it can do so and preach and hear confessions reasonably well after six months.'[12] He felt anxious about the indigenous languages and the future of the apostolate to the Indians if no solution was to be found.

Nine months later, the rector of Cuzco, Diego Alvarez de Paz, expressed the very opposite opinion. According to him, even if 70 per cent of the Jesuits had to learn indigenous languages – since Indians made up the majority of the population – this requirement did not apply to the remaining 30 per cent.[13] He wanted tasks to be divided among those who evangelized the Indians, those who governed, and those who undertook spiritual activities. Preference for Indian ministry should govern the choice of the Jesuits who became missionaries. Applying a general rule to all the members of the province would simply not work. In Paz's opinion, there should be a hierarchy of Jesuits' 'occupations' within the Society. He wrote further that 'ministry to the Indians requires little study, because it is not necessary to tell them about subtle concepts or preach Holy Scripture. On the contrary, one does better and more appropriately to employ a simpler, everyday language for them. By contrast, ministry to the Spanish requires study. The preacher has to be heard and the confessor cannot make mistakes.'[14]

This was not the only intellectual rift between the missionaries and the rest of the Peruvian province. Diego Alvarez de Paz believed that there was a difference between them from a spiritual and disciplinary point of view as well. He wrote, 'Ours who go on too many missions acquire an abstracted and unquiet spirit, which is so far from devotion, and so little concerned with religious discipline and prayer, that when they come back nobody recognizes them and can straighten them out again.'[15] He thought that ministry to the Indians was a waste of personnel because, 'for the sake of the Indians' care, the province is deprived of people who could serve it in much more important matters, and they are sent to very distant missions, concerning the benefit to which I can say nothing because I have never participated in them. But I have heard very diverse opinions among Ours: some say the benefit is very great, and others say the contrary, and thus there is little we can do.'[16]

These doubts about remote missions applied to those being founded in the provinces of Tucuman (present-day Argentina) and Chile. Diego Alvarez de Paz had fewer doubts about the 'flying' missions, for which 'a large number of people is not necessary, because the fruits of the missions are not as great as they imagine over there [that is, in Rome]. That is beyond doubt because of the very meagre capacity of these people.'[17] Therefore, it was not necessary for all Jesuits to learn the indigenous languages. The rector of Cuzco could not understand why the fathers who devoted themselves to the missions wanted to apply the language rules so passionately. He wrote, 'They are so fooled by this order and so blind that they are convinced there is nothing more pleasing to God than to hear the confessions of four little Indians.'[18] In his opinion, these laws brought about a division between the missionaries and the rest of the Society. The first 'have a privileged air about them, and think they are the only ones who belong to the Society, and that the others do not belong to it.'[19] This debate reveals how knowledge of indigenous languages clearly determined missionaries' specialization. The Jesuits' individual destinies were directly influenced by the policy of learning local languages for the purpose of evangelization. It was owing to this link that we can observe the same reluctance among their students.

Contempt for the Missions

Examples confirm a lack of vocation for mission work among some of the Jesuits in Peru. In 1617, General Muzio Vitelleschi reacted concerning 'Father Sebastián Ferrufiño, who appealed to a relative of his, an inquisitor, to get away with certain things, such as permission not to go to Juli and not to learn the language as the others do.'[20] It is difficult to say whether attempting to avoid mission work was common, and documents concerning Ferrufiño's career give no indication of whether he ever worked with Indians.[21] In 1637, Juan Ternino wrote that he desired to join the Chilean missions and explained that 'those who want to undertake this activity are very few.'[22] In 1616 the procurator of the province in Rome, Juan Vázquez, tried to explain to the Roman authorities the negative view of mission work:

The mindset of these people, their ministry, is held in little esteem in the eyes of lay people, and, consequently, in the eyes of Ours, who apply themselves with more enthusiasm and facility to the brilliant dealings of Spaniards. That is the reason why it is so difficult for many of them to learn the language and to devote themselves to Indians. And even if the superiors order them to acquire some proficiency, sometimes they lack authority. If they are not vigilant in getting rid of the other hindrances and occupations, nobody will learn the language. This ministry also needs men realistic and humble enough to despise brilliant and reputable things and to devote themselves to despised and very lowly things. Fathers who do care for such things are men of great virtue and talent in the eyes of God. And they should be the same in the eyes of their superiors. They are the ones who work, because they know the language and are busy day and night. On the contrary, those who do not know it stay in their rooms or talk with their friends, or are out visiting all day long.[23]

Table 27.1
Jesuits and the Indian apostolate in the Peruvian province, 1576–1637

	1576	1583	1595	1601	1613	1637
Jesuits in the province (A)	73	136	244 (242)	280 (279)	367 (365)	490 (488)
Jesuits in the Indian apostolate (B)	23	13	38	49	70	152
American-born Jesuits in the province	10	25	38	38	77	187
as % of A	13.7	18.4	15.7	13.6	21.1	38.3
American-born Jesuits in the Indian apostolate	8	6	11	8	17	81
as % of B	34.8	46.1	28.9	16.7	26.1	63.3

Note: The numbers in parentheses refer to individuals about whom information is available in the documents. The place of birth of some individuals is unknown.

In the opinion of Alonso Ruiz, prejudices against the ministry to the Indians were very common among *criollos*. He wrote in 1585, 'Some of these *criollos*, as they call them here, even if they know the language better than those who come from Spain, use it with reluctance. And if they know one language they do not apply themselves well to another, even though it is easier for them because their ears are used to it.'[24]

However, *criollos* were not the only Jesuits who lacked a missionary vocation. In 1596, General Acquaviva wrote about the desire expressed by some Europeans to go back to Europe: 'I think the first reason for this desire is that work with the Indians is not sufficiently pleasant and satisfying. That is why they do not want to learn their language. And this kind of work does not make them happy.'[25] The opposition between *criollos* and Spaniards, frequently remarked upon in the historiography, does not seem to be borne out in this case. The two groups seem to have shared a reluctance for mission work. After a long period of discrimination, the position of *criollos* in the Peruvian province rose to one of great prominence, in the first third of the seventeenth century (table 27.1). They made up only 13.7 per cent of the province in 1576 and 21.1 per cent in 1613, but by 1637 the figure had risen to 38.3 per cent. The percentage of *criollo* participation in missionary activities was always greater than their proportion in the Society as a whole: in 1637, 63.3 per cent of the Jesuits who were or had been engaged in missionary activity were American-born. But figures have nothing to do with vocation; they show only that missionary activity had become almost compulsory for Jesuits sixty years after the arrival of the Society in Peru.

Seen in the context of increased local recruiting, this reluctance for mission work demonstrates that the Society's missionary project was not in keeping with colonial society's expectations of them. How to resolve this lack of vocation for mission ministry? The Society of Jesus tried to find a way of motivating students to study indigenous languages. In theory, Jesuits professed the fourth vow after they had finished their studies; the highest status in the hierarchy of the order was reserved for those who had studied philosophy for three years and theology for four years. To encourage vocations to the missions, the missionary provinces could apply more lax rules than those found in European colleges. In 1642 the provincial congregation of Peru reacted to a modification of the 1619 rules for instruction and asked for its suppression: 'It has been suggested that it was advisable to implore our father general to stop the privilege that has been granted to this province. The question is whether mediocre results are sufficient for one to be advanced from the cycle of arts to theology and from one year to the other. The aim of this is to promote to the fourth vow those who possess distinguished knowledge of the languages and who are eminent "workers" with Indians. Owing to this privilege, some of them have reached this level.'

Fifteen fathers among twenty-four asked for the suppression of the privilege, because students had started to abuse it and begun to study much less than before. Their thinking was, '[If] mediocrity is enough, then I will learn the language and be able to make the profession,'[26] wrote the superiors in a letter to the general in 1642. In their opinion the privilege was being abused:

Here the practice has been different. They are advanced showing mediocre results and without knowing the language, though keeping in mind that they have to learn it. They actually learn it later, and they are moved on by having preached a sermon committed to memory and perhaps well done, but without understanding what they are saying. It is clear that this is a fraudulent use of the aforementioned privilege and of the intention of our Father. Because the result is that they know neither the language nor theology at the level the *Constitutions* require. This is an abuse of the privilege, and that is why it ought to be suppressed.[27]

As far as I know, no work has been done on the differences between European and Latin American theological training and learning. The unique practices in Jesuit education in the Peruvian province, which I have pointed out here, would make for an interesting contrast with European practices. A similar situation existed in other parts of the Americas. For example, in late sixteenth-century Brazil, as Charlotte de Castelnau-L'Estoile discusses elsewhere in this volume, exceptional missionaries could replace Latin with the study of Tupí. Clearly, being a Jesuit did not have the same meaning everywhere in the world. In the case of Peru, students' attempts to thwart indigenous language instruction and avoid missionary assignments seemed to be clear and real. One of the more important reasons for these difficulties was that knowledge of indigenous languages was considered practical knowledge, a mere skill, and not genuine scholarly knowledge. If indigenous language–learning had an application in a geographical place (i.e., in the *doctrinas*), it did not necessarily play a consistent role in a Jesuit's education or career over time. Even if the *Constitutions* stressed the importance of learning local languages, the text did not mention when they had to be learned. It is logical that adaptations of the rule should be decided on a case-by-case basis by the father generals, but the generals were not always able to preserve the unity of Jesuit training throughout the world. Such limitations are logical for a living, expanding institution such as the Society of Jesus.

Many conclusions come to mind after this short presentation of the problem, and I would like briefly to touch upon some of them. First of all, the refusal to learn indigenous languages reveals that there were differing opinions among the Jesuits themselves as to the Society's missionary and apostolic vocation – both between the Jesuits in Europe and those in Latin America, and between missionaries and urban Jesuits within Peru itself. It shows that the question, What are we here for? would not receive a simple answer among the Jesuits of seventeenth-century Peru. A Jesuit could ask, Are we here to teach, and to take care of Spaniards' souls, and spread among them the new ideas of the Council of Trent? Or he could ask, Are we here to take care of Indians' souls and convert those who are still unbelievers? All these activities continued, in spite of the contradictions and differing attitudes within the Society. The contradictions nevertheless reveal the difficult relationship that existed between missions and colonial society, and between the rules and precepts of Rome and local expectations of the Society of Jesus. Second, *criollos* and Spaniards seemed to share a negative view of missionary activity, a finding demonstrating that religious orders were often places of mutual acculturation and dialogue rather than cultural confrontation. One of the reasons might be that in the seventeenth century a large number of Europeans finished their studies in Lima and at a very young age, and therefore became as familiar with the *criollo* world as those who were born there. Finally, for us the idea of a unified Society of Jesus becomes difficult to preserve given the challenges of the new social and geographical realities faced by the Jesuits. Although the Society has often been portrayed as monolithic and rigidly homogeneous, further study of the differing educational methods and approaches to ministry throughout the Jesuits' worldwide enterprise will reveal a multifaceted and often contradictory series of attitudes – and a 'corporate culture' that is far from uniform.

NOTES

1 ARSI FG 1488/II/24 fol. 1: 'la teologia aca sera muda para predicar el evangelio y
   instituir en christianas costumbres a los yndios que es el principal asunto y fin de
   esta provincia.'

2 *M Peru.* 1:266: 'Los de acá saben todos la lengua y están hechos a la tierra; y
   mortificados bien y fundados en virtud, haran buenos conpañeros para los que de
   alla vinieren.' For Pizarro, see ibid., 1:258–9.

3 Blas Valera entered the Society upon its arrival in Peru in 1568. José de Acosta, who
   came only in 1574, was not the first provincial to open the doors of the Society to
   mestizos, as Bernard Lavallé has asserted, *Recherches sur l'apparition de la conscience créole dans la vice-royauté du Pérou: L'antagonisme hispano-créole dans
   les ordres religieux (XVIe–XVIIe)* (Lille, 1982), p. 691.

4 Acts of the first congregation of Cuzco, 11 December 1576, *M Peru.* 2:68: 'Duas
   illas in hoc latissimo Regno generales linguas, quichuam et aymaram, cum
   fructificaturo in Domino necessariae omnino sint, Nostris studiose esse discendas.
   Quod sane fiet rudimenta quidem earum, et quae artis praeceptionibus constant,
   in collegiis discendo: mox vero, perfectam earum facultatem in ipsis indorum
   doctrinis, usu et exercitatione assidua, comparando. Id enim ex doctrinis indorum
   et facilius et commodius hauriri posse; neque ad ministerium sermonis ullam aliam
   esse magis compendiariam et aptiorem viam.'

5 Annual Letter, by José de Acosta, Lima, 11 April 1579, *M Peru.* 2:619: 'tienen
   gran exercicio de la lengua y cada día se juntan una o dos horas a conferir haciendo
   diversos exercicios de componer, traducir, etc., con esto tenemos ya experiencia que
   en quatro o cinco meses aprenden la lengua de los indios los Nuestros, de suerte que
   pueden bien confessar y cathequizar, y dentro de un año pueden predicar, y assi ay
   allí cinco de los Nuestros que predican con gran facilidad y abundancia, y en esto se
   pone diligencia, porque se ve por experiencia que consiste en ello la conversión de
   los indios.'

6 Bonaventura Beati to Marcantonio Beati, Chuquiabo, 1625, ARSI FG 1488/IV/3:
   'Gia ho finito li studii, gia ho finito la terza probazione; gia ha un'anno che com-
   mincai a imparar la lingua Aymara, per auto si questa gentilità; sia lodato Iddio,
   ancorche non senza difficoltà per star nelli principii, confesso e predico nella lingua
   degl'Indii; e con la gracia del señore, il travaglio in dies, sara minore. e quando
   fosse maggiore; per tan buon Dio tutto si puo passare. Di sanità lodato Iddio mi
   trovo molto bene; e meglio che in Italia. Piaccia a Iddio la sappi impiegare bene nel
   suo santo servicio. Fra pochi giorni andró in missione, e sará la prima volta; Mi
   trovo hora nel Collegio di Chuquiabo; havendo stato 10 mesi nella Residenza de
   Giuli imparando la lingua, doppo havermi partito di Lima; dove tenni la 3a pro-

bacione finiti li studii. Plura nellem pero non posso ser piú longo perche le continue confessioni non mi danno luogo.'

7 *M Mex.* 1:420.

8 Claudio Acquaviva to Baltasar Piñas, provincial of Péru, 21 November 1583, *M Peru.* 3:289: 'El orden que se ha dado a la Provincia de México acerca de aprender los Nuestros las lenguas de los gentiles entre los quales se hallan cuya copia se enbía con esta, desseo que Vuestra Reverencia haga tanbién guardar en esa provincia.'

9 Nicolas Mastrilo Durán to Acquaviva from Juli, where he is the superior, 15 March 1601, *M Peru.* 7:278: 'Los ministerios de los indios en las casas donde el Superior no sabe lengua, van con tanta floxedad que no parecen colegios de la Compañía.'

10 Ibid.

11 Ibid.: 'Añado que en esta Provincia no puede aver paz, si no ay igualdad en el trabajo, porque acontesce cada día y cada noche que los que saben la lengua trabajan notablemente y los que no la saben, como la ocupación de españoles es muy poca, están todo el día estudiando, o en buena conversación con seglares.'

12 Ibid.: 'La lengua es cosa muy fácil y que quienquiera que aprenderla quisiere, podrá salir con ella, y muy razonable, para predicar y confesar en 6 meses.'

13 His arguments are founded on the notion that the specialization of individuals should be according to their preferences and their talents – a notion that was applied, in his opinion, in the European provinces. Indeed, the *Constitutions* of the Society recommend that superiors select individuals for particular apostolates according to their personal qualities: 'Aussi, pour mener à bien ces missions, en y envoyant les uns et non pas les autres, en confiant à ceux-ci une charge et à ceux-là d'autres charges, est-il non seulement très important mais capital que le supérieur ait une pleine connaissance des inclinations et des motions de ceux dont il a la charge.' See Ignatius of Loyola, *Constitutions,* in *Ecrits,* ed. Pierre-Antoine Fabre (Paris, 1991), p. 414.

14 *M Peru.* 7:616: 'El ministerio de los indios a menester muy poco tiempo de studios, pues no hay de decilles conceptos ni predicalles escritura, sino aquel habla mejor y más a provecho que usa de cosas más llanas y manuales que se pueden decir de repente, y el ministerio de españoles no es así, sino que es necessario estudiar para que el predicador sea oído y para que el confessor no yerre.'

15 *M Peru.* 7:607: 'De continuar mucho las misiones, cobran los Nuestros un spíritu tan distraído, tam inquieto, tam enemigo de recogimiento y poco aplicado a oración y a disciplina religiosa, que quando buelven no ay quien los conozca ni quien los endereze.'

16 *M Peru.* 7:617: 'Por acudir a los indios se priva la Provincia de sujetos que la podrían ayudar en cosas de mayor importancia y los embían a missiones muy apartadas, de cuyo fructo no puedo dar parecer por no aver estado en donde se

hazen y oír muy diversas opiniones entre los Nuestros: unos dizen son de mucho fructo y otros que de muy poco, y así tenemos pocas ayudas.'

17 *M Peru*. 7:607: 'Para este ministerio no son menester muchos sujetos, praecipue que el fructo que de él se coje no es tan grande como por allá suena, y esto no es cosa que tiene duda y la poca capacidad de esta gente lo da bien a entender.'

18 *M Peru*. 7:611: 'Están tam engañados con esta ordenación y tan ciegos, que se persuaden que no ay en qué entender ni cosa que agrade a Dios, sino confessar a quatro indieçuelos.'

19 *M Peru*. 7:618: 'Casi todos tienen un modo de privilegiados y que ellos solos son los de la Compañía y los demás no.'

20 7 August 1617, ARSI Peru 1A fol. 114: 'Piensase que el Padre Sebastian Ferrufino se vale de un pariente suyo inquisidor para salir con algunas cosas, como seria para no ir a Juli a deprender la lengua como otros, ordenarse antes de acabar sus studios, darsele el officio de ministro o Procurador de Provincia, a Vuestra Reverencia toca verificar la verdad que esto tenga y remediarlo como conviene.'

21 Sebastián Ferrufiño came from Seville and entered the Society in 1603, according to the catalogue of 1607. At that time he was 25 years old and lived in Lima at the San Martín college. He had just begun his studies (ARSI Peru 4I fols 103v–124). In 1613 he was a priest but had not yet made his profession. He lived in the college of Lima, where he had been a minister and a procurator. There is no mention of any contact with indigenous people.

22 Lima, 1 April 1637, ARSI FG 1488/IV/4: Juan Ternino asks the general for permission to go to the Chilean missions with books 'acomodados para un misionero a que yo tengo interior y exterior propension, e inclinacion lo uno por aver tan pocos que quieran ocuparse en este ministerios, lo otro por lograr y no perder lo que Nro Señor me a dado en que sepa las dos lenguas del Piru, aymara y quichua ... Son muy pocos los que quieren emplearse en esto.'

23 ARSI Congr. 55 fol. 128r–v: 'La cabeça desta gente haze de poca estima su ministerio delante de los ojos de los seglares y por consiguiente de los nuestros, que con mas gusto y facilidad se aplican al trato lucido de los españoles. De aqui se saca la raiz de la dificultad que muchos tienen en aprender la lengua, y en aplicarse a los yndios, y aunque los superiores procuran aplicarlos, a vezes no son poderosos, y si no son vigilantes en quitar los estorvos y ocupaciones diferentes, no abra quien la aprenda. Sacase tambien que este ministerio a menester hombres humildes y desengañados, para dexar lo lucido y honrado, y para aplicarse a lo menospreciado y abatido, con que se dexa entender que los padres que se dedican a ello, son hombres de mucha virtud, y merito para con Dios, y lo deven ser para con los superiores. Son los que trabajan, porque con saber lengua, se ocupan de dia y de noche sin descanso y los que no saben lengua se estan en su celda, o estan parlando con sus amigos, o visitando todo el dia.'

24 Alonso Ruiz to Acquaviva, Cuzco, 26 December 1585, *M Peru.* 3:723: 'Una cosa
    deseo y la he dicho al Padre Provincial, que también la desea, que se diesse orden
    para que los que entran acá se aplicassen a la ayuda de los naturales, porque muchos
    dellos, después de averles dado estudios la Compañía, no ay quien les applique a
    indios, sino a españoles, y plega a Dios que no les mueva la honra o el menos
    trabajar, y aunque con lo que Vuestra Paternidad de parte de Su Sanctidad y suya ha
    escrito y encomendado, se comiençan a alentar más, pero represéntaseme que
    ayudaría mucho si Vuestra Paternidad ordenasse que ni se admittan a Ordenes ni se
    incorporen del todo en la Compañía por professos y coadjutores formados los que
    no se aplicaren de veras a este ministerio, y que sea este un modo de probación aun
    en el tercero año, porque algunos destos criollos, que assi se llaman por acá, aunque
    sepan mejor la lengua que los que vienen de España, violentamente se applican a
    esto, y si saben una lengua, mal se applican a otra, siéndoles a ellos más fácil por
    tener hecho el oído.'
25 Instructions to the Visitor of the Province of Peru, October, 1596, *M Peru.* 6:222:
    'La razón particular deste deseo creo que es que la ocupación con los indios no es
    tan gustosa ni aplausible, y por esto no se aficionan a aprender su lengua, y ansí no
    tienen empleo proporcionado para vivir contentos.'
26 Provincial Congregation, 1642, ARSI Congr. 71 fol. 108: 'mediocridad me vasta,
    y despues aprendere la lengua, y con esto haré la profession.'
27 Ibid.: 'Pero aca se ha practicado differentemente, por que sin saberla van pasando
    con la mediocridad, intuitu de que aprenderan despues la lengua, y despues la
    aprenden muy de cumplimiento, y an pasado con que predique un sermon tomado de
    memoria, y quiça trabajado destro, y sin entender lo que dize. Y esto claro es, que es
    en fraude del dicho privilegio, y de la mentalidad de Nuestro Padre pues se queda
    sin saber la lengua, y sin saber theologia con las calidades, que la constitucion pide,
    y esto es abuso del privilegio y gracia y como tal se debe quitar.'

28 / The Uses of Shamanism: Evangelizing Strategies and Missionary Models in Seventeenth-Century Brazil

CHARLOTTE DE CASTELNAU-L'ESTOILE

'We should not despair of the Indians' salvation': José de Acosta began his book *De procuranda Indorum salute* (1588) with this striking sentence, which is both an expression of the difficulties that missionaries had to face while evangelizing the Indians in America and a missionary plan of action.[1] This statement by the Peruvian Jesuit is somehow surprising: it reveals the confusion and distress the fathers felt in the face of their mission.

In Brazil, the first American region in which the Jesuits founded a province,[2] the difficulty of converting the Indians quickly became a common grievance in documents written by the fathers of the Society. The apparent absence of beliefs and rituals among the Tupí Indians was first seen as an advantage by the missionaries, who were eager to fill this 'blank page,' but soon it came to be regarded as an obstacle. In 1557, less than ten years after his arrival, the provincial Manoel da Nóbrega, in *Dialogue on the Conversion of the Gentile*,[3] summed up an opinion that was widespread among the Jesuits in his province: 'As these pagans worship nothing, and believe nothing, all that you tell them amounts to nothing.' It was not an intellectual deficiency that made the Jesuits regard the Tupí Indians as unfit for evangelization; on the contrary, the fathers praised their capacity for understanding. What puzzled the Jesuits was the Indians' fickleness, the facility they had for adopting and then shortly afterwards rejecting the beliefs and rituals the missionaries were teaching them.[4]

The Jesuits' acknowledgment of the situation to a certain extent called their mission into question, but it also gave them an incentive to try to find new evangelizing methods.[5] The enticement of the Indians through music and dance, which were their basic method of expression, immediately became the most viable option. In 1550 the Jesuits had children, specifically orphans, come from Lisbon to dance and sing, in hopes of transporting the Indian children. The fathers tried to adapt themselves to the Indians' taste; accordingly, those more fluent in the Tupí language adopted the Tupí prophets' lengthy preaching method of catechesis instead of the traditional missionary dialogue. But the limitations of this seduction rapidly became clear. Although the Indians appreciated the fathers' rituals, they were not thoroughly converted, and as soon as they became adults they would run away to the forest and revert to their own customs.

Accordingly, by the end of the 1550s a policy of coercion and domination was established under the influence of the new governor of the colony, Mem de Sá. The Jesuits founded their own missionary *aldeias*, which were villages close to Portuguese settlements that assembled Indians from various regions in one place. The Indians were forced to give up their relatively nomadic way of life and live under the control of a missionary. They had to work and were required to abandon whatever customs were considered incompatible with Christianity.

For the missionaries, the alternatives were either to transform the Indians by force so as to evangelize them later, or adapt to Indian customs as a way of seducing and then converting them. Although the former method was the most common among the missionaries in Brazil – at least officially – there were always some missionaries in the province who decided to adapt their evangelization strategy to Indian customs. Since this second method was more controversial, it was less documented in the archives of the Roman General Curia, which are more or less the only surviving archives on the Jesuits' activities in Brazil. Indeed, adaptation belonged to the experience in the field, and was something that did not have to be mentioned to the distant central hierarchy. We therefore have few clues to follow and must read behind the lines in documents in order to resurrect unrecognized and forgotten Jesuits and attempt to understand their methods of adaptation to the Tupí Indians in Brazil.

Francisco Pinto was a Jesuit in Brazil who was killed in 1608 by some Indians from Sierra d'Ibiapaba, in the area of today's Ceará (Northeastern Brazil), after many years of service as a missionary.[6] His extraordinary mastery of the Tupí language and above all his reputation as a 'Master of the Rain,' gained among the Indians of Rio Grande do Norte (the Potiguar), made him unique. His relics, which were carefully guarded by the Indians, would reap the benefits of this reputation long after his death. Who was this strange missionary? What was his evangelizing method? How did the Indians see him? And how did the Society view him?

From Missionary to *Caraiba*

The 1598 catalogue of personnel in the Brazilian province provides several clues about Francisco Pinto, and allows us to characterize him as a missionary typical of the province.[7] Pinto was born in the Azores in 1552, and he entered the

Society in 1568 in Salvador de Bahia. He had gone to Brazil as a child with his parents, where he studied in the Jesuit college of Olinda, in Pernambuco. As far as the Jesuits were concerned, Pinto was a Portuguese, even though he had not travelled to Brazil as a missionary and had been educated in Brazil rather than Portugal. In 1578, after ten years of formation, he was ordained a priest and declared fit to serve. He was sent to a Jesuit *aldeia*, or missionary village.

The catalogue specifies that Francisco Pinto served as a missionary among the Indians for twenty years; this work was what he specialized in, not an occasional duty. While to Europe it appeared that all Jesuits overseas were missionaries working with the Indians, the reality in the Brazilian field was rather different. Only certain fathers specialized in the missions to the indigenous people. These missionaries (about twenty in the province in 1598) had a well-defined profile, and Pinto is a perfect representative of the group. He was trained in moral rather than speculative theology, he was a spiritual coadjutor, and he was fluent in the Tupí language. Indeed, satisfying this linguistic criterion was so indispensable that the term used for addressing a missionary was 'língua.' The missionaries' position was somewhere in the middle of the Jesuit hierarchy in the province.[8]

In 1598, Francisco Pinto was the superior of the Espírito Santo *aldeia*, not far from the college of Salvador de Bahia. Life in the *aldeia* is seldom described in the documents; it was probably very hard, and a far cry from the security of the colleges, which offered a way of life much closer to that of the European colleges. In 1598, of 164 members of the province, only 23 resided in the *aldeias*. In spite of the *aldeias'* being only a short distance from Portuguese cities, the isolation and discomfort of the life there was keenly felt by the missionaries. Some young students who were sent to an *aldeia* spoke of their repulsion (*asco*, according to the texts) and thought of it as a place in which to lose both religious ardour and virtue.

More precisely, life among the Indians consisted of a number of spiritual tasks: teaching catechism twice a day, celebrating mass on Sunday, and administering the sacraments to the dying. Since the *aldeia* was a place for civilizing the Indians, the missionary was also in charge of controlling the houses and supervising the men's daily work. For this task of 'temporal administration,' he was empowered to administer punishment to his flock, which had to be carried out by an Indian.

The life of the missionaries in the *aldeias* had very little to do with the heroic image of missionary life. It was a routine and dreary job. From time to time, the ordinary course of events might be interrupted by a letter from the college, a visit, or a celebration of the patron saint. Young students from the Society came regularly to spend shorter or longer periods of time there, in order to be initiated into the missionary life among the *línguas*. In 1598, Francisco Pinto was in charge of training at his mission a young brother who was 18 years old and also from the Azores. From time to time the fathers of the *aldeias* went back to the college in order to renew their vows, make the Spiritual Exercises, strengthen their ties with the Jesuit community, and rekindle their sometimes quenched ardour.

This is a typical portrait of the fathers of the *aldeias*, of whom Francisco Pinto is a supremely characteristic representative. But in many respects Pinto was exceptional, especially owing to his profound knowledge of the Indian language and customs. In 1598 the Jesuit provincial was ordered by the military chief of Pernambuco to send him 'a father well experienced in the language and conversion of the gentile.' The provincial chose Father Francisco Pinto, 'one of the best *línguas* in this province, known and respected as such by the Indians.'[9] Pinto had distinguished himself as one of the best specialists among the missionaries, and was regarded as such by the Jesuit hierarchy and by the Indians.

In the second catalogue of the province, 1598, which provides evaluations of the competencies and talents of the Jesuits, we discover that Pinto stood out among specialized missionaries, and earned a series of very positive assessments.[10] His evaluators stressed his high intellectual competency: 'He has good knowledge of Latin and cases of conscience; he is excellent in Brazilian.'

This last praise was exceptional, and very few fathers listed in the 1598 catalogue were in a position to deserve it. Linguistic facility was quickly recognized as essential for a good missionary to the Indians, but not all missionaries spoke the 'Brazilian' language well. In a letter to Rome in 1584, a superior who had just arrived described the various levels of linguistic competency in great detail. He explicitly linked language ability to the novice's level of skill during apprenticeship. Those who learn the language late 'succeed only in understanding it and talking a little so that they can hear confession.' For others, 'this language is almost a native tongue, and they know manners and ways of speaking.' This formulation is interesting because it shows that it was not sufficient merely to know the language, but to speak it fluently. In fact, the difficulty with Tupí was in learning and mastering idiomatic expressions. The superior insisted that the missionaries could acquire a real influence over the Indians only through a full mastery of Tupí: '[These fathers] enjoy favour, efficiency, and authority among the Indians, which enables them to preach to them about the things of the faith, and they know how to persuade them to remain calm and satisfied.'[11] This passage recalls the provincial's judgment concerning Pinto: namely, that his mastery of the Brazilian language endowed him with authority and prestige among the Indians. The Jesuits were perfectly aware, then, of the importance of linguistic mastery for the transmission of the Christian faith and for the establishment of social and political domination.

Francisco Pinto was therefore considered by his superiors an 'expert' on Indian matters. An undated document signed by Pinto, in which he described Tupí matrimonial customs, attests to his familiarity with Indian culture.[12] Understanding these customs was essential for understanding native marital unions and for considering the compatibility of Indian conjugal mores with the Christian sacrament of marriage. On this question, information and reflections were exchanged on both sides of the ocean, among experts in canon law, theology, and Tupí customs. Pinto was the only one of these interlocutors who was a man of practical experience, a simple missionary.[13]

Pinto's exceptional skills helped him move away from the anonymity of being a father in an *aldeia*. He was assigned peacemaking missions, including one in 1598 in Rio Grande do Norte, on the border of the territory colonized by the Portuguese, and one farther north, towards Maranhão, during which he was killed (in January 1608) by the Gê Indians, the enemies of the Tupí. These missions were penetrations into the hinterland (*o sertão*), into unconquered territories where the Indians were still free. They aimed to bring 'peace' to the Indians, which meant transforming them into allies of the Portuguese power and thereby extending the territory of the colony. In 1596 the Jesuits were designated by new legislation enacted by Philip II to accompany these penetrations as part of the struggle against Indian hunters and slave raiders.[14]

After the 1598 expedition Pinto's track can be followed more clearly, thanks to various documents. They indicate that Pinto's activity among the Indians was not that of an ordinary missionary. His words, his relationship with the Indians, and even his violent death were closer to those of a Tupí prophet. Like other Native American societies, the Tupí had intermediaries between the supernatural and human worlds. These intermediaries had specific gifts such as the ability to cure, foretell the future, and master the weather.[15] Among these shamans, some were distinguished by outstanding eloquence. They were called *caraiba* and had great power and prestige. In 1585 the Jesuit Fernão Cardim described them as 'Masters of the Word:' '[The Indians] think so highly of those who speak well that they call them masters of the word. These men are invested with a power of death and life, and they shall bring about wherever they want with no contradiction.'[16]

After the 1598 expedition among the Potiguar, Francisco Pinto took on the role of a 'Master of the Word' and was regarded as such by the Indians. Like a *caraiba*, he travelled from village to village. He would preach all day long in the main square of the villages:

We passed though the *aldeias* we saw on our way. In each I delivered my 'sermon,' as was the custom, in the central square. There gathered not only the leaders, but the whole *aldeia*, without a person missing. The order in which I spoke to them was as follows: first,

I told them who we were, and then why we came, that it was for two reasons: to give them peace and to teach them their Creator; because they did not know him, and they were blind and did not understand the immortality of their souls and the fact that in the other life there was glory for the good and punishment for the evil. I continued with these questions until nighttime, when I retired exhausted.[17]

The theme of the immortality of the soul could sound relatively close to the Tupí belief in a Land without Evil, that is, a fertile land in which everything would grow without labour, a land that would belong to great warriors after death, or to the living, who could reach it after a long journey. As a Master of the Word, Pinto was hardly allowed to stop talking: 'They greatly enjoy speaking with me, and it appeared that the one who did not speak with me remained inconsolable, so it was necessary to converse and speak with them, with one or the other, all day long.'[18]

Francisco Pinto thus enjoyed a prestige similar to that of a prophet among the Indians: he was famous all over the *sertão*, he received presents, and he was even carried from one village to another in a hammock, which was strictly forbidden by the Jesuit hierarchy. His mastery of the word endowed him with other prestigious qualities. For example, his reputed supernatural powers were great enough to gain him a reputation as a 'Master of the Rain.' In this very dry region of the *nordeste* of Brazil, the power to make rain entailed the mastery of fertility, which was a *caraiba* characteristic. Finally, he shared the risk of being put to death with these prophets, who were sometimes worshipped, sometimes hated.[19] He received death threats several times and was finally killed by Indian enemies during his last expedition.

The career of this missionary who became a shaman-prophet is exceptional but not unique. There were similar cases in Brazil, such as that of Pero de Correia, who was also killed by the Indians, in 1553. Neither was the acquisition of shamanistic titles by Europeans a monopoly of the Jesuits in Brazil. Even Indian hunters tried to play the role, and in other missionary contexts friars acted as a kind of sorcerer – practices that would make very relevant comparisons with Jesuit examples.[20] Pinto's case is quite well documented, especially in various sources that allow us to witness sometimes contradictory opinions, and that give us insight into an Indian version of events. Since Pinto was an intermediary between two worlds, neither of which was monolithic, we can attempt to discover the meaning of his activity in each of these worlds – Indian and European.

A Controversial Evangelization Strategy

How could a Jesuit explain his transformation into an Indian prophet? In his narratives to his superiors, Pinto deciphered his activity among the Indians so as to help his Jesuit readers understand what was happening. These explanations sound also like justifications of his own way of evangelizing. Indians had to be taken to God slowly and progressively. First, they should be seduced and attracted by means of indigenous practices, which could be given a Christian meaning later. Baptism would conclude this slow process. Three examples will serve to illustrate the strategy and its justification.

When recounting his preaching on the creation of the soul and immortality, Pinto insisted on its effect on the Indians:

> To those who listened, these things seemed in the beginning like a dream, but at least they remained well disposed, with a desire to hear them again, and little by little these things came to have such an impression on them that they responded with these words: 'Oh my father, this is very good, I rejoice in this, I am satisfied with your words; your word filled me, your word nourished me, I have already swallowed it once, I will not spit it out of my soul.' With these and other similar words, they expressed as best they could their contentment and the satisfaction they received from [hearing such things].[21]

Pinto noticed that the Indians yielded to the flood of Jesuit words, and also that they were seduced but not convinced. According to his account, the Indians literally swallowed the words of the father, and by this act of verbal cannibalism assimilated and appropriated them. Pinto gives here a clear and extraordinary example of ontological predation, to use a modern anthropological term.[22] Indians did not respond to Jesuit preaching through adhesion or belief, but by 'gulping down.' Pinto declared himself perfectly satisfied with the Indian response to this oratorical seduction. For this missionary, then, the goal of his preaching was not to convert the Indians but to immerse and impress them. Pinto's incisive comment demonstrates the depth of his knowledge of Tupí culture. Apparently without negative judgment, he recognized the specificity of Tupí customs, based on exchange, receptivity, and malleability. He regarded the way in which the Indians received the Christian message as somehow suitable; although very different from what Europeans expected, the Indian response to the Christian message should not be condemned. Most of the Jesuits in Brazil distrusted the Indians' enthusiasm and fickleness with respect to Christianity, and saw these as reasons to despair of them. Pinto, by contrast, wholeheartedly adopted the Tupí way of oratorical exchange, and seemed satisfied with being able to speak and be heard as a Master of the Word.

The episode of the rain miracle, related by Pinto in a 1600 letter, illustrates the ambiguity of his situation and of his allowing the Indians to regard him as a shaman.[23] An Indian asked Father Pinto to make the rain come, because 'he thought I was some sort of saint,' the Jesuit wrote. The missionary set him straight, telling him that he only interceded with the Creator. At that very moment, it started raining. In this episode, the missionary offers both the Jesuit (God creates everything) and the Indian (sorcerers as masters of the rain) versions of this miracle. As a linguistic and cultural translator, he mastered both cultural languages. But in this episode he went beyond words by acting in both worlds: as an intercessor and as a great shaman. He was aware that the Indians regarded him as a sort of 'saint,' and actually played on the ambiguity of the word. In sixteenth-century Brazil, it had two meanings – the traditional Christian one, in which a saint is an intercessor between mortals and the Lord, and also the meaning embodied by the *caraiba*. Indeed, the Jesuits called the Tupí prophetic movements 'santitade' and they translated the word 'caraiba' into 'santos.'[24] In the Indians' eyes, Pinto did not prevent himself from being regarded as a 'sort of saint,' that is, as a *caraiba*. Pinto hoped that the Indians ultimately would recognize their real Creator and give up their own sorcerers; the truth would be reached through error. The best justification of this indirect method seemed to have been the coming of the rain, which he saw as a sort of divine approbation.

The last example of this missionary strategy and its justification is the exceptional celebration held to welcome Pinto and his companion to an Indian *aldeia* they reached during their last expedition in 1607. The description of this feast, which lasted two days and nights and was filled with continuous song, dance, and present-giving, shows that they were greeted as very prestigious *caraiba*. Pinto's companion, Luiz Figueira, tried to justify Pinto's acceptance of honours that were so incompatible with Jesuit humility: 'Blessed be the Lord, who let these barbarians know and worship his servant although they do not know him.'[25] This sentence shows all the ambiguity of the situation, in which Indians and Jesuits interacted according to two different modes. The Indian songs and dances were part of the prophetic ritual, a way of communicating with the spirits. In accepting these excessive manifestations, the Jesuits accepted the role of shaman conferred on them by the Indians. But Figueira underscores that the missionaries did not forget they were only God's servants. The purpose is once more to emphasize that although the action of the missionaries was indigenous, their intent remained Christian. To participate in such celebration was indirectly to honour God.

Pinto chose to adapt the Christian message to Indian customs and hide the Christian meaning behind an indigenous appearance. He spoke and acted like an Indian prophet, but he chose his examples carefully, to remain in keeping with religious doctrine. His actions could be interpreted in two ways; their Christian meaning was less obvious but would eventually prevail. Pinto's method here was rather different from the usual Jesuit method, which was to capitalize on the rivalry between the Christian and Indian supernatural worlds. The Jesuits would compete against Indian sorcerers, and the missionaries would almost systematically win these sorcery contests by demonstrating the superiority of their God. Pinto's method was a more refined way of leading the Indians to the Christian God: instead of trying to combat the Indian sorcerers, he acted as one of them. Such a method involved an extraordinary empathy with Indian culture, made possible by Pinto's knowledge of the Indian language.

For these Indians, who neither were Christian nor had yet submitted to Portuguese domination, Pinto chose an evangelizing method that adapted the Christian message to the culture of those he sought to convert.[26] This kind of method, based on openness to other people, became a Jesuit specialty and was repeated in many other missionary contexts. It explicitly relied on the authority and experience of the Church Fathers, but it also involved Ignatian spiritual principles. According to Ignatius, God could be found in all things – even, indirectly, in pagan customs – and Satan's cunning must be harnessed to the effort to convert, transforming people's minds from the inside.[27]

Although the adaptation method was common among the Jesuits, it still raised legitimacy issues. How far can adaptation to a different cultural and religious environment go? How far can you get to know other people without losing your own identity? All missionary situations raised the basic and crucial problem of where to locate the border between the missionary world and the indigenous universe – and how to avoid falling headlong into the latter.

In Brazil, the adaptation question is linked to the issue of cultural hierarchy. As defined by European church intellectuals of the era, Brazilian Indians belonged to the lowest category of barbarians. Culturally, they were considered close to animals, below human politics and religion, without writing or history. Adaptation to Indian customs was therefore illegitimate. Becoming a *caraiba* was not like becoming a Brahman. For sixteenth-century Jesuits, all customs were not equal.[28]

Finally, the adaptation question was also political. Such a method was favoured where the Europeans did not have political power. Where they were the rulers, the resort to force and coercion was encouraged. In Brazil, at the time of the creation of the Jesuit *aldeias*, the Jesuit hierarchy decided that the first step in the evangelization process would be to impose political domination. Using coercion they would change the Indians, who, as part of their transformation into civilized Christians, would have to give up traditions such as consumption of human flesh, continual warfare, polygamy, nudity, sorcerers, and nomadism.[29] So how could a Jesuit who in many ways behaved like a sorcerer be tolerated by the other Jesuits?

But although the eradication of indigenous customs was the method that, officially, succeeded in this Jesuit province of Brazil, it involved certain difficulties. Espousing the complete transformation of the indigenous people raised the issue of their 'conservation,' as the Jesuits put it. Indeed, the Jesuits realized how hard it was for the Indians to survive in the artificial *aldeias* they had created. Many Indians died there or tried to escape. The drop in the demography was mainly due to disease (Indians without any immune defences against European sicknesses were brought close to Portuguese settlements). But according to the Indians and some Jesuits, it was also connected to the prohibition of the Indians' customs. In 1609, just after Pinto's death, a document drafted within the province suggested that some of these prohibitions be abolished. Some of the customs that were not in contravention of Christianity (such as the periodical moving of villages) should be maintained: 'By custom, the Indians often move their *aldeias* in order to maintain themselves .... The Indians can die simply as a result of their melancholy. It is therefore not good for us to deprive them of those of their customs that do not violate the laws of God, such as crying, singing, or drinking in moderation.'[30] As this excerpt suggests, there was controversy in the province over missionary methods. Although the prevailing method was still to transform the Indians as a way of christianizing them, there were always some missionaries who tried to adapt their evangelization to Indian customs.

The Brazil Jesuits were not the only ones to hesitate between these two methods. The difficulty of deciding whether to abolish or maintain indigenous customs is epitomized in the figure of José de Acosta. He supported coercion for barbarians belonging to the third category in his *Historia natural y moral*, but defended adaptation in his *De procuranda Indorum salute*. Relying on a proto-anthropological perspective that is both religious and cultural, Acosta noted the difficulty of converting American Indians. He suggested some sort of 'tolerance' regarding Indian practices, and the adoption of Indian customs as a way of bringing the people slowly to conversion.[31]

In Brazil the opposition between the two ways of converting was not highly theoretical, and a choice was often made on pragmatic grounds. The missionaries would use one method rather than the other depending on their own capacity (knowledge of the Tupí language) or the situation (whether they were in an area clearly dominated by the Portuguese or not). Some of them would even embrace both methods and use one after the other, as did José de Anchieta, who was called 'the Brazilian apostle' by his companions after his death in 1597.

Seen in this context, Francisco Pinto's way of proceeding was only marginally unusual, and it was probably regarded by him as a temporary measure, and something for which there was no better alternative. It was made possible by specific geopolitical realities in the *nordeste* of Brazil in the early seventeenth century: Portuguese dominion was being challenged by Indian opposition as well as French competition. For his Jesuit confrères, Pinto's method was on the fringe of political peril and cultural illegitimacy. Although he was not completely condemned, he aroused suspicion. As early as 1600, Pinto was asked by his superiors to leave the Potiguar. He was then restricted to the Pernambuco college, where he became a minister, despite his eagerness to carry on his mission and the shortage of missionaries in the area.[32] He was kept away from the Indians except in cases of real necessity, such as in 1602, when he was allowed to leave his college to pacify the Potiguar, who were threatening to rebel because the colonial authorities had cheated them. This commission illustrates, once again, Pinto's great charisma among the Indians.[33]

Pinto's activity, therefore, could be regarded as an evangelizing strategy that was common among Jesuit missionaries but that he carried a little farther than usual, owing to the specific political and cultural situation and to his extraordinary mastery of Tupí culture. Nevertheless, the adaptation represents not merely a clever strategy planned by a Jesuit; it was also the result of an interaction between Indians and Europeans in which the Indians were themselves agents.

Indigenous Agency

In the texts dealing with Pinto's expeditions, the Indians are often represented as the ones who take the initiative. They ask the missionary to go from one village to another, to fix crosses, or to make the rain come. They are not an undefined collective group, but specific individuals with names (Big Shrimp, Blue Snake) and functions (principals or shamans, slaves or women). The Indians are far from passive, and it seems clear that Pinto became a shaman under their influence. The Jesuit cautiously mentions the Indian initiative to his own superiors, claiming that he has not taken the step on his own but has had no choice but to respond to Indian demands. This way of representing things probably reflected the real situation. What does the transformation of a missionary into a shaman mean from the indigenous point of view?

For an indigenous version of the facts, the historian invariably faces a lack of documents. The Pinto episode, however, can be documented by some indirect Indian sources. A few Indians who knew Pinto, or who took part in his expeditions, became sources of information for the two French Capuchins Claude d'Abbeville and Yves d'Evreux, who arrived in Maragnan (Maranhão) in 1612. We can cautiously use these Indians' comments, which survive thanks to the Capuchins' work, as a way of understanding the Indian views of the episode. Both Capuchins gave a version of Pinto's last expedition and death. Both of them condemned this father as a double impostor, to the Europeans and to the

Indians. If the condemnation comes from the French Capuchins, the well-documented portrait of Pinto relies on Indian testimonies.[34]

In his *Histoire de la mission des pères capucins en l'Isle de Maragnan et terres circonvoisines*, published in Paris in 1614, Claude d'Abbeville devotes a chapter to a character whose name and function are kept silent but who can easily be identified as Pinto:[35] 'Histoire d'un certain personnage qui se disoit estre descendu du ciel.' According to the Capuchin, Pinto's transformation into a *caraiba* went even beyond what the Jesuit sources admitted. Pinto is presented as completely ambivalent, divided between the Indian and European worlds. Though 'le personnage' was Portuguese, he spoke like an Indian: 'Il avoit pris tant de peine à apprendre les langues desdits Indiens, qu'il la parloit aussi parfaitement, que s'il eust esté de leur pays.' He enjoyed great authority over the Indians, who worshipped him: 'La fatigue d'un si long et si pénible voyage chemin n'estoit comme rien à ces pauvres gens, tant ils aimoient et chérissoient ce personnage qui les conduisoit, ayant acquis un tel renom entre eux qu'ils le tenoient pour un tres-grand prophète.'

According to the informants, Pinto did not give up his missionary role, and told the Indians he was there 'pour les instruire au christianisme et vivre parmi eux comme de bons amis.' Still, he let them believe that he did not have a completely human nature: 'Il leur donnoit à entendre, et les faisoit croire, soit par charme, soit par piperie, qu'il n'estoit pas homme nay de pere, ne de mere comme les autres, ains qu'il estoit sorti de la bouche de Dieu le Pere, lequel l'avoit envoyé du Ciel icy bas pour leur venir annoncer sa parole.' He enjoyed supernatural powers and commanded fertility: 'Il disoit que c'estoit luy qui faisoit fructifier la terre, qu'il leur envoyaoit à cet effect le soleil, et la pluie; bref qu'il leur donnoit tous les biens et nourritures qu'ils avoient.'

In this French-Tupí version of Pinto's story, the Jesuit appears as a cross between a *caraiba* and a missionary. He has become a Tupí prophet while remaining a missionary. What for the Jesuits was a straightforward missionary expedition is presented here as a migration motivated by the search for a Land without Evil. In this version, the 'personnage' enjoys his role as an exceptional shaman, and comes across as going far beyond what was cited as acceptable from a religious point of view in the Jesuit documents instructing Pinto. But the two portraits – that in the Jesuit documents and that in d'Abbeville – do not contradict each other. On the contrary, they interact and create the complex figure of a man who was both a missionary and a *caraiba*, and who mastered both Indian and Christian cultures, playing dangerously with both of them until his death.

The Indian version related by d'Abbeville showed that the Indians believed in Pinto and assimilated him to a new variety of powerful *caraiba*, all the while still considering him a missionary. They followed him because they thought he would lead them to a better world. To account for this indigenous belief, we can analyse it in the light of situations studied by anthropologists of contemporary Tupí societies. Of course, we should not be misled into thinking that present-day Tupí are identical to the Potiguar of the early seventeenth century. But we can note some similar mechanisms in empirical situations that can be compared in spite of chronological and spatial distances. There is, for instance, Carlos Fausto's analysis of the reaction of the Parakana, a tupinophone group in Amazonia, when they faced their 'discoverer' in the early 1970s.[36] João Carvalho was a member of the Agency for Indigenous Affairs, a *sertanista*[37] who knew how to speak the Tupí language and how to dance and sing. The Parakana began to regard him as a shaman and asked him to raise someone from the dead. This story of a transformation of a twentieth-century man of European descent into a shaman can help shed light on the indigenous perception of Pinto's transformation in the seventeenth century.

Like the Parakana in the early 1970s, the Potiguar in the 1600s were in a 'contact situation' with Europeans – that is, it was a time of uncertainty and ignorance characterized by reciprocal observation, without any relationship of dominance or defeat. The beginning of the seventeenth century witnessed an explosion of prophetic movements among the indigenous peoples, and many migrations took place, including the one in which Pinto participated.

During that time of uncertainty, a recurrent and lasting view among native peoples was that Europeans held supernatural powers. Although attributing this idea to the native peoples might seem suspect, since the idea itself has fuelled destructive European imperialism, the notion was very common in contact situations between Europeans and Indians, and especially among tupinophone groups. According to Carlos Fausto, it corresponded to 'some deep-rooted cultural assumptions about life, power and death among the natives.'

This assimilation had something to do with the creative power of the Europeans and their possession of objects. The Indians demanded a great number of objects, and at the meeting stage the role played by some objects owned by Europeans is famous. The missionaries always brought objects with them, including weapons, even though they denounced the self-interest and constant dissatisfaction of the Indians. For the Indians, these weapons not only were worthy in themselves but enshrined the shamanistic power of their owner-producer. The Indian demand for objects played a role in Pinto's transformation into a shaman. During the 1607 expedition, the Potiguar called Pinto 'Senhor das cosas,' Lord of Objects, because he distributed a large number of axes and hooks. Since every European who owned objects was a potential shaman, the Indians would test the extent of his power. When an Indian asked Pinto in 1600 to make the rain come, he was measuring the father's shamanistic abilities. Far from being naivety, it was a 'cognitive practice,' as Fausto said of the Parakana's asking João Carvalho to resuscitate a dead body. In both cases, the Indians needed to understand who the newcomer was, and were attempting to figure out a new situation created by the presence of the European.

Since these Europeans, Pinto in the early seventeenth century and Carvalho in the 1970s, were *sertanistas* – that is, good Tupí speakers, dancers, and singers – they were ready to adapt themselves to the Indians' demands up to a certain point. This was where the two men's destinies took a different path. Asked by the Indians to make a specific person come to life again, Carvalho answered that 'he was no shaman.' Pinto went farther than Carvalho: he made the rain come. The Jesuit shared with the Indians the same belief in a supernatural world. The miracle of the rain was made possible in both universes, the early modern Christian one and the Tupí one. There was sufficient resonance between Indian demand and missionary supply to make Pinto become a great *caraiba* whose fame spread throughout the *sertão*. Pinto was not playing on the Indians' credulity, and he was not more cynical than Carvalho. His own world and that of the Indians simply had more in common with each other than either did with that of a 1970s Brazilian civil servant.

Pinto's shamanistic power was at the junction of a Jesuit strategy and an Indian demand. His ambivalent role was the result both of the excellent knowledge he had acquired of the Indians during his long service among them and of the ability of the Indians to accept and integrate exogenous elements. It was also the result of a specific empirical situation born of uncertainty, in which Indian and Jesuit actors could still enjoy some *marge de manœuvre*. Pinto's history is therefore not only a Jesuit story of adaptation to a different cultural environment to ease the course of evangelization, but also an Indian story of reception and assimilation of novelty in an uncertain context.

A Saint for Pagan Indians

Pinto's history does not end with his death; his double life continued after 1608. The Indians began to worship his bones at the same time that the Jesuits hesitated about what reputation to grant him for posterity.

For the Indians of the *nordeste*, Pinto's death was not a break. He was killed by some enemies, but he remained an exceptional shaman, and his bones still mastered the powers he had while he was alive, especially the power to make rain. In 1615, while passing through the Ibiapaba hills on his way to Maranhão, Father Manuel Gomes tried to recover some pieces of Pinto's bones in order to bring them to the college in Bahia.[38] The Indians of Ibiapaba refused categorically to cede the bones of Father Pinto, since, they claimed, the bones brought rain and sun on their demand. To ensure that the Portuguese would not seize the bones, the Indians unearthed the body of Francisco Pinto and hid it elsewhere. So the Portuguese left empty-handed, but not before being arrested by the Indians, who, dressed in their war gear, searched them thoroughly in order to check that there was not a single bone missing. We will not consider here whether the worship of the bones was a purely indigenous belief or a sign of acculturation to the European cult of relics.[39] What is important is that even in death Father Pinto was still considered 'Amanajira,' Master of the Rain, and was venerated as such.

For the Jesuit cultural world, on the contrary, Pinto's violent death was marked by a curious silence, even though his death could potentially have led to his being named a martyr, and so restored some legitimacy to this suspect priest. The majority of the Jesuits in the province made no attempt to make him a martyr, nor to use him as a missionary model. Significantly, they did not find it necessary to write a biography on this missionary killed by the Indians, even though his kind of tragic death was relatively rare in the history of the province. This lacuna is even more peculiar given that the province was in search of a saint at that particular moment, and the pious life history was a literary genre much in vogue.[40] The absence of a Jesuit biography means that Francisco Pinto was not a possible candidate for canonization in the seventeenth-century Luso-Brazilian context.

Instead, the province promoted José de Anchieta, 'the Brazilian apostle' (d. 1597), for canonization, and, beginning in the mid-seventeenth century, another missionary figure, João de Almeida, who was the exact opposite of Pinto. This English Jesuit struggled to learn the Tupí language, and fought with sorcerers in order to make headway against the shamans. He was a devoted missionary, but had no specific empathy with the Indians. The differences between the two missionaries make it clear that Pinto was not considered a model. At the end of João de Almeida's biography, published in 1658, Father Vasconcelos, the historian of the province, supplied a list of sixty-four names – 'Illustrious men whose virtue flourished in the Brazilian province' – in which Father Pinto was mentioned for being venerated among the Indians of the Ceará rather than for his virtues.[41]

Some Brazilian Jesuits, however, attempted to promote this unusual figure and his unorthodox methods. In a few scattered documents can be found writings about Pinto's death, the Indians' veneration, and the miracle of the rain. On the basis of these texts, Pinto was mentioned in some martyrologies, such as *Societas Iesu usque ad sanguinis et vitae profusionem militans* by Mathias Tanner, published in Prague in 1675. In the militant context of the Central

European Catholic Counter Reformation, Francisco Pinto was presented as a martyr for the faith killed by cruel barbarians. Such an image was rather different from the conception the Brazilian province had of him as a shamanistic and controversial missionary.

We cannot analyse here the variety of posthumous readings of Pinto. But it is important to note that authors preserved his memory as long as the Jesuit provinces in Brazil and Amazonia were in existence. Indeed, the chronicler José de Morais made him a key figure in his history of the province of Maragnan, written in 1759.[42] This series of supporters must be understood as evidence of a minority trend in the Brazilian provinces in favour of adaptating Christianity to indigenous culture.

Pinto's advocates in the province failed to persuade the Jesuit hierarchy to promote him as a missionary model. In the face of this refusal, they created the multifaceted figure of a saint for the pagans. Father Manuel Gomes, the relics' hunter, concluded the story of his attempt to recover some of the Jesuit's bones by saying, 'To honour his servants when they are about to be forgotten, God has them worshipped by pagans.'[43] Gomes countered the Jesuits' rejection of Pinto's memory just ten years after his death by developing the fact that the Indians still worshipped him. He underscored the divine favour that granted Pinto the power to make the rain come: God wanted Pinto to be a saint for the pagans, that is, a *caraiba* for non-Christian Indians. This amounts to saying that Pinto was a *caraiba* owing to God's grace. The controversial strategy used by the missionary is herewith completely justified.

Pinto's story illustrates the Jesuits' great faculty for transforming and adapting themselves to different worlds. Nevertheless, this missionary crossed a line: he entered the Indian world. His uncommon example shows how the undertaking to evangelize the lowest barbarians, as they were called in Acosta's terminology, could sometimes have an adverse impact on the Europeans. This kind of experiment is not the subject of the controversies in other, more prestigious mission fields, where written and printed documents were more common than in Brazil. Although there was no real controversy here, Pinto was set aside and his missionary experiment was never referred to as a model.

A methodological observation is that historians of the Society of Jesus need to invest time in studying marginal figures, despite the scarcity of sources, so as to understand hidden aspects of the memory of the Society. By remembering those who were meant to be forgotten, we can learn more about the variety of missionary behaviours and practices that were adopted when the Jesuits faced the challenge of evangelizing the Indians of the New World.

NOTES

I am grateful for comments on previous versions of this text to Manuela Carneiro da
Cunha and the participants at the WHALA Seminar at Chicago University in April
2001, to Pierre-Antoine Fabre and Dominque Julia, and to the participants in the Boston
Conference, especially Gauvin Bailey. I would like also to thank Claire Julhiet and Ines
Zupanov for their help in translating my text into English.

 1 José de Acosta, *De procuranda Indorum salute*, ed. Luciano Pereña, 2 vols (Madrid,
   1987).
 2 On the Society of Jesus in Brazil, see the classic work by Serafim Leite, *História
   da Companhia de Jesús no Brasil*, 10 vols (Lisbon and Rio de Janeiro, 1938–50)
   (hereafter *HCJB*).
 3 Manoel da Nóbrega, *Dialogo sobre a conversao do gentio,* ed. Serafim Leite
   (Lisbon, 1954). See the recent study by Thomas Cohen, ' "Who Is My Neighbor?"
   The Missionary Ideals of Manuel da Nóbrega,' in *Jesuit Encounters in the New
   World: Jesuit Chroniclers, Geographers, Educators, and Missionaries in the
   Americas, 1549–1767*, ed. J.A. Gagliano and C.E. Ronan (Rome, 1997), pp. 209–28.
 4 See the analysis by Eduardo Viveiros de Castro, an anthropologist specializing in
   current Tupí societies, ' "Le marbre et le myrte: De l'inconstance de l'âme
   sauvage,' in *Mémoires de la tradition*, ed. A. Molinié and A. Becquelin (Nanterre,
   1993).
 5 On the Jesuits' mission plan, see Charlotte de Castelnau-L'Estoile, *Les ouvriers
   d'une vigne stérile. Les jésuites et la conversion des Indiens au Bresil, 1580–1620*
   (Lisbon and Paris, 2000).
 6 My interest in Pinto started with a basic biographical investigation that covered only
   part of the topic: ' "Un maître de la parole indienne Francisco Pinto (1552–1608),
   missionnaire au Brésil" ' in *Arquivos do Centro Cultural Calouste Gulbenkian
   Biographies*, vol. 39 (Lisbon and Paris, 2000), pp. 45–60; and 'Un maestro della
   parola indiana Francisco Pinto (1552–1608),' *Etnosistemi processi e dinamiche
   culturali, Missioni percorsi tra antropologia e storia* 9:9 (January 2002): 26–36. I
   am grateful to Claudia Mattalucci for her remarks on Pinto's case study. I was not
   able to use here Cristina Pompa's *Religião como tradução. Misionarios, Tupi e
   Tapuia no Brasil colonial* (São Paulo, 2003), as it appeared after the final version of
   this article. Pompa's work deals at length with the figure of Pinto.
 7 Catalogue of the Jesuit personnel of the Brazilian province, 1598, ARSI Bras. 5-1
   fols 35–46v. All the information in the 1598 catalogue is presented in tabular form
   in Castelnau-L'Estoile, *Les ouvriers*, pp. 545ff. See the entry on Francisco Pinto in
   the first catalogue: 'Oppidum Spiritus Sancti [annexum huic Collegio Bahiaensis].
   P. Franciscus Pintus superior ex Insula Terceira annorum 46 mediocri valetudine
   admissus in Societatem anno 1568 studuit linguae latinae annos 3 totidem casibus

conscientiae et annos iam fere 20 in Indorum conversione se exercet coadjutor spiritualis formatus ab anno 1588.'

8 Temporal coadjutors were in charge of the organization of the material life of the Jesuit group; spiritual coadjutors were priests and took care of the spiritual life. However, having made only the vows of coadjutors, they were appointed as auxiliaries and did not belong to the elite of the province, which consisted of priests professed of the four vows. Provincials and rectors were not spiritual coadjutors.

9 Letter on the pacification of Rio Grande do Norte, included in a letter of Pero Rodrigues, 19 May 1599, ARSI Bras. 15 fol. 477r–v, published in *HCJB*, I, pp. 521–5.

10 This is the entry on Pinto from the second catalogue, under rubric 62 of the secret section of the catalogue: 'Ingenio, prudentia, rerumque experientia bona. Profecit bene in lingua latina et casibus conscientiae. Optime in brasilica. Habet talentum ad audiendas confessiones et ad Indorum conversionem. Cholericus melancholicus.'

11 ARSI Lus. 68 fols 410–11 (1 December 1584): 'tienen mucha gracia, efficacia y autoridad con los indios para hazerles praticas de la cosas de la fe y les persuaden todo lo que es menester para tenerlos quietos y contentos.'

12 Pareceres sobre os casamentos dos Indios do Brasil, Evora, Biblioteca Publica, Cod. CXVI/I-33 fols 131–4, published in *HCJB*, II, pp. 625–6.

13 Other Jesuits in the province who sent information on the subject were 'intellectual' figures, fully professed fathers, or Jesuits with supervisory responsibilities: José de Anchieta, who trained at the University of Coimbra; Inácio Tolosa, a doctor of theology from the University of Evora; and the Italian Leonardo Arminio, professor of theology at the college in Bahia. In Europe, the theologians were among the prominent figures of Iberian neo-scholastic thought: Fernão Peres, Gaspar Gonçalves, and Luis de Molina.

14 'me pareceo emcarregar por hora, em quanto eu nom ordenar outra cousa, aos religiosos de la Companhia de Jesus o cuydado de fazer deçer este gentio do sertão, e o enstruir nas cousas de religião xpãa, e domesticar, emsinar, e encaminhar no q convem ao mesmo gentio, assi nas cousas de su salvação, como na vivenda comun, e tratamento com os povadores, e moradores daquellas partes …': law of 26 July 1596 on Indian freedom, quoted in Georg Thomas, *Politica indigenista dos portugueses no Brasil, 1500–1640* (São Paulo, 1982), pp. 225–6. The colonists and the civil power strenuously fought this law, which was abolished in 1610.

15 See the classic work by Hélène Clastres, *La Terre sans mal. Le prophétisme tupiguarani* (Paris, 1975); and Isabelle Combès, ' "Dicen que por ser ligero": Cannibales, guerriers et prophètes chez les anciens Tupi Guarani,' *Journal de la Société des américanistes* 83 (Paris, 1987): 93–106. See also Carlos Fausto's works, which historicize Tupí prophetism more fully, by insisting on the role of the Conquest and its traumatic effects in bringing about the multiplication of prophetic movements in sixteenth- and seventeenth-century Brazil: Carlos Fausto, 'Fragmentos de historia e

cultura tupinamba. Da etnologia como instrumento critico de conhecimento etno-
historico,' in *Historia dos Indios no Brasil*, ed. Manuela Carneiro da Cunha (São
Paulo, 1992), pp. 381–96, and *Inimigos fieis; historia, guerra e xamanismo na
Amazônia* (São Paulo, 2001).

16 Fernão Cardim, *Tratados da terra e gente do Brasil* (São Paulo, 1980), p. 152:
'Estimam tanto um bom lingua que lhe chamam o senhor da falla. Em sua mão tem
a morte e a vida, e os levará por onde quizer sem contradição.'

17 Francisco Pinto, letter on mission among the Potiguar, 1599, ARSI Bras. 15-II fols
473–8, published in *HCJB*, I, pp. 514–28: 'viemos pellas Aldeas que de caminho
podiamos ver em todas fazia minhas práticas em seus terreiros como he costume
aonde se aiuntarão não somente os principaes mas toda a aldea sem ficar ninguém.
A ordem que tinha em lhes falar era esta: primeiro lhes dezia que éramos, depois ao
que hyamos que erão duas cousas, a 1ª darlhes as pazes, e a outra darlhes a
conhecer seu criador ao qual por não conhecerem estavão cegos nem entendião a
immortalidade de sua alma nem como na outra vida avia glória para os bons, e
castigos para os maos: nisto me detinha até a boca da noite em que depois de
cansado me recolhia' (p. 523).

18 Pinto, letter on mission among the Potiguar, 1600, ARSI Bras. 3 (1) fols 177–179v:
'folgavão muito de falar comigo e parece que quem não falava comigo não hia
consolado; e asi me hera necessario estar todo dia tratando e falando ora com huns
ora com outros.'

19 Carlos Fausto insists on the ambivalent figure of the prophet, who can be either
healer or bearer of disease. The death penalty for prophets was not rare. In Pinto's
case, the presence of the French in the region can also explain the death of the
Jesuit.

20 See, for instance, Carmen Bernand, 'Le chamanisme bien tempéré: Les jésuites et
l'évangélisation de la Nouvelle Grenade,' *MEFRIM* 101 (1989): 789–815. But in the
New Granada example, friars were engaged in a competitive contest with sorcerers,
and there was not a complete metamorphosis into shaman.

21 *HCJB*, I, p. 523: 'Aos ouvintes no princípio parecia hum sonho estas cousas, mas ao
menos ficavão dispostos com dezejos de as tornar a ouvir e pouco a pouco vierão a
fazer nellas tanta impressão que me respondião com estas palavras: ó meu pay como
está isso bom, folgo muito com isso, estou muito contente de tuas palavras,
encheome a tua falla, fartoume tua palavra, iá huma vez a enguli, não a tornarei a
deitar fora da minha alma. Com estas e semelhantes palavras declaravão o melhor
que podião seu contentamento e satisfação que recebião.'

22 Viveiros de Castro has explained the success of the Jesuits as owing to a parallel
between a love of the word among the Tupínambá that was itself connected to
cannibalism, and the Jesuit technique of rhetorical seduction. His conclusion can
appropriately be applied to the pacification of Potiguar: 'One way or the other, the

Tupinamba ended up dying (and came to an end), because of the mouths of either their enemies or the fathers of the Society of Jesus' (E. Viveiros de Castro, *From the Enemy's Point of View: Humanity and Divinity in an Amazonian Society* [Chicago, 1992], pp. 279–80).

23 ARSI Bras. 3 (1) fols 177–179v (Pernambuco, 17 January 1600).

24 On the translation of *caraiba* by 'saint' or 'saintliness,' see Clastres, *La Terre sans mal*, p. 47; and 'saincts caraïbes' in Isabelle Combès, *La tragédie cannibale chez les anciens Tupi-Guarani* (Paris, 1992), Act IV.

25 Relação da missão do Maranhão, 1608: 'Bendito seja o Senhor que permitte que estes barbaros sem o conhecer a Elle conheção e honrem a seus servos so pello serem' (Antonio Serafim Leite, *Luiz Figueira; A sua vida heroica e a sua obra literaria* [Lisbon, 1940], p. 121).

26 This method relied on the concept of 'accommodation,' which has a traditional theological meaning (attribution of a new meaning, unintended by the author, to a passage in scripture), and, finally, means adapting the methods of conversion to the culture of those being converted. See Ines G. Zupanov, *Disputed Mission: Jesuit Experiments and Brahmanical Knowledge in Seventeenth-Century India* (Oxford and New Delhi, 1999); and Sabine MacCormack, *Religion in the Andes: Vision and Imagination in Early Colonial Peru* (Princeton, 1991).

27 Ignatius of Loyola, letter no. 32, to Paschase Broët and Alfonso Salmerón, Rome, September 1541, *MI Epp* 1:179–81.

28 In *Natural and Moral History of the Indies*, José de Acosta summed up three different methods of conversion for three types of barbarians. For the third type, illiterates without law and who were hunters and gatherers, conversion had to be through the use of force, for the barbarians' own good in being rescued from damnation; local religious practices had to be destroyed. On Acosta, see Pagden Anthony, *The Fall of Natural Man: The American Indian and the Origin of Comparative Ethnology* (Cambridge, 1986); and MacCormack, *Religion in the Andes.*

29 See the famous letter by Nóbrega of 8 May 1558 to the provincial, Miguel Torres, in Portugal, in which Nóbrega explains the goal of the *aldeias, M Bras.* 2:445–59.

30 BNVE Ges. 1255 (38), Algumas advertencias para a provincia do Brasil: 'Os indios conforme a seu costume, mudan as aldeias muitas vezes porque assi se conservão mais. Como os indios para morrerem basta tomaren melanconia ec. Parece que não he bem tirar-lhe os nossos seus costumes que se não encontrão com a lei de Deus, como chorar, cantar e beberem com moderação.' For an analysis of that text, see Castelnau-L'Estoile and Carlos Alberto de M.R. Zeron, '"Une mission glorieuse et profitable": Réforme missionnaire et économie sucrière dans la province jésuite du Brésil au début du XVIIe siècle,' *Rev. syn.* 120, pp. 335–58.

31 Acosta uses the term 'tolerance' in its sixteenth-century restrictive sense of 'bearing with.' To understand the contradiction, we must remember that these two books had

very different functions: the *Historia*, written in vernacular, addresses a wide audience and pursues a scientific goal, whereas the *De procuranda*, written in Latin, addresses a smaller audience, of ecclesiastical people. It is not a theoretical but a pragmatic work. I thank Sabine MacCormack for this insight regarding Acosta.

32 In a private letter to the general, Pinto mentioned that he was waiting for orders to go back to Rio Grande do Norte to live with the Potiguar; the letter represented an attempt to go around the local officials, who had forced him to stay at the college (ARSI Bras. 3 (1) fols 177–179v [Pernambuco, 17 January 1600]).

33 Luiz Figueira mentions the story in the Annual Letter, 1602–3; see Leite, *Luiz Figueira,* p. 93.

34 There are only a few copies left of Yves d'Evreux's work, which was censored right after its publication in 1615. Hélène Clastres published a very abbreviated version in *Voyage au Nord du Brésil* (Paris, 1985).

I warmly thank Franz Obermeier for these significant quotations from the censored part of Evreux's book: 'ie rapporteray l'Histoire d'un Pere Jesuite, Indien de nation sorti de leurs Colleges bastis en ces terres du Bresil, quelques annees auparavant que nous allassions à Maragnan' (S fol. 302r); 'Ce Pere Jesuite, comme ils m'ont raconté, vint, iusqu'à la montagne de Camoussy [aujourd'hui Camocim], où il fut fleché & tué par les habitans du lieu, & lors toute sa compagnie se sauva comme elle peut, & son compagnon avec eux, allans qui deçà, qui delà, & ces deux ieunes hommes sus mentionnez [scil. Sebastien et Gregoire, deux indiens plus tard venus au Maragnan] prindrent le chemin de l'Isle' (S fol. 302v) (Franz Obermeier, *Französische Brasilienreiseberichte im 17. Jahrhundert. Claude d'Abbeville: Histoire de la mission, 1614. Yves d'Evreux: Suitte de l'Histoire, 1615* [Bonn, 1995], p. 268).

35 Claude d'Abbeville, *Histoire de la mission des pères capucins en l'Isle de Maragnan et terres circonvoisines* (Paris, 1614), chap. 12. Like Franz Obermeirer, Serafim Leite identified the character of 'le personnage' in d'Abbeville with Pinto, although the Jesuit historian is disturbed by the figure of the missionary shaman, in *HCJB,* III, pp. 8–9: 'a pesar de confusa, e misturando factos diferentes, a narrativa do Capuchincho tem todos os indicios de ter o P Francisco Pinto como nucleo central, ainda que diluido na erronea interpretação dos seus informadores.'

36 The idea is not to underestimate the significance of the indigenous history and adopt a static structuralist vision. The event as well as the way it was seen structurally must be taken into account. That is what I understood from the highly suggestive works by Carlos Fausto, who 'tried to read chronicles using recent ethnograpic materials' and looked for a logical continuity in the functioning of Tupí societies nowadays and in the sixteenth and seventeenth centuries (Fausto, 'Fragmentos,' and 'The Bones Affair: Knowledge Practices in Contact Situations Seen from an Amazonian Case,' *Journal of the Royal Anthropological Institute* 10 [December 2002]:

669–90). I am grateful to Carlos Fausto for our conversations on Pinto and Carvalho, but I alone am responsible for these rather bold comparisons.

37 This word means those who know the *sertão* well, specialists in the contact with the Indians. Significantly, Luiz Figueira also used this word for Pinto, whom he called 'o padre sertanista' (Leite, *Luiz Figueira*, p. 120).

38 BNL 29 no. 31, letter from Manuel Gomes, Lisbon, 2 July 1621.

39 See Manuela Carneiro da Cunha, 'Da guerra das relíquias ao quinto império, importação e exportação da história no Brasil,' *Novos estudos do Cebrap* 44 (1996): 73–87. See also my article 'Le partage des reliques. Les Potiguar, les jésuites et les os du Père Pinto (Brésil, XVIIe siècle),' in *Reliques et corps saints*, ed. Philippe Boutry and Dominique Julia (forthcoming).

40 As in the case of Father Anchieta, who died in 1597; the first life history was written in 1598, the second in 1606. See *Primeiras biografias de José de Anchieta*, ed. Helio Vitti (São Paulo, 1988).

41 Simão de Vasconcelos, *Vida do Padre João de Almeida da Companhia de Jesus na provinicia do Brasil* (Lisbon, 1658): 'Breve catalogo dos varoens insignes da Companhia de Jesus que floreceram em virtude na Provincia do Brasil … O P Francisco Pinto varom esforçado e conhecido em toda a Provincia, e tam venerado dos Indios da Capitania do Siara, em cujo sertam a maos dos gentios Tapuias deu a vida em huma gloriosa Missam de obedencia.'

42 José de Morais, *Historia da Companhia de Jesus na extinta provincia do Maranhão e Para pelo Pe José de Morais da mesma Companhia* (Alhambra, 1759; Rio de Janeiro, 1987).

43 BNL 29 no. 31, letter from Manuel Gomes, Lisbon, 2 July 1621, fol. 119v: 'assi honra Deus a seus servos, que quando paresem, que hão de ficar sepultados no esquesimento os fas reverensiar e estimar da propia gentilidade.'

29 / Jesuits, Too: Jesuits, Women Catechists, and Jezebels in Christian-Century Japan

HARUKO NAWATA WARD

The Jesuit Determination Not to Proceed with Women

From its inception, the Society of Jesus affirmed its identity as a body of clerics regular engaged in pastoral ministry.[1] Active apostolate and male gender became the quintessential marks of the order. The Jesuits decided early that they would perpetually forgo the establishment of a second order for women and the regular spiritual direction of women.

Ignatius of Loyola's personal encounter with Isabel Roser and her companions led to this decision.[2] Isabel had been a benefactor of Ignatius long before he founded the Society of Jesus in 1540. She heartily embraced the Jesuit active apostolate as her own vocation. After corresponding with Ignatius for twenty years, the widowed Isabel and her companions finally left their home in Barcelona, and arrived in Rome in 1543, where she immediately began working alongside Ignatius and the Society. Sometime later Isabel appealed to Pope Paul III to order Ignatius to accept her vows, and the pope complied. On Christmas Day, 1545, Isabel Roser, Lucrezia di Brandine, and Francisca Cruyllas pronounced solemn vows of obedience to Ignatius.

Isabel's zeal and companionship overwhelmed Ignatius, who quickly realized that working with a 'female branch' distracted the male Jesuits from their more important ministries. Ignatius too petitioned the pope, who reversed his previous order, and on 3 November 1546 the pope ordered that these three women transfer their vows of obedience from Ignatius to the diocesan bishop. As a result, Isabel Roser and her companions became enclosed nuns, as was the norm for religious women in post-Tridentine Europe.[3] In May 1547, Ignatius petitioned the pope for the perpetual release of the Jesuits from the spiritual direction of women. The Jesuit determination not to proceed with women members was secured in the papal bull *Licet debitum* of 1549 and firmly set forth in the *Constitutions* of 1552.[4]

The 'problem' of women identifying themselves as Jesuits occurred again and again in history.[5] Yet the Jesuits never wavered in their decision not to recognize women as members of the Society, with one exception. In 1554, Ignatius admitted Princess Juana de Austria as a scholastic member of the Society on the condition that her membership be kept an absolute secret.[6] Juana was to be referred to by her pseudonym of Mateo Sánchez. It seems that in this case Ignatius's compromise was politically motivated, Princess Juana being a daughter of Emperor Charles V and regent for her brother King Philip II of Spain. At court, the crypto-Jesuit Princess Juana provided powerful protection for the Jesuits and intervened on their behalf until her death in 1573. No other women were ever made members of the Society.[7]

As the Jesuit mission spread throughout the world, the missionaries found women who responded to the Jesuit active vocation outside Europe.[8] The Jesuits dealt cautiously with these women. On the one hand, they often made use of and relied on native women's talents and resources in their overseas missions. On the other hand, in their reports to Rome the missionaries carefully dissociated themselves from women so as not to be charged with violating the constitutions. Women pursued their vocations, and often formed their own societies on the Jesuit model, and were successful in their ministries.

The Jesuit Ways of Accommodation in the Japan Mission

After the arrival of Francis Xavier in 1549, Christianity enjoyed rapid growth in Japan, but owing to a systematic nation-wide persecution, the Christians were forced underground by 1650. This span of a hundred years is known as the Christian Century.[9] The Jesuits dominated the initial christianization effort in Japan: a papal brief of 1585 assured the Jesuits under Portuguese patronage a monopoly in the mission to Japan for the first fifty years. A brief of 1608 reversed this decision and allowed the mendicants entry.[10] By this time the Jesuits had gained a remarkable number of converts belonging to all social classes. For multiple and complex reasons, Japan rejected Christianity and the West. The Christian Century ended with a total banishment of anyone and anything Christian from Japanese soil for the next 250 years.

The Jesuits of Japan's Christian Century practised 'cultural accommodation' or persuasion rather than the forced conversion of the Spanish conquistadors.[11] Following the model of Francis Xavier, many missionaries in Japan, such as Gnecchi-Soldo Organtino, first followed the method of accommodation in their work in the field, and later Alessandro Valignano, Visitor to the East, articulated and developed this method as suitable also for the Jesuit mission in China.[12]

Scholars have noted the Jesuit creation of a new class of Japanese catechists as a good example of accommodation. The European classifications 'temporal coadjutor,' 'scholastic,' and 'lay brother' could not be applied directly to these native catechists.[13] Adapting a Buddhist term, the Jesuits in Japan called the Japanese evangelical preachers *dōjuku*.[14] Buddhist *dōjuku* were trainees who served at the bottom of the priestly hierarchy. They lived with and assisted the priests in both physical and spiritual matters. The major responsibilities of the Jesuit *dōjuku* were to preach and teach catechism in Japanese, help compose and translate literature, and interpret and serve as intermediaries for the European members of the Society. *Dōjuku* were unmarried itinerant full-time evangelists. *Kanbō* represented another Jesuit appropriation of a Buddhist term and referred to another class of Japanese catechists. *Kanbō* were married stationary bi-vocational pastors who maintained a place of worship and cared for the Japanese Christians where there were no resident priests.

Both *dōjuku* and *kanbō* engaged in 'priestly functions' such as assisting the *padres* at mass, and, in the *padres'* absence, leading Sunday services, baptizing, and burying the dead. They also heard confessions of the sick and dying. In Europe it was accepted practice for persons in danger of death to confess their sins to a layperson when no priest was available. The non-sacramental confessions to *dōjuku* and *kanbō* became important in Japan, especially during the period of persecution. The Jesuit press in Japan published instructional leaflets for the use of catechists who baptized and heard confessions in the absence of priests. *Baputesuma no sazukeyō* (How to Baptize), published in Amakusa in 1593, instructed the catechist on how to help the sick and the dying.[15] The catechist was to review the basic teachings of Christianity, invite the dying person to examine his or her conscience, encourage the person towards true contrition, and declare to the person that God will accept his or her soul even without the actual sacrament of confession. Because the *padres* were increasingly scarce in the field, *dōjuku* and *kanbō* played a significant role in the Jesuit mission. The number of *dōjuku* increased from 100 in 1580 to 284 in 1603.[16]

The Women Catechists

Women catechists played a role as important as that of men catechists in the Jesuit mission in Japan.[17] No official documents ever mentioned that women were entrusted with apostolic work, and very little of these women's own accounts survived the persecution. But in the writings of the Jesuits who worked with these women are traces of their existence.

Table 29.1
Women catechists in Christian-Century Japan

Name	Dates	Baptism	Vows	Titles	Ministry	Areas
Catharina of Bungo	?–?	?	na	mother, teacher	teaching, preaching, baptizing, rescuing, practising charity, making pilgrimage	Usuki, Kurume
Catharina of Tanba	c.1520–c.1587	c. 1550, Cosme de Torres	na	widow, mother of seminarians	preaching, persuading, making trip to annual confession, serving as companion to Hosokawa Tama Gracia	Yamaguchi, Tanba, Miyako, Osaka
Kiyohara Ito Maria	?–?	1587, Cespedes	1587, vow of chastity	teacher, mother of soul	catechizing, teaching, persuading, baptizing, translating, mediating, hearing confession	Osaka, Miyako
Naitō Julia	c.1530–28 Mar. 1627	1596, Organtino	1600, 3 vows	founding superiora, 'padres' apostle'	Miyako no bikuni	Osaka, Miyako, Manila
Iga Maria	c.1583–9 Oct. 1639	?	1608, 3 vows	beata	Miyako no bikuni	Osaka, Miyako, Manila
Nakashima Magdalena	c.1577–15 May 1622	?	1602, 3 vows	beata, assistant of Naitō Julia	Miyako no bikuni	Osaka, Miyako, Manila
Park Marina	c.1572–15 May 1636	1600	1612, 3 vows	war captive, beata, visionary	Miyako no bikuni	Korea, Osaka, Miyako, Manila
Lucia	? – 3 Mar. 1636	1596	c.1635, 3 vows	maid, beata	Miyako no bikuni	Osaka, Miyako, Manila
Mencia	c.1574–1641	1596	? 3 vows	beata, 2nd superiora	Miyako no bikuni	Osaka, Miyako, Manila

Table 29.1
Women catechists in Christian-Century Japan (*concluded*)

Name	Dates	Baptism	Vows	Titles	Ministry	Areas
Lucia de la Cruz	1580–12 Aug. 1656	?	1606, 3 vows	*beata*, visionary	Miyako no bikuni	Osaka, Miyako, Manila
Tecla Ignacia	1579–Dec.1656	1584	1600, 3 vows	*beata*, 3rd *superiora*, visionary	Miyako no bikuni	Osaka, Miyako, Manila
Kyōgoku Maria	c.1543–1618	1581	1606–7, confirmation	'padres' apostle'	preaching, persuading, mass converting	Osaka, Tango, Wakasa
Kyakujin Magdalena	?–? (active in 1580s–1590s)	?	na	mirror	catechizing, teaching, providing information at Hideyoshi's women's quarters	Osaka, Miyako
Mecia of Miyako	?–? c.1591–2	?	na	widow	leading house congregation, providing escape route for abused women with Kiyohara Ito Maria	Miyako
Leanor of Shishi	c.1541–64		na	teacher of catechism	serving as local leader	Gotō Island
Magdalena of Wakamatsu	?–? (active in 1587)		na	mother, teacher, shelter	serving as local leader	Gotō Island
Ota Julia	?–? c.1597 c.1600 c.1612	?	na	'saint' captive of war in Korea	persuading at Ieyasu's court, persuading in exile	Korea, Tokyo Ōshima, Niijima, Kōzujima

According to the documents, the women catechists functioned very much as the men catechists, but without receiving the title *dōjuku* or *kanbō*. The women preached evangelical sermons, disputed with Buddhist priests, taught catechism and other Christian literature, translated and wrote Christian literature, persuaded and helped women and men convert to Christianity, baptized, heard confessions, cared for their flocks, and formed women's societies. They often interpreted for and served as intermediaries between women kept in confinement and other women, as well as between Jesuit fathers and brothers. Above all, the women saw themselves as working within the 'company' of the Jesuits.

I have found evidence of about a dozen well-known and numerous lesser-known Japanese women catechists. The names, dates, and major activities of the better-known of these catechists are listed in table 29.1. Here I will highlight the ministries of three of them: Kiyohara Ito Maria, Naitō Julia, and Kyōgoku Maria.

Kiyohara Ito Maria (c. 1565–?)

Ito was born to the aristocratic family of Kiyohara.[18] Her father, Kiyohara Edataka (1520–90), was a Confucian scholar and professor at the emperor's court. He was converted to Christianity around 1563, but seems to have apostatized by the time of his death in 1590. Ito's own dates of birth and death are unknown.

Ito's history as a woman catechist began in 1587. She was chief lady-in-waiting to Lady Hosokawa Tama (1563–1600) and a governess in the Hosokawa residence in Osaka. Hosokawa Tama's husband, Lord Hosokawa Tadaoki (1563–1645), was an extremely jealous man. Tama was a daughter of Akechi Mitsuhide, the assassin of the former unifier, Oda Nobunaga, and was considered potentially dangerous to the new unifier, Toyotomi Hideyoshi. For these two reasons, Lord Tadaoki placed Tama under strict confinement and surveillance, and Ito provided the sole contact between Tama and the outside world.

Tama became interested in Christianity, and on Easter, 1587, while her husband was away at a battle, she and her ladies-in-waiting secretly left her residence and visited the Jesuit church in Osaka. Tama interrupted the sermon, disputed with the preacher from her Zen Buddhist point of view, asked many doctrinal questions, and returned home much intrigued. This was the only occasion on which Tama left her household compound until her death in a fiery siege in 1600.

After Tama returned home from the church that Easter Day, she maintained communication with the church via Ito. Ito would go to catechism classes and masses in Tama's stead, and bring back reports of what she had learned to Tama. Through Ito, Tama asked the Jesuits for some Christian literature so that she could examine Christianity further. Ito would take Tama's questions, arising from her study, to the *padres*, and bring back their answers. Among the questions were some having to do with interpretations of Latin and Portuguese phrases. Ito also memorized parts of the Latin liturgy and taught Tama prayers, as well as describing the life in the church and teaching Tama how Christians should behave. Within a few months, Ito was baptized as Maria. Ito Maria persuaded the other sixteen ladies-in-waiting to become candidates for baptism. Kiyohara Ito Maria became like a *kanbō*, or resident pastor, in the Hosokawa compound. Tama too strongly desired to be baptized, but she was not able to return to the church.

Meanwhile, the first wave of persecution had begun. In late July 1587, Toyotomi Hideyoshi issued the *Edict of Expulsion of the Padres* and prohibited Christian conversion. The Jesuits in Osaka decided to hide on some nearby islands, and before fleeing they instructed Ito Maria in the formula of baptism. On 17 August 1587, Ito Maria baptized Lady Tama. Luís Fróis, a Jesuit missionary and historian, described the scene: 'Because it was a cause of great danger for [Tama] to leave the household at that time, the fathers resolved to teach Maria, her servant and kinsperson, the form and words of holy baptism and more requirements for this ministry, with the intention that she would baptize her in her residence. And thus well instructed inside her private room, on her knees with her hands elevated, [Tama] received holy baptism at Maria's hands in front of an image before which she prayed continuously. The name Gracia was given to her.'[19]

Immediately after administering baptism to Tama Gracia, Kiyohara Ito Maria affirmed her sense of vocation to this new ministry by going to the Osaka church, making a confession, and taking a vow of chastity. Fróis recorded Ito Maria's words, spoken to Father Cespedes at the church:

Great is the mercy of God, who grants this honour to me. This is appropriate for the priests, but God chose me instead, such an unworthy one, as an instrument so that I would baptize my Lady with my own hands. Already she regards me with a special respect as a mother of her soul. From now on, I want to leave behind the things of the world (she being still a young woman with such good natural qualities). Therefore, I vow to God from now on to live in chastity until death. For this I beseech you that you grant me that I may shave my head (as in Japan this was a sign of renunciation of the world).[20]

Fróis describes Ito Maria almost in the way he would a Jesuit coadjutor, when he quotes her as expressing a great desire 'to minister to and strengthen her women companions in this persecution.'[21]

Ito Maria's administering of baptism was remarkable on two grounds. First, the Jesuits' act of entrusting a baptism to a woman was extraordinary. Later, in 1593, a Jesuit manual for catechists stated, 'It is the norm that a man should baptize rather than a woman if possible.'[22] Second, in the stratified society of early modern Japan, for a maidservant to act thus as her lady's superior was extraordinary. Only the Christian understanding of the equality of all believers before God made this possible.

Ito Maria's preparation as a catechist for Tama Gracia was sufficient for her subsequent independent ministry. From Tama Gracia's own letter, quoted by Fróis, we know that in the following months, on her own initiative, Ito Maria baptized Tama Gracia's toddler son, Okiaki João (1583–1615), who was gravely ill: 'After the departure of the Fathers there has been no lack of trials for me, but in everything God has favoured and supported me. My second son (a babe of three years) was very ill, and when there was no longer any hope of his recovery, I, dreading greatly the loss of his soul, consulted with Maria what to do, and we found that the best remedy would be to entrust him to the God who has created him. Maria therefore secretly baptized him and christened him John, and from that very day he began to recover, and he is completely cured.'[23] Ito Maria did not need permission from the *padres* of the Osaka church, who were now in hiding, but used her own discretion.

Tama Gracia consulted and listened to Ito Maria as her teacher and the mother of her soul on all matters of faith. She also consulted Ito Maria about how to deal with the physical and sexual abuse she and her maidservants were subjected to by her husband. Ito Maria dealt with Lord Tadaoki assertively and rejected his demand to hand over Luisa, a beautiful maidservant. She then set up an underground escape route between the churches in Osaka and Kyoto for Luisa and other maidservants abused by Lord Tadaoki. The escape route was intended also for the use of Tama Gracia herself in case she decided to leave.

Even though the name of Ito Maria disappears from Jesuit accounts after 1589, there are later references to a maidservant of Tama Gracia who ministered to her in her seclusion. In 1596, nine years after Tama Gracia's baptism, there was a woman catechist in the Hosokawa residence to whom Tama Gracia made a confession: 'Since thus far she had received no instruction for the sacrament of penance, she called to her her maidservant, in whom she confided much. She confessed all her sins to her, and asked her, because she herself was able to feel deeply, that she confess this to the father rector of Miyako in her name and obtain the penance and absolution from him … [The father rector] sent to her by the words of the maidservant a method by which she can request contrition and forgiveness of her sins, instructing her in faith and hope, which she must place in God.'[24] Thus Tama Gracia confessed to her maidservant, from whose mouth came words of forgiveness as though her maidservant were her confessor.

Technically the catechist-confessors in the Jesuit overseas missions were translators. In Brazil, women occasionally served as translators for the Jesuit confessors. However, they seem to have provided the faithful with more than just a literal translation of the priests' words. Concerning such addition by a woman catechist to the pastoral advice, a Jesuit wrote in 1552, 'I think she is a better confessor than I am.'[25] In Tama Gracia's case, Fróis raised no objection to the woman catechist's performing this semi-sacramental function in the place of the priest-confessor.

Kiyohara Ito Maria's story is important because it illustrates how women came to affirm their identity as catechists and what kind of vows they might have taken. It indicates that they might have engaged in a wide range of pastoral ministries, including administering the sacrament of baptism. It illuminates how women took up the ministry of penance, and how their ministry was regarded by both participants and observers as no less of a sacramental ministry than that of the ordained clergy. My next example shows how a woman catechist formed a women's society on the Jesuit model.

Naitō Julia (c. 1566–1627)

Naitō Julia was a sister of Naitō Tokuan João (?–1626), a nobleman, once the lord of Kameyama and Yagi in Tanba.[26] Her Japanese name is not known. She was born in about 1566, was widowed by 1588, and was a Buddhist nun of the Jōdo (Pure Land) school in Kyoto for the next sixteen years. Julia became the head of the nunnery and preached regularly in the name of Amida Buddha. She was well known and trusted by women of the noble class as their teacher of Buddhism. After studying the beliefs and practices of Christianity, she was converted and baptized by Father Organtino in 1596. Immediately after her baptism, Naitō Julia became an evangelical preacher. In about 1600, Julia founded a society of women catechists in Kyoto, known as the Miyako no bikuni, or Beatas of Miyako. The Jesuit historian Francisco Colín described its founding: '[Julia] decided to establish a solitary way of life for Christian women, who, in contrast to the [Buddhist nuns], would dedicate themselves totally to the service of the true God. She realized this plan with help from the counsel and opinion of Fathers [Organtino and Morejon], who were working as evangelists at the court. Along with five companions, who shaved their heads and [dressed] in black religious habit, she took the three vows of poverty, chastity, and obedience at the hands of the fathers. Lady Julia composed the Rule.'[27]

The involvement of the two Jesuit priests in the foundation of Julia's society is clear, but Colín was careful to state that it was not the Jesuit fathers themselves who founded this women's order. Colín noted that the community was not recognized by the pope, but that apart from that formality it lacked nothing for enabling its members to live a perfect life very similar to that lived in orders approved by the Holy See.[28]

It seems, though, that Julia desired to found a Society of Jesus for women, to work side by side with the Jesuits in apostolic ministry. Her house stood next to the Jesuit house in Kyoto, and the Jesuit priests heard the women's confessions regularly. Colín continued: 'In their institution and way of living [or way of proceeding] they tried to conform to that of the Society of Jesus, which is the salvation of souls. Julia's principal work was teaching Christian Doctrine to pagan ladies and exhorting them to convert to our holy faith. Because in Japan it was the custom for upper-class ladies and their daughters not to go out to see men, even clerics, and because the demon took advantage of this custom and closed the door of conversion to these ladies, God took Lady Julia as an instrument to open it.'[29]

In her ministry dedicated to the salvation of souls, Naitō Julia was able to make use of the network among noblewomen that she had established as a Buddhist abbess. Her companions, such as Iga Maria (1575–1639), also converted many noblewomen from Buddhism to Christianity. In order to do this, women catechists needed to be able to explain the doctrinal differences between Christianity and the Japanese religions. To meet this need, in around 1605, Fabian Fukan (1565–1621), then a Jesuit brother, wrote *Myōtei mondō* as a manual for women catechists.[30] The work is basically a Christian catechism, with its middle portion devoted to arguments against the different schools of Buddhism, Taoism, Confucianism, and Shintoism. *Myōtei mondō* adapted the Buddhist literary genre of *futari bikuni* (two-nun dialogue) in its dialogue between Yūtei, a noble Christian nun, and Myōshū, a noble widow nun of the Jōdo school.[31]

Naitō Julia's success in converting many famous women of high social status, such as the daughter of Oda Nobunaga, the first unifier, greatly offended the Buddhist clerics. The Jesuits hid Julia in the remote southern region in 1601–4 to enable her to avoid physical attacks by angry Buddhist clerics. Naitō Julia subsequently came back to Kyoto to continue her ministry.

In 1612, Tokugawa Ieyasu, the third unifier, issued the first of the series of *Decrees Prohibiting Christianity*. In 1613 the governor of Kyoto ordered the Jesuit Kyoto church as well as the house of the Miyako no bikuni to be burned down. The women catechists were told to renounce the Christian faith or be sold into brothels. Naitō Julia hid nine younger members of the community and refused any compromising of her faith. She and eight other older women were arrested and publicly tortured. The missionary eyewitness accounts of this incident were immediately sent to Europe and translated for the Catholics in England, who were also facing persecution:

Into which [rice sacks] presently the officers did thrust them, and bynd them so hard that they could neyther move hand nor foote and then they tyed them to staves and so carried them upon their shoulders through the streets accompanied with many armed men. The people came all out of their houses to see them, some mocking at them and abusing them, others admiring at their constancy. They put them in a publike place without the Citty, where they use to execute justice upon malefactors, and their they remayned all that day and the next, exposed to the could and snowy weather.[32]

Covered with snow 'Julia and her companions did not seem to feel the cold at all as if they were in the celestial temple.'[33] Piled up in the rice sacks, 'the servants of God began to sing sweet canticles and psalms of praise of our Lord with great awe.' When a kind Jōdo priest covered Julia's sack with his coat and tried to persuade her to invoke the name of Buddha, she yelled back and spat upon him. Luzia de la Cruz was taken by her relatives by force to her father's house. She 'went all the way crying out aloud, *I am a Christian, I am a Christian.*'[34] As soon as she was freed, she ran back, stepped back into the sack herself, and lay down with her companions so that people would not think she had apostatized. During nine days of torture, not one of the women recanted.

The Tokugawa shogunate issued the second *Statement on the Expulsion of the Padres* on 28 January 1614. The governor of Kyoto decided to expel the Miyako no bikuni from Japan. The ship left Nagasaki on 8 November 1614, carrying Naitō Julia and 14 other women catechists; 23 European and Japanese Jesuits, including Father Morejon; 15 *dōjuku*; and some well-known Christian families such as the Takayamas and Naitōs. It arrived in Manila on 21 February 1615.

In the Philippines, Naitō Julia and her women went into seclusion. They lived in a house next to the Jesuit house and church in the village of San Miguel. Julia died in 1627. The Miyako no bikuni, now completely enclosed, continued until 1656, when its last two members, Tecla Ignacia and Luzia de la Cruz, died.[35] The Jesuits provided splendid funerals for these former women catechists, at the Jesuit college in Manila, as though they were their own members.

Kyōgoku Maria (c. 1543–1618)

My third example suggests how successful the women catechists were in their ministry of persuasion and in their networking with one another. Kyōgoku Yōfukuin Maria was a daughter of Asai Hisamasa, a high-ranking samurai family.[36] She was married to Kyōgoku Takayoshi, of the prestigious Kyōgoku family, whom the Asai family served. She was baptized with her husband in the Jesuit church in Kyoto in 1581. Like Hosokawa Tama Gracia, she was very learned in Zen. Before accepting Christian doctrine concerning the immortality of the soul and judgment after death, she engaged in a disputation with a Japanese Jesuit brother that lasted forty days. Soon after her baptism Kyōgoku Maria was widowed. In 1582, Hideyoshi, the second unifier, forcibly took her daughter Tatsuko as a concubine. Maria was confined with her daughter in the women's quarters of Hideyoshi's castle in Osaka. In her confinement she studied some Christian literature, including *The Imitation of Christ*, which she requested and received from the Jesuit rector.[37]

Hideyoshi's death in 1598 led to her release, and in around 1600, Kyōgoku Maria began to be named in Jesuit documents as a woman catechist. In fact, between 1600 and 1609, Maria was the best-known woman catechist in the Kyoto-Osaka area. The Jesuit reports in 1601–2 attributed the conversion of nine hundred women and men, partly from the noble class and partly commoners, solely to the persuasion of Kyōgoku Maria.[38] She also 'recruited two female teachers of Christian Doctrine to work with her.'[39]

Kyōgoku Maria and her teachers worked in concert with Naitō Julia and the Miyako no bikuni. Maria helped Naitō Julia escape the physical attacks of the Buddhist monks,[40] and a Jesuit account referred to Maria as Julia's 'best friend.' Another Jesuit account paired Maria and Julia, calling them '*padres*' apostles.'[41] Jesuit reports often singled out Maria and Julia as excellent 'coadjutors' of the Jesuits.[42]

Maria used every occasion to minister for the salvation of souls, even when her other daughter, Magdalena, who was a Christian, died in 1606.[43] Magdalena was married to a high-ranking government official, Kuchiki Nobutsuna. Maria dissuaded her son-in-law from arranging for a large-scale Buddhist funeral for Magdalena, and instead sponsored a solemn mass in the new church in Kyoto. Maria worked closely on this occasion with the Jesuit brother Fabian Fukan. Fabian, the author of *Myōtei mondō*, the manual for women catechists, preached an eloquent sermon, as a result of which there were several conversions among the nobility.

Because this funeral mass impressed many and aroused the curiosity of non-Christians, the opposition of the Buddhist priests and rulers at the court to Christian conversion increased. Magdalena's father-in-law, Kuchiki Mototsuna, demanded that Maria's sons force their mother, Maria, to renounce her Christian faith.[44] Both Naitō Takatsugu and Takatomo, who were nominal Christians, were pressured to move Maria into seclusion. Sometime in 1606–7, Maria and her ladies-in-waiting received the sacrament of confirmation from Bishop Cerqueira, and Maria retired to Wakasa under Takatsugu's protection.

In 1609, Maria moved again to a remote area in Tango under Takatomo's patronage. Old and infirm, Maria did not abandon her identity as a woman catechist. She invited some Jesuits from Kyoto to Tango, and the arrival of the priests brought a sudden recovery from her sickness and a joyous celebration of confession and communion. This visit of the Jesuits produced many converts among Maria's relatives.[45] The Jesuit report in 1612, the last to mention Maria, described her as a spiritual leader of Christian women in the Kyōgoku residence.[46] Maria died in a small hut belonging to a Buddhist nunnery in Tango in 1618.

In the Jesuit reports from Kyoto telling of Maria's retirement to Wakasa, an unnamed woman catechist was introduced, of whom it was said that the fathers 'used her to preach to those persons who could not come to our house and to whom we could not go according to the custom.'[47] This woman catechist preached to and baptized a noble woman patron of the church secretly in her house and gave her a new Christian name, Maria. It seems likely that this unnamed woman catechist was one of the many whom Kyōgoku Maria trained.

The Jesuit Way of Proceeding with the Women Catechists in Japan

The stories of Kiyohara Ito Maria, Naitō Julia, Kyōgoku Maria, and their fellow women catechists reveal several important features of the Jesuit mission in Christian-Century Japan. First, the evidence is clear that there existed a female equivalent of the male catechists, and that they ministered and acted as Jesuit coadjutors not only in women's circles but also in a wider arena. Second, for women who had no opportunity to receive the sacraments, pastoral nurture, and instruction from the priests, the ministry of women catechists was essential. Third, there were Christian women's circles that supported the leadership of the women catechists, and that were mobilized to rescue women who were being abused. Fourth, women catechists were able to draw upon their former religious training in Buddhism in their new Christian ministry. And fifth, the activities of the women catechists challenged the Japanese social and political order. Kiyohara Ito Maria, a subordinate, taught and provided spiritual guidance to Lady Hosokawa Tama Gracia. Naitō Julia's and Kyōgoku Maria's resistance to Buddhist priests and the Tokugawa government was perceived as insubordination, and this perception added to the fervour with which Christians were persecuted.

The Jesuit missionaries in Japan appreciated the women catechists' contributions and recorded their activities. However, they were not ready to embrace a cutting-edge ecclesiology by admitting to themselves that the women were serving as their co-ministers. There were two basic differences between the Jesuit way of proceeding with the women catechists and with the men catechists in Japan. First, the Jesuits expected the women to provide their own financial support, whereas the men were employed by the Society. Both *dōjuku* and *kanbō* were 'maintained at the cost of the Society.'[48] They received compensation, some housing benefits or necessities of life, and 'attire' in which to perform their ministerial tasks.[49] Second, the Jesuits never allowed women catechists to study in their seminaries or colleges. The men were able to advance in the Society if they were willing to take vows. If they were able to master Latin, they could even become priests beginning in 1601. Women catechists were willing to take vows and learned some Latin on their own, but there was no way in which they could enter the seminaries for more advanced training.

In Christian-Century Japan, laymen and male catechists made the Spiritual Exercises in order to discern their Christian calling.[50] Some scattered records indicate that women catechists also made the Spiritual Exercises.[51] It is not certain whether the 'reduced' version, without the election of a way of life, was used for women, as it was in Europe.[52] Japanese women catechists' affirmation of their 'election' was proved only by their action. And their contribution was not marginal to but vital in the Jesuit mission.

The Jesuits and the Japanese Jezebels

It is important to remember that in Japan, Christian conversions did not take place in a religious vacuum. Christian life was lived on a soil fertile with many religious traditions. The Christian Century, marked by the active apostolate of women catechists, was also the golden age of active Buddhist nuns, called Kumano bikuni. These nuns were itinerant or stationary preachers. They taught the ways of women's salvation when Japanese Buddhism as a whole condemned women to eternal suffering in a lake of blood. The Jesuits in general considered the women leaders of Japanese religions enemies of God and demonized them as witches. Some Kumano bikuni ministered to such women, for example the divorced queen of the famous Christian daimyo, Ōtomo Sōrin Francisco. The Jesuits idealized Sōrin Francisco as the most Christian king of Christian-Century Japan,[53] and disparagingly called this queen 'Jezebel' because she was a powerful Shinto priestess as well as a supporter of the Kumano school of Buddhism. In both their view of the women catechists and their denunciation of witches, the Jesuits of Christian-Century Japan proved to be men of their own time.

Historiography shows that women's participation in Jesuit ministries has been marginalized. One reason for this marginalization is the assumption on the part of scholars that, owing to the constitutional restriction, women did not participate in Jesuit activities. Another is that historians have paid more attention to the Society's polity and theory than to descriptions of its practice. The first conference on the Jesuits at Boston College, in 1997, did not include a session on women. The second conference, in 2002, did have such a session. That was an improvement, but the approach still reflected the traditional pejorative labelling of women who embraced Jesuit apostolic aspiration as 'Jesuitesses.'[54] In view of the title of the conference, 'The Jesuits II,' we could begin to call these women 'Jesuits, too.'

John W. O'Malley notes the presence of women in Jesuit ministries, in his acclaimed 1993 book *The First Jesuits*, and comments, 'In general, the Jesuits' practice in dealing with women was much better than their talk about it.'[55] In his view, the Jesuits' positive attitude towards the women in their care was manifested in the fact that they 'made no distinction in their ministries between the sexes.' Jesuit ministry to women thrived in many places. With regard to the Jesuits' attitude towards women as co-ministers, O'Malley notes: 'Without hesitation they enlisted women to help them and entrusted them with responsible positions, including guiding other women into a deeper spiritual life. As with men, they led them in the *Exercises*, and outside the *Exercises* they taught them how to meditate.' This sounds as though the Jesuits fully accepted women catechists as their co-workers and had a clear sense of their vocation. In reality they accepted them only to a limited degree, as these examples from Japan have shown.

O'Malley defends the early Jesuits, who 'inherited' a vocabulary 'inadequate for the reality they lived, or at least wanted to live.'[56] It is true that in both their 'praise' and their 'blame' of women, the Jesuits remained the product of early modern Europe. Yet it was the Jesuits who recognized the remarkableness of women religious leaders in their missions around the world. It was they who preserved information on these women, when no other sources even recorded their existence. The Jesuit mission histories, letters, and reports have turned out to be a rich source for today's historians of women. Through the eyes of the Jesuits, who worked with women catechists and witnessed their apostolate with amazement, we catch glimpses of them. And the women catechists are only a few of the many women who appear in the Jesuit writings. Women carved out unique and creative ways of proceeding in Christian ministry in the sixteenth and seventeenth centuries, and twenty-first-century historians have the exciting task of combing through the Jesuit sources in order to tell their stories.

NOTES

1 On the formation of a Jesuit identity, see John Patrick Donnelly, 'The New Religious Orders, 1517–1648,' in *Handbook of European History, 1400–1600*, ed. Thomas A. Brady et al., vol. 2 (Leiden, 1995), pp. 290–4; Donnelly, 'Religious Orders of Men, Especially the Society of Jesus,' in *Catholicism in Early*

Modern History: A Guide to Research (St Louis, 1988), pp. 147–53; and O'M. *First.*

2 Hugo Rahner, *Saint Ignatius Loyola: Letters to Women*, trans. Kathleen Pond and S.A.H. Weetman (New York, 1960), pp. 251–95. A cynical treatment of this episode and its historical consequences is found in Jean Lacouture, 'No Women Need Apply,' in his *Jesuits: A Multibiography*, trans. Jeremy Leggatt (Washington, 1995), pp. 136–60.

3 It took the three women some time to find places to which their vocations suited them. Lucrezia moved from a convent in Rome to another in Naples. Francisca became a nun in the Hospital of the Cross in Barcelona. Isabel did not immediately relinquish her active apostolate in Rome, but established an orphanage there. In 1550 she took the veil in the Franciscan convent of Holy Jerusalem in Barcelona, and remained in the contemplative life until her death in 1555. On enclosure, see *The Canons and Decrees of the Council of Trent*, trans. and ed. H.J. Schroeder (Rockford, IL, 1978), pp. 217–32. A significant amount of literature has been produced on the limited vocational choices for women in early modern Europe, for example *Women in Reformation and Counter-Reformation Europe: Public and Private Worlds*, ed. Sherrin Marshall (Bloomington, 1989).

4 See especially Ignatius of Loyola, *The Constitutions of the Society of Jesus*, trans. George E. Ganss (St Louis, 1970), secs 262–3 (p. 588).

5 For some examples of European women who aspired to the Jesuit active apostolate, such as Mary Ward and Angela Merici, see Elizabeth Rapley, *The Dévotes: Women and Church in Seventeenth-Century France* (Montreal, 1990). Rapley seems to be the first historian to name these women 'catechists' (pp. 7, 51, 114, 117).

6 Rahner, *Letters,* pp. 52–67.

7 For a discussion of another Spanish woman catechist with strong Jesuit self-identity, see Elizabeth Rhodes, *This Tight Embrace: Luisa de Carvajal y Mendoza (1566–1614)* (Milwaukee, 2000).

8 For an example from the Jesuit mission in Argentina, see Alicia Fraschina's article in this volume. Studies are needed of such 'native' women catechists as Candida Xu in the China mission and the two Catalinas in the Vietnamese mission.

9 This term was crystallized by C.R. Boxer, *The Christian Century in Japan, 1549–1650* (Berkeley, 1967).

10 *Ex pastoralis officio* of 1585 secured Japan for the Jesuit mission under the Portuguese *padroado real. Sedis Apostolicae providentia* of 1608 allowed mendicant orders under the Spanish *patronato* to enter Japan from the Philippines. See Boxer, *The Christian Century*, pp. 239, 241.

11 For a positive assessment of Jesuit 'adaptability,' see Boxer, *The Christian Century*, pp. 209–30; and Andrew Ross, 'Alessandro Valignano: The Jesuits and Culture in the East,' in O'M. *Jes. Cult.*, pp. 336–51. For a discussion of the limitations of Jesuit tolerance of other cultures, see J.F. Moran, *The Japanese and*

the Jesuits: Alessandro Valignano in Sixteenth-Century Japan (London, 1993), pp. 161–77.

12 Although Xavier was the first Christian missionary to enter Japan, his stay there was brief, from 1549 to 1552. Organtino lived as though he were a Japanese throughout his long ministry in Japan, from his entry in 1567 to his death in Nagasaki in 1609. Luís Fróis, the author of *História de Japão*, was also a field missionary who practised accommodation. He remained active in Japan from his entry in 1563 to his death in Nagasaki in 1597, except when he accompanied Visitor Valignano as interpreter-amanuensis-secretary to Macao in 1592–5. Valignano visited Japan three times, in 1579–82, 1590–2, and 1598–1603. He never acquired the Japanese language.

13 For the Jesuit ranks, see *Constitutions*, ed. Ganss, p. 81; and Josef Franz Schütte, *Valignano's Mission Principles for Japan*, vol. 1 (St Louis, 1983), part 1, p. 252.

14 For an evaluation of the Jesuit adaptation of the *dōjuku* system, see Jesús López-Gay, 'Las organizaciones de laicos en el apostolado de la primitiva misión del Japón,' *AHSI* 36 (1967): 3–31; Alessandro Valignano, *Sumario de las cosas de Japon (1583)*, ed. José Luis Alvarez-Taladriz, Monumenta Nipponica Monographs 9 (Tokyo, 1954), nn 188–97; Hubert Cieslik, 'Laienarbeit in der alten Japan-Mission,' in *Das Laienapostolat in den Missionen: Festschrift Prof. Dr. Johannes Beckmann SMB zum 60. Geburtstag dargeboten von Freunden und Schülern*, ed. Johann Specker and Walbert Bühlmann (Schöneck-Beckenried, Switzerland, 1961), pp. 99–129; Boxer, *The Christian Century*, pp. 222–6; Schütte, *Valignano's Mission Principles*, part 1, pp. 251–2; and Moran, *The Japanese and the Jesuits*, pp. 161–88. For the term *kanbō*, see Shinzo Kawamura, 'Making Christian Lay Communities during the "Christian Century" in Japan,' dissertation, Georgetown University, 1999, pp. 176–83, 338; and Gonoi Takashi, 'Kirishitan jidai no kanbō ni tsuite' [on *kanbō* of the Kirishitan period], *Kirishitan kenkyū* 19 (1979): 248–54.

15 *Byōnin o tasukuru kokoroe* [How to help the sick], in *Kirishitansho; haiyasho*, ed. Ebisawa Arimichi, H. Cieslik, Doi Tadao, and Ōtsuka Mitsunobu, Nihon shisō taikei 25 (Tokyo, 1970), pp. 84–101. Another manual, *Konchirisan no ryaku* [A brief summary of contrition], attributed to Bishop Cerqueira around 1603, was orally transmitted from catechist to catechist among the secret Christians throughout the persecution period. The text is found in *Konchirisan no ryaku* [Abbreviated manual on contrition], ed. Kataoka Yakichi, in *Kirishitansho; haiyasho*, ed. Ebisawa et al., pp. 362–80.

16 López-Gay, 'Las organizaciones de laicos,' pp. 21, 28. Bishop Cerqueira ordained fourteen Japanese men as priests between 1601 and 1614. See Moran, *The Japanese and the Jesuits*, p. 162. During the period of persecution and the total absence of ordained priests, these Japanese catechists maintained the underground church.

17 For a fuller discussion of this topic, see Haruko Nawata Ward, 'Women and the

Jesuits in the Christian Century in Japan (1549–1650),' dissertation, Princeton Theological Seminary, 2001.

18 On the Kiyohara family, see Matsuda Kiichi, *Kinseishoki nihonkankei nanbanshiryō kenkyū* [Study of European primary sources on early modern Japan] (Tokyo, 1983), pp. 720–1.

19 Luís Fróis, *História de Japaō*, ed. José Wicki, 5 vols (Lisbon, 1976), IV, p. 495. Unless otherwise indicated, translations are my own.

20 Fróis, *História*, vol. 4, p. 496.

21 Ibid., p. 495.

22 *Byōnin o tasukuru kokoroe* (n15 above), p. 85.

23 *Cartas que os padres e irmãos da Companhia de Jesus escreverão dos reynos de Iapão e China aos da mesma Companhia da India e Europa, desdo anno de 1549 ate o de 1580*, vol. 2 (Evora, 1598; facs. ed. Nara, 1992), fol. 220v. I am quoting Boxer's English translation, found in C.R. Boxer, 'Hosokawa Tadaoki and the Jesuits, 1587–1645,' in his *Portuguese Merchants and Missionaries in Feudal Japan, 1543–1640* (Aldershot, UK, 1986), pp. 88–9.

24 John Hay, *De rebvs Iaponicis, Indicis, et Pervanis epistolae recentiores a Ioanne Hayo Dalgatiensi Scoto Societatis Iesu in liberum unum coaceruatae* (Antwerp, 1605; facs. ed. Nara, 1977), pp. 455–6.

25 O'M. *First*, p. 152.

26 For a detailed study of Naitō Julia and the Miyako no bikuni, see Kataoka Rumiko, *Kirishitan jidai no joshi shūdōkai: Miyako no bikunitachi* [Women's society in the Kirishitan period: the Miyako no bikuni], Kirishitan bunka kenkyū 14 (Tokyo, 1976).

27 Francisco Colín, *Labor evangélica de los obreros de la Compañía de Jesús en las Islas Filipinas* (1663), ed. Pablo Pastells, vol. 3 (Barcelona, 1902), p. 500.

28 Colín, *Labor evangélica,* p. 551.

29 Ibid., pp. 550–1.

30 See the critical edition of Fabian Fukan's *Myōtei mondō* by Ide Katsumi and Ebisawa Arimichi, in *Kirishitan kyōrisho*, ed. Ebisawa Arimichi et al., Kirishitan bungaku sōsho, Kirishitan kenkyū 30 (Tokyo, 1993), pp. 287–417, 434–58. On *Myōtei mondō*, see Ebisawa's introduction in *Kirishitansho; haiyasho* (n15 above), pp. 613–15, 637–8, and in *Nanban kōhaiki, Jakyōtaii, Myōtei mondō, Ha Daiusu*, ed. Ebisawa, Tōyō bunko 14 (Tokyo, 1964), pp. 115–18, 275–7; and also Ebisawa, 'Kaidai: Myōtei mondō,' in *Kirishitan kyōrisho*, ed. Ebisawa et al., pp. 509–12. On Fabian Fukan, see George Elison, *Deus Destoyed: The Image of Christianity in Early Modern Japan* (Cambridge, MA, 1973), pp. 142–84; Ide Katsumi, 'Habian to Myōtei mondō,' *Kikan nihon shisōshi* 6 (January 1978): 52–5; Ide, 'Haikyōsha Fukansai Fabian no shōgai hosetsu' [Additional information on the apostate Fukansai Fabian], *Shigaku* 48:1 (1977): 24–5; Ide, *Kirishitan shisōshi kenkyū*

josetsu: Nihonjin no kirisutokyō juyō [A history of Kirishitan thought: acceptance of Christianity by the Japanese people] (Tokyo, 1995), pp. 262–3; and Hubert Cieslik, 'Fabian Fukan den nōto' [Notes for the biography of Fabian Fukan], *Kirishitan bunka kenkyūkai kaihō* 15: (December 1972): 244–50.

31 It is most likely that Fabian produced this work while acting as a spiritual director under the supervision of Fathers Organtino and Morejon for the Miyako no bikuni. It is also likely that he used some members of Naitō Julia's society as the model for his Yūtei and Myōshū. Fabian later apostatized, and he left the Society of Jesus in 1608 to live with a former member of the Miyako no bikuni. He became a well-known author of anti-Christian literature.

32 Pedro Morejon, *A Brief Relation of the Persecution Lately Made against the Catholike Christians, in the Kingdome of Japonia, 1619*, trans. W.W. Gent, 1619, English Recusant Literature 213 (London, 1974), pp. 156–7.

33 Colín, *Labor evangélica*, p. 502.

34 Morejon, *A Brief Relation*, p. 157.

35 See the accounts of Luzia de la Cruz (1580–1656) and Tecla Ignacia (1579–1656) in Colín, *Labor evangélica*, pp. 507–47 and 547–62 respectively. On the life of the Miyako no bikuni in exile in the Philippines, see Ward, 'Women and the Jesuits,' pp. 124–67.

36 For Maria's biography, see Shibuya Mieko, 'Kyōgoku Maria fujin' [Lady Kyōgoku Maria],' in *Kirishitan ronbunshū rekishi, bunka, kotoba: Aoyama Gen kyōju tainin kinen* [Anthology of essays on Kirishitan: history, culture and languages; festschrift for Professor Aoyama Gen on his retirement] (Nagoya, 1999), pp. 39–63.

37 In his annual report of 1596, Fróis listed *Catechism, Guide for Confession*, and *Book of Meditations* ('P. Rector misit ei tres libros, Catechismum, Rationem confitendi, & librum Meditationum') as among these books. See Hay, *De rebvs Iaponicis,* p. 469.

38 Fernão Guerreiro, *Relação Anual das coisas que fizeram os padres da Companhia de Jesus nas suas missões do Japão, China … nos anos de 1600 a 1609*, 3 vols (Lisbon and Evora, 1603–11; repr. Coimbra, 1930), I, p. 219.

39 Hay, *De rebvs Iaponicis*, p. 618.

40 Guerreiro, *Relação Anual*, vol. 2, p. 74.

41 Daniello Bartoli, *Istoria della Compagnia di Gesú il Giappone: Secunda parte dell'Asia* (written in 1660), 8 vols in 2 (Naples, 1857–8), IV, pp. 196–7.

42 Guerreiro, *Relação Anual*, vol. 1, p. 219; vol. 2, p. 75.

43 Ibid., vol. 3, pp. 117–20.

44 Ibid., pp. 212–13.

45 João Rodriguez Giram, *Lettera Annua del Giappone del 1609 e 1610* (Rome, 1615), p. 130.

46 João Rodriguez Giram, *Lettera Annua del Giappone del M.DC.XII* (Rome, 1615), p. 126.

47 Guerreiro, *Relação Anual*, vol. 3, p. 214.
48 Boxer, *The Christian Century*, p. 223. O'M. *First*, pp. 147–8, lists two important restrictions that the Jesuits in Europe imposed on women. First, 'Jesuits admitted only males to their schools.' Second, 'they [laid] down for themselves some restrictions on hearing the confessions of women' because they feared that their familiarity with women would give rise to accusations of impropriety. For the women catechists, these two restrictions posed serious hurdles. Without higher education, women catechists' avenues in ministry remained limited. And not being allowed to secure Jesuit confessors on a regular basis, women were always reminded that their vocational identity as Jesuit co-ministers was marginal in Jesuit eyes.
49 Fróis, *História*, vol. 2, p. 369: '*sobrepeliz.*'
50 Ignacio Iparraguirre, *Historia de los Ejercicios de San Ignacio desde la muerte de San Ignacio hasta la promulgación del directorio oficial (1556–1599)*, vol. 2 (1955) of his *Historia de la práctica de los Ejercicios Espirituales de San Ignacio de Loyola*, 3 vols (Rome and Bilbao, 1946–73), pp. 209–12.
51 Kataoka, *Kirishitan jidai no joshi shûdôkai* (n26 above), p. 179.
52 Iparraguirre, *Historia de los Ejercicios*, pp. 225–31.
53 On Ōtomo-Nata Jezebel, Kumano bikuni, Shinto priestesses, and the 'Blood Bowl sutra,' see Ward, 'Women and the Jesuits,' pp. 236–79.
54 The session title was 'Almost Jesuitesses: Exploiting Opportunities on the Margins of the Society.'
55 O'M. *First*, p. 75.
56 Ibid.

30 / Clockwork and the Jesuit Mission in China

CATHERINE PAGANI

The history of Western-style clockwork in China is connected to the Jesuit presence at court. In 1601, Matteo Ricci (1552–1610) gave the first mechanical clock to the Chinese emperor, and from then on elaborate timepieces figured prominently in Sino-Jesuit interaction. The missionaries used these highly desired objects to gain imperial favour and thus obtain access to the highest reaches of Chinese society. But their role in the history of horology in China went further: they also introduced the theory and mechanics of the Western clock to the Chinese, serving as clock- and watchmakers within the court. This would be the Jesuits' lasting contribution to Chinese culture, since this technology, which forms the foundation of many other machines, had far-reaching implications. For the Jesuits, the European technology housed within appealing decorative cases made these *zimingzhong*, or 'self-sounding bells,' so named for their ability to chime on their own, the perfect link between science and art, both of which were in demand by the emperors, and ensured the missionaries nearly two hundred years of access to the Chinese court. To them, the Western mechanical clock was more than an object representing the latest European innovations: it was their key in a vast, closed empire that held the potential for countless religious conversions.

In this article I examine the Jesuit contribution to clock-making in China by offering a new interpretation of the mechanical clock within this inter-cultural context. The issues surrounding the introduction and development of clock-making parallel the successes and failures of the missions in China. Conflicts that arose between technology and catechism, and over whether to serve the emperor or God, illustrate the larger battles fought with other missionary groups in the Celestial Empire, with the pope in Rome, and among the missionaries themselves. In this way, clockwork may be seen as a microcosm of the Jesuit experience in seventeenth- and eighteenth-century China. But for the missionaries the clock also carried a deeper significance. By the time of Ricci's arrival in the Far East, clocks and clock-makers had been used in Europe as a metaphor for God and the creation; for the Jesuits, the clock went beyond its role as a technological artefact and represented the higher beliefs they hoped to instil in the Chinese.

The real success of the Jesuit missions in the Far East is due to the zeal and insight of Alessandro Valignano (1539–1606), an Italian Jesuit who was appointed by the Society as Visitor-General to the Indies in 1573, and who laid the foundations for the unique Jesuit approach to proselytizing in China. Detained at Macao on his way to Japan in 1578, Valignano had the opportunity to ponder the problems the Jesuits were having in establishing themselves in China. Valignano was the first to realize that if the enterprise were to be a success, the missionaries would have to learn Chinese and devote their entire lives to these missions. His missionary strategy, put into action by Matteo Ricci, who arrived at Macao in 1582, consisted of four main components: accommodation or adaptation to Chinese culture; propagation of the faith from the 'top down,' that is, by reaching the upper classes first; the use of science to aid in the propagation of the faith; and an openness to Chinese values and customs. It was these policies that set the Jesuits apart from other contemporary missionary groups, such as the Dominicans and Franciscans, and ensured Jesuit successes in China.[1]

Of the methods Ricci used in his efforts to enter the Chinese Empire and set up residence at the capital, two are of particular importance. The first was cultural accommodation, as advocated by Ignatius of Loyola, which Ricci employed very effectively, by giving Chinese names to the religious figures in his translation of the catechism, for example, and by allowing the Chinese who came to Christian services to continue to honour Confucius. Ricci's concept of accommodation focused on Confucius as the central figure in a Chinese-Christian synthesis developed as a means of adapting Christianity to Chinese culture, specifically to Confucian discourses on human nature,[2] and is reflected in the first Chinese catechism, *Tianzhu shiyi* (The True Meaning of the Lord of Heaven), written by Ricci and Michele Ruggieri (1543–1607) in 1584. The policy continued into the seventeenth century with the publication in 1623 of *Xingxue cushu* (A Brief Outline of the Study of Human Nature) by Giulio Aleni (1582–1649), and the *Confucius Sinarum philosophus*, a Jesuit translation of three of the Four Books of Confucianism, of 1687. This method of making and holding converts would later become the main issue of debate between the Jesuits and other missionaries, and would lead to fervent anti-Jesuit criticism.

Ricci's second method, termed *propagatio fidei per scientias* (propagating the faith through science), would become the focus of the Jesuits' proselytizing strategies in China. Trained in such areas as mathematics, astronomy, geometry, and cartography, the Jesuits utilized their knowledge to enable them to make more conversions.[3] Although this method was unsuitable for large-scale proselytization, it was useful to them in wooing influential Chinese scholars. Discussions would begin with scientific principles and then turn to aspects of the faith. Eventually, it came to be understood that an acceptance of Western science went hand in hand with an acceptance of Christianity.

The growing Chinese interest in science aided and shaped this strategy. As the Ming empire entered a period of decline, scholars seeking a cause for the dynasty's problems targeted the writings of the early Ming philosopher Wang Yangming (1472–1528) as the source of the problem. The Chinese literati of the early seventeenth century rejected Wang's notion that the source of moral action came from within one's own body and looked for more practical, outward solutions in the form of *shixue*, 'solid learning' or 'concrete studies.' This existing Chinese interest made the Jesuit strategy of using science to make converts all the more important, for it allowed them to reach the influential literati and created an environment in which these scholars were receptive to Jesuit ideas. In response, the order sought men for the China mission who were trained specifically in the areas of science and technology.

The Jesuits were ideal communicators of information on European science because the order itself stressed training in this area.[4] Members both taught and studied alongside the best scientific minds of Europe; and certainly the men sent to China were well versed in current theory.[5] In addition to theoretical knowledge, the Jesuits brought tangible examples of European science to engage the interest of the Chinese, thus taking advantage of an already present Chinese curiosity in objects from the West.[6] The most important of these were elaborate mechanical clocks.

Ricci had discovered the value of European goods in securing a place for the missionaries when he used Western objects to facilitate his journey to Beijing and obtain his audience with the Wanli emperor (r. 1573–1620) in 1601. Among the presents Ricci brought were a crucifix, a statue of the Virgin Mary, a clavichord, and two glass prisms.[7] Much was made in Ricci's diary of the emperor's interest in two chiming clocks, which he said were especially prized. Ricci's accounts were intended to elicit support for his missions and therefore may not be seen as truly accurate reporting of imperial attitudes; however, contemporary Chinese sources and extant objects show that there was indeed a genuine imperial interest in European clocks. In his diary, Ricci wrote of the emperor one day demanding these curiosities: 'Where is that clock, I say, where is that clock that rings of itself; the one the foreigners were bringing here to me, as they said in their petition?'[8] In his *Description of the Empire of China*, published in the first half of the eighteenth century, Jean-Baptiste du Halde attributed Ricci's success in reaching the emperor and establishing himself at the imperial court to these two pieces of mechanics; these soon led to a vast collection of elaborate clocks, which were 'of the newest Invention, and most curious workmanship.'[9]

The practice of presenting clocks to the Wanli emperor begun by Ricci continued with Nicolas Trigault (1577–1628). Trigault was charged with obtaining not only funds for the mission, but books and other objects of value from Europe that could be used to interest members of the Chinese bureaucracy. He was a remarkable man, who acquired a number of clocks for the Chinese court. In 1613 he left China for Rome, later to continue his voyage to the courts in the other major cities in Europe in order to publicize the missions. This trip was the most famous of the so-called missionary propaganda tours.[10] When Trigault departed from Lisbon for China (in 1617), he carried with him not only ample funds for the missions, but a great number of gifts for the emperor, the most numerous among them being elaborate clocks. One of the more complicated pieces he received came from Ferdinand II of Bavaria (1578–1637), elector and archbishop of Cologne. This most unusual clock depicted the Nativity. According to Trigault, the entire scene was 'marvellously enacted by little figures in gilded copper' and contained a number of elements, including Magi paying homage by bending their bodies, and animals that appeared to 'woo the Holy Child with their breath.' From a golden globe placed above, the Holy Father looked down. An ingenious mechanism in one part of the globe allowed two little angels to ascend and descend continuously. 'Throughout the scene,' Trigault continued, 'St. Joseph rocks the cradle and at the same time, most wonderful of all, an instrument plays a lullaby of its own accord.'[11] Unfortunately, this piece has not survived.

Ricci attributed the Chinese imperial interest in elaborate clockwork to the fact that the Chinese seemed to prefer 'that which comes from without to that which they possess themselves, once they realize the superior quality of the foreign product.' He continued, 'Their pride, it would seem, arises from an ignorance of the existence of higher things and from the fact that they find themselves far superior to the barbarous nations by which they are surrounded.'[12] Here, the 'foreign product' included maps and clocks; the 'higher things' were the doctrines of Christianity. In so reporting, Ricci hoped to give legitimacy in Europe to one of his proselytizing strategies: that of using European science to secure a foothold in China. This 'foreign product,' in fact, did allow the missionaries to reside in Beijing, and eventually they were granted a special residence and church in the Forbidden City.[13]

From the time the first clocks were brought to China from Europe around

1582, the Chinese were at a loss as to how to repair and maintain them. Matteo Ricci was instrumental in remedying this deficiency by initiating a long-standing cooperative effort between Jesuit and Chinese scholars. As a result, the Jesuits were able to exert an influence on both the theory and the practice of horology in China, first through the publication in Chinese of Western horological principles, and then in the staffing of the imperial clock-making workshop.

The Jesuits actively promoted European scientific knowledge, and during this period important treatises on Western mechanical technology were published in Chinese. Ricci was assisted in the translation into Chinese of European works on geometry, trigonometry, mathematics, astronomy, and hydraulics, and even Euclid's *Elements*, by the scholar Xu Guangqi (1562–1633).[14] Xu also co-authored, with the Jesuit mechanician Sabatino de Ursis (1575–1620), *Taixi shuifa* (Hydraulic Machinery of the West), published in 1612, for which Xu also wrote the preface. Following this came Guilio Aleni's (1582–1649) *Xixue fan* (A Sketch of Western Learning) in 1623.[15]

Shortly thereafter, in 1627, a pivotal work was published on the principles of European engineering and mechanics, *Yuanxi qiqi tushuo* (Diagrams and Explanations of Wonderful Machines of the Far West). This work, which provided Chinese names for Western mechanical terms and was the first to describe a European-style verge-and-foliot escapement, was co-authored by the Swiss missionary Johannes Schreck (1576–1630) and the Chinese scholar Wang Zheng (1571–1644).[16] In the same year, Wang also published a shorter volume, *Zhuqi tushuo* (Diagrams and Explanations of a Number of Machines), in which is found the earliest account in Chinese of the verge-and-foliot escapement, here applied to a clock by Wang. This clock is notable in that it also contained at the back a traditional Chinese type of timekeeper.[17]

However, it was not enough to supply mechanical theory: practical skills were necessary to keep the pieces already in the imperial collection in good repair. The history of Western clock-making at the Chinese court begins in the first years of the seventeenth century, when the emperor assigned four eunuchs from the College of Mathematics at the palace to study the art of clock maintenance and repair with Ricci. Ultimately the eunuchs were unable to cope with the demands of the imperial court. They believed they could not keep such complex mechanical objects running without the help of the Jesuit fathers, and the missionaries were often called to the palace to conduct repairs. The Wanli emperor, therefore, arranged to have the Jesuits at court look after the clocks.[18] The four eunuchs at the palace who received instruction under Ricci began an association between the Chinese and the Jesuit missionaries that would continue for nearly two centuries. Eventually the Jesuits were able to call upon professional clock-makers, who were then made part of the China mission.[19] So strong was this connection that into the nineteenth century, Ricci was regarded by the clock-makers of Shanghai as their patron saint of sorts, being known as 'Li Madou pusa,' the Bodhisattva Matteo Ricci.[20]

Sometime in the late seventeenth century, the Kangxi emperor (r. 1662–1722) established a number of *zuofang* (workshops) that manufactured luxury and more utilitarian goods for palace use, operating under the administration of the Imperial Household.[21] Modelled after Louis XIV's Académie Royale des Sciences from Jesuit reports, these workshops employed craftsmen from throughout China. One of the workshops was devoted to Western-style clocks. The Office of 'Self-Ringing Bells' (*Zimingzhongchu*) is mentioned in palace documents of 1689 and 1692,[22] the suggestion being that it was established around the same time that the palace workshops were formally organized. This workshop was the predecessor of the *Zuozhongchu*, Office of Clock Manufacture. The *Zuozhongchu* was not formally named until 1723, and remained active until at least 1879, when the last dated inventory of clocks was compiled.[23] By the time of Qianlong's rule (1736–95), the workshop was well established, with the Jesuits still working closely with the Chinese. Although this workshop was only one of many set up at the palace to produce goods for imperial use, ultimately it would prove to be the most significant: it allowed the Jesuits to introduce yet another (and highly practical) area of European science and technology to the Chinese that was soon disseminated to other parts of the country with the growth of a native clock-making industry. European science and technology had now fully penetrated the court circle (see figs 30.1, 30.2).

The missionaries were vital to the success of the clock-making workshop. In the course of staffing the imperial workshops, they created some rather extraordinary pieces that, it was said, in Europe would be considered masterpieces. Such clever constructions include an automaton in the form of a walking lion that Father Gilles Thébault (1703–66) was able to construct using the most basic of horological principles, and Father Valentin Chalier's (1697–1747) alarm clock, which the emperor kept in his own apartments. Father Sigismondo (1713–67) had planned to make an extraordinary automaton in human form that would be able to walk in a natural manner. It was feared that, should Sigismondo succeed (as he was expected to do), Qianlong would then demand of the missionary, 'You've made it walk, now make it talk.'[24]

One very high-profile piece was made in celebration of the empress dowager's sixtieth birthday, which fell on 6 January 1752. The attention given to this object in the Jesuit letters is not surprising: not only were the Jesuits made a part of this important occasion, an involvement reaffirming their close connection to Qianlong, but they were presenting a marvellous example of their skill to a very important recipient. Their work, as suggested in their letters, could compete with

30.1. *Zitan* wood, enamel, and jade clock in the form of a two-storey building.
Ht 152 cm. Imperial clock-making workshop. Qianlong period, 18th century.
Palace Museum, Beijing.

The Jesuits used their knowledge of mechanics and clockwork technology to gain
access to the Chinese court. By the late seventeenth century, the Kangxi emperor
(r. 1662–1722) had become so enamoured of these objects that he established a palace
workshop to produce elaborate clocks for him. Under the rule of the Qianlong emperor
(r. 1736–1795), this horological workshop was further expanded, and by the
late eighteenth century it was making dozens of clocks annually for imperial use.

30.2. Clock of gilt bronze made for the birthday of the Qianlong emperor (birthday
not specified). Ht 97 cm. Guangzhou, 18th century. Palace Museum, Beijing.
As a result of the increased demand for clocks both inside and outside the court
circle, manufacturing centres developed in the cities of Guangzhou and Suzhou.
The technology that had begun at the court with Matteo Ricci instructing four palace
eunuchs in the early seventeenth century had been disseminated to other parts of the
empire by the second half of the eighteenth century.

'the most curious and the rarest items from the four corners of the earth,' thereby confirming the triumph of European (and therefore missionary) ingenuity and enterprise in far-off China.

The hemicyclical mechanical theatre stood about three feet high and had three scenes painted in perspective. A Chinese figure holding an inscription wishing the emperor long life stood at the back; and in front of each scene, Chinese figures held in their left hands small gilt-copper bowls that were struck with a small hammer held in the right. The Jesuit Jean-Joseph-Marie Amiot continues his description:

This theatre ... was supposed to have been built on the edge of water. At the front was a lake, or more accurately, a basin from the middle of which rose a jet of water that cascaded down. A mirror represented the basin, and filaments of glass, blown by a very able artisan, were so slender; they imitated a jet of water so well that one was deceived even at a short distance. Around the basin was a dial with letters on it [European and Chinese]. A goose and two ducks frolicked in the middle of the water. The two ducks paddled around, and the goose marked the present hour with its beak. The dial moved by means of springs that ran a clock in the machine. A magnet, which was also hidden and made the dial move, was followed by the goose, which was made mostly of iron.

When the hour was about to strike, the statue that carried the inscription in its hand left its compartment at the back of the theatre and with deep respect showed its inscription; then the six other statues played an air by striking each on its basin the note assigned to it as many times and for as long as was determined by the music. With this done, the figure carrying the inscription gravely returned, not to come out again until the next hour.

This machine so pleased the emperor that he wanted to show his appreciation to the foreigners [the Europeans]; he gave them a gift that amounted to at least the cost that would have been paid for its construction. The honour thus given to us here is more precious than the greatest riches.[25]

So that he could enjoy it often, the emperor later had the machine placed in the Yuan Ming Yuan, his summer palace, which he visited frequently. This was exactly what the Jesuits had hoped would happen; as Amiot wrote, 'It is thus that we try, in the interest of religion, to win the goodwill of the prince and to make our services to him useful and necessary so as to engage him and make him favourable towards the Christians, so that he will persecute them less, and give the priests the freedom to make known Jesus Christ to those who will pay heed to them.'[26]

It can be argued that by giving clocks to the Chinese emperor, Ricci and subsequent missionaries were simply following an established European gift-giving practice. By the sixteenth century in Europe, the clock had become a standard presentation gift among various courts.[27] Clocks symbolized the well-regulated state, and their artistry and technology made them showcases of the high level of skill attained: they were the 'pride of princely ostentation.'[28] That being so, it is not surprising that the Jesuits would choose for their gifts to the Chinese court objects that were already deemed highly appropriate at home and that were representative of the latest technology and finest craftsmanship Europe had to offer. As well, by the time Ricci arrived in China, clocks had already been given to foreign dignitaries. Honorariums from Holy Roman Emperor Maximilian II (1527–76) to the Turks in the mid-sixteenth century took the form of natural objects, such as spices and precious stones, and the finest crafted objects that could not be found, at least of similar quality, in Ottoman Turkey; in the 1560s, clocks made in Augsburg formed an important part of these honorariums.

But for the Jesuits, the giving of clocks must have carried a deeper significance. In European society, the clock's steadfastness and regularity were seen as instilling order in a chaotic world, and allowed comparisons to be made with universal harmony, the state, and the Creator. Philosophical writings connected the clock-maker and the clock with the Creator and the world.

In the late thirteenth century, the religious establishment used the clock to support the notion that the world was a perpetual machine, and thus was eternal. Furthermore, an understanding of mechanics would lead to an understanding of higher principles. Bonaventure (1221–74), in his *Retracing the Arts to Theology* of 1250–3, wrote that 'the illumination of mechanical knowledge is the path to the illumination of the Sacred Scripture.'[29] The mechanician in Bonaventure's writing is analogous to God, for 'every artificer ... aims to produce a work that is beautiful, useful, and enduring ... so that he may derive *praise, benefit*, or *delight* therefrom,' for the same 'reason that God made the soul rational, namely, that of its own accord, it might *praise* Him, *serve* Him, [and] *find delight* in Him.'[30] By the fifteenth century, God was regarded as the eternal clock-maker. Like the horologist who had envisioned his product in full from the start, God had his fully conceived eternal plan that unfolded like the running of a clock.[31]

This metaphor of the Creator as clock-maker was at the centre of the mechanical philosophy of the seventeenth century. Proponents, particularly René Descartes (1596–1650) and Robert Boyle (1627–91), applied this theory to non-mechanical things by equating the body with a machine.[32] Boyle likened the Creator to the clock-maker and the universe to clockwork. A favourite image in Boyle's conception of the world as a machine was the monumental clock of Strasbourg Cathedral, built in 1352–4.[33] Its notable features included images of the Virgin and Child, the Three Magi, and the well-known mechanical rooster that could crow and flap its wings.[34] Just as the Strasbourg clock continued to run without the intervention of its builder, so, too, would the universe, which was made by

God, and would continue to run according to God's laws but without his intervention. The Strasbourg clock also illustrates the more tangible connections between the clock and the church, since many of the great public clocks were installed in cathedrals. Thus, with all its European socio-religious associations, the clock as an appropriate gift for the Chinese emperor in its potential for aiding the missions could hardly have escaped Jesuit notice.

When the Jesuits arrived in China, they found mechanisms in the form of water-clocks and sand-clocks that were not strictly speaking mechanical clocks in the European sense.[35] What they were seeing was a technology at the end of a long period of development, and limited in its wider applications. Although the European clocks were at that time relatively inaccurate, they would eventually far surpass the water- and sand-driven mechanisms.[36] Therefore of value to the missions were men trained in horology, who could instruct the Chinese in clock-making, construct pieces according to the emperor's wishes, and make much-needed repairs to those pieces already in China. In fact, the Jesuits' skills as watchmakers were desired by the Chinese emperors second only to their knowledge of astronomy and mathematics.[37]

When the Kangxi emperor, intrigued by the foreign watches, decided to set up his Office of Self-Ringing Bells (*Zimingzhongchu*) in the late seventeenth century,[38] the missionaries were ideally placed to 'illuminate the Sacred Scripture' as they 'illuminated mechanical knowledge' in accordance with Bonaventure's philosophies.

The issue of whether or not to serve the Chinese emperor was addressed by Ricci, who in his proselytizing strategies had stressed focusing on the highest reaches of Chinese society. His method of using science to spread the faith enabled the Jesuits to place themselves well at the court. In theory, the plan could hold nothing but success; in reality, it was fraught with frustration, disappointment, and conflict. Serving the emperor, especially for those skilled in mechanics, involved an enormous amount of time. Many of the missionaries' letters tell of the long hours they were required to spend repairing and constructing mechanical objects that left them little time to use their knowledge to aid in explaining some of the higher principles of the faith.[39] A frustrated Father Jean Walter (1708–59) wrote, 'The tastes of this prince vary, like the seasons, so to speak. It was for music and jets of water, today it is for machines and buildings ... The same tastes may come back, and every day we must be on our guard so that we are not taken by surprise.'[40] In 1704, Father Jean de Fontaney (1643–1710) wrote to the 'Confesseur du Roy,' Father La Chaise, about the amount of work that Father Jartoux, a mechanician and horologer, and Father Brocard, a painter, were required to do for the Kangxi emperor. Such were their tasks that they were 'not allowed the time to proclaim Jesus Christ, and make him known to the officials of the palace.'[41] The situation did not improve under the Qianlong emperor. In a letter of 15 September 1769 written by Father de Ventavon to Father du Brasard, de Ventavon relates that he was obliged to be of service at the palace every day and so had no time to breathe. But, he continues, 'the princes and the nobles of the empire appealed to the Europeans to take care of their watches and clocks, of which there are a great number here, and there were only two of us who were in a position to accommodate them, a father of the Propaganda and myself. Now and again we find ourselves, I would not say, occupied with the work but overwhelmed by it.'[42] Many other accounts in the letters of the Jesuits tell of their enduring hardships for the sake of the success of the mission. Jean-Denis Attiret (1702–68) wrote to M. d'Assaut in 1743:

To be chained to one sun or another; to labour on Sundays and feast days in order to pray to God; to paint almost nothing that is not in his taste or character; to have a thousand other encumbrances that would be too long to explain to you: all of this would send me quickly on the way to Europe if I did not believe that my brush is used for the good of religion and to make the emperor favourable towards the missionaries who preach it, and if I did not see paradise at the end of my pains and my labours. This is the only attraction that makes me serve the emperor.[43]

Compounding matters were the conflicts that arose between the Jesuits and the church, and among the missionaries themselves.

A particularly sensitive issue was the growing controversy surrounding the Jesuit practice of adapting certain aspects of the faith to Chinese culture, so that Christianity would appear less foreign and those Chinese who converted would still be able to show respect for the important native rituals. The European clock-makers, both Jesuit and non-Jesuit, were particularly affected, because their knowledge of mechanics often required that they engage in activities other than simply constructing clocks. They were criticized by some as compromising the faith and engaging in counter-Christian practices.

A clear illustration is a disagreement that arose between a certain Father Angelo, a Franciscan who likely came to China with the Mezzabarba Legation in 1720, and Father Matteo Ripa (1682–1745), a secular priest who served as a painter and engraver to the court from 1710 to 1723. Although neither Angelo nor Ripa was a Jesuit, they worked alongside Jesuit clock-makers; and the issues they faced may be seen as representative of the experiences felt by the missionary clock-makers at the Chinese court.

Angelo was presented to the court in 1721 and became one of the emperor's clock-makers. Father Angelo was apparently quite skilled but was prevented from displaying his talents fully, because Ripa felt that if he did he would be contributing to idolatry among the Chinese. A passage from Ripa's *Memoirs* illustrates the conflicts within the missionary ranks:

[In 1723] His Majesty had taken it into his head to have a fountain constructed which should never cease to play. We were accordingly asked by command, whether any of us were able to contrive it ... Father Angelo, through me as an interpreter, replied without hesitation, that he felt equal to the task. ... Father Angelo had already begun a design to be submitted to the Emperor, when I was informed that the fountain required by the superstitious monarch owed its origin to the following circumstance. His Majesty demanded of a certain Bonze, who was believed to be possessed of miraculous powers, how his dynasty should be rendered perpetual – and the Bonze had replied that this might be attained whenever a fountain should be constructed whose waters should never cease to flow upon the figure of a dragon. Those who gave me this information, deeming it wrong to encourage such heathen superstition, had unanimously declared that they were unable to execute the work ... I deemed it my duty to prevent Father Angelo from undertaking the work, especially as by means of polite excuses and suitable representations he could avoid it without giving offence. Accordingly I communicated my opinion to Father Angelo, and found much difficulty in inducing him to adopt it.[44]

Not long afterward, the emperor asked Angelo if he would assist in constructing bronze bells for a temple. Ripa objected to this as well, for the bells were probably for use in 'temples of idols,' and therefore felt it his duty to save Angelo from committing 'the sin of idolatry.' Father Angelo did not share Ripa's views, for, according to Ripa, 'as [Angelo] was well informed in mechanics, so he was deficient in theology and philosophy.' Ultimately, the two men were unable to work around their opposing viewpoints. Father Angelo 'became greatly incensed, saying that I had deprived him of the honour of being employed in the service of His Majesty, and immediately went away to our residence at Haetien, declaring that he would no longer live in the same house with me, and that for the future he would have some other interpreter.'[45]

In practical as well as philosophical terms, the European mechanical clock was of great value to the missions and was far from being merely a technological artefact. It figured prominently in both Jesuit proselytization strategies: using science to gain access to influential scholars, and cultural accommodation, which, in Ricci's form, allowed the practice of certain Chinese rites in order to make the doctrines of Christianity seem less foreign to converts. The clock proved to be an ideal choice of gift for the Chinese emperors, who collected these objects in great numbers and eventually established imperial workshops for their manufacture. Clock-making, along with skills in other areas such as astronomy, contributed to the favour the Jesuits enjoyed, and gave them an access to the Chinese emperor that would allow them, in theory, to convert the empire of China from the top down.

But the clock's value to the Jesuits was not only that it promoted European science; it also represented the higher principles of the faith and had strong associations to Christianity in the form of concepts that would have been familiar to the Jesuits and that appealed to them. The clock gave order to chaos, and the relationship between the clock-maker and the clock was analogous to that between God and creation. In bringing the technology to China, teaching the skill to the Chinese, and making clocks themselves, the Jesuits were serving a higher purpose. 'Divine Wisdom,' according to Bonaventure, '[is] to be found in the illumination of the mechanical arts, the sole purpose of which is the *production of works of art*.'[46] So by offering to instruct the Chinese in clock-making, the Jesuits were also aiding their conversion to Christianity: making clocks became a spiritual exercise. As Bonaventure continues: 'In this illumination we can see the ... *Incarnation of the Word* ... and the *union of the soul with God*. And this is true if we consider the *production*, the *effect*, and the *advantage* of the work, or if we consider the *skill of the artist*, [and] *the quality of the effect produced*.'[47] It could not have been coincidental that theologians placed an emphasis on mechanical principles to illustrate higher matters of the faith, and that the Jesuits placed an emphasis on these same arts in their proselytization strategies.

But the Jesuits' success in securing a place for the missions using such skills as clock-making contributed to inter-missionary rivalries that fuelled the Rites Controversies of the seventeenth and eighteenth centuries. Debate over and criticism of Jesuit activity in China connected with Ricci's cultural accommodation policies also owe something to the Jesuits' positions as clock-makers and mechanicians. Conflicts in ideology between technology and catechism, and over whether to serve the emperor's needs or not, were realities in the lives of the makers at court. The mechanical clock may thus be seen as a microcosm of Jesuit activity in China; more important, it also served as an expression of the scientific and religious aspects of European culture that the Jesuits sought to introduce to the Chinese court.

NOTES

1 For a discussion of these elements and their role in defining Jesuit corporate culture, see Nicolas Standaert, 'Jesuit Corporate Culture As Shaped by the Chinese,' in O'M. *Jes. Cult.*, pp. 352–63.

2 Qiong Zhang has examined Ricci's method of cultural accommodation in 'Transla-

tion as Cultural Reform: Jesuit Scholastic Psychology in the Transformation of the Confucian Discourse on Human Nature,' in O'M. *Jes. Cult.*, pp. 364–79, and 'Cultural Accommodation or Intellectual Colonization? A Reinterpretation of the Jesuit Approach to Confucianism,' dissertation, Harvard University, 1996.

3 Klaus Maurice, 'Propagatio fidei per scientias: Jesuit Gifts to the Chinese Court,' in *The Clockwork Universe*, ed. Klaus Maurice and Otto Mayr (Washington and New York, 1980), p. 31.

4 Maurice, 'Propagatio,' p. 30.

5 One of the main controversies of the seventeenth century was between proponents of the geocentric universe belonging to the long-held Aristotelian-Ptolemaic world view, and proponents of the heliocentric universe of Copernicus. Galileo, whose discoveries corroborated the heliocentric view, for twenty years had known the Jesuit Christoph Clavius (Klau, 1537–1612), the eminent mathematician who oversaw the final reform of the Gregorian calendar. Clavius was at the celebrated Collegio Romano and had taught Ricci. Although Clavius was not ready to accept Galileo's theories fully, he did confirm the accuracy of some of Galileo's observations. Unfortunately, with Clavius's death in 1612, Galileo lost an important ally; shortly thereafter, the church denounced Galileo's theories, and he was publicly condemned in 1633.

   This condemnation was enormously restrictive for the Jesuits, who were well aware of Galileo's findings. Ordered not to expound the theory of heliocentrism (although they found that it made more and more sense in explaining natural phenomena), they compromised by telling the Chinese of the work of the Danish astronomer Tycho Brahe (1546–1601), who supported the Ptolemaic view of the sun as circling the earth but had the other planets circle the sun (the Tychonic system). There were obvious limitations to this theory, and on occasion the Jesuits used the controversial ideas of Copernicus. It was not until 1670, however, that the Jesuits openly taught the Copernican model to the Chinese. It is interesting to note that the six large cast-bronze instruments for the astronomical observatory in Beijing set up in 1669 by Ferdinand Verbiest (1623–88), at that time the director of the Imperial Board of Astronomy, were based on designs by Brahe. These instruments still stand there today. On Brahe, see J.R. Christianson, *On Tycho's Island: Tycho Brahe and His Assistants, 1570–1601* (Cambridge, 2000); Kitty Ferguson, *The Nobleman and His Housedog: Tycho Brahe and Johannes Kepler: The Strange Partnership That Revolutionised Science* (London, 2002); and Kenneth J. Howell, *God's Two Books: Copernican Cosmology and Biblical Interpretation in Early Modern Science* (South Bend, IN, 2002).

6 He Zhe, 'Qingdai de Xifang zhuanjiaoshi yu Zhongguo wenhua' [Western missionaries and Chinese culture in the Qing dynasty], *Gugong bowuyuan yuankan* 1983

no. 2:17–26; Ju Deyuan, 'Qingdai Yesuhuishi yu xiyang qiqi' [The Jesuits and strange Western objects of the Qing dynasty], part 1, *Gugong bowuyuan yuankan* 1989 no. 1: 3–16; part 2, ibid., no. 2:13–23; and Zhang Yinlin, 'Ming Qing shi ji xixue shu ru Zhongguo kaolu' [History of the penetration of Western science and technology into China in the Ming and Qing dynasties], *Qinghua xuebao* 1924 no. 1:38.

7 Matteo Ricci, *China in the Sixteenth Century: The Journals of Matteo Ricci, 1583–1610*, ed. Nicolas Trigault, trans. Louis J. Gallagher (New York, 1953), p. 313.

8 Ricci, *China*, p. 369.

9 Jean-Baptiste du Halde, *A Description of the Empire of China and Chinese-Tartary, Together with the Kingdoms of Korea, and Tibet: Containing the Geography and History (Natural as well as Civil) of Those Countries. Enrich'd with General and Particular Maps, and Adorned with a Great Number of Cuts. From the French of P.J.B. Du Halde, Jesuit: with Notes Geographical, Historical, and Critical; and Other Improvements, Particularly in the Maps, by the Translator*, 2 vols (London, 1738–41), II, p. 127.

10 Maurice, 'Propagatio,' p. 32.

11 Alfred Chapuis and Edmond Droz, *Automata: A Historical and Technological Study* (Neuchâtel and New York, 1958), pp. 79–80.

12 Ricci, *China*, pp. 22–3.

13 Kenneth Scott Latourette, *A History of Christian Missions in China* (New York, 1929), p. 121; and Bernward H. Willeke, *Imperial Government and Catholic Missions in China during the Years 1784–1785* (New York, 1948), p. 7. There were four churches in which the missionaries were allowed to reside, two of which were established prior to this edict. In 1653, Lodovico Buglio set up the Dongtang, or Eastern Church, located in Dongtangzi Hutong or Ganyu Hutun (Hutong). It came to be known as the Lesser Portuguese Church at the end of the Qianlong period. The Nantang, or Southern Church, was established in 1650 by Adam Schall von Bell. Also known at the time as the German Convent, it was located to the east of the Xuanwu Gate. At the end of the Qianlong period, it was known as the Greater Portuguese Church. The Beitang, or Northern Church, also known as the French Convent, was dedicated in 1703 and built by the French Jesuits under Gerbillon. Known for its fine library, it was located outside Xi'an men. The Xitang, or Western Church, also called the Italian Convent or the Church of the Propaganda, was established under Pedrini in 1723 and was located on the main thoroughfare of Xizhi men. Of this church, Matteo Ripa noted in his memoirs that early in 1722 he and the Italian Jesuits had been staying at the imperial residence known as the Changchun yuan, approximately two hours' journey from Pekin; these Jesuits were ordered to stay in Pekin with the

French or Portuguese Jesuits, a situation that prompted Ripa 'to seize the opportunity, and attempt to establish a house in Peking for the use of the missionaries sent by the Propaganda' (Matteo Ripa, *Memoirs of Father Ripa, during Thirteen Years' Residence at the Court of Peking in the Service of the Emperor of China; with an Account of the Founding of the College for the Education of Young Chinese at Naples*, trans. Fortunato Prandi [London, 1844], p. 118). For more information on these churches, see Fu Lo-shu, *A Documentary Chronicle of Sino-Western Relations (1644–1820)*, Association for Asian Studies Monograph 22, vol. 2 (Tucson, 1966), p. 591 n24; W. Devine, *The Four Churches of Peking* (London, 1930); and *Lettres édifiantes et curieuses, écrites des missions étrangères, par quelques missionnaires de la Compagnie de Jésus*, 30 vols (Paris 1708–44), IX, p. 377.

The Yongzheng emperor, in an edict of 1724 prohibiting Christianity, forced the missionaries to leave their churches. This had more effect on the provincial churches, since the missionaries who served at the court as mathematicians, astronomers, and artists were spared. See Willeke, *Imperial Government*, p. 10.

14 Xu most likely would have learned something about clock-making from his association with Ricci.

15 A mathematician and geographer, Aleni was a prolific writer and had an excellent knowledge of Chinese. In addition to his scientific works, he published a world atlas, compiled with Yang Tingyun, based on Matteo Ricci's world map along with the notes made by other Jesuits. See L. Carrington Goodrich, *Dictionary of Ming Biography*, ed. L. Carrington Goodrich and Chaoying Fang, vol. 1 (New York and London, 1976), pp. 2–5.

16 Schreck was well versed in the sciences of medicine, mathematics, and natural philosophy. In Italy, Schreck was a member, along with Galileo (1564–1642), of the Cesi Academy, and was a friend of Johannes Kepler (1571–1630). See Joseph Needham, Wang Ling, and Derek J. de Solla Price, *Heavenly Clockwork: The Great Astronomical Clocks of Medieval China* (Cambridge, 1960; 2nd ed., with supplement by John H. Combridge, 1986), p. 145.

17 Needham et al., *Heavenly Clockwork*, pp. 146–7.

18 Ricci, *China*, pp. 373, 392, 536.

19 Needham et al., *Heavenly Clockwork*, p. 148.

20 Joseph Needham, *Science and Civilisation in China* (Cambridge, 1954), IV ii 2, 532. All clock-makers belonged to a guild. All guild members were required to participate in religious ceremonies associated with their particular guild. These ceremonies were often designed as worship of the guild's founder, which may explain the 'deification' of Ricci, he being the first to introduce Western clock-making to the Chinese court. Guilds will be discussed in greater detail below.

21 Gao Zhentian, 'Kangxidi yu Xiyang zhuanjiaoshi' [The Kangxi emperor and Western missionaries], *Lishi dang'an* 1986 no. 1:187–91; and Liu Yufang,

'Qinggong zuozhongchu' [The clock-making workshop of the Qing palace],
Gugong bowuyuan yuankan 1989 no. 4:49–54.

22 Zhang Tangrong, *Qinggong shuwen* [Detailed account of the Qing Imperial Palace]
(Taibei, 1969), pp. 316–18.

23 *Zuozhongchu zhongbiao xishu qingce* [Accurate list of the detailed count of clocks
of the Office of Clock Manufacture] from the *Yuanmingyuan chengnei zuozhongchu
zhongbiaodeng xiang qingce* [Accurate list of the clocks, watches, etc., of the
Yuanmingyuan and Inner City Office of Clock Manufacture], Beijing, Number
One Historical Archives, #404 (Guangxu 5/12/20).

24 Jean-Joseph-Marie Amiot, letter of 1754, in *Lettres édifiantes et curieuses, écrites
des missions etrangères. Mémoires de la Chine*, new ed., 26 vols (1771–81), XXIII,
p. 362.

25 Jacques Philibert Rousselot de Surgy, *Memoires géographiques, physiques et
historiques. Sur l'Asie, l'Afrique, & l'Amerique. Tirés des Lettres Édifiantes, & des
Voyages des Missionaires Jésuites*, vol 2 (Paris, 1767), pp. 271–4. This letter, with
slight changes as indicated by the square brackets, is found in *Lettres édifiantes*
(1771–81), vol. 23, pp. 176–8. This letter was also published in *Lettres édifiantes*
(1708–44), vol. 28 (1758), where the date of the event is given incorrectly as
6 January 1750.

26 *Lettres édifiantes* (1771–81), vol. 23, p. 178.

27 'The Court: Source of Support and Challenge,' in *The Clockwork Universe*, ed.
Maurice and Mayr, p. 212.

28 Otto Mayr, 'A Mechanical Symbol for an Authoritarian World,' in *The Clockwork
Universe*, ed. Maurice and Mayr, p. 1.

29 Bonaventure, *Retracing the Arts to Theology, or Sacred Theology, the Mistress
among the Sciences,* trans. in *Philosophy in the Middle Ages,* ed. Arthur Hyman and
James J. Walsh (Indianapolis, 1983), p. 466.

30 Condensed from Bonaventure, *Retracing the Arts to Theology*, secs 13–14.

31 These notions were expounded by Nicolaus Cusanus (1401–64) in his *De visione
Dei* of 1458.

32 Galileo was the first to propose a mechanical philosophy in *The Assayer* of 1623.
See Descartes's *Principles of Philosophy* (1644); and Boyle's *The Excellency and
Grounds of the Corpuscular or Mechanical Philosophy* (1674). For a deeper discus-
sion of clockwork in this context, see Otto Mayr, *Authority, Liberty, and Automatic
Machinery in Early Modern Europe* (Baltimore, 1986).

33 Robert Boyle, *The Works of the Honourable Robert Boyle, in Six Volumes*, ed.
Thomas Birch (London, 1772). See *Usefulness of Natural Philosophy* (II, p. 39) and
Final Causes of Natural Things (V, p. 443).

34 After the mechanism of the first clock failed, a second clock was constructed there
in 1574, and included with it were paintings of such scenes as the Creation, sculp-

tures, and various automata. See *The Clockwork Universe*, Maurice and Mayr, p. 17, fig. 6 for an illustration of the second Strasbourg clock.

35 The Chinese also used incense-clocks, as Ricci was aware. He mentions the water-clocks in his diary, but also those which use 'the fire of certain perfumed fibres made all of the same size.' In the same passage, Ricci tells of sand-clocks. All of these were considered 'very imperfect.' See Pasquale M. d'Elia, *Fonti ricciane. Documenti originali concernenti Matteo Ricci e la storia delle prime relazioni tra l'Europa e la Cina. 1579–1615*, 3 vols (Rome, 1942–9), I, p. 33. A recent work on incense-clocks in the Far East is Silvio Bedini's *The Trail of Time: Time Measurement with Incense in East Asia* (Cambridge, 1994).

36 See the first chapter of David S. Landes, *Revolution in Time: Clocks and the Making of the Modern World* (Cambridge, MA, and London, 1983).

37 Beginning with Adam Schall von Bell (1592–1666) in 1644, a succession of Jesuits held the important position of director of the Imperial Board of Astronomy. He was succeeded by Johannes Schreck (1576–1630), followed by Ferdinand Verbiest (1623–88), Thomas Grimaldi (1639–1712), Ignatius Kögler (1680–1746), Augustus von Hallerstein (1703–74), Felix da Rocha (1713–81), Joseph Raux (1754–1801), and the Portuguese P. Serra, who was the last European to hold the post. See Fu, *A Documentary Chronicle* (n13 above), pp. 476, 505; and Louis Pfister, *Notices biographiques et bibliographiques sur les jésuites de l'ancienne mission de Chine, 1552–1773*, 2 vols (Shanghai, 1932). In cartography, the Jesuits undertook to map the empire in 1708, a ten-year project, the result of which was later engraved for printing under the direction of the missionary Matteo Ripa (1682–1745). See, for example, Henri Bernard, 'Les étapes de la cartographie scientifique pour la Chine et les pays voisins depuis le XVIe jusqu'à la fin du XVIIIe siècle,' *Monumenta Serica* 1 (1935): 462; and Ju Deyuan, 'Qing qintian jianzheng Liu Songling' [August von Hallerstein, the director of the Board of Astronomy of the Qing dynasty], *Gugong bowuyuan yuankan* 1985 no. 1:53–62.

38 Zhang, *Qinggong shuwen* (n22 above), pp. 316–18.

39 It was not just the sciences but the arts that proved to be useful, and the order sent missionaries who were competent in the arts. See, for example, Cécile and Michel Beurdeley, *Castiglione: Peintre jésuite à la cour de Chine* (Fribourg, 1971); George Loehr, 'Missionary Artists at the Manchu Court,' *Transactions of the Oriental Ceramic Society* 34 (1962–3): 51–7; Loehr, 'European Artists at the Chinese Court,' in *The Westward Influence of the Chinese Arts from the 14th to the 18th Century,* ed. William Watson (London, 1972), pp. 33–42; John E. McCall, 'Early Jesuit Art in the Far East,' *Artibus Asiae* 11 (1948): 45–69; Paul Pelliot, 'La peinture et la gravure européennes en Chine au temps de Matthieu Ricci,' *T'oung Pao* 20 (1921): 183–274; and Michael Sullivan, *The Meeting of Eastern and Western Art* (London, 1972).

40 *Lettres édifiantes* (1771–81), vol. 23, p. 364.

41 *Lettres édifiantes* (1708–44), vol. 8, p. 88.

42 *Lettres édifiantes* (1771–81), vol. 24, p. 110.

43 Ibid., vol. 22, p. 518.

44 Ripa, *Memoirs*, pp. 127–8.

45 Ibid., pp. 128–9.

46 Bonaventure, *Retracing the Arts to Theology*, p. 465.

47 Ibid.

PART SIX

Expulsions, Suppressions, and the Surviving Remnant

Marc Fumaroli introduces this part of our volume by sketching in broad strokes the situation that give rise to the suppression of the Society in France in 1763–4, and made the general suppression almost inevitable. He rightly observes that, although the Society had already been brutally disbanded in Portugal and in the Portugese dominions overseas, it was the suppression in France that led almost ineluctably to the event of 1773. In France, the Jesuits were caught between enemies on the far right, the Jansenists, and enemies on the far left, the *philosophes* – an impossible situation, made worse by some of their own missteps. The rage the Jesuits' enemies on the left directed against them would be unleashed in even greater fury during the French Revolution against the institution they saw the Society as representing, the church itself.

Richard Clay brings these events down to concrete reality and gives them a new dimension with his account of the dispersal and destruction of Jesuit artistic objects in France, first in the wake of the suppression and then in the wake of the Revolution. His piece can be seen as a sad codicil to Part Two, which expounded on the creation of the Jesuits' artistic corpus.

The Jesuits were proud of what they had accomplished for the native peoples in their Reductions in Latin America, but these settlements had long been a source of resentment and suspicion in certain quarters and, along with the mission to the imperial court in Beijing, an object of attack for the enemies of the Society. Dauril Alden here relates in vivid detail the operations of four officials of the Portuguese crown that resulted in the destruction of the Reductions in territories claimed by Portugal, a harbinger of the destruction of the Reductions in Spanish territories just a few years later and, more devastating still, of the suppression of the Society itself in Portuguese and Spanish lands. In that last, Portugal and Spain provided a model for France to follow.

In recent years we have become familiar with the story of Matteo Ricci and of Jesuit beginnings in the court of Beijing. We know in general terms the blow dealt by the papal decision in the early eighteenth century against 'Chinese Rites.' What Ronnie Po-chia Hsia provides below is a detailed account of a lesser-known aspect of the history of the Jesuits in China, the decline of the mission in the decades after the papal edict. For reasons internal to Catholic polity and inherent in the character of Chinese culture, the mission was doomed, it seems, even before 1773.

These first four essays in Part Six offer glimpses into the darkest hours of Jesuit history and suggest that the whole enterprise was moving towards oblivion almost without leaving a trace, a victim of, among other things, 'the Enlightenment.' The last three are not so dark. Larry Wolff writes about Roger Boscovich, who, as noted in the introduction to Part Three, was surely the most celebrated Jesuit scientist of the eighteenth century and perhaps the most important and distinguished of all Jesuit scientists. Wolff is able to illustrate, especially by making use of a diary Boscovich kept during a trip in 1762 through southeastern Europe, how Boscovich had appropriated many of the ideals and prejudices that we identify with the Enlightenment. He thereby provides further grounds for exploring the idea of a 'Catholic Enlightenment' and for considering how that might have played itself out in the Society of Jesus.

The next two essays reveal that, even after the suppression, the Society or its influence survived, sometimes in unexpected ways and places. With María Antonia de Paz y Figueroa, a Jesuit 'beata' who was allowed to wear the Jesuit cassock, Alicia Fraschina shows how after the suppression one woman successfully undertook the mission of keeping the Spiritual Exercises alive and of working for the restoration of the Society. In 1814 the Society was in fact restored by an official act of Pope Pius VII. That act almost certainly would not have been possible if the Society had not vestigially survived in two highly unlikely places – Russia and the United States, the subject of Daniel L. Schlafly, Jr's, essay, a fitting piece, we believe, with which to end our volume.

31 / Between the Rigorist Hammer and the Deist Anvil: The Fate of the Jesuits in Eighteenth-Century France

MARC FUMAROLI
de l'Académie Française

It is sad in a volume about the Jesuits' contribution to culture, sciences, and the arts to have to include accounts of the Society's doom in the twilight of the era. It was in fact the Jesuits' active and conspicuous contributions to these fields in the eighteenth century that summoned against them a convergence of hatreds so momentous that within a few years it succeeded in eliminating them from the French and then from the European stage. Even if the first deadly thunderbolt was flung against the Jesuits in Portugal in 1759, their fate in eighteenth-century Europe was definitively sealed when France, the key nation on the Continent, decided in 1763 to get rid of them.

It is not by chance, then, that before narrating the suppression of the order, John McManners's recent and authoritative survey of the Catholic church in France in that century describes the Jesuits' extensive presence in the realm: their educational empire with its network of Marian congregations, their output of printed books, and their influential learned periodical, the *Journal de Trévoux*.[1] Such social power exercised by a single religious order directly attached to its superior general in Rome and thence to the pope could not but be felt by local bodies inside and outside the Gallican church to be 'an empire within the realm.' The old and renewed passion, which then found the name of 'patriotism' and which would give such an impetus to the French Revolution, boiled behind the old arguments and traditional procedures used by the Jesuits' foes to eliminate these 'aliens' from their native land.

Only the absolute authority of the seventeenth-century French kings had been able to restrain the deep resentment felt against these brilliant and successful intruders. The Bourbon monarchs, from Henri IV to Louis XIV, were anxious to tame their difficult *noblesse de robe et d'épée*, and therefore were badly in need of the civilizing process carried on by the fashionable Jesuit colleges and their Marian congregations for laymen. Still, from the time the Jesuits first moved into the kingdom in 1561, right at the beginning of the Wars of Religion, this resentment and the corresponding argumentative weaponry never ceased to grow among the Gallican clergy as well as among several powerful quarters of French lay society. Among these lay critics stood the magistrates of the *parlements*, always prone to assert their self-proclaimed right to restrain the royal power within the 'fundamental laws' of the kingdom. From the start they saw arbitrariness in the royal will that established the Jesuit colleges as rivals of the French universities.

It is significant that even during the long and staunchly pro-Jesuit reign of Louis XIV, at a time when the *parlements* were somewhat cowed, none of the prestigious royal academies created or renewed by Colbert ever elected one Jesuit to its membership, in spite of the literary, scholarly, and scientific achievements and celebrity of so many French Jesuits. The Académie Française deeply resented the obligation imposed upon it by the king to receive as honorary members his Jesuit confessors, Fathers La Chaise and Le Tellier. This tacit public ostracism, never commented on, says much about the breadth of the common mistrust of the incurably 'alien' Society of Jesus, which was after all founded by a Spanish enemy and was blindly devoted by a special vow to an Italian pope.

In fact the Society had never taken full and definitive legal root in the kingdom. The Edict of Rouen of 1603, almost contemporary with the Edict of Nantes, submitted the re-establishment of the Jesuits in France to more severe and restrictive conditions than those of the provisional 'toleration' conceded to the Protestants. Never had the *parlements* declared the Jesuit *Constitutions* to be in conformity with Gallican laws. Never had royal *Lettres patentes* deigned to give definitive and sound status to an order conditionally tolerated since 1603. From the time of the Edict of Rouen, as before their expulsion in 1594, the Jesuits depended on the personal goodwill of the royal dynasty and therefore on the capacity of the reigning king to assert it against the anti-Jesuit grain.

The impressive fecundity of the Jesuit order in France hung by this single thread. But the French Jesuits themselves and the immense majority of the French, however Gallican and unfriendly to them, did not see this fundamental weakness of the order, so much were they accustomed after two centuries to a more or less wary cohabitation warranted by the ostensible favour of the successive Bourbon kings. But the Society had accumulated enemies perfectly aware of this invisible weakness, who only awaited the right hour to strike.

As it happened, the right hour came in 1757, when Louis XV's prestige and authority were severely damaged by military defeats during the Seven Years' War and when he badly needed his *parlements* to approve new taxes. The stubborn anti-Jesuit energies, until then divided among themselves and successfully contained by the royal power, burst forth. The permanent Gallican passion against papal temporal encroachments, the *parlements'* renewed assertiveness against royal absolutism, and the Jansenist theological horror of the Jesuits' Molinism all merged for the first time and fought the order with one will, finding public opinion massively on their side. The prosecution was channelled into the most subtle manoeuvres among the *parlements*, Versailles, and Rome, and into the most intricate legal procedures inside the *parlements*. It lasted six years, with a constant acceleration towards the final denouement.

The French Jesuits had made extraordinary efforts to nationalize and, so to speak, gallicanize themselves. The most authoritative *Histoire de France,* published in 1714, was written by Gabriel Daniel, a Jesuit. Father Louis Malbourg was called a 'Gallican Jesuit' because of his numerous and learned defences of Louis XIV's ecclesiological positions against those of Pope Innocent XII. The contribution of French Jesuits to the illustration and diffusion of French literary culture had been overwhelming, as instanced in French Jesuits such as Dominique Bonhours and in the more general teaching in the Jesuit colleges of French language and of French authors, most notably Corneille. Despite all this, the ultra-sensitive French national identity, frustrated by the weaknesses of Louis XV, came to define itself more violently than ever by opposition to these ultramontane and intrusive monks. Such was the common prejudice the professed anti-Jesuits could rely on and exacerbate at will. Without this prevalent mood of national hostility, their tremendous offensive against the very existence of the order would never have had a chance to prevail upon the will of Louis XV, inheritor of the Bourbon covenant with the Society of Jesus. The king's confessor, Father Desmarets, was a Jesuit, as had been the rule of the court since the days of Henri IV. It may be said that the king's final surrender to the strategy of the Jesuits' foes was a foretaste of his grandson's backtracking in the wake of the French Revolution.

Who were, then, these 'professed anti-Jesuits'? A small 'Jansenist party,' entrenched in the Gallican clergy and in the *parlements*. This party had lost all its doctrinal battles since the time of its appearance under Richelieu, and the Roman Curia, under pressure from the French court, had several times solemnly condemned its creed as semi-heretical. Under Louis XV, in 1713, the buildings of Port-Royal-des-Champs, the party's shrine, had been demolished. But the resilience of this little church within the church was prodigious. When a rift arose between the *parlements* and the royal power, the few Jansenist magistrates were ready to take the lead and make of the Jesuit case a trial of strength.

The archbishop of Paris, Christophe de Beaumont, used the uncharitable blackmail of threatening to refuse the sacraments in order to exact from the dying rebels their formal approval of the anti-Jansenist papal bull *Unigenitus*

(1713). The prelate intended to eradicate definitively the Jansenists, just as Louis XIV had done with the Calvinists. The Gallican Parlement of Paris was incensed by this brutal zeal. The Jansenist party there had no difficulty in convincing its Gallican colleagues that the Jesuits were the masterminds of this unchristian moral harassment. Their clandestine journal, *Les nouvelles ecclésiastiques*, widely distributed and read, kept the sacred flame of wrath burning.

Several events, contemporary with the decline of royal prestige, offered to the Jansenist magistrates the providential opportunity to renew on a larger scale and with stunning success the anti-Jesuit Gallican assaults of the sixteenth and early seventeenth centuries, before the Edict of Rouen. On 5 January 1757, Louis XV was stabbed in the courtyard of Versailles by a certain Robert François Damiens from Arras. The king recovered rapidly, but the national emotion was understandably immense. It reminded every French citizen of former assassinations of kings. Damiens's judges concluded that he was an isolated fanatic, but leaks from the inquiry fuelled a violent polemic against his imagined instigators.

Damiens had been a pupil at the Jesuit college in Arras ten years earlier. It was much too easy to conclude that he was another Jacques Clement, who murdered Henri III, or another Jean Chastel, who tried to murder Henri IV, or another François Ravaillac, who succeeded in 1610. Was it not the moral theology of the Jesuits to advise and condone the assassination of so-called unjust kings? This Jansenist thesis received widespread assent.

In spite of the fact that Damiens himself claimed to have been inflamed to kill by what he had heard from Jansenist magistrates about the ferocity of Christophe de Beaumont and the support he received from the king, public prejudice tended to agree with the Jansenist version, publicized by the *Nouvelles ecclésiastiques* and numerous pamphlets.

From that point forward national pride had found the scapegoat for its wounds. When in January 1759 the news arrived in Paris of the strangulation and burning at the stake of Father Gabriele Malagrida in Lisbon and of Pombal's ignominious expulsion of the Jesuits from Portugal, who were accused of attempting to assassinate King José I, the Parisians raised shouts of triumph and set bonfires throughout the capital.

Two years later, on 8 May 1761, the same public acclaim welcomed the decision of the Parlement of Paris against the French Jesuits, in a notorious case that had dragged on since 1755, to the dismay of the Jesuits and the delight of their foes. The English, at war with France, had captured several French vessels bearing merchandise sent by the Jesuits' West Indies mission on the island of Martinique, which was in payment of a debt to their commercial correspondents in Marseille. Instead of deploring a French loss, public opinion in France saw in this seizure a sudden light thrown on the scandalous origins of the supposed wealth accumulated by the Jesuit 'Fifth Column.'

The visitor-general and apostolic prefect of Martinique, Father Antoine de Lavalette (or Valette), was the mastermind of an ingenious system of closed economy and speculation on the exchange rates of money. The system was disrupted by the seizure of the vessels, and the Marseille and Nantes correspondents, compelled to declare bankruptcy, demanded justice and their money back. But from whom? From Lavalette and the mission in the West Indies? From the French assistancy of the Jesuits? From the whole Society of Jesus? The case passed from the provincial and obscure consular courts to the Parlement of Paris, where it offered a wonderful opportunity to the Jansenist magistrates to throw light on the international structure of the Society and to substantiate the accusations of lax morals levelled against it since Pascal's *Provincial Letters*.

In order to make his charge worse against the defendants, the lawyer for the plaintiffs had been allowed by the authors to use in manuscript the monumental indictment against the Jesuit order *Histoire génerale de la Compagnie de Jésus en France*, compiled by two Jansenist magistrates, Le Paige and Condrette, which would be published in 1761. The lawsuit therefore was turned into a public case against the Society on the grounds not only of its un-French essence but also of the basically unlawful and offensive character of its existence on French soil.

Relying on the propitious trend created by this legal case, the Abbé de Chauvelin, another Jansenist magistrate, took the decisive step on 8 May 1761. He raised before the Parlement of Paris the political and legal question that had been simmering since 1603, concerning the presence of the Jesuits in France. His indictment of this international order culminated in a word that sounded familiar to all readers of Montesquieu: 'Is it possible that here exists, or even to imagine, an authority more extensive, more arbitrary, more *despotic*?' Then he added, 'These same Jesuits direct within the realm the education and consciences of the subjects of the king, these men, who by their state of life, by their vows, by their *Constitutions* cannot be and are not in reality anything other than the blind and passive instrument of one arbitrary and *despotic* will, of a foreign General who must always reside in Rome.'[2] With a single word the Jansenist Chauvelin sounded against the Jesuits both the Gallican chord of French freedom from Rome and the Enlightenment chord of political liberty from absolutism.

This sound was heard from afar by non-Jansenist ears. The following year, 1762, the *procureur général* of the Parlement of Rennes, Louis René de la Chalotais, who was then a spokesman for the Breton nobility embattled against Versailles, published his *Compte rendu des Constitutions des jésuites*, in which he likened the organization of the order to the 'oriental despotism' described by Montesquieu and its spirit to the religious 'fanaticism' described by Voltaire. This was the only contribution of the 'parti de la philosophie' to the Jansenist anti-Jesuit battle, but it drummed up new troops for the fray.

The court at Versailles tried everything to neutralize the offensive of the Parlement of Paris, which had leagued with almost all the provincial *parlements* in favour of suppressing the 'illegal' and 'threatening' Jesuits. The enfeebled king was more than reluctant to do harm to the Jesuits, but the financial situation and the mood of public opinion compelled him to come to terms with the iron will of the magistrates.

Several compromises suggested by Versailles and the majority of the Gallican bishops were considered and submitted to Pope Clement XIII and to the general of the order, Lorenzo Ricci. Neither would accept the total nationalization of the French Jesuits and the consequent parcelling out of the Society itself. But, besieged by his magistrates and faced with the fait accompli effected by them in several of their jurisdictions, the king by imperceptible degrees bowed. In 1763, in exchange for the Parlement's ratification of a raise in taxes, he had to issue an edict suppressing the Society of Jesus in France. This same year the Treaty of Paris, disastrous for French interests, put a shameful end to the Seven Years' War.

The classic study by Dale Van Kley has established overwhelming evidence of a clever Jansenist conspiracy leading the judicial machine step by step to the destruction of the Society in the Kingdom of France. There is a sort of cold refinement in the style of this masterly revenge. The list of Jesuit 'errors' compiled by Le Paige for the Parlement of Paris, for example, is an implicit reply to the list of errors of Jansen and Quesnel enumerated in the papal bulls that condemned their doctrine. The Jansenists had won. The victory was won in the name of ancient grievances, in the name of the past. But the scheme had succeeded because the schemers had flattered the modern passions of Enlightened France, its Gallican patriotism, its anti-clerical bent, and its growing dissatisfaction with the absolutist monarchy.

The Encyclopaedists, enrolled since 1750 by Voltaire in his crusade against 'l'Infâme,' that is, principally, the Catholic church and its Judaeo-Christian faith and priesthood, stayed silent during the process of the suppression of the Jesuits, except for the outsider, La Chalotais. Voltaire, who loved his deceased Jesuit teacher of humanities at the Collège-Louis-le-Grand, Father Charles Porée, and who had often been reviewed favourably in the Jesuits' *Journal de Trévoux*, nevertheless did not take sides with Porée's imperilled colleagues. The suppression of the Jesuits was in his view a big and welcome blow to the church in general. But he hated the 'Jansenist party' and feared that its revival could become extremely dangerous for 'the philosophers' if it took a lasting hold on the *parlements*. With a perfect sense of timing he chose to launch in 1762 his own 'party of philosophy' against the Jansenist Parlement of Toulouse, inciting it with his pamphlets on the famous 'Callas affair.'

In 1767, Voltaire's Parisian lieutenant, d'Alembert, published anonymously the letter *Sur la destruction des jésuites en France*. This text had been devised jointly with Voltaire. With urbane condescension, the 'philosopher' places laurels on the tomb of the ex-Jesuits, extolling in them everything the Jansenists had denounced in the Jesuits' *Constitutions* as deviations from the monastic norm: first, the long length of the novitiate, two years, which allowed Jesuit superiors enough time in which to assign to each of the novices the occupation for which he was best suited, and allowed these future Jesuits enough time to test themselves; second, the exemption from devotional exercises and communal recitation of the Divine Office, which gave them all enough leisure to study and made the Society a cornucopia of 'science and lights.'[3] D'Alembert also praised their morals, who were uniformly severe on themselves but adjusted to the human weaknesses of others and thus prepared to regulate by persuasion and not by force, as evident in the smoothly run human society in Paraguay.

'This masterpiece of human industry in the realm of politics' was thus the very opposite of the Jansenist ethos, which imposed rigorous ethical standards on everyone while suppressing for everyone any reasonable hope of reward.[4] With the most biting irony, the 'philosopher' suggested, therefore, that the Jansenists had done the dirty job of suppressing the only religious order that could disturb and seriously rival, by its own Catholic Enlightenment, the 'party of philosophy.' Now the time had come for philosophical 'reason' to crush the 'Cossacks' and the 'Pandours' of the tiny and obscurantist 'Jansenist party.'

Behind d'Alembert's quarrel with the Jansenists over the now suppressed Jesuits stood the question of 'culture, science, and the arts,' that is, the essence of the Enlightenment. For d'Alembert and Diderot, of the *Encyclopédie*, there was no doubt that human 'reason' had fuelled the progress of 'culture, science, and the arts,' and the task of philosophy was further to promote it. From d'Alembert's and Voltaire's viewpoint, the learning of the Jesuit mathematicians, physicists, ethnologists, dramatists, musicians, poets, orators, and educators – their 'science and lights' – far from being objectionable per se, were an integral part of the Enlightenment: the pity was that these achievements served too well the cause of the chief obstacle to the lay Enlightenment, the Catholic church.

For the Jansenists, on the contrary, and notably for Pascal, culture, science, and the arts were 'divertissements' that turned sinners away from the only serious object deserving attention, salvation. It may seem that such a stance was hopeless in the fashionable Paris of the Enlightenment, but Voltaire's lay

Enlightenment was one thing, Rousseau's lay Enlightenment another thing altogether.

In 1751 the Citizen of Geneva published his *Discours sur les sciences et les arts*, in which he treated culture as a symptom of moral corruption and a fallacious remedy for the misery of modern man. It is the same Rousseau who replied to d'Alembert in 1758, with his *Lettre sur les spectacles*, that the art of theatre, so favoured by the 'philosophers' and by the Jesuits, was in fact, as the Jansenist Pierre Nicole had said long before, a poison for the soul and for a healthy society.

Voltaire, who liked to see himself as the legitimate heir of Racine on the French stage, reacted bitterly to that 'obscurantist' thesis. The Ferney Patriarch was even more angered to find in Rousseau's *Emile* the eloquent 'profession of faith of the Savoy vicar,' in which the supreme cognitive power in man was removed from frail 'reason' and attributed to the 'heart,' the only source of morals and religion. And the heart, according to Rousseau's spokesman, felt with compelling evidence that natural morality and religion and the ones revealed by Christ were identical.

Although, at first glance, at the time no common ground could be imagined between Rousseau and the Jansenist party, it soon became obvious that their views about religion and culture could well coalesce. In Pascal's *Pensées*, it is the heart, not the arrogant Cartesian 'reason,' that is the seat of faith. In the last years of the *ancien régime*, Catholic apologetics had already turned itself towards a neo-Augustinianism indebted to both Pascal and Rousseau.

In his *Génie du christianisme*, published in 1802, at the same time as the concordat between the French Republic and the papacy, Chateaubriand revived with striking eloquence the Christian-Rousseauan-Pascalian apologetics of the heart against the philosophers' reason. But he rescues 'culture, science, and the arts' from the indictment of Rousseau and Pascal to present them as legitimate offsprings of the restless Christian 'heart.'

In the meantime, the French Revolution had given to the question of culture, science, and the arts its full political significance. The Jansenist enthusiast asceticism and Rousseau's Spartan republicanism had been associated with and compromised in the bloody Jacobin experiment of 1792–4. Nevertheless, although it had evaporated as a 'party,' Jansenism survived in nineteenth-century France as a spirit, often and subtly associated with Rousseauan themes, in the minds of the major liberal writers and thinkers such as Chateaubriand, Lamennais, Tocqueville, and Sainte-Beuve.

To these Catholic liberals, the return of the Society of Jesus in France under the restoration of the Bourbon monarchy, after a half-century of absence, did not appear as a renewal of Renaissance humanism or a revival of the Catholic

Enlightenment but as the reinforcement of an anti-liberal outlook. It explains why even today the anti-Jesuit masterpiece of Sainte-Beuve, *Port-Royal,* retains its place as a lay Bible of French national consciousness.

NOTES

1 John McManners, *Church and Society in Eighteenth-Century France: The Religion of the People and the Politics of Religion* (Oxford, 1998), pp. 423–530.
2 See Dale Van Kley, *The Janenists and the Expulsion of the Jesuits from France, 1757–1765* (New Haven and London, 1975), p. 111.
3 See Van Kley, *The Jansenists,* p. 216.
4 See ibid., p. 217.

32 / The Expulsion of the Jesuits and the Treatment of Catholic Representational Objects during the French Revolution

RICHARD CLAY

In this essay I focus on how the suppression of the Jesuits in the 1760s and the religious policies of later governments, during the French Revolution, affected Jesuit visual signs in the church of the Maison Professe on the rue St-Antoine in Paris. The dispersal and destruction of many Jesuit representational objects is explored below, but so too is the remarkable survival of other such objects *in situ*. While separated by more than a quarter of a century, the suppression of the Jesuits and the French Revolution were connected, not only in terms of the treatment afforded to certain categories of representational objects in each case but also in the 'imaginary' of some late eighteenth-century French people. As is shown below, pamphlets and speeches kept the Jesuits in the public sphere in the late 1780s and the 1790s, despite the absence of the Society of Jesus from France.[1]

In 1755 the business dealings of a Jesuit, Père Antoine de Lavalette, based in Saint-Domingue, went disastrously wrong, generating enormous debts. When creditors pursued their claims for compensation in the Parlement of Paris, a powerful law court, Jansenist lawyers succeeded in putting the whole Society of Jesus on trial, challenging its right to remain in the region.[2] The king was resistant to proposals to expel the Jesuits.[3] Nevertheless, he did eventually issue a royal edict ordering suppression in November 1764.[4] By mid-April 1762, however, the future of the contents of Jesuit buildings in Paris was already in doubt.

Anticipating the Parlement's sequestration of their property, the Jesuits took advantage of the court's recess in mid-April 1762 and began to burn documents and sell off kitchen implements, linen, and furniture.[5] Following its return, the Parlement sent hussars to the Maison Professe in Paris, on 23 April 1762; papers were seized and seals were placed on the buildings.[6] Ostensibly, these measures were meant to protect property that could be used to pay the creditors who had originally brought a case in the Parlement against the Jesuits. But the Parlement did not actually order the Jesuits' suppression in the Parisian region until 6 August 1762, several months later.[7] In the meantime, placing seals and making inventories signified to the public the law court's control over Jesuit spaces and over the Society's future. By treating Jesuit property as if suppression was a fait accompli early in 1762, the Parlement put pressure on the king to give in to the momentum of anti-Jesuit policies.

Following its ruling on the expulsion of the Jesuits, the Parlement ordered all members of the Society of Jesus to leave their buildings, and Jesuits' goods were seized ready for sale.[8] Sensitive to the potential interpretation of removals as profanation, the Parlement requested the assistance of the local clergy in selecting objects that had to stay in Jesuit churches in order to guarantee their decency for future worship.[9] In Paris, this policy might have helped to pacify wealthy and powerful Catholics, mainly from the exclusive Marais district, who were attending services that the visiting clergy of St-Paul and St-Sulpice were holding in the church of the former Maison Professe.[10] Yet sale of the church's non-essential silverware in particular still constituted a potential means of paying the Jesuits' litigious creditors. After all, as Brice noted in his 1752 guidebook to Paris, the Maison Professe contained more silverware than any other church in Paris.[11] But the selective sale or melting down of Jesuit silverware also gave the Society's enemies a non-economic advantage – it disrupted Jesuit resistance. On 31 August 1762 the Parlement specifically ordered that all silver from the chapels and rooms of Jesuit congregations was to be melted down into specie.[12] The congregations were confraternities of laymen, and removing all their silverware rendered their chapels unsuitable for worship. Thus, members were prevented from continuing religious practices that were at the heart of specifically Jesuit forms of sociability that could focus resistance to the Parlement's anti-Jesuit policies. As Henri Lefebvre has noted, a space's use signifies its meanings, so disrupting the congregations also helped to de-signify the church on the rue St-Antoine as a Jesuit space.[13]

Yet the Parlement was not thorough in removing non-silver Jesuit representational objects from the church of the Maison Professe. Despite being condemned as artistically 'pitiable' by the influential writer Piganiol de la Force,[14] statues of the celebrated Jesuit saints Ignatius of Loyola and Francis Xavier remained on the facade of the church until the 1790s.[15] Inside the church, imagery not only signified the space's connections with the Society of Jesus, but also visually repudiated several of the centuries-old accusations that the Parlement had recently re-mobilized against the Jesuits.[16] Vinache's figure *Religion Trampling Idolatry* rebutted accusations of erroneous Jesuit use of images. N.S. Adam's figure *Religion Teaching a Young American* challenged claims that Jesuits were too willing to accommodate pagan customs in their foreign missions.[17] The chapels on either side of the high altar, where Louis XIII's and Louis XIV's hearts were buried, visually resisted suggestions that the Jesuits were guilty of lese-majesty and were ultra-papists who posed a potentially regicidal threat to the French monarchy. Simon Voüet's painting of the assumption of the royal saint, St Louis, was at the centre of the high altar. The altar's lower level was flanked by sculptures of the Jesuits' founder, St Ignatius of Loyola; his trusted lieutenant, St Francis Xavier; the key royal saint, Louis; and the founder of the French monarchy, Charlemagne.[18] The signifying scheme of the high altar thus reiterated the close links between royalty and the Jesuits. The church's iconographical scheme posed a dilemma to the Jesuits' opponents, constituting a formidable visual riposte to the Society's enemies; still, it was necessary to the building's preparedness for ongoing non-Jesuit religious use by the priests of St-Paul and St-Sulpice.

Initially, Jesuit signifiers were simply left in place, probably owing to the expense of removing them.[19] However, once Louis XV bought the ex-Jesuit church and gave it to the Chanoines Réguliers de Ste-Catherine in 1767,[20] designification of the space as Jesuit could no longer be delayed. Following the demolition of their own buildings to make way for a market in 1782, the Chanoines Réguliers moved their living quarters and their worship to the rooms and church of the former Maison Professe.[21] The Chanoines Réguliers removed the keystone of the church's iconographical scheme, the high altar, with its Jesuit sculptures.[22] A new, less ostentatious high altar 'à la Roman' was introduced instead,[23] and the choir was widened.[24] The relative aesthetic simplicity of the new altar, compared with the baroque intricacies of its predecessor, might have been intended to signify a return to the austere spiritual simplicity of the early church that many contemporaries contrasted with the alleged spiritual laxity of Jesuits.[25] It was more problematic to remove the bronze bas-relief by Duval that represented the Jesuit saint Ignatius of Loyola kneeling in prayer at the foot of the cross on which Christ was crucified.[26] The sculpture was placed above the altar of the chapel in which the male members of the powerful Condé family were buried. It might have been religious and personal respect for the Condé family's continued use of the chapel for an annual mass held for the repose of the soul of Le Grand Condé[27] that ensured that the image of St Ignatius remained in place. Furthermore, unlike removing the high altar, transforming the signifying scheme of the Chapelle du Condé risked mobilizing opposition on artistic grounds, because it was highly esteemed.[28] Other Jesuit signifiers, however, were removed from the Maison Professe. A painting by Michel Corneille of St Francis Xavier entitled *Taking the Faith to the Indies* was rolled up and left in a corner of the church.[29] A similar obscurity kept a painting of St Ignatius of

Loyola out of public view in one of the rooms of the former Maison Professe.[30] The new clergy of the former Maison Professe had almost entirely 'de-Jesuitized' the space by the time of the French Revolution.

With the removal of all but one of the church's specifically Jesuit signifiers, the royal chapels and the sculptures representing the dangers of idolatry and the legitimacy of missionary work ceased to be readily legible as refutations of accusations made against the Society of Jesus. Rather, as a result of the changing visual and discursive contexts in which their meanings were constructed, the images were transformed into rebuttals of the *philosophes'* critiques of the church's uneasy relationship with the Crown and of Catholicism's alleged 'superstition.'[31] Incorporating new elements into the church's iconographical scheme served to further dilute significations of the Jesuits' earlier presence and to clearly signify the new ownership of the space. In 1782 the Chanoines Réguliers had the tombs of Pierre d'Orgemont, Cardinal de Birague, and his wife, Valentine Dalbiani, moved to the church of the former Maison Professe.[32] Two marble fonts, a bas-relief representing St Louis along with 'two other seigneurs,' and another bas-relief depicting a monk and two sergeants-at-arms were introduced into the nave.[33] The treasury was enriched with a vermeil relic of the church's new patron saint, St Catherine, and two other reliquaries, one of St James and the other of St Louis. The Chanoines Réguliers had bought the latter two objects from the Jesuits following the Society's suppression, having chosen to purchase non-Jesuit relics.[34] Finally, in 1787, two paintings by the young artist Touzé, representing St Catherine of Alexandria and St Louis respectively,[35] were placed in the choir along with another image of St Catherine.[36]

The introduction of new images into other parts of the former Maison Professe also contributed to the building's re-signification. In 1773, when the former Jesuit library was handed over to the Parisian municipality to house the city's collection of books, a painting was installed above the stairs outside the library, signifying the space's new secular and municipal functions and meanings.[37] The painting, by the academic artist Hallé, was entitled *Peace Bringing Abundance and the Arts to the Town Hall*.[38] Ostensibly, Hallé's painting celebrated the end of the Seven Years' War in 1763, in representing the arts in Paris as benefiting from the peace dividend afforded by the relaxation of royal wartime spending constraints.[39] But the image made an alternative and anti-Jesuit reading available to its well-educated audience of library-goers. After all, in 1763 the last members of the Society of Jesus left Paris, meaning that there was finally peace between Jansenists and Jesuits as well as between France and foreign powers. As a result of the religious peace, the fruits of the famously erudite Jesuits' love of the literary arts (their library) were surrendered to the Town Hall. Thus, in more than one sense, peace had indeed brought abundance and the arts to the municipality – the theme of Hallé's painting. After the suppression, removing particular kinds of representational objects, introducing new ones, and changing spaces' functions thus signified that the library and church of the former Maison Professe were non-Jesuit spaces.

The only historian to focus on the material consequences of the Jesuits' expulsion from France, Jacques Bonzon, argued that the sale of Jesuit goods stemmed from the Parlement's urge to 'turn everything into money,' regardless of artistic or intellectual value.[40] Bonzon accused the Parlement of a philistinism that, he claimed, was avoided during the French Revolution by the preservation of many confiscated Catholic objects in secular museums and depots. Of course, in the 1760s, many Jesuit objects were sold or literally turned into money by being melted down. But the decision of the Parlement of Paris to sell rather than melt down so much of the silverware from the former Maison Professe indicates an understanding that a large market for art objects existed, and that this market recognized the artistic value of the silverware as justifying prices that exceeded the objects' material value. The *parlementaires*, unlike later revolutionary pres- ervationists, also privileged the religious value of Catholic representational objects, allowing municipal officers to have the first choice of former Jesuit goods that they deemed might be suitable for their town's churches. The prices charged to the municipal officers were related to the goods' material value rather than to their cost on the open art market, where prices were inflated by purchas- ers' willingness to pay extra for added artistic value.[41] Accordingly, the Parlement's policies on the sale of Jesuit objects might be regarded not as demonstrating a philistine disregard for artistic and intellectual value but as constituting a vote of confidence in the connoisseurial sophistication of the art market and the impor- tance of objects' religious value. Certainly, the Parlement's policies towards former Jesuit objects after June 1763 cannot have been motivated by cupidity, as Bonzon suggested, because the king had ruled that money raised from sales would be given to a body beyond the Parlement's usual jurisdiction – the Catholic church in France.[42] It might have been hoped that such a policy would placate French Catholics, who were by no means unanimous in their support for the Jesuits' expulsion and the resulting treatment of sacred objects.

Some individuals clearly bought Jesuit objects following the suppression because the goods were of religious value and signifiers of loyalty to the much- maligned Society of Jesus. For example, the aristocrat the Marquis Lefranc de Pompignan bought more than twenty-five silver objects from the Maison Professe in Paris.[43] The marquis was an *amateur* who collected secular art, but the Jesuit silver was not destined for his collection.[44] Instead, the marquis, a known supporter of the Jesuits, bought the silverware for religious use in a chapel at his home.[45] The timing of the blessing of the chapel, in October 1762,[46] suggests that the space had been prepared in order to guarantee the ongoing religious veneration of the sacred Jesuit objects it contained. The Parlement's drive to de-Jesuitize did not extend to preventing such semi-private use of former Jesuit objects bought by supporters of the Society of Jesus. Nevertheless, the fact that the Catholic church in France profited from the dispersal of Jesuit goods into non-Jesuit churches, the chapels of individual Catholics, and private art collections did not placate opposition to the sales.

As late as 1790, when Jacques Desenne wrote to the revolutionary National Assembly, he used the treatment of Jesuit art in the aftermath of the Society's expulsion in the 1760s to warn against the nationalization of all church property in France. Nationalization had been made law on 2 November 1789, as a means of raising revenue for an almost bankrupt French state.[47] Desenne wrote: 'See what has become of the riches of the most powerful religious body that we had in France [the Jesuits]. No sooner was it destroyed than its immense spoils disappeared from before all eyes.'[48] As a result of nationalization, church goods, especially those made of metal and belonging to contemplative religious communities that were closed in February 1790,[49] did disappear 'from before all eyes' – the objects were melted down or sold to private individuals.[50] Desenne's warning that church goods could disappear from sight following nationalization supports Bonzon's later claim that successive revolutionary governments' policies on church goods were repetitions on a larger scale of that associated with the suppression of the Jesuits more than a quarter of a century earlier.[51] The methods employed during the revolutionary suppressions were certainly similar to those of the Jesuit precedent – the authorities put seals on goods, made inventories, and began sales, visibly signifying secular control over Catholic spaces.[52] But the scale of the revolutionary suppression of religious communities was much larger than that of the suppression of the Jesuits, and involved tens of thousands more objects. Furthermore, the aims of the revolutionary legislators were very different from those of the earlier *parlementaires*, and the profits accrued by suppression went to the nation's coffers and not those of the church or litigious individuals.

While the art market had been able to soak up objects sold following the suppression of the Jesuits, the scale of the revolutionary suppressions from 1790 on was so great that art prices suffered massive deflation. Connoisseurs began to warn that the national patrimony was being dispersed to undiscerning collectors, many of them foreign.[53] In response, the National Assembly formed the Commission of Monuments in November 1790, charged with preserving artistically valuable objects for the nation.[54] The Commission, later replaced by the Temporary Committee of the Arts, used secular criteria based on objects' perceived aesthetic or historical value to select those goods worthy of preservation in depots and, subsequently, the new museums.[55] But such secular preservations were small consolation to Catholics witnessing what they regarded as the systematic profanation of sacred objects. Occasionally, the revolutionary authorities ceded nationalized goods from suppressed communities to parishes, signifying the state's desire to accommodate the church. For example, marble from the high altar of the church of the former Maison Professe was given to the clergy of St-Eustache when the church's incumbent clergy, the Chanoines Réguliers, were suppressed in 1790.[56] Nevertheless, following the establishment of the French Republic on 22 September 1792,[57] and the launching of a de-christianizing campaign in September 1793,[58] increasing numbers of representational objects from churches of size and status comparable to that of the Maison Professe were either destroyed or removed for secular storage. Yet, while a number of major sculptures and marbles were moved from the former Maison Professe to the new Museum of Monuments,[59] many of the royalist and Catholic objects that had been in the church since before the Jesuits' suppression were not sold, altered, or destroyed. Why?

In August 1791, workmen charged with removing bronze from nationalized buildings, for use by the army, declared that they wished to melt down the Maison Professe's only remaining Jesuit image, Duval's bas-relief representing St Ignatius of Loyola praying before Christ on the cross. The Commission of Monuments successfully argued that the piece should stay *in situ*, in the Condé chapel, because 'the merit of the work infinitely surpasses the value of the material.'[60] While Sarrazin's bronze statues of angels, and figures from Birague's tomb were taken to the foundry, the Commission of Monuments lobbied successfully for the goods' preservation on aesthetic grounds, taking the case all the way to the National Convention.[61] The Commission of Monuments also resisted iconoclasm in the former Maison Professe that did not stem from the state's need for metal. Reporting to the Commission on 6 December 1791, Lemmonier warned that the church had become 'a store open to workers and other people who are less than indifferent towards the conservation of works of art.'[62] Lemmonier said that the workers were guilty of 'degradations, negligence, and other abuses of which we have proof.'[63] To illustrate his point, he placed on the table a part of the tomb of Birague from the Maison Professe and called for the church's monuments to be surrounded with barriers and planks 'to defend them from the accidents to which they are exposed.'[64] Subsequently, the threats posed to the building's monuments by zealous or merely careless workers were addressed by ensuring that such people did not use the space.

By early 1792, Ameilhon, the municipal librarian and a member of the Commission of Monuments, had succeeded in having the whole of the church of the Maison Professe transformed into a store for books.[65] From the start of the

Revolution, many other churches and chapels had been used as meeting-rooms for local government Sections. As political and religious discourse became more radical, members of the Sections regularly called for alterations to the signifying schemes in such churches.[66] However, while local committees met in one of the rooms of the Maison Professe,[67] members of the general public were not using the church itself, and as a result there were no calls from the Section for alterations to the signifying scheme on political or religious grounds.[68] As had been the case in the 1760s, during the Revolution it was the transformation of the Maison Professe, this time into a store for books rather than into a non-Jesuit church, that helped to ensure the preservation of many of the building's representational objects.

Once the de-christianizing regime had fallen from power in 1794, several Parisian churches were re-consecrated for renewed Catholic use, and their representational objects began to be slowly returned from the homes of Catholics who had privately preserved them, and from the secular depots and museums.[69] However, the church of the former Maison Professe had no clergy until 1802 and therefore no official body to legitimately demand the return of objects that had been removed.[70] Even when the church had a clergy again, in 1803, the deaf and dumb sculptor Deseine still needed to publish a pamphlet to urge the return of the 'superb tomb, known under the name of the Chapelle des Condé,' to the 'church of the old Jesuits.'[71] Deseine argued that Liberty without Christianity is anarchic and immoral; a return to a Catholic moral framework was needed for maintaining peace and order. He claimed that Catholics regarded a tomb with piety and recognition, and that these sentiments, promoted by observing exemplary tomb sculpture, were the 'basis of public bliss.'[72] Yet although Deseine's request was not granted,[73] such was the extent of the artistic survivals in the church of the former Maison Professe that Legrand and Landon's guide to Paris of 1808 still described the space as 'a superb museum.'[74] Almost all Jesuit buildings had been emptied of their representational objects in the 1760s, and thousands of non-Jesuit churches and chapels throughout France had been de-christianized in the 1790s. Yet the interior of the church of the former Maison Professe retained visual signifiers of Catholicism even before the building's re-consecration, and its Jesuit past was still publicly signified until the bas-relief of St Ignatius of Loyola was finally moved to the Museum of Monuments, probably in early 1797.[75]

In 1797, Catholicism was officially tolerated, but the Jesuits had once again become a focus of heated political discourse. Pro-Catholic royalist murder squads in Lyon had been seeking to wreak their revenge on revolutionaries associated with republicanism and de-christianization. The royalists called themselves the 'Compagnie de Jéhu' after the Old Testament king who killed Jezebel, her children, and all those people whom she had persuaded to worship the allegedly false god Baal.[76] But republican orators, eager to distinguish between royalist Catholics they despised and pro-revolutionary Catholics they tolerated, called the Lyonnaise rebels the 'Compagnie de Jésus' – the name of the Jesuits.[77] Given that one of the principal charges against the Jesuits in the 1760s had been their alleged disrespect for the king, it is ironic that revolutionaries named royalist Catholics in Lyon after the Jesuits in order to vilify them and distinguish them from republican Catholics. Almost thirty-five years after the suppression of the Jesuits, the Society of Jesus, while rarely visually signified in public, remained a resource for French people's imagination and representation of the struggle between the Catholic religion and a state that by then was a secular republic.

Yet the belated removal of the final Jesuit monument from the church of the former Maison Professe in Paris came a few months after the revolutionary discourse on the 'Compagnie de Jésus' had reached its peak. When the Jesuit monument was eventually removed, it was because Alexandre Lenoir wanted to incorporate into his museum's collection a sculpture that he considered historically and aesthetically valuable. Despite the fact that the Society of Jesus remained very much a part of the contemporary political 'imaginary,' the secular revolutionary space of the museum presented the bas-relief featuring St Ignatius as a politically unproblematic aesthetic object the meanings of which related to France's past and not its revolutionary present. Having saved the St Ignatius of Loyola bas-relief from removal to the foundry on at least one occasion, the relatively recent official privileging of the object's aesthetic value eventually was responsible for the loss by the church of the former Maison Professe of its last monumental Jesuit signifier.

NOTES

1 While I do not discuss pamphlets from the late 1780s that focused on the Jesuits' alleged role in contemporary freemasonry, Jacques Lemaire has examined such sources. See Jacques Lemaire, *Les origines françaises de l'antimaçonnisme (1744–1787)* (Brussels, 1985), pp. 76–8. For an example of a book dealing exclusively with Jesuit subject-matter in this period, see Abbé Grosier, *Mémoires d'un société célèbre, considérée comme corps littéraire et académiques: Depuis le commencement de ce siècle: ou mémoires des jésuites sur les sciences, les belles-lettres et les arts* (Paris, 1792).

2 See Dale Van Kley, *The Jansenists and the Expulsion of the Jesuits from France, 1757–1765* (New Haven and London, 1975), pp. 90–104.

3 Van Kley, *The Jansenists*, pp. 113–16, 137, 163, 167.

4 Ibid., p. 190.

5 See E. de Ménorval, *Les jésuites de la rue Saint-Antoine. L'église de Saint-Paul–Saint-Louis et le lycée Charlemagne* (Paris, 1872), p. 122.

6 De Ménorval, *Les jésuites*, p. 122. The decision to send hussars to the Jesuits' buildings, rather than the civilian *econemes sequestres* appointed to administer the property of the Jesuits, signified the Parlement's suspicion that the threat of force might be needed to enforce its rulings in Jesuit spaces.

7 Ibid., pp. 122–3. The Parlement's *arrêt* was distributed to the public on 13 August 1762.

8 Ibid., p. 123. The homelessness of the Jesuits was the theme of a derisive game that Bachaumont reported as being played in the Foire St-Ovid in Paris. Small wax figures dressed as Jesuits had a snail's shell at their base. The player used a system of strings to return the Jesuit to his shell (ibid., p. 125).

9 *Extrait des registres du parlement. Du 31 Août 1762* (Paris, 1762), pp. 2–3.

10 Many aristocrats had townhouses in the Marais district and used the Jesuit church on the nearby rue St-Antoine; see Denise Maynial, *Saint-Paul–Saint-Louis* (Paris, n.d.), p. 3. Regarding the use of the space by the clergy of St-Paul and St-Sulpice, see Jacques Bonzon, *La vente d'une congrégation sous Louis XV: Suppression des jésuites* (Paris, 1901), p. 134.

11 Brice, *Description nouvelle de ce qu'il y a de plus remarquable dans la ville de Paris*, vol. 1 (Paris, 1752), p. 183. In a later guide, Piganiol de la Force noted that few churches in the whole of Christendom could claim such riches of silverware; see Piganiol de la Force, *Description historique de la ville de Paris et de ses environs*, 10 vols (Paris, 1765), V, p. 6.

12 *Extrait des registres du parlement. Du 31 Août 1762*, p. 1.

13 Henri Lefebvre, *The Production of Space* (Oxford, 1991), pp. 11, 17.

14 Piganiol de la Force, *Description*, vol. 5, p. 4.

15 De Ménorval, *Les jésuites*, p. 150.

16 The 1765 edition of Piganiol de la Force's guide to Paris included a lengthy discussion of the suppression of the Jesuits, noting that from late 1761 until 5 March 1762 members of the Parlement of Paris were checking all books written by Jesuits for passages that encouraged a number of crimes, including blasphemy, sacrilege, perjury, theft, homicide, parricide, and occultism; see Piganiol de la Force, *Description*, vol. 8, p. 347. Regarding precedents for such accusations, see Van Kley, *The Jansenists*, pp. 31, 33.

17 The Parlement's inquiry into the Jesuits' publications accused the Society of Jesus of replacing religion with 'all sorts of superstitions, favouring magic, blasphemy, irreligion, and idolatry' ('toutes sortes de superstitions, en favorisant la magie, le blasphême, l'irreligion et l'idolâtrie'); see Piganiol de la Force, *Description*, vol. 8, p. 350.

18 See *Saint-Paul–Saint-Louis: Les jésuites à Paris. Musée Carnavalet, 12 mars – 2 juin 1985* (Paris. 1985).

19 Piganiol de la Force had previously noted that the main obstacle to removing the figures of St Ignatius of Loyola and St Francis Xavier from the facade was the operation's cost (*Description*, vol. 5, p. 4). Removing the other Jesuit signifiers from within the church would also have been expensive.

20 See de Ménorval, *Les jésuites*, p. 138.

21 The former Maison Professe was renamed St-Louis de la Couture Ste-Catherine in 1777 (*Saint-Paul–Saint-Louis*, p. 85). Regarding the circumstances of the community's transferral to the former Maison Professe, see J.G. Legrand and C.P. Landon, *Description de Paris et de ses édifices, avec un précis historique et des observations sur le caractère de leur architecture, et sur les principaux objets d'art et de curiosité qu'ils renferment* (Paris, 1808), p. 76.

22 The catalogue for the Musée Carnavalet's exhibition on the church noted that the original high altar had 'disappeared' but did not state when (*Saint-Paul–Saint-Louis*, p. 34). However, comparison of the updated descriptions of the church in successive editions of the same eighteenth guidebook makes it clear that the new altar had not been introduced by 1749 (before the suppression of the Jesuits) but was in place by 1770. See M. D*** [Antoine-Nicolas Dezaillier d'Argenville], *Voyage pittoresque de Paris, ou Indication de tout ce qu'il ya de plus beau dans cette ville, en peinture, sculpture et architecture* (Paris, 1749), p. 253; (Paris, 1770), pp. 157, 160; (Paris, 1778), p. 237. It seems most likely that the old altar was replaced soon after the king's gift of the church to the Chanoines Réguliers de Ste-Catherine in 1767.

23 Dezaillier, *Voyage* (1770), p. 253; (1778), p. 237. See also M. Thiéry, *Guide des amateurs et des étrangers voyageurs a Paris, ou Description raisonée de cette ville, des sa banlieue, et de tout ce qu'elles contiennent de remarquable*, vol. 1 (Paris 1787), p. 699.

24 *Saint-Paul–Saint-Louis*, p. 32.

25 For a discussion of alleged Jesuit laxity, see Dale K. Van Kley, *The Religious Origins of the French Revolution: From Calvin to the Civil Constitution of the Clergy, 1560–1791* (New Haven and London, 1996).

26 See Piganiol de la Force, *Description*, vol. 5, p. 11.

27 Regarding the annual mass, held on 1 September, see ibid., p. 379.

28 Alexandre Tuetey noted that Piganiol de la Force had cited Bernini's appreciation of the chapel's monuments in support of his own high estimation of them; see Alexandre Tuetey, *Procès-verbaux de la Commission des Monuments, 1790–1794*, vol. 1 (Paris, 1869), p. 47 n1. In his inventory of 8 January 1791, the municipal officer Roard noted that the bas-relief featuring St Ignatius of Loyola was still in place and described the chapel's aesthetic qualities as 'miraculeux'; see Henri Stein, *Etat des objets d'arts placés dans les monuments religieux et civils de Paris au début*

de la Révolution française (Paris, 1890), p. 126. In contrast, Piganiol de la Force complained that the high altar was so low one could not properly distinguish the celebrant on entering the church. He added that the figure of St Louis in the Voüet painting was so feminized as to be regularly mistaken for an image of the Virgin Mary (*Description*, vol. 5, p. 6). Piganiol's views on the forms and functions of art in Paris remained influential throughout the eighteenth century. For example, his guide was referred to in a letter written by Mercier for the Commission of Monuments, probably in An II. See Archives Nationale F 17 1036A dossier 6 no. 102.

29 The municipal officer Roard recorded the painting as being in this state when he made an inventory of the church's contents on 24 September 1790. The image of a Jesuit saint was the only painting that had been rolled for storage in the building by the Chanoines Réguliers. See Stein, *Etat*, p. 123.

30 Ibid., p. 122.

31 Ironically, as Dale Van Kley has argued, it was partly because Jesuit writers focused almost exclusively on the threat posed by the *philosophes* to Catholicism during the suppression crisis of the 1760s that they failed to mount an effective defence of themselves (*The Jansenists*, pp. 139–62). Following the king's gift of the former Maison Professe to the Chanoines Réguliers, one of their number, R.P. Bernard, gave a discourse of thanks in the church and took the opportunity to note that the church's ceremonies were always 'free of superstition, the true spirit of which one takes care to teach the people' ('exemptes de superstition, sur le véritable espirit desquelles on a soin d'instruite le peuple'); see R.P. Bernard, *Discours sur l'obligation de prier pour les rois, prononcé dans l'Eglise des chanoines réguliers de Saint Louis de la culture, le 5 Septembre 1769, par R.P. Bernard, chanoine régulier, prieur-curé de Nanterre* (Paris 1769), p. 41.

32 De Ménorval, *Les jésuites*, p. 137.

33 The bas-reliefs were described as 'curious gothics' in Roard's inventory of January 1791 (Stein, *Etat*, p. 129). Introducing a new image of St Louis might have compensated for the transferral into the refectory of the old high altar's painting by Voüet that represented the saintly king (Dezaillier, *Voyage* [1778], p. 241). R.P. Bernard's discourse on the biblically justified need to pray for all kings, given in the church and then published in 1767, certainly indicated that the Chanoines Réguliers were eager to publicly signify their support for the Crown (*Discours*).

34 Thiéry, *Guide*, p. 701.

35 Ibid., p. 700. These paintings were later exhibited at the Salon of 1791 (*Saint-Paul–Saint-Louis*, p. 90).

36 The artist was unknown by Roard when he made an inventory of the church in 1790 (Stein, *Etat*, p. 122).

37 The contents of the Jesuits' library had been sold sometime in the period 1762–5. See Piganiol de la Force, *Description*, vol. 8, p. 381.

38 Thiéry, *Guide*, p. 704.

39 This painting (14 ft × 10 ft) had been shown in the Salon of 1767; see *Diderot. Oeuvres tome IV, esthétique-théâtre*, ed. Laurent Versini (Paris, 1996), pp. 535–7.

40 Bonzon, *La vente*, p. 41.

41 *Extrait des registres du parlement. Du 31 Août 1762*, p. 3.

42 The royal ordinance was issued to this effect on 14 June 1763 (Bonzon, *La vente*, pp. 47–8).

43 See Le Chanoine Fernand Pottier, *Les châsses et reliquaries de Pompignan autres-fois de la Maison Professe des jésuites de Paris* (Montauban, 1901).

44 Pottier, *Les châsses*, p. 8.

45 Voltaire attacked Le Franc de Pompignan for his connections with the clergy, including the bishop of Amiens, who was a supporter of the pro-Jesuit Christophe de Beaumont, bishop of Paris; see ibid., p. 7.

46 Ibid., p. 7 n2.

47 See Colin Jones, *The Longman Companion to the French Revolution* (London, 1995), p. 240.

48 'Voyez ce que sont devenues les richesses du Corps Religieux le plus puissant qu'ait eu la France [the Jesuits]. A peine est-il détruit et déja ses immenses dépouiles ont disparu à tous les yeux'; see Jean-Baptiste Desenne, *Mémoire à l'Assemblée nationale, pour les créanciers des jésuites* (Paris, 1790), pp. 1–2.

49 The contemplative religious communities were suppressed by the law of 13 February 1790 (Jones, *The Longman Companion*, p. 240).

50 Other metal goods were also removed from churches as a result of the National Assembly's order in September 1789 that the clergy surrender all silverware not required for 'decent worship'; see John McManners, *The French Revolution and the Church* (London, 1969), p. 9. Some clergy had already begun to surrender silverware before the National Assembly's order; See Richard Clay, 'Saint-Sulpice de Paris: Art, Politics, and Sacred Space in Revolutionary Paris, 1789–1795' *Object* 1 (London, 1998): 5–23. Similar voluntary contributions to the national government had been made before the Revolution. For example, on 26 April 1760 the clergy of St-Sulpice surrendered silverware to a royal treasury stretched by the expenses of the Seven Years' War; see Charles Hamel, *Histoire de l'église de Saint-Sulpice* (Paris, 1900), p. 201 n1.

51 In relation to the suppression of the Jesuits, Bonzon wrote, 'What was the final result of this operation, a first attempt, the general repetition of which, the integral proscription of religious orders, thirty years later, the Revolution must attempt' ('Quel fut le sort final de cette opération, premier essai, répétition générale de la proscription intégrale des ordres religieux qui, trente ans après, doit tenter la Révolution') (*La vente*, pp. 5–6). However, it is important to note that the suppression of the Jesuits was itself justified and administered with reference to precedents

set during earlier suppressions of other orders. In a ruling made by the Crown regarding the administration of the suppression of the Jesuits, it was noted that it should be carried out 'following the forms that were already practised in parallel cases' ('suivant des formes qui s'étoient déja pratiquées en pareil cas'); see *Lettres patentes du roi, en interprétation de celles du 2 février 1763, concernant l'abbréviation des Procédures, et la diminution des frais dans la discussion des biens des jésuites. Données à Versailles, le cinq mars 1763* (Paris 1763), p. 2.

52 See Clay, 'Signs of Power: Iconoclasm in Paris, 1789–1795,' dissertation, University of London, 1999.

53 See Edouard Pommier, 'Le théorie des arts,' in *Aux armes et Aux arts! Les arts pendant la Révolution, 1789–1799*, ed. Philippe Bordes and Régis Michel (Paris, 1988), pp. 167–99.

54 'Détails sur le travail des Comités de l'assemblée rélativement à tout le mobilier des maisons ecclésiastiques, et réligeuses et notament à tous monumens [*sic*]' (1790), Archives Nationale N. F17 1036A.

55 For a discussion of the committees' work, see Clay, *Signs of Power*. For a discussion of the formation of the new museums, see A. McClellan, *Inventing the Louvre: Art, Politics, and the Origins of the Modern Museum in Eighteenth-Century Paris* (London, 1994).

56 For example, the secular authorities ceded marbles and pedestals from the new high altar of the former Maison Professe to the clergy of St-Eustache in 1791. See Sigismond Lacroix, *Actes de la Commune de Paris pendant la Révolution*, ser. 1 7 vols, ser. 2 8 vols (Paris, 1920), ser. 2, VII, p. 306

57 Following the suspension of the monarchy in August 1792, royalist signs were proscribed. For a discussion of anti-monarchical iconoclasm and bibliographical details, see Clay, *Signs of Power*, chaps 4–6.

58 De-christianization involved the suppression of signs of Catholicism. For a discussion of anti-Catholic iconoclasm and bibliography, see ibid., chaps 5–6.

59 Several sculptures from the church of the former Maison Professe entered the Museum of Monuments in 1791–3. One of the statues was a marble representing St Francis Xavier. It is likely that the sculpture came from the facade of the church, as no mention of such a statue was made in the exhaustive inventories of 1790 and 1791. Other sculptures moved to the museum included a wooden crucifix attributed to Sarrazin, two gilded bronze bas-reliefs of Christ in the tomb by Germain Pilon, and four columns of marble. See Louis Corajod, *Alexandre Lenoir, son journal et le musée des monuments français*, 3 vols (Paris, 1878), I, pp. 9, 12, 15; II, p. 258.

60 'Le mérite de l'ouvrage surpasse infiniment la valeur de la matière' (Tuetey, *Procès-verbaux de la Commission des Monuments*, p. 47).

61 It was the painter Jacques-Louis David who brought the matter before the Convention and succeeded in saving the statues on 7 April 1793; ibid., p. 202 n3. In a report

to the Committee of Public Instruction, in 1795, Alexandre Lenoir, who ran the Museum of Monuments, noted that he had recently once again saved the tomb of Birague from the foundry; see *Inventaire générale des richesses d'art de la France*, 3 vols (Paris, 1883–97), I, p. 25.

62 'Un magasin ouvert à des ouvriers et autres personnes au moins indifférents à la conservation des chefs-d'oeuvre de l'art' (Tuetey, *Procès-verbaux de la Commission des Monuments*, p. 61). The choir and nave of the church were being used to store goods destined for local indigents; see Alexandre Tuetey, *Répertoire générale des sources manuscrites de l'histoire de Paris pendant la Révolution française*, vol. 3 (Paris, 1890), document 1998.

63 'Les dépredations, les néglicences et autres abus dont on a des preuves' (Tuetey, *Procès-verbaux de la Commission des Monuments*, p. 61).

64 'Les défendent des accidents auxquels elles sont exposées' (ibid.).

65 At one point the collection included more than one million texts; see de Ménorval, *Les jésuites*, p. 142.

66 Calls for the republicanization or de-christianization of churches in Paris that had public functions other than serving as local government meeting-rooms (for example, Temples of Reason or Temples of the Supreme Being) were common at this time; see Clay, *Signs of Power*, chaps 5–6.

67 Roard noted that fourteen paintings were in the 'salle de la Section' of the former Maison Professe in October 1790 (Stein, *Etat*, p. 122).

68 Perhaps the church was positively associated with that foundational revolutionary event the fall of the nearby Bastille, the archives of which were subsequently stored in the former Maison Professe. See Lacroix, *Actes de la Commune*, ser. 1, vol. 1, p. 596; ser. 2, vol. 1, p. 100.

69 For a discussion of the return to churches of Catholic objects that had been officially or unofficially preserved, see Clay, *Signs of Power*, chaps 5–6.

70 On the return of the church to Catholics, see *Saint-Paul–Saint-Louis*, p. 8.

71 '[Ce] superbe tombeau, connu sous le nom de chapelle des Condé' should be returned to the 'église des anciens Jésuites' (Deseine, *Lettre sur la sculpture destiné à orner les temples consacrés au culte catholique, et particulièrement sur les tombeaux, adressée au Général Bonaparte, premier consul de la République française* [Paris, Floréal an X], p. 19).

72 'Piété et la reconnoissance sont les bases de la félicité publique' (Deseine, *Lettre sur la sculpture*, p. 19).

73 On 8 March 1816, the Prince de Condé wrote personally to Alexandre Lenoir, who ran the Museum of Monuments, to ask that the Condé tomb from the 'église des Grands-Jésuites' be returned to the church. See *Inventaire générale des richesses*, vol. 1, p. 429.

74 See Legrand and Landon, *Description*, p. 76.

75 On 19 September 1796, Alexandre Lenoir, who ran the Museum of Monuments, asked that the remaining portion of the Condé tomb join the rest of the Condé monument already in the museum. See *Inventaire générale des richesses*, vol. 1, p. 57.

76 See G. Lenotre, *La Compagnie de Jéhu. Episodes de la réaction lyonnaise, 1784–1899* (Paris, 1931), p. 125. Châlier, the republican whose bloody regime the Compagnie were avenging, can be seen as an equivalent of Jezebel, and his supporters as being those who, in joining the revolutionary Cult of the Supreme Being, had worshipped a false god.

77 See Lenotre, *La Compagnie de Jéhu*; and Marie-Joseph Chénier, *Rapport fait à la Convention nationale au nom des comités de Salut public et de Sûreté générale par Marie-Joseph Chénier, Député du Département de Seine et Oise. Dans le séance du 6 Messidor, an III* (Paris, c. 1795); and Chénier, *Rapport fait à la Convention nationale au nom des comités de Salut public et de Sûreté générale. Séance du 29 Vendémiaire, l'an quatrième de la République française, une et indivisible* (Paris, c. 1795).

33 / The Gang of Four and the Campaign against the Jesuits in Eighteenth-Century Brazil

DAURIL ALDEN

In 1750 the courts of Lisbon and Madrid agreed to a landmark treaty that was intended to end their bitter, long-lasting territorial rivalry in South America. By that agreement, known as the Treaty of Limits, the Treaty of Madrid, or the Treaty of 1750, they agreed to exchange key territories and to establish by joint boundary teams their common boundary in that continent.[1] No one had a greater stake in the success or failure of that agreement than the Jesuits and their Amerindian neophytes. During the critical 1750s, however, several key figures, the members of the Gang of Four, exploited a series of contretemps in the implementation of the treaty in order to discredit the Society of Jesus and prepare the way for the expulsion of that vaunted order from the Lusitanian world. The gang was headed by Portugal's dominant royal minister, Sebastião José de Carvalho e Melo, best known as the Marquis of Pombal. His cohorts included two energetic colonial governors who were high commissioners charged with implementation of the treaty, and a self-serving, fault-finding bishop who became interim governor of northern Brazil.

The new agreement was secretly negotiated over a three-year period of exceptional cordiality between the two Iberian courts. It specifically superseded the only extant boundary treaty between them, the famed Treaty of Tordesillas (1494), which established a polar line of demarcation between their respective territories in South America. Lands situated to the east of that line were considered to be Portuguese; those to the west, Castilian. The Spaniards believed the line entered the continent near the mouth of the Amazon and exited close to the port of Santos, south of Rio de Janeiro. The Portuguese, on the other hand, insisted that it extended far to the south and included part of the estuary of the Río de la Plata as well as present-day Uruguay. During the ensuing centuries Portuguese and Brazilian pathfinders, Indian slavers, and gold seekers consistently ignored the line. Accordingly, Portugal claimed far more territory in South

America than Tordesillas authorized. Furthermore, in 1680 the Portuguese government aggressively asserted its claim to the Platine estuary by establishing the fortress of the Holy Sacrament, Colônia do Sacramento, opposite Buenos Aires.[2]

Colônia became a notorious smuggling base, a lucrative source of illicit silver from the highlands of Upper Peru (Bolivia). For nearly a century it remained an object of acrimonious contention between the two Iberian powers. Iberian diplomats devised the 1750 treaty in order to end that hostility. Their agreement contained three key provisions: 1) in accordance with the principle of *uti possidetus*, Spain recognized nearly all the territory that Portugal actually occupied in South America; 2) the two powers agreed to assign joint teams of technicians to survey their common boundary by following the banks of rivers and high-ground summits throughout the continental interior. One team would begin in the Amazon, the others in what is today Brazil's southernmost state, Rio Grande do Sul. The marking of the common frontier in both arenas would be supervised by high commissioners representing each of the two governments; 3) in the most critical provision of the treaty, Portugal would surrender Colônia do Sacramento and its claims to the Platine estuary in exchange for the transfer of seven Spanish Jesuit Guaraní missions, or *reducciones*, and their supporting lands east of the Uruguay River in what is now western and central Rio Grande do Sul.[3]

Predictably, once the treaty's key provisions became known, grave misgivings were expressed in both empires. One of the first officials in Brazil to learn about the treaty was Gomes Freire de Andrade.[4] Gomes Freire, the first of the Gang of Four, was the son of a senior bureaucrat and soldier who had long served the Portuguese crown. One of his ten siblings succeeded their father as military commandant of southern Portugal; another became Portugal's ambassador to Vienna during the crucial 1750s; two joined religious orders. Gomes Freire and another brother were administrators in Brazil. Beginning in 1733, he became governor of the city and environs of Rio de Janeiro. Later his authority was enlarged, and he was made administratively responsible for all of southern and western Brazil.

Gomes Freire had no affection for the Jesuits. In June 1750 he wryly expressed surprise that the Madrid Jesuits had not prevented the drafting of the treaty. He warned Lisbon that the Jesuits in the mission lands had never welcomed outsiders, not even bishops or governors. The Governor predicted that they would not willingly relinquish their control over the *reducciones*. He opined that the Jesuits would pose obstacles to the implementation of the treaty because they had invariably incited the Amerindians against the Portuguese in Brazil. He reported to his Lisbon superiors rumours that the Paraguayan Jesuits were embittered about the prospective loss of their missions, and were contending that these missions did not belong to the king but had been acquired by 'Jesuit sweat.'[5] Such were the beginnings of the development of the theory of Jesuit conspiracy that, despite the absence of any factual foundation, would gain increasing acceptance within both Iberian governments during the ensuing decade.

The thirty Jesuit *reducciones* belonging to the province of Paraguay had long been a source of rumour and controversy in both Spanish and Portuguese South America. The seven missions, planted east of the Uruguay River between 1687 and 1706, were the easternmost salient of that province, which embraced portions of modern Argentina, Paraguay, and Uruguay, as well as southernmost Brazil.[6] The seven were the successors of an earlier group established in the same area in the 1620s and 1630s. Their predecessors had been destroyed by aggressive Portuguese slavers, or *bandeirantes*, whose attacks succeeded until the Jesuits gained papal permission to arm and train their neophytes. In 1641 the *bandeirantes* were shockingly defeated by newly equipped Guaraní warriors, and thereafter turned elsewhere in their quest for wealth, leaving behind a venerable tradition of Indian achievement and hatred of the Portuguese. During the next century the Spanish crown repeatedly utilized Guaraní militia to restore civil order in turbulent Paraguay and to besiege the Portuguese in Colônia.

Spanish settlers both feared and resented that militia. They complained of Jesuit inhospitality in the mission properties, where it was believed that the fathers secretly operated gold mines and gunpowder plants. They also resented the Jesuits' economic competition, especially their sales of yerba mate tea to markets throughout southern and western Spanish America and even to Spain, and they contended that the Guaraní were undertaxed. Such grievances prompted the dispatch of a magistrate to Paraguay to investigate their merits in the 1730s. He found the Jesuits faultless. In 1743 the Crown reaffirmed its satisfaction with the Jesuits' conduct.[7]

The missionaries were therefore stunned when they learned that Spain had agreed to the transfer of the mission lands. As they recognized, not only were the eastern seven missions affected, but so too several of the Paraná *reducciones*, situated west of the Uruguay. The Guaraní inmates of the seven were given the choice either of becoming subjects of the hated Portuguese or of abandoning their homes, churches, ranches, and orchards, and their dead. Their compliance with conditions set forth in the treaty would compel them to start over in some unspecified region west of the Uruguay River where they were bound to encounter hostile Amerindian rivals of the Guaraní. Their abandonment of the original mission sites meant surrendering what generations of Indians had built in return for the Crown's proferred pittance.

Nevertheless, when Father General François Retz, nearing the end of a generalate that had begun in 1730, learned of the exchange, he sensed an opportunity to restore the Society's tarnished image. He therefore enjoined the superior of the missions to instruct 'all the Jesuits who have worked in these areas [to] use their influence so that the Indians immediately hand over their territory to the Portuguese ... without resistance, without evasions, and without pretexts.'[8] His successor, Ignazio Visconti, went even further: first, he named an outsider, a Peruvian-born father, to become Paraguay's new provincial in the hope that he would not become emotionally involved in the defence of the *reducciones*; second, he appointed a special commissioner, Father Lope Luis Altamirano, and equipped him with extraordinary authority to implement the transfer as speedily as possible; and third, he admonished the Spanish king's confessor to abstain from involving himself in the sure-to-be-contested transfer.[9]

In April 1751 more than seventy veteran missionaries from the thirty missions assembled to consider their options. Recognizing that the Guaraní would likely resist abandoning their homes, they decided upon two responses. The first was to encourage an aggressive letter-writing campaign to Madrid by concerned municipalities and royal officials throughout the Viceroyalty of Peru protesting the treaty. The second was to dispatch a special procurator to Rome to inform the general that they considered their province to be in peril. Unfortunately for the Jesuits, their agent never reached his destination: when he arrived in Rio de Janeiro, he was turned back by Gomes Freire on the ground that he was about to reveal state secrets.[10]

On 27 January 1752 the Spanish frigate *Jasón* brought to the Plata the Spanish southern boundary teams, the Spanish high commissioner, the Peruvian-born Marquis of Valdelirios, and the Jesuit commissioner, Father Altamirano. In Buenos Aires they conferred with the governor, Don José de Andonaegui, and with senior Jesuits, who urged that additional time be granted to conduct the relocation, an appeal that was denied.[11] Subsequently, Father Altamirano was sent to the missions to expedite their transfer. His visitation became a disaster and an embarrassment for the Society.

Not until September 1752 did the two high commissioners and their staffs gather on the coast south of Rio Grande do Sul's Lagoa dos Patos. There the first stone markers were laid with appropriate ceremonies. Then the commissioners retired respectively to Montevideo and Colônia to await developments. Not surprisingly, when the first boundary team, escorted by troops from both nations, reached the cattle station of Santa Tecla in central Rio Grande, they were met by a detachment of about fifty Guaraní warriors, who informed them that while the Spanish members were free to advance, the Portuguese were not. Such a response had been anticipated. Rather than fight, the boundary party beat a hasty retreat – all the way to the Plata.[12]

Gomes Freire was not surprised. He wrote Portugal's colonial minister that he was familiar with the Jesuits' pattern of duplicity, and that even the Jesuit commissioner Altamirano conceded that only force could compel compliance.[13] The result was the first military campaign. At the beginning of May 1754, Don José de Andonaegui set forth from Montevideo with two thousand men and a large number of cattle and horses. His destination was the Uruguay River, and his task was the investment of the westernmost of the seven missions. In effect, he was to assume a blocking position while Gomes Freire advanced from the Lagoa dos Patos to occupy the remaining missions.

The result was a fiasco. Andonaegui, a tired, 75-year-old cyclops, encountered spirited Indian resistance in the first mission he approached, at a cost of 260 casualties. Poor pasturage cost him many of his livestock. Dispirited, he ordered a full retreat. Meanwhile, Gomes Freire's army of one thousand found its way blocked by two thousand warriors assembled from five of the *reducciones*. After months of stalemate, he accepted a humiliating agreement with the defenders and likewise withdrew.[14]

Obviously, explanations were in order. Gomes Freire insisted that his withdrawal was inevitable once Andonaegui had left the field, since the full force of the resisters then fell upon him. Both commissioners knew very well why the Spanish commander had failed to do his duty: he was married to a Canary Islander who came from a pro-Jesuit family and who had a Jesuit confessor in Buenos Aires. Obviously, they said, he had been Jesuited. And both embarrassed commissioners assured their governments that, since the Guaraní could not possibly have acted on their own, the devious Jesuits were behind their resistance.[15]

The royal ministers in both kingdoms were sympathetic with the plight of their field commanders. They accepted unverified field reports that the Jesuits were erecting powerful fortresses within the mission lands, that they commanded thousands of well-trained warriors, and that their goal was not to safeguard the Amerindians' homes but to protect their own hidden gold mines.

The second phase of the so-called Guaraní war was swift and decisive. In the beginning of 1756 the combined Luso-Spanish army advanced from the Lagoa dos Patos in a northwesterly direction. On 10 February they discovered a large group of Guaraní confined to a primitive fort on high ground about halfway between the town of Rio Grande and the cattle station of Santa Tecla. After their demands to surrender had been rejected, they cannoned the fort relentlessly. Within an hour and a quarter the fort had been demolished and more than 1,500 of its defenders had perished. Among the survivors, 154 became prisoners of war; uncounted others fled. European casualties were minimal. By June 1756, mopping up operations in the mission lands had been completed and the indigenous population dispersed, and the way was cleared for the southernmost boundary team to proceed with its work.[16]

Meanwhile, as Gomes Freire's reports concerning the allegedly sinister Jesuitical machinations in Rio Grande do Sul reached Lisbon, they were matched by similar allegations emanating from northern Brazil. These came from two other members of the Gang of Four, the newly arrived bishop of Pará and the incoming governor of the State of Maranhão, who was also high commissioner for the boundary treaty in the north. The State of Maranhão consisted of two large administrative units, the captaincies of Maranhão and Grão Pará. The latter was embraced by the vast valley of the Amazon and its numerous tributaries. A half-dozen religious orders functioned in the State, led by the Society of Jesus, which had organized the vice-province of Maranhão in the 1720s, as separate from the Brazil province. In the 1750s the vice-province, numbering about 150 subjects, consisted of two colleges, several lesser houses, and 19 of the 63 missions, or *aldeias*, the religious orders maintained in the Amazon, as well as others in adjacent Maranhão. In the Amazon the Jesuit missions were situated along the great river's southern banks and on its major northward-flowing tributaries.

As had happened in Paraguay, the Jesuits in the far north also had endured a long and turbulent relationship with the settlers and some of their governors. In the Paraguayan capital of Asunción, angry settlers had driven the Jesuits out on four occasions. The same had occurred twice during the seventeenth century in parts of the State. Following the second uprising, the Crown not only restored the Society but, in 1686, issued the famous mission ordinances, which gave the Jesuits pre-eminent influence in shaping Indian-European relations in the State. Those ordinances remained in force until the 1750s, when they were abrogated.

As in Paraguay, the stream of rumour-based settlers' complaints against the religious, especially the Jesuits, never ceased to flow. There, too, allegations of misdeeds by the religious orders triggered a series of investigations by special magistrates sent from Portugal. One took place in Maranhão in 1721. On that occasion the examining judge found that violations of Indian rights were so prevalent the king would be best advised to grant a general pardon and to replace ransomed Indians, actually slaves, with imported Africans. Those recommendations were never implemented, and complaints against the missionaries intensified in the succeeding decades coincidentally with the development of Maranhão's first major export – wild cacao. It was during those decades that Paulo da Silva Nunes, a relentless settler lobbyist, repeatedly memorialized the Crown against the Society's economic operations. He contended that the reason why most colonists remained abjectly poor, in spite of the State's growing trade with the kingdom, was that the missionaries, especially the Jesuits, were insatiably ambitious and greedy. Their missions, he insisted, were not simply evangelical enterprises but commercial operations from which they reaped vast profits at the expense of the king and his loyal subjects. Once again, such complaints triggered a special investigation, and once again the missionaries were found guiltless.[17]

Nevertheless, the secret royal instructions issued in 1751 to the State's new governor warned him to be on guard against anticipated misbehaviour by the orders, especially the Jesuits. The recipient of those instructions was the second member of the Gang of Four, Francisco Xavier de Mendonça Furtado. Mendonça Furtado, younger brother of the head of the Gang, Pombal, was born in Lisbon in 1700. Nothing is known concerning his activities until 1735, when he was sent as a military officer from Rio de Janeiro to the beleaguered Platine outpost of Colônia, then under siege by Spanish colonial and Guaraní militia forces. He remained there for nearly two years before being sent on another assignment in northeastern Brazil, after which he sailed back to Lisbon. No trace of his activities between 1736 and 1749 remains. But in the latter year he became one of four candidates to conduct a voyage to India, but was passed over in favour of a more experienced officer. Two years later the king sent him to Belém, the capital of the State of Maranhão.[18]

Mendonça Furtado's instructions disclosed that the Crown intended to abolish Indian slavery in the State and to substitute African slavery in its place. Although the Jesuits had always been champions of Indian freedom in Brazil, the colonial minister warned Mendonça Furtado that, out of self-interest, the fathers would likely oppose the abolition of Indian slavery. They were to be reminded that the king expected them to be the first to obey his wishes, especially because most of their extensive landed properties had been acquired without explicit royal approval. Moreover, they were to be notified that the king no longer wished them to retain temporal responsibility for the *aldeias*, as the ordinances of 1686 had stipulated, but to restrict themselves to spiritual supervision. The Indians would then be allowed to govern themselves. It was left to Governor Mendonça Furtado to determine when the transformation of the missions should occur. He was expected to take that step after consulting with the bishop of Pará, Dom Miguel de Bulhões, the third member of the Gang.[19]

Dom Miguel hailed from a small lagoon town about 135 miles northwest of Lisbon. His family may have been of Dutch origin. One of his brothers became a prominent sea captain on the Brazil run for better than a quarter-century. Dom Miguel, however, became a Dominican priest in 1722. In the 1730s he was admitted to the elite Portuguese Academy of History, where he most likely met Pombal, another of its fifty select members. There he became admired for his oratorical skills. He displayed his talent in 1746, when he preached the sermon that accompanied the 221st *auto-de-fé* of the Lisbon branch of the Inquisition. That year he was named to a sinecure, the bishopric of Malacca, but he never sailed to Asia. Instead, two years later, he became the third bishop of Pará, thanks to the influence of two powerful court Jesuits. He reached his new see in Belém, Pará, in 1749, two years before Mendonça Furtado's arrival.[20]

Less than two months after Governor Mendonça Furtado landed there, he submitted the first of many reports to his Lisbon superiors. Like the lobbyist Silva Nunes, whose writings were clearly known to him, he charged that the primary reason for the backwardness of the State was the overwhelming power of the religious orders. He was convinced that they exercised complete control over the backlanders, particularly the Amerindians, and that their domination of the State's commerce deprived the settlers of the workers they required to sustain their plantations. Moreover, just as the Spanish Jesuits spoke to their neophytes in Guaraní, a language most settlers did not understand, the Portuguese Jesuits in the north insisted on communicating with their Indians by means of a hybrid tongue, the *língua geral*, which most Portuguese-speaking settlers did not comprehend. The governor was convinced that the primary cause of the State's backwardness lay with the 1686 mission ordinances, which enabled the missionaries to behave as tyrants towards the king's subjects. He urged the Crown to designate 'a good Christian, a disinterested, independent' official who could intercede on behalf of the Indians and protect them from missionary abuses. Having heard from settlers that the missionaries were maintaining an army of three thousand bowmen in the interior, he also called for military reinforcements. That was the beginning of the myth that the Jesuits in Brazil and adjacent Spanish America constituted a threatening armed state in defiance of the Iberian crowns.[21]

In subsequent dispatches Mendonça Furtado intensified his verbal assault against the Jesuits. Those he sent in 1754 were replete with long-standing settlers' allegations against the religious orders and radical proposals to end their 'formidable' power. He emphasized that it was necessary to reform the Jesuits first, since they were the pacesetters. The best way to eliminate their 'absolute and most prejudicial' power was to confiscate their properties, convert them into settlements administered by soldiers, distribute their lands to the impoverished settlers, and confine an allowable number of Jesuits to their urban colleges, where they might subsist on modest royal stipends. [22]

Although Mendonça Furtado's criticisms had been focused on all the religious orders in the State, they became more specifically directed against the Jesuits when he and his large entourage ascended the Amazon in October 1754, the beginning of what proved to be a succession of frustrating, fruitless efforts to rendezvous with the Spanish high commissioner, who was supposed to ascend the Orinoco River, cross over to the Rio Negro, a northern Amazonian tributary, and meet the Portuguese commissioner at a Carmelite mission. With 1,025 men, including 511 Indian oarsmen who propelled 23 large canoes, the governor took two and a half months to reach his destination.

Each week his reports to his acting replacement, Bishop Bulhões, and to Lisbon were filled with complaints. They particularly concerned the propensity of the Amerindians to desert his service and fade into the forests, and the scarcity of provisions, especially the basic staple, manioc, best known to us in its commercial form as tapioca, which he expected the missions to provide. Although shirking had long characterized Indian-European relations in the Amazon and would continue to do so long afterwards, the governor was convinced that the Jesuits were deliberately inducing the Indians to flee. Ignoring the fact that the Lower Amazon had been devastated during the 1740s by a succession of smallpox and measles epidemics that had killed thousands, mostly Indians, he attributed the food shortages to the refusal of the Jesuits to supply his needs.[23] After learning of Gomes Freire's problems in Rio Grande do Sul, he became convinced that the Jesuits were actively frustrating the implementation of the boundary treaty.

As the months passed, Mendonça Furtado's health deteriorated and his frustration mounted, prompting him to manufacture new grievances against the Jesuits. He accused those on the Madeira River, a western and southern tributary of the Amazon, of engaging in unauthorized communication with Spanish Jesuits in present-day Ecuador. It was while he was supervising the secularization of one Jesuit mission on that river that the governor was shocked by two discoveries. The first was a spectacular demonstration arranged by the resident German-born Jesuit father, who welcomed him by discharging his mission's two small-bore cannon. Proud of his antique weapons, Anselmo Eckhart also fired them to celebrate the Nativity, to toast the birthday of Portugal's reigning monarch, and to bid adieu to the departing governor. After witnessing such firepower, the alarmed governor warned Lisbon that even in the remote Upper Amazon the Jesuits were armed! He neither knew nor cared that the weapons had been authorized by the previous king, in 1724, for the purpose of frightening away marauding hostile Indians. But he was equally disturbed when he observed in the chapel of the same former mission a set of weighing scales next to the altar. They were used to record the amount of forest products each Indian had gathered during his daily foraging. However, in the troubled mind of the suspicious governor the presence of such a contrivance conjured up Christ's exhortation against the money-changers in the temple and further convinced him that the Jesuits had abandoned their spiritual calling and embraced Mammon.[24]

Mendonça Furtado certainly had no difficulty in convincing Bishop Bulhões of the seriousness of his suspicions. The bishop, an ambitious, self-serving opportunist, who governed the State during the governor's absences, initially maintained cordial relations with Jesuits in the field and with those who had been his benefactors at court. Beginning in 1754, however, he sent voluminous reports to both the governor and the court in which he labelled the Jesuits in northern Brazil as 'arrogant,' 'contumacious,' 'despotic,' 'obstinate,' 'prideful,' defiant, excessively ambitious, and disloyal. Like Mendonça Furtado, he condemned the orders for their commercial activities in the State, and he shared with the governor his conviction that the Jesuits were deliberately hiding both the Indians and the foodstuffs he needed.[25]

Much of Bishop Bulhões's venom was directed against Francisco Toledo, a member of the Brazil province whom Father General Ignazio Visconti had sent to the vice-province in 1755 as a troubleshooter, bearing the title Visitor and Vice-Provincial.[26] Bulhões was certain that Toledo's appearance was intended to strengthen the Jesuits' opposition to his directives, which, he invariably insisted, were merely executions of the king's commands. Yet when the Visitor pressed him to display his orders calling for the removal of four Jesuits from the vice-province, Bulhões refused to comply.[27]

The four Jesuits, the first of twenty-one who would be recalled from Maranhão over the next three years, were the first the Crown ever banished from Brazil.[28] One was an experienced German-born father, Roque Hundertpfundt. His offence came to light during interrogations of colonists who had attended a party on a plantation outside the capital. During the frivolity that accompanied the consumption of beverages, someone suggested that the State of Maranhão would be more likely to thrive under French than Portuguese rule. When that statement was revealed to a suspicious cleric during confession, he rushed to the bishop, who ordered the arrest of twenty-three persons of both sexes. The zealous bishop became certain that those who had been at the party were engaged in a treasonable conspiracy. He identified Father Hundertpfundt as 'the chief conspirator' because he had administered the Spiritual Exercises to some of them.

In late 1756, shortly after many of these state prisoners had been sent to fortress dungeons near Lisbon, Mendonça Furtado returned to the capital to supervise a series of measures that would directly – and adversely – affect the Jesuits in the State. First, the settlers were encouraged to invest in and trade with a newly established government monopoly company that would supply African slaves and Portuguese manufactures to the State's consumers, and buy their exports. It was expected that the company would weaken the role of the religious orders, especially the Jesuits, in the State's economy.[29] Second, a papal brief condemning Indian slavery was finally broadcast, having been issued in 1741.[30]

The two Gang members pretended it was primarily directed against the Jesuits, even though the Society's leaders had long called for such a condemnation. Third, in accordance with Lisbon's orders, all the State's Indians were declared free persons. But because neither the bishop nor the governor believed the Indians had the capacity for self-rule, their communities were assigned to new military supervisors called directors, precisely what the colonists had long been advocating. Fourth, at a special meeting held in the Jesuit college of Santo Alexandre in Belém in February 1757, the heads of the orders were notified that they would no longer possess temporal authority over the Indians, and that their missions would be transformed into secular communities, each of which would be symbolically renamed after a Portuguese city or town. That measure was intended to efface the memory of their evangelical origin and to bond them with communities in the kingdom. A few days later, at another special meeting, the bishop triumphantly informed the heads of the orders that their members were now parish priests and therefore subject to his discipline. All but one leader acquiesced. The defiant one was the Jesuit visitor, Francisco Toledo.[31]

The bishop's challenge and Toledo's response, which was consistent with the Society's constitutions, was the beginning of a stepped-up campaign against the Jesuits. When Toledo withdrew his subjects from the former missions, the government insisted that all appurtenances, including sacred vessels, remain on the sites, since they properly belonged to the Amerindians. For a similar reason the governor embargoed forest products the Jesuits were attempting to ship to the kingdom. In addition, both he and the bishop insisted that tithes be paid on everything produced by Jesuit properties, with the proceeds remitted to the royal treasury. In May and again in June 1757, Mendonça Furtado sent the court lengthy assessments of the economic role of the Society of Jesus in the State. He asserted that for decades the order had acquired 'immense capital' through its illicit activities and had deprived the Crown of vast revenues to which it was properly entitled. Although he claimed that his calculations were based on Jesuit accounts, he submitted none. The admittedly fragmentary Jesuit accounts that survive, as well as the government's own customs records, belie his exaggerated contentions. But that did not deter the governor from renewing his contention that the Jesuits were guilty of heinous crimes, including treason, sedition, insubordination, defiance, despotism, and greed.[32]

The inevitable consequence of this intense campaign was Lisbon's call for 'violent reprisals' against the Jesuits. That call was issued in early July 1757. By the last months of the year, fifteen Jesuits, including the vice-provincial, two college rectors, and the provincial procurator (the economus of today), and several foreign-born missionaries were banished to the kingdom. They were the harbingers of the hundreds who would follow within the next several years.

The removal of key Jesuits from the vice-province and of others from the Brazil province were the first steps in the government's campaign to destroy the Society of Jesus within the Portuguese assistancy. That campaign was orchestrated by the last member of the Gang of Four – its leader, Sebastião José de Carvalho e Melo, the future Marquis of Pombal. Like Mendonça Furtado, his younger brother by a year, he was born in Lisbon.[33] Their family, members of the lesser, country nobility, had for centuries served the church and the Crown. Many, like Pombal himself, were informers for the Holy Office of the Inquisition. Indeed, his younger brother Paulo would become the kingdom's Grand Inquisitor. Several brothers pursued military careers, as did Pombal until the mid-1730s, when he resigned from the army after having been passed over for promotion. Three years later, in 1738, he succeeded an elder cousin as envoy extraordinary to the Court of St James, one of only a half-dozen diplomatic posts maintained by Portugal. He was attached to the London embassy until 1745, when he was transferred to Vienna. Having been conveniently widowed when his wealthy first wife died in 1738 and left him her substantial estate, he took a second wife, affiliated with Austria's leading field marshal, soon after reaching the Habsburg capital. They quickly produced three of their five children, perhaps his greatest accomplishment during his service abroad.

In 1749, Pombal was recalled to Lisbon, where Portugal's long-time sovereign, João V (1706–50) was near death. His successor, José I, took the unexpected, indeed surprising step of naming Pombal one of the kingdom's three secretaries of state. Precisely who bears the credit or the blame for that appointment has long been debated. Jesuit and pro-Jesuit scholars have long contended that he owed his appointment to palace Jesuits. That contention fits their depiction of Pombal as a duplicitous turncoat who later savaged the very men who had advanced his career. But there is no persuasive evidence that supports such an interpretation. It is true, however, that Pombal had enjoyed a long and cordial correspondence with court Jesuits during his years abroad, as did many other Portuguese officials. But there is no evidence that he was secretly plotting against the Society during the years before he became a royal minister.[34]

During the first years of the new regime, Pombal worked tirelessly to gain the inexperienced king's trust and to install at all levels of government, both at home and abroad, men who would recognize him as their protector. Such men – especially the diplomats, magistrates, military officers, and prelates such as Bishop Bulhões – became key instruments in his personal quest for absolute power. As said, there is no evidence that, in 1750, Pombal planned an assault against the Jesuits, but the secret instructions issued to his brother, Mendonça Furtado, the next year portended the stream of vilification against the Society that would follow. It is true, of course, that Pombal was not the author of the instructions to Mendonça Furtado, but their hostile tone far more closely reflected his own attitude towards the religious orders, beginning in the 1750s, than it did that of the colonial secretary who actually signed them.

Beginning in 1752, Pombal received regular reports from the other three members of the Gang, Gomes Freire in the south and Bishop Bulhões and Governor Mendonça Furtado in the north, that the Jesuits were deliberately obstructing the will of the king's ministers and must be sharply disciplined if not exterminated, to use the Portuguese word, from the Lusitanian world. By 1755 he had reached the conclusion that the Society of Jesus was a potential danger to the imposition of absolutist authority and must therefore be eliminated. What deterred him from proceeding then was a wholly unexpected, catastrophic event, the earthquake of 1 November that year, which levelled the city of Lisbon, killing thousands of persons, disrupted government operations, and caused severe damage to Portuguese communities from the central parts of the kingdom to its Mediterranean coast. It was Pombal who assumed unchallenged leadership after the earthquake and was able to consolidate his unrivalled authority as Portugal's chief minister.[35]

Within the next two years Pombal moved to distance the Jesuits from the rulers and the populace they had so long served. In 1757 there occurred a popular revolt in the northern city of Porto in protest against a new government wine company. Despite the absence of evidence, the Jesuits were accused of fomenting that tumult. On 19 September of that year, precisely the date on which the group of Jesuits in Pará were notified of their impending banishment, the royal confessors were barred from the imperial palace, so that the king became entirely isolated from all informants except those to whom his ministers permitted access.

Further measures soon followed. The first was the publication of a white paper, entitled 'Short Account of the Republic Which the Jesuits Have Established in the Spanish and Portuguese Dominions of the New World,' the release of which was timed for 3 December, a noteworthy day in the history of the Society. The 'Short Account,' that 'little book of lies' as José Caeiro, the foremost Jesuit chronicler of those troubled times, has called it, was the first of a series of increasingly damning anti-Jesuit publications issued by the government over the next decade. It was a bill of particulars concerning alleged Jesuit misdeeds in South America since the signing of the Treaty of Madrid. And it was based on reports from the three Gang members whose accounts we have considered. Jesuits were charged with having mobilized large armies in both the north and the south to prevent the implementation of the treaty. In Greater Paraguay their thirty missions constituted a formidable and independent republic in which, as in the Amazon, Indians were deprived of their lands and the fruits thereof. The

Indians were enslaved and exploited to enrich the missionaries, who barred the settlers and the king's ecclesiastical and lay representatives from contact with them. From the Amazon to Rio Grande do Sul, engineers, posing as Jesuits, manned the ramparts with powerful artillery. In short, the Society's installations in the continental interior constituted a state within a state, a threat to the Iberian empires' very survival.[36]

Reputedly, twenty thousand copies of the 'Short Account,' translated into the major European languages, were disseminated to prominent ecclesiastical and lay figures in Portugal and throughout the Continent. In May 1758 the supreme pontiff yielded to Pombaline pressure and designated a Portuguese cardinal, a kinsman and one of Pombal's lackeys, as papal reformer of the Society in the kingdom. The cardinal was charged with verifying the charges of Bishop Bulhões and Governor Mendonça Furtado that the Society was guilty of engaging in commercial activities contrary to 'all laws divine and human.' One week after his ceremonial visit to the Professed House of São Roque, the reformer found the Society guilty, even though he had not scrutinized a single Jesuit account. In June, Jesuits throughout the kingdom were forbidden to preach or hear confessions. On the night of 3 September 1758, José I became the victim of a failed assassination attempt. Three of Portugal's wealthiest but most heavily indebted aristocratic families were implicated. Since Jesuits had been their spiritual advisers, and since the Jesuits were known to sanction regicide, they too came under suspicion. Early in January 1759 the purported regicides were barbarously executed in a theatrical display of Pombaline power and personal vengeance. The same month, the Society's properties in the kingdom were confiscated by the Crown. Its justification for doing so was that Jesuits were believed responsible for the embarrassing missions war and, indirectly, for the attack on the king's life. Jesuits residing in the kingdom were immediately placed under house arrest. There remained only one additional step in the government's campaign against the Society of Jesus: on 3 September 1759, the first anniversary of the real or feigned attack on José I, Portugal, the nation that had first welcomed the Jesuits and first sent them overseas, became the first European power to oust them from its domains.

Thus the labours of the Gang of Four concluded triumphantly. To be sure, they possessed many collaborators in the anti-Jesuit campaign, including magistrates, prelates, soldiers, and others who slavishly carried out the instructions of their patrons. The patrons gained important rewards for their roles in orchestrating the demise of the Jesuits in the Lusitanian world. In 1758, Gomes Freire became a count, though he scarcely had time to enjoy his good fortune before his death on 1 January 1763. In 1759, Francisco Xavier de Mendonça Furtado returned to Lisbon, where he became colonial secretary, a post he held until he succumbed to a fatal stroke in 1769. His cohort, Miguel de Bulhões, became bishop of Leiria, in north-central Portugal, where he remained until his demise in 1779. Sebastião José de Carvalho e Melo, the chief of the Gang, successively Count of Oeiras and, beginning in 1770, Marquis of Pombal, was dismissed from office in 1777 as soon as his master died. He successfully withstood investigations of his conduct in office and died of natural causes in 1782.

As for the Jesuits – those who yielded to pressure and left the order; those who survived arrest, transport, capture by Algerian corsairs, and banishment to the Pontifical States; those who endured years of confinement in military dungeons in the Portuguese kingdom – theirs is a fascinating story, one best left for another occasion.

NOTES

This essay is derived from chapters of a book in progress, 'The Destruction of an Enterprise: The Jesuits in the Portuguese World and Beyond, 1750–1777,' to be published by Harvard University Press. The title was inspired by the author's correspondence with Father John W. O'Malley, to whom this essay is dedicated, and who employed this designation for the organizers of the first Boston College conference on the Jesuits in 1997.

1 Guillermo Kratz, *El tratado hispano-portugues de limites de 1750 y sus consequencias* ... (Rome, 1954); Luís Ferrand de Almeida, *Alexandre de Gusmão, o Brasil e o tratado de Madrid (1735–1750)* (Coimbra, 1990); Jorge Couto, 'O tratado de limites de 1750 na perspectiva portuguesa,' in Congresso Internacional de Historia, *El tratado de Tordesillas y su epoca*, vol. 3 (n.p., n.d.), pp. 1593–1610.

2 For an introduction to the voluminous literature on Colônia, see Luís Ferrand de Almeida, 'A Colónia do Sacramento e a formação do sul do Brasil,' in his *Páginas dispersas: Estudos de história moderna de Portugal* (Coimbra, 1995), pp. 163–82.

3 The text of the treaty can be found in many places, including Archivo General de la Nación, Argentina, *Campaña del Brasil: Antecedentes coloniales*, 3 vols (Buenos Aires, 1931–41), II, pp. 5–15.

4 No adequate biography of Gomes Freire exists, but see Robert Allan White, 'Gomes Freire de Andrada: Life and Times of a Brazilian Colonial Governor, 1688–1763,' PhD dissertation, University of Texas, 1972.

5 Gomes Freire de Andrade to Marco António de Azevedo Coutinho, 12 June 1750, *Alexandre de Gusmão e o tratado de Madrid*, ed. Jaime Cortesão, 9 vols in 5 parts (Rio de Janeiro, 1952–63), part 4, vol. 2, pp. 412–13.

6 There is a voluminous literature on the missions. One of their finest scholars was Guillermo Furlong [Cardiff]; see his *Missiones y sus pueblos de Guaraníes* (Buenos Aires, 1962). For a bibliography of recent literature, see Thomas Whigham, 'Para-

guay's *Pueblos de Indios*: Echos of a Missionary Past,' in *The New Latin American Mission History*, ed. Erick Langer and Robert H. Jackson (Lincoln, NE, 1995), pp. 157–88. See also Barbara Ganson, *The Guaraní under Spanish Rule in the Río de la Plata* (Stanford, 2003).

7 Magnus Mörner, 'The Cedula Grande of 1743,' *Jahrbuch fur geschichte von staat, wirtschaft und gesellschaft Lateinamerikas* 4 (Koln, 1967), pp. 489–505. See also Mörner, 'The Guaraní Missions and the Segregation Policy of the Spanish Crown,' *AHSI* 30 (July–December 1961): 367–86; James Scholfield Saeger, 'Origins of the Rebellion of Paraguay,' *Hispanic American Historical Review* 52:2 (May 1972): 215–29; and Adelberto López, *The Revolt of the Comuñeros, 1721–1735: A Study in the Colonial History of Paraguay* (Cambridge, MA, 1976).

8 Sélim Abou, *The Jesuit 'Republic' of the Guaranís (1609–1768) and Its Heritage*, trans. Lawrence J. Johnson (New York, 1997), pp. 101–2. This work contains outstanding illustrations and superior maps.

9 Ignazio Visconti to Manuel Querini (provincial, Paraquaria), 21 July 1751, in Robert Lacombe, *Guaranis et jésuites: Un combat pour la liberté* (Paris, 1993), pp. 263–4.

10 For local Jesuit responses, see Francisco Mateos, 'El tratado de límites entre España y Portugal de 1750 y las misiones del Paraguay (1751–1753),' *Missionalia hispánica* 6 (1949): 319–78.

11 Cardiff, *Missiones*, pp. 649–50.

12 Ferrand de Almeida, *O tratado de Madrid* (n1 above), pp. 149–51.

13 Freire de Andrade to Diogo de Mendonça Corte Real, 3 April 1953, in Eduardo de Castro e Almeida, comp., *Inventário dos documentos relativos ao Brasil existentes no arquivo de marinha e ultramar de Lisboa*, 8 vols (Lisbon and Rio de Janeiro, 1913–36), VIII, p. 278.

14 Mateos, 'El tratado de límites,' pp. 296–305; Cardiff, *Misiones*, pp. 666–8. Kratz, *Tratado*, pp. 115–16, is less satisfactory. On the truce, see Castro e Almeida, *Inventário*, vol. 8, pp. 411–12.

15 Freire de Andrade to Sebastião José de Carvalho e Melo, 24 September 1754, in *Alexandre de Gusmão*, ed. Cortesão, vol. 5, pp. 423–4.

16 Kratz, *Tratado*, pp. 149–61, and sources too numerous to list.

17 Dauril Alden, 'Indian versus Black Slavery in the State of Maranhão during the Seventeenth and Eighteenth Centuries,' in *Iberian Colonies, New World Societies: Essays in Memory of Charles Gibson*, ed. Richard L. Garner and William B. Taylor (n.p., 1985), pp. 71–102; Alden, *The Making of an Enterprise: The Society of Jesus in Portugal, Its Empire, and Beyond, 1540–1750* (Stanford, 1996), chaps 17, 19, and 23.

18 Petition of Francisco Xavier de Mendonça Furtado to the Crown, [1749], in Castro e Almeida, *Inventário*, vol. 8, p. 82; Overseas Council to the king, 14 March 1749,

Lisbon, Arquivo Histórico Ultramarino, Papeis Avulsas, India, maço 61; *Gazeta de Lisboa*, 22 April 1751, announcing his appointment to Brazil's State of Maranhão.

19 'Instrução q. V. Mag.^{de} he servido mandar dar a Francisco X'er de Mendonça ..., 30 May 1751, repr., among other places, in Marcos Carneiro de Mendonça, comp., *A Amazônia na era Pombalina: Correspondência inédita do governador e capitão-general do estado do Grão Pará e Maranhão Francisco Xavier de Mendonça Furtado, 1751–1759*, 3 vols (Rio de Janeiro, 1963) (hereafter *CMF*), I, pp. 26–38.

20 M. Lopes de Almeida, comp., *Notícias históricas de Portugal e Brasil*, 2 vols (Coimbra, 1961–4), I, pp. 165, 181, 239, 245, 252, 281, 291; II, pp. 5, 26, 38, 52, 78; Caesar Augusto Marquis, 'Vida e feitos de Dom Frei Miguel de Bulhões e Souza. 3° bispo do Gram-Pará,' *Revista do Instituto histórico e geográfico brasileiro* 50:3 (1877): 143–56; Manoel Ferreira Leonardo (the bishop's secretary), 'Relação da viagem e entrada, ue fez o excelentissimo e reverendissimo senhor d. Fr. Miguel de Bulhoens e Sousa ...' (Lisbon, 1749), copy in the John Carter Brown Library, Brown University, pp. 69–100.

21 Mendonça Furtado to Carvalho e Melo, 21 and 28 November and 29 December 1751, in *CMF*, I, pp. 63–81, 143–8.

22 Mendonça Furtado to Carvalho e Melo, 26 January 1754, in *CMF*, II, pp. 465–70; [Mendonça Furtado], 'Memoria das fazendas ... que têm os padres da Companha nesta capitania do Pará,' 8 February 1754, ibid., pp. 485–9; Mendonça Furtado to Carvalho e Melo, 18 February 1754, ibid., pp. 498–505.

23 On smallpox epidemics in Brazil, see Dauril Alden and Joseph C. Miller, 'Out of Africa: The Slave Trade and the Transmission of Smallpox to Brazil, 1560–1831,' in *Health and Disease in Human History: A Journal of Interdisciplinary History Reader*, ed. Robert I. Rotberg (Cambridge, MA, 2000), pp. 203–30. A recent discussion of the governor's first expedition is Augusto Titarelli, 'A expedição das demarcaçöes: Notas de viagem,' in Comissão Nacional para as Comemorações dos Descobrimentos Portugueses, *Amazónia felsínea* (Lisbon, 1999), pp. 153–72.

24 Mendonça Furtado to Carvalho e Melo, 20 July 1755, in *CMF*, II, pp. 781–2; the same to the same, 13 October 1756, ibid., III, pp. 985–7.

25 Dom Miguel de Bulhões to Mendonça Furtado, 5 November 1754, 22 January, 12 August, 24 September, 14 October, and 29 December 1755, BNL Col. Pomb. Cod. 627 fols 41r–v, 86r–v, 224r–226r, 234r, 244r, and 256v–257r; Bulhões to Carvalho e Melo, 19 September 1754, Lisbon, Arquivo Nacional da Torre do Tombo, Ministerio do Reino 598.

26 Serafim Leite, *História da Companhia de Jesús no Brasil*, 10 vols (Lisbon and Rio de Janeiro, 1938–50), IX, pp. 156–62.

27 Bulhöes to Mendonça Furtado, 12 August 1755, BNL Col. Pomb. 627 fols 224r–226r.

28 [Domingos Antonio], *Collecção dos crimes e decretos pelos quaes vinte e hum jesuítas foraõ mandados sahir no estado do Gram Pará e Maranhaõ antes do*

extermino geral de toda a Companhia de Jesus daquelle estado (*ca. 1780*), ed.
Serafim Leite (Coimbra, 1947).

29 For background to the establishment of the company, see Alden, 'Indian versus
Black Slavery,' pp. 98–9.

30 The text of the bull of 20 December 1756 is given in the *Collecção de negocios de
Roma no reinado de el-rey Dom José I, 1755–1775*, 3 vols and supplement (Lisbon,
1874–5), I, pp. 9–14.

31 José Caeiro, *Jesuitas no Brasil e da India na persequição do marquês de Pombal
(século xviii)*, trans. Manoel Martins (Bahia, 1936), pp. 428–41.

32 Mendonça Furtado to Tomé Joaquim da Costa Corte Real (colonial secretary),
23 May 1757, *Anais da biblioteca e arquivo do Pará* 4 (Belém, 1905): 212–20; the
same to Carvalho e Melo, 16 June 1757, BL 20997 fols 173v–179v, published in
CMF, III, pp. 1098–1104.

33 The most recent (of many) biographies of Pombal is Kenneth Maxwell, *Pombal:
Paradox of the Enlightenment* (Cambridge, 1995).

34 Rocha Martins, *O marquês de Pombal: Pupilo dos Jesuitas* (Lisbon, 1924); but cf.
*Marquês de Pombal e a Companhia de Jesus: Correspondência inédita ao longo de
115 cartas (de 1743 a 1751)*, ed. António Lopes (São João de Estoril, 1999).

35 For a recent assessment, see Kenneth Maxwell, 'The Earthquake of 1755 and Urban
Recovery under the Marquês de Pombal,' in *Out of Ground Zero: Case Studies in
Urban Reinvention*, ed. Joan Ockman (New York, 2002), n.p.

36 A convenient text of the 'Relação Abreviada' is in José Caeiro, *História da expulsão
da Companhia de Jesus da província de Portugal (séc. xviii)*, 3 vols (Lisbon, 1991–9),
I, appendix.

34 / Twilight in the Imperial City: The Jesuit Mission in China, 1748–60

RONNIE PO-CHIA HSIA

In the 1740s, China was perhaps closer to Europe than ever before, thanks to the Jesuits. Only a few years earlier, in 1735, Jean-Baptiste du Halde, prefect of the Paris Maison Professe, had published in Paris a four-volume work that quickly became an authoritative text on China. This work, *Description géographique, historique, chronologique et politique de l'Empire de la Chine et de la Tartarie chinoise*, was translated into English in 1741 and into German in 1747. To no small extent it contributed to the Sinophilia of mid-eighteenth-century Europe. This French father was not an ex-missionary, however, but one of the chief editors of the best-known missionary series of all times, the *Lettres édifiantes et curieuses*, published in thirty-four volumes between 1703 and 1776.[1] Pious and curious news from China became à la mode: the persecution of the Manchu nobleman Sounou and his Christian sons, especially Prince Joseph (Urchen) and Jean (Sourghien), by the Yongzheng emperor, first reported by the French Jesuit Dominique Parrenin from Beijing, acquired novelistic proportions (617 pages) in four instalments of the *Lettres* between 1724 and 1734.[2] Capturing the imagination of Catholic Europe, the fate of Sounou and his sons inspired at least nine tragedies performed in the Jesuit colleges of the German provinces between 1731 and 1754.[3]

The story of Sounou involved a complex plot with scores of characters and many narrative streams. Its main theme was Christian martyrdom, set in remote, exotic China; its heroes were the extended family of a Manchu noble clan of imperial blood; its plot unfolded in disgrace, persecution, perseverance, and final deliverance. As with any complicated story, there was a central idea: the new emperor Yongzheng, unlike his tolerant and open-minded father Kangxi (r. 1662–1723), the subject of much Jesuit encomium, disliked Christianity and was angry that converts were found among high-ranking Manchu noblemen. Steadfastly refusing to abjure, the men and women of the household endured prison, exile, even death, chastisements inflicted by the cruel pagan emperor. The story of Sounou's kin did not end in unmitigated tragedy. After the death of Yongzheng in 1734, his son, the Qianlong emperor (r. 1734–94), pardoned Sounou's descendants and permitted them to return from exile in Mongolia to China proper, thus ending the decade-long story of Christian martyrdom.

Just as intellectual and fashionable Europe was experiencing a China wave, tragedy hit much closer to home. In December 1747 two Jesuit missionaries in Suzhou, the Italian Tristan de Attemis and the Portuguese Antonio Joseph Henriques, were denounced by a Christian apostate and arrested by the local magistrate. Their imprisonment came in the wake of the execution of five Dominicans and their Chinese catechist in Fujian province the year before, an event that signalled a crisis for the China mission. In spite of the Chinese Rites controversy, the failure of papal legations, the prohibition of Christianity by Emperor Kangxi in 1717, the exile of all missionaries in the provinces to Guangzhou, and their expulsion to Macao by Yongzheng in 1732, the Catholic church had not suffered major persecutions prior to 1746. True, imperial edicts banned European missionaries from the provinces, permitting them to reside and exercise their religion only in Beijing, in consideration of the services they rendered to the emperor as court astronomers, musicians, and technicians. In practice, the emperors tolerated a small native Christian community in Beijing; and provincial officials were less than rigorous in their pursuit of foreign missionaries, who continued to slip into China and minister to Christian communities in secret.

The arrests of 1746–7 formed a watershed in that the anti-Christian laws in the Qing empire were carried out rigorously and European missionaries were executed for the first time. The martyrdom of the five Spanish Dominicans in 1747 was followed by the executions of the two Jesuits on 12 September 1748; they were the first Jesuit martyrs since the foundation of the China mission in 1584.[4] Perhaps the greatest blow to the Jesuit mission was the realization of the fathers at court of their powerlessness, in failing to have the executions commuted to lighter sentences, a tactic that had worked in the past, by means of petitions to influential courtiers and bribery for lower officials. Long before the suppression of the Society in Portugal and France, which had been the two major patrons of the China mission, and the dissolution of the Society in 1773, the Jesuit mission had entered a crisis.

By the 1740s the Jesuit mission in China had passed its prime. After increasing steadily during the seventeenth century, the number of Christian converts reached an estimated peak of 200,000 around 1700.[5] This increase reflected the prestige of Christianity in the wake of the so-called 1692 Edict of Toleration under

Kangxi. The Chinese Rites controversy, or, more precisely, the prohibition of Christianity in the provinces by Kangxi, put an abrupt end to growth in the number of conversions. The numbers declined. By 1740 the estimated number of Christians stood at 120,000. This absolute decline was even more drastic, given that the eighteenth century witnessed a rapid population growth; the population of China more than doubled, from 160 million to 350 million, between 1700 and 1800.[6]

A larger blow to the China mission was the change in the profile of the converts. With a few notable and highly publicized exceptions, elite converts became fewer. In a 1726 letter, the French Jesuit Antoine Gaubil wrote that of the four thousand converts in Beijing, one could find only four or five low-ranking mandarins and two or three literati; the rest were poor folks. 'One baptizes only poor folks,' lamented Gaubil. 'The literati and those highly placed who had wanted to become Christians abandoned us the moment we published the *decrets*, in accordance with the order of the supreme pontiff, even with the permissions granted by the patriarch, M. Mezzabarba.'[7] Gaubil then identified the crucial factor: 'The emperor does not love our religion.' After Kangxi, the court Jesuits no longer harboured hopes of an imperial conversion. Yongzheng's hostility had been replaced by Qianlong's indifference, which did not spare the mission from sporadic persecution.

In any event, there was plenty of evidence to show a changing sociology of conversion. In 1715 the French Jesuit F.X. Dentrecolles reported from Jiangxi that most Christians counted among the working poor, and many were forced to sell off their children in times of dire need. Although some literati befriended him, Dentrecolles added, all refused baptism.[8] In Beijing, the Belgian Jesuit François Noël confirmed Gaubil's picture in the annual report of 1730: most Christians were commoners, with the exception of one Manchu nobleman at court; the very few mandarin Christians were all colleagues of the Jesuits at the Bureau of Mathematics.[9] This new sociology of conversion brought to the fore two areas of concern, the first involving the baptism of abandoned infants, and the second, the conversion of sectarians.

If the literati and mandarins occupied a less prominent place in eighteenth-century Jesuit mission discourses, abandoned infants assumed a new rhetorical significance. Summarizing the work of different Jesuit missionaries of the French mission in 1726, Gaubil reported on the zeal of Father Maurice du Baudory, in Guangzhou, who baptized 2,500 infants in two short years. Without the persecutions, Gaubil speculated, the Jesuits would have been able to send 20,000 infants to heaven.[10] The practice of baptizing abandoned infants in Guangzhou was initiated in 1719 by Philippe Cazier, a Belgian Jesuit, who laboured there between 1711 and 1722. A long letter by his colleague, du Baudory, described in detail this work of charity. Alongside the official Beijing Foundling Hospital, funded by the emperor, the Jesuits established their own such hospital, discreetly staffed by native catechists. In 1719, when they began their work, they baptized 136 infants; in 1721, they baptized 241; in 1721, the number grew to 267; and by 1724 it had reached 300. In addition to taking in infants to their Maison de la Miséricorde, the Jesuits paid the director of the Foundling Hospital to allow them access. Catechists visited there periodically to baptize moribund infants, thereby assuring them an immediate path to heaven, and those who survived their illnesses were targeted for adoption by Christian families. Far fewer infants were brought directly to the Jesuit church: du Baudory himself baptized only 45 in 1723. All in all, this was work that cost a sizeable subsidy for the payment of Chinese catechists and gentiles who brought infants to the missionaries.[11]

By any measure, abandoned infants vastly outnumbered adults in the catalogue of salvation. In 1734 the French Jesuits in Beijing baptized 2,000 infants ('une bonne oeuvre, bien solide') but only a few more than 200 adults;[12] in 1741, they baptized 1,500 infants and 250 adults.[13] Their achievements in saving the souls of these little ones became marks of distinction for some missionaries. The two septuagenarians of the French Jesuit mission, Dentrecolles and Parrenin, both of whom died in 1741 (at the ages of 79 and 76 respectively), had each baptized more than 10,000 abandoned infants in their forty-odd years of missionary work in China.[14] This was not only a work of charity, but a source of polemics for the Jesuits against their enemies. Describing an endowment for the purpose to his brother, Gaubil wrote in 1722: 'With the donations of charitable people, we established a foundation in our church that procured the entry into paradise every year of more than 380 little infants. Certainly we have no need to fear that even the Jansenists would want to send them to hell, on the pretext that being baptized by the Jesuits is committing an unforgivable sin.'[15] In times of adversity, the large numbers of saved infants affirmed the purpose of the mission. When the persecutions of 1748–52 were barely subsiding, Gaubil reflected on the work of the mission: 'At Beijing, in spite of the aversion of the emperor to our religion, every year we manage to baptize and send to paradise a very large number of abandoned or moribund small infants of idolaters. Very few of these abandoned infants escape; almost all die. For several years the number of these baptized infants has increased to more than 6,000 in Beijing. One cannot contradict the fact that this is one of the best and most solid good works in this country, equal to the printing and distributing of large numbers of books of religion.'[16]

Making the best of adversity, the Jesuits of the Portuguese vice-province also prized their work with abandoned infants. The persecutions of 1748 had made the baptism of these poor creatures dangerous for Christian catechists. So the

Portuguese mission turned to paying Chinese workers, who collected the infants every morning from the city gates, to baptize the moribund.[17]

Infanticide had a long history in imperial China. Despite periodic prohibitions by central governments and the lamentations of local mandarins, the widespread belief in reincarnation and pragmatic calculations in household management helped to make infant abandonment acceptable, even if deplored. In 1659, during the early Qing, an edict outlawing infanticide was promulgated. The first foundling hospital in Beijing opened in 1661; others were established in urban areas, especially in the densely urbanized and prosperous Jiangnan region. Mercantile and gentry elites often took the initiative; imperial and magisterial support came in fits and starts.[18]

Although Matteo Ricci had observed the practice of infanticide, especially of infant girls, no mention is made of baptizing these poor souls in his journal.[19] There seems to have been no effort to baptize abandoned infants during the early mission; at least nothing is mentioned in the Annual Letters of the tumultuous 1640s by António de Gouvea.[20] Nor do the Annual Letters of the 1650s and 1660s mention baptisms of abandoned children. While numbers of baptisms are given here and there, more significance is attached to specific cases of edification and to the conversion of literati and mandarins.[21] Jesuit involvement with the baptizing of abandoned infants did not begin until the 1680s, when it paralleled a growing consciousness among the Qing elites of the need to address this social problem.

In 1684, Ferdinand Verbiest mentioned a confraternity among Chinese Christians in the capital devoted to the work of baptizing abandoned infants.[22] Some 5,800 baptisms were performed that year on moribund infants, more than ten times the number of adult baptisms.[23] As many as 40 infants were found daily at the eight gates of the imperial capital.[24] But the new Jesuit initiative provoked a counteraction. Projects for saving these infants were undertaken by mandarins and the wealthy, who collected donations enabling abandoned infants to be brought to Buddhist monasteries for care. According to the Jesuits, the Buddhist monks tried to prevent Christians from baptizing the children. And when large numbers of moribund infants died after baptism, the Buddhist monks complained to the magistrates, who asked the Jesuits to desist.[25] The Portuguese Jesuit Pereira, music tutor to Emperor Kangxi, brought up the subject with the emperor after a lesson on 6 March 1685, and explained the need to save these souls.[26] The Jesuits were apparently allowed to continue their practice.

By the 1690s, abandoned infants formed a new category in the growing Chinese Church Militant. A Triennial Report covering the years 1694–6 lamented that more than 40,000 infants were abandoned every year out of poverty and illegitimacy; most perished in water or were killed by animals, and a few ended up in Buddhist monasteries. In Beijing alone, the members of the Portuguese vice-province baptized between 2,600 and 3,400 during those years.[27] News of this reserve army of Christian souls reached Europe with the publication of the letters by Dentrecolles after 1726, in *Neue Weltbott* (published in Augsburg and Vienna) and *Lettres édifiantes*.[28] Interestingly, Jesuit-sponsored work among abandoned infants coincided with an effort by the Qing state to centralize charity. In 1724, Yongzheng recognized and endowed the Beijing Foundling Hospital, thus promoting the official sponsorship of foundling hospitals and other charitable institutions.[29]

All this points to a reasonable conjecture: that the baptism of abandoned infants might have been undertaken initially by Chinese Christians as part of a much larger trend towards elite mobilization for charity in late imperial China. A significant role was played by Christian Chinese physicians, who secretly baptized moribund infants brought to their care.[30] In any case, so as to avoid arousing suspicion the Jesuits themselves baptized comparatively few of these infants; paid Chinese catechists and gentiles (during periods of persecution) undertook the bulk of the work.

While infanticide represented a general demographic phenomenon, foundling hospitals and the baptism of abandoned children were almost exclusively urban developments. The 1752 Annual Letter of the Portuguese vice-province shows an interesting set of statistics: in Beijing (the college and the residence) in that year the Jesuits baptized 113 adults, 449 children of Christians, and 1,327 abandoned infants. In the three missions in Zhili province, in the environs of Beijing, which were administered by the Jesuits, there were 229 adult and 1,307 (750 were children of Christians) child baptisms. No baptisms of abandoned children were recorded. Likewise, figures from Huguang (the only information from the provinces) did not indicate the baptism of abandoned infants. Aside from the obvious urban-rural or capital-provincial differences, the statistics point to another reasonable conjecture: that the high proportion of children of Christians among the baptized reflected a stabilizing of the convert population. Chinese Christians were becoming a self-replenishing group.

Just how important abandoned infants were in the overall economy of the Jesuit mission is reflected in table 34.1. But beyond percentages, the presence of abandoned infants loomed large in the Jesuit discourse on conversion and mission during the eighteenth century. It was a central concern in the long correspondence between the Silesian Jesuit Florian Bahr in Beijing and his patron, Maria Theresia, countess of Fugger-Wellenburg, in Augsburg and Munich, between 1739 and 1762. Having first learned of the practice in a letter from Bahr, the countess wrote on 31 October 1740 begging for more details. Were the

Table 34.1
Percentage of abandoned infants among those baptized by Jesuits in the China mission, 1685–1752

1685	1694	1695	1696	1726	1734	1741	1752
93	87	81	88	81	91	86	92[a]

[a]Abandoned infant and adult baptisms only; the figure is lowered to 68% if the children of Christians are included.
Source: Data from (1685) Beijing, BA Jesuítas na Asia 49-V-19 fol. 597r; (1694, 1695, 1696) Beijing (Portuguese vice-province), BA Jesuítas na Asia 49-V-22 fols 610r–611v; (1726) Jesuit college, Hangzhou, for 1 September 1725 to 31 August 1726, BA Jesuítas na Asia 49-V-21 fols 158v–159r; (1734, 1741) Le P. Antoine Gaubil, S.J., Correspondance de Pékin, 1722–1759, ed. Renée Simon (Geneva, 1970), pp. 387, 536; (1752) Litterae annuae, 1752, Dillingen, Fugger-Archiv, published in R. Po-chia Hsia, The Countess, The Jesuits, and the Orphans: Maria Theresia von Fugger-Wellenburg (1690–1762) and the Jesuit Mission in China and Vietnam (Nettetal, 2006), document 72.

children abandoned at night, and every night? How many were there? Were all of them baptized, and by whom? Were they left to rot away and die after Holy Baptism? Why were not all abandoned children baptized, and how could one help? 'You see the concerns of a woman, which extend even to the end of the world,' pleaded the countess.[31]

Bahr's reply to the countess, written one year later, on 9 November 1740, shows that he had anticipated her questions before her letter arrived from Europe.[32] Bahr informed the countess that his particular duty was teaching catechism to children and teenagers.[33] While that task gave him great satisfaction, 'the other part of innocent youth, namely, those poor children, abandoned and deprived of all human help, is more difficult to reach with help in the present circumstances. Not all our effort suffices to help them, nor are all our tears capable of sufficiently lamenting their abandonment.'[34] At all eight gates of the Imperial City, one found abandoned infants every night, some dead, others still alive. Bahr wrote that he would not speak of the fact that perhaps only one in ten of these infants was baptized by the Jesuits, until now; nor would he speak of the fact that many European benefactors had donated money so that the Jesuits could man five of the eight gates 'to baptize these abandoned orphans at night, in order to guarantee their eternal life after such an early loss of their earthy life.' No, he would not speak of these things; he would speak only of a Chinese Christian, arrested at the gate while baptizing these poor souls and sentenced to wearing a heavy cangue, or wooden board, around his neck for a month at the Hata Gate (Hai Tai Men). The Chinese Christians were now afraid to baptize the children, and many souls had been lost. Forced to adopt an emergency measure, the Jesuits were paying money to heathens to save the souls of these exposed children.

The small sums given to support the baptisms of abandoned infants by Countess Maria Theresia had turned into an endowment of 16,000 florins by 1745. The rhetoric of salvation of the souls of the innocents evoked a powerful response in Catholic Europe. Through Bahr's letters and the countess's mediation, Empress Amalia, the widow of Holy Roman Emperor Carl Albrecht, also offered the Jesuit mission in China an annual pledge of 150 florins, payable from a capital of 3,000 florins, specifically to pay for the baptisms of abandoned infants.[35]

Infanticide was a desperate response to poverty and overpopulation. The Jesuit mission in China, and Chinese Christianity as a whole, steadily descended the social ladder in eighteenth-century China after the prohibition of Chinese rites. As conversions were concentrated more exclusively within the ranks of commoners, the Christian mission ran into greater risk of association with rebellious sectarianism. Owing to the Jesuits' foreign status, rituals, and organization, some Chinese elites had accused them of organizing clandestine sects and fomenting rebellions even in the early seventeenth century. The polemic with Buddhism, initiated by Matteo Ricci and his supporters in the first years of the seventeenth century, provoked the 1616 anti-Christian campaign. The compilation of anti-Christian writings entitled *Poxie ji* by the lay Buddhist Xu Changzhi in 1640 preserved in the form of a printed text the common association of Christianity with rebellious sects. While Buddhist polemic against Christianity seemed to have faded after 1640, the specific association of Christianity with sectarianism lingered in elite thought. In 1664–5 the mandarin Yang Guangxian, not known for any particular Buddhist allegiance, attacked Jesuit astronomy and Christianity from the point of view of ultra-Confucian orthodoxy.

The subject of the relations between Christianity and Chinese sectarianism remains largely under-explored. Xenophobia was a factor contributing to the association of the two in some people's minds, but by no means the decisive factor. An important question is the extent to which Christianity represented an attractive belief and ritual system for potential adherents of folk religion. Another crucial problem is the similarity between Christianity – in its religious rituals and soteriology – and lay Buddhist, Taoist, and other Chinese popular sects. Despite the famous treatise by Yang Tingyun (Michele, 1557–1627) distinguishing Christianity from heterodox sects, *Xiaoluan Bu Bingming Shou* (The Owl and the Phoenix Do Not Sing Together, 1616), in which Yang listed fourteen differences between Christian orthodoxy and sectarian heterodoxy, the Western religion was never cleansed of the odour of sectarianism.[36] Several cases from the period 1680s–1740s show that elite suspicion was not completely without grounds.

One case, from the 1680s, was from a village called Vam gan chin (Wan an zhen), in the district of Hutum (Hudong), about twenty leagues from Kiamchu (Jiangzhou). It involved the leaader of a sect who, along with his disciples, was persuaded to receive baptism, and afterwards mixed Christian doctrines with the fables of his sect.

In his district is a heavily populated village called Vam gan chin, where dwelt a diabolical man by the name of Liu, the leader of a false sect. This man had come there because the mandarins were pursuing him, and he dissimulated in such a manner that he deceived the fathers, who had been there before the persecution, and who administered Holy Baptism to him and many of his disciples. After receiving baptism he began to look through our books and add our mysteries to his fables, fabricating new dogmas and new prayers, with which for more than twenty years he deceived the fathers, who did not presume to look for the poison hidden in such a gilded vessel.[37]

The poison was not discovered until the Jesuit José Soares visited the man at his home and found blasphemous images and the like. The man claimed to be the Third Person of the Trinity, called upon the Holy Ghost, and presented himself as the bridge to heaven for his followers. The most interesting point is not the infiltration of Christianity by a sect leader and his followers but the appropriation of Christian symbols, rituals, and doctrines to elaborate a basic set of sectarian soteriological rituals and practices. The process was similar to that in the appropriation of Buddhist doctrines and sutras, first in the creation of the Lo Jiao (named after the founder of the Wuwei, or Do Nothing, sect in the 1510s), and later in the development of millenarian popular sects that created their own *bao juan* (precious scrolls) from terms, figures, and doctrines borrowed from Buddhist sutras.[38]

Missionary work among the boat people of Huguang (the Donting and Poyang lakes are the largest inland lakes in China) and along the Grand Canal was especially sensitive. The Jesuits attracted a number of sectarians from the White Lotus and the Lo Jiao, two of the most prominent sectarian groups in late imperial China. In 1730, for example, while ministering in the Donting Lake, the French Jesuit Etienne Le Couteux baptized a household of more than twenty who were all formerly White Lotus sectarians.[39] In 1734, sectarian rebels in Shandong and Henan proclaimed themselves Christians, thereby causing considerable trouble for the local missionaries.[40]

In the Annual Letter for 1752, written by Florian Bahr, there is a sombre assessment of the situation facing the China mission:

The conditions this year have been the same as last year – that our mission has suffered no open persecutions, and we can hope to have peace in the future. When I speak of peace, I do not mean the liberty to preach the true law [i.e., the gospel], but rather a cessation of persecution, or, more likely, neglect by our persecutors. Not only in Beijing but also in the provinces where the persecution was the fiercest, our holy law has suffered no tribulations, though not to the extent that one can say the mission enjoys full security ... The concern these days lies not so much in the empty suspicion of an imagined rebellion, which the enemies of our law claimed during the last persecution, but rather in the real danger of an uproar throughout the empire, which has made things very troublesome in several provinces. Near the city of Jin Zhou Fu in Huguang province, many rebels had been hiding for some years, and among them, it was said, were several descendants of the previous dynasty. In conspiracy with other malcontents in other provinces, these rebels planned an uprising in five provinces (Huguang, Henan, Jiangxi, Jiannan, and Zejiang), and vowed that after killing the body of the empire, they would take its head, in Beijing, and thus overthrow the Manchu regime. Thanks to God's providence, a few days before the capital of Huguang province was to be burned and the imperial tax office plundered, one of the ringleaders was caught, and confessed under torture. From that time on no day has passed without someone getting caught, tortured, or executed; and there will be no end to the search until the chief ringleader has been caught.[41]

Bahr describes further how the searches pose a grave danger for European missionaries, and have caused the Austrian Jesuit Gottfried von Laimbeckhoven, who was working in the province, the endless misery of having to evade government troops. The reason is that 'some of the rebels claimed under interrogation that [their] leader was a prince of the previous dynasty, who had sojourned in Europe, and that from him the rebels in the mountains received daily directions and commands through the clouds, to the effect that he [the prince himself] would come the following winter with a large army to aid the rebels.'[42]

This story is corroborated by extensive reports in official Qing sources, specifically the memorials and edicts gathered in the Veritable Records (*shilu*) of the Qianlong reign. An intriguing point was the terminology used by the rebels: Tiantang (Heaven) as the name for one of their mountain strongholds, and Tai Xiyang (Great Western Ocean) as the abode of the Ming Pretender. The first term, 'Tiantang,' appeared in some sectarian precious scrolls as denoting heaven or paradise; it was also the term used by the Catholic mission to denote the Christian paradise. 'Tai Xiyang' had referred to the Far West, or Europe, since the late Ming. The interesting point in the government investigation was that although the provincial officials raised the connection of Europeans/Christians to the rebellion, the Qianlong emperor himself pointed out the error of identifying the two.[43]

If the Jesuit mission attracted no more than temporary suspicion during the hunt for the rebel leader, its fortunes still depended on an emperor who prized the Jesuits only as skilled artisans and interpreters. It was this same emperor, Qianlong, who had permitted the persecutions of 1746–8. In a 1748 letter to

Countess Maria Theresia in Munich, Florian Bahr, who was a court musician in Beijing, could not suppress his bitterness: 'The continuous persecutions of three years have ruined the mission; this Chinese Empire, which was so highly praised in books because of its laws, customs, and politics, has now, however, earned the name of a barbarian empire. Both the emperor and the mandarins who carry out his edicts are treating their own Chinese Christians in an extremely brutal manner; the treatment of foreigners is even more severe, and has completely overthrown the former well-treatment of Europeans.' The only consolation for Bahr was God's just punishment, in sending plagues and disasters to China: 'Famine, floods, drought, and rebellions are signs of God. Our emperor could have been, without doubt, the most fortunate emperor in the world, ruling over this prosperous empire, enjoying limitless wealth. But he has not improved a bit and has thrown himself entirely into this tragedy. Today God will change the heart of this obstinate emperor and send multiple disasters to his empire.'[44] These harsh words from Bahr had particular significance, because he was the only Jesuit in Beijing who engaged full time in pastoral work, since the emperor almost never summoned him for his musical duties; his confrères were first and foremost courtiers in the Forbidden Palace.

The Kangxi emperor, praised as a tolerant and wise philosopher-king ruling over a prosperous and ancient civilization in the earlier Jesuit discourse on China, had been succeeded by his favourite grandson, Qianlong, who is represented in the later Jesuit discourse as a barbarous tyrant who persecutes Christianity. Florian Bahr died in 1771 in Beijing; two years later the Society of Jesus was dissolved by the papacy. Deprived of their ecclesiastical mother, the fathers stayed on, themselves orphans in the court of a pagan emperor, Qianlong, who was both the chastiser of Christianity and the protector of the ex-Jesuits. The last of these Jesuits, such as the Portuguese José Bernardo de Almeida (1728–1805), who was the final Jesuit president of the Bureau of Mathematics, survived even Qianlong and died during the early years of Jiaqing. The patterns of the Jesuits' work of evangelization – baptizing abandoned infants, encountering secret sects, and facing persecution by a hostile state – already discernible in the mid-eighteenth century, would recur to trouble the Christian mission from the re-establishment of the Society to the end of the nineteenth century.

NOTES

1 *Lettres édifiantes et curieuses, écrites des missions étrangères, par quelques missionnaires de la Compagnie de Jésus*, 34 vols (Paris, 1703–76).

2 *Lettres édifiantes*, vol. 17, pp. 1–162; vol. 18, pp. 33–121, 248–311; vol. 19, pp. 1–205; vol. 20, pp. 1–45; vol. 22, pp. 44–98.

3 Adrian Hsia, 'The Transformation of Chinesia from Jesuitical Fiction to Jesuit College Drama: A Preliminary Survey,' *Sino-Western Cultural Relations Journal* 17 (1995): 14–16, 24–6.

4 See 'Relation d'une persecution générale qui s'est élevé contre la religion chrétienne dans l'Empire de la Chine en 1746,' ed. Jean-Gaspard Chanseaume, in *Lettres édifiantes*, vol. 27, pp. 279–412. For the Spanish account of the persecution in Fujian, see José Maria Gonzalez, *Misiones dominicanas en China (1700–1750)*, 2 vols (Madrid, 1958), I, pp. 359ff. For a study using official Qing sources, see Zhang Ze, *Qingdai jin jiao qi de Tianzhujiao* (Taibei, 1992), pp. 66–71.

5 *Handbook of Christianity in China*, vol. 1, *635–1800*, ed. Nicolas Standaert (Brill, 2001), pp. 382–4.

6 James Z. Lee and Wang Feng, *One Quarter of Humanity: Malthusian Mythology and Chinese Realities, 1700–2000* (Cambridge, MA, 1999), p. 27.

7 *Le P. Antoine Gaubil, S.J., Correspondance de Pékin, 1722–1759,* ed. Renée Simon (Geneva, 1970), p. 128.

8 *Lettres édifiantes*, vol. 13, pp. 315–27.

9 Ibid., vol. 6, pp. 87–90.

10 *Gaubil correspondance*, ed. Simon, p. 129.

11 *Lettres édifiantes*, vol. 16, pp. 300–17.

12 *Gaubil correspondance*, ed. Simon, p. 387.

13 Ibid., p. 536.

14 Ibid., pp. 535, 541.

15 Ibid., p. 43.

16 Ibid., p. 720.

17 *Litterae annuae*, 1752, Dillingen, Fugger-Archiv, published in R. Po-chia Hsia, *The Countess, the Jesuits, and the Orphans: Maria Theresia von Fugger-Wellenburg (1690–1762) and the Jesuit Mission in China and Vietnam* (Nettetal, 2006), document 72.

18 Angela K.C. Leung, 'Shiqi shihba shiji Changjiang xiayou zhi yüyingtang,' in *Zhongguo haiyang fazhan shi lunwen ji*, vol. 1 (Taibei, 1994), pp. 97–130; Leung, 'L'acceuil des enfants abandonnés dans la Chine du Bas-Yangtze aux XVIIe et XVIIIe siècles,' *Etudes chinoises* 4:1 (1985): 15–54; Leung, *Shishan yu jiaohua: Ming-Qing di cishan zuzhi* [Charity and moral transformation: Philanthropic organizations of the Ming and Qing periods] (Taibei, 1997).

19 *Fonti ricciane. Storia dell'introduzione del cristianesimo in Cina*, ed. Pasquale M. d'Elia, 3 vols (Rome, 1942–9), I, document 158, p. 99.

20 António de Gouvea, *Cartas ânuas da China (1636, 1643 a 1649)*, ed. Horácio P. Araújo (Lisbon, 1998).

21 This statement is based on the *Litterae annuae* of 1657–60, written by André Ferrão, Manoel Jorge, and Gabriel de Magalhães, in BA Jesuítas na Asia 49-V-14.

22 BA Jesuítas na Asia 49-V-19 fol. 597r.

23 Ibid., fols 597r, 634r, 652r.

24 Ibid., fol. 620r–v.

25 Ibid., fols 620v, 652r–v.

26 Ibid., fol. 639v.

27 BA Jesuítas na Asia 49-V-22 fols 610r–611v.

28 *Neue Weltbott*, vol. 1, part 8, no. 189 (1726); and *Lettres édifiantes*, vol. 20 (1731).

29 Leung, *Shishan yu jiaohua* (n18 above), pp. 96–100.

30 *Gaubil correspondance*, ed. Simon, pp. 512, 525.

31 Hsia, *The Countess* (n17 above), document 9.

32 This letter is not extant in the Fugger-Archiv. It is published in *Neue Weltbott*, vol. 4, 2. Halfband, no. 630.

33 Bahr published two works in Chinese, one a biography of St John Nepomuc and the other *Sheng yong xu jie*, an explanation of the prayers for the daily Marian devotions. See Xu Zongzi, *Ming Qing jian Yesuhui shi yizhu tiyao* (Shanghai, 1949; repr. Taibei, 1958), p. 414.

34 On abandoned infants, see *Neue Weltbott*, vol. 4 no. 630, fols 75ff.

35 Hsia, *The Countess*, document 78.

36 For a summary of Yang's arguments, see R. Po-chia Hsia, 'Etre chinois et chrétien: Religion et identité en Chine aux XVIIe et XVIIIe siècles,' in *Religion et identité*, ed. Gabriel Audisio (Aix-en-Provence, 1998), pp. 241–8. For Yang Tingyun, see Nicolas Standaert, *Yang Tingyun, Confucian, and Christian in Late Ming China* (Leiden, 1988).

37 BA Jesuítas na Asia 49-V-19 fols 660r–661v.

38 For an overview, see Richard H. Shek, 'Religion and Society in Late Ming: Sectarianism and Popular Thought in Sixteenth and Seventeenth Century China,' dissertation, University of California–Berkeley, 1980; and B.J. ter Haar, *The White Lotus Teachings in Chinese Religious History* (Leiden, 1992).

39 *Lettres édifiantes*, vol. 22, pp. 157–60.

40 *Gaubil correspondance*, ed. Simon, p. 382.

41 Hsia, *The Countess*, document 72.

42 Ibid.

43 For further source references, see ibid., notes to document 72.

44 Ibid., document 72.

35 / Boscovich in the Balkans: A Jesuit Perspective on Orthodox Christianity in the Age of Enlightenment

LARRY WOLFF

In 1760, Ruggiero or Roger Boscovich, or, in Croatian, Ruđer Bošković, the most celebrated Jesuit scientist of the eighteenth century, travelled to London and was elected to the Royal Society. In 1761, at the age of 50, he set out for Constantinople, intending to witness the transit of Venus, though in the end he arrived too late. In 1762, therefore, he departed from Constantinople, making an unusual overland voyage through southeastern Europe, with plans to visit Poland and ultimately St Petersburg, where he had also recently been elected to the Academy of Sciences. He thus travelled in Ottoman Europe, crossing the eastern ranges of the Balkan Mountains and passing through the territories of Thrace, Bulgaria, and Moldavia. Boscovich did not fail to make scientific observations as he travelled, concerning geography and astronomy, but he also kept a diary of his more personal impressions in southeastern Europe. He particularly recorded the details of his encounters with the Orthodox religion in this region, so the diary reveals his religious perspective on other denominations. It was published in French translation in 1772, in German translation in 1779, and in the original Italian in 1784, *Giornale di un viaggio da Constantinopoli in Polonia*.

Judging from his scientific activities and the recognition they received, the historian would have no hesitation in recognizing Boscovich as a Jesuit of the Enlightenment. His encounters with Orthodoxy suggest that his religious perspective was also, in significant respects, influenced by enlightened values. The case of Boscovich, especially as he appears in his travel diary, thus offers insight into the question of what it meant to be an enlightened Jesuit in the eighteenth century.

The bias of the Enlightenment against the Jesuits was virtually a cultural obsession, and it contributed to the smug consensus that eventually welcomed the suppression of the order in 1773. The case of Jean-Baptiste Girard, a Jesuit accused in 1731 of seducing a young woman while acting as her confessor, was transformed into a pornographic cartoon of clerical hypocrisy in 1748 in the novel *Thérèse philosophe* by the Marquis d'Argens. The intellectuals of the Enlightenment tended to caricature the Society as a fount of fanaticism and bigotry, but also of hypocrisy and depravity.[1] Even Jesuit erudition was regarded with contempt by those who advocated a new enlightened spirit of philosophical criticism. Yet recent scholarship has suggested that the picture was more complex, and that the Jesuits were, in fact, sometimes implicated and even integrated in the project of the Enlightenment itself. Marc Fumaroli has argued that enlightened perspectives in the eighteenth century were often nourished by Jesuit education, especially in rhetoric. 'Voltaire was perfectly aware,' writes Fumaroli, 'of the covert debt owed by his philosophical party to his beloved and admired teachers at the Collège-Louis-le-Grand.' Steven J. Harris and Marcus Hellyer have remarked on the important Jesuit presence in the scientific world of the eighteenth century, participating in experiments and explorations that were central to the concerns of the Enlightenment.[2]

Boscovich was the most famous of many Jesuit scientists, and was fully involved in the Newtonian, and even Galilean, legacy: a mathematician, physicist, and astronomer, studying such subjects as telescopes, optics, sunspots, aurora borealis, the theory of matter, the sphericity of the earth, and the orbits of the planets. To be a Jesuit scientist of the Enlightenment inevitably involved some tensions, and Boscovich found himself sometimes frustrated and uncomfortable with his Jesuit colleagues at the Collegio Romano in Rome. He maintained a tense scientific balance when he wrote about astronomical theory without fully embracing Copernicanism and without completely ruling out the possibility of a stationary earth. He was sometimes at odds with French *philosophes* such as d'Alembert, who disagreed with him on specific scientific issues but also were hostile to Jesuits in general. Boscovich himself was not necessarily enthusiastic about the *philosophes*, as when he wrote that he 'abhorred' Rousseau for his pointless paradoxes and 'total lack of reasoning.' Yet the values of the Enlightenment were unquestionably relevant to Boscovich in his scientific career, and his voyage through the Orthodox world in 1762 revealed that his Roman Catholic perspective on other religions was far from fanatical. If, as Fumaroli has provocatively suggested, one may contemplate the notion of 'Voltaire-jésuite,' one may reciprocally propose the possibility of 'Boscovich-philosophe.'[3]

This study of Boscovich travelling through southeastern Europe poses the question of how he perceived religious difference, and how he appreciated the significance of the Christian schism between Roman Catholicism and Greek Orthodoxy. Samuel Huntington has argued that that schism was fundamental for defining separate civilizations, by setting up a 'clash of civilizations' between the West and the Orthodox world. The voyage of Boscovich, in the context of

35.1. Boscovich in the Balkans: The voyage of Boscovich across Ottoman Europe in 1762 began in Istanbul (Constantinople). He travelled north from Kirkkilise to Karnobat in Bulgaria, and crossed the Danube at Galatz. He paused at Jassy (Iaşi) in Moldavia, and then travelled on to cross the Dniester and enter the Polish-Lithuanian Commonwealth at Zaleszczyki. From there he made the short trip to join the Jesuit community at Kamieniec.

other eighteenth-century travels through the Orthodox world, allows one to consider whether such a clash of civilizations was meaningfully apparent to intellectuals of the Enlightenment. At the same time, Boscovich, when he travelled through Thrace, Bulgaria, and Moldavia, participated in the cultural process by which the Enlightenment was mapping the continent of Europe according to a modern differentiation between Western Europe and Eastern Europe based on the secular principle of 'civilization.' Boscovich was a particularly apt observer of such European boundaries, between Roman Catholicism and Greek Orthodoxy, between Western Europe and Eastern Europe, because he himself was a native of Dubrovnik, or Ragusa, on the eastern coast of the Adriatic Sea. Though educated in Rome at the Collegio Romano, and fundamentally a man of Latin and Italian culture, he was able to understand the Slavic language spoken in Bulgaria because of the linguistic relation to his own original Slavic tongue.[4] Ragusa was a Roman Catholic city on the Adriatic, but it stood in close proximity to the territories of Bosnia and Serbia, which included large Orthodox populations, though subject to the Ottoman Empire. The interest and sensitivity of Boscovich when he encountered the Orthodox world in southeastern Europe was partly conditioned by his own origins and identity.

The voyage of 1762 was undertaken by Boscovich in the company of the departing English ambassador to Constantinople, James Porter, and his travelling party, including an Ottoman guide. Boscovich, in his diary, recorded details of religion and society in the villages and towns through which he passed, and thus produced a kind of religious geography of this region. In fact, he was himself a scientific geographer, who had been involved in surveying the Roman papal state in Italy. Now, however, he was functioning as a social scientist, informing himself about local religion and making use of the special instrument that made him uniquely sensitive to his social environment in southeastern Europe: his native Slavic language. His representation of the religious landscape may be considered in the context of contemporary enlightened perspectives on Orthodox religion. His Jesuit outlook may further encourage comparison, across the early modern centuries, to that of the sixteenth-century Jesuit Antonio Possevino, who probably knew more about Orthodoxy than anyone in the Catholic world at that time. Possevino visited Moscow in 1581 and published his *Moscovia* in 1586. As a Jesuit of the Catholic Reformation, Possevino may be contrasted with Boscovich, a Jesuit of the Enlightenment.

In Thrace: 'Everything among Men Is Relative'

The first reference to Orthodoxy in the diary came with the introduction of the Ottoman guide, or *mihmandar*, assigned by the sultan to accompany foreign ministers, such as James Porter, and to provide for their travel and accommodation. 'The *mihmandar* assigned to His Excellency was Haji Abdullah, Haji for having made the pilgrimage to Mecca,' noted Boscovich. 'He was born in the Morea of Greek Christian parents, and still as a child was made a slave in the recent conquest of that realm, was educated in the Mohammedan religion, but nevertheless still retains the Greek language.'[5] Haji Abdullah was therefore Orthodox by birth, and a convert to Islam. His case illustrated the plasticity of religion and identity in southeastern Europe. Boscovich, as he would soon have occasion to demonstrate, had retained the Slavic language of his own childhood in spite of a long career on the Italian side of the Adriatic.

The case of Haji Abdullah might have been especially interesting to Boscovich in view of the fact that the Jesuit's own religious origins have been disputed. His mother was of Italian descent and Roman Catholic, but his Slavic father, Nicholas Boscovich, from Hercegovina, may have been Orthodox. While descent from an Orthodox father would hardly have affected the way Boscovich was viewed by his eighteenth-century contemporaries in the Roman Catholic world, the issue has become more problematic in modern times, when religion has been perceived as a national marker in the Yugoslav and post-Yugoslav context. While the Jesuit Boscovich has been patriotically regarded as a part of the national intellectual legacy in Croatia, the possibility of an Orthodox father would carry the inconvenient implication that the Croatian hero was in part, by descent, a Serb.[6] Boscovich, though he came from Ragusa and designated his native language as Slavic, did not actually identify himself as either Serbian or Croatian. He did attribute his volatile temper to his 'Dalmatian' character, and is supposed to have quoted St Jerome in reciting the Confiteor: 'Parce mihi Domine, quia Dalmata sum.' Have mercy on me God, I am Dalmatian.[7]

On 25 May 1762, the first day out of Constantinople, travelling in Thrace, Boscovich and his Christian party stayed in a village that included some Christian Greek families. The travellers were lodged in the houses of the Greeks, and Boscovich remarked upon the Orthodox icons: 'In these Greek houses there were images of saints on paper, quite ugly and horrible [*ben brutte e orride*].' The houses themselves were 'extremely poor,' and the icons were perpetually illuminated by the light of an 'ugly and dirty lamp.'[8] Boscovich's aesthetic distaste for Orthodox religious art in the Byzantine style was entirely consistent with the aesthetic judgment of other travellers of the Enlightenment. John Glen King, the British Anglican chaplain in St Petersburg in the 1760s, had the very same reaction to Russian icons:

It might be expected that valuable paintings should also make a part of the riches of a church, in which religious pictures are not only an indispensable ornament, but are necessary in its worship ... Yet the same cause has not been so lucky as to produce one good painter or one capital picture in Russia: on the contrary these are the most wretched dawbings that can be conceived ... Nor shall we wonder that the national taste should be so depraved as to bear, nay, perhaps be delighted with such miserable performances, without colouring, drawing, or perspective, if we reflect that that people were for ages sunk in ignorance, and looked upon the making [of] pictures rather as a manufacture than fine art, which requires the exertion of superior genius and talents.[9]

The Jesuit Roman Catholic judgment of Boscovich was thus extremely close to the Anglican verdict of King; the two men were equally incapable of recognizing the aesthetic virtues of Orthodox religious art.

Their convergent views corresponded to a generally 'enlightened' perspective, rather than a denominationally religious perspective, on Orthodoxy, for Boscovich, just like King, saw the quality of the icons in relation to the backwardness of the social and economic context. King explained that Russians could not appreciate art because they were 'for ages sunk in ignorance,' while Boscovich saw the artistic failure of the icons in relation to the dirt and poverty of domestic life in southeastern Europe. Such perceptions of backwardness were crucial for the Enlightenment's construction of the difference in civilization between Western Europe and Eastern Europe, and Boscovich brought that enlightened perspective to his view of Orthodox religion.

Five days later, on 30 May, Boscovich was in Kirkkilise (today Kirklareli in Turkey), a largely Turkish village with some Greek families. The travellers considered staying in a Greek house, but finally decided that it was too dirty:

The mistress of the house said to the ambassador, who understands and speaks Greek optimally, that she could not understand how her house could not seem beautiful and magnificent to us, that she believed that in all the world there was no more beautiful and magnificent house than her own. That is a matter of education and the lack of ideas, and it is very true that everything among men is relative [*ogni cosa fra gli uomini è rispettiva*]. We went afterwards to see the house of the Greek priest, which was larger, but almost equally dark and incomparably more filthy [*incomparabilmente più sudicia*]. The room that was least unfit served as the church, which we could have had with the rest of the house, but even that was quite sordid.[10]

The travellers ended up sleeping in a tent, but Boscovich, in the course of considering and rejecting the houses of the Greek woman and the Greek priest, had the opportunity to confirm his perspective on the backwardness of the Orthodox community in southeastern Europe. Lack of education and lack of cleanliness formed a comprehensive picture of social backwardness.

Even more striking was his ironic perspective on how the ignorant Greeks failed to recognize the miserable condition of their own circumstances. It was almost a Voltairean parable, as in *Candide*, when the Château Thunder-ten-tronckh appeared to its residents, including Candide, to be the best of all possible châteaux in the best of all possible worlds. Just so, did the house of the Greek woman appear magnificent to her, and presumably the church of the Greek priest, sordid in the eyes of Boscovich, appeared perfectly suitable from the local Orthodox perspective, and perhaps the best of all possible churches. Boscovich may well have read *Candide*, which had been only just published in 1759. In fact, in November 1759, Boscovich came to Paris, the centre of French enlightened culture, and stayed for six months, sometimes attending meetings of the Académie des Sciences.

Boscovich in southeastern Europe learned the enlightened lesson that 'everything among men is relative.' Strikingly, the Jesuit seemed to see the implicit relevance of this lesson even for matters of religion, as in the case of the village Orthodox church. This view was radically different from Possevino's sixteenth-century Counter-Reformation understanding of the theological difference between Roman Catholicism and Byzantine Orthodoxy. For Boscovich, in fact, the character of Orthodoxy hardly seemed to be a matter of theology at all; the diary attributed an inferior character to Orthodoxy based on standards of poverty, ignorance, and dirtiness, rather than theology. Boscovich simply implied that the Greek Orthodox priest of Kirkkilise would be as deluded as the Greek woman if he believed that his sordid little church was beautiful and magnificent. The crucial issue was the difference between civilization and backwardness, as in the Enlightenment's distinction between Western Europe and Eastern Europe.

In Bulgaria: 'To Show Our Faces Completely Uncovered'

At the end of May, approaching Bulgaria, Boscovich watched local people flying kites and remarked that 'this children's amusement, so common in the Christian world [*in Cristianità*], has extended even to these regions.'[11] Boscovich, in his mental geography, preserved a sense of difference between the Christian world, his own world, and the Muslim world of the Ottoman Empire, which also included a Christian Orthodox population. On 1 June he arrived at the Bulgarian village of Canara, entering a new ethnographic domain, of Orthodox Bulgarians rather than Orthodox Greeks, but remaining still within the Muslim world of the Ottoman Empire. The houses of the Bulgarians were, he noted, 'very poor but very clean' – apparently an improvement over the houses of the Greeks, which had seemed to him both poor and dirty.[12] Boscovich, as he travelled, thus made several sorts of overlapping differentiations in his mental mapping: a political distinction between the Christian world and the Muslim Ottoman Empire, a socioeconomic comparison between the civilization of Western Europe and the backwardness of Eastern Europe, and a religious evaluation of the difference between Roman Catholicism and Greek Orthodoxy.

The Bulgarians were evangelized by both Byzantine and Roman missionaries in the ninth century, and ultimately accepted Christianity from Constantinople, along with the Slavonic liturgy created by Cyril and Methodius. Bulgaria was conquered by the Ottomans at the end of the fourteenth century, and, though there was some conversion to Islam and some colonial settlement of Muslim Turks, the Bulgarians largely preserved their Orthodox Christianity, under the spiritual leadership of the autocephalous archbishopric of Ohrid in Macedonia. Administratively, Bulgaria formed part of the *beylerbeylik* (governor generalcy) of Rumeli, and was divided by *vilayet* (province) and *sanjak* (district) according to the design of Ottoman government. In their religious and legal condition, the Bulgarians belonged to the Orthodox *millet* (religious community). In the eighteenth century, Bulgarians were still ruled politically by the Turkish sultan, while the Greek patriarch in Constantinople exercised ever greater religious prerogatives over the Bulgarians, culminating in the abolition of the Ohrid archbishopric in 1767. Yet the Bulgarian modern national revival may be dated to 1762, the same year that Boscovich travelled through the country. In 1762, in a monastery on Mount Athos, a Bulgarian monk, Father Paisii Hilendarski, composed his *Slavo-Bulgarian History of the Bulgarian Peoples, Their Emperors, and Their Saints*, celebrating the glory of medieval Bulgaria.

Boscovich himself was aware of the Slavic character of the Bulgarians, as linguistically and ethnographically distinct from that of the Greeks and the Turks he had hitherto encountered on his voyage. In Canara he recognized his own Slavic linguistic relation to the Bulgarian population, and made use of the approximate common language to learn more about Orthodoxy.

The language of the country is a dialect of the Slavic language, and since it is also my native language of Ragusa I could make myself understood and understand something of what they were saying. The religion is Christian, and their priests depend on the bishops, who recognize the patriarch of Constantinople. The priest holds the parish as if on lease from his bishop. The priest of Canara was a young man of 25 years, married, who already had children ... He was paid a piastre for every death, 10 for every baptism, 15 for every marriage, and had various other occasional earnings. He read his liturgy in Greek, but his ignorance and that of all these poor people is incredible. They do not know anything about their religion except the fasts and the festivals, the Sign of the Cross, the worship of some images which one sometimes finds among them, quite horrible and ugly, and the name of being a Christian ... They do not know either the Pater Noster, or the Credo, or the essential mysteries of the religion. They told me that their priest does not give any instruction to the people or the children, and each father instructs his own children. They nevertheless appeared to me very good people [*buonissima gente*].[13]

Boscovich, the scientist, here pursued an empirical study of the Orthodox religion in Bulgaria, based on the collection of data, presented in precise numbers, and obtained through the methodology of his serendipitous linguistic affinity with the villagers. His observations in the diary amounted to a sort of natural history of religion in southeastern Europe, for he took note of Muslims and Jews as well as Orthodox Christians.

The Orthodox priest was, of course, a married priest, with children, a fact that was noted by Boscovich with interest but without evident disapproval. Rather, for the Jesuit, the crucial issues of religious difference were ignorance and poverty, matters of civilization. Once again he noted the ugliness of Orthodox icons. Greater emphasis, however, was placed on the ignorance that Boscovich discovered in the Orthodox priest, a specifically religious ignorance of, for instance, the Pater Noster and the Credo. Yet the Jesuit said nothing about the theological issues of the Credo, about the *filioque* clause that separated Roman Catholicism from Byzantine Orthodoxy. Boscovich did not bother to qualify the priest or the community as 'schismatic,' according to the conventional formula of the Vatican. For in Boscovich's diary the distinction of Orthodoxy was not primarily theological but a matter of civilization, evaluated according to a secular standard even when measuring religious ignorance. Furthermore, in spite of his distaste for Rousseau, the ignorance of the Bulgarians was sympathetically interpreted by Boscovich as Rousseauist simplicity: 'They nevertheless appeared to me very good people.' If Boscovich was influenced by any sense of Jesuit mission, it was not about the propagation of the Roman Catholic faith, but much more a matter of education.

This same emphasis on the ignorance of the Orthodox world was evident in other enlightened travel accounts. William Coxe, an Anglican clergyman in Russia in the 1770s, made observations similar to those of the Jesuit Boscovich in Bulgaria.

The parochial clergy, who may, and ought to be, the most useful members of society, are in Russia the refuse of the people. It is literally true that many of them cannot even read, in their own language, the Gospel which they are commissioned to preach, but deliver from memory the service, a chapter of the New Testament, or part of a homily, which they repeat every Friday and Sunday. Nor is it in the least surprising that some are so illiterate, when we consider the scanty maintenance which they derive from their profession ... As the parish-priests are undoubtedly the principal sources from which instruction must be generally diffused among the lower class of people, if they, who ought to enlighten others, are so ignorant, how gross must be the ignorance of their parishioners! In no instance, perhaps, has the empress contributed more towards civilizing her people, than by instituting seminaries for the children of priests, by endeavouring to promote among the clergy a zeal for liberal science, and to rouse them from that profound ignorance in which they are plunged.[14]

Coxe made the connection between the ignorance of the Orthodox clergy and the ignorance of society at large, and he explicitly formulated this as a problem of civilization with his tribute to the empress, Catherine the Great, for her efforts at 'civilizing her people' by educating the clergy. The problem of ignorance and the program of education were concerns of the Enlightenment throughout Europe. In the case of Boscovich, it is possible that his sense of Jesuit mission made him especially sensitive to issues of education. Yet he used the issue of education as a secular standard by which to evaluate religious character in southeastern Europe.

On 13 June, in the mixed Turkish and Bulgarian village of Jenibazar, Boscovich received the same impression of Orthodox ignorance: 'Examining the various Christians of the place, I saw clearly that there was nothing Christian about them except the name and the baptism, for they know nothing but the Sign of the Cross. They do not even know the Pater Noster.'[15] On 15 June, in another Turkish and Bulgarian village, Boscovich was able to make a more detailed analysis of Orthodox Bulgarian ignorance:

There came towards us the Greek *papas*, or rather priest, and with the aid of my Slavic language I managed to understand that there were two priests in the village … For as much as I could recognize, the ignorance even of the priests is extreme. I had in my hand Suetonius, which I was then reading to divert myself, and there were pictures of the emperors. He asked me what it was, and when I told him it was the lives of the Roman emperors, he said, 'Ah! Constantine.' He told me they had no knowledge of any emperor other than Constantine. He had no knowledge of Rome, of the pope, or of any controversy of religion, and he asked me if there were priests in Rome. This great ignorance I confirmed also by using more than one interpreter so as not to rely only on what I understood myself. He was surprised that I was without a beard, and that the ambassador was too. For in those parts all men, priests and peasants, have beards, and it is shameful not to have one. He asked me if anyone had ordered me to shave, as a penance, and he was astonished when I told him that it was a common usage in our countries, and that not even bishops, kings, or emperors had beards. When he showed his astonishment, I told him that we wanted to show our faces completely uncovered.[16]

Here Boscovich gave a very clear idea of what it meant for him to 'examine' the ignorance of his interlocutor. With Suetonius in hand, Boscovich displayed a purely secular standard of erudition and ignorance, perhaps influenced by the traditional Jesuit emphasis on the classical curriculum. The ignorance of the Orthodox priest was demonstrated, paradoxically, by his failure to recognize the pagan emperors of Suetonius.

Boscovich made no mention of schism, as if aware that here, on the local level, the historical schism could have little meaning to an Orthodox priest who had never heard of the pope. The priest, as a paragon of ignorance, was unaware of 'any controversy of religion,' and seemed to understand the Roman Catholicism of Boscovich as a matter more of facial hair than of papal authority. The Jesuit accordingly declined to enter into any discussion with his Orthodox interlocutor, or even reflection in his personal diary, about the strictly religious difference between Orthodoxy and Catholicism. When asked about clean-shaven Roman Catholic chins, Boscovich replied with symbolic significance that 'we wanted to show our faces completely uncovered.' It was an enlightened affirmation of Rousseauist transparency. Boscovich declared his own identity, the self versus the other, the Jesuit face to face with an Orthodox priest, the clean-shaven enlightened intellectual in dialogue with the bearded and ignorant Bulgarian. Yet they communicated in a sort of linguistic fraternity, for they spoke related Slavic languages. For Boscovich, the most celebrated Jesuit scientist of the century, the encounter with Orthodoxy in Bulgaria became an occasion for defining his own identity, for recognizing his own uncovered face as reflected in the gaze of the other.

In Moldavia: 'A Land of Ignorance and Barbarism'

On his voyage Boscovich had the opportunity to reflect upon his own Jesuit identity in sharply contrasting opposition to the Orthodox clergy, but southeastern Europe also offered a multiplicity of religions and cultures as the context for this dualist polarity. In Bulgaria, in the town of Karnobat, Boscovich happened upon a trade fair, 'to which people came from as far as Constantinople, Turks, Greeks, and Jews, bringing the usual thousand things.' There may have been a thousand things for sale, but there were also in evidence at least three religions distinct from his own Roman Catholicism. Boscovich ended up sleeping in the house of a Turkish officer of the Janissaries. In a Balkan mountain village of Turks and Bulgarians, 'we found the people to be very good [*buonissima*].' In this case Boscovich was further impressed by the harmony between Muslims and Christians: 'The Bulgarians told us that they live in optimal agreement with the Turks; they even make mixed marriages.' A party of music-making gypsies also appeared on the scene. In another village there were Turks who seemed 'most humane' (*umanissimi*) and 'most civil' (*civilissimi*). Boscovich and his party were assigned lodgings in Jewish houses, but as these were 'poor and dirty,' the travellers transferred themselves to more appealing Armenian houses.[17]

While noting all this religious and ethnographic variety, Boscovich in Bulgaria remained aware that he was within the Ottoman Empire and therefore outside the Christian world. As the travellers made their way north through the Dobruja region, moving parallel to the coast of the Black Sea, they worried about finding fresh water, and Boscovich made technological observations on the digging of wells. Some local wells seemed especially familiar: 'There are many such also in Christendom [*in Cristianità*].'[18] He thus discovered points of comparison between the Christian and Muslim worlds, but he was conscious of the difference.

Boscovich identified the border between the Christian and Muslim worlds as the Danube River, separating Bulgaria from Moldavia. For Moldavia and Wallachia, the Romanian principalities, though ultimately under the sovereignty of the Ottoman sultan, were autonomously ruled by Greek Orthodox princes from the Phanariot Greek community in Constantinople. In the eighteenth century these Phanariot princes often purchased their appointments from the Ottoman Porte, and then ruled exploitatively over the Romanian populations in order to profit by the investment. The historian Barbara Jelavich has commented that 'what the Phanariot rulers accomplished was the establishment of a Byzantine island within the Ottoman empire.'[19] For Boscovich this Byzantine island, though emphatically Orthodox, belonged to the Christian world.

Boscovich encountered a Romanian community on the southern shore of the Danube even before entering Moldavia. He noted the presence of 'Christians who were speaking the Wallachian language, quite different from the Bulgarian.' It was a variant of Romanian, and Boscovich recognized the affinity to Latin of a Romance language. The Orthodox priest of the village appeared to Boscovich all too similar to the Bulgarian Orthodox priests of his earlier acquaintance – 'the *papas*, whom we found ignorant like the others.' Boscovich tested the learning of the priest by a secular classical standard, and found that 'his entire knowledge of ancient history consisted of knowing that there had been a certain great monarch named Constantine.'[20] In the observations of an enlightened Jesuit, Orthodoxy among the Romanians, as among the Bulgarians, presented the same features of ignorant backwardness.

On 23 June, Boscovich crossed the Danube and entered Moldavia. In the town of Galatz (Galati today, in Romania) the travellers were promptly lodged in an Orthodox monastery. It was a reminder that though this might be the Christian world, it was the Orthodox Christian world:

Moldavia is an entirely Christian province, governed by a Greek prince, chosen by the Porte ... The dominant religion is the Greek of the Schismatic Patriarch of Constantinople, though in various parts there are also some Catholic churches under the protection of Poland. In Galatz there was one not long ago, but now there is no longer any Catholic church or priest. There are, however, seven Greek Christian churches, and here, after the sojourn in Constantinople and after such a long voyage, we began to see crosses displayed in public and bell towers, and we heard the sound of the bells.[21]

In Moldavia the visible and audible tokens of Christendom were welcome to Boscovich, even though they were Orthodox in form and affiliation. The Greek patriarch in Constantinople was qualified as the 'Schismatic Patriarch,' as if that were his formal title, though Boscovich, describing his travels in Bulgaria, did not label the local Orthodox believers as schismatics.

In Moldavia, Boscovich claimed to discern an improved level of civilization, evident even in the Orthodox monastery where he was lodging. The monastery, 'although it is poor by comparison with the buildings of the civilized countries [*paesi colti*] of Europe, nevertheless appears magnificent after the houses, or rather huts, of the villages of Bulgaria.'[22] The standard by which Boscovich judged was entirely secular, a standard of civilization as measured by the quality of construction. That standard, furthermore, was relative, inasmuch as he could compare degrees of poverty and magnificence, from Bulgaria, to Moldavia, to the civilized lands of Europe, presumably Western Europe. In recognizing these degrees of more or less civilization, Boscovich clearly articulated the modern conceptual framework of backwardness and development with reference to Eastern Europe.

'We visited various churches that were rather dirty inside with the most miserable pictures,' reported Boscovich, predictably, about the Orthodox churches of Galatz. 'We found the sacred books in Greek characters printed in Venice.' As before, the Jesuit's observations of religious difference were negative only with reference to the secular issue of cleanliness and the artistic quality of the icons. Boscovich also encountered a Roman Catholic missionary priest in Galatz, who seemed to be manoeuvring on behalf of Catholicism without the authority of Rome: 'He seemed to me a fanatical man, whose brain had been turned.'[23] This was harsher than the judgment of ignorance that Boscovich generally applied to the Orthodox priests he met, and the term 'fanatical,' with reference to Roman Catholic missionary zeal, was very close in spirit to that of the Enlightenment of Voltaire. Boscovich himself, in his diary, never betrayed the slightest hint of interest in proselytizing among the Orthodox of southeastern Europe.

Furthermore, even the Christian world of Moldavia could be unfavourably compared to the Muslim world on the other side of the Danube. Boscovich found that the Turks who had accompanied the travellers from Constantinople now eagerly crossed the river to Galatz, 'to enjoy some days of liberty with women and wine, as in that city there is an incredible libertinism most shameful for Christendom [*vergognosissimo pel Cristianesimo*].' He reported that 'there are taverns everywhere, and every tavern has women who publicly prostitute themselves with impudence and inexpressible public scandal.'[24] In the observations of the Jesuit traveller, the boundary between the Christian and Muslim worlds, at the Danube, was not necessarily a notable moral boundary.

At Jassy (today (Iaşi), the capital of Moldavia, Boscovich was welcomed by the Greek Phanariot prince, Gregory Callimachus, who spoke to the Jesuit in Greek, through an interpreter, and offered coffee and sweets. 'I was truly surprised,' remarked Boscovich, 'not expecting on any account such refinements in such a land.' He claimed to be no less surprised at being welcomed as an intellectual (*letterato*), 'in a land of ignorance and barbarism.'[25] Again, Boscovich was sensitive to the sliding scale of backwardness and development in Eastern Europe, with the measure of civilization, in this case, being nothing other than the recognition of his own intellectual reputation. Yet Moldavia was nevertheless a land of ignorance and barbarism, and the former epithet was completely consistent with his judgments about the Orthodox clergy. Clearly, Boscovich saw the alleged ignorance of Orthodoxy as integrally related to the more general ignorance that he attributed to the lands of southeastern Europe. His seeming disparagement of the Orthodox religion was only one aspect of the cultural geography deriving from his travels in the region.

Boscovich met two Franciscans and a Polish Jesuit in Jassy, the representatives of Roman Catholicism, and they explained that 'the free exercise of the Catholic religion was not forbidden, but there are a thousand vexations of every kind' harassing the Roman Catholics. For instance, 'if they make a bell a little bigger, the schismatics want to take it by force for their own churches.' Noting the tension between Roman Catholics and Orthodox 'schismatics' in Christian Moldavia, Boscovich came to the dispassionate conclusion that the embroilment of the Catholics and the Orthodox in Jassy was 'for motives of interest, and not of religion,' centring on disputes over pieces of property, such as the bells.[26]

When Boscovich left Jassy, the prince showed regret at his departure, and expressed the wish he could stay longer, 'for at least five or six months.' Boscovich tactfully pleaded the marching orders from his superiors in Rome. He was, however, touched by the warmth of Gregory Callimachus, and recorded in his diary an exclamation of pity –'Povero Signore!' – for a prince who held his throne only at the pleasure of the sultan in Constantinople. Boscovich feared that the prince might be removed from his office and recalled to Constantinople, reduced to the condition of 'private life among the Turks, who regard and treat their Christian subjects incomparably worse than we do our Jews in the Ghetto.'[27] One hardly knows which to find more remarkable: the Jesuit's sympathy for the Orthodox Christian subjects of the sultan, or his explicitly parallel sympathy for the Jews of the Roman Ghetto. If Boscovich came to southeastern Europe with enlightened inclinations of sympathy towards other religions and denominations, the experience of travel had clearly exercised a powerfully reinforcing effect on this aspect of his character as a Jesuit of the Enlightenment.

In Poland: 'Notwithstanding the Difference of Religions'

On 12 July, while travelling through Moldavia towards Poland, Boscovich reached the little town of Ciarnuz on the Pruth River. This was the kernel of the future city of Czernowitz, which in the nineteenth century would become an important site of German Jewish culture within the Habsburg monarchy. In 1762 there were only twenty houses in the village, but that was sufficient to enable Boscovich to sample once again the religious heterogeneity of Eastern Europe: 'The greater part of the inhabitants are Greek Schismatic Christians, but there are many Jews who practise commerce on that frontier, and some of us had our quarters in their houses. There were three houses of Turkish merchants.'[28] Boscovich does not say whether he himself lodged with Orthodox Christians, Turkish Muslims, or Jews, but he seemed to have reached a state of ecumenical readiness for any of the above, with cleanliness the chief consideration for choosing among the options.

In fact, he was hurrying to reach the Commonwealth of Poland-Lithuania, because he knew there was a Jesuit college in Kamieniec (today Kamianets-Podilsky in Ukraine), and he hoped to obtain there medical attention for an injured leg. On 15 July the travellers crossed the Dniester River, the border between Moldavia and the Commonwealth. On one side, they took leave of the *mihmandar* who had accompanied them from Constantinople. On the other side, they arrived in the town of Zaleszczyki, newly founded by Stanisław Poniatowski, the father of Stanisław August, who would be elected king of Poland two years later. They visited Poniatowski's own palace, which was still under construction, but sufficiently finished for Boscovich to admire 'an optimal apartment furnished according to the usage of the civilized countries of Europe,' which was a great relief 'after such a long stretch of uncivilized barbarism.'[29] He did not mean to suggest that Poland itself was already one of the civilized countries of Europe, but rather that it was possible, in Poland, to furnish a room according to the civilized standard. Again he invoked the sliding scale of civilization, but if Poland seemed an improvement over Moldavia, which was already an improvement over Bulgaria, Boscovich did not attribute this to the dominant place of Catholicism in the Commonwealth.

The Commonwealth of Poland-Lithuania, though religiously diverse, recognized Roman Catholicism as the religion of state. Yet, in evaluating the refinement of Zaleszczyki, Boscovich seemed most impressed by the immigrant community of German Protestants, including the Protestant minister, 'young, quite polite, and full of erudition.' It was the leading Protestants who welcomed Boscovich 'with a thousand courtesies [*politezze*], notwithstanding the difference of religions and my condition as a Jesuit, which has not prevented me from receiving a great many courtesies in England and Holland.'[30] For Boscovich the standard of civilized conduct clearly transcended denominational distinctions. He expected civilized Protestants to overlook his Jesuit condition and treat him as an enlightened member of the Republic of Letters, and presumably he himself was prepared to do the same when confronted with men of other religions or denominations.

Nevertheless, he hurried onward, leaving Zaleszczyki for Kamieniec, eager to be among Jesuits; he was worried about his leg and the possiblity of gangrene. He spent one night on the road, on the way to Kamieniec: 'The next morning I arrived. My own people [*i miei*], one of whom I had known in Rome, treated me with all possible attention. But since there was no good doctor there, because he was away, and no good surgeon, I fell, to my great misfortune, into the hands of a most ignorant [*ignorantissimo*] man of his trade, who ruined me completely.'[31] He moved on to Warsaw, still recovering, but gave up on his plan to visit St Petersburg. What was striking about his misfortune at the Jesuit college in Kamieniec was that, having left behind the Muslim world of Ottoman Bulgaria and the Orthodox principality of Moldavia, and having finally arrived among 'my own people,' not just Catholics but Jesuits, he failed to find satisfaction. If a man was ignorant, he was ignorant regardless of the religious circumstances, and the practitioner at the Jesuit college was very ignorant indeed. This concluding episode in Boscovich's voyage illuminated the entire course of the journey by clarifying the secular meaning of 'ignorance,' the term Boscovich had employed from his very first encounters with Orthodox Christianity. His was not a bigoted disparagement of another religion for religious motives, but rather a part of the enlightened cultural geography by which he attempted to make sense of the worlds he witnessed, Muslim or Christian, Orthodox or Catholic, as he made his voyage and kept his diary.

The Last Jesuits

In 1582, Antonio Possevino, a Jesuit of the Catholic Reformation, prepared a treatise for Ivan the Terrible in Moscow entitled 'The Chief Points on Which the Greeks and the Muscovites Differ from the Latins in the Faith,' and featuring 'A

Brief, Clear, and Firm Refutation of the Errors of the Greeks and the Muscovites.' Possevino recognized the importance of theology: 'The fundamental
difference between the peoples of the East and Catholics is that the former,
rashly and in contravention of decisions taken in preceding Councils, have come
to the conclusion that an addition has been made to the Creed; namely, that the
Holy Ghost proceeds from the Father and from the Son.'[32] This was precisely the
sort of issue that did not even rate a mention in the diary of Boscovich two
centuries later. Boscovich was seemingly indifferent to the theological distinction between Roman Catholicism and Greek Orthodoxy, and, in his encounters
with Orthodox priests, he was obviously uninterested in any sort of 'firm
refutation of the errors of the Greeks.' In his account of Orthodoxy in Thrace,
Bulgaria, and Moldavia, Boscovich seemed to anticipate the principles of modern social science: making the observations of an anthropologist or sociologist of
religion, attempting to understand the significance of religious difference according to the social and cultural context. As a scientist of the Enlightenment, he was
gathering empirical evidence and looking for principles of explanation.

As a Jesuit of the Enlightenment, however, he seemed to anticipate the spirit
of modern ecumenism. When he wrote about the Bulgarians, 'They nevertheless
appeared to me very good people,' he meant, in spite of their ignorance, not in
spite of their Orthodoxy. The sympathetic engagement of Boscovich in Bulgaria
in the eighteenth century might call to mind the experience of Angelo Giuseppe
Roncalli as apostolic visitor and delegate in Bulgaria between 1925 and 1934.
For the future Pope John XXIII, the assignment to Bulgaria was intended as a
banishment to obscurity for his incipient liberalism, but Roncalli discovered a
tremendous sympathy for the Orthodox Bulgarians, and this interlude in his
career has been summed up as an 'apprenticeship' in ecumenism.[33]

Boscovich, when he finally published his travel account in the original Italian
in 1784, twenty years after his voyage and three years before his death, was
already, in some sense, putting his religious and cultural reflections before the
modern public. He was not publishing, as so often before, for the benefit of
scientific circles, and neither was he writing for his fellow Jesuits, since the
Society had been suppressed in 1773, and the Jesuits no longer existed as such.
In the twenty years since Boscovich had made his voyage, the Russian armies of
Catherine the Great had invaded the Ottoman Empire in southeastern Europe,
along the route he himself had travelled. Catherine attempted to make Greek
Orthodoxy the basis of insurrection against the sultan, and she envisioned in her
'Greek Project' the restoration of an Orthodox empire based in Constantinople.
In the 1770s the American colonies rose up against England and fought for their
independence, an enterprise that Boscovich thoroughly approved.[34] Though he
died in 1787, two years before the French Revolution, the world of the 1780s,

in which he published his travel account, was already buzzing with modern debates concerning political despotism, religious oppression, and national independence. When publishing the diary of 1762, twenty years later in 1784, Boscovich felt obliged to add a footnote to his mention of the Jesuit college at Kamieniec: 'When I was writing this diary, the order still existed, as may be seen from the dates.'[35] This remarkable annotation, suggesting as it did that the world might already have forgotten the Jesuits ten years after their suppression, underlined the fact that Boscovich was aware of publishing for a generationally transformed public in 1784. He saw himself as belonging to the generation of the last Jesuits. He may have seen his diary as offering some religious reflections from the Jesuit legacy to the modern public of future generations, which, as far as he knew, would regard the Jesuits entirely as past history.

Boscovich in the Balkans was fascinated by Orthodoxy, but the focus of his observations was not religious difference. He took stock of the Orthodox clergy with Suetonius in his hand. In the spirit of the Enlightenment, distinguishing between Eastern Europe and Western Europe, Boscovich judged the backwardness of the former according to the presumptive 'civilization' of the latter. The diary of his voyage through the Orthodox world was a study in poverty and dirtiness, the ugliness of the icons and the ignorance of the clergy. These same judgments on Orthodoxy appeared in accounts composed by other eighteenth-century travellers, a convergence suggesting that the Jesuit perspective of Boscovich was largely aligned with the values of the Enlightenment in this regard. At the same time, it was fully consistent with the Jesuit legacy to attempt to evaluate Orthodoxy in terms of ignorance and education. Boscovich, with his remarkable observation that 'everything among men is relative,' showed what it meant for a celebrated Jesuit scientist to articulate an enlightened perspective, even beyond his specifically scientific concerns, and address religious issues as a Jesuit of the Enlightenment.

NOTES

1 Robert Darnton, *The Forbidden Best-Sellers of Pre-Revolutionary France* (New York, 1995), pp. 91–2

2 Marc Fumaroli, 'The Fertility and the Shortcomings of Renaissance Rhetoric: The Jesuit Case,' in O'M. *Jes. Cult.*, p. 100; Marcus Hellyer, 'Jesuit Physics in Eighteenth-Century Germany: Some Important Continuities,' ibid., pp. 538–54; and Steven J. Harris, 'Boscovich, the "Boscovich Circle," and the Revival of Jesuit Science,' in *R.J. Boscovich: Vita e attività scientifica: His Life and Scientific Work*, ed. Piers Bursill-Hall (Rome, 1993), pp. 527–48.

3 Gennaro Barbarisi, 'Il letterato Boscovich,' in *Bicentennial Commemoration of*

R.G. Boscovich: Proceedings, ed. M. Bossi and P. Tucci (Milan, 1988) p. 169; Germano Paoli, 'Boscovich and Enlightenment,' ibid., pp. 227–35; John Pappas, 'Les relations entre Boscovich et d'Alembert,' ibid., pp. 121–48; Luigi Pepe, 'Boscovich and the Mathematical Historiography of His Time: An Unpublished Letter by d'Alembert,' in *R.J. Boscovich*, ed. Bursill-Hall, pp. 491–509; Roger Hahn, 'The Ideological and Institutional Difficulties of a Jesuit Scientist in Paris,' ibid., pp. 1–12; Marc Fumaroli, 'Voltaire jésuite,' *Commentaire* 69 (1995): 107–14.

4 Larry Wolff, *Inventing Eastern Europe: The Map of Civilization on the Mind of the Enlightenment* (Stanford, 1994), pp. 171–83; Elizabeth Hill, 'Roger Boscovich: A Biographical Essay,' in *Roger Joseph Boscovich*, ed. Lancelot Law Whyte (London, 1961), pp. 17–101; Ante Kadić, 'A Literary and Spiritual Profile of Boscovich,' in *R.J. Boscovich*, ed. Bursill-Hall, pp. 13–25; Sante Graciotti, 'Le idee e l'arte del letterato Boscovich,' ibid., pp. 27–39; P. Casini, 'Boscovich, Ruggiero Giuseppe,' in *Dizionario biografico degli Italiani*, vol. 13 (Rome, 1971), pp. 221–30.

5 Ruggiero Giuseppe Boscovich, *Giornale di un viaggio da Costantinopoli in Polonia dell'abate Ruggiero Giuseppe Boscovich* (Milan, 1966), p. 14.

6 Hill, 'Roger Boscovich,' p. 17; Kadić, 'A Literary and Spiritual Profile,' p. 13.

7 Paoli, 'Boscovich and Enlightenment,' p. 229.

8 Boscovich, *Giornale*, p. 17.

9 John Glen King, *The Rites and Ceremonies of the Greek Church in Russia: Containing an Account of Its Doctrine, Worship, and Discipline* (London, 1772; repr. New York, 1970), p. 33.

10 Boscovich, *Giornale*, p. 31.

11 Ibid., p. 33.

12 Ibid.

13 Ibid., pp. 34–5.

14 William Coxe, *Travels in Poland and Russia*, vol. 1, from *Travels into Poland, Russia, Sweden, and Denmark*, 5th ed. (London, 1802; repr. New York, 1970), pp. 142–4.

15 Boscovich, *Giornale*, pp. 59–60

16 Ibid., p. 62.

17 Ibid., pp. 42, 50, 64.

18 Ibid., p. 68.

19 Barbara Jelavich, *History of the Balkans: Eighteenth and Nineteenth Centuries* (1983; Cambridge, 1996), p. 104.

20 Boscovich, *Giornale*, p. 74.

21 Ibid., pp. 79–80.

22 Ibid., p. 80.

23 Ibid., pp. 81–3.

24 Ibid., p. 82.

25 Ibid., p. 106.
26 Ibid., p. 108
27 Ibid., p. 111.
28 Ibid., p. 121.
29 Ibid., p. 125.
30 Ibid., p. 126.
31 Ibid., p. 128.
32 Antonio Possevino, *The Moscovia*, trans. Hugh Graham (Pittsburgh, 1977), pp. 80–3.
33 Paul Johnson, *Pope John XXIII* (Boston, 1974), pp. 44–60.
34 Kadić, 'A Literary and Spiritual Profile,' p. 23.
35 Boscovich, *Giornale*, p. 122.

36 / A Jesuit *Beata* at the Time of the Suppression in the Viceroyalty of Río de la Plata: María Antonia de Paz y Figueroa, 1730–1799

ALICIA FRASCHINA

My purpose in this essay is to describe and analyse the experience and practices[1] of María Antonia de San José, a *beata*, or woman living under informal religious vows of the Society of Jesus, in the southernmost part of the colonial Spanish Empire in the second half of the eighteenth century. By the end of her life she had become a social agent with her own identity.[2] I shall examine how she successfully constructed her identity and space, how she became part of the network of solidarity that developed among supporters of the Jesuits, and how she designed strategies and practices that enabled her to make use of the limited freedom allowed to women at that time.

In order to overcome the marginalization of Spain in both the European and the international sphere, Pedro Rodríguez de Campomanes, the president of the Council of Castile, carried out a series of reforms in which secularization occupied a prominent place.[3] The royal decree of 1767 expelling the Society of Jesus from all Spanish-held lands helped to achieve this secularization.

The decree had diametrically opposite consequences for the parties involved. For the Spanish crown, it was a fundamental step in implementing its regalist policy towards the church.[4] For the Jesuits, it meant expatriation. Forced out of Río de la Plata – the region specifically dealt with in this essay – 455 Jesuits sought refuge in the Pontifical States, where they had to rebuild their lives in the midst of constant uncertainty.[5]

After the expulsion and suppression of the Society of Jesus, the life of María Antonia de San José, a *beata* of the Society, suffered a dramatic change. Details on the first years of her life are scarce. Tradition has it that she was born in Santiago del Estero, in the department of Córdoba del Tucumán, which was part of the Viceroyalty of Peru at the time. She belonged to the Paz y Figueroa family, some of whose members were American-born grantees, soldiers, and members of the town council.[6] At 15, when most of the young women of her age and social rank either married or, in a few cases, entered a convent, María Antonia took the Jesuit cassock and made informal vows of poverty and chastity 'before the altars,'[7] since the Jesuits had no third order or female branch. She would be a *beata*[8] in the Society of Jesus: her actions would be circumscribed neither by monastic life nor by family obligations. Within her social space, she had achieved a perfectly well defined place: for the rest of her days, she would work alongside the Jesuit fathers, helping them in the administering of the Spiritual Exercises and sharing their immense prestige in the region, where they ran large estancias and had organized settlements of indigenous people.[9] In the city they had built a church, a chapel for the native people, a school, and a retreat house.[10] The last was her home for more than fifteen years; there, she helped the fathers give the Ignatian Spiritual Exercises.

For María Antonia de San José, the expulsion of the Jesuits had a dual impact: on the one hand, it caused her anguish and pain[11] – an anguish that marked her whole life – and on the other, it provided her with new options and served as an impetus to future activities.

In the same year in which the Jesuits were expelled, she devoted herself to organizing the giving of the Spiritual Exercises in the space she had known and lived in since her birth, the town of Santiago del Estero and two small neighbouring villages. Two Mercedarian friars preached the series of Exercises,[12] since women were not allowed to preach publicly. She remained in her native town for six years, a decision perhaps based on prudence, since the bishop, Manuel Abad Illana, was firmly anti-Jesuit.[13] But in 1771 a new prelate arrived in the diocese. María Antonia saw the chance to expand her area of influence and to request permission to carry on with her work. She left her home town and went north to seek out the new bishop. At that moment she made an important decision: she would be a pilgrim and an apostle.

She wore and carried with her a number of items that would serve to introduce her and make her intentions clear. She took the wooden cross that was to accompany her throughout her life, the same one the Jesuits had used when visiting the sick and hearing confessions.[14] She also took with her an image of Our Lady of Sorrows,[15] who would become the 'abbess' of a number of her retreat houses, and a Jesuit cloak that one of the priests had given her at the time of the expulsion of the order.[16]

The many public testimonials on her behalf and her abundant correspondence for nearly two decades,[17] mainly with the former Jesuit, and her compatriot, Father Gaspar Juárez,[18] who lived in Rome, and with Ambrosio Funes,[19] a well-known resident of the city of Córdoba and a former student of Father Juárez, give a good indication of the objective of her missionary activities over the years. Actually, she had two objectives: one explicit and the other private. The first one, which she repeatedly expressed, was 'to achieve the greater glory of God and the good of souls,'[20] 'to maintain the Holy Exercises of the Glorious St Ignatius of Loyola so that this beneficial work would not be lost to the world,'[21] 'to reform customs,'[22] and 'to convert sinners.'[23]

The other objective, which is revealed in her correspondence with Father Juárez and Funes, to whom she appears to have expressed her most intimate concerns, was the restoration of the order. She wanted to see the Jesuits 'restored in honour and exultation,'[24] and she was adamant that she wanted them 'wearing their own cassocks.'[25] Alternating between trust in God and awareness of the uncertainty of human actions, she took the necessary steps to keep the Ignatian spirit alive throughout the Viceroyalty of Río de la Plata.

From then on, her activities were directed towards achieving this objective. Her bishop gave her permission to organize the giving of the Spiritual Exercises, to beg publicly for alms to support the retreatants, and to establish retreat houses, of which she might be the abbess.[26] For two years she travelled through the northern and central regions of the present territory of Argentina; she organized the Spiritual Exercises in the cities of Tucumán, Salta, Valle de Catamarca, and La Rioja. In 1777 and 1778 she lived in Córdoba,[27] where the Jesuits had been an important presence. There, in the seventeenth century, the Jesuit fathers had founded Monserrat College and the first university in the region. This university was attended by students from Córdoba and Buenos Aires, Salta, Santa Fe, and Santiago del Estero.[28] It was a fertile environment, in which useful, lifelong relationships were built. There María Antonia became part of a network of solidarity centred around former Jesuits now relocated in the Pontifical States,[29] former Jesuits who even managed to obtain for her a *carta de hermandad* issued in Russia, where the Jesuits were still active.[30] She formed a close friendship with Ambrosio Funes and, through him, with the people of Córdoba and other cities in the viceroyalty. She became part of a transatlantic network that carried on an active correspondence for more than twenty years, during which time the members exchanged words of affection, spiritual aid, money, gold, indulgences, devotional images, reports of the new itineraries of some of the members, stories, and explanations of what was going on in Europe – the French Revolution, the synod of Pistoia, which threatened papal authority – and in America – the implementation of the Bourbon reforms.[31]

While Father Juárez was attempting to adjust to his new situation in Rome by devoting himself to the celebration of the Divine Office and writing about the Virgin and American flora,[32] and Funes was suffering under the new colonial order in Córdoba, which had replaced the one set up largely by the Jesuits,[33] María Antonia de San José arrived in Buenos Aires, in September 1779, determined to pursue her goals.[34]

At the time, Buenos Aires was undergoing unprecedented physical, demographic, economic, and political growth. In accordance with the plan of the Bourbon reforms, the city was being transformed from a peripheral city of the Viceroyalty of Peru into the capital of the new Viceroyalty of Río de la Plata. An Enlightenment culture was emerging that was leading some inhabitants towards a secular cosmovision, while others remained loyal to the principles of scholasticism.[35]

It was in this Buenos Aires, in the midst of this complete transformation, that María Antonia arrived. The presence of the Bourbon state was even stronger here than in the interior of the viceroyalty. She had to form new alliances in order to adapt to the new situation, and her adjustment was long and difficult.[36] On her arrival, she and her group of women companions from Santiago del Estero were insulted, stoned, and accused of being witches.[37] The viceroy, Juan José de Vértiz, rejected her request for permission to organize the giving of the Spiritual Exercises, for he correctly perceived that what she was proposing 'smacked of Jesuitism.'[38] The two retreat houses the Jesuits had run in Buenos Aires prior to the expulsion had, in accordance with the new rationality, been turned into an orphanage and a prison for women.[39]

Shortly after María Antonia's arrival, a new bishop, Friar Sebastián Malvar, a Franciscan, took office. He had frequent confrontations with the viceroy and became a well-known public figure. Although the two authorities at first agreed to reject María Antonia's requests, within a year the bishop had become her closest ally. He granted her permission to carry out her work, shared meals with the retreatants, made himself available to her, offered her monetary assistance, and even asked for her advice and support.[40] Perhaps the underlying situation of conflict between the two centres of power – the secular and the religious – was one of the reasons the bishop so strongly supported María Antonia. She, fully aware of her plight, used the situation to her advantage.

Four years after María Antonia's arrival in Buenos Aires, some 25,000 persons had made the Spiritual Exercises in the two houses she had rented for the purpose,[41] a height never achieved in the city during the Jesuit period. To realize her desire, she had to choose an appropriate location, find priests to preach the Spiritual Exercises, and beg for alms in the city and in the rural areas – since the retreatants were not required to pay a fee,[42] and the income from the estancias that had supported the Exercises was no longer available.[43] She also had to make repeated requests that the formalities in Europe be streamlined – the petition of favour from the Holy See had to be submitted through Father Juárez to the Council of the Indias; that indulgences be granted to the retreatants; and that she be allowed to appoint both her own female successor and the director of the retreat house.[44]

Finally, in 1792, after buying and being granted some land,[45] María Antonia applied to Viceroy Arredondo and the city council for permission to build the Casa y Beaterio de Ejercicios Espirituales, or House of the Spiritual Exercises and Home for Beatas. After twenty-five years of hard work she was on the verge of fulfilling her dream of having her own space. She submitted her highly ambitious plan, which included a chaplain's house, with an entry hall and kitchen, a living area for the porter, an interior chapel, twenty-four cells on the main and second floors, and interior courtyards for the retreatants; a large refectory, a pantry, a bread-making room, a kitchen, and a courtyard for the retreatants' servants; twenty-seven cells for the *beatas*, together with a pantry and refectory, two courtyards, and a choir, also for them; infirmaries for the servants and *beatas*; three cells for temporary guests; a lower choir; a visitors' parlour; a porter's office; a church; and ovens.[46]

She had to negotiate the building of the Casa, since the city representative and the members of the city council, though they accepted her plan, also raised objections and specified that certain requirements must be met: a public church could not be built, and the new retreat house would also have to serve as a detention centre for women sent there by the ecclesiastical and civil judges. At the financial level, the authorities insisted that some buildings must be designed to produce income, and they promised to raise the 70,000 pesos that 'must be available' in Córdoba and Buenos Aires, an amount that, having belonged to the Jesuits, was in the hands of the Committee of Administration of the Jesuits' Assets.[47] This amount would be in addition to the 18,000 pesos that had been offered by Bishop Malvar, her unconditional benefactor.[48]

The Casa was built according to the approved plan, but the city authorities never produced the 70,000 pesos, nor did the bishop keep his promise, because, as he himself reported from his new see of Santiago de Galicia, 'he saw his name neither on the building itself nor on the requested permits.'[49] The retreat house and *beaterio* – which was huge by the standards of Buenos Aires – was built with the charitable contributions of the people.[50] It also benefited from a vast network of assistance, which extended as far as Paraguay, where the Jesuits had had a very strong presence.[51]

The nature and degree of María Antonia's success – seventy thousand retreatants were reported during her lifetime,[52] and the buildings were grand – lead one to wonder why the people involved did what they did. What arose to account for the success of a *woman* in a patriarchal society; a *layperson* trying to carry out an essentially religious work; a *beata* in a dissolved order; and *a person abandoned financially* by both church and secular authorities, after they had promised her large sums of money?

In response, I shall simply put forward a hypothesis. In her daily activities,

María Antonia established her identity in accordance with what she had experienced in her youth and with what her fellow human beings expected and needed from her. She built up for herself and took on the roles given to her by those to whom she ministered. She became a 'vehicle of God,' like other *beatas* in both Europe[53] and America;[54] practised Ignatian 'indifference';[55] and considered herself 'chosen by God,' a God who had 'created her through his goodness,'[56] and given her 'the gift of moving hearts.'[57]

Her contemporaries regarded her as a 'mediator of divine graces.' When they suffered dangerous illnesses or a difficult childbirth, they asked her for the crucifix with a Christ child that she wore around her neck, 'her' Manolito (Jesus Emmanuel), who would perform a miracle.[58]

She was an 'apostle,' that is, she brought the word of God to people who had been virtually abandoned by the rest of the clergy since the departure of the Jesuits.[59]

She considered herself an heir of the Jesuits, and even wrote to Father Juárez: 'Jesus Christ is the one who directs my steps to gather the grain that Your Grace is not permitted to gather because of your profession. And since this grain has been abandoned for so many years, it is being collected now in abundance.'[60]

She used the power of images and material objects to emphasize her words.[61] In her retreat houses, she set up oratories and placed devotional images of Jesus the Nazarene, St Ignatius, St Stanislas, St Cajetan, and Our Lady of Sorrows.

She organized street processions, ordered masses to be sung in honour of St Joseph and St Ignatius,[62] obtained indulgences from the bishops of Buenos Aires and from the Holy See – through former Jesuits living in Rome – for the poor,[63] for her benefactors,[64] for those celebrating the feasts of the Most Holy Virgin,[65] and for the retreatants.[66]

She made sure that the food in her retreat house was good and abundant, to the point that she was able to share it with prisoners and beggars.[67]

She organized series of the Spiritual Exercises for the people of the city and the countryside, for men and women of all social segments, for 'Spaniards,' mestizos, and Africans, for priests, and for aspirants to the priesthood.[68]

All her activities were marked by a strong Ignatian stamp:[69] the Spiritual Exercises, the devotional practices, the adapting to the specific needs of each human being, the helping 'souls' – that is, the soul and the body, as evidenced by her corporal works of mercy – and the spreading of the consolation of God's Word throughout the globe, 'even to Flanders, if necessary,' as she said in her letters.[70]

The expulsion of the Jesuits meant that some of the spaces of power and influence carved out and occupied by the fathers were left empty. One of these lacunae, the giving of the Spiritual Exercises, was filled by the *beata* María

Antonia de San José. She rose from being a woman in a subordinate position, dependent on an all-male order, and limited to domestic chores in an absolutely restricted private space to becoming one who created and carried out a leadership role, which she assumed in full awareness, considering herself an heir of the expelled order in her organization of the Spiritual Exercises and the pious public manifestations accompanying them.

Her membership in the network of solidarity that developed around the expelled Jesuits expanded her sphere of influence to unimaginable lengths. The founding of a Casa de Ejercicios and *beaterio* in the fastest-growing southern city under Bourbon influence was the result of her clear sense of mission, her ability to negotiate, and the economic independence afforded her by the charity of the people.

She introduced substantial innovations in the Casa: far from reflecting the existing social class system, it was a place where the Spiritual Exercises made by the women were shared with retreatants from the most diverse social backgrounds and ethnic groups.

She achieved all this despite being immersed in a highly patriarchal society, which had questioned both her ability and her intentions. This same society denied her the funding she had been promised, and forced her to provide rooms for women sent to her by the civil and ecclesiastical judges.

A biography of María Antonia that circulated throughout Europe in several languages during her lifetime was largely based on her letters, but in an effort to 'protect her,' it described her in terms of the prevalent stereotype: a poor, obscure, and powerless woman.[71] Her achievements were interpreted by her contemporaries from the perspective of faith. They defined her as 'chosen by God,'[72] a person whose miracles and prodigious works none the less had to be kept quiet. Only after her death, in his eulogy, did the Dominican friar Julián Perdriel recognize her publicly as 'the Xavier of the West.'[73]

María Antonia de San José died in her retreat house in Buenos Aires on 7 March 1799.[74] Only one section of the Casa had been completed by then. In Europe the possible restoration of the Jesuit order had been rumoured, and it actually took place in 1814. She, however, who had so strongly desired and intuited this outcome, could not be present for it. When the Jesuits returned to Río de la Plata in 1836, the University of Córdoba was being run by the secular clergy;[75] the estancias had been ruined; the missions among the indigenous people had all but disappeared.[76] In Tucumán, Salta, Córdoba, and Buenos Aires, however, a *beata* from a small, impoverished city in the interior of the viceroyalty had managed to keep Ignatian spirituality alive by organizing the Spiritual Exercises and forging unexpected ties that had undermined the effectiveness of the royal decree expelling the Jesuits. This decree, although it had been completely effective in almost all the things it had proposed to do – expel the Jesuits from the Spanish colonies, confiscate their property for the use of the state, and transfer their retreat houses and missions to the secular clergy or other orders – had not totally eliminated the Jesuit heritage in the southernmost part of the Spanish Empire.

NOTES

I am indebted to Asunción Lavrin and Ricardo Cicerchia for helping me in my research work on nuns and *beatas* in Buenos Aires.

1 My approach has been inspired by the work of Michel de Certau, *La escritura de la historia* (Mexico City, 2nd ed. 1993); and Roger Chartier, *Escribir las prácticas. Foucault, de Certau, Marin* (Buenos Aires, 1996), especially 'Estrategias y tácticas. De Certau y las artes de hacer,' pp. 55–72.

2 For these concepts, see Roger Chartier, *El mundo como representación. Historia cultural: Entre práctica y representación* (Barcelona, 2nd ed. 1995), especially 'Prólogo a la edición española,' pp. i–xii, and 'Debates e interpretaciones,' pp. 13–104.

3 See Pedro Rodríguez Campomanes, *Reflexiones sobre el comercio español a Indias* (Madrid, 1908), pp. 230–51.

4 See Alberto de la Hera, *Iglesia y Corona en la América española* (Madrid, 1992), pp. 396–500.

5 José Andrés-Gallego, 'Consecuencia de la expulsión de los jesuitas en América: Primer balance,' in *Congreso internacional, Jesuitas 400 años en Córdoba*, 4 vols (Córdoba, Argentina, 1999), II, pp. 149–75; and Hugo Storni, 'Jesuitas argentinos exiliados por Carlos III en 1767,' *Archivum* 9 (Buenos Aires, 1967): 39–56.

6 See Justo Beguiriztain, 'Disquisiciones y aclaraciones sobre patria, linaje y fecha de nacimiento de la Beata de los Ejercicios,' *Estudios* 68 (1942): 220–9. After careful research I have concluded that, in the absence of sources, it cannot be known for certain who her parents were, though it is known, on the basis of several testimonials, that she was a member of the Paz and Figueroa family.

7 See Julián Perdriel, 'Oración fúnebre pronunciada por el R.P. Fray Julián Perdriel, prior del Convento de Predicadores de Buenos Aires, en las solemnes exequias que se celebraron en la iglesia de Santo Domingo por el alma de la señora beata doña María Antonia de la Paz, el día 12 de julio de 1799,' in José María Blanco, *Vida documentada de la Sierva de Dios María Antonia de la Paz y Figueroa, fundadora de la Casa de Ejercicios de Buenos Aires* (Buenos Aires, 1942), pp. 380–99.

8 'Lay pious houses for men and women called *beaterios* appear in Spanish records as early as 1406, but more commonly lay pious women called *beatas* either followed the eremitic tradition, took third order vows with a regular order, became affiliated with a particular convent, lived quietly alone or congregated with other women in

their own homes. Until the Council of Trent they were generally not cloistered, having more freedom than nuns to become teachers, writers, preachers, alms collectors, nurses, prophetesses, and prayer leaders at funerals. *Beatas* occupied an ambivalent position because they attempted to create a viable space for women that encompassed both the sacred and the worldly and yet remained separate from the strict enclosure of the convent and the responsibilities of the household … Tridentine reforms placed *beaterios* under the direct authority of the regular clergy' (Nancy van Deusen, 'Defining the Sacred and the Worldly: *Beatas* and *Recogidas* in Late-Seventeenth-Century Lima,' *Colonial Latin American Historical Review* 6 [Fall 1997]: 441–77).

The development of *beatas* and *beaterios* in Latin America diverged over time and space. For Río de la Plata, more research must be done; at present we know only that there were *beatas* in various towns. For Santiago del Estero, see Luis Allen Lascano, 'Historia de la Compañía de Jesús en Santiago del Estero, capital del Tucumán, siglos XVI–XVII,' *Archivum* 9 (1967): 154–5; for La Rioja, Raul Molina, 'La educación de la mujer en el siglo XVII y comienzos del siguiente. La influencia de Da. Marina de Escobar,' *Historia* 5 (Buenos Aires, 1956): 11–32; for Córdoba, Joaquín Gracia, *Los jesuitas en Córdoba* (Buenos Aires and Mexico City, 1940): 472–3; for Santa Fe, Guillermo Furlong, *Historia del Colegio del Salvador, 1617–1841* (Buenos Aires, 1944), p. 24; and for Buenos Aires, R. Lafuente Machain, *Buenos Aires en el siglo XVIII* (Buenos Aires, 1980) p. 244.

9 See Lascano, 'Historia de la Compañía,' pp. 151–3; Jorge Troisi Melam, 'Los colegios de la provincia del Paraguay y sus esclavos,' in *Congreso internacional* (n5 above), vol. 1, pp. 339–52.

10 Archivo de la Provincia de Santiago del Estero, 'Testimonio de los inventarios que se practicaron al tiempo del secuestro que se hizo de los Regulares Expulsos de este Colegio de Santiago del Estero, año 1767,' Leg. 4, expediente 21, in Lascano, 'Historia de la Compañía,' p. 158. See also Carlos Leonhart, 'Ensayo histórico sobre las Casas de Ejercicios en la Argentina y apostolado de la Venerable Madre Sor María Antonia de la Paz,' *Estudios* 31 (1922): 215–24.

11 Archivio di Stato di Roma, Amministrazione Camerale del Patrimonio ex Gesuitico, buste 7–8, corrispondenza riguardante l'esecuzione del breve di soppressione, 1773–5 (hereafter ASR), about 300 pages, letters from María Antonia de San José and Don Ambrosio Funes to the former Jesuit Gaspar Juárez. ASR, María Antonia de San José to Gaspar Juárez, 6 December 1783, fols 47–9: 'Extraño mucho que no sospeche V.M. cual sea la causa de mis fatigas y crueles penas … Pues ¿cuál ha de ser sino ver la Compañía de mi Manuelito o de mi Jesús retirada, extrañada y desterrada de estos países en los últimos confines del mundo? Este es mi tormento, este es mi desconsuelo.'

12 ASR, María Antonia to Juárez, 26 May 1785, fol. 135; Archivo del Convento de la

Merced, Córdoba, Argentina, Libro 18 fol. 108. The *beata* María Antonia de San José was granted a *carta de hermandad* by the Mercedarian order.

13 See Cayetano Bruno, 'El Doctor Don Manuel Abad Illana, decimocuarto obispo del Tucumán,' in *Historia de la Iglesia en la Argentina*, 12 vols (Buenos Aires, 1966–81), VIII, pp. 157–60.

14 See Guillermo Furlong, 'Un valioso documento sobre la Madre Antula,' *Estudios* 2 (Buenos Aires, 1947): 363–78.

15 Archivo General de la Nación, Buenos Aires, Argentina (hereafter AGN), Sala IX 5.9.3, Intendencia de Córdoba, Auto del obispo del Tucumán para la Beata Madre María Antonia, 1773.

16 In 'El estandarte de la mujer fuerte,' in Blanco, *Vida documentada* (n7 above), p. 423.

17 ASR (n11 above); see also Pedro Grenón, *Los Funes y el Padre Juárez*, 2 vols (Buenos Aires, 1920). Grenón compiled the letters Juárez sent over a thirty-year period to Gregorio and Ambrosio Funes in Córdoba.

18 See Guillermo Furlong, *Gaspar Juárez y sus 'Noticias Fitológicas,' 1789* (Buenos Aires, 1954). Father Gaspar Juárez was born in Santiago del Estero on 11 June 1730. He became a Jesuit in 1748 and was professor of philosophy, theology, and canon law at the University of Córdoba.

19 See Enrique Udaondo, *Diccionario biográfico colonial* (Buenos Aires, 1975). Ambrosio Funes studied at Monserrat College and eventually became 'procurador de la ciudad, diputado del Real Consulado, alcalde de primer voto, gobernador interino de Córdoba.' For a description of the society of Córdoba, see Lilians Betty Romero Cabrera, *La casa de Allende y la clase dirigente, 1750–1810* (Córdoba, 1993). Ambrosio Funes became a member of the Allende family through his marriage.

20 AGN Sala IX 31.3.1, Solicitud que dirigió María Antonia de San José al Ilustrísimo Señor Malvar, obispo de Buenos Aires, 1784; and ASR, María Antonia to Juárez, 7 August 1787, fols 237–8.

21 AGN Sala IX 5.9.4, Intendencia de Córdoba, 1774–9, María Antonia de San José, beata de la Compañía, to Viceroy Cevallos, 6 August 1777.

22 AGN Sala IX 31.3.1, Licencia del obispo de Tucumán, don Manuel de Moscoso y Peralta, a María Antonia de San José, 1773.

23 María Antonia to Father Toro, a Mercedarian friar, October 1783, in Blanco, *Vida documentada*, p. 170.

24 Ambrosio Funes to Juárez, 6 August 1784, ibid., p. 191.

25 María Antonia to A. Funes, ibid., p. 319.

26 AGN Sala IX 5.9.3, Intendencia de Córdoba, Auto del obispo de Tucumán, don Manuel de Moscoso y Peralta, Licencia para la Beata María Antonia de San José, 11 September 1773.

27 ASR, María Antonia to Juárez, 26 May 1785, fols 133–8.

28 See María Cristina Vera de Flachs, *Finanzas, saberes y vida cotidiana en el Colegio Monserrat. Del Antiguo al Nuevo Régimen* (Córdoba, 1999).

29 The membership of the former Jesuits from Río de la Plata, of María Antonia, of Funes, and of some neighbours from Buenos Aires and Córdoba, is registered in the letters at the ASR; Grenón, *Los Funes*; and Blanco, *Vida documentada*.

30 ASR, Carta de Hermandad to María Antonia de San José by Gabriel Lenkiewicz, vicar of the Society of Jesus, 18 April 1786, Alba Russia, fol. 163. For the activities of the Jesuits in Russia and their regard for María Antonia, see Juárez to Don Isidoro Lorea, 8 May 1789, in Grenón, *Los Funes*, vol. 1, pp. 147–56.

31 Consider for example, ASR, María Antonia to Juárez, 28 November 1781, fols 23–6; ASR, A. Funes to Juárez, 1 November 1789, fols 275–89; Juárez to A. Funes, 12 September 1792, in Grenón, *Los Funes*, vol. 2, pp. 1–12.

32 See, for example, Juárez to A. Funes, 11 May 1790, in Grenón, *Los Funes,* vol. 1, pp. 198–219.

33 See, for example, ASR, Funes to Juárez, 1 November 1789, fols 275–98.

34 AGN Sala IX 31.3.1, expediente 45, 1784, Informe del Ilustrísimo Señor Malvar, obispo de Buenos Aires, a petición de María Antonia de San José.

35 See Ricardo Cierchia, *Historia de la vida privada en la Argentina* (Buenos Aires, 1998), pp. 33–53. See also José Carlos Chiaramonte, *Ciudades, provincias, estados: Orígenes de la nación Argentina (1800–1846)* (Buenos Aires, 1997).

36 ASR, María Antonia to Juárez, 7 August 1780, fols 1–5: 'Se me proponen varios impedimentos: el mundo está un poco alterado, los superiores no muy flexibles, los vecinos vacilando sobre mi misión, otros la reputan de fatua, en suma, cooperan a ello rumores frívolos, empero la Providencia del Señor hará llanos todos los caminos que a primera vista parecen insuperables.'

37 Don Isidoro Lorea, a neighbour from Buenos Aires, to Father Diego Iribarren, a former Jesuit, at Faenza, 1 October 1788, in Blanco, *Vida documentada*, pp. 287–92.

38 ASR, 'Carta de un Ilustre Caballero Americano, natural de Córdoba del Tucumán a un sujeto residente en Roma,' Córdoba, 7 October 1784. It is Juárez's version of a letter sent to him by A. Funes.

39 ASR, María Antonia to Juárez, 25 January 1783, fols 39–42.

40 ASR, A. Funes to Juárez, 7 October 1784, fols 117–28.

41 ASR, María Antonia to Juárez, 25 January 1783, fols 39–42.

42 AGN Sala IX 31.3.1, expediente 45, Informe del Obispo Malvar para la Curia Romana, 15 January 1784.

43 See Gracia, *Los jesuitas en Córdoba* (n8 above), pp. 534–5.

44 ASR, María Antonia to Juárez, 26 May 1785, fols 133–8.

45 AGN, 'Venta y donación de don Antonio Alberti a favor de la Madre Beata Sor María Antonia de San Joseph,' Registro de Escribano 2, 1793, fols 91v–94v.

46 AGN, 'Testimonio del expediente promovido por la Madre Beata Doña María Antonia de San Joseph sobre permiso para edificar una Casa y Beaterio de Ejercicios Espirituales en esta capital de Buenos Aires,' 26 September 1793, Sala IX 31.6.5, expediente 934. The plan is in AGN Mapoteca II-14-16.

47 See Ernesto Maeder, 'La Administración de las Temporalidades Rioplatenses. Balance de una gestión,' in *Congreso internacional*, vol. 2, pp. 215–37.

48 Don Cornelio Saavedra to María Antonia, 10 November 1795, in Blanco, *Vida documentada*, p. 352.

49 Ibid.

50 Archivo Histórico de la Provincia de Buenos Aires, Real Audiencia, 'Recurso de fuerza por la Priora de la Casa de Ejercicios Espirituales de las Providencias expedidas por el Discreto Provisor sobre la Elección de Eclesiástico,' Leg. 7.5.11.11, 1801.

51 Archivo Nacional de Asunción, Paraguay, v 19, 2–10, 1787, Sección Histórica, in Blanco, *Vida documentada*, p. 355.

52 N.N. [A. Funes] to a Jesuit [Juárez], n.d. [c. 1787], in Blanco, *Vida documentada*, p. 278.

53 See Blanca Gari, 'Margarita y el saber. Senderos de conocimiento y libertad en el "Espejo de las almas simples" de Margarita Porete,' in *Las sabias mujeres*, vol. 2, *Siglos III–XVI*, ed. María del Mar Graña Cid (Madrid, 1995), pp. 87–101. See also Gabriella Zarri, 'Living Saints: A Typology of Female Sanctity in the Early Six-teenth Century,' in *Women and Religion in Medieval and Renaissance Italy*, ed. Daniel Bornstein and Roberto Rusconi (Chicago, 1996), pp. 219–303.

54 See Ellen Gunnarsdottir, 'Una visionaria barroca de la provincia mexicana: Francisca de los Angeles (1674–1744),' in *Monjas y beatas. La escritura femenina en la espiritualidad barroca novohispana. Siglos XVII y XVIII*, ed. Asunción Lavrin y Rosalva Loreto López (Mexico City, 2002), pp. 205–62. See also Fernando Iwasaki Cauti, 'Mujeres al borde de la perfección: Rosa de Santa María y las alumbradas de Lima,' *Hispanic American Historical Review* 73:4 (1993): 581–613.

55 ASR, María Antonia to Juárez, 28 November 1781, fols 23–6. 'Dedicando todas mis acciones a la disposición del Altísimo, viviré siempre por estos reinos, hasta que dicho Señor disponga aquello que fuese su santa voluntad.' Idem., the same to the same, 25 January 1783, fols 39–42: 'Me ha agradado mucho el consejo que Vuestra Merced me da de abandonarme absolutamente a la Providencia Divina por los caminos visibles que me insinúa, y así el Señor decidirá de mis futuros destinos, de sus medios, de su duración, entre tanto abra margen para los otros establecimientos que planeo.'

56 ASR, María Antonia to Juárez, 28 November 1781, fols 23–6.

57 'El estandarte de la mujer fuerte,' María Antonia de San José's biography, written by an unknown person in Europe, from the letters sent by María Antonia herself, by A. Funes, and by some others in Río de la Plata. This biography, a *vita*, was translated into various languages and circulated in Europe during the *beata*'s lifetime. See Blanco, *Vida documentada*, p. 427.

58 ASR, María Antonia to Juárez, 4 January 1786, fols 157–62.

59 See Roberto Di Stefano, 'Abundancia de clérigos, escasez de párrocos: Las contradicciones del reclutamiento del clero en el Río de la Plata (1770–1840),' *Boletín del Instituto de historia argentina y americana 'Dr. E. Ravignani'* 16–17 (1997–8): 33–59.

60 ASR, María Antonia to Juárez, 5 September 1782, fols 31–8. She was considered an heir of the Jesuits by some other people. Abad Don Juan del Prado, in a letter dated 8 April 1786, reproduces some words from Don Pedro Arduz, a former coadjutor of the Society, sent to him in Italy on 10 October 1785: 'De nuestra Beata doña María Antonia de San José digo que esta Señora es un vivo despertador de nuestra memoria ... está substituyendo la falta de la Compañía ... Está la Compañía en espíritu en esta pequeña máquina de Doña María Antonia, como lo está en la Rusia y lo estuvo aquí en 1766' (Blanco, *Vida documentada*, p. 260).

61 For the crucial use of images by the Society, see Bail. 'Style.' For the use of images among the laity, see Chiara Frugoni, 'Female Mystics, Visions, and Iconography,' in *Women and Religion*, ed. Bornstein and Rusconi (n53 above), pp. 130–64.

62 ASR, María Antonia to Juárez, 22 August 1785, fols 147–52.

63 ASR, the same to the same, 7 December 1784, fols 101–4.

64 ASR, the same to the same, 14 December 1786, fols 199–200.

65 ASR, the same to the same, 7 August 1787, fols 237–8.

66 ASR, the same to the same, 28 November 1781, fols 23–6.

67 Ibid.

68 ASR, María Antonia to Juárez, 9 October 1780, fols 19–22; ibid., the same to the same, 28 November 1781, fols 23–6.

69 For an analysis of the Ignatian stamp, see John W. O'Malley, 'Some Distinctive Characteristics of Jesuit Spirituality in the Sixteenth Century,' in *Jesuit Spirituality: A Now and Future Resource*, ed. O'Malley et al. (Chicago, 1990), pp. 1–20.

70 ASR, María Antonia to Juárez, 3 July 1788, in Blanco, *Vida documentada*, p. 282.

71 'El estandarte de la mujer fuerte' (see n57 above), pp. 421–35. Blanco sets out the itinerary of this biography, which was translated into French, Italian, Spanish, and German. For the role of the clergy as mediator in the *vitae*, see Kathleen Myers, 'The Mystic Triad in Colonial Mexican Nuns' Discourse: Divine Author, Visionary Scribe, and Clerical Mediator,' *Colonial Latin American Historical Review* 6:4 (Fall 1997): 479–524; and Myers, *Word from New Spain: The Spiritual Autobiography of*

Madre María de San José (1656–1719) (Liverpool, 1993), especially 'Introduction' and 'Bibliographical Essay.' Father Gaspar Juárez wrote about María Antonia's biography; see the letter from Juárez to A. Funes, 12 July 1791: 'Acabo de saber que muchos retazos de estas [cartas], juntamente con los de la Beata, de su vida, y de la Catalina se han impreso en francés, en un libro cuyo título es *El Estandarte de la Mujer Fuerte*. Por "Mujer Fuerte" entiende a la Beata cuyos ministerios y Ejercicios es su principal asunto. Yo no he visto todavía el Libro, pero ya ha venido a Roma, y quien lo ha leído, me lo ha dicho' (Grenón, *Los Funes*, vol. 1, p. 289).

72 ASR, N.N. [A. Funes] to Juárez, 7 November 1784, fols 85–95: 'Nos vimos obligados a reconocer en ella una fuerza divina ... era el *Dedo de Dios* [underlined in the original text] quien movía principalmente esta grande obra.'

73 Perdriel, 'Oración fúnebre' (n7 above), pp. 380–99.

74 AGN, Testamento de María Antonia de San José, Beata, Registro de Escribano 2, 1799, fols 562–83.

75 See Silvano G.A. Benito Moya, *Reformismo e ilustración. Los Borbones en la Universidad de Córdoba* (Córdoba, 2000).

76 See Ernesto J.A. Maeder, *Misiones del Paraguay. Conflictos y disolución de la sociedad güaraní (1768–1850)* (Madrid, 1992); and Magnus Mörner, 'La expulsión de los jesuitas,' in *Historia de la Iglesia en Hispanoamérica y Filipinas (siglos XV–XIX)*, ed. Pedro Borges, 2 vols (Madrid, 1992), I, pp. 245–60.

37 / The Post-Suppression Society of Jesus in the United States and Russia: Two Unlikely Settings

DANIEL L. SCHLAFLY, JR

When Pope Pius VII formally restored the Society of Jesus with the promulgation of *Sollicitudo Omnium Ecclesiarum* on 7 August 1814, there were about 600 Jesuits. By 1820, they numbered about 1,300; in 1850, 4,600; and in 1900, 15,073, when they had returned to almost all their former territories and were reaching out to new missions.[1] This resurgence was especially dramatic in that the 1773 suppression had been the final chapter of a protracted and successful campaign against the Jesuits by partisans of the Enlightenment, who saw them as the fanatical and unscrupulous shock troops of bigotry and reaction, and by Portugal, France, Spain, and other courts, who long had resented the powerful and independent Jesuit presence in their domains.[2]

How could this remarkable revival have occurred? A major reason was the successful Jesuit response to the suppression, as core Jesuit values and structures, especially the educational methodology of the *Ratio studiorum*, proved resilient even under adverse conditions. Two examples are imperial Russia and colonial and early federal Maryland, settings quite different both from each other and from the traditional Jesuit milieu of the Catholic monarchies of Western and Central Europe.

When *Dominus ac Redemptor* was proclaimed on 21 July 1773, Catherine II of Russia's subjects included 201 Jesuits with four colleges and several missions and residences acquired in the First Partition of Poland the previous year. She was the heir to Peter the Great's tradition of what Michael Cherniavsky called 'autocratic rule, truly secular and truly absolute in the sense of owing nothing to anyone outside of himself and limited by nothing outside of himself.'[3] As Catherine put it, the sovereign was simply 'chef de son Eglise.'[4] Hence, during her reign, as earlier under the regent Sophia and Peter the Great[5] and later under Paul I and Alexander I, the Jesuits in the empire depended absolutely on the will of the sovereign.

Historically, Russia saw the Roman Catholic church, particularly the Society of Jesus, as agents of Western national, cultural, religious, and even military aggression, exemplified by the invasion of Dmitrii the Pretender, accompanied by Jesuit advisers, in the early seventeenth century.[6] By the late eighteenth century, however, Russia was more open to the Western learning and superior Western education the Jesuits could provide. St Petersburg's large foreign community included many Catholics, whose numbers were augmented by émigrés fleeing the French Revolution. Catherine set an example by her own patronage of European arts and culture, and the Westernized element of the nobility, many of whom knew foreign languages and had studied and travelled abroad, were eager to provide a Western education for their children.[7]

Late colonial America also presented challenges and opportunities for the Society in the suppression era. Jesuits had been in Maryland since 1634, and the colony's old Catholic families supported the order, sent their sons to short-lived Jesuit schools there and to established Jesuit colleges on the Continent, and generated a number of vocations.[8] But overall in the thirteen colonies Catholics were a scattered and often distrusted minority, perhaps thirty thousand in a population of three million, with Jesuits often seen as the epitome of the Old World autocracy, rigidity, and intolerance that American Protestants attributed to the Roman church. As John Adams wrote to Thomas Jefferson on 16 May 1816, 'If ever a congregation could merit eternal perdition on earth and in heaven, it is this company of Loyola.'

But immediately following this statement, Adams noted a crucial difference between Protestant America and Orthodox Russia: 'Our system, however, of religious liberty must offer them an asylum.'[9] Although in 1773 this 'system of religious liberty' lacked the formal protection of the Constitution and Bill of Rights, nothing in the American colonies approached imperial Russia's concept of absolute subordination of religion to the whims of an autocrat.

The American cultural and educational landscape also was different from Russia's. Even though colonial and early federal America had dozens of academies and colleges,[10] many foreign observers compared it unfavourably to Europe. Father Giovanni (John) Grassi, S.J., president of Georgetown in 1812–17, commented that 'in America there is a certain superficial smattering of knowledge, perhaps more extensive and more widespread than elsewhere.'[11]

What was the impact of *Dominus ac Redemptor* on the large Jesuit community in the Russian Empire and the twenty-one Jesuits scattered in the Maryland and Pennsylvania missions? The unusual form in which the brief of suppression was promulgated meant that Catherine II's refusal to accept it in her domains, despite Jesuit pleas that she do so, allowed the Society to continue as an organized community.[12] The empress described the Jesuits as 'the wisest and most submissive citizens of Belarus,'[13] not only valuing their educational reputation but also looking to the order to foster the loyalty of the Polish nobility in the newly annexed provinces. Catherine also wanted to assert her independence of the papacy and the anti-Jesuit Bourbon courts who opposed her foreign goals, and realized that the Society had no choice but to be the willing instrument of her policies if it was to survive.

In a letter sent on 6 October 1773 to 'Messers. the missioners in Maryland & Pensilvania [*sic*],' the vicar apostolic in London informed them of 'the total dissolution of the Society of Jesus' and asked them to sign and return an enclosed 'declaration of your obedience & submission,'[14] which all twenty-one did, on a document received by the Propaganda archives in Rome in 1774.[15] The former Jesuits remained at their posts, now holding the Society's properties as private individuals; as John Carroll noted in a 28 February 1779 letter to John Plowden, 'no such division of property has taken place here, as you mention in Egnld: on the contrary, everything has hitherto been conducted as heretofore.'[16] European monarchs saw suppression or, in the case of Catherine II and Frederick II, protection of the Jesuits as an affair of state; John Carroll, for example, left a vivid description of the expulsion of Jesuits and the seizure of their college in Bruges by imperial forces.[17] But in America, the existence or non-existence of the Society did not concern the civil authorities, and an ex-Jesuit was still a citizen who could function as a priest and hold property.

The continued benevolence of Catherine II, Paul I, and, until 1815, Alexander I meant that their Jesuit subjects not only could maintain their pre-suppression status but also, depending on the signals from Rome, could ordain priests, recruit novices, welcome former Jesuits from outside the empire, re-establish the Society's governing structure, and expand their educational, parochial, and missionary work in Belarus and beyond. Thus, Stanisław Siestrzencewicz-Bohusz, archbishop of Mohylew, whom Catherine had given full authority over all Latin-rite Catholics in the empire in 1773 with strict instructions not to try to implement the suppression of the Jesuits or to interfere with their work,[18] ordained twenty Jesuits to the priesthood in 1776.[19] As word of the Society's survival in Belarus spread, former members from Poland, Germany, France, Bohemia, Spain, and Italy came to resume their Jesuit vocations;[20] others renewed their vows while remaining abroad.[21] A novitiate was opened at the college in Połock in 1780, and courses in theology for scholastics were begun that year, followed by courses in philosophy in 1782 and a tertiership house in 1784, so a complete program of formation was provided.[22]

A general congregation held in Połock in October 1782 elected Stanisław Czerniewicz, then provincial of the surviving community in Belarus, 'Vicar General for life, with all the powers of a Father General until a Father General is elected with the restoration of the Universal Society.'[23] General congregations in 1785, 1799, 1802, and 1805 followed traditional Jesuit procedures for electing superiors and resolving issues.[24] On 17 March 1801, Pope Pius VII's brief *Catholicae fidei* officially confirmed the existence of the Society in the Russian Empire, which Pius VI had done less formally on several occasions; Vicar-General Franciszek Kareu now assumed the title of Father General.[25] Although papal approval extended only to the tsar's domains, the Jesuits there now had not only a full-fledged system of governance and formation but also an entity with which groups of former Jesuits elsewhere could and did affiliate before the universal restoration in 1814. Thus, as early as 1793, ex-Jesuits in Parma began functioning as a religious community with approval from Połock,[26] in 1804 in the Kingdom of the Two Sicilies,[27] in 1803 in England,[28] in 1805 in the United States,[29] and in 1804–5 in Holland and Belgium.[30]

Meanwhile in the United States, John Carroll in 1782, while grateful that former Jesuits there had escaped the fate of their brethren 'in almost every other country … [who] have scarce a miserable pittance,' argued strongly for 'establishing a system of administration … to provide an equitable support for all the present labourers in Christ's vineyard and to transmit that same support to their successors in the ministry.' This would preserve 'the Catholick clergy's estates from alienation, waste and misapplication.'[31]

As a result, in three meetings between 27 June 1783 and 11 October 1784, the former Jesuits of the Maryland mission organized the Chapter of the Clergy to maintain spiritual order and manage the Jesuit property wisely, and elected the former superior of the Maryland mission, John Lewis, as superior of the new body; John Carroll succeeded him the following year and served until 1806.[32] The Chapter was formally incorporated under the laws of Maryland in 1792.[33] The Chapter members declared that they would 'to the best of their powers promote and effect an absolute and entire restoration of the Society of Jesus,'[34] although Carroll initially was less sanguine about this prospect.[35]

On 25 April 1803 several former Jesuits and new candidates wrote to Carroll, consecrated bishop of Baltimore in 1790, requesting aggregation with the 'Russian' Society,[36] and in a letter sent to the then father general, Gabriel Gruber, a month later, 25 May, Carroll and his coadjutor, Leonard Neale, asked that 'the many who requested' to serve again in 'the genuine form … of the former Society' be admitted.[37] On 13 March 1804, Gruber agreed to admit 'however many seek union with us,' whether former Jesuits or not; promised to send men 'if not from here, then certainly from England'; and authorized Carroll to name a superior for the American Society.[38] Between June and October 1805, the new superior, Robert Molyneux, and four others, although not Carroll, renewed their vows.[39] With the opening of a novitiate at Georgetown in October 1806 and the arrival of eight Jesuits from the Russian Empire between 1806 and 1811, the American Society was well established when Grassi described the Te Deum led by Bishop Neale at Georgetown on 9 December 1814, after news of *Sollicitudo Omnium Ecclesiarum* reached the United States.[40]

Education was the crucial factor for the Society's success in the Russian Empire. Although the curriculum at Połock and the other Belarusian colleges still was largely that prescribed by the 1599 *Ratio studiorum*, they and Jesuit schools elsewhere had begun to give a greater place to vernacular languages, the sciences, and other 'modern' subjects.[41] Catherine II, impressed by her visit to the Połock college in May 1780,[42] invited Jesuits to participate in discussions of general school reform in 1784,[43] and gave them supervision of primary school reform in Belarus in 1786.[44] Emperor Paul I (r. 1796–1801) wrote to Gruber in 1800, 'I can see no other way to stem the wave of impiety, illuminism, and Jacobinism in my Empire than by entrusting the education of youth to the Jesuits,'[45] and that same year granted the Society permission 'to open schools as they see fit' and administration of the giant St Catherine's Roman Catholic church in St Petersburg.[46]

A free day school, the Pauline College, and a boarding school for nobles, the Noble Pension, were opened in 1801 and 1803 respectively in the Russian capital and flourished until the Jesuits were abruptly expelled from Moscow and St Petersburg in December 1815.[47] Students in the Pauline College, most of whom came from the capital's large expatriate community, had to take Russian and either French or German, history, and mathematics in all six classes, and natural sciences and 'mechanics' in the last two, in addition to the Latin language and literature emphasized by the *Ratio*.[48]

In the Noble Pension, three-quarters of whose students were Orthodox, many from the most prominent families,[49] although Latin was taught, French was emphasized from the first year on and Russian from the third. Mathematics, history, dancing, fencing, drawing, music, philosophy, physics, architecture, and law also were offered.[50] Both Catholic and Orthodox students were taught Bellarmino's catechism, but starting in 1806, the latter were instructed in doctrine separately by Russian priests.[51]

This marked divergence from the norms of the *Ratio* demonstrated the Society's ability to adapt to the needs of the time. The Jesuits also publicly demonstrated their loyalty to the empire and invited such distinguished visitors as the sister of then Empress Elizabeth to public performances and examinations.[52] Jesuit influence peaked in 1812, when Alexander I raised Połock to the status of academy with sole supervision over all the Jesuit schools of the empire.[53] The Society also found support in émigré circles in the capital, among sympathetic conservative aristocrats, and among noblewomen who converted to Catholicism.[54] Jesuit missions in Moscow, Riga, Saratov, South Russia, and Siberia, including a few small schools, were short-lived and incidental to the Society's educational work in St Petersburg and Belarus.[55]

Education was not as central to Jesuit survival in America as in the Russian Empire, but here adaption of the *Ratio* to unique local circumstances also helped win local support. Two small schools in Maryland operated briefly in the seventeenth century, and another from 1740 to 1749. Far more influential for the permanent foundation of Jesuit education the United States was the model of Jesuit recusant colleges at Saint-Omer and Bruges, where Carroll and many other Maryland Catholics had studied.[56] In 1783, Carroll wrote that 'the object nearest to my heart is to establish a college ... which might at the same time be a Seminary,'[57] and in 1786–7 he persuaded the Chapter of the Clergy to support the concept.[58] The prospectus approved by the Chapter stated that the school 'will be superintended by those ... [with] Experience in similar Institutions' and conduct students 'through the several Branches of Classical Learning.' A clear deviation from the *Ratio*, however, was the listing of subjects as 'READING, WRITING, ARITHMETIC, the easier Branches of the MATHEMATICS, and the GRAMMAR of our NATIVE TONGUE,' which would 'be attended to no less than the LEARNED LANGUAGES [Latin and Greek],' and the appeal to 'Students of EVERY RELIGIOUS PROFESSION.'[59] Classes at the Georgetown Academy, with two students, actually began in 1792.[60]

The 1798 prospectus put primary emphasis on 'the study of dead languages, that foundation of universal knowledge'; 'the English and French languages come next.' In addition to the subjects proposed in 1787, 'geography, the use of globes, and the art of an elegant elocution' were offered, with plans to add 'history, moral and natural philosophy, and Spanish.' As before, non-Catholic students were welcomed.[61] By 1814, Georgetown claimed to teach '*English, Latin, Greek*, and all other branches of classical education, *Sacred and Profane History, Geography, Use of Globes, Arithmetic, Book Keeping, Algebra, Geometry, Trigonometry, Mensuration, Navigation, Surveying, Astronomy, Fluxions*, and the other parts of *Mathematics* in general,' plus '*Natural* and *Experimental Philosophy*' and 'Italian and Spanish.'[62]

Like the Jesuit schools in Russia, Georgetown, except for short periods, welcomed non-Catholics and shaped its curriculum to meet the needs of its clientele. The majority of its students came from the Washington-Maryland area, most of them the sons of merchants and planters, with a fair number from the families of government officials and politicians.[63]

Unlike at the Jesuit schools in St Petersburg, however, no Jesuits taught at Georgetown until 1806, although three of the first four presidents were former Jesuits; enrolment fluctuated wildly until the late 1820s,[64] and there were constant financial problems.[65] The arrival of Jesuits from the 'Russian' Society, especially the talented Giovanni Grassi, after 1806 and vocations from the United States, however, created a solid Jesuit base for the future. In 1808, for example, four Jesuit novices were available to teach 'Latin, Greek, French, writing, arithmetic, and mathematics.'[66]

Mindful of the negative image many Americans had of the Catholic church, and of the Society of Jesus in particular, a special effort was made, as in Russia, to cultivate public figures and demonstrate a patriotic spirit. Thus, faculty and students turned out to welcome George Washington with flowery speeches when he visited Georgetown in 1797, and mourned his death in 1799 with a solemn church service,[67] just as two years later the Jesuit community in St Petersburg stood on the steps of St Catherine's next to the college building to watch Paul I's funeral cortège pass by.[68] An even more striking example of deliberate Americanization was the close imitation of the Great Seal of the United States in the Georgetown college seal, designed in 1798 by President William Du Bourg and still used today.[69] After the 1805 restoration, the American Jesuits continued their parish and mission work, but, as in the Russian Empire, education was the major focus.

Emperor Alexander I, initially favourable to the Jesuits, expelled them abruptly from St Petersburg and Moscow in December 1815, charging they had 'begun to use the trust accorded them for evil ends,' especially in converting Orthodox to Catholicism,[70] although Jesuit resistance to Alexander's educational plans and ecumenical religious projects were more important in the decision.[71] Too, the general restoration of the Society in 1814 meant that Russia lost its leverage as the Jesuits' sole protector. In 1820 the Society was expelled from the rest of the empire, not to return to Russia as an organized body until 1992. An autocrat's whim could save the Jesuits, but it also could destroy them, at least in Russia.

The 'Russian Society' was crucial, not just for Jesuit survival, but also for the dramatic revival of the order in the nineteenth century. After 1773 it gave former Jesuits the opportunity to live, study, and work as Jesuits, constituted a centre with which ex-Jesuits outside Russia could affiliate before the 1814 restoration, and sent men out to America and elsewhere starting in 1794. After 1820, the 320 Jesuits then in the empire made their mark throughout the world as missionaries, teachers, rectors, provincials, and, with Jan Roothaan, as father general from 1829 to 1853.[72] Several came to America, most notably Franciszek (Francis) Dzierożyński, who arrived at Georgetown in 1821 and served ably as superior of the Maryland mission during a very trying period.[73]

In a 7 March 2002 letter to a Moscow conference jointly organized by the Jesuit Historical Institute in Rome and the Institute of Universal History of the Russian Academy of Sciences, Father General Peter-Hans Kolvenbach formally thanked Russia for the survival of the Society after the 1773 suppression. But imperial patronage alone does not explain the success the Society enjoyed for a time in Russia and in the same era in America, nor its dramatic revival after 1814. Just as important was the remarkable continuity, particularly in the educational methodology of the *Ratio studiorum*, throughout the suppression era. The order's legendary centralized and hierarchical structure served it well, by enabling it to use its international membership wherever they would be most effective. At the same time, the Jesuits demonstrated considerable flexibility and adaptability to local circumstances, again most obviously in modifications of the *Ratio*. The achievements of the Slovene Gabriel Gruber in Slovenia, Austria, Moravia, Połock, and St Petersburg and of the Italian Giovanni Grassi in Italy, Połock, and the United States are but two of many examples. The strength of the Society of Jesus can be seen in the era of its greatest misfortune as well as in that of its greatest glory.

NOTES

1 Figures from J.B. Goetstouwers, *Synopsis historiae Societatis Jesu* (Louvain 1950), p. 711.
2 The Jesuits were expelled from Portugal and its possessions beginning in 1759, from France in 1764, from Spain and Naples in 1767, and from Parma in 1768; see ibid., pp. 314, 332, 355–6. For a comprehensive discussion of the suppression in the context of overall papal policy, see Ludwig von Pastor, *The History of the Popes*, trans. E.F. Peeler et al., vols 35–8 (St Louis, 1950–2).
3 Michael Cherniavsky, *Tsar and People* (New Haven, 1961), p. 90.
4 Quoted in Igor Smolitsch, *Geschichte der russischen Kirche* (Leiden, 1964), p. 141.
5 For the Jesuits and Russia in this era, see Jan Joseph Santich, *Missio Moscovitica: The Role of the Jesuits in the Westernization of Russia, 1582–1689* (New York 1995); and Antonín Florovský, *Čeští jesuité na Rusi* (Prague, 1941).
6 See Daniel L. Schlafly, Jr, 'Roman Catholicism in Today's Russia: The Troubled Heritage,' *Journal of Church and State* 39 (Autumn 1997): 681–96; and *The Modern Encyclopedia of Russian and Soviet History*, s.v. Jesuits in Russia.
7 Leonide Ignatieff, 'French Emigrés in Russia, 1789–1825: The Interaction of Cultures in Time of Stress,' dissertation, University of Michigan, 1963, pp. 175–99; Léonce Pinguad, *Les français en Russie et les russes en France: L'ancien régime – l'émigration – les invasions* (Paris, 1886); Schlafly, 'True to the *Ratio studiorum*? Jesuit Colleges in St Petersburg,' *History of Education Quarterly* 37:4 (Winter 1997): 426–7; Denise Eeckhaute, 'A propos de la pédagogie en Russie au début du XIXe siècle,' *Cahiers du monde russe et soviétique* 11 (April–June 1970): 244–58.
8 The fullest account is Thomas Hughes, *History of the Society of Jesus in North*

America, Colonial and Federal, 3 vols in 4 parts (London 1907–17). For the period 1634–1773, see vol. 1, pp. 141–562; vol. 2, pp. 3–609.

9 Quoted ibid., vol. 2, p. 604.

10 Robert Emmet Curran, *The Bicentennial History of Georgetown University*, vol. 1, *From Academy to University, 1789–1889* (Washington, 1993), pp. 11–12

11 Giovanni Grassi, *Notizie varie sullo stato presente della repubblica degli Stati-Uniti dell'America Settentrionale del P. Giovanni Grassi, della Compagnia di Gesù*, 3rd ed (Turin, 1822), p. 42. This judgment was seconded by the first Russian diplomat in America, Andrei Iakolevich Dashkov, who wrote in 1820 that schools, literature, and the arts in America were still 'in their infancy' (untitled manuscript f. 907 op. 1 d. 122, Moscow, Gosudarstvennyi arkhiv Rossisskoi Federatsii, 30v).

12 On the Jesuit survival under Catherine despite the papal brief, see Marek Inglot, *La Compagnia di Gesù nell'Impero Russo e la sua parte nella restaurazione generale della Compagnia* (Rome, 1997), pp. 43–63. A *Supplex libellus* submitted to Catherine by the Jesuits of Belarus in 1773 urging her to implement *Dominus ac Redemptor* effectively refutes the charge often made at the time and later that the Jesuits tried to evade the papal order; repr. ibid., pp. 263–5. See also William James, 'Paul I and the Jesuits in Russia,' dissertation, University of Washington, 1977, pp. 13–19.

13 Quoted in Paul Pierling, *La Russie et la Saint-Siège*, 5 vols (Paris, 1896–1912), V, p. 113.

14 Georgetown University Special Collections (hereafter GUSC), Maryland Province Archives (hereafter MPA), Box 2, folder 8, 2R2 1/2.

15 Reproduced in Hughes, *The History of the Society of Jesus in North America*, vol. 3, *Documents*, part 2, facing p. 607.

16 *The John Carroll Papers*, ed. Thomas O'Brien Hanley, 3 vols (Notre Dame, 1976), I, pp. 52–3.

17 Ibid., vol. 1, pp. 32–45.

18 André Arvaldis Brumanis, *Aux origines de la hiérarchie latine en Russie: Mgr Stanislas Siestrzencewicz-Bohusz: Premier archevêque-métropolitain de Mohilev (1731–1826)* (Louvain, 1968), pp. 42–3.

19 Inglot, *La Compagnia di Gesù nell'Impero Russo*, p. 71.

20 Ibid., pp. 86–7 and passim.

21 List of names, ibid., pp. 318–25.

22 Ibid., pp. 86, 89.

23 'Vicarium Generalem perpetuum cum plena potestate Praepositi Generalis donec, restituta Universa Societate, Praepositus Generalis eligeretur' (ibid., p. 88; Goetstouwers, *Synopsis*, p. 378).

24 Goetstouwers, *Synopsis*, pp. 378, 386, 394, 402.

25 A full description of the stages in this process can be found in Inglot, *La Compagnia di Gesù nell'Impero Russo,* pp. 125–64.

26 Ibid., pp. 166–79.

27 Ibid., pp. 191–200.

28 Ibid., pp. 214–29.

29 Ibid., pp. 228–37.

30 Ibid., pp. 237–44.

31 *The John Carroll Papers*, ed. Hanley, vol. 1, pp. 59–63.

32 Ibid., pp. 71–7; Hughes, *The History of the Society of Jesus in North America*, vol. 3, *Documents*, part 2, pp. 617–19; 'List of Superiors in Mission & Province of Maryland from 1634 to 1879,' GUSC, MPA, Box 2, folder 9, 2T3.

33 'An Act for Securing Certain Estates and Property for the Support and Uses of Ministers of the Roman Catholic Religion,' copy in GUSC, MPA, Box 23, folder 18. Reprinted in Hughes, *The Society of Jesus in North America*, vol. 3, *Documents*, part 2, pp. 722–6.

34 'Proceedings of a Meeting of Deputies from the Several Districts of the Clergy in Pennsylvania and Maryland Begun at the Whitemarsh Nov 6, 1783,' GUSC, MPA, Box 2, folder 5, 2N4.

35 In a 15 December 1785 letter to John Plowden, Carroll wondered whether 'our Governments here or almost any one in Europe would allow of the dependence such as formerly existed, on a General residing in Rome?' (*John Carroll Papers*, ed. Hanley, vol. 1, p. 197).

36 Hughes, *The History of the Society of Jesus in North America*, vol. 3, *Documents*, part 2, p. 816.

37 Ibid., pp. 818–19.

38 Quoted in Inglot, *La Compagnia di Gesù nell'Impero Russo*, pp. 231–2; the text of Carroll's 21 June 1805 letter to Molyneux appointing him superior is in Hughes, *The Society of Jesus in North America*, vol. 3, *Documents*, part 2, p. 820.

39 Inglot, *La Compagnia di Gesù nell'Impero Russo*, pp. 232–3. The restored American Jesuits remained in close contact with their brethren in the Russian Empire and expressed gratitude for their brethren's role in the preservation of the Society. A unique expression of this is a short play (undated) with Latin dialogue and English stage directions apparently performed by Georgetown students in the suppression era. In it the Jesuit general is portrayed as Jesus brought before the pope, cast as Pilate, with European monarchs as the Jews calling for Jesus' crucifixion and the generals of other religious orders placing a crown of thorns on the Jesuit general and dividing his clothing. Catherine the Great speaks the lines of Pilate's wife: 'Nihil tibi et justo illi multae enim passus [*sic*] sum hodie per visum' (Have nothing to do with this just man. Because of him I have suffered much in a dream). After he is

scourged and handed over to be crucified, the general proclaims, 'Post tres dies resurgam' (After three days I will rise again) (GUSC, MPA, Box 57, folder 13, 202 M1).

40 Giovanni Grassi, 'Diary,' GUSC, Georgetown University Archives (hereafter GUA), Catholic Historical mss, Box 10, folder 13:11, entry for 9 December 1814. The celebration was also described by Father John McElroy, S.J., 'Notes of Fr. John McElroy,' GUSC, MPA, Box 10, 12A5, entry for 10 December 1814.

41 See, for example, Robert Schwickerath, *Jesuit Education: Its History and Principles* (St Louis, 1903); Allan P. Farrell, *The Jesuit Code of Liberal Education: Development and Scope of the Ratio Studiorum* (Milwaukee, 1933); and Frederick Artz, *The Development of Technical Education in France, 1500–1800* (Cambridge, MA, 1966). For adaptations in Poland, see Stanislas Bednarski, 'Déclin et renaissance de l'enseignement des jésuites en Pologne,' *AHSI* 2 (1933): 199–233. For the curriculum at Połock and other Jesuit schools in Belarus, see Inglot, *La Compagnia di Gesù nell'Impero Russo*, p. 95; and James, 'Paul I and the Jesuits in Russia,' p. 58. In Połock, for example, Polish was taught and, after the First Partition, Russian as well (ibid., p. 62). For a discussion of Połock as a model for state school reforms under Alexander I, see Sabina Pavone Taviani, 'Accademia di Polock, collegi gesuiti e reforme statali in Russia all'inizio del XIX secolo,' *Orientalia Christiana periodica* 61:1 (1995): 163–94. Comprehensive tables of the subjects taught and the daily and weekly schedules for various classes at Połock and other Jesuit schools in Belarus after 1773 can be found in Tamara Borisovna Blinova, *Iezuity v Belarusi: Rol' iezuitov v organizatsii obrazovaniia i prosveshcheniia* (Grodno, 2002), pp. 391–408.

42 Stanislas Zalenski, *Les jésuites de la Russie-Blanche*, trans. A. Vivier, 2 vols (Paris, 1886), I, pp. 471–2.

43 Inglot, *La Compagnia di Gesù nell'Impero Russo*, pp. 96–7.

44 Eduard Winter, *Russland und das Papsttum*, 3 vols (Berlin, 1960–72), II, p. 101.

45 Gabriel Gruber to Monsignor Marotti, 11/23 November 1800, quoted in Ivan Gagarin, 'L'Empereur Paul et le P. Gruber,' *Etudes* 23:3 (1873): 46.

46 Quoted in M.-J. Rouët de Journel, *Un collège de jésuites à Saint-Pétersbourg, 1800–1816* (Paris, 1922), p. 20.

47 For a description of these schools, see Rouët de Journel, *Un collège de jésuites*; and Schlafly, 'True to the *Ratio studiorum*?'

48 'Ordre des leçons et division du temps dans les écoles de la Compagnie de Jésus,' reproduced in Rouët de Journel, *Un collège de jésuites*, pp. 55–64.

49 'Élèves du collège de St. Pétersbourg,' typescript compiled by M.-J. Rouët de Journel, based in part on research by Paul Pierling, Meudon, France, Bibliothèque Slave, Carton 'Jésuites de Russie.'

50 Gabriel Gruber's 'Plan d'éducation au Pensionnat des nobles,' reproduced in Rouët de Journel, *Un collège de jésuites*, pp. 104–10.

51 Rouët de Journel, *Un collège de jésuites*, pp. 114–16; Mikhail Moroshkin, *Iezuity v Rossii s tsartsvovaniia Ekateriny II-i i do nashego vremeni*, 2 vols (St Petersburg 1870), II, p. 127.

52 Schlafly, 'True to the *Ratio studiorum*? pp. 431–2.

53 See Daniel Beauvois, 'Les jésuites dans l'Empire russe (1772–1820,' *Dix-huitième siècle* 8 (1976): 262–6.

54 See Rouët de Journel, *Un collège de jésuites*, passim; Schlafly, 'De Joseph de Maistre à la "Bibliothèque rose"; le catholicisme chez les Rostopčin,' *Cahiers du monde russe et soviétique* 11 (January–March 1970): 93–109; and Ekaterina Nikolaevna Tsimbaeva, *Russkii katolitsizm: Zabytnoe proshloe rossiikogo liberalizma* (Moscow, 1999), pp. 56–68. Tsimbaeva provides a list of most of the nineteenth-century converts, pp. 164–6.

55 On Siberia, see Anna Peck, 'Between Russian Reality and Chinese Dream: The Jesuit Mission in Siberia, 1812–1820,' *Catholic Historical Review* 87:1 (January 2001): 17–33.

56 Curran, *From Academy to University*, pp. 4–7.

57 Carroll to John Plowden, 26 September 1783, *The John Carroll Papers*, ed. Hanley, vol. 1, p. 78.

58 Curran, *From Academy to University*, pp. 10–15.

59 'Proposals for Establishing an Academy at George-Town, Patowmack-River, Maryland' (1787), GUSC, MPA, Box 19, folder 6. Text reproduced without heading in John M. Daley, *Georgetown University: Origin and Early Years* (Washington, 1957), pp. 34–5.

60 Curran, *From Academy to University*, p. 34.

61 'College of George-Town (Potomack) in the State of Maryland, United States of America' (1798), GUSC, MPA, Box 19, folder 6.

62 'Georgetown College, District of Columbia, under the Direction of the Incorporated Catholic Clergy of Maryland' (1814), GUSC, MPA, Box 19, folder 6.

63 Tabulations based on incomplete records in Curran, *From Academy to University*, pp. 408–10.

64 Yearly figures, ibid., pp. 397–8. A graphic picture of the constant comings and goings of students can be seen in the 'Rector's Entrance Book, 1809–1858,' GUSC, GUA.

65 Curran, *From Academy to University*, pp. 31–101.

66 Quoted in Daley, *Georgetown University*, p. 131.

67 Ibid., pp. 94–7, 104.

68 James, 'Paul I and the Jesuits in Russia,' pp. 237–8.

69 It depicts the same eagle with the shield of union on his breast surrounded by thirteen stars, with a cross and a globe replacing the arrows of war, and the olive branch of peace in his talons (Curran, *From Academy to University*, p. 49, depicted

on 123). An almost identical seal was later adopted by St Louis College, and five other American Jesuit colleges incorporated American eagles into their seals as well.

70 *Polnoe sobranie zakonov: Poveleniem gosudaria Nkolaia Pavlovicha sostavlennoe: Sobranie pervoe s 1649 po 12 dekabria 1825 goda*, 46 vols (St Petersburg, 1830), XXXIII, pp. 408–9, no. 26,032.

71 See James Flynn, 'The Role of the Jesuits in the Politics of Russian Education,' *Catholic Historical Review* 56 (July 1970): 249–65; and Judith Zacek, 'The Russian Bible Society and the Catholic Church,' *Canadian Slavic Studies* 5 (Spring 1970): 35–50.

72 Examples from Inglot, *La Compagnia di Gesù nell'Impero Russo*, pp. 258–62.

73 See Anthony J. Kuzniewski, 'Francis Dzierozynski and the Jesuit Restoration in the United States,' *Catholic Historical Review* 74:1 (1992): 51–73.

Appendix

Jesuit Opera in Seventeenth-Century Vienna: *Patientis Christi memoria* by Johann Bernhard Staudt (1654–1712)

T. FRANK KENNEDY, S.J.

The following were program notes for the production of Staudt's Patientis Christi memoria *at St Mary's Chapel, Boston College, 8 June 2002. A digital videodisc (DVD) of that performance, with subtitles in English, has been included with this volume. The Latin text of the opera, with an English translation, follows the program notes.*

In the autumn of 1995, in a conversation I had with Mme Catherine Massip, the librarian of the Music Section of the Bibliothèque Nationale in Paris, we both wondered why all the music manuscripts and prints associated with the pre-suppression Society of Jesus had disappeared. Musicologists had recovered a great deal of documentary evidence about the rich musical tradition of the old Jesuit colleges and chapels, but little of the music itself. At the time, we were discussing the autograph manuscript of the Johannes Kapsberger opera of 1622, the *Apotheosis of Sts Ignatius and Francis Xavier*, which somehow found its way into the Bibliothèque Nationale's holdings, and to my knowledge is the first complete score of the Jesuit operas to be rediscovered.[1] Then in 1996 the first recording of a small chamber opera, *San Ignacio,* from the Jesuit missions of Paraguay, appeared, having been teased out of a collection of manuscripts discovered in the remote Bolivian town of Concepción.[2] Both Mme Massip and I had agreed at the end of our conversation that the music most probably exists, and that we simply have not found it yet or, more likely, have not yet recognized the various parts of the music we have found as belonging to this great tradition. Musicologists such as Bernardo Illari from the University of North Texas, Víctor Rondón from the University of Chile, Franz Körndle from the Friederich-Schiller-Universität Jena, and David Crook from the University of Wisconsin are gradually and painstakingly recovering the musical notation of the Jesuit enterprise.

Along with the work of these scholars, we can add that the Jesuit college dramatic productions in Vienna seem to be the next point of recovery of Jesuit music. Although the music connected with the Jesuit dramatic productions in late sixteenth-, seventeenth-, and eighteenth-century Vienna has not gone unremarked by Austrian historians, hardly any of their work has been noted and expanded upon by musicologists. To my surprise, two years ago, when I met Ms Rosemary Moravec, a librarian in the manuscript collection of the Austrian National Library in Vienna who for many years before her transfer to that collection had worked in the music collection, I learned of an extensive body of Jesuit music outside the music collection in Vienna. After her transfer Ms Moravec started looking at a large number of manuscripts of dramatic compositions that had previously belonged either to the Jesuit college or to the Professed House in Vienna. Most of these dramas contain musical notation, some simply for choruses at important points in the drama; some with whole scenes set to music; others, a smaller number, with the entire work set to music.

There are 236 drama manuscripts in the Austrian National Library that pertain to Jesuit drama in German-speaking lands. More than 117 of these manuscripts are of dramas that were produced in Vienna in the last quarter of the seventeenth century, especially under the patronage of Kaiser Leopold and his wife, Eleonora. The other Jesuit school dramas in the collection pertain to Prague, Dillingen, Olmütz, Graz, Bohemia, Passau, Bruges, Innsbruck, Klagenfurt, Linz, Augsburg, and – the most significant number after those pertaining to the city of Vienna – Munich, 18 dramas in the National Library. The collection is a treasure trove of material for both music historians and historians of the drama.

The DVD in this volume contains a recording of *Patientis Christi memoria,* or *The Memory of the Suffering Christ,* one of the thirty-nine dramas set to music by Johann Bernhard Staudt (1654–1712) while he was the chorus director at the Professed House in Vienna, from 1684 until his death in 1712. Staudt was born in Wiener Neustadt in 1654, and from 1666 to 1670 he was a boarding student at the Jesuit college in Vienna. In the academic year 1667–8 he attended lectures at the university as well. On the front of the DVD is a drawing of the Üniversitätskirche, which is the Jesuit church in the Ignaz Seipel Platz. It is also the church in which Brother Andrea Pozzo, the famous Jesuit painter, is buried; it is the last church Pozzo worked on. To the right of the church is the old Jesuit college, and in that building is the theatre in which this piece was first performed. To the left of the Jesuit church is the famous Aula Magna of the university, where many celebrated first performances were held. A generation later saw and heard Franz Joseph Haydn's *Creation* first performed there. As yet, there is no knowledge of Staudt's whereabouts and activities in the years 1670–84, but in 1684 he became the music master for the students at his old college, and also was named a 'freeman' of the city, a title indicating the respect he commanded in Vienna.[3]

Unfortunately, Staudt's reputation as a well-respected musician has not seemed to survive intact. Though I suspect listeners and viewers will be charmed by this little chamber opera, what has come down to us in modern dictionaries of music history, and unfortunately been repeated over and over, is a line from an Austrian scholar named Waltraute Kramer[4] who in her 1961 dissertation, entitled 'The Music in Viennese Jesuit Drama 1677–1711,' glibly states that Staudt is 'a technically well trained writer, prolific but deadened by routine.' After quoting that line, most other scholars comment that, after all, since these dramas were didactic in purpose, it is no surprise that they were routinely repetitive, and, ultimately, no offence should be taken. Listeners can agree or disagree, but one of the lessons the early music movement has taught us forty years after Dr Kramer's comment is that we need to move beyond the concept of a closed musical canon, beyond the notion that only the great works of any age are passed on and are worthy of our listening. What I sense from the rather thin body of Jesuit music dramas or operas that we have been able to hear and study, is that, if in the seventeenth century the genre seems to be a conservative one, or does not change as radically or as quickly as opera in the public theatre does, that is because its purpose is different. These works are not first and foremost for entertainment; they teach, and on many levels – on the level of the music, on the level of the style of the text and poetry, and on the level of the life-lessons offered to the students. The *Patientis Christi memoria* and similar works were also reinforcements or reminders for the adults present at the performances. For late twentieth- and early twenty-first-century observers didactic is a negative word, but the actual vision here is broad. We also need to keep in mind that in 1961, when Kramer was writing, nobody knew how to perform this music; the score looked so simple. It is only the recovery of baroque performance practice traditions during the last thirty years that enables listeners today to recognize that these works are anything but boring.

The author of the text of *Patientis Christi memoria* is unknown. Thirty-four of the 39 music dramas that Johann Staudt composed for were text settings of works by Father Johann Baptist Adolph (1657–1708), but Adolph entered the Society of Jesus in 1677 and was not assigned to the college in Vienna until after the 1685 date of *Patientis Christi memoria*, so the text cannot be his. The other great Jesuit dramatic writer of the seventeenth century in Vienna was the Austrian Nicholas Avancini (1611–86), but though he evidently kept writing dramatic texts while he was provincial superior and even as general assistant in Rome, in none of his collected works, some of which have been printed, does *Patientis Christi memoria* appear.[5] Father Adolph's plays seem to address more broadly the issues of society and its culture; they are often referred to as the culmination of Jesuit dramatic art in their baroque display of pomp and power.[6] The text of the *Patientis*, on the other hand, more resembles the type of play that Father Avancini composed – allegorical in nature, and often emphasizing a moral teaching. If Avancini did not compose this text – by 1685 he was already a general assistant in Rome – then his strong influence on the actual Jesuit composer can be felt in the style and presentation of *Patientis Christi memoria.*

The sources of the text are Sacred Scripture, *De sacra virginitate* by St Augustine, and freely composed poetic verses using metric schemes associated with the metres of Horace's *Odes*, especially the greater sapphic metre, most often a four-foot verse. See Durities Cordis's opening words: 'Quae scena tristis? Saxis in istis, / Funesta dolore, acerba maerore, / Plena panditur atroce' (What is this sad scene? In this rocky place, deadly with pain, bitter with mourning, full of gloom, it is revealed). Or, Memoria Passionis's lines: 'Esto memor Creatoris, / Tanta vi, qui te amoris' (Be mindful of the Creator, who loves you with such great force). A small part of the text of Augustine's *De sacra virginitate* is used as a background for the actual dramatic text. The full passage is spoken before the beginning of the drama, but even here there is a slight adaptation: in Augustine's text the second-person verb forms are plural, in the opera, singular.

The quotations from Sacred Scripture are also adaptations. In the Latin text the scripture references are incomplete – the chapter is referred to, but never the verse. There is a sense that the librettist is using his memory of scripture to fit the general outline of the story. Compassio's first line, from Jeremiah 2, 'You Heavens, wonder greatly about this,' is joined with a line from 1 Peter 3, 'The just one has died for the unjust.' Sometimes a part of a line and sometimes several lines are quoted from a chapter, but often not in the order in which they appear in scripture. For instance, in the Epilogus, Genius Christi sings from Isaiah 49, but the verses are out of order, abbreviated, and put together again: the order is verse 16 first, then half of verse 22, then the last phrase (6 words) of verse 19, and finally verse 23, but only the third, fifth, and sixth phrases of the the six-phrase verse. Pietas Christiana follows with a quotation from Habakkuk 3, where there is a word play with the original Hebrew verb *Y'shua,* 'to cause to save': the word 'saviour' is used, but in the Vulgate the Hebrew *Y'shua* becomes 'Jesus,' and in the original program of 1685 the words 'God' and 'Jesus' appear in capitals, 'DEO' and 'JESU.' In this libretto there is also a wonderful juxtaposing of Old and New Testament texts. In the middle of Inductio I, Memoria Passionis sings a line from John 2, 'Ipse est propitiatio pro peccatis nostris' (He is the very atonement for our sins), along with a line from 3 Kings (1 Chronicles) 22, 'Pone sermones ejus in corde (Take his utterances to heart)': in the quotation from Chronicles, King David is ordering the building of the temple, while in the quotation from John the reference is to Jesus as the temple, in the sense of 'mercy seat.' The juxta-positions point towards reconciliation of texts, perhaps proofs of scriptural truths. Depending on one's perspective, the combination of scriptural phrases in this libretto could be seen as accommodation, or simply clarification, or both. Often the combination or rearrangement of verses creates a new contex-tual meaning without negating the context or meaning of the original.

Patientis Christi memoria is an allegorical play. Who are the characters? Memoria Passionis (the Memory of the Passion) is central to the drama. He is dressed in rags; no one wants to notice him (countertenor). Durities Cordis (Hardness of Heart), also a major character, is selfish, and closed in his invul-nerability. He is really quite unattractive, but in the end he turns into another character, Fortitudo (Courage). His is a bass role, in a strange love/conversion story. Pietas Christiana (Christian Duty) is also a central character, the Chris-tian of all time and every place. Also a countertenor, he is of course dressed like us. Dolor (Pain) and Compassio (Compassion) belong together; they are a soprano and tenor respectively and are supports to Memoria Passionis. Justitia (Justice) joins Pain and Compassion in Inductio III. In Inductio I, Genius Christi (the Spirit of Christ) quotes Isaiah 63, the 'Song of the Suffering Servant.' The image of blood, the central conceit of the opera, is taken from Isaiah 63. Yahweh himself treads the wine press in Isaiah 63. The Lord treads the nations, represented by Edom and Bozrah, and in *Patientis Christi memo-ria,* once again the Old and New Testament images are joined: Yahweh and Jesus.

Though this work is a small, tiny piece, baroque musical forms are well in evidence – recitative and arioso passages, as well as more developed baroque musical forms. While most of the piece is in an arioso style, there are more formally organized sections. Dolor and Compassio respond to Durities Cordis with a lovely little duet that has some beautiful simple imitation, or counter-point. The first real aria belongs to Genius Christi in Inductio I. It is easy to notice because Staudt has added string accompaniment to the continuo, and he also uses ritornello form as a compositional procedure. Basic procedures of the baroque era, ritornello and fugue are evident throughout the work. Durities Cordis also has a real aria with a string ritornello accompaniment. He sings, 'I want favours, I do not want sorrows.' Staudt uses the strings within the musical structure sparingly and always to indicate serious business. The Epilogus uses a large ritornello that punctuates what amounts to a love duet between Pietas Christiana and Genius Christi. But this love duet takes place only after the earlier love/reconciliation duet of Memoria Passionis and Pietas Christiana in Inductio II. Memoria Passionis sings, 'Do you love me?' and Pietas Christiana responds, 'One thing I ask is you alone, without which I cannot breathe, I want you in my heart, where I cherish only you.'

As I have mentioned, this opera uses as its central conceit the verse from Isaiah 63 sung by Genius Christi, in Inductio I. It invokes the God of Isaiah 63, the one dressed in the blood-red garments of him who treads the wine press. Thus, the blood of Christ in his sacrifice on Calvary, the blood of Christ of the Eucharistic celebration is the conceit – the total generosity of Christ, his blood poured out. This conceit represents our reflection before Christ's tomb on Holy Saturday. As in the Middle Ages, the shape of the high altar was meant to call up the tomb of Christ, so in our production we begin with a procession to the tomb of Christ. The processional music is by a slightly older contemporary of Staudt named Johann Heinrich Schmelzer (1620–80), and this particular sonata, no. 4, is from his collection of sonatas for a single violin, which were the first solo sonatas published in Vienna by a non-Italian.[7] He was also the first non-Italian *Kapellmeister* at the Viennese court. It was during this period that Viennese humanism came of age.

NOTES

1 Johannes Hieronymous Kapsberger, *Apotheosis sive consecratio SS. Ignatii et Francisci Xaverii*, BNP, Département de musique, Res F. 1075.

2 Both the *Apotheosis* and the *San Ignacio* have recently been released: Dorian Recordings #DOR-93243. The Dorian Recordings catalogue can be seen at www.dorian.com or info@dorian.com.

3 Walter Pass, 'Staudt, Johann Bernhard,' in *The New Grove Dictionary of Music and Musicians*, 2nd ed., ed. Stanley Sadie and John Tyrell, 29 vols (London, 2002), XXIV, pp. 301–2.

4 Waltraute Kramer, 'Die Musik im Wiener Jesuitendrama von 1677–1711,' dissertation, University of Vienna, 1961.

5 Ludwig Koch, *Jesuiten-Lexikon: Die Gesellschaft Jesu einst und jetzt* (Paderborn, 1934), pp. 15 and 142–3; I, and Somm. *Bib.,* 'Adolph Johann B.,' I, cols 53–4, and 'Avancinus, Nikolaus,' I, cols 668–80.

6 Pass, 'Staudt,' p. 302.

7 Rudolf Schnitzler, 'Schmelzer, Johann Heinrich,' in *The New Grove Dictionary*, vol. 22, pp. 526–8.

Patientis Christi memoria
by Johann Bernhard Staudt, 21 April 1685: Text

Inspice vulnera pendentis, sanguinem morientis, pretium redimentis, cica-
trices resurgentis. Caput habet inclinatum ad osculandum, cor apertum ad
diligendum, brachia extensa ad amplexandum, totum corpus expositum ad
redimendum. Haec quanta sint cogitate, ut totus vobis figatur in corde, qui
totus pro vobis fixus fuit in Cruce (*S. Augustinus de Virginitate*).
[Gaze on the wounds of him hanging there, the blood of him dying, the cost
of him redeeming, the scars of him rising. He holds his head inclined to kiss,
his heart open to love, his arms extended to embrace, his whole body exposed
to redeem. Consider how great these things are, that all be fixed in your
heart, just as all has been fixed for you on the cross (St Augustine, *On Holy
Virginity*).]

Inductio I

Memoria Passionis Dominicae a duritie humani exclusa peregrino in cultu oberrat.
[The Memory of the Passion of the Lord, shut out by human hardness, wanders in the
habit of a pilgrim.]

Dolor.	Venite gentes, et accurrite populi de longe (Isa. 49?).
	[Come you nations, hasten from afar you peoples.]
Compassio.	Obstupescite Caeli super hoc (Jer. 2).
	Mortuus est justus pro injustus (1 Pet. 3).
	[You Heavens, wonder greatly about this.
	The just one has died for the unjust.]
Dolor. Compassio.	Et non est qui recogitet in corde (Isa. 57).
	Non est usque ad unum (Ps. 13).

[And there is no one who takes it to heart.
There is not even one.]

Durities Cordis.   Quae scena tristis? Saxis in istis,
Funesta dolore, acerba maerore,
Plena panditur atroce.
Squallent, gemiscunt cuncta,
Lamenta personant.
Justi cruorem fusum
Hic luctus intonat.
Ad tela provocat
Maeroris haec procella,
Ad bella stimulant
Emortui Trophaea.
[What is this sad scene? In this rocky place,
deadly with pain, bitter with mourning,
full of gloom, it is revealed.
They mourn, they all groan,
they cry loudly the laments.
Here the lamentation thunders over
the blood poured out of the just one.
This storm of mourning
calls to arms.
The trophies of the one who died
call to war.]

Dolor. Compassio.   Magna opera Domini (Ps. 110).
Quae posuit prodigia super terram (Ps. 45).
Languores nostros ipse tulit, et dolores nostros ipse portavit
(Isa. 53).
[Great are the works of the Lord.
What wonders he placed on earth.
For he has borne our griefs and carried our sorrows.]

Durities Cordis.   Pudenda fraus doloris
Ut corda vulneres,
Scenas struis maeroris
Ut pectus occupes.
Non movebor, non terrebor,
Cor obserabo, fraudes vitabo,
Pectus contra obarmabo, concitabo.
[By the shame-causing deceit of pain
that you wound hearts with,

	by the scenes of heaped up grief
	that you seize the breast with,
	I will not be disturbed, I will not be terrified.
	I will silence my heart, I will shun the deceits.
	I will arm and rouse up my breast against these.]
Memoria Passionis.	Quae est haec ira furoris? (Deut. 29).
	Doloris? Amaroris?
	[What is this wrath of fury?
	Is it of pain? Is it of bitterness?]
Durities Cordis.	Conculcabo, concremabo
	Maesta Crucis labara.
	[I will tread under foot, I will burn up
	the sorrowful standards of the cross.]
Memoria Passionis.	Quiescat ira tua, et esto placabilis (Exod. 33).
	Salutis instrumenta sunt,
	Quae cernis hoc in colle,
	Haec Numen ipsum pertulit,
	Inferret ut te Caelo.
	[Let your anger subside and be easily appeased.
	These are the instruments of salvation,
	which you see on this hill,
	These the Divine himself has borne,
	that he may carry you to heaven.]
Durities Cordis.	Tace, obmutesce (Mark 9).
	Meminisse nolo Tragodiae,
	Assueta laetiori.
	[Be quiet, be dumb.
	I do not want to remember tragic scenes.
	Accustom me to more joyful ones.]
Dolor.	Recludo fontes gaudij
	Jocosque cordis pando.
	[I reveal the sources of joy
	and I throw open the jokes of the heart.]
Mem. Pass. *Compass.*	Amara, quo sunt dulcia,
	Despecta fortunata.
	[Bitter things in which there are sweet things,
	things despised can bring great fortune.]
Genius Christi.	Torcular calcavi solus, et de gentibus non est
	vir mecum (Isa. 63).

[I have trodden the wine press alone, and of the people no one was with me.]

Memoria Passionis.   Respice in faciem Christi tui (Ps. 83).

[Look upon the face of your anointed.]

Compassio. Dolor.   Qui dedit Redemptionem semetipsum pro nobis
(1 Tim. 2).

[Who gave his very self as a ransom for us.]

Durities Cordis.   Opprobrium hominum est, et abjectio plebis (Ps. 21).

[He is the reproach of men and the one rejected by the people.]

Memoria Passionis.   Ipse est propitiatio pro peccatis nostris (John 2).

Pone sermones ejus in corde (3 Kings 22).

[He is the very atonement for our sins.

Take his utterances to heart.]

Durities Cordis.   Non recipiam eum (Luke 9).

Volo favores; nolo dolores;

Luctus exspirent, joci respirent,

Nolo dolores.

[I will not accept him.

I want favours, I do not want sorrows;

let mourning die, let jokes be a relief.]

Memoria Passionis.   Esto memor Creatoris

Tanta vi, qui te amoris,

Passionis per dolores,

Animique amarores

Ream culpae liberavit.

Et haeredem adoptavit.

[Be mindful of the Creator,

who loves you with such great force,

that through the sorrows of the Passion,

and the bitterness in his soul,

He has freed the prisoner of sin

and made him an adopted heir.]

Durities Cordis.   Usquequo affligis animam meam? (Job 19).

Sine spe, recede a me.

[To what point will you afflict my soul?

Without hope, stand back from me.]

Memoria Passionis.   Ah! ama me, et pro te

Passi memoriam recipe me.

[Ah! Love me, and receive me,

the memory of him who suffered for you.]

Durities Cordis.	Nolo te.
	[I do not want you.]
Memoria Passionis.	Ah! ama me.
	[Ah! Love me.]
Durities Cordis.	In corde nolo te.
	Sine spe, recede a me.
	[I do not want you in my heart,
	Without hope, stand back from me.]
Memoria Passionis.	Haeccine reddis Domino tuo? (Deut. 23).
	[Will you not give that which is due to your Lord?]
Mem. Pass.	Eris deserta, quia oblita es salvatoris tui; et fortis adjutoris
Dolor. Compass.	tui non es recordata (Isa. 17).
	[You will be desolate, for you have forgotten the God of your
	salvation; and you have not remembered your strong helper.]
Dolor.	Rumpator furore, angatur timore.
	[Broken by fury, he is tormented by fear.]
Compassio.	Tabescat maerore, amarore.
	[May he pine away with sorrow, with bitterness.]
Dolor. Compassio.	Noluit benedictionem et elongabitur ab eo.
	Dilexit maledictionem et venit ei (Ps. 108).
	[He refused blessing, it will be far from him!
	He loved cursing, and it came to him.]

Inductio II

Oberranti passionis Memoriae occurrit pietas Christiana, eique cor suum in jugem offert mansionem.
[Christian Duty engages in the wandering of the Memory of the Passion, and his heart offers him an eternal resting place.]

Memoria Passionis.	Ah! veniat dies, qua(e) fessae sit quies;
	Humano in corde, flagrante amore,
	Irarum post fluctus, post animi luctus;
	Ah! veniat dies, qua(e) fessae sit quies.
	[Ah! Let the day come on which there is rest for the weary,
	in the human heart, with burning love,
	after the waves of furies, after the grieving of the soul.
	Ah! Let the day come on which there is rest for the weary.]
Pietas Christiana.	Exardesce caeli flamma,

Cor ignesce DEUM ama,
Ab amore sauciatum,
Clavis, spinis, vulneratum.
Ama hunc salutis spe, qui pro te,
Totum, totum dedit se.
[Burn with the flame of heaven,
catch fire heart, and love God,
who was mortally wounded by love,
pierced with nails and thorns.
Love him with the hope of salvation, the one that for you,
totally, totally gave himself.]

Memoria Passionis.   Vox dilectae audita est!
[The voice of the beloved is heard!]

Pietas Christiana.   Ubi es? Veni! veni!
Tibi dixit cor meum, exquisivit te facies mea (Ps. 26).
Quare sic attenuaris? (2 Kings 13).
[Where are you? Come! Come!
My heart spoke to you,
my face has sought you.
Why are you so haggard?]

Memoria Passionis.   Christo dolente, gemente me,
Humano a corde, amante se
Illudor et spernor,
Excludor undique.
[With Christ suffering, with me groaning,
with him loving with his human heart,
I am mocked and I am scorned,
I am shut out on all sides.]

Pietas Christiana.   Ecce paratum cor meum (Ps. 107).
Inhabita in saeculum saeculi (Ps. 36).
[Behold my ready heart.
Live in it forever.]

Memoria Passionis.   Amas me?
[Do you love me?]

Pietas Christiana.   Te unam requiro, qua sine non spiro,
In corde te volo, quo totam te colo.
[One thing I ask is you alone, without which I cannot
breathe,
I want you in my heart, where I cherish only you.]

Inductio III

Memoria passionis Christianam Pietatem remuneratura, appensis in statera Justitiae passionis instrumentis. Ecclesiam super omnes inimicos exaltat; atque post multos triumphos, stabili tranquillitate perfruituram demonstrat.
[The Memory of the Passion will repay Christian Duty, having weighed the instruments of the Passion in the scales of justice. He elevates the church above all her enemies, and after many triumphs, reveals that she will fully enjoy stable tranquillity.]

Memoria Passionis.	Ostendam tibi bonum (Exod. 33).
	Quod oras, quod gemens imploras.
	[I will show you the good,
	that which you pray for, and in mourning you beg for.]
Justitia. Compass.	Pones inimicos tuos scabellum pedum tuorum (Ps. 109).
Dolor.	[You make your enemies your footstool.]
Fortitudo.	Arcum conteres, et confringes arma, et scuta combutes igni
	(Ps. 45).
	Donec auferatur luna (Ps. 71).
	[You will break the bow, shatter the spear and burn the shields
	with fire –
	until the moon be no more.]
Pietas Christiana.	Quam bonus Israel DEUS (Ps. 72).
	Conturbatae sunt gentes, et inclinata regna (Ps. 45).
	Quid retribuam Domino pro omnibus his? (Ps. 115).
	[How good is the God of Israel.
	The nations rage, the kingdoms totter.
	What return shall I make to the Lord for all these things?]
Memoria Passionis.	Noli oblivisci omnes retributiones (Ps. 102).
	[Forget not all his benefits.]
Pietas Christiana.	Misericordias Domini in aeternum cantabo (Ps. 88).
	[I will sing of the mercies of the Lord forever.]
Memoria Passionis.	Majora horum faciet (John 14).
	[And greater works than these will he do.]
Chorus.	Nominabitur enim tibi, Nomen tuum a DEO sempiternum, pax
	justitiae, et honor Pietatis (Bar. 5).
	[For your name will forever be called by God, the peace of justice
	and the glory of godliness.]

Epilogus

Christianae Pietatis in patientem Christum affectus, ac firma in exercituum Domino, pacisque Principe fiducia.
[The feelings of Christian Duty before the suffering Christ, and his steadfast confidence in the armies of the Lord of Hosts and the Prince of Peace.]

Pietas Christiana.	O amor! O pondus meum! (St Augustine).
	O vita! O pax! O salus mea!
	[O Love! O my Treasure!
	O Life! O Peace! O my Salvation!]
Genius Christi.	In manibus meis descripsi te: muri tui coram oculis meis semper.
	Ecce levabo ad gentes manum meam, et exaltabo signum meum,
	et longe fugabuntur, qui absorbebant te. Vultu demisso adorabunt
	te, ut sciat omnis caro, quia ego Dominus, super quo non
	confundentur qui exspectant eum (Isa. 49).
	[I have written you on the palms of my hands, your walls are
	always before me. Behold I will lift up my hand to the nations,
	and raise my signal to the peoples, and those who swallowed you
	up will be chased far away. With their faces to the ground they
	shall bow down to you, that all flesh may know that I am the
	Lord, and they who wait for Him shall not be put to shame.]
Pietas Christiana.	In Domino gaudebo, et exultabo in DEO JESU meo (Hab. 3).
	Quia factus est spes mea et turris fortitudinis et facie inimici
	(Ps. 60).
	Quando in die malorum protexit me et exaltavit caput meum
	super inimicos meos (Ps. 26).
	[I will rejoice in the Lord and rejoice in God, my Saviour, who is
	my hope and tower of strength in the face of my enemy.
	Since he protected me in the day of trouble, and he has lifted up
	my head above my enemies round about me.]
Omnes.	Beata gens, cujus est Dominus DEUS ejus, populus
	Quem elegit in haereditatem sibi (Ps. 32).
	Quem morte redemit,
	Quem orco exemit,
	Quem vindex defendit,
	Et hostes peremit.
	Cui lauros paravit,
	Post belli procellas
	Quem pace beabit.

Haec quanta sint cogitate, ut totus vobis figatur in corde,
qui totus pro vobis fixus fuit in cruce (St Augustine).
[Blessed is the nation whose God is the Lord, the people
whom he has chosen as his heritage,
whom he has redeemed by his death,
whom he has freed from hell,
whom the avenger has defended.
And he has annihilated the enemy
whose triumphs he has procured
after the tempests of war,
which he will bless with peace.
Consider how great these things are, that all be fixed in your
    heart,
just as all has been fixed for you on the cross (St Augustine,
    On Holy Virginity).]

Omnia ad Majorem DEI patientis Gloriam.
[All things for the greater glory of the suffering God.]

Index

work on Quechua, 586; clarity of, 589, 600n104

Arte de la lengua general del Reyno de Chile (Febrés), 501, 508

Arte y gramática general de la lengua que corre en todo el Reyno de Chile (Valdivia), 501, 508

art history: interdisciplinary methods needed in, 113–14, 144; neglect of catechisms and emblems in, 124

artillery instruction, and Newtonian concepts, 395

Artillery Lessons (Cerdá), 395

artillerymen, mathematics for, 393

artisans: African, in Peru, 242; daily life of, 76; Marian congregation of, 68; participation of in festivals, 78

Art of Poetry (Horace), 121

Ascension of Christ (Silveira), 206

Aschhausen, Johann Gottfried von (bishop of Bamberg), 294, 296

Asclepi, Giuseppe Maria, S.J., 417

Ashrea, or The Grove of Beatitude, 93

Asquasciati, Francesco, 436n51, 443n121

Assumption, of Mary: testimony to, 174. *See also* Mary, St; Our Lady of the Assumption

assumption, of St Louis, painting of, 693

Astete, Gaspar de, 37

Astráin, Antonio, 11

'astrological chiromancy,' 385

astrology: and astronomy, 376, 389n15; attitude towards, 384–5; books opposing, 373; condemnation of, 373, 386; false vs. true, 378; historical circumstances fostering belief in, 387n6; Jesuit teaching of, 289, 371–86; judicial or judiciary, 372, 374, 375, 379; justification for teaching of, 374–80; lecture notes from courses in,

371–2, 374, 388nn11, 12; licit vs. illicit, 372, 377, 379; natural, 372, 379, 385; and navigation, 379–83, 385; as science, 376–7; and study of sphere, 387n2; superstitious vs. scientific, 377, 378; teaching of as good pedagogy, 381

astronomical miracles: eclipse of sun at Crucifixion, 301; rainbow, 293, 297–8; star of Bethlehem, 296, 297, 301; sun standing still or reversing course, 291, 293, 296–7, 301, 305

astronomy, 392, 393; and astrology, 376, 389n15; Boscovich's involvement with, 739; Catholic, 296; Galileo's work in, 324–5, 397; history of, 396; Jesuit, attack on in China, 732; Jesuit involvement in, 289, 292, 668, 671; and mathematics, 307; and navigation, 395, 396, 398n1; and observatory in Spain, 392, 393; role of Christoph Clavius in, 292, 296; teaching of, 357, 362, 367n16, 371, 372, 393; translation of texts on, 662; Wendlingen's observations, 394

Asunción (Paraguay), Jesuits driven out of, 712

Athalie (Racine), 544

atheists, opposition of to Boscovich's theory, 406

Atienza, Juan de, S.J., 582

atmosphere: height of, 437n55; lunar, 438n65

atmospheric phenomena, recitations on, 544

Attemis, Tristan de, 726

Attiret, Jean-Denis, S.J., painter and missionary, 104, 262; brush used for good of religion by, 669

attraction, law of, 425, 433n28

communal meal, of Jesuits and indigenous peoples in Peru, 595n48

communion, 159, 160; frequent, 177; provision of for slaves, 242

communion rail, *142*; as barrier, 139

'Compagnie de Jéhu,' and French royalist cause, 698

'Compagnie de Jésus,' used as accusation against Lyonnaise rebels, 699

Compañía. *See* La Compañía

Compassion (character in opera), 790–1

compline, 457

Compte rendu des Constitutions des jésuites (La Chalotais), 686–7

Concepción (Bolivia), manuscripts found in, 787

concertations, 75

concordat, between France and papacy, 689

Condé: chapel for at Maison Professe, 693, 697; inadequate support of Bourges by, 18

Condrette (Jansenist magistrate), 686

conduct, rules of, 579; written about by native speakers of Aymara, 587. *See also* 'way of proceeding,' Jesuit

conférences (reading together as group), 75

confession(s): alleged domination of conscience by Jesuits in, 51; as commandment of the church, 118; frequent, 119; heard by lay catechists, 640, 641, 646; hearing of, xxvii, xxxv, xxxvi, 55, 159, 578, 581; of indigenous peoples, 607, 608; as instrument of blackmail, 56; manuals for, in indigenous languages, 584, 596n65, 602; preparation for, xxiv; restitution of in Flanders, 137; for slaves, 242; Valdivia's catechetical work on, 501; of women, 41, 42

confessionals: in Antwerp churches, 137, 139, *140*, 160; in Jesuit church in Castro (Chile), 217; requirement for, 119; resistence to grates in, 147n22

confessor(s): alleged manipulation or misconduct by, 51, 711, 738–9; angels flanking chair of, 139; Jesuit, specially sought, 41; linguistic facility needed by, 603, 605, 607, 619; as one who cannot make mistakes, 607; role of, 55; royal, 8–9, 393, 400n6, 683, 684, 710, 719; in a rural church, 119; of Teresa of Avila, 41; to the wife of a Spanish commander, 711; woman catechist praised as, 646

confirmation, of converts in Japan, 649

confraternities: in Chile, 498–9; in China, devoted to baptism of abandoned infants, 729; French seizure of silver from chapels of, 692; lectures for, 160; Marian congregations as continuation of, 3. *See also* Marian congregations; sodalities

Confraternity of Christian Doctrine, iconography of, 195

Confucianism: arguments against, 647; ultra-orthodox version of, 732

Confucius, honoured by Chinese Christians, 659

Confucius Sinarum philosophus (Jesuit translation of the Four Books of Confucianism), 25, 659

Congolese language, 25

'Congrégation des Messieurs,' 68

Congregation for Christian Instruction (Antwerp), 115

Congregation for the Doctrine of the Faith, complaints filed with, 55–6

congregationists (members of Marian congregation): adult education course

for, 68–72; books shared by, 73;
importance of edifying conversation
in, 69; library access of, 72; participation in festivals by, 70–1; reading
practices of, 70, 74, 75; self-improvement fostered in, 75

Conimbricenses (Coimbra Latin commentators), 327

conscience(s): and Acosta's political
views, 584; alleged Jesuit domination
of, 51; examination of, 73, 241; of
indigenous peoples, 596n65; knowledge of cases of, 619; as opera character, 505; penetration of by funeral
commemoration of Philip III, 533;
of students, shaped by rhetoric, 538

consideration, virtue of, depicted in
Milan Cathedral, 535

consolation, spiritual, xxvii, xxxv, xxxvi;
importance of, 579

Constantine (emperor), 747, 749

Constantinople: Boscovich in, 738, 742,
750; Bulgarians as having accepted
Christianity from, 745; patriarch of,
749, 750; Phanariot Greek community
in, 749; proposed restoration of
Orthodox empire based in, 754

Constanz, Jiři, S.J., 27, 31

Constitutions, Jesuit, 358, 454; and
censorship process, 337, 346; changes
in, xxiii; and choice of apostolate,
613n13; clarity and arrangement of,
589, 600n104; despotism alleged in,
686; escape clauses in, xxvi; examination of conscience prescribed in, 73;
and finding God in all things, xxxiii;
and Gallican laws in France, 683; and
learning required in Jesuit formation,
610, 611; missions emphasized in,
xxv; and prohibition of women

members, 639; purported secret
version of, 55; request for change in,
56; schools not mentioned in, xxx;
and universality of apostolate, 361

Constitutions, of Seminary of Nobles,
393, 401–2n15

contemplation: and action, Jesuit combination of, 42, 175; of the cross, 93; of
light, 93; objectives of, 36; of time,
104

Contento mundis, 241

continuity principle, 429, 434n31,
435n44, 438n68

Contra os juízos dos astrólogos (Against
the Judgments of Astrologers) (de
Beja), 373

conversation: and cultivation of widows,
51; private, winning souls through,
144; with women, potential misinterpretation of, 42

conversation, in French Marian congregations: and acceptance in new social
milieu, 77; and *honnêteté*, 69; self-
improvement fostered by, 75; topics
used in, 81n30

conversion: art fostering process of, 114;
coercion vs. accommodation in, 617,
625, 639; of 'Durities Cordis' in opera,
790; gradual, of Andean people, 584;
of indigenous peoples, 616–17; of
individuals, 114, 159, 611; to Islam,
742, 745; Jesuit discourse on, 730; of
philosophers by argumentation, 171; of
Protestants, 113, 171, 175; in Russia,
776; of sinners, 760; strategies of, 133.
See also proselytism

conversion, in Japan: from Buddhism to
Christianity, 647; forbidden, 644; by
women catechists, 643, 647, 649

conversion/converts, in China: anti-Jesuit